eleventh edition
VOLUME

D1483826

AMERICA

A Narrative History

David Emory Shi

W. W. NORTON & COMPANY, INC.
New York · London

W. W. Norton & Company has been independent since its founding in 1923, when William Warder Norton and Mary D. Herter Norton first published lectures delivered at the People's Institute, the adult education division of New York City's Cooper Union. The firm soon expanded its program beyond the Institute, publishing books by celebrated academics from America and abroad. By midcentury, the two major pillars of Norton's publishing program—trade books and college texts—were firmly established. In the 1950s, the Norton family transferred control of the company to its employees, and today—with a staff of four hundred and a comparable number of trade, college, and professional titles published each year—W. W. Norton & Company stands as the largest and oldest publishing house owned wholly by its employees.

Copyright © 2019, 2016, 2013, 2010, 2007, 2004, 1999, 1996, 1992, 1988, 1984 by W. W. Norton & Company, Inc.

All rights reserved
Printed in Canada

Editor: Jon Durbin
Associate Managing Editor: Melissa Atkin
Editorial Assistant: Lily Gellman
Managing Editor, College: Marian Johnson
Managing Editor, College Digital Media: Kim Yi
Production Managers: Ashley Horna and Benjamin Reynolds
Media Editor: Carson Russell
Media Project Editor: Rachel Mayer
Media Associate Editor: Sarah Rose Aquilina
Media Editorial Assistant: Alexandra Malakhoff
Marketing Manager, History: Sarah England Bartley
Design Director: Hope Goodell Miller
Photo Editor: Travis Carr
Composition: SixRedMarbles / Jouve – Brattleboro, VT
Manufacturing: Transcontinental Interglobe

Permission to use copyrighted material is included on page A157.

The Library of Congress has cataloged the Full, One-Volume, Edition as follows:

Names: Shi, David Emory, author.
Title: America : a narrative history / David Emory Shi.
Description: Eleventh edition. | New York : W. W. Norton & Company, 2019. |
   Includes bibliographical references and index.
Identifiers: LCCN 2018046039 | ISBN 9780393689693 (hardcover : alk. paper)
Subjects: LCSH: United States—History—Textbooks.
Classification: LCC E178.1 .T55 2019 | DDC 973—dc23 LC record available at
   https://lccn.loc.gov/2018046039

ISBN this edition: 978-393-66894-0

W. W. Norton & Company, Inc., 500 Fifth Avenue, New York, NY 10110-0017
wwnorton.com
W. W. Norton & Company Ltd., 15 Carlisle Street, London W1D 3BS
1 2 3 4 5 6 7 8 9 0

FOR
GEORGE B. TINDALL (1921–2006)
HISTORIAN, COLLEAGUE, FRIEND

DAVID EMORY SHI is a professor of history and the
president emeritus of Furman University. He also
taught for seventeen years at Davidson College,
where he chaired the history department, served as
the Frontis Johnson Professor of History, and won the
Distinguished Teaching Award. He is the author of
several books on American cultural history, including
the award-winning *The Simple Life: Plain Living and
High Thinking in American Culture, Facing Facts:
Realism in American Thought and Culture, 1850–1920,*
and *The Bell Tower and Beyond: Reflections on Learning
and Living.*

CONTENTS

25 The New Deal, 1933–1939 1166

26 The Second World War, 1933–1945 1208

PART SEVEN THE AMERICAN AGE 1271

27 The Cold War and the Fair Deal, 1945–1952 1274

28 America in the Fifties 1318

29 A New Frontier and a Great Society, 1960–1968 1368

30 Rebellion and Reaction, 1960s and 1970s 1424

31 Conservative Revival, 1977–1990 1482

32 Twenty-First-Century America, 1993–Present 1528

MAPS

PREFACE

This Eleventh Edition of *America: A Narrative History* improves upon a textbook celebrated for its compelling narrative history of the American experience. Over the past thirty years, I have sought to write an engaging book centered on political and economic developments animated by colorful characters, informed by balanced analysis and social texture, and guided by the unfolding of key events. Those classic principles, combined with a handy size and low price, have helped make *America: A Narrative History* one of the most popular and well-respected textbooks in the field.

This Eleventh Edition of *America* features important changes designed to make the text more teachable and classroom friendly. The overarching theme of the new edition is the importance of immigration to the American experience. Since 1776, the United States has taken in more people from more nations than any other country in the world. By welcoming newcomers, America has enriched its economy, diversified its people and culture, and testified to the appeal of a democracy committed to equal opportunity and equal treatment. Writer Vivian Gornick, the daughter of Russian Jewish immigrants, cherished the ethnic mosaic of her childhood New York City neighborhood: "The 'otherness' of the Italians or the Irish or the Jews among us lent spice and interest, a sense of definition, an exciting edge to things that was openly feared but secretly welcomed." At times, however, the nation's Open Door policy has also generated tension, criticism, prejudice, and even violence. Those concerned about immigration, past and present, have complained about open borders and called into question the nation's ability to serve as the world's "melting pot." The shifting attitudes and policies regarding immigration have testified to the continuing debate over the merits of newcomers. Immigration remains one of the nation's most cherished yet contested values, and as such it deserves fresh emphasis in textbooks and classrooms.

While an introductory textbook must necessarily focus on major political, constitutional, diplomatic, economic, and social changes, it is also essential that it convey how ordinary people managed everyday concerns—housing, jobs, food, recreation, religion, and entertainment—and surmounted exceptional challenges—depressions, wars, and racial injustice.

I have continued to enrich the political narrative by incorporating more social and cultural history into this new edition. The text has been updated to include the following key new discussions:

- **Chapter 1** "The Collision of Cultures" highlights President John F. Kennedy's emphasis on the United States as "a nation of immigrants," and revised assessments of Christopher Columbus's roles as colonial governor, ship captain, and slave trader.
- **Chapter 2** "England's Colonies" includes expanded coverage of the various factors that led Europeans to relocate to the American colonies, new discussion of the varied fates of British convicts and others who were sent involuntarily to America, the experience of indentured servants, and expanded focus on Chief Powhatan and his response to English colonists who were determined to "invade my people."
- **Chapter 3** "Colonial Ways of Life" features fresh insights into nativism and xenophobic sentiment toward German immigrants in the American colonies, including anti-immigrant comments from Benjamin Franklin in Pennsylvania; and discussion of the plight of immigrant women who worked in Virginia's textile factories.
- **Chapter 4** "From Colonies to States" includes new assessment of the small, but distinctive French immigration to North America before 1750; new focus on the massive surge in immigration and slave imports after the French and Indian War; and, new treatments of the first Revolutionary battles.
- **Chapter 5** "The American Revolution" features new discussion of the system of enslaved labor during the War of Independence, the discriminatory legal status of African Americans, and British characterizations of American colonies as the "land of the free and the land of the slave." There is also a profile of Thomas Jeremiah, a South Carolina "boatman" whom colonial authorities executed after he alerted enslaved blacks that British soldiers were coming to "help the poor Negroes." The chapter also includes a new photo depicting free black soldiers fighting in the Revolution.
- **Chapter 6** "Strengthening the New Nation" expands discussion of the delegates to the Constitutional Convention and their involvement with slavery; features debates over immigration in the new nation, offers new perspective on Alexander Hamilton's development as an immigrant to the

United States. It includes new photos of the uniform Rule of Naturalization in 1790, southern writer Eliza Yonge Wilkinson, and women's activist Judith Sargent Murray.

- **Chapter 7** "The Early Republic" includes expanded treatment of the Lewis and Clark expedition, of the strategic significance of the Louisiana Purchase, and the legacy of the War of 1812. It also features new coverage of Thomas Jefferson's writings on race and frank discussion of his sexual relationship with slave Sally Hemings; includes new photos of a Sacagawea dollar and an anti-Jefferson cartoon.
- **Chapter 8** "The Emergence of a Market Economy" includes new discussions on anti-Catholic and anti-Irish sentiments during the first half of the nineteenth century, the changing dynamics among immigrants of different nationalities, and the challenges immigrant workers faced in forming unions. New photos that depict symbols of organized labor and of Irish immigration have been added.
- **Chapter 9** "Nationalism and Sectionalism" features a revised profile of John Quincy Adams and fresh coverage of Henry Clay.
- **Chapter 10** "The Jacksonian Era" includes expanded coverage of Andrew Jackson's Indian Removal policy, the Deposit and Distribution Act, the Specie Circular, and the Eaton Affair—including a new image of Peggy Eaton.
- **Chapter 11** "The South, Slavery, and King Cotton" highlights the changing dynamics between slave labor and immigrant labor in the Old South, new coverage of sexual violence upon female slaves in the New Orleans slave trade and other regions, and a new photo depicting the vitality of African American religion.
- **Chapter 12** "Religion, Romanticism, and Reform" includes revised discussions of religious awakenings, Mormonism, and transcendentalism, with expanded focus on transcendentalist Henry David Thoreau and Christian revivalist Peter Cartwright. The chapter also features social developments in women's rights and the transition from gradualism to abolitionism among those opposed to slavery.
- **Chapter 13** "Western Expansion" includes a new biographical sketch of John A. Sutter, the Swiss settler who founded a colony of European emigrants in California and created a wilderness empire centered on the gold rush. It also contains expanded content on Irish and German immigrants in the Saint Patrick's Battalion in the Mexican army. The chapter also reveals the development of John C. Calhoun's race-based ideology following the Texas Revolution and includes a new photograph of the Donner party.

- **Chapter 14** "The Gathering Storm" features new discussion of the California gold rush's impact on the Native American population, new biographical material on Presidents James Buchanan and Abraham Lincoln, and expanded coverage of the Lincoln-Douglas debates.
- **Chapter 15** "The War of the Union" discusses the substantial immigrant participation in the Civil War, features a new biographical sketch and photo of Private Lyons Wakeman—a young woman who disguised herself as a man in order to fight in the Union army. Also added is new discussion of African American rebellions in the South.
- **Chapter 16** "The Era of Reconstruction" explains changing immigration policy in the context of the Naturalization Act of 1870; offers new treatments of Indian policies, Congressional Reconstruction, and the legacies of Reconstruction.
- **Chapter 17** "Business and Labor in the Industrial Era" includes broader discussion of immigrant women, the contributions of inventors like Croatian immigrant Nikola Tesla, and examines the relationship between immigration—especially Chinese immigration—and the railroad boom beginning in the 1860s. Increased discussion of immigrants and the settlement house movement, union organizers such as Eugene Debs, and textile mill and factory strikers.
- **Chapter 18** "The New South and the New West" expands explanation of the spread of institutional racial segregation and of the emergence of the southern tobacco industry after the Civil War.
- **Chapter 19** "Political Stalemate and Rural Revolt" includes new photos of Charles Guiteau, who assassinated President James Garfield, and of the unemployed protesters who marched in Coxey's Army protesting the recession of the late nineteenth century.
- **Chapter 20** "Seizing an American Empire" includes expanded content and a new photo regarding Japanese immigration to the United States.
- **Chapter 21** "The Progressive Era" features increased discussion of the social gospel movement and the women's suffrage movement, new biographical material on Presidents Taft, Roosevelt, and Wilson, and expanded focus on the racial biases of the Wilson administration.
- **Chapter 22** "America and the Great War" includes expanded coverage of immigrants, including Italian American Tony Monanco, who fought in World War I; new coverage of Woodrow Wilson's prosecution of immigrants who spread the poison of disloyalty during the war; nativism's ties to racism and eugenics; and increased discussion about the Palmer raids.

- **Chapter 23** "A Clash of Cultures" includes new discussion of flappers, the sexual revolution, and the new woman; revised treatments of Albert Einstein, scientific developments, and the impact of the radio; and, fresh insights into Ernest Hemingway and the "Lost Generation."
- **Chapter 24** "The Reactionary Twenties" expands discussion of reactionary conservatism and restrictive immigration policies; extends content on the revival of the Ku Klux Klan, prohibition, racial progressivism, and President Herbert Hoover's financial and social policies. There are new photos depicting the Johnson-Reed Act, Hoover's "Keep Smiling" slogan, and the Bonus Army.
- **Chapter 25** "The New Deal" features expanded coverage of the New Deal's impact on women and Native Americans; there is new material on President Franklin Delano Roosevelt's relationship with his wife Eleanor Roosevelt.
- **Chapter 26** "The Second World War" includes expanded coverage of social and racial prejudice against African Americans and Japanese Americans; features a new discussion of army enlistment after the attack on Pearl Harbor; and new photos depicting the Battle of the Bulge and A. Philip Randolph.
- **Chapter 27** "The Cold War and the Fair Deal" includes discussion of the Immigration and Nationality (McCarran-Walter) Act of 1952 within the contexts of the Red Scare and McCarthyism.
- **Chapter 28** "America in the Fifties" highlights the emergence of a "car culture," expanded discussion of the communist politics of Cuba, and bolstered coverage regarding Elizabeth Eckford, the student who attempted to enter Little Rock High School in Arkansas after the desegregation of public schools.
- **Chapter 29** "A New Frontier and a Great Society" includes fresh coverage of the Immigration and Nationality Services Act of 1965, of the Logan Act regarding communication with foreign governments, and of U.S. Attorney General Robert Kennedy. It also features new set pieces highlighting the work of organizers Audre Lorde and Angela Davis, both of whom were involved with the Black Panther party.
- **Chapter 30** "Rebellion and Reaction" features new discussions on the founding of the United Farm Workers and the organizing efforts of Dolores Huerta and Cesar Chavez, including Chavez's twenty-five-day hunger strike in 1968 and the pathbreaking worker's rights negotiations with grape growers in the 1970s. It also includes a new set piece spotlighting feminist pioneer and *Ms.* magazine founder Gloria Steinem, and another covering clinical psychology professor Timothy Leary's crusade on behalf of psychedelic drugs.

- **Chapter 31** "Conservative Revival" includes expanded discussion of the Carter administration, new coverage of the Immigration Act of 1990, and revised treatment of George H. W. Bush's presidency.
- **Chapter 32** "Twenty-First-Century America" includes new coverage and photos of the Black Lives Matter movement, the 2016 election, and the Me Too movement. New Trump administration coverage includes the efforts to restrict immigration and movement (travel ban, family separation, and increased border security); the proposed ban of transgender service members; and Supreme Court appointments.

In addition, I have incorporated throughout this edition fresh insights from important new books and articles covering many significant topics. Whether you consider yourself a political, social, cultural, or economic historian, you'll find new material to consider and share with your students.

As part of making the new editions even more teachable and classroom friendly, the new Eleventh Edition of *America: A Narrative History* also makes history an immersive experience through its innovative pedagogy and digital resources. Norton InQuizitive for History—W. W. Norton's groundbreaking, formative, and adaptive new learning program—enables both students and instructors to assess learning progress at the individual and classroom level. The Norton Coursepack provides an array of support materials—free to instructors—who adopt the text for integration into their local learning-management system. The Norton Coursepack includes valuable assessment and skill-building activities like new primary source exercises, review quizzes, and interactive map resources. In addition, we've created new Chapter Overview videos that give students a visual introduction to the key themes and historical developments they will encounter in each chapter (see pages xvi–xx for information about student and instructor resources).

MEDIA RESOURCES FOR INSTRUCTORS AND STUDENTS

America's new student resources are designed to develop more-discriminating readers, guiding students through the narrative while simultaneously developing their critical thinking and history skills.

The comprehensive ancillary package features a groundbreaking new formative and adaptive learning system, as well as innovative interactive resources, including maps and primary sources, all designed to help students master the Focus Questions in each chapter and continue to nurture their work as historians. W. W. Norton is unique in partnering to develop these resources exclusively with subject-matter experts who teach the course. As a result, instructors have all the course materials needed to manage their U.S. history survey class, whether they are teaching face-to-face, online, or in a hybrid setting.

New! History Skills Tutorials

With the Eleventh Edition we've expanded our digital resources to include a new series of tutorials to build students' critical analysis skills. The History Skills Tutorials combine video and interactive assessments to teach students how to analyze documents, images, and maps. By utilizing a three-step process, students learn a framework for analysis through videos featuring David Shi; then are challenged to apply what they have learned through a series of interactive assessments. The History Skills Tutorials can be assigned at the beginning of the semester to prepare students for analysis of the sources in the textbook and beyond, or they can be integrated as remediation tools throughout the semester.

New! Chapter Overview Videos

New Chapter Overview Videos, featuring author David Shi, combine images and primary sources to provide visual introduction to the key themes and historical developments students will encounter in each chapter. These are in addition to the Author Videos in which David Shi explains essential developments and difficult concepts, with available closed captioning.

Norton InQuizitive for History

This groundbreaking formative, adaptive learning tool improves student understanding of the Focus Questions in each chapter. Students receive personalized quiz questions on the topics with which they need the most help. Questions range from vocabulary and concepts to interactive maps and primary sources that challenge students to begin developing the skills necessary to do the work of a historian. Engaging game-like elements motivate students as they learn. As a result, students come to class better prepared to participate in discussions and activities.

STUDENT SITE

Free and open to all students, the Student Site includes additional resources and tools.

- **Author Videos:** These segments include the NEW! Chapter Overview Videos and feature David Shi discussing essential developments and difficult concepts from the book.
- **Online Reader:** This resource offers a collection of primary source documents and images for use in assignments and activities.
- **iMaps:** Interactive maps allow students to view layers of information on each map with accompanying printable **Map Worksheets** for offline labeling.

NORTON EBOOKS

Norton Ebooks give students and instructors an enhanced reading experience at a fraction of the cost of a print textbook. Students are able to have an active reading experience and can take notes, bookmark, search, highlight, and even read offline. As an instructor, you can add your own notes for students to see as they read the text. Norton Ebooks can be viewed on—and synced between—all computers and mobile devices. The ebook for the Eleventh Edition includes imbedded Author Videos, including the new Chapter Overview Videos; pop-up key term definitions; and enlargeable images and maps.

NORTON LMS RESOURCES

Easily add high quality Norton digital media to your online, hybrid, or lecture course—all at no cost. Norton Coursepacks work within your existing learning-management system; there's no new system to learn, and access is free and easy. Content is customizable and includes:

- **Author Videos:** These segments include the NEW! Chapter Overview Videos and illuminate key events, developments, and concepts in each chapter by bringing the narrative to life with additional context and anecdotes.
- **Primary Source Exercises:** These activities feature primary sources with multiple-choice and short-response questions to encourage close reading and analysis.

- **iMaps:** These interactive tools challenge students to better understand the nature of change over time by allowing them to explore the different layers of maps from the book. Follow-up map worksheets help build geography skills by allowing students to test their knowledge by labeling.
- **Review Quizzes:** Multiple-choice and true/false questions allow students to test their knowledge of the chapter content and then identify where they need to focus their attention to better understand difficult concepts.
- **Online Reader:** This resource includes about 1,000 additional primary sources (textual and visual). These are also available grouped by **Research Topic** for further investigation and writing assignments.
- **Flashcards:** This tool aligns key terms and events with brief descriptions and definitions.
- **Forum Prompts:** Three to five suggested topics per chapter offer additional opportunities for class discussion.

INSTRUCTOR'S MANUAL

The Instructor's Manual for *America: A Narrative History*, Eleventh Edition, is designed to help instructors prepare lectures. It contains chapter summaries; chapter outlines; lecture ideas; in-class activities; discussion questions; and a NEW! Quality Matters correlation guide.

TEST BANK

The Test Bank contains over 2,000 multiple-choice, true/false, and essay questions. The questions are aligned with the chapter's Focus Questions and classified according to level of difficulty, and Bloom's Taxonomy, offering multiple avenues for content and skill assessment. All Norton Test Banks are available with ExamView Test Generator software, allowing instructors to easily create, administer, and manage assessments.

CLASSROOM PRESENTATION TOOLS

- **Lecture PowerPoint Slides:** These ready-made presentations feature images and maps from the book as well as bullet points to encourage student comprehension and engagement.

- **Image Files:** All images and maps from the book are available separately in JPEG and PowerPoint format for instructor use.
- **Norton American History Digital Archive:** The archive includes over 1,700 images, audio and video files that are arranged chronologically and by theme.

PRIMARY SOURCE READERS TO ACCOMPANY *AMERICA: A NARRATIVE HISTORY*

- **NEW!** Seventh Edition of *For the Record: A Documentary History of America*, by David E. Shi and Holly A. Mayer (Duquesne University), is the perfect companion reader for *America: A Narrative History*. *For the Record* now features 268 primary-source readings from diaries, journals, newspaper articles, speeches, government documents, and novels, including several readings that highlight the substantially updated theme of immigration history in this new edition of *America*. If you haven't scanned *For the Record* in a while, now would be a good time to take a look.
- **Norton Mix: American History** enables instructors to build their own custom reader from a database of nearly 300 primary- and secondary-source selections. The custom readings can be packaged as a standalone reader or integrated with chapters from *America* into a custom textbook.

ACKNOWLEDGMENTS

This Eleventh Edition of *America: A Narrative History* has been a team effort. Several professors who have become specialists in teaching the introductory survey course helped create the Test Bank, instructor resources, and interactive media:

David Cameron, Lone Star College–University Park

Brian Cervantez, Tarrant County College–Northwest Campus

Manar Elkhaldi, University of Central Florida

Christina Gold, El Camino College

Maryellen Harman, North Central Missouri College

David Marsich, Germanna Community College

Lise Namikas, Baton Rouge Community College

Matthew Zembo, Hudson Valley Community College

The quality and range of the professorial reviews on this project were truly exceptional. The book and its accompanying media components were greatly influenced by the suggestions provided by the following instructors:

Milan Andrejevich, Ivy Tech College–South Bend

Carol A. Bielke, San Antonio Independent School District

April Birchfield, Asheville-Buncombe Technical Community College

Howard Bodner, Houston Community College

Matt Brent, Rappahannock Community College

Sharon J. Burnham, John Tyler Community College

Michael Collins, Texas State University

Scott Cook, Motlow State Community College

Carrie Coston, Blinn College

Nicholas P. Cox, Houston Community College

Tyler Craddock, J. Sargeant Reynolds Community College

Carl E. Creasman Jr., Valencia College

Stephen K. Davis, Texas State University

Frank De La O, Midland College

Jim Dudlo, Brookhaven College

Robert Glen Findley, Odessa College

Brandon Franke, Blinn College

Chad Garick, Jones County Junior College

Christopher Gerdes, Lone Star College–Kingwood and CyFair

Mark S. Goldman, Tallahassee Community College

Abbie Grubb, San Jacinto College—South Campus

Devethia Guillory, Lone Star College–North Harris

Jennifer Heth, Tarrant County College–South Campus

Justin Hoggard, Three Rivers College

Andrew G. Hollinger, Tarrant County College

David P. Hopkins Jr., Midland College

Justin Horton, Thomas Nelson Community College

Theresa R. Jach, Houston Community College

Robert Jason Kelly, Holmes Community College

Jennifer Lang, Delgado Community College

Nina McCune, Baton Rouge Community College

Richard Randall Moore, Metropolitan Community College–Longview

Ken S. Mueller, Ivy Tech College–Lafayette

Lise Namikas, Colorado State University–Global

Brice E. Olivier, Temple College

Candice Pulkowski, The Art Institutes

Shane Puryear, Lone Star College–Greenspoint and Victory Centers

Carey Roberts, Liberty University

John Schmitz, Northern Virginia Community College–Annandale

Greg Shealy, University of Wisconsin–Madison

Thomas Summerhill, Michigan State University

Scott M. Williams, Weatherford College

Christopher Thomas, J. Sargeant Reynolds Community College

Laura Matysek Wood, Tarrant County College–Northwest

Crystal R. M. Wright, North Central Texas College

As always, my colleagues at W. W. Norton shared with me their dedicated expertise and their poise amid tight deadlines, especially Jon Durbin, Melissa Atkin, Lily Gellman, Carson Russell, Sarah Rose Aquilina, Ben Reynolds, Sarah England Bartley, Hope Goodell Miller, Travis Carr, and Marne Evans. In addition, Jim Stewart, a patient friend and consummate editor, helped winnow my wordiness.

Finally, I have dedicated this Eleventh Edition of *America* to George B. Tindall, my friend and co-author, who until his death in 2006, shared his wisdom, knowledge, wit, and humor with me. Although few of his words remain in this book, his spirit continues to animate its pages.

AMERICA

16 The Era of Reconstruction
1865–1877

***A Visit from the Old Mistress* (1876)** This powerful painting by Winslow Homer depicts a plantation mistress visiting her former slaves in the postwar South. Although their living conditions are humble, these freedwomen stand firmly and eye-to-eye with the woman who had kept them in bondage.

I n the spring of 1865, the terrible conflict was finally over. The war to restore the Union transformed American life. The United States was a "new nation," said an Illinois congressman, because it was now "wholly free." At a cost of some 750,000 lives and the destruction of the southern economy, the Union had won the war, and almost 4 million enslaved Americans had seized their freedom. But the end of slavery did not bring the end of racism, nor did it bring equality to people of color.

The defeated Confederates had seen their world turned upside down. The abolition of slavery, the disruptions to the southern economy, and the horrifying human losses had destroyed the plantation system and upended racial relations in the South. "Change, change, indelibly stamped upon everything I meet, even upon the faces of the people!" marveled Alexander Stephens, vice president of the Confederacy. His native region now had to come to terms with a new era and a new order as the U.S. government set about "reconstructing" the South and policing defiant ex-Confederates. Diarist Mary Chesnut expressed the angry frustration felt by the southern white elite when she wished that "they were *all* dead—all Yankees!"

Freed slaves felt just the opposite. Yankees were their saviors. The ratification of the Thirteenth Amendment to the U.S. Constitution in December 1865 ended all doubt about the status of former slaves by abolishing slavery everywhere. No longer would enslaved workers be sold and separated from their families or prevented from learning to read and write or attending church. "I felt like a bird out of a cage," said former slave Houston Holloway of Georgia, who had been sold to three different owners during his first twenty years. "Amen. Amen. Amen. I could hardly ask to feel any better than I did that day."

Few owners, however, willingly freed their slaves until forced to by the arrival of Union soldiers. A North Carolina planter pledged that he and other

focus questions

1. What major challenges did the federal government face in reconstructing the South?

2. How and why did Reconstruction policies change over time?

3. In what ways did white and black Southerners react to Reconstruction?

4. What were the political and economic factors that helped end Reconstruction in 1877?

5. What was the significance of Reconstruction on the nation's future?

whites "will never get along with the free negroes" because they were an "inferior race." Similarly, a Mississippi planter predicted that "these niggers will all be slaves again in twelve months." When a South Carolina white man caught an enslaved mother and her children running toward freedom, he "drew his bowie-knife and cut her throat; also the throat of her boy, nine years old; also the throat of her girl, seven years of age; threw their bodies into the river, and the live baby after them."

Such brutal incidents illuminate the extraordinary challenges the nation faced in "reconstructing" and reuniting a ravaged and resentful South while helping to transform ex-slaves into free workers and equal citizens. It would not be easy. Rebels had been conquered, but they were far from being loyal Unionists.

Although the Reconstruction era lasted only twelve years, from 1865 to 1877, it was one of the most challenging and significant periods in U.S. history. At the center of the debate over how best to restore the Union were questions of continuing significance: Who is deserving of citizenship and what does it entail? What rights should all Americans enjoy? What role should the federal government play in ensuring freedom and equality? Those questions are still shaping American life nearly 150 years later.

THE WAR'S AFTERMATH IN THE SOUTH

In the spring of 1865, Southerners were emotionally exhausted; a fifth of southern white males had died in the war; many others had been maimed for life. In 1866, Mississippi spent 20 percent of the state's budget on artificial limbs for Confederate veterans.

Property values had collapsed. In the year after the war ended, eighty-one plantations in Mississippi were sold for less than a tenth of what they had been worth in 1860. Confederate money was worthless; personal savings had vanished; tens of thousands of horses and mules had been killed in the fighting; and countless farm buildings and agricultural equipment had been destroyed.

Many of the largest southern cities—Richmond, Atlanta, Columbia—were devastated. Most railroads and many bridges were damaged or destroyed, and Southerners, white and black, were homeless and hungry. Along the path that General William Tecumseh Sherman's Union army had blazed across Georgia and the Carolinas, one observer reported in 1866, the countryside "looked for many miles like a broad black streak of ruin and desolation." Burned-out Columbia, South Carolina, said another witness, was "a wilderness of ruins"; Charleston, the birthplace of secession, had become a place of "vacant houses,

Richmond after the Civil War Before evacuating Richmond, Virginia, the capital of the Confederacy, Rebels set fire to warehouses and factories to prevent them from falling into Union hands. Pictured here is one of Richmond's burned districts in April 1865. Women in mourning attire walk among the shambles.

of widowed women, of rotting wharves, of deserted warehouses, of weed-wild gardens, of miles of grass-grown streets, of acres of pitiful and voiceless barrenness."

Between 1860 and 1870, northern wealth grew by 50 percent while southern wealth dropped 60 percent. Emancipation wiped out $4 billion invested in slavery, which had enabled the explosive growth of the cotton culture. Not until 1879 would the cotton crop again equal the record harvest of 1860. Tobacco production did not regain its prewar level until 1880. The sugar crop of Louisiana did not recover until 1893, and the rice economy along the coast of South Carolina and Georgia never regained its prewar levels of production or profit.

In 1860, just before the Civil War, the South had generated 30 percent of the nation's wealth; in 1870, it produced but 12 percent. Amanda Worthington, a planter's wife from Mississippi, assessed the damage: "None of us can realize that we are no longer wealthy—yet thanks to the Yankees, the cause of all unhappiness, such is the case."

Resentment in the South boiled over. Union soldiers were cursed and spat upon. A Virginia woman expressed a spirited defiance common among her Confederate friends: "Every day, every hour, that I live increases my hatred and detestation, and loathing of that race. They [Yankees] disgrace our common humanity. As a people I consider them vastly inferior to the better classes of our slaves." Fervent southern nationalists implanted in their children a similar hatred of Yankees and a defiance of northern rule.

Rebuilding the former Confederate states would not be easy, and the issues related to Reconstruction were complicated and controversial. For example, the process of establishing new state governments required first determining the official status of the states that had seceded: Were they now conquered territories? If so, then the Constitution assigned Congress authority to re-create their state governments. But what if, as Abraham Lincoln argued, the Confederate states had never officially left the Union because the act of secession was itself illegal? In that circumstance, the president would be responsible for re-forming state governments.

Whichever branch of government—Congress or the presidency—directed the reconstruction of the South, it would have to address the most difficult issue: What would be the political, social, and economic status of the freedpeople? Were they citizens? If not, what was their status?

What the former slaves most wanted was to become self-reliant, to be compensated for their labor, reunite with their family members, gain education for their children, enjoy full political participation, and create their own community organizations and social life. Most southern whites were just as determined to prevent that from happening.

DEBATES OVER POLITICAL RECONSTRUCTION

Reconstruction of former Confederate states actually began during the war and went through several phases, the first of which was called Presidential Reconstruction. In 1862, President Lincoln had named army generals to serve as temporary military governors for conquered Confederate areas. By the end of 1863, he had formulated a plan to reestablish governments in states liberated from Confederate rule.

LINCOLN'S PLAN In late 1863, President Lincoln issued a Proclamation of Amnesty and Reconstruction, under which former Confederate states could re-create a Union government once a number equal to 10 percent of those who had voted in 1860 swore allegiance to the Constitution. They also received a presidential pardon acquitting them of treason. Certain groups, however, were denied pardons: Confederate government officials; senior officers of the Confederate army and navy; judges, congressmen, and military officers of the United States who had left their posts to join the rebellion; and, those who had abused captured African American soldiers.

CONGRESSIONAL PLANS A few conservative and most moderate Republicans supported Lincoln's program that immediately restored pro-Union southern governments. Radical Republicans, however, argued that Congress, not the president, should supervise Reconstruction.

The **Radical Republicans** favored a drastic transformation of southern society that would grant ex-slaves full citizenship. They believed that all people, regardless of race, were equal in God's eyes. They wanted no compromise with the "sin" of racism.

They also hoped to replace the white, Democratic planter elite with a new generation of small farmers. "The middling classes who own the soil, and work it with their own hands," explained Radical leader Thaddeus Stevens, "are the main support of every free government."

THE WADE-DAVIS BILL In 1864, with the war still raging, the Radicals tried to take charge of Reconstruction by passing the Wade-Davis Bill, named for two leading Republicans. In contrast to Lincoln's 10 percent Reconstruction plan, the Wade-Davis Bill required that a *majority* of white male citizens declare their allegiance to the Union before a Confederate state could be readmitted.

The bill never became law, however, for Lincoln vetoed it. In retaliation, Radicals issued the Wade-Davis Manifesto, which accused Lincoln of exceeding his constitutional authority. Unfazed by the criticism, Lincoln continued his efforts to restore the Confederate states to the Union. He also rushed assistance to the freedpeople in the South.

THE FREEDMEN'S BUREAU In early 1865, Congress approved the Thirteenth Amendment to the Constitution, officially abolishing slavery in the United States, and it became law in December. Yet what did freedom mean for the former slaves, most of whom had no land, no home, no food, no jobs, and no education? "What is freedom?" asked Congressman James A. Garfield, a former Union general and a future U.S. president, in 1865. "Is it the bare privilege of not being chained? If this is all, then freedom is a bitter mockery, a cruel delusion." The debate over what freedom should entail became the central issue of Reconstruction. "Liberty has been won," Senator Charles Sumner noted. "The battle for Equality is still pending."

Freedmen's school in Virginia Throughout the former Confederate states, the Freedmen's Bureau set up schools for former slaves, such as this one.

To address the complex issues raised by emancipation, Congress on March 3, 1865, created the **Freedmen's Bureau** to assist the suffering "freedmen and their wives and children." It was the first federal effort to provide help directly to people rather than to states. And its task was daunting. When General William T. Sherman learned that his friend, General Oliver O. Howard, had been appointed to lead the Freedmen's Bureau, he warned: "It is not . . . in your power to fulfill one-tenth of the expectations of those who framed the Bureau."

Undeterred by such realities, in May 1865, Howard declared that freed slaves "must be free to choose their own employers, and be paid for their labor." He sent agents to the South to negotiate labor contracts between freed people and white landowners, many of whom resisted. The Bureau also provided the former slaves with medical care and food and clothing, and helped set up schools. Northern missionary societies also established schools for former slaves. As a Mississippi freedman explained, education "was the next best thing to liberty."

By 1870, the Freedmen's Bureau was supervising nearly 4,000 new schools serving almost 250,000 students. The Freedmen's Bureau also helped former slaves reestablish connection with their family members and to legalize marriages that had been banned prior to the war.

SELF-SUSTAINING FREEMEN
In July 1865, hundreds of freed slaves gathered on St. Helena Island off the South Carolina coast. There, Virginia-born freeman Martin Delaney, the highest-ranking officer in the U.S. Colored Troops, addressed them. Before the Civil War, he had been a prominent abolitionist in the North. Now, Major Delaney assured the gathering that slavery had indeed been "absolutely abolished." But abolition, he stressed, was less the result of Abraham Lincoln's leadership than it was the outcome of former slaves and free blacks like him undermining the Confederacy. Slavery was dead, and freedom was now in their hands. "Yes, yes, yes," his listeners shouted.

Major Martin Delaney Delaney urged former slaves to achieve economic self-sufficiency.

Delaney then noted that many of the white planters in the area claimed that the former slaves were lazy and "have not the intelligence to get on for yourselves without being guided and driven to the work by [white] overseers." Delaney dismissed such assumptions as lies intended to restore a system of forced labor for blacks. He then told the freed slaves that their best hope was to become self-sustaining farmers: "Get a community and get all the lands you can—if you cannot get any singly." He added that if they could not become economically self-reliant, they would find themselves slaves again.

Several white planters attended Delaney's talk, and an army officer at the scene reported that they "listened with horror depicted in their faces." The planters predicted that such speeches would incite "open rebellion" among southern blacks.

DEATH OF A PRESIDENT The possibility of a lenient federal Reconstruction of the Confederacy would die with Abraham Lincoln. The president who yearned for a peace "with malice toward none, with charity for all" offered his last view of Reconstruction in the final speech of his life.

On April 11, 1865, Lincoln rejected calls for a vengeful peace. He wanted "no persecution, no bloody work," no hangings of Confederate leaders, and no extreme efforts to restructure southern social and economic life. Three days later, on April 14, Lincoln and his wife Mary Todd attended a play at Ford's Theatre in Washington, D.C.

With his trusted bodyguard called away to Richmond, Lincoln was defenseless as twenty-six-year-old John Wilkes Booth, an actor and rabid Confederate, slipped into the unguarded presidential box and shot the president in the head. As Lincoln slumped forward, Booth pulled out a knife, stabbed the president's military aide, and jumped from the box to the stage, breaking his leg in the process. He then mounted a waiting horse and fled the city. Lincoln died nine hours later.

At the same time that Booth was shooting the president, other Confederate assassins were hunting Vice President Andrew Johnson and Secretary of State William H. Seward. Johnson escaped injury because his would-be assassin got drunk in the bar of the vice president's hotel. Seward and four others, including his son, however, suffered severe knife wounds when attacked at home.

The nation was stunned and leaderless. At the funeral service in the East Room of the Executive Mansion (White House), General Ulysses Grant, hardened by war, openly wept. Vice President Andrew Johnson was sworn in as the new president, but for a time chaos reigned. Secretary of War Edwin Stanton, not knowing if the assassination was a prelude to a Confederate invasion, summoned Grant to defend the government in Washington, D.C. Eleven days later, Union troops found Booth hiding in a northern Virginia tobacco barn, where he was shot and killed. Booth whispered as he lay dying, "Tell my mother I died for my country."

Paying respect The only photograph of Lincoln in his coffin, displayed here in New York's City Hall rotunda.

The nation extracted a full measure of vengeance from the conspirators. Three of Booth's collaborators were convicted by a military court and hanged, as was Mary Surratt, who owned the Washington boardinghouse where the assassinations had been planned.

The outpouring of grief after Lincoln's death was overwhelming. Planned victory celebrations were canceled. Even a Richmond, Virginia, newspaper called the assassination the "heaviest blow which has fallen on the people of the South."

Lincoln's body lay in state for several days in Washington, D.C., before being transported 1,600 miles for burial in Springfield, Illinois. In Philadelphia, 300,000 mourners paid their last respects; in New York City, 500,000 people viewed the president's body. On May 4, Lincoln was laid to rest.

JOHNSON'S PLAN President Lincoln's shocking death propelled Andrew Johnson of Tennessee, a pro-Union Democrat, into the White House. Johnson had been added to Lincoln's National Union ticket in 1864 solely to help the president win reelection. Humorless, insecure, combative, and self-righteous, Johnson hated both the white southern elite and the idea of racial equality. He also had a weakness for liquor. At the inaugural ceremonies in 1865, he had delivered his vice-presidential address in a state of slurring drunkenness.

Like Lincoln, Johnson was a self-made man. Born in 1808 in a log cabin near Raleigh, North Carolina, he lost his father when he was three and never attended school. His illiterate mother apprenticed him to a tailor to learn a trade. He ran away from home at thirteen and eventually landed in Greeneville, nestled in the mountains of East Tennessee, where he became a tailor. He taught himself to read, and his sixteen-year-old wife showed him how to write and do some basic arithmetic.

Over time, Johnson prospered and acquired five slaves, which he sold in 1863. A natural leader, he eventually served as the mayor, a state legislator, governor, congressional representative, and U.S. senator. A friend described the trajectory of Johnson's life as "one intense, unceasing, desperate upward struggle" during which he identified with the poor farmers and came to hate the "pampered, bloated, corrupted aristocracy" of wealthy planters.

During the Civil War, Johnson called himself a Jacksonian Democrat "in the strictest meaning of the term. I am for putting down the [Confederate] rebellion, because it is a war [of wealthy plantation owners] against democracy." Yet Johnson also shared the racist attitudes of most southern whites. "Damn the negroes," he exclaimed during the

Andrew Johnson A pro-Union Democrat from Tennessee, Johnson became president after Abraham Lincoln was assassinated during his vice presidency.

war. "I am fighting those traitorous aristocrats, their masters." Impoverished whites, Johnson maintained, were most hurt by the slave system, and he was an unapologetic white supremacist. "White men alone must manage the South," he declared.

As a states' rights Democrat, Johnson also insisted that the federal government be as small and inactive as possible. He strongly opposed Republican economic policies designed to spur industrial development.

In May 1865, Johnson issued a new Proclamation of Amnesty that excluded not only those ex-Confederates whom Lincoln had barred from voting or holding office but also anyone with property worth more than $20,000. Johnson was determined to keep the wealthiest Southerners from regaining political power.

Surprisingly, however, by 1866 Johnson had pardoned some 7,000 former Confederates and eventually pardoned most of the white "aristocrats" he claimed to despise. What brought about this change of heart? Johnson had decided that he could buy the political support of prominent Southerners by pardoning them, improving his chances of reelection.

Johnson's Restoration Plan mandated the appointment of a Unionist as provisional governor in each southern state. Each governor was to call a convention of men elected by "loyal" (not Confederate) voters. Johnson's plan required that each state convention ratify the Thirteenth Amendment. The president also encouraged giving a few blacks voting rights, especially those who had some education or had served in the military, so as to "disarm" the "Radicals who are wild upon" giving *all* African Americans the right to vote. Except for Mississippi, each former Confederate state held a convention that met Johnson's requirements but ignored his suggestion about voting rights for blacks.

FREEDMEN'S CONVENTIONS Neither Lincoln nor Johnson saw fit to ask freedpeople in the South what they most needed. So the former slaves—men and women—took matters into their own hands. They met and marched, demanding not just freedom but citizenship and full civil rights, land of their own, and voting rights. Especially in and around large cities such as New Orleans, Mobile, Norfolk, Wilmington, Nashville, Memphis, and Charleston, former slaves organized regular meetings, chose leaders, protested mistreatment, learned the workings of the federal bureaucracy, and sought economic opportunities.

During the summer and fall of 1865, liberated slaves and Northern African Americans ("missionaries") organized freedmen's conventions (sometimes called Equal Rights Associations). Often led by ministers, they met in state capitals "to impress upon the white men," as the Reverend James D. Lynch told the Tennessee freedmen's convention, "that we are part and parcel of the American republic." As such they were eager to counter the whites-only state conventions being organized under Johnson's Reconstruction plan. Virtually all the freedmen's conventions forged resolutions that stressed their desire for free public education, their need for paying jobs and their own land, and their insistence on full civil rights—especially voting rights.

The North Carolina freedmen's convention elected as its president James Walker Hood, a free black from Connecticut. In his acceptance speech, he emphasized their goals: "We and the white people have to live here together. . . . We have been living together for a hundred years and more, and we have got to live together still; and the best way is to harmonize our feelings as much as possible, and to treat all men respectfully." Hood then demanded three constitutional rights for African Americans: the right to testify in courts, serve on juries, and "the right to carry [a] ballot to the ballot box."

In sum, the freedmen's conventions demanded that their voices be heard in Washington and southern state capitals. As the Virginia freedmen's convention asserted, "Any attempt to reconstruct the states . . . without giving to American citizens of African descent all the rights and immunities accorded to white citizens . . . is an act of gross injustice."

THE RADICALS REBEL President Johnson's initial assault on the southern planter elite pleased Radical Republicans, but not for long. The most extreme Radicals, led by Thaddeus Stevens of Pennsylvania and Charles Sumner of Massachusetts, wanted Reconstruction to provide social and political equality for black people. They resented Johnson's efforts to bring the South back into the Union as quickly as possible.

Stevens argued that the Civil War had been fought to produce a "*radical revolution*" in southern life: The "whole fabric of southern society must be changed" to "revolutionize southern institutions, habits, and manners." The Confederate states were, in his view, "conquered provinces" to be readmitted to the Union by the U.S. Congress, not the president. Johnson, however, balked at such an expansion of federal authority. He was committed to the states' rights to control their affairs.

Former Confederates agreed with Johnson. After the war, most white Southerners could not forget the war or their defeat, and they resented and resisted the North's efforts to reconstruct their homeland. As a North Carolinian muttered in 1866, he felt the "bitterest hatred toward the North." He and others wanted to rebuild the new South as it had been before the war, the fabled "Old South," and they were determined to do so in their own way and under their own leadership.

They saw no need for their beloved region to be "reconstructed" by outsiders. As a southern white woman lamented, "Think of all our sacrifices—of broken hearts, and desolated homes—or our *noble, glorious* dead—and say for what? *Reconstruction!* How the very word galls."

So when the U.S. Congress met in December 1865, for the first time since the end of the war, the new southern state governments looked remarkably like the former Confederate governments. Southern voters had refused to extend voting rights to the newly freed slaves. Instead, they had elected former Confederate leaders as their new U.S. senators and congressmen. Georgia, for example, had elected Alexander Stephens, former vice president of the Confederacy.

Across the South, four Confederate generals, eight colonels, six Confederate cabinet members, and several Confederate legislators were also elected. Outraged Republicans denied seats to all such "Rebel" officials and appointed a Joint Committee on Reconstruction to develop a new plan to bring the former Confederate states back into the Union.

The Joint Committee discovered that white violence against blacks was widespread. A former slave in Shreveport, Louisiana, testified that whites still bullwhipped blacks as if they were slaves. He estimated that 2,000 freedpeople had been killed in Shreveport in 1865.

In May and July of 1866, white mobs murdered African Americans in Memphis and New Orleans. General Grant reported that Memphis was "a scene of murder, arson, rape & robbery in which the victims were all helpless and unresisting negroes, stamping lasting disgrace upon the [white] civil authorities that permitted them." Memphis authorities arrested no one responsible for the mayhem.

The massacres, Radical Republicans argued, resulted from Andrew Johnson's lenient policy toward white supremacists. Senator Charles Sumner cried, "Who can doubt that the President is the author of these tragedies?" The race riots helped spur the passage and ratification of the Fourteenth Amendment (1868), extending federal civil rights protections to African Americans.

BLACK CODES The violence against southern blacks was triggered in part by black protests over restrictive laws passed by the new all-white southern state legislatures in 1865 and 1866. These **black codes,** as a white Southerner explained, would ensure "the ex-slave was not a free man; he was a free Negro." A Northerner visiting the South observed that the new black codes would guarantee that "the blacks at large belong to the whites at large."

Black codes varied from state to state. In South Carolina, African Americans were required to remain on their former plantations, forced to labor from dawn to dusk. Mississippi declared that black people could not hunt or fish, making them even more dependent on their white employers.

Some black codes recognized black marriages, but prohibited interracial marriage. The Mississippi codes stipulated that "no white person could intermarry with a freedman, free negro, or mulatto." Violators faced life imprisonment.

The codes also prohibited African Americans from voting, serving on juries, or testifying against whites. They could own property, but they could not own farmland in Mississippi or city property in South Carolina. In Mississippi, every black male over the age of eighteen had to be apprenticed to a white, preferably a former slave owner. Any blacks not apprenticed or employed by January 1866 would be jailed as "vagrants." If they could not pay the vagrancy fine—and most of them could not—they were jailed and forced to work for whites as convict laborers in "chain gangs."

In part, states employed this "convict lease" system as a means of increasing government revenue and cutting the expenses of housing prisoners. At its worst, however, convict leasing was one of the most exploitive labor systems in history, as people convicted of crimes, mostly African Americans who were often falsely accused, were hired out by county and state governments to work for individuals and businesses—coal mines, lumber camps, brickyards, railroads, quarries, mills, and plantations. Convict leasing, in other words, was a thinly disguised form of neo-slavery.

The black codes infuriated Republicans. "We [Republicans] must see to it," Senator William Stewart of Nevada resolved, "that the man made free by the Constitution of the United States is a freeman indeed." And that is what they set out to do.

JOHNSON'S BATTLE WITH CONGRESS Early in 1866, the Radical Republicans openly challenged Andrew Johnson over Reconstruction policies. Johnson started the fight when he vetoed a bill renewing funding for the Freedmen's Bureau. The Republicans could not overturn the veto. Then, on February 22, 1866, Johnson criticized the Radical Republicans for promoting black civil rights. Moderate Republicans thereafter deserted the president and supported the Radicals. Johnson had become "an alien enemy of a foreign state," Thaddeus Stevens declared.

In mid-March 1866, the Radical-led Congress passed the pathbreaking Civil Rights Act, which declared that "all persons born in the United States," including the children of immigrants, but excluding Native Americans, were citizens entitled to "full and equal benefit of all laws."

The legislation infuriated Johnson. Congress, he fumed, could not grant citizenship to blacks, who did not deserve it. Claiming that the proposed Civil

Rights Act discriminated against the "white race," Johnson vetoed it, but this time, on April 6, 1866, Republicans overrode the veto.

It was the first time in history that Congress had overturned a presidential veto of a major bill. From that point on, President Johnson steadily lost both public and political support. A New Yorker noted in his diary that "the feud between Johnson and the 'Radicals' grows more and more deadly every day." General Ulysses S. Grant told his wife that Johnson had become "a national disgrace."

FOURTEENTH AMENDMENT To remove all doubt about the legality of the new Civil Rights Act, Congress passed the **Fourteenth Amendment** to the U.S. Constitution in June 1866. It guaranteed citizenship not just to freemen but also to immigrant children born in the United States. Taking direct aim at the black codes, it also prohibited any efforts to violate the civil rights of "citizens," black or white; to deprive any person "of life, liberty, or property, without due process of law"; or to "deny any person . . . the equal protection of the laws."

With the Fourteenth Amendment, Congress gave the federal government responsibility for protecting (and enforcing) civil rights. The amendment was ratified by three-quarters of the states in 1868. All states in the former Confederacy were required to ratify the amendment before they could be readmitted to the Union and to Congress.

President Johnson urged the southern states to refuse to ratify the amendment. He predicted that the Democrats would win the congressional elections in November and then nix the new amendment. But Johnson was steadily losing support in the North. New York newspaper editor Horace Greeley called Johnson "an aching tooth in the national jaw, a screeching infant in a crowded lecture room."

"(?) Slavery Is Dead (?)" (1867)
Thomas Nast's cartoon argues that southern blacks were still being treated as slaves despite the passage of the Fourteenth Amendment. This detail illustrates a case in Raleigh, North Carolina: a black man was whipped for a crime despite federal orders specifically prohibiting such forms of punishment.

JOHNSON VERSUS RADICALS To win votes for Democratic candidates in the 1866 congressional elections, Johnson went on a speaking tour of the Midwest during which he denounced Radical Republicans as traitors who should be hanged. His partisan speeches backfired, however.

In Cleveland, Ohio, Johnson described the Radical Republicans as "factious, domineering, tyrannical" men, and exchanged hot-tempered insults with a heckler. At another stop, while the president was speaking from the back of a railway car, the engineer mistakenly pulled the train out of the station, making the president appear quite the fool. Republicans charged that such unseemly incidents confirmed Johnson's image as a "ludicrous boor" and a "drunken imbecile."

Voters agreed. The 1866 congressional elections brought a devastating defeat for Johnson and the Democrats; in each house, Radical Republican candidates won more than a two-thirds majority, the margin required to override presidential vetoes. Congressional Republicans would now take over from the president the process of reconstructing the former Confederacy.

CONGRESS TAKES CHARGE On March 2, 1867, Congress passed, over President Johnson's vetoes, the First Reconstruction Act, which included three crucial laws creating what came to be called **Congressional Reconstruction**: the Military Reconstruction Act, the Command of the Army Act, and the Tenure of Office Act.

The Military Reconstruction Act was the capstone of the Congressional Reconstruction plan. It abolished the new governments "in the Rebel States" established under Johnson's lenient Reconstruction policies. In their place, Congress established military control over ten of the eleven former Confederate states. (Tennessee was exempted because it had already ratified the Fourteenth Amendment.) The other ten states were divided into five military districts, each commanded by an army general who acted as governor.

Yet only 10,000 federal troops, mostly African Americans, were expected to police those sprawling "military districts." There were never enough soldiers to enforce Congressional Reconstruction. The entire state of Mississippi, for instance, had fewer than 400 soldiers to ensure compliance.

The Military Reconstruction Act required each former Confederate state to create a new constitution that guaranteed all adult males the right to vote— black or white, rich or poor, landless or property owners. Women—black or white—were still not allowed to vote.

The act also stipulated that the new constitutions were to be drafted by conventions elected by male citizens "of whatever race, color, or previous condition." Once a majority of voters ratified the new constitutions, the state legislatures had to ratify the Fourteenth Amendment; once the amendment became part of the Constitution, the former Confederate states would be entitled to representation in Congress. Several hundred African American delegates participated in the constitutional conventions.

The Command of the Army Act required that the president issue all army orders through General-in-Chief Ulysses S. Grant. (The Radicals feared that President Johnson would appoint anti-black generals to head the military districts who would be too lenient toward whites who defied efforts to "reconstruct" the South.)

The Tenure of Office Act stipulated that the Senate must approve any presidential effort to remove federal officials whose appointments the Senate had confirmed. Radicals intended this act to prevent Johnson from firing Secretary of War Edwin Stanton, the president's most outspoken critic in the cabinet.

Congressional Reconstruction embodied the most sweeping peacetime legislation in American history to that point. It sought to ensure that freed slaves could participate in the creation of new state governments in the former Confederacy. As Thaddeus Stevens explained, the Congressional Reconstruction plan would create a "perfect republic" based on the principle of *equal rights* for all citizens. "This is the promise of America," he insisted. "No More. No Less."

IMPEACHING THE PRESIDENT The first two years of Congressional Reconstruction produced dramatic changes in the South, as new state legislatures rewrote their constitutions and ratified the Fourteenth Amendment. Radical Republicans now seemed fully in control of Reconstruction, but one person still stood in their way—Andrew Johnson. During 1867 and early 1868, more and more Radicals decided that the president must be removed from office.

Johnson himself opened the door to **impeachment** (the formal process by which Congress charges the president with "high crimes and misdemeanors") when, in violation of the Tenure of Office Act, he fired Secretary of War Edwin Stanton, who had refused to resign from the cabinet despite his harsh criticism of the president's Reconstruction policy. Johnson, who considered the Tenure of Office Act an illegal restriction of presidential power, fired Stanton on August 12, 1867, and replaced him with Ulysses S. Grant.

The Radicals now saw their chance. By removing Stanton without congressional approval, Johnson had violated the Tenure of Office Act.

On February 24, 1868, the Republican-dominated House passed nine articles of impeachment (that is, specific charges against the president), most of which dealt with Stanton's firing and all of which were flimsy (two more

Trial of Andrew Johnson In this *Harper's Weekly* illustration, Johnson is seated at the center of the foreground among his defense committee. The galleries of the Senate are packed with men and women watching the trial.

charges were added later). In reality, the essential grievance against the president was that he had opposed the policies of the Radical Republicans. According to Secretary of the Navy Gideon Welles, Radicals were so angry at Johnson that they "would have tried to remove him had he been accused of stepping on a dog's tail."

The first Senate trial of a sitting president began on March 5, 1868. It was a dramatic spectacle before a packed gallery of journalists, foreign dignitaries, and political officials. Newspaper reporters clogged the halls. As the proceedings began, acid-tongued Stevens warned the president: "Unfortunate, unhappy man, behold your doom!"

The five-week trial came to a stunning end when the Senate voted 35–19 for conviction, only *one* vote short of the two-thirds needed for removal. Senator Edmund G. Ross, a young Radical from Kansas, cast the deciding vote in favor of acquittal, knowing that his vote would ruin his political career. He had decided that the evidence against Johnson was both insufficient for conviction and overtly partisan. "I almost literally looked down into my open grave," Ross explained afterward. "Friendships, position, fortune, everything that makes life desirable . . . were about to be swept away by the breath of my mouth."

Angry Radicals thereafter shunned Ross. He lost his reelection campaign and died in near poverty.

In the end, the effort to remove Johnson was a grave political mistake, for it weakened public support for Congressional Reconstruction. The Richmond *Daily Dispatch* stressed that Johnson's acquittal was "a terrible rebuke on the Radical party, and diminished its physical support (it never had any other)." Nevertheless, the Radical cause did gain Johnson's private agreement to stop obstructing Congressional Reconstruction. (He would later break his word by turning a deaf ear to pleas for federal support in suppressing Klan violence.)

General Grant urged Johnson to let him exert more federal force in the South. To that end, he forwarded to the president a letter from a Tennessee legislator that documented gangs of whites "scouring the country by night—causing dismay & terror to all—Our civil authorities are powerless." Johnson declared that it was a local issue. Federal troops should stay out of it.

Grant refused to take no for an answer. He continued to barrage Johnson with fresh evidence of white efforts to terrorize freedpeople. "If Civil Government fails to protect the Citizen," Grant argued, "Military government should supply its place."

REPUBLICAN RULE IN THE SOUTH In June 1868, congressional Republicans announced that eight southern states could again send delegates to Congress. The remaining former Confederate states—Virginia, Mississippi, and Texas—were readmitted in 1870, with the added requirement that they ratify the **Fifteenth Amendment**, which would give voting rights to African American men. As Frederick Douglass, himself a former slave, had declared in 1865, "slavery is not abolished until the black man has the ballot."

The Fifteenth Amendment prohibited states from denying a citizen's right to vote on grounds of "race, color, or previous condition of servitude." But Susan B. Anthony and Elizabeth Cady Stanton, leaders of the movement to secure voting rights for women, insisted that the amendment should have included women. As Anthony stressed in a famous speech, the U.S. Constitution refers to: "We, the people; not we, the white male citizens; nor yet we, the male citizens; but we, the whole people, who formed the Union—women as well as men."

Radical Republicans tried to deflect the issue by declaring that it was the "Negro's hour." Women, both black and white, would have to wait—another fifty years for voting rights, as it turned out.

The Fifteenth Amendment ignited a violent backlash in the South. The idea of the federal government guaranteeing the right of freedmen to vote deepened resentment of Reconstruction. In Georgia, white officials devised new ways to restrict black voting, such as poll taxes and onerous registration procedures. Other states followed suit.

Four months after the Fifteenth Amendment became the law of the land, Congress also passed the Naturalization Act of 1870. For the first time, it extended the process whereby immigrants had gained citizenship to include *"aliens of African nativity and to persons of African descent."* Efforts to include Asians and Native Americans in the new naturalization law were defeated, however.

BLACK LIFE UNDER RECONSTRUCTION

When a federal official asked Garrison Frazier, a former Georgia slave, if he and others wanted to live among whites, Frazier said that they preferred "to live by ourselves, for there is a prejudice against us in the South that will take years to get over." In forging new lives, Frazier and many other former slaves set about creating their own social institutions.

FREED BUT NOT EQUAL African Americans were active agents in affecting the course of Reconstruction. It was not an easy process, however, because whites, both northern and southern, still practiced racism. A northern journalist traveling in the South after the war reported that the "whites seem wholly unable to comprehend that freedom for the negro means the same thing as freedom for them."

Once the excitement of freedom wore off, most southern blacks realized that their best chance to make a living was by working for pay for their former owners. In fact, the Freedmen's Bureau and federal soldiers urged and even ordered them to sign labor contracts with local whites. Many planters, however, conspired to control the amount of wages paid to freedmen. "It seems humiliating to be compelled to bargain and haggle with our own servants about wages," complained a white planter's daughter.

A Man Knows A Man A black soldier for the Union with an amputated leg clasps hands with a white amputee in this 1865 cartoon. The caption read: "Give me your hand, comrade! We have each lost a leg for the good cause; but, thank God, we never lost heart."

White Southerners also used terror, intimidation, and violence to suppress black efforts to gain social and economic equality. In many respects, the war had not ended, as armed men organized to thwart federal efforts to reconstruct the South. In July 1866, a black woman in Clinch County, Georgia, was arrested and given sixty-five lashes for "using abusive language" during an encounter with a white woman. The Civil War brought freedom to enslaved African Americans, but it did not bring them protection against exploitation or abuse.

After emancipation, Union soldiers and northern observers often expressed surprise that the freed slaves did not leave the South. But why would they leave what they knew so well? As a group of African Americans explained, they did not want to abandon "land they had laid their fathers' bones upon." A Union officer noted that southern blacks seemed "more attached to familiar places" than any other group in the nation.

Participation in the Union army or navy had given many freedmen training in leadership. Indeed, black military veterans would form the core of the first generation of African American political leaders in the postwar South. Military service also gave many former slaves their first opportunities to learn to read and write and alerted them to new possibilities for economic advancement, social respectability, and civic leadership. In addition, fighting for the Union cause instilled a fervent sense of nationalism. A Virginia freedman explained that the United States was "now *our* country—made emphatically so by the blood of our brethren."

BLACK CHURCHES AND SCHOOLS African American religious life in the South was transformed during and after the war. Many former slaves identified with the biblical Hebrews, who were led out of slavery into the "promised land." Emancipation demonstrated that God was on *their* side. Before the war, slaves who attended white churches were forced to sit in the back. After the war, with the help of many northern Christian missionaries, both black and white, ex-slaves established their own churches that became the crossroads for black community life.

Ministers emerged as social and political leaders. One could not be a real minister, one of them claimed, without looking "out for the political interests of his people." Many African Americans became Baptists or Methodists, in part because these were already the largest denominations in the South, and in part because Baptists and Methodists reached out to the working poor. In 1866 alone, the African Methodist Episcopal (AME) Church gained 50,000 members. By 1890, more than 1.3 million African Americans in the South had become Baptists, nearly three times as many as had joined any other denomination.

The First African Church On the eve of its move to a new building, the First African Church of Richmond, Virginia, was featured in a short article, including illustrations such as this one, in *Harper's Weekly*, in June 1874.

African American communities also rushed to establish schools. Starting schools, said a former slave, was the "first proof" of freedom. Before the Civil War, most plantation owners had denied an education to their slaves to keep them from reading abolitionist literature and organizing uprisings. After the war, the white elite worried that education would distract poor whites and blacks from their work in the fields or encourage them to leave the South in search of better social and economic opportunities.

The opposition of southern whites to education for blacks made public schools all the more important to African Americans. South Carolina's Mary McLeod Bethune rejoiced in the opportunity: "The whole world opened to me when I learned to read." She walked five miles to school as a child, earned a scholarship to college, and went on to become the first black woman to found a school that became a four-year college: Bethune-Cookman University, in Daytona Beach, Florida.

POLITICS AND AFRICAN AMERICANS With many ex-Confederates denied voting rights, new African American voters helped elect some 600 blacks—most of them former slaves—as state legislators under Congressional Reconstruction. In Louisiana, Pinckney Pinchback, a northern free black and former Union soldier, was elected lieutenant governor. Several other African Americans were elected to high state offices. There were two black senators in Congress, Hiram Revels and Blanche K. Bruce, both Mississippi natives who had been educated in the North, while fourteen black congressmen served in the U.S. House of Representatives.

The election of black politicians appalled southern whites. Democrats claimed that Radicals were trying to "organize a hell in the South" by putting "the Caucasian race" under the rule of "their own negroes." Southern whites complained that freed slaves were illiterate and had no civic experience or appreciation of political issues and processes. In this regard, however, blacks were no different from millions of poor or immigrant white males who had been voting and serving in office for years.

Some freedmen frankly confessed their disadvantages. Beverly Nash, an African American delegate to the South Carolina convention of 1868, told his colleagues, "We are not prepared for this suffrage [the vote]. But we can learn. Give a man tools and let him commence to use them, and in time he will learn a trade. So it is with voting."

African American political figures of Reconstruction Blanche K. Bruce (left) and Hiram Revels (right) served in the U.S. Senate. Frederick Douglass (center) was a major figure in the abolitionist movement.

LAND, LABOR, AND DISAPPOINTMENT Many ex-slaves argued that what they needed most was land. A New Englander traveling in the postwar South noted that the "sole ambition of the freedman" was "to become the owner of a little piece of land, there to erect a humble home, and to dwell in peace and security at his own free will and pleasure."

In several southern states, former slaves had been "given" land by Union armies after they had taken control of Confederate areas during the war. Andrew Johnson, however, reversed such transfers of white-owned property to former slaves. In South Carolina, the Union general responsible for evicting former slaves urged them to "lay aside their bitter feelings, and become reconciled to their old masters." But the assembled freedmen shouted "No, never!" and "Can't do it!" They knew that ownership of land was the foundation of their freedom. They may have had no deeds or titles for the land they now worked, but it had been "earned by the sweat of *our* brows," said a group of Alabama freedmen. "Our wives, our children, our husbands, has been sold over and over again to purchase the lands we now locates on," a Virginia freedman noted. "Didn't we clear the land and raise de crops? We have a right to [that] land."

Thousands of former slaves were forced to return their farms to white owners. In addition, it was virtually impossible for former slaves to get loans to buy farmland because few banks were willing to lend to blacks. Their sense of betrayal was profound. An ex-slave in Mississippi said that he and others were left with nothing: "no *land*, no *house*, not so much as a place to lay our head."

As former slaves were stripped of their land, they had little choice but to become farmworkers under a new system: **sharecropping**. White landowners would provide land, seed, and tools to poor laborers in exchange for a *share* of the crop. This essentially re-enslaved the workers because, as a federal army officer said, no matter "how much they are abused, they cannot leave without permission of the owner." If they left, they would forfeit their portion of the crop. Workers who violated the terms of the contract could be evicted from the plantation, leaving them jobless and homeless—and subject to arrest. Across the former Confederacy, the growth of

Sharecroppers A family is shown outside their Virginia home in this 1899 photograph, taken by Frances Benjamin Johnston, one of the earliest American female photojournalists.

sharecropping revealed that most white plantation owners and small farmers were determined to control African Americans as if they were still enslaved. And if bad weather or insects or disease stunted the harvest, it pushed the sharecropper only deeper in debt.

Many freed blacks preferred sharecropping over working for wages, since it freed them from day-to-day supervision by white landowners. Over time, however, most sharecroppers, black and white, found themselves trapped, deep in debt to the landowner, with little choice but to remain tied to the same discouraging system of dependence that, over the years, felt much like slavery. As a former slave acknowledged, he and others had discovered that "freedom could make folks proud but it didn't make 'em rich."

TENSIONS AMONG SOUTHERN BLACKS African Americans in the postwar South were by no means a uniform community. They had their own differences and disputes, especially between the few who owned property and the many who did not. In North Carolina, for example, less than 7 percent of black people owned land by 1870.

Affluent northern blacks and the southern free black elite, most of whom were city dwellers and "mulattos" (people of mixed racial parentage), often opposed efforts to redistribute land to the freedmen, and many insisted that political equality did not mean social equality. As an African American leader in Alabama stressed, "We do not ask that the ignorant and degraded shall be put on a social equality with the refined and intelligent." In general, however, unity prevailed, and African Americans focused on common concerns. "All we ask," said a black member of the state constitutional convention in Mississippi, "is justice, and to be treated like human beings."

BLACKS IN POLITICS Many African Americans served in state governments with distinction. Nonetheless, the scornful label "black Reconstruction," used by critics then and since, distorts African American political influence. Such criticism also overlooks the political clout of the large number of white Republicans, especially in the mountain areas of the Upper South, who also favored the Radical plan for Reconstruction.

Only South Carolina's Republican state convention had a black majority. Louisiana's was evenly divided racially, and in only two other state conventions were more than 20 percent of the members black: Florida and Virginia. The Texas convention was only 10 percent black, and North Carolina's was 11 percent—which did not stop a white newspaper from calling it a group of "baboons, monkeys, mules . . . and other jackasses."

Freedmen voting in New Orleans The Fifteenth Amendment, ratified in 1870, guaranteed at the federal level the right of citizens to vote regardless of "race, color, or previous condition of servitude." But former slaves had been registering to vote—and voting in large numbers—in some state elections since 1867, as in this scene.

"CARPETBAGGERS" AND "SCALAWAGS" Unreconstructed white Southerners dismissed whites who served in the new Republican southern state governments as "carpetbaggers" or "scalawags." Carpetbaggers, critics argued, were the 30,000 scheming Northerners, mostly young men, who rushed South with their belongings in cheap suitcases made of carpeting ("carpetbags") to grab political power or buy plantations.

Some of the Northerners who migrated south were corrupt opportunists. However, most were Union military veterans drawn to the South by the desire to rebuild the region's devastated economy. Many other so-called carpetbaggers were teachers, social workers, attorneys, physicians, editors, and ministers motivated by a genuine desire to help free blacks and poor whites improve their lives.

For example, Union general Adelbert Ames, who won the Medal of Honor, stayed in the South after the war because he felt a "sense of Mission with a large M" to help former slaves develop healthy communities. He served as the military governor of Mississippi before being elected a Republican U.S. senator in 1870.

Southern Democrats especially hated the scalawags, or southern white Republicans, calling them traitors to their region. A Nashville newspaper editor

Carpetbagger The cartoonist's caption to this critique of carpetbaggers reads: "The bag in front of him, filled with others' faults, he always sees. The one behind him, filled with his own faults, he never sees."

described them as the "merest trash." Most scalawags had been Unionists opposed to secession. They were prominent in the mountain counties of Georgia, Tennessee, and Alabama. Among the scalawags were several distinguished figures, including former Confederate general James Longstreet, who decided that the Old South must change its ways. He became a successful cotton broker in New Orleans, joined the Republican party, and supported Radical Reconstruction.

Another unlikely scalawag was Joseph E. Brown, the Confederate governor of Georgia, who urged Southerners to support Republicans because they were the only source of economic investment in the devastated region. What the scalawags had in common was a willingness to work with Republicans to rebuild the southern economy.

SOUTHERN RESISTANCE AND WHITE "REDEMPTION"

Most southern whites viewed secession as a noble "lost cause." They used all means possible—legal and illegal—to "redeem" their beloved South from northern control, Republican rule, and black equality. An Alabama planter admitted that southern whites simply "can't learn to treat the freedmen like human beings."

White southern ministers assured their congregations that God endorsed white supremacy. In an attempt to reunite the Protestant denominations of the North and South, many northern religionists became "apostles of forgiveness" for their southern white brethren. Even abolitionists such as the Reverend Henry Ward Beecher, whose sister Harriet Beecher Stowe had written *Uncle Tom's Cabin* (1857), called for southern whites—rather than federal officials or African Americans themselves—to govern the South after the war.

With each passing year during Reconstruction, African Americans suffered increasing exploitation and abuse. The black codes created by white state governments in 1865 and 1866 were the first of many efforts to deny equality. Southern whites disrupted black Republican meetings, targeted black and

RECONSTRUCTION, 1865–1877

States with Reconstruction governments
1868 Date of readmission to the Union
1870 Date of reestablishment of conservative Democratic rule
2 Military districts set up by the Reconstruction Act of 1867
Means by which Slavery was Abolished
▲ Emancipation Proclamation, 1863
■ State action
◆ Thirteenth Amendment, 1865

- How did the Military Reconstruction Act reorganize governments in the South in the late 1860s and 1870s?
- What did the former Confederate states have to do to be readmitted to the Union?
- Why did "Conservative" white parties gradually regain control of the South from the Republicans in the 1870s?

white Republican leaders for beatings or killings, and, in general, prevented blacks from exercising their political rights. Hundreds were killed across the South and many more injured in systematic efforts to "keep blacks in their place," as whites repeatedly explained.

In Texas, a white farmer, D. B. Whitesides, told a former slave named Charles Brown that his newfound freedom would do him "damned little good . . . as I intend to shoot you"—which he did, shooting Brown in the chest as he tried to flee. Whitesides then rode his horse beside Brown and asked, "I got you, did I Brown?" "Yes," a bleeding Brown replied. "You got me good." Whitesides yelled that the wound would teach "niggers [like you] to put on airs because you are free."

"Worse Than Slavery" This Thomas Nast cartoon condemns the Ku Klux Klan for promoting conditions "worse than slavery" for southern blacks after the Civil War.

Such ugly incidents revealed a harsh truth: the death of slavery did not mean the birth of true freedom for African Americans. For a growing number of southern whites, resistance to Radical Reconstruction became more and more violent. Several secret terrorist groups, including the Ku Klux Klan, the Knights of the White Camelia, the White Line, and the White League emerged to harass, intimidate, and even kill African Americans.

The **Ku Klux Klan** (KKK) was formed in 1866 in Pulaski, Tennessee. The name *Ku Klux* was derived from the Greek word *kuklos*, meaning "circle" or "band"; *Klan* came from the English word *clan*, or family. The Klan, and other groups like it, began initially as a social club, with spooky costumes and secret rituals. But its members, most of them former Confederate soldiers, soon began harassing blacks and white Republicans. General Philip Sheridan, who supervised the district that included Louisiana and Texas, said that Klansmen were terrorists intent on suppressing black political participation.

These groups' motives varied—anger over the Confederate defeat, resentment against federal soldiers occupying the South, complaints about having to pay black workers, and an almost paranoid fear that former slaves might seek revenge against whites. Klansmen marauded at night on horseback, spreading rumors, issuing threats, and burning schools and churches. "We are going to kill all the Negroes," a white supremacist declared during one massacre.

THE LEGACY OF CONGRESSIONAL RECONSTRUCTION

One by one, the Republican state governments were overturned. Yet they left behind an important accomplishment: the new constitutions they created remained in effect for years, and later constitutions incorporated many of their most progressive features.

Some of the significant innovations brought about by the Republican state governments protected black voting rights and restructured legislatures to reflect shifting populations. More state offices were changed from appointed to elective positions to weaken the "good old boy" tradition of rewarding political supporters with state government jobs.

In South Carolina, former Confederate leaders opposed the Republican state legislature not simply because of its black members but because poor whites were also enjoying political clout for the first time, thereby threatening the dominance of wealthy white plantation owners and merchants.

Given the hostile circumstances under which Republican state governments operated in the South, their achievements were remarkable. They rebuilt an extensive railroad network and established public school systems funded by state governments and open to all children, although the buildings were segregated by race. Some 600,000 black pupils had enrolled in southern schools by 1877.

The Radicals also gave more attention to the poor and to orphanages, asylums, and institutions for the deaf and blind of both races. Much needed infrastructure—roads, bridges, and buildings—was repaired or rebuilt. African Americans achieved rights and opportunities that would repeatedly be violated in coming decades but would never completely be taken away, at least in principle, such as equality before the law and the rights to own property, attend schools, learn to read and write, enter professions, and carry on business.

Yet government officials also engaged in corrupt practices. Bribes and kickbacks, whereby companies received government contracts in return for giving government officials cash or stock, were commonplace. In Louisiana, a twenty-six-year-old carpetbagger, Henry Clay Warmoth, somehow turned an annual salary of $8,000 into a million-dollar fortune during his four years as governor. (He was eventually impeached and removed from office.) "I don't pretend to be honest," he admitted. "I only pretend to be as honest as anybody in politics."

As was true in the North and the Midwest, southern state governments awarded money to corporations, notably railroads, under conditions that invited shady dealings and outright corruption. Some railroad corporations received state funds but never built railroads, and bribery was rampant. But the Radical Republican regimes did not invent such corruption, nor did it die with them. Governor Warmoth recognized as much: "Corruption is the fashion" in Louisiana, he explained.

THE GRANT ADMINISTRATION

Andrew Johnson's crippled presidency created an opportunity for Republicans to elect one of their own in 1868. Both parties wooed Ulysses S. Grant, the "Lion of Vicksburg" credited by most with the Union victory in the Civil War. His falling-out with President Johnson, however, had pushed him toward the Republicans, who unanimously nominated him as their presidential candidate.

THE ELECTION OF 1868 The Republican party platform endorsed Congressional Reconstruction. More important, however, were the public expectations driving the candidacy of Ulysses S. Grant, whose slogan was "Let us have peace." Grant promised that, if elected, he would enforce the laws and promote prosperity for all.

"This is a white man's country," the Democrats claimed, so "let white men rule." They charged that the Radical Republicans were subjecting the South "to military despotism and Negro supremacy." They nominated Horatio Seymour, the wartime governor of New York and a passionate critic of Congressional Reconstruction, who dismissed the Emancipation Proclamation as "a proposal for the butchery of women and children." His running mate, Francis P. Blair Jr., a former Union general from Missouri who had served in Congress, attacked Grant for exercising military tyranny "over the eight millions of white people in the South, fixed to the earth with his bayonets." An unapologetic racist, Blair denounced Republicans for promoting equality for "a semi-barbarous race" who sought to "subject the white women to their unbridled lust." This belief that black men were sexual predators lying in wait for white women was a false stereotype throughout the South with horrifying consequences: it was often used as a justification for lynchings.

"The Working-Man's Banner" This campaign banner makes reference to the working-class origins of Ulysses S. Grant and his vice-presidential candidate, Henry Wilson, by depicting Grant as a tanner of hides and Wilson as a shoemaker.

A Democrat later said that Blair's "stupid and indefensible" remarks cost Seymour a close election. Grant won all but eight states and swept the electoral college, 214–80, but his popular majority was only 307,000 out of almost 6 million votes. More than 500,000 African American voters, mostly in the South, accounted for Grant's margin of victory (he won only a minority of white votes nationwide), and many of them risked their lives supporting him. Klan violence soared during the campaigning, and hundreds of freedpeople paid with their lives. Still, the efforts of Radical Republicans to ensure voting rights for southern blacks had paid off. As Frederick Douglass explained, "the Republican party is the ship and all else is the sea" as far as black voters were concerned.

Grant, the youngest president up to that time (forty-six years old at his inauguration), was a courageous defender of Congressional Reconstruction, but he was not a great president. He later admitted that he took office "without any previous experience either in civil or political life. I thought I could run the government of the United States as I did the staff of my army. It was my mistake, and it led me into other mistakes."

Grant passively followed the lead of Congress and was often blind to the political forces and self-serving influence peddlers around him. He showed poor judgment in his selection of cabinet members, often favoring friendship, family, loyalty, and military service over integrity and ability.

During his two terms in office, his seven cabinet positions changed twenty-four times. Some of the men betrayed his trust and engaged in criminal behavior. His former comrade in arms and close friend, General William T. Sherman, said he felt sorry for Grant because so many supposedly "loyal" Republicans used the president for their own selfish gains. Carl Schurz, a Union war hero who became a Republican senator from Missouri, expressed frustration that Grant was misled by cunning advisers who "prostituted" his administration.

Yet Grant excelled at bringing diversity to the federal government. During his two presidential terms, he appointed more African Americans, Native Americans, Jews, and women than any of his predecessors, and he fulfilled his campaign pledge to bring the nation "peace and prosperity."

THE FIFTEENTH AMENDMENT President Grant viewed Reconstruction of the South as the nation's top priority, and he doggedly insisted that freedpeople be allowed to exercise their civil rights without fear of violence. On March 30, 1870, Grant delivered a speech to Congress in which he celebrated the ratification of the Fifteenth Amendment, which gave voting rights to African American men nationwide. "It was," he declared, "...the most important event that has occurred since the nation came into life...the realization of the Declaration of Independence." Frederick Douglass appreciated Grant's efforts: "To Grant, more than any other man, the Negro owes his enfranchisement."

But the Fifteenth Amendment ignited a violent backlash in the South. The idea of the federal government guaranteeing the right of freedmen to vote deepened resentment of Reconstruction. In Georgia, white officials devised new ways to restrict black voting, such as poll taxes and onerous registration procedures. Other states followed suit.

Four months after the Fifteenth Amendment became the law of the land, Congress also passed the Naturalization Act of 1870. For the first time, it extended the process whereby immigrants had gained citizenship to include *"aliens of African nativity and to persons of African descent."* Efforts to include Asians and Native Americans in the new naturalization law were defeated, however.

THE UNION LEAGUE The Fifteenth Amendment had enormous political consequences. Southern whites feared nothing more than black voters, while Republicans were eager to recruit them. To do so, Republicans organized Union Leagues throughout the former Confederacy. Republicans had founded the Union League (also called the Loyal League) in 1862 to rally voters behind Lincoln, the war, and the party. By late 1863, the league claimed more than 700,000 members in 4,554 councils across the nation.

In the postwar South, the leagues operated like fraternities, with formal initiations and rituals and secret meetings to protect the freedpeople from being persecuted by angry white Democrats. They met in churches, schools, homes, and fields, often hearing from northern speakers who traveled the South extolling the Republican party and encouraging blacks to register and vote. By the early 1870s, the Union League in the South had become one of the largest black social movements in history. With the help of the Union Leagues, some 90 percent of southern freedmen registered to vote, almost all of them as Republicans, and they voted in record numbers (often as high as 80–90 percent). In Mississippi and South Carolina, black registered voters outnumbered whites.

Voting was not easy for freedmen, however, because most white Southerners were eager to deny them the vote. "All the blacks who vote against my ticket shall walk the plank," threatened former Georgia governor Howell Cobb, a Democrat who had been a Confederate general. Angry whites persecuted, evicted, or fired African American workers who "exercised their political rights," as a Union officer reported from Virginia.

Black Republicans were at times equally coercive. "The Negroes are as intolerant of opposition as the whites," a white South Carolina Democrat observed. They shunned, expelled, and even killed any "of their own" who "would turn democrats." He added that freedwomen were as partisan as the men—and as intolerant of opposition: the "women are worse than the men, refusing to talk to or marry a renegade [black Democrat], and aiding [men] in mobbing him."

Yet the net result of the Union Leagues was the mobilization of African American voters whose numbers enabled black men to win elected offices for the first time in the states of the former Confederacy. Francis Cardozo, a black minister who served as president of the South Carolina Council of Union Leagues, declared in 1870 that the state had "prospered in every respect" as a result of the enfranchisement of black voters enabled by the Union Leagues.

INDIAN POLICY President Grant was almost as progressive in his outlook toward Native Americans as he was toward African Americans. In 1869, he appointed General Ely Parker, a Seneca chief trained as an attorney and engineer, as the new Commissioner of Indian Affairs, the first Native American to hold the position.

Parker had served as Grant's military secretary during the war. Now, as commissioner, Parker faced formidable challenges in creating policies for the 300,000 Indians across the nation, many of whom continued to be pressured by white settlers, miners, railroads, and telegraph companies to give up their ancestral lands.

Working with Parker, Grant created a new Peace Policy toward Native Americans. "The Indians," he observed, "require as much protection from the whites as the white does from the Indians." He did not want the army "shooting these poor savages; I want to conciliate them and make them peaceful citizens." His own experiences had shown that the "Indian problem" was in fact the result of "bad whites." Grant believed that lasting peace could only result from Indians abandoning their nomadic tradition and relocating to government reservations, where federal troops would provide them "absolute protection."

Grant also promised to end the chronic corruption whereby congressmen appointed cronies as licensed government traders with access to the Indian reservations. Many of the traders used their positions to swindle the Native Americans out of the federally supplied food, clothing, and other provisions intended solely for the reservations. One of the accused traders was the president's brother.

To clean up the so-called Indian Ring, Grant moved the Bureau of Indian Affairs out of the control of Congress and into the War Department. He also created a ten-man Board of Indian Commissioners, a new civilian agency whose mission was to oversee the operations of the Bureau of Indian Affairs to ensure that corruption was rooted out. Grant then appointed Quakers as reservation traders, assuming that their honesty, humility, and pacifism would improve the distribution of government resources. "If you can make Quakers out of the Indians," Grant told them, "it will take the fight out of them. Let us have peace." Yet Quakers proved no more able to manage Indian policy than government bureaucrats could.

Like other presidents, Grant discovered that there often emerged a gap between the policies he created and the implementation of them by others. Many of the officers and soldiers sent to the West to "pacify" Indian peoples in the Great Plains displayed an attitude toward Native Americans quite different from Grant's. For example, it was General Philip Sheridan who coined the infamous statement: "The only good Indians I know are dead." He dismissed Indians as "the enemies of our race and of our civilization" and called for a campaign of "annihilation." Native Americans who refused to move to government-mandated reservations should be killed, he argued. General William T. Sherman agreed. He stressed to Sheridan that "the more [Indians] we kill this year, the less we would have to kill next year."

Such attitudes led the abolitionist Wendell Phillips to ask why Indians were one of the only groups still denied citizenship. His answer was clear: "The great poison of the age is race hatred" directed at both African Americans and Native Americans. Most white Americans, however, did not care that racism was at work. "Wendell Phillips' new nigger," the editors of the *New York Herald* observed with disdain, "is the 'noble red man.'" Phillips responded, "We shall never be able to be just to other races . . . until we 'unlearn' contempt" for others different from us.

SCANDALS President Grant's naive trust in people led his administration to stumble into a cesspool of scandal. Perhaps because of his own disastrous efforts as a storekeeper and farmer before the Civil War, Grant was awestruck by men of wealth. As they lavished gifts and attention on him, he was lured into their webs of self-serving deception.

In the summer of 1869, two unprincipled financial schemers, Jay Gould and James Fisk Jr., both infamous for bribing politicians and judges, plotted with Abel Corbin, the president's brother-in-law, to "corner" (manipulate) the nation's gold market. They intended to create a public craze for gold by purchasing massive quantities of the precious metal to drive up its value.

The only danger to the complicated scheme lay in the possibility that the federal Treasury would burst the bubble by selling large amounts of its gold, which would deflate its market value. When Grant was seen in public with Gould and Fisk, people assumed that he supported their scheme. As the false rumor spread in New York City's financial district that the president endorsed the run-up in gold, its value soared.

On September 24, 1869—soon to be remembered mournfully as Black Friday—the Gould-Fisk scheme worked, at least for a while. Starting at $150 an ounce, the price of gold rose, first to $160, then $165, leading more and more investors to join the stampede.

Then, around noon, Grant and his Treasury secretary realized what was happening and began selling government gold. Within fifteen minutes, the price plummeted to $138. Schemers lost fortunes amid the chaotic trading. Some ruined traders wept. One fainted, and still another felt the need to commit suicide. Soon the turmoil spread to the entire stock market, claiming thousands of victims. As Fisk noted, each man was left to "drag out his own corpse."

For weeks after the gold bubble collapsed, financial markets were paralyzed and business confidence was shaken. Congressman James Garfield wrote privately to a friend that President Grant had compromised his office by his "indiscreet acceptance" of gifts from Fisk and Gould and that any investigation of Black Friday would lead "into the parlor of the President." One critic announced that U.S. Grant's initials actually stood for "uniquely stupid."

The plot to corner the gold market was only the first of several scandals that rocked the Grant administration. The secretary of war, it turned out, had accepted bribes from merchants who traded with Indians at army posts in the West. And in St. Louis, whiskey distillers bribed federal Treasury agents in an effort to avoid paying excise taxes on alcohol. Grant's personal secretary participated in the scheme, taking secret payments in exchange for confidential information. Grant, spotlessly honest himself, urged Congress to investigate. "Let no guilty man escape," he stressed. "No personal considerations should stand in the way of performing a public duty."

Various congressional committees uncovered no evidence that Grant was personally involved. His poor choice of associates, however, earned him widespread criticism. Democrats scolded Republicans for their "monstrous corruption and extravagance" and reinforced public suspicion that elected officials were less servants of the people than they were self-serving bandits.

LIBERAL REPUBLICANS With the end of slavery, the Republican party lost its cohesion. Disputes over political corruption and the fate of Reconstruction helped divide Republicans into two warring factions: the Liberals (or Conscience Republicans) and Stalwarts (or Grant Republicans). Liberal Republicans, led by Senator Carl Schurz, embraced free trade and opposed any government regulation of business and industry while championing gold coins as the only reliable currency.

Liberal Republicans thirsted to oust the "tyrannical" Grant from the presidency and end Reconstruction. They wanted to lower the tariffs lining the pockets of big corporations and promote "civil service reforms" to end the "partisan tyranny" of the "patronage system" whereby new presidents rewarded the "selfish greed" of political supporters with federal government jobs.

Liberal Republicans charged that Grant and his cronies were pursuing policies and making decisions solely to benefit themselves. They also opposed Grant's efforts to suppress racism and Ku Klux Klan terrorism. As the *Nation* magazine stressed, "Everybody is heartily tired of discussing [the Negro's] rights." They believed there was no more need for federal intervention in the South. "The removal of white prejudice against the negro depends almost entirely on the negro himself" rather than the presence of federal troops. The abolitionist leader Wendell Phillips was horrified by the possibility that Liberal Republicans might oust Grant, for to him their party was "nothing but Ku-Klux-Klanism disguised."

THE 1872 ELECTION In 1872, the breakaway Liberal Republicans, many of whom were elitist newspaper editors suspicious of the "working classes," held their own national convention in Cincinnati, during which they accused the Grant administration of corruption, incompetence, and "despotism." They then committed political suicide by nominating Horace Greeley, the editor of the *New York Tribune* and a longtime champion of causes ranging from abolitionism, socialism, vegetarianism, and spiritualism (communicating with the dead).

E. L. Godkin, the editor of the *Nation* magazine and a Liberal Republican sympathizer, could not imagine voting for Greeley, whom he dismissed as "a conceited, ignorant, half-cracked, obstinate old creature." Greeley's image as an eccentric who repeatedly reversed his political positions was matched by his record of hostility to Democrats, whose support the Liberal Republicans needed if they were to win.

Southern Democrats, however, liked Greeley's criticism of Reconstruction. His newspaper, for example, claimed that "ignorant, superstitious, semi-barbarian" former slaves were "extremely indolent, and will make no exertion beyond what is necessary to obtain food enough to satisfy their hunger." Moreover, Radical Republicans had given the vote to "ignorant" former slaves whose "Nigger Government" exercised "absolute political supremacy" in several states and was transferring wealth from the "most intelligent" and "influential" southern whites to themselves.

Most Northerners, however, were appalled at Greeley's candidacy. By nominating Greeley, said the *New York Times*, the Liberal Republicans and Democrats had killed any chance of electoral victory.

In the 1872 balloting, Greeley carried only six southern states and none in the North. Grant won thirty-one states and tallied 3,598,235 votes to Greeley's 2,834,761. An exhausted Greeley confessed that he was "the worst beaten man who ever ran for high office." His wife died six days before the election, and he died three weeks later.

Grant was delighted that the "soreheads and thieves who had deserted the Republican party" were defeated, and he promised to avoid the "mistakes" he had made in his first term.

THE MONEY SUPPLY Complex financial issues—especially monetary policy—dominated Grant's second term. Prior to the Civil War, the economy operated on a gold standard; state banks issued paper money that could be exchanged for an equal value of gold coins. So both gold coins and state bank notes circulated as currency. **Greenbacks** (so called because of the dye color used on the printed dollars) were issued by the federal Treasury during the Civil War to help pay for the war.

When a nation's supply of money grows faster than the economy itself, prices for goods and services increase (inflation). This happened when the greenbacks were issued. After the war, the U.S. Treasury assumed that the greenbacks would be recalled from circulation so that consumer prices would decline and the nation could return to a "hard-money" currency—gold, silver, and copper coins—which had always been viewed as more reliable in value than paper currency.

The most vocal supporters of a return to hard money were eastern creditors (mostly bankers and merchants) who did not want their debtors to pay them in paper currency. Critics of the gold standard tended to be farmers and other debtors. These so-called soft-money advocates opposed taking greenbacks out of circulation because shrinking the supply of money would bring lower prices (deflation) for their crops and livestock, thereby reducing their income and making it harder for them to pay their long-term debts. In 1868 congressional supporters of such a soft-money policy—mostly Democrats—forced the Treasury to stop withdrawing greenbacks.

President Grant sided with the hard-money camp. On March 18, 1869, he signed the Public Credit Act, which said that investors who purchased government bonds to help finance the war effort must be paid back in gold. The act led to a decline in consumer prices that hurt debtors and helped creditors. It also ignited a ferocious political debate over the merits of hard and soft money that would last throughout the nineteenth century—and beyond.

FINANCIAL PANIC President Grant's effort to withdraw greenbacks from circulation unintentionally helped cause a major economic collapse. During 1873, two dozen overextended railroads stopped paying their bills, forcing Jay Cooke and Company, the nation's leading business lender, to go bankrupt and close its doors on September 18, 1873.

The shocking news created a snowball effect as other hard-pressed banks began shutting down. A Republican senator sent Grant an urgent telegram from New York City: "Results of today indicate imminent danger of general national bank panic."

The resulting **Panic of 1873** triggered a deep depression. Tens of thousands of businesses closed, 3 million workers lost jobs, and those with jobs saw their wages slashed. In major cities, the unemployed and homeless roamed the streets and formed long lines at soup kitchens.

The depression led the U.S. Treasury to reverse course and begin printing more greenbacks. For a time, the supporters of paper money celebrated, but in 1874, Grant overruled his cabinet and vetoed a bill to issue even more greenbacks. His decision pleased bankers and other lenders but ignited a barrage of criticism. A Tennessee Republican congressman called the veto "cold-blooded murder," and a group of merchants in Indiana charged that Grant had sold his soul to those "whose god is the dollar."

A Visit from the Ku Klux Klan African Americans in the South lived in constant fear of racial violence, as this 1872 engraving from *Harper's Weekly*, published to elicit northern sympathy, illustrates.

In the end, Grant's decision only prolonged what was then the worst depression in the nation's history. It also brought about a catastrophe for Republicans in the 1874 congressional elections, as Democrats blamed them for the economic hard times. In the House, Republicans went from a 70 percent majority to a 37 percent minority. They maintained control of the Senate but were placed on the defensive.

WHITE TERROR President Grant initially fought to enforce federal efforts to reconstruct the postwar South, but southern resistance to "Radical rule" increased and turned brutally violent. In Grayson County, Texas, a white man and two friends murdered three former slaves because they wanted to "thin the niggers out and drive them to their holes."

Klansmen focused their program of murder, violence, and intimidation on prominent Republicans, black and white—elected officials, teachers in black schools, state militias. In Mississippi, they killed a black Republican leader in front of his family. Three white scalawag Republicans were murdered in Georgia in 1870, and that same year an armed mob of whites assaulted a Republican political rally in Alabama, killing four black participants and wounding fifty-four. An Alabama Republican pleaded with President Grant to intervene.

"Give us poor people some guarantee of our lives," G. T. F. Boulding wrote. "We are hunted and shot down as if we were wild beasts."

In South Carolina, white supremacists were especially violent. In 1871, some 500 masked men laid siege to the Union County jail and eventually lynched eight black prisoners. In March 1871, Klansmen killed thirty African Americans in Meridian, Mississippi.

At Grant's urging, Republicans in Congress responded with three Enforcement Acts (1870–1871). The first of these measures imposed penalties on anyone who interfered with any citizen's right to vote. The second dispatched federal supervisors to monitor elections in southern districts where political terrorism flourished. The third, called the Ku Klux Klan Act (1871), outlawed various activities of the KKK—forming conspiracies, wearing disguises, resisting officers, and intimidating officials. It also allowed the president to send federal troops to any community where voting rights were being violated. When some Republicans balked at such federal intrusions into states' rights to police their elections, Grant appeared in person before Congress to urge passage of the Klan Act.

Once the legislation was approved, Grant sent Attorney General Amos Akerman, a Georgian, to recruit prosecutors and marshals to enforce it. The Klan, Akerman reported, "was the most atrocious organization that the civilized part of the world has ever known." Its violent acts "amount to war." In South Carolina alone, Akerman and federal troops and prosecutors convinced local juries to convict 1,143 Klansmen. By 1872, the Klan was effectively killed by Grant's stern actions.

In general, however, the Enforcement Acts were not consistently enforced. As a result, the violent efforts of southern whites to thwart Reconstruction escalated.

On Easter Sunday 1873 in the black Republican township of Colfax, Louisiana, a mob of 140 white vigilantes, most of them ex-Confederate soldiers led by Klansmen, used a cannon, rifles, and pistols to attack a group of black Republicans holed up in the courthouse, slaughtering eighty-one and burning the building. When federal troops arrived, an officer reported that they found heaps of black bodies being picked over by dogs and buzzards. "We were unable to find the body of a single white man," he said. Many of the dead "were shot in the back of the head and neck." Most had "three to a dozen wounds."

President Grant told the Senate that the "monstrous" Colfax Massacre was unprecedented in its "barbarity." He declared parts of Louisiana in a state of insurrection and imposed military rule. Federal prosecutors used the Enforcement Acts to indict seventy whites, but only nine were put on trial and just three convicted—but of "conspiracy," not murder.

SOUTHERN "REDEEMERS" The Klan's impact on southern politics varied from state to state. In the Upper South, it played only a modest role in helping Democrats win local elections. In the Lower South, however, Klan violence had more serious effects. In overwhelmingly black Yazoo County, Mississippi, vengeful whites used terrorism to reverse the political balance of power. In the 1873 elections, for example, the Republicans cast 2,449 votes and the Democrats 638; two years later the Democrats polled 4,049 votes, the Republicans 7. Once Democrats regained power, they ousted black legislators, closed public schools for black children, and instituted poll taxes to restrict black voting.

The activities of white supremacists disheartened black and white Republicans alike. "We are helpless and unable to organize," wrote a Mississippi scalawag. We "dare not attempt to canvass [campaign for candidates], or make public speeches." At the same time, Northerners displayed a growing weariness with using federal troops to reconstruct the South. "The plain truth is," noted the *New York Herald*, "the North has got tired of the Negro."

President Grant, however, desperately wanted to use more federal force to preserve peace. He asked Congress to pass new legislation that would "leave my duties perfectly clear." Congress responded with the Civil Rights Act of 1875, which said that people of all races must be granted equal access to hotels and restaurants, railroads and stagecoaches, theaters, and other "places of public amusement."

Unfortunately for Grant, the new anti-segregation law provided little enforcement authority. Those who felt their rights were being violated had to file suit in court, and the penalties for violators were modest. In 1883, the U.S. Supreme Court, in an opinion arising from five similar cases, struck down the Civil Rights Act on the grounds that the Fourteenth Amendment focused only on the actions of state governments; it did not have authority over the policies of private businesses or individuals. Chief Justice Joseph Bradley added that it was time for blacks to assume "the rank of a mere citizen" and stop being the "special favorite of the laws." As a result, the *Civil Rights Cases* (1883) opened the door for a wave of racial segregation that washed over the South during the late nineteenth century.

Republican political control in the South and public interest in protecting civil rights gradually loosened during the 1870s as all-white "Conservative" parties mobilized the anti-Reconstruction vote. They called themselves Conservatives to distinguish themselves from northern Democrats. Conservatives—the so-called **redeemers** who supposedly "saved" the South from Republican control and "black rule"—used the race issue to excite the white electorate and threaten black voters. Where persuasion failed to work, Conservatives used trickery to rig the voting. As one Conservative boasted, "The white and black Republicans may outvote us, but we can outcount them."

Republican political control ended in Virginia and Tennessee as early as 1869 and collapsed a year later in Georgia and North Carolina, although North Carolina had a Republican governor until 1876. Reconstruction lasted longest in the

Lower South, where whites abandoned Klan robes for barefaced intimidation in paramilitary groups such as the Mississippi Rifle Club and the South Carolina Red Shirts. The last Radical Republican regimes ended, however, after the elections of 1876, and the return of the old white political elite further undermined the country's commitment to Congressional Reconstruction.

THE SUPREME COURT Key rulings by the U.S. Supreme Court further eroded Congressional Reconstruction by weakening the effects of the Thirteenth and Fourteenth Amendments. For instance, the *Slaughterhouse Cases* (1873) limited the "privileges or immunities" of U.S. citizenship as outlined in the recently ratified Fourteenth Amendment.

In 1869, the Louisiana legislature had granted a single company a monopoly of the livestock slaughtering business in New Orleans as a means of protecting public health. Competing butchers sued the state, arguing that the monopoly violated their "privileges" as U.S. citizens under the Fourteenth Amendment and deprived them of property without due process of law.

In a 5–4 decision, the Court ruled that the monopoly did not violate the Fourteenth Amendment because its "privileges and immunities" clause applied only to U.S. citizenship, not state citizenship. States, in other words, retained legal jurisdiction over their citizens, and federal protection of civil rights did not extend to the property rights of businesses.

Dissenting Justice Stephen J. Field argued that the Court's mistaken ruling rendered the Fourteenth Amendment a "vain and idle enactment" with little scope or authority. By designating the rights of state citizens beyond the jurisdiction of federal law, the *Slaughterhouse Cases* unwittingly opened the door for states to discriminate against African Americans.

Three years later, in *United States v. Cruikshank* (1876), the Supreme Court further eroded the protections of individuals embedded in the Fourteenth Amendment by overturning the convictions of William Cruikshank and two other white men who led the Colfax Massacre. In doing so, the Court argued that the equal protection and due process clauses in the Fourteenth Amendment governed only state actions, not the behavior of individuals. Furthermore, the prosecution's failure to prove racial intent placed the convictions outside the reach of the Equal Protection Clause of the Fourteenth Amendment.

In Chief Justice Morrison Waite's view, the duty to protect the "equality of the rights of citizens" had been "originally assumed by the States; and it still remains there." He and the other justices thus struck down the Enforcement Acts, ruling that the states, not the federal government, were responsible for protecting citizens from attack by other private citizens.

Taken together, the *Slaughterhouse* and *Cruikshank* cases so gutted the Fourteenth Amendment that freedpeople were left even more vulnerable to

THE ELECTION OF 1876

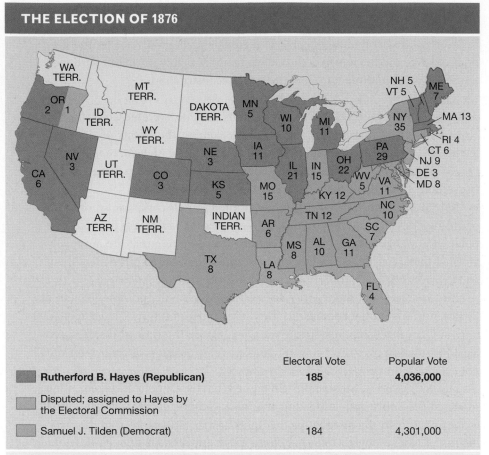

	Electoral Vote	Popular Vote
Rutherford B. Hayes (Republican)	**185**	**4,036,000**
Disputed; assigned to Hayes by the Electoral Commission		
Samuel J. Tilden (Democrat)	184	4,301,000

- Why did the Republicans pick Rutherford Hayes as their presidential candidate?
- Why were the electoral votes of several states disputed?
- What was the Compromise of 1877?

violence and discrimination. The federal government was effectively abandoning its role in enforcing Reconstruction.

THE CONTESTED ELECTION OF 1876 President Grant wanted to run for an unprecedented third term in 1876, but many Republicans had lost confidence in his leadership. In the summer of 1875, he acknowledged the inevitable and announced that he would retire. James Gillespie Blaine of Maine, former Speaker of the House, initially seemed the likeliest Republican to succeed Grant, but his candidacy crumbled when newspapers revealed that he had secretly promised political favors to railroad executives in exchange for shares of stock in the company.

The scandal led the Republican convention to select Ohio's favorite son, Rutherford B. Hayes. A former Union general who had been wounded five times during the Civil War, Hayes had served three terms as governor of Ohio. He was a civil service reformer eager to reduce the number of federal jobs subject to political appointment. But his chief virtue was that he offended neither Radicals nor reformers. As a journalist put it, he was "obnoxious to no one."

Hayes called for reforming the civil service to eliminate cronyism and corruption within his administration and promised to reject a second term for himself. The Republican platform criticized the "corrupt centralism" of the Grant administration that had infested the federal government with "incapacity, waste, and fraud."

The Democratic convention was uncharacteristically harmonious. On the second ballot, the nomination went to Samuel J. Tilden, a wealthy corporate lawyer and reform governor of New York.

The 1876 campaign avoided controversial issues. In the absence of strong ideological differences, Democrats highlighted the Republican scandals. Republicans responded by repeatedly waving "the bloody shirt," linking the Democrats to secession, civil war, and the violence committed against Republicans in the South. As Robert G. Ingersoll, the most celebrated Republican public speaker of the time, insisted: "The man that assassinated Abraham Lincoln was a Democrat. . . . Soldiers, every scar you have on your heroic bodies was given you by a Democrat!"

Early election returns pointed to a victory for Tilden. Nationwide, he outpolled Hayes by almost 300,000 votes, and by midnight following Election Day, Tilden had won 184 electoral votes, just 1 short of the total needed for victory. Overnight, however, Republican activists realized that the election hinged on 19 disputed electoral votes from Florida, Louisiana, and South Carolina.

The Democrats needed only one of the challenged votes to claim victory; the Republicans needed all nineteen. Republicans in the three states had engaged in election fraud, while Democrats had used violence to keep black voters at home. All three states, however, were governed by Republicans who appointed the election boards, each of which reported narrow victories for Hayes. The Democrats immediately challenged the results.

In all three states, rival election boards submitted conflicting vote counts. Weeks passed with no solution. On January 29, 1877, Congress appointed an electoral commission to settle the dispute. Finally, on March 1, 1877, the commission voted 8–7 in favor of Hayes. The next day, the House of Representatives declared Hayes president by an electoral vote of 185–184.

Tilden decided not to protest the decision. His campaign manager explained that they preferred "four years of Hayes's administration to four years of civil war."

Hayes's victory hinged on the defection of key southern Democrats, who, it turned out, had made secret deals with the Republicans. On February 26, 1877, prominent Ohio Republicans and powerful southern Democrats had struck a private bargain—the **Compromise of 1877**—at Wormley's Hotel in Washington, D.C. The Republicans promised that if Hayes were named president, he would remove the last federal troops from the South.

For his part, President Grant was eager to leave the White House: "I never wanted to get out of a place as much as I did to get out of the Presidency." Others were sorry to see him leave. T. Jefferson Martin spoke for many African Americans when he wrote Grant upon his retirement: "As a colored man I feel in duty bound to return you my greatful [sic] and heartfelt thanks, for your firm, steadfast, and successful administrations of our country, both as military chieftain and civil ruler of this nation. . . . My dear friend of humanity."

THE END OF RECONSTRUCTION In 1877, the Democrat-controlled House of Representatives refused to fund federal troops in the South after July, and President Hayes withdrew U.S. soldiers from Louisiana and South Carolina, whose Republican governments collapsed soon thereafter. In the congressional elections of 1878, Hayes admitted that the balloting in southern states was corrupted by "violence of the most atrocious character," but he was not about to send federal troops again.

Over the next thirty years, federal protection of black civil rights in the South crumbled. As Henry Adams, a former Louisiana slave, observed in 1877, "The whole South—every state in the South—has got [back] into the hands of the very men that held us as slaves." New white state governments rewrote their constitutions, ousted the "carpetbaggers, scalawags, and blacks," and cut spending. "The Yankees helped free us, so they say," a former North Carolina slave named Thomas Hall remembered, "but [in 1877] they let us be put back in slavery again."

THE "LOST CAUSE" While white conservatives were reasserting control and reinforcing white supremacy, novelists, poets, and former Confederate leaders were fashioning what came to be called the **Lost Cause narrative**, a sanitized version of history in which a romanticized Confederacy could do no wrong during the "War of Northern Aggression."

Nostalgic apologists for secession glamorized the old plantation culture and insisted that the Civil War had little to do with slavery and everything to do with a noble defense of states' rights and the southern homeland against the aggressions of a tyrannical Republican party. As Jefferson Davis claimed in 1881, the loyal and faithful slaves in the South were "contented with their lot" in 1861.

President Lincoln, however, hoodwinked them into believing they would be better off free and "sent them out to devastate their benefactors [owners]."

The Lost Cause myth also demonized abolitionists and idealized the leadership of Confederate generals Robert E. Lee ("the soldier who walked with God") and Stonewall Jackson, deifying them as chivalrous pillars of southern virtue who fought bravely and ethically against far larger Union armies led by ruthless outlaws such as Ulysses S. Grant and William T. Sherman.

To bolster this intentional reimagining of southern history, communities erected scores of monuments and memorials glorifying Confederate leaders. On Memorial Day 1890, for example, more than 100,000 people gathered in Richmond, Virginia, to celebrate the unveiling of a massive statue of General Lee seated on his celebrated warhorse, "Traveler." What the speakers at the event failed to mention was that Lee, before his death in 1871, had urged southerners *not* to create such memorials to a cause that was "lost" on the battlefields.

RECONSTRUCTION'S SIGNIFICANCE

The collapse of Congressional Reconstruction in 1877 had tragic consequences, as the white South aggressively renewed traditional patterns of discrimination against African Americans. Black activist W. E. B. DuBois called the effort to make slaves into citizens a "splendid failure."

Yet for all its unfulfilled promises, Congressional Reconstruction did leave an enduring legacy—the Thirteenth, Fourteenth, and Fifteenth Amendments. If Reconstruction's experiment in interracial democracy failed to provide true social equality or substantial economic opportunities for African Americans, it did create the essential constitutional foundation for future advances in the quest for equality and civil rights—and not just for African Americans, but for women and other minority groups.

Until the pivotal Reconstruction era, the states were responsible for protecting citizens' rights. Thereafter, thanks to the Fourteenth and Fifteenth Amendments, blacks had gained equal rights (in theory), and the federal government had assumed responsibility for ensuring that states treated blacks equally. A hundred years later, the cause of civil rights would be embraced again by the federal government—this time permanently.

CHAPTER REVIEW

SUMMARY

- **Reconstruction Challenges**   With the defeat of the Confederacy, the federal government had to develop policies and procedures to address a number of vexing questions: What was the status of the defeated states and how would they be reintegrated into the nation's political life? What would be the political status of the former slaves and what would the federal government do to integrate them into the nation's social and economic fabric?

- **Reconstruction over Time**   Abraham Lincoln and his successor, Southerner Andrew Johnson, wanted a lenient plan for Reconstruction. *Johnson's Restoration Plan (1865)*, like Lincoln's, said that when ten percent of a former Confederate state's voters swore a loyalty oath to the Union, that state could be readmitted. The *Freedmen's Bureau* helped to educate and aid freed slaves, negotiate labor contracts, and reunite families. Lincoln's assassination led many Northerners to favor the *Radical Republicans*, who wanted to end the grasp of the old plantation elite on the South's society and economy. Whites resisted and established *black codes* to restrict the freedom of former slaves. *Congressional Reconstruction* responded by stipulating that former Confederate states had to ratify the *Fourteenth (1868)* and *Fifteenth Amendments (1870)* to the U.S. Constitution to protect the rights of African Americans. Congress also passed the Military Reconstruction Act, which used federal troops to enforce the voting and civil rights of African Americans.

- **Views of Reconstruction**   After the war, land ownership reverted to the old white elite, reducing newly freed blacks to *sharecropping*. African Americans enthusiastically participated in politics, with many serving as elected officials. Along with white southern Republicans (scalawags) and northern carpetbaggers, they worked to rebuild the southern economy. Many white Southerners, however, supported the *Ku Klux Klan*'s violent intimidation and Conservative control of southern state governments.

- **Political and Economic Developments and the End of Reconstruction**   Scandals during the Grant administration involving an attempt to corner the gold market plus the *Panic of 1873* and disagreement over whether to continue the use of *greenbacks* or return to the gold standard, eroded northern support for the status quo in government and weakened Reconstruction. Southern white *redeemers* were elected in 1874, successfully reversing the political progress of Republicans and blacks. In the *Compromise of 1877*, Democrats agreed to the election of Republican Rutherford B. Hayes, who put an end to the Radical Republican administrations in the southern states.

- **The Significance of Reconstruction**   Southern state governments quickly renewed long-standing patterns of discrimination against African Americans, but the Fourteenth and Fifteenth Amendments remained enshrined in the Constitution, creating the essential constitutional foundation for future advances in civil rights.

Chronology

1865	Congress sets up the Freedmen's Bureau
April 14, 1865	Lincoln assassinated
1865	Johnson issues Proclamation of Amnesty
	All-white southern state legislatures pass various black codes
1866	Ku Klux Klan organized
	Congress passes the Civil Rights Act
1867	Congress passes the Military Reconstruction Act
1868	Fourteenth Amendment is ratified
	The U.S. House of Representatives impeaches President Andrew Johnson; the Senate fails to convict him
	Grant elected president
	Eight former Confederate states readmitted to the Union
1870	Fifteenth Amendment ratified
	First Enforcement Acts passed in response to white terror in the South
1872	Grant wins reelection
1873	Panic of 1873 triggers depression
1877	Reconstruction ends; Hayes becomes president

Key Terms

Radical Republicans p. 733

Freedmen's Bureau p. 734

Johnson's Restoration Plan p. 738

black codes p. 740

Fourteenth Amendment (1866) p. 742

Congressional Reconstruction p. 743

impeachment p. 744

Fifteenth Amendment (1870) p. 746

sharecropping p. 751

Ku Klux Klan (KKK) p. 756

greenbacks p. 764

Panic of 1873 p. 765

redeemers p. 768

Compromise of 1877 p. 772

Lost Cause narrative p. 772

 INQUIZITIVE

Go to InQuizitive to see what you've learned—and learn what you've missed—with personalized feedback along the way.

part five

GROWING PAINS

The defeat of the Confederacy in 1865 restored the Union and, in the process, helped accelerate America's transformation into an agricultural empire and an industrial powerhouse. A stronger sense of nationalism began to temper the regional conflicts of the prewar era. During and after the Civil War, the Republican-led Congress pushed through legislation to promote industrial and commercial development and western expansion at the same time that it was "reconstructing" the former Confederate states. The United States forged a dynamic new industrial economy serving an increasingly national and international market for

American goods. Food production soared, as did exports to foreign countries. Railroads formed a spider web of economic development that created truly national markets. Yet the progress was tarnished by the relentless relocation of Native Americans onto reservations and the reckless exploitation of the continent's natural resources.

Fueled by innovations in mass production and mass marketing, and by advances in transportation and communications such as transcontinental railroads and transatlantic telegraph systems, huge corporations began to dominate the economy. As social theorist William Graham Sumner remarked, the process of industrial development "controls us all because we are all in it. It creates the conditions of our own existence, sets the limits of our social activity, and regulates the bonds of our social relations."

Late nineteenth-century American life drew much of its energy from the mushrooming industrial cities. "This is the age of cities," declared midwestern writer Hamlin Garland. "We are now predominantly urban." Yet the transition from an economy made up of mostly small local and regional businesses to one dominated by large-scale national and international corporations affected rural life as well.

As early as 1869, novelist Harriet Beecher Stowe reported that the "simple, pastoral" America "is a thing forever gone. The hurry of railroads and the rush and roar of business" had displaced the Jeffersonian ideal of America as a nation of small farms.

She exaggerated, of course. Small farms and small towns survived the impact of the Industrial Revolution, but farm folk, as one New Englander stressed, now had to "understand farming as a business; if they do not it will go hard with them." The friction between the new forces of the national marketplace and the traditional folkways of small-scale family farming generated social unrest and political revolts during the last quarter of the nineteenth century.

The clash between tradition and modernity, sleepy farm villages and bustling cities, peaked during the 1890s, one of the most strife-ridden decades in American history. A deep economic depression, political activism by farmers, and violent conflicts between industrial workers and employers transformed the presidential campaign of 1896 into a clash between rival visions of America's future.

The Republican candidate, William McKinley, campaigned on modern urban and industrial values. William Jennings Bryan, the nominee of the Democratic and the Populist parties, was an eloquent defender of America's rural past. McKinley's victory proved to be a turning point in American political and social history. By 1900, the United States had emerged as one of the world's greatest industrial powers, and it would thereafter assume a new leadership role in world affairs—for good and for ill.

17 Business and Labor in the Industrial Era

1860–1900

Carnegie Steel Company Steelworkers operate the massive and dangerous Bessemer converters at Andrew Carnegie's steel mill in Pittsburgh, Pennsylvania.

Although the Civil War devastated the South, it provided a powerful stimulant to the northern economy. The wartime need to supply the Union armies with shoes, boots, uniforms, weapons, supplies, food, wagons, and railroads ushered in an era of unprecedented industrial development. The scope of the war favored large-scale businesses and hastened the maturation of a truly national economy. As an Indiana congressman told business leaders in 1864, the war had sparked the development of "resources and capabilities such as you never before dreamed you possessed."

During the war, the number of manufacturing companies in the United States almost doubled. In 1865, Ohio senator John Sherman wrote a letter to his brother, William T. Sherman, the celebrated Union general, in which he observed that the northern states had emerged from the war "unimpaired." The process of mass-producing mountains of goods for the war effort had given a widened "scope to the ideas of leading capitalists, far higher than anything undertaken in this country. They talk of millions as confidently as before [they talked] of thousands."

Between the end of the war and 1900, America experienced explosive growth, the fastest in history to that point. The nation's population tripled, agricultural production more than doubled, and manufacturing output grew *six* times over. When the Civil War ended, there was not a single industrial corporation listed on the New York Stock Exchange. By 1900, there were dozens of them employing hundreds of thousands of managers, clerks, and workers. In the thirty-five years after the Civil War, the United States achieved

focus questions

1. What factors stimulated the unprecedented industrial and agricultural growth in the late nineteenth century?

2. Who were the entrepreneurs who pioneered the growth of Big Business? What were their goals, and what strategies did they use to dominate their respective industries?

3. What role did the federal government play in the nation's economic development during this period?

4. Analyze the ways in which the class structure and lives of women changed in the late nineteenth century.

5. Assess the efforts of workers to organize unions to promote their interests during this era.

the highest rate of economic growth in the world, and by 1900, American industries and corporate farms dominated global markets in steel, oil, wheat, and cotton.

Such phenomenal growth led to profound social changes, the most visible of which was the sudden prosperity of large industrial cities such as Pittsburgh, Chicago, and Cleveland. Millions of young adults left farms and villages to work in factories, mines, and mills and to revel in city life. In growing numbers, women left the "cult of domesticity" and entered the urban-industrial workplace as clerks, typists, secretaries, teachers, nurses, and seamstresses.

While a few made fortunes, most laborers remained in unskilled, low-wage jobs. The world of *Big Business*, a term commonly used to refer to the giant corporations that emerged after the Civil War, was as untamed and reckless as the cow towns and mining camps of the West were. New technologies and business practices outpaced the ability of the outdated legal system to craft new laws and fashion ethical norms to govern the rapidly changing economy. Business owners took advantage of this lawless environment to build fortunes, destroy reputations, exploit workers and the environment, and gouge consumers. Yet out of the scramble for profits emerged an undreamed-of prosperity and a rising standard of living that became the envy of the world.

Along with great wealth came great poverty, however. In a capitalist economy, people with different talents, opportunities, and resources receive unequal rewards from their labors. And, in a capitalist democracy like America, the tensions between equal political rights and unequal economic status generate social instability. In the decades after the Civil War, the overwhelming influence exercised by the business tycoons spurred the formation of labor unions and farm associations. Increasingly, tensions erupted into violent clashes that required government intervention and produced class conflict.

INDUSTRIAL AND AGRICULTURAL GROWTH

Several factors converged during the second half of the nineteenth century to accelerate the nation's industrial development. Perhaps most important was the expansion of transportation systems—canals, steamboats, railroads, and the development of instantaneous communication networks enabled first by the telegraph, and later, the telephone. All together, these innovations combined to create a truly national marketplace for the sale and distribution of goods and services.

In addition, America enjoyed the benefits of its vast natural resources: land, forests, minerals, oil, coal, water, and iron ore. At the same time, a rising tide of immigrants created an army of low-wage, high-energy workers while expanding the pool of consumers eager to buy new products. Between 1865 and 1900, more than 15 million newcomers arrived in the United States.

A new generation of outsized business leaders drove the transition to an urban-industrial society. Admirers called them captains of industry, while critics called them robber barons because they controlled the flow of money and commerce.

Whatever the label, the post–Civil War tycoons were determined to create large enterprises never before imagined. Intelligent, ambitious, bold, and energetic, they were exemplars of free enterprise and self-reliance who were convinced that what was good for their businesses was good for the country. Hated, feared, envied, or admired, they were the catalysts for a new America of cities and factories, prosperity amid poverty, and growing social strife and political corruption.

Bigness was the driving goal of industrial capitalism. Daring entrepreneurs took advantage of new money-making opportunities, technologies, and political lobbying (including bribery) to build gigantic corporations that dominated industries such as oil refining, steel, sugar, and meatpacking.

Ingenuity became America's economic trademark. The promoters of Big Business ruthlessly improved efficiency and productivity, cut costs, bought politicians, and suppressed competition. These predatory men—Cornelius Vanderbilt, John D. Rockefeller, Andrew Carnegie, and J. P. Morgan, among others—wanted to *dominate* their industries. When Vanderbilt, a developer first of steamboats and then railroads, learned that some rivals had tried to steal one of his properties, he penned a brief message: "Gentlemen: You have undertaken to cheat me. I will not sue you, for law takes too long. I will ruin you." And he did.

CORPORATE AGRICULTURE

At the same time that the manufacturing sector was experiencing rapid growth, the agricultural economy was shifting to a large-scale industrial model of operation. Giant corporate-owned "bonanza farms" spread across the West. They were run like factories by professional, college-educated managers, who would hire hundreds of migrant workers who used mechanized equipment to harvest crops, usually wheat or corn destined for eastern or foreign markets.

The farm sector stimulated the industrial sector—and vice versa. In the West, bonanza farms using the latest machinery and scientific techniques became internationally famous for their productivity. On one bonanza farm in North Dakota, a single field of wheat encompassed 13,000 acres. For farmers in the High Plains, wheat became a perennial cash crop, and American-grown wheat was exported around the world. Another bonanza farm in South Dakota employed more than 1,000 migrant workers to tend 34,000 acres. Such agribusinesses were the wave of the future.

By 1870, the United States had become the world's leading agricultural producer. With the growth of the commercial cattle industry, the process of slaughtering, packing, and shipping cattle, hogs, and sheep evolved into a major industry, especially in Chicago, the nation's fastest-growing city and the largest slaughterhouse in the world.

TECHNOLOGICAL INNOVATIONS

America has always nurtured a culture of invention and innovation. Abraham Lincoln had often praised the nation's peculiar talent for "discoveries and inventions," which became commonplace in the decades after the Civil War. Inventors, scientists, research laboratories, and business owners developed labor-saving machinery and mass-production techniques that spurred dramatic advances in efficiency, productivity, and the size of industrial enterprises.

New technologies Business executives watch Alexander Graham Bell at the New York end of the first long-distance telephone call to Chicago, 1892.

Such innovations helped businesses turn out more products more cheaply, thus enabling more people to buy more of them. Technological advances created *economies of scale*, whereby larger business enterprises, including huge commercial farms, could afford expensive new machinery and large workforces that boosted their productivity.

After the Civil War, technological improvements spurred phenomenal increases in industrial productivity. The U.S. Patent Office, which had recorded only 276 inventions during the 1790s, registered almost 235,000 new patents in the 1890s, many of them issued to women and African Americans. New Yorker Beulah Louisa Henry accounted for almost 50 of those patents, most of them improvements on household goods. The list of innovations produced in the late nineteenth century included barbed wire, mechanical harvesters, reapers and combines, refrigerated railcars, air brakes for trains, steam turbines, typewriters, sewing machines, vacuum cleaners, ice cream churns, and electric motors.

BELL'S TELEPHONE Few inventions could rival the importance of the telephone. In 1875, twenty-eight-year-old Alexander Graham Bell began experimenting with the concept of a "speaking telegraph," or talking through wires. The following year, he developed a primitive "electric speaking telephone" that enabled him to send a famous message to his assistant in another room: "Mr. Watson, come here, I want to see you." In 1876, Bell patented his device and started the American Telephone and Telegraph Company (AT&T), to begin manufacturing telephones. Five years later, he perfected the long-distance telephone lines that revolutionized communication. By 1895, more than 300,000 telephones were in use. Bell's patent became the most valuable one ever issued.

TYPEWRITERS AND SEWING MACHINES Other inventions changed the nature of work. Typewriters, for example, transformed the operations of business offices. Because managers assumed that women had greater

Office typists In new roles enabled by typewriters, women served as clerks or secretaries at many offices, such as the Remington Typewriter Company, pictured here.

dexterity in their fingers and because women were paid less than men on the assumption that they were not supporting a household, employers hired them to operate typewriters. Clerical positions soon became the fastest-growing job category for women.

Likewise, the introduction of sewing machines for the mass production of clothing and linens opened new, though often exploitative, employment opportunities to women. So-called sweatshops emerged in the major cities, where large numbers of mostly young immigrant women worked long hours in cramped, stifling conditions.

THOMAS EDISON   No American inventor was more influential or prolific than Thomas Alva Edison. As a boy in Michigan, he loved to "make things" and "do things." His mother homeschooled him and allowed him to explore the outdoors and perform what he called chemical "experiments." Edison later said his mother "let me follow my bent." His "bent" was toward telegraphy and electricity. He built his own telegraph set and dreamed of being a telegraph operator sending messages in Morse code.

When Edison was twelve, he began working for the local railroad, selling newspapers, food, and candy. "Being poor," he explained, "I already knew that money is a valuable thing." One day he was late for the train and ran after it. A conductor reached down and lifted him into the train by his ears. Edison felt something snap in his head, and soon he was nearly deaf. Despite his hearing loss, however, he said that his work as a trainboy "was the happiest time of my life."

In 1862, early in the Civil War, the solitary Edison fastened on his real passion: being a telegraph operator, first in Cincinnati, then in Louisville and Boston. The clicking telegraph key enabled him to listen to others and tinker with the equipment.

Despite having no formal scientific education, Edison became a mechanical genius. In January 1869, at the age of twenty-one, he announced that he would "hereafter devote his full time to bringing out his inventions." He moved to New York City to be closer to the center of America's financial district; there he developed dozens of new machines, including a "stock market ticker" to report the transactions on Wall Street in real time. Soon, job offers and what he referred to as "real money" flooded his way. Edison, however, had a different goal: to become a full-time inventor.

In 1876, he moved into what he called his "science village" in Menlo Park, New Jersey, twenty-five miles southwest of New York City. There, in the nation's first industrial research laboratory, Edison and his assistants created the phonograph in 1877 and a long-lasting electric lightbulb in 1879. He also improved upon the telephone.

By the ripe age of thirty, Edison was the nation's foremost inventor. Altogether, he created or perfected hundreds of new devices and processes, including the storage battery, Dictaphone, mimeograph copier, electric motor, and motion picture camera and projector.

He soon became world famous. A magazine saluted him as the "Wizard of Menlo Park" and called him one of the "wonders of the world." President Rutherford B. Hayes invited him to the White House, and Congress honored him. Until Edison's inventions came along, the availability of daylight determined much about how people lived and worked. With the lightbulb, the distinction between night and day virtually disappeared.

GEORGE WESTINGHOUSE AND ELECTRIC POWER Before the 1880s, kerosene and gas lamps illuminated the nation after dark. All that changed in 1882, when the Edison Electric Illuminating Company launched the electric utility industry. Several companies that made lightbulbs merged into the Edison General Electric Company in 1888, later renamed General Electric.

The use of direct electrical current, however, limited Edison's lighting system to a radius of about two miles. To cover greater distances required an alternating current, which could be transmitted at high voltage and then stepped down by transformers. George Westinghouse, inventor of the railway air brake, developed the first alternating-current electric system in 1886, and he thereafter set up the Westinghouse Electric Company to manufacture the equipment.

Edison resisted the new method as too risky, but the Westinghouse system won the "battle of the currents," and the Edison companies had to switch over to AC (alternating current) from DC (direct current). In 1887, a twenty-eight-year-old Croatian immigrant named Nikola Tesla, who had briefly worked with Thomas Edison before the two parted ways, set up laboratories in New York where he invented the alternating-current (AC) motor, which he sold to George Westinghouse, who improved it, and the company began selling dynamos.

The invention of dynamos (electric motors) dramatically increased the power, speed, and efficiency of machinery. Electricity enabled factories to be located anywhere; factories and mills no longer had to cluster around waterfalls and coal deposits to have a ready supply of energy. Electricity also spurred urban growth by improving lighting, facilitating the development of trolley and subway systems, and stimulating the creation of elevators that enabled the construction of taller buildings.

THE RAILROAD REVOLUTION

More than any other industry, railroads symbolized the impact of innovative technologies on industrial development and the maturation of a truly national economy. No other form of transportation played so large a role in the development of the interconnected national marketplace.

In 1888, William Cox, a Nebraska writer, reported that "a new railway has been commenced and completed" across the state, opening "up a great new artery of traffic, and bringing in its train joy and gladness for thousands of people." The new rail line was "building up three new villages along the way, and infusing new life and activity into a fourth." The railroads, he concluded, were providing America with a pathway to progress, profit, and modernity.

TRAINS AND TIME Railroads compressed time and distance. They moved masses of people and goods faster, farther, and cheaper than any other form of transportation. The railroad network prompted the creation of uniform national and international time zones and spurred the use of wristwatches, for the trains were scheduled to run on time. Towns that had rail depots thrived; those that did not died. The stations were the lifelines connecting small towns with the outside world. A town's connection to a railroad, observed Anthony Trollope, a British writer touring the United States, was "the first necessity of life, and gives the only hope of wealth."

Although the first great wave of railroad building occurred in the 1850s, the most spectacular growth took place after the Civil War. By 1897, the national rail network grew to nearly 200,000 miles, from a system of about 35,000 miles of track in 1865. Alongside each mile of track, a network of telegraph poles and wires were installed. Transportation and communication thus combined to forge a truly national economy.

TRAINS AND THE INDUSTRIAL ERA Railroads were America's first truly big business, the first beneficiaries of the great financial market known as Wall Street in New York City, the first industry to have operations in several states, and the first to develop a large-scale management bureaucracy.

The railroad boom was the catalyst for America's transition to an urban-industrial economy. From the 1860s to the 1960s, most people entered or left a city through its railroad stations. Trains opened the West to economic development, enabled federal troops to suppress Indian resistance, ferried millions of immigrants from New York City and other East Coast ports, helped transform commercial agriculture into a major international industry, and transported raw materials to factories and finished goods to retailers.

Railroads were expensive, however. Locomotives, railcars (called "rolling stock"), and the construction of track, trestles, and bridges required enormous investments. The railroad industry was the first to contract with "investment banks" to raise capital by selling shares of stock to investors. Railroads also stimulated other industries through their purchases of iron and steel, coal, timber, leather (for seats), and glass. In addition, railroad companies were the nation's largest employers.

THE DOWNSIDE OF THE RAILROAD BOOM Many railroad developers, however, cared more about making money than safety. Companies often overlooked dangerous working conditions that caused thousands of laborers to be killed or injured. Too many railroads were built; by the 1880s, there were twice as many as the economy could support.

Some railroads were poorly or even criminally managed and went bankrupt. Those that succeeded often broke the rules. Railroad lobbyists helped to corrupt state and federal legislators by "buying" the votes of politicians with cash or shares of stock. Charles Francis Adams Jr., head of the Union Pacific Railroad, admitted, "Our method of doing business is founded upon lying, cheating, and stealing—all bad things."

BUILDING THE TRANSCONTINENTALS

For decades, visionaries had dreamed of the United States being the first nation to build a railroad spanning a continent. In the 1860s, the dream became reality as construction began on the first of four rail lines that would bridge the nation—and, as one promoter boasted, establish "our empire on the Pacific."

THE "WORK OF GIANTS" The transcontinental railroads were, in the words of General William T. Sherman, the "work of giants." Their construction required heroic feats by the surveyors, engineers, and laborers who laid the rails, built the bridges, and gouged out the tunnels through rugged mountains.

The first transcontinental railroads were much more expensive to build than the shorter "trunk" lines in the East. Because the western routes passed through vast stretches of unpopulated plains and deserts, construction materials as well as workers and supplies had to be hauled long distances. Locomotives, railcars, rails, ties, spikes, and much more were often transported by ships from the East Coast to San Francisco and then moved by train to the remote construction sites.

The construction process was like managing a moving army. Herds of cattle, horses, mules, and oxen had to be fed and tended. Huge mobile camps, called

"Hell on Wheels," were built to house the crews and moved with them as the tracks progressed. The camps even included tents for dance halls, saloons, gambling, and prostitution. Nightlife was raucous. As a British reporter wrote, "Soldiers, herdsmen, teamsters, women, railroad men, are dancing, singing, or gambling. There are men here who would murder a fellow-creature for five dollars. . . . Not a day passes but a dead body is found somewhere in the vicinity with pockets rifled of their contents."

THE PACIFIC RAILWAY ACT (1862) Before the Civil War, construction of a transcontinental line had been delayed because northern and southern congressmen clashed over the choice of routes. Secession and the departure of southern congressmen for the Confederacy in 1861 finally permitted Republicans in Congress to pass the Pacific Railway Act in 1862. It authorized construction along a north-central route by two competing companies: the Union Pacific Railroad (UP) westward from Omaha, Nebraska, across the prairie, and the Central Pacific Railroad (CP) eastward from Sacramento, California, through the Sierra Nevada. Both companies began construction during the war, but most of the work was done after 1865.

Building a railroad across the continent entailed feats of daring, engineering, and construction. Laying rail around and through the mountains required extensive use of dynamite and required costly bridges and tunnels. Harsh weather led to frequent seasonal disruptions, and many workers were killed or injured over the course of construction. At times, some 15,000 people, mostly men, worked for each of the railroad companies as they raced each other to complete their tasks. The company that laid the most track in the shortest time would be awarded more money by Congress.

The competition led both companies to cut corners. Collis Huntington, one of the CP owners, confessed that his goal was to build "the cheapest road that I could . . . so that it moves ahead fast." If bridges or trestles collapsed under the weight of freight trains, they could be fixed later. Mark Hopkins, one of Huntington's partners, agreed, noting that his goal was to build as "poor a road as we can."

RAILROAD WORKERS The UP crews were composed largely of young, unmarried former Civil War soldiers, both Union and Confederate, along with ex-slaves and Irish and German immigrants. The CP crews were mainly young Chinese workers lured to America by the California gold rush or by railroad jobs. Most of these "coolie" laborers were single men eager to earn money to take back to China. The term coolie derived from the Hindu word for manual laborer, but in the western United States it came to be a derogative term for

Chinese railroad workers Using horse-drawn carts, picks, shovels, and dynamite, Chinese laborers played a large role in constructing the transcontinental Central Pacific Railroad track.

workers willing to work for wages so low that they hurt all laborers. Their temporary status and dreams of a good life made them more willing than American laborers to endure the low pay, dangerous working conditions, and intense racial prejudice.

What distinguished Chinese from other laborers was their ability to work together in accomplishing daunting tasks. Mark Twain described them as "quiet, peaceable, tractable, free from drunkenness, and they are as industrious as the day is long. A disorderly Chinaman is rare, and a lazy one does not exist."

LAYING TRACK The process of building the rail lines involved a series of sequential tasks. First came the surveyors, who selected and mapped the routes and measured grade changes. Engineers then designed the bridges, trestles, tunnels, and snowsheds. Tree cutters and graders followed by preparing the rail beds. Wooden cross ties were then placed in the ground and leveled before thirty-foot-long iron rails weighing 560 pounds were laid atop them. Next came spikers, who used special hammers to wallop two-pound spikes attaching the rails to the ties. Finally, workers shoveled gravel between the ties to stabilize them.

This huge undertaking encountered constant interruptions: terrible weather, late deliveries of key items, accidents, epidemics, and Indian attacks. Arthur Ferguson, a supervisor who kept a journal, frequently noted the hazards of constructing the first transcontinental in 1868:

> May 17—Two more men drowned in the river yesterday.
>
> June 4—At about sunrise, were attacked by Indians and succeeded in shooting one.
>
> June 21—Indians killed two men. Both had been horribly mutilated about the face by cuts made by a knife or a tomahawk.
>
> June 30—Four men were killed and scalped today about two miles above camp.

It was not only Native American warriors doing the killing, however. Workers often fought and killed each other. On June 7, Ferguson recorded that "two men were shot this evening in a drunken row—one was instantly killed, and the other is not expected to live."

The Union Pacific meets the Central Pacific On May 10, 1869, the celebration of the first transcontinental railroad's completion took place in Promontory, Utah.

THE RACE TO THE FINISH   The drama of constructing the first transcontinental railroad seized the nation's imagination. Every major newspaper carried stories about the progress of the competing companies. Finally, on May 10, 1869, former California governor Leland Stanford, one of the owners of the Central Pacific, drove a gold spike to complete the line at Promontory Summit in the Utah Territory north of the Great Salt Lake. The Union Pacific had built 1,086 miles of track compared with the Central Pacific's 689, much of it mountainous.

"In one sense," gushed the *Cincinnati Gazette*, the transcontinental railroad "is as great an achievement as the war, and as grand a triumph." The golden spike used to connect the final rails symbolized the uniting of East and

TRANSCONTINENTAL RAILROAD LINES, 1880s

- What was the route of the first transcontinental railroad, and why was it not in the South?
- Who built the railroads? How were they financed?

West. Soon the process would be repeated, as other companies constructed more lines across the continent.

By connecting the nation from ocean to ocean, the railroads became the basis of a truly national market for goods and services, including tourism. In 1872, Congress established Yellowstone National Park. Within ten years, railroads had brought a burgeoning tourist business to the nation's first national park in remote northwest Wyoming, then a territory.

As they pushed into sparsely populated western states and territories, the railroad companies became the region's primary real estate developers. They transported millions of settlers from the East, many of them immigrants eager to buy land. The railroads changed the economic, political, and physical landscapes of the nation and enabled the United States to emerge as a world power.

THE RISE OF BIG BUSINESS

The emergence of Big Business was one of the most significant developments in American history. Corporations grew increasingly larger and more powerful, transacting business across the nation and abroad. At the same time, business leaders exerted unprecedented influence and even bribery to influence governors, legislators, Congress, and presidents.

The growing political power of Big Business had negative effects that did not go unnoticed. "The growing wealth and influence of our large corporations," warned the *New York Times*, "is one of the most alarming phenomena of our time. Our public companies already wield gigantic power, and they use it like unscrupulous giants."

THE GROWTH OF CORPORATIONS

As businesses grew, they took one of several different forms. Some were owned by an individual; others were partnerships involving several owners. Increasingly, however, large companies that served national and international markets were converted into corporations—legal entities that separate the *ownership* of an enterprise from the *management* of its operations.

Once a corporation was registered ("chartered" or "incorporated") with a state government, it could raise money to operate ("capital") by selling shares of stock—representing partial ownership of the company—to people not otherwise involved with it. Shareholders elected a board of directors who appointed and evaluated the corporation's executives ("management"). One of the most important benefits of an incorporated business corporation is "limited legal liability": stockholders share in its profits but cannot be held liable for its debts if it fails.

FIGHTING COMPETITION

Competition is supposed to be the great virtue of capitalism, since it forces businesses to produce better products at the lowest cost. As many businesses became giant corporations, however, some owners came to view competition as a burden. Financier J. P. Morgan, for example, claimed that "bitter, destructive competition" always led to "destruction and ruin."

To eliminate cutthroat competition and thereby stabilize production, wages, and prices, rival companies selling similar products often formed "pools" whereby they secretly agreed to keep production and prices at specified levels. Such pools rarely lasted long, however, because one or more participants usually violated the agreement. The more effective strategy for the most aggressive companies was to drive the weaker companies out of business—or buy them out.

Strategies like these, and the methods used to carry them out, led critics to call the corporate titans robber barons. When asked how people might react to the shady methods he used to build his network of railroads, William Henry Vanderbilt famously replied, "The public be damned!"

THE BARONS OF BUSINESS

Most of the men who created large businesses in the late nineteenth century yearned to become rich and influential, and many religious leaders urged them on. "To secure wealth is an honorable ambition," stressed Russell Conwell, a prominent Baptist minister. "Money is power," he explained, and "every good man and woman ought to strive for power, to do good with it when obtained. I say, get rich! get rich!"

The industrial and financial giants personified the values that Conwell celebrated. They were men of grit and genius who found innovative—and at times unethical and illegal—ways to increase production and eliminate competition. They were also mercilessly adept at cutting costs and lowering prices.

Several business barons stood out for their extraordinary accomplishments: John D. Rockefeller and Andrew Carnegie for their innovations in organization, J. Pierpont Morgan for his development of investment banking, and Richard Sears and Alvah Roebuck for their creation of mail-order retailing.

John D. Rockefeller Co-founder of the Standard Oil Company.

JOHN D. ROCKEFELLER Born in New York in 1839, John D. Rockefeller moved as a child to Cleveland, Ohio. Raised by his mother, he developed a single-minded passion for systematic organization. As a young man, he decided to bring order and rationality to the new boom-and-bust oil industry. He was obsessed with precision, efficiency, tidiness—and money.

The railroad and shipping connections around Cleveland made it a strategic location for serving the booming oil fields of nearby western Pennsylvania. The first oil well in the United States began operating in 1859 in Titusville, Pennsylvania, and led to the Pennsylvania oil rush of the 1860s. Because oil could be refined into kerosene, which was widely used for lighting, heating, and cooking, the economic importance of the oil rush soon outstripped that of the California gold rush ten years earlier. Well before the end of the Civil War, oil refineries sprang up in Pittsburgh and Cleveland. Of the two cities, Cleveland had better rail service, so Rockefeller focused his energies there.

In 1870, Rockefeller teamed with his brother William and two other businessmen, Henry M. Flagler and Samuel Andrews, to establish the **Standard Oil Company** of Ohio. Although the company quickly became the largest oil refiner in the nation, John Rockefeller wanted to take control of the entire industry, in large part because he believed his competitors were inefficient and distracting.

During the 1870s, Rockefeller used various schemes to destroy his competitors. Early on, he pursued a strategy called **horizontal integration**, in which a dominant corporation buys or forces out most of its competitors. Rockefeller viewed competition as a form of warfare. In a few cases, he hired former competitors as executives, but only "the big ones," he said, "those who have already proved they can do a *big business*. As for the others, unfortunately they will have to *die*."

By 1879, Standard Oil controlled more than 90 percent of the nation's oil refining business. Still, Rockefeller's goal was a **monopoly**, a business so large that it controls an entire industry.

The rise of oil Crowding this Pennsylvania farm are wooden derricks that extracted crude oil.

In pursuing a monopoly, Rockefeller methodically reduced expenses by improving productivity, squeezing suppliers, and eliminating any hint of waste. He was determined to avoid letting any of his suppliers earn "a profit" from him. Because Standard Oil shipped so much oil by rail, Rockefeller forced railroads to pay him secret rebates on the shipments, enabling him to spend less for shipping than his competitors did.

Most important, instead of depending upon the products or services of other firms, known as middlemen, Standard Oil eventually owned everything it needed to produce, refine, and deliver oil—from wells to the finished product. The company had its own pipelines, built factories to make its own wagons and storage barrels, did its own hauling, and owned its own storage tanks and tanker ships. In economic terms, this business strategy is called **vertical integration**.

During the 1870s, Standard Oil bought so many of its competitors that it developed nearly a monopoly over the industry. Many state legislatures responded by outlawing the practice of one corporation owning stock in competing ones. In 1882, Rockefeller tried to hide his monopoly by organizing the Standard Oil Trust.

A **trust** gives a corporation (the trustee) the legal power to manage another company. Instead of owning other companies outright, the Standard Oil Trust controlled more than thirty companies by having their stockholders transfer their shares "in trust" to Rockefeller and eight other trustees. In return, the stockholders received *trust certificates*, which paid them annual dividends from the trust's earnings. During the Gilded Age, however, Americans began to call any huge corporation a trust.

The formation of corporate trusts generated intense criticism. In 1890, Congress passed the Sherman Anti-Trust Act, which declared that efforts to monopolize industries and thereby "restrain" competition were illegal. But the bill's language was so vague that its regulations were toothless.

State laws against monopolies were more effective than the Sherman Act. In 1892, Ohio's Supreme Court ordered the Standard Oil Trust dissolved. Rockefeller then developed another way to maintain control of his companies: a **holding company**, which is a corporation that controls other companies by "holding" most or all of their stock certificates. A holding company produces nothing itself; it simply owns a majority of the stock in other companies.

Rockefeller was convinced that ending competition was a good thing for the nation. Monopolies, he insisted, were the natural result of capitalism at work. "It is too late," he declared in 1899, "to argue about the advantages of [huge] industrial combinations. They are a necessity." That year, Rockefeller brought his empire under the direction of the Standard Oil Company of New Jersey, a gigantic holding company. By 1904, Rockefeller controlled almost 85 percent of the petroleum industry.

Andrew Carnegie Scottish immigrant who established the Carnegie Steel Company and became the wealthiest man in the world.

ANDREW CARNEGIE Like John D. Rockefeller, Andrew Carnegie, who created the largest steel company in the world, rose to wealth from boyhood poverty. Born in Scotland, the son of weavers, he migrated with his family in 1848 to western Pennsylvania. At age thirteen, he quit school and went to work twelve hours a day in a textile mill. In 1853, he became personal secretary to Thomas Scott, then district superintendent of the Pennsylvania Railroad and later its president. When Scott was promoted, Carnegie became superintendent. During the Civil War, when Scott became assistant secretary of war in charge of transportation, Carnegie went with him to Washington, D.C., and helped develop a military telegraph system.

Carnegie worked his way up—from telegraphy to railroading to bridge building, and then to steelmaking and investments. In the early 1870s, he decided "to concentrate on the manufacture of iron and steel and be master in that." A tiny man (barely five feet tall), Carnegie wanted to tower over the steel industry, just as Rockefeller was doing with oil.

Until the mid–nineteenth century, steel, which is stronger and more flexible than iron, could be made only from wrought iron (expensive since it had to be imported from Sweden) and could only be manufactured in small quantities. Bars of wrought iron were heated with charcoal over several days to add carbon and produce steel. It took three tons of coke, a high-burning fuel derived from coal, to produce one ton of steel.

That changed in the 1850s, when England's Sir Henry Bessemer invented the **Bessemer converter**, a process by which high-quality steel could be produced more quickly by blasting oxygen through the molten iron in a furnace. In the early 1870s, Carnegie decided to concentrate on the manufacture of steel because Bessemer's process had made it so inexpensive to produce—and the railroad industry required massive amounts of it.

As more steel was produced, its price dropped and its industrial uses soared. In 1860, the United States produced only 13,000 tons of steel. By 1880, production had reached 1.4 million tons annually. Between 1880 and 1900, Carnegie dominated the steel industry, acquiring competitors or driving them out of business by cutting prices and taking their customers. By 1900, the United States was producing more steel than Great Britain and Germany combined.

Carnegie insisted upon up-to-date machinery and equipment; he expanded production quickly and cheaply by purchasing struggling companies and preached continuous innovation to reduce operating costs. He also employed vertical integration to gain control of every phase of the steel business. He owned coal mines in West Virginia, bought vast deposits of iron ore in Michigan and Wisconsin, and transported the ore in his own ships across the Great Lakes and then by rail to his steel mills in Pittsburgh.

By 1900, the **Carnegie Steel Company**, with 20,000 employees, was the largest industrial company in the world. Carnegie's mills operated nonstop with two daily twelve-hour shifts, the only exception being the Fourth of July. "The old nations of the world," Carnegie observed, creep on at a snail's pace." America, however, "thunders past with the speed of an express [train]." Yet the frenzied pursuit of progress often made for dangerous working conditions. In a single

J. Pierpont Morgan Despite his privileged upbringing and financial success, he was self-conscious about his deformed nose, caused by chronic skin diseases.

month, seven workers were killed at Carnegie's mills. There were no safety regulations, only production goals.

J. PIERPONT MORGAN Unlike John D. Rockefeller and Andrew Carnegie, J. Pierpont Morgan was born to wealth in Connecticut. His father was a partner in a large English bank. After attending school in Switzerland and college in Germany, Morgan was sent in 1857 to work in New York City for a new enterprise started by his father, **J. Pierpont Morgan and Company**. The firm, under various names, invested European money with American businesses. It grew into a financial power by helping competing corporations merge and by purchasing massive amounts of stock in American companies and selling them at a profit.

Morgan, like Rockefeller and Carnegie, believed in freewheeling capitalism but hated competition. In his view, high profits required order and stability, and stability required consolidating competitors into trusts that he could own and manipulate.

Early on, Morgan recognized that railroads were essential to the nation's economy and growth, and by the 1890s, he controlled a sixth of the nation's railway system. But his crowning triumph was the consolidation of the steel industry. After a rapid series of mergers, he bought Carnegie's steel and iron holdings in 1901. Morgan added scores of related companies to form U.S. Steel Corporation, the world's first billion-dollar corporation, employing 168,000 people. It was the climactic event in the efforts of the great financial capitalists to reduce competition and forge monopolies.

SEARS AND ROEBUCK After the Civil War, American inventors helped manufacturers produce many new products. But the most important economic challenge was enabling the millions who lived on isolated farms and in small towns to buy the same goods available in cities.

A traveling salesman from Chicago named Aaron Montgomery Ward decided that he could reach more people by mail than on foot and thus eliminate the middlemen whose services increased the retail price of goods. Beginning in the early 1870s, Montgomery Ward and Company began selling goods at a 40 percent discount through mail-order catalogs.

By the end of the century, a new retailer had come to dominate the mail-order industry: Sears, Roebuck and Company, founded by two midwestern entrepreneurs, Richard Sears and Alvah Roebuck. The Sears, Roebuck catalog in 1897 was 786 pages long. It featured groceries, drugs, tools, furniture, household products, musical instruments, farm implements, shoes, clothes, books, and sporting goods. The company's ability to buy goods in high volume from wholesalers enabled it to sell items at prices below those offered in rural general stores. By 1907,

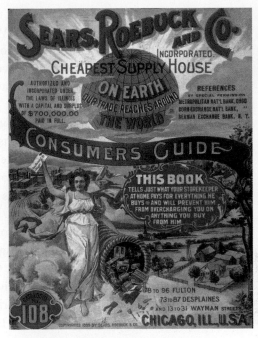

Cover of the 1897 Sears, Roebuck and Company catalog Sears, Roebuck's extensive mail-order business and discounted prices allowed its many products to reach customers in cities and in the backcountry.

Sears, Roebuck and Company, headquartered in Chicago, had become one of the largest businesses in the nation.

The Sears catalog helped transform the lives of millions of people. With the advent of free rural mail delivery in 1898, families on farms and in small towns and villages could purchase by mail the products that had been either prohibitively expensive or available only to city dwellers. By the turn of the century, 6 million Sears catalogs were being distributed each year, and the catalog had become the most widely read book in the nation after the Bible.

THE GOSPEL OF WEALTH The aggressive captains of industry were convinced that they benefited the public by accelerating America's transformation into an industrial colossus. In their eyes, it was a law of societal evolution that those most talented at producing wealth should accumulate enormous fortunes.

Some of them, however, insisted that great wealth brought great responsibilities. In his essay "The Gospel of Wealth" (1889), Andrew Carnegie argued that "not evil, but good, has come to the [Anglo-Saxon] race from the accumulation of wealth by those who have the ability and energy that produces it." Carnegie and John D. Rockefeller gave away much of their money, mostly to support education and medicine.

By 1900, Rockefeller had become the world's leading philanthropist. "I have always regarded it as a religious duty," he said late in life, "to get all I could honorably and to give all I could." He donated more than $500 million during his lifetime, including tens of millions to Baptist causes and $35 million to found the University of Chicago. His philanthropic influence continues today through the Rockefeller Foundation.

As for Carnegie, after retiring from business at age sixty-five, he declared that the "man who dies rich dies disgraced." He thereafter devoted himself to dispensing his $400 million fortune. Calling himself a "distributor" of wealth, he gave huge sums to numerous universities, built 2,500 public libraries, and helped fund churches, hospitals, parks, and halls for meetings and concerts, including New York City's Carnegie Hall.

THE ALLIANCE OF BUSINESS AND POLITICS

Most of the businesses developed by Andrew Carnegie, John D. Rockefeller, and others had cozy relationships with local, state, and federal government officials, a process of buying influence ("lobbying") that continues to this day. Big Business has legitimate political interests, but at times it exercises a corrupt influence on government. Nowhere was this more evident than during the decades after the Civil War.

REPUBLICANS AND BIG BUSINESS During and after the Civil War, the Republican party and state and federal governments grew increasingly allied with Big Business. A key element of this alliance was tariff policy. Since 1789, the federal government had imposed **tariffs**—taxes on imported goods—to raise revenue and to benefit American manufacturers by penalizing foreign competitors. In 1861, as the Civil War was starting, the Republican-dominated Congress enacted the Morrill Tariff, which doubled tax rates on hundreds of imported items, to raise money for the war and reward businesses that supported the Republican party.

After the war, President Ulysses S. Grant and other Republican presidents and Congresses continued the party's commitment to high tariffs despite

Celebrating Big Business A lavish dinner celebrated the merger of the Carnegie and Morgan interests in 1901. The shape of the banquet table is meant to symbolize a rail.

complaints that the tariffs increased consumer prices at home by restricting foreign imports and thereby relieving American manufacturers of the need to keep prices down. Farmers in the South and Midwest especially resented tariffs because, while they had to sell their crops in an open world market, they had to buy manufactured goods whose prices were artificially high because of tariffs.

During the Civil War, Congress passed other key economic legislation. The Legal Tender Act of 1862 authorized the federal government to issue paper money ("greenbacks") to help pay for the war. Having a uniform paper currency across the nation was essential to a modern economy. To that end, the National Banking Act (1863) created national banks authorized to issue greenbacks, which discouraged state banks from continuing to print their own money.

Congress also took steps to tie the new western states and territories into the national economy. The U.S. government owned vast amounts of western land, most of it acquired from the Louisiana Purchase of 1803, the Oregon Treaty with Britain in 1846, and the lands taken from Mexico in 1848 after the Mexican-American War. In the Homestead Act of 1862, Congress provided free 160-acre (or even larger) homesteads to settlers in the West, including single women and freed slaves. Their only requirement was to "improve" the

Homesteaders An African American family poses outside their log and sod cabin.

land for five years. By encouraging western settlement, the Homestead Act created markets for goods and services and spurred railroad construction to connect scattered frontier communities with major cities. Still, half the homesteads failed within a few years.

The Morrill Land-Grant College Act of 1862 transferred to each state 30,000 acres of federal land for each member of Congress the state had. The sale of those lands provided funds for states to create colleges of "agriculture and mechanic arts," such as Iowa State University and Kansas State University. The land-grant universities were created specifically to support economic growth by providing technical training needed by farmers and rapidly growing industries such as mining, steel, petroleum, transportation, forestry, and construction (engineering).

LAISSEZ-FAIRE Equally important in propelling the postwar economic boom was what governments did *not* do. There were no sweeping investigations of business practices, no legislation to protect workers and consumers, and no effective regulatory laws or commissions. Elected officials deferred to business leaders.

In general, Congress and presidents opposed government regulation of business and accepted the traditional economic doctrine of **laissez-faire**, a French phrase meaning "let them do as they will." Business leaders spent time—and money—ensuring that government officials stayed out of their businesses. For their part, politicians were usually eager to help the titans of industry in exchange for campaign contributions—or bribes.

AN INDUSTRIAL SOCIETY

Industrialization transformed not only the economy and the workplace, but also the nation's social life. Class divisions became more visible. The growing gap between rich and poor was like "social dynamite," said the Reverend Josiah Strong in 1885. Massachusetts reformer Lydia Maria Child reported that the rich "do not intermarry with the middle classes; the middle classes do not intermarry with the laboring class," nor did different classes "mix socially."

THE WAYS OF THE WEALTHY

The financiers and industrialists who dominated social, economic, and political life in post–Civil War America amassed so much wealth and showed it off so publicly that the period is still called the Gilded Age. To "gild" something is to cover it with a thin layer of gold, giving it the appearance of having greater value than it warrants. The name derived from a popular novel by Mark Twain and Charles Dudley Warner, *The Gilded Age: A Tale of Today*, which mocked the crooked dealings of political leaders and the business elite.

In 1861, the United States had only a few dozen millionaires. By 1900, there were more than 4,000. Most of them were white Protestants who voted Republican. A few were women, including Madam C.J. Walker (born Sarah Breedlove, the daughter of former Louisiana slaves), who created specialized hair products for African Americans.

Many of the *nouveaux riches* (French for "newly rich") indulged in "conspicuous consumption," competing to host the fanciest parties and live in the largest and most extravagant houses. One tycoon gave a lavish dinner to honor his dog and presented it with a $15,000 diamond necklace. At a party at New York's Delmonico's restaurant, guests smoked cigarettes wrapped in $100 bills.

When not attending parties, the rich were relaxing in mansions overlooking the cliffs at Newport, Rhode Island, atop Nob Hill in San Francisco, along Chicago's Lake Shore Drive and New York City's Fifth Avenue, and down the "Main Line" in suburban Philadelphia. "Who knows how to be rich in America?" asked E. L. Godkin, a magazine editor. "Plenty of people know how

The nouveaux riches Members of a New York City high-society club pose for a photograph at the James Hazen Hyde Ball in 1905.

to get money, but . . . to be rich properly is, indeed, a fine art. It requires culture, imagination, and character."

A GROWING MIDDLE CLASS

It was left to the fast-growing middle class to practice traditional virtues such as self-discipline, restraint, simplicity, and frugality. The term *middle class* had first appeared in the 1830s and had become commonplace by the 1870s, as more and more Americans came to view themselves as members of a distinct social class between the ragged and the rich. The middle class, explained the Chicago writer George Ade, meant those people who "are neither poverty-stricken nor offensively rich."

Most middle-class Americans working outside the home were salaried employees of large businesses who made up a new class of "white-collar" professionals: editors, engineers, accountants, supervisors, managers, marketers, and realtors. Others, mostly unmarried women, were clerks, secretaries, salespeople, teachers, and librarians.

During the 1870s, the number of office clerks quadrupled, and the number of accountants and bookkeepers doubled. At the same time, the number of attorneys, physicians, professors, journalists, nurses, and social workers also rose dramatically. The number of women working for wages outside the home tripled between 1870 and 1900, when 5 million women (17 percent of all women) held full-time jobs. This development led one male editor to joke that he was being drowned "by the rising tide of femininity."

MIDDLE-CLASS WOMEN The growing presence of middle-class women in the workforce partly reflected the increasing number of women who were gaining access to higher education. Dozens of women's colleges were founded after the Civil War, and many formerly all-male colleges began admitting women. By 1900, a third of college students were women. "After a struggle of many years," a New York woman boasted, "it is now pretty generally admitted that women possess the capacity to swallow intellectual food that was formerly considered the diet of men exclusively."

To be sure, college women were often steered into "home economics" classes and "finishing" courses intended to perfect their housekeeping or social skills. Still, the doors of the professions—law, medicine, science, and the arts—were at least partially opened to women during the Gilded Age.

In this context, then, the "woman question" that created so much public discussion and controversy in the second half of the nineteenth century

College women By the end of the century, women made up more than a third of college students. Here, an astronomy class at New York's Vassar College is underway in 1880.

involved far more than the issue of voting rights; it also concerned the liberation of at least some women from the home and from long-standing limits on
their social roles. "If there is one thing that pervades and characterizes what
is called the 'woman's movement,'" E. L. Youmans, a prominent science writer,
remarked, "It is the spirit of revolt against the home, and the determination to
escape from it into the outer spheres of activity."

NEURASTHENIA Women who tried to escape the cult of domesticity
often paid a high price. Many contracted a peculiar and baffling affliction,
which male physicians called *neurasthenia*, an energy-draining psychological and physical disorder whose symptoms included insomnia, hysteria,
headaches, depression, and a general state of fatigue. Although neurasthenia
plagued both genders, it most often affected college-educated women frustrated by the lack of meaningful career options for them.

Some doctors sought to use the prevalence of neurasthenia to force women
back into the cult of domesticity. Neurologist George M. Beard concluded—
incorrectly—that women were "more nervous, immeasurably, than men" and
that female neurasthenics tended to be "overly active" outside the home. This
explanation led one doctor to insist that the malady provided the best "argument against higher education of women."

Many women objected to such arguments. Charlotte Perkins Gilman wrote
her short story "The Yellow Wallpaper" to expose the horrors of the "rest cure"
she was subjected to at age twenty-seven. A doctor had ordered her to "live as
domestic a life as possible; have your child with you all the time; lie down an
hour after each meal; have but two hours intellectual life a day; and *never touch
pencil, brush, or pen as long as you live*." This excruciating regimen, Gilman
explained, took her "as near lunacy as one can."

The neurasthenia epidemic was responsible for an unexpected business
development. In 1886, John Stith Pemberton, a former Confederate cavalry
officer, introduced a new therapeutic elixir called Coca-Cola. During the final
days of the war, Pemberton had been slashed in the chest by a Union saber.
To relieve his pain, he took morphine, only to become addicted, as did many
other wounded soldiers. As a licensed pharmacist in civilian life, living in
Columbus, Georgia, he experimented with various "opium-free" pain reliev-
ers in liquid form. While combining residue from coca leaves (the source of
cocaine) and kola nuts (a source of caffeine), he happened upon a syrup that
relieved his pain and headaches in general.

Pemberton took the sample to Jacobs Pharmacy in Atlanta in 1886, and,
after mixing it with carbonated water, citric acid, and sugar, discovered that it

was more a tasty drink full of fizz and zest than a medicinal syrup. So Jacobs Pharmacy began selling it at the soda fountain. To boost sales, Pemberton boasted that it served as a "valuable brain tonic": it would cure headaches, relieve exhaustion, and calm nerves.

Pemberton, still addicted to morphine, died of stomach cancer two years later, but an Atlanta business executive named Asa Candler arranged to buy the rights to Coca-Cola. By 1895, Candler could announce in the company's annual report that "Coca-Cola is now drunk in every state and territory in the United States." Ads for the soft (nonalcoholic) drink promised that it was a particularly beneficial nerve tonic for neurasthenic "ladies, and all those whose sedentary employment causes nervous prostration."

The formula for the most popular drink in the world remains a closely held secret. However, the small amount of cocaine in the original mixture was removed over a century ago, when some whites claimed that its abuse "by the negroes of the South" provided a "direct incentive to the crime of rape."

COCA-COLA
SYRUP ⚹ AND ⚹ EXTRACT.

For Soda Water and other Carbonated Beverages.

This "INTELLECTUAL BEVERAGE" and TEMPERANCE DRINK contains the valuable TONIC and NERVE STIMULANT properties of the Coca plant and Cola (or Kola) nuts, and makes not only a delicious, exhilarating, refreshing and invigorating Beverage, (dispensed from the soda water fountain or in other carbonated beverages), but a valuable Brain Tonic, and a cure for all nervous affections — SICK HEAD-ACHE, NEURALGIA, HYSTERIA, MELANCHOLY, &c.

The peculiar flavor of COCA-COLA delights every palate; it is dispensed from the soda fountain in same manner as any of the fruit syrups.

J. S. Pemberton;
↪ Chemist, ↩
Sole Proprietor, Atlanta, Ga.

Coca-Cola In his advertisement for Coca-Cola syrup and extract, John Stith Pemberton describes the beverage not only as one that "delights every palate," but also as a cure for all "nervous affections."

JANE ADDAMS Social worker Jane Addams struggled with neurasthenia. After graduating in 1881 from Rockford College in Illinois, she found few opportunities to use her degree and lapsed into a state of depression during which she developed an intense "desire to live in a really *living* world."

Addams's desire to engage "real life" eventually led her to found Hull House in Chicago. There, she and other social workers helped immigrants adapt to American life and mentored young women to "learn of life from life itself." Addams and others helped convince many middle-class women to enter the "real" world. By 1890, *Arena* magazine would urge progressive-minded people to recognize the traditional view of "women as homebodies" for what it was: "hollow, false, and unreal."

Jane Addams She believed that social service requires a "scientific" observation of one's community in order to "see the needs" and provide data for legislative reform.

LADIES' HOME JOURNAL

Many women, however, identified more with the domestic life that was the focus of numerous mass-circulation magazines, the most popular of which was the *Ladies' Home Journal*. By 1910, it had almost 2 million subscribers, the largest circulation of any magazine in the world.

Edward Bok became editor of *Ladies' Home Journal* in 1889 at age twenty-six. Under his direction, the magazine provided a "great clearing house of information" to the rapidly growing urban middle class, including sections on sewing, cooking, religion, politics, and fiction.

Bok was no activist for gender equality; "my idea," he stressed, "is to keep women in the home." There, he believed, they would maintain a high moral tone for society, for women were "better, purer, conscientious, and morally stronger than men." Bok saw the middle-class woman as the "steadying influence" between the "unrest among the lower classes and [the] rottenness among the upper classes."

Bok's view of the ideal life for a woman included "a healthful diet, simple, serviceable clothing, a clean, healthy dwelling-place, open-air exercise, and good reading." He preached contentment rather than conspicuous consumption, a message directed not just to middle-class readers but also to the working poor. In a Christmas editorial, though, Bok recognized that "it is a hard thing for those who have little to believe that the greatest happiness of life is with them: that it is not with those who have abundance."

THE WORKING CLASS

Railroads, factories, mills, mines, slaughterhouses, and sweatshops had growing needs for unskilled workers, which attracted new groups to the workforce, especially immigrants and women and children. In addition, millions of rural folk, especially young people, formed a migratory stream from the agricultural regions of the South and Midwest to cities and factories across the country.

Although wage levels rose during the Gilded Age, there was a great disparity in the pay received by skilled and unskilled workers. During the economic recessions and depressions that occurred about every six years, unskilled workers were the first to be laid off or to have their wages slashed. In addition, working conditions were difficult and often dangerous for those at the bottom of the occupational scale. The average workweek was fifty-nine hours, or nearly six 10-hour days.

American industry had the highest rate of workplace accidents and deaths in the world, and there were virtually no safety regulations. Few machines had safety devices; few factories or mills had fire escapes. Respiratory diseases were common in mines, textile mills, and unventilated buildings. Between 1888 and 1894, some 16,000 railroad workers were killed and 170,000 maimed in on-the-job accidents. The United States was also the only industrial nation with no insurance program to cover medical expenses for on-the-job injuries.

WORKING WOMEN Mills, mines, factories, and large businesses needed far more unskilled workers than skilled ones. Employers often recruited women and children for the unskilled jobs because they were willing to work for lower wages than men. In addition to operating sewing machines or tending to textile machines spinning yarn or thread, women worked as maids, cooks, or nannies. In the manufacturing sector, women's wages averaged $7 a week, compared to $10 for unskilled men.

CHILD LABOR Young people had always worked in America; farms required everyone to pitch in. In the late nineteenth century, however, millions of children took up work outside the home, sorting coal, stitching clothes, shucking oysters, peeling shrimp, canning food, blowing glass, tending looms, and operating other kinds of machinery. **Child labor** increased as parents desperate for income put their children to work. By 1880, one of every six children under age fourteen was working full-time; by 1900, the United States had almost 2 million child laborers.

In Pennsylvania, West Virginia, and eastern Kentucky, soot-smeared boys worked in the coal mines. In New England and the South, children labored in dusty textile mills where, during the night shift, they had water thrown in their faces to keep them awake. In the southern mills, a fourth of the employees were below age fifteen, and children as young as eight often worked twelve hours a day, six days a week. As a result, they received little or no education.

Children in industry These four young boys performed the dangerous work of mine helpers in West Virginia around 1900.

Factories, mills, mines, and canneries were especially dangerous for children, who suffered three times as many accidents as adult workers and higher rates of respiratory diseases. A child working in a southern textile mill was only half as likely to reach the age of twenty as a child who did not.

ORGANIZED LABOR The efforts of the working poor to form unions to improve their pay and working conditions faced formidable obstacles during the Gilded Age. Many executives fought against unions. They "blacklisted" union organizers by circulating their names to keep them from being hired, fired labor leaders, and often hired "scabs" (nonunion workers) to replace workers who went on strike. Another factor impeding the growth of unions was that many workers were immigrants who spoke different languages and often distrusted people from other ethnic groups. Nonetheless, with or without unions, workers began to stage strikes that often led to violence.

THE MOLLY MAGUIRES During the early 1870s, violence erupted in the eastern Pennsylvania coalfields, when a secret Irish American group called the Molly Maguires took economic justice into their own hands. The Mollies took their name from an Irish patriot who had led the resistance against the British. Outraged by dangerous working conditions in the mines and the owners' brutal efforts to suppress union activity, the Mollies used intimidation, beatings, and killings to avenge the wrongs done to Irish workers.

Their terrorism reached its peak in 1874–1875, prompting mine owners to hire men from the Pinkerton Detective Agency (commonly referred to as Pinkertons) to stop the movement. One of the agents who infiltrated the Mollies uncovered enough evidence to have the leaders indicted for the coalfield murders. In 1876, twenty-four Molly Maguires were convicted by a non-Irish jury; ten were hanged.

THE GREAT RAILROAD STRIKE (1877) After the financial panic of 1873, the major rail lines, fearful of a recession, had slashed workers' wages by 35 percent. In July 1877, the companies announced another 10 percent wage cut, which led most of the Baltimore and Ohio (B & O) railroad workers at Martinsburg, West Virginia, to walk off the job, which shut down rail traffic. Initially, John Garrett, the president of the B & O, was confident the protest would quickly subside. Because "labor lacked unity," he commented, "strikes had easily been broken and the men easily replaced."

Garrett was wrong. The railroad strike spread to hundreds of other cities and towns. In San Francisco, local grievances led raging trainmen, who blamed Asians for taking white jobs, to set fire to Chinese neighborhoods. Across the

"The Chinese Must Go" In this advertisement for the Missouri Steam Washer, the American-made washing machine drives a Chinese laundryman back to China, playing on the growing anti-Chinese sentiments in the 1880s.

nation, tens of thousands of railroad workers walked off the job, and the subsequent violence left more than 100 people dead, many more wounded, and resulted in millions of dollars in damaged property.

In Pittsburgh, thousands of striking workers burned 39 buildings and destroyed more than 1,000 railcars and locomotives. The strikers also assaulted workers who refused to join them. Hundreds of looters—men, women, and children—risked their lives to grab anything of value from the freight cars before they were put to the torch. A huge crowd filled nearby hillsides and cheered as the Pennsylvania Railroad, "that damned monopoly," went up in flames.

The **Great Railroad Strike of 1877** was the first nationwide labor uprising, and it revealed how polarized the relationship between the working poor and company executives had become. Governors mobilized state militia units to suppress the rioters.

In Philadelphia, the militia dispersed a crowd at the cost of twenty-six lives, but looting and burning continued until President Rutherford B. Hayes dispatched federal troops to put down the "insurrection." It was the first time federal troops in large numbers had suppressed civilian strikers. Eventually the disgruntled workers, lacking organized bargaining power, had little choice but to return to work.

The strike had failed, but for many it raised the possibility of what a Pittsburgh newspaper saw as "a great civil war in this country between labor and capital." Many workers felt that violence was their only option. "The working people everywhere are with us," a unionist told a reporter. "They know what it is to bring up a family on ninety cents a day, to live on beans and corn meal week in and week out, to run in debt at the [company] stores until you cannot get trusted any longer, to see the wife breaking down . . . and the children growing sharp and fierce like wolves day after day because they don't get enough to eat."

Equally disturbing to those in positions of corporate and political power was the presence of many women among the protesters. A Baltimore journalist noted that the "singular part of the disturbances is the very active part taken by the women, who are the wives and mothers of the [railroad] firemen."

President Hayes wrote in his diary, "The strikes have been put down by *force*. But now for the *real* remedy. Can't something be done by education of the strikers, by judicious control of the capitalists, by wise general policy, to end or diminish the evil?" It was a fair question that largely went unanswered.

THE SAND-LOT INCIDENT In California, the national railroad strike indirectly gave rise to a working-class political movement. In 1877, a meeting held in a sandy San Francisco vacant lot to express sympathy for the railroad strikers ended with white laborers attacking Chinese workers who were passing by. In the so-called Sand-Lot Incident, the Chinese were handy scapegoats for frustrated whites who believed the Asians had taken their jobs.

Such anti-Chinese sentiment soon drove an Irish immigrant delivery-man in San Francisco, Denis Kearney, to organize the Workingmen's Party of California, whose platform called for the United States to stop Chinese immigration. Kearney lectured about the "foreign peril" and blasted the railroad barons for exploiting the poor. Although Kearney failed to build a lasting movement, his anti-Chinese theme became a national issue. In 1882, Congress voted to prohibit Chinese immigration for ten years.

THE NATIONAL LABOR UNION As the size and power of corporations increased, efforts to build a national labor union movement gained momentum. During the Civil War, because of the increased demand for skilled labor, so-called craft unions made up of workers expert at a particular handicraft or trade grew in strength and number. Yet there was no overall connection among such groups until 1866, when the **National Labor Union (NLU)** convened in Baltimore.

The NLU was more interested in improving workplace conditions than in bargaining about wages. The group promoted an eight-hour workday, workers' cooperatives (in which workers, collectively, would create and own their own large-scale manufacturing and mining operations), "greenbackism" (the printing of paper money to inflate the currency and thereby relieve debtors), and equal voting rights for women and African Americans.

Like most such organizations in the nineteenth century, however, the NLU did not allow women as members. It also discriminated against African American workers, who were forced to organize unions of their own. W. E. B. DuBois, an outspoken black civil rights activist, charged that the "white worker did not want the Negro in his unions, did not believe in him as a man."

After the NLU's head, William Sylvis, died suddenly in 1869, its support declined, and by 1872 the union had disbanded. It was, however, influential in persuading Congress to enact an eight-hour workday for federal employees and to repeal the 1864 Contract Labor Act, which had been passed to encourage the importation of laborers by allowing employers to pay for the passage of foreign workers to America. In exchange, the workers were committed to work for a specified number of years. Employers had taken advantage of the Contract Labor Act to recruit foreign laborers willing to work for lower wages than their American counterparts.

THE KNIGHTS OF LABOR In 1869, another national labor group emerged: the Noble Order of the **Knights of Labor**. Even as trade unions collapsed during the depression of the 1870s, it grew rapidly.

The Knights of Labor endorsed most of the reforms advanced by previous workingmen's groups, including the elimination of convict-labor competition, the establishment of the eight-hour day, and the greater use of paper currency. One reform the group pursued was equal pay for equal work by men and women.

The Knights of Labor wanted to transform capitalism. "We do not believe," a Knights leader explained, "that the emancipation of labor will come with increased wages and a reduction in the [working] hours of labor; we must go deeper than that, and this matter will not be settled until the wage system is abolished."

The Knights of Labor did not believe in organizing members according to their particular trade. The organization allowed as members all who had ever worked for wages, except lawyers, doctors, bankers, those who sold liquor, and the Chinese, whom they viewed as "coolies." By recruiting all types of workers, black or white, men or women, the Knights became the nation's largest labor union, but they also struggled with internal tensions.

In 1879, Terence V. Powderly, the thirty-year-old mayor of Scranton, Pennsylvania, became head of the Knights of Labor. He stressed winning political control of the communities where union workers lived, and the Knights owed their greatest growth to strikes that occurred under his leadership. In the

Knights of Labor This national labor organization was the most egalitarian union during the Gilded Age.

early 1880s, they increased their membership from about 100,000 to more than 700,000. As Powderly explained, the Knights were the "connecting link between all branches of honourable toil."

MOTHER JONES One of the most colorful labor agitators was a remarkable woman known simply as Mother Jones. Dressed in matronly black dresses and hats, she was a tireless champion of the working poor who used fiery rhetoric to excite crowds and attract attention. She led marches, dodged bullets, served jail terms, and confronted business titans and police. In 1913, a district attorney called her the "most dangerous woman in America."

Mother Jones The Irish-born teacher turned celebrated union activist and progressive is pictured here campaigning for the rights of workers at the White House in 1924.

Born in Cork, Ireland, in 1837, Mary Harris was the second of five children in a poor Catholic family that fled the Irish potato famine at midcentury and settled in Toronto. In 1861, she moved to Memphis, Tennessee, and began teaching. There, as the Civil War was erupting, she met and married George Jones, an iron molder and staunch union member. They had four children, but in 1867, disaster struck. A yellow fever epidemic devastated Memphis, killing Mary's husband and children.

The grief-stricken thirty-seven-year-old widow moved to Chicago and took up dressmaking, only to see her shop, home, and belongings destroyed in the Great Fire of 1871. Having lost her family and her finances, and angry at the social inequality and injustices she saw around her, Mary Jones drifted into the labor movement and soon emerged as its most passionate advocate. Chicago was, at the time, the seedbed of labor radicalism, and the union culture nurtured in her a lifelong dedication to the cause of wage workers and their families.

Declaring herself the "mother" of the fledgling labor movement, she joined the Knights of Labor as an organizer and public speaker. In the late 1880s she became an ardent advocate for the United Mine Workers (UMW), various other unions, and the Socialist party. For the next thirty years, she crisscrossed the nation, recruiting union members, supporting strikers (her "boys"), raising funds, walking picket lines, defying court injunctions, berating politicians, and spending time in prison. She became a living legend. By 1900, Jones was the most famous woman in the labor union movement. "Whenever trouble broke out against the miners," a union leader explained, "Mother Jones went there."

Wherever Mother Jones went, she promoted higher wages, shorter hours, safer workplaces, and restrictions on child labor. During a miners' strike in West Virginia, she was arrested, convicted of "conspiracy that resulted in murder," and sentenced to twenty years in prison. The outcry over her plight helped spur a Senate committee to investigate conditions in the coal mines. The governor set her free.

In 1903, Mother Jones organized a highly publicized weeklong march of child workers from Pennsylvania to the New York home of President Theodore Roosevelt. The children were physically stunted and mutilated, most of them missing fingers or hands from machinery accidents. Roosevelt refused to see them, but as Jones explained, "Our march had done its work. We had drawn the attention of the nation to the crime of child labor." Shortly thereafter, the Pennsylvania state legislature raised the legal working age to fourteen.

Mother Jones's commitment never wavered. At age eighty-three, she was arrested and jailed after joining a miners' strike in Colorado. At her funeral, in 1930, a speaker urged people to remember her famous rallying cry: "Pray for the dead and fight like hell for the living."

ANARCHISM One of the many challenges facing the labor union movement during the Gilded Age was growing hostility from middle-class Americans who viewed unionized workers, especially those involved in clashes with police, as violent radicals or anarchists. Anarchists believed that powerful capitalists bribed elected officials to oppress the working poor. They dreamed of the elimination of government altogether, and some were willing to use bombs and bullets to achieve their goal.

Many European anarchists, mostly Germans or Italians, immigrated to the United States during the last quarter of the nineteenth century. Although most disavowed violence, the terrorists among them ensured that the label "anarchist" provoked frightening images in the minds of many. Anarchists dreamed of labor unions replacing governments, enabling workers to rule.

Labor-related violence increased during the 1880s as the gap between the rich and working poor widened. Between 1880 and 1900, some 6.6 million hourly workers participated in more than 23,000 strikes nationwide. Chicago was a hotbed of unrest and a magnet for immigrants, especially German and

Irish laborers, some of whom openly endorsed violence to ignite a working-class uprising. The Chicago labor movement's foremost demand was for an eight-hour workday. What came to be called the **Haymarket riot** grew indirectly out of prolonged agitation for this goal.

THE HAYMARKET RIOT (1886) In 1886, some 40,000 Chicago workers went on strike in support of an eight-hour workday. On May 3, violent clashes between strikers and nonunion scabs hired to replace the striking workers erupted outside the McCormick Harvesting Machine Company plant. The police arrived, shots rang out, and two strikers were killed. The killings infuriated leaders of the anarchist movement, who organized a mass protest at Haymarket Square, near Chicago's city center, the following night, May 4.

The rally was peaceful, but the speeches were not. After listening to speakers complain about low wages and long working hours, the crowd of angry laborers was beginning to break up when more than a hundred police arrived and ordered them to disperse. At that point, someone threw a bomb into the ranks of blue uniforms that left dozens maimed or killed. The police then fired into the fleeing crowd, resulting in more casualties. Four workers and seven policemen were killed, and over a hundred more were wounded in what journalists called America's first terrorist bombing.

The next day, Chicago's mayor banned all labor meetings, and newspapers printed sensational headlines about anarchists terrorizing the city. "There are no good anarchists except dead anarchists," the *St. Louis Globe-Democrat* raged. One New York newspaper demanded stern punishment for "the few long-haired, wild-eyed, bad-smelling, atheistic, reckless foreign wretches" who promoted such unrest.

During the summer of 1886, seven anarchist leaders, all but one of them German-language speakers, were sentenced to death despite the lack of evidence linking them to the bomb thrower, whose identity was never determined. After being sentenced to be hanged, Louis Lingg declared that he was innocent but was "in favor of using force" to end the abuses of the capitalist system.

Lawyers for the anarchists appealed the convictions to the Illinois Supreme Court, and petitioners from around the world appealed for clemency. One of the petitioners was Samuel Gompers, the founding president of the American Federation of Labor (AFL). "I abhor anarchy," Gompers stressed, "but I also abhor injustice when meted out even to the most despicable being on earth."

On November 10, 1887, Lingg committed suicide in his cell, using a dynamite blasting cap hidden in a cigar. That same day, the governor commuted the sentences of two convicted conspirators to life imprisonment. The next day, the four remaining condemned men were hanged.

One of those executed was Albert Parsons, an Alabama-born socialist-anarchist journalist and labor organizer, the only English-speaker among those convicted. Orphaned at age five, he had been raised by a slave named Esther before joining his older brother in Texas. As a fifteen-year-old, he joined his brother's Confederate unit, the Lone Star Grays, and fought in the Civil War. After the war, he reversed himself and championed "the political rights of the negro people" and the Republican party. He later joined the Socialist party and published a militant newspaper, *The Spectator*. Doing so earned him "idolization" from African Americans and death threats from unreconstructed white Texans, who called him a scalawag traitor. He was shot in the leg, beaten, and threatened with lynching.

Such violent acts led Parsons to move to Chicago in 1873 with his wife Lucy, a former slave who had become a women's rights activist and union organizer. In Chicago, Parsons joined the Knights of Labor and published *The Alarm*, a newspaper aimed at the working poor.

During the early 1880s, Albert and Lucy Parsons embraced anarchism, explaining that the movement "believes in peace, but not at the expense of liberty." Albert denounced all "political laws as violations of the laws of nature, and the rights of men." From his prison cell in 1886, he penned a message to his friends and followers: "Lay bare the inequities of capitalism; expose the slavery of law; proclaim the tyranny of government; denounce the greed, cruelty, abominations of the privileged class who riot and revel on the labor of their wage-slaves."

Some 200,000 people lined the streets of Chicago as the caskets of Parsons and the other condemned men were paraded before burial. To labor militants around the world, the executed anarchists were working-class martyrs; to the police and the economic elite in Chicago, they were demonic assassins.

A BACKLASH AGAINST UNIONS After the Haymarket riot, tensions between workers and management reached a fever pitch across the nation. In 1886 alone, there were 1,400 strikes involving 700,000 workers. But the violence in Chicago also triggered widespread hostility to the Knights of Labor and labor groups in general. Despite his best efforts, union leader Terence Powderly could never separate in the public mind the Knights from the anarchists, since one of those convicted of conspiracy in the bombing was a member of the union.

Powderly clung to leadership until 1893, but after that the union evaporated. Yet the Knights did attain some lasting achievements, including an 1880 federal law providing for the arbitration of labor disputes, and the creation of the federal Bureau of Labor Statistics in 1884. Another of their successes was the Foran Act of 1885, which, though poorly enforced, penalized employers who imported immigrant workers. By their example, the Knights spread the idea of unionism and initiated a new type of organization: the industrial union, which included all skilled and unskilled workers within a particular industry.

GOMPERS AND THE AFL The craft (or trade) unions, representing skilled workers, generally opposed efforts to unite with industrial unionism. Leaders of the craft unions feared that doing so would mean the loss of their identity and bargaining power. Thus, in 1886, delegates from twenty-five craft unions organized the **American Federation of Labor (AFL)**. It was a federation of many separate national unions, each of which was largely free to act on its own in dealing with business owners.

Samuel Gompers served as president of the AFL from its founding until his death in 1924. Born in England, he came to the United States as a teenager, joined the Cigar Makers' Union in 1864, and became president of his New York City local union in 1877. Unlike Terence Powderly and the Knights of Labor, Gompers focused on concrete economic gains—higher wages, shorter hours, and better working conditions.

The AFL at first grew slowly, but by the turn of the century, it claimed 500,000 members. In 1914, it had 2 million, and in 1920, it reached a peak of 4 million. But even then, the AFL included less than 15 percent of the nation's nonagricultural workers. In fact, all unions, including the so-called railroad brotherhoods that were unaffiliated with the AFL, accounted for little more than 18 percent of the total workforce.

Organized labor's strongholds were in transportation and the building trades. Most of the larger manufacturing industries—including steel, textiles, tobacco, and meatpacking—remained almost untouched. Gompers never opposed industrial unions, and several became important affiliates of the AFL: the United Mine Workers, the International Ladies Garment Workers, and the Amalgamated Clothing Workers.

Two incidents in the 1890s stalled the emerging industrial-union movement: the **Homestead Steel strike** of 1892 and the **Pullman strike** of 1894. These conflicts represented a test of strength for the organized labor movement. They also served to reshape the political landscape.

THE HOMESTEAD STEEL STRIKE The Amalgamated Association of Iron and Steel Workers, founded in 1876, was the nation's largest craft union. At the massive steel mill owned by Andrew Carnegie at Homestead,

Pennsylvania, along the Monongahela River near Pittsburgh, the union had enjoyed friendly relations with management until Henry Clay Frick became chief executive in 1889 and the company's second largest shareholder. Frick prided himself on being the most anti-labor executive in the nation.

A showdown was delayed until 1892, however, when the union contract came up for renewal. Carnegie, who had previously expressed sympathy for the unions, went on a hunting trip in his native Scotland, intentionally leaving Frick to handle the difficult negotiations. He was "sure you will win."

Carnegie knew what was in the works: a cost-cutting reduction in the number of highly paid skilled workers through the use of labor-saving machinery, even though the corporation was enjoying high profits. It was a deliberate attempt to smash the union. "Am with you to the end," Carnegie wrote to Frick. William Jones, the mill manager, opposed cutting wages because "our men are working hard and faithfully. . . . Now, mark what I tell you. Our labor is the cheapest in the country."

Jones's protests did little good. As negotiations dragged on, the company announced on June 25 that it would stop negotiating with the 3,800 workers in four days unless an agreement were reached. A strike—or, more properly, a lockout in which management closed down the mill to force the union to make concessions—would begin on June 29. Frick told journalists that he was determined to have "absolute control of our plant and business."

Frick ordered construction of a twelve-foot-high fence crowned with barbed wire around the plant and equipped it with watchtowers, searchlights, rifle slits, and high-pressure water cannons. He also hired a private army of 316 Pinkerton agents to protect "Fort Frick."

Before dawn on July 6, 1892, the "Pinkertons" floated up the Monongahela River on two barges pulled by a tugboat. Thousands of unionists and their supporters, many of them armed, were waiting on shore. A fourteen-hour gun battle ensued. Seven workers and four Pinkertons were killed, and dozens were wounded. Hundreds of women on shore shouted, "Kill the Pinkertons!"

In the end, the Pinkertons surrendered and were marched away to taunts from crowds lining the streets. But the celebrations were short-lived. A week later, the Pennsylvania governor dispatched 4,000 state militiamen to Homestead, where they surrounded the mill and dispersed the picketing workers. Frick then hired strikebreakers to operate the mill. He refused to resume negotiations: "I will never recognize the union, never, never!"

The strike dragged on until November, but by then the union was dead and its leaders had been charged with murder and treason. The union cause was not helped when Alexander Berkman, a Lithuanian anarchist, tried to assassinate Frick in his office on July 23, shooting him twice in the neck and stabbing him three times. Despite his wounds, Frick fought back fiercely and, with the help of staff members, subdued the would-be assassin.

After that incident, much of the sympathy for the strikers evaporated. As a union leader explained, Berkman's bullets "went straight through the heart of the Homestead strike." Penniless and demoralized, the workers ended their walkout on November 20 and accepted the company's harsh wage cuts. Only a fifth of the strikers got their jobs back; the rest were "blacklisted" to prevent other steel mills from hiring them.

Carnegie and Frick, with the support of local, state, and national officials, had eliminated the union. After the Homestead strike, none of Carnegie's steel plants employed unionized workers. Within a few years, Carnegie could confide to a friend that he was "ashamed to tell you" how large his profits were from the Homestead plant.

But his reputation was ruined. "Three months ago Andrew Carnegie was a man to be envied," wrote a St. Louis newspaper. "Today he is an object of mingled pity and contempt." The editor called him a "moral coward." A "single word from him [in Scotland] might have saved the bloodshed—but the word was never spoken."

With each passing year, Carnegie nursed regrets about how Frick had handled the Homestead strike. In the end, Frick split with Carnegie after learning that his boss had been telling lies about him and making "insults" about his character. Frick told Carnegie that he had grown "tired of your business methods, your absurd newspaper interviews and personal remarks and unwarranted interference in matters you know nothing about." When Carnegie sought to reconcile with his former lieutenant, Frick told the messenger: "You can say to Andrew Carnegie that I will meet him in hell where we are both going."

THE PULLMAN STRIKE The Pullman strike of 1894 paralyzed the economies of the twenty-seven states and territories in the western half of the nation. It involved a dispute at Pullman, Illinois, a "model" industrial suburb of Chicago owned by the Pullman Palace Car Company, which made passenger train cars (called "Pullmans" or "sleeping cars").

Employees were required to live in the town's 1,400 cottages, which had been built to high standards, with gas heat and indoor plumbing. With 12,000 residents, the town boasted a library, a theater, a school, parks and playgrounds, and a glass-roofed shopping mall owned by the company. There were no saloons, social clubs, newspapers, or private property not owned by the company. No political activities were allowed.

As a "company town," Pullman was of much higher quality than the villages in the South owned by textile mills. Yet over time, many workers came to resent living under the thumb of the company's owner, George Pullman.

Eugene V. Debs Founder of the American Railway Union, and later the presidential candidate for the Socialist Party of America.

During the depression of 1893, Pullman laid off 3,000 of his 5,800 employees and cut wages 25 to 40 percent for the rest, but he did not lower rents for housing or the price of food in the company store. In the spring of 1894, desperate workers joined the American Railway Union, founded the previous year by Eugene V. Debs.

Debs was a child of working-class immigrants in Indiana. He had quit school at age fourteen to work for an Indiana railroad before becoming a union organizer. After serving in the state legislature, he became a tireless spokesman for labor radicalism, and he worked to organize all railway workers—skilled or unskilled—into the American Railway Union, which soon became a powerful example of his idea of "One Big Union."

Debs was impossible to dislike. Even his enemies acknowledged that he was a truly good person. His essential goodness prompted him to intervene in the Pullman controversy. He urged the angry workers to obey the laws and avoid violence. After George Pullman fired three members of a workers' grievance committee, the workers went on strike on May 11, 1894.

In June, after Pullman refused Debs's plea for a negotiated settlement, the Railway Union workers stopped handling trains containing Pullman railcars. By the end of July, they had shut down most of the railroads in the Midwest and cut off all traffic through Chicago. To keep the trains running, railroad

The Pullman Strike Federal troops guarding the railroads, 1894.

executives hired strikebreakers, and the U.S. attorney general, swore in 3,400 special deputies to protect them. Yet angry workers still assaulted strikebreakers and destroyed property.

Finally, on July 3, President Grover Cleveland sent 2,000 federal troops into the Chicago area, claiming it was his duty to ensure delivery of the mail. Meanwhile, the attorney general convinced a federal judge to sign an *injunction* (an official court decree) prohibiting the labor union from interfering.

On July 13, the union called off the strike. A few days later, a court cited Debs for violating the injunction and sentenced him to serve six months in jail. Eugene Debs emerged from jail the most famous labor leader in the United States. While a prisoner, he had become a socialist who would run for president five times.

In 1897, George Pullman died of a heart attack, and the following year, the city of Chicago annexed the town of Pullman. A reporter for the *Nation* noted that despite the town's attractive features, what the workers wanted most was the chance to own a house of their own. "Mr. Pullman," he explained, "overlooked this peculiar American characteristic."

THE LATTIMER MASSACRE In August 1897, the Lehigh and Wilkes-Barre Coal Company laid off anthracite coal workers from the Lattimer mine near Hazleton, Pennsylvania. Those who remained had to accept wage cuts, longer workdays, increased costs for company-owned housing and goods from the company-owned store, and increasingly dangerous working conditions. An average of three workers were killed in accidents every two days. Immigrants were assigned the most dangerous jobs.

Such conditions finally provoked a strike by many of the 10,000 workers, most of whom were from central or eastern Europe: Poland, Slovakia, Hungary, Lithuania, and Germany. Speaking for the workers, the *Hazleton Evening Standard* issued a blunt warning: "The day of the slave driver is past, and the once ignorant foreigner will no longer tolerate it." Initially, management agreed to raise wages, only to renege on the offer. As the strike continued, the mine owners asked county sheriff James L. Martin to disperse the workers.

On September 10, Martin organized a posse of 150 armed men paid by the mine owners. They soon confronted several hundred unarmed strikers marching peacefully to the Lattimer mine, where they intended to convince Italian workers to join them. They carried an American flag.

Sheriff Martin ordered the marchers to disperse and tried to seize their flag. When a scuffle ensued, a deputy shouted, "Shoot the sons of bitches." The posse opened fire, killing nineteen unarmed miners. At least thirty-nine others were wounded. Most of them had been shot in the back. The flag bearer was the first man killed.

Accounts of the Lattimer Massacre circulated quickly throughout the state and nation. Thousands attended the funerals of the slain workers as newspapers expressed widespread revulsion at the "butchery." One Pittsburgh headline read: "Massacre of Slavs—In the Free-est Country under the Sun—People Are Shot like Dogs."

In early 1898, Sheriff Martin and seventy-three of his deputies were tried for murder. Martin expressed surprise, explaining that he and his men had shot "only foreigners." In his closing remarks to the jury, the district attorney noted that if the deputies "had protected the lives of these poor creatures of God with the same solicitude they displayed in protecting the property of the employers there would be no case here today." All of the accused were acquitted. Within weeks after the massacre, 15,000 miners joined the United Mine Workers union.

THE WESTERN FEDERATION OF MINERS At the same time that Eugene Debs was mobilizing a socialist-based working-class movement, militant labor leaders in the West were organizing the Western Federation of Miners (WFM). The WFM represented smelter workers and "hard-rock" miners who worked deep underground harvesting copper, gold, silver, and lead in Montana, Colorado, Idaho, Utah, and the Dakotas.

Almost from its birth in 1883 in Butte, Montana, the WFM was viewed as a radical labor union. The Western Federation was at the center of violent confrontations with unyielding mine operators who mobilized secret spies, private armies, state militias, and even federal troops against it.

That several dozen miners were killed in clashes with management helps explain why the WFM grew especially militant. At its 1901 convention, it was proclaimed that a "complete revolution of social and economic conditions" was "the only salvation of the working classes." WFM leaders demanded the abolition of the wage system. By the spring of 1903, the WFM was the most militant labor organization in the country.

The group's most outspoken leader was William "Big Bill" Haywood. Born in Salt Lake City, Utah, he went to work in Nevada silver mines at age nine. He later was a homesteader and surveyor before becoming a socialist miner and joining the union in 1896; by 1902, he was its primary spokesman, featuring a face "like a scarred battlefield."

Haywood and the WFM promoted industrial unionism, recruiting both skilled and unskilled workers. The organization also welcomed members of all races and ethnic groups—men and women. Perhaps most controversial was Haywood's advocacy of strikes over negotiations, a militant stance that few other unions adopted.

THE INTERNATIONAL WORKERS OF THE WORLD In 1905, Big Bill Haywood, Eugene Debs, Daniel De Leon (head of the Socialist Labor party), Mother Jones, Lucy Parsons, and two dozen other prominent socialists and union leaders met secretly in Chicago to form the **International Workers of the World (IWW)**. It would be a giant global "revolutionary labor union" ("One Big Union") open to all workers, skilled or unskilled, man or woman, child or adult, native or immigrant, black or white—as long as they renounced capitalism. Their purpose was to provide an alternative to the American Federation of Labor, which excluded unskilled laborers.

The "Wobblies," as IWW members were called, sought to destroy the capitalist system and "take possession of the means of production." Workers would then elect their workplace managers. De Leon argued that the IWW "must be founded on the class struggle" and "the irrepressible conflict between the capitalist class and the working class." The Wobblies were disproportionately immigrants and migrant workers, the unskilled, unorganized, unrepresented, and unwanted among the working poor.

Not surprisingly, the IWW generated intense criticism. The *Los Angeles Times*, for example, claimed that a "vast number of IWWs are non-producers.

IWW stands for I won't work, and I want whisky. . . . The average Wobbly, it must be remembered, is a sort of half wild animal. He lives on the road, cooks his food in rusty tin cans . . . and sleeps in "jungles," barns, outhouses, freight cars. . . . They are all in all a lot of homeless men wandering about the country without fixed destination or purpose, other than destruction."

Like other radical groups, the IWW was split by sectarian disputes. Debs and De Leon withdrew because the IWW refused to affiliate with their rival socialist parties.

Bill Haywood held the IWW together, recruiting tens of thousands of new members from lumberyards, farms, and factories. Tall, handsome, and muscular, he commanded attention and respect. He despised the AFL and its conservative labor philosophy. Samuel Gompers, he claimed, was "a squat specimen of humanity" with "small snapping eyes, a hard cruel mouth," and a personality that was "vain, conceited, petulant and vindictive." Instead of following Gompers's advice to organize only skilled workers, Haywood persisted in his dream of an all-inclusive union dedicated to a socialism "with its working clothes on."

Haywood and the Wobblies, however, recruited members with the least power and influence, chiefly the migrant workers in the West and immigrants in the East. Always ambivalent about diluting their revolutionary principles, Wobblies scorned the usual labor agreements even when they participated in them. They engaged in spectacular battles with employers but scored few victories while arousing hysterical opposition. They were branded anarchists, bums, and criminals.

The largest and most successful IWW strike was against a textile mill in Lawrence, Massachusetts, in 1912, when it announced an across-the-board cut in wages. Haywood and others, including young Elizabeth Gurley Flynn, the "Joan of Arc of the working class," forged an unlikely coalition of thousands of mostly immigrant women workers. Their ranks included Italians, Germans, French Canadians, Poles, Lithuanians, Russians, Greeks, as well as those from a dozen other countries. Representing almost half the mill's workforce, the strikers spoke as many as fifteen different languages.

The IWW organizers shrewdly captured public support by portraying the strike as a plea for basic human rights. As Flynn insisted, "Better to starve fighting than to starve working!" Striking mill girls carried picket signs announcing: "WE WANT BREAD AND ROSES, TOO." The strikers won the fight, as the owners of the American Woolen Company agreed to wage increases, overtime pay, and other benefits. "Labor has seldom, if ever, won so complete a victory," journalist Lincoln Steffens wrote in the *New York Globe*.

ECONOMIC SUCCESS AND EXCESS

For all the stress and strain caused by swift industrialization and labor union responses, American productivity soared in the late nineteenth century. By 1900, the United States was producing a third of the world's goods, and millions of immigrants continued to risk all in hopes of chasing the American dream. Corporate empires generated enormous fortunes for a few and real improvements in the quality of life for many. The majority of workers now labored in factories and mines rather than on farms.

The urban-industrial revolution and the gigantic new corporations it created transformed the size, scope, and power of the American economy, for good and for ill. As the twentieth century dawned, an unregulated capitalist economy had grown corrupt and recklessly out of balance—and only government intervention could restore economic fairness and social stability.

CHAPTER REVIEW

SUMMARY

- **The Causes of Industrial Growth**   During the late nineteenth century, agricultural and industrial production increased sharply. The national railroad network grew to nearly 200,000 miles, the most extensive in the world. The surge of industrialization expanded the use of electrical power and the application of scientific research to industrial processes. The *Bessemer converter* allowed for the mass production of steel.

- **The Rise of Big Business**   Many businesses grew to enormous size and power—and often ignored ethics and the law in doing so. Entrepreneurs like John D. Rockefeller, Andrew Carnegie, and J. Pierpont Morgan were extraordinarily skilled at gaining control of particular industries. Companies such as *Standard Oil* and *Carnegie Steel* practiced both *vertical integration*, through which they controlled all the enterprises needed to produce and distribute their products, and *horizontal integration*, in which they absorbed or eliminated their competitors. To consolidate their holdings and sidestep laws prohibiting *monopolies*, they created *trusts* and eventually *holding companies*. *J. Pierpont Morgan and Company*, an investment bank, pioneered methods for consolidating corporations and eliminating competition.

- **The Alliance of Business and Politics**   The federal government encouraged economic growth after the Civil War by imposing high *tariffs* on imported products, granting public land to railroad companies and settlers in the West, establishing a stable currency, and encouraging the creation of land-grant universities to spur technical innovation and research. Equally important, local, state, and federal governments made little effort to regulate the activities of businesses. This *laissez-faire* policy allowed entrepreneurs to experiment with new methods of organization but also created conditions for rampant corruption and abuse.

- **A Changed Social Order**   While the business and financial elite showed off their new wealth with extravagant homes and parties, the urban and industrial work-force was largely composed of unskilled workers. *Child labor* sometimes involved children as young as eight working twelve-hour days. Business owners and managers showed little concern for workplace safety, and work-related accidents and diseases were common. With industrialization and the rise of Big Business also came an increase in the number of people who considered themselves middle class. Growing numbers of women went to college, took business and professional jobs, and participated in other public activities.

- **Organized Labor**   It was difficult for unskilled workers to organize effectively into unions, in part because of racial and ethnic tensions among laborers, language barriers, and the efforts of owners and supervisors to undermine unionizing efforts. Business owners often hired "strikebreakers," usually desperate immigrant workers who were willing to take jobs at the prevailing wage. Nevertheless, several unions did advocate for workers' rights at a national level. After the violence associated with the *Great Railroad Strike of 1877, Haymarket riot (1886)*, the *Homestead Steel strike (1892)*, and the *Pullman strike (1894)*, many Americans grew fearful of unions and viewed them as politically radical.

CHRONOLOGY

1859	First oil well is struck in Titusville, Pennsylvania
1861	Congress creates the Morrill Tariff
1869	First transcontinental railroad is completed at Promontory Summit, Utah
1876	Alexander Graham Bell patents his telephone
1877	Great Railroad Strike
1879	Thomas A. Edison makes the first durable incandescent lightbulb
1882	John D. Rockefeller organizes the Standard Oil Trust
1886	American Federation of Labor is organized
1892	Homestead Steel strike
1894	Pullman strike
1901	J. Pierpont Morgan creates the U.S. Steel Corporation

KEY TERMS

Standard Oil Company p. 796

horizontal integration p. 796

monopoly p. 796

vertical integration p. 797

trust p. 797

holding company p. 798

Bessemer converter p. 799

Carnegie Steel Company p. 799

J. Pierpont Morgan and Company p. 800

tariff p. 802

laissez-faire p. 805

child labor p. 811

Great Railroad Strike of 1877 p. 814

National Labor Union (NLU) p. 815

Knights of Labor p. 815

Haymarket riot (1886) p. 819

American Federation of Labor (AFL) p. 821

Homestead Steel strike (1892) p. 821

Pullman strike (1894) p. 821

International Workers of the World (IWW) p. 827

 INQUIZITIVE

Go to InQuizitive to see what you've learned—and learn what you've missed—with personalized feedback along the way.

18 The New South and the New West

1865–1900

Mining on the Comstock (1877) The Comstock Lode was one of the largest gold and silver mines in America, yielding more than $300 million over two decades. This illustration shows a cutaway of the Comstock Lode, revealing the complex network of shafts and supports, as well as the various tasks performed by miners.

A fter the Civil War, the devastated South and the untamed West were the most distinctive sections of the nation. Both eluded mapping or measuring, for they resided within powerful myths as much as physical regions.

Both also provided enticing frontiers for economic enterprise. The South had to be rebuilt, while the sparsely settled territories and states west of the Mississippi River were ripe for the development of farms, businesses, railroads, and towns. Bankers and financiers in America and Europe invested heavily in both regions, but especially in the Far West between the Mississippi River and California.

Americans had long viewed the Great Plains as suitable only for Indians. After 1865, however, the federal government encouraged western settlement and economic development in what was called Indian Country. Two thirds of Native Americans in 1865 still lived on the Great Plains.

The construction of transcontinental railroads, the military conquest of the Indians, and the policy of distributing 270 million acres of government-owned lands at little or no cost to settlers, including women, African Americans (after the passage of the 14th Amendment), and immigrants. Free land and the possibility of finding gold or silver or starting a business lured millions of pioneers and enterprising capitalists westward. Charles Goodnight, a Texas cattle

focus questions

1. In what ways did a "New South" emerge in the late nineteenth century?

2. What was the crop-lien system in the South? Explain how it shaped the region after the Civil War.

3. How and why did white southerners adopt Jim Crow segregation laws and take away African Americans' right to vote at the end of the nineteenth century?

4. Who were the various groups of migrants to the West after the Civil War? Why did they move there?

5. Describe the experiences of miners, farmers, ranchers, and women in the West in the late nineteenth century.

6. How did the federal government's post–Civil War policies in the West affect Native Americans?

7. How did the South and West change by 1900?

rancher, recalled that "we were adventurers in a great land . . . fresh and full of the zest of darers." By 1900, a New West and a New South had emerged, and eleven new states had been created out of the western territories.

THE MYTH OF THE NEW SOUTH

After the Civil War, the South fought an ideological civil war over its future. Southerners devastated by defeat found solace in the "Lost Cause"—nostalgia for the mythic Old South of white-columned plantations, white supremacy, and cotton-generated wealth produced by enslaved black people. As one southerner said, his native region remained "old-fashioned, medieval, provincial, worshipping the dead."

At the same time, no region has inspired a more tenacious pride of place. Mississippi writer Eudora Welty once explained that in the South, "feelings are bound up with place." *Home* and *history* are two of the most revered words in southern life. Nineteenth-century southerners did not simply live in the present and dream of the future. They were forever glancing backward in the process of moving forward. As William Faulkner recognized in his novel *Intruder in the Dust (1948)*, "The past isn't dead. It's not even past."

Some prominent southerners, however, looked more to the future. They called for a *New* South in which the Old South agricultural economy worked by slaves and dominated by the planter elite would be replaced by a society of small farms owned by blacks and whites. The New South would also boast a growing industrial sector, and race relations would become harmonious.

The champion of the New South ideal was Henry Woodfin Grady, the powerful editor of the *Atlanta Constitution* newspaper. In 1886, Grady told a New York City audience he was glad that the Union was saved and slavery was abolished, but he insisted that the "South has nothing for which to apologize . . . The South has nothing to take back." The Old South was dead, but there "is now a New South of union and freedom—that South, thank God, is living, breathing, and growing every hour."

Grady claimed that the New South was becoming "a perfect democracy" of small farms complemented by mills, mines, factories, and cities, "a hundred farms for every plantation, fifty homes for every palace, and a diversified industry that meets the complex needs of this complex age." The postwar South, Grady claimed, would no longer be dominated by the planter aristocracy or dependent upon cotton and slave labor. No section of the nation "shows a more prosperous laboring population than the Negroes of the South; none in fuller sympathy with the employing and land-owning class." Without acknowledging his exaggeration, he insisted that the "relations of the Southern people with the Negro are close and cordial."

Many southerners shared Grady's progressive vision. The Confederacy, they concluded, had lost the war because it had relied too much on King Cotton—and slavery. In the future, the New South needed to follow the North's example ("out-Yankee the Yankees") and develop a strong industrial sector to go with its agricultural foundation. New South advocates also stressed that more-efficient farming, which used the latest machinery and technical expertise, was essential, and that widespread vocational training was urgently needed. They asserted that racial harmony built upon black peoples' acceptance of white supremacy (a peculiar kind of "perfect democracy") would provide a stable social environment for economic growth.

TEXTILE MILLS The chief accomplishment of the New South's effort to industrialize was a dramatic expansion of the region's **textile industry**, which produced cotton thread, bedding, and clothing. From 1880 to 1900, the number of red-brick cotton mills in the South grew from 161 to 400, the number of mill workers (mostly whites, with women and children outnumbering men) increased fivefold, and the demand for cotton products rose eightfold. By 1900, the South had surpassed New England as the largest producer of cotton fabric in the nation.

Thousands of dirt-poor farm folk—many of them children—rushed to take jobs in the mills. Seventy percent of mill workers were younger than twenty-one, and many were under fourteen. A dawn-to-dusk job in a mill paying 50¢ a day "was much more interesting than one-horse farming," noted one worker, "because you can meet your bills." Those bills were usually paid to the mill owner, who, like a feudal baron, provided housing, food, and supplies to the workers in his village—for a fee.

Over time, mill owners hired and paid the village schoolteachers, doctors, and ministers. They organized dances and concerts and created sports leagues. Their paternalistic social system was in part intended to create a sense of community so strong that workers would never be tempted to organize labor unions.

THE TOBACCO INDUSTRY Tobacco growing and cigarette production also soared. Essential to the rise of the tobacco industry was the Duke family of Durham, North Carolina. Soon after the Civil War ended, Washington Duke

Southern smokes Allen & Ginter, a major tobacco manufacturer, was acquired by the American Tobacco Company. This advertisement, featuring black laborers in the tobacco fields, plays to southern nostalgia for the "Old Dominion" before the Civil War.

took his barn load of tobacco, dried it, and, with the help of his two sons, hitched up his wagon and traveled the state, selling tobacco in small pouches. By 1872, the Dukes had a modern cigarette factory producing 125,000 pounds of tobacco annually.

Washington's son, James Buchanan Duke, wanted even greater success. He spent lavishly on advertising and perfected the mechanized mass production of cigarettes. He also undersold competitors and cornered the supply of ingredients needed to make cigarettes.

His primary competitors eventually agreed to join forces with him, and in 1890 Duke brought most of them into the **American Tobacco Company**, which controlled 90 percent of the nation's cigarette production. He was well on his way to becoming one of the wealthiest and most powerful men in the nation.

OTHER NEW SOUTH INDUSTRIES Effective use of other natural resources also helped revitalize the South along the Appalachian chain from West Virginia to Alabama. Coal production grew from 5 million tons in 1875 to 49 million tons by 1900. At the southern end of the mountains, Birmingham, Alabama, sprang up in large part because of the massive deposits of iron ore in the surrounding ridges, leading boosters to label the steelmaking city the "Pittsburgh of the South."

Urban and industrial expansion as well as rapid population growth created a need for housing. In response to the demand, logging and lumber production became the fastest-growing industry in the South after 1870. Northern investors bought vast forests of yellow pine and set about clear-cutting them and hauling the logs to new sawmills, where they were milled into lumber for the construction of homes and businesses.

By 1900, southern lumber had surpassed textiles in annual economic value. Still, for all its advances, the South continued to lag behind the rest of the nation in industrial development and educational attainment.

THE REDEEMERS Henry Grady's vision of a New South celebrated the **redeemers**, the conservative, pro-business, white politicians in the Democratic party who had embraced the idea of industrial progress grounded in white supremacy. Their supporters referred to them as redeemers because they supposedly saved ("redeemed") the South from Yankee domination, and what they called "black rule," during Reconstruction.

The redeemers included lawyers, merchants, railroad executives, and entrepreneurs who wanted a more diversified economy. They also sought cuts in state taxes and expenditures, including those for public-school systems started after the war. "Schools are not a necessity," claimed a Virginia governor. Black children, in particular, suffered from such cutbacks. The redeemers did not want educated African Americans. "What I want here is Negroes who can make cotton," explained a white planter, "and they don't need education to help them make cotton."

The Failings of the New South

Despite the development of mills and factories, the South in 1900 remained the least industrial, least urban, least educated, and least prosperous region in the nation. Per capita income in the South was only 60 percent of the national average, and the region remained dependent on the North for investment capital and manufactured goods.

Cotton remained king, although it never regained the huge profitability it had generated in the 1850s. By the 1880s, southern farmers, black and white, were producing as much cotton as they had before the war but were earning far less money because the world price for cotton had declined.

SOUTHERN POVERTY Henry Grady hoped that growing numbers of southern farmers would own their own land by the end of the nineteenth century. But the opposite occurred. A prolonged decline in crop prices made it more difficult than ever to buy and own land. By 1900, an estimated 70 percent of farmers did not own the land they worked.

THE CROP-LIEN SYSTEM Because few southern communities had banks after the Civil War, people had to operate with little or no cash. Many rural areas adopted a barter economy in which a "crossroads" merchant would provide food, clothing, seed, fertilizer, and other items to poor farmers "on credit" in exchange for a share (or "lien") of their crops when harvested.

Southern farmers, white and black, who participated in the **crop-lien system** fell into three categories: small farm owners, sharecroppers, and tenants. The farms owned by most southerners were small and did not generate much income. As a result, even those who owned farms had to pledge a portion of their future crop to the local merchant in exchange for supplies, clothing, and food.

The crop-lien system was self-destructive. Planting cotton or tobacco year after year stripped the soil of its fertility and stability and led to disastrous erosion of farmland during rainstorms. Topsoil washed into nearby creeks, collapsing riverbanks and creating ever-deepening gullies. In addition, landowners required croppers and tenants to grow a "cash crop" exclusively, usually cotton or tobacco. By permitting only these cash crops, landowners prevented croppers and tenants from growing their own vegetable gardens; they had to get their food from the local merchant in exchange for promised cotton.

"Free slaves" Sharecroppers painstakingly pick cotton while their white overseer watches from atop his horse.

Because most farmers did not own the land they worked, the cabins they lived in, or the tools they used, they had little incentive to enrich the soil or maintain buildings and equipment. According to a study of southern agriculture in 1897, "The tenant is interested only in the crop he is raising, and makes no effort to keep up the fertility of the land." The tenant system had been "more wasteful and destructive than slavery was anywhere."

The crop-lien system was a post–Civil War version of economic slavery for poor white people as well as black. The landowner, or merchant (often the same person), decided what crop would be planted and how it would be cultivated, harvested, and sold. In good times, croppers and tenants barely broke even; in bad times, they struggled to survive.

Those who worked the farms developed an intense suspicion of their landlords, who often swindled them by not giving them their fair share of the crops. Landowners kept the books, handled the sale of crops, and gave the cropper or tenant his share of the proceeds after deducting for all the items supplied during the year, plus interest that ranged, according to one newspaper, "from

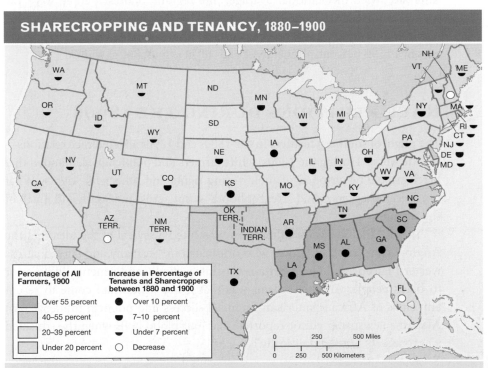

SHARECROPPING AND TENANCY, 1880–1900

Percentage of All Farmers, 1900
- Over 55 percent
- 40–55 percent
- 20–39 percent
- Under 20 percent

Increase in Percentage of Tenants and Sharecroppers between 1880 and 1900
- ● Over 10 percent
- ◗ 7–10 percent
- ▾ Under 7 percent
- ○ Decrease

- Why was there a dramatic increase in sharecropping and tenancy in the late nineteenth century?
- Explain why the South had more sharecroppers than other parts of the country.

24 percent to grand larceny." Often, the cropper or tenant received nothing but a larger debt to be rolled over to the next year's crop. Over time, the high interest charged on the credit offered by the local store or landowner, coupled with sagging prices received for cotton and other crops, created a hopeless cycle of debt among small farmers, sharecroppers, and share tenants.

FALLING COTTON PRICES As cotton production soared during the last quarter of the nineteenth century, the price paid for raw cotton fell steadily. "Have you all felt the effects of the low price of cotton?" Mary Parham of Amite, Louisiana, wrote to her father in 1892. "It nearly ruined us. I did not get my house built. The farmers are very blue here. But [they are] getting ready to plant cotton again." As the price of cotton dropped, desperate farmers planted even more cotton, which only accelerated the decline in price from 11.77¢ per pound in the 1870s to 7.72¢ in 1896.

The average annual income of white southerners in 1900 was about half that of whites outside the South. Eleven percent of whites in the South were illiterate, twice the national average. The region's poorest people were the 9 million former slaves and their children. Per capita black income in 1900 was a third of what was earned by southern whites, and the black illiteracy rate was nearly 50 percent, almost five times higher than that of whites.

RACE RELATIONS DURING THE 1890S

The plight of southern farmers in the 1880s and 1890s affected race relations—for the worse. During the 1890s, white farmers and politicians demanded that black people be stripped of their voting rights and other civil rights. What northern observers called "Negrophobia" swept across the South and much of the nation.

In part, the new wave of racism represented a revival of the idea that the Anglo-Saxon "race" of whites who originated in Germany and spread across western Europe and Great Britain was intellectually and genetically superior to black people. Another reason was that many whites had come to resent any signs of African American financial success and political influence. An Alabama newspaper editor reported that "our blood boils when the educated Negro asserts himself politically."

DISENFRANCHISING AFRICAN AMERICANS By the 1890s, a new generation of African Americans born and educated since the Civil War was determined to gain complete equality. They were more assertive and less patient than their parents. "We are not the Negro from whom the chains of slavery fell a quarter century ago, most assuredly not," a black editor announced. A growing number of young white adults, however, were equally determined to keep all "Negroes in their place."

Mississippi took the lead in stripping blacks of their voting rights. The so-called **Mississippi Plan**, a series of amendments to the state constitution, set the pattern of disenfranchisement that nine more states would follow. The Mississippi Plan of 1890 first instituted a residence requirement for voting—two years in the state, one year in a local election district—aimed at African American tenant farmers who were in the habit of moving each year in search of better economic opportunities. Second, Mississippi disqualified black people from voting if they had committed certain crimes. Third, in order to vote, people had to have paid all taxes on time, including a so-called poll tax specifically for voting—a restriction that hurt both poor blacks and poor whites. Finally, all voters had to be able to read or at least "understand" the U.S. Constitution. White registrars decided who satisfied this requirement and usually discriminated against black people.

Other states had variations on the Mississippi Plan. In 1898, Louisiana inserted into its state constitution the "grandfather clause," which allowed illiterate whites to vote if their fathers or grandfathers had been eligible to vote on January 1, 1867, when African Americans were still disenfranchised. By 1910, Georgia, North Carolina, Virginia, Alabama, and Oklahoma had incorporated the grandfather clause. Also in the solidly Democratic South, every southern state created a Democratic primary process to select candidates. Most of the primaries excluded African American voters, and rarely was a Republican vote cast. Hence, the overwhelmingly Democratic region came to be called the "Solid South."

When such "legal" means were not enough to ensure their political dominance, white Democratic candidates turned to fraud and violence. Benjamin Tillman, the white supremacist who served as South Carolina's governor from 1890 to 1894, maintained that his state's problems were caused by white farmers renting their land to "ignorant lazy negroes." With such racist comments, he gained the support of poor whites. To ensure his election, he and his followers effectively eliminated the black vote. He admitted that "we have done our level best [to prevent black people from voting]. . . . We stuffed ballot boxes. We shot them. We are not ashamed of it."

By the end of the nineteenth century, widespread racial discrimination—segregation of public facilities, political disenfranchisement, and vigilante justice—had elevated government-sanctioned bigotry to an official way of life in the South. Tillman bluntly declared in 1892 that black people "must remain subordinate or be exterminated."

The efforts to suppress the black vote succeeded. In 1896, Louisiana had 130,000 registered black voters; by 1900, it had only 5,320. In Alabama in 1900, the census data indicated that 121,159 black men were literate; only 3,742, however, were registered to vote. By that year, black voting across the South had declined by 62 percent, the white vote by 26 percent.

THE SPREAD OF SEGREGATION At the same time that southern blacks were being shoved out of the political arena, they were also being segregated socially. The symbolic first target was the railroad passenger car. In 1885, novelist George Washington Cable noted that in South Carolina, black people "ride in first-class [rail] cars as a right" and "their presence excites no comment." Likewise, in New Orleans a visitor was surprised to find that "white and colored people mingled freely." From 1875 to 1883, in fact, any local or state law requiring racial segregation violated the federal Civil Rights Act.

In 1883, however, the U.S. Supreme Court ruled that the Civil Rights Act of 1875 was unconstitutional. In an 8-1 opinion written by Justice Joseph P. Bradley, the Court declared that neither the 13th nor the 14th Amendment gave Congress the authority to pass laws dealing with racial discrimination by private citizens or businesses. The judges explained that individuals and organizations could engage in acts of racial discrimination because the Fourteenth Amendment specified only that "no State" could deny citizens equal protection of the law.

Justice John Marshall Harlan offered a famous dissent to the Court's decision. A Kentuckian who had once owned slaves but had served in the Union army, he had opposed the emancipation of slaves and the Fourteenth and Fifteenth Amendments. After the war, however, the violent excesses of the Ku Klux Klan had convinced him to rethink his attitudes. He became a Republican in 1868 and was named to the Supreme Court by President Rutherford B. Hayes in 1877.

Harlan now argued that the 13th and 14th Amendments, as well as the Civil Rights Act of 1875, were designed to ensure African Americans the same access to public facilities that white citizens enjoyed. The federal government, he insisted, had both the authority and the responsibility to protect citizens from any actions that deprive them of their civil rights. To allow private citizens and enterprises to practice racial discrimination would "permit the badges and incidents of slavery" to remain.

The Court's interpretation in what came to be called the Civil Rights Cases (1883) left as an open question the validity of state laws requiring segregated public facilities under the principle of "separate but equal," a slogan popular in the South referring to the argument that racial segregation laws were legal as long as the segregated facilities were equal in quality.

In the 1880s, Florida, Tennessee, Texas, and Mississippi required railroad passengers to ride in racially segregated cars. When Louisiana followed suit in 1890 with a similar law, black people challenged it in the case of *Plessy v. Ferguson* (1896).

The case originated in New Orleans when Homer Adolph Plessy, an "octoroon" (a racist term for a person having *one-eighth* African ancestry), refused to leave a whites-only railroad car and was convicted of violating the law.

In arguments presented to the U.S. Supreme Court, Plessy's attorney contended that the Louisiana law sought "to debase and distinguish against the inferior race." He then asked the justices to imagine a future dictated by such statutes: "Was there any limit to such laws? Why not require all colored people to walk on one side of the street and whites on the other?" The Court disagreed, ruling that states had a right to create laws segregating public places such as schools, hotels, and restaurants.

The only justice to dissent was again John Marshall Harlan, who stressed that the Constitution is "color-blind, and neither knows nor tolerates classes among citizens. In respect of civil rights, all citizens are equal before the law." He argued that the *Plessy* ruling violated both the Thirteenth and Fourteenth Amendments. The former "not only struck down the institution of slavery" but also "any burdens or disabilities that constitute badges of slavery or servitude." The Fourteenth Amendment "added greatly to the dignity and glory of American citizenship, and to the security of personal liberty . . . The arbitrary separation of citizens, on the basis of race . . . is a badge of servitude wholly inconsistent with the civil freedom and the equality before the law established by the Constitution. It cannot be justified on any legal grounds."

Harlan feared that the Court's ruling would plant the "seeds of race hate" under "the sanction of law." That is precisely what happened. The ruling legitimized the widespread practice of racially **separate but equal** facilities. In 1900, the editor of the *Richmond Times* insisted that racial segregation "be applied in every relation of Southern life. God Almighty drew the color line, and it cannot be obliterated. The negro must stay on his side of the line, and the white man must stay on his side, and the sooner both races recognize this fact and accept it, the better it will be for both."

The new regulations came to be called "Jim Crow" laws. The name derived from "Jump Jim Crow," a song-and-dance caricature of African Americans made popular in the 1830s by Thomas Rice, a New York songwriter/dancer and comedian who performed in blackface makeup. By the 1890s, the term *Jim Crow* had become a derisive expression meaning "Negro." Signs reading "whites only" or "colored only" above restrooms and water fountains emerged as hallmarks of the Jim Crow system.

The lynching of Henry Smith Despite a lack of evidence, Smith was convicted of murdering a white girl in Paris, Texas. A large crowd assembled to watch her family torture Smith on a platform labeled "Justice." After Smith was burned alive, the townspeople kept his charred teeth and bones as souvenirs.

Racist customs dating to before the Civil War were revived. If whites walked along a sidewalk, blacks were expected to step aside and let them pass. There were racially separate funeral homes, cemeteries, churches, and water fountains. When a white deacon in a Mississippi church saw a black man in the sanctuary, he asked: "Boy, what you doin' in there? Don't you know this is a white church?" The black man replied: "Boss, I'm here to mop the floor." The white man paused and said, "Well, that's all right then, but don't let me catch you prayin'."

Widespread violence accompanied the Jim Crow laws. From 1890 to 1899, the United States averaged 188 racial lynchings per year, 82 percent of which occurred in the South. Lynchings usually involved a black man (or men) accused of a crime, often rape. White mobs would seize, torture, and kill the accused. Large crowds, including women and children, would watch amid a carnival-like atmosphere. The governor of Mississippi declared that "if it is necessary that every Negro in the state will be lynched, it will be done to maintain white supremacy."

MOB RULE IN NORTH CAROLINA In the late 1890s, a resurgent and often violent white supremacy movement emerged in the coastal port town of Wilmington, North Carolina, with about 20,000 residents. In 1894

Wilmington insurrection A mob of white supremacists pose with their rifles before the demolished printing press of the *Daily Record*, an African American newspaper.

and 1896, black voters, a majority in the city, elected African Americans to various municipal offices, infuriating the white elite. "We will never surrender to a ragged raffle of Negroes," warned Alfred Waddell, a former congressman and Confederate colonel, "even if we have to choke the Cape Fear River with [black] carcasses." It was not an idle threat.

On the morning of November 10, 1898, some 2,000 white men and teens rampaged through the city's streets. Armed with rifles, pistols, and even a Colt machine gun capable of firing 420 bullets per minute, they destroyed the offices of the *Daily Record*, the black-owned newspaper, then moved into African American neighborhoods, killing dozens and destroying homes and businesses.

The mob then stormed the city hall, declared that Colonel Waddell was the new mayor, and forced African American business leaders and elected officials to resign and board northbound trains. The self-appointed city government issued a "Declaration of White Independence" that stripped black people of their jobs and voting rights. Desperate black residents appealed to the governor and to President William McKinley, but received no help. The Wilmington insurrection marked the first time that a lawfully elected municipal government had been overthrown in the United States.

THE AFRICAN AMERICAN RESPONSE

By the end of the nineteenth century, white supremacy had triumphed across the South. Some African Americans chose to leave in search of equality and opportunity. Those who stayed and resisted white supremacy—even in self-defense—were ruthlessly suppressed. When a white woman, Mrs. Pines, struck her black maid, Sarah Barnett, with a stick, Barnett fought back.

Infuriated, Pines's husband shot Barnett through the shoulder. She survived, only to be convicted of assault and jailed. Another black domestic servant, Ann Beston, stabbed and killed her abusive mistress in Rome, Georgia. A mob lynched her.

Most African Americans had no choice but to adjust to the realities of white supremacy and segregation. "Had to walk a quiet life," explained James Plunkett, a Virginian. "The least little thing you would do, they [whites] would kill ya." Survival required black people to wear a mask of deference and discretion and to behave in a "servile way" when shopping at white-owned stores. News of lynchings, burnings, and beatings sent chilling reminders of the dangers they constantly faced.

Black novelist Richard Wright remembered how in his native Mississippi the "sustained expectation of violence" at the hands of whites induced a "paralysis of will and impulse" in him and others. It unconsciously affected his speech, movements, and manners around whites. "The penalty of death awaited me if I made a false move."

Yet accommodation did not mean surrender. African Americans constructed their own lively culture. Churches continued to provide an anchor for black communities and were often the only public buildings blacks could use for large gatherings, such as club meetings, political rallies, and social events. For men especially, churches offered leadership roles and political status. Being a deacon was one of the most prestigious roles a black man could achieve. As in many white churches, men preached and governed church affairs; the women often did everything else.

Religious life provided great comfort to a people worn down by the daily hardships and abuses associated with segregation. As the Reverend Benjamin Mays explained, he and his black neighbors in South Carolina "believed that the trials and tribulations of the world would be all over when one got to heaven. Beaten down at every turn by the white man, as they were, Negroes could perhaps not have survived without this kind of religion."

One irony of Jim Crow segregation was that it opened up new economic opportunities for African Americans. Black entrepreneurs emerged to provide essential services to the black community—insurance, banking, barbering, funerals, hair salons. Black people also formed their own social and fraternal clubs and organizations, all of which provided fellowship, mutual support, and opportunities for service.

Middle-class African American women formed a network of social clubs that served as engines of community service across the South and the nation. They cared for the aged, infirm, orphaned, and abandoned, provided homes for single mothers and nurseries for working mothers, and sponsored health clinics and classes in home economics.

In 1896, the leaders of women's clubs formed the National Association of Colored Women. The organization's first president, Mary Church Terrell, told the members they had an obligation to serve the "lowly, the illiterate, and even the vicious to whom we are bound by the ties of race and sex, and put forth every effort to uplift and reclaim them." Courageous African American women declared that black men were not providing sufficient leadership. An editorial in the *Woman's Era* called for "timid men and ignorant men" to step aside and let the women show the way.

IDA B. WELLS One of the most outspoken African American activists was Ida B. Wells. Born into slavery in 1862 in Mississippi, she attended a school staffed by white missionaries. In 1880, she moved to Memphis, Tennessee, where she taught in segregated schools and gained entrance to the social life of the African American middle class.

In 1883, after losing her seat on a railroad car because she was black, Wells became the first African American to file a suit challenging such discrimination. The circuit court decided in her favor and fined the railroad, but the Tennessee Supreme Court overturned the ruling. Wells thereafter discovered "[my] first and [it] might be said, my only love"—journalism—which she used to fight for justice. She became editor of *Memphis Free Speech*, a newspaper that focused on African American issues.

In 1892, after three of her friends were lynched by a white mob, Wells launched a crusade against lynching. Angry whites responded by destroying her office and threatening to lynch her. She moved briefly to New York and then settled in Chicago, where she continued to criticize Jim Crow laws and fought for the restoration of black voting rights. "Somebody must show that the Afro-American race is more sinned against than sinning," she explained, "and it seems to have fallen upon me to do so." She helped found the National Association for the Advancement of Colored People (NAACP) in 1909 and worked for women's suffrage. In promoting racial equality, Wells often found herself in direct opposition to Booker T. Washington, the most influential African American leader of the time.

Ida B. Wells While raising four children, Wells sustained her commitment to ending racial and gender discrimination and lynching.

BOOKER T. WASHINGTON Born a slave in Virginia in 1856, the son of a black mother and a white father, Booker T. Washington at sixteen had enrolled at Hampton Normal and Agricultural Institute, one of several colleges for ex-slaves created during Reconstruction. There he met the school's founder, Samuel Chapman Armstrong, who preached moderation and urged the students: "Be thrifty and industrious," "Command the respect of your neighbors by a good record and a good character," "Make the best of your difficulties," and "Live down prejudice." Washington listened and learned.

Nine years later, Armstrong received a request from a group in northern Alabama starting a black college called Tuskegee Institute. The college needed a president, and Armstrong urged them to hire Washington. At twenty-five years old, Washington was, according to Armstrong, "a very capable mulatto, clear headed, modest, sensible, polite, and a thorough teacher and superior man."

Young Washington got the job and quickly went to work. The first students had to help construct the first buildings, making the bricks themselves. As the years passed, Tuskegee Institute became celebrated as a college dedicated to discipline and vocational training.

Over time, Washington became a skilled fundraiser, gathering substantial gifts from wealthy whites, most of them northerners. The complicated racial dynamics of the late nineteenth century required him to walk a tightrope between being candid and being an effective college president. He learned to act like a fox, masking his militancy to maintain the support of whites. As the years passed, the pragmatic Washington became a source of inspiration and hope to millions of blacks.

Washington's recurring message to black students focused on the importance of gaining "practical knowledge." In part to please his white donors, he argued that African Americans should not focus on fighting racial segregation.

Booker T. Washington Founder of the Tuskegee Institute, a historically black vocational training school. He went on to become the nation's most prominent African American leader.

They should instead work hard and avoid stirring up trouble. Their priority should be self-improvement rather than social change. Washington told them to begin "at the bottom" as well-educated, hardworking farmers, not as social activists.

Yet Washington's emphasis on economic self-sufficiency did not satisfy many white racists. Thomas Dixon, a North Carolina Baptist minister, state legislator, and novelist, complained that Washington was teaching students "to be masters of men, to be independent, to own and operate their own industries," all of which would "destroy the last vestige of dependence on the white man for anything."

Washington ignored such critics. In a famous speech at the Cotton States and International Exposition in Atlanta in 1895, he urged the African American community not to migrate to northern states or to other nations but to "Cast down your [water] bucket where you are—cast it down in making friends . . . of the people of all races by whom we are surrounded. Cast it down in agriculture, mechanics, in commerce, in domestic service, and in the professions." Fighting for "social equality" and directly challenging white rule would be "the extremest folly," and any effort at "agitation" would, he warned, backfire. African Americans first needed to become self-sufficient economically. Civil rights would have to wait.

W. E. B. DU BOIS Other African American leaders disagreed with Booker T. Washington's accommodationist strategy. W. E. B. Du Bois emerged as Washington's foremost rival. A native of Massachusetts, Du Bois recalled that he first experienced racial prejudice as a student at Fisk University in Nashville, Tennessee. He later studied in Germany before becoming the first African American to earn a doctoral degree from Harvard. In addition to promoting civil rights, he authored more than twenty books.

In *The Souls of Black Folk*, Du Bois highlighted the "double consciousness" felt by African Americans: "One ever feels his two-ness—an American, a Negro; two souls, two thoughts, two unreconciled strivings; two warring

W. E. B. Du Bois A fierce advocate for black education and civil rights.

ideals in one dark body, whose dogged strength alone keeps it from being torn asunder." He spent his career exploring this double consciousness and how it inevitably set black people apart. A young white visitor to Mississippi in 1910 noticed that nearly every black person he met had "two distinct social selves, the one he reveals to his own people, the other he assumes among the whites."

Soon after Du Bois began teaching at Atlanta University in 1897, he launched a public assault on Booker T. Washington's strategy for improving the quality of life for African Americans. Du Bois called Washington's celebrated 1895 speech "the **Atlanta Compromise**" and said that he would not "surrender the leadership of this race to cowards" who, like Washington, "accepted the alleged inferiority of the Negro" so blacks could "concentrate all their energies on industrial education, the accumulation of wealth, and the conciliation of the South." Du Bois stressed that African American leaders should adopt a strategy of "ceaseless agitation" directed at ensuring the right to vote and winning civil equality. The education of black people, he maintained, should not be merely vocational but comparable to that enjoyed by the white elite, and it should help develop bold leaders willing to challenge Jim Crow segregation and discrimination.

The dispute between Washington and Du Bois came to define the tensions that would divide the twentieth-century civil rights movement: militancy versus conciliation, separatism versus assimilation, social justice versus economic self-reliance. What Du Bois and others did not know was that Washington secretly worked to challenge segregation and disenfranchisement, stop brutal lynchings, and increase funding for public schools. He often acted privately because he feared that public activism would trigger violence against Tuskegee and himself.

In the end, Washington wanted to engender in his students a confident faith in molding a better future. He counseled them to grasp hope rather than hate, and told racist whites that "you can't keep another man in the ditch without being in the ditch yourself."

THE SETTLING OF THE NEW WEST

Like the South, the West has always been a region wrapped in myths and stereotypes, many of them reinforced even today by popular novels, movies, and television shows. The vast land west of the Mississippi River contains remarkable geographic extremes: majestic mountains, roaring rivers, deep-sculpted canyons, searing deserts, grassy plains, and dense forests. The Civil War and Reconstruction were remote events that hardly touched the lives of the

Indians, Mexicans, Asians, farmers, ranchers, trappers, miners, and Mormons scattered through its plains, valleys, and mountains.

Between 1870 and 1900, Americans settled more land in the West than they had in the centuries before 1870. By 1900, a third of the nation lived west of the Mississippi River, and the New West came to symbolize economic opportunity and personal freedom. On another level, however, the economic exploitation of the West was a story of irresponsible behavior and abuse of nature that scarred the land, decimated its wildlife, and nearly exterminated much of Native American culture—and Native Americans.

THE WESTERN LANDSCAPE After midcentury, farmers and their families began spreading west across the Great Plains—western Kansas, Nebraska, Oklahoma, northern Texas, the Dakotas, eastern Colorado, Wyoming, and Montana. From California, miners moved eastward to Utah and Nevada, drawn by one new discovery after another. From Texas, nomadic cowboys migrated northward annually onto the plains and even across the Rocky Mountains into the Great Basin of Utah and Nevada.

The settlers encountered challenges markedly different from those they had left behind. The Great Plains had little rainfall and few rivers or trees, which rendered useless the familiar trappings of the pioneer—the axe, the log cabin, the rail fence—as well as traditional methods of tilling the soil.

For a long time, the region had been called the Great American Desert; in the minds of most Americans it was unfit for human habitation, and, therefore, it was the perfect refuge for any Indians who refused to accept the white way of life. But that view changed in the last half of the nineteenth century.

With the completion of the transcontinental railroads, the diminishing threat of Indian violence, and a seemingly limitless supply of natural resources, it soon became clear that the New West held the key to national prosperity. Capitalists made huge profits investing in western mines, cattle, railroads, buffalo hides, and commercial farms. Agriculture expanded westward as the development of new techniques of dry farming and irrigation made the Great American Desert fruitful, after all.

THE MIGRATORY STREAM A nonstop stream of migrants flowed into what had been the largely Indian and Hispanic West. As millions of whites, Native Americans, African Americans, Mexicans, South Americans, and European and Chinese immigrants intermingled, they transformed western life and culture.

The largest number of foreign immigrants came from northern Europe and Canada. In the northern plains (the Dakotas, Minnesota, Montana, and

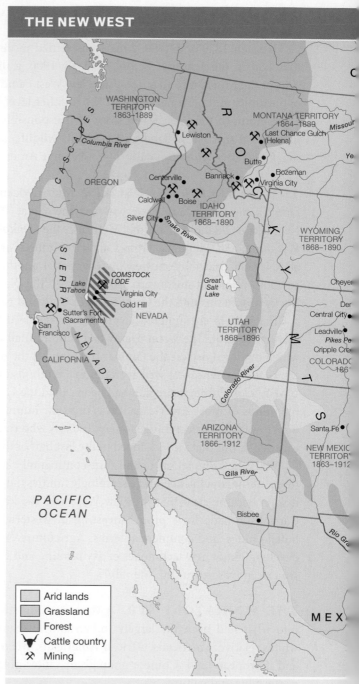

THE NEW WEST

WASHINGTON TERRITORY 1863–1889

CASCADES

Columbia River

Lewiston

OREGON

Centerville

Caldwell   Boise

Silver City

IDAHO TERRITORY 1868–1890

Snake River

ROCKY

MONTANA TERRITORY 1864–1889

Last Chance Gulch (Helena)

Butte

Bannack   Bozeman

Virginia City

Missouri

Ye

SIERRA NEVADA

Lake Tahoe

COMSTOCK LODE

Virginia City

Gold Hill

Sutter's Fort (Sacramento)

San Francisco

NEVADA

CALIFORNIA

Great Salt Lake

UTAH TERRITORY 1868–1896

Colorado River

ARIZONA TERRITORY 1866–1912

Gila River

PACIFIC OCEAN

Bisbee

WYOMING TERRITORY 1868–1890

Cheyer

Der

Central City

Leadville
Pikes Pe
Cripple Cre

COLORADO 186

Santa Fe

NEW MEXIC TERRITORY 1863–1912

Rio Gr

M T S

MEX

Legend:
- Arid lands
- Grassland
- Forest
- Cattle country
- Mining

- What were the main industries of the New West?
- How did mining transform the ecology of the New West?

CANADA

Yellowstone River

Miles City

DAKOTA TERRITORY 1863–1889

Deadwood Gulch

BLACK HILLS

Missouri River

Centerville

MINNESOTA

Lake Superior

WISCONSIN

Lake Michigan

MI

Platte River

NEBRASKA TERRITORY 1863–1867

Ogallala

Omaha

IOWA

Chicago

ILLINOIS

IN

Republican River

KANSAS

Abilene

Ellsworth

Dodge City

Wichita

Caldwell

Kansas City

Sedalia

St. Louis

Ohio River

KY

MISSOURI

Arkansas River

TERRITORY 876

UNORGANIZED TERRITORY

ARKANSAS

Mississippi River

TN

MS

TEXAS

Chisholm Trail

Western Trail

Colorado River

Sedalia Trail

Brazos River

Centerville

LOUISIANA

Red River

Pecos River

Caldwell

Austin

San Antonio

Galveston

New Orleans

Corpus Christi

O

GULF OF MEXICO

0   100   200 Miles

0   100   200 Kilometers

Wyoming) Germans, Scandinavians, and Irish were especially numerous. In Nebraska in 1870, a quarter of the 123,000 residents were foreign-born. In North Dakota in 1890, immigrants composed 45 percent of the residents.

Compared with European immigrants, those from China and Mexico were much less numerous but nonetheless significant. More than 200,000 Chinese arrived in California between 1876 and 1890, joining some 70,000 others who had come earlier to build railroads and work in mining communities. Chinese were frequently discriminated against and denied citizenship rights—and they became scapegoats whenever there was an economic downturn.

THE AFRICAN AMERICAN MIGRATION After the collapse of Radical Republican rule in the South, thousands of African Americans began migrating westward; some 6,000 black southerners arrived in Kansas in 1879, and as many as 20,000 followed the next year. They were called **Exodusters** because they were making their exodus from the South in search of a haven from racism and poverty.

Nicodemus, Kansas By the 1880s, this African American colony had become a thriving town of Exodusters. Here, its residents are photographed in front of the First Baptist Church and general store.

The foremost promoter of black migration to the West was Benjamin "Pap" Singleton. Born a slave in Tennessee in 1809, he escaped and made his way to Michigan. After the Civil War, he returned to Tennessee and decided that African Americans could never gain equal treatment if they stayed in the former Confederacy. When he learned that land in Kansas was selling for $1.25 an acre, he led a party of 200 colonists to the state in 1878, bought 7,500 acres that had been an Indian reservation, and established the Dunlop community.

Over the next several years, thousands of African Americans followed Singleton to Kansas, leading many southern leaders to worry about the loss of black laborers. In 1879, white southerners closed access to the Mississippi River and threatened to sink all boats carrying blacks to the West.

By the early 1880s, however, the exodus of black southerners had petered out. Many were unprepared for the harsh living conditions. Their Kansas homesteads were often not large enough to be self-sustaining, and most black farmers were forced to supplement their income by hiring themselves out to white ranchers. Drought, grasshoppers, prairie fires, and dust storms led to frequent crop failures and bankruptcy.

The sudden influx of so many southern blacks also taxed their resources and patience. There were not enough houses, stores, or construction materials; few government services; and rarely enough water. Many African American pioneers in Kansas abandoned their land and moved to cities in the state.

By 1890, some 520,000 African Americans lived west of the Mississippi River. As many as 25 percent of the cowboys who participated in the Texas cattle drives were African Americans, as were many federal horse soldiers in the West.

WESTERN MINING   After the Civil War, the dream of striking it rich by finding gold or silver continued to be the most powerful lure to the West. The nature of mining, however, had changed drastically. Like much of western agriculture, mining had become a mass-production industry. Individual prospectors gave way to large mining companies.

The miners who first rushed to California in 1849 had sifted gold dust and nuggets out of riverbeds by means of "placer" mining, or "panning." Once the placer deposits were exhausted, however, efficient mining required large-scale operations, massive machinery, and substantial capital investment. Companies shifted from surface digging to hydraulic mining, dredging, or deep-shaft "hard-rock" mining.

Industrial miners used huge hydraulic cannons to strip canyon walls of rock and topsoil in a search for veins of gold or silver. The dirt and debris unearthed by the water cannons covered rich farmland downstream and created sandbars that clogged rivers and killed fish. All told, some 12 billion tons of earth were blasted out of the Sierra Nevada and washed into local rivers.

California farmers in the fertile Central Valley bitterly protested the damage done by the powerful industrial mining operations. In 1878, they formed the Anti-Debris Association, but their efforts to pass state legislation restricting hydraulic mining repeatedly failed because mining companies controlled the votes.

The group then turned to the courts. On January 7, 1884, they won their case when federal judge Lorenzo Sawyer, a former miner, outlawed the dumping of mining debris where it could reach farmland or navigable rivers. *Woodruff v. North Bloomfield Gravel Mining Company* became the nation's first major environmental legal victory. As a result of the ruling, hydraulic mining dried up, leaving abandoned equipment, ugly ravines, ditches, gullies, and mountains of discarded rock and gravel.

MINING BOOMTOWNS Tombstone, Arizona, was a major silver mining site in the 1870s. Within its fourth year of existence, it was the fastest-growing **boomtown** in the Southwest. It boasted a bowling alley, four churches, a school, two banks, three newspapers, and an ice cream parlor alongside 110 saloons, 14 gambling halls, and numerous dance halls and brothels.

Deadwood, Dakota Territory A gold-rush town in 1876, before the Dakotas became states.

Other famous mining boomtowns included Virginia City in Nevada, Cripple Creek and Leadville in Colorado, and Deadwood in the Dakota Territory. These were male-dominated communities with a substantial population of immigrants from China, Chile, Peru, Mexico, France, Germany, Scotland, Wales, Ireland, and England.

Ethnic prejudice was as common as violence in mining towns. Chinese, for example, were banned from laboring in the mines but were allowed to operate laundries and work in boardinghouses. Mexicans often suffered the worst treatment. "Mexicans have no business in this country," a Californian insisted. "The men were made to be shot at, and the women were made for our purposes."

Most boomtowns lasted only a few years. Once the mines played out, the people moved on. In 1870, Virginia City, Nevada, then called the richest city in America, had a population of 20,000. Today, it has fewer than 1,000 residents.

New discoveries of gold and silver occurred through the late nineteenth century. The **Comstock Lode** was found near Gold Hill, Nevada, on the eastern slope of the Sierra Nevada near the California border. Henry Comstock, a Canadian-born fur trapper, gave the discovery (actually made by other prospectors in 1859) his name. The Comstock Lode, a seam of gold and silver more than fifty feet wide and thousands of feet deep, was the most profitable mine in history to that point.

The rapid growth of mining spurred the creation of territorial governments and cries for statehood. But after Colorado's admission into the Union in 1876, there was a long pause in admitting new states because of party divisions in Congress; Democrats refused to create states out of territories that were dominated by Republicans. After the sweeping Republican victory in the 1888 legislative races, however, Congress admitted North and South Dakota, Montana, and Washington as states in 1889, and Idaho and Wyoming in 1890. Utah entered the Union in 1896 (after the Mormon church agreed to abandon the practice of polygamy). Oklahoma became a state in 1907, and in 1912, Arizona and New Mexico became the forty-seventh and forty-eighth contiguous states. (The final two, Alaska and Hawaii, were added fifty years later.)

LIFE IN THE NEW WEST

In the 1880s, James H. Kyner, a railroad builder in Oregon, described "an almost unbroken stream of emigrants from horizon to horizon." These "hardy, optimistic folk" traveled in wagons, on horses, and on foot, "going west to seek their fortunes and to settle an empire." Most thought little about forcing out the Native Americans, Chinese workers, and Hispanic cowboys who were there first. Americans claimed a special destiny to settle, develop, and dominate the entire continent.

To encourage new settlers in the West, the federal government, as noted in the previous chapter, helped finance the construction of four transcontinental railroads, dispatched federal troops to conquer Indians and relocate them to reservations, and sold government-owned land at low prices—or granted it to railroad companies as a means of rapidly populating areas served by trains. The transcontinental railroads received some 200 million acres of government land.

Herding cattle Cowboys on horseback herd cattle into a corral beside the Cimarron River in 1905.

Over time, the railroads sold much of the land to create towns and ranches. The arrival of trains was the lifeblood of the western economy.

The surge of western migration displayed some of the romantic qualities so often depicted in novels, films, and television shows. Those who braved harsh conditions and uncertain circumstances were, indeed, courageous and tenacious. Cowboys and Indians, outlaws and vigilantes, and farmers, ranchers, and herders populated the plains, while miners and trappers led nomadic lives in the hills and backwoods.

These familiar yet often romanticized images tell only part of the story, however. Drudgery and tragedy were commonplace. In contrast to the Hollywood versions of the West, settlers were a diverse lot: they included women as well as men, African Americans, Hispanics, Asians, and European immigrants. The feverish quest for quick profits also helped fuel a boom-and-bust economic cycle that injected chronic instability into the society and politics of the region.

The abuse, displacement, and relocation of Native Americans, and rapidly dwindling buffalo herds coincided with a burgeoning cattle industry in the West. Cattle were herded into the grasslands where buffalo once had roamed.

For many years, wild cattle first brought to America by the Spanish had competed with buffalo in the borderlands of Texas and Arizona. Breeding them with Anglo-American domesticated cattle produced the hybrid Texas longhorn. Tough, lean, and rangy, the longhorn were noted more for speed and endurance than for yielding choice steak. By the time the Confederacy surrendered, millions of longhorn were wandering freely across Texas. They had marginal economic value because the largest urban markets for beef were so far away—that is, until the railroads arrived.

THE CATTLE BOOM At the end of the Civil War, Kansas Pacific Railroad crews were beginning to lay rails in the buffalo country of the southern plains, between St. Louis and Kansas City. A few entrepreneurs began to imagine how the extension of the railroad might "establish a market whereby the Southern [cattle] drover and Northern buyer would meet upon an equal footing."

That junction was Abilene, in eastern Kansas, a "very small, dead place, consisting of about one dozen log huts." Once the rail lines reached Kansas from Missouri, Joseph G. McCoy, an Illinois livestock dealer, recognized the possibilities of driving vast herds of cattle raised in Texas northward to Kansas, where they would be loaded onto freight cars and sent to the rest of the nation.

In 1867, McCoy bought 250 acres in Abilene and built a stockyard, barn, office building, livestock scales, hotel, and a bank. He then sent an agent to Texas to convince the owners of herds bound north to go through Abilene. When the cattle reached Abilene in August 1867, they were loaded onto railcars and shipped to Chicago stockyards, where they were slaughtered and then sent (as sides of beef) around the nation.

Abilene flourished, and by 1871, an estimated 700,000 steers passed through the town every year. Moreover, the ability to ship large numbers of cattle by rail transformed ranching into a huge national industry and turned Kansas into a major economic crossroads.

Other cattle towns sprouted along the rail line: Ellsworth, Wichita, Caldwell, Dodge City. None lasted more than a few years. Once people bought farms nearby, they lobbied successfully to stop the Texas herds from coming through their area.

In response, cattlemen developed new routes north to new cow towns and rail hubs in Colorado, Wyoming, and Montana. Soon, those states had their own cattle ranches. By 1883, there were half a million cattle in eastern Montana alone, as the disappearing buffalo herds gave way to steers and sheep.

Cattle ranchers were forced to meet and develop their own code of laws and ways to enforce them. As cattle often wandered onto other ranchers' land, cowboys would "ride the line" to keep the animals off the adjoining ranches. In the spring, the cowboys would "round up" the herds, which invariably got mixed up, and sort out ownership by identifying the distinctive ranch symbols "branded," or burned, into the cattle.

All that changed in 1873, when Joseph Glidden, an Illinois farmer, developed the first effective and inexpensive form of barbed-wire fencing. Soon the **open range**, where a small rancher could graze his cattle anywhere, was no more. Barbed-wire fences triggered "range wars," where small ranchers fought to retain the open range. The widespread use of barbed wire also ravaged Native American culture by denying Indians access to their ancestral lands.

Fencing immediately converted free-range prairie into pastures, putting smaller-scale cattle ranchers out of business. Many former ranchers became cowboys working for wages. Cattle raising, like mining, evolved from a romantic adventure into a business dominated by "cattle barons" and large corporations. As one cowboy lamented, "times have changed."

CHICAGO The rise of the cattle industry helped make Chicago the fastest-growing city in the nation. Located on Lake Michigan and served by several rivers and nine railroads in 1865, Chicago was the gateway to the western economy. It was a crossroads where city and frontier intersected. Its lumber yards, grain elevators, stockyards, and slaughterhouses became magnets for immigrants seeking jobs.

Chicago was the catalyst for much of the West's development. "The Great Grey City, brooking no rival," wrote Frank Norris in his novel *The Pit* (1903), "imposed its dominion upon a reach of country larger than many a kingdom of the Old World. For thousands of miles beyond its confines its influence was felt."

The meatpacking industry in places like Cincinnati and Chicago had started not with cattle but with hogs, in part because pork could be preserved longer (with salt and smoking) than beef. Since colonial days, pork packing had been one of the earliest and most important frontier industries. Hogs reproduce much faster than cattle, and they thrive on corn. As a nineteenth-century economist explained, "What is a hog, but fifteen or twenty bushels of corn on four legs?"

In 1850, Chicago slaughterhouses butchered and packed 20,000 hogs. By contrast, Cincinnati (called "Porkopolis") processed 334,000 each year. That changed as the federal government ordered vast quantities of pork for its armies. By 1862, Chicago had displaced Cincinnati as the world's largest pork-processing center. By the 1870s, thanks to the railroad connections, the city was processing more than 2 million hogs per year. The use of ice cut from frozen Lake Michigan and placed in freight trains enabled Chicago pork to be shipped all the way to the East Coast.

But there was no ice in the summer. This challenge led Gustavus F. Swift to begin experimenting with ways to "refrigerate" railcars year round. Within a few years, Swift and his main competitor, Philip Armour, had developed refrigerated freight cars that enabled them to ship processed meat, rather than live hogs and cattle.

This key innovation enabled Chicago to add beef packing to its hog-processing operations. "The refrigerator car," announced Swift and Company, "is one of the vehicles on which the packing industry has ridden to greatness." By the end of the nineteenth century, the economies of scale enjoyed by the four dominant Chicago meatpacking corporations drove most local butchers across the nation out of business.

Swift and Armour became two of the richest men in the world. They soon branched out and became traders in grain—wheat and corn. They also built packing plants in cattle towns such as Kansas City and Omaha, and soon were processing almost half as much meat as Chicago.

FARMING ON THE PLAINS

Farming in the harsh weather of the Great Plains was brutal. A New York newspaper publisher traveling to California described the region as "a treeless desert" that baked during the day and was "chill and piercing" at night. Still, people made the dangerous trek, lured by inexpensive federal land and mis-leading advertisements celebrating life on the plains. One woman said she was "glad to be leaving" her farm in Missouri: "We were going to a new land and get rich." Few got rich, however.

HOMESTEADERS The first homesteaders in the Great Plains were mostly landless folk eager to try farming. Many had never used a hoe or planted a seed. "I was raised in Chicago without so much as a back yard to play in," said a Montana homesteader, "and I worked 48 hours a week for $1.25. When I heard you [a married couple] could get 320 acres just by living on it, I felt that I had been offered a kingdom." By 1900, the federal government had awarded some 270 million acres to 1.6 million people.

Yet they faced a grim struggle. Although land was essentially free through the Homestead Act (1862), horses, livestock, wagons, wells, lumber, fencing, seed, machinery, and fertilizer were not. Freight rates and interest rates were criminally high. Declining crop prices produced chronic indebtedness, leading strapped farmers to embrace virtually any plan to increase the money supply and

Innovative farming Powered by more than a dozen horses and driven by two men, this early-nineteenth-century "combine" machine could, at the same time, cut, thresh, bag, and weigh wheat.

thus pay off their debts with inflated currency. The virgin land itself, although fertile, resisted planting; the heavy sod woven with tough grass roots broke many a plow. Since wood and coal were rare on the prairie, pioneer families initially had to use buffalo chips (dried dung from buffaloes and cattle) for fuel.

Farm families also fought constant battles with tornadoes, hailstorms, windstorms, droughts, prairie fires, blizzards, wolves, and hostile Indians. Swarms of locusts often clouded the horizon; a Wichita newspaper reported in 1878 that they destroyed "every plant that is good for food or pleasant to the eyes." In the late 1880s, a prolonged drought forced many homesteaders to give up. In the end, two thirds of the people who gained land under the Homestead Act failed to become self-sustaining farmers.

COMMERCIAL FARMING Eventually, as the railroads brought lumber from the East, farmers could upgrade their houses built of sod ("Kansas brick") into more-comfortable wood-framed dwellings. New machinery and equipment, for those who could afford them, improved productivity. In 1868, James Oliver, a Scottish immigrant living in Indiana, made a sturdy chilled-iron "sodbuster" plow that greatly eased the task of preparing land for planting. New threshing machines, hay mowers, planters, manure spreaders, and other equipment also lightened the burden of farm labor but often deepened the debts that farmers owed.

Although the overall value of farmland and farm products increased, small farmers did not keep up. Their numbers grew in size but decreased in proportion to the population at large. Wheat in the western states, like cotton in the antebellum South, was the export crop that spurred economic growth. Few small farmers prospered, however, and by the 1890s, they were in open revolt against the "system" of corrupt processors (middlemen) and "greedy" bankers and railroaders who they believed conspired against them.

WOMEN IN THE WEST The West remained a largely male society. Most women in mining towns provided domestic services: cooking, cleaning, doing laundry. They were as valued as gold, since many mining towns had a male-to-female ratio as high as 9 to 1.

In both mining and farming communities, women were prized as spouses, in part because farming required help. But women pioneers continued to face many of the same legal barriers and social prejudices prevalent in the East.

Women of the frontier A woman and her family in front of their sod house. The difficult life on the prairie led to more egalitarian marriages than were found in other regions of the country because women had to play so many roles.

A wife could not sell property without her husband's approval. Texas women could not sue except for divorce, nor could they serve on juries, act as lawyers, or witness a will.

The constant fight for survival west of the Mississippi, however, made men and women there more equal partners than was typical in the East. Many women who lost their mates to the deadly toil of "sod busting" assumed responsibility for their farms. In general, women on the prairie became more independent than women leading domestic lives back East. A Kansas woman recalled "that the environment was such as to bring out and develop the dominant qualities of individual character. Kansas women of that day learned at an early age to depend on themselves—to do whatever work there was to be done, and to face danger when it must be faced, as calmly as they were able."

It was not coincidental, then, that the new western territories and states were among the first to allow women to vote and hold office—in the hopes that by doing so, they would attract more women settlers. In 1890, Wyoming was admitted to the Union as the first state that allowed women to vote. Utah, Colorado, and Idaho followed soon thereafter.

THE FATE OF WESTERN INDIANS

As settlers spread across the continent, some 250,000 Native Americans, many of them originally from east of the Mississippi, were forced into what was supposed to be their last refuge, the Great Plains and mountain regions of the Far West.

By signing the 1851 Fort Laramie Treaty, Plains Indians accepted tribal boundaries and allowed white pioneers to travel across their lands. Yet as the numbers of white settlers increased, fighting resumed.

INDIAN RELATIONS IN THE WEST From the early 1860s until the late 1870s, the trans-Mississippi West, often called "Indian Country," raged with the so-called **Indian wars**. Although the U.S. government had signed numerous treaties with Indian nations giving them ownership of reservation lands for "as long as waters run and the grass shall grow," those commitments were repeatedly violated by buffalo hunters, miners, ranchers, farmers, railroad surveyors—and horse soldiers.

In the 1860s, the federal government ousted numerous tribes from lands they had been promised would be theirs forever. A Sioux chieftain named Spotted Tail expressed the anger felt by many Indians when he asked, "Why does not the Great Father [U.S. president] put his red children on wheels so that he can move them as he will?"

In the two decades before the Civil War, the U.S. Army's central mission in the West was to protect pioneers traveling on the major Overland Trails. During and after the war, the mission changed to ensuring that Native Americans stayed on the reservations and that settlers or miners did not trespass on Indian lands.

Emigrants, however, repeatedly violated the agreements. The result was simmering frustration punctuated by outbreaks of tragic violence. In the summer of 1862, an uprising by Sioux warriors in the Minnesota Valley resulted in the deaths of 644 white traders, settlers, government officials, and soldiers. It was the first of many clashes between settlers and miners and the Indians living on reservations.

THE SAND CREEK MASSACRE   Two years later, a horrible incident occurred in Colorado as a result of the influx of white miners. After Indians murdered a white family near Denver, John Evans, the territorial governor, called on whites to "kill and destroy" the "hostile Indians on the plains." At the same time, Evans persuaded "friendly Indians" (mostly Cheyenne and Arapaho) to gather at "places of safety" such as Fort Lyon, in southeastern Colorado near the Kansas border, where they were promised protection.

Despite that promise, at dawn on November 29, 1864, while most of the Indian men were off hunting, Colonel John M. Chivington's 700 militiamen attacked a camp of Cheyennes and Arapahos along Sand Creek, about forty miles from Fort Lyon. Black Kettle, the chief, waved first an American flag and then a white flag, but the soldiers paid no heed. Over seven hours, the Colorado militiamen slaughtered, scalped, and mutilated 165 peaceful Indians—men, women, children, and the elderly. Chivington, a former abolitionist and Methodist minister (the "Fighting Parson"), had told his men to "kill and scalp all [Indians], big and little, you come across."

In his report to army officials, Chivington claimed a great victory against 1,000 entrenched Cheyenne warriors. He was greeted as a hero back in Denver. "Colorado soldiers have again covered themselves in glory," the *Rocky Mountain News* initially proclaimed.

Then the truth about Sand Creek began to come out. Captain Silas Soule had witnessed the massacre, but, along with his company of soldiers, had disobeyed orders to join the attack. "I refused to fire and swore [to my men] that none but a coward" would shoot unarmed women and children.

Three weeks after the massacre, Soule wrote a letter to a superior officer revealing what had actually happened: "Hundreds of women and children were coming toward us, and getting on their knees for mercy," only to be murdered and "have their brains beat out by men professing to be civilized."

Far from being a hero, Soule added, Chivington encouraged the slaughter through his *lack* of leadership: "There was no organization among our troops, they were a perfect mob—every man on his own hook." He predicted that "we will have a hell of a time with Indians this winter" because of the Sand Creek Massacre.

Congress and the army launched lengthy investigations, and Captain Soule was called to testify in January 1865. The eventual congressional report concluded that Chivington had "deliberately planned and executed a foul and dastardly massacre," murdering "in cold blood" Indians who "had every reason to believe they were under [U.S.] protection." An army general described the massacre as the "foulest and most unjustifiable crime in the annals of America."

Chivington resigned from the militia to avoid a military trial. He soon became the Denver sheriff. On April 23, 1865, Soule was shot and killed in Denver. One of his murderers—never prosecuted—was identified as one of Chivington's soldiers.

SPREADING CONFLICT The **Sand Creek Massacre** ignited warfare that raged across the central plains for the next three years, forcing the federal government to dispatch troops to the West. Arapaho, Cheyenne, and Sioux war parties attacked ranches and stagecoach stations, killing hundreds of white men and kidnapping many white women and children. The government responded by authorizing the recruitment of soldiers from among Confederate military prisoners (called "white-washed Rebels") and the creation of African American cavalry regiments.

In 1866, Congress passed legislation establishing two "colored" cavalry units and dispatched them to the western frontier. The Cheyenne nicknamed them "buffalo soldiers" because they "fought like a cornered buffalo; who, like a buffalo, had suffered wound after wound, yet had not died; and who, like a buffalo, had a thick and shaggy mane of hair."

The buffalo soldiers were mostly Civil War veterans from Louisiana and Kentucky. They built and maintained forts, mapped vast areas of the Southwest, strung hundreds of miles of telegraph lines, protected railroad construction crews, subdued hostile Indians, and captured outlaws and rustlers (horse and cattle thieves). Eighteen buffalo soldiers won Congressional Medals of Honor.

INDIAN RELOCATION A congressional committee in 1865 gathered evidence on the Indian wars and massacres. Its 1867 "Report on the Condition of the Indian Tribes" led to the creation of an Indian Peace Commission charged with removing the causes of the wars.

Congress decided that this would be best accomplished by persuading nomadic Indians yet again to move to out-of-the-way federal reservations where they could take up farming that would "civilize" them. They were to give up their ancestral lands in return for peace so that whites could move in. In 1870, Native Americans outnumbered white people in the Dakota Territory by 2 to 1; by 1880, whites, mostly gold prospectors, would outnumber Indians by more than 6 to 1. The U.S. government had decided it had no choice but to gain control of the region—by purchase if possible, by force if necessary.

In 1867, a conference at Medicine Lodge, Kansas, ended with the Kiowas, Comanches, Arapahos, and Cheyennes reluctantly agreeing to move to western Oklahoma. The following spring, the western Sioux (the Lakotas) signed the Treaty of Fort Laramie (1868). They agreed to settle within the huge Black Hills Reservation in southwestern Dakota Territory, in part because they viewed the Black Hills as sacred ground.

GRANT'S INDIAN POLICY In his inaugural address in 1869, President Ulysses S. Grant urged Congress to adopt more-progressive policies toward Native Americans: "The proper treatment of *the original inhabitants of this land*" should enable the Native Americans "to become *citizens* with all the rights enjoyed by every other American."

Grant's noble intentions, however, ran afoul of longstanding prejudices and the unrelenting efforts of miners, farmers, railroaders, and ranchers to trespass on Indian lands and reservations. The president recognized the challenges; Indians, he admitted, "would be harmless and peaceable if they were not put upon by whites." Yet he also stressed that protecting the new transcontinental railroad was his top priority. In the end, however, Grant told army officers that "it is much better to support a peace commission than a [military] campaign against Indians."

Periodic clashes brought demands for military action. William T. Sherman, commanding general of the U.S. Army, directed General Philip Sheridan, head of the military effort in the West, to "kill and punish the hostiles [Indian war parties], capture and destroy the ponies" of the "Cheyennes, Arapahos, and Kiowas."

Neither Sherman nor Sheridan agreed with Grant's peace policy. In their view, the president's naive outlook reflected the distance between the Great Plains and Washington, D.C. Sherman ordered Sheridan to force all "nonhostile" Indians onto federal reservations, where they would be provided land for farming, immediate rations of food, and supplies and equipment (a promise that was rarely kept).

Some Native Americans refused to be moved again. In the southern plains of New Mexico, north Texas, Colorado, Kansas, and Oklahoma, Native Americans, dominated by the Comanches, focused on hunting buffalo. Armed clashes occurred with increasing frequency until the Red River War of 1874–1875, when Sheridan's soldiers won a series of battles in the Texas Panhandle. The defeated Comanches, Cheyennes, Kiowas, and Arapahos were forced onto reservations.

CUSTER AND THE SIOUX Meanwhile, trouble was brewing again in the northern plains. White prospectors searching for gold were soon trespassing on Sioux hunting grounds in the Dakota Territory despite promises that the army would keep them out. Ohio senator John Sherman warned that nothing would stop the mass migration of pioneers across the Mississippi River: "If the whole Army of the United States stood in the way, the wave of emigration would pass over it to seek the valley where gold was found."

The massive gold rush convinced some Indians to make a last stand. As Red Cloud, a Sioux chief, said, "The white men have crowded the Indians back year by year, and now our last hunting ground, the home of my people, is to be taken from us. Our women and children will starve, but for my part I prefer to die fighting rather than by starvation." Another prominent Sioux war chief, Sitting Bull, told Indians living on the Black Hills reservation that "the whites may get me at last, but I will have good times till then."

George A. Custer The reckless and glory-seeking lieutenant colonel of the U.S. Army.

In 1875, Lieutenant Colonel George Armstrong Custer, a veteran Indian fighter driven by headstrong ambition and reckless courage, led 1,000 soldiers into the Black Hills, where he announced the discovery of gold near present-day Custer, South Dakota. The news set off a massive gold rush, and within two years, the mining town of Deadwood overflowed with 10,000 miners.

The undermanned army units in the area could not keep the miners from violating the rights guaranteed to the Sioux by federal treaties. President Grant and federal authorities tried to convince the Sioux to sell the Black Hills to the government for $6 million. Sitting Bull told the American negotiator to tell "the Great Father [Grant] that I do not want to sell any land to the government."

With that news, Custer was sent back to the Black Hills, this time to find roving bands of Sioux and Cheyenne warriors and force them back onto reservations. If they resisted, he was to kill them. It would not be easy. As General William T. Sherman said, the Sioux were the "most brave and warlike Savages of this Continent."

The colorful Custer, with his curly, golden hair and buckskin outfits, stood out among his horse soldiers. Free-spirited and fun-loving, he was one of the few soldiers who fought for the fun of it; to him, war was "glorious." President Grant, however, noted that Custer was "not a very level-headed man."

During the Civil War, Custer had earned a battlefield promotion to brevet general (a way of honoring gallantry without conferring the actual rank) at the age of twenty-three and had played an important role in the Union victory at Gettysburg by leading a gallant cavalry charge. Now he was preparing to attack the wandering bands of Sioux hunting parties, even though he recognized that intruding American miners had caused the renewal of warfare. As he told reporters, "We are goading the Indians to madness by invading their hallowed [hunting] grounds."

What became the **Great Sioux War** was the largest military campaign since the end of the Civil War. The war lasted fifteen months and entailed fifteen battles in present-day Wyoming, Montana, South Dakota, and Nebraska. In the end, more soldiers than Indians were killed, but the Native Americans were defeated.

In June 1876, after several indecisive encounters, Custer found a large encampment of Sioux and their Northern Cheyenne and Arapaho allies on the Little Bighorn River in the southeast corner of the Montana Territory. Ignoring the warnings of his scouts, Custer split his force in two and attacked a Sioux village on June 25. "Hurrah boys, we've got them," he shouted, not realizing how outnumbered they were. Within minutes, the horse soldiers were surrounded by 2,500 warriors led by the fierce Crazy Horse, who deemed it "A good day to fight, a good day to die!"

After a half hour, the 210 horse soldiers, their ammunition exhausted, were all dead. Custer laughed as he fired his last bullet; he was then felled by shots to his head and heart. Also dead were two of his brothers, a brother-in-law, and a nephew. Afterward, Cheyenne women pierced Custer's eardrums with sewing needles because he had failed to listen to their warnings to stay out of their ancestral lands.

Battle of Little Bighorn, 1876 Amos Bad Heart Bull, an Oglala Sioux artist and historian, painted this scene from the battle.

The Sioux had won their greatest battle, but doing so helped ensure that they would lose the war. Upon learning of the Battle of Little Bighorn ("Custer's Last Stand"), President Grant and Congress abandoned the peace policy and dispatched more supplies and troops to the plains. General Philip Sheridan now planned for "total war." Former Confederates wrote to President Grant to offer their services.

Under Sheridan's leadership, the army quickly regained the offensive and relentlessly pursued the Sioux and Cheyenne across Montana. Warriors were slain, villages destroyed, and food supplies burned. Iron Teeth, a Cheyenne woman, recalled an attack in November 1876: "They killed our men, women, and children." She ran away with her three daughters, while her husband and two sons remained to fight. "My husband," she remembered, "was walking, leading his horse, and stopping at times to shoot. Suddenly, I saw him fall. I started to go back to him, but my sons made me go on." The last time she saw her husband, he was dead in the snow.

Forced back onto reservations, the remaining Native Americans soon were struggling to survive. Many died of starvation or disease. By the end of 1876, the chiefs living on the Dakota reservation agreed to sell the Black Hills to the U.S. government.

In the spring of 1877, Crazy Horse and his people surrendered. The Great Sioux War was over, but the fate of Native Americans remained uncertain.

THE DEMISE OF THE BUFFALO The collapse of Indian resistance resulted as much from the decimation of the buffalo herds as from the actions of federal troops. In 1750, an estimated 30 million buffalo inhabited the plains. The herds were so vast that one traveler said they changed the color of the landscape, "blackening the whole surface of the country." By 1850, there were fewer than 10 million; by 1900, only a few hundred remained. (Today there are about 200,000.) What happened to them?

The conventional story focuses on intensive harvesting of buffalo by white commercial hunters after the Civil War. The construction of railroads through buffalo country brought hundreds of hunters who shipped huge numbers of hides to the East, where consumers developed a voracious demand for buffalo robes, buffalo leather, and trophy heads. The average commercial hunter killed 100 buffalo a day. "The buffalo," reported an army officer, "melted away like snow before a summer's sun."

The story is more complicated, however. A prolonged drought during the late 1880s and 1890s severely reduced the grasslands upon which the animals depended. At the same time, the buffalo had to compete for food with other grazing animals; by the 1880s, more than 2 million horses were roaming buffalo lands.

The Plains Indians themselves, empowered by horses and rifles and spurred by profits reaped from selling hides and meat to white traders, accounted for much of the devastation of the buffalo herds after 1840. If there had been no white hunters, the buffalo would probably have lasted only another thirty years because their numbers had been so greatly reduced by other factors. Whatever the reasons, the disappearance of the buffalo gave the Plains Indians little choice but to settle on government reservations.

THE LAST RESISTANCE In the Rocky Mountains and west to the Pacific Ocean, the story of courageous yet hopeless resistance to white intruders was repeated again and again. Indians were the last obstacle to white western expansion, and they suffered as a result.

The Blackfeet and Crows had to leave their homes in Montana. In a war along the California-Oregon boundary, the Modocs held out for six months in 1871–1872 before they were overwhelmed. In 1879, the Utes were forced to give up their vast territories in western Colorado. In Idaho, the peaceful Nez Perce bands refused to surrender land along the Salmon River, and prolonged fighting erupted there and in eastern Oregon.

In 1877, Joseph, a Nez Perce chief, led some 650 of his people on a 1,300-mile journey through Montana in hopes of finding safety in Canada.

Chief Joseph Leader of the Nez Perce, he was recognized as a strong, eloquent voice against the injustices suffered by Native Americans.

Just before reaching the border, they were caught by U.S. soldiers. As he surrendered, Joseph delivered an eloquent speech: "I am tired of fighting. Our chiefs are killed. . . . The old men are all dead. . . . I want to have time to look for my children, and see how many of them I can find. . . . My heart is sick and sad. From where the sun now stands I will fight no more forever." The Nez Perce requested that they be allowed to return to their ancestral lands in western Idaho, but they were forced to settle in the Indian Territory (Oklahoma), where many died of malaria.

A generation of Indian wars virtually ended in 1886 with the capture of Geronimo, a powerful chief of the Chiricahua Apaches, who had outridden, outwitted, and outfought American forces in the Southwest for fifteen years. General Nelson A. Miles, commander of the soldiers who captured Geronimo, called him "one of the brightest, most resolute, determined-looking men that I have ever encountered."

THE GHOST DANCE The last major clash between Indians and American soldiers occurred near the end of the nineteenth century. Late in 1888, Wovoka (or Jack Wilson), a Paiute in western Nevada, fell ill. In a delirium, he imagined being in the spirit world, where he learned of a deliverer coming to rescue the Indians and restore their lands. To hasten their deliverance, he said, the Indians must perform a ceremonial dance wearing "ghost shirts" enlivened by sacred symbols that would make them bulletproof. The Ghost Dance craze fed upon old legends of the dead reuniting with the living and bringing prosperity and peace.

The **Ghost Dance movement** spread rapidly. In 1890, the western Sioux adopted the practice with such passion that it alarmed white authorities. "Indians are dancing in the snow and are wild and crazy," reported a government agent at the Pine Ridge Reservation in South Dakota. "We need protection and we need it now." The Indian Bureau responded by banning the Ghost Dance ceremony on Lakota reservations, but the Indians defied the order.

On December 29, 1890, a bloodbath occurred at an Indian camp in South Dakota, along a frozen creek called Wounded Knee. U.S. soldiers ordered the Indians to surrender their weapons. "They called for guns and arms," remembered White Lance, "so all of us gave the guns and they were stacked up in the center." Convinced that there were more weapons, the soldiers began searching in tipis. The medicine man began dancing the Ghost Dance when a shot rang out. Overeager soldiers began firing indiscriminately into a group of Indians.

More than 150 unarmed Indians, men, women, and children died in the Battle of Wounded Knee. Twenty-five soldiers were also killed, most by friendly fire. Major General Nelson A. Miles, the regional commander, wrote his wife that hopes for a peaceful settlement had dissolved into a "most abominable, criminal military blunder and a horrible massacre of women and children."

Miles relieved Colonel James W. Forsyth of his command and ordered an immediate inquiry into what had happened, for he was convinced that Forsyth's actions were "about the worst I have ever known." Yet the court of inquiry exonerated Forsyth and covered up the massacre, much to the chagrin of General Miles. Some twenty soldiers received the Congressional Medal of Honor.

A CENTURY OF DISHONOR The Indian wars ended with characteristic brutality and misunderstanding. General Philip Sheridan, overall commander of U.S. troops, was acidly candid in summarizing how whites had treated the Indians: "We took away their country and their means of support, broke up their mode of living, their habits of life, introduced disease and decay among them, and it was for this and against this that they made war. Could anyone expect less?"

Many politicians and religious leaders condemned the persistent mistreatment of Indians. In his annual message of 1877, President Rutherford B. Hayes joined the protest: "Many, if not most, of our Indian wars have had their origin in broken promises and acts of injustice on our part." Helen Hunt Jackson, a novelist and poet, focused attention on the Indian cause in *A Century of Dishonor* (1881), a book that powerfully detailed the sad history of America's exploitation of Native Americans.

In part as a reaction to Jackson's book, U.S. policies gradually improved but did little to enhance the Indians' difficult living conditions and actually helped destroy remnants of their culture. The reservation policy inaugurated by the Peace Commission in 1867, though partly humanitarian in motive,

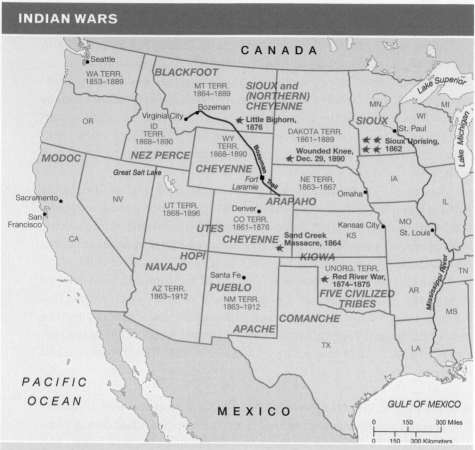

INDIAN WARS

- What was the Great Sioux War?
- What happened at the Little Bighorn battle, and what were the consequences?
- Why were hundreds of Native Americans killed at Wounded Knee?

also saved money; housing and feeding Indians on reservations cost less than fighting them.

Well-intentioned but biased white reformers sought to "Americanize" Indians by forcing them to become self-reliant farmers owning their own land rather than allowing them to be members of nomadic bands or tribes holding property in common. Such reform efforts produced the **Dawes Severalty Act** of 1887 (also called the General Allotment Act), the most sweeping policy directed at Native Americans in U.S. history. Sponsored by Senator Henry L. Dawes of Massachusetts, it divided tribal lands and "allotted" them to individuals, granting 160 acres to each head of a family and lesser amounts to others.

White Bear, a Kiowa chief, said that his people did "not want to settle down in houses you [the federal government] would build for us. I love to roam over the wild prairie. There I am free and happy." But his preferences were ignored. Between 1887 and 1934, Indians lost an estimated 86 million of their 130 million acres. As Henry Teller, a congressman from Colorado, pointed out, the allotment policy was designed solely to strip the "Indians of their lands and to make them vagabonds on the face of the earth."

THE END OF THE FRONTIER

The end of Native American resistance was one of several developments that suggested the New West was indeed different from the Old West. Other indicators of the region's transformation led some scholars to conclude that American society itself had reached a turning point.

FREDERICK JACKSON TURNER The 1890 national census data indicated that the frontier era was over; Americans had spread across the entire continent. This news led Frederick Jackson Turner, a historian at the University of Wisconsin, to announce in 1893 his "frontier thesis," which argued that more than slavery or any other single factor, "the existence of an area of free land, its continuous recession, and the advance of American settlement westward, explain American development." The experience of taming and settling the frontier, he added, had shaped the national character in fundamental ways. It was

> to the frontier [that] the American intellect owes its striking characteristics. That coarseness and strength combined with acuteness and acquisitiveness; that practical, inventive turn of mind, quick to find expedients; that masterful grasp of material things, lacking in the artistic but powerful to effect great ends; that restless, nervous energy; that dominant individualism, working for good and for evil, and withal that buoyancy and exuberance which comes with freedom—these are traits of the frontier, or traits called out elsewhere because of the existence of the frontier.

Now, however, Turner stressed, "the frontier has gone and with its going has closed the first period of American history."

Turner's view of the frontier gripped the popular imagination. But the frontier experience that he described was in many respects a self-serving myth involving only Christian white men and devoid of towns and cities, which grew *along* with the frontier—not *after* it had been tamed. He virtually ignored the role of women, African Americans, Native Americans, Hispanics, and Asians in shaping the western United States. Moreover, Turner downplayed the vivid evidence of greed, exploitation, and frequent failure in the settling of the West.

He also implied that America would be fundamentally different after 1890 because the frontier experience was essentially over. In many respects, however, the West has retained the qualities associated with the rush for land, gold, timber, and water rights. The mining frontier, as one historian recently wrote, "set a mood that has never disappeared from the West: the attitude of every extractive industry—get in, get rich, get out."

DISCONTENTED FARMERS By 1900, both the South and West were quite different from what they had been in 1865. In both cases, changed economic conditions spurred the emergence of a New South and a New West.

In the West, mechanized commercial agriculture changed the dynamics of farming. By the end of the nineteenth century, many homesteaders had been forced to abandon their farms and become wage-earning laborers, migrant workers moving with the seasons to different states to harvest crops produced

Chinese immigrants in Wyoming These Chinese immigrants were paid lower wages than their white counterparts in the mines of Rock Springs, Wyoming. They continued to work in the mines through a wave of anti-Chinese violence that included the Rock Springs massacre of 1885.

on large commercial farms or ranches. They were often treated as poorly as the white and black sharecroppers in the South. One western worker complained that the landowner "looked at me, his hired hand, as if I was just another workhorse."

As discontent rose among farmers and farmworkers in the South and the West, many joined the People's party, whose followers were known as Populists, a grassroots social and political movement that was sweeping the poorest rural regions of the nation. In 1892, a Minnesota farm leader named Ignatius Donnelly told Populists at their national convention: "We meet in the midst of a nation brought to the verge of moral, political, and material ruin." He affirmed that Populism sought "to restore the Government of the Republic to the hands of the 'plain people' with whom it originated."

The Populist movement would tie the South and West together in an effort to wrest political control from Republicans in the Northeast and Midwest. That struggle would come to define the 1890s and determine the shape of twentieth-century politics.

CHAPTER REVIEW

SUMMARY

- **The New South**   Many southerners embraced the vision of the *New South* promoted by Henry Grady and others, who called for a more diverse economy with greater industrialization, more vocational training, and widespread acceptance of white supremacy in social relations. But agriculture—and especially cotton—still dominated the southern economy, much as it had before the Civil War. Under the *crop-lien system*, large landowners rented land to cash-poor tenant farmers or sharecroppers (the latter usually African Americans) in return for a "share" of the cotton they grew each year. The crop-lien system kept millions in debt and limited where they could live and how they could make a living.

- **Jim Crow Policies in the South**   During the 1890s, southern states disenfranchised the vast majority of African American voters and instituted a series of policies known as Jim Crow laws segregating blacks and whites in public facilities. State governments across the South passed a series of measures that included poll taxes, grandfather clauses, literacy tests, and residency requirements, making voting nearly impossible for most African Americans and some poor whites. Disenfranchisement was followed by legalized segregation (*separate but equal*), ruled constitutional by the Supreme Court in *Plessy v. Ferguson* (1896). African Americans who resisted were often the target of violence at the hands of whites, the most gruesome form being organized lynching. African Americans in the South responded by turning inward and strengthening their own social institutions.

- **Western Migrants**   Life in the West was often harsh, but the promise of cheap land or wealth from mining drew settlers from the East. Although most westerners were white Protestant Americans or immigrants from Germany and Scandinavia, Mexicans, African Americans (the *Exodusters*), and Chinese, as well as many other nationalities, contributed to the West's diversity. About three fourths of those who moved to the West were men.

- **Miners, Farmers, Ranchers, and Women**   Many migrants to the West were attracted to opportunities to mine, ranch, farm, or work on the railroads. Miners were drawn to the discovery of precious minerals such as silver at the *Comstock Lode* in Nevada in 1861. But most miners and cattle ranchers did not become wealthy, because mining and raising cattle, particularly after the development of barbed wire and the end of the *open range*, became large-scale enterprises. Farmers on the Great Plains were able to produce wheat for export, but declining grain prices and the need for expensive machinery and transportation meant that only large-scale farms owned by a wealthy few could sustain real profits.

- **Indian Wars and Policies**   By 1900, Native Americans were no longer free to roam the plains, as the influx of miners, ranchers, farmers, and soldiers had curtailed their traditional way of life. Instances of armed resistance, such as the

Great Sioux War (1876–1877), were crushed. Beginning in 1887 the *Dawes Severalty Act* forced Indians to relinquish their traditional culture and adopt the "American way" of individual landownership. The prevailing attitude of most whites in the West was to displace or exterminate the Native Americans. After the *Sand Creek Massacre* in 1864 conflicts between U.S. Army units and Native Americans, called the *Indian Wars*, continued for most of the century. The last major conflict at Wounded Knee resulted from the *Ghost Dance movement*.

- **The South and West in 1900**   In 1893, Frederick Jackson Turner, a prominent historian, declared that the frontier era was over. He argued that the western-moving frontier of white settlement had been the nation's primary source of democratic politics and rugged individualism. By 1900, the West resembled the South, where agricultural resources were concentrated in the hands of a few. In the 1890s, poor farmers in the West joined with tenant farmers in the South to support the People's party or the Populist party.

CHRONOLOGY

1862	Congress passes the Homestead Act
1864	Sand Creek Massacre
1876	Battle of Little Bighorn
1880s	Henry Grady spreads the New South idea
1890	Battle of Wounded Knee
1893	Frederick J. Turner outlines his "frontier thesis"
1896	*Plessy v. Ferguson* mandates "separate but equal" racial facilities

KEY TERMS

textile industry p. 835

American Tobacco Company p. 836

redeemers p. 837

crop-lien system p. 838

Mississippi Plan (1890) p. 841

separate but equal p. 843

Atlanta Compromise (1895) p. 850

Exodusters p. 854

boomtown p. 856

Comstock Lode p. 857

open range p. 860

Indian wars p. 864

Sand Creek Massacre (1864) p. 866

Great Sioux War p. 869

Ghost Dance movement p. 872

Dawes Severalty Act (1887) p. 874

 INQUIZITIVE

Go to InQuizitive to see what you've learned—and learn what you've missed—with personalized feedback along the way.

19 Political Stalemate and Rural Revolt

1865–1900

New York, 1911 This scene of early-twentieth-century life in New York City by George Wesley Bellows captures people of all walks of life converging on a busy, vibrant downtown intersection.

W ithin three decades after the Civil War, American life had experienced a stunning transformation. An agricultural society long rooted in the soil and little involved in global issues had become an urban and industrialized nation deeply entwined in world markets and international politics.

The period from the end of the Civil War to the beginning of the twentieth century witnessed a widening social, economic, and political gap between the powerful and the powerless, the haves and have-nots. It was labeled the **Gilded Age** for its greed and vulgarity, as the newly rich flaunted their enormous personal wealth—the same wealth that financed extensive political and corporate corruption.

Urban America

Between 1865 and 1900, the United States became a nation dominated by rapidly growing cities. The urban population skyrocketed from 8 million to 30 million. European and Asian immigrants, as well as migrants from America's rural areas, streamed into cities, attracted by plentiful jobs. Many had been pushed off the land with the adoption of new agricultural machinery that sharply reduced the need for farmworkers. Four men could now perform the farmwork that earlier had required fourteen.

focus questions

1. What were the effects of urban growth during the Gilded Age? What problems did it create?

2. Who were the "new immigrants" of the late nineteenth century? How were they viewed by American society?

3. How did urban growth and the increasingly important role of science influence leisure activities, cultural life, and social policy in the Gilded Age?

4. How did the nature of politics during the Gilded Age contribute to political corruption and stalemate?

5. How effective were politicians in developing responses to the major economic and social problems of the Gilded Age?

6. Why did the money supply become a major political issue, especially for farmers, during the Gilded Age? How did it impact American politics?

By the end of the nineteenth century, much of the West was taking an urban form, with new towns forming around mines and railroad junctions. Still other migrants, bored by rural or small-town life, moved to cities in search of more excitement. Whatever the reasons, America increasingly became an urban society. "We cannot all live in cities," cautioned Horace Greeley, the New York newspaper editor and 1872 Democratic presidential candidate, "yet nearly all seem determined to do so."

While the Far West had the greatest proportion of urban dwellers, concentrated in cities such as San Francisco and Denver, the Northeast and Midwest held far more people in huge cities—New York, Boston, Philadelphia, Pittsburgh, Chicago, Cincinnati, St. Louis, and others. Most city dwellers had little or no money and nothing but their labor to sell. And they were forced to live in congested, germ-ridden hovels that seemed like prison cells.

Fortunately, during the last quarter of the nineteenth century, researchers made discoveries that improved living conditions, public health, economic productivity, and communications. Advances in modern science stimulated public support for higher education but also opened up doubts about many long-accepted "truths" and religious beliefs. During the second half of the nineteenth century, more and more people began to question the literal truth of the Bible.

GROWTH IN ALL DIRECTIONS Advances in technology helped city buildings hold their surging populations. In the 1870s, heating innovations such as steam radiators made the construction of much larger apartment buildings financially feasible, because expensive coal-burning fireplaces and chimneys were no longer required in each apartment. Before the 1860s, few structures had been more than five or six stories. During the 1880s, engineers developed cast-iron and steel-frame construction techniques that allowed for taller structures—"skyscrapers." When the Otis Elevator Company installed the first electric elevator in 1889, taller buildings were immediately more practical to design and inhabit.

Cities grew out as well as up, as horse-drawn streetcars and commuter railways allowed people to live farther away from their downtown workplaces. In 1873, San Francisco became the first city to use cable cars that clamped onto a moving underground cable driven by a central power source. Some cities ran steam-powered trains on elevated tracks, but by the 1890s, electric trolleys were preferred. Mass transit received an added boost from underground subway trains built in Boston, New York City, and Philadelphia.

Commuter trains and trolleys allowed a growing middle class of business executives and professionals (accountants, doctors, engineers, sales clerks,

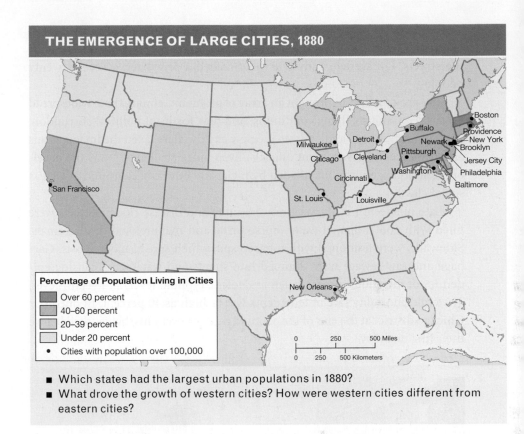

THE EMERGENCE OF LARGE CITIES, 1880

Percentage of Population Living in Cities
- Over 60 percent
- 40–60 percent
- 20–39 percent
- Under 20 percent
- • Cities with population over 100,000

■ Which states had the largest urban populations in 1880?

■ What drove the growth of western cities? How were western cities different from eastern cities?

teachers, store managers, and attorneys) to retreat from crowded downtowns to quieter, tree-lined "streetcar suburbs." But the working poor, many of them immigrants or African Americans, could rarely afford to leave the inner cities. As their populations grew, cities became dangerously congested and plagued with fires, violent crimes, and diseases. New York City, for instance, doubled in size between 1860 and 1890, so fast that basic services could not keep up.

CROWDS, DIRT, AND DISEASE The wonders of big cities—electric lights, streetcars, telephones, department stores, theaters, and many other attractions—lured rural dwellers bored by isolated farm life. Yet they often traded one set of problems for another. In New York City in 1900, some 2.3 million people—two thirds of the city's population—lived in overcrowded apartments called **tenements**, where residents, many of them immigrants, were packed like sardines in poorly ventilated and dimly lit apartments.

Tenement buildings were usually five to six stories tall, lacked elevators, and were jammed so tightly together that most of the apartments had little or no natural light or fresh air. They typically housed twenty-four to thirty-two families, usually with lots of children who had few places to play except in the streets. On average, only one toilet (called a *privy*) served every twenty people.

The growth of cities brought an array of problems, among them widespread poverty, unsanitary living conditions, and new forms of political corruption. How to feed, shelter, and educate the new city dwellers taxed the imaginations and resources of government officials. Even more challenging was the development of neighborhoods divided by racial and ethnic background as well as social class.

Late nineteenth-century cities were filthy and disease ridden. Streets were filled with contaminated water, horse urine and manure, and dead animals. Sidewalks were festooned with tobacco spit, which spread tuberculosis. Garbage and raw sewage were dumped into streets and waterways, causing epidemics of infectious diseases such as cholera, typhoid fever, and yellow fever. The child-mortality rate in tenements was as high as 40 percent. In one poor Chicago district at the end of the century, three of every five babies died before their first birthday.

Urbanization and the environment Garbage carts retrieved trash in New York City, starting in the late-nineteenth century.

Sanitary reformers—public health officials and engineers—eventually created regulations requiring more space per resident as well as more windows and plumbing facilities. Reformers also pushed successfully for modern water and sewage systems and for regular trash collection. They lobbied to ban slaughterhouses and hogs and cattle within city limits, and to replace horse-drawn trolleys with electric-powered streetcars.

THE NEW IMMIGRATION

America's roaring prosperity and promise of political and religious freedom attracted waves of immigrants from every part of the globe after the Civil War. By 1900, nearly 30 percent of city residents were foreign-born. Most of those newcomers were desperately poor people eager to pursue the American dream. They brought with them a distinctive work ethic. Working only to survive is often wretched. Working for a better life for oneself and one's children and grandchildren gives labor a fierce dignity. That dignity, infused with an optimistic energy and aspiration, endowed the new immigrants with resilience and determination. In providing much-needed labor for the growing economy, however, the influx of immigrants also sparked racial and ethnic tensions.

A SURGE OF NEWCOMERS FROM EUROPE Immigration has always been one of the most powerful and controversial forces shaping American development. This was especially true between 1860 and 1900, as more and more foreigners, most of them young and poor, arrived from eastern and southern Europe. The number of immigrants rose from just under 3 million annually in the 1870s to more than 5 million per year in the 1880s. Nearly 9 million came to the United States annually in the first decade of the twentieth century. In 1890, four out of five New Yorkers were foreign-born, a higher proportion than in any city in the world. Chicago was not far behind.

Rapidly growing industries—including mines, railroads, mills, and factories—sought low-wage workers; they sent agents abroad to lure immigrants to the United States. Under the Contract Labor Act of 1864, the federal government helped pay for immigrants' travel expenses to America. The law was repealed in 1868, but not until 1885 did the government stop companies from importing foreign laborers, a practice that put immigrant workers under the control of their employers.

The so-called "old immigrants" who came before 1880 were mainly Protestants and Roman Catholics from northern and western Europe. Germans were the single largest ethnic population in America by 1900, most of them eventually settling in the Midwest. By 1910, some 490 German-language newspapers were being published in the United States.

The traditional pattern of immigration changed, however, as the proportion of immigrants from southern and eastern Europe, especially Russia, Poland, Greece, and Italy, rose during the last quarter of the nineteenth century. After 1890, these "**new immigrants**" made up a majority of arrivals. Their languages and cultural backgrounds were markedly different from those of previous immigrants or of most native-born Americans. The dominant religions of the new immigrants, for example, were Judaism, Eastern Orthodox, and Roman Catholicism, whereas Protestants still formed a large majority of the U.S. population.

While many immigrants gravitated to large cities—New York, Boston, Philadelphia, Chicago—others headed West upon arriving in New York. By 1890, an estimated 45 percent of people living in North Dakota were foreign-born. In South Dakota, California, and Washington, nearly 30 percent of residents

Ellis Island To accommodate the soaring numbers of immigrants passing through New York City, Congress built a reception center on Ellis Island, near the Statue of Liberty. Pictured here is its registry room, where immigrants awaited close questioning by officials.

were immigrants, and in virtually all the western states the foreign-born were over 20 percent of the population.

The South, however, remained unattractive to immigrants. The percentage of foreign-born residents in the states of the former Confederacy declined between 1860 and 1900. By 1910, only 2 percent of southerners were immigrants compared to the national average of 15 percent. Newcomers avoided the South because of its low wages, racial dynamics, and widespread poverty.

In 1907, Congress appointed the Dillingham Commission to examine the changes in immigration patterns. In its lengthy report, released in 1911, the commission concluded that immigrants from southern and eastern Europe posed a social and cultural threat to America's future. They were "far less intelligent than the old, approximately one-third of all those over 14 years of age when admitted being illiterate. Racially, they are for the most part essentially unlike the British, German and other peoples who came during the prior period to 1880, and generally speaking they are actuated in coming by different ideals."

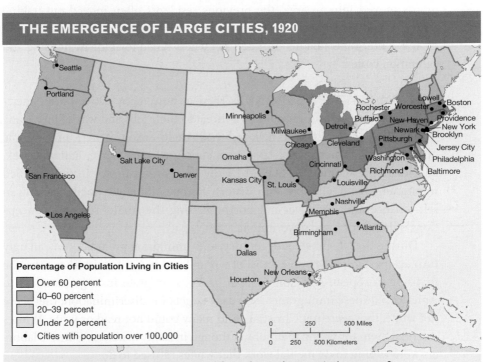

THE EMERGENCE OF LARGE CITIES, 1920

Percentage of Population Living in Cities

- Over 60 percent
- 40–60 percent
- 20–39 percent
- Under 20 percent
- • Cities with population over 100,000

0   250   500 Miles

0   250   500 Kilometers

- How did technology change urban life in the early twentieth century?
- What was the role of mass transit in expanding the urban population?
- How did the demographics of the new cities change between 1880 and 1920?

Immigrants were usually desperately poor and needed to find jobs—quickly. Many were greeted at the docks by family and friends, others were met by representatives of immigrant-aid societies or by company agents offering low-paying and often dangerous jobs in mines, mills, sweatshops, and on railroads.

Since most immigrants knew little if any English and nothing about American employment practices, they were easy targets for exploitation. Many lost a healthy percentage of their wages to unscrupulous hiring agents in exchange for a bit of whiskey and a job. Companies eager for workers gave immigrants train tickets to inland cities such as Buffalo, Pittsburgh, Cleveland, Chicago, Milwaukee, Cincinnati, and St. Louis.

As strangers in a new land, most immigrants wanted to live in neighborhoods populated by people from their homeland. The largest cities had vibrant immigrant districts with names such as Little Italy, Little Hungary, and Chinatown, where immigrants sustained their native religions and customs and spoke and read newspapers in their native languages.

But they paid a price for such community solidarity. When new immigrants moved into an area, the previous residents often moved out, taking with them whatever social prestige and political influence they had achieved. Living conditions often deteriorated as owners failed to abide by housing and sanitation codes.

THE NATIVIST RESPONSE Then, as now, many native-born Americans saw the newest immigrants as a threat to their jobs and way of life. Many "**nativists**" were racists who believed that "Anglo-Saxon" Americans—people of British or Germanic ancestry—were superior to the Slavic, Italian, Greek, and Jewish newcomers. A Stanford University professor, for instance, called immigrants from southern and eastern Europe "illiterate, docile, lacking in self-reliance and initiative, and not possessing the Anglo-Teutonic conceptions of law, order, and government."

During the late nineteenth century, anti-immigrant prejudice took an ugly turn against Chinese people, most of whom lived in California. They were the first non-European and non-African group to migrate in large numbers to America. Chinese immigrants were easy targets for discrimination; they were not white, they were not Christian, and many could not read or write. Whites resented them for taking their jobs, although in many instances Chinese laborers were willing to do menial work that whites refused to do.

John Jeong, a young Chinese immigrant, arrived in San Francisco and quickly encountered ethnic persecution. As he and others made their way to the Chinatown neighborhood in an open carriage, "some white boys came up and started throwing rocks at us." Another Chinese newcomer experienced similar treatment. Whenever he and his friends strayed outside their own neighborhood, "whites would attack you with stones."

White Californians demanded an end to Chinese immigration. Until 1875, however, immigration policies had been left up to the states. In that year, however, Congress passed the Page Act, the first federal law intended to restrict "undesirable" immigration. It prohibited Asian prostitutes, convicts, and anyone entering the country under an arrangement of "forced labor" (a form of slavery).

Seven years later, in 1882, anti-Chinese sentiment on the West Coast led Congress to pass the **Chinese Exclusion Act**. It was the first federal

Chinese Exclusion Act Chinese caricature "John Chinaman" is escorted out of America by Lady Liberty with his ironing board and opium pipe, while other accepted minorities look on.

law to restrict the immigration of free people on the basis of race and class. The act, which barred Chinese laborers ("yellow hordes") from entering the country for ten years, was periodically renewed before being extended indefinitely in 1902. With the Chinese Exclusion Act, the golden door welcoming foreigners to the United States began to close. Not until 1943 were barriers to Chinese immigration finally removed.

Chinese were not the only group targeted. In 1887, Protestant activists in Iowa formed the American Protective Association (APA), a secret organization whose members pledged never to employ or vote for a Roman Catholic. Working often within local Republican party organizations, the APA quickly enlisted 2.5 million members and helped shape the 1894 election results in Ohio, Wisconsin, Indiana, Missouri, and Colorado.

In 1891, nativists in New England formed the Immigration Restriction League to, in their words, "save" the Anglo-Saxon "race" from being "contaminated" by "alien" immigrants, especially Roman Catholics and Jews. The League convinced Congress to ban illiterate immigrants. Three presidents vetoed such bills: Grover Cleveland in 1897, William H. Taft in 1913, and Woodrow Wilson in 1915 and 1917. The last time, however, Congress overrode the veto, and illiterate immigrants were banned.

CULTURAL LIFE

The flood of people into cities brought changes in recreation and leisure. Middle- and upper-class families, especially those in streetcar suburbs, often spent free time together at home, singing around a piano, reading, or playing games. In congested urban areas, politics as a form of public entertainment attracted large crowds. New forms of mass entertainment—movie theaters; vaudeville shows featuring singers, dancers, and comedians; art museums; symphonies; sporting events; Wild West shows, and circuses—drew a broad cross-section of residents. In large cities, new streetcar transit systems allowed people to travel easily to sporting events, and rooting for the home baseball team helped unify a city's ethnic and racial groups and social classes. By the end of the century, sports of all kinds had become a major part of popular culture.

Urbanization and technological progress also contributed to the prestige of modern science. By encouraging what one writer called a "mania for facts," scientists generated changes throughout social, intellectual, and cultural life. Scientific research led to transformational technologies such as electric power and lights, telephones, phonographs, motion pictures, bicycles, and automobiles.

Vaudeville For as little as 1¢ for admission, vaudeville shows aimed to please the tastes of their wildly diverse audience with a great range of entertainment.

Mulberry Street, 1900 This colorized photograph captures the many Italian immigrants who made Mulberry Street in downtown New York City their home at the turn of the century. Horse-drawn carts weave through crowds shopping, socializing, and people gazing.

Although only men could vote in most states, both men and women flocked to hear candidates speak at political meetings. In the largest cities, membership in a political party offered many social benefits. As labor unions became increasingly common, they too took on social roles for working-class men.

SALOONS The most popular leisure destinations for urban wage workers were **saloons**, beer gardens, and dance halls. By 1900, the United States had more saloons (over 325,000) than grocery stores and meat markets. New York City alone had 10,000 saloons, 1 for every 500 residents.

Saloons were the workingman's social club and were especially popular among immigrants seeking companionship in a strange land. In cities such as New York, Boston, Philadelphia, and Chicago, the customers were disproportionately Irish, German, and Italian Catholics. Politics was often the topic of intense discussions in saloons; in New York City in the 1880s, saloons doubled as polling places, where patrons could cast their votes in elections. One journalist called the saloon "the social and intellectual center of the neighborhood."

Men also went to saloons to check job postings, participate in labor unions, cash paychecks, mail letters, read newspapers, and gossip. Patrons could play chess, billiards, darts, cards, dice, or even handball, since many saloons included gymnasiums. Because saloons were heated and had restrooms, they served as refuges for the homeless, especially in the winter.

Although saloons were for men only, women and children could use a side door to buy a pail of beer to carry home (a task called "rushing the growler"). Some saloons also provided "snugs," separate rooms for women customers. "Stall saloons" included "wine rooms" where prostitutes worked.

LEISURE FOR WORKING WOMEN Married working-class women had even less free time than working-class men did. Many were working for pay themselves, and even those who were not were frequently overwhelmed by housework and child-rearing responsibilities. As a social worker noted, "The men have the saloons, political clubs, trade-unions or [fraternal] lodges for their recreation . . . while the mothers have almost no recreation, only a dreary round of work, day after day, with occasionally doorstep gossip to vary the monotony of their lives."

Married working-class women often used the streets and alleys as their public space. Washing clothes, supervising children at play, or shopping at the local market provided opportunities for socializing.

Single women, many of whom worked as housekeepers ("maids") and had more leisure time than working mothers, flocked to dance halls, theaters,

Steeplechase Park, Coney Island, Brooklyn, New York Members of the working class could afford the inexpensive rides at this popular amusement park.

amusement parks, and picnic grounds. With the advent of movie theaters, the cinema became the most popular form of entertainment for working women. As an advertisement promised, "If you are tired of life, go to the movies. If you are sick of troubles rife, go to the picture show. You will forget your unpaid bills, rheumatism and other ills, if you stow your pills and go to the picture show."

THE IMPACT OF DARWINISM

Virtually every field of thought felt the impact of natural scientist Charles Darwin's controversial *On the Origin of Species* (1859), one of the most influential books ever written. Basing his conclusions on extensive yet "imperfect" field research done around the world, Darwin showed how the chance processes of evolution give energy and unity to life. At the center of his concept was "natural selection." He demonstrated that most organisms produce many more offspring than can survive. Those offspring with certain favorable characteristics adapt and live, while others die from starvation, disease, or predators.

This "struggle for existence" in a crowded world drove the process of natural selection, Darwin said. Over many millions of years, modern species "evolved" from less complex forms of life; individuals and species that had characteristics advantageous for survival reproduced, while others fell by the wayside. As Darwin wrote, "the vigorous, the healthy, and the happy survive and multiply."

Darwin's theory of biological evolution was shocking because most people still embraced a literal interpretation of the biblical creation story, which claimed that God created all species at the same moment and they remained the same thereafter. Although Darwin had trained for the ministry and was reluctant to be drawn into religious controversy, his biological findings suggested to many, then and since, that there was no providential God controlling the universe. People were no different from plants and animals; they too evolved by trial and error rather than by God's purposeful hand. What came to be called *Darwinism* spelled the end of a God-given world.

Charles Darwin Darwin's scientific theories influenced more than a century of political and social debate.

Many Christians charged that Darwin's ideas led to atheism, a denial of the existence of God, while others found their faith severely shaken. Most of the faithful, however, came to reconcile science and religion. They decided that the process of evolutionary change in nature must be God's doing.

SOCIAL DARWINISM Although Darwin's theory of evolution applied only to biological phenomena, many applied it to human society. Englishman Herbert Spencer, a leading social philosopher, was the first major prophet of what came to be called **social Darwinism**.

Spencer argued that human society and its institutions, like the organisms studied by Darwin, evolved through the same process of natural selection. The "survival of the fittest," in Spencer's chilling phrase, was the engine of social progress. By encouraging people, ideas, and nations to compete with one another for dominance, society would generate "the greatest perfection and the most complete happiness."

Charles Darwin dismissed Spencer's social theories as "unconvincing." He did not believe that the evolutionary process in the natural world had any relevance to human social institutions. Others, however, eagerly endorsed social Darwinism. E. L. Youmans, founding editor of *Popular Science Monthly*, became the foremost champion of Spencer's ideas in America. He claimed that in the United States, *Darwinism* really meant *Spencerism*, the "anti-philanthropic, anti-meddling side" of Spencer's philosophy. If, as Spencer believed, society naturally evolved for the better through "survival of the fittest," then interference with human competition in the marketplace was a serious mistake because it would help "unfit" people survive, and thereby hinder progress.

Social Darwinism implied the need for hands-off, laissez-faire government policies; it argued against the regulation of business or of required minimum standards for sanitation and housing. To Spencer, the only acceptable charity was voluntary, and even that was of dubious value. Spencer warned that "fostering the good-for-nothing [people] at the expense of the good, is an extreme cruelty" to the health of civilization.

For Spencer and his many American supporters, successful businessmen and corporations provided proof of the concept of survival of the fittest. Oil tycoon John D. Rockefeller revealed his embrace of social Darwinism when he told his Baptist Sunday-school class that the "growth of a large business is merely a survival of the fittest. . . . This is not an evil tendency in business. It is merely the working-out of a law of nature and a law of God."

Spencer's chief American academic disciple, William Graham Sumner, taught at Yale University, where he preached the gospel of natural selection. Sumner's most lasting contribution, made in his book *Folkways* (1907), was to argue that it would be a mistake for government to try to promote equality, since doing so would interfere with the "survival of the fittest."

REFORM DARWINISM Sumner's efforts to use Darwinism to promote "rugged individualism" and oppose government regulation of business prompted an alternative use of Darwinism in the context of human society. What came to be called **reform Darwinism** found its major advocate in Lester Frank Ward, a government employee who fought his way up from poverty and never lost his empathy for the underdog.

Ward's *Dynamic Sociology* (1883) singled out one aspect of evolution that both Darwin and Spencer had neglected: the human brain. True, as Sumner claimed, people, like animals, compete. But, as Ward explained, people also collaborate. Unlike animals, people can plan for a distant future; they have minds capable of shaping and directing social change. Far from being the helpless object of irresistible evolutionary forces, Ward argued, humanity could actively control social evolution through long-range planning.

Ward's reform Darwinism held that *cooperation*, not *competition*, would better promote social progress. Government, in Ward's view, should pursue two main goals: alleviating poverty, which impeded the development of the mind, and promoting the education of the masses. Intellect, informed by science, could foster social improvement. Reform Darwinism would prove to be one of the pillars of the progressive movement during the late nineteenth century and after.

REALISM IN LITERATURE AND ART

Before the Civil War, Romanticism had dominated American literature and painting. Romantics such as the New England transcendentalists believed that fundamental truths rested in the unseen world of ideas and spirit. They used their excursions in nature—woods, fields, valleys, and mountains—as a springboard to the sacred, taking notice of the divinity residing in outdoor scenes: a solitary encounter with a deer or a fox or a hemlock, or wading in a creek or swimming in a pond.

That changed during the second half of the nineteenth century, however, as a new generation of writers and artists calling themselves "realists" began to challenge the "sentimentality" and the nature-worshipping credo of the Romantic tradition. A writer in *Putnam's Monthly* noted in 1854 a growing emphasis on "the real and the practical." This emphasis on "realism" matured into a full-fledged cultural force during the late nineteenth century, as more and more writers and artists focused on depicting the actual aspects of urban-industrial

America: scientific research and technology, factories and railroads, cities and immigrants, labor unions and social tensions.

For many Americans, the horrors of the Civil War had led to a less romanticized and more realistic view of life. An editor attending an art exhibition in 1865 sensed "the greater reality of feeling developed by the war. We have grown more sober, perhaps, and less patient of romantic idealism."

Another factor contributing to the rise of realism was the impact of modern science. "This is a world of reality," admitted a Romantic writer, "and romance breaks against the many hard facts." The "stupendous power of Science," announced one editor, would rid American thought of "every old-time idea, every trace of old romance and art, poetry and romantic or sentimental feeling" and wash away the "ideal . . . and visionary."

Embracing realism, as writer Fanny Bates stressed, meant that stories and novels should be fed by fact and enlivened by textured social details. Authors should cast a roving eye on the scenes and concerns of daily life, peering into apartments, houses, shops, and factories—telling about life as it *is*, rather than how it should be. The tone of such writing and art appealed especially to people living in busy, swarming cities, people "whose lives are crowded with a variety of interests."

The worship of money was the most common theme in realistic novels, short stories, and portraits during the Gilded Age. In William Dean Howells's *The Rise of Silas Lapham* (1885), Bromfield Corey announces that money "is the romance, the poetry of our age." Lily Bart, the heroine of Edith Wharton's *The House of Mirth* (1905), declares that she "must have a great deal of money" to be happy.

City streets, sidewalks, and parks provided countless scenes of *real* life to depict on canvas and in words. Novelist Henry James said that the daily urban scene unleashed a "flood of the real" to study and portray. John Sloan, a New York City painter, chose his subjects by spying on people from his Manhattan studio. He confided in his diary that he was addicted to "watching every bit of human life" through his windows and along the sidewalks.

Others shared Sloan's "spectatorial" sensibility. "My favorite pastime," writer Theodore Dreiser remembered, "was to walk the city streets and view the lives and activities of others." In Dreiser's influential novel *Sister Carrie* (1900), Carrie Meeber uses her "gift of observation" to view strangers through the open windows of shops, offices, and factories, imagining what "they deal with, how they labored, to what end it all came."

The realists' emphasis on closely observing everyday life grew out of the scientific spirit. Just as scientists sought verifiable facts and transformed them into knowledge, cultural realists studied the world around them and expressed

Stag at Sharkey's (1909) New York painter George Bellows witnessed such fierce boxing matches across the street from his studio, at the saloon of retired heavyweight boxer "Sailor" Sharkey. Bellows is one of the most famous artists from the Ashcan School, which was committed to capturing the gritty reality of the urban scene.

it in art and literature. Like a gust of fresh air, they made Americans aware of the significance of their everyday surroundings, in all their beauty and ugliness.

GILDED AGE POLITICS

The Gilded Age displayed more political corruption than political innovation. In 1879, Woodrow Wilson, then a young college graduate, described the political system as having "no leaders, no principles." Wilson's foremost critic, Theodore Roosevelt, agreed with him about the venality of Gilded Age politics. "When they call the roll in the Senate," he quipped, "the senators don't know whether to answer 'present' or 'not guilty.'"

Political parties were more powerful than presidents during the Gilded Age, and business tycoons were more powerful than parties. So-called captains of industry regularly used their wealth to "buy" elections and favors at all levels of government. Jay Gould, one of the most aggressive railroad tycoons, admitted that he elected "the [New York] legislature with my own money."

"Special interests," businesses that bought political and legislative favors from government officials, dominated Gilded Age politics. By the end of the nineteenth century, however, new movements and parties were pushing to reform the excesses and injustices created by a political system that had grown corrupt in its efforts to support the special interests of Big Business. As reformer Lyman Abbott maintained, "Politically America is a democracy; industrially America is an aristocracy."

LOCAL POLITICS AND PARTY LOYALTIES Perhaps the most important feature of Gilded Age politics was its local focus. Most political activity occurred at the state and local levels. Unlike today, the federal government was an insignificant force in the daily lives of most citizens, in part because it was so small. In 1871, the entire federal civilian workforce totaled 51,000 (most of them postal workers), of whom only 6,000 actually worked in Washington, D.C. Not until the twentieth century did the importance of the federal government begin to surpass that of local and state governments.

Americans during the Gilded Age were intensely loyal to their chosen political party, which they joined as much for the fellowship and networking connections as for its positions on issues. Unlike today, party members paid dues to join, and party leaders regularly demanded large campaign contributions from the captains of industry and finance. Collis Huntington, a California railroad tycoon, admitted that bribery in the form of campaign contributions was expected: "If you have to pay money to have the right thing done, then it is only just and fair to do it." Roscoe Conkling, a powerful Republican senator from New York, was equally candid: "Of course, we do rotten things in New York. . . . Politics is a rotten business." Democrat Horatio Seymour, a presidential candidate in 1868, explained that "our people want men in office who will not steal, but who will not interfere with those who do."

In cities crowded with new immigrant voters, politics was usually controlled by "rings"—small groups who shaped policy and managed the nomination and election of candidates. Each ring typically had a powerful "boss" who used his "machine"—a network of neighborhood activists and officials—to govern.

Colorful, larger-than-life figures such as New York City's William "Boss" Tweed shamelessly ruled, plundered, and occasionally improved municipal government, often through dishonest means and frequent bribes. Until his arrest in 1871 and his conviction in 1873, Tweed used the Tammany Hall ring to dominate the nation's largest city. The Tammany Hall political machine doled out contracts to business allies and jobs to political supporters. In the late 1870s one of every twelve New York men worked for the city government. The various city rings and bosses were often corrupt, but they did bring structure, stability, and services to rapidly growing inner-city communities, many of them composed of immigrants newly arrived from Ireland, Germany, and, increasingly, from southern and eastern Europe.

William "Boss" Tweed A larger-than-life political boss was New York City's William "Boss" Tweed, whose powerful connections made "no prison big enough to hold the Boss."

The party in power expected the government employees it appointed to become campaign workers and to do the bidding of **party bosses**. Those bosses in "smoke-filled back rooms" often decided who the candidates would be and commanded loyalty and obedience by rewarding and punishing their party members. They helped settle local disputes, provided aid for the poor, and distributed government jobs and contracts to loyal followers and corporate donors through the **patronage** system. President Ulysses S. Grant's secretary told a Republican party boss that he hoped "you will distribute the patronage in such a manner as will help the Administration."

Throughout the Gilded Age, almost every government job—local, state, and federal—was subject to the latest election results. As a Democratic party official in New York City admitted, "You can't keep a [political] organization together without patronage. Men ain't in politics for nothin'. They want to get somethin' out of it."

The jobs (patronage) given to party loyalists covered a wide range, from cabinet posts to courthouse clerk positions. The largest single source of political jobs was the postal service, which accounted for over half of all federal civilian employees. Those who were awarded government jobs were expected to contribute a percentage of their salary to the political party.

The corruption associated with the patronage system eventually drew criticism from civil service reformers, progressives who pushed through legislation designed to limit such patronage. As replacement they advocated a "merit system" for government employment based on ability and experience.

NATIONAL POLITICS Several factors gave national politics in the Gilded Age its distinctive texture. First in importance was the close division between Republicans and Democrats in Congress. Because neither party was dominant, they both avoided controversial issues or bold initiatives for fear of losing a close election. Yet, paradoxically, voter intensity at all levels peaked during the Gilded Age at the same time that many divisive issues were suppressed or ignored. Voter turnout was commonly about 70 to 80 percent. (By contrast, the turnout for the 2016 U.S. presidential election was 61 percent.)

Most voters cast their ballots for the same party year after year. Party loyalty was often an emotional choice. In the 1870s and 1880s, for example, people continued to fight the Civil War during political campaigns. Republican candidates regularly "waved the bloody shirt," accusing Democrats of having caused "secession and civil war," while Republicans took credit for abolishing slavery and saving the Union.

Democrats, especially in the South, where they monopolized political power after 1877, responded by reminding voters that they stood for limited government, states' rights, and white supremacy. Republicans tended to favor high tariffs on imports, but many Democrats also supported tariffs if they benefited the dominant businesses in their districts or states. Third parties, such as the Greenbackers, Populists, and Prohibitionists, appealed to specific interests and issues, such as currency inflation, railroad regulations, or legislation to restrict alcohol consumption.

Party loyalties reflected religious, ethnic, and geographic divisions. After the Civil War, the Republican party remained strongest in New England, upstate New York, Pennsylvania, Ohio, and the Midwest. Republicans tended to be Protestants of English or Scandinavian descent. As the party of Abraham Lincoln (the "Great Emancipator") and Ulysses S. Grant, Republicans could also rely upon the votes of African Americans in the South (until their right to vote was taken away by Jim Crow laws) and the support of a large bloc of Union veterans of the Civil War, who were organized into a powerful national interest group called the Grand Army of the Republic.

The Democrats were a more diverse coalition of conservative southern whites, northern Catholics of Irish or German backgrounds, and others repelled by the Republicans' claim to be the "party of morality." As one Chicago Democrat explained, "A Republican is a man who wants you t' go t' church every Sunday. A Democrat says if a man wants to have a glass of beer on Sunday he can have it."

During the 1880s, Protestant Republicans infuriated many immigrants and Catholics of Irish, Italian, or German background by promoting efforts to limit or prohibit the consumption of alcoholic beverages. They also pushed for nativist policies designed to restrict immigration and the employment of foreigners.

Many Irish, Germans, and Italians brought with them to America robust drinking traditions that upset many Protestant Republicans who considered saloons the central social evil around which all others revolved.

Carrie Nation, the most colorful member of the Women's Christian Temperance Union (WCTU), became a national celebrity known for her attacks on saloons with a hatchet. Saloons, she argued, stripped a married woman of everything by turning husbands into alcoholics, as had happened with Nation's first husband: "Her husband is torn from her, she is robbed of her sons, her home, her food, and her virtue."

Between 1869 and 1913, from the first term of Ulysses S. Grant through the election of William Howard Taft, Republicans monopolized the White House except for two nonconsecutive terms of New York Democrat Grover Cleveland. Otherwise, national politics was remarkably balanced. Between 1872 and 1896, *no* president won a majority of the popular vote. In each of those presidential elections, sixteen states invariably voted Republican and fourteen, including every southern state (the "Solid South"), voted Democratic. That left six "swing" (closely contested) states to determine the outcome. Two of those states, New York and Ohio, decided the election of eight presidents from 1872 to 1908.

All presidents during the Gilded Age, both Republican and Democrat, deferred to their party leaders in the Senate and House of Representatives. They believed that Congress, not the White House, should formulate major policies that the president would implement. As Senator John Sherman of Ohio stressed, "The President should merely obey and enforce the law" as laid out by Congress.

HAYES TO HARRISON

Both Republicans and Democrats had their share of officials willing to buy and sell government jobs or legislative votes. Yet as early as the 1870s, in response to the corruption uncovered in the Grant administration, each party developed factions promoting honesty in government. The struggle for "clean" government became one of the foremost issues of the Gilded Age.

HAYES AND CIVIL SERVICE REFORM

President Rutherford B. Hayes brought to the White House in 1877 both a lingering controversy over the disputed election results (critics called him "His Fraudulency" or "His Accidency") and an uprightness in sharp contrast to the scandals of Grant's presidency. Hayes appointed a Democrat as postmaster general in an effort to clean up an agency infamous for trading jobs for political favors.

The son of an Ohio farmer, Hayes was wounded four times in the Civil War. He went on to serve in Congress and as governor of Ohio. Honest and conservative, he was, said a Republican journalist, a "third-rate nonentity" whose only virtue was that he was "obnoxious to no one."

Hayes had been the compromise presidential nominee of two factions fighting for control of the Republican party, the so-called Stalwarts and Half-Breeds, led, respectively, by Senators Roscoe Conkling of New York and James G. Blaine of Maine. The Stalwarts had been "stalwart" in their support of President Grant during the furor over the misdeeds of his cabinet members. Further, they had mastered the patronage system (spoils system) of distributing political jobs to party loyalists. The Half-Breeds supposedly were only *half* loyal to Grant and *half* committed to reform of the spoils system. But in the end, the two factions existed primarily to advance the careers of Conkling and Blaine, who detested each other.

To his credit, President Hayes tried to stay above the petty bickering. He joined the growing public outrage over the era's astonishing corruption, admitting that his party "must mend its ways" by focusing on Republican principles rather than fighting over the spoils of office. It was time "for **civil service** [government jobs] **reform**." He appointed a committee to consider a merit

"The Bosses of the Senate" This 1889 cartoon bitingly portrays the period's corrupt alliance between big business and legislators.

system for hiring government employees. In a dramatic gesture, Hayes also fired Chester A. Arthur, a Stalwart Republican who ran the New York Customs House, because he had abused the patronage system in ways that promoted "ignorance, inefficiency, and corruption."

Hayes's commitment to cleaning up politics enraged Republican leaders. In 1879, Ohio congressman James Garfield warned Hayes that "if he wishes to hold any influence" with fellow Republicans, he "must abandon some of his notions of Civil Service reform." For his part, Hayes confessed that he had little hope of success because he was "opposed by . . . the most powerful men in my party."

On economic issues, Hayes held to a conservative line that would guide his successors—from both parties—for the rest of the century. His answer to demands for expansion of the nation's money supply (which would become one of the leading issues of the late nineteenth century) was a resounding no: he vetoed the Bland-Allison Act (1878), a bipartisan effort to increase the supply of silver coins. (More money in circulation was generally believed to raise farm prices and help those trying to pay off debts.) Hayes believed only in "hard money"—gold coins.

When the Democrat-controlled Congress convinced many Republicans to help overturn Hayes's veto, the president confided in his diary that he had become a president without a party. In 1879, with a year still left in his term, Hayes was ready to leave the White House. "I am now in my last year of the Presidency," he wrote a friend, "and look forward to its close as a schoolboy longs for the coming vacation."

GARFIELD, ARTHUR, AND THE PENDLETON ACT

With Hayes choosing not to pursue a second term, the Republican presidential nomination in 1880 was up for grabs. In the end, the Stalwarts and Half-Breeds were forced to select a compromise candidate, Congressman James A. Garfield.

Born in an Ohio log cabin, Garfield had been a minister, a lawyer, professor, and a college president before serving in the Civil War as a Union army general. In an effort to please the Stalwarts and also win the crucial swing state of New York, the Republicans named Chester A. Arthur, whom Hayes had fired as head of the New York Customs House, as their candidate for vice president.

The Democrats, even more divided than the Republicans, selected Winfield Scott Hancock, a retired Union general who had distinguished himself at the Battle of Gettysburg but had done little since. Ulysses S. Grant had known Hancock for forty years. He described him as "a weak, vain man. He is the most selfish man I know. He could never endure to have anyone else receive any credit."

In large part, the Democrats had selected Hancock to help deflect the Republicans' "bloody-shirt" attacks on Democrats as the party of the Confederacy. Yet Hancock undermined that effort by supporting southern efforts to strip blacks of voting rights.

In an election marked by widespread bribery, Garfield eked out a popular-vote plurality of only 39,000, or 48.5 percent out of some 9 million votes. He won a more comfortable margin of 214 to 155 in the electoral college. Republicans took control of Congress as well. As the country entered the last decades of the century, Garfield would be the last president born in a log cabin.

Embedded in the voting, however, was a worrisome pattern: the Democrats won all the southern states, and the Republicans won all the northern states. Politically, the Civil War was not over. Moreover, in presidential elections during the rest of the nineteenth century, if the Republicans lost New York State, they would lose the White House. Securing the nation's most-populous state thus became central to Republican strategy.

A PRESIDENCY CUT SHORT In his 1881 inaugural address, President Garfield gave an impassioned defense of civil rights, arguing that the "elevation of the negro race from slavery to the full rights of citizenship is the most important political change we have known since the adoption of the Constitution of 1787." The end of slavery, he said, "has added immensely to the moral and industrial forces of our people. It has liberated the master as well as the slave from a relation which wronged and enfeebled both." He also confirmed, however, that the Republicans had ended efforts to reconstruct the former Confederacy. Southern blacks were on their own now; they had been "surrendered to their own guardianship."

Garfield was old-school in many respects. He opposed labor unions, opposed the idea of an eight-hour workday, and viewed voting rights for women as "atheistic, and destructive of marriage and family." Presidents, he argued, should continue to defer to Congress, and the federal government should simply "keep the peace" and stay out of the way of the states. Outgoing President Hayes said Garfield "was not executive in his talents—not original, not firm, not a moral force. He leaned on others."

In the continuing feud between the Half-Breed and Stalwart factions of the Republican party, Garfield chose the Half-Breeds. He appointed

James G. Blaine as secretary of state over the objection of Ulysses S. Grant, leading the former president to tell reporters that Garfield "is a man without backbone. A man of fine ability but lacking stamina. He wants to please everybody." As far as Blaine was concerned, Grant confessed that he did "not like the man, have no confidence in his friendship nor in his reliability."

Garfield would have no time to prove himself as president, however. On July 2, 1881, after only four months in office, he was walking through the Washington, D.C., railroad station when he was shot twice by Charles Guiteau, a thirty-nine-year-old Republican office seeker. "My God," the president cried out, "What is this?" before slumping to the floor, bleeding heavily. Guiteau had earlier visited Garfield to ask for a job in the U.S. consulate in Paris, only to be rejected. As a policeman wrestled the assassin to the ground, Guiteau shouted: "Yes! I have killed Garfield! [Chester] Arthur is now President of the United States. I am a Stalwart!" That declaration would eventually destroy the Stalwart wing of the Republican party.

On September 19, after seventy-nine days of struggle, Garfield died of infection resulting from inept medical care. Former president Grant cried when he heard the news, explaining that Garfield's death had "produced a shock upon the public mind but little less than that produced by the assassination of Mr. Lincoln."

During a sensational ten-week trial, Guiteau claimed that God had ordered him to kill the president. His dastardly deed so incensed Americans that two men, one of them Guiteau's jailer, separately tried to shoot him but missed. The jury refused to believe that he was insane and pronounced him "devilishly depraved" and guilty of murder. On June 30, 1882, Guiteau was hanged; an autopsy revealed that his brain was diseased.

"A Model Office-Seeker" This 1881 cartoon depicts Charles J. Guiteau, who was convicted of assassinating President James A. Garfield. In one hand, he brandishes a pistol, and in the other, a paper that reads: "an office or your life!"

THE CIVIL SERVICE COMMISSION In their grief over Garfield's death, Americans blamed Roscoe Conkling and the Stalwart Republicans for inciting Guiteau. A *New York Tribune* headline read: "MURDERED BY THE SPOILS SYSTEM!"

People saw little potential in the new president, Chester A. Arthur, who had been Roscoe Conkling's trusted lieutenant. Grant wrote an associate that he did not "expect much from this administration." Yet Arthur surprised most political observers by distancing himself from Conkling and the Stalwarts and becoming a civil service reformer. Throughout his presidency, he kept a promise not to remove any federal office holder purely for political reasons. He also made cabinet appointments based on merit rather than partisanship. One of Arthur's former New York associates, a Stalwart, grumbled that "he has done less for us than Garfield, or even Hayes."

Little is known about President Chester Arthur. Unlike most presidents, there is no library or museum dedicated to his career. Just before he died, he had all his official papers and correspondence burned. He wanted obscurity and he got it. What we do know is that he did not invest much time in his role as chief executive. He worked only from ten to four each day and took Sundays and Mondays off. One of his clerks noted that Arthur "never did today what he could put off until tomorrow."

In 1883, momentum against the spoils system generated by Garfield's assassination enabled George H. Pendleton, a Democratic senator from Ohio, to convince Congress to establish a Civil Service Commission, the first federal regulatory agency. Because of the Pendleton Civil Service Reform Act, at least 15 percent of federal jobs would now be filled based on competitive tests (the merit system) rather than political favoritism. In addition, federal employees running for office were prohibited from receiving political contributions from government workers.

The Pendleton Act was a limited first step in cleaning up the patronage process. It was sorely needed, in part because the federal government was expanding rapidly. By 1901, there would be 256,000 federal employees, five times the number in 1871. A growing portion of these federal workers were women, who by 1890 held a third of the government's clerical jobs.

THE CAMPAIGN OF 1884

Chester Arthur's efforts to clean up the spoils system might have attracted voters, but they did not please Republican leaders. So in 1884, the Republicans dumped the ailing Arthur (he had contracted a kidney disease) and chose as their nominee James Gillespie Blaine of Maine, the handsome, colorful secretary of state.

Blaine inspired the party faithful with his electrifying speeches, and he knew how to make backroom deals. One critic charged that Blaine "wallowed in spoils like a rhinoceros in an African pool." Newspapers soon uncovered evidence of his corruption in the so-called Mulligan letters. They revealed that Congressman Blaine had secretly sold his votes on measures favorable to a railroad corporation.

During the presidential campaign, more letters surfaced linking Blaine to shady deal making. In one of them, Blaine told the recipient: "Burn this letter!" For the reform element of the Republican party, this was too much, and many independent-minded Republicans refused to endorse Blaine's candidacy. "We are Republicans but we are not slaves," said one of the independents. He insisted that the party of Lincoln must recommit itself to "retrenchment, purity and reform." Party regulars scorned such critics as "goo-goos"—the "good-government" crowd who were outraged by the corrupting influence of money in politics. The editor of a New York newspaper jokingly called the anti-Blaine Republicans **Mugwumps**, after an Algonquian Indian word meaning "big chief."

The Mugwumps, a self-appointed group of reformers dedicated to promoting honest government, saw the election as a "moral rather than political" contest. Centered in the large cities and major universities of the northeast, the Mugwumps were mostly professors, editors, and writers. Like the Liberal Republicans before them, the Mugwumps sought to reform the patronage system by declaring that *all* federal jobs would be filled solely on the basis of merit. The rise of the Mugwumps, as well as growing national concerns about political corruption, prompted the Democrats to nominate New Yorker Grover Cleveland, a massive figure with a bull neck, strong jaw, and an overflowing moustache that made him resemble a walrus.

Cleveland had first attracted national attention in 1881, when he was elected mayor of Buffalo on an anti-corruption platform. Elected governor of New York in 1882, he continued to build a reform record by fighting New York City's corrupt Tammany Hall ring. As mayor and as governor,

Grover Cleveland As president, Cleveland made the issue of tariff reform central to the politics of the late 1880s.

he repeatedly vetoed bills that he felt served private interests at the expense of the public good. He supported civil service reform, opposed expanding the money supply, and preferred free trade rather than high tariffs.

Although Cleveland was known for his honesty and integrity, two personal issues hurt him: the discovery that he had paid for a substitute to take his place in the Union army during the Civil War, and a juicy sex scandal that erupted when a Buffalo newspaper revealed that Cleveland, a bachelor, had seduced an attractive widow named Maria Halpin, who named him the father of her baby born in 1874. Cleveland had refused to marry her but had discreetly provided financial support for the child.

The escapades of Blaine and Cleveland inspired some of the most colorful battle cries in political history: "Blaine, Blaine, James G. Blaine, the continental liar from the state of Maine," Democrats chanted. Republicans countered with "Ma, ma, where's my Pa? Gone to the White House—Ha! Ha! Ha!" Near the end of the nasty campaign, Blaine and his supporters committed two fateful blunders in the crucial state of New York.

The first occurred at New York City's fashionable Delmonico's restaurant, where Blaine went to a private dinner with 200 of the nation's wealthiest business leaders to ask them to help finance his campaign. Accounts of the unseemly event appeared in the newspapers for days afterward. One headline blared: "Blaine Hobnobbing with the Mighty Money Kings!" The article explained that the banquet was intended to collect contributions for a "Republican corruption fund."

Blaine's second blunder occurred when a Protestant minister visiting Republican headquarters in New York referred to the Democrats as the party of "rum, Romanism, and rebellion [the Confederacy]." Blaine, who was present, let pass the implied insult to Catholics—a fatal oversight, since he had cultivated Irish American support with his anti-English talk and repeated references to his mother being a Catholic. Democrats claimed that Blaine was, at heart, anti-Irish and anti-Catholic.

The two incidents may have tipped the election. The electoral vote was 219 to 182 in Cleveland's favor, but the popular vote ran far closer: Cleveland's plurality was fewer than 30,000 votes out of 10 million cast. Cleveland won New York by only 1,149 votes out of 1,167,169 cast. Blaine and his supporters charged that the Democrats had paid so many voters in New York that it had cost the Republican the White House. Yet Blaine refused to challenge the results, in part because the Republicans were buying votes too. Doing so, explained a journalist, "is considered a necessary part of 'practical politics,' and to be applauded in proportion to their success." By hook or by crook, a Democrat was back in the White House.

CLEVELAND'S REFORM EFFORTS

During his first few months in office, President Cleveland struggled to keep Democratic leaders from reviving the patronage system. In a letter to a friend, the new president reported that he was living in a "nightmare," that "dreadful, damnable, office-seeking hangs over me and surrounds me" and that it made him "feel like resigning." Democratic newspapers heaped scorn on him for refusing to award federal jobs to his supporters. One accused Cleveland of "ingratitude" toward those who had "delivered the vote." Despite the president's best efforts, about two thirds of the 120,000 federal jobs went to Democrats as patronage during his administration.

Cleveland was an old-style Democrat who believed in minimal government activity. During his first term, he vetoed over 400 acts of Congress, more than twice as many as all previous presidents combined. In 1887, he illustrated his "do as little as possible" philosophy by vetoing a congressional effort to provide desperate Texas farmers with seeds in the aftermath of a terrible drought. "Though the people support the government, the government should not support the people," Cleveland asserted.

RAILROAD REGULATION For all his commitment to limited government, President Cleveland urged Congress to adopt an important new policy: federal regulation of the rates charged by interstate railroads (those whose tracks crossed state lines) to ship goods, crops, or livestock. States had adopted laws regulating railroads since the late 1860s, but in 1886 the Supreme Court declared in *Wabash, St. Louis, and Pacific Railroad Company v. Illinois* that no state could regulate the rates charged by railroads engaged in interstate traffic. Because most railroads crossed state lines, Cleveland urged Congress to close the loophole.

Congress followed through, and in 1887, President Cleveland signed an act creating the **Interstate Commerce Commission (ICC)**, the first federal agency designed to regulate business activities. The law empowered the ICC's five members to ensure that railroad freight rates were "reasonable and just." But one senator called the new agency "a delusion and a sham" because its members tended to be former railroad executives. Moreover, the commission's actual powers were weak when challenged in the courts by railroads. Over time, the ICC came to be ignored, and the railroads continued to charge high rates while making secret pricing deals with large shippers.

TARIFF REFORM AND THE ELECTION OF 1888 President Cleveland's most dramatic challenge to Big Business focused on **tariff reform**. During the late nineteenth century, the government's high-tariff policies, shaped largely by the Republican party, had favored American manufacturers by effectively shutting out foreign imports, thereby enabling U.S. corporations to dominate the marketplace and charge higher prices for their products. Tariffs on some 4,000 imported items had also brought in more revenue from foreign manufacturers than the federal government spent. As a result, the tariff revenues were producing an annual government surplus, which proved to Cleveland and the Democrats that the rates were too high.

In 1887, Cleveland argued that Congress should reduce both the tariff rates ("the vicious, inequitable and illogical source of unnecessary taxation . . . [and] a burden upon the poor") and the number of imported goods subject to tariffs, which would enable European companies to compete in the American marketplace (and bring down prices for consumers). His outspoken stance set the stage for his reelection campaign in 1888.

To oppose Cleveland, the Republicans, now calling themselves the GOP (Grand Old Party) to emphasize their longevity, turned to the obscure Benjamin Harrison, a Civil War veteran whose greatest attributes were his availability and the fact that he was from Indiana, a pivotal state in presidential elections. The grandson of President William Henry Harrison, he had a modest political record; he had lost a race for governor and had served one term in the U.S. Senate (1881–1887). Stiff and formal, Harrison was labeled the "human iceberg."

Theodore Roosevelt held Harrison in contempt, once calling him a "cold-blooded, narrow-minded, prejudiced, obstinate, timid old psalm-singing Indianapolis politician." In the eyes of the party leadership, however, Harrison had the most important attribute: he would do as he was told.

The Republicans enjoyed a huge advantage in campaign funding, as business executives contributed generously to their campaign. Still, the outcome was incredibly close. Cleveland won the popular vote by the thinnest of margins—5,540,329 to 5,439,853—but Harrison carried crucial New York State and the electoral college by 233 to 168. "Providence," said the new president, "has given us the victory." Matthew Quay, the powerful Republican boss of Pennsylvania who managed Harrison's campaign, knew better. Harrison, he muttered, "ought to know that Providence hadn't a damned thing to do with it! [A] number of men were compelled to approach the penitentiary to make him President."

Quay's decision to distribute campaign money in key states and to promise federal jobs to loyalists also helped Republicans gain control of the House and the Senate. As the Republicans prepared for the inauguration, *Frank Leslie's Illustrated Newspaper*, co-edited by Harrison's son Russell, made clear the new president's priorities: "This is to be a businessman's Administration," and "businessmen will be thoroughly well content with it."

REPUBLICAN ACTIVISM UNDER HARRISON

President Benjamin Harrison owed a heavy debt to military veterans, whose votes had been critical to his election, and he paid it by signing the Dependent Pension Act, which doubled the federal pensions paid to veterans between 1889 and 1893.

The Republicans also took advantage of their control of Congress to pass a cluster of significant legislation in 1890: the Sherman Anti-Trust Act; the Sherman Silver Purchase Act; the McKinley Tariff Act; and, the admission of Idaho and Wyoming into the Union—all on the heels of North and South Dakota, Montana, and Washington becoming states in 1889.

The Sherman Anti-Trust Act, named for Ohio senator John Sherman, prohibited powerful corporations from "conspiring" to establish monopolies or "restrain trade" in their industries. It made the United States the first nation in the world to outlaw monopolistic business practices.

Though badly needed, the Sherman Anti-Trust Act was a toothless hoax intended to make it appear that Congress was clamping down on the gigantic corporations that were dominating more and more industries. That it passed

"COMING OUT" FOR HARRISON.
Protected Monopolist.—Chuck in your votes there, and don't forget that you 're "working for—Kane !"

"'Coming Out'—For Harrison" This 1888 cartoon depicts efforts by employers to force the working class to vote for the Republican party ticket, including presidential nominee Benjamin Harrison.

BILLION- DOLLARISM) HOLE

A billion-dollar hole In an attack on Benjamin Harrison's spending policies, Harrison is shown pouring Cleveland's huge surplus down a hole.

without any opposition suggested that the bill was mostly for show. Critics called it the "Swiss Cheese Act" because it had so many loopholes in its language. As the *New York Times* recognized in 1890, the "so-called Anti-Trust law" was passed "to deceive the people" and prepare the way for a much higher tariff bill. Senator Sherman, the article added, supported this "humbug" of a law so that party spokesmen "might say 'Behold! We have attacked the trusts. The Republican Party is the enemy of all such rings.'"

The Sherman Anti-Trust Act was rarely enforced, in large part because of its vague definitions of trusts and monopolies. From 1890 to 1901, only eighteen lawsuits were instituted, four of which were filed against labor unions rather than corporations, claiming that striking workers were conspiring to restrain trade.

The Sherman Silver Purchase Act (1890), which required the Treasury to purchase 4.5 million ounces of silver each month to convert into dollar coins, was an effort by the Republicans to please the six new western states that had numerous silver mines. The bill's sponsor, Senator John Sherman, admitted that he proposed the bill only to defuse cries for the "unlimited coinage" of silver. "I voted for it," he confessed, "but the day it became law I was ready to repeal it." The Sherman act helped set the stage for the "money problem" to eclipse all others during the financial panic that would sweep the country in 1893.

As for tariff policy, Republicans viewed their victory as a mandate to reward the support of large corporations by raising tariff rates even higher. Piloted through Congress by Ohio representative William McKinley, the McKinley Tariff Act of 1890 raised duties (taxes) on imported manufactured goods to their highest level and added many agricultural products to the tariff list to appease farmers. Its passage encouraged many businesses to raise prices, because their European competitors were now effectively shut out of the U.S. market. The *New York Times* expressed the indignation of many voters when it charged in a huge headline: "MCKINLEY'S PICKPOCKETS [WERE] PAYING A PARTY DEBT" to large corporate donors by passing the new tariff bill.

The Republican efforts to reward Big Business backfired, however. In the November 1890 congressional elections, Democrats regained control of the House by a 3 to 1 margin. William McKinley, who had sponsored the tariff bill, lost his seat (although the following year he would be elected Ohio's governor). In the Senate, the Republican majority was reduced to four. Republicans were "astounded and dazed" by their election losses. Even more worrisome was the emergence of the Populists, a new political party representing disgruntled farmers and wage laborers. Revolution was in the air.

FARMERS AND THE "MONEY PROBLEM"

More than tariffs, trusts, and efforts to clean up political corruption, national politics during the Gilded Age was preoccupied with monetary issues. The nation's money supply had not grown along with the expanding economy and population. From 1865 to 1890, the amount of money in circulation (both coins and paper currency) actually *decreased* about 10 percent.

Such currency deflation raised the cost of borrowing money as the shrinking money supply enabled lenders to hike interest rates on loans. Creditors—bankers and others who loaned money—supported a "sound money" policy limiting the currency supply as a means of increasing their profits. By contrast, farmers, ranchers, miners, and others who had to borrow money to make ends meet claimed that the sound money policy lowered prices for their crops and herds and drove them deeper into debt. Farmers in the Midwest, Great Plains, and South, and miners in the West, demanded more paper money and the increased coinage of silver, which would inflate the currency supply, raise commodity prices, and provide them with more income.

"King of the World" Reformers targeted the growing power of monopolies, such as John D. Rockefeller's Standard Oil.

In 1873, the Republican-controlled Congress had declared that only gold, not silver, could be used for coins. This decision (called "the Crime of '73" by critics) occurred just when silver mines in the western states had begun to increase their production and deposits of gold were drying up.

In 1874, several farm organizations across the nation had organized the independent Greenback party to promote the benefits of paper money over gold and silver coins; "Greenbackers" won fifteen seats in Congress in 1878, illustrating the significance of currency issues to voters. Although the Greenback party died out in 1889, the demands for increasing the money supply ("inflation") survived. All six western states admitted to the Union in 1889 and 1890 had substantial silver mines, and their new congressional delegations—largely Republican—wanted the federal government to buy more silver for minting as coins.

AGRICULTURAL UNREST The congressional elections revealed a deep-seated unrest in the farming communities of the South, on the plains of Kansas and Nebraska, and in the mining towns of the Rocky Mountain region. Over the previous twenty years, corn prices had fallen by a third, wheat by more than half, cotton by two-thirds. The drastic decline in prices was caused by overproduction and growing international competition in world food markets. The vast new lands brought under cultivation in the plains as a result of the extension of rail lines and the use of new farm machinery poured an ever-increasing supply of grain (corn, wheat, oats, etc.) into world markets, driving prices down.

Meanwhile, farmers in the South and West had become increasingly indebted to local banks or merchants who loaned them money at high interest rates to buy seed, fertilizer, tools, and other supplies. As prices for their crops dropped, however, so did the income the farmers received, thus preventing them from paying their debts on time.

In response, most farmers had no choice but to grow even more wheat, cotton, or corn, but the increased supply pushed down prices and incomes even further. High tariffs on imported goods also hurt farmers because they allowed U.S. companies to raise the prices of manufactured goods needed by farm families.

Besides bankers, merchants, and high tariffs, struggling farmers blamed the railroads, warehouse owners, and food processors—the so-called middlemen—who helped get crops and livestock to market. Farmers especially resented that railroads, most of which had a monopoly over the shipping of grain and animals, charged such high rates to ship agricultural products.

At the same time that farm income was dropping, successive years of parched summers and bitterly cold winters had destroyed harvests in many states. "This season is without parallel in this part of the country," reported the

"I Feed You All!" (1875) The farmer is the cornerstone of American society, according to this Granger-inspired poster. Without the food he produces, no man in any occupation can do his job—including the railroad magnate (left) and warehouse owners who try to exploit him.

editor of a Nebraska agricultural journal in 1891. "The hot winds burned up the entire crop, leaving thousands of families wholly destitute" and vulnerable to the "money loaners and sharks" charging criminal rates of interest. In a slap at the cutthroat capitalism justified by the heartless logic of social Darwinism, the editor dismissed the popular slogan "survival of the fittest" as a "satanic creed" that means "slavery to millions."

In drought-devastated Kansas in 1890, Populists won five congressional seats from Republicans. In early 1891, the newly elected Populists and Democrats took control of Congress just as an acute economic crisis appeared on the horizon: farmers' debts were mounting as crop prices continued to fall.

THE GRANGER MOVEMENT When the Department of Agriculture sent Oliver H. Kelley on a tour of the South in 1866, he was struck by the social isolation of people living on small farms. To address the problem, Kelley helped found the National Grange of the Patrons of Husbandry, better known as the Grange (an old word for places where crops were stored).

The Grange grew quickly, reaching a membership of 858,000 men and women by 1875. It started out offering social events and educational programs for farmers and their families, but as it grew, it began to promote *cooperatives* where farmers could join together to store and sell their crops to avoid the high fees charged by brokers and other middlemen.

In five Midwest states, Grange chapters persuaded legislatures to pass "Granger laws" establishing state commissions to regulate the prices charged by railroads and grain warehouses (called "elevators"). Farmers rented space in the grain elevators to store their harvested crop before it was sold and shipped by railroads. Many elevator operators were corrupt, however. They secretly conspired with their competitors to "fix" the storage rates charged farmers. Railroads also squeezed the farmers. Since they usually had a monopoly in a given agricultural community, railroads could charge whatever they wanted to ship grain, and they discriminated in favor of the largest farms.

To address the concerns of grain growers, the Illinois legislature in 1871 established regulations prohibiting railroads from charging different freight rates and establishing rates for grain elevator storage. The state created a Board of Railroad and Warehouse Commissioners to enforce the new regulations. Other states passed similar laws.

Railroad and warehouse owners challenged and often defied the laws, arguing that efforts to regulate them were forms of socialism. In *Munn v. Illinois* (1877), however, the Supreme Court ruled 7–2 that the Constitution sanctioned regulation of businesses that operated in the public interest. In response to the Court's decision, Chicago grain elevators lowered their storage fees. Nine years later, however, the Court threw out the *Munn* ruling, finding in *Wabash v. Illinois* that only Congress, not states, could regulate industries involved in *interstate* commerce.

FARMERS' ALLIANCES   The Granger movement failed to address the foremost concerns of struggling farmers: declining crop prices and the inadequate amount of money in circulation. As a result, people shifted their allegiance to a new organization called the Farmers' Alliance. Like the Grange, the Farmers' Alliances organized social and recreational activities for small farmers and their families while also emphasizing political action and economic cooperation to address the hardships caused by chronic indebtedness, declining crop prices, and droughts.

Emerging first in Texas, the Southern Alliance movement swept across the South, Kansas, Nebraska, and the Dakotas. By 1890, the white Alliance movement had about 1.5 million members nationwide. The Southern Alliance refused to allow blacks to join, not only because of racism but also because most black farmers were tenants and sharecroppers rather than landowners. Although many landless farmers supported the Alliances, the majority of members were landowners who sold their crops in the marketplace. In 1886, a white minister in Texas responded to the appeals of African American farmers by organizing the Colored Farmers' National Alliance. By 1890, it would claim more than 1 million members.

In the states west of the Mississippi River, political activism intensified after record blizzards in 1887, which killed most of the cattle and hogs across the northern plains, and a prolonged drought two years later that destroyed millions of acres of corn, wheat, and oats. Distressed farmers lashed out against what they considered to be a powerful conspiracy of eastern financial and industrial interests, which they variously called "monopolies," "the money power," or "Wall Street." As William Jennings Bryan, a Democratic congressman from Nebraska, explained: "We simply say to the East: take your hands out of our pockets and keep them out."

The Alliances called for the federal government to take ownership of the railroads and create an income tax on wealthy Americans. They also organized economic cooperatives to bind together their collective strength in negotiations with warehouse operators and railroads. In 1887, Charles W. Macune, the Southern Alliance president, explained that "the Alliance is the people and the people are together." He exhorted Texas farmers to create their own Alliance Exchange to free themselves from dependence on commercial warehouses, grain elevators, and banks. Members of the Alliance Exchange would act collectively, pooling their resources to borrow money from banks and purchase their goods and supplies from a new corporation created by the Alliance in Dallas. The exchange would also build warehouses to store and market members' crops. With these crops as collateral, members would receive loans to buy household goods and agricultural supplies. Once the farmers sold their crops, they would pay back the loans provided by the Alliance warehouse.

This *cooperative* scheme collapsed when Texas banks refused to accept paper money. Undaunted, Alliance members then focused on what Macune called a subtreasury plan, whereby farmers would store their crops in federally funded and *government*-run warehouses and obtain cash loans for up to 80 percent of the crops' value. Besides providing immediate cash, the subtreasury warehouses would allow farmers the option of storing a crop in hopes of getting a better price later.

Despite the strong support from farmers, however, Congress nixed the subtreasury plan in 1890. Its defeat, as well as setbacks to other Alliance proposals, convinced many farm leaders that they needed more political power to secure the reforms necessary to save the agricultural sector: railroad regulation, currency inflation, state departments of agriculture, anti-trust laws, and more accessible farm-based credit (loans).

The Alliance welcomed rural women and men over sixteen years of age who displayed a "good moral character," believed in God, and demonstrated "industrious habits." About one fourth of Alliance members were women. A North Carolina woman relished the "grand opportunities" the Alliance provided women, allowing them to emerge from household drudgeries. "Drudgery, fashion, and gossip," she declared, "are no longer the bounds of woman's sphere." One Alliance publication made the point explicitly: "The Alliance has come to redeem woman from her enslaved condition, and place her in her proper sphere." Many women assumed key leadership roles in the "grand army of reform."

NEW THIRD PARTIES The Alliances called for third-party political action to address their concerns. In 1890, farm activists in Colorado joined with miners and railroad workers to form the Independent party, and Nebraska farmers formed the People's Independent party. Leonidas Polk, a former Confederate general who was the head of the North Carolina Alliance, traveled to Kansas and was so impressed by the size of the open-air farm rallies that he declared that farmers across the nation "have risen up and inaugurated a movement such as the world has never seen."

In the South, the Alliance movement elected four Democrats as governors, forty-four as congressmen, and several as U.S. senators, as well as seven pro-Alliance state legislatures. Among the most respected of the Southern Alliance leaders was Thomas E. Watson, a lawyer from Georgia. The son of prosperous slaveholders who had lost everything after the Civil War, Watson took the lead in urging black and white tenant farmers to join forces. "You are [racially] kept apart," he told blacks and whites, "that you may be separately fleeced of your earnings." He insisted on cooperation by black and white farmers to resist the power of the wealthy political elite in the South.

In Kansas, Mary Elizabeth Lease emerged as a fiery speaker for the farm protest movement. Born in Pennsylvania to Irish immigrants, Lease migrated to Kansas, taught school, raised a family, and failed at farming in the mid-1880s. She then studied law and became one of the state's first female attorneys.

A proud, tall, and imposing woman with a magical voice, Lease began giving rousing speeches during the 1890s on behalf of struggling farmers. "The people are at bay," she warned; "let the bloodhounds of money beware." She urged angry farmers to take control "with the ballot if possible, but if not that way then with the bayonet."

Like so many Alliance supporters, Lease viewed eastern financiers as the enemy. "Wall Street owns the country. It is no longer a government of the people, by the people, and for the people, but a government of Wall Street, by Wall Street, and for Wall Street. The great common people of this country are slaves, and monopoly is the master." The two political parties "lie to us" in blaming farmers for overproduction, "when 10,000 little children starve to death every year in the United States."

Mary Elizabeth Lease A charismatic leader in the farm protest movement.

THE 1892 ELECTION In 1892, Alliance leaders organized a convention in Omaha, Nebraska, at which they formed the **People's party (Populists)**. The delegates approved a platform that called for unlimited coinage of silver, a *progressive* income tax whose rates would rise with income levels, and federal ownership of the railroads and telegraph systems. The Populists also endorsed the eight-hour workday and new laws restricting "undesirable" immigration, for fear that the "pauper and criminal classes of the world" were taking Americans' jobs. "We meet in the midst of a nation brought to the verge of moral, political, and material ruin," the Populists announced. "The fruits of toil of millions are boldly stolen to build up colossal fortunes for a few. . . ." They called for the "power of government" to be expanded to assault "oppression, injustice, and poverty."

The Populist party's platform turned out to be more exciting than its presidential candidate: Iowa's James B. Weaver, a former Union army officer who had headed the Greenback party ticket twelve years earlier. The major parties renominated the same candidates who had run in 1888: Democrat Grover Cleveland and Republican president Benjamin Harrison. Each major candidate

The Populist party A Populist gathering in Callaway, Nebraska, 1892.

received more than 5 million votes, but Cleveland won a majority of the electoral college. Weaver received more than 1 million votes and carried Colorado, Kansas, Nevada, and Idaho. Alabama was the banner Populist state of the South, with 37 percent of its vote going to Weaver.

THE DEPRESSION OF 1893 AND THE "FREE SILVER" CRUSADE

While farmers were funneling their discontent into politics, a fundamental weakness in the economy was about to cause a major collapse and a social rebellion. Just ten days before Grover Cleveland was inaugurated in the winter of 1893, the Philadelphia and Reading Railroad declared bankruptcy, setting off a national financial crisis, now called the **Panic of 1893**. It grew into the worst depression the nation had ever experienced.

Other overextended railroads collapsed, taking many banks with them. European investors withdrew their funds from America. A quarter of unskilled urban workers lost their jobs, many others had their wages cut, and by the fall of 1893, more than 600 banks had closed and 15,000 businesses had failed. Farm foreclosures soared in the South and West, and by 1900, a third of all American farmers rented their land rather than owned it.

By 1894, the nation's economy had reached bottom. But the depression lasted another four years, with unemployment hovering at 20 percent. In New York City, the rate was close to 35 percent.

President Cleveland's response was recklessly conservative: he convinced Congress to return the nation's money supply to a gold standard by repealing the Sherman Silver Purchase Act of 1890, a move that made the depression worse. The weak economy needed *more* money in circulation, not *less*. Investors rushed to exchange their silver dollars for gold, further constricting the money supply.

Hard times triggered a wave of labor unrest. In 1894, some 750,000 workers went on strike. One protest group, called Coxey's Army, was led by "General" Jacob S.Coxey, a wealthy Ohio quarry owner turned Populist who demanded that the federal government provide the unemployed with meaningful work. Coxey, his wife, and their son, Legal Tender Coxey, rode in a carriage ahead of some 400 protesters who marched hundreds of miles to Washington, D.C., where police arrested Coxey for walking on the grass. Although his ragtag army dispersed peacefully, the march, as well as the growing strength of Populism, struck fear into the hearts of many conservatives.

Republicans portrayed Populists as "tramps" and "hayseed socialists" whose election would endanger the capitalist system. The Populists responded by charging that Americans were divided into "tramps and millionaires."

Coxey's Army, 1894 A subset of Coxey's Army, mid-march, on the outskirts of Washington D.C. Coxey's economic ideology was popular with immigrants.

In this climate of class warfare and social anxiety, the 1894 congressional elections devastated President Cleveland and the Democrats, who were blamed for the economic crisis. The Republicans gained 118 seats in the House, the largest increase ever. Only in the solidly Democratic South did the party retain its advantage. The Populists emerged with six senators and seven representatives, and they expected the festering discontent in rural areas to carry them to national power in 1896. Their hopes would be dashed, however.

SILVERITES VERSUS GOLDBUGS Cleveland's decision to repeal the Sherman Silver Purchase Act created an irreparable division in his party. One pro-silver Democrat labeled the president a traitor. Politicians from western states with large silver mines increased their demands for the "unlimited" coinage of silver, presenting a strategic dilemma for Populists: should the party promote the long list of reforms it had originally advocated, or should it try to ride the silver issue into power?

Presidential campaign badges
On the left wings of the "goldbug" and "silverite" badges are McKinley (top) and Bryan (bottom), with their running mates on the right.

Although flooding the economy with silver coins would probably not have provided the benefits its advocates claimed, the "free silver" crusade had taken on powerful symbolic overtones. Over the protests of more-radical members, Populist leaders decided to hold their 1896 nominating convention *after* the two major-party conventions, confident that the Republicans and Democrats would at best straddle the silver issue and enable the Populists to lure away pro-silver advocates from both.

The major parties, however, took opposite positions on the currency issue. The Republicans, as expected, nominated William McKinley, a former congressman and governor of Ohio, on a platform committed to gold coins as the only form of currency. A small but vocal group of "Silver Republicans" from western states, led by Senator Henry Teller of Colorado, were so upset that they stormed out of the convention. After the convention, a friend told McKinley that the **"money problem"** would determine the election. He was right.

The Democratic convention, held in Chicago, was one of the great turning points in political history. The pro-silver, largely rural delegates surprised the party leadership and the "Gold Democrats," or "goldbugs," by capturing control of the convention.

WILLIAM JENNINGS BRYAN Thirty-six-year-old William Jennings Bryan of Nebraska gave the final speech at the Democratic convention before the presidential balloting began. A fiery evangelical moralist, Bryan was a two-term congressman who had lost a race for the Senate in 1894, when Democrats by the dozens were swept out of office. In the months before the convention, he had traveled throughout the South and West, speaking passionately for the unlimited coinage of silver, attacking Cleveland's "do-nothing" response to the depression, and endorsing both Democrats and Populists who embraced the cause of "free silver."

Bryan was a compelling speaker, a crusading preacher in the role of a Populist politician. In his carefully crafted and well-rehearsed convention speech, he claimed that two ideas about the role of government were competing for the American voter. The Republicans, he said, believed "that if you just legislate to make the well-to-do prosperous, that their prosperity will leak through on those below." The Democrats, by contrast, believed "that if you legislate to make the masses prosperous their prosperity will find its way up and through every class that rests upon it." For his part, Bryan spoke for the "producing masses of this nation" against the eastern "financial magnates" who had "enslaved" them by manipulating the money supply to ensure high interest rates.

William Jennings Bryan His "cross of gold" speech at the 1896 Democratic Convention roused the delegates and secured him the party's presidential nomination.

As Bryan brought his electrifying twenty-minute speech to a climax, he fused Christian imagery with Populist anger:

I come to speak to you in defense of a cause as holy as the cause of liberty—the cause of humanity. . . . We have petitioned, and our petitions have been scorned. . . . We have begged, and they have mocked when our calamity came. We beg no longer; we entreat no more; we petition no more. We defy them!

Bryan then identified himself with Jesus Christ. Sweeping his fingers across his forehead, he shouted: "You shall not press down upon the brow of labor this crown of thorns. You shall not crucify mankind upon a cross of gold!"— at which point he extended his arms straight out from his sides, as if he were being crucified. His riveting performance worked better than even he could have imagined. As he strode triumphantly off the stage, the delegates erupted in wild applause. "Everybody seemed to go mad at once," reported the *New York World*.

For their part, the Republicans were not amused by Bryan's antics. A Republican newspaper observed that no political movement had "ever before spawned such hideous and repulsive vipers." Theodore Roosevelt claimed that Bryan was a demagogue with an "unsound mind" who was promoting mob rule by "the shiftless and the disorderly and the criminal and the semi-criminal" elements of society.

The next day, Bryan won the presidential nomination on the fifth ballot, but in the process the Democratic party was fractured. Disappointed Democrats who had supported Grover Cleveland dismissed Bryan as a fanatic and a socialist. They were so alienated by his positions and his rhetoric that they walked out of the convention and nominated their own candidate, Senator John M. Palmer of Illinois. "Fellow Democrats," Palmer announced, "I will not consider it any great fault if you decide to cast your vote for William McKinley."

When the Populists gathered in St. Louis for their nominating convention two weeks later, they faced an impossible choice. They could name their own candidate and divide the pro-silver vote with the Democrats, or they could endorse Bryan and probably lose their identity. In the end, they backed Bryan but chose their own vice-presidential candidate, Thomas E. Watson, and invited the Democrats to drop their vice-presidential nominee. Bryan refused.

THE ELECTION OF 1896 The election of 1896 was one of the most dramatic in history, in part because of the striking contrast between the candidates and in part because the terrible economic depression made the stakes so high. One observer said that the campaign "took the form of religious frenzy." Indeed, Bryan campaigned like the evangelist he was. He was the first major candidate since Andrew Jackson to champion the poor, the discontented, and the oppressed. He excited struggling farmers, miners, and union members. And he was the first leader of a major party to call for the expansion of the federal government to help the working class.

No one loved campaigning more than Bryan. He traveled some 18,000 miles by train, delivering impassioned speeches in 26 states and 250 cities and towns. His populist crusade was for whites only, however. Like so many otherwise progressive Democratic leaders, Bryan never challenged the practices of racial segregation and violence against blacks in the solidly Democratic South. And he alienated many working-class Catholics in northern states by supporting prohibition of alcoholic beverages.

McKinley, meanwhile, stayed at home and kept his mouth shut, letting other Republicans speak for him. He knew he could not compete with Bryan as a speaker, so he conducted a "front-porch campaign," welcoming some 750,000 supporters who came to his home in Canton, Ohio, during the campaign. He gave only prepared statements to the press, most of which warned middle-class voters of the perils of Bryan's "dangerous" ideas. McKinley's brilliant campaign manager, Mark Hanna, shrewdly portrayed Bryan as a "Popocrat" (Populist Democrat), a radical whose "communistic spirit" would ruin the capitalist system and stir up a class war. Hanna convinced the Republican party to declare that it was "unreservedly for sound money"—meaning gold coins.

By appealing to such fears, the Republicans raised vast sums from corporations and wealthy donors to finance an army of 1,400 speakers who traveled the country promoting McKinley. It was the most sophisticated—and expensive—presidential campaign in history to that point.

In the end, Bryan won the most votes of any candidate in history— 6.5 million—but McKinley won even more: 7.1 million. The better-organized and better-financed Republicans won the electoral college vote by 271 to 176.

Bryan carried most of the West and all the South but found little support in the North and East. In the critical Midwest, from Minnesota and Iowa eastward to Ohio, he did not win a state. His evangelical Protestantism repelled many Roman Catholic voters, who were normally drawn to the Democrats. Farmers in the Northeast, moreover, were less attracted to radical reform than were farmers in the West and South. Workers in the cities found it easier to identify with McKinley's focus on reviving the industrial economy than with

THE ELECTION OF 1896

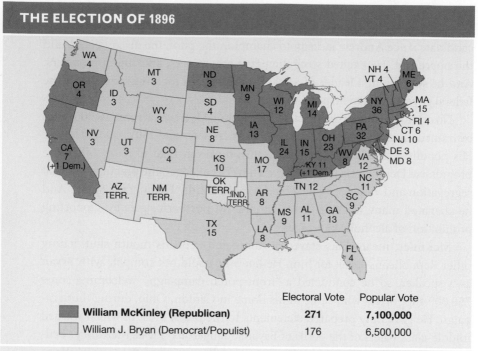

	Electoral Vote	Popular Vote
■ **William McKinley (Republican)**	**271**	**7,100,000**
☐ William J. Bryan (Democrat/Populist)	176	6,500,000

- How did Bryan's "cross of gold" speech divide the Democratic party?
- How did McKinley's campaign strategy differ from Bryan's?
- Why was Bryan able to carry the West and the South but unable to win in cities and the Northeast?

Bryan's farm-based, free-silver evangelism. Of the nation's twenty largest cities, Bryan won only New Orleans.

Although Bryan lost, he launched the Democratic party's shift from pro-business conservatism to its eventual twentieth-century role as a party of liberal reform. The Populist party, however, virtually disintegrated. Having won a million votes in 1896, it collected only 50,000 in 1900. Conversely, McKinley's victory climaxed a generation-long struggle for political control of an industrialized urban America. The Republicans would be dominant for sixteen years.

By 1897, when McKinley was inaugurated, prosperity was returning. Economic recovery came in part from the inflation of U.S. currency, which bore out the arguments of the Greenbackers and silverites that the nation's money supply had been inadequate during the Gilded Age. Inflation came, however, not from the influx of more greenbacks or silver dollars but from a flood of gold discovered in South Africa, northwest Canada, and Alaska. In 1900, Congress passed, and McKinley signed, a bill affirming that the nation's money supply would be based only on gold.

Even though the Populist movement faded after William Jennings Bryan's defeat, most of the ideas promoted by Bryan Democrats and Populists, dismissed as too radical in 1896, would be implemented over the next two decades by a more diverse coalition of Democrats and Republicans who would call themselves "progressives." The volcanic turmoil of the 1890s set the stage for the twentieth century's struggles and innovations.

CHAPTER REVIEW

SUMMARY

- **America's Move to Town**   America's cities grew in all directions during the *Gilded Age (1860–1896)*. Electric elevators and steel-frame construction allowed architects to extend buildings upward, and mass transit enabled the middle class to retreat to suburbs. Crowded *tenements* bred disease and crime and created an opportunity for urban *party bosses* to accrue power, in part by distributing various forms of assistance to the poor.

- **The New Immigration**   By 1900, an estimated 30 percent of Americans living in major cities were foreign-born, with the majority of *new immigrants* coming from eastern and southern Europe rather than western and northern Europe, as did most immigrants of generations past. Their languages, culture, and religion were quite different from those of native-born Americans. Beginning in the 1880s, *nativists* advocated restrictive immigration laws and won passage of the *Chinese Exclusion Act (1882)*.

- **Changes in Culture and Thought**   Many areas of American life underwent profound changes during the Gilded Age. The growth of large cities led to the popularity of vaudeville and Wild West shows and to the emergence of spectator sports. Charles Darwin's *On the Origin of Species* shocked people who believed in a literal interpretation of the Bible's account of creation. Proponents of *social Darwinism* applied Darwin's theory of evolution to human society by equating economic and social success with "survival of the fittest."

- **Gilded Age Politics**   Huge corporations corrupted politics bought political influence. Political activity was still concentrated at the state and local, rather than federal, levels. Americans were intensely loyal to the two major parties, whose local "bosses" and "machines" won votes by distributing *patronage* jobs and contracts to members, as well as charitable relief. The major parties were so balanced that neither wanted to risk alienating voters by taking bold stands.

- **Corruption and Reform**   National politics during the Gilded Age focused on tariffs, the regulation of corporations, currency issues, and *civil service reform*. The passage of the Pendleton Civil Service Reform Act in 1883 began the professionalization of federal workers. In the 1884 presidential election, Republicans favoring reform, the *Mugwumps*, helped elect Democrat Grover Cleveland. As president, he signed the 1887 act creating the *Interstate Commerce Commission (ICC)* to regulate railroads. In 1890, under President Benjamin Harrison, Republicans passed the Sherman Anti-Trust Act, the Sherman Silver Purchase Act, and the McKinley Tariff Act.

- **Inadequate Currency Supply and Unhappy Farmers** Over the course of the late nineteenth century, the *money problem* had become a central political issue. The supply of money had not increased as the economy had grown. Many farmers believed that the coinage of silver, rather than a gold standard system, would result in inflation, which in turn would increase the value of their crops and reduce their debts. Farmers and others dissatisfied with the Republican and Democratic parties formed a series of political parties and alliances, one of which, the *People's party (Populists)*, briefly operated as a national third party. The *Panic of 1893* created a devastating depression. In the election of 1896, the Democratic party nominated William Jennings Bryan, who adopted the coinage of silver as his crusade. He was opposed by Republican William McKinley, who supported the gold standard. McKinley won the election in part by appealing to the growing number of city dwellers and industrial workers.

CHRONOLOGY

1859	Charles Darwin's *On the Origin of Species* is published
1882	Congress passes the Chinese Exclusion Act
1883	Congress passes the Pendleton Civil Service Reform Act
1886	Supreme Court issues *Wabash, St. Louis, and Pacific Railroad Company v. Illinois* decision
1887	Interstate Commerce Commission is created
1890	Congress passes the Sherman Anti-Trust Act, the Sherman Silver Purchase Act, and the McKinley Tariff Act

KEY TERMS

Gilded Age p. 881

tenements p. 883

new immigrants p. 886

nativists p. 888

Chinese Exclusion Act (1882) p. 889

saloons p. 891

social Darwinism p. 894

reform Darwinism p. 895

party bosses p. 899

patronage p. 899

civil service reform p. 902

Mugwumps p. 907

Interstate Commerce Commission (ICC) p. 910

tariff reform p. 909

People's party (Populists) p. 919

Panic of 1893 p. 920

money problem p. 923

 INQUIZITIVE

Go to InQuizitive to see what you've learned—and learn what you've missed—with personalized feedback along the way.

part six

MODERN AMERICA

The United States entered the twentieth century on a wave of unrelenting change. The nation was on the threshold of modernity, which both excited and scared Americans. Old truths and beliefs clashed with unsettling scientific discoveries and social practices. People debated the legitimacy of Darwinism, the existence of God, the dangers of jazz, and the federal effort to prohibit the sale of alcoholic beverages.

The advent of automobiles and airplanes helped shrink distance, and such communications innovations as radio and film helped strengthen the sense that America now had a *national* culture. William McKinley was the first president to ride in an automobile, to appear in motion pictures, and to use the telephone to plot political strategy.

Spurred by its growing industrial power, the United States began to emerge from its isolationist shell. Previously, presidents and statesmen had sought to insulate America from the intrigues and conflicts of European powers. As early as 1780, John Adams had warned against U.S. involvement in Europe's affairs. "Our business with them, and theirs with us," he wrote, "is commerce, not politics, much less war."

With only a few exceptions, statesmen during the nineteenth century followed such advice. Noninvolvement in foreign wars and nonintervention in the internal affairs of foreign governments formed the pillars of U.S. foreign policy. During the 1890s, however, expanding commercial interests led Americans to broaden their global commitments.

Imperialism was the focus of the major European powers, and a growing number of expansionists demanded that the United States join in the hunt for new territories and markets beyond North America. Others believed America should support democratic ideals abroad. Such mixed motives helped spark the Spanish-American War (more recently called the War of 1898) and justify the resulting acquisition of colonies. Entangling alliances with European powers soon followed.

The outbreak of the Great War in Europe in 1914 posed an even greater challenge to America's tradition of nonintervention. The prospect of a German victory over the French and British threatened the balance of power in Europe, which had long ensured the security of the United States. By 1917, it appeared that Germany might triumph and menace the Western Hemisphere. When German submarines began sinking American merchant ships, President Woodrow Wilson's patience ran out, and in April 1917, the United States entered the Great War.

Wilson's crusade to transform international affairs in accordance with his idealistic principles dislodged American foreign policy from its isolationist moorings. It also spawned a prolonged debate about the nation's role in world affairs—a debate that World War II would resolve (for a time) on the side of internationalism.

While the United States was becoming a formidable military power, cities and factories were sprouting across the nation's landscape, and an abundance of jobs and affordable farmland attracted millions of foreign immigrants. They were not always welcomed, nor were they readily assimilated. Ethnic and racial strife grew, as did labor agitation.

In the midst of such social turmoil and unparalleled economic development, reformers made their first sustained attempt to adapt political and social institutions to the realities of the industrial age. The worst excesses of urban-industrial development—corporate monopolies, child labor, political corruption, hazardous working conditions, urban ghettos—were finally addressed. During the Progressive Era (1890–1920), local, state, and federal governments sought to rein in industrial capitalism and develop a more rational and efficient public policy.

A conservative Republican resurgence challenged the notion of the new regulatory state during the 1920s, and free enterprise and corporate capitalism enjoyed a dramatic revival. But the stock market crash of 1929 helped propel the United States and the world into the worst economic downturn in history. The severity of the Great Depression renewed demands for federal programs to protect the general welfare. The many New Deal initiatives and agencies instituted by President Franklin Delano Roosevelt and his Democratic administration created the framework for a welfare state that has since served as the basis for public policy.

The New Deal revived public confidence and put people back to work, but it took a second world war to end the Great Depression and restore full employment. The necessity of mobilizing the nation to support the war also accelerated the growth of the federal government, and the unparalleled scope of the war helped catapult the United States into a leadership role in world politics. The development of atomic bombs ushered in a new era of nuclear diplomacy that held the fate of the world in the balance. For all the new creature comforts associated with modern life, Americans in 1945 found themselves living with an array of new anxieties.

20 Seizing an American Empire

1865–1913

The Charge of the Rough Riders of San Juan Hill **(1898)** Before Frederic Remington
became a professional artist, he had unsuccessful forays into hunting, ranching, and
even the saloon business in the West. His intimacy with the Western way of life, along
with his technical skill and keen sense of observation, were not lost on Theodore
Roosevelt, who invited Remington to travel with the Rough Riders during the Spanish-
American War.

After the Civil War, a mood of isolationism—a desire to stay out of conflicts elsewhere in the world—dominated American public opinion. The nation's geographic advantages encouraged this attitude: oceans to the east and west, and militarily weak neighbors in the Western Hemisphere. That the powerful British navy protected the shipping lanes between the United States and the British Isles gave Americans a heightened sense of security.

By the end of the nineteenth century, however, people had become aware that America was a world power with global responsibilities and imperial ambitions. As a Kentucky newspaper editor proclaimed in 1893, the United States was "the most advanced and powerful" nation in the world, an "imperial Republic" destined to shape the "future of the world." The *Washington Post* agreed, saying that "the Taste of Empire is in the mouth of the people."

While still wanting to stay out of European conflicts, a growing number of Americans urged officials to acquire territory outside North America. The old idea of "manifest destiny"—that the United States had been blessed by God (was "destined") to expand its territory westward across the continent—broadened America's reach into other regions of the Western Hemisphere and as far as the Pacific and Asia. Americans embraced a new form of expansionism that sought distant territories as colonies," with no intention of admitting them to the nation as states. The new manifest destiny, in other words, became a justification for imperialism.

focus questions

1. What factors motivated America's new imperialism after the Civil War?

2. How and why did America expand its influence in the Pacific before the Spanish-American War (War of 1898)?

3. What were the causes of the Spanish-American War (War of 1898)? What were its major events?

4. What were the consequences of the Spanish-American War (War of 1898) for American foreign policy?

5. What reasons were behind Theodore Roosevelt's rapid rise to the presidency? What were the main elements of his foreign policies?

6. How did presidents Roosevelt, Taft, and Wilson expand America's international involvement?

As historian Frederick Jackson Turner had proclaimed in 1893, continental expansion was complete, so Americans needed new frontiers in which to exercise their "expansive character" and to spread their democratic ideals, capitalist investments, and Christian beliefs.

Manifest destiny also took on a racial meaning. Many Americans agreed with future president Theodore Roosevelt that the United States needed to expand "on behalf of the *destiny* of the [Anglo-Saxon] race." Roosevelt and others believed that the Americans and British were at the top of the racial pyramid, superior to all others in intellect, ambition, and creativity.

Political and business leaders argued that America's rapid industrial development required the addition of foreign territories—by conquest if necessary—to gain easier access to vital raw materials such as rubber, tin, copper, palm oil, and various dyes. At the same time, manufacturers and commercial farmers had become increasingly dependent on international trade, which required an expanded force of warships to protect growing numbers of oceangoing U.S. freighters. And a modern, steam-powered navy needed bases in the Caribbean and Pacific, where its warships could replenish their supplies of coal and water.

For these and other reasons, America expanded its military presence and territorial possessions. In 1898, as the result of a one-sided war against Spain, the United States, born in a revolution against British colonial rule, would become an imperial ruler of colonies around the world. Motivated by a mixture of moral and religious idealism, assumptions of Anglo-Saxon racial superiority, and naked greed, the expansionist push also provoked strong opposition.

Most Americans, however, sided with future president Theodore Roosevelt, who in his 1896 book *The Winning of the West* declared that the conquest of the "backward peoples" of the world, like the defeat of the Indians in the American West, benefited "civilization and the interests of mankind."

Toward the New Imperialism

Writing in 1902, the British economist J. A. Hobson declared that imperialism was "the most powerful factor in the current politics of the Western world." The United States was a latecomer to the global **imperialism** long practiced by European powers. By the 1880s, the British, French, Belgians, Italians, Dutch, Spanish, and Germans had subjugated most of Africa and Asia. Often competing with one another for territories, they had established colonial governments to rule over the native populations and exploited the colonies economically. Each imperial nation dispatched missionaries to convert conquered peoples to Christianity. By 1900, some 18,000 Protestant and Catholic evangelicals were scattered around the world.

A small yet influential group of American officials demanded expansion beyond North America. In addition to Theodore Roosevelt, they included naval captain Alfred Thayer Mahan, president of the U.S. Naval War College, and Senators Albert J. Beveridge of Indiana and Henry Cabot Lodge of Massachusetts. Referring to European imperialism, Lodge said, "We must not be left behind."

In 1890, Mahan published *The Influence of Sea Power upon History, 1660–1783*, in which he argued that national greatness flowed from naval power, as the British had demonstrated. Mahan insisted that modern industrial development required a powerful navy centered on huge battleships, foreign commerce, colonies to provide raw materials and new markets, and global naval bases.

Mahan championed America's "destiny" to control the Caribbean Sea, build a canal across Central America to connect the Atlantic and Pacific Oceans, acquire Hawaii and the Philippine Islands, and spread Christian values and American investments across the Pacific. His ideas were widely circulated. By 1896, the United States had built eleven new battleships, making its navy the third most powerful in the world, behind those of Great Britain and Germany.

Claims of racial superiority reinforced the new imperialist spirit. Many Americans and Europeans readily assumed that the Anglo-Saxon race was dominant and others were clearly inferior (Indians, Africans). Such racist notions were given "scientific" authority by researchers at universities throughout Europe and America.

Prominent Americans used the arguments of social Darwinism to justify economic exploitation and territorial conquest abroad and racial segregation at home. Among nations as among individuals, they claimed, only the strongest survived. John Fiske, a Harvard historian, proclaimed the superior character of Anglo-Saxon institutions and peoples. The English-speaking "race," he argued, was destined to dominate the globe and transform the institutions, traditions, language, and even the blood of the world's "backward" races.

Such theories were often used to justify armed conquest. Theodore Roosevelt, for example, loved war and considered it necessary to maintain racial supremacy. He described warfare as the best way to promote "the clear instinct for race selfishness" and stressed that "the most ultimately righteous of all wars is a war with savages."

All these factors helped excite imperialist fervor in the United States during the late nineteenth century. As a Kentucky newspaper editor proclaimed in 1893, the United States was "the most advanced and powerful" nation in the world, an "imperial Republic" destined to shape the "future of the world." The *Washington Post* agreed: "The taste of Empire is in the mouth of the people."

EXPANSION IN THE PACIFIC

For John Fiske and other imperialists, Asia offered an especially attractive target. In 1866, Secretary of State William H. Seward had predicted that the United States must inevitably impose its economic domination "on the Pacific Ocean, and its islands and continents." To take advantage of the Asian markets, Seward believed that the United States first had to remove foreign powers from its northern Pacific coast and gain access to the region's valuable ports. To that end, he tried to acquire British Columbia, sandwiched between Russian-owned Alaska and the Washington Territory.

Late in 1866, while encouraging British Columbia to consider becoming a U.S. territory, Seward learned of Russia's desire to sell Alaska. He leaped at the opportunity, thinking the purchase might help his efforts to acquire British Columbia. In 1867, the United States bought Alaska for $7.2 million, thus removing the threat of Russian imperialism in North America. Critics scoffed at "Seward's folly," but the Alaska Purchase proved to be the best bargain since the Louisiana Purchase, in part because of its vast deposits of gold and oil.

Seward's successors at the State Department sustained his expansionist vision. Their major focus was acquiring key ports in the Pacific Ocean. Two island groups occupied especially strategic positions: Samoa and Hawaii (the Sandwich Islands). Both had major harbors, Pago Pago and Pearl Harbor, respectively. In the years after the Civil War, American interest in those islands deepened.

SAMOA In 1878, the Samoans granted the United States a naval base at Pago Pago and extraterritoriality for Americans (meaning that in Samoa, Americans remained subject only to U.S. law), exchanged trade concessions, and called for the United States to help resolve any disputes with other nations. The following year, the German and British governments worked out similar arrangements with other islands in the Samoan group. There matters rested until civil war broke out in Samoa in 1887. A peace conference in Berlin in 1889 established a protectorate over Samoa, with Germany, Great Britain, and the United States in an uneasy partnership administering the island nation.

HAWAII The Hawaiian Islands, a unified kingdom since 1795, had a sizable population of American Christian missionaries and a profitable crop, sugarcane. In 1875, Hawaii had signed a reciprocal trade agreement allowing its sugar to enter the United States duty free in exchange for a promise that none of its territory would be leased or granted to a third power.

"Our New Senators" Mocking the Alaska Purchase, this political cartoon shows President Andrew Johnson and Secretary of State William H. Seward welcoming two new senators from Alaska: an Eskimo and a penguin.

This agreement led to a boom in sugar production based on cheap immigrant labor, mainly Chinese and Japanese workers, and American sugar planters soon formed an economic elite. By the 1890s, the native Hawaiian population had been reduced to a minority by smallpox and other diseases, and Asian immigrants had become the largest ethnic group.

Beginning in 1891, Queen Liliuokalani, the Hawaiian ruler, tried to restrict the growing political power of American planters. Two years later, however, Hawaii's white population (called *haoles*) overthrew the monarchy with the help of U.S. Marines brought in by John L. Stevens, the U.S. ambassador. Stevens reported that the "Hawaiian pear is now fully ripe, and this is the golden hour

Queen Liliuokalani The Hawaiian queen sought to preserve her nation's independence.

for the United States to pluck it." Within a month, a committee representing the *haoles* asked the U.S. government to annex the islands. President Benjamin Harrison sent an annexation treaty to the Senate just as he was leaving the presidency in early 1893.

To investigate the situation, the new president, Grover Cleveland, sent a special commissioner to Hawaii, who reported that the Americans in Hawaii had acted improperly and that most native Hawaiians opposed annexation. Cleveland tried to restore the queen to power but met resistance from the *haoles*. On July 4, 1894, the government they controlled created the Republic of Hawaii, which included in its constitution a provision for American annexation.

In 1897, when William McKinley became president, he was looking for an excuse to annex the islands. "We need Hawaii," he claimed. "It is [America's] manifest destiny." The United States annexed Hawaii in the summer of 1898 over the protests of native Hawaiians.

THE SPANISH-AMERICAN WAR (THE WAR OF 1898)

The annexation of Hawaii set in motion efforts to create a much larger American presence in Asia. Ironically, this imperialist push originated in Cuba, a Spanish colony ninety miles south of Florida. Even more ironically, the chief motive for intervention in Cuba was outrage at Spain's brutal imperialism.

"FREE CUBA" Throughout the second half of the nineteenth century, Cubans had repeatedly revolted against Spanish rule, only to be ruthlessly suppressed. As one of Spain's oldest colonies, Cuba was a major market for Spanish goods. Powerful American sugar and mining companies had also invested heavily in

Cuba. In fact, the United States traded more with Cuba than Spain did, and American owners of sugar plantations in Cuba had grown increasingly concerned about the security of their investments.

On February 24, 1895, Cubans began a guerrilla war against Spanish troops. During what became the Cuban War for Independence (1895–1898), tens of thousands of Cubans died in Spanish detention camps.

Americans followed the conflict through the newspapers. Two of the largest newspapers, William Randolph Hearst's *New York Journal* and Joseph Pulitzer's *New York World*, were then locked in a fierce competition for readers. Each strove to outdo the other with sensational headlines about Spanish atrocities, real or invented.

Hearst explained that the role of newspapers was not simply to report on events but to shape public opinion and legislation. Newspapers, he boasted, had the power to "declare wars" by their sensational story making. Editors sent their best reporters to Cuba and encouraged them to distort, exaggerate, or even make up stories to attract more readers. Hearst's efforts to manipulate public opinion was called **yellow journalism**.

In addition to boosting the *Journal*'s circulation, Hearst wanted a war against Spain to propel the United States to world-power status. Once war was declared, he took credit for it; one headline blared, "HOW DO YOU LIKE THE JOURNAL'S WAR?" Many Protestant ministers and publications also campaigned for war, in part because of antagonism toward Catholic Spain.

THE POLITICAL PATH TO WAR At the outset of the Cuban War for Independence, President Grover Cleveland tried to protect U.S. business interests while avoiding military involvement. Public sympathy for the rebel cause prompted growing concern in Congress, however. By concurrent resolutions on April 6, 1896, the House and Senate endorsed granting official recognition to the Cuban rebels.

After his inauguration in March 1897, President William McKinley continued the official policy of neutrality while taking a sympathetic stance toward the rebels. McKinley, a Civil War veteran, did not want war. "I have been through one war," he said. "I have seen the dead piled up, and I do not want to see another." Later that year, Spain offered Cubans autonomy (self-government without formal independence) in return for ending the rebellion, but the Cubans rejected the offer.

Early in 1898, two events pushed Spain and the United States into a war that neither wanted. On January 25, the **U.S. battleship *Maine*** docked in Havana, the Cuban capital, supposedly on a courtesy call. On February 9, the *New York*

"$50,000 Reward!" As if the news of the *Maine* sinking were not disturbing enough, the *New York Journal* sensationalized the incident by offering a $50,000 reward for the perpetrator—the equivalent of $1.3 million today.

Journal released the text of a letter from Dupuy de Lôme, Spanish ambassador to the United States, to a friend in Havana, summarizing McKinley's annual message to Congress. In the **de Lôme letter**, the Spaniard called McKinley "weak and a bidder for the admiration of the crowd, besides being a would-be politician who tries to leave a door open behind himself while keeping on good terms with the jingoes [warmongers] of his party."

Six days later, at 9:40 on the night of February 15, the *Maine* exploded. Within minutes, its ruptured hull filled with water. Many sailors, most of whom were asleep, drowned as the ship sank. Of the 354 on board, 260 died. (Half of the sailors were foreign-born immigrants.) Years later, the sinking was ruled an accident resulting from an on-board coal explosion, but in 1898, those eager for war were convinced that the Spanish had sunk the ship.

Theodore Roosevelt, the assistant secretary of the navy, called the sinking "an act of dirty treachery" and told a friend that he "would give anything if President McKinley would order the fleet to Havana tomorrow." The United States, he insisted, "needs a war," and he hoped it would "come soon."

Congress authorized $50 million to prepare for combat, but McKinley, who assumed that the sinking was an accident, resisted demands for war while negotiating with the Spanish. He also avoided interacting with Roosevelt, who he said was "too pugnacious."

As the days passed, Roosevelt told his war-hungry friends that McKinley had "no more backbone than a chocolate éclair." With Roosevelt's encouragement, the public's antagonism toward Spain grew, stirred by the popular saying, "Remember the *Maine*, to Hell with Spain!"

At first, the Spanish government grudgingly agreed to every major American demand, but the weight of public opinion, the outcry from Democratic leaders, and the influence of Republican jingoists eroded McKinley's neutrality.

On April 11, McKinley asked Congress for authority to use the armed forces to end the fighting in Cuba. On April 20, Congress declared Cuba independent from Spain and demanded the withdrawal of Spanish forces. The Spanish government quickly broke diplomatic ties with the United States. After U.S. ships began blockading Cuban ports, Spain declared war on April 24. The next day, Congress passed its own declaration of war. The **Teller Amendment** to the war resolution denied any U.S. intention to annex Cuba.

"We are all jingoes now," trumpeted the *New York Sun*, and the head jingo is the Hon. William McKinley." McKinley called for 125,000 volunteers to supplement the 28,000 men already serving in the U.S. Army. Among the first to enlist was Theodore Roosevelt, who resigned from his government post and told his tailor to make him a dashing army uniform. To him, combat would help America reclaim "the stern and manly qualities which are essential to the well-being of a masterful race."

Never had an American war generated such unexpected and far-reaching consequences. McKinley soon saw it as an opportunity to acquire overseas territories. (What had long been called the Spanish-American War has been renamed the War of 1898 because it involved not just Spanish and American combatants, but Cubans, Filipinos, and Puerto Ricans.)

"A SPLENDID LITTLE WAR"

The war with overmatched Spain lasted only 114 days, but it set the United States on a course that would transform its role in the world. The conflict was barely under way before the U.S. Navy produced a spectacular victory 7,000 miles away at Manila Bay in the Philippine Islands, a colony controlled by Spain for more than 300 years. Just before war was declared, Roosevelt, who was still assistant secretary of the navy, ordered Commodore George Dewey, commander of the U.S. Asiatic Squadron, to engage Spanish warships in the Philippines in case of war in Cuba.

Dewey arrived in Manila Bay on April 30 with six modern warships, which quickly destroyed or captured the outdated Spanish vessels there. An English reporter called it "a military execution rather than a real contest." News of the battle set off wild celebrations in America.

THE SPANISH-AMERICAN WAR IN THE PACIFIC (THE WAR OF 1898)

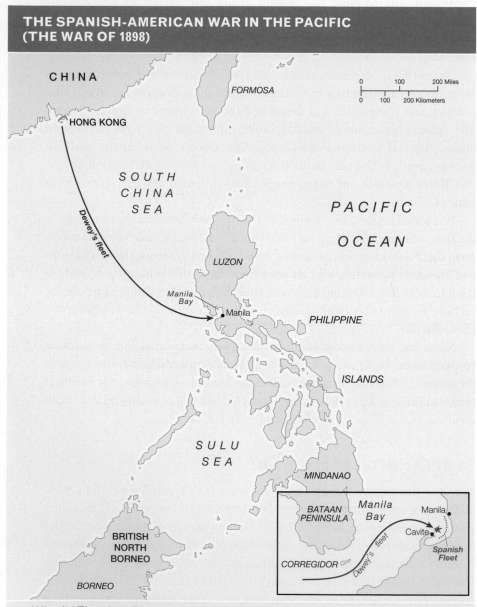

- Why did Theodore Roosevelt order Commodore Dewey to take Manila?
- What role did Filipino nationalist leader Emilio Aguinaldo play?
- Why were many Americans opposed to the acquisition of the Philippines?

Dewey, however, had no soldiers to go onshore. He and his fleet stayed for several months waiting for reinforcements while German and British warships cruised offshore, ready to seize the Philippines if the United States did not.

In the meantime, Emilio Aguinaldo, leader of the Filipino nationalist movement, declared the Philippines independent on June 12, 1898. With Aguinaldo's help, Dewey's forces entered Manila on August 13 and accepted the surrender of the Spanish troops, who had feared for their lives if they surrendered to the Filipinos.

News of the American victory sent President McKinley in search of a map to locate the islands now occupied by U.S. soldiers and sailors. Senator Lodge was delighted with the news from the Philippines: "We hold the other side of the Pacific," he bragged, "and the value to this country is almost beyond imagination. We must on no account let the [Philippine] islands go," for they provided access to "the vast markets furnished by the millions of people in the East." McKinley agreed, stressing that "we must keep all we get."

THE CUBAN CAMPAIGN At the start of the war, the Spanish army in Cuba was five times as large as the entire U.S. Army. McKinley's call for volunteers, however, inspired nearly a million men to enlist. Among the new recruits were some 10,000 African American soldiers, mostly northerners determined to "show our loyalty to our land." In the Jim Crow South, however, blacks were less eager to enlist because, as a Richmond newspaper editor observed, they suffered "a system of oppression as barbarous as that which is alleged to exist in Cuba."

In the meantime, the U.S. Navy blockaded the Spanish fleet inside Santiago Harbor while some 17,000 American troops hastily assembled at Tampa, Florida. One prominent unit was the First Volunteer Cavalry, better known as the Rough Riders, a special regiment made up of former Ivy

African American troops in Cuba
Soldiers stand in formation wearing old wool uniforms unsuited to Cuba's tropical heat.

League athletes; Irish policemen; ex-convicts; cowboys from Oklahoma and New Mexico; Texas Rangers; and Cherokee, Choctaw, Chickasaw, Pawnee, and Creek Indians. All were "young, good shots, and good riders."

The Rough Riders are best remembered because Theodore Roosevelt was second in command. One Rough Rider said that Roosevelt was "nervous, energetic, virile [manly]. He may wear out some day, but he will never rust out."

When the 578 Rough Riders, accompanied by a gaggle of reporters and photographers, landed on June 22, 1898, at the undefended southeastern tip of Cuba, chaos followed. Except for Roosevelt's horse, most of the unit's horses and mules had been mistakenly sent elsewhere, leaving the Rough Riders to become the "Weary Walkers." Nevertheless, land and sea battles around Santiago quickly broke Spanish resistance.

On July 1, about 7,000 U.S. soldiers took the fortified village of El Caney. While a much larger force attacked San Juan Hill, a smaller unit, led by Roosevelt on horseback and including the Rough Riders on foot, prepared to seize nearby Kettle Hill. Situated in a field of tall grass, the frustrated Americans were being shot by Spanish snipers while waiting to attack. Captain Bucky O'Neill decided to boost morale by strolling among the men while smoking a cigarette. When one of them shouted, "Captain, a bullet is sure to kill you," O'Neill replied, "Sergeant, the Spanish bullet ain't made that will kill me"—whereupon a Spanish bullet struck him in the jaw, killing him instantly.

O'Neill's death prompted Roosevelt to mount his horse and order his men to rise and charge the Spaniards. Although shot in the arm, Roosevelt kept moving, and his headlong gallop toward the Spanish lines made him a home-front legend. The *New York Times* reported that he had led the charge with "bulldog ferociousness." Roosevelt boasted that nobody "else could have handled this regiment quite as I handled it."

Being a military hero was Roosevelt's lifelong dream. According to the *New York World,* he had become "more talked about than any man in the country." Roosevelt crowed that he had "killed a Spaniard with my own hand—like a jack rabbit" and requested a Congressional Medal of Honor for his exploits. It did not come. (President Bill Clinton finally awarded the medal posthumously in 2001.)

While Colonel Roosevelt was basking in the glory of battle, other U.S. soldiers were less enthusiastic about modern warfare. Walter Bartholomew, a private from New York, reported that the war was so "much more hideous than my wildest imagination that I have not yet recovered from the shock." A soldier standing beside him had "the front of his throat torn completely

Colonel Roosevelt With hand on hip, Roosevelt led the Rough Riders in Cuba. He recruited most of his regiment from Arizona, New Mexico, and Texas because the southwestern climate resembled that of Cuba.

off" by a Spanish bullet. As his unit was charging up San Juan Hill, they "became totally disorganized and thrown into utter confusion" amid the intense shooting. He discarded all he carried except for his rifle "in the mad scramble to get out of the valley of death." While stopping to shoot, he saw the 24th Regiment of Colored Infantry racing up the hill and decided to follow their lead, "so excited that I forgot to fire my gun, and I actually charged clean up to the top of the hill without shooting, in as great panic as if I had been retreating."

SPANISH DEFEAT AND CONCESSIONS On July 3, the Spanish warships trapped at Santiago attempted to evade the American fleet blockading the harbor. But they were quickly destroyed; 474 Spaniards were killed or wounded, while the Americans suffered only two casualties. Spanish officials surrendered on July 17. On July 25, an American force moved into Spanish-held Puerto Rico, meeting only minor resistance.

The next day, the Spanish government sued for peace. A cease-fire agreement was signed on August 12. In Cuba, the Spanish formally surrendered and sailed for home. Excluded from the ceremony were the Cubans, for whom the war had supposedly been fought.

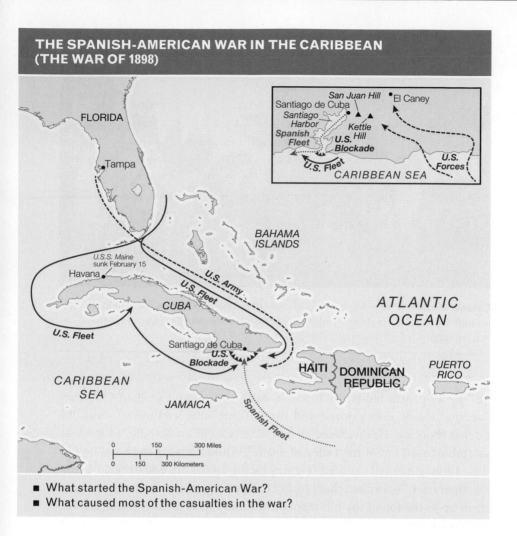

THE SPANISH-AMERICAN WAR IN THE CARIBBEAN (THE WAR OF 1898)

- What started the Spanish-American War?
- What caused most of the casualties in the war?

On December 10, 1898, the United States and Spain signed the Treaty of Paris. Under its terms, Cuba was to become independent and the United States was to annex Puerto Rico and Guam (a Spanish-controlled island between Hawaii and the Philippines) as new American territories. The United States would continue to occupy Manila, pending a transfer of power to the U.S. government in the Philippines. Thus the Spanish Empire in the Americas, initiated by the voyages of Christopher Columbus some four centuries earlier, came to a humiliating end. The United States was ready to create its own empire.

During the four-month War of 1898, more than 60,000 Spanish soldiers and sailors died of wounds or disease—mostly malaria, typhoid, dysentery, or yellow fever. Some 10,500 Cubans died. Among Americans, 5,462 died, but only 379 in battle; most died from disease. At such a cost, the United States imposed its will as a great power, with all the benefits—and burdens—that come with being an imperial nation.

Halfway through the fighting, John Hay, the U.S. ambassador to Great Britain who would soon become secretary of state, wrote to Roosevelt, calling the conflict "a splendid little war, begun with the highest motives, carried on with magnificent intelligence and spirit, favored by that fortune which loves the brave." By contrast, Spaniards referred to the war as "The Disaster," because the humiliating defeat called into question Spain's status as a world power. "Everything is broken in this unhappy country," a Spanish newspaper reported.

CONSEQUENCES OF VICTORY

Victory in the War of 1898 boosted American self-confidence and reinforced the self-serving belief that the United States had a manifest destiny to reshape the world in its own image.

In 1885, the Reverend Josiah Strong wrote a best-selling book titled *Our Country* in which he used a Darwinian argument to strengthen the appeal of manifest destiny. The "wonderful progress of the United States," he boasted, was an illustration of Charles Darwin's concept of "natural selection," since Americans had demonstrated that they were a "superior" civilization that represented "the largest liberty, the purest Christianity, the highest civilization" in the world, a race of superior people destined to "spread itself over the earth."

Europeans agreed that the United States had now made a forceful entrance onto the world stage. The *Times* of London announced that the American victory over Spain must "effect a profound change in the whole attitude and policy of the United States. In the future America will play a part in the general affairs of the world such as she has never played before."

TAKING THE PHILIPPINES

The United States soon substituted its own imperialism for Spain's. If the war had saved many lives by ending the insurrection in Cuba, it had also led the United States to take many lives in suppressing the anti-colonial insurrection in the Philippines. The acquisition of America's first imperial colonies created a host of moral and practical problems, from the difficulties of imposing U.S. rule on native peoples to those of defending far-flung territories.

MCKINLEY'S MOTIVES The Treaty of Paris had left the political status of the Philippines unresolved. American business leaders wanted the United States to keep the islands so that they could more easily penetrate the markets of nearby China. As Mark Hanna, President McKinley's top adviser, stressed, controlling the Philippines would enable the United States to "take a large slice of the commerce of Asia." American missionary organizations, mostly Protestant, also favored annexation; they viewed the Philippines as a base from which to bring Christianity to "the little brown brother."

Not long after the United States took control, American authorities ended the Roman Catholic Church's status as the Philippines' official religion and made English the official language, thus opening the door for Protestant missionaries in the region.

These factors helped convince McKinley of the need to annex "those darned islands." He explained that

> one night late it came to me this way—I don't know how it was, but it came: (1) that we could not give them back to Spain—that would be cowardly and dishonorable; (2) that we could not turn them over to France or Germany—our commercial rivals in the Orient—that would be bad business and discreditable; (3) that we could not leave them to themselves—they were unfit for self-government—and they would soon have anarchy and misrule over there worse than Spain's was; and (4) that there was nothing left for us to do but to take them all, and to educate the Filipinos, and uplift and civilize and Christianize them, and by God's grace do the very best we could by them, as our fellowmen for whom Christ also died. And then I went to bed, and went to sleep and slept soundly.

In this brief statement, McKinley had summarized the motivating ideas of American imperialism: (1) national glory, (2) commerce, (3) racial superiority, and (4) evangelism. American negotiators in Paris finally offered Spain $20 million for the Philippines, Puerto Rico, and Guam, which would serve as a coaling station for ships headed across the Pacific.

Meanwhile, in addition to annexing Hawaii in 1898, the United States also claimed Wake Island, between Guam and Hawaii, which would become a vital link in a future transpacific telegraph cable. In 1899, Germany and the United States agreed to divide the Samoa Islands.

DEBATING THE TREATY By early 1899, the Senate had yet to ratify the Treaty of Paris with Spain because of growing opposition to a global American empire. Anti-expansionists argued that annexing the former Spanish colonies would violate the longstanding American principle embodied in the Constitution that people should be self-governing rather than colonial subjects. Senator Albert Beveridge of Indiana, however, argued that the ideal of democracy "applies only to those who are capable of self-government." In his view, the Filipinos were incapable of governing themselves. His friend Theodore Roosevelt put it more bluntly. The Filipinos, he declared, were "wild beasts" who would benefit from American-imposed discipline: "There must be control! There must be mastery!"

The opposition might have killed the treaty had not the most prominent Democratic leader, William Jennings Bryan, argued that ending the war would open the way for the future independence of the Philippines. His position convinced enough Senate Democrats to support the treaty on February 6, 1899, by the narrowest of margins: only one vote more than the necessary two thirds majority.

President McKinley, however, had no intention of granting independence to the Philippines. He insisted that the United States take control of the islands as an act of "benevolent assimilation" of the native population. A California newspaper gave a more candid explanation: "WE DO NOT WANT THE FILIPINOS. WE WANT THE PHILIPPINES."

Many Filipinos had a different vision. In January 1899, they declared again their independence and named twenty-nine-year-old Emilio Aguinaldo president. The following month, an American soldier outside Manila fired on Aguinaldo's nationalist forces, called *insurrectos*, killing two. The next day, the U.S. Army commander, without investigating the shooting, ordered his troops to assault the *insurrectos*, thus igniting a full-scale conflict that continued for weeks. General Elwell S. Otis rejected Aguinaldo's proposals for a truce, saying that "fighting, having begun, must go on to the grim end." He would accept only unconditional surrender.

On June 2, 1899, the Philippine Republic declared war against the United States. Since the *insurrectos* more or less controlled the Philippines outside Manila, what followed was largely a war of conquest at odds with the founding principle of the United States: that people have the right to govern themselves. The war would rob the Filipinos of the chance to be their own masters.

THE PHILIPPINE-AMERICAN WAR (1899-1902) The effort to crush Filipino nationalism lasted three years and involved some 126,000 U.S. troops, four times as many as had been sent to liberate Cuba. It cost the American government $600 million and took the lives of 200,000 Filipinos (most of them civilians) and 4,234 American soldiers.

Turmoil in the Philippines Emilio Aguinaldo (seated third from right) and other leaders of the Filipino insurgence.

It was a brutal conflict fought in tropical heat and humidity. Racism spurred numerous atrocities by the Americans, many of whom referred to the Filipinos as "niggers." U.S. troops burned villages, tortured and executed prisoners, and imprisoned civilians in overcrowded concentration camps. A reporter for the *Philadelphia Ledger* noted that U.S. soldiers had "killed to exterminate men, women, children, prisoners and captives, active insurgents and suspected people from lads of ten up, the idea prevailing that the Filipino as such was little better than a dog." One U.S. soldier from Indiana celebrated the slaughter of an entire village in retaliation for the murder of an American: "I am in my glory when I can sight my gun on some dark skin and pull the trigger."

Both sides used torture to gain information. A favorite method employed by Americans was the "water cure," a technique to simulate drowning developed in the Spanish Inquisition during the sixteenth century. (Today it is called waterboarding.) A captured insurgent would be placed on his back on the ground. While soldiers stood on his outstretched arms and feet, they pried his mouth open and held it in place with a bamboo stick. They then poured salt water into the captive's mouth and nose until his stomach was bloated, whereupon they would stomp on his abdomen, forcing the water, now mixed with gastric juices, out of his mouth. They repeated the process until the captive told the soldiers what they wanted to know—or died. "It is not civilized warfare," wrote the *Philadelphia Ledger*, "but we are not dealing with civilized people."

"The water cure" American soldiers torture a Filipino prisoner during the Philippine-American War.

Thus did the United States destroy a revolutionary movement modeled after America's own struggle for independence. Organized Filipino resistance collapsed by the end of 1899, but sporadic clashes continued for months thereafter. On April 1, 1901, Aguinaldo swore an oath accepting the authority of the United States over the Philippines.

Against this backdrop, the debate over imperialism continued in the United States. In 1899, several groups combined to form the **American Anti-Imperialist League**. Andrew Carnegie footed the bills for the League and even offered $20 million to buy independence for the Filipinos. Other prominent anti-imperialists included Mark Twain, college presidents Charles Eliot of Harvard and David Starr Jordan of Stanford, and social reformer Jane Addams. Even former presidents Grover Cleveland and Benjamin Harrison urged President McKinley to withdraw U.S. forces from the Philippines.

The conflict to suppress Filipino independence had become "a quagmire," said Mark Twain, and the United States should "not try to get them under our heel" or intervene "in any other country that is not ours." He "opposed" the American eagle "putting its talons on any other land." Harvard philosopher

William James was even more emphatic, arguing that imperialism had caused the United States to "puke up its ancient soul."

Senator George Frisbie Hoar led the opposition in Congress to annexation of the Philippines. Under the Constitution, he pointed out, "no power is given the Federal government to acquire territory to be held and governed permanently as colonies" or "to conquer alien people and hold them in subjugation."

U.S. INTERESTS IN THE PACIFIC

Dates indicate year of acquisition or occupation by the United States.

■ Why was President McKinley eager to acquire territory in the Pacific and the Caribbean?

■ What kind of political system did the U.S. government create in Hawaii and in the Philippines?

■ How did Filipinos and Hawaiians resist the Americans?

Ministers denounced imperialism as un-Christian. Charles Ames, a prominent Unitarian leader, predicted that American imperialism would "put us into a permanent attitude of arrogance, testiness, and defiance towards other nations. . . . We shall be one more bully among bullies." Southern Democrats feared that giving civil rights to people of color would undermine white supremacy in America.

Samuel Gompers, the union leader, opposed converting the former Spanish colonies into American colonies because he was convinced that immigrants would lower wage levels: "If these new islands are to become ours . . . can we hope to close the floodgates of immigration from the hordes of Chinese and the semisavage races coming from what will then be part of our own country?"

ORGANIZING THE NEW COLONIES

In the end, the imperialists won the debate. Senator Albert J. Beveridge boasted in 1900: "The Philippines are ours forever. And just beyond the Philippines are China's illimitable markets. . . . The power that rules the Pacific is the power that rules the world." He added that the U.S. economy was producing "more than we can consume, making more than we can use. Therefore we must find new markets for our produce." American-controlled colonies would make the best new markets. Without acknowledging it, Beveridge and others were using many of the same arguments that England had used in founding the American colonies in the seventeenth century.

On July 4, 1901, the U.S. military government in the Philippines gave way to civilian control, and William Howard Taft became the civil governor. In 1902, Congress passed the Philippine Government Act, which declared the islands an "unorganized territory"—in essence, it became an American colony not a territory eligible for statehood. In 1917, the Jones Act affirmed America's intention to grant the Philippines independence, but that would not happen until 1946.

Closer to home, Puerto Rico had been acquired in part to serve as a U.S. outpost guarding the Caribbean Sea. On April 12, 1900, the Foraker Act established a government on the island, and its residents were declared citizens of the Commonwealth of Puerto Rico, not Spain; they were made dual citizens of the United States 1917. (As residents of a territory, not a state, Puerto Ricans cannot vote in American presidential elections. They pay billions each year in various federal taxes, but not the personal income tax.)

In Cuba, the United States finally fulfilled the promise of independence after restoring order, organizing schools, and improving sanitary conditions. The problem of widespread disease prompted the work of Dr. Walter Reed. Named head of the Army Yellow Fever Commission in 1900, he proved that

"Well, I hardly know which to take first!" With a growing appetite for foreign territory, Uncle Sam browses his options: Cuba Steak, Puerto Rico Pig, Philippine Floating Islands, and others. An expectant President McKinley waits to take his order.

mosquitoes carry yellow fever. The commission's experiments led the way to effective control of the disease worldwide.

In 1900, on President McKinley's order, Cubans drafted a constitution modeled on that of the United States. The following year, however, the Platt Amendment sharply restricted the Cuban government's independence by requiring that Cuba never sign a treaty with a third power, that it keep its debt within the government's power to repay it out of ordinary revenues, and that it acknowledge the right of the United States to intervene whenever it saw fit. Finally, Cuba had to sell or lease to the United States lands to be used for coaling or naval stations, a stipulation that led to a U.S. naval base at Guantánamo Bay that still exists today.

IMPERIAL RIVALRIES IN EAST ASIA

While the United States was conquering the Philippines, other nations were threatening to carve up China. After Japan defeated China in the First Sino-Japanese War (1894–1895), European nations set out to exploit the weakness of the virtually defenseless nation. By the end of the century, Russia, Germany, France, and Great Britain had each established spheres of influence in China—territories that they controlled but did not formally annex.

In 1898 and again in 1899, the British asked the American government to join them in preserving the territorial integrity of China against further imperialist actions. Both times, however, the Senate rejected the request because the United States as yet had no strategic investment in the region. The American outlook changed with the defeat of Spain and the acquisition of the Philippines. Instead of acting jointly with Great Britain, however, the U.S. government decided to act alone (unilaterally) in implementing the British policy.

What came to be known as the **Open Door policy** was outlined in Secretary of State John Hay's Open Door Note, dispatched in 1899 to his European counterparts. Without consulting the Chinese, Hay announced that China should remain an "open door" to European and American trade and that other nations should not try to take control of Chinese ports or territory. None of the European powers except Britain accepted Hay's principles, but none rejected them, either. So, Hay announced that all major powers involved in China had accepted the policy.

The Open Door policy was rooted in the desire of American businesses to exploit and ultimately dominate Chinese markets. It also appealed to those who opposed imperialism because it pledged to keep China from being carved up by powerful European nations.

The policy had little legal standing, however. When the Japanese became concerned about growing Russian influence in Manchuria (in northeast China) and asked how the United States intended to enforce the policy, Hay replied that America was "not prepared . . . to enforce these views." So the situation would remain for forty years, until continued Japanese military expansion in China would bring about a diplomatic dispute with America that would lead to war.

THE BOXERS A new Asian crisis arose in 1900 when Chinese nationalists known to the Western world as Boxers—they called themselves the "Fists of Righteous Harmony"—rebelled against foreign involvement in China, especially Christian missionary efforts, and laid siege to foreign embassies in Peking (now known as Beijing). An expedition of British, German, Russian, Japanese, and American soldiers was organized to rescue the international diplomats and their staffs. Hay, fearful that the intervention might become an excuse for other nations to dismember China, took the opportunity to

Intervention in China After quelling the Boxer Rebellion, U.S. troops march in the Forbidden Palace, the imperial palace in the Chinese capital of Beijing.

refine the Open Door policy. The United States, he said, sought a solution that would "preserve Chinese territorial and administrative integrity" as well as "equal and impartial trade with all parts of the Chinese Empire." Six weeks later, the foreign military expedition reached Peking and ended the Boxer Rebellion.

ROOSEVELT'S "BIG-STICK" DIPLOMACY

On September 6, 1901, while President McKinley was shaking hands in a reception line at the Pan-American Exposition in Buffalo, New York, a twenty-eight-year-old unemployed anarchist, approached with a concealed gun and fired twice at point-blank range. One bullet was deflected by the president's coat button and breastbone, but the other tore through his abdomen and lodged in his back. McKinley urged police not to "hurt" his assailant; he is "just some poor misguided fellow."

For several days, doctors issued optimistic reports about McKinley's condition, but after a week, the president knew he was dying. "It is useless, gentlemen," he told the doctors. "I think we ought to have a prayer." Then he said, "Goodbye, goodbye to all." Leon Czolgosz (pronounced CHOL-gosh) was convicted of murder and executed in an electric chair, a new invention.

Vice President Theodore Roosevelt became president on September 14, 1901. His infusion of "manly energy" would transform the modern presidency. The nation had emerged from the War of 1898 a world power with major international responsibilities. To ensure that Americans accepted their new global role, Roosevelt stretched both the Constitution and executive power to the limit. In the process, he pushed a reluctant nation onto center stage of world affairs.

A "ROCKET" RISE TO PROMINENCE

Born in 1858, "Teedie" Roosevelt enjoyed a privileged life in New York City. He visited Europe as a child, studied with a personal tutor, spoke German fluently, and graduated from Harvard with honors in 1880. A frail, puny boy, nearly blind in one eye and weakened by chronic asthma, he followed his father's order to "make your own body." He compulsively lifted weights in a gym his father installed in their mansion, wrestled, hiked, rowed, swam, boxed, played tennis, rode horses, became a crack shot with rifles and pistols, and climbed mountains, all in an effort to build himself into an intellectual athlete.

Roosevelt transformed himself into a barrel-chested man of almost super-human energy who fiercely championed the "strenuous life." He told his children that he would rather see them dead than grow up to be "weaklings" and "sissies."

Roosevelt was a fearless "he-man" who also displayed extraordinary intellectual curiosity. At Harvard, he spoke up so often in class that one professor felt forced to remind his impetuous student, "See here, Roosevelt. Let *me* talk. I'm running this course." He became a voracious reader and talented writer, a natural scientist, a dedicated bird watcher, a renowned historian and essayist, and a zealous moralist who divided the world into two camps: good and evil.

Roosevelt's zest for life and his combative spirit were contagious, and he was ever eager to express an opinion on any subject. After young Roosevelt participated in a buffalo hunt in the Dakotas, one of the cowboys said: "There goes the most remarkable man I ever met. Unless I am badly mistaken, the world is due to hear from him one of these days."

Within two years after graduating from Harvard, Roosevelt, a reform-minded Republican, won election as the youngest member of the New York legislature. He could not be bought, nor did he tolerate the excesses of the spoils system. "Though I am a strong party man," he warned, "if I find a corrupt public official, I would take off his head."

With the world seemingly at his feet, however, disaster struck. In 1884, his mother, Mittie, only forty-eight years old, died of typhoid fever. Eleven hours later, his "bewitchingly pretty," twenty-two-year-old wife, Alice, died in his arms of kidney failure, having given birth to their only child just two days earlier. The "light has gone out of my life," Roosevelt noted in his diary. The double funeral service for his wife and mother was so emotional that the officiating minister wept throughout his prayer.

Shaken by his "strange and terrible fate," Roosevelt turned his newborn daughter over to his sister, quit his political career, sold the family house, and moved to a cattle ranch in the Dakota Territory, where he stayed for two years. He threw himself into roping and branding steers, shooting buffalo and bears, capturing outlaws, fighting Indians, and reading by campfire. He was, by his own admission, a poor shot, a bad roper, and an average rider, but he loved his western life. He would write in his memoirs that "I owe more than I can express to the West."

Back in New York City, Roosevelt remarried and ran unsuccessfully for mayor in 1886. He later served as a U.S. Civil Service commissioner and as the city's police commissioner. In 1896, he campaigned energetically for William McKinley, and the new president rewarded him with the position of assistant secretary of the navy. Roosevelt lusted to be "one of the governing class," so he took full advantage of the celebrity he had gained with the Rough Riders in Cuba to win the governorship of New York in 1898. By then, he had become the most visible young Republican in the nation. Two years later, Republican leaders were urging him to become the vice-presidential running mate for McKinley, who was hoping for a second presidential term.

FROM VICE PRESIDENT TO PRESIDENT

In the 1900 presidential contest, the Democrats turned again to William Jennings Bryan, who wanted to make American imperialism the "paramount issue" of the campaign. The platform condemned the conflict with Filipino nationalists as "an unnecessary war" that had placed the United States "in the false and un-American position of crushing with military force the efforts of our former allies to achieve liberty and self-government."

The Republicans renominated McKinley and named Roosevelt, now known as "Mr. Imperialism," their candidate for vice president. Roosevelt, who despised Bryan, crisscrossed the nation condemning Bryan's "communistic and socialistic doctrines" that promoted higher taxes and the unlimited coinage of silver. In the end, McKinley and Roosevelt won by 7.2 million to 6.4 million popular votes and 292 to 155 electoral votes. Bryan even lost Nebraska, his home state.

On September 14, 1901, McKinley died from his assassin's bullet. "Now look," exclaimed Mark Hanna, who had been McKinley's political manager, "that damned cowboy is President of the United States!"

Six weeks short of his forty-third birthday, Roosevelt, known affectionately as TR, was the youngest man to become president. But he had more experience in public affairs than most new presidents, and more vitality than any. One observer compared his boundless personality and energy to Niagara Falls—"both great wonders of nature." TR's glittering spectacles, glistening teeth, and overflowing enthusiasm were like divine gifts to political cartoonists, as was his motto, an old African proverb: "Speak softly, and carry a big stick."

THE BIG STICK IN THE CARIBBEAN SEA

Big-stick diplomacy President Theodore Roosevelt wields "the big stick," symbolizing his aggressive diplomacy. As he stomps through the Caribbean, he drags a string of American warships behind him.

Roosevelt's unshakable self-righteousness led him to cast nearly every issue in moral and patriotic terms. He was the first truly activist president. The presidency was, as he put it, a "bully pulpit"—an inviting platform for delivering fist-pumping speeches on the virtues of honesty, courage, and civic duty.

Like many of his political friends and associates, Roosevelt was convinced that the "civilized" and "barbarian" people of the world faced inevitable conflict, not unlike the fate of the Native Americans pushed off their ancestral lands by Americans. In 1899, he argued that the United States needed to conquer other regions of the world to bring "law, order, and righteousness" to "backward peoples." He believed that American imperialists would be missionaries of civic virtue, spreading the merits of their "race" to "savages."

THE PANAMA CANAL After the Spanish-American War (the War of 1898), one issue overshadowed every other in the Caribbean: the proposed Panama Canal. By enabling ships to travel from the Pacific Ocean directly into the Gulf of Mexico, such a canal would cut the travel distance between San Francisco and New York City by almost 8,000 miles.

The nation of Panama had been a major concern of Americans since the late 1840s, when it became an important overland link in the sea route from the East Coast to the California goldfields. Two treaties dating from that period loomed as obstacles to the construction of a canal. The Bidlack Treaty (1846) with Colombia (then called New Granada) guaranteed Colombia's control over Panama. In the Clayton-Bulwer Treaty (1850), the British had agreed to acquire no more Central American territory, and the United States joined them in agreeing to build or fortify a canal only by mutual consent.

Secretary of State John Hay asked the British for consent to build a canal. The outcome was the Hay-Pauncefote Treaty of 1901. Other obstacles remained, however. From 1881 to 1887, a French company led by Ferdinand de Lesseps, who had engineered the Suez Canal in Egypt, had already spent nearly $300 million and some 20,000 lives to dig a canal a third of the way across Panama, which was still under Colombian control. The company convinced the United States to purchase the partially completed canal.

In return for acquiring a canal zone six miles wide, the United States agreed to pay Colombia $10 million. The U.S. Senate ratified the Hay-Herrán Treaty in 1903, but the Colombian Senate held out for $25 million. As President Roosevelt raged against the "foolish and homicidal corruptionists in Bogotá," the Panamanians revolted against Colombian rule.

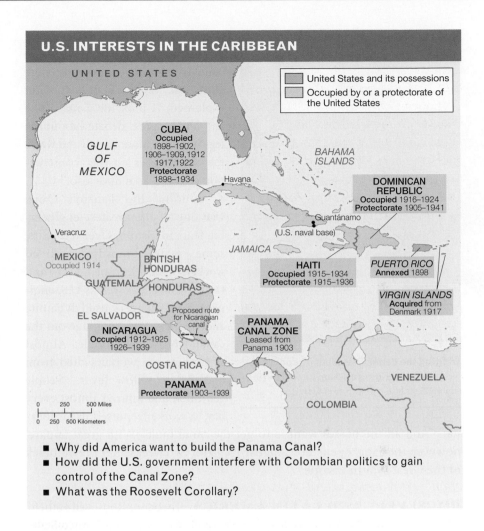

U.S. INTERESTS IN THE CARIBBEAN

UNITED STATES

- United States and its possessions
- Occupied by or a protectorate of the United States

GULF OF MEXICO

CUBA
Occupied
1898–1902,
1906–1909, 1912
1917, 1922
Protectorate
1898–1934

Havana

BAHAMA ISLANDS

DOMINICAN REPUBLIC
Occupied 1916–1924
Protectorate 1905–1941

Guantánamo
(U.S. naval base)

Veracruz

JAMAICA

MEXICO
Occupied 1914

BRITISH HONDURAS

GUATEMALA

HONDURAS

HAITI
Occupied 1915–1934
Protectorate 1915–1936

PUERTO RICO
Annexed 1898

VIRGIN ISLANDS
Acquired from Denmark 1917

EL SALVADOR

Proposed route for Nicaraguan canal

NICARAGUA
Occupied 1912–1925
1926–1939

PANAMA CANAL ZONE
Leased from Panama 1903

COSTA RICA

VENEZUELA

PANAMA
Protectorate 1903–1939

COLOMBIA

0   250   500 Miles

0   250   500 Kilometers

- Why did America want to build the Panama Canal?
- How did the U.S. government interfere with Colombian politics to gain control of the Canal Zone?
- What was the Roosevelt Corollary?

President Roosevelt aided the Panamanian rebels and signed a treaty with the newly independent nation that extended the Canal Zone from six to ten miles wide.

For a $10 million down payment and $250,000 a year, the United States received "in perpetuity the use, occupation and control" of the fifty-mile-long Canal Zone. Not everyone applauded the president's actions. A Chicago newspaper attacked him for his "rough-riding assault upon another republic over the shattered wreckage of international law." The U.S. attorney general, asked to supply a legal opinion upholding Roosevelt's actions, responded wryly, "No, Mr. President, if I were you I would not have any taint of legality

Digging the canal President Theodore Roosevelt operating a steam shovel during his 1906 visit to the Panama Canal.

about it." He then added, "You were accused of seduction and you have conclusively proved that you were guilty of rape." Roosevelt later explained, "I took the Canal Zone and let Congress debate [about the legitimacy of his actions]; and while the debate goes on the [construction of the] Canal does also."

Building the Panama Canal was one of the greatest engineering feats in history. Over ten years, some 60,000 mostly unskilled workers from Europe, Asia, and the Caribbean, as well as U.S. engineers and managers, used dynamite and steam shovels to gouge out the canal from dense jungle. Almost a third of the workers died from malaria or yellow fever. "People get killed and injured almost every day," a worker reported in his journal. "And all the bosses want is to get the canal built." With great fanfare, however, the canal opened on August 15, 1914, two weeks after the outbreak of the Great War in Europe.

ROOSEVELT AND LATIN AMERICA Theodore Roosevelt's "theft" of the Panama Canal Zone created decades of ill will toward the United States throughout Latin America. Constant interference from both the United States and European countries only aggravated tensions. A frequent excuse for intervention was to promote a safe and stable environment for American businesses, including the collection of debts owed by Latin American governments. The Latin Americans responded with the Drago Doctrine (1902), named after Argentinian foreign minister Luis María Drago, which prohibited armed intervention by other countries to collect debts.

In December 1902, however, German and British warships blockaded Venezuela to force the repayment of debts in defiance of both the Drago Doctrine and the Monroe Doctrine, the U.S. policy dating to 1823 that prohibited European intervention in the Western Hemisphere. Roosevelt decided that if the

United States were to keep European nations from intervening militarily in Latin America, "then sooner or later we must keep order [there] ourselves."

In 1904, a crisis over the debts of the Dominican Republic prompted Roosevelt to send two warships to the island nation and issue what came to be known as the **Roosevelt Corollary** to the Monroe Doctrine: the principle, in short, that in certain circumstances, the United States was justified in intervening in Latin America to prevent Europeans from doing so. Thereafter, U.S. presidents would repeatedly use force to ensure that Latin American nations paid their debts.

RELATIONS WITH JAPAN

While wielding a "big stick" in Latin America, Roosevelt was playing the role of peacemaker in East Asia. In 1904, the rivalry between Russia and Japan flared into the Russo-Japanese War over Japan's attempts to expand its influence in China and Korea.

On February 8, Japanese warships devastated the Russian fleet. The Japanese then occupied the Korean peninsula and drove the Russians back into Manchuria. When the Japanese signaled that they would welcome a negotiated settlement, Roosevelt sponsored a peace conference in Portsmouth, New Hampshire. In the Treaty of Portsmouth, signed on September 5, 1905, Russia acknowledged Japan's "predominant political, military, and economic interests in Korea." (Japan would annex the kingdom in 1910.) Both powers agreed to leave Manchuria.

Japan's show of strength raised concerns among U.S. leaders about the security of the Philippines. During the Portsmouth talks, Roosevelt sent William Howard Taft to meet with the Japanese foreign minister. They negotiated the Taft-Katsura Agreement of July 29, 1905, in which the United States accepted Japanese control of Korea in exchange for Japan acknowledging U.S. control of the Philippines. Three years later, the Root-Takahira Agreement, negotiated by Secretary of State Elihu Root and the Japanese ambassador to the United States, reinforced the Open Door policy by supporting "the independence and integrity of China."

Behind the outward appearances of goodwill, however, lay distrust. For many Americans, the Russian threat in East Asia gave way to concerns about the "yellow peril." Racial conflict on the West Coast, especially in California, helped sour relations with Japan. In 1906, San Francisco's school board ordered students of Asian descent to attend a separate public school from "Americans." When the Japanese government protested, President Roosevelt persuaded the

Japanese immigration Japanese immigrants arrive at the Immigration Station on Angel Island in San Francisco, California. Many other Japanese immigrants settled in Hawaii.

school board to change its policy, but only after making sure that Japanese authorities would stop encouraging unemployed Japanese "laborers" to go to America. This "Gentlemen's Agreement" of 1907 halted the influx of Japanese immigrants to California.

THE GREAT WHITE FLEET

After Theodore Roosevelt's election to a full term as president in 1904, he celebrated America's rise as a world power. In 1907, without consulting Congress or his cabinet, he sent the entire U.S. fleet of warships, by then second in strength only to Britain's Royal Navy, on a fourteen-month world tour to demonstrate America's power and to show that "the Pacific is as much our home waters as the Atlantic."

At every port of call—down the Atlantic coast of South America, then up the Pacific coast, out to Hawaii, and down to New Zealand and Australia— the "Great White Fleet" of eighteen gleaming battleships, eight armored cruisers, and assorted support ships, received a rousing welcome. The triumphal procession continued to Japan, China, and the Philippines, then to Egypt, through the Suez Canal and across the Mediterranean Sea before steaming back to Virginia in early 1909, just in time to close Roosevelt's presidency.

Roosevelt's success in expanding U.S. power abroad would have mixed consequences, however, because underlying his imperialism was a militantly racist view of the world. Roosevelt and others believed that the world included "civilized" societies, such as the United States, Japan, and the nations of Europe, and those they described as "barbarous," "backward," or "impotent." It was the responsibility of the "civilized" nations to exercise control of the "barbarous" peoples, by force if necessary.

TAFT'S "DOLLAR DIPLOMACY" Republican William Howard Taft, who succeeded Roosevelt as president in 1909, continued to promote America's economic interests abroad, practicing what Roosevelt called "**dollar diplomacy**." Taft used the State Department to help American companies and banks invest in foreign countries, especially East Asia and the less developed nations of Latin America and the Caribbean. To ensure the stability of those investments, Taft did not hesitate to intervene in nations experiencing political and economic turmoil. In 1909, he dispatched U.S. Marines to support a revolution in Nicaragua. Once the new government was formed, Secretary of State Philander C. Knox helped U.S. banks negotiate loans to prop it up. Two years later, Taft again sent American troops to restore political stability. This time they stayed for more than a decade.

WILSON'S INTERVENTIONISM In 1913, the new Democratic president, Woodrow Wilson, attacked dollar diplomacy as a form of economic imperialism. He promised to treat Latin American nations "on terms of equality and honor." Yet Wilson, along with William Jennings Bryan, his secretary of state, dispatched American military forces to Latin America more often than Taft and Roosevelt combined. Wilson argued that the United States must intervene to stabilize weak governments in the Western Hemisphere to keep European nations from doing so.

In 1915, when the Dominican Republic refused to sign a treaty that would have given the United States a "special" role in governing the island nation, Wilson sent Marines to establish a military government and suppress anti-American rebels. That same year, Wilson intervened in Haiti, next door to the Dominican Republic. He admitted that his actions were "high-handed" but argued that they were justified because the "necessity for exercising control there is immediate, urgent, imperative." Others disagreed. As the *New York*

Times charged, Wilson's frequent interventions made Taft's dollar diplomacy look like "ten cent diplomacy."

THE UNITED STATES IN MEXICO Mexico was a much thornier problem for Woodrow Wilson. In 1910, Mexicans had revolted against the dictatorship of Porfirio Díaz, who had given foreign corporations a free rein in developing the nation's economy. After occupying Mexico City in 1911, the victorious rebels began squabbling among themselves. The leader of the rebellion, Francisco Madero, was overthrown by his chief of staff, General Victoriano Huerta, who assumed power in early 1913 and then had Madero and thirty other political opponents murdered.

President Wilson refused to recognize "a government of butchers." Huerta ignored the criticism and established a dictatorship. Wilson decided that Huerta must be removed and ordered U.S. warships to halt shipments of foreign weapons to the new government. Meanwhile, several rival revolutionary Mexican armies, the largest of which was led by Francisco Pancho Villa, began trying to unseat Huerta.

On April 9, 1914, nine American sailors were arrested in Tampico, Mexico, while trying to buy supplies. Mexican officials quickly released

Intervention in Mexico U.S. Marines enter Veracruz, Mexico, in 1914.

them and apologized to the U.S. naval commander. There the incident might have ended, but the imperious U.S. admiral demanded that the Mexicans fire a twenty-one-gun salute to the American flag. After they refused, Wilson sent U.S. troops ashore at Veracruz on April 21, 1914. They occupied the city at a cost of 19 American lives; at least 300 Mexicans were killed or wounded.

For seven months, the Americans governed Veracruz. They left in late 1914 after Huerta was overthrown by Venustiano Carranza. Still, the problems south of the border continued. In 1916, Pancho Villa launched raids into Texas and New Mexico in a deliberate attempt to trigger U.S. intervention. On March 9, he and his men attacked Columbus, New Mexico, three miles across the border. His army of 500 revolutionaries burned the town and killed seventeen Americans.

A furious Wilson sent General John J. Pershing to Mexico with 6,000 soldiers. For nearly a year, Pershing's troops chased Villa's army through the mountains of northern Mexico. As Pershing muttered, "It's like trying to chase a rat in a cornfield." In 1917, the American troops were ordered home. The elusive Villa, meanwhile, named his mule "President Wilson." By then, however, Wilson paid little notice, for he was distracted by a much greater threat: war in Europe.

CHAPTER REVIEW

SUMMARY

- **Toward the New Imperialism**   Near the end of the nineteenth century, the popular idea that America had a manifest destiny to expand its territory abroad, combined with industrialists' desire for new markets for their goods, helped to fuel America's new *imperialism*. White Americans believed that their advanced industrial development proved their racial superiority, and by conquering "backward peoples," the United States was simply enacting the theory of survival of the fittest. American evangelical Protestants also thought they had a duty to Christianize and "uplift" people throughout the world.

- **Expansion in the Pacific**   Business leaders hoped to extend America's commercial reach across the Pacific to exploit vast Asian markets. The Alaska Purchase (1867) initiated the effort to acquire Pacific ports. American planters in the Kingdom of Hawaii developed a thriving sugar industry using Asian laborers, which increased Hawaii's commercial connections to the United States. In 1894, Hawaii's minority white population *(haoles)* ousted the native Hawaiian queen, declared a republic, and requested that Hawaii be annexed by the United States. In 1898, President William McKinley agreed to annex the islands.

- **The Spanish-American War (The War of 1898)**   When Cubans revolted against Spanish colonial rule in 1895, many Americans supported their demand for independence. *Yellow journalism* sensationalizing the Spanish suppression of the revolt further aroused Americans' sympathy. Early in 1898, the publication of the *de Lôme letter*, followed by the sinking of the *U.S. battleship Maine* in Havana Harbor, helped propel America into war with Spain. In declaring war, Congress passed the *Teller Amendment* denying any territorial ambitions in Cuba. The war lasted only 114 days. Under the Treaty of Paris ending the war, Cuba became independent and the United States annexed Spain's other Caribbean possession, Puerto Rico, which it had occupied. In the Spanish colony of the Philippine Islands, America's Pacific naval fleet under Commodore George Dewey defeated the Spanish fleet in the Battle of Manila Bay.

- **Consequences of Victory**   A vicious guerrilla war followed in the Philippines when Filipinos rebelled against American control. The rebellion was suppressed, and President McKinley announced that the United States would annex the Philippines. The *American Anti-Imperialist League* and others argued that acquiring overseas territories violated American principles of self-determination and independence. In the end, the imperialists won the debate, and Congress set up a government in the Philippines and in Puerto Rico. The United States also annexed Hawaii, Guam, Wake Island, and some of the Samoa Islands during or shortly after the Spanish-American War (the War of 1898). In East Asia, Secretary of State John Hay promoted the *Open Door policy (1899)* of preserving China's territorial integrity and equal access by all nations to trade with China.

- **Theodore Roosevelt and Big-Stick Diplomacy** Theodore Roosevelt pursued an imperialist foreign policy that confirmed the United States' new role as a world power. He helped negotiate the treaty that ended the Russo-Japanese War, seized control of the Panama Canal, and sent the navy's fleet of new battleships around the world as a symbol of American might. He also proclaimed the *Roosevelt Corollary (1904)* to the Monroe Doctrine, asserting that the United States would intervene in Latin America as necessary to prevent European intervention.

- **Taft and Wilson's Interventionism Abroad** William Howard Taft and Woodrow Wilson continued Roosevelt's pattern of intervening in the internal affairs of other nations, especially in Latin America and the Caribbean. What Taft called *dollar diplomacy* involved the U.S. government fostering American investments in less developed nations and then using U.S. military force to protect those investments. Wilson's frustrations at the instability of the Mexican government led him to intervene there with American troops twice. In both cases, the presence of U.S. soldiers only deepened the resentment of "Yankee imperialism" throughout Latin America.

CHRONOLOGY

1894	Republic of Hawaii is proclaimed
1898	U.S. battleship *Maine* explodes in Havana Harbor
	The Spanish-American War (War of 1898)
	United States annexes Hawaii
1899	U.S. Senate ratifies the Treaty of Paris, ending the War of 1898
1899–1902	Insurgents resist U.S. conquest of the Philippines
	President McKinley assassinated; Roosevelt becomes president
1914	Panama Canal opens
1909–1917	U.S. military interventions in Mexico and Latin America

KEY TERMS

imperialism p. 936

yellow journalism p. 941

U.S. battleship *Maine* p. 941

de Lôme letter (1898) p. 942

Teller Amendment (1898) p. 943

American Anti-Imperialist League p. 953

Open Door policy (1899) p. 957

Roosevelt Corollary (1904) p. 965

dollar diplomacy p. 967

 INQUIZITIVE

Go to InQuizitive to see what you've learned—and learn what you've missed—with personalized feedback along the way.

21 The Progressive Era

1890–1920

"Votes For Us When We Are Women!" Parades organized by women's suffrage groups attracted women of all ages and social classes. Here, from a patriotically outfitted automobile, some young suffragists ask their many spectators for "votes for us when we are women."

Theodore Roosevelt's emergence as a national leader coincided with the onset of what historians have labeled the Progressive Era (1890–1920), an extraordinary period of social activism and political innovation during which compelling public issues forced profound changes in the role of government and presidential leadership. Millions of middle-class progressives believed that America was experiencing a disruptive crisis of democracy because of the urban-industrial revolution. Widespread inner-city poverty, children laboring in unregulated mines and factories, tainted food, miserable working conditions, and low pay, progressives insisted, required bold action by churches, charitable organizations, experts, and individuals—and an expanded role for governments.

One of the major concerns was continuing evidence of fraudulent conduct by elected officials. As Amos Pinchot, a progressive attorney and reformer from New York City, said, corruption was "destroying our respect for government, uprooting faith in political parties, and causing every precedent and convention of the old order to strain at its moorings."

The widening gap between rich and poor during the Gilded Age had become another major issue. Walter Weyl, a progressive economist, insisted that "we shall not advance far in working out our American ideals without striking hard at . . . inequality." Political equality, he added, "is a farce and a peril unless there is at least some measure of economic equality." The growth of industries like railroading, steel, coal, and oil had attracted waves of poor farm

focus questions

1. What were the motives of progressive reformers?

2. Which sources of thought and activism contributed to the progressive movement?

3. What were the specific goals of progressive reformers and how did they address them?

4. What contributions did Presidents Theodore Roosevelt and William Howard Taft make to the progressive movement? How and why did these men come to disagree about the best ways to advance progressive ideals?

5. Which policies of President Woodrow Wilson were influenced by the progressive movement? How and why did they differ from the policies of Roosevelt and Taft?

folk and foreign immigrants to cities, where basic social services—food, water, housing, education, sanitation, transportation, and medical care—could not keep pace with the rate of urban growth.

Between 1890 and 1920, progressive reformers attacked the problems created by political corruption, unregulated industrialization, and unplanned urbanization. They insisted that something must be done to control the powerful corporations that dominated the economy and corrupted U.S. political life.

By the beginning of the twentieth century, **progressivism** had become the most dynamic social and political force in the nation. In 1910, Woodrow Wilson told a gathering of clergymen that progressivism had generated "an extraordinary awakening in civic consciousness."

THE PROGRESSIVE IMPULSE

Progressives were liberals, not revolutionaries. Liberalism in the twentieth century referred to those who believed that governments must exercise greater power on behalf of society in regulating the behavior of businesses and ensuring the welfare of the people. They wanted to reform and regulate capitalism, not destroy it. Most were Christian moralists who felt that politics had become a contest between good and evil, honesty and corruption. What they all shared was the assumption that governments—local, state, and national—must become more active in addressing the problems created by rapid urban and industrial growth.

Progressivism was more a widespread impulse supported by elements of both major political parties than it was a single movement with a common agenda. Theodore Roosevelt called it the "forward movement" because it promoted positive changes led by people "who stand for the cause of progress, for the cause of the uplift of humanity and the betterment of mankind."

Unlike Populism, whose grassroots appeal centered on farming regions in the South and Midwest, progressivism was a national movement. It was based in large cities but also popular in rural areas. Progressive activists came in all stripes: men and women; Democrats, Republicans, Populists, and socialists; labor unionists and business executives; teachers, engineers, editors, and professors; social workers, doctors, ministers, and journalists; farmers and homemakers; whites and blacks; clergymen, atheists, and agnostics. Their combined efforts led to significant social reforms and government regulations of businesses.

To make governments more efficient and businesses more honest, progressives drew upon the new "social sciences"—sociology, political science, psychology, public health, and economics—being developed at research universities. The progressive approach was to appoint social scientists to "investigate, educate, and legislate." Urban reformer Florence Kelley voiced the era's widespread belief that once people knew "the truth" about social ills, "they would act upon it."

Yet progressivism also had flaws, inconsistencies, and hypocrisies. Progressives' "do-good" perspective was often limited by racial and ethnic prejudices, as well as by social and intellectual snobbery. The goals of upper-class white progressives rarely included racial equality, for example. Many otherwise progressive people, including Theodore Roosevelt and Woodrow Wilson, believed in the supremacy of the "Anglo-Saxon race." They assumed that the forces shaping modern society were too complicated for the "ignorant" masses to understand, much less improve, without direction by those who knew better.

THE SOURCES OF PROGRESSIVISM

During the last quarter of the nineteenth century, progressives began to attack corrupt political bosses and irresponsible corporate barons. They sought a more honest and efficient government, more-effective regulation of big businesses ("the trusts"), and better living and working conditions for the laboring poor. Only by expanding the scope of local, state, and federal governments, they believed, could these goals be attained.

ECONOMIC DEPRESSION AND DISCONTENT More than any factor, the devastating economic depression of the 1890s ignited the progressive spirit of reform. The depression brought massive layoffs; nearly a quarter of the adults in the workforce lost their jobs.

Although the United States boasted the highest per capita income in the world ($428 in 1900; about $15,000 today), it also had some of the highest concentrations of poverty. In 1900, the U.S. population numbered 82 million, of which an estimated 10 million were living in poverty. The devastating effects of the depression prompted many upper-middle-class urban reformers—lawyers, doctors, executives, social workers, teachers, professors, journalists, and college-educated women—to organize efforts to help those in need and thereby keep them from becoming social revolutionaries or anarchists.

POPULISM Populism was another thread in the fabric of progressivism. The Populist party platforms of 1892 and 1896 included reforms intended to give more power to the people, such as the "direct election" of U.S. senators by voters rather than by state legislatures. Although William Jennings Bryan's loss in the 1896 presidential campaign ended the Populist party as a serious political force, many reforms pushed by Populists were implemented by progressives.

"HONEST GOVERNMENT" The Mugwumps—"gentlemen" reformers who had fought the patronage system and insisted that government jobs be awarded on the basis of merit—supplied progressivism with another key goal: the "honest government" ideal. Over the years, the good-government movement expanded to address persistent urban issues such as crime, unequal access to electricity, clean water and municipal sewers, mass transit, and garbage collection.

SOCIALISM The Socialist Party of America, supported mostly by militant farmers and German/Jewish immigrants, served as the radical wing of progressivism. Socialists focused on improving working conditions and closing the widening income gap between rich and poor through progressive taxation, whereby tax rates would rise with income. Most progressives were capitalist reformers, not socialist radicals. They rejected the extremes of both socialism and laissez-faire individualism, preferring a new, regulated capitalism "softened" by humanitarianism.

Ludlow Street cellar habitation
This December 1895 photograph from Jacob Riis's *How the Other Half Lives* revealed the cramped and unsanitary living conditions faced by many immigrants living in tenements on New York City's lower East Side.

MUCKRAKING JOURNALISM
Progressivism depended upon the press—newspapers and magazines—to inform the public about political corruption and social problems. The so-called **muckrakers** were America's first investigative journalists. Their aggressive reporting played a crucial role in educating readers about political and corporate wrongdoing and revealing "how the other half lives," the title of an influential exposé of the terrible living conditions experienced by immigrants in New York City, written by the Danish immigrant photojournalist Jacob Riis.

The muckrakers got their nickname from Theodore Roosevelt, who said that crusading journalists were "often indispensable to . . . society, but only if they know when to stop raking the muck." By uncovering political corruption and writing about social ills, muckrakers gave journalism a new political role. Roosevelt, both as governor of New York and as president of the United States, frequently used muckrakers to drum up support for his policies; he corresponded with them, invited them to the White House, and used their popularity to help shape public opinion.

The golden age of muckraking began in 1902, when Samuel S. McClure, owner of *McClure's* magazine, recruited idealistic journalists to expose corruption in politics and corporations. McClure claimed that the "vitality of democracy" depended upon educating the public about "complex questions." *McClure's* and other muckraking magazines investigated corporate monopolies and crooked political machines while exposing the miserable conditions in which the working poor lived and labored.

Muckrakers Lincoln Steffens, Ray Stannard Baker, and Ida Tarbell led the way in promoting reforms of all sorts. Steffens focused his investigative reporting on political corruption while Baker concentrated on railroad abuses. Ida Tarbell, whose father's small oil business was destroyed by John D. Rockefeller, spent years investigating and writing about the unethical and illegal means by which Rockefeller had built his gigantic Standard Oil Trust. At the end of her series of nineteen articles in *McClure's*, she asked readers: "And what are we going to do about it?" She stressed that it was "the people of the United States, and nobody else, [who] must cure whatever is wrong in the industrial situation."

Muckraking became the heart of progressivism. Without the muckrakers, progressivism would never have achieved widespread popular support. Investigative journalism became such a powerful force for change that one editor said that Americans were benefiting from "Government by Magazine."

Ida Tarbell An author, teacher, and pioneer of investigative journalism in the United States.

Religious Activism and Social Responsibility

Still another stream flowing into progressivism was religious activism directed at achieving social justice—the idea that society had an ethical obligation to help its poorest and most vulnerable members. A related ideal was the **social gospel**, the belief that religious institutions and individual Christians must help bring about the "Kingdom of God" on earth.

Rugged individualism may have been the path to wealth, they argued, but "Christian socialism" offered hope for unity among all classes. "Every religious and political question," said George Herron, a religion professor at Grinnell College, "is fundamentally economic." And the solution to economic tensions was social solidarity.

In many respects, in fact, the progressive movement formed a new phase of Christian spiritual revival, an energetic form of public outreach focused not so much on individual conversion and salvation as on social reform. "We believe," as the Religious Education Association explained, "that the age of sheer individualism is past, and the age of social responsibility has arrived."

THE SOCIAL GOSPEL During the last quarter of the nineteenth century, many churches and synagogues began emphasizing community service to address the needs of the unfortunate. New organizations made key contributions to the movement. The Young Men's Christian Association (YMCA) and a similar group for women, the YWCA, both entered the United States from England in the 1850s and grew rapidly after 1870. The Salvation Army, founded in London in 1878, came to the United States a year later.

The YMCA and YWCA combined religious evangelism with social services and fitness training in community centers, which were segregated by race and gender. Intended to provide low-cost housing and exercise in a "safe Christian environment" for young men and women from rural areas or foreign countries, the YMCA/YWCA centers often included libraries, classrooms, and kitchens. "Hebrew" counterparts—YMHAs and YWHAs—provided similar facilities in cities with large Jewish populations. Salvation Army centers offered soup kitchens to feed the poor and day nurseries for the children of working mothers.

The major forces behind the social gospel movement were Protestants and Catholics who charged that Christianity had become too closely associated with the upper and middle classes. In 1875, Washington Gladden, a pastor in Springfield, Massachusetts, published *Working People and Their Employers* (1876), which argued that true Christianity was based on the principle that "thou shalt love thy neighbor as thyself." Gladden rejected the view of social

Darwinists that the poor and disabled deserved their fate and should not be helped. He argued that helping the poor was an essential element of the Christian faith. To that end, he became the first prominent religious leader to support the rights of workers to form unions. He also condemned racial segregation and discrimination against immigrants.

Gladden's efforts helped launch a new era in which churches engaged with the problems created by a rapidly urbanizing and industrializing society. He and other social gospelers reached out to the working poor who lived in grossly substandard housing, lacked the legal right to form unions, and had no insurance for on-the-job accidents.

Walter Rauschenbusch, a German-born Baptist minister serving immigrant tenement dwellers in the Hell's Kitchen neighborhood of New York City, became the greatest champion of the social gospel. In 1907, he published *Christianity and the Social Crisis*, in which he argued that "whoever uncouples the religious and social life has not understood Jesus." The Christian emphasis on personal salvation, he added, must be linked with an equally passionate commitment to social justice. Churches must embrace "the social aims of Jesus," for Christianity was intended to be a "revolutionary" faith.

In Rauschenbusch's view, religious life needed the social gospel to revitalize it and make it socially relevant: "We shall never have a perfect social life, yet we must seek it with faith." His message resonated with Theodore Roosevelt, Woodrow Wilson, and many others. Years later, Rev. Martin Luther King Jr. said that *Christianity and the Social Crisis* "left an indelible imprint on my thinking."

SETTLEMENT HOUSES Among the most visible soldiers in the social gospel movement were those who volunteered in innovative community centers called settlement houses. Hull House was a dilapidated two-story redbrick mansion converted into a settlement house in a shabby immigrant Chicago neighborhood. Two college-educated women from privileged Illinois backgrounds, Jane Addams and Ellen Gates Starr, organized a progressive reform community there to address the needs of the unskilled working poor, especially newly arrived European immigrants. Some 50,000 working poor circulated through Hull House in its first year. By 1940, the annual number was 320,000.

Addams and Starr were driven by an "impulse to share the lives of the poor" and to make social service "express the spirit of Christ." Besides a nursery for the infant children of working mothers, Hull House also sponsored health clinics, lectures, music lessons and art studios, men's clubs, an employment bureau, job training, a gymnasium, a coffeehouse, a savings bank, and a public bath. Classes were offered in acting, weaving, carpentry, art history, phi-

Jane Addams By the end of the century, thanks to the efforts of Jane Addams and others, religious groups were joining the settlement house movement.

losophy, and music. All residents were treated as equals. By the early twentieth century, there were hundreds of settlement houses in cities across the United States, most of them in the Northeast and Midwest.

Addams and other settlement house leaders soon realized, however, that their work was like bailing out the ocean with a teaspoon. They thus added political reform to their agenda and began lobbying for city parks and playgrounds, neighborhood clean-up days, and laws and regulations to improve living conditions in poor neighborhoods.

Florence Kelley, a graduate of Cornell University and Northwestern University School of Law, served as a staff member at Hull House. As a researcher for the Illinois Bureau of Labor Statistics, she visited Chicago's tenements and sweatshops to document the exploitation of desperately poor women and children. Her pathbreaking book, *Hull-House Maps and Papers* (1895), contained her research results as well as essays by social scientists. The book supplemented tenement tours that Kelley organized for state legislators and inspired new city ordinances and workplace regulations.

As her influence grew in Chicago, Jane Addams served on governmental and community boards, focusing her radiant personality and powerful convictions on improving public health and food safety. She pushed for better street lighting and police protection in poor neighborhoods, and sought to reduce the misuse of narcotics. An ardent pacifist and outspoken advocate for *suffrage* (voting rights) for women, Addams would become the first American woman to win the Nobel Peace Prize.

THE WOMAN'S SUFFRAGE MOVEMENT

From 1880 to 1910, the number of employed women tripled from 2.6 million to 7.8 million. As college-educated women became more involved in the world of work and wages, the suffrage movement grew.

In 1869, Susan B. Anthony and Elizabeth Cady Stanton had founded the National Woman Suffrage Association (NWSA) in New York City to promote a **women's suffrage** amendment to the Constitution. They condemned both the Fourteenth and Fifteenth Amendments for limiting voting rights to men only. They also campaigned for new laws requiring higher pay for working women and making it easier for abused wives to get divorces.

Other suffrage activists insisted that pursuing multiple issues hurt their cause, however. In 1869, Julia Ward Howe and Lucy Stone formed the American Woman Suffrage Association (AWSA). Based in Boston, it focused solely on voting rights and included men among its leaders.

In 1890, the two groups united as the National American Woman Suffrage Association (NAWSA). That same year, the Wyoming Territory became a state—the first to give full voting rights to women. It was in the territories and states west of the Mississippi River that the suffrage movement had its earliest successes. In those areas, where Populism found its strongest support, women were more engaged in grassroots political activities than they were in

East meets West San Francisco suffragists calling for a constitutional amendment marched across the country in 1915 to deliver a petition with more than 500,000 signatures to Congress in Washington, D.C. Along the way, they were warmly received by other suffragists, like those of New Jersey, pictured here.

the East. In addition, the mostly male settlers in the western territories hoped that providing suffrage would encourage more women to settle in the region.

For these reasons and others, the West was the region most supportive of women's rights. Between 1890 and 1896, the suffrage cause won three more victories in western states—Utah, Colorado, and Idaho. In 1912, five more western states embraced women voters: Washington, California, Arizona, Kansas, and Oregon. Yet not until New York acted in 1917 did a state east of the Mississippi River allow women to vote in all elections.

Many advocates for women's suffrage argued that the right to vote and hold office was a matter of simple justice: women were just as capable as men of exercising the rights and responsibilities of citizenship. Others insisted that women were morally superior to men and would better promote the welfare of society as a whole. One activist explicitly linked women's suffrage with the social gospel, declaring that women followed the teachings of Christ more

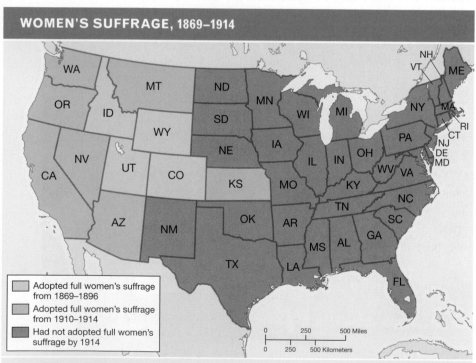

WOMEN'S SUFFRAGE, 1869–1914

Adopted full women's suffrage from 1869–1896

Adopted full women's suffrage from 1910–1914

Had not adopted full women's suffrage by 1914

- Which states first gave women the right to vote?
- Why did it take fifty-one years—from Wyoming's grant of full suffrage to women until ratification of the Nineteenth Amendment—for women to receive the right to vote in both state and national elections?
- How was suffrage part of a larger women's reform movement?

faithfully than men did. If they were elected to public office, they would "far more effectively guard the morals of society and the sanitary conditions of cities."

The women's suffrage movement was not free from social, ethnic, and racial prejudices. After the Civil War, suffragists had hoped that the Fifteenth Amendment, which guaranteed voting rights for African American men, would aid their own efforts to gain the vote. Some believed that they should be granted the vote before freedmen. The majority of men, however, still insisted that women stay out of politics because it would supposedly corrupt their moral purity.

At the end of the nineteenth century, suffragists lashed out at Congress for allowing illiterate immigrant men to vote but not well-educated women. Carrie Chapman Catt, who became president of the National American Woman Suffrage Association in 1900, warned of the danger that "lies in the votes possessed by the males in the slums of the cities, and the ignorant foreign [immigrant] vote." She added that the nation, with "ill-advised haste," had given "the foreigner, the Negro and the Indian" the vote but still withheld it from white women. Throughout the country, most suffrage organizations barred African American women from joining.

PROGRESSIVES' AIMS AND ACHIEVEMENTS

The progressive movement grew out of what Theodore Roosevelt called the public's "fierce discontent with evil" at the start of the twentieth century. Progressives focused on numerous social and political ills, from corrupt politicians to too-powerful corporations, from economic distress on small farms and in big cities to the general feeling that "the people" had lost control of the nation to the special interests—businesses and their leaders who were solely interested in "money-getting" at the expense of public welfare.

POLITICAL REFORMS

Progressivism set in motion the two most important political developments of the twentieth century: the rise of direct democracy and the expansion of federal government power. In his monthly articles in *McClure's* magazine, Lincoln Steffens, a leading muckraker, regularly asked: "Will the people rule? Is democracy possible?" Steffens and other progressives often stressed that the way to improve America's democracy was to make it even more democratic.

To empower citizens to clean up the political system, progressives pushed to make the political process more open and transparent. One proposal was the *direct primary*, which would allow all members of a political party to vote on the party's nominees, rather than the traditional practice in which an inner circle of party leaders chose the candidates, often behind closed doors. In 1896, South Carolina became the first state to adopt a statewide primary. Within twenty years, nearly every state had done so.

Progressives also developed other ways to increase public participation in the political process ("direct democracy") so as to curb the influence of corporate bosses on state legislatures. In 1898, South Dakota became the first state to adopt the *initiative* and *referendum*, procedures that allowed voters to create laws directly rather than having to wait for legislative action. Citizens could sign petitions to have a proposal put on the ballot (the initiative) and then vote it up or down (the referendum). Still another progressive innovation was the *recall*, whereby corrupt or incompetent elected officials could be removed by a public petition and vote. By 1920, nearly twenty states had adopted the initiative and referendum, and nearly a dozen had sanctioned the recall procedure.

Progressives also fought to change how U.S. senators were elected. Under the Constitution, state legislatures elected senators, a process frequently corrupted by lobbyists and vote buying. In 1900, for example, Senate investigators revealed that a Montana senator had given more than $100,000 in secret bribes to members of the legislature that chose him. In 1913, thanks to the efforts of progressives, the **Seventeenth Amendment**, providing for the direct election of senators, was ratified and became law.

THE EFFICIENCY MOVEMENT

A second major theme of progressivism was the "gospel of efficiency." The champion of progressive efficiency was Frederick Winslow Taylor, an industrial engineer who became a celebrated business consultant, helping factory owners implement "scientific management."

The nation's first "efficiency expert," Taylor showed employers how to cut waste and improve productivity. By breaking down work activities (filling a wheelbarrow, driving a nail, shoveling coal) into a sequence of mechanical steps and using stopwatches to measure the time it took each worker to perform each step, Taylor established detailed performance standards (and cash rewards) for each job classification, specifying how fast people should work and when they should rest. His book, *The Principles of Scientific Management* (1911), influenced business organizations for decades.

The goal of what came to be called **Taylorism** was to usher in a "mental revolution" in business management that would improve productivity and profits, raise pay for the most efficient workers, and reduce the likelihood of worker strikes. As Taylor wrote, "Men will not do an extraordinary day's work for an ordinary day's pay."

Many workers, however, resented Taylor's innovations, seeing them as just a tool to make people work faster at monotonous tasks. "We object to being reduced to a scientific formula," an Iowa machinist thundered. Yet Taylor's "scientific" approach to industrial management became one of the most important contributions to capitalist economies in the twentieth century and brought solid, measurable improvements in productivity.

Political progressives applied Taylorism to the operations of government by calling for the reorganization of state and federal agencies to eliminate duplication, to establish clear lines of authority, and to replace political appointees with trained specialists. By the early twentieth century, many complex functions of government had come to require specialists with technical expertise. As Woodrow Wilson wrote, progressive ideals could be achieved only if government agencies at all levels were "informed and administered by experts." Many cities set up "efficiency bureaus" to identify government waste and apply more cost-effective "best practices."

MUNICIPAL REFORM Two Taylorist ideas to reform city and county governments emerged in the first decade of the new century. One, the commission system, was first adopted in 1901 by the city of Galveston, Texas, after the local government collapsed following a devastating hurricane and tidal wave that killed more than 8,000 people—the largest natural disaster in American history. The commission system placed ultimate authority in a board composed of commissioners who combined both legislative and executive powers in heading up city departments (sanitation, police, utilities, and so on). By 1911, over sixty cities had adopted the commission system of government.

Even more popular was the city-manager plan, under which an appointed administrator ran a city or county government in accordance with policies set by the elected council and mayor. Staunton, Virginia, adopted the first city-manager plan in 1908.

Yet the efforts to make local governments more "businesslike" and professional had a downside. Shifting control from elected officials representing individual neighborhoods to at-large commissioners and nonpartisan specialists separated local government from party politics, which for many working-class voters had been their primary civic activity. In addition, running a city like a business led commissioners and managers to focus on reducing expenses rather than expanding services, even when such expansion was clearly needed.

THE WISCONSIN IDEA At the state level, the ideal of efficient government run by nonpartisan experts was pursued most notably by progressive Republican governor Robert M. La Follette of Wisconsin. "Fighting Bob" La Follette declared war on "vast corporate combinations" and political corruption by creating a nonpartisan state government that would become a "laboratory for democracy." He established a Legislative Reference Bureau, which provided elected officials with nonpartisan research, advice, and help in drafting legislation. La Follette used the bureau's reports to enact such reforms as the direct primary, stronger railroad regulation, the conservation of natural resources, and workmen's compensation programs to support people injured on the job. The "Wisconsin idea" was widely copied by other progressive governors.

REGULATION OF BUSINESS Of all the problems facing American society, one towered above all: how to regulate giant corporations. The threat of corporate monopolies increased during the depression of the 1890s as struggling companies were gobbled up by larger ones. Between 1895 and 1904, some 157 new holding companies gained control of 1,800 different businesses. Almost 50 of these giant holding companies controlled more than 70 percent of the market in their respective industries. In 1896, fewer than a dozen com-

Friends of the working class (Left to right) American labor leader Andrew Furuseth, Governor Robert M. La Follette, and muckraker Lincoln Steffens.

panies other than railroads were worth $10 million or more. By 1903, that number had soared to 300.

Concerns over the concentration of economic power in trusts and other forms of monopolies had led Congress to pass the Sherman Anti-Trust Act in 1890, but it proved ineffective. In addition, government agencies responsible for regulating businesses were often headed and staffed by men who had worked in the very industries they were appointed to regulate. Congress, for instance, named retired railroad executives to the Interstate Commerce Commission (ICC), which had been created to regulate railroads. The issue of regulating the regulators has never been fully resolved.

Social Justice

The progressive movement also set its sights on improving social justice for the working poor, the jobless, and the homeless. In addition to their work in settlement houses and other areas, many progressives formed advocacy organizations such as the National Consumers League, led by Florence Kelley, which promoted safer and less exploitative working conditions for women by educating consumers about harsh working conditions in factories and mills and the widespread use of child workers.

Other organizations, such as the General Federation of Women's Clubs, insisted that civic life needed female leadership. Women's clubs across the country sought to clean up slums by educating residents about personal and household hygiene (what women reformers called "municipal housekeeping"), urging construction of sewer systems, and launching public-awareness campaigns about the connection between unsanitary tenements and disease. Women's clubs also campaigned for child-care centers, kindergartens, government inspection of food processing plants, stricter housing codes, laws protecting women in the workplace, and more social services for the poor, sick, disabled, and abused. Still others addressed prostitution and alcohol abuse.

THE CAMPAIGN AGAINST DRINKING Middle-class women were the driving force behind efforts to stop the sale and consumption of alcoholic beverages. Founded in Cleveland, Ohio, in 1874, the Women's Christian Temperance Union (WCTU) became the largest women's group in the nation, boasting 300,000 members. While some members were motivated by Protestant beliefs that consuming alcohol was a sin, most saw excessive drinking, especially in saloons, as a threat to social progress and family stability.

By attacking drunkenness and closing saloons, temperance reformers hoped to (1) improve family life by preventing domestic violence, (2) reduce

Frances Willard Founder of the WCTU who lobbied for women's suffrage.

crime in the streets, and (3) remove one of the worst tools of corruption—free beer on Election Day, which was used to "buy" votes among the working class. As a Boston sociologist concluded, the saloon had become "the enemy of society because of the evil results produced upon the individual."

Initially, WCTU members met in churches to pray and then marched to saloons to try to convince their owners to close. They promoted *temperance*—the reduction of alcohol consumption. But they also urged individuals to embrace *abstinence* and refuse to drink any alcoholic beverages.

Under the leadership of Frances Willard, president of the WCTU between 1879 and 1898, the organization began promoting legislation to ban alcohol ("prohibition"). Willard also pushed the WCTU to lobby for an eight-hour workday, the regulation of child labor, government-funded kindergartens, the right to vote, and federal inspections of the food industry.

The battle against alcoholic beverages took on new strength in 1893 with the formation of the Anti-Saloon League, an organization based in churches that pioneered the strategy of the single-issue political pressure group. The bipartisan league, like the WCTU, initially focused on closing down saloons rather than abolishing alcohol. Eventually, however, it decided to force the prohibition issue into the forefront of state and local elections. At its "Jubilee Convention" in 1913, the league endorsed an amendment to the Constitution prohibiting the manufacture, sale, and consumption of alcoholic beverages, which Congress approved in 1917.

LABOR LEGISLATION In 1890, almost half of wage workers toiled up to twelve hours a day—sometimes seven days a week—in unsafe, unsanitary, and unregulated conditions for extremely low wages. Legislation to ensure better working conditions and limit child labor was perhaps the most significant reform to emerge from the drive for progressive social justice.

At the end of the nineteenth century, fewer than half of working families lived solely on the husband's earnings. Many married women engaged

Child labor Child workers shuck oysters in 1913 at the Varn & Platt Canning Company in Bluffton, South Carolina.

in "homework"—making clothes, selling flower arrangements, preparing food for others, and taking in boarders. Children of poor families frequently dropped out of school and went to work in factories, shops, mines, mills, and canneries, and on farms. In 1900, some 1.75 million children between the ages of ten and fifteen were working outside the home.

Many progressives argued that children, too, had rights. In southern textile mills, a third of the workers were children. In several southern states, children worked sixty-six hours a week. "I regard my employees," a manager said, "as I regard my machinery. So long as they can do my work for what I choose to pay them, I keep them, getting out of them all I can." The National Child Labor Committee campaigned for laws prohibiting the employment of children. Within ten years, most states had passed such laws, although some were lax in enforcing them.

Reformers also sought to regulate the length of the workday for women, in part because some working mothers were pregnant and others had children at home with inadequate supervision. Spearheaded by Florence Kelley,

National Consumers' League exhibit
To raise awareness about labor reform, everyday objects are displayed alongside descriptions of the poor working conditions and exploitation that went into their manufacture.

progressives convinced many state governments to ban the hiring of children below a certain age, and to limit the hours that women and children could work.

It took a tragedy, however, to spur meaningful government regulation of dangerous workplaces. On March 25, 1911, a fire broke out at the Triangle Shirtwaist factory (called a "sweatshop" because of its cramped, unventilated work areas) in New York City. Escape routes were limited because the owners kept the stairway door locked to prevent theft, and 146 workers trapped on the upper floors of the ten-story building died or leaped to their deaths. The victims were mostly young, foreign-born women in their teens, almost all Jewish, Italian, or Russian immigrants. In the fire's aftermath, dozens of city and state regulations dealing with fire hazards, dangerous working conditions, and child labor were enacted across the nation. After stalling for years, the owners of the Triangle Shirtwaist company finally paid $75 to the families of each employee who died.

The Supreme Court was inconsistent in its rulings on state labor laws. In *Lochner v. New York* (1905), the Court declared that a state law limiting bakers to a sixty-hour workweek was unconstitutional because it violated workers' rights to accept any job they wanted, no matter how bad the working conditions or how low the pay. Three years later, in *Muller v. Oregon* (1908), the Court changed its mind. Based on evidence that long working hours increased the chances of health problems, the Court approved an Oregon law restricting the workday to no more than ten hours for women.

THE "PROGRESSIVE" INCOME TAX   The cost of fighting the Civil War had led the federal government to institute the first income tax, but it was repealed in 1872. Thereafter, it relied on tariff revenues (45 percent) and taxes on liquor and tobacco (43 percent) to fund the government.

Progressives, however, believed that a "progressive" federal income tax—so called because the tax rates "progress," or rise, as income levels rise, thus forcing the rich to pay more—would close the gap between rich and poor. Such a graduated (or progressive) tax system was the climax of the movement's commitment to a more equitable distribution of wealth.

The progressive income tax was an old idea. In 1894, William Jennings Bryan had persuaded Congress to approve a 2 percent tax on corporations and individuals earning more than $4,000 a year (the approximate equivalent of $110,000 today). Soon after the tax became law, however, the Supreme Court, in *Pollock v. Farmers' Loan Company* (1895), declared it unconstitutional, claiming that only the states could levy income taxes.

Still, progressives continued to believe that a graduated income tax would help slow the concentration of wealth in the hands of the richest Americans. In 1907, President Theodore Roosevelt announced his support. Two years later, his successor, William Howard Taft, endorsed a constitutional amendment allowing such a tax, and Congress agreed. This taxation became law in 1913 with state ratification of the **Sixteenth Amendment**.

PROGRESSIVISM UNDER ROOSEVELT AND TAFT

Most progressive legislation originated at the state and local levels. Federal reform efforts began in earnest only when Theodore Roosevelt (TR) became president in 1901. "A great democracy," he said, "has got to be *progressive* or it will soon cease to be great or a democracy."

Unlike his predecessor, William McKinley, who was unwilling to confront business leaders, Theodore Roosevelt thrived on confrontation. One journalist described him as "impetuous, impatient, and wholly lacking in tact." TR was a force of nature, an American original blessed with a triumphant grin and an oversized intellect and ego. His contradictions were maddening, but his exuberance, charm, energy, and humor made up for them. Woodrow Wilson confessed after meeting Roosevelt, "You can't resist the man."

On his first day in the White House, Roosevelt announced that he intended to use the presidency as his "bully pulpit." He would educate Americans about the new realities facing their society at the beginning of the new century. He tackled his duties with self-described "strenuosity."

Rising before dawn each day, TR ran like a fever and frenzy over his daily schedule. He led cabinet members on skinny-dipping swims in the Potomac River; invited distinguished guests to wrestle or box with him, or to fight with wooden swords or climb trees; and organized pillow fights with his children in the White House. His outsized personality, said a friend, "so crowds the room that the walls are worn thin and threaten to burst outward."

Roosevelt loved power, for he was certain that he knew best how to lead the nation. Congress, he had decided, had grown too dominant and too corrupt. He therefore abandoned the Gilded Age tradition in which presidents had deferred to Congress. In his view, the problems caused by explosive industrial growth required substantial responses, and he was unwilling to wait for Congress to act. "I believe in a strong executive [president]," he asserted. "I believe in power." During his administration, the president, not Congress, became the primary source of policymaking.

Like his hero Abraham Lincoln, Roosevelt believed that great presidents must take "noble risks," even if it meant stretching the limits of the Constitution. People quickly noticed his expansive view of presidential powers. Joseph "Joe" Cannon, the Republican Speaker of the House, complained that Roosevelt had "no more use for the Constitution than a tomcat has for a marriage license."

TAMING BIG BUSINESS Roosevelt was the first president to use executive power to rein in Big Business. As governor of New York, he had pushed for legislation to regulate sweatshops, institute state inspections of factories and slaughterhouses, and limit the workday to eight hours. He believed in capitalism and the accumulation of wealth, but he was willing to adopt radical methods to ensure that the social unrest caused by the insensitivity of business owners to the rights of workers and the needs of the poor did not mushroom into a revolution.

TR applauded the growth of industrial capitalism but declared war on the "wealthy criminal class" and its corruption and cronyism, or the awarding of political appointments, government contracts, and other favors to politicians' personal friends. He endorsed a **Square Deal** for "every man, great or small, rich or poor." His Square Deal program featured the "Three Cs": greater government *control* of corporations, enhanced *conservation* of natural resources, and new regulations to protect *consumers* against contaminated food and medications.

CURBING THE TRUSTS In December 1901, just a few months after entering the White House, President Roosevelt declared that it was time to deal with the "grave evils" resulting from huge corporations exercising dominance over their industries and the nation's economic life. In his view, the federal government had the right and the obligation to curb the excesses of Big Business.

Roosevelt believed that governments must ensure fairness. To that end, he declared war against the robber barons who displayed "swinish indifference" to the public good and the "unscrupulous politicians" whose votes could be bought and sold by corporate lobbyists.

Early in 1902, the president shocked the business community when he ordered his attorney general to break up the Northern Securities Company. Organized by Wall Street titan J. Pierpont Morgan, this immense holding company comprised a vast network of railroads and steamships in the Pacific Northwest.

Morgan could not believe the news. He rushed to the White House and told the president, "If I have done anything wrong, send your man to my man and they can fix it up." Roosevelt retorted, "That can't be done." His attorney general, who also attended the meeting, told Morgan: "We don't want to 'fix it up.' We want to stop it." Morgan then asked Roosevelt if he planned to attack his other trusts, such as U.S. Steel and General Electric. "Certainly not," Roosevelt replied, "unless we find out that . . . they have done something wrong." After Morgan left, the president told the attorney general to file the anti-trust paperwork.

In 1904, the Supreme Court would rule in a 5–4 decision that the Northern Securities Company was indeed a monopoly and must be dismantled, thereby opening the way for more-aggressive enforcement of the Sherman Anti-Trust Act (1890). Roosevelt recognized the benefits of large-scale capitalism, and thought that the rise of Big Business was the inevitable result of the industrial era. He did not want to destroy the titans of industry and finance, but he insisted that they be regulated for the public good.

Altogether, Roosevelt approved about twenty-five anti-trust suits against oversized corporations. He also sought stronger regulation of railroads. By their very nature, railroads often exercised a monopoly over the communities they served, enabling them to gouge customers. In 1903, the Elkins Act made it illegal for railroads to give secret rebates (cash refunds) on freight charges to high-volume business customers. That same year, Congress approved Roosevelt's

Square Deal This 1906 cartoon likens Roosevelt to the Greek legend Hercules, who as a baby strangled snakes sent from hell to kill him. Here, the serpents are pro-corporation senator Nelson Aldrich and Standard Oil's John D. Rockefeller.

request that a federal Department of Commerce and Labor be formed, within which a Bureau of Corporations would monitor big businesses.

THE 1902 COAL STRIKE On May 12, 1902, more than 100,000 members of the United Mine Workers (UMW) labor union walked off the job in Pennsylvania and West Virginia. The overworked and underpaid miners were seeking a wage increase and a shorter workday. The union also sought official recognition by the mine owners, who refused to negotiate and instead chose to shut down the coal mines. The miners, mostly immigrants from southern and eastern Europe, were in a bind. One owner expressed the ethnic prejudices shared by many of his colleagues when he proclaimed, "The miners don't suffer—why, they can't even speak English."

By October, the lengthy shutdown had caused the price of coal to soar, and hospitals and schools reported empty coal bins as winter approached. In many northern cities, poor households had run out of coal. "The country is on the verge of a vast public calamity," warned Walter Rauschenbusch. The Reverend Washington Gladden led a petition drive urging Roosevelt to mediate the strike.

The president invited leaders of both sides to a conference in Washington, D.C., where he appealed to their "patriotism, to the spirit that sinks personal considerations and makes individual sacrifices for the public good." The mine owners, however, refused to speak to the UMW leaders.

Roosevelt was so infuriated by what he called the "extraordinary stupidity" of the "wooden-headed" and "arrogant" owners that he wanted to grab their spokesman "by the seat of his breeches" and "chuck him out" a window. Instead, he threatened to declare a national emergency so that he could take control of the mines and use soldiers to run them. When a congressman questioned the constitutionality of such a move, Roosevelt roared, "To hell with the Constitution when the people want coal!"

The president's threat worked; the strike ended on October 23. The miners won a nine-hour workday and a 10 percent wage increase. Roosevelt was the first president to use his authority to referee a dispute between management and labor—believing that both sides deserved a fair hearing. His predecessors had responded to strikes by sending federal troops to shoot union activists.

ROOSEVELT'S REELECTION

Theodore Roosevelt's forceful leadership won him friends and enemies. As he prepared to run for reelection in 1904, he acknowledged that the "whole Wall Street crowd" would do all they could to defeat him. Nevertheless, he won the Republican nomination.

Roosevelt's duality Theodore Roosevelt depicted as an "apostle of prosperity" (top) and as a Roman tyrant (bottom). Roosevelt's energy, self-righteousness, and impulsiveness elicited conflicting reactions.

The Democrats, having lost twice with William Jennings Bryan, essentially gave the election to Roosevelt and the Republicans by nominating the virtually unknown Alton B. Parker, chief justice of the New York Supreme Court. Parker was the dullest—and most forgettable—presidential candidate in history. One journalist dubbed him "the enigma from New York." The most interesting item in Parker's campaign biography was that he had trained his pigs to come when called by name.

The Democrats suffered their worst election defeat in thirty-two years. After winning the electoral vote 336 to 140, Roosevelt told his son it was his "greatest triumph." Having succeeded to the presidency after William McKinley's assassination, he had now won election on his own and, in his view, had a mandate to do great things. On the eve of his inauguration in March 1905, he announced: "Tomorrow I shall come into office in my own right. Then watch out for me!"

PROGRESSIVE REGULATION Theodore Roosevelt launched his second term with an even stronger commitment to regulating corporations and their corrupt owners who exploited workers and tried to eliminate competition. His comments irked many of his corporate contributors and congressional Republican leaders. Said Pittsburgh steel baron Henry Frick, "We bought the son of a bitch, and then he did not stay bought."

To promote the "moral regeneration of business," Roosevelt first took aim at the railroads. In 1906, he persuaded Congress to pass the Hepburn Act, which gave the federal Interstate Commerce Commission the power to set maximum freight rates for the railroad industry.

Under Roosevelt's Square Deal programs, the federal government also assumed oversight of key industries affecting public health: meat-packers, food processors, and makers of drugs and patent medicines. Muckraking journalists had revealed all sorts of unsanitary and dangerous activities in the preparation of food and drug products. Perhaps the most powerful blow against these abuses was struck by Upton Sinclair's novel *The Jungle* (1906), which told the story of a Lithuanian immigrant working in a filthy Chicago meatpacking plant:

> It was too dark in these storage places to see well, but a man could run his hand over these piles of meat and sweep off handfuls of the dried dung of rats. These rats were nuisances, and the packers would put poisoned bread out for them, they would die, and then rats, bread, and meat would go into the hoppers [to be ground up] together.

After reading *The Jungle*, Roosevelt urged Congress to pass the Meat Inspection Act of 1906. It required the Department of Agriculture to inspect every

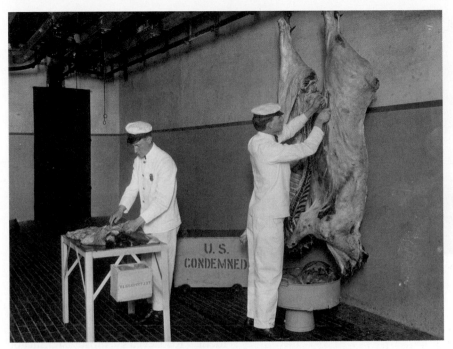

Bad meat Government inspectors examine sides of beef at a meatpacking plant.

hog and steer whose carcass crossed state lines. The Pure Food and Drug Act (1906), enacted the same day, required the makers of prepared food and medicines to host government inspectors—and label the ingredients in their products.

ENVIRONMENTAL CONSERVATION Theodore Roosevelt was passionately committed to environmental conservation. An avid outdoorsman, hunter, and naturalist, he championed efforts to protect wilderness areas and manage the nation's natural resources. He created fifty federal wildlife refuges, approved five new national parks and fifty-one federal bird sanctuaries, and designated eighteen national monuments, including the Grand Canyon.

In 1898, Roosevelt had endorsed the appointment of his friend Gifford Pinchot, the nation's first professionally trained forest manager, as head of the Department of Agriculture's Division of Forestry. Pinchot, like Roosevelt, believed in economic growth as well as environmental preservation. Pinchot said that the conservation movement promoted the "greatest good for the greatest number for the longest time."

Yosemite Valley A couple playfully poses atop Glacier Point Rock in Yosemite National Park in 1902.

Roosevelt and Pinchot used the Forest Reserve Act (1891) to protect 172 million acres of federally owned forests from loggers. The owners of lumber companies were furious, but the president held firm, declaring, "I hate a man who skins the land."

Overall, Roosevelt set aside more than 234 million acres of federal land for conservation purposes and created forty-five national forests in eleven western states. As Pinchot recalled, "Launching the conservation movement was the most significant achievement of the TR Administration, as he himself believed."

ROOSEVELT AND RACE President Roosevelt's most significant domestic policy failures were his refusal to endorse women's suffrage and to confront racism. Like Populists, progressives worked to empower "the people." For many of them, however, "the people" did not include African Americans, Native Americans, or some immigrant groups. Most white progressives ignored or even endorsed the passage of Jim Crow laws in the South that prevented blacks from voting and subjected them to rigid racial separation.

Hundreds of African Americans were being lynched each year across the South, where virtually no blacks were allowed to serve on juries or work in law enforcement. A white candidate for governor in Mississippi in 1903 announced that he believed "in the divine right of the white man to rule, to do all the voting, and to hold all the offices, both state and federal." The South, wrote W. E. B. Du Bois, then a young black sociologist at Atlanta University, "is simply an armed camp for intimidating black folk."

At the same time, few progressives questioned the many informal and private patterns of segregation and prejudice in the North and West. "The plain fact is," journalist Ray Stannard Baker admitted in 1909, "most of us in the North do not believe in any real democracy between white and colored men." Roosevelt once confided to a friend that African Americans "are altogether inferior to whites."

Theodore Roosevelt and Booker T. Washington Roosevelt addresses the National Negro Business League in 1900 with Washington seated to his left.

Yet he had made a few exceptions. On October 16, 1901, Roosevelt took the unprecedented step of inviting Booker T. Washington, the nation's most prominent black leader, to the White House for dinner. White southerners exploded with fury. The *Memphis Scimitar* screamed that inviting a "nigger" to dine in the White House was "the most damnable outrage that has ever been perpetrated by a citizen of the United States." South Carolina senator Benjamin R. Tillman threatened that "a thousand niggers in the South will have to be killed to teach them 'their place' again."

Roosevelt gave in to the criticism. Never again would he host a black leader. During a tour of the South in 1905, he pandered to whites by highlighting his own southern ancestry (his mother was from Georgia) and expressing his admiration for the Confederacy and Robert E. Lee. His behavior, said an African American leader, was "national treachery to the Negro."

THE BROWNSVILLE RIOT In 1906, a violent racial incident occurred in Brownsville, Texas, where a dozen or so members of an African American army regiment shot several whites who had been harassing them outside a saloon. One white bartender was killed, and a police officer was seriously wounded. An investigation concluded that the soldiers were at fault, but no one could identify the shooters and none of the soldiers was willing to talk.

Roosevelt responded by dishonorably discharging the entire regiment of 167 soldiers, several of whom had been awarded the Congressional Medal of Honor for their service in Cuba during the War of 1898. Critics flooded the White House with angry telegrams. Secretary of War William H. Taft urged the president to reconsider, but Roosevelt refused to show any mercy to "murderers, assassins, cowards, and comrades of murderers." (Sixty years later, the U.S. Army "cleared the records" of the black soldiers.)

TAFT AND RETRENCHMENT

After his 1904 election victory, Theodore Roosevelt had said he would not run for president again, in part because he did not want to be the first president to serve the equivalent of three terms. "No president has ever enjoyed himself as much as I enjoyed myself," he reflected. "I have used every ounce of power there was in the office, and I have not cared a rap for the criticisms of those who spoke of my 'usurpation of power.'" The strength of the United States depended upon having a "strong central executive," he declared. For now, he was ready to leave the White House and go hunting for big game in Africa.

Unlike most retiring presidents, however, Roosevelt would leave with regret, for he was loved by his party, who gave him a roaring ovation at the 1908 Republican nominating convention. When the cheers subsided, he urged the delegates to nominate his long-time friend, Secretary of War William Howard Taft, which they did on the first ballot.

The Democrats again chose William Jennings Bryan, who still retained a faithful following. Taft promised to continue Roosevelt's policies, and the Republican platform endorsed the president's progressive program. The Democratic platform echoed the Republican emphasis on regulation of business but called for a lower tariff. Bryan struggled to attract national support and was defeated for a third time, as Taft swept the electoral college, 321 to 162.

A LIFE OF PUBLIC SERVICE On paper, William Howard Taft was superbly qualified to be president. Born in Cincinnati in 1857, the son of a prominent attorney who had served in President Grant's cabinet, Taft had graduated second in his class at Yale University and become a leading legal scholar, serving on the Ohio Supreme Court. In 1900, President McKinley appointed him the first American governor-general of the Philippines, and three years later Theodore Roosevelt named him secretary of war. Taft supervised the construction of the Panama Canal and organized the relief effort after the San Francisco earthquake of 1906.

Until becoming president, Taft had never held elected office, nor was he ever sure he wanted to be chief executive. His preference was to be a justice on the U.S. Supreme Court. Running for president, he once confessed, was "a nightmare," for politics "makes me sick."

Unlike the robust, athletic Roosevelt, Taft struggled most of his life with obesity, topping out at 332 pounds. A special bathtub had to be installed in the White House to accommodate him. While serving as governor-general of the Philippines, he had cabled Secretary of War Elihu Root from Manila: "Took long horseback ride today, feeling fine." Root cabled back: "How is the horse?"

William Howard Taft Speaking at Manassas, Virginia, in 1911.

Theodore Roosevelt, Taft explained, "loves the woods, he loves hunting; he loves roughing it, and I don't." His primary sin, he confessed, was laziness. He often fell asleep at cabinet meetings, White House banquets, and public events. Although good-natured and easygoing, Taft as president never managed to escape the shadow of his charismatic predecessor. "When I hear someone say 'Mr. President,'" he confessed, "I look around expecting to see Roosevelt."

Taft was a cautious, conservative progressive who embraced "strict construction" of the Constitution, which meant that he believed the founders had intentionally limited the powers of each of the three government branches—executive, legislative, and judicial. Unlike Roosevelt, who insisted that the president could take any action not explicitly prohibited by the Constitution, Taft argued that the president's authority should be limited to what the Constitution specified and that the president should have no role in the development of legislation, which was solely the responsibility of Congress.

Taft explained that his focus was to "complete" the programs and policies Roosevelt had initiated. He vowed to preserve capitalism by protecting "the right of private property" and the "right of liberty." In practice, this meant that he was even more determined than Roosevelt to support "the spirit of commercial freedom" against monopolistic trusts, but he was not interested in pushing for additional reforms or exercising extraordinary presidential power.

Taft viewed himself as a judge-like administrator, not an innovator. (After leaving the White House, he got the job he had always wanted: chief justice of the U.S. Supreme Court.) He was neither as energetic nor as wide-ranging as Roosevelt in his role as a reformer president—a difference that would lead to a fateful break between the two men.

TAFT AND THE TARIFF President Taft displayed his credentials as a progressive Republican by supporting *lower* tariffs on imports; he even called a special session of Congress to address the matter. But he proved less skillful than Roosevelt in dealing with Congress. Taft also discontinued Roosevelt's practice of using interviews with journalists to influence congressmen by wielding his "big stick through the press."

In the end, Taft's failure of leadership allowed Congress to pass the flawed Payne-Aldrich Tariff (1909), which did little to change federal policies. Taft's failure to gain real reform and his lack of a "crusading spirit" angered progressive, pro-Roosevelt Republicans, whom Taft called "assistant Democrats." He gravitated to the "Old Guard" Republican conservatives.

Roosevelt was not happy; nor were other Republican progressives. William Allen White, a prominent newspaper editor in Kansas, concluded that Taft, a "genial, chuckling, courteous, kindly gentleman," was at heart "a deep-dyed political and economic conservative, and bull-headed at that."

THE BALLINGER–PINCHOT CONTROVERSY In 1910, the split between the conservative and progressive Republican factions was widened into a chasm by the Ballinger-Pinchot controversy. President Taft's secretary of the interior, Richard A. Ballinger, opened to commercial development millions of acres of federal lands that Roosevelt had ordered protected. Chief of forestry Gifford Pinchot complained about the "giveaway," but Taft refused to intervene, calling Pinchot a "radical and a crank." When Pinchot made his opposition public early in 1910, the president fired him. In doing so, Taft ignited a feud with Roosevelt that would eventually end their friendship—and cost him reelection.

THE TAFT–ROOSEVELT FEUD In 1909, soon after Taft became president, Roosevelt and his son Kermit had sailed to Africa, where they would spend nearly a year hunting big-game animals. (When business tycoon J. Pierpont Morgan heard about the extended safari, he expressed the hope that "every lion would do its duty" by eliminating Roosevelt). Roosevelt had left the White House assuming that Taft would continue to promote a progressive agenda. But by filling the cabinet with corporate lawyers and firing Gifford Pinchot, Taft had, in Roosevelt's view, failed to "carry out my work unbroken."

Roosevelt's rebuke of Taft was in some ways undeserved. Taft had at least attempted tariff reform, which Roosevelt had never dared. Although Taft had fired Pinchot, he had replaced him with another conservationist. Taft's administration actually preserved more federal land in four years than Roosevelt's had in nearly eight, and it filed twice as many anti-trust suits, including one that led to the breakup of the Standard Oil Company in 1911. Taft also supported giving women the right to vote and workers the right to join unions.

None of that satisfied Roosevelt, however. On August 31, 1910, the former president, eager to return to the political spotlight, gave a speech at Osawatomie, Kansas, in which he announced his latest progressive proposals—his "New Nationalism." Roosevelt explained that he wanted to go beyond ensuring a Square Deal in which corporations were forced to "play by the rules"; he now promised to "change the rules" to force large corporations to promote social welfare and serve the needs of working people.

To save capitalism from the threat of a working-class revolution, Roosevelt called for tighter federal regulation of "arrogant" corporations that too often tried to "control and corrupt" politics; for a federal income tax (the Sixteenth Amendment had still not become law); and for federal laws regulating child labor. "What I have advocated," he explained, "is not wild radicalism. It is the highest and wisest kind of conservatism."

Political giants A cartoon showing Roosevelt charging through the air at Taft, who is seated on a mountaintop.

Then, on February 24, 1912, Roosevelt announced that he would challenge Taft for the Republican presidential nomination. He dismissed the "second-rate" Taft as a "hopeless fathead" and "flubdub" who had "sold the Square Deal down the river." Taft responded by calling Roosevelt a "dangerous egotist" and a "demagogue." Thus began a bitter war in which Roosevelt had the better weapons, not the least of which was his love of a good fight.

By 1912, a dozen or so states were letting citizens vote for presidential candidates in party primaries instead of following the traditional practice in which party leaders chose the nominee behind closed doors. Roosevelt decided that if he won big in the Republican primaries, he could claim to be "the people's choice." Yet even though he won all but two primaries, including the one in Taft's home state of Ohio, his popularity was no match for Taft's authority as party leader. In the thirty-six states that chose candidates by conventions dominated by party bosses, the Taft Republicans prevailed. At the Republican National Convention, Taft won easily.

Sideshow Ted This 1912 cartoon criticizes the Bull Moose party for being just a sideshow (with suffragists selling lemonade outside) and points out the menacing ego of Roosevelt himself.

Roosevelt was furious. He denounced Taft and his supporters as thieves and stormed out of the convention along with his delegates—mostly social workers, teachers, professors, journalists, and urban reformers, along with a few wealthy business executives.

THE PROGRESSIVE PARTY Six weeks later, Theodore Roosevelt urged his supporters to reconvene in Chicago to create the **Progressive party**. There they enthusiastically nominated him as their candidate. He assured the delegates that he felt "fit as a bull moose," leading journalists to nickname the new party the "Bull Moose party."

Progressives adored Roosevelt because he showed what a government dedicated to the public good might achieve. When Roosevelt closed his acceptance speech by saying, "We stand at Armageddon [the climactic encounter between Christ and Satan], and we battle for the Lord," the delegates stood and began singing the hymn, "Onward, Christian Soldiers." One reporter wrote that the "Bull Moose" movement was not so much a party as it was a political crusade, and Roosevelt was its leading evangelist.

The Progressive party platform, audacious for its time, revealed Roosevelt's growing liberalism. It supported a minimum "living wage" for hourly workers; an eight-hour workday; women's suffrage and "an equal voice with women in every phase of party management"; campaign finance reform; and a system of "social security" insurance to protect people against sickness, unemployment, and disabilities. It also pledged to end the boss system governing state and local politics and destroy the "unholy alliance between corrupt business and corrupt politics." Conservative critics called Roosevelt a socialist, a revolutionist, and a "monumental egotist."

Roosevelt charged that President Taft was not a progressive because he had tried to undo land conservation efforts and had failed to fight for social justice or against the special interests. Instead, Roosevelt said that Taft had aligned himself with the privileged political and business leaders who steadfastly opposed "the cause of justice for the helpless and the wronged."

WOODROW WILSON: A PROGRESSIVE SOUTHERNER

The fight between William Howard Taft and Theodore Roosevelt gave hope to the Democrats, whose presidential nominee, New Jersey governor Woodrow Wilson, had enjoyed remarkable success in his brief political career. Until his nomination and election as governor in 1910, Wilson had been a college professor and then president of Princeton University, where he had become a popular speaker promoting progressive political reforms and government regulation of corporations.

Wilson had never run for political office or worked in business. He was a man of books and ideas, with a keen intellect and "a first class mind" bolstered by an analytical temperament, a tireless work ethic, an inspiring speaking style, and a strong conviction that he knew what was best for the nation.

TO SERVE HUMANITY Born in Staunton, Virginia, in 1856, the son, grandson, nephew, and son-in-law of Presbyterian ministers, Thomas Woodrow Wilson had grown up in Georgia and the Carolinas during the Civil War and Reconstruction. The South, he once said, was the only part of the nation

Woodrow Wilson The first president to hold a doctoral degree.

where nothing had to be explained to him. Tall and slender, with a long, chiseled face, he developed an unquestioning religious faith. Convinced that God had selected him to serve humanity, he often displayed an unbending self-righteousness that would prove to be his undoing as president. As Ray Stannard Baker observed, Woodrow Wilson was "a lonely man, outwardly cold and remote, inwardly molten passion, and an unparalleled tenacity of faith, an unequaled constancy of courage."

Wilson graduated from Princeton in 1879. After law school at the University of Virginia, he briefly worked as an attorney before enrolling at Johns Hopkins University to study history and political science. He earned one of the nation's first doctoral degrees, became an expert in constitutional government, and served as a popular professor at several colleges before becoming president of Princeton in 1902.

Eight years later, Wilson accepted the support of New Jersey Democrats for the gubernatorial nomination. He harbored higher ambitions, however. If he could become governor, he said, "I stand a very good chance of being the next President of the United States." Like Roosevelt, Wilson was intensely ambitious and idealistic; he felt destined to preside over America's emergence as the greatest world power.

After winning the governorship by a landslide, Wilson persuaded the state legislature to adopt an array of progressive reforms to curb the power of party bosses and corporate lobbyists. "After dealing with college politicians," he joked, "I find that the men who I am dealing with now seem like amateurs."

Wilson soon attracted national attention. At the 1912 Democratic convention, he faced stiff competition from several veteran party leaders for the presidential nomination. With the support of William Jennings Bryan, however, he won on the forty-sixth ballot.

THE 1912 ELECTION The 1912 presidential campaign was one of the most exciting in history. It involved four strong candidates: Democrat

Woodrow Wilson, Republican William Howard Taft, Socialist Eugene V. Debs, and Progressive Theodore Roosevelt. For all their differences, the candidates shared a basic progressive assumption that modern social problems could be resolved only through active governmental intervention.

No sooner did the formal campaign open than Roosevelt's candidacy almost ended. While on his way to deliver a speech in Milwaukee, Wisconsin, he was shot by John Schrank, a deranged man who believed that any president seeking a third term should be killed. The bullet went through Roosevelt's overcoat, a steel eyeglasses case, and fifty-page speech, then fractured a rib before nestling just below his right lung, an inch from his heart.

THE ELECTION OF 1912

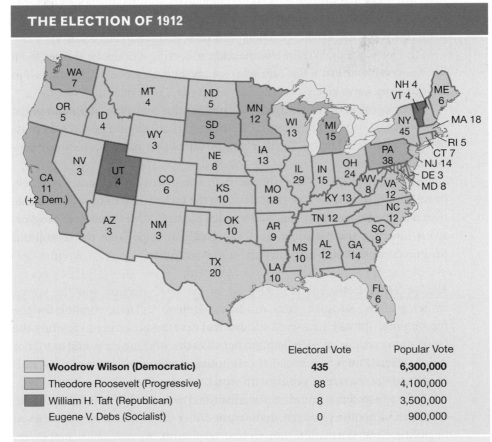

	Electoral Vote	Popular Vote
Woodrow Wilson (Democratic)	**435**	**6,300,000**
Theodore Roosevelt (Progressive)	88	4,100,000
William H. Taft (Republican)	8	3,500,000
Eugene V. Debs (Socialist)	0	900,000

- Why was Taft so unpopular?
- How did the split between Roosevelt and Taft give Wilson the presidency?
- Why was Wilson's victory in 1912 especially significant?

Refusing medical attention, Roosevelt insisted on delivering his eighty-minute speech to 10,000 supporters. In a dramatic gesture, he showed the audience his bloodstained shirt and punctured text, explaining that "the bullet is in me now, so I cannot make a very long speech." Then, grinning, he vowed, "It takes more than this to kill a bull moose." When he finished, he went directly to a hospital.

As the campaign developed, Taft quickly lost ground and essentially gave up. "There are so many people in the country who don't like me," he lamented. The contest settled into a debate over Roosevelt's New Nationalism and Wilson's **New Freedom**. The New Freedom, designed by Louis Brandeis, favored small government and states' rights, arguing that federal intervention should be a last resort. It aimed to restore economic competition by eliminating *all* trusts rather than just those that misbehaved. Where Roosevelt admired the power and efficiency of law-abiding corporations, no matter how large, Brandeis and Wilson were convinced that huge, "heartless" industries needed to be broken up.

On Election Day, Wilson won handily, collecting 435 electoral votes to 88 for Roosevelt and just 8 for Taft, who said he had only one consolation: "No candidate was ever elected ex-President by such a large majority."

After learning of his election, Wilson told the chairman of his campaign committee, "I owe you nothing. God ordained that I should be the next president of the United States. Neither you nor any other mortal could have prevented that."

Had the Republicans not divided their votes between Taft and Roosevelt, however, Wilson would have lost. His was the victory of a minority candidate over a divided opposition. Since all four candidates called themselves progressives, however, the president-elect expressed his hope "that the thoughtful progressive forces of the nation may now at last unite."

EUGENE DEBS The real surprise of the 1912 election was the strong showing of the Socialist party candidate, Eugene V. Debs, running for the fourth time. The tall, blue-eyed idealist had devoted his career to fighting the "monstrous system of capitalism" on behalf of the working class, first as a labor union official, then as a socialist promoting government ownership of railroads and the sharing of profits with workers.

Debs promoted a brand of socialism that was flexible rather than rigid, Christian rather than Marxist, democratic rather than totalitarian. He believed in political transformation, not violent revolution. As one of his supporters said, "That old man with the burning eyes actually believes that there can be such a thing as the brotherhood of man. And that's not the funniest part of it. As long as he's around I believe it myself."

Debs became the symbol of a diverse movement that united West Virginia coal miners, Oklahoma sharecroppers, Pacific Northwest lumberjacks, and immigrant workers in New York City sweatshops. One newspaper described "The Rising Tide of Socialism" in 1912, as some 1,150 Socialists won election to local and state offices across the nation, including eighteen mayoral seats.

To many voters, the Socialist party, whose 118,000 dues-paying members in 1912 were double the number from the year before, offered the only real alternative to a stalemated political system in which the two major parties had few real differences. A business executive in New York City explained that he had become a Socialist "because the old parties [Democrats and Republicans] were flimflamming us all the time."

Fear of socialism was also widespread, however. Theodore Roosevelt warned that the rapid growth of the Socialist party was "far more ominous than any Populist or similar movement in the past."

In 1912, Debs crisscrossed the nation giving fiery speeches. He dismissed Roosevelt as "a charlatan, mountebank [swindler], and fraud" whose progressive promises were nothing more than "the mouthings of a low and utterly unprincipled self-seeker and demagogue." Debs won more than 900,000 votes, twice as many as he had received four years earlier.

A BURST OF REFORM BILLS

On March 4, 1913, a huge crowd surrounded the Capitol in Washington, D.C., to watch Woodrow Wilson's inauguration. At the White House, President Taft told his successor, "I'm glad to be going—this is the lonesomest place in the world."

In his speech, the new president declared that it was not "a day of triumph" but "a day of dedication." Blessed with Democratic majorities in the House and Senate, Wilson promised to lower "the stiff and stupid" Republican tariff, create a new national banking system, strengthen anti-trust laws, and establish an administration "more concerned about human rights than about property rights."

Wilson worried about being compared to Roosevelt: "He appeals to their imagination; I do not. He is a real, vivid person. . . . I am a vague, conjectural [philosophical] personality, more made up of opinions and academic prepossessions than of human traits and red corpuscles."

Roosevelt had been a strong president by force of personality; Wilson became a strong president by force of conviction. "I have a strong instinct for leadership," he stressed, and he sincerely believed he was being directed by

God. (A Maryland congressman told a bartender that Wilson "gives me the creeps," for I don't "know whether God or him was talking.").

Despite their differences, Wilson and Roosevelt, the two progressive presidents, shared a belief that national problems demanded national solutions. Together they set in motion the modern presidency, expanding the scope of the executive branch at the expense of Congress.

Like Roosevelt, Wilson was an activist president: He was the first to speak to the nation over the radio and to host weekly press conferences. A brilliant, intense man, the first president with a doctoral degree, Wilson was a spellbinding speaker with a fervent sense of destiny.

As a political scientist, Wilson was an expert at the processes of government. During his first two years, he pushed through Congress more new bills than any previous president. Like "most reformers," however, Wilson "had a fierce and unlovely side," according to the president of Harvard University. The new president found it hard to understand—much less work with—people who disagreed with him.

His victory, coupled with majorities in the House and Senate, gave Democrats effective national power for the first time since the Civil War—and also gave southerners a significant national role for the first time since the war. Five of Wilson's ten cabinet members were born in the South.

COLONEL HOUSE Woodrow Wilson's closest adviser was "Colonel" Edward M. House of Texas, who held no official government position but was the president's constant companion, a "small, frail, courteous bright-eyed man with a gentle voice and winning manners." House was one of the most skilled political operators in history, working mostly behind the scenes to excite and mobilize others. He and Wilson developed the most famous political partnership of the twentieth century. The president described House as "my second personality. He is my independent self. His thoughts and mine are one." Wilson told House that he thanked "God every day that I have so generous" a friend and adviser.

House helped steer Wilson's proposals through a Congress in which southerners, by virtue of their seniority, held the lion's share of committee chairmanships. As a result, much of the progressive legislation of the Wilson era would bear the names of southern Democrats.

THE TARIFF AND THE INCOME TAX Like Taft, Wilson pursued tariff reform, but with greater success. By 1913, the federal tariff included hundreds of taxes on different imported goods, from oil to nails. The president believed that U.S. corporations were misusing the tariff to keep out foreign competitors and to create monopolies that held consumer prices artificially high.

To lower tariff rates and thereby lower consumer prices, Wilson summoned Congress for what came to be the longest special session in history. Over that eighteen months, Wilson addressed Congress in person—the first president to do so since John Adams.

The new tariff bill passed the House easily. The crunch came in the Senate, where swarms of lobbyists grew so thick, Wilson said, "a brick couldn't be thrown without hitting one of them." By publicly criticizing the "industrious and insidious" tariff lobby, Wilson finally convinced Congress to support his approach.

The Underwood-Simmons Tariff Act (1913) lowered tariff rates on almost 1,000 imported products. To compensate for the reduced tariff revenue, the bill created the first income tax allowed under the newly ratified Sixteenth Amendment: the initial tax rates were 1 percent on income more than $3,000 ($4,000 for married couples) up to a top rate of 7 percent on annual income of $500,000 or more. Most workers paid no income tax because they earned less than $3,000 a year.

THE FEDERAL RESERVE ACT No sooner did the new tariff pass than the administration proposed the first major banking reform since the Civil War. Ever since Andrew Jackson had killed the Second Bank of the United States in the 1830s, the nation had been without a central bank. Instead, the money supply was chaotically "managed" by thousands of local and state banks.

Such a decentralized system was unstable and inefficient. During financial panics, fearful depositors eager to withdraw their money would create "runs" that often led to the failure of smaller banks because they would run out of cash. The primary reason for a new central bank was to prevent such panics, which had occurred five times since 1873. President Wilson believed the banking system needed a central reserve agency that, in a crisis, could distribute emergency cash to stressed banks. Any new system, however, must be overseen by the government rather than by bankers themselves (the "money power"). He wanted a central bank that would benefit the entire economy, not just the large banks headquartered on Wall Street in New York City.

After much dickering, Congress passed the **Federal Reserve Act** on December 23, 1913. It created a national banking system with twelve regional districts, each of which had its own Federal Reserve Bank owned by member banks in the district. All nationally chartered banks had to be members of the Federal Reserve System. State-chartered banks—essentially unregulated— did not (and, indeed, two thirds of the nation's banks chose not to become members of the Federal Reserve System). The twelve regional Federal Reserve banks were supervised by a central board of directors in Washington, D.C.

The overarching purpose of the Federal Reserve System was to adjust the nation's currency supply to promote economic growth and ensure the stability and integrity of member banks. When banks ran short of cash, they could borrow from the Federal Reserve. Each of the new regional banks issued Federal Reserve notes (currency) to member banks in exchange for their loans. By doing so, "the Fed," as the system came to be called, promoted economic growth and helped preserve the stability of banks during panics. The Federal Reserve board required member banks to have a certain percentage of their total deposits in cash on hand ("reserve") at all times.

One conservative Republican called the Federal Reserve Act "populistic, socialistic, half-baked, destructive, and unworkable." The system soon proved its worth, however, and the criticism eased. The Federal Reserve Act was the most significant new program of Wilson's presidency.

ANTI-TRUST ACTIONS Woodrow Wilson made "trust-busting" the focus of his New Freedom program. Giant corporations had continued to grow despite the Sherman Anti-Trust Act (1890) and the Bureau of Corporations, the federal watchdog agency created by Theodore Roosevelt.

The **Clayton Anti-Trust Act** of 1914 exempted labor unions from anti-trust laws and revived the Populists' demand that companies, such as railroads, be prohibited from charging different prices to different customers. It also banned corporate directors from serving on the boards of competing companies.

Wilson decided to make a strong **Federal Trade Commission (FTC)** the cornerstone of his anti-trust program. Created in 1914, the five-member FTC replaced Theodore Roosevelt's Bureau of Corporations and assumed powers to define "unfair trade practices" and issue "cease and desist" orders when it found evidence of such practices. Wilson explained that the purpose of the FTC was to "destroy monopoly and maintain competition as the only efficient instrument of business liberty." His goal was to prevent monopolistic trusts, not to regulate them.

WILSON DECLARES VICTORY

In November 1914, just two years after his election, President Wilson announced that he had accomplished his major goals. Through his effective leadership, he had fulfilled his audacious promises to lower the tariff, create a national banking system, and strengthen the anti-trust laws. The New Freedom was now complete, he wrote, for he had no desire to continue increasing the power of the federal government. "The history of liberty," he stressed, "is the history of the limitation of governmental power, not the increase of it." As the *New York Times* acknowledged, "this Congress has a President on its back, driving it pitilessly. . . . Never were Congressmen driven so, not even in the days of [TR] and the 'big stick.'"

Wilson's victory declaration bewildered many progressives, especially those who had long advocated additional social-justice legislation that the president had earlier supported. Herbert Croly, editor of the *New Republic* magazine, wondered how the president could assert "that the fundamental wrongs of a modern society can be easily and quickly righted as a consequence of [passing] a few laws." Wilson's about-face, he concluded, "casts suspicion upon his own sincerity [as a progressive] or upon his grasp of the realities of modern social and industrial life."

PROGRESSIVISM FOR WHITES ONLY African Americans continued to resent the racial conservatism of most progressives. Carter Glass, the Virginia senator largely responsible for developing the Federal Reserve Act in 1913, was an enthusiastic supporter of his state's efforts to disenfranchise black voters. When questioned by a reporter about being a racist progressive, Glass embraced the label: "Discrimination! Why that is exactly what we propose. To remove every Negro voter who can be gotten rid of."

Similarly, Woodrow Wilson shared many of the racist attitudes common at the time. As a student at Princeton, he had dismissed African Americans as "an ignorant and inferior race." As a politician, Wilson courted African American voters, but he rarely consulted or associated with black leaders.

Josephus Daniels, a North Carolina newspaper editor who became Wilson's secretary of the navy, was a white supremacist who stressed that "the subjection of the negro, politically, and the separation of the negro, socially, are paramount to all other considerations in the South." For Daniels and other southern progressives, "progress" was possible only if blacks were "kept in their place."

Daniels and other cabinet members racially segregated the federal employees in their offices, dining halls, and restrooms. Wilson endorsed the policy, claiming that racial segregation "is not humiliating but a benefit." To him, "separate but equal" was the best way to resolve racial tensions. He was the first president since the Civil War who openly endorsed discrimination against African Americans.

In November 1914, a delegation of concerned African American leaders met with Wilson to ask how a "progressive" president could adopt such "regressive" policies. Wilson responded that both races benefited from the policies because they eliminated "the possibility of friction." William Monroe Trotter, a

New freedom, old rules Woodrow Wilson and his wife Edith ride in a carriage with African American drivers.

Harvard-educated African American newspaper editor who had helped found the National Association for the Advancement of Colored People (NAACP), scolded the president: "Have you a 'new freedom' for white Americans, and a new slavery for 'your Afro-American fellow citizens'? God forbid."

A furious Wilson told the visitors to leave, saying their unchristian "tone offends me." In 1916, when Wilson campaigned for a second term, not a single African American leader endorsed him. "You have grievously disappointed us," W. E. B. Du Bois said.

THE VOTE FOR WOMEN Activists for women's suffrage were also disappointed in President Wilson. Despite having two daughters, Eleanor and Jessie, who were suffragists, he insisted that the issue of women's voting rights should be left to the states rather than embodied in a constitutional amendment.

Wilson's lack of support led some leaders of the suffrage movement to revise their tactics. Alice Paul was a New Jersey–born Quaker and Swarthmore College graduate who earned a master's degree from the University of Pennsylvania before becoming a social worker. In 1910, she returned to the United States from her work with militant suffragists in England, where she had engaged in hunger strikes and been jailed. She joined the National American Woman Suffrage Association (NAWSA) and urged activists to use more aggressive tactics: picketing state legislatures, "punishing" politicians who failed to endorse suffrage, chaining themselves to public buildings, inciting police to arrest them, and launching hunger strikes. Eventually, NAWSA decided Paul was too militant and expelled her from their ranks. She responded in 1913 by forming the Congressional Union for Woman Suffrage and starting the *Suffragist* magazine.

Alice Paul Sewing a suffrage flag— orange and purple, with stars—that she and other suffragists often waved at strikes and protests.

Early that March, Paul organized 5,000 suffragists to protest at Wilson's inauguration. The protesters were well-dressed and well-behaved but their critics were not. Spectators "taunted, spat upon, and roughed up" marchers, while police did little to control the crowds. Wilson ordered his driver to avoid the rally, for he could not stand hearing "women speak in public."

A few days later, Paul and three others met President Wilson in the White House. They warned that if he continued to oppose an amendment providing the vote to women, then thousands of suffragists would campaign against his reelection. "If they did that," Wilson replied, "they would not be as intelligent as I believe they are." He regretted their "unladylike" behavior.

Four years later, having formed the National Woman's Party, Paul urged suffragists to do something even more dramatic: picket the White House. Beginning on January 11, 1917, from 10 A.M. to 5 P.M., five days a week, amid rain, sleet, and snow, Paul and her followers (the "Silent Sentinels") took turns carrying signs reading: "MR. PRESIDENT! HOW LONG MUST WOMEN WAIT FOR LIBERTY?"

They picketed for six months, until Wilson ordered their arrest. Some sixty middle-class suffragists were jailed. At their trials, the women found their voices. Florence Bayard Hilles, daughter of a former secretary of state, expressed the outrage felt by all suffragists: "What a spectacle it must be to the thinking people of this country to see us urged to go to war for democracy in a foreign land and to see women thrown into prison who plead for the same cause at home."

Paul was sentenced to seven months in prison. She went on a hunger strike, leading prison officials to force-feed her raw eggs through a rubber tube inserted in her nose. She recalled, "It was shocking that a government of men could look with such extreme contempt on a movement that was asking nothing except such a simple little thing as the right to vote." Buffeted by negative press coverage and public criticism, Wilson pardoned Paul and the other activists.

PROGRESSIVISM RENEWED By 1916, Woodrow Wilson's determination to win reelection revived his commitment to progressive activism. The president nominated Bostonian Louis D. Brandeis, the "people's attorney," to the Supreme Court. Brandeis was not just a famed defender of unions against big businesses; he would also be the first Jewish member of the Supreme Court. Progressives viewed the nomination as a "landmark in the history of American democracy." Others disagreed. Former president Taft dismissed Brandeis as "a muckraker, an emotionalist for his own purposes, a socialist . . . who is utterly unscrupulous." The Senate, however, confirmed Brandeis's appointment. Justice Oliver Wendell Holmes Jr., the leading figure on the court, sent Brandeis a one-word telegram: "WELCOME."

FARM LEGISLATION President Wilson also urged Congress to pass the first federal legislation directed at assisting farmers. The Federal Farm Loan Act became law in 1916. Under the control of the Federal Farm Loan Board, twelve Federal Land banks offered loans to farmers for five to forty years at low interest rates. At about the same time, a dream long advocated by Populists—federal loans to farmers on the security of their crops stored in warehouses—finally came to fruition when Congress passed the Warehouse Act of 1916.

Farmers also benefited from the Smith-Lever Act of 1914, which provided programs to educate farmers about new machinery and new ideas related to agricultural efficiency, and the Smith-Hughes Act (1917), which funded agricultural and mechanical education in high schools. Farmers with newfangled automobiles had more than a passing interest as well in the Federal Highways Act of 1916, which helped finance new roads, especially in rural areas.

LABOR LEGISLATION One of the long-standing goals of progressive Democrats was a *federal* child-labor law. When Congress passed the Keating-

Owen Act in 1916, banning products made by child workers under fourteen from being shipped across state lines, Wilson expressed doubts about its constitutionality but eventually signed it. Less than two years later, however, the Supreme Court ruled the Keating-Owen Act unconstitutional in *Hammer v. Dagenhart* (1918), declaring that only states had the right to regulate working hours.

Another landmark law was the Adamson Act of 1916, which resulted from a threatened strike by railroad unions demanding an eight-hour day and other concessions. Wilson, who objected to some of the unions' demands, nevertheless asked Congress to approve the Adamson Act. It required time-and-a-half pay for overtime work beyond eight hours and appointed a commission to study working conditions in the railroad industry.

Assessing Progressivism

Progressivism—and its notion that the nation's quality of life could be improved by government action—reached its peak during Woodrow Wilson's two terms as president. After decades of political upheaval and social reform, progressivism had shattered the laissez-faire notion that government had no role in protecting the public welfare through regulating the economy or by improving the American quality of life. Progressives demonstrated that people of good will could make a difference in improving social conditions for all.

Progressives established the principle that governments—local, state, and federal—had a responsibility to ensure that Americans were protected from abuse by powerful businesses and corrupt politicians. As a Texas progressive said in 1910, most Americans now acknowledged that governments must protect "the weak against the encroachments of the strong."

Ultimately, progressivism faded as an organized political movement because international issues pushed aside domestic concerns. By 1916, the optimism of a few years earlier had disappeared in the wake of the Great War in Europe. The twentieth century, which had dawned with such bright hopes, held in store episodes of unprecedented brutality that would call into question whether progress was even possible anymore.

CHAPTER REVIEW

SUMMARY

- **The Progressive Impulse**   Progressives were mostly middle-class idealists of both political parties who promoted reform and government regulation to ensure social justice. Many progressives wished to restrict the powers of local political machines and establish honest and efficient government. They called for legislation to end child labor, promote workplace safety, ban the sale of alcoholic beverages, regulate or eliminate trusts and other monopolies, and grant *woman suffrage*.

- **The Varied Sources of Progressivism**   Many religious reformers, such as those involved in the *social gospel* movement, urged their fellow Protestants to reject social Darwinism and do more to promote a better life for the urban poor. The settlement house movement spread through urban America as college-educated middle-class women formed community centers in poverty-stricken neighborhoods. Progressives drew inspiration from the women's suffrage movement, as more women became involved in social reform efforts and in the workplace. Many progressive ideas arose from the efforts of reformers to end political corruption. Progressives, while not radicals, also responded to the growing socialist movement and its calls for economic justice for the working class. *Muckrakers*—investigative journalists who exposed political and corporate corruption—further fueled the efforts to address abuses of power in American society.

- **Progressives' Aims and Achievements**   Progressives focused on stopping corruption in politics. In 1912, they advanced reforms, such as the direct primary; the initiative, referendum, and recall at the state level; and the direct election of U.S. senators through the passage of the *Seventeenth Amendment (1913)*. Other progressives focused on incorporating new modes of efficiency and scientific management in business, known as *Taylorism*, into government. Their efforts inspired many cities and counties to adopt the commission system and the city-manager plan. Still other progressives focused on legislation and regulatory oversight to control or eliminate trusts and other forms of monopolies.

- **Progressivism under Roosevelt and Taft**   The administrations of Theodore Roosevelt and William H. Taft increased the power of the presidency and the federal government to regulate corporations and improve the lives of many Americans. Roosevelt promoted his *Square Deal* program, which included regulating trusts through the creation of the Bureau of Corporations, arbitrating the 1902 coal strike, persuading Congress to regulate the railroads through the Elkins and Hepburn Acts, and to clean up the meat and drug industries with the Meat Inspection and Pure Food and Drug Acts. Roosevelt also initiated an environmental conservation campaign to preserve the nation's natural resources.

- **Woodrow Wilson's Progressivism**   Wilson's *New Freedom* program included lower tariffs and anti-trust regulations. He also established a central banking

system with the *Federal Reserve Act (1913)*, and launched a rigorous anti-
program with the passage of the *Clayton Anti-Trust Act (1914)* and the creatio
of the *Federal Trade Commission (1914)*. But Wilson opposed a constitutional
amendment guaranteeing women's suffrage. A southerner, he believed African
Americans were inferior, and he imposed segregation in federal offices.

CHRONOLOGY

1901	William McKinley is assassinated
	Theodore Roosevelt becomes president
	Galveston, Texas, adopts the commission system of city government
1902	Justice Department breaks up the Northern Securities Company
1903	Congress passes the Elkins Act and creates the Bureau of Corporations
1906	Upton Sinclair's *The Jungle* is published
	Congress passes the Meat Inspection Act and the Pure Food and Drug Act
1909	William Howard Taft inaugurated
1911	Frederick Taylor's *The Principles of Scientific Management* is published
1912	Woodrow Wilson wins four-way presidential election
1913	Alice Paul and 5,000 suffragists protest Wilson's inauguration
	Sixteenth and Seventeenth Amendments ratified
1914	Congress passes the Clayton Anti-Trust Act

KEY TERMS

progressivism p. 974

muckrakers p. 976

social gospel p. 978

women's suffrage p. 981

Seventeenth Amendment (1913) p. 984

Taylorism p. 984

Sixteenth Amendment (1913) p. 991

Square Deal p. 992

Progressive party p. 1004

New Freedom p. 1008

Federal Reserve Act (1913) p. 1011

Clayton Anti-Trust Act (1914)
p. 1012

Federal Trade Commission (1914)
p. 1012

 INQUIZITIVE

Go to InQuizitive to see what you've learned—and learn what you've
missed—with personalized feedback along the way.

America and the Great War

1914–1920

Make American History In this U.S. Navy recruiting poster in New York City, a sailor encourages a young man to play an active role in the Great War.

Throughout the nineteenth century, the Atlantic Ocean had protected America from wars fought on the continent of Europe. During the early twentieth century, however, the nation's global isolation ended. Ever-expanding world trade entwined U.S. interests with the world economy. In addition, the development of steam-powered ships and submarines meant that foreign navies could directly threaten U.S. security.

At the same time, the election of Woodrow Wilson in 1912 brought to the White House a self-righteous moralist determined to impose his standards on what he saw as renegade nations. This combination of circumstances made the outbreak of the "Great War" in Europe in 1914 a profound crisis for the United States. The first world war would become the defining event of the early twentieth century.

For almost three years, President Wilson maintained America's stance of "neutrality" toward the war while providing increasing amounts of food and supplies to Great Britain and France. In 1917, however, German submarine attacks on U.S. ships forced Congress to declare war.

Once America entered the war, almost 5 million men joined the military, including 400,000 African Americans. The departure of so many men from civilian life opened up new jobs across the nation for men and women. Recruited by businesses, some 1.6 million mostly rural African Americans moved to cities outside the South to work in defense industries in what was called the Great Migration. The prospect of higher-paying jobs stimulated

focus questions

1. What caused the outbreak of the Great War, and why did the United States join the conflict? What was distinctive about the fighting on the Western Front?

2. How did the Wilson administration mobilize the home front? How did these mobilization efforts affect society?

3. What were the major events of the war after the United States entered the conflict? How did the American war effort contribute to the defeat of the Central Powers?

4. How did Wilson promote his plans for a peaceful world order as outlined in his Fourteen Points?

5. What were the consequences of the war at home and abroad?

the mass migration, but African Americans were also eager to get away from the often violent racism and rigid Jim Crow segregation they suffered under in the southern states.

An Uneasy Neutrality

Woodrow Wilson once declared that he had "a first-class mind." He was indeed intelligent, thoughtful, principled, and courageous. Upon learning of death threats against him, for example, he refused to change his schedule of public appearances. "The country," he explained, "cannot afford to have a coward for President."

For all his accomplishments and abilities, however, Wilson had no experience or expertise in international relations before becoming president. "It would be an irony of fate," he confessed, "if my administration had to deal chiefly with foreign affairs." Ironic or not, when war erupted in Europe during the summer of 1914, he shifted his attention from the New Freedom's progressive reforms to foreign affairs.

Wilson believed God was directing him to help create a new world order governed by morality and ideals rather than by selfish national interests. Both Wilson and William Jennings Bryan, his first secretary of state, believed that America had a God-given duty to promote democracy and Christianity around the world. "Every nation of the world," Wilson declared, "needs to be drawn into the tutelage [guidance] of America."

The Great War

Woodrow Wilson faced his greatest challenge beginning in the summer of 1914, when the "dreadful conflict" in Europe exploded suddenly, like "lightning out of a clear sky," as a North Carolina congressman said. Unfortunately, the outbreak of war coincided with a sharp decline in the health of Wilson's wife Ellen, who died on August 6, 1914. "God has stricken me," the president wrote a friend, "almost beyond what I can bear."

Wilson would also have trouble bearing the horrors of the war. Lasting more than four years, from 1914 to 1918, the so-called Great War (a future generation would call it the First World War) would involve more nations and cause greater destruction than any previous conflict: 20 million military and civilian deaths, and 21 million more wounded. The Great War would topple monarchs, destroy empires, create new nations, and set in motion a series of events that would lead to an even costlier war in 1939.

CAUSES The Great War resulted from long-simmering national rivalries and ethnic conflicts in Europe, as powerful imperial nations competed for foreign colonies and military supremacy. There had not been a major European war in more than forty years, but the great powers, driven by a lusty sense of hypernationalism aggravated by ethnic hatreds and racist beliefs, had been preparing for one. Germany's determination to have its "place in the sun" at the expense of Great Britain was only one of several threats to peace and stability.

Growing tensions during the early twentieth century spawned a furious arms race and the creation of two competing military alliances: the **Central Powers** (Germany, Austria-Hungary, Bulgaria, and Turkey [the Ottoman Empire]), and the **Allied Powers** (France, Great Britain, and Russia). The participants in these two alliances pledged to come to the defense of their members should they be attacked, thus dividing Europe into two armed camps.

Although Europe was officially at peace in 1914, most nations had initiated universal military conscription (the "draft"). In May, Colonel Edward M. House, President Wilson's closest adviser, traveled to Europe and reported that the "situation is extraordinary. It is jingoism [violent nationalism] run stark mad. . . . There is too much hatred, too many jealousies" among the major powers. He predicted "an awful cataclysm" because the German system represented "militarism run mad."

At the core of the tensions was the "powder keg of Europe," the Austro-Hungarian (Habsburg) Empire, an unstable collection of eleven nationalities whose leaders were determined to suppress their southern neighbor and long-standing enemy, Serbia. Serbian nationalists (Pan-Slavists) had long hoped to create "Yugoslavia," a nation encompassing all ethnic Slavic peoples from throughout the Austro-Hungarian Empire. Russia, home to millions of Slavs, supported the Pan-Slavic movement.

A recklessly militaristic Germany, led by Kaiser (Emperor) Wilhelm II, had been a latecomer to industrialization and nationalism, having become a united nation only in 1871. Its leaders yearned to catch up with Great Britain and France. By 1892, German steel production had surpassed that of Britain and by 1910 had doubled it. Germany had also created its own colonial empire in Africa and Asia while building a navy powerful enough to challenge British supremacy on the seas and an army capable of defeating its old enemies, the Russian Empire and France. Now, Kaiser Wilhelm wanted to be like Napoléon Bonaparte, a military conqueror.

These factors—militarism, alliances, imperialism, and nationalism—created a combustible situation. All that was needed to ignite it was a spark.

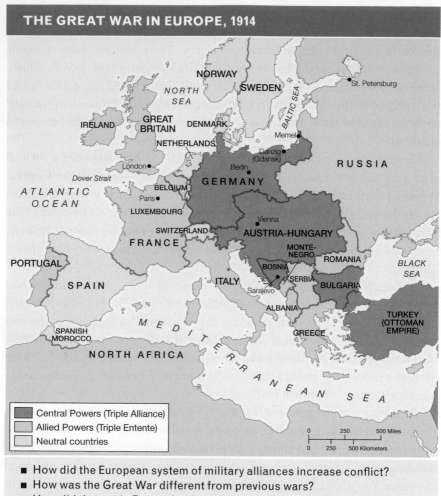

THE GREAT WAR IN EUROPE, 1914

- Central Powers (Triple Alliance)
- Allied Powers (Triple Entente)
- Neutral countries

0   250   500 Miles

0   250   500 Kilometers

- How did the European system of military alliances increase conflict?
- How was the Great War different from previous wars?
- How did the war in Europe lead to ethnic tensions in the United States?

FIGHTING ERUPTS That spark came in the Balkan Peninsula, a volatile region of southeastern Europe on the southern border of the Austro-Hungarian Empire. There, for centuries, the Austrian and Russian monarchies and the Ottoman Empire had competed for influence and control. Six years before, in 1908, Austria had annexed Bosnia from the Ottoman Empire, infuriating Serbian nationalists.

On June 28, 1914, the heir to the Austro-Hungarian throne, Archduke Franz Ferdinand, and his pregnant wife Sophie, visited Sarajevo (the capital of Austrian-controlled Bosnia). When the Archduke's driver took a wrong turn and was forced to back the motorcar slowly down a crowded street, Gavrilo Princip, a nineteen-year-old Serbian nationalist, shot the imperial couple at point-blank range. They both died.

To avenge the murders, Austria-Hungary, with Germany's approval, resolved to bring Serbia under its control—or destroy it. To that end, it bullied and humiliated Serbia by issuing deliberately unreasonable ultimatums. Serbia agreed to most of them, but Austria-Hungary prepared for war anyway. Russia responded by mobilizing its army to defend Serbia, triggering reactions by other members of the rival European military alliances. In late 1918, when the war ended, an Austrian diplomat confessed, "We began the war, not the Germans."

Germany, expecting a limited war and quick victory, declared war on Russia on August 1, 1914, and on France two days later. German troops then invaded neutral Belgium to get at France, murdering or deporting thousands of Belgian civilians in the process. The "rape of Belgium" brought Great Britain into the war on August 4 on the **Western Front**, the line of fighting in northern France and Belgium.

On the evening of August 4, as five global empires—Austria-Hungary, France, Germany, Great Britain, and Russia—mobilized for war, the British foreign minister, Sir Edward Grey, expressed the fears of many when he observed that "the lamps are going out all over Europe; we shall not see them lit again in our time."

On the sprawling Eastern Front, Russian armies clashed with German and Austro-Hungarian forces as well as those of the Turkish (Ottoman) Empire. Within five weeks of the assassination in Sarajevo, a "great war" had consumed all of Europe. In 1915, Italy would join the Allied Powers in fighting Germany and Austria-Hungary.

AN INDUSTRIAL WAR

The Great War required the total mobilization of economies and civilians, as well as soldiers and sailors. Of the approximately 70 million soldiers and sailors who fought on both sides, more than half were killed, wounded, imprisoned, or unaccounted for.

The staggering human casualties and physical destruction resulted from powerful new weapons, which dramatically changed the nature of warfare. Machine guns, submarines, aerial bombing, poison gas, flame throwers, land mines, mortars, long-range artillery, and armored tanks produced horrifying casualties and widespread destruction. On August 22, 1914, for example, the French army lost 27,000 men. An average of 900 Frenchmen and 1,300 Germans died *every* day on the Western Front.

TRENCH WARFARE In the early weeks of the war, German armies swept quickly across Belgium and northeastern France, only to bog down in nightmarish **trench warfare** that came to symbolize a brutal war of futility. Both sides dug in and fought a grinding war of attrition, gaining little territory in the process. The U.S. ambassador in London cabled President Wilson that the "horror" of the war "outruns all imagination."

During 1914–1915, the two sides built a network of zigzagging trenches from the coast of Belgium some 460 miles across northeastern France to the border of Switzerland. Some trenches measured forty feet deep and swarmed with rats and lice. "When all is said and done," grumbled an English infantry officer, "the war was mainly a matter of holes and ditches."

Soldiers often ate, slept, lived, and died without leaving their underground homes. A French soldier described life in the trenches as a "physical, almost animal" existence in which "the primitive instincts of the race have full sway: eating, drinking, sleeping, fighting—everything but loving."

The object was not so much to gain ground as to inflict death and destruction on the enemy until its resources were exhausted. In one assault against the Germans in Belgium, the British lost 13,000 men in three hours—and gained

Trench warfare Soldiers eat amid the reek of death and threat of enemy fire in a frontline trench in France.

only 100 yards. As the war ground on, both sides found themselves using up their available men, resources, courage, and cash. The Great War, mourned a German soldier, had become the "grave of nations."

Throughout 1914, both sides talked about the "glory" and "glamour" of war. Captain Julian Grenfell, a poet, was giddy after his first combat. "I adore war," he wrote his parents. "It is like a big picnic. . . . I've never been so well or so happy. The fighting-excitement vitalizes everything, every sight and action. One loves one's fellow man so much more when one is bent on killing him." Five months later, a piece of shrapnel hit Grenfell in the head; he died thirteen days later.

As the casualties soared, notions of romantic glory died with them. British poet Wilfred Owen called the idealization of combat "the old Lie." (He would be killed in action in 1918, just a week before the war ended.) The traditional glorification of military combat disintegrated as soldiers died like cattle in a slaughterhouse.

From 1914 to 1918, the opposing armies in northeastern France attacked and counterattacked along the Western Front, gaining little ground while casualties soared into the millions. Time and again, inept generals sent their troops "over the top," climbing up and out of waterlogged trenches carrying sixty pounds of gear. Many of the soldiers died as they reached the top of the ladders. Of the 800 men in one British regiment who went over the top at Somme, 266 were killed and 446 wounded—a casualty rate of 89 percent.

The soldiers who made it out of the trenches had to slog across "No Man's Land" between the opposing entrenchments. Their lives depended on navigating through webs of barbed wire and devastating fire from machine guns and high-powered rifles, all the while being showered by constant artillery shelling. During the Battle of Verdun, which lasted from February to December 1916, some 32 million artillery shells streaked across the landscape—1,500 shells for every square yard of that battlefield in northeastern France. The casualties were so numerous that French soldiers began to mutiny.

The hellish nature of trench warfare posed extraordinary psychological challenges for the combatants on both sides. Thousands of soldiers fell victim to "shell shock," now known as post–traumatic stress disorder. "It was a horrible thing," explained a nurse. "They became quite unconscious, with violent shivering and shaking." In 1916, a British officer ordered his unit to "fix bayonets" and prepare to charge out of the trenches when he sounded his whistle. One of his men recalled standing "beside a young chap called Lucas, and he was a bundle of nerves. . . . He could hardly hold his rifle, never mind fix [attach] his bayonet. So I fixed mine and then I said, 'Here you are, Lucas,' and I fixed it for him." They then clambered out of the trench and began moving

Total ruin German soldiers stand before the French Fort Souville between the Battles of Verdun in September 1916. The constant artillery fire gouged out huge craters and destroyed whole forests.

forward. "There were shell-holes everywhere . . . and there were lads falling all over the place" as German machine guns mowed them down. "Lucas went down."

An American journalist reported that the massive casualties changed the way men looked at war. In earlier conflicts, soldiers were eager to fight and confident they would return unscathed. Now, the new recruits seemed to have "left hope behind" and were confident that they were "going to their death."

In 1917, George Barnes, a British official whose son had been killed in the war, went to speak at a military hospital in London, where injured soldiers were being fitted with artificial limbs. At the appointed hour, the men, in wheelchairs and on crutches, all with empty sleeves or pants, arrived to hear the speaker. Yet when Barnes rose to talk, he found himself speechless—literally. As the minutes passed, tears rolled down his cheeks. Finally, without having said a word, he simply sat down. What the mutilated soldiers heard was not a war-glorifying speech but the muted pity of grief. The war's mindless horrors had come home.

INITIAL AMERICAN REACTIONS

When war erupted in Europe, American officials were stunned. One of Wilson's cabinet members remembered that "the end of things had come. I stopped in my tracks, dazed and horror-stricken." But shock mingled with relief that a wide ocean stood between America and the killing fields. President Wilson, an avowed pacifist, maintained that the United States "was too proud to fight" in Europe's war, "with which we have nothing to do, whose causes cannot touch us." He repeatedly urged Americans to remain "neutral in thought as well as in action." Privately, however, he sought to ensure that the United States could provide Great Britain and France as much financial assistance and supplies as possible.

That most Americans wanted the nation to stay out of the fighting did not keep them from choosing sides. More than a third of the nation's citizens were first- or second-generation immigrants still loyal to their homelands. Nine million German-born Americans lived in the United States in 1914, and there were more than 500 German-language newspapers across the country. Most of the 4.5 million Irish-born Americans detested England, which had ruled Ireland for centuries. For the most part, these groups supported the Central Powers, while others, largely of British origin, supported the Allied Powers.

One of the few issues that Woodrow Wilson and Theodore Roosevelt agreed on was the need to stamp out what they called "Hyphenism" and replace it with "100 Percent Americanism." The one way to destroy America, Roosevelt charged, would be to "permit it to become a tangle of squabbling nationalities, an intricate knot of German-Americans, Irish-Americans, English-Americans, French-Americans, Scandinavian-Americans, or Italian-Americans, each preserving its separate nationality, each at heart feeling more sympathy with Europeans of that nationality, than with the other citizens of the American Republic." There is no such thing as "a hyphenated American," he argued, "who is a good American."

SUPPORTING THE ALLIES By the spring of 1915, the Allied Powers' need for food, supplies, and weapons had generated an economic windfall for U.S. businesses, bankers, and farmers. Exports to France and Great Britain quadrupled from 1914 to 1916, and America's manufacturing capacity soon surpassed that of Great Britain, the world's leader. Farm income soared 25 percent. The Allies, especially Britain and France, needed loans from U.S. banks and "credits" from the U.S. government, which would allow them to pay for their purchases later.

Early in the war, Secretary of State William Jennings Bryan, a strict pacifist, took advantage of President Wilson's absence from Washington following the death of Ellen, the First Lady, to tell J. Pierpont Morgan, the world's richest banker, that loans to any nations at war were "inconsistent with the true spirit of neutrality."

Upon his return to the White House, an angry Wilson reversed Bryan's policy by removing all restrictions on loans to the warring nations. The president was determined that America avoid the war's horrors while reaping its economic benefits. Banks and other investors would eventually send more than $2 billion to the Allies before the United States entered the fighting while offering only $27 million to Germany. What Bryan feared, and what Wilson did not fully realize, was that the more Britain and France borrowed and purchased, the harder it became for America to remain neutral.

Despite the disproportionate financial assistance provided to the Allies, the Wilson administration maintained its stance of neutrality for thirty months. In particular, Wilson tried valiantly to defend the age-old principle of "freedom of the seas," arguing that the ships of neutral nations had the right to trade with warring nations without fear of being attacked.

On August 6, 1914, Bryan urged the warring countries to respect the rights of neutral nations to ship goods across the Atlantic. The Central Powers agreed, but the British refused. In November, the British ordered the ships of neutral nations to submit to searches to discover if cargoes were bound for Germany. A few months later, the British announced that they would seize any ships carrying goods to Germany.

"The Sandwich Man" To illustrate America's biased brand of neutrality, this political cartoon shows Uncle Sam wearing a sandwich board that advertises the nation's conflicting desires.

AMERICAN VOLUNTEERS The United States provided more than material aid to the Allies. Thousands of men and women volunteered in the British, Canadian, and French militaries, the French Foreign Legion, the American Ambulance Field Corps, military hospitals, and various refugee relief organizations. In October 1914, the first American Red Cross ship arrived in France, carrying 170 doctors and nurses.

Some volunteers sought adventure or glory. Others were eager to fight German imperialism, and still others sought to repay France for its support for America during the Revolutionary War. Almost 300 volunteers served as pilots in an all-American aviation unit in France called the Lafayette

Escadrille. Some 4,000 Native Americans, still not granted citizenship in the United States, volunteered in the Canadian Expeditionary Force. Theodore Roosevelt's son Kermit used his father's help to gain a commission as a captain in the British Expeditionary Force in France. By 1916, some 45,000 Americans were serving as volunteers in Allied hospitals in France and England, or as soldiers or pilots on the Western Front.

Poet Alan Seeger, a Harvard graduate living in Paris when the war started, volunteered in the French Foreign Legion. He did so for "a chance to live life free from stain and that rare privilege of dying well."

After months of living and fighting in disgusting trenches, however, Seeger saw little glory in the conflict. As a "poor common soldier," he wrote, his role was "simply to dig himself a hole in the ground and to keep hidden in it as tightly as possible. Continually under the fire of the opposing [artillery] batteries, he is yet never allowed to get a glimpse of the enemy. Exposed to all the dangers of war, but with none of its enthusiasms or splendid *élan* [spirit], he is condemned to sit like an animal in its burrow and hear the shells whistle over his head and take their little daily toll from his comrades."

While awaiting combat, Seeger wrote his famous poem, "I Have a Rendezvous with Death," with its oft-quoted lines: "I have a rendezvous with death/ On some scarred slope or battered hill/When Spring comes round again this year/And the first meadow-flowers appear."

On July 4, 1916, Seeger died well, as the romantic he was, "smiling and without regret," at the Battle of the Somme in northern France. Just weeks before, he had written that the volunteers fighting in France "did not pursue worldly rewards; they wanted nothing more than to live without regret, brothers pledged to the honor implicit in living one's own life and dying one's own death." In his view, death was not "terrible after all. It may mean something more wonderful than life."

NEUTRAL RIGHTS AND SUBMARINE ATTACKS With its warships bottled up by a British blockade of its ports, the German government announced a "war zone" around the British Isles. All ships in those waters would be attacked by submarines, the Germans warned, and "it may not always be possible to save crews and passengers."

The German use of submarines, or **U-boats** (*Unterseeboot* in German), violated the long-established wartime custom of stopping an enemy vessel and allowing the passengers and crew to board lifeboats before sinking it. During 1915, German U-boats sank 227 British ships in the Atlantic Ocean and North Sea.

The United States called the attacks "an indefensible violation of neutral rights," and Wilson warned that he would hold Germany to "strict accountability" for the loss of lives and property. Then, on May 7, 1915, a German submarine off the Irish coast sank the British ship **Lusitania**, the foremost luxury liner in the world. Of the 1,198 persons on board who died, 128 were Americans. Fifty of the dead were infants.

The sinking of the *Lusitania*, asserted Theodore Roosevelt, called for an immediate declaration of war. Wilson, however, urged patience: "There is such a thing as a man being too proud to fight. There is such a thing as a nation being so right that it does not need to convince others by force that it is right."

Roosevelt dismissed the president's words as "unmanly," called the president a "jackass," and threatened to "skin him alive if he doesn't go to war." General John Pershing, who would later command U.S. forces in France, told his wife that Wilson was a "weak, chicken-hearted, white-livered" president. Wilson privately admitted that the fainthearted language had "occurred to me while I was speaking, and I let it out. I should have kept it in."

Wilson's earlier threat of "strict accountability" now required a tough response. On May 13, Secretary of State Bryan demanded that the Germans stop unrestricted submarine warfare, apologize, and pay the families of those killed on the *Lusitania*. The Germans countered that the ship was armed (which was false) and secretly carried rifles and ammunition (which was true); they further declared it was transporting hundreds of Canadian soldiers (which was true). On June 9, Wilson dismissed the German claims and reiterated that the United States was "contending for nothing less high and sacred than the rights of humanity."

Bryan resigned as secretary of state in protest of Wilson's pro-British stance. Upon learning of Bryan's departure, Edith Bolling Galt, soon to be Wilson's second wife, shouted: "Hurrah! Old Bryan is out!" She called the former secretary of state an "awful Deserter." The president confided that he viewed Bryan as a "traitor."

Stunned by the global outcry over the *Lusitania* sinking, the German government told its U-boat captains to stop attacking passenger vessels. Despite the order, however, a German submarine sank the British liner *Arabic*, and two Americans on board were killed. The Germans paid a cash penalty to the families of the deceased and issued what came to be called the *Arabic* Pledge on September 1, 1915: "Liners will not be sunk by our submarines without warning and without safety of the lives of non-combatants, provided that the liners do not try to escape or offer resistance."

In early 1916, Wilson again sent Colonel Edward House to London, Paris, and Berlin in hopes of stimulating peace talks, but the mission failed. So the killing continued. On March 24, 1916, a U-boat sank the French passenger ferry *Sussex*, killing eighty passengers and injuring two Americans. After

Wilson threatened to end relations with Germany, its leaders again promised not to sink merchant and passenger ships. The *Sussex* Pledge implied the virtual abandonment of submarine warfare. Colonel House noted in his diary that Americans were "now beginning to realize that we are on the brink of war and what war means."

PREPARING FOR WAR The sinking of U.S. passenger vessels triggered efforts to strengthen the army and navy in case the nation was forced into war. On December 1, 1914, a "preparedness" movement, led by Theodore Roosevelt and Henry Cabot Lodge, created the National Security League to convince Congress and the president to begin preparing for war. The growing scope of the conflict in Europe and the quarrels over trading with belligerent nations contributed to a demand in the United States for a stronger army and navy.

After the *Lusitania*'s sinking, Wilson asked the War and Navy Departments to develop plans for a $1 billion military expansion. Many Americans—pacifists, progressives, and midwestern Republicans—opposed the preparedness effort, seeing it as a propaganda campaign to benefit businesses that made weapons and other military equipment. Some charged that Wilson was secretly plotting to enter the war.

Others, however, insisted that Wilson's proposal fell short of what the nation needed in the likelihood that it was drawn into the war. The secretary of war and his assistant resigned in protest.

Yet the Germans kept pushing Americans toward war. German spies and saboteurs organized numerous explosions in the United States in their efforts to stop the flow of military supplies to France, Great Britain, and Russia. In the predawn hours of July 30, 1916, German agents dynamited the "Black Tom" munitions depot in New York Harbor at Jersey City, where more than 1,000 tons of ammunition and explosives were stored.

The explosion killed seven people, injured hundreds, blew out windows in Times Square and St. Patrick's Cathedral, jolted millions out of their beds, caused damages totaling half a billion dollars, and raked the Statue of Liberty with shrapnel. Fires smoldered for days, and more than 200 rail cars were destroyed.

Despite opposition, Congress in 1916 passed the National Defense Act, which provided for the expansion of the U.S. Army from 90,000 to 223,000 men over the next five years. While some complained that Wilson wanted to "drag this nation into war," the president told an aide that he was determined not to "be rushed into war, no matter if every damned congressman and senator stands up on his hind legs and proclaims me a coward."

Opponents of preparedness insisted that the expense of military expansion should rest upon the wealthy munitions makers who were profiting from trade with the Allies. Congress decided to use the income tax as its weapon to deter war-related profiteering. The Revenue Act of 1916 doubled the income tax rate from 1 to 2 percent, created a 12.5 percent tax on munitions makers, and added a new tax on "excessive" corporate profits. The new taxes were the culmination of the progressive legislation that Wilson had approved to strengthen his chances in the upcoming presidential election. Fearing that Theodore Roosevelt would be the Republican presidential candidate, Colonel House believed that the "Democratic Party must change its historic character and become the progressive party in the future."

THE 1916 ELECTION

As the 1916 election approached, Theodore Roosevelt hoped to become the Republican nominee. But his decision in 1912 to run as a third-party candidate had alienated many powerful members of his party, and his eagerness to enter the war scared many voters. So instead, the Republicans nominated Supreme Court Justice Charles Evans Hughes, a progressive who had served as governor of New York from 1907 to 1910.

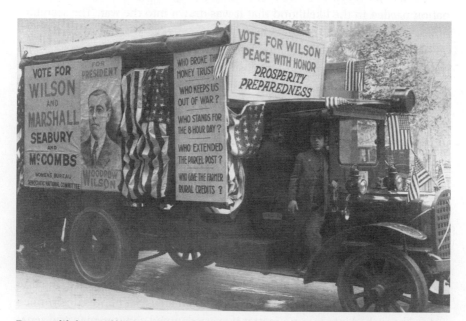

Peace with honor Wilson's neutrality policies proved popular in the 1916 campaign.

The Democrats, staying with Wilson, adopted a platform centered on social-welfare legislation and prudent military preparedness. The peace theme, refined in the slogan "He kept us out of war," became the campaign's rallying cry, although the president acknowledged that the nation could no longer refuse to play the "great part in the world which was providentially cut out for her. . . . We have got to serve the world." Colonel House was more blunt. He told Secretary of State Robert Lansing that they "could not permit the Allies to go down in defeat, for if they did, we would follow."

The two candidates were remarkably similar. Both Wilson and Hughes were sons of preachers; both were attorneys and former professors; both had been progressive governors; both were known for their integrity. Hughes called for higher tariffs, attacked Wilson for being hostile to Big Business, and implied that Wilson was not neutral enough in responding to the war. Roosevelt called the bearded Hughes a "whiskered Wilson." Wilson, however, proved to be the better campaigner—barely.

By midnight on election night, Wilson went to bed assuming that he had lost. Roosevelt was so sure Hughes had won that he sent him a congratulatory telegram. At 4 A.M., however, the results from California showed that Wilson had eked out a victory in that state by only 4,000 votes, and thus had become the first Democrat to win a second consecutive term since Andrew Jackson in 1832. His pledge of "peace, prosperity, and progressivism" won him the western states, Ohio, and the solidly Democratic South.

AMERICA GOES TO WAR

After his close reelection, Woodrow Wilson again urged the warring nations in Europe to negotiate a "peace without victory," but to no avail. A French official spoke for many European leaders when he said that Wilson's notion of peace without victory was like "bread without yeast."

On January 31, 1917, German military leaders renewed unrestricted submarine warfare in the Atlantic, for they had come to believe that victory depended on their cutting off the trans-Atlantic supply lines from America and Canada to the European allies. Now, all American vessels headed for Britain, France, or Italy would be sunk without warning. "This was practically ordering the United States off the Atlantic," said William McAdoo, Wilson's secretary of the Treasury.

Germany's decision, Colonel House wrote in his journal, left Wilson "sad and depressed," for the president knew it meant war. For their part, the German leaders underestimated the American reaction. The United States, the German military newspaper proclaimed, "not only has no army, it has no artillery, no means of transportation, no airplanes, and lacks all other instruments of modern warfare." When his advisers warned that German submarines might cause the United States to enter the war, Kaiser Wilhelm scoffed, "I don't care."

THE ZIMMERMANN TELEGRAM On February 3, President Wilson informed Congress that he had formally ended diplomatic relations with the German government to preserve the "dignity and honor of the United States." Three weeks later, on February 25, he learned that the British had intercepted a coded telegram from Germany's foreign minister, Arthur Zimmermann, to the German ambassador in Mexico City. The telegram said that Germany would begin "unrestricted submarine warfare on February 1." If war erupted with the United States, the ambassador was instructed to offer the Mexican government an alliance: If the United States entered the war in Europe, Mexican forces would invade the United States. In exchange, Germany would return to Mexico its "lost territory in Texas, New Mexico, and Arizona."

On March 1, newspapers broke the news of the notorious **Zimmermann telegram**. The Mexican government immediately disavowed any support for the Germans. Infuriated Americans called for war. A New York newspaper said the Zimmermann telegram was "final proof that the German government has gone stark mad."

AMERICA ENTERS THE WAR In March 1917, German submarines torpedoed five U.S. ships in the North Atlantic. For Wilson, this was the last straw. On April 2, he called on Congress to declare war against the German Empire and its allies.

In one of his greatest speeches, Wilson acknowledged that it was "a fearful thing to lead this great peaceful people into war," but "the world must be made safe for democracy." He warned that it would require mobilizing "all the material resources of the country," and he called for 500,000 men to bolster the armed forces. The nation's motives, he insisted, were pure. The United States was entering the war not so much to defend its honor as to lead a "great crusade" for the "ultimate peace of the world and for the liberation of its peoples."

Congress erupted with approval. Wilson told an aide how surreal it was to watch the legislators stand and applaud the decision for war. "My message today was a message of death for our young men. How strange it seems to applaud that." He then sat down and sobbed. Two days later, the Senate passed the war resolution by a vote of 82 to 6. The House followed, 373 to 50, and Wilson signed the measure on April 6.

Opposing the war resolution were thirty-two Republicans, sixteen Democrats, one Socialist, and one independent. Among the "No" votes was

Republican Jeannette Rankin of Montana, the first woman elected to the House of Representatives. "Peace is a woman's job," she explained. "You can no more win a war than you can win an earthquake. I want to stand by my country, but I cannot vote for war."

Like Rankin, Wilson had doubts about joining the war. The president feared—accurately, as it turned out—that waging war and stamping out dissent would destroy the ideals and momentum of progressivism: "Every reform we have made will be lost if we go into this war." Yet in the end, he saw no choice.

America's long embrace of isolationism was over. The nation had reached a turning point in its relations with the world that would test the president's political and diplomatic skills—and his stamina.

MOBILIZING A NATION

In April 1917, the U.S. Army remained small, untested, and poorly armed. With just 127,000 men, it was only the seventeenth largest army in the world. Now the Wilson administration needed to recruit, equip, and train an army of millions and transport them across an ocean infested with German submarines. On May 18, 1917, Congress passed the Selective Service Act, which instructed local boards to register men ages twenty-one to thirty for the draft (later expanded to eighteen to forty-five years old). Community draft boards were supposed to be impartial; many were not. An Atlanta board exempted 526 out of 815 white men but only 6 out of 202 black men.

RECRUITING AN ARMY Many men did not wait to be drafted; they rushed to enlist. Even recently arrived immigrants felt inspired to fight. Tony Monanco, a "diminutive Italian" who worked as a water boy, showed up early one morning at the recruiting office in Buffalo, New York. When a clerk asked him what he wanted, Monanco replied, "My name is Tony Monanco. I have been in this country six months. Give me a gun."

Twenty percent of those who joined the army were immigrants. Some 31 percent of them were illiterate. Polish immigrants were especially eager to serve because of their harsh treatment by the Germans over the years. Although they represented only 4 percent of the national population, some 40 percent of the first 100,000 U.S. service enlistees were Polish.

The challenge of training recruits of many different languages led the army to create the Foreign-Speaking Soldier Subsection to bridge the communication gap. An army officer said the foreign-born recruits "obeyed orders better and were less complaining than the native-born Americans."

MANAGING THE HOME FRONT Mobilizing the nation for war led to an unprecedented expansion of federal authority. Congress passed the Lever Act, which gave the president authority to manage the nation's supplies of food and fuels (oil and gasoline), and to take over factories, railroads, mines, warehouses, and telephone and telegraph systems. Federal agencies could also set prices for wheat and coal. "Laissez faire is dead," rejoiced a progressive. "Long live social control."

Soon after the United States declared war, President Wilson called for complete economic mobilization and created new agencies to coordinate the effort. The War Industries Board (WIB) soon became the most important of all the federal mobilization agencies. Bernard Baruch, a savvy financier, headed the WIB, which had the unprecedented authority to ration raw materials, construct factories, and set prices.

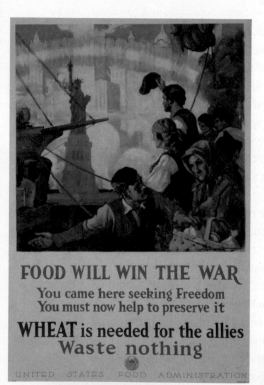

FOOD WILL WIN THE WAR
You came here seeking Freedom
You must now help to preserve it
WHEAT is needed for the allies
Waste nothing
UNITED   STATES   FOOD   ADMINISTRATION

The immigrant effort This Food Administration poster emphasizes that "wheat is . . . for the allies," an important message to immigrants from Germany and Austria.

Wilson appointed business magnate Herbert Hoover to lead the new Food Administration, whose slogan was, "Food will win the war." The bureau's purpose was to increase agricultural production while reducing civilian food consumption, because Great Britain and France needed massive amounts of corn and wheat. Hoover organized a huge group of volunteers who fanned out across the country to urge families and restaurants to participate in "Wheatless" Mondays, "Meatless" Tuesdays, and "Porkless" Thursdays and Saturdays. In crises such as war, Hoover declared, democracies must show "a willingness to yield to dictatorship."

The Great War would cost the U.S. government $30 billion, which was more than thirty times the federal budget in 1917. In addition to raising taxes to finance war efforts, the Wilson administration launched a nationwide campaign to sell "liberty bonds," government certificates that guaranteed the purchaser a fixed rate of return.

The government recruited dozens of celebrities to promote bond purchases, arguing that a liberty bond was both patriotic and a smart investment. Even the Boy Scouts and Girl Scouts sold bonds, using advertising posters that said, "Every Scout to Save a Soldier." By war's end, the government had sold more than $20 billion in bonds, most of which were purchased by banks and investment houses rather than by individuals.

A NEW LABOR FORCE Removing 4.7 million people from the workforce to serve in the armed forces created an acute labor shortage. It was made worse because the European war shut off the flow of immigration to the United States. To address the shortfall of workers, women were encouraged to take jobs that had been held primarily by men.

Initially, most women had supported the war effort in traditional ways. They helped organize fund-raising drives, donated canned food and war-related materials, volunteered for the Red Cross, and joined the army nurse corps. As the scope of the war widened, however, women were recruited to

At the munitions factory Women played crucial roles in the war effort. Here, women use welding torches to fabricate bombs.

work on farms, loading docks, and railway crews, as well as in the armaments industry, machine shops, steel and lumber mills, and chemical plants. "At last, after centuries of disabilities and discrimination," noted a speaker at a Women's Trade Union League meeting in 1917, "women are coming into the labor [force] and festival of life on equal terms with men."

The changes turned out to be limited and brief, however. About a million women participated in "war work," but most were young, single, and already working outside the home. Most returned to their previous jobs once the war ended. In fact, after the war, male-dominated unions encouraged women to go back to domestic roles. The Central Federated Union of New York insisted that "the same patriotism which induced women to enter industry during the war should induce them to vacate their positions after the war."

The Great War also generated dramatic changes for many minority groups. Hundreds of thousands of African American men joined the military, where they were required to serve in racially segregated units commanded by white officers, as in the Civil War half a century earlier.

Segregation in the military Most African American enlistees served in support units because whites believed them unfit for combat, despite evidence of black military contributions since the Revolution. Here, soldiers in the 92nd Infantry Division (one of the few "colored" units sent overseas) march in Verdun, France.

On the home front, northern businesses sent recruiting agents into the largely rural and agricultural southern states to find workers for factories and mills. For the first time, such employment efforts were directed at African Americans as well as whites. More than 400,000 black southerners, mostly sharecroppers, joined what came to be known as the **Great Migration**, a mass movement of people that would continue through the 1920s and reshape the political and social chemistry of northern and western cities. By 1930, the number of African Americans living in the North had tripled that of 1910. A rural people had become urban; an oppressed people had gained opportunities for equality.

Recruiting agents and newspaper editors, both black and white, portrayed the North and West as the "land of promise" for African American southerners. Jobs in northern steel mills, factories, and railroads were plentiful, and paid well by southern standards, and racism was less obvious and violent—at least at first. A black migrant from Mississippi wrote from Chicago in 1917 that he wished he had moved north twenty years earlier. "I just begin to feel like a man [here]," he explained. "It's a great deal of pleasure in knowing that you have some privilege. My children are going to the same school with the whites, and I don't have to be humble to no one."

Many Mexican Americans found similar opportunities to improve their status. Some joined the military. David Barkley Hernandez had to drop his last name when he enlisted in San Antonio, Texas, because the local draft board was not accepting Mexicans. In 1918, just two days before the war ended, he died in France while returning from a dangerous mission behind German lines. Hernandez became the first person of Mexican descent in the U.S. Army to win the Congressional Medal of Honor.

Even more Mexicans pursued economic opportunities created by the war effort. Between 1917 and 1920, some 100,000 job-hungry Mexicans crossed the border into the United States.

The newcomers were often resented, however. J. Luz Saenz, a Mexican American man from Texas, noted in his diary that it took only three days after he was discharged from the army to have whites "throw us out from restaurants and deny us service as human beings." In 1917, more than forty African Americans and nine whites were killed during a riot in a weapons plant in East St. Louis, Illinois. Two years later, a Chicago race riot left twenty-three African Americans and fifteen whites dead.

WAR PROPAGANDA The war effort also led the government to mobilize public opinion. On April 14, 1917, eight days after the declaration of war, President Wilson established the Committee on Public Information

(CPI), composed of the secretaries of state, war, and the navy. Its executive director, George Creel, convinced Wilson that the best way to influence public opinion was with propaganda. To that end, Creel organized a public relations campaign to explain the Allies' war aims to the people.

Creel organized the CPI into four divisions. The Speaking Division recruited 75,000 public lecturers known as "Four-Minute Men" for their ability to compress the war's objectives into a few words. They gave some 7.5 million speeches to civic groups, churches, synagogues, fraternal lodges, union halls, colleges, and schools. The Film Division produced short films celebrating the U.S. war effort. The Foreign Language Division monitored U.S. newspapers published in languages other than English, and the Division of Pictorial Publicity recruited an army of artists to produce patriotic posters.

Creel insisted his committee's work was not simply propaganda, but he admitted his job was to shape public perceptions. The CPI was "a plain publicity proposition, a vast enterprise in salesmanship, the world's greatest adventure in advertising."

A LOSS OF CIVIL LIBERTIES Once the United States entered the war, Americans equated anything German with disloyalty. Towns, streets, businesses, and even families with German names were renamed. Berlin, Iowa, became Lincoln, and East Germantown, Indiana, became Pershing, in honor of the military leader. Many quit drinking beer because German Americans owned most of the breweries. Symphonies refused to perform music by Bach and Beethoven, schools canceled German language classes, and grocers renamed *sauerkraut* "liberty cabbage." Mobs killed several German Americans accused of spying. Dozens of others were tarred and feathered.

President Wilson had predicted as much. "Once [we] lead this people into war," he said, "they'll forget there ever was such a thing as tolerance." What Wilson did not say was that he would lead the effort to suppress civil liberties, for, as he claimed, subversive forces in a nation at war must be "crushed out." Theodore Roosevelt likewise denounced the "whole raft of sexless creatures" who opposed going to war. Former secretary of state Elihu Root, an attorney, was equally direct: "There are men walking about the streets . . . who ought to be taken out at sunrise tomorrow and shot for treason."

In passing the Espionage and Sedition Acts, Congress authorized the most outrageous violations of civil liberties since the 1798 Alien and Sedition Acts. The Espionage Act of 1917 stipulated that anyone who helped the enemy, encouraged insubordination, disloyalty, or refusal of duty in the armed services, or interfered with the war effort in other ways, could be imprisoned for up to twenty years.

A year later, Congress amended the Espionage Act with the Sedition Act. It outlawed saying, writing, or printing anything "disloyal, profane, scurrilous, or abusive" about the American form of government, the Constitution, or the army and navy.

The effort to squelch free speech provoked sharp criticism. Senator George Norris, a progressive Republican from Nebraska, wondered why the nation should fight a war for democracy abroad if Congress were going to interfere "with the very fundamental principles of human liberty and human freedom on which our great Commonwealth is founded."

The Supreme Court endorsed the Espionage and Sedition Acts in two rulings issued after the war ended. *Schenck v. United States* (1919) reaffirmed the conviction of Charles T. Schenck, head of the Socialist party, for circulating anti-war leaflets among members of the armed forces. Justice Oliver Wendell Holmes wrote the unanimous opinion that freedom of speech did not apply to words that represented "a clear and present danger to the safety of the country." In *Abrams v. United States* (1919), the Court upheld the conviction of a man who had distributed pamphlets opposing military intervention in Russia to thwart the Communist revolution.

Keep out of it In this 1918 war poster, the kaiser—with his famous moustache and spiked German helmet—is depicted as a spider, spinning an invisible web to catch the stray words of Allied civilians.

During the U.S. involvement in the war, courts convicted 1,055 people under the Espionage Act. Most were simply critics of the war. On June 16, 1918, Socialist leader Eugene V. Debs, the 63-year-old pacifist who had run against Wilson in 1912, gave a speech in Canton, Ohio, in which he stressed that the war was inherently unfair. It was, he said, "the working class who fight all the battles, the working class who make the supreme sacrifices, the working class who freely shed their blood and furnish the corpses, have never yet had a voice in either declaring war or making peace. It is the ruling class that invariably does both. They alone declare war and they alone make peace."

Government agents recorded the speech, and two weeks later they arrested Debs. After being convicted of violating the Espionage Act for expressing sympathy for men jailed for encouraging others to avoid the draft, he was sentenced to ten years in prison. He told the court he was exercising his rights of free speech under the First Amendment and would always criticize wars imposed by the "master" class: "While there is a lower class, I am in it. While there is a criminal element, I am of it. While there is a soul in prison, I am not free." In 1919, the Supreme Court unanimously approved Debs's conviction.

Debs was sent first to the West Virginia State Prison, then to the federal penitentiary near Atlanta. The West Virginia warden wrote to the Atlanta warden: "I never in my life met a kinder man [Debs]. He is forever thinking of others, trying to serve them, and never thinking of himself." In the federal prison, he charmed prisoners and guards alike and radiated warmth and fellowship. In 1920, the Socialist party nominated him for the fifth time as its presidential candidate. Even though he was a prisoner, he would receive more than 900,000 votes.

THE "POISON OF DISLOYALTY" President Wilson was equally resolute in prosecuting immigrants who supported America's enemies. From colonial days, Americans had always recruited, yet feared, immigrants. Now, fear took over. As Wilson warned, "there are citizens of the United States, I blush to admit, born under other flags . . . who have poured the poison of disloyalty into the very arteries of our national life. . . . Such creatures of passion, disloyalty, and anarchy must be crushed out."

Others were determined to shut off immigration altogether, especially from southern and eastern Europe. In 1916, Madison Grant, a New York attorney, published a hugely influential book, *The Passing of the Great Race*. Grant was a fervent eugenicist (a believer in the pseudoscience of racial breeding). During the early twentieth century, the popularity of eugenics prompted thirty states to pass laws requiring compulsory sterilization of the insane, the "feebleminded," the "dependent," and the "diseased."

In *The Passing of the Great Race*, Grant claimed that racial purity was the foundation of great nations. Yet America's once-dominant Nordic stock, he warned, was committing "race suicide" by interbreeding with African Americans and an "increasing number of the weak, the broken, and the mentally crippled of all the races drawn from the lower stratum of the Mediterranean basin and the Balkans, together with hordes of the wretched, submerged populations of the Polish Ghettos." He railed against "the maudlin sentimentalism" that welcomed these "worthless race types" from Europe, for they were "sweeping the nation toward a racial abyss."

Such notions led Congress in 1917 to revive the idea of requiring a literacy test of immigrants. Three times before, Congress had passed similar legislation, only to see Presidents Cleveland, Taft, and Wilson (1915) veto it. Now, in response to theories of racial superiority and pleas from labor union leaders concerned about an influx of unskilled "aliens," overwhelming majorities in both the House and Senate overrode Wilson's veto of the first widely restrictive immigration law. (Wilson had argued that literacy had nothing to do with a person's character).

The Immigration Act of 1917 required immigrants over 16 years old to take a literacy test to demonstrate basic reading ability in any language. It also increased the "head tax" immigrants paid upon arrival to $8 (about $160 today) and allowed immigration officials to exercise more discretion in excluding newcomers. It specifically denied entry to "idiots, imbeciles, feeble-minded persons, epileptics, insane persons, paupers, beggars, vagrants, alcoholics, prostitutes, persons afflicted with disease, criminals, polygamists, and anarchists."

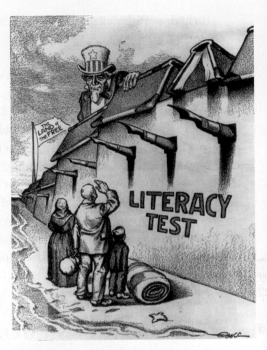

The Americanese Wall In this cartoon responding to the Immigration Act of 1917, sponsored by Congressman John Burnett of Alabama, Uncle Sam looms behind a "Literacy Test" wall fortified with the points of pens and books for battlements. He tells the immigrant family looking up at him: "You're welcome in—if you can climb it!"

Finally, the Immigration Act of 1917 was much more restrictive than the 1882 Chinese Exclusion Act because it excluded *all* Asians except Japanese and Filipinos. In 1907, the Japanese Government had voluntarily limited Japanese immigration to the United States in the so-called Gentlemen's Agreement with President Roosevelt. Because the Philippines was a U.S. colony, its citizens were U.S. nationals and could travel freely to the United States.

Senator Ellison "Cotton Ed" Smith, a South Carolina Democrat who chaired the Immigration Committee, stressed "the necessity for a pure, homogeneous American people." He and other advocates of the literacy test believed it would reduce the number of immigrants from eastern and southern Europe by more than 40 percent. In reality, only a small number of immigrants were turned away because of illiteracy. Still, America's open-door tradition was closing.

WAGING WAR ON LABOR President Wilson was concerned about the loyalty of other Americans, too. Hundreds of local and state officials belonged to the Socialist party, which opposed U.S. involvement in the war. And thousands of wage workers were "Wobblies," members of the radical Industrial Workers of the World (IWW), who supported the battle between labor and management, not the war in Europe.

The IWW was devastated by the Great War, when hundreds of Wobblies were jailed, beaten, shot, and tortured for opposing the conflict. Federal agents raided forty-eight IWW offices across the country. They confiscated filing cabinets filled with correspondence and records and arrested 165 Wobblies. A hundred were eventually tried for sedition, and all were convicted and imprisoned.

THE AMERICAN ROLE IN THE WAR

In 1917, America's war strategy focused on helping the struggling French and British armies on the Western Front. The Allied leaders stressed that they needed at least a million U.S. troops, but it would take months to recruit, equip, and train that many new soldiers.

On December 21, 1917, French premier Georges Clemenceau urged the Americans to rush their army, called the American Expeditionary Force (AEF), to France. "A terrible blow is imminent," he told a journalist about to leave Paris. "Tell your Americans to come quickly." Clemenceau was referring to the likelihood of a massive German attack, made more probable by the end of the fighting on the Eastern Front following the Bolshevik Revolution in Russia in November 1917.

THE BOLSHEVIK REVOLUTION Among the many casualties of the Great War, none was greater than the destruction of the Russian Empire and its incompetent monarchy. It was the first nation to crack under the prolonged strain of the war.

Ravaged by widespread starvation and united by a desire for change, the Russian people launched a revolution in the bitterly cold winter of 1917. On February 23, crowds of women factory workers gathered in the streets of the capital, Petrograd (formerly St. Petersburg). More workers, male and female, joined in. On March 1, the rebels formed a "provisional government," eventually led by Alexander Kerensky, who demanded that the inept tsar, Nicholas II, give up the throne.

On March 2, 1917, Nicholas II, having presided over a war that had ruined his nation's economy and transportation system, abdicated his throne and turned the nation over to the provisional government. Within months, Russia was a republic committed to continuing the war.

The fall of the tsar created the illusion that all the major Allied powers— including Russia—were now fighting for the ideals of constitutional democracy. Through the summer and into the fall of 1917, Woodrow Wilson and his advisers assumed that Kerensky would democratize Russian institutions, rebuild morale, and make Russia a worthy partner in making the world safe for democracy.

That illusion was shattered after the Germans helped an exiled Marxist radical named Vladimir Ilyich Lenin board a sealed train to Russia from Switzerland. For years, Lenin had been biding his time, waiting for the war to devour the German and Russian monarchs.

The Germans hoped that Lenin would cause turmoil in his homeland. He did much more than that. As the train left Zurich, he leaned out a window to say goodbye to a friend. "Either we'll be swinging from the gallows in three months," he predicted, "or we shall be in power."

On the night of April 16, 1917, the forty-seven-year-old Lenin, a man of iron will and ruthless determination, arrived in Petrograd. A huge crowd welcomed him. Climbing atop an armored car, he pledged to withdraw Russia from the hated war and to eliminate private property. "The people," he shouted, "need peace, the people need bread, the people need land." The provisional government, he charged, "gives you war, hunger, no bread. We must fight for the social revolution" until the "complete victory of the proletariat. Long live the worldwide Socialist revolution!"

Lenin saw power lying in the streets, waiting to be picked up. To do

Vladimir Lenin Communist revolutionary who led the Bolsheviks in seizing power and ultimately establishing the Soviet Union.

so, he mobilized the Bolsheviks, a group of cold-blooded Communist revolutionaries convinced that they were in the vanguard of the irresistible force of history. The Bolsheviks promised to end Russia's involvement in the war and to institute a Communist system of government.

During the night of October 25, armed Bolsheviks took over train stations, post offices, and telegraph offices. Others stormed the Petrograd Winter Palace, seized power from the provisional government, established a dictatorship, and called for a quick end to the war. As a disillusioned Bolshevik noted, Lenin's dictatorship, "a government that promised freedom for all working people, had created a tyranny" that soon unleashed a reign of terror.

For the first time in history, a government—the Bolsheviks—announced that it was both infallible and rooted in atheism. Lenin pledged to hang, shoot, and destroy anyone foolish enough to oppose the revolution. He took control of banks, businesses, church properties, and great landed estates, censored newspapers, shut down the legal system, jailed opponents, and created a brutal secret police force. "To us," Lenin announced, "all is permitted. . . . Blood? Let there be blood."

The Bolshevik Revolution triggered a chaotic civil war throughout Russia, with the anti-Bolshevik White army fighting the Communist Red army—and many other groups choosing or switching sides. In mid-August 1918, President Wilson, horrified at the idea of a Communist Russia, sent 8,000 U.S. soldiers to Siberia. The Siberian Expeditionary Force went to Vladivostok on Russia's Pacific coast, ostensibly to retrieve military supplies sent to the prerevolutionary Russians. Its commanding general pledged to take no part in any "crusade" against Bolshevism.

Walter Lippmann, editor of the *New Republic* magazine, warned Wilson that he should stick to his original position of "no interference in Russia's internal affairs" and not embroil U.S. troops in the Russian civil war. Yet Wilson intervened anyway. After nineteen months of unsuccessful military efforts against the Bolsheviks, U.S. troops returned to America in April 1920. Thereafter, Russian Communists steadfastly believed that America had tried to overturn their revolution.

FOURTEEN POINTS Woodrow Wilson was determined to ensure that the Great War would be the last world war. To that end, in September 1917, he appointed a group of 150 experts in politics, history, geography, and foreign policy, called the Inquiry, to draft a peace plan. America, according to Wilson, had no selfish goals; it was simply "one of the champions of the rights of mankind." Drawing upon the Inquiry's advice, Wilson developed the

Fourteen Points, a comprehensive list of provisions intended to shape the peace treaty and the postwar world.

Wilson made a dramatic presentation of his Fourteen Points to a joint session of Congress on January 8, 1918, describing his proposal as "the only possible program" for peace. The first five points endorsed the open conduct of diplomacy rather than backroom deals and secret treaties, the recognition of neutral nations' right to continue maritime commerce in time of war ("freedom of the seas"), the removal of international trade barriers ("free trade"), and the worldwide reduction of armaments.

Most of the other points dealt with territorial claims. Wilson demanded that, in redrawing the map of Europe, the victors follow the principle of "self-determination," allowing overlapping nationalities and ethnic groups to develop their own independent, democratic nations. Point thirteen created a new nation for Poland, long dominated by the Russians in the east and the Germans in the west. Point fourteen, the capstone of Wilson's postwar scheme, called for a permanent "league" of nations to preserve global peace.

Overall, the reaction was positive. The headline of a *New York Times* editorial proclaimed: "The President's Triumph." When the Fourteen Points were made public, however, African American leaders asked the president to add a fifteenth point: an end to racial discrimination. Wilson did not respond.

Meanwhile, the war ground on with no diplomatic solution in sight. In Germany, food and fuel shortages led to growing discontent. Workers went on strike, and soldiers and sailors mutinied and deserted. "The Monarchy," said a German official, "is lurching toward the edge of the abyss."

RUSSIA SURRENDERS Conditions were even worse in Russia. When Vladimir Lenin took power in 1917, some 4 million ill-clad, poorly equipped, and half-starved Russian soldiers had been killed or wounded in the war. Lenin declared that the world would be freed from war only by a global revolution in which capitalism was replaced by communism. To that end, he wanted Russia out of the war as soon as possible.

On March 3, 1918, Lenin signed a humiliating peace agreement with Germany, the Treaty of Brest-Litovsk. The treaty forced Russia to transfer vast territories to Germany and Turkey and to recognize the independence of the Ukraine region, thereby depriving Russia of much of its population, coal and wheat production, and heavy industry. In addition, Russia had to pay $46 million to Germany. Lenin was willing to accept such a harsh peace because he needed to concentrate on the ongoing Russian civil war.

With Russia out, the Germans could focus on the Western Front. Erich Ludendorff, the German army commander, said the ability to move hundreds of thousands of soldiers from the Russian front to France would give him numerical superiority for the first time and enable him to "deal an annihilating blow to the British before American aid can become effective."

AMERICANS ON THE WESTERN FRONT On March 21, 1918, the Germans began the first of several offensives in France and Belgium designed to win the war before the American Expeditionary Force could arrive. By May, the Germans had advanced within fifty miles of Paris, and the British Fifth Army was destroyed.

In early April, however, the Germans suddenly lost their momentum. On April 5, the German commander called a halt because so many soldiers were exhausted and demoralized, convinced, as one officer admitted, that their "hope [for victory] had been dashed" by their inability to sustain the supply lines needed for such a widespread advance.

In May, French and British leaders pressed Wilson to hurry troops into the fighting. By the end of the month, some 650,000 American soldiers were in Europe. In June, they were ready to fight.

At the month-long Battle of Belleau Wood, which began on June 2, U.S. forces commanded by General John J. "Black Jack" Pershing joined the French in driving the Germans back. A French officer remarked that the Americans were providing "a wonderful transfusion of blood" for the Allied cause.

During the ferocious fighting, a French officer urged an American unit to retreat. In a famous exchange, U.S. Marine Captain Lloyd W. Williams refused the order, saying: "Retreat? Hell, we just got here." Two days later, in the midst of an intense German bombardment, an American sergeant rallied his men by barking, "Come on, you sons-of-bitches! Do you want to live forever?"

AN AMERICAN HERO Among the millions who served in the Great War, one stood out: Sergeant Alvin York, an American original. Born in 1887, he was a tall, red-haired, freckle-faced pacifist from the mountains in north-central Tennessee, near the Kentucky border. He and his deeply religious, dirt-poor family lived in a log cabin whose windswept walls were papered with pages torn from mail-order catalogs. York left school after the third grade to help support the family by working in his father's blacksmith shop. As a teen, he went through a "wild" phase, but his hijinks ended when he succumbed to the appeals of an evangelist on New Year's Day in 1915. Thereafter, he swore off "smoking, drinking, gambling, cussing, and brawling."

When the United States entered the war in 1917, York, the best shot in Tennessee, wanted no part of it. He worshiped the Bible, especially the sixth commandment that said, "Thou shalt not kill." So when York registered for the draft, he wrote on the form, "I don't want to fight." The government thought otherwise. In November 1917, he was told to report to Camp Gordon in Georgia.

After basic training, as his unit prepared to head overseas, York stayed up all night praying. By morning, he had made up his mind: "I begun to understand that no matter what a man is forced to do, so long as he is right in his own soul, he remains a righteous man. I knowed I would go to war." Once in France, York became embroiled in the forty-seven-day-long Meuse-Argonne offensive in the Argonne Forest in October 1918. The fighting, a journalist

Sergeant Alvin York The World War I hero who, when registering for the draft, said he did not want to fight.

reported, was "as bloody and difficult as any the war has seen."

On the Western Front, York's platoon was told to assault three dozen German machine guns perched along a ridge. A storm of bullets stymied the Americans, killing or wounding every officer and leaving York in charge of seven privates who were trapped in "No Man's Land."

York began to return fire, for "I was cornered. It was either them or me." Every time a German helmet popped up, he shot with deadly accuracy. Then, a German officer and five soldiers rose from a trench twenty-five yards away and charged York, who dropped his rifle and pulled out a pistol. He shot the last man first, then the next farthest from him, and the next, just like "the way we shoot wild turkeys at home." York killed all six, which led others to surrender.

By then, York had killed twenty-eight Germans and captured thirty-five machine guns. He and his surviving comrades then marched their prisoners to the rear, capturing and killing more Germans along the way. When a lieutenant counted the prisoners, the number was 132.

Word spread quickly that York had singlehandedly "captured the whole damned German army." The Allied nations showered him with their highest

Meuse-Argonne Offensive Soldiers of the 23rd Infantry, 2nd Division, fire machine guns at the Germans from what was left of the Argonne Forest in France.

military honors, and the United States awarded him the Congressional Medal of Honor. After appearing before Congress, York returned to his simple home along the Tennessee-Kentucky border.

ENDING THE WAR In a massive Allied offensive, begun on September 26, 1918, U.S. troops joined British and French armies in a drive toward Sedan, France, and its strategic railroad, which supplied the German army occupying northern France. With 1.2 million soldiers involved, it was the largest U.S. action of the war, and it resulted in 117,000 casualties, including 26,000 dead. The Allied offensive sent the outnumbered Germans reeling in retreat. "America," wrote German general Erich Ludendorff, "became the decisive power in the war."

On October 6, the German government asked Wilson for peace negotiations based on his Fourteen Points. British and French leaders accepted the plan as a basis of negotiations, but with two significant reservations. The British insisted on the right to discuss limiting freedom of the seas to preserve their naval dominance, and the French demanded massive reparations (payments to the victors by the defeated nations) from Germany and Austria for war damages.

THE GERMAN COLLAPSE By the end of October 1918, Germany was on the verge of collapse. Revolutionaries rampaged through the streets. Sailors mutinied. Germany's allies (Bulgaria, Turkey, and Austria-Hungary) dropped out of the war, and military leaders demanded that the civilian government ask for an armistice (cease-fire agreement). On November 9, the German kaiser resigned, and a republic was proclaimed.

Early on the morning of November 11, an official cease-fire took effect. The Germans were required to evacuate all captured territory and turn over 150,000 railroad freight cars, 5,000 locomotives, 5,000 trucks, 1,700 warplanes, and 25,000 machine guns. In exchange, they were assured that President Wilson's Fourteen Points would be the basis for the upcoming peace conference.

Six hours later, at the eleventh hour of the eleventh day of the eleventh month, and after 1,563 days of terrible warfare, the most needless of wars was finally over. That morning, Harry Truman, an artillery officer who would become America's president in 1945, could see in the distance a seated German soldier manning a machine gun. At 11 A.M., the German stood, took off his helmet, bowed toward the American lines, and walked away.

From Europe, Colonel Edward House sent Wilson a telegram: "Autocracy [government by an individual with unlimited power] is dead; long live democracy and its immortal leader." The end of the war triggered frenzied celebrations throughout the world. "The world awakes," wrote African American activist W. E. B. Du Bois. "The long, horrible years of dreadful night are passed. Behold the sun!" Wilson was not as joyful. The Great War, he said, had dealt a grievous injury to civilization "which can never be atoned for or repaired."

American casualties A Salvation Army worker writing a letter home for a wounded soldier.

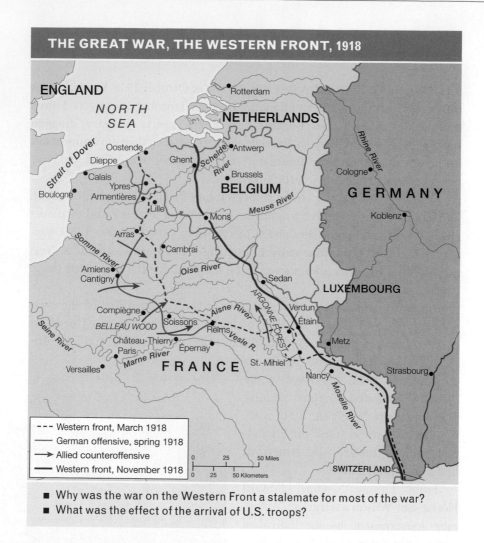

THE GREAT WAR, THE WESTERN FRONT, 1918

--- Western front, March 1918
— German offensive, spring 1918
→ Allied counteroffensive
— Western front, November 1918

0   25   50 Miles
0   25   50 Kilometers

■ Why was the war on the Western Front a stalemate for most of the war?
■ What was the effect of the arrival of U.S. troops?

The United States had lost 53,402 servicemen in combat during its nineteen months in the war. Another 63,114 U.S. soldiers and sailors died of various diseases, the largest number of those casualties the result of the deadly influenza epidemic that swept across the world in 1918. Some 200,000 Americans were wounded. Germany's war dead totaled 1.6 million; France lost nearly 1.4 million, Great Britain 658,000, and Russia 1.7 million.

While decimating a generation of young men, the war also ruined the economies of Europe. The new Europe would be very different: much poorer,

Armistice Night in New York (1918) George Luks, known for his vivid paintings of urban life, captured the unbridled outpouring of patriotism and joy that extended into the night of Germany's surrender.

more violent, more polarized, more cynical, less sure of itself, and less capable of decisive action. The United States, for good or ill, emerged as the world's dominant power.

THE POLITICS OF PEACE

On June 25, 1918, Colonel House wrote Woodrow Wilson from France, urging him to take charge of the peacemaking process. "It is one of the things with which your name should be linked during the ages." House was right. Wilson and the peace agreement ending the Great War would be forever linked, but not in the positive light they assumed.

In the making of the peace agreement, Wilson showed himself both at his best and worst. The Fourteen Points embodied his vision of a better world governed by fairer principles. In promoting his peace plan, he felt guided "by the hand of God." A peacekeeping "League of Nations" was, in his view, the key element to a "secure and lasting peace" and the "most essential part of the peace settlement." If the diplomats gathering to draft the peace treaty failed to follow his plans to reshape the world in America's image, he warned, "there will be another world war" within a generation. In the end, however, Wilson's grand efforts at global peacemaking failed—not abroad—but at home, and because of his own faults.

WILSON'S KEY ERRORS

Whatever the merits of President Wilson's peace plan, his efforts to implement it proved clumsy and self-defeating. He made several decisions that would come back to haunt him. First, against the advice of his staff and of European leaders, he decided to attend the peace conference in Paris that opened on January 18, 1919. Never before had a president left the United States for such a prolonged period (six months). During his time abroad, Wilson lost touch with political developments at home.

His second error of judgment involved politics. In the congressional election campaign of 1918, Wilson defied his advisers and political tradition by urging voters to elect a Democratic Congress as a sign of their approval of his policies in handling the war—and the peace. He "begged" the public not to "repudiate" his leadership.

Republicans, who for the most part had backed Wilson's war measures, were not pleased. Theodore Roosevelt called Wilson's self-serving appeal "a cruel insult to every Republican father or mother whose sons have entered the Army or Navy." Voters were not impressed, either, especially western farmers upset with government price ceilings placed on wheat.

In the elections, the Democrats lost control of both houses of Congress. It was a bad omen for Wilson's peacemaking efforts, since any treaty to end the war would have to be approved by at least two thirds of the Senate, now controlled by Republicans. Roosevelt said that Wilson could no longer claim "to speak for the American people." The former president and his friend Henry Cabot Lodge thereafter did their best to undermine Wilson's negotiating strength with the Allies.

Meanwhile, Wilson had dispatched Colonel House and several aides to Europe to begin convincing Allied leaders to embrace the Fourteen Points. The lopsided losses in the elections, said House, "made his difficulties enormously greater." Gordon Auchincloss, House's son-in-law who assisted him in Europe, displayed the brash confidence of many American diplomats when he boasted that "before we get through with these fellows over here, we will teach them how to do things and to do them quickly." It would not be so easy.

Wilson's efforts were further weakened when he refused to appoint a prominent Republican to the peace delegation. House had urged him to appoint Roosevelt or Lodge, the president's archenemy and the leading Republican in Congress, but Wilson refused. In the end, he appointed Harry White, an obscure Republican. Former president William Howard Taft groused that Wilson's real intention in going to Paris was "to hog the whole show."

Wilson's participation in the Paris Peace Conference would be an opportunity for him to convince Europe to follow him in creating a very different postwar world. As Wilson prepared to head for Europe, muckraking journalist Ray Stannard Baker wrote that the president "has yet to prove his greatness. The fate of a drama lies in its last act, and Wilson is now coming to that."

Initially, Wilson's entrance on the European stage in December 1918 was triumphant. Millions of grateful Europeans greeted him as an almost mystical hero, even as their savior. An Italian mayor described Wilson's visit as the "second coming of Christ." Others hailed him as the "God of peace."

The adoration reinforced Wilson's belief that only he could guide the peacemaking efforts. Claiming that he was now "at the apex of my glory in the hearts of these people," Wilson was committed to shaping a peace treaty and postwar world based on principles of justice, fairness, and self-determination.

Fit for a messiah Woodrow Wilson rode down the Champs-Élysées in Paris as the crowds showered him with flower petals and cheered, *"Vive Wilson! Vive l'Amérique! Vive la liberté!"*

From such a height, there could only be a fall. Although popular with the European people, Wilson had to negotiate with tough-minded, wily statesmen who resented his efforts to forge a peace settlement modeled on American values. That Wilson had not bothered to consult them about his Fourteen Points proposal before announcing it to the world did not help. In the end, the European leaders would force the American president to abandon many of his ideals.

THE PARIS PEACE CONFERENCE

The Paris Peace Conference lasted from January to June 1919. The participants had no time to waste. The German, Austro-Hungarian, and Ottoman Empires were in ruins. Across much of Europe, food was scarce and lawlessness rampant. The threat of revolution hung over Central Europe as Communists jostled to take control of the defeated, war-torn nations.

The peace conference dealt with immensely complex and controversial issues (including the need to create new nations and redraw the maps of Europe and the Middle East) that required both political statesmanship and technical expertise. The British delegation alone included almost 400 members, many of them specialists in political geography or economics.

THE BIG FOUR From the start, the Paris Peace Conference was controlled by the Big Four: the prime ministers of Britain, France, and Italy, and the president of the United States. Neither Germany nor its allies were allowed to attend. Communist Russia was also not invited.

Georges Clemenceau, the seventy-seven-year-old French premier known as "The Tiger," had little patience with President Wilson's idealistic preaching. In response to Wilson's claim that "America is the only idealistic nation in the world," Clemenceau grumbled that talking with Wilson was like talking to Jesus Christ. "God gave us the Ten Commandments and we broke them," the French leader sneered. "Wilson gave us the Fourteen Points—we shall see."

The Big Four fought in private and in public. The French and British, led by Prime Minister David Lloyd George, insisted that Wilson agree to their proposals to weaken Germany economically and militarily, while Vittorio Orlando, prime minister of Italy, focused on gaining territories from defeated Austria.

THE LEAGUE OF NATIONS Although suffering from chronic health issues, including hypertension and blinding headaches, Wilson lectured the other statesmen about the need to embrace his beloved **League of Nations**, which he insisted must be the "keystone" of any peace settlement. He believed that a world peace organization would abolish war by settling international disputes and mobilizing united action against aggressors. Article X of the charter, which Wilson called "the heart of the League," allowed member nations to impose military and economic sanctions, or penalties, against military aggressors. The league, Wilson predicted, would have such moral influence that it would make military action to preserve peace unnecessary.

On February 14, 1919, Wilson presented the final draft of the league covenant to the Allies and left Paris for a ten-day visit home, where he faced growing opposition among Republicans. The League of Nations, Theodore Roosevelt complained, would revive German militarism and undermine American morale. "To substitute internationalism for nationalism," Roosevelt argued, "means to do away with patriotism."

Henry Cabot Lodge, chairman of the Senate Foreign Relations Committee, who despised Wilson, also opposed the League of Nations because, he claimed, it would potentially involve sending U.S. troops to foreign conflicts without Senate approval. On March 3, 1919, Lodge presented a resolution on the Senate floor that the "League of Nations in the form as now proposed . . . should not be accepted by the United States." He then announced that thirty-seven Republicans endorsed his resolution—more than enough to block ratification of Wilson's treaty.

The Treaty of Versailles

Henry Cabot Lodge's preemptive action undermined President Wilson's leverage with the British and French. So, too, did a potent virus and the strain of overwork that weakened Wilson physically. When he returned to Paris in the spring of 1919, his European colleagues maneuvered him into concessions that mocked his ideals.

Wilson yielded to French demands that Germany transfer territory to France on its west and to Poland on its east and north. In other territorial matters, Wilson had to abandon his principle of national self-determination. As Secretary of State Robert Lansing correctly predicted, preaching self-determination would only "raise hopes which can never be realized." (Wilson later told the Senate that he wished he had never said that "all nations have a right to self-determination.")

In their efforts to allow for some degree of ethnic self-determination in multiethnic regions, the statesmen at Versailles transformed Europe from a continent of empires to one of nations. They created Austria, Hungary, Poland, Yugoslavia, and Czechoslovakia in Central Europe and four new nations along the Baltic Sea: Finland, Estonia, Lithuania, and Latvia.

The victorious Allies, however, did not create independent nations out of the colonies of the defeated and now defunct European empires. Instead, they assigned the former German colonies in Africa and the Turkish colonies in the Middle East to France and Great Britain for an unspecified time, while Japan took control of the former German colonies in the Pacific.

The issue of reparations—payments by the vanquished to the victors—triggered bitter arguments. The British and the French (on whose soil much of the war was fought) wanted Germany to pay the entire cost of the war, including their military veterans' pensions.

On this point, Wilson made perhaps his most fateful concessions. Although initially opposed to reparations, he eventually agreed to a crucial clause that forced Germany to accept responsibility for the war and its entire expense. The "war guilt" clause so offended Germans that it became a major factor in the rise of Adolf Hitler and the Nazi party during the 1920s. Wilson himself privately admitted that if he were a German, he would refuse to sign the treaty.

Colonel Edward House privately blamed Wilson for many problems associated with the treaty, saying that the president "speaks constantly of teamwork but seldom practices it." Wilson was "becoming stubborn and angry, and he never was a good negotiator."

On May 7, 1919, the victorious powers presented the treaty to the German delegates, who returned three weeks later with 443 pages of criticism. Among other things, they noted that Germany would lose 13 percent of its territory, 10 percent of its population, and all its colonies in Asia and Africa. The German president called the treaty's terms "unrealizable and unbearable." He resigned rather than sign it.

A few minor changes were made, but when the Germans still balked, the French threatened to launch a new military attack. Finally, on June 28, 1919, the Germans gave up and signed the treaty in the glittering Hall of Mirrors at Versailles, the magnificent palace built by King Louis XIV in the late seventeenth century. Thereafter, the agreement was called the **Treaty of Versailles**. It was signed exactly five years after the assassination of Archduke Franz Ferdinand.

None of the peacemakers was fully satisfied with the treaty. As France's Georges Clemenceau observed, "it was not perfect," but it was, after all, the "result of human beings. We did all we could to work fast and well." British diplomat Harold Nicolson predicted that historians would "come to the conclusion that we were very stupid men [in creating the Versailles Treaty]. I think we were."

When Adolf Hitler learned of the treaty's provisions, he vowed a ghastly and pitiless revenge. "It cannot be that two million Germans have fallen in vain," he screamed during a speech in Munich in 1922. "We demand vengeance!"

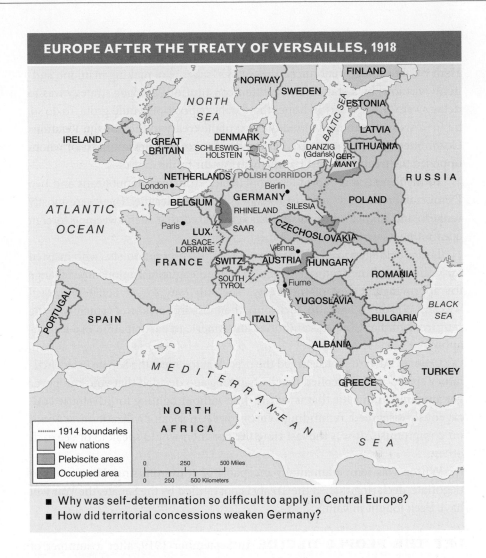

EUROPE AFTER THE TREATY OF VERSAILLES, 1918

Legend:
- ·········· 1914 boundaries
- New nations
- Plebiscite areas
- Occupied area

0   250   500 Miles
0   250   500 Kilometers

■ Why was self-determination so difficult to apply in Central Europe?

■ How did territorial concessions weaken Germany?

THE TREATY DEBATE On July 8, 1919, Woodrow Wilson arrived back in Washington, D.C., to pursue Senate approval of the treaty. Before leaving Paris, he had assured a French diplomat that he would not allow changes to the treaty: "The Senate must take its medicine." Thus began one of the most partisan and bitterly personal disputes in history.

On July 10, Wilson called upon both parties to accept their "great duty" and ratify the treaty. He then grew needlessly confrontational, dismissing critics as "blind and little provincial people." The world, he claimed, was relying on the United States to sign the treaty: "Dare we reject it and break the heart of the world?"

Yes, answered Senate Republicans, who had decided that Wilson's commitment to the League of Nations was a reckless threat to America's independence. Henry Cabot Lodge denounced the treaty's "scheme of making mankind suddenly virtuous by a statute or a written constitution." Lodge's strategy was to delay a vote on the treaty in hopes that public opposition would grow. To do so, he took six weeks to read aloud the text of the treaty to the Foreign Relations Committee. He then organized a parade of expert witnesses, most of whom opposed the treaty, to appear at the hearings on ratification.

In the Senate, a group of "irreconcilables," fourteen Republicans and two Democrats, refused to support membership in the league. They were mostly western and midwestern isolationists who feared that such sweeping foreign commitments would threaten domestic reforms.

Lodge belonged to a larger group called the "reservationists," who insisted upon limiting American participation in the League of Nations in exchange for approving the rest of the treaty. The only way to get Senate approval was for Wilson to agree to revisions, the most important of which was the requirement that Congress authorize any American participation in a league-approved war.

Colonel Edward House urged the president to "meet the Senate in a conciliatory spirit." Wilson replied that he had long ago decided that you "can never get anything in this life that is worthwhile without fighting for it." House courageously disagreed, reminding Wilson that American civilization was "built on compromise." It was the last time the two men would speak to or see each other.

Wilson was temperamentally incapable of compromising. He refused to negotiate, declaring that "if the Treaty is not ratified by the Senate, the War will have been fought in vain."

LET THE PEOPLE DECIDE In September 1919, after a summer of fruitless debate, an exhausted Wilson decided to take his case directly to the voters. On September 2, against doctor's orders and the advice of his wife and aides, he boarded a train and left Washington for a grueling 10,000-mile tour through the Midwest to the West Coast. He planned to visit twenty-nine cities and deliver nearly 100 speeches on behalf of the treaty.

No president had ever made such an effort to win public support. Enormous crowds greeted him in Columbus, Kansas City, Des Moines, Omaha, and other stops. In St. Louis, Wilson said that he had returned from Paris "bringing one of the greatest documents of human history," which was now in danger of being rejected by the Senate. He pledged to "fight for a cause . . . greater than the Senate. It is greater than the government. It is as great as the cause of mankind."

Despite suffering from pounding headaches, Wilson spoke as many as four times a day. By the time his train reached Spokane, Washington, he was visibly fatigued. Still, he kept going, through Oregon and California. Some 200,000 people greeted him in Los Angeles.

Then disaster struck. After delivering an emotional speech on September 25, 1919, in Pueblo, Colorado, Wilson collapsed from severe headaches. His left side was paralyzed, and one side of his face was palsied, limp, and expressionless. "I seem to have gone to pieces," he sighed. The presidential train, its blinds drawn, raced back to Washington, D.C.

A STRICKEN PRESIDENT A week later, the president suffered a stroke (cerebral hemorrhage) that left him paralyzed on his left side and partially blind; he could barely speak. Ray Stannard Baker visited Wilson in the White House and came away stunned. The president, Baker gasped, had become "a broken, ruined old man, shuffling along, his left arm inert, the fingers drawn up like a claw, the left side of his face sagging frightfully. His voice is not human: it gurgles in his throat."

For five months, from the autumn of 1919 and into early 1920, the president lay in bed while his doctor issued reassuring medical bulletins. Wilson "lived on, but oh, what a wreck of his former self!" said a White House staff member. "He had changed from a giant to a pygmy." If a document needed Wilson's signature, his wife guided his hand, leading a senator to complain that the nation now had a "petticoat government."

Secretary of State Robert Lansing urged the president's aides to declare him disabled and appoint Vice President Thomas Marshall in his place. They angrily refused. Soon thereafter, Wilson replaced Lansing.

Wilson became emotionally unstable and began displaying signs of paranoia. A visitor found the president bitter and brooding, full of self-pity and anger. For the remaining seventeen months of his second term, Wilson's wife, along with aides and trusted cabinet members, kept him isolated from all but the most essential business. When a group of Republican senators visited the White House, one of them said: "Well, Mr. President, we have all been praying for you." Wilson replied, "Which way, Senator?"

THE TREATY UNDER ATTACK Such humor was rare, however. President Wilson's hardened arteries seemed to have hardened his judgment as well. For his part, Henry Cabot Lodge pushed through the Senate fourteen changes (the number was not coincidental) in the draft of the Treaty of Versailles.

The exiled Colonel Edward House became so concerned that he wrote Edith Wilson a letter in which he said how "vital" it was for some form of the treaty to be approved, since the president's "place in history is in the balance." House pleaded for Wilson to negotiate a compromise. The First Lady refused to share his concerns with her husband.

In the end, Wilson rejected any proposed changes to the treaty. As a result, his supporters in the Senate were thrown into an unlikely alliance with the irreconcilables, who opposed the treaty under *any* circumstances. The final Senate vote in 1920 on Lodge's revised treaty was 39 in favor and 55 against. On the question of approving the original treaty without changes, the irreconcilables and the reservationists, led by Lodge, combined to defeat ratification, with 38 for and 53 against.

Woodrow Wilson's grand effort at global peacemaking had failed. (He did receive the Nobel Peace Prize for his efforts.) When told of the final Senate vote, he said it "would have been better if I had died last fall."

After refusing to ratify the treaty, Congress tried to declare an official end to the war by a joint resolution on May 20, 1920, which Wilson vetoed. It was not until July 2, 1921, four months after he had left office and almost eighteen months after the fighting had stopped, that another joint resolution officially ended the state of war with Germany and Austria-Hungary. Separate peace treaties with Germany, Austria, and Hungary were ratified on October 18, 1921. By then, Warren G. Harding was president.

The U.S. failure to ratify the Versailles Treaty was a defining moment in world history, for it helped trigger a chain of events that would contribute to a second world war twenty years later. The United States never joined the League of Nations. With Great Britain and France too exhausted and too timid to keep Germany weak and isolated, a dangerous power vacuum would emerge in Europe, one that Adolf Hitler and the Nazis would fill.

STUMBLING FROM WAR TO PEACE

In America, celebrations over the war's end soon gave way to widespread inflation, unemployment, labor unrest, socialist and Communist radicalism, race riots, terrorist bombings, and government tyranny. With millions of servicemen returning to civilian life, war-related industries shutting down, and wartime price controls ending, unemployment and prices for consumer goods spiked.

Bedridden by his stroke, President Wilson became increasingly distant, depressed, and peevish. His administration was in disarray, he had never been so unpopular, and the Democratic party was floundering along with him.

THE SPANISH FLU Beginning in 1918, many Americans confronted an infectious enemy that produced far more casualties than the war and in much shorter time. It became known as the "Spanish" influenza (although it did not originate in Spain), a new and deadly strain of the virus that within months swept across the globe.

The disease appeared in January 1918 at an overcrowded Kansas army camp and spread quickly to Europe with the U.S. troops. By June, the pandemic stretched from Algeria to New Zealand, India and the Pacific islands. Its initial outbreak lasted a year and killed between 50 million and 100 million people worldwide, far more than were killed in the Great War. In the United States alone, it infected 26 million people, some 670,000 of whom died, more than ten times the number of U.S. combat deaths in France. The public health system was strained to the breaking point. Hospitals ran short of beds, nurses, and doctors; funeral homes ran out of coffins.

Fear seized the population. Schools and churches closed, and people ignored desperate appeals for hospital volunteers for fear of becoming infected themselves. In Goldsboro, North Carolina, Dan Tonkel remembered, "We were actually almost afraid to breathe. You were afraid to go out. The fear was so great people were actually afraid to leave their home . . . afraid to talk to one another."

Influenza epidemic Office workers wearing gauze masks during the Spanish flu epidemic of January 1918.

By the spring of 1919, the pandemic had run its course. Although another outbreak occurred in the winter of 1920, people had grown more resistant to it. No disease in human history—indeed, no war, famine, or natural catastrophe—had killed so many in such a short time.

SUFFRAGE AT LAST As the first outbreak of the Spanish flu was ending, women finally gained a constitutional guarantee of their right to vote. After six months of delay, debate, and failed votes, Congress passed the **Nineteenth Amendment** in the spring of 1919 and sent it to the states for ratification.

Tennessee's legislature was the last of thirty-six state assemblies to approve the amendment, and it did so in dramatic fashion. As thousands of supporters and opponents mobilized in Knoxville, the state capital, the outcome was uncertain.

The initial vote was 48–48. Then a twenty-four-year-old Republican legislator named Harry T. Burn changed his no vote to yes at the insistence of his strong-willed mother, Phoebe Ensminger Burn. She had written her son a note admonishing him to be a "good boy" and vote for suffrage. "Don't keep them in doubt!" He did as she directed, and the Nineteenth Amendment became

Their first votes Women of New York City's East Side vote for the first time in the presidential election of 1920.

official on August 18, 1920, making the United States the twenty-second nation to allow women's suffrage. Josephine Pearson, the most vocal Tennessee anti-suffragist, labeled Burn a "traitor to manhood's honor."

Women's suffrage was the climactic achievement of the Progressive Era. Suddenly, 9.5 million women were eligible to vote in national elections; in the 1920 presidential election, they would make up 40 percent of the electorate. "The greatest thing to come out of the war," said suffragist Carrie Chapman Catt, "was the emancipation of women, for which no man fought."

Carrie Chapman Catt The women's suffrage leader is pictured here speaking on the telephone at her desk.

ECONOMIC TURBULENCE

As consumer prices rose, discontented workers, released from wartime controls on wages, grew more willing to go on strike. In 1919, more than 4 million hourly wage workers, 20 percent of the workforce, participated in 3,600 strikes. Most wanted nothing more than higher wages and shorter workweeks, but their critics linked them with the worldwide Communist movement. Charges of a Communist conspiracy were greatly exaggerated, however. In 1919, fewer than 70,000 people nationwide belonged to the Communist party.

The most controversial labor dispute was in Boston, where police went on strike on September 9, 1919. Massachusetts governor Calvin Coolidge mobilized the National Guard to maintain order. After four days during which looters panicked the city, the striking police offered to return, but Coolidge ordered that they all be fired. When labor leaders appealed for their reinstatement, Coolidge responded in words that made him an instant national hero: "There is no right to strike against the public safety by anybody, anywhere, any time."

RACE RIOTS The end of the Great War brought fresh hopes that African Americans might gain full equality. John M. Ross, a black officer, stressed that fighting the war had given him "a greater feeling of pride in the achievements of my race, and a hope that this great country of ours will give every man in it a square deal, no matter what his race or color may be." Others were more skeptical. Herbert Seligmann, a journalist who served on the board of the NAACP, maintained that the war "has meant a vital change in the position of the Negro and in his own feeling about the position." Yet Seligmann warned that "if the white man tries to 'show the nigger his place' by flogging and lynching him, the Negro, when the government does not defend him, will purchase arms to defend himself."

Seligmann's greatest fear was realized. The end of the war brought a wave of racist assaults. As more and more African Americans, including many of the 367,000 who were war veterans, developed successful careers and asserted their civil rights, resentful whites reacted with an almost hysterical brutality. In 1919 alone, seventy-six black people, including nine military veterans, were killed by southern whites.

What African American leader James Weldon Johnson called the Red Summer (*red* signifying blood) began in July, when a mob of whites invaded the black neighborhood in Longview, Texas, angry over rumors of interracial dating. They burned shops and houses and ran several black residents out

Safe, briefly Escorted by a police officer, an African American family moves its belongings from their home, likely destroyed by white rioters, and into a protected area of Chicago.

of town. A week later, in Washington, D.C., false reports of black assaults on white women stirred up white mobs, and gangs of rioters waged a race war in the streets until soldiers and driving rains ended the fighting.

The worst was yet to come. In late July, 38 people were killed and 537 injured in five days of rioting in Chicago, where some 50,000 African Americans, mostly migrants from the South, had moved during the war, leading to tensions with local whites over jobs and housing. White unionized workers especially resented black workers who were hired as strikebreakers.

Altogether, twenty-five race riots erupted in 1919, and eighty African Americans were lynched, including eleven war veterans. In August, the NAACP sent President Wilson a telegram "respectfully enquiring how long the Federal Government under your administration intends to tolerate anarchy in the United States?" The White House chose not to reply.

The riots were indeed a turning point for many African Americans, but not a happy one. "We made the supreme sacrifice," a black veteran told poet-journalist Carl Sandburg. "Now we want to see our country live up to the Constitution and the Declaration of Independence." Another ex-soldier noted how much the war experience had changed the outlook of black people: "We were determined not to take it anymore."

Many blamed the riots on socialist and Communist agitators. "Reds Try to Stir Negroes to Revolt," and "Radicals Inciting Negro to Violence," cautioned the *New York Times* in July 1919. The *New York Tribune* followed suit, announcing that a "Plot to Stir Race Antagonism in United States Charged to Soviets." By December 1919, the *Times* had decided that "no element in this country is so susceptible to organized propaganda . . . as the least informed class of Negroes." It warned that "Bolshevist[s] . . . are winning many recruits among the colored races."

THE FIRST RED SCARE With so many people convinced that the strikes and riots were inspired by Communists and anarchists (two different groups that shared a hatred for capitalism), a New York journalist reported that Americans were "shivering in their boots over Bolshevism, and they are far more scared of [Vladimir] Lenin than they ever were of the [German] Kaiser. We seem to be the most frightened victors the world ever saw."

Fears of revolution led to what came to be called the **First Red Scare**. It was fueled by the violent actions of a few militants. In early 1919, the Secret Service discovered a plot by Spanish anarchists to kill President Wilson and other government officials. In April 1919, postal workers intercepted nearly forty homemade mail bombs addressed to government officials. One mail bomb, however, blew off the hands of a Georgia senator's maid.

In June, a twenty-four-year-old Italian anarchist named Carlo Valdinoci used a suitcase filled with dynamite to blow up Attorney General A. Mitchell Palmer's home in Washington, D.C. The bomb exploded prematurely when Valdinoci tripped and fell as he approached the house. A neighbor, Assistant Secretary of the Navy Franklin Roosevelt, was walking with his wife Eleanor when the bomb exploded. The blast shattered windows and knocked neighbors out of their beds. Valdinoci's collarbone landed on the Roosevelts' front steps, and his scalp ended up on their roof. Valdinoci had become the nation's first suicide bomber.

The bombing transformed Attorney General Palmer. "I remember . . . the morning after my house was blown up, I stood in the middle of the wreckage of my library with Congressmen and Senators, and without a dissenting voice they called upon me in strong terms to exercise all the power that was possible . . . to run to earth the criminals who were behind that kind of outrage."

At the same time, other anarchist bombers were setting off explosives in New York City, Boston, Pittsburgh, Philadelphia, Cleveland, and Washington, D.C. Palmer, who had ambitions to succeed Wilson as president, concluded that a "Red Menace," a Communist "blaze of revolution," was "sweeping over every American institution of law and order."

In August 1919, Palmer appointed a twenty-four-year-old attorney named J. Edgar Hoover to lead the new General Intelligence Division within the Justice Department to collect information on radicals. Hoover and others in the Justice Department worked with a network of 250,000 informants in 600 cities, all of them members of the American Protective League, which had been founded during the war to root out "traitors" and labor radicals.

On November 7, 1919, in what came to be called the "Palmer raids," federal agents rounded up 450 alien "radicals," most of whom were law-abiding Russian immigrants. All were deported to Russia without a court hearing. On January 2, 1920, federal agents and police in dozens of cities arrested 5,000 more suspects. The raids were disasters. Poor communications, faulty planning, and murky intelligence created chaos and confusion. Meanwhile, however, panic about possible foreign terrorists and American radicals erupted across the nation. Vigilantes driven by fear, prejudice, and ignorance took matters into their own hands.

At a patriotic pageant in Washington, D.C., a sailor shot a spectator who refused to rise for "The Star-Spangled Banner"; the crowd cheered. In Hammond, Indiana, a jury took two minutes to acquit a man who had murdered an immigrant for yelling "To hell with the U.S." In Waterbury, Connecticut, a salesman was sentenced to six months in jail for saying that Lenin was "one of the brainiest" of the world's leaders.

By the summer of 1920, the Red Scare had begun to subside. But it left a lasting mark by strengthening the conservative crusade for "100 percent Americanism" and new restrictions on immigration.

EFFECTS OF THE GREAT WAR

The extraordinary turbulence in 1919 and 1920 was an unmistakable indication of how the Great War had changed the shape of modern history. It had destroyed old Europe—its cities, people, economies, and four grand empires. The war also changed Europe's self-image as the center of civilized Western culture. Winston Churchill, the future British prime minister, called postwar Europe "a crippled, broken world."

Peace brought festering resentment among the vanquished. Most Germans and Austrians believed they were the victims of a harsh peace, and many wanted revenge. At the same time, the war had hastened the Bolshevik Revolution that caused Russia to exit the war, abandon its western European allies, and, in 1922, reemerge as the Union of Soviet Socialist Republics (USSR). Thereafter, Soviet communism would be one of the most powerful forces shaping the twentieth century.

Postwar America was a much different story. For the first time, the United States had decisively intervened in a major European war. After a sharp but brief postwar recession, the economy entered a period of unprecedented prosperity. During the twenties, the United States became the world's dominant power. What came to be called the "American Century" was at hand.

CHAPTER REVIEW

SUMMARY

- **An Uneasy Neutrality**   After war erupted in Europe in 1914, the *Western Front* bogged down in horrific *trench warfare*, in which both sides were stalemated yet absorbed horrific losses. The Wilson administration declared the United States neutral but allowed businesses to extend loans to the warring nations, principally the *Allied Powers* (Britain, France, and Russia), to purchase food and military supplies. Very little aid was provided the *Central Powers* (Germany, Austria-Hungary, and Turkey). Americans were outraged by the Germans' use of submarine (*U-boat*) warfare, especially after the sinking of the *Lusitania*. In 1917, submarine attacks and the publication of the *Zimmermann telegram*, which revealed that Germany had tried to encourage Mexico to wage war against the United States, led America to enter the Great War.

- **Mobilizing a Nation**   The Wilson administration drafted young men into the army and created new agencies such as the War Industries Board and the Food Administration to coordinate industrial production and agricultural consumption. As white workers left their factory jobs to join the army, hundreds of thousands of African Americans relocated from the rural South to the urban North as part of the *Great Migration (1914–1920)*. Many white southerners and Mexican Americans also migrated to industrial centers. One million women participated in war work but were encouraged to leave those jobs as soon as the war ended. The federal government severely curtailed civil liberties, and the Espionage and Sedition Acts of 1917 and 1918 criminalized opposition to the war.

- **The American Role in Fighting the War**   Communists seized power in November 1917 in Russia and negotiated a separate peace treaty with Germany, thus freeing the Germans to focus on the *Western Front*. By 1918, however, the arrival of U.S. troops turned the tide of the war. German leaders sued for peace, and an armistice was signed on November 11, 1918. Wilson insisted that the United States wanted a new democratic Europe. His *Fourteen Points (1918)* speech outlined his ideas for a League of Nations to promote peace.

- **The Fight for the Peace**   At the Paris Peace Conference, President Wilson was only partially successful. The *Treaty of Versailles (1919)* did create a *League of Nations* but included a "war guilt clause" that forced Germany to pay reparations for war damages to France and Britain. In the end, Wilson's illness following a stroke, his refusal to compromise on the terms of the treaty, and his alienation of Republican senators resulted in the Senate voting against ratification.

- **Lurching from War to Peace** The United States struggled with its new status as the leading world power and with changes at home. As wartime industries shifted to peacetime production, wage and price controls ended. As former soldiers reentered the workforce, unemployment rose and consumer prices increased, provoking labor unrest. Many believed these problems were part of a Bolshevik plot. Several incidents of domestic terrorism provoked what would be known as the *First Red Scare (1919–1920)*, during which the Justice Department illegally arrested and deported suspected radicals, most of whom were immigrants. At the same time, race riots broke out as resentful white mobs tried to stop African Americans from exercising their civil rights. The summer of 1919 also brought the ratification of the *Nineteenth Amendment (1919)*, which gave women the right to vote once ratified by the states in 1920.

CHRONOLOGY

1914	The Great War (World War I) begins in Europe
1915	The *Lusitania* is torpedoed by a German U-boat
February 1917	Germany announces unrestricted submarine warfare
March 1917	Zimmermann telegram disclosed
April 1917	United States enters the Great War
January 1918	Woodrow Wilson delivers Fourteen Points speech
November 11, 1918	Representatives of warring nations sign armistice
1919	Paris Peace Conference convenes
	Race riots break out during the Red Summer
1919–1920	First Red Scare
1920	The Senate rejects the Treaty of Versailles
	The Nineteenth Amendment is ratified by the states

KEY TERMS

Central Powers p. 1023

Allied Powers p. 1023

Western Front p. 1025

trench warfare p. 1026

U-boats p. 1031

Lusitania p. 1032

Zimmermann telegram p. 1036

Great Migration p. 1041

Fourteen Points (1918) p. 1049

League of Nations p. 1058

Treaty of Versailles (1919) p. 1060

Nineteenth Amendment (1920) p. 1066

First Red Scare (1919–1920) p. 1069

 INQUIZITIVE

Go to InQuizitive to see what you've learned—and learn what you've missed—with personalized feedback along the way.

23 A Clash of Cultures
1920–1929

Nightclub **(1933)** The roar of the twenties subsided for some at the heart of it all. In this painting by American artist Guy Pène du Bois, flappers and their dates crowd into a fashionable nightclub, yet their loneliness amid the excitement is deafening.

The decade between the end of the Great War and the onset of the Great Depression at the end of 1929 was perhaps the most dynamic in American history. It was a period punctuated by rapid urbanization, technological innovation, widespread prosperity, social rebelliousness, cultural upheaval, and political conservatism.

The Eighteenth Amendment ("Prohibition") outlawed alcoholic beverages in 1920, setting off an epidemic of lawbreaking throughout the twenties, as many people defied the ban, smuggling, producing, and consuming "bootleg" liquor in violation of the law. At the same time, the Nineteenth Amendment allowed women to vote and to experience many freedoms previously limited to men. Despite some improvement in employment opportunities, Jim Crow laws continued to prevent most African Americans in the South, women and men, from voting.

Cultural conflicts resulted largely from tensions between rural and urban ways of life. For the first time in the nation's history, more people lived in cities than in rural areas, but old farm folkways lived on for almost half the population.

While the urban middle class prospered, farmers suffered as the wartime boom in exports of grains and livestock to Europe ground to a halt. Four million people moved from farms to cities, in part because of the better quality of life and in part because of the prolonged agricultural recession. Amid this massive population shift, bitter fights erupted between traditionalists and modernists, small towns and big cities, as old and new values fought a cultural civil war that continues today.

The postwar wave of strikes, bombings, anti-Communist hysteria, and race riots created a widespread sense of alarm that led many to cling to traditional

focus questions

1. Assess the impact of the consumer culture during the 1920s. What contributed to its growth?

2. What were the other major social and cultural trends and movements that became prominent during the twenties? How did they challenge traditional standards and customs?

3. What does "modernism" mean in intellectual and artistic terms? How did the modernist movement influence American culture in the early twentieth century?

religious beliefs and "native" ways of life. America during the twenties, said one social commentator, was the most "volcanic of any area on earth." All the changes created what one historian called a "nervous generation" of Americans "groping for what certainty they could find."

MODERNITY VERSUS TRADITION During the twenties, the new and unusual clashed openly with the conventional and commonplace. Modernists and traditionalists waged cultural warfare with one another, one group looking to the future for inspiration and the other looking to the past for guidance.

The scope and pace of societal changes were bewildering, as a national entertainment culture emerged. Radio networks and motion pictures, mass ownership of automobiles, and national chain stores, combined with the soaring popularity of spectator sports and the rise of mass marketing and advertising, transformed America into the world's leading consumer society. The culture of mass consumption ignited the growth of middle-class urban life while assaulting traditional virtues such as frugality, prudence, and religiosity.

In the political arena, reactionaries and rebels battled for control. The brutal fight between Woodrow Wilson and the Republican-led Senate over the Treaty of Versailles, coupled with the administration's crackdown on dissenters and socialists, had weakened an already fragmented progressivism. As reformer Amos Pinchot bitterly observed, President Wilson had "put his enemies in office and his friends in jail." By 1920, many disillusioned progressives had grown skeptical of any politician claiming to be a reformer or an idealist. Social reformer Jane Addams sighed that the 1920s, dominated politically by a Republican party devoted to the interests of Big Business, were "a period of political and social sag."

The desire to restore traditional values and social stability led voters to elect Republican Warren G. Harding president in 1920. He promised to return America to "normalcy." Both major parties still included progressive wings, but they were shrinking. The demand for honest, efficient government and public services remained strong; the impulse for social reform, however, shifted into a drive for moral righteousness and social conformity. By 1920, many progressives had withdrawn from public life.

Mainstream Americans were also shocked by "modernist" forms of artistic expression and sexual liberation. Mabel Dodge Luhan, a leading promoter of modern art and literature, described the literary and artistic rebels that emerged during and after the war as being determined to overthrow "the old order of things."

In sum, postwar life in America and Europe was fraught with turbulent changes, contradictory impulses, superficial frivolity, and seething tensions.

As French painter Paul Gauguin acknowledged, the upheavals of cultural modernism and the chaotic aftermath of the war produced "an epoch of confusion."

THE NATION IN 1920

The 1920 census reported that 106 million people lived in the United States, a third of the number today. More than half were under the age of twenty-five. The average life expectancy was just fifty-six years for men and fifty-eight for women.

American society remained overwhelmingly white—90 percent. (Persons of Latino origin were considered white.) African Americans were 9 percent, and Native Americans and Asian Americans made up most of the rest. Almost half the white population were immigrants or the children of immigrants, the highest percentage since the late eighteenth century.

For the first time, more than half the population resided in "cities" of more than 2,500 residents. Some 16 million Americans lived in the ten largest cities, such as New York, Boston, Chicago, and Philadelphia. The South remained the most rural and poorest region. Only half of southern farmers owned their land, compared to three quarters of farmers in the rest of the nation. The others were either tenants who rented or sharecroppers who gave the landowner a share of the harvested crop in exchange for access to land. Most sharecroppers, especially black sharecroppers, remained grimly poor, in large part because of low crop prices during the twenties.

A "NEW ERA" OF CONSUMERISM

America experienced so many dramatic changes during the twenties that people referred to it as a "New Era." Following the brief postwar recession in 1920–1921, economic growth soared to record levels. Jobs were plentiful, the nation's total wealth almost doubled, and wage workers enjoyed record-breaking increases in average income. By 1929, the United States enjoyed the highest standard of living in the world.

Construction led the way. By 1921, a building boom was under way that would last the rest of the decade. At the same time, the remarkable growth of the automotive industry created an immediate need for roads, highways, service stations, and "motels" (motor hotels). New construction and new cars stimulated other industries such as lumber, steel, concrete, rubber, gasoline, and furniture.

Technology also played a key role in the prosperity by enabling mass production through the assembly-line process. Manufacturing grew more mechanized and efficient. Powerful new machines (electric motors, steam turbines, dump trucks, tractors, bulldozers, steam shovels) and more-efficient ways of operating farms, factories, plants, mines, and mills generated dramatic increases in productivity. In 1920, the nation's factories produced 5,000 electric refrigerators; in 1929, they produced almost a million.

THE FLORIDA LAND RUSH While production and consumption were soaring, so were get-rich-quick schemes, the most outlandish of which was the Florida real estate boom. One of the least developed states on the Atlantic coast suddenly became the nation's fastest-growing state, in part because it was the only state without an income tax or inheritance tax, and in part because widespread ownership of automobiles made it possible for masses of people to vacation in the "winter playground of America."

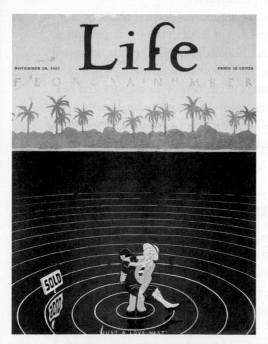

Florida land boom This 1925 *Life Magazine* cover lampoons the get-rich-quick schemes triggered by the Florida land boom of the 1920s. It looks as though these buyers were sold a damper piece of real estate than they had bargained for.

Like prospectors during the California gold rush, speculators and developers swooped into the "Land of Flowers" and bought, cleared, tamed, subdivided, and sold parcels of land so fast they could not keep up with the paperwork. Miami, the "Magic City," was the fastest-growing community in the nation. From 1,700 residents in 1900, its population mushroomed to 111,000 by 1925. One reporter gushed that Miami was "growing so fast it creaks." A beachfront property that sold for $35,000 went for $1 million just three years later.

An advertisement for Florida made it sound like Shangri-la: "Florida is bathed in passionate caresses of the southern sun. It is laved by the limpid waves of the embracing seas, wooed by the glorious Gulf Stream. . . . Florida is an emerald kingdom . . . clothed in perpetual verdure and lapt in the gorgeous folds of the semi-tropical zone."

By the end of 1925, some 20 million parcels were for sale in Florida, enough for every adult in the nation. Hundreds of thousands of people, mostly northerners, invested in Florida real estate sight unseen, but what they were told was prime property often turned out to be swamp land. Fraudulent sales made people hesitant to join the stampede. Soon, analysts predicted the Florida land bubble would burst. "The rise in Florida [land values] will continue as long as northern money is sent to Florida," said the Ohio state commerce director, "and the end will be that of every boom, where few prosper and many hold the bag at the end."

As he predicted, in mid-1926, the Florida real estate bubble imploded. Too much growth too fast had caused unexpected problems. Railroads struggling to supply food to the state's rapidly growing population announced they were no longer transporting construction supplies, leaving thousands of homes unfinished. In July, *The Nation* magazine reported: "The world's greatest poker game, played with building lots instead of chips, is over. And the players are now cashing in or paying up." A devastating hurricane that roared across South Florida in September only deepened the pain.

By 1928, much of Florida was a wasteland. A journalist described the damage: "Dead subdivisions line the highway, their pompous names half-obliterated on crumbling stucco gates. Lonely, white-way lights stand guard over miles of cement sidewalks, where grass and palmetto [trees] take the place of homes that were to be. . . . Whole sections of outlying subdivisions are composed of unoccupied houses, through which one speeds on broad thoroughfares as if traversing a city in the grip of death." The collapse of the Florida land boom proved to be but an audition for the great stock market bubble that would burst at the end of 1929.

A GROWING CONSUMER CULTURE

In the late nineteenth century, the U.S. economy had been driven by commercial agriculture and large-scale industrial production—the building of railroads and bridges, the manufacture of steel, and the construction of housing and businesses in cities. During the twenties, an explosion of new consumer goods made available through a national marketplace revolutionized the lives of the middle class.

The success of mass production made mass consumerism more important than ever. A 1920 newspaper editorial insisted that the American's "first importance to his country is no longer that of citizen but that of *consumer*." To keep factory production humming required converting once-frugal people into enthusiastic shoppers. "People may ruin themselves by saving instead of spending," warned one economist.

During the Great War, the government had urged Americans to work long hours, conserve resources, and live simply. After the war, a new **consumer culture** encouraged carefree spending. "During the war," a journalist noted in 1920, "we accustomed ourselves to doing without, to buying carefully, to using

A modern home This 1925 Westinghouse advertisement urges homemakers to buy its "Cozy Glow, Jr." heater and "Sol-Lux Luminaire" lamp, among other new electrical appliances that would "do anything for you in return."

economically. But with the close of the war came reaction. A veritable orgy of extravagant buying is going on. Reckless spending takes the place of saving, waste replaces conservation."

To keep people buying, businesses developed new ways for consumers to finance purchases over time ("layaway") rather than pay cash up front ("buy now, pay later"). Traditional notions such as paying with cash and staying out of debt were now dismissed as needlessly old-fashioned. Consumer debt almost tripled. By 1929, almost 60 percent of purchases were made on the installment plan.

Advertising became a huge enterprise, especially with the advent of the radio, which aired its first commercial in 1922. President Calvin Coolidge declared that advertising had become "the most potent influence in adopting and changing the habits and modes of life, affecting what we eat, what we wear, and the work and play of the whole nation."

The visibility of ads helped shape how people behaved and how they defined the pursuit of happiness. Zelda Sayre Fitzgerald, the writer and wife of popular novelist F. Scott Fitzgerald, recalled that "we grew up founding our dreams on the infinite promises of American advertising." In a 1923 interview, she embraced the culture of consumption: "I don't mean that money means happiness, necessarily. But having things, just things, objects, makes a woman happy. The right kind of perfume, the smart pair of shoes." Her husband chimed in: "Women care for 'things,' clothes, furniture, for themselves . . . and men [do too], in so far as they contribute to their vanity." The Fitzgeralds spoke for many Americans who assumed that social status was measured in dollars.

New weekday radio programs popular with middle-class housewives, for example, were often sponsored by national companies advertising laundry detergent and hand soap—hence the term *soap operas*. Because women purchased two thirds of consumer goods, advertisers aimed commercials at them.

The huge jump in the use of electricity was also a transformational force. In 1920, only 35 percent of homes had electricity; by 1930, the number was 68 percent. Similar increases occurred in the number of households with indoor plumbing, washing machines, and automobiles. Moderately priced creature comforts and conveniences such as flush toilets, electric irons and fans, hand-held cameras, wristwatches, cigarette lighters, vacuum cleaners, and linoleum floors, became more widely available, especially among the urban middle class. As always, the poor, with little discretionary income, remained on the margins.

THE RISE OF MASS CULTURE

The consumer culture helped create a marketplace of retail stores and national brands (Kellogg's Corn Flakes, General Electric toasters, etc.) in which local and regional businesses were increasingly squeezed out by giant department stores and "chain" stores. By the 1920s, Woolworth's, for example, had 1,500 stores across the country; Walgreen's had 525. National retailers bought goods in such large quantities that they were able to get discounted prices that they passed on to consumers.

Mass advertising and marketing campaigns increasingly led to a *mass culture*: more and more people saw the same advertisements and bought the same products at the same stores. They also read the same magazines, listened to the same radio programs, drove the same cars, adored the same sports stars and celebrities, and watched the same movies.

MOVIE-MADE AMERICA   In 1896, a New York City audience viewed the first moving-picture show. By 1924, there were 20,000 theaters nationwide showing 700 new "silent" films a year, and the movie business had become the chief form of mass entertainment. Hollywood, California, emerged as the international center of movie production, grinding out Westerns, crime dramas, murder mysteries, and the comedies of Mack Sennett's Keystone Company, in which a raft of slapstick comedians, notably London-born Charlie Chaplin, perfected their art, transforming it into a form of social criticism.

Movie attendance during the 1920s averaged 80 million people a week. It surged even more after 1927 with the appearance of movies with sound ("talkies"). Americans spent ten times as much on movies as they did on tickets to baseball and football games.

Movies did much more than entertain, however. They helped expand the consumer culture by setting standards and tastes in fashion, music, dancing, and hairstyles. As producer-director D.W. Griffith claimed in 1917, "The cinema is the agent of Democracy. It levels barriers between races and classes."

Popular films also helped stimulate the sexual revolution. One boy admitted that the movies taught him how "to kiss a girl on her ears, neck, and cheeks, as well as on the mouth." A researcher

Charlie Chaplin An English-born actor who rose to international fame as the "Tramp," pictured above in the 1921 silent film *The Kid*.

concluded that movies made young Americans more "sex-wise, sex-excited, and sex-absorbed" than previous generations.

RADIO Radio broadcasting enjoyed even more spectacular growth. Between 1920 and 1930, the number of families owning a radio soared from 15,000 to nearly 14 million. Almost two thirds of homes had at least one radio.

The radio changed the patterns of everyday life. At night after dinner, families gathered to listen to music, speeches, news broadcasts, weather forecasts, and comedy shows. One ad claimed that the radio "is your theater, your college, your newspaper, your library."

In 1920, some 41 million radios were manufactured in the United States. Calvin Coolidge was the first president to address the nation by radio, and his monthly talks paved the way for Franklin Delano Roosevelt's influential "fireside chats" during the thirties.

Radio transformed jazz music into a national craze. Big band leaders Paul Whiteman, Guy Lombardo, Duke Ellington, Glenn Miller, and Tommy and Jimmy Dorsey regularly performed live over the radio. Country music also developed a national following as a result of radio broadcasts. In 1925, WSM,

Radio broadcasting Radio players act out 'Rip Van Winkle' in a sound effects studio during a broadcast from Schenectady, New York.

a station in Nashville, Tennessee, began offering a weekly variety show, *The Grand Ole Opry*, which featured an array of country music stars.

FLYING MACHINES Advances in transportation were as significant as the impact of commercial radio and movies. In 1903, Wilbur and Orville Wright, owners of a bicycle shop in Dayton, Ohio, had built and flown the first "flying machine" at Kitty Hawk, North Carolina.

The development of airplanes advanced slowly until the outbreak of war in 1914, when Europeans began using the airplane as a military weapon. When the United States entered the war, it had no combat planes; American pilots flew British or French warplanes. An American aircraft industry arose during the war but collapsed in the postwar demobilization. Under the Kelly Act of 1925, however, the federal government began to subsidize the industry through airmail delivery contracts. The Air Commerce Act of 1926 provided federal funds for the advancement of air transportation and navigation, including the construction of airports.

The aviation industry received a huge psychological boost in May 1927 when twenty-six-year-old Charles A. Lindbergh Jr., a St. Louis–based pilot blessed with extraordinary courage and endurance, won a $25,000 prize by making the first *solo* transatlantic flight, traveling from New York City to Paris in thirty-three and a half hours through thunderstorms, ice clouds, and dense fog.

A handsome, daring college dropout, Lindbergh oversaw a fanatical effort to reduce the weight of his plane to accommodate the 2,500 pounds of fuel—heavier than the plane itself—needed for the crossing. He used a wicker basket for a seat, removed the radio, and modified the tail section to make the plane hard to control so as to ensure he did not fall asleep.

When Lindbergh, known as the "Lone Eagle," landed in France, 150,000 people greeted him with thunderous cheers. The New York City parade honoring his accomplishment surpassed the celebration of the end of the Great War. A new dance, the Lindy Hop, was named for him, and a popular song, "Lucky Lindy," celebrated his "peerless, fearless" feat. (When Lindbergh met Britain's King George V soon after his long flight, the monarch asked him, "How did you pee?" "In paper cups," the pilot answered.) Lindbergh's flight redefined the potential of "flying machines" to transform transportation and compress distance.

No sooner did Lindbergh return to America than promoters began looking for a female pilot to equal his feat. In June 1928, Kansas-born Amelia Earhart, who had dropped out of college during the Great War to nurse wounded soldiers, joined two male pilots in being the first woman to cross the Atlantic

Amelia Earhart The pioneering aviator would tragically disappear in her 1937 attempt to fly around the world.

in an airplane—as a passenger. "Stultz did all the flying — had to," she said. "I was just baggage, like a sack of potatoes. Maybe someday I'll try it alone."

Thereafter, Earhart launched a national organization of female pilots, solo piloted a plane non-stop coast to coast across the United States, and set several speed records for women pilots. In 1932, Earhart climbed into her candy apple red Lockheed Vega and equaled Lindbergh by flying solo from Canada to Northern Ireland in fifteen hours, thereby becoming one of the most famous women in the world.

In 1937, Earhart set out with a male navigator to fly around the globe at the equator, long before radar was developed. They would use the sun and stars to guide them the 30,000 miles. Just before taking off, she told reporters, "I won't feel completely cheated if I fail to come back." While crossing the South Pacific, she lost radio contact and was never heard from again.

THE CAR CULTURE By far the most significant economic and social development of the early twentieth century was the emergence of a car-centered culture. The motor car came to symbolize the twentieth-century machine age, which transported people into modernity. In 1924, when asked about the changes transforming American life, a resident of Muncie, Indiana, replied: "I can tell you what's happening in just four letters: A-U-T-O."

In 1900, the United States had produced 5,000 automobiles. By 1910, that number had spiked to 137,000. Ten years later, there were 8.1 million cars motoring across America, and half of all families owned at least one.

The first cars were handmade, expensive, and designed for the wealthy. Henry Ford changed all that beginning in 1903 by pledging to build "a car for the multitude." He vowed "to democratize the automobile. When I'm through, everybody will be able to afford one, and about everyone will have one."

Ford's Model T, the celebrated "Tin Lizzie," appeared in 1908 at a price of $850 (about $22,000 today). By 1924, as a result of Ford's increasingly efficient production techniques, the same car sold for $290 (less than $4,000 today). The Model T, "built to last forever," changed little from year to year, and it came in one color: black. Selling millions of identical cars at a small profit allowed Ford to keep prices low and wages high—the perfect formula for a mass-consumption economy.

Other automakers followed Ford's production model. By 1929, there were more than 23 million registered cars and trucks. The automobile revolution was in part propelled by the discovery of vast oil fields in Texas, Oklahoma, Wyoming, and California. By 1920, the United States produced two thirds of the world's oil and gasoline. By 1930, an estimated 10 percent of America's workforce was centered on the production of automobiles.

Ford Motor Company's Highland Park plant, 1913 Gravity slides and chain conveyors contributed to the mass production of automobiles.

The automobile industry also became the leading example of modern, mechanized, mass-production techniques. Ford's Highland Park plant outside Detroit was the largest factory in the world. It employed 68,000 workers and used a moving conveyor system that pulled the car chassis down an assembly line of sequential workstations. Each worker performed a single task, such as installing a fender or a wheel, as the car-in-process moved down the line. Through this monotonous yet efficient technique, a new car could be pieced together in ninety-three minutes.

Just as the railroad helped transform the pace and scale of life in the late nineteenth century, the automobile changed social life during the twentieth century. Americans developed a love affair with cars. In the words of one male driver, young people viewed the car as "an incredible engine of escape" from parental control and a safe place to "take a girl and hold hands, neck, pet, or . . . go the limit."

Cars and networks of new roads enabled people to live farther away from their workplaces, thus encouraging suburban sprawl. Cars also helped fuel the economic boom of the 1920s by creating tens of thousands of new jobs and a huge demand for steel, glass, rubber, leather, oil, and gasoline. The car culture stimulated road construction, and dotted the landscape with gasoline stations, traffic lights, billboards, and motor hotels. By 1929, the federal government was constructing 10,000 miles of paved highways each year.

SPECTATOR SPORTS Automobile ownership and rising incomes changed the way people spent their leisure time. Americans fell in love with spectator sports; people in cities could drive into the countryside, visit friends and relatives, and go to ballparks, stadiums, or boxing rings.

Baseball had become the "national pastime." With larger-than-life heroes such as New York Yankee legends George Herman "Babe" Ruth and Henry Louis "Lou" Gehrig, baseball teams attracted intense interest and huge crowds. Ruth may well have been the most famous athlete of all time. In 1920, more than a million spectators attended his games.

Two years later, the Yankees built a new stadium, dubbing it the "House That Ruth Built." They went on to win World Series championships in 1923, 1927, and 1928. More than 20 million people attended professional games in 1927, the year that Ruth, the "Sultan of Swat," set a record by hitting sixty home runs. Because baseball remained a segregated sport, so-called Negro Leagues were organized for African Americans.

Football, especially at the college level, also attracted huge crowds. It, too, benefited from outsized heroes such as running back Harold Edward "Red" Grange of the University of Illinois, the first athlete to appear on the cover

Babe Ruth The star pitcher and outfielder won the hearts of fans, first with the Boston Red Sox, then the New York Yankees, and, finally, the Boston Braves. Here, he autographs bats and balls for soldiers at basic training camp.

of *Time* magazine. In a 1924 game against the University of Michigan, the "Galloping Ghost" scored a touchdown the first four times he carried the ball. After Illinois won, students carried him on their shoulders for two miles across the campus. When Grange signed a contract with the Chicago Bears in 1926, he single-handedly made professional football competitive with baseball as a spectator sport.

What Ruth and Grange were to their sports, William Harrison "Jack" Dempsey was to boxing. In 1919, he won the world heavyweight title from Jess Willard, a giant of a man weighing 300 pounds and standing six and a half feet tall. Dempsey knocked him down seven times in the first round. Willard gave up in the fourth round, and Dempsey became a dominant force in boxing. The "Manassa Mauler" was especially popular with working-class men, for he had been born poor and lived for years as a hobo, wandering the rails in search of work and challenging toughs in bars to fight for money.

Dempsey was more than a champion; he was a hero to millions. In 1927, when James Joseph "Gene" Tunney defeated Dempsey, more than 100,000 people attended, including 1,000 reporters, 10 state governors, and numerous Hollywood celebrities. Some 60 million people listened to the fight over the radio.

THE "JAZZ AGE"

While the masses of Americans devoted their free time to spectator sports, radio programs, and movies, many young people, especially college students, focused on social and cultural rebellion—trying daring new fads and fashions, new music, new attitudes, and new ways of having fun.

F. Scott Fitzgerald became the self-infatuated "voice of his generation" after his best-selling first novel, *This Side of Paradise* (1920), portrayed rowdy student life at Princeton University, which he had attended. "No one else," Fitzgerald announced, "could have written so searchingly the story of the youth of our generation." Fitzgerald fastened upon the "**Jazz Age**" as the evocative label for the rebelliousness and spontaneity displayed by American youth during the "greatest, gaudiest spree in history."

THE BIRTH OF JAZZ

F. Scott Fitzgerald's Jazz Age label referred to the popularity of jazz music, a dynamic blend of several musical traditions. It had first emerged as piano-based "ragtime" at the end of the nineteenth century. Thereafter, African American musicians such as Jelly Roll Morton, Duke Ellington, Louis Armstrong, and Bessie Smith (known as the "Empress of the Blues") combined the energies of ragtime with the emotions of the blues to create *jazz*, originally an African American slang term meaning sexual intercourse. With its improvisations, variations, and sensual spontaneity, jazz appealed to people of all ethnicities and ages because it celebrated pleasure and immediacy.

Louis Armstrong, an inspired trumpeter with a unique, froggy voice, was the Pied Piper of jazz, an inventive and freewheeling performer who reshaped the American music scene. Born in a New Orleans shack in 1900, the grandson of slaves, he was abandoned by his father and raised by his prostitute mother, who was just fifteen when he was born. As a youth, he experienced the mean and ugly side of America. "I seen everythin' from a child comin' up," he said once. "Nothin' happen I ain't never seen before."

Then he found music, using his natural genius to explore the fertile possibilities of jazz. As a teen, he sneaked into music halls to watch Joe "King" Oliver and other early jazz innovators. In 1922, Armstrong moved to Chicago, where he delighted audiences with his passionate trumpet performances and open-hearted personality. He radiated a joy that reflected his faith in the power of music and laughter to promote racial harmony.

The culture of jazz quickly spread from its origins in New Orleans, Kansas City, Memphis, and St. Louis to the African American neighbor-

Duke Ellington and his band Jazz emerged in the 1920s as a uniquely American expression of the modernist spirit. African American artists bent musical conventions to give freer rein to improvisation and sensuality.

hoods of Harlem in New York City and Chicago's South Side. Large dance halls met the demand for jazz music and the dances it inspired, like the Charleston and the Black Bottom. Affluent whites flocked to the dance halls as well as to "black" nightclubs and "jazz joints." People spoke of "*jazzing* something up" (invigorating it) or "jazzing around" (acting youthfully and energetically).

Many Americans, however, were not fans of jazz ("the devil's music") or the suggestive dances it inspired. Dr. Francis E. Clark, a Christian moralist, denounced "indecent dance" as "an offense against womanly purity." In 1921, the *Ladies' Home Journal* discouraged jazz dancing because of its "direct appeal to the body's sensory centers," and Princeton professor Henry van Dyke dismissed jazz as "merely an irritation of the nerves of hearing, a sensual teasing of the strings of physical passion."

Such criticism, however, failed to stem the growing worldwide popularity of jazz. As celebrated symphony conductor Leopold Stokowski acknowledged, "Jazz has come to stay because it is an expression of the times, of the breathless, energetic, superactive times in which we are living."

A SEXUAL REVOLUTION?

What was most shocking during the Jazz Age was a defiant sexual revolution among young people, especially those on college campuses. "None of the Victorian mothers—and most of the mothers were Victorian—had any idea how casually their daughters were accustomed to being kissed," wrote F. Scott Fitzgerald in *This Side of Paradise*.

During the twenties, Americans learned about the hidden world of "flaming youth" (the title of a popular novel): wild "petting parties," free love, speakeasies, "joyriding," and skinny-dipping. A promotional poster for the 1923 silent film *Flaming Youth* asked: "How Far Can a Girl Go?" Other ads claimed the movie appealed especially to "neckers, petters, white kisses, red kisses, pleasure-mad daughters, [and] sensation-craving mothers."

THE IMPACT OF SIGMUND FREUD The increasingly frank treatment of sex resulted in part from the influence of Sigmund Freud, the Austrian founder of modern psychoanalysis. Freud explored the human psyche, determined to legitimize psychoanalysis as a professional field anchored in clinical research. Yet he was a reckless and unethical scientist. He lied, manipulated or invented data, made unsubstantiated assertions, and stole ideas from others. He also relied upon a handful of questionable clinical cases to justify his insistence that the mind is baffling in its opaqueness and unpredictability, mysteriously "conflicted" by often unconscious efforts to repress powerful impulses and sexual desires ("libido"). Yet Freud created a new vocabulary for mapping the inner lives of people, explaining the complex dynamics of the ego, the id, and, after 1914, the superego.

Freud dismissed all forms of traditional religion as irrational responses to infantile fears and father worship. "Science," he stressed, "is no illusion," but religious faith was an illusion—and nothing more. Freud came to see psychoanalysis as the modern successor to religion. It could provide the answers to the fundamental questions that for thousands of years religion had claimed authority over: How should we live? Why does happiness elude us? What really matters?

In 1899, the cocaine-addicted Freud (cocaine was then legal) had published *The Interpretation of Dreams*, a pathbreaking book that stressed the crucial role of the subconscious in shaping behavior and moods. He claimed that dreams provide the "royal road to the unconscious" by revealing the psyche as a roiling snake pit of "repressed" sexual yearnings and aggressions, many of which result from early childhood experiences with repressed erotic feelings toward our parents. Dreams, slips of the tongue, and neurotic symptoms,

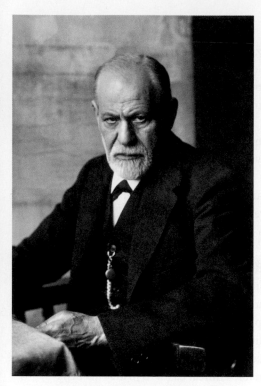

Sigmund Freud Founder of modern psychoanalysis, in 1926.

Freud concluded, were the mind's most important activity, for they reveal what we truly desire. The role of psychotherapy was thus to help patients discover their hidden selves and suppressed desires.

Women and men, Freud argued, are endowed with equal sexual energy, and human behavior is driven by a variety of intense sexual desires, repressed memories, and efforts to release pent-up aggression. These natural human conflicts cause unhappiness because people desire more pleasures than they can attain.

It did not take long for Freud's ideas to penetrate society at large. By 1909, when he first visited the United States to lecture at Clark University in Massachusetts, he was surprised to find himself famous "even in prudish America." Books, movies, and plays included frequent references to his ideas and phrases (Oedipus complex, penis envy, the death drive, the superego, talk therapy), and some of the decade's most popular magazines—*True Confessions, Telling Tales,* and *True Story*—focused on Freud-inspired romance and sex. Likewise, the most popular female movie stars—Madge Bellamy, Clara Bow, and Joan Crawford—projected images of sensual freedom, rebellious energy, and feisty independence.

Traditionalists bristled at the scandalous behavior of rebellious young women. "One hears it said," lamented a Baptist magazine, "that the girls are actually tempting the boys more than the boys do the girls, by their dress and conversation."

Psychoanalysis, whose purpose is to explain activities in the mind, soon became the world's most celebrated—and controversial—technique for helping troubled people come to grips with the psychic demons haunting them by using "talk therapy"—getting patients to tell the story of their lives, inner frustrations, and repressed fears and urges. By 1916, there were some 500 psychoanalysts in New York City alone.

For many young Americans, Sigmund Freud seemed to provide scientific justification for rebelling against social conventions and indulging in sex. Some oversimplified his theories by claiming that sexual pleasure was essential for emotional health, that all forms of sexual activity were good, and that all inhibitions about sex were bad.

MARGARET SANGER AND BIRTH CONTROL Perhaps the most controversial women's issue of the Jazz Age was birth control. Christians— both Protestants and Catholics—opposed it as a violation of God's law. Other crusaders viewed it differently.

Margaret Sanger, a nurse and midwife in the working-class tenements of Manhattan, saw many young mothers struggling to provide for their families. One of eleven children born to Irish immigrants, she herself had experienced the poverty often faced by large immigrant families. "Our childhood," she remembered, "was one of longing for things that were always denied."

In her work, Sanger witnessed the consequences of unwanted pregnancies, miscarriages, and amateur abortions. To her, the problems had an obvious solution: *birth control*, a term she and friends coined in 1914.

In 1911, Sanger and her husband joined the Socialist party, and their home became a gathering place for journalists, anarchists, labor leaders, and reformers. The party hired Sanger to promote women's suffrage, but she decided that birth control was more important to poor women than the vote. In 1912, she began to distribute birth-control information to working-class women and resolved to spend the rest of her life helping women gain control of their bodies. To do so, she began publishing a magazine called *Woman Rebel* in which she promoted women's suffrage, workers' rights, and contraception.

In 1916, Sanger was arrested and charged with disseminating obscenity through the mail, but the case was eventually dropped. She then opened the nation's first birth-control clinic, in Brooklyn, serving 464 clients before police shut it down.

Margaret Sanger The American sex educator, nurse, and birth control activist.

In 1921, Sanger organized the American Birth Control League, which in 1942 would change its name to Planned Parenthood. The Birth Control League distributed information to doctors, social workers, women's clubs, the scientific community, and to thousands of women.

Sanger, however, alienated supporters of birth control by endorsing sterilization for the mentally incompetent and for people with certain hereditary conditions. Birth control, she stressed, was "the most constructive and necessary of the means to racial health."

Although Sanger did not succeed in legalizing the distribution of contraceptives and contraceptive information through the mail, she laid the foundation for such efforts. In 1936, a federal court ruled that physicians could prescribe contraceptives. Before Sanger died in 1966 at the age of eighty-seven, the U.S. Supreme Court, in *Griswold v. Connecticut* (1965), declared that women had a constitutional right to use contraceptives as a form of birth control.

THE "NEW WOMEN" New clothing fashions reflected the rebellion against traditional female roles in an especially powerful way. Emancipated "new women" seized the right to vote while discarding the confining wardrobe of their "frumpy" mothers—pinched-in corsets and choking girdles, layers of petticoats, and floor-length dresses. In 1919, skirt hems were typically six inches above the ground; by 1927, they were at the knee. The Utah legislature in 1921 debated a bill that would have jailed women wearing "skirts higher than three inches above the ankle."

The shortest skirts were worn by so-called **flappers**, impetuous young women eager to defy prevailing social conventions. F. Scott Fitzgerald defined the flappers (the name derived from the flapping sound made by the unfastened rubber galoshes they wore over their shoes in wet weather) as "young things with a splendid talent for living." Usually thin, long-legged, and precocious, flappers were daring pleasure-seekers who loved short dresses and plunging necklines while wearing minimal underclothing, gauzy fabrics, sheer stockings,

The "new woman" of the 1920s
Two risk-taking flappers dance atop the Hotel Sherman in Chicago, 1926.

dangling pearl necklaces, and plenty of makeup. They often joined young men in smoking cigarettes, drinking, gambling, and shaking and shimmying to the sensual energies of jazz music.

Flappers attracted enormous attention in part because they were both defiantly independent and desperately seductive. After interacting with flappers in New York City, British novelist Elinor Glyn asked: "Has the American girl no innate modesty—no sub-conscious self-respect, no reserve, no dignity?" Others, however, embraced "flapperism." Charles W. Hoffman, a Cincinnati judge, celebrated the flapper for "standing on her own feet, with the right to be free from the pretentious mastery of men." When a Pennsylvania high school PTA met to pass restrictions on the behavior of student flappers, girls in the crowd shouted defiance: "I can show my shoulders, I can show my knees, I'm a free-born American, and can show what I please."

Flappers were hell-bent on defying traditional standards for women. They wanted more out of life than conventional marriage and motherhood. Their carefree rebelliousness was fun-loving, self-indulgent, and often self-destructive. F. Scott Fitzgerald claimed that his beautiful, brazen, "wild-eyed" wife, Zelda, was the "First American Flapper." Scott and Zelda seemed fated to excite and destroy one another. The daughter of a strict Alabama Supreme Court justice, deservedly celebrated for her beauty and charm, she was wild to the point of exhaustion, flirting with men and drinking herself into a haze. As Scott told a friend, Zelda was "very beautiful and very wise and very brave . . . but she's a perfect baby and a more irresponsible pair than we'll be will be hard to imagine." He and Zelda fought constantly. Stimulated by bootleg gin and her mischievous personality, Zelda loved doing "crazy things": dancing in New York City fountains, stripping off her clothes in the middle of Grand Central Station, and greeting the dawn in all-night cafes.

In her "Eulogy on the Flapper," Zelda explained that the flapper "flirted because it was fun to flirt and wore a [then scandalous] one piece bathing suit because she had a good figure, she covered her face with powder and paint because she didn't need it, and she refused to be bored chiefly because she wasn't boring."

The craziness of flappers shocked and scared observers. A Catholic priest in Brooklyn complained that the rebelliousness of young women during the 1920s had provoked a "pandemonium of powder, a riot of rouge, and a moral anarchy of dress."

NOT SO NEW WOMEN Most women in the 1920s were not flappers, however. Lillian Symes, a longtime activist, stressed that her "generation of feminists" had little in common with the "spike-heeled, over-rouged flapper

The beautiful and the damned In an outfit typical of flappers, Zelda Fitzgerald poses with her husband, author F. Scott Fitzgerald, on the Riviera.

of today." Although more middle-class women attended college in the 1920s than ever before, a higher percentage of them married soon after graduation than had been the case in the nineteenth century.

Women were discouraged from enrolling in coeducational colleges and universities, however. Male doctors warned that mixed-gender classrooms hindered childbearing potential in women by "forcing their blood to nourish their brain instead of their ovaries." Prolonged academic study made women "mannish."

The conservative political mood helped steer women who had worked for the war effort back into their traditional roles as homemakers, and college curricula began to shift accordingly. At Vassar College, an all-women's school outside New York City, students took domestic courses such as "Husband and Wife," "Motherhood," and "The Family as an Economic Unit."

At the same time, fewer college-educated women pursued careers outside the home. The proportion of physicians who were women fell during the twenties, and similar reductions occurred among dentists, architects, and chemists. A student at all-female Smith College in Massachusetts expressed frustration "that a woman must choose between a home and her work, when a man may have both. There must be a way out, and it is the problem of our generation to find the way."

As before, most women who worked outside the home labored in unskilled, low-paying jobs. Only 4 percent of working women were salaried professionals. Some moved into new vocations, such as accounting assistants and department-store clerks. The number of beauty shops soared from 5,000 in 1920 to 40,000 in 1930, creating jobs for hair stylists, manicurists, and cosmeticians.

The majority of women, however, remained either full-time wives and mothers or household servants. The growing availability of electricity and electrical appliances—vacuum cleaners, toasters, stoves, refrigerators, washing machines, irons—made housework easier. Likewise, "supermarkets" offered year-round access to fruits, vegetables, and meats, which greatly reduced the traditional tasks of food preparation—canning, baking bread, and plucking chickens.

African American and Latino women faced the greatest challenges. As a New York City newspaper observed, they did the "work which white women will not do." Women of color usually worked as maids, laundresses, or seamstresses, or on farms.

THE COLOR LINE Racism also continued to limit the freedom of women. For example, in 1919, an interracial couple from Ayer, Massachusetts, Mabel Puffer, a wealthy college graduate, and Arthur Hazzard, a handyman, decided to get married in Concord, New Hampshire. They checked into separate rooms in a hotel, then walked three blocks to the courthouse to apply for a marriage license, only to be told that there was a five-day waiting period. So they waited and made preparations for the wedding. The mayor of Concord agreed to perform the service.

When news of the interracial couple strolling the streets of Concord reached the Boston newspapers, the headline in the *Boston Traveller* read: "Will Marry Negro in 'Perfect Union': Rich Ayer Society Woman Determined to Wed Servant Although Hometown Is Aflame with Protest." The news outraged many residents of Ayer. The next day, the *Boston Evening Globe* ran the now provocative story on its front page. The headline was sensational: "Hope to Prevent White Woman Wedding Negro: Two Friends of Mabel E. Puffer Have Gone to Concord, N.H."

Suddenly, the mayor of Concord announced he could not perform the wedding. The betrothed couple, after being turned down several times, finally found a minister willing to marry them. But the night before the wedding, the Ayer police chief arrested Hazzard on a charge of "enticement" and took Puffer into custody because she had been deemed "insane." The nation that Woodrow Wilson had led into war to "make the world safe for democracy" remained an unsafe place for those bold enough to cross the color line.

AFRICAN AMERICAN LIFE

The most significant development in African American life during the early twentieth century was the **Great Migration** northward from the South. The mass movement accelerated in 1915–1916, when rapidly expanding war industries needed new workers. It continued throughout the twenties, as almost a million African Americans, mostly sharecroppers, boarded trains bound for what they called the "promised land" up north.

Many landed in large cities—New York City, Chicago, Detroit, Cleveland, Washington, D.C., Philadelphia, and others—producing dramatic social, economic, and political changes. In 1900, only 740,000 African Americans lived outside the South, just 8 percent of the nation's black population. By 1970, more than 10.6 million African Americans lived outside the South, 47 percent of the nation's total.

They were lured by what writer Richard Wright called the "warmth of other suns"—better living conditions and better-paying jobs. In the North, for the most part, they were able to speak more freely and were treated better than in the South, although not equally, and educational opportunities for children were much better. Collectively, blacks gained more political leverage by settling in populous states like New York, Pennsylvania, Ohio, and Illinois, with many electoral votes. The political effects of the Great Migration were evident in 1928 when a Chicago Republican, Oscar De Priest, became the first black elected to Congress since Reconstruction and the first ever from a northern district.

The Migration of the Negro, Panel No. 1 In Jacob Lawrence's series of paintings, African Americans leave the South for jobs in cities like New York, Chicago, and St. Louis.

The difficult decision to leave their native South ended one set of troubles but created others. "Never in history," said Richard Wright, "has a more utterly unprepared folk wanted to go to the city." The new arrivals were strangers in a strange land, and they were not always welcomed. In densely populated northern cities, blacks who moved into established neighborhoods sometimes clashed with local ethnic groups, especially Irish and Italians who feared that the newcomers would take their jobs. Many southern blacks, ignorant of city ways, were taken advantage of by white landlords, realtors, and bankers; they were often forced into substandard and segregated housing and were paid lower wages than whites.

But northern discrimination still paled beside the injustices of the segregated South. "If all of their dream does not come true," a black newspaper in Chicago stressed, "enough will come to pass to justify their actions." Black poet Langston Hughes spoke for many when he wrote that he was "fed up / With Jim Crow laws, / People who are cruel / And afraid, / Who lynch and run, / Who are scared of me / And me of them." Over time, the transplanted African Americans built new lives, new churches, new communities, new families, even new cultures.

THE NAACP The mass migration of southern blacks northward helped spur the creation of the **National Association for the Advancement of Colored People (NAACP)**, founded in 1910 by African American activists and white progressives. W. E. B. Du Bois became the organization's director of publicity and research and editor of its journal, *The Crisis*.

The NAACP focused its political strategy on legal action to bring the Fourteenth and Fifteenth Amendments back to life. One early victory came with *Guinn v. United States* (1915), in which the Supreme Court struck down Oklahoma's efforts to deprive African Americans of the vote. In *Buchanan v. Warley* (1917), the Court invalidated a residential segregation ordinance in Louisville, Kentucky. In 1919, the NAACP launched a national campaign against lynching. An anti-lynching bill to make mob murder a federal crime passed the House in 1922 but was defeated by southerners in the Senate.

THE HARLEM RENAISSANCE So many African Americans converged in New York City during the twenties that they inspired the **Harlem Renaissance**, the nation's first black literary and artistic movement. It started in the community of Harlem in northern Manhattan. In 1890, one in seventy people in Manhattan had been African American; by 1930, it was one in nine.

The "great, dark city" of Harlem, in poet Langston Hughes's phrase, contained more blacks per square mile than any urban neighborhood in the nation.

Their numbers generated a sense of common identity, power, and distinctive self-expression that transformed Harlem into the cultural capital of African American life. Writer James Weldon Johnson described "Black Manhattan" as a "typically Negro" community of 175,000 in that it featured "movement, color, gaiety, singing, dancing, boisterous laughter, and loud talk."

Dotted with lively taverns, lounges, supper clubs, dance halls, and saloons ("speakeasies") where writers and painters listened to jazz and drank illegal booze, Harlem became what journalists called the "Nightclub Capital of the World." Hughes explained that Harlem writers and artists were ready "to express our individual dark-skinned selves without fear or shame. If white people are pleased, we are glad. If they are not, it doesn't matter. We know we are beautiful. And ugly too."

Alain Locke, the first black Rhodes Scholar, was the guiding spirit of the "new" African American culture. Tiny in stature—he was less than five feet tall and weighed 95 pounds—Locke played a herculean role as the champion of the Harlem Renaissance. In 1925, for example, he announced that the Harlem Renaissance was led by a self-confident "new Negro" who no longer felt subservient to white culture or imprisoned by a sense of grievance against the Jim Crow system of white supremacy. Blacks, he argued, could shape their future by using the arts to transform their present.

Alain LeRoy Locke The philosopher and writer called "Dean" of the Harlem Renaissance sits at a desk in his office at Howard University.

In poetry and prose, Harlem Renaissance writers celebrated African American culture, especially jazz and the blues, which featured deep emotional roots in black history. As Hughes wrote, "I am a Negro—and beautiful. . . . The night is beautiful. So [are] the faces of my people." But while Hughes loved Africa and its cultural heritage, his outlook emphatically "was not Africa. I was [shaped by] Chicago and Kansas City and Broadway and Harlem."

Women were active in the Harlem Renaissance. In January 1925, a thirty-four-year-old African American woman named Zora Neale Hurston

Into Bondage This painting (left) by Aaron Douglas exemplifies how black artists in the Harlem Renaissance used their African roots and collective history as inspiration. **Realization** This sculpture (right) by Augusta Savage reflects her mission to challenge negative views of African Americans.

arrived in Harlem from Eatonville, an all-black community in rural central Florida. An aspiring writer and inventive storyteller, she became the first African American to enroll at Barnard College, the woman's college of Columbia University, where she majored in cultural anthropology.

Hurston had mastered the art of survival by learning to reinvent herself as the need arose. Motherless at nine and a runaway at fourteen, she became a calculating opportunist blessed with remarkable willpower. She came to Harlem to immerse herself in the "clang and clamor" of city life.

Within a few months, Hurston was behaving, in her words, as the queen of the Harlem Renaissance, writing short stories and plays about the "Negro furthest down" while positioning herself at the center of the community's raucous social life. Her outspokenness invited controversy, as when she claimed that she "did not belong to the sobbing school of Negrohood who hold that nature somehow has given them a lowdown dirty deal and whose feelings are all hurt about it." Hurston went on to become an anthropologist, folklorist, and novelist, expert at describing the ways in which African Americans in the Lower South forged cohesive communities in the face of white bigotry and violence. She also spoke out on behalf of poor African Americans who, "having nothing, still refused to be humble."

James Weldon Johnson coined the term *Aframerican* to designate Americans with African ancestry and to emphasize that blacks were no longer divided by their heritage; they were proud to be Americans who happened to have African ancestry. Black sculptor Augusta Savage explained that African Americans for three centuries had shared the "same cultural background, the same system, the same standard of beauty as white Americans. . . . It is impossible to go back to primitive [African] art for our models."

By 1930, Harlem Renaissance writers had produced dozens of novels and volumes of poetry, several Broadway plays, and a flood of short stories, essays, and films. A people capable of producing such great art and literature, Johnson declared, should never again be "looked upon as inferior."

GARVEYISM The celebration of black culture found much different expression in what came to be called **black nationalism**, which promoted black separatism from mainstream American life. Its leader was Marcus Garvey, who claimed to speak for all 400 million blacks worldwide. In 1916, Garvey brought to Harlem the headquarters of the Universal Negro Improvement Association (UNIA), which he had started in his native Jamaica two years before.

Garvey insisted that blacks had *nothing* in common with whites and called for racial separation. "The black skin," he stressed, "is not a badge of shame, but rather a glorious symbol of national greatness." Garvey urged African Americans to cultivate black solidarity and "black power."

The UNIA quickly became the largest black political organization in U.S. history. By 1923, Garvey claimed the UNIA had as many as 4 million members served by 800 offices. His goal was to build an all-black empire in Africa. To that end, he called himself the "Provisional President of Africa," raised funds to send Americans to Africa, and expelled any UNIA member who married a white.

Marcus Garvey The Jamaican-born founder of the Universal Negro Improvement Association and leading spokesman for "black nationalism."

Garvey's message of black nationalism and racial solidarity appealed especially to poor blacks in northern cities, but he also had supporters across the rural South. Garveyism, however, appalled some black leaders. W. E. B. Du Bois labeled Garvey "the most dangerous enemy of the Negro race. . . . He is either a lunatic or a traitor." An African American newspaper pledged to help "drive Garvey and Garveyism in all its sinister viciousness from the American soil."

Garvey's crusade collapsed in 1923 when he was convicted of fraud for overselling shares of stock in a steamship corporation, the Black Star Line, which he had founded to transport American blacks to Africa. Sentenced to five years in prison, he was pardoned in 1927 by President Calvin Coolidge on the condition that he be deported to Jamaica. Upon arrival there, he received a hero's welcome. Garvey died in obscurity in 1940, but the memory of his movement kept alive an undercurrent that would re-emerge in the 1960s under the slogan "black power."

THE MODERNIST REVOLT

During the twenties, a cultural civil war erupted between modernists eager to "make it new" and traditionalists anchored in what experimental poet Ezra Pound called "a botched civilization." Modernists were intellectuals, writers, and artists who used new modes of expression and behavior to illustrate that they were living in an era of confusion and possibility that demanded new ways of thinking and behaving. They saw the start of the twentieth century as a historical hinge opening the way for a new world view that rejected conventional notions of reality and values (progress, reason, and even God).

The modernists adopted radical new forms of artistic expression. In 1922, Irish modernist James Joyce published his pathbreaking novel *Ulysses,* and Anglo-American poet T. S. Eliot wrote "The Waste Land," in which he claimed to speak for a postwar culture in crisis.

Critics charged that Eliot, Joyce, and other self-described modernists were "ruining" literature. Modernists fought back, claiming that they were simply acknowledging the arrival of an unsettling new way of viewing life and expressing its raucous energies.

ALBERT EINSTEIN

During a century remarkable for its disruptive discoveries and technological advances, one modernist genius stands out: Albert Einstein, who precipitated a fundamental change in understanding the operations of the universe. Many of his greatest innovations emerged from his remarkable ability to *picture,* in the

Albert Einstein One of the most influential scientists of the twentieth century, Einstein received a Nobel Prize.

inner recesses of his mind, the strange effects of natural forces, from the infinitesimally small to the infinitely large. "Imagination," he concluded, "is more important than knowledge." His "thought experiments" blossomed into theories about the fluid interplay of space, time, matter, energy, and gravity that caused traditional notions of a stable universe to wobble.

In 1905, the German-born Einstein, then a twenty-six-year-old physicist working in Switzerland, published several papers that changed science forever while at times defying common sense. The first paper, which would earn him the Nobel Prize in 1921, revealed that nothing could travel faster than light and that light was not simply a wave of continuous energy but a stream of tiny particles, called *quanta* (now called *photons*). This breakthrough would provide the theoretical basis for quantum physics and lead to new electronic technologies such as television, laser beams, and semiconductors used to make computers and cell phones.

In his second research paper, Einstein confirmed the existence of molecules and atoms by showing how their random collisions explained the jerky motions of minute particles in water.

His third paper overturned traditional notions of the universe. It grew out of one of his favorite thought experiments: If you were in a train that neared the speed of light, would time and space behave differently?

Einstein's reflections led to his special theory of relativity, which explains that no matter how fast one is moving toward or away from a source of light, the speed of that light beam will appear the same, a constant 186,000 miles per second. Space and time, however, will appear *relative* to the speed of light. So if a train were traveling at the speed of light, time would slow down from the perspective of those watching, and the train itself would get shorter and heavier. Space and time, in other words, are not independent of one another. They instead form the fabric of space-time within which matter resides.

It took Einstein ten more years to devise a *general theory of relativity*. He was sitting in a chair in his office "when all of a sudden a thought occurred to me. If a person falls freely, he will not feel his own weight." He later called it the "happiest thought in my life."

The resulting general theory of relativity maintains that the fundamental concepts of space, time, matter, and energy are not distinct, independent entities with stable and permanent dimensions, as Sir Isaac Newton had assumed in the eighteenth century. Instead, they are interacting elements constantly changing one another. Gravity, therefore, is not a force transmitted across space-time like magnetism. Gravity is the geometry of that space-time itself that keeps planets in their orbits around the sun. Space-time, in other words, is dynamic and elastic, much like the behavior of a bowling ball on the surface of a trampoline. Gravity can stretch and grow or collapse into a black hole of infinite density.

Einstein's discoveries revolutionized the way scientists perceived the universe. A British newspaper said the general theory of relativity was "one of the most momentous . . . pronouncements of human thought."

AN AGE OF RELATIVISM Just as Darwinism became not just a biological theory but also a social, economic, and political point of view, so too did Einstein's concept of relativity shape many of the intellectual, cultural, and social currents of the twentieth century. People oversimplified his theory by claiming that there were no absolute standards; all was "relative." During the twenties, the idea of "relativity" emerged in discussions of topics such as sexuality, the arts, and politics; there was less faith in absolutes.

In 1920, an American journalist said that Einstein's theories had moved physics into the region of "metaphysics, where paradox and magic take the place of solid fact . . . and common sense." The farther scientists reached out into the universe and into the microscopic world of the atom, the more traditional certainties dissolved.

MODERNIST ART AND LITERATURE

The scientific breakthroughs associated with Sigmund Freud, Albert Einstein, and others helped to inspire and shape a "modernist" cultural revolution. **Modernism** as a movement appeared first in the capitals of Europe in the 1890s. By the second decade of the twentieth century, cultural modernism had spread to the United States.

Put most simply, modernism was the widespread awareness that new ideas and ways of doing things were making a sharp break with tradition, and that new technologies, modes of transportation and communication, and scientific discoveries were transforming the nature of everyday life and the way people "saw" the world.

The horrors of the Great War accelerated and expanded the appeal of modernism. To be modern was to take chances, violate artistic rules and moral restrictions, and behave in deliberately shocking ways. "Art," said a modernist painter, "is meant to disturb."

Modernism was loosely based on three unsettling assumptions: (1) God did not exist; (2) reality was not rational, orderly, or obvious; and, in the aftermath of the Great War, (3) social progress could no longer be taken for granted. These premises led writers, artists, musicians, designers, and architects to rebel against good taste, old-fashioned morals, and old-time religion.

Modernists refused to be conventional. Poet Ezra Pound, a militant propagandist for the modernist movement, believed that he and other cultural rebels were "saving civilization" from the dictatorship of tradition: "We are restarting civilization."

Like many previous cultural movements, modernism involved a fresh way of *seeing* the world, led by a new intellectual and cultural elite determined to capture and express the hidden realm of imagination and dreams. Doing so, however, often made their writing, art, music, and dance difficult to understand, interpret, or explain. "The pure modernist is merely a snob," explained a British writer.

But for many modernists, being misunderstood was a badge of honor. American experimentalist writer Gertrude Stein, for example, declared that a novel "which tells about what happens is of no interest." Instead of depicting real life or telling recognizable stories in books such as *Three Lives* and *Tender Buttons*, she was interested in playing with language. Words, not people, are the characters in her writings, although in her private life she became famous for hosting in her Paris salon the leading modernists from around the world.

Until the twentieth century, most writers and artists had taken for granted an accessible, identifiable world that could be readily observed, scientifically explained, and accurately represented in words or paint or even music. Modernists, however, applied Einstein's ideas about relativity to a world in which reality no longer had an objective or recognizable basis. They agreed with Freud that reality was an intensely inward and subjective experience— something deeply personal that was to be imagined and expressed by one's

Russian Ballet **(1916)** Jewish American artist Max Weber's painting is a modernist take on a traditional subject. Splicing the scene of the performance into overlapping planes of jarring colors, this painting exemplifies the impact of psychoanalysis and the theory of relativity on the arts.

innermost being. Walter Pach, an early champion of modern art, explained that modernism resulted from the discovery of "the role played by the unconscious in our lives."

For modernists such as Spanish painter Pablo Picasso and Irish writer James Joyce, art involved an unpredictable journey into the realm of individual fantasies and dreams, exploring and expressing the personal, the unknown, the primitive, the abstract. Modernist artists discarded literal representation of recognizable subjects in favor of vibrant color masses, simplified forms, or geometric shapes.

THE ARMORY SHOW The crusade to bring European-inspired modernism to the United States reached a climax in the **Armory Show** of 1913, the most scandalous event in the history of American art. Mabel Dodge, one of the organizers, wrote to Gertrude Stein that the exhibition would cause "a riot and revolution and things will never be the same afterwards."

The Armory Show, officially known as the International Exhibition of Modern Art, opened February 17, 1913, in the vast 69th Army Regiment Armory in New York City. It featured 1,200 works and created an immediate sensation. One prominent critic grumbled that modernism "is nothing else than the total destruction of the art of painting." The *New York Times* warned visitors that they would enter "a stark region of abstractions" at the "lunatic asylum" show that was "hideous to our unaccustomed eyes."

The experimentalist ("avant-garde") artists whose works were on display (including painters Vincent Van Gogh, Paul Gauguin, Henri Matisse, Paul Cezanne, and Picasso) were "in love with science but not with objective reality," the *Times* critic complained, and had produced paintings "revolting in their inhumanity." Former president Theodore Roosevelt dismissed the show as "repellent from every standpoint."

Yet it also generated excitement. "A new world has arisen before our eyes," announced an art magazine. "To miss modern art," a critic stressed, "is to miss one of the few thrills that life holds." From New York, the show went to Chicago and Boston, where it aroused similar responses and attracted overflow crowds.

After the Armory Show, many people discovered a new faith in the disturbing powers of art. "America in spite of its newness," predicted Walt Kuhn, a painter who helped organize the exhibition, "is destined to become the coming center" of modernism. Indeed, the Museum of Modern Art, founded in New York City in 1929, came to house the world's most celebrated collection of avant-garde paintings and sculpture.

POUND, ELIOT, AND STEIN The leading American champions of modern art and literature lived in England and Europe: Idaho-born Ezra Pound and St. Louis–born T. S. Eliot in London, and Californian Gertrude Stein in Paris. They were self-conscious revolutionaries concerned with creating strange, new, and often beautifully difficult forms of expression, and they found more inspiration and more receptive audiences in Europe.

As the foreign editor of the Chicago-based *Poetry* magazine, Pound became the cultural impresario of modernism. In bitter poems and earnest essays denouncing war and commercialism, he displayed an uncompromising urgency to transform the literary landscape. An English poet called him a "solitary volcano." Eliot claimed that Pound was single-handedly responsible for the modernist movement in poetry.

Pound recruited, edited, published, and reviewed the best among the modernist writers, improving their writing, bolstering their courage, and propelling their careers. In his own poetry, he expressed the feeling of many that the Great War had wasted a generation of young men who died in defense of a "botched civilization."

One of the young American writers Pound took under his wing was Eliot, who had recently graduated from Harvard. Within a few years, Eliot surpassed Pound to become the leading American modernist.

Eliot's epic 433-line poem *The Waste Land* (1922), which Pound edited, became a monument of modernism. It expressed a sense of postwar disillusionment and melancholy that had a powerful effect on other writers. As a poet and critic for the *Criterion*, a poetry journal that he founded in 1922, Eliot became the arbiter of modernist taste in Anglo-American literature.

Gertrude Stein was the self-appointed champion of the American modernists living in Paris. Long regarded as simply the literary eccentric who wrote, "Rose is a rose is a rose is a rose," Stein was in fact one of the chief promoters of the triumphant subjectivity undergirding modernist expression. She sought to capture in words the equivalent of abstract painting and its self-conscious revolt against portraying recognizable scenes from real life. Stein hosted a cultural salon in Paris that became a gathering place for American and European modernists.

THE "LOST GENERATION" The arts and literature of the twenties were also greatly influenced by the dreadfulness of the Great War. F. Scott Fitzgerald wrote in *This Side of Paradise* that the "sad young men" who had fought to "make the world safe for democracy" had "grown up to find all Gods dead, all wars fought, all faiths in man shaken."

Cynicism had supposedly displaced idealism in the wake of the war's horrific senselessness. Frederic Henry, a character in Ernest Hemingway's novel *A Farewell to Arms* (1929), declares that "abstract words such as *glory, honor, courage* . . . were obscene" in the context of the war's colossal casualties.

Hemingway, Fitzgerald, and other young modernists were labeled the **Lost Generation**—those who had lost faith in the values and institutions of Western civilization and were frantically looking for new gods to worship. In 1921, Gertrude Stein told Hemingway that he and his dissolute friends who had served in the war as soldiers or ambulance drivers "are a lost generation." When Hemingway objected, she held her ground. "You are [lost]. You have no respect for anything. You drink yourselves to death."

In his first novel, *The Sun Also Rises* (1926), Hemingway used the phrase "lost generation" in the book's opening quotation. The novel centers on Jake Barnes, a young American castrated by a war injury. His impotence leads him to wander the cafes and nightclubs of postwar Europe with his often-drunk friends, who acknowledge that they are all wounded and sterile in their own way. They have lost their innocence, their illusions, and their motivation to do anything with their lives.

Hemingway sought "in all my stories to get the feeling of the actual life across—not just to depict life—but to actually make it alive. So that when you have read something by me you actually experience the thing."

Hemingway's friend and rival, Fitzgerald, shared a similar goal. He was the self-appointed chronicler of the Lost Generation. Like his fictional characters, Fitzgerald blazed up brilliantly, delighted in the hard-drinking, party-going pace of the Jazz Age, and then flickered out in a fog of drunkenness. (He would die in 1940 at age forty-four.) A fellow writer called Fitzgerald "our darling, our genius, our fool." He used his writings to depict the frivolity of the "upper tenth" of American society and to reveal his own shortcomings and failures, guilt and shame.

In 1924, while drafting *The Great Gatsby*, Fitzgerald announced his intention to "write a novel better than any novel ever written in America." The novel dealt with the misfortunes of the fortunate: self-indulgent and self-destructive wealthy people who drank and partied as a means of medicating themselves to the pointlessness of their shallow lives.

What gave depth to the best of Fitzgerald's stories was what a character in *The Great Gatsby* called "a sense of the fundamental decencies" amid all the superficial merriment and fanatical materialism—and a sense of impending doom in a world that had lost its meaning through the disorienting discoveries of modern science and the horrors of war.

Just six months after the stock market crashed in October 1929, Zelda Fitzgerald experienced the first of several nervous breakdowns triggered by schizophrenia and punctuated by attempted suicide. She and Scott, drinking heavily and fighting viciously, experienced the "crack up" of their hopes and sanity at the same time that the world careened into the Great Depression.

The gaiety of the Jazz Age, F. Scott Fitzgerald noted, "leaped to a spectacular death in October 1929" with the collapse of the stock market. In 1931, he recalled that the Roaring Twenties "was an age of miracles, an age of art, it was an age of excess, and it was an age of satire." It "bore him up, flattered him and gave him more money than he had dreamed of, simply for telling people that he felt as they did, that something had to be done with all the nervous energy stored up and unexpended in the War."

To be sure, the twenties roared only for a small group of affluent Americans, but those years involved something soon inconceivable—the belief in freedom at all costs; freedom for the sake of nothing but the enjoyment of one's freedom; freedom that endowed life with vitality, ingenuity, and openness to new experience that had defined the American myth since colonial days.

The title of one of Fitzgerald's earliest novels seemed to have predicted the collapse of the Jazz Age and all of its hollowness and aimlessness. It was called *The Beautiful and the Damned* (1922).

CHAPTER REVIEW

SUMMARY

- **A "New Era" of Consumerism** The American economy grew at its fastest rate in history during the 1920s, led by an explosion in mass production and sales of new consumer goods. Innovations in production, advertising, and financing, and a sharp rise in the use of electricity, enabled and encouraged millions of Americans to purchase automobiles, radios, and other electrical appliances. Ford Motor Company pioneered mass production using moving assembly lines, a highly efficient method that helped make its cars affordable for a majority of Americans. The new *consumer culture* valued leisure, self-expression, and self-indulgence. During the twenties, consumer debt tripled. Innovations in communications (especially the growth in radio ownership), transportation, finance, and advertising also brought about a mass culture, as more and more Americans purchased national brand-name items from retail chain stores, listened to the same radio shows, watched the same movies, and followed the lives and careers of national celebrities and superstars.

- **The "Jazz Age"** Other new social and cultural trends and movements rapidly challenged the traditional order. The carefree fads and attitudes of the 1920s, perhaps best represented by the frantic rhythms of jazz music, led writer F. Scott Fitzgerald to call the decade the *Jazz Age*. A "new woman" appeared, best represented by *flappers*—impetuous young women eager to define their own identity by challenging prewar restrictions with their short hemlines, drinking, smoking, and open discussions of sex. The majority of women, however, remained full-time housewives and mothers or domestic servants, and fewer young women pursued professional careers. With the *Great Migration* continuing, African Americans in northern cities felt freer to speak out against racial injustice and express pride in their race. The *Harlem Renaissance* movement gave voice to African American literature and music. Racial separatism and *black nationalism* grew popular under the leadership of Marcus Garvey, while other African Americans joined white supporters in the *National Association for the Advancement of Colored People (NAACP)* and supported its efforts to undo racism through education, legislation, and court challenges.

- **The Modernist Revolt** Some American artists and intellectuals alienated by the horrors of the Great War and the collapse of many traditional ideals coalesced into what was called the *Lost Generation*. Others were attracted to *modernism*, a movement that had begun in Europe before the Great War and reflected new developments in science, particularly Albert Einstein's theory of relativity and Sigmund Freud's exploration of how the subconscious mind shapes human behavior. To be "modern" meant to break free of tradition, violate restrictions, shock the public, and make one's works difficult to explain or interpret. Americans were first exposed to modern art in a substantial way with the *Armory Show* of 1913.

CHRONOLOGY

1903	Wright Brothers fly first motorized airplane
	Ford Motor Company is founded
1910	National Association for the Advancement of Colored People (NAACP) is founded
1913	Armory Show introduces Americans to modern art
1916	Marcus Garvey brings Universal Negro Improvement Association to New York
1920	Prohibition begins
	F. Scott Fitzgerald's *This Side of Paradise* is published
	Warren G. Harding is elected president
1921	Albert Einstein receives Nobel Prize in physics
1922	First radio commercial is aired
1927	Charles A. Lindbergh Jr. makes first solo transatlantic airplane flight

KEY TERMS

consumer culture p. 1080

Jazz Age p. 1089

flappers p. 1094

Great Migration p. 1097

National Association for the Advancement of Colored People (NAACP) p. 1099

Harlem Renaissance p. 1099

black nationalism p. 1102

modernism p. 1105

Armory Show p. 1107

Lost Generation p. 1109

 INQUIZITIVE

Go to InQuizitive to see what you've learned—and learn what you've missed—with personalized feedback along the way.

24 The Reactionary Twenties

Black Tuesday In this photograph, crowds panicked by the news of the plummeting stock market take to Wall Street on the morning of Tuesday, October 29, 1929. An account of the crash in the *New York Times* reported that "the streets were crammed with a mixed crowd—agonized little speculators, . . . sold-out traders, . . . inquisitive individuals and tourists seeking . . . a closer view of the national catastrophe. . . . Where was it going to end?"

The self-indulgent excesses of the Lost Generation and the frivolities associated with the Jazz Age made little sense to average Americans during the twenties. Most were not disillusioned, self-destructive, or defiantly modernist. The majority still led traditional lives; they aggressively defended established values, old certainties, and the comfort of past routines, and they were shocked by the decade's social turmoil and cultural rebelliousness.

In national politics, the small-town backlash against modern city life—whether represented by immigrants plotting revolution, liberal churches embracing evolution, or jazzed-up flappers swilling cocktails—mirrored Republican efforts to reverse the progressivism of Theodore Roosevelt and Woodrow Wilson.

By 1920, the progressive political coalition that had reelected Wilson in 1916 had fragmented. The growing middle class had become preoccupied less with reform than with enjoying America's economic prosperity, the outcome of increased mass production, mass consumption, and labor-saving electrical appliances.

Many Americans traced the germs of dangerous radicalism (the Red Scare) to cities teeming with immigrants and foreign ideas such as socialism, communism, anarchism, and labor union militancy. Others feared the erosion of traditional religious beliefs in the face of secular modernism. People were convinced that dangers from abroad and at home must be vigorously resisted. This reactionary conservatism of the 1920s fed on the popularity of **nativism**—the prejudice against immigrants from countries outside

focus questions

1. How did the reactionary conservatism during the 1920s manifest itself in social life and governmental policies?

2. To what extent did the policies of the Republican party dominate the federal government during the twenties? In what ways were these policies a rejection of progressivism?

3. What were the major causes of the Great Depression?

4. How did the Great Depression impact the American people?

5. In what ways did Hoover fail to address the human distress caused by the Great Depression?

of western Europe—and a militant Protestantism that sought to restore the primacy of traditional Christian morality.

REACTIONARY CONSERVATISM AND IMMIGRATION RESTRICTION

After the end of the Great War, masses of people emigrated from Europe to the United States. Between 1919 and 1924, more than 600,000 people from southern and eastern Europe, most of them Italians, entered the United States, along with 150,000 Poles and 50,000 Russians. At the same time, some 150,000 Mexicans crossed the border; most settling in the Southwest and California. In the early 1920s, more than half of the white men and a third of the white women working in mines, mills, and factories were immigrants. Some had retained a passion for socialism or anarchism—as well as a willingness to use violence to achieve their political goals.

Nativists alarmed by the surge in immigration realized the literacy test added in 1917 was not excluding enough newcomers, for between 1920 and 1921 some 1,235,000 foreigners entered the United States. Fears of an invasion of foreign radicals led Congress to pass the Emergency Immigration Act of 1921, which limited *total* immigration to 150,000 a year and restricted new-comers from each European country to 3 percent of the total number of that nationality represented in the 1910 census.

Three years later, Congress responded to complaints that too many eastern and southern Europeans were still being admitted by passing the **Immigration Act of 1924** (the Johnson-Reed Act). The bill, set to take effect

Immigration Act of 1924 This immigration chart illustrates the nationalities of the foreign-born population in the United States in 1920, which formed the basis of the quota system introduced in the Johnson-Reed Act.

in 1929, reduced the number ("quota") of visas from 3 to 2 percent of the total number of people of each nationality in the United States as of the 1890 rather than the 1910 national census, since there were far fewer eastern and southern Europeans in the nation in 1890. It also banned almost all immigrants from Asia.

The purpose of placing a numerical ceiling or quota on immigrants was to shrink the total number of newcomers, to favor immigrants from northern and western Europe, and to reduce those from southern and eastern Europe, especially Jews, Italians, Poles, Turks, and Russians. The plan was clearly discriminatory since it favored some peoples over others. Congressman Fred S. Purnell of Indiana urged legislators to stop the "stream of irresponsible and broken wreckage that is pouring into the lifeblood of America the social and political diseases of the Old World."

Senator Ellison D. "Cotton Ed" Smith, a South Carolina Democrat, likewise asserted that it was long past time "to shut the door. We have been called the melting pot of the world . . . we had allowed influences to enter our borders that were about to melt the pot in place of us being the melting pot. Americanize what we have, and save the resources of America for the natural increase of our population."

H. L. Mencken, the celebrated columnist for the *Baltimore Evening Sun*, attacked the Immigration Act because its primary purpose was "to hobble and cage the citizen of newer [racial] stocks in a hundred fantastic ways." Immigrants from southern and eastern Europe were being treated as domestic enemies, he charged, even though they were benefiting the nation. "The fact that they increase [in number] is the best hope of civilization in America. They shake the old race out of its spiritual lethargy, and introduce it to disquiet and experiment. They make for a free play of ideas."

Such arguments had no effect on President Calvin Coolidge. "America," he emphasized, "must be kept for Americans." He readily signed the immigration restriction bill, which remained in force until 1965. Its impact was immediate. Under the quota system, more than 50,000 Germans could enter the nation annually, while fewer than 4,000 Italians were allowed, compared to the more than 2 million Italians who had arrived between 1910 and 1920. Not even Adolf Hitler's persecution of Jews could persuade Congress to raise the quota for European refugees.

The Immigration Act of 1924, however, placed no quota on immigrants from countries in the Western Hemisphere, particularly Mexico. Responding to the lobbying efforts of railroads and commercial farm owners in the West, Congress sought to ensure an adequate supply of low-paid laborers from Mexico, Puerto Rico, and Cuba. An unexpected result of the 1924 immigration act was that people of Latin American descent became the fastest-growing ethnic minority during the twenties.

The number of Mexicans living in Texas increased tenfold between 1900 and 1930 in response to the needs of Texas farmers for "stoop" laborers hired to harvest cotton and other crops. "Cotton picking suits the Mexican," was the common assertion among Texas growers. Because migrant workers were less likely to have established "roots" in the United States and because they were willing to move with the seasons, farm owners came to prefer them over black or Anglo tenants and farm laborers.

SACCO AND VANZETTI The nativism embedded in the new immigration laws reinforced the connection between European immigrants and political radicalism. That connection erupted in the most widely publicized criminal case of the twenties.

Sacco and Vanzetti The trial and conviction of these working-class Italian immigrants became a public spectacle amid the growing mood of nativism.

On May 5, 1920, two Italian immigrants who described themselves as revolutionary anarchists eager to topple the American government were arrested outside Boston, Massachusetts. Shoemaker Nicola Sacco and fish peddler Bartolomeo Vanzetti were accused of stealing $16,000 from a shoe factory and killing the paymaster and a guard. Both men were armed with loaded pistols when arrested, both lied to the police, and both were identified by eyewitnesses. The stolen money, however, was never found, and several people claimed that they were with Sacco and Vanzetti far from the scene of the crime when it occurred.

The **Sacco and Vanzetti case** occurred at the height of Italian immigration to the United States and against the backdrop of numerous terror attacks by anarchists, some of which Sacco and Vanzetti had participated in. The charged atmosphere, called "the Red hysteria" by one journalist, ensured that the men's trial would be a public spectacle.

In July 1921, Sacco and Vanzetti were convicted and sentenced to death. Their legal appeals lasted six years before they were electrocuted on August 23, 1927, still claiming innocence. To millions around the world, they became victims of capitalist injustice. People still debate their guilt or innocence.

THE NEW KLAN The most violent of the reactionary conservative movements during the twenties was a revived Ku Klux Klan, the infamous post–Civil War group of racists that had re-created itself in 1915 in conjunction with the widely popular film *Birth of a Nation*. Produced and directed by D. W. Griffith, son of a Confederate army officer, the movie was set during Reconstruction and based on a novel, *The Clansman: An Historical Romance of the Ku Klux Klan* (1905), written by Thomas Dixon, a Princeton classmate of Woodrow Wilson. The president hosted a special showing of the film at the White House and was reported to have said, "It is like writing history with lightning. And my only regret is that it is all so terribly true."

Thanks in part to Wilson's endorsement, *Birth of a Nation* became the most popular movie up to that time. The film rewrote southern history, portraying Klansmen as crusading heroes and newly freed slaves as working with unprincipled carpetbaggers and scalawags to corrupt state governments.

During the film's ballyhooed opening in Atlanta, William J. Simmons, an Atlanta physician, announced the founding of the second Ku Klux Klan. This new version—the Invisible Empire of the Knights of the Ku Klux Klan—was, by 1920, a *nationwide* organization devoted to "the maintenance of White Supremacy" and "100 percent Americanism." Only "natives"—meaning white, "Anglo-Saxon," evangelical Protestants born in the United States—could be members. At its peak in 1924, the new Klan numbered more than 4 million

Ku Klux Klan rally In 1925, the KKK marched down Pennsylvania Avenue in Washington, D.C.

members, making it the largest far-right movement in history. (It is no coincidence that 1924 was the same year in which numerous states erected memorial statues celebrating Confederate generals such as Robert E. Lee.)

Shrouded in secrecy and costumed in white sheets and spooky hats, the Klan was both bizarre and mainstream, sponsoring baseball teams, college fraternities, and county fairs. It even hosted beauty pageants where young women competed to be "Miss 100 Percent America."

Klan leader Hiram Wesley Evans explained that the organization embodied "an idea, a faith, a purpose, an organized crusade" against "that which is corrupting and destroying the best in American life." It embraced militant patriotism, restrictions on immigration and voting, and strict personal morality. It opposed illegal ("bootleg") liquor and labor unions and preached hatred against African Americans, Roman Catholics, Jews, immigrants, Communists, atheists, prostitutes, and adulterers.

The Klan became infamous for its blanket assaults on various categories of Americans. As a member stressed, "Every criminal, every gambler, every thug . . . every wife beater . . . every moonshiner, every crooked politician . . . is fighting the Klan." The United States was no melting pot, shouted Imperial Wizard William J. Simmons: "It is a garbage can! . . . When the hordes of aliens walk to the ballot box and their votes outnumber yours, then that alien horde has got you by the throat."

In the Southwest, Klansmen directed their anger at Mexicans; in the Pacific Northwest, Japanese people were the enemy; in New York, the targets were primarily Jews and Catholics. Klan members were elected governor in Oregon, Texas, and Colorado; others were mayors in Portland, Oregon, and Portland, Maine. The Klan became so "respectable" in the eyes of many that none of the presidents during the twenties—Wilson, Coolidge, or Hoover—spoke out against it.

White-robed bigotry also became big business. Members of local "klaverns" paid a $10 initiation fee and $5 in annual dues; they were required to buy an official Klan robe, a pointed hood, and other accessories. Protestant ministers received free membership. Whole families attended Klan gatherings, "klasping" hands while listening to violent speeches, watching fireworks, and burning crosses. A Colorado judge said that his neighbors had "paid ten dollars to hate somebody [by joining the Klan], and they were determined to get their money's worth."

In Texas, Klan members used harassment, intimidation (often in the form of burning crosses), beatings, and "tar and feathers" to discipline alcoholics, gamblers, adulterers, and other sinners. In the spring of 1922 alone, the Dallas Klan flogged sixty-eight men.

The reborn Klan grew rapidly, especially in the rural Midwest. During the twenties, 40 percent of its "Anglo-Saxon" members were in three midwestern states: Illinois, Indiana, and Ohio. Only 16 percent of registered Klansmen were in the former Confederate states. Recruiters, called Kleagles, were told to "play upon whatever prejudices were most acute in a particular area."

Most Klan members were small farmers, sharecroppers, or wage workers, but the organization also attracted clergymen, engineers, doctors, lawyers, accountants, business leaders, and teachers. As a prominent southern journalist observed, the new Klan was "anti-Negro, anti-alien, anti-red, anti-Catholic, anti-Jew, anti-Darwin, anti-Modern, anti-Liberal; Fundamentalist, vastly Moral, militantly Protestant."

African Americans grew increasingly concerned about Klan violence. The Chicago *Defender*, the African American newspaper with the widest circulation in the nation, urged its readers to fight back against Klansmen trying to "win what their fathers [in the Civil War] lost by fire and sword."

David C. Stephenson, the Grand Dragon of Indiana and a sly con man, became so influential in electing local and state officials (the "kluxing" of America, as he called it) that he boasted, "I am the law in Indiana!" Klan-endorsed candidates won the Indiana governorship and controlled the state legislature.

At the 1924 Republican State Convention, Stephenson patrolled the aisles with a pistol. He later confessed that he "purchased the county and state officials." Stephenson, who had grown wealthy by skimming from the dues he collected from Klan members as well as selling robes and hoods, planned to run for president.

In August 1925, some 25,000 Klansmen paraded down Pennsylvania Avenue in the nation's capital, dressed in their white-hooded regalia. The Klan's influence began to crumble, however, after Stephenson was arrested and sentenced to life in prison in 1925 for kidnapping, raping, and mutilating a twenty-eight-year-old female Klan staff member, who then committed suicide.

Stephenson assumed the governor would pardon him. When that did not happen, he told police about the widespread political bribery he had engaged in. As a result, the governor, the Indianapolis mayor, the county sheriff, congressmen, and other officeholders were indicted. Many ended up in prison.

News of the scandal caused Klan membership to tumble. More than a dozen Klan offices and meeting places across the country were bombed, burned, or blasted by shotguns. Several states passed anti-Klan laws and others banned the wearing of masks and burning of crosses. By 1930, nationwide Klan membership had dwindled to 100,000, mostly southerners.

Yet the impulse underlying the Klan lived on, fed by deep-seated fears and hatreds that have yet to disappear. On Memorial Day in 1927, a throng of 1,000 white-robed Klansmen paraded through the Jamaica neighborhood in Queens, a borough of New York City. A confrontation with police grew into a brawl, and six Klansmen were arrested. Another "berobed" man was jailed for "refusing to disperse," although the charge was later dropped. His name was Fred C. Trump, the twenty-one-year-old son of German immigrants, who later would father a son named Donald, a future president.

FUNDAMENTALISM

While the Klan fought against what they viewed as the nation's "growing immorality" and the "alien menace" they also defended "old-time religion" against dangerous ideas circulating in progressive or liberal Protestant churches. The most threatening of those ideas were that the Bible was not literally the word of God and that Charles Darwin's theories of biological evolution were true. Conservative Protestants embraced a militant fundamentalism, distinctive for its hostility toward such liberal beliefs and its insistence on the literal truth of the Bible.

The result was a religious civil war that divided congregations and entire denominations. A burst of Protestant fundamentalism swept the country, largely as a conservative reaction to the spread of modernism in mainline Protestantism, which sought to accommodate Christian teaching with modern science.

In a famous 1922 sermon titled "Shall the Fundamentalists Win?" Harry Emerson Fosdick, the progressive pastor at New York City's First Presbyterian Church, dismissed biblical fundamentalism as "immeasurable folly." The Bible, he explained, was not literally the "word of God" but a representation of God's wonders. Christianity had nothing to fear from Darwinian evolution or modern science, he argued, for liberal Christianity "saves us from the necessity of apologizing for immature states in the development of the biblical revelation." Fosdick, an outspoken critic of racism and social injustice, outraged fundamentalists, who launched an effort to "try" him for heresy. He decided to resign instead.

Among national leaders, however, only the "Great Commoner," William Jennings Bryan, the former Democratic congressman, secretary of state, and three-time presidential candidate, had the support, prestige, and eloquence to transform fundamentalism into a popular crusade. Bryan was a strange bird, a liberal progressive and pacifist Populist in politics and a right-wing religious crusader who believed in the literal Bible.

Bryan supported new state laws banning the teaching of evolution in public schools. He passionately condemned Darwin's theory of evolution, which suggested that human beings had evolved from monkeys and apes. "Darwinism is not science at all," he maintained. "It is guesses strung together."

THE SCOPES TRIAL During the 1920s, bills banning the teaching of Darwinian evolution in public schools were introduced in numerous state legislatures, but the only victories came in the South—and there were few of them. Miriam "Ma" Ferguson, the first woman governor of Texas (her husband "Pa" Ferguson had earlier been impeached as governor), outlawed school textbooks that included sections on Darwinism. "I am a Christian mother who believes that Jesus Christ died to save humanity," she declared, "and I am not going to let that kind of rot go into Texas schoolbooks."

The dramatic highpoint of the fundamentalist war on Darwinism came in Tennessee, where in 1925 the legislature outlawed the teaching of evolution in public schools and colleges. In the small mining town of Dayton, in eastern Tennessee, civic leaders eager to create money-making publicity for their depressed economy persuaded John T. Scopes, a twenty-four-year-old substitute high-school science teacher, to become a test case against the new law. He was arrested for "teaching" Darwin's theory of evolution.

Monkey trial In this snapshot of the courtroom, John T. Scopes (far left) clasps his face in his hands and listens to one of his attorneys (second from right). Clarence Darrow (far right), too, listens on, visibly affected by the sweltering heat.

The **Scopes Trial** did indeed bring worldwide publicity to Dayton, but not the kind town leaders had anticipated. Before the start of the trial on July 10, 1925, the sweltering streets of Dayton overflowed with sightseers, evangelists, atheists, and some 200 newspaper and radio reporters. Main Street merchants festooned their shop windows with pictures of apes and monkeys lampooning Darwinian evolution. A man tattooed with Bible verses preached on a street corner while a live piano-playing monkey was paraded about town. Ministers harangued passersby about the evils of coffee, ice cream, and Coca-Cola ("a hell-sent narcotic").

The two warriors pitting science against fundamentalism were both national celebrities: William Jennings Bryan, who had offered his services to the prosecution, and Chicagoan Clarence Darrow, the nation's foremost defense attorney and a tireless defender of the rights of the working class, who had volunteered to defend Scopes.

Temperatures surpassed 100 degrees as the trial began. Bryan insisted that the trial was about a state's right to determine what was taught in the public schools. It was a "contest between evolution and Christianity, a duel to the death." Darrow countered: "Scopes is not on trial. Civilization is on trial." His goal was to prevent "bigots and ignoramuses from controlling the education of the United States" by proving that America was "founded on liberty and not on narrow, mean, intolerable and brainless prejudice of soulless religio-maniacs."

On July 20, the seventh day of the trial, the defense called Bryan as an expert witness on biblical interpretation. Darrow began by asking him about biblical stories. Did he believe that Jonah was swallowed by a whale and that Joshua made the sun stand still? Yes, Bryan replied, as beads of sweat streamed down his face. All things were possible with God.

Darrow pressed on relentlessly. What about the great flood and Noah's ark? Was Eve really created from Adam's rib? Bryan hesitated, and the crowd grew uneasy as the hero of fundamentalism crumpled in the heat. Bryan appealed to the judge, claiming that the Bible was not on trial, only to have Darrow yell: "I am examining you on your fool ideas that no intelligent Christian on earth believes." A humiliated Bryan claimed that Darrow was insulting Christians. Darrow, his thumbs clasping his colorful suspenders, shot back: "You insult every man of science and learning in the world because he does not believe in your fool religion." At one point, the men lunged at each other, prompting the judge to adjourn court for the day.

Journalist H. L. Mencken called the legal proceedings a "universal joke." Bryan, he said, was a "charlatan, a mountebank, a zany," and the residents of Dayton ("Monkey Town") were "gaping primates" and "rustic ignoramuses."

As the trial ended, the judge said that the only question for the jury was whether John T. Scopes had taught evolution. No one had denied that he had done so. The jurors did not even sit down before deciding, in nine minutes, that Scopes was guilty. But the Tennessee Supreme Court, while upholding the anti-evolution law, waived Scopes's $100 fine on a technicality. Both sides claimed victory.

Five days after the trial ended, the sixty-five-year-old Bryan died in his sleep. Scopes left Dayton to study geology at the University of Chicago; he became a petroleum engineer.

The Scopes Trial symbolized the waning of an old order in America and the rise of a *modern* outlook—more pluralistic, diverse, and skeptical, more tolerant of controversial ideas, and less obsessed with intellectual control. Still, the debate between fundamentalism and modernism continues today.

PROHIBITION

William Jennings Bryan died in 1925 knowing that one of his crusades had succeeded: On December 18, 1917, Congress had sent to the states the Eighteenth Amendment. Ratified by all but two states by January 1919, the amendment banned "the manufacture, sale, and transportation of intoxicating liquors," effective one year later. The movement to prohibit the sale of beer, wine, and liquor forged an unusual alliance between rural and small-town Protestant evangelicals and urban political progressives: between believers in religious fundamentalism who opposed drinking as sinful and progressive social reformers, mostly women, who were convinced that **Prohibition** would reduce prostitution, domestic abuse, and workplace violence. The result was the largest social reform movement since abolitionism.

Alcohol-related problems were widespread. Per capita beer consumption between 1840 and 1910 had soared more than 1,000 percent. Excessive drinking, said the *Nashville Banner*, was the largest "producer of disease, crime, and poverty."

During the Great War, rationing dictated the need to use grain for food rather than for making booze. That, combined with a backlash against the majority of beer brewers because of their German background, transformed the cause of Prohibition into a virtual test of American patriotism.

Billy Sunday, a Christian evangelist who described himself as a "temperance Republican down to my toes," told 10,000 people gathered at his tabernacle that the age of righteousness was at hand: "Men will walk upright now; women will smile and the children will laugh." Former president William Howard Taft, soon to be chief justice of the Supreme Court, had a different perspective. "No tendency is quite so strong in human nature," he said, "as the desire to lay down rules of conduct for other people."

Ethnic and social prejudices drove the Prohibition crusade. The head of the Anti-Saloon League, for example, declared that German Americans "eat like gluttons and drink like swine." For many such nativists, in fact, the primary goal of Prohibition was to police the behavior of the foreign-born, the working class, African Americans, and poor whites.

Many leaders of the Prohibition movement also supported immigration restrictions. Charles Eliot, president of Harvard University, declared that alcoholism "threatened the destruction of the white race." Likewise, Frances Willard, head of the Women's Christian Temperance Union, believed Prohibition was essential in the war against foreign invaders, many of whom were Catholics. "Alien illiterates rule our cities today," she exclaimed. "The saloon is their place; the toddy stick [a utensil used to make toddy, a hot rum drink] their sceptre."

Prohibition took effect in January 1920. For a time, it worked. Neighborhood saloons closed, and drinking among the working poor dropped by half. With each passing month, however, people found ways to defy the law. Passenger ships anchored just off-shore to serve as floating saloons, and commercial bootleggers sprouted like mushrooms.

Over time, Prohibition proved to be a colossal and costly failure. In 1923, a federal agent said it would take a visitor in any city less than thirty minutes to find a drink. In New Orleans, he added, it would take only thirty-five seconds.

The National Prohibition Act of 1919 (commonly called the Volstead Act) outlined the rules and regulations needed to enforce the Eighteenth Amendment. Yet it had so many loopholes that it virtually guaranteed failure. Technically, it never stated that *drinking* alcohol was illegal, only the manufacture, distribution, and sale of alcoholic beverages.

All's fair in drink and war Torpedoes filled with malt whiskey were discovered in New York Harbor in 1926, an elaborate attempt by bootleggers to smuggle alcohol during Prohibition. Each "torpedo" had an air compartment so it could be floated to shore.

In addition, individuals and organizations were allowed to keep and drink any liquor owned on January 16, 1919. Not surprisingly, people stocked up before the law took effect. The Yale Club in New York City stored so much liquor that it never ran out during the thirteen years of Prohibition. Farmers were allowed to "preserve" their fruits by fermenting them, which resulted in barns stockpiled with "hard cider" and homemade wine. So-called medicinal liquor remained legal, which meant that physicians (and even veterinarians) wrote numerous prescriptions for "medicinal" brands such as Old Grand-Dad and Jim Beam whiskies.

Thousands of people set up home breweries, producing 700 million gallons of beer in 1929 alone. Wine was made just as easily, and "bathtub gin" was the simplest of all, requiring little more than a one-gallon still and some fruit, grain, or potatoes. Two thirds of illegal liquor came from Canada, with most of the rest from Mexico or overseas. Yet this bootleg alcohol became notoriously dangerous. Tens of thousands were killed or disabled by deadly batches of illegal liquor, whose alcohol content usually exceeded that in wine and beer.

The new law was too sweeping to enforce and too inconveniencing for most Americans to respect. It also had unexpected consequences. The loss of liquor taxes cost the federal government 10 percent of its annual revenue, and the closing of breweries, distilleries, and saloons eliminated thousands of jobs. Prohibition also spurred a dramatic increase in the size and scope of the federal government. Enforcement agents had to be hired, prisons needed to be built to house violators, federal police powers were expanded, and civil liberties were violated.

Yet for all the increases in federal power, Congress never supplied adequate funding to implement the Volstead Act. The Prohibition Unit, a new agency within the U.S. Treasury Department, had 3,000 employees to police the nation, five times the number at the new Federal Bureau of Investigation. Yet their numbers were not nearly enough to enforce Prohibition. New York's mayor said it would require 250,000 police officers in his city alone. In working-class and ethnic-rich Detroit, the bootleg industry was second in size only to the auto industry. In Virginia, jails could not contain the 20,000 Prohibition-related arrests each year.

Moreover, many prominent Americans regularly broke the anti-liquor law. President Warren G. Harding stashed a whiskey flask in his golf bag and regularly drank and served bootleg liquor in the White House, explaining that he was "unable to see this as a great moral issue." The largest bootlegger in Washington, D.C., reported that "a majority of both houses" of Congress were regular customers. Secretary of Commerce Herbert Hoover often slipped into the Belgian Embassy to satisfy his thirst for fine wines.

The efforts to defy Prohibition generated widespread police corruption and boosted organized crime. Many activities and images associated with the Roaring Twenties were fueled by bootleg liquor supplied by crime syndicates and sold in saloons called speakeasies, which police often ignored in exchange for bribes. Well-organized crime syndicates controlled the entire stream of liquor's production, pricing, distribution, and sales. As a result, the Prohibition era was a thirteen-year orgy of unparalleled criminal activity. By 1930, more than one third of federal prisoners were Prohibition violators.

Although total alcohol consumption did decrease during the twenties, as did the number of deaths from alcohol abuse, in many cities drinking actually *increased* during Prohibition. New York City's police commissioner estimated that there were 32,000 speakeasies in the city in 1929. There had been only 15,000 saloons when Prohibition started. As humorist Will Rogers quipped, "Prohibition is better than no liquor at all."

Outlawing alcohol became a prime example of unintended consequences. Prohibition, for example, generated enormous income for organized crime. The most notorious Prohibition-era gangster was Alphonse Capone, the son of poor Italian immigrants. As a teenager, he shined shoes on a street corner in Brooklyn, New York, where he saw local mobsters at work. Soon, he organized a ring to extort money from other shoeshine boys.

In 1917 a neighborhood gangster hired Capone as bartender and bouncer at the Harvard Inn on Coney Island. One night, Capone insulted a woman at the bar. Her brother punched Capone, then slashed him across the face with a knife, leaving three scars that inspired his nickname, "Scarface." By 1925, Capone had assumed control of a mob in Chicago.

Two years later, Capone's bootlegging, prostitution, and gambling empire brought him an annual income of $60 million. His army of 700 gangsters was involved in 200 murders (none solved). The worst was the St. Valentine's Day Massacre, when his hit men, disguised as cops, drove up to a garage where seven members of a rival gang were awaiting a shipment of bootleg liquor. Capone's men murdered them with machine guns.

Capone, however, was a hero to many. He dressed in expensive, colorful suits; rode in a custom-built, armor-plated Cadillac with bulletproof glass; telephoned his mother and wife every day; gave huge tips to waiters, news-boys, and hat-check girls; and provided a soup kitchen that served 3,000 of Chicago's poorest residents daily. When criticized for his shady dealings, he claimed to be providing the public with the goods and services it demanded: "Some call it bootlegging. Some call it racketeering. I call it business. They say I violate the prohibition law. Who doesn't?"

Capone neglected to add that he had also beaten to death several police officers; ordered the execution of dozens of rivals; and bribed may-ors, judges, and police officers. Law-enforcement officials led by FBI agent Eliot Ness began to smash Capone's bootlegging operations in 1929. In the end, he was convicted on charges of tax evasion and sentenced to eleven years in prison. After only eight years, however, he died in prison of cardiac arrest.

A Republican Resurgence

After the Great War, most Americans had endured enough of Wilson's cru-sading idealism and spurned any leader who promoted sweeping reforms. Wilson, who despite his poor health wanted a third presidential term, recog-nized the shifting public mood. "It is only once in a generation," he remarked, "that a people can be lifted above material things. That is why conservative government is in the saddle two-thirds of the time."

Progressivism lost its momentum for several reasons. For one thing, its leaders were no more. Theodore Roosevelt died in 1919, just as he was begin-ning to campaign for the Republican presidential nomination, and Wilson's stroke had left him broken physically and mentally.

In addition, organized labor resented the Wilson administration's crackdown on striking workers in 1919–1920. Farmers in the Great Plains and West thought wartime price controls had discriminated against them. Liberal intellectuals became disillusioned with grassroots democracy because of popular support for Prohibition, the Ku Klux Klan, and religious fundamentalism.

After the war, most people were preoccupied with pursuing their own concerns as the nation made the transition from war to peace. And finally, progressivism had already accomplished its major goals: Prohibition and the women's vote.

Progressivism did not disappear, however. Progressive Republicans and Democrats dominated key leadership positions in Congress during much of the 1920s. The progressive impulse for honest, efficient government and regulation of business remained strong, especially at the state and local levels, where efforts to improve public education, public health, and social-welfare programs gained momentum. At the national level, however, conservative Republicans returned to power eager to reduce the size and scope of the federal government—and the presidency.

HARDING AND "NORMALCY" In 1920, Republican leaders turned to a likeable mediocrity as their presidential candidate: Warren G. Harding, a dapper, silver-haired U.S. senator from Ohio. One Republican senator explained that the party chose Harding not for his abilities or experience (which were minimal) but because he was from a key state and looked presidential. Harding, he said, was "the best of the second–raters." Harding admitted as much. When he asked his campaign manager, Harry Daugherty, if he had the abilities to be president, Daugherty laughed: "The day of giants in the presidential chair is passed."

Even Harding's wife, Florence, was wary. After learning that her husband had been nominated, she told a journalist, "I can see but one word written over the head of my husband if he is elected—and that word is tragedy." The irreverent H. L. Mencken was much less sympathetic: "No other such complete and dreadful nitwit is to be found in the pages of American history."

Harding set the anti-Wilson, anti-internationalism tone of his campaign when he pledged to "safeguard America first . . . to exalt America first, to live for and revere America first." America, Harding concluded, needed not "heroics, but healing; not nostrums, but normalcy; not revolution, but restoration; not agitation, but adjustment; not surgery, but serenity; not the dramatic, but the dispassionate."

Harding's clumsy speechmaking and ornate prose caused Mencken to explode in protest: "He writes the worst English I have ever encountered.

It reminds me of a string of wet sponges; it reminds me of tattered washing on the line; it reminds me of stale bean-soup, of college yells, of dogs barking idiotically through endless nights. It is so bad that a sort of grandeur creeps into it." Harding must have agreed, for he became the first president to hire a full-time speechwriter.

At their convention, the Democrats quickly rejected Wilson's desire for a third term and chose Ohioan James Cox, a former newspaper publisher and three-term governor of the state. For vice president, they selected New Yorker Franklin Delano Roosevelt, who as assistant secretary of the navy occupied the same position his Republican cousin Theodore Roosevelt had once held. Handsome, vigorous, and a stirring speaker, he would deliver more than 1,000 speeches during the campaign.

Cox's campaign was disorganized and underfunded, however, and the Democrats struggled against the conservative postwar mood. In the words of progressive journalist William Allen White, Americans were "tired of issues, sick at heart of ideals, and weary of being noble."

Harding won big, getting 16 million votes to 9 million for Cox, and the Republicans increased their majority in both houses of Congress. Harding's victory led Clarence Darrow to quip that he had grown up hearing that "anybody can become president. I'm beginning to believe it." Franklin Roosevelt predicted that the Democratic party could not hope to return to power until the Republicans led the nation "into a serious period of depression and unemployment." He was right.

The one-sided election was significant in another way: it was the first presidential contest in which women voted in all forty-eight states. (In the 1916 presidential election, about thirty states had permitted women to participate.) Still, not all women found voting easy. In North Carolina, Blanche Benton remembered that many men "said if their wives voted, they would leave them. Even my mother didn't want to vote the first time." She told the *Charlotte Observer* that many women voted like their husbands or fathers in the beginning, but she voted her conscience. "My husband, he said to vote the way I wanted, and he would vote the way he wanted."

"JUST A PLAIN FELLOW" Harding's vanilla promise of a **"return to normalcy"** reflected his unexceptional background and limited abilities. One of his speechwriters admitted that Harding was both "indolent" and "ignorant of most of the big questions that would confront him." A farmer's son and newspaper editor, Harding described himself as "just a plain fellow" who was "old-fashioned and even reactionary in matters of faith and morals" and had pledged "total abstinence" from alcohol.

In fact, however, Harding drank outlawed liquor in the White House, smoked and chewed tobacco, hosted twice-weekly poker games, had numerous affairs, and even fathered children with women other than his domineering wife, Florence Harding, whom he called "the Duchess." The president's dalliances brought him much grief, however. One of his mistresses blackmailed him, demanding money for her silence—which she received. Another, after his death in 1923, wrote a tell-all account of their affair titled *The President's Daughter*.

The public, however, saw Harding as a handsome, charming politician who looked the part of a leader. Yet privately, he worried about his limitations. "I am not fit for this office and should never have been here," he once admitted. "I cannot hope to be one of the great presidents, but perhaps I may be remembered as one of the best loved."

Harding in office had much in common with Ulysses S. Grant. His cabinet, like Grant's, mixed some of the "best minds" in the party with a few of the worst. Charles Evans Hughes, like Grant's Hamilton Fish, became a distinguished secretary of state. Herbert Hoover in the Commerce Department, Andrew W. Mellon in the Treasury, and Henry C. Wallace in the Agriculture Department made policy on their own. Other cabinet members and administrative appointees, however, were not so conscientious. The secretary of the interior landed in prison, and the attorney general narrowly escaped serving time. Many lesser offices went to members of the "Ohio gang," a group of Harding's drinking buddies.

Harding was no reformer. He set out to reverse the progressive activism of Woodrow Wilson and Theodore Roosevelt and reassert the primacy of Congress over the presidency. He and his lieutenants dismantled or neutralized many progressive regulatory laws and agencies. His four Supreme Court appointments were all conservatives, including Chief Justice William Howard Taft, who announced that he had been "appointed to reverse a few decisions." During the 1920s, the Taft-led court struck down a federal child-labor law and a minimum-wage law for women, issued numerous injunctions against striking unions, and passed rulings limiting the powers of federal agencies that regulated big businesses.

ANDREW MELLON AND THE ECONOMY The Harding administration inherited a slumping economy burdened by high wartime taxes and a national debt that had ballooned from $1 billion in 1914 to $27 billion in 1920 because of the expenses associated with the war. Unemployment was at nearly 12 percent.

The Ohio gang President Warren G. Harding (third from right) surrounded himself with a network of friends, often appointing them to public office despite their inferior qualifications.

To generate economic growth, Secretary of the Treasury Andrew Mellon, at the time the third-richest man in the world behind John D. Rockefeller and Henry Ford, developed the Mellon plan, which called for reducing federal spending and lowering tax rates. To implement the plan, Mellon persuaded Congress to pass the landmark Budget and Accounting Act of 1921, which created a Bureau of the Budget to streamline the process of preparing an annual federal budget to be approved by Congress. The bill also created a General Accounting Office to audit spending by federal agencies. The act fulfilled a long-held progressive desire to bring greater efficiency and nonpartisanship to the budget preparation process.

The brilliant but cold Mellon (his son described him as a "thin-voiced, thin-bodied, shy and uncommunicative man") also proposed sweeping tax reductions. By 1918, the wartime tax rate on the highest income bracket had risen to 73 percent. Mellon believed the high rates were pushing wealthy Americans to avoid paying taxes by investing their money in foreign countries or tax-free government bonds. His policies systematically reduced tax rates while increasing tax revenues. He convinced Congress to cut the top rate from 73 percent in 1921 to 24 percent in 1929, and rates for individuals with the lowest incomes were also cut substantially, helping the working poor. By 1929, barely 2 percent of American workers had to pay any income tax.

At the same time, Mellon helped Harding reduce the federal budget. Government expenditures fell, as did the national debt, and the economy soared. Unemployment plummeted to 2.4 percent in 1923. Mellon's supporters labeled him the greatest Treasury secretary since Alexander Hamilton in the late eighteenth century.

In addition to tax cuts, Mellon promoted the long-standing Republican policy of high tariffs on imported goods. The Fordney-McCumber Tariff of 1922 increased rates on imported chemical and metal products to help prevent the revival of German corporations that had dominated those industries before the Great War. To please commercial farmers, the new act included tariffs on agricultural imports.

REDUCED REGULATION The Republican economic program also sought to dismantle or neutralize many progressive regulatory laws and agencies. President Harding appointed commissioners to federal agencies who would promote "regulatory capitalism" and policies "friendly" to business interests. Republican senator Henry Cabot Lodge, who influenced Harding's choices to lead the regulatory agencies, boasted that "we have torn up Wilsonism by the roots."

RACIAL PROGRESSIVISM In one area, however, conservative Warren G. Harding abandoned his conventional views and proved to be more progressive than Woodrow Wilson. He reversed Wilson's segregationist policy of excluding African Americans from federal government jobs. He also spoke out against the vigilante racism that had flared up across the country during and after the war.

In his first speech to a joint session of Congress in 1921, Harding insisted that the nation must deal with the festering "race question." He attacked the Ku Klux Klan for fomenting "hatred and prejudice and violence" and urged Congress "to wipe the stain of barbaric lynching from the banners of a free and orderly, representative democracy." Harding supported an anti-lynching bill that passed the House, but it was killed by southern Democrats in the Senate.

In October 1921, Harding became the first president to deliver a speech focused on race in the former Confederacy. In Birmingham, Alabama, to celebrate the city's fiftieth anniversary, the president shocked whites among the

100,000 in attendance by demanding complete economic and political rights for African Americans: "I say let the black man vote when he is fit to vote; prohibit the white man voting when he is unfit to vote." As whites in the segregated audience responded with icy silence, Harding abandoned his prepared text and lectured them: "Whether you like it or not, our democracy is a lie unless you stand for that equality." He then stressed that he did not endorse "social equality" for blacks and whites, by which he meant intermarriage and the desegregation of schools, restaurants, hotels, and other public places: "Racial amalgamation can never come in America."

After reading the text of the president's speech, Marcus Garvey, president of the Universal Negro Improvement Association, sent a telegram to Harding in which he applauded his speech "on behalf of four hundred million negroes of the world." Garvey added that "all true negroes are against social equality, believing that all races should develop on their own social lines. Only a few selfish members of the negro race believe in the social amalgamation of black and white." Harding's unprecedented speech also delighted W. E. B. Du Bois, head of the NAACP. Writing in *The Crisis*, he stressed that Harding's address, "like sudden thunder in blue skies, ends the hiding and drives us all into the clear light of truth."

Few southerners agreed, however. Pat Harrison, a Democratic senator from Mississippi, warned that if Harding's speech "were carried to its ultimate conclusion, that means that the black man can strive to become president of the United States!" Likewise, Senator J. Thomas Heflin of Alabama reminded the president that white southerners "hold to the doctrine that God Almighty has fixed the limits and boundaries between the two races, and no Republican living can improve upon His work."

SETBACKS FOR UNIONS Urban workers shared in the affluence of the 1920s. "A workman is far better paid in America than anywhere else in the world," a French visitor wrote in 1927, "and his standard of living is enormously higher." Nonfarm workers gained about 30 percent in real wages between 1921 and 1928, but farm income rose only 10 percent, and organized labor suffered. Although President Harding endorsed collective bargaining and tried to reduce the twelve-hour workday and six-day workweek to give the working class "time for leisure and family life," he ran into stiff opposition in Congress. The widespread strikes of 1919 had created fears that unions promoted radical socialism.

Between January 1920 and August 1921, the national unemployment rate jumped from 2 percent to 14 percent, and industrial production fell by 23 percent. The brief postwar depression so weakened unions that in 1921 business groups in Chicago designated the **open shop** to be the "American plan" of employment. Unlike the closed shop, which forced businesses to hire only union members, the open shop gave an employer the right to hire anyone.

Employers often required workers to sign "yellow-dog" contracts, which forced them to agree not to join a union, leaving them feeling as mistreated as a yellow dog. Owners also used spies, blacklists, and intimidation to block unions. Some employers tried to kill the unions with kindness by introducing programs of "industrial democracy" guided by company-sponsored unions, or various schemes of "welfare capitalism," such as profit sharing, bonuses, pensions, health programs, and recreational activities.

Such anti-union efforts paid off for employers. Union membership dropped from about 5 million in 1920 to 3.5 million in 1929 as industrial production soared and joblessness fell to 3 percent. But the anti-union effort, led by businesses that wanted to keep wages low and unions weak, unwittingly helped create a "purchasing-power crisis" whereby the working poor were not earning enough to buy the goods being churned out by increasingly productive industries. In fact, large groups of hourly workers, such as miners and textile mill hands, saw their income *drop*. Executives used company profits to pay dividends to stockholders, invest in new equipment, and increase their own salaries, while doing little to help wage earners. In 1929, corporate executives, an estimated 5 percent of the nation's workforce, received one third of the nation's income.

In other words, the much-trumpeted "new economy" was not benefiting enough working-class Americans to be sustainable. Wage levels did not give the masses enough purchasing power to sustain economic growth. This would be a major cause of the Great Depression, as the Republican formula of high tariffs, low and stagnant wages, low taxes, little regulation, and anti-unionism would eventually implode.

ISOLATIONISM IN FOREIGN AFFAIRS

In addition to the Senate's rejection of American membership in the League of Nations, the postwar spirit of isolation found other expressions. George Jean Nathan, a drama critic, expressed the sentiments of many when he announced that the "great problems of the world—social, political, economic and theological—do not concern me in the slightest. . . . What concerns me alone is myself, and the interests of a few close friends."

Yet the desire to stay out of foreign wars did not mean that the United States could ignore its expanding global interests. The Great War had made the United States the world's chief banker, and American investments and loans enabled foreigners to purchase U.S. exports.

WAR DEBTS AND REPARATIONS Nothing did more to heighten America's isolationism—and anti-American feelings among Europeans—than the complex issue of paying off war debts. In 1917, when France and Great Britain ran out of money to pay for military supplies, the U.S. government had advanced them massive loans, first for the war effort and then for postwar reconstruction projects.

Most Americans expected the debts to be repaid, but Europeans thought differently. The European Allies had held off the German invasion at great cost while the United States was raising an army in 1917. The British also noted that after the American Revolution, the newly independent United States had repudiated old debts to British investors. The French likewise pointed out that they had never been repaid for helping the Americans win the Revolution.

Throughout the 1920s, the British and French were in a complex financial bind. To get U.S. dollars with which to pay their war-related debts, European nations had to sell their goods to the United States. However, soaring American tariff rates made imported European goods more expensive for wage-stagnant U.S. consumers, so the war-related debts became harder to pay. The French and British insisted that they could repay their debts only if they could collect the $33 billion in reparations owed them by Germany. The German economy, however, was in shambles.

Twice during the 1920s, the financial strain on Germany brought the structure of international payments to the verge of collapse. Both times the international Reparations Commission called in private American bankers to work out rescue plans. Loans provided by U.S. banks thus propped up the German economy so that Germany could pay its reparations to Britain and France, thereby enabling them to pay their debts to the United States.

ATTEMPTS AT DISARMAMENT After the Great War, many Americans decided that the best way to keep the peace was to limit the size of armies and navies. The United States had no intention of maintaining a large army after 1920, but under the shipbuilding program begun in 1916, it had constructed a powerful navy second only to that of Great Britain. Although neither the British nor the Americans wanted a naval armaments race, both were worried about the growth of Japanese power in Asia and the Pacific.

To address the problem, President Harding in 1921 invited diplomats from eight nations to the Washington Naval Conference in Washington, D.C., at which Secretary of State Charles Evans Hughes made a blockbuster proposal. The only way out of an expensive naval arms race, he declared, "is to end it now" by eliminating scores of existing warships. He pledged that America would junk thirty battleships and cruisers and then named thirty-six British and Japanese warships that would also be destroyed. The stunned audience stood and roared its approval. In less than fifteen minutes, one journalist reported, Hughes had destroyed more warships "than all the admirals of the world have sunk in a cycle of centuries." The delegates at the Washington Naval Conference (1921–1922), spent months ironing out the final details of the agreement, which finally took effect in 1922.

Representatives from the United States, Britain, Japan, France, and Italy signed the Five-Power Treaty (1922), which limited the size of their navies. It was the first disarmament treaty in history. The agreement also, in effect, divided the world into spheres of influence: U.S. naval power became supreme in the Western Hemisphere, Japanese power in the western Pacific, and British power from the North Sea to Singapore.

THE KELLOGG-BRIAND PACT During and after the Great War, many Americans embraced the fanciful idea of abolishing war with a stroke of a pen. In 1921, a wealthy Chicagoan founded the American Committee for the Outlawry of War. "We can outlaw this war system just as we outlawed slavery and the saloon," said an enthusiastic convert.

The seductive notion of simply abolishing war culminated in the signing of the Kellogg-Briand Pact. In 1927, French foreign minister Aristide Briand proposed to U.S. Secretary of State Frank B. Kellogg that the two countries agree never to go to war against each other.

Kellogg countered with a plan to have *all* nations sign the pact. The General Treaty for Renunciation of War as an Instrument of National Policy, or the Kellogg-Briand Pact, signed on August 27, 1928, declared that the signatories renounced war "as an instrument of national policy." Eventually, sixty-two nations, including all the great powers, signed the pact, but all reserved the right of "self-defense." The U.S. Senate ratified the agreement by a vote of 85 to 1.

A senator who voted for "this worthless, but perfectly harmless peace treaty" wrote a friend later that he feared it would "confuse the minds of many good people who think that peace may be secured by polite professions of neighborly and brotherly love." In a more pointed assessment, British writer George Orwell said that outlawing war was one of those "ideas so absurd only an intellectual could believe them."

The treaty went into effect July 24, 1929, after which Japan invaded Manchuria (1931); Italy invaded Ethiopia (1935); Japan invaded China (1937); Germany invaded Poland (1939); the Soviet Union invaded Finland (1939); Germany invaded Denmark, Norway, Belgium, the Netherlands, Luxembourg, and France, and attacked Great Britain (1940); and Japan attacked the United

States (1941), culminating in a global war that resulted in more than 60 million deaths. All these nations had signed the Kellogg-Briand Pact. So much for outlawing war.

THE WORLD COURT The isolationist mood in the United States was no better illustrated than in the repeated refusal by the Senate to approve American membership in the World Court, formally called the Permanent Court of International Justice, at The Hague in the Netherlands. Created in 1921 by the League of Nations, the World Court was intended to arbitrate disputes between nations. During the 1920s, Presidents Harding, Coolidge, and Hoover had each asked the Senate to approve American membership in the World Court, but the legislative body refused, for the same reasons that it had refused to sign the Versailles treaty: it did not want the United States to be bound in any way by an international organization.

IMPROVING RELATIONS IN LATIN AMERICA The isolationist attitude during the 1920s led Republican presidents Harding, Calvin Coolidge, and Herbert Hoover to soothe tensions with America's neighbors to the south. The Harding administration agreed in 1921 to pay $25 million that the republic of Colombia had demanded for America having seized the Panama Canal Zone. In 1924, American troops left the Dominican Republic after eight years of intervention. U.S. Marines left Nicaragua in 1925 but returned a year later at the outbreak of disorder and civil war. There, in 1927, the Coolidge administration brought both parties into an agreement for U.S.-supervised elections, but one rebel leader, César Augusto Sandino, held out, and the marines stayed until 1933.

The troubles in Nicaragua increased strains between the United States and Mexico. Relations had already soured after repeated Mexican threats to expropriate American oil properties in Mexico. In 1928, however, the U.S. ambassador negotiated an agreement protecting American rights acquired before 1917. Expropriation did in fact occur in 1938, but the Mexican government agreed to reimburse American owners.

THE HARDING SCANDALS

As time passed, President Harding found himself increasingly distracted by scandals within his administration. Early in 1923, the head of the Veterans Bureau resigned when faced with an investigation for stealing medical and hospital supplies intended for former servicemen. A few weeks later, the legal adviser to the bureau killed himself.

Soon thereafter, it was revealed that Jesse Smith, a colleague of Attorney General Harry M. Daugherty, was illegally selling federal paroles, pardons, and judgeships from his Justice Department office. When Harding learned of his escapades, he called Smith to the Oval Office and dressed him down. The next day, Smith killed himself in Daugherty's apartment. Then, Daugherty was accused of selling, for his personal gain, German assets seized after the war. When asked to testify about the matter, he refused on the grounds that doing so might incriminate him.

The most serious scandal was the **Teapot Dome Affair**. The Teapot Dome was a government-owned oil field in Wyoming managed by the Department of the Interior. Secretary of the Interior Albert B. Fall, deeply in debt and eight years overdue in paying his taxes, began selling the oil to close friends who were executives of petroleum companies. In doing so, Fall took bribes of

Teapot Dome scandal In this 1924 political cartoon, Republican officials try to outrun the Teapot Dome scandal, represented by a giant steamrolling teapot, on an oil-slicked highway.

about $400,000 from an oil tycoon. Convicted of conspiracy and bribery and sentenced to a year in prison, Fall was the first former cabinet official to serve time because of misconduct in office.

How much Harding knew of the scandals is unclear, but he knew enough to be troubled. "My God, this is a hell of a job!" he confided to a journalist, "I have no trouble with my enemies; I can take care of my enemies all right. But my damn friends, my God-damn friends. . . . They're the ones that keep me walking the floor nights!"

In 1923, Harding left on what would be his last journey, a trip to the West Coast and the Alaska Territory. Along the way, he asked Herbert Hoover, the secretary of commerce, what he should do about the Fall scandal. Hoover gave the correct response: "Publish it, and at least get credit for integrity on your side." Before Harding had time to act, he suffered an attack of food poisoning in Seattle. After showing signs of recovering, he died in San Francisco. He was fifty-seven years old.

Largely as a result of Harding's corrupt associates, his administration came to be viewed as one of the worst in history. Even Hoover admitted that Harding was not "a man with either the experience or the intellectual quality that the position needed."

More recent assessments, however, suggest that the scandals obscured Harding's accomplishments. He led the nation out of the turmoil of the postwar years and helped create the economic boom of the 1920s. He endorsed diversity and civil rights and was a forceful proponent of women's rights. Yet even Harding's foremost scholarly defender admits that he lacked good judgment and "probably should never have been president."

COOLIDGE CONSERVATISM

The news of President Harding's death reached Vice President Calvin Coolidge when he and his wife were visiting his father in Plymouth Notch, Vermont. "Guess we'd better have a drink," said Coolidge upon being awakened to learn the news. At 2:47 A.M. on August 3, 1923, Colonel John Coolidge, a farmer, merchant, and notary public, issued the presidential oath of office to his son by the light of a kerosene lamp.

Calvin Coolidge, born on the fourth of July in 1872, was a throwback to an earlier era. A puritan in his personal life, he was horrified by the jazzed-up Roaring Twenties. He believed in the ideals of personal integrity and devotion to public service, and, like Harding, he was an evangelist both for capitalism and minimal government regulation of business.

A DO-NOTHING PRESIDENT—BY DESIGN Although Coolidge had won every political race he had entered, he had never loved the limelight. Shy and awkward, he was a man of famously few words—hence his nickname, "Silent Cal." After being reelected president of the Massachusetts State Senate in 1916, he gave a four-sentence inaugural address that concluded with, "above all things, be brief." He later explained that he had "never been hurt by what he had not said."

Coolidge demanded that his wife, Grace, a gregarious college graduate of "vastly different temperament and taste," speak less and do less than he did. He prohibited her from giving interviews, driving a car, flying in an airplane, cutting her hair, smoking in public, or giving opinions on national affairs.

Grace Coolidge accepted her subordinate role. She once proudly revealed that she never entered the President's office and "knew nothing of what took place there."

Coolidge's conventional views about gender roles did not faze most voters. Most people liked his uprightness and personal humility. He was a simple, direct man who championed self-discipline and hard work. Alice Roosevelt Longworth, the outspoken daughter of Theodore Roosevelt, said the atmosphere in the Coolidge White House compared to that of Harding was "as different as a New England front parlor is from the back room in a speakeasy." Coolidge, she quipped, looked like he had been "weaned on a pickle."

Calvin Coolidge "Silent Cal" was so inactive as president that when he died in 1933, American humorist Dorothy Parker remarked, "How could they tell?"

As a state senator in Massachusetts, Coolidge had often aligned himself with Republican progressives. He voted for women's suffrage, a state income tax, a minimum wage for female workers, and salary increases for public school teachers. By the time he entered the White House, however, he had abandoned most of those causes.

Coolidge was determined *not* to be an activist president. He noted that his greatest accomplishment was "minding my own business," and he believed that "four-fifths of our troubles would disappear if we would sit down and keep still." Following his own logic, he insisted on twelve hours of sleep *and* a lengthy afternoon nap. Journalist H. L. Mencken claimed that Coolidge "slept more than any other president."

EVANGELIST FOR CAPITALISM Even more than Harding, Coolidge linked the nation's welfare with the success of Big Business. "The chief business of the American people is business," he preached. "The man who builds a factory builds a temple. The man who works there worships there." Coolidge famously claimed that "wealth is the *chief* end of man."

With the help of Treasury secretary Andrew Mellon and Republican-controlled Congresses, Coolidge continued Harding's efforts to lower tax rates. Where Harding had sought to balance the interests of labor, agriculture, and industry, Coolidge focused on promoting industrial development by limiting federal regulation of business and industry. The nation had too many laws, Coolidge insisted, and "we would be better off if we did not have any more." True to his word, he vetoed fifty acts of Congress. After having dinner with the president at the White House, Colonel House, the prominent Democrat, decided that Coolidge "has more ability than I had given him credit for, but he has little imagination and no initiative. He will make a safe President," but would not do "anything brilliant or spectacular."

Coolidge was also "obsessed" with reducing federal spending, even to the point of issuing government workers one pencil at a time—and only after they turned in the stub of the old pencil. His penny-pinching, pro-business stance led the *Wall Street Journal* to rejoice: "Never before, here or anywhere else, has a government been so completely fused with business."

THE ELECTION OF 1924 Calvin Coolidge restored the dignity of the presidency while holding warring Republican factions together. He easily gained the party's 1924 presidential nomination. Soon thereafter, he invited reporters to the White House. One reporter asked, "Have you any statement on the campaign?" Coolidge said, "No." Another reporter tried: "Can you tell us about the world situation?" Again the president said, "No." After someone asked about Prohibition, the reply was the same: "No." As the frustrated reporters left, Coolidge yelled, "Now remember—don't quote me."

Meanwhile, the Democratic party's nominating convention in New York City illustrated the deep divisions between urban and rural America. One of the leading contenders, lawyer William McAdoo, Woodrow Wilson's son-in-law, was endorsed by the Ku Klux Klan. The other front-runner, New York governor Al Smith, was an Irish Catholic who led the party's anti-Klan, anti-Prohibition wing.

Neither McAdoo nor Smith could gain the nomination. The fragmented Democrats took a record 103 ballots over sixteen broiling summer days before deciding on a compromise candidate: John W. Davis, a little-known lawyer from West Virginia who could nearly outdo Coolidge in his conservatism.

While the Democrats bickered, rural Populists and urban progressives decided to abandon both major parties, as they had done in 1912. Reorganizing the old Progressive party, they nominated Wisconsin's Robert M. "Fighting Bob" La Follette. As a Republican senator, La Follette had voted against the 1917 declaration of war against Germany. Now, in addition to the progressives, he won the support of the Socialist party and the American Federation of Labor.

In the 1924 election, Coolidge swept both the popular and electoral votes. Davis and the Democrats took only the southern states, and La Follette carried only Wisconsin, his home state. The popular vote went 15.7 million for Coolidge, 8.4 million for Davis, and 4.8 million for La Follette—the largest popular vote ever polled by a third-party candidate up to that time. Coolidge viewed his landslide as a mandate to continue his efforts to shrink the federal government. If it disappeared, he predicted, most voters "would not detect the difference."

Coolidge's victory represented the height of postwar political conservatism. Business executives interpreted the election results as an endorsement of their influence on government policy, and Coolidge saw the economy's surging prosperity as confirmation of his support of Big Business. The United States, he proclaimed in his 1925 inaugural address, had reached "a state of contentment seldom before seen." His duty was to do nothing that might undermine such contentment.

THE RISE OF HERBERT HOOVER

During the twenties, the drive for industrial efficiency, which had been a prominent theme among progressives, powered the wheels of mass production and consumption and became a cardinal belief of Republican leaders. Herbert Hoover, secretary of commerce in the Harding and Coolidge cabinets, embodied the dream of organizational efficiency, for he himself was a remarkable success story.

Born into a devout Quaker family in Iowa in 1874, he was orphaned at age nine, and raised by stern uncles in Iowa and Oregon. He was a shy "loner" who studied geology and mechanical engineering at Stanford University, where he determined that he was smarter, more energetic, and more disciplined than others. After graduating, he became a world-renowned mining engineer, harvesting gold in Australia, coal in China, and zinc in Burma. He went on to prosper as an oil tycoon and financial wizard, and was a multimillionaire before the age of forty.

Hoover's meteoric success and ruthless genius for managing difficult operations bred in him a self-confidence verging on conceit. In his twenties, he began planning to be president of the United States.

A PROGRESSIVE CONSERVATIVE With the outbreak of war in 1914, Herbert Hoover exchanged his career in private business for one in public service. He organized the evacuation of tens of thousands of Americans stranded in Europe by the German invasion of France, then led a massive program to provide food to 7.5 million starving civilians in German-occupied Belgium.

The "Great Humanitarian" also applied his managerial skills to the Food Administration and served with the U.S. delegation at the Versailles peace conference. Hoover idolized Woodrow Wilson and supported American membership in the League of Nations. Franklin Roosevelt, then assistant secretary of the navy, stood in awe of Hoover. In 1920, Roosevelt said that Hoover was "certainly a wonder [boy], and I wish we could make him President of the United States. There would not be a better one."

Hoover, however, soon disappointed Roosevelt by declaring himself a Republican "progressive conservative." In a book titled *American Individualism* (1922), Hoover said he wanted to promote a "rugged individualism" directed at promoting the greater good, not selfishness. He wanted government officials to encourage business leaders to forgo "cutthroat competition" and engage in "voluntary cooperation" by forming trade associations that would share information and promote standardization—all in an effort to increase efficiency and productivity.

As secretary of commerce during the 1920s, Hoover transformed the small department into the government's most dynamic agency. He looked for new markets for business, created a Bureau of Aviation to promote the new airline industry, and established the Federal Radio Commission. When the Mississippi River flooded in 1927, devastating much of the Midwest and Gulf states, Hoover organized the massive recovery effort, despite President Coolidge's indifference.

THE BUSINESS OF FARMING During the 1920s, agriculture remained the weakest sector of the economy. The wartime boom fed by agricultural exports lasted into 1920 before commodity prices collapsed as European agricultural production returned to prewar levels. Lower prices for crops

Farming technology Mechanization became increasingly important in early twentieth-century agriculture. Here, farmers pose alongside their new equipment.

persisted into 1923, and after that, improvement was spotty. A bumper cotton crop in 1926 resulted only in a price collapse and an early taste of depression in much of the South, where foreclosures and bankruptcies spread.

The most successful farms, like the most successful corporations, were getting larger, more efficient, and more mechanized. By 1930, about 13 percent of all farmers had tractors; the proportion was even higher on the western plains. Better plows, harvesters, combines, and other machines improved crop yields, fertilizers, and methods of animal breeding.

Most farmers, however, were struggling to survive. They asked for help, and in 1924, Senator Charles L. McNary of Oregon and Representative Gilbert N. Haugen of Iowa introduced the first McNary-Haugen bill, which sought to secure "equality for agriculture in the benefits of the protective tariff."

The proposed bill called for surplus American crops to be sold on the world market. The goal was to raise prices at home so that farmers would have the same purchasing power relative to the prices they had enjoyed between 1909 and 1914, a time viewed as a golden age of American agriculture.

The McNary-Haugen bill passed Congress in 1927 but was vetoed by President Coolidge, who dismissed it as unsound and unconstitutional. The process was repeated in 1928. In a broader sense, however, McNary-Haugenism did not fail. The debates over the bill made the "farm problem" a national issue and defined it as a matter of managing surpluses. Moreover, the evolution of the McNary-Haugen plan revived the idea of a political alliance between the rural

South and the West, a coalition that in the next decade would have a dominant influence on national farm policy.

THE 1928 ELECTION: HOOVER VERSUS SMITH On August 2, 1927, while on vacation in the Black Hills of South Dakota, President Coolidge announced, "I do not choose to run for President in 1928." His unexpected decision reflected his continuing grief at the death of his sixteen-year-old son in 1924 from an infected foot. He also was wary of becoming the longest-serving president in history, fearing that critics would claim he was pursuing a dictatorship.

Coolidge's decision cleared the way for Herbert Hoover to win the Republican nomination. The party's platform took credit for the nation's longest period of sustained prosperity, the government's cost cutting, debt and tax reduction, and the high tariffs ("as vital to American agriculture as . . . to manufacturing") designed to "protect" American businesses from foreign competition.

The Democrats nominated four-term New York governor Alfred E. Smith, called the "Happy Warrior" by Franklin D. Roosevelt in his nominating speech. The candidates presented sharply different images: Hoover, the successful businessman and bureaucratic manager from an Iowa farm, and Smith,

Campaign sheet music The sheet music for the Democratic nominee, Alfred E. Smith (left), and the Republican nominee, Herbert Hoover (right), drew on popular tunes and motifs of the time.

a professional Irish American politician from New York City's Lower East Side. To working-class Democrats in northern cities, Smith was a hero, the poor grandson of Irish Catholic immigrants who had become governor of the most populous state. His outspoken criticism of Prohibition also endeared him to the Irish, Italians, Germans, and others.

On the other hand, as the first Roman Catholic nominated for president by a major party, a product of New York's machine-run politics, and a "wet" on Prohibition (in direct opposition to his party's platform), Smith represented all that was opposed by southern and western rural Democrats—as well as most rural and small-town Republicans. A Kansas newspaper editor declared that the "whole puritan civilization, which has built a sturdy, orderly nation, is threatened by Smith." The Ku Klux Klan issued a "Klarion Kall for a Krusade" against him, mailing thousands of postcards proclaiming that "Alcohol" Smith, the Catholic New Yorker, was the Antichrist. While Hoover stayed above the fray, Smith was forced to deal with constant criticism.

No Democrat could have beaten Hoover in 1928, however. The nation was prosperous and at peace, and Hoover seemed the best person to sustain the good times. He was perhaps the best-trained economic mind ever to run for president, and he was widely viewed as a brilliant engineer and humanitarian, a genius "who never failed."

Herbert Hoover "I have no fears for the future of our country," Hoover told the nation at his inauguration in 1929.

On Election Day, Hoover, the first Quaker to be president, won in a landslide, with 21 million popular votes to Smith's 15 million and an electoral college majority of 444 to 87. Hoover even penetrated the Democrats' Solid South, winning Virginia, North Carolina, Tennessee, Florida, and Texas. Republicans also kept control of both houses of Congress.

Hidden in the results, however, was a glimmer of hope for Democrats. Overall, Smith's vote total, especially strong in the largest cities, doubled that of John Davis four years earlier. In 1932, Franklin D. Roosevelt would build upon that momentum to win back the presidency for the Democrats.

Calvin Coolidge was skeptical that Hoover could sustain the good times. He quipped that the "Wonder Boy" had offered him "unsolicited advice for six years, all of it bad." Coolidge's doubts about Hoover's political abilities would prove accurate, as the new president would soon confront an economic earthquake that would test all of his skills—and expose his weaknesses.

1929—A Turning Point

Rarely had a new president entered office with greater expectations. In fact, Herbert Hoover was worried that people mistakenly viewed him as "a superman; that no problem is beyond my capacity."

He was right to be concerned. People saw in him a dedicated public servant whose proven organization skills and business savvy would ensure continued prosperity. In 1929, Americans were fully employed and earning record levels of income. But that was about to change.

The Onset of the Great Depression

Herbert Hoover's election boosted the hopes of Wall Street investors in what had come to be called "the Great Bull Market." Since 1924, the prices of stock shares invested in U.S. companies had steadily risen. Beginning in 1927, prices soared further on wings of reckless speculation. In 1919, some 317 million shares of stock changed hands; in 1929, the number was more than a billion. Treasury secretary Andrew W. Mellon's tax reductions had given people more money, and much of it went into the stock market. In April 1929, Hoover voiced concern about the "orgy of mad speculation" and urged investors to be more cautious—while privately telling his broker to sell many of his stock holdings. He saw disaster coming.

THE STOCK MARKET What made it so easy for so many to invest in stocks was the common practice of buying "on margin"—that is, an investor could make a small cash down payment (the "margin") on shares of stock and borrow the rest from a bank or a stockbroker, who held the stock certificates as security in case the share price plummeted. If stock prices rose, as they did in 1927, 1928, and most of 1929, the investor made enough profits to pay for the "margin loan" and reinvest the rest.

Yet if the stock price declined and the buyer failed to pay off the broker's loan, the broker could sell the stock at a much lower price to cover the loan.

By August 1929, stockbrokers were lending investors more than two thirds of the face value of the stocks they were buying. Yet few people seemed concerned about the growing bubble, and stock prices kept rising.

There were signs that the economy was weakening. By 1927, steel production, residential construction, and automobile sales were slowing, as was the rate of consumer spending. By mid-1929, industrial production, employment, and other measures of economic activity were also declining. Still, the stock market rose.

Then, in early September 1929, the stock market fell sharply. By the middle of October, world exchanges had gone into a steep decline. Still, most investors remained upbeat. The nation's foremost economist, Irving Fisher of Yale University, told investors on October 17, "Stock prices have reached what looks like a permanently high plateau."

THE CRASH The next week, however, stock market values wobbled, then tumbled again, triggering a wild scramble among terrified investors. As they rushed to sell their shares, the decline in stock prices accelerated. On what came to be called Black Tuesday, October 29—the worst day in the stock market's history—prices went into free fall, and brokers found themselves flooded with stocks they could not sell. On that day, investors lost $15 billion. By the end of the month, they had lost $50 billion.

Suddenly, the carefree indulgences of the Jazz Age had ended with the nerve-shattering crash on Wall Street. Fear and uncertainty spread like a virus across the nation and the world.

Rumors circulated of fortunes lost and careers ruined. Investors who had borrowed heavily to buy stocks were now forced to sell their holdings at huge losses so they could pay their debts. Some stockbrokers and investors committed suicide. In New York, the president of a bankrupt cigar company jumped off a hotel window ledge, and two business partners joined hands and leaped to their deaths from a room at the Ritz Hotel. Room clerks in Manhattan hotels started asking registering guests if they wanted a room for jumping or sleeping.

The economy began to sputter. In 1930, at least 26,355 businesses shut down; even more failed the following year. The resulting economic slowdown became so severe and long-lasting that it came to be known as the Great Depression.

The collapse of the stock market did not *cause* the **Great Depression**, however. Rather, it revealed that the prosperity of the 1920s had been built on weak foundations. As F. Scott Fitzgerald observed in *Echoes of the Jazz Age* (1931), the twenties were an "age of excess" that could not last.

The stock market crash had the added effect of creating a psychological panic that accelerated the economic decline. Frightened of losing everything,

Bank run As news of the Great Crash spread across the world, people rushed to banks to withdraw their money. The line at this branch of the American Union Bank wraps around the building.

people rushed to remove their money from banks and the stock market. This only made things worse. By 1932, more than 9,000 banks had closed as the nation's economy experienced a shocking collapse.

WHY THE ECONOMY COLLAPSED

What were the underlying *causes* of the Great Depression? Most scholars emphasize a combination of interrelated elements. The once-roaring economy had actually begun to fall into a recession months *before* the stock market crash because of *overproduction* and *underconsumption*. During the twenties, manufacturing production increased 43 percent, but the purchasing power of consumers did not grow nearly as fast. In essence, the economy was turning out more products than consumers could buy, and too many people had been borrowing too much money for unproductive purposes, such as speculating in the stock market.

At the same time, many business owners had taken large profits while denying wage increases to employees. By plowing profits into executive salaries, stock dividends, and business expansion, employers created an imbalance between production and consumption. Because union membership had plummeted, organized labor no longer exerted as much leverage with management over wage increases. Two thirds of families in 1929 earned less than $2,000 annually, an amount said by economists to provide "only basic necessities."

As the stock market was crashing, factories were reducing production or shutting down altogether. From 1929 to 1933, U.S. economic output dropped by almost 27 percent, triggering layoffs and firings. And by 1933, a quarter of the workforce was jobless.

At the same time, the farm sector stagnated. Farm incomes had soared during the Great War because the European nations needed American grains, beef, and pork. Eager to sustain their prosperity, farmers took out mortgages to buy more acreage or equipment to boost output. However, without European demand, increased production during the twenties led to *lower* prices for grains and livestock. To make matters worse, record harvests in the summer and fall of 1929 caused prices for corn, wheat, and cotton to fall precipitously, pinching the income of farmers who had taken on mounting debts.

GOVERNMENT'S ROLE Government policies also contributed to the Depression. Like most Republican presidents, Herbert Hoover supported raising tariffs on imported goods to keep out foreign competition.

The Smoot-Hawley Tariff of 1930, authored by Republicans Reed Owen Smoot and Willis C. Hawley, sought to help the farm sector by raising tariff duties on agricultural products imported into the United States. As so often happens, however, a swarm of corporate lobbyists convinced Congress to add thousands of nonagricultural items to the tariff bill. The average tariff rate jumped from an already high 25 percent to 50 percent, making it the highest in history.

More than 1,000 economists petitioned Hoover to veto the bill because its logic was flawed: By trying to "protect" farmers from foreign competition, it would actually raise prices on most raw materials and consumer products. And by reducing European imports into the United States, the bill would make it much harder for France, Great Britain, and Germany to make enough money to repay their war debts.

On June 17, 1930, however, Hoover, pressured by Republicans, signed the bill, causing another steep drop in the stock market. As predicted, the Smoot-Hawley Tariff prompted other countries to retaliate by passing tariffs of their own, thereby making it more difficult for American farms and businesses to sell their products abroad. U.S. exports plummeted along with international trade in general, worsening the Depression.

Another factor contributing to the Great Depression was the stance of the Federal Reserve Board, the government agency that served, then and now, as a "central bank" by managing the nation's money supply and adjusting interest rates. Instead of expanding the money supply to generate growth, the Federal Reserve tightened it out of concern for possible inflation in consumer prices. Between 1929 and 1932, the money supply shrank by a third, leading almost 10,000 small banks to close—and take millions of their depositors with them into bankruptcy.

EUROPE'S IMPACT The Depression was also fueled by the chaotic state of the European economy, which had never fully recovered from the Great War or from the punitive provisions of the Versailles treaty. During the late 1920s, nations such as Great Britain, France, Spain, and Italy slowed their purchases of American goods as their economies began recovering. Meanwhile, the German economy continued to flounder, drained by the war reparations it was forced to pay France and Great Britain.

A related factor was the inability of the victorious Allied nations to pay their war debts to each other—and to the United States. The American government insisted that the $11 billion it had loaned the Allies be repaid, but Great Britain and France had no money. They were forced to borrow billions of dollars from U.S. banks, which only increased their overall indebtedness. After the stock market crash, American banks could no longer prop up the European economies.

The Federal Reserve's tight monetary policy also slowed the amount of American money going abroad. The German economy, which had grown dependent on loans from American banks, was devastated as American loans dried up. Then the Smoot-Hawley Tariff made it even more difficult for European nations to sell their products in the United States. As the European economy stumbled, it subsequently deepened the American depression.

THE HUMAN TOLL OF THE DEPRESSION

The Great Depression was an international catastrophe that brought the worst of times. No business slump had been so deep, so long, or so painful. By 1932, one of every four Americans was unemployed, most of them wage workers. In many large cities, nearly *half* the adults were out of work. Millions of others saw their working hours and wages reduced. Some 500,000 people lost homes or farms because they could not pay their mortgages.

Amid such turmoil, the carefree optimism and indulgence of the twenties disappeared. Grassroots protests erupted; hungry people looted grocery stores, angry mobs stopped sheriffs from foreclosing on farms, and judges were threatened at bankruptcy hearings.

THE FARMERS' HOLIDAY ASSOCIATION

In Iowa in 1932, a growing number of farmers were unable to make their mortgage payments. Before long, sheriffs were showing up at farms with fore-closure papers. Frustrated farmers formed the Farmers' Holiday Association to make their case for government assistance. If their demands were not met, they threatened to go on strike ("holiday"), withholding their crops, milk, and livestock from the nation's markets. Before the Association could mobilize, however, scattered groups of farmers took direct action, blockading roads and preventing the movement of milk and grains.

Some launched a "Cornbelt Rebellion," invading courthouses and intimi-dating judges. On April 27, 1933, angry farmers broke through a line of dep-uties outside the O'Brien County Court House, entered the courtroom, and demanded that the judge stop signing farm eviction orders. When he refused, they dragged him outside along with the county sheriff and deputies, and forced them to kneel and kiss the U.S. flag. A few days later, a mob almost lynched still another judge.

Iowa's governor responded by mobilizing the National Guard and declar-ing martial law in several rural counties. The lawlessness subsided, and the farm protest movement gave way to hopes for agricultural improvement under a new presidential administration.

RISING UNEMPLOYMENT AND DEMANDS FOR ASSISTANCE

As the economy spiraled downward, growing numbers of city workers were fired or had their wages cut. Unemployment soared to 4 million in 1930, to 8 million in 1931, and to 12 million by 1932.

As record numbers found themselves out of work and money, many people grew desperate. "Hold-ups and killings are becoming more frequent," a man wrote in his diary, "and it becomes dangerous to walk the streets." Unemployed city dwellers became street-corner merchants. Some 6,000 jobless New York-ers sold apples on street corners to survive. Their motto was, "Buy an apple a day and eat the Depression away."

Many struggling business executives and professionals—lawyers, doctors, dentists, accountants, stockbrokers, teachers, nurses, and engineers—went with-out food and medical care to save money and avoid the humiliation of "going on relief"—seeking assistance from churches, charitable organizations, and soup kitchens. The sense of shame cut across class lines. In *The Grapes of Wrath* (1939), John Steinbeck's novel about the victims of the Depression, a poor but proud woman is disgraced by accepting "charity" from the Salvation Army: "We was hungry. They made us crawl for our dinner. They took our dignity."

HUNGER Surveys of children in the nation's public schools in 1932 showed that one-quarter suffered from malnutrition. The U.S. Public Health Service revealed that the families of unemployed workers had 66 percent more illnesses than those of employed workers. In 1931, New York City hospitals reported about 100 cases of death by starvation.

Millions lined up at neighborhood soup kitchens or breadlines, where churches and charities distributed free food and water. In Detroit, "we saw the city at its worst," wrote Louise V. Armstrong. "We saw a crowd of some fifty men fighting over a barrel of garbage which had been set outside the back door of a restaurant. American citizens fighting over scraps of food like animals!"

HOMELESSNESS The contraction of the economy squeezed homeowners who had monthly mortgages to pay. A thousand Americans per day lost their homes to foreclosure, and millions were forced to move in with relatives or friends. At first, those made homeless by the Depression were placed in almshouses, also called *poorhouses* or *workhouses*.

By 1933, however, the swelling numbers of homeless people overwhelmed the public facilities. People were forced to live in culverts, under bridges, on park benches, and in doorways and police stations. To make matters worse, the poor were subject to frequent abuse and arrest. Fourteen states banned paupers from voting.

Millions of homeless people, mostly men, took to living on the road or the rails. These hobos walked, hitch-hiked, or sneaked onto empty railway cars and rode from town to town. One railroad, the Missouri Pacific, counted 200,000 vagrants living in its empty boxcars in 1931. The following year, the Southern Pacific Railroad reported that it had evicted 683,457 people from its freight trains. A black military veteran recalled life as a hobo: "Black and white, it didn't make any difference who you were, 'cause everybody was poor. . . . They didn't have no mothers

The morning news in a Chicago shantytown In response to the economic devastation of the Great Depression, numerous shantytowns emerged in cities across the country to house the homeless.

or sisters, they didn't have no home; they were dirty, they had overalls on, they didn't have no food, they didn't have anything."

In New York City, hundreds of homeless people lived on subway trains. One of them, Karl Monroe, an unemployed reporter, discovered that he could pay a nickel and ride the subway all night, sleeping in his seat. "A good corner seat" on a subway train, he explained, "gives the rider a chance to get a fair nap, and the thing can be repeated endlessly." In 1932, the *New York Times* reported the arrest of fifty-four men for "idling" in a subway. Most of them celebrated, for in going to jail they would get free meals and a bed.

DESPERATE RESPONSES As always, those hardest hit were the most disadvantaged groups—immigrants, the elderly, women, children, farmers, the urban unemployed, migrant workers. Desperate conditions led desperate people to do desperate things. Crime soared, as did street-corner begging, homelessness, and prostitution.

Although the divorce rate dropped, in part because couples could not afford to live separately or pay legal fees, many jobless husbands simply deserted their wives and children. "You don't know what it's like when your husband's out of work," a woman told a reporter. "He's gloomy and unhappy all the time. Life is terrible. You must try all the time to keep him from going crazy."

With their future so uncertain, married couples often decided not to have children, and birth rates plummeted. Many struggling parents sent their children to live with relatives or friends. Some 900,000 children simply left home and joined the growing army of homeless migrants. During the Great Depression, for the first time ever, more people left the United States than arrived as immigrants.

PLIGHT OF WORKING WOMEN The Depression put women in a peculiar position. By 1932, an estimated 20 percent of working women were unemployed, a slightly lower percentage than men. Because women held a disproportionate number of the lowest-paying jobs, they were often able to keep them. Even so, many women also had the added burden of keeping their families together emotionally. Magazines published numerous articles about the challenge of maintaining households when the husband had been "unmanned" by losing his job.

As the Depression deepened, however, married women became the primary targets of layoffs. The reasoning being that a married woman—who presumably had a husband to take care of her—should not "steal" a job from a man who may be a husband and father. In a desperate attempt to create jobs for unemployed men, many employers and even whole states

Just dropping off a résumé In October 1938, when the federal government opened six custodian positions, 15,000 African American women lined up overnight to turn in their applications. Pictured here is a policeman leaping over a hedge to keep the crowd under control.

adopted policies barring married women from employment. For example, three fourths of the public school systems across the nation during the Great Depression fired women teachers who got married. As a legislator commented, the working woman in Depression-era America was "the first orphan in the storm."

It was acceptable for single white women to find jobs that were considered to be in the realm of "women's work": as salesgirls, beauticians, schoolteachers, secretaries, and nurses. The job market for African American women was even more restricted, with most of them limited to working as maids, cooks, or laundresses.

MINORITIES Most African Americans during the thirties still lived in the states of the former Confederacy, where the farm-dominated economy was depressed before 1929 and worsened during the Great Depression. Most

African Americans in the South still earned their meager livelihoods as tenants and sharecroppers. Pervasive racial discrimination consigned them to the most menial, lowest-paying jobs.

They also continued to be victims of violence and intimidation. Jim Crow laws still excluded most African Americans from voting, and public places like hotels and trains were segregated. Black people were among the hardest hit by the Depression. As a blues song called "Hard Times Ain't Gone Nowhere" revealed, "Hard times don't worry me; I was broke when it first started out." Some 3 million blacks in the rural South lived in cramped cabins without electricity, running water, or bathrooms.

In the mills, factories, mines, and businesses of the North, the philosophy of "last hired, first fired" meant that the people who could least afford to be jobless were fired first. Black workers who had left the South to take factory jobs in the North were among the first to be laid off. And this group had the highest rate of joblessness in the early years of the Great Depression. "At no time in the history of the Negro since slavery," reported the Urban League, "has his economic and social outlook seemed so discouraging." Churches and other charity organizations gave aid to the needy, but some refused to provide support for minority groups.

Impoverished whites in western states found themselves competing with Latino and Asian farmhands for seasonal work on large corporate farms. As a consequence, many Chinese, Japanese, and Filipino farm laborers moved to cities. Mexicans, who had come to the United States during the 1920s, were also mostly migrant workers, traveling from farm to farm to work during harvest and planting seasons. They settled in California, New Mexico, Arizona, Colorado, Texas, and the midwestern states. As economic conditions worsened, government officials called for the deportation of Mexican-born Americans to avoid the cost of providing them with public services. By 1935, more than 500,000 Mexican Americans (250,000 from Texas alone) were deported along with their American-born children.

Everywhere one looked in the early 1930s, people were suffering. City, county, and state governments proved incapable of managing the misery. As Americans turned to the federal government for answers, Herbert Hoover, the "Great Engineer," struggled to provide them.

FROM HOOVERISM TO THE NEW DEAL

The Great Depression revealed Herbert Hoover to be a brilliant mediocrity. His initial response to the crisis was denial; there was no calamity, he insisted. All that was needed, he and others in his administration argued, was to let the economy cure itself. The best policy, Treasury secretary Andrew Mellon advised, would be to "liquidate labor, liquidate stocks, liquidate the farmers, liquidate real estate." Letting events run their course, he claimed, would "purge the rottenness out of the [capitalist] system."

Mellon's do-nothing approach did not work, however. Falling wages and declining land and home values made it even harder for struggling farmers, businesses, and households to pay their bills. With so many people losing jobs and income, consumers and businesses simply could not buy enough goods and services to reenergize the economy.

Hoover's Efforts at Recovery

As the months passed, President Hoover proved less willing than Andrew Mellon to sit by and let events take their course. He invited business, labor, government, and agricultural leaders to a series of conferences in which he urged companies to maintain employment and wage levels, asked unions to end strikes, and pleaded with state governors to accelerate planned construction projects so as to keep people working. He also formed committees and commissions to study various aspects of the economic calamity.

UPBEAT MESSAGES President Hoover became an ineffective cheerleader for capitalism. In early May 1930, he told the U.S. Chamber of Commerce that he was "convinced we have passed the worst and with continued effort we shall rapidly recover." A few weeks later, Hoover assured a group of bankers that the "depression is over." His administration also circulated upbeat slogans such as "Business IS Better" and "Keep Smiling."

Uplifting words were not enough, however, and Hoover never felt comfortable reassuring a desperate nation. His recurring statement—"No one is actually starving. The hoboes . . . are better fed than they have ever been"—was hardly helpful, or, as it turned out, accurate.

SHORT-SIGHTED TAX INCREASES The Great Depression was the greatest national emergency since the Civil War, and the nation was woefully unprepared to deal with it. As personal income plummeted, so did government tax revenues. President Hoover insisted on trying to balance the federal budget by raising taxes and cutting budgets—precisely the wrong prescription. He pushed through Congress the Revenue Act of 1932, the largest—and most poorly timed—peacetime tax increase in history, raising the top rate from 24 percent to 63 percent. By taking money out of consumers' pockets, the higher taxes accelerated the economic slowdown. People had less money to spend when what the economy most needed was increased consumer spending.

HOOVER'S REACTION TO THE SOCIAL CRISIS By the fall of 1930, many cities were buckling under the strain of lost revenue and human distress. State and local governments cut spending, worsening the economic situation, and the federal government had no programs to deal with homelessness and joblessness. Shantytowns sprouted in vacant lots. People called their makeshift villages *Hoovervilles* to mock the president. To keep warm, they wrapped themselves in newspapers, calling them *Hoover blankets.*

The president's unwillingness to address the social crisis reflected his fear that the nation would be "plunged into socialism" if the government provided direct support to the poor. He still trumpeted the virtues of self-reliance, claiming that government assistance would rob people of the desire to help themselves.

Hoover hoped that the "natural generosity" of the American people and charitable organizations would be sufficient, and he believed that volunteers (the backbone of charity organizations) would relieve the social distress. But his faith in traditional "voluntarism" was misplaced. Local and state relief

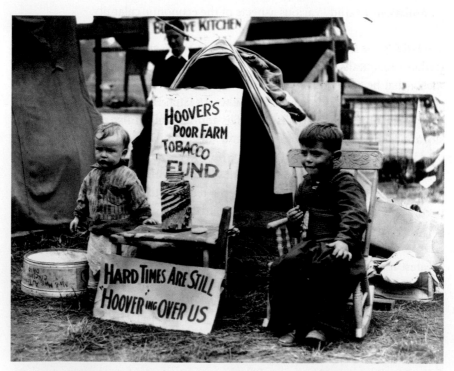

Young and hungry Two children beg for change in "Hooverville" homeless camp.

agencies were overwhelmed by the crisis, as were churches and charitable organizations like the Salvation Army and the Red Cross.

RISING CRITICISM OF HOOVER

That the economic collapse was so unexpected and intense made people all the more insecure and anxious, and Herbert Hoover increasingly became the target of their frustration. The Democrats shrewdly exploited his predicament. In November 1930, they gained their first national off-year election victory since 1916, winning a majority in the House and a near majority in the Senate.

Hoover refused to see the elections as a warning. Instead, he grew more resistant to calls for federal intervention. The *New York Times* concluded that Hoover had "failed as a party leader. He has failed as an economist. . . . He has failed as a business leader. . . . He has failed as a personality because of [his] awkwardness of manner and speech and lack of mass magnetism." When Hoover asked Treasury Secretary Andrew Mellon for a nickel to phone a friend, the secretary replied, "Here are two nickels—call all of them."

CONGRESSIONAL INITIATIVES With a new Congress in session in 1932, demands for federal action forced President Hoover to do more. That year, Congress approved his request to create the **Reconstruction Finance Corporation (RFC)** to make emergency loans to banks, life-insurance companies, and railroads. If the federal government could help huge banks and railroads, asked New York Democratic senator Robert F. Wagner, why not "extend a helping hand to that forlorn American, in every village and every city of the United States, who has been without wages since 1929?" Hoover, however, signed only the Emergency Relief Act (1932), which authorized the RFC to make loans to states for infrastructure projects. Critics called the RFC a "breadline" for businesses while the unemployed went hungry.

VETERANS IN PROTEST Fears of organized revolt arose when almost 20,000 Great War veterans and their families converged on the nation's capital in the spring of 1932. The "**Bonus Expeditionary Force**" pressed Congress to pay the cash bonuses owed to nearly 4 million veterans, many of them now homeless and jobless. In 1924, Congress had passed the Adjusted Compensation Act, which agreed to pay veterans in 1945 a bonus for their war service. Now, in 1932, the House authorized the payments immediately, but the Senate said no because they would have forced a tax increase.

Most of the veterans went home. The rest, along with their families, having no place to go, camped in vacant federal buildings and in a shantytown within sight of the Capitol. They became the first large-scale example of nonviolent protest in the nation's capital.

Eager to remove the veterans, Hoover persuaded Congress to pay for their train tickets home. More left, but hundreds stayed, hoping to meet with the president. Late in July, Attorney General William D. Mitchell ordered the government buildings cleared.

The secretary of war dispatched 700 soldiers to remove the "Bonus Army." The soldiers, commanded by the army chief of staff, General Douglas MacArthur, used horses, tanks, tear gas, and bayonets to disperse the unarmed veterans and their families. Then, exceeding orders, the soldiers burned the makeshift camp. Fifty-five veterans were injured and 135 arrested. The grandstanding MacArthur held a press conference at which he assured the nation that he had suppressed the "insurrectionists" who were spreading a "spirit of revolution."

The attack on the Bonus Army was a public relations disaster and led even more people to view Hoover and the Republicans as heartless. Unbeknownst to the nation, the president had sent a message to MacArthur ordering him not to send his troops in. Hoover, however, perhaps out of embarrassment, took responsibility for MacArthur's assault on the Bonus Army: "Thank God," he declared, "we still have a government in Washington that knows how to deal with a mob."

The Democratic governor of New York was horrified by the assault on the Bonus Army. "Well," Franklin Roosevelt told an aide, "this elects me" as the next president. (The veterans finally received their "bonus" payment in 1936.)

HOOVER'S PREDICAMENT The stress of the nation's plight sapped Hoover's health and morale. "I am so tired," he said, "that every bone in my body aches." When aides urged him to be more of a public leader, he replied, "I have no Wilsonian qualities." He hated giving speeches, and when he did he came across as cold and uncaring. He also got along badly with journalists, who often highlighted his sour demeanor and dull, monotone voice. A sculptor claimed that "if you put a rose in Hoover's hand, it would wilt."

The organizational genius who had promised Americans "permanent prosperity" lost the respect of most Americans and for many became a laughingstock. Unemployment continued to rise, wage levels continued to fall, and millions struggled simply to survive. In the end, Hoover failed because he never understood or acknowledged the seriousness of the nation's economic problems and social distress.

THE 1932 ELECTION In June 1932, glum Republicans gathered in Chicago to nominate Herbert Hoover for a second term. By contrast, the Democrats arrived in Chicago a few weeks later confident that they would nominate the next president. Fifty-year-old New York governor Franklin Delano Roosevelt won on the fourth ballot.

Roosevelt—charming, witty, energetic, and eloquent—broke precedent by traveling to Chicago to accept the nomination in person. He told the cheering delegates: "I pledge you, I pledge myself to a *new deal* for the American people" that would "break foolish traditions" and create a new, enlightened administration "of competence and courage." The contest against Hoover, he said, would be "more than a political campaign; it is a call to arms."

Throughout the campaign, Roosevelt stressed that the struggling economy required new ideas and aggressive action. "The country needs, and . . . the country demands bold, persistent experimentation," he said. "Above all, try something." There were "many ways of going forward," but "only one way of standing still."

In contrast to Roosevelt, Hoover lacked vitality and vision. He warned that Roosevelt's proposals for unprecedented government action "would destroy the very foundations of our American system." The election, he said, was a battle "between two philosophies of government" that would decide "the direction our nation will take over a century to come."

On Election Day, voters swept Roosevelt into office, 23 million to 16 million. In 1928, Hoover had carried forty states; four years later, he won but six. Roosevelt had promised Americans a vague "New Deal." Now he had to fashion one.

CHAPTER REVIEW

SUMMARY

- **The Reactionary Twenties**   With the end of the Great War, a renewed surge of immigration led to another wave of *nativism*. To Americans who feared that many immigrants were political radicals, the *Sacco and Vanzetti case (1921)* confirmed their suspicions. Nativists persuaded Congress to restrict future immigration, particularly from eastern and southern Europe, in the *Immigration Act of 1924*. Other reactionary movements reflected the feeling of many white Protestants that their religion and way of life were under attack. A revived Ku Klux Klan promoted hatred of Catholics, Jews, immigrants, Communists, and liberals, as well as African Americans. Fundamentalist Protestants campaigned against teaching evolution in public schools. Their efforts culminated in the 1925 *Scopes Trial*. Along with progressive reformers, conservative Protestants supported the nationwide *Prohibition (1920–1933)* of alcoholic beverages. Union membership declined in the 1920s as businesses adopted new techniques (such as the *open shop*) to resist unions.

- **Republican Resurgence**   Although the Eighteenth Amendment (paving the way for Prohibition) and the Nineteenth Amendment (guaranteeing women's right to vote) marked the culmination of progressivism, the movement lost much of its appeal as disillusionment with the Great War and its results created a public preference for disarmament and isolationism, stances reflected in the Five-Power Treaty of 1922. Warren G. Harding's landslide presidential victory in 1920 was based on his call for a *return to normalcy*. Harding and his fellow Republicans, including his vice president and successor, Calvin Coolidge, followed policies advocated by Secretary of the Treasury Andrew Mellon that emphasized lowering taxes and government spending as well as raising tariffs to protect domestic industries. The plan revived the economy. Harding died suddenly in 1923. Coolidge restored trust in the presidency and won reelection in a landslide in 1924. In the 1928 presidential election, Herbert Hoover, secretary of commerce under Harding and Coolidge, won a third straight decisive victory for the Republicans.

- **The Great Depression**   The 1929 stock market crash revealed the structural flaws in the economy, but it was not the only cause of the *Great Depression (1929–1941)*. During the twenties, business owners did not provide adequate wage increases for workers, thus preventing consumers' "purchasing power" from keeping up with increases in production. The nation's agricultural sector also suffered from overproduction. Government policies—such as high tariffs that helped to reduce international trade and the reduction of the nation's money supply as a means of dealing with the financial panic—worsened the emerging economic depression.

- **Hoover's Failure**   Hoover's philosophy of voluntary self-reliance prevented him from using federal intervention to relieve the nation's suffering. When thousands of out-of-work veterans of the Great War protested in Washington, D.C., demanding that Congress pay the cash bonus owed them, their efforts ended in violence. In March 1933, Franklin D. Roosevelt assumed the presidency and set in motion a New Deal that entailed scores of new federal agencies and programs designed to end the depression and put people back to work.

CHRONOLOGY

1920   Prohibition begins

Warren G. Harding is elected president

1921   Congress passes Emergency Immigration Act

Washington Naval Conference

1922   Five-Power Treaty

1923   Teapot Dome scandal becomes public

President Harding dies in office and is succeeded by Calvin Coolidge

1924   Congress passes restrictive Immigration Act (Johnson-Reed Act)

Coolidge is reelected president

1925   Scopes "monkey trial"

1928   Herbert Hoover is elected president

1929   Stock market crashes in late October

1930   Smoot-Hawley Tariff

1932   Reconstruction Finance Corporation (RFC) created

Franklin D. Roosevelt elected president

KEY TERMS

nativism p. 1115

Immigration Act of 1924 p. 1116

Sacco and Vanzetti case (1922) p. 1119

Scopes Trial (1925) p. 1124

Prohibition (1920–1933) p. 1126

return to normalcy p. 1131

open shop p. 1136

Teapot Dome Affair (1923) p. 1140

Great Depression (1929–1941) p. 1150

Reconstruction Finance Corporation (1932) p. 1161

Bonus Expeditionary Force (1932) p. 1161

 INQUIZITIVE

Go to InQuizitive to see what you've learned—and learn what you've missed—with personalized feedback along the way.

25 The New Deal
1933–1939

Construction of a Dam **(1939)** One of the most famous and controversial of the
artists commissioned by the New Deal's Works Progress Administration was William
Gropper, the son of Jewish immigrants who became a Communist sympathizer during
the twenties and thirties. In 1939, he painted this mural displayed in the Department
of the Interior building in Washington, D.C. Based on his observations of dam
construction on the Columbia and Colorado Rivers, Gropper illustrates the sense of
triumph and brotherhood that emerged from the New Deal's massive public projects
during the Great Depression.

The Great Depression was not simply an American event; it was a worldwide economic disaster whose global scale increased its severity and complicated efforts to address its impact. In 1929, Europe was still reeling from the financial effects of the Great War. Once the American economy tumbled, it sent shock waves throughout the world. Economic distress fed the rise of totalitarian regimes—fascism and Nazism in Italy and Germany, communism in the Soviet Union. "Capitalism is dying," theologian Reinhold Niebuhr proclaimed. "Let no one delude himself by hoping for reform from within."

Yet that is exactly what Franklin Delano Roosevelt sought to do in 1933. He would save capitalism by transforming it from within. Like his cousin and hero, Theodore Roosevelt, he believed that the basic problem of twentieth-century life was the excessive power of large corporations. Only the federal government and an active president could regulate corporate capitalism for the public benefit.

Few leaders have taken office in more dire circumstances. Yet within days of becoming president, Roosevelt, often called FDR, took dramatic steps that forever changed the scope and role of the federal government while keeping the nation from fragmenting. He believed that America's democratic form of government had the responsibility to help people who were in distress. With the help of a supportive Congress, he set about enacting dozens of measures to relieve human suffering and promote economic recovery.

FDR was an inspiring personality, overflowing with cheerfulness, strong convictions, and an unshakeable confidence in himself and in the resilience of the American people. He was not committed to any particular ideology; instead, he was a pragmatist willing to try different approaches. As a consequence, his program for economic recovery, the New Deal, was a series

focus questions

1. What were the accomplishments and criticisms of the First New Deal?

2. Analyze why FDR launched a Second New Deal in 1935. How did it differ from the first?

3. What was the purpose and structure of the Social Security system?

4. How did the New Deal transform the role of the federal government in American life?

of trial-and-error actions rather than a comprehensive scheme. None of the many initiatives worked perfectly, and some failed miserably. Yet their combined effect restored hope and energy to a nation eager for dynamic leadership.

ROOSEVELT'S NEW DEAL

Franklin Roosevelt promised voters a "New Deal," and within hours of being inaugurated, he and his aides set about creating a "new order of competence and courage." The federal government assumed responsibility for national economic planning and for restoring prosperity and ensuring social security—for all. What Roosevelt called the "forgotten man" (by which he meant the working poor, both men and women) would no longer be forgotten.

ROOSEVELT'S RISE Born in 1882, the only child of wealthy, aristocratic parents, young Franklin Roosevelt enjoyed a pampered life. He was educated by tutors at Springwood, a Hudson River manor near Hyde Park, north of New York City. At age fourteen, he boarded his father's private railroad car and traveled to Massachusetts, where he enrolled in the exclusive Groton school. He then attended Harvard College and Columbia University Law School, where he did not earn a degree. While a law student in 1905, he married Anna Eleanor Roosevelt, his distant cousin and the favorite niece of President Theodore Roosevelt. Eleanor's father, Elliott, was Theodore's alcoholic brother who died in 1894 at age thirty-four.

In 1910, twenty-eight-year-old Franklin Roosevelt won a Democratic seat in the New York State Senate. Tall, handsome, and athletic, he seemed destined for greatness. In 1913, President Woodrow Wilson appointed him assistant secretary of the navy. Seven years later, Roosevelt became James Cox's vice presidential running mate on the Democratic ticket.

TRIAL BY FIRE Then a tragedy occurred. In 1921, at age thirty-nine, Franklin Roosevelt contracted polio, an infectious neuromuscular disease that left him permanently disabled. He would never walk again unaided. Roosevelt fought back, however. For seven years, with his wife Eleanor's help, he strengthened his body to compensate for his disability. The exhausting daily exercise and the awareness that his disability would be permanent transformed him. Polio paralyzed his legs but expanded his sympathies. He became less pompous, more considerate, more focused, and more able to identify with the problems of people facing hard times.

Roosevelt had a remarkable ability to make people feel at ease and to express his genuine concern about their troubles. The aristocrat had developed the common touch as well as a great talent for public relations, but he also was vain and calculating and a clever manipulator. In other words, he was a consummate politician.

A PEOPLE'S PRESIDENT FDR was neither a masterful administrator nor a deep thinker. One of his closest aides said the president never "read a serious book." He did, however, have many virtues: courage, good instincts, unrelenting optimism, and a charming personality.

He loved talking to voters and reporters, and he was determined to help those who could not help themselves. Colonel Edward House, the veteran Democratic counselor, explained that Woodrow Wilson "liked humanity as a whole and disliked people individually." Roosevelt, by contrast, was "genuinely fond of people and shows it."

What truly set him apart was his willingness to experiment with using government power and resources to address the pressing problems generated by the Great Depression. FDR initially embraced the orthodoxy of a balanced budget and complained about a "bloated bureaucracy," for example, only to incur more budget deficits than all his predecessors combined as he expanded the scope of the federal government.

THE 1933 INAUGURATION Inaugurated in March 1933, Franklin Delano Roosevelt assumed leadership during a profound national crisis that threatened the very fabric of American capitalism and unleashed the possibility of widespread civil unrest. "The situation is critical, Franklin," journalist Walter Lippmann warned. "You may have to assume dictatorial powers"—as had happened in Germany, Italy, and the Soviet Union.

Roosevelt did not become a dictator, but he did take extraordinary steps while assuring Americans "that the only thing we have to fear is fear itself." He confessed in his inaugural address that he did not have all the answers, but he did know that "this nation asks for action, and action now." He asked Congress for "a broad Executive power to wage a war against the emergency" just as "if we were in fact invaded by a foreign foe." Roosevelt's uplifting speech won rave reviews. Nearly 500,000 Americans wrote letters to the new president, and even the pro-Republican *Chicago Tribune* praised his "courageous confidence."

THE FIRST HUNDRED DAYS In March 1933, President Roosevelt confronted four major challenges: reviving the industrial economy, addressing the needs of record numbers of jobless and homeless Americans, rescuing the ravaged farm sector, and reforming those defects of the capitalist system that had contributed to the Depression. He quickly addressed all those challenges—and more.

The new president admitted that he would try several different "experiments." Some would succeed, and others would fail, but the important thing was to do something bold—and fast. It was no time for timid leadership or paralyzing doubts. The defining characteristic of Roosevelt's approach to presidential leadership was *action*.

To advise him, Roosevelt assembled a "brain trust" of specialists—professors, journalists, economists, social workers, and others. "I'm not the smartest fellow in the world," Roosevelt admitted, "but I sure can pick smart colleagues."

The president and his advisers settled on a three-pronged strategy to revive the economy and help those in need. First, they would tackle the banking crisis and provide short-term emergency relief for the jobless. Roosevelt said, "Our greatest primary task is putting people to work." Second, the New

Franklin Delano Roosevelt Preparing to deliver the first of his popular "fireside chats" to a national radio audience. This message focused on measures to reform the American banking system.

Dealers—men and women (professors, journalists, economists, social workers, and political appointees) who swarmed to Washington during the winter of 1933—would encourage agreements between management and unions designed to keep businesses from failing. Third, they would raise depressed commodity prices (corn, cotton, wheat, beef, pork, etc.) by paying farmers "subsidies" to *reduce* the sizes of their crops and herds so that prices would *rise* and thereby increase farm income over time, even if it meant higher food prices for consumers.

The new Congress was ready to take action. From March 9, when the session opened, to June 16, the so-called First Hundred Days, Congress approved fifteen major pieces of legislation proposed by Roosevelt. Several of these programs comprised what came to be called the **First New Deal** (1933–1935).

Shoring Up the Financial System

Money is the lubricant of capitalism, and money was fast disappearing from circulation by 1933. Since the stock market crash of 1929, panicky depositors had been withdrawing their money from banks and the stock market—and hoarding gold. Taking so much money out of circulation worsened the Depression and brought the banking system to the brink of collapse. Throughout the twenties, an average of almost 700 banks a year had failed. After 1929, that number had doubled and then tripled.

BANKING REGULATION On March 5, 1933, his first full day in office, Franklin Roosevelt called on Congress to convene in emergency session. He asked the legislators to pass the Emergency Banking Relief Act, which declared a four-day bank holiday to allow the financial panic to subside. (A sulking Herbert Hoover criticized the move as a "reckless" step toward "gigantic socialism.") For the first time, all U.S. banks closed their doors.

Roosevelt's financial experts drafted the Emergency Banking Act of 1933 to restore confidence in banks and inject $2 billion of new cash into the economy. On March 12, in the first of his many radio "fireside chats" to the nation, the president assured his 60 million listeners that it was safer to "keep your money in a reopened bank than under the mattress." The following day, people took their money back to the banks. "Capitalism was saved in eight days," said one of Roosevelt's advisers.

On June 5, 1933, Roosevelt shocked the financial world and earned the scorn of bankers by taking the United States off the gold standard, whereby the amount of dollars in circulation was governed by the amount of gold in government vaults. Dropping the gold standard enabled the president to increase the currency supply and ward off deflation while encouraging the public to spend, which would foster economic growth. As it turned out, the sooner countries abandoned the gold standard, the more quickly their economies recovered. By 1936, most nations had done so.

On June 16, Roosevelt signed the Glass-Steagall Banking Act of 1933. It created the **Federal Deposit Insurance Corporation** (FDIC), which insured customer bank accounts up to $2,500, thus reducing the likelihood of future panics. The Glass-Steagall Act also called for the separation of commercial banking from investment banking to prevent banks from investing the savings of depositors in the risky stock market. Only banks that specialized in investment could trade shares in the stock market after 1933. In addition, the Federal Reserve Board was given more authority to intervene in future financial emergencies. These steps effectively ended the banking crisis.

The galloping snail A vigorous Roosevelt drives Congress to action in this *Detroit News* cartoon from March 1933.

REGULATING WALL STREET Before the Great Crash in 1929, there was little government oversight of the securities (stocks and bonds) industry. In 1933, President Roosevelt's administration developed two important pieces of legislation intended to regulate the operations of the stock market and eliminate fraud and abuses.

The Securities Act of 1933 was the first major federal legislation to regulate the sale of stocks and bonds. It required every corporation that issued stock for public sale to disclose all relevant information about the operations and management of the company so that investors could know what they were buying. The second bill, the Securities Exchange Act of 1934, established the **Securities and Exchange Commission** to enforce the new laws and regulations governing the issuance and trading of stocks and bonds.

THE FEDERAL BUDGET As part of the breathless pace of the First Hundred Days, FDR convinced Congress to pass the Economy Act allowing him to cut government workers' salaries, reduce payments to military veterans for non-service-connected disabilities, and reorganize federal agencies—all designed to reduce government expenses. He then took the dramatic step of ending Prohibition—in part because it was so widely violated, in part because most Democrats wanted to end it, and in part because he wanted to regain the federal tax revenues from the sale of alcoholic beverages. The Twenty-First Amendment, ratified on December 5, 1933, ended Prohibition.

Helping the Unemployed and Homeless

Another top priority was relieving the human distress caused by joblessness and homelessness. Herbert Hoover had stubbornly refused to help the unemployed and homeless, since he assumed that individual self-reliance, acts of charity, and the efforts of local organizations (the Red Cross, churches, and "city missions") would be sufficient.

The Roosevelt administration, however, knew that the numbers of people in need far exceeded the capacity of charitable organizations and local agencies. As Harry L. Hopkins, an aide to Roosevelt, said, "Hunger is not debatable." With a sense of urgency that Herbert Hoover had never summoned, President Roosevelt pushed through a series of programs that created what came to be called the "welfare state." He did not believe that the government should give suffering people cash (called a "dole"), but he insisted that the federal government help the unemployed and homeless by providing them jobs. For the first time, the federal government took responsibility for assisting the most desperate Americans.

PUTTING PEOPLE TO WORK The Federal Emergency Relief Administration (FERA), headed by Harry L. Hopkins, was Roosevelt's first effort to deal with massive unemployment. It sent money to the states to spend on the unemployed and homeless. After the state-sponsored programs proved inadequate, Congress created the Civil Works Administration (CWA) in November 1933. It marked the first large-scale *federal* effort to put people directly on the government payroll at competitive wages: 40¢ an hour for unskilled workers, $1 for skilled.

The CWA provided 4 million federal jobs during the winter of 1933–1934 and organized a variety of useful projects: repairing 500,000 miles of roads, laying sewer lines, constructing or improving more than 1,000 airports and 40,000 public schools, and providing 50,000 teaching jobs that helped keep small rural public schools open. When the program's cost soared, however,

Roosevelt ordered the CWA dissolved. By April 1934, 4 million workers were again unemployed.

THE CCC The most successful New Deal jobs program was the Civilian Conservation Corps (CCC), managed by the War Department. It built 2,500 camps in forty-seven states to house up to half a million unemployed, unmarried young men ages seventeen to twenty-seven. They worked as "soil soldiers" in national forests, parks, and recreational areas, and on soil-conservation projects. The CCC also recruited 150,000 jobless military veterans and 85,000 Native Americans, housing them in separate camps. Women were excluded from working in the CCC; African Americans and Native Americans were housed in segregated facilities.

CCC workers had to be between 60 and 78 inches tall, weigh more than 107 pounds, and have at least six teeth. They were to be paid $1 a day for no more than nine months so as to make room for others. Critics charged that the CCC would undermine wage gains made by the labor union movement, but

Federal relief programs Civilian Conservation Corps enrollees in 1933, on a break from work. Directed by army officers and foresters, the CCC camps were operated like military bases.

Roosevelt responded that the young men selected for the program would be those who "have no chance to get a job." Congress passed the CCC bill only after Oscar De Priest, an African American legislator from Illinois, introduced an amendment requiring that the agency not discriminate on account of race, color, or creed.

Over the next nine years, the 2.5 million CCC enrollees were provided shelter in barracks, given uniforms, food, and a small wage of $30 a month ($25 of which had to be sent home to their families). The young men could also earn high-school diplomas.

CCC workers cleared brush; constructed roads, bridges, campgrounds, fire towers, fish hatcheries, and 800 parks; planted 3 *billion* trees; taught farmers how to control soil erosion; built 13,000 miles of trails, including the Appalachian Trail from Georgia to Maine; and fought fires.

Roosevelt, a dedicated conservationist, loved to visit the CCC camps. He saw the New Deal as an opportunity to reinvigorate the movement to preserve America's natural resources. He believed that a "nation that destroys its soils destroys itself. Forests are the lungs of our land, purifying the air and giving fresh strength to our people." His policies would "not only preserve the existing forests, but create new ones," he boasted. After sharing a meal with a group of CCC workers, he told them, "I wish I could spend a couple of months here myself." By 1942, when the CCC was dismantled, some 3 million young men had passed through the program.

SAVING HOMES In 1933, an estimated 1,000 homes or farms were being foreclosed upon each day because people could not pay their monthly mortgages. President Roosevelt convinced Congress to create the Home Owners' Loan Corporation, which helped people refinance their mortgages at lower interest rates. In 1934, Roosevelt created the Federal Housing Administration (FHA), which offered mortgages of much longer duration (twenty years) to reduce monthly payments. Prior to that, typical home mortgages had terms of less than ten years.

REVIVING THE INDUSTRIAL SECTOR The centerpiece of the New Deal's efforts to revive the industrial economy was the National Industrial Recovery Act (NIRA) of 1933. It created massive public-works construction projects funded by the federal government. The NIRA started the Public Works Administration (PWA), granting $3.3 billion for the construction of government buildings, highways, bridges, dams, port facilities, and sewage plants. Among its noteworthy projects were the Blue Ridge Parkway in North Carolina and the Grand Coulee Dam in Washington State. The PWA also built forty-seven public housing projects for low-income Americans, all of them segregated by race.

A second, more controversial part of the NIRA created the **National Recovery Administration** (NRA), headed by Hugh S. Johnson, a hard-drinking retired army general known for his administrative expertise. The NRA represented a radical shift in the federal government's role in the economy. Never before in peacetime had Washington bureaucrats taken charge of setting prices, wages, and standards for working conditions.

The primary purpose of the NRA was to promote economic growth by ignoring anti-trust laws and allowing executives of competing businesses to negotiate among themselves and with labor unions to create "codes of fair competition" that would set prices, production levels, minimum wages, and maximum hours within each industry, no matter how small. In New York City, for example, women who made their living as burlesque-show strippers agreed to an NRA code limiting the number of performers on stage and the number of performances they could provide each night.

The NRA codes also included "fair labor" policies long sought by unions and social progressives: a national forty-hour workweek with a maximum eight-hour workday, minimum weekly wages of $13 ($12 in the South, where living costs were lower), and a ban on the employment of children under the age of sixteen. The NRA also guaranteed the right of workers to organize unions.

For a time, the downward spiral of wages and prices subsided. As soon as economic recovery began, however, small business owners complained that the NRA's price-fixing robbed small producers of the chance to compete with large corporations. And because NRA wage codes excluded agricultural and domestic workers (at the insistence of southern Democrats), few African Americans derived any benefit. When the Supreme Court declared the NRA unconstitutional in May 1935 for assigning lawmaking powers to the NRA in violation of the Constitution's allocation of such authority only to Congress, few regretted its demise.

Despite being declared unconstitutional, some NRA policies that remained in place had lasting effects. New workplace standards, such as the forty-hour workweek; a national minimum wage; and restrictions that ended child labor were part of the NRA legacy. Its endorsement of collective bargaining spurred the growth of unions. Yet, as 1934 ended, industrial recovery was still feeble.

AGRICULTURAL ASSISTANCE In addition to rescuing the banks and providing jobs to the unemployed, Franklin Roosevelt created the Farm Credit Administration to help farmers deal with their debts and lower their mortgage payments to avoid bankruptcy.

The **Agricultural Adjustment Act** of 1933 created the Agricultural Adjustment Administration (AAA), which sought to raise prices for crops and herds by paying farmers to cut production. The money came from a tax on the businesses that processed food crops and certain agricultural commodities—cotton gins, flour mills, and slaughterhouses.

By the time the AAA was created, however, the spring planting season was under way. The prospect of another bumper cotton crop forced the AAA to pay farmers to "plow-under" the sprouting seeds in their fields. To destroy a growing crop was a "shocking commentary on our civilization," Agriculture Secretary Henry A. Wallace admitted. "I could tolerate it only as a cleaning up of the wreckage from the old days of unbalanced production."

Moreover, in an effort to raise pork prices, some 6 million baby pigs were slaughtered and buried to raise prices. By the end of 1934, the AAA efforts had worked. Wheat, cotton, and corn production had declined, and prices for those commodities had risen. Farm income increased by 58 percent between 1932 and 1935.

A NEW ROLE FOR GOVERNMENT At the end of the First Hundred Days of Franklin Roosevelt's presidency, the principle of an *activist* federal government had been established. While journalists characterized the AAA, NRA, CCC, CWA, and other New Deal programs as "alphabet soup," and conservative critics warned that Roosevelt was leading America toward fascism or communism, the president had become the most popular man in the nation.

DUST BOWL MIGRANTS At the same time that the agricultural economy was struggling, a terrible drought created an ecological catastrophe known as the **Dust Bowl**. Colorado, New Mexico, Kansas, Nebraska, Texas, Arkansas, and Oklahoma were hardest hit. With little rain for months, crops withered, and income plummeted. Strong winds swept across the treeless plains, scooping up tons of parched topsoil into billowing dark clouds, called black blizzards, which engulfed farms and towns. By 1938, topsoil had disappeared from more than 25 million acres of prairie land.

Farmers could not pay their debts, and banks foreclosed on family farms. Suicides soared, and millions abandoned their farms and headed toward California, where jobs were said to be plentiful. Disparagingly called "Okies" or "Arkies," most of the Dust Bowl refugees were from Arkansas, Texas, Missouri, and Oklahoma. During the 1930s and 1940s, some 800,000 people, mostly whites, headed to the Far West.

Without money to pay rent or a mortgage, homeless migrants set up squatter camps, often called Little Oklahomas alongside highways or close to towns

"Okies" on the run A sharecropping family reaches its destination of Bakersfield, California, in 1935, after "we got blowed out in Oklahoma."

where they could get food and supplies. When one crop was harvested, the migrants moved on to the next, carrying their belongings with them.

Most of them went to California's urban areas—Los Angeles, San Diego, or San Francisco. Others moved into the San Joaquin Valley, the state's agricultural heartland. There they discovered that California was no paradise. Most had to work as farm laborers. Living in tents or crude cabins, they suffered from exposure to the elements, poor sanitation, and social abuse. As one transplanted worker from Oklahoma reported, when the big farmers "need us they call us *migrants*, and when we've picked their crop, we're *bums* and we got to get out."

THE TENNESSEE VALLEY AUTHORITY Early in his presidency, Franklin Roosevelt declared that the "South is the nation's number one economic problem." Indeed, since the end of the Civil War, the economy and quality of life in the southern states had lagged far behind the rest of the nation. That gap only widened during the Great Depression.

To help, Roosevelt created one of the most innovative programs of the First New Deal: the Tennessee Valley Authority (TVA), which brought electrical power, flood control efforts, and jobs to Appalachia, the desperately poor mountainous region that stretched from West Virginia through western Virginia and North Carolina, Kentucky, eastern Tennessee, and northern Georgia and Alabama.

By 1940, the TVA, a multipurpose public corporation, had constructed twenty-one hydroelectric dams that created the "Great Lakes of the South" in Kentucky, Tennessee, North Carolina, Georgia, and Alabama, and produced enough electricity to power the entire region, at about half the average national rate. The TVA also dredged rivers to allow for boat and barge traffic, promoted soil conservation and forestry management, attracted new industries, and improved schools and libraries. It provided 1.5 million isolated farms with electricity and indoor plumbing.

Norris Dam The massive dam in Tennessee, completed in 1936, was essential in creating jobs and expanding electricity under the TVA.

Progress often comes at a cost. Many New Deal programs helped some people and hurt others. Tough choices had to be made. Building those huge dams in Appalachia and the resulting lakes meant displacing thousands from homes and villages that were destroyed to make way for progress. "I don't want to move," said an elderly East Tennessee woman. "I want to sit here and look out over these hills where I was born. My folks are buried down the road a piece, and our babies are over there on the hill under the cedars."

Yet overall, the First New Deal programs—and Roosevelt's leadership—had given Americans a renewed faith in the future. In the congressional elections of 1934, the Democrats increased their majority in Congress.

ELEANOR ROOSEVELT One of the reasons for FDR's popularity was his energetic wife, Eleanor, who would prove to be one of the most influential leaders of the twentieth century. Never had a First Lady been so engaged in public life or so widely beloved. She was her husband's moral compass, prodding him about social-justice issues while steadfastly supporting his political ambitions and policies.

THE TENNESSEE VALLEY AUTHORITY

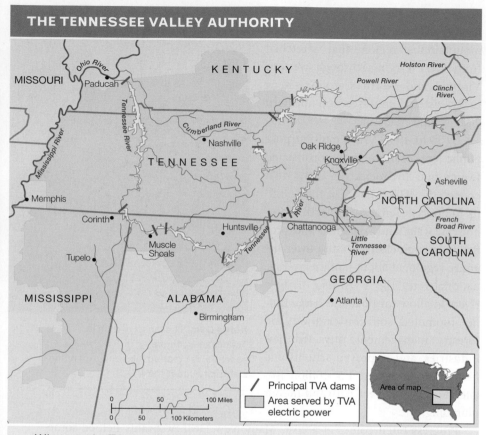

Legend:
- / Principal TVA dams
- Area served by TVA electric power
- Area of map

- What was the Tennessee Valley Authority?
- Why did Congress create it?
- How did it transform the Tennessee Valley?

Born in 1884 in New York City, Eleanor married her distant cousin Franklin in 1905, only to learn that his domineering mother, Sara Delano Roosevelt, would always be the most important woman in his life. (Sara once had workers erect a ladder to Franklin's boarding school window so that she could climb up and care for him during an illness.) "He might have been happier with a wife who was completely uncritical," Eleanor wrote later. "That I was never able to be, and he had to find it in other people."

Eleanor was dedicated to humanitarian causes from an early age. Before her marriage to Franklin, she was a precocious progressive: she worked in the Rivington Street settlement house in Manhattan and joined the National Consumers League. After the Great War, she participated in the International Congress of Working Women and the Women's International League for Peace and Freedom, endorsing efforts to address widespread poverty among women around the world. She joined the League of Women Voters in 1920.

While raising six children, she worked tirelessly on behalf of women, African Americans, and youth, giving voice to the voiceless and hope to the hopeless. Her compassion resulted in large part from the self-doubt and loneliness she had experienced as the ignored child of an alcoholic father and an aloof mother. Throughout her life, she fought a paralyzing fear of being unloved.

Eleanor Roosevelt Intelligent, principled, and a political figure in her own right, she is pictured here addressing the Red Cross Convention.

In September 1918, the Roosevelts' marriage changed forever when Eleanor, while unpacking Franklin's suitcase after a trip, discovered love letters he had exchanged with Lucy Mercer, her friend and personal secretary. As Eleanor read the letters, "the bottom dropped out" of her world.

Tart-tongued Alice Roosevelt Longworth—the daughter of Theodore Roosevelt, and Eleanor's cousin—actually nurtured the extramarital affair, hosting Mercer and Franklin for secret dinners. She later explained that Franklin "deserved a good time," for, after all, "he was married to Eleanor."

Eleanor offered Franklin a divorce, but he knew that would end his political future since divorce was not a socially accepted practice at the time. So they decided to maintain their marriage as a political partnership. As their son James said, the relationship became an "armed truce"—more a merger than a marriage. Eleanor later observed that she could "forgive, but never forget," but she never truly forgave or forgot.

Franklin and Eleanor were both concerned for each other's happiness while acknowledging their inability to provide it. In the White House, they lived apart, rarely seeing each other except for formal occasions and public events. As Eleanor confided to a friend, "There is no fundamental love to draw on," no passion or intimacy, "just respect and affection."

Over time, Eleanor compensated for her cooled relationship with Franklin by nurturing "a life of my own" and forming "special friendships" with men and women. Earl Miller, a handsome, athletic New York state trooper, served as her bodyguard when Franklin was governor of New York. He coached her in horseback riding, tennis, swimming, and target shooting. Eleanor's son James described the relationship as possibly the "one real romance in mother's life outside of marriage," adding that Miller "encouraged her to take pride in herself, to be herself, to be unafraid of facing the world. . . . Above all, he made her feel that she was a woman."

Lorena "Hick" Hickok, the first female journalist to have her byline featured on the front page of the *New York Times* and the only female reporter on Franklin's 1932 "Roosevelt Special" campaign train, had asked the Associated Press to assign her to cover the First Lady. Within weeks, the women fell deeply in love, and Eleanor proudly wore an emerald ring Hick had given her as proof of their special relationship. "Remember," Eleanor told Hick in early 1933, "no one is just what you are to me."

By then, Hickok had quit her job in order to become Eleanor's nearly constant traveling companion. When separated, they wrote letters, more than 3,000 of them during their thirty-year-long relationship. "I wish I could lie down beside you tonight & take you in my arms," Eleanor wrote Hick one night. The two women became so infatuated that Eleanor convinced Hick to move into the White House, assuming a post in the Federal Emergency Relief Administration.

Hickok and Eleanor Here, Hickok and Roosevelt walk side by side during an inspection trip to Puerto Rico.

During the summer of 1933, Eleanor and Hick drove around New England in a blue convertible, surprising desk clerks at motels when they showed up without reservations. Two years later, however, Eleanor ended their relationship, explaining that "you have a feeling for me which I may not return in kind."

While redefining the role of the First Lady, Eleanor Roosevelt became an outspoken and relentless social activist: she was the first woman to address a national political convention, write a nationally syndicated newspaper column, and hold press conferences. She crisscrossed the nation, speaking in support of the New Deal, meeting with African American leaders, supporting equal access for women in the workforce and in labor unions, and urging Americans to live up to their humanitarian ideals. She helped convince her husband to reverse Woodrow Wilson's policy of segregation of federal government agencies and offices.

In 1933, Eleanor convened a White House conference on the emergency needs of women. It urged the Federal Emergency Relief Administration (FERA) to ensure that "women are employed wherever possible." Within six months, some 300,000 women were at work on various federal government projects.

Eleanor Roosevelt had become, said a journalist, "the most influential woman of our times." A popular joke claimed that the president's nightly prayer was "Dear God, please make Eleanor a little tired." In fact, however, he was deeply dependent on his wife. She was the impatient agitator dedicated to what *should* be done; he was the calculating politician focused on what *could* be done.

Women and FERA, 1934 Federal Emergency Relief Administration enrollees take a break to gather on Reunion Day at a FERA camp for women in Arcola, Pennsylvania.

THE NEW DEAL UNDER FIRE

By 1934, Franklin Roosevelt had become the best loved and most hated president of the twentieth century. He was loved because he believed in and fought for the common people. The president, said a southern white tenant farmer, "is as good a man as ever lived." A textile mill worker reinforced the point by declaring that Roosevelt "is the biggest-hearted man we ever had in the White House." Where Herbert Hoover received an average of 400 letters a day as president, Roosevelt got more than ten times as many.

He was also loved for what a French leader called his "glittering personality." Roosevelt, with his famously arched eyebrows, upturned chin, and twinkling eyes, radiated optimism and confidence, courage in a crisis, and a self-assurance bordering on arrogance. "Meeting him," said British prime minister Winston Churchill, "was like uncorking a bottle of champagne." Roosevelt, he added, was "the greatest man I have ever known."

Roosevelt was the most visible and accessible of all U.S. presidents. Twice a week he held press conferences, explaining new legislation, addressing questions and criticisms, and winning over most journalists while befuddling his opponents. Huey Long, a Democratic senator from Louisiana and one of Roosevelt's harshest critics, complained that the president could charm a snake: "You go in there [the White House] and see FDR wanting to tear him apart. You come out whistling 'Dixie.'"

But even Roosevelt's charm had its limits. He was despised by business leaders and political conservatives who believed the New Deal and the higher taxes it required were moving America toward socialism. Some called Roosevelt a "traitor to his [aristocratic] class."

Others, on the left, hated him for not doing enough to end the Depression. By the mid-1930s, the early New Deal programs had slowed the economy's downward slide, but prosperity remained elusive. "We have been patient and long suffering," said a farm leader. "We were promised a New Deal. . . . Instead, we have the same old stacked deck."

In many respects, the contrasting opinions of Roosevelt reflected his own divided personality and erratic management style. He was both a man of idealistic principles and a practical politician prone to snap judgments, capable of both compromise and contradictory actions. He once admitted to an aide that to implement the New Deal he had to "deceive, misrepresent, leave false impressions . . . and trust to charm, loyalty, and the result to make up for it. . . . A great man cannot be a good man."

Continuing Hardships

Economic growth during FDR's first term averaged 9 percent, a peacetime record, but extensive suffering persisted. As late as 1939, some 9.5 million workers (17 percent of the labor force) remained unemployed.

IMMIGRATION AND THE GREAT DEPRESSION   There was no New Deal for immigrants. Hard times had always provoked anti-immigration feelings, and the Great Depression was no exception. Nativist prejudices prevailed as people blamed "aliens" for taking "Americans jobs." In 1935, the *New York American* newspaper declared that "existing immigration laws ought to be strengthened not weakened."

Congressman Martin Dies of Texas, a powerful Democrat, blamed the Depression itself on immigration. "If we had refused admission to the 16,500,000 foreign-born who are living in this country today, we would have no unemployment problem to distress and harass us." Dies was an ardent nativist who viewed immigration as the nation's greatest threat. "There is no middle ground or compromise" on the issue, he argued. "Either we are for or against America. If we are for America, we must be for the exclusion of these new-seed immigrants and the deportation of those unlawfully here."

Opposing such efforts was Congressman Vito Marcantonio, the son of Italian immigrants whose New York City district was filled with immigrants from Italy and Puerto Rico. "Let us legislate not by hysteria but with common sense," he told the House of Representatives. Marcantonio expressed his sorrow and disbelief that congressmen "would dare talk disparagingly about any racial group in the United States where, after all, we are all of alien stock." His strenuous opposition to "anti-immigrant bills" prevented their passage during the mid-1930s, a development all the more remarkable for the failure of Franklin Roosevelt to speak out on the issue. Fearful of losing Democratic support in the South, he refused to take political risks by protecting immigrants.

AFRICAN AMERICANS AND THE NEW DEAL   The New Deal also had blind spots. Franklin Delano Roosevelt was never as progressive on social issues as most people assumed. A northern senator was shocked to hear the president speak of "the nigger vote." FDR showed little interest in the plight of African Americans, even as black voters were shifting from the Republicans (the "party of Lincoln") to the Democrats. And like Woodrow Wilson before him, he failed to address long-standing patterns of racism and segregation in the South for fear of angering conservative southern Democrats in Congress.

As a result, many New Deal programs discriminated against African Americans. As Mary White Ovington, treasurer of the National Association for the Advancement of Colored People (NAACP), stressed, the racism in any agency "varies according to the white people chosen to administer it, but always there is discrimination."

For example, the payments from the AAA to farm owners to take land *out* of production in an effort to raise prices for farm products forced hundreds of thousands of tenant farmers and sharecroppers, both black and white, off the land. In addition, FHA refused to guarantee mortgages on houses purchased by blacks in white neighborhoods, and both the CCC and the TVA practiced racial segregation within their facilities.

The NAACP waged an energetic campaign against racial prejudice throughout the 1930s, as did Eleanor Roosevelt, and the president did appoint more African Americans to significant government positions than had any of his predecessors. One of the most visible was Mary McLeod Bethune, the

"There's no way like the American way" Margaret Bourke-White's famous 1937 photograph of desperate people waiting in a disaster-relief line in Louisville, Kentucky, captures the continuing racial divide of the era and the elusiveness of the "American dream" for many minorities.

child of slaves from South Carolina, who had founded Bethune-Cookman College in Daytona Beach, Florida, and served as head of the NAACP in the 1920s. In 1935, Roosevelt named her director of the Division of Negro Affairs within the National Youth Administration, an agency that provided jobs to unemployed young Americans. Bethune worked with other black staffers in New Deal agencies to form an informal "Black Cabinet" to ensure that African Americans had equal access to federal programs.

COURT CASES AND CIVIL LIBERTIES Racial prejudice in the South remained unabated. In a 1931 Alabama case, an all-white jury, on flimsy, conflicting testimony, convicted nine black boys and young men, ranging in age from thirteen to twenty-one, of raping two white women while riding a freight train. Eight of the "Scottsboro Boys" were sentenced to death as white spectators cheered. In his award-winning novel *Native Son* (1940), African American writer Richard Wright recalled the "mob who surrounded the Scottsboro jail with rope and kerosene."

The injustice of the Scottsboro case sparked protests throughout the world. The two white women, it turned out, had been selling sex to white and black teens on the train. One of the women eventually recanted and began appearing at rallies on behalf of the defendants.

No case in legal history produced as many trials, appeals, reversals, and retrials as the Scottsboro case. Further, it prompted two important rulings. In *Powell v. Alabama* (1932), the U.S. Supreme Court overturned the original

Scottsboro case Haywood Patterson (center), one of the defendants in the case, with his attorney, Samuel Leibowitz (left) in Decatur, Alabama, in 1933.

convictions and ordered new trials because the judge had not ensured that the accused were provided adequate defense attorneys. In *Norris v. Alabama* (1935), the Court ruled that the systematic exclusion of African Americans from Alabama juries had denied the Scottsboro defendants equal protection under the law—a principle that had widespread impact on state courts by opening up juries to African Americans.

Although Alabama eventually dropped the charges against the four youngest Scottsboro defendants and granted paroles to the others, their lives were ruined. The last defendant left prison in 1950.

NATIVE AMERICANS AND THE DEPRESSION The Great Depression also ravaged Native Americans. Some were initially encouraged by President Roosevelt's appointment of John Collier as commissioner of the Bureau of Indian Affairs (BIA). Collier steadily increased the number of

"Indian New Deal" Arrayed in traditional dress, several Hopi Native American chiefs visiting from Arizona are honored at a ceremony of the new Interior Department building in Washington, D.C. Seated left to right: Chief Loma Haftowa, Chief Kol Chaf Towa, and United States Indian Commissioner John Collier.

Native Americans employed by the BIA and ensured that all Indians gained access to New Deal relief programs.

Collier's primary objective, however, was passage of the Indian Reorganization Act. Designed to reinvigorate Native American cultural traditions by restoring land to tribes, the proposed law would have granted them the right to start businesses, establish self-governing constitutions, and receive federal funds for vocational training and economic development. The act that Congress passed, however, was a much-diluted version, and the "Indian New Deal" brought only partial improvements. It did, however, spur several tribes to revise their constitutions so as to give women the right to vote and hold office.

CULTURAL LIFE DURING THE DEPRESSION

One might have expected the onset of the Great Depression to have deepened the despair of the writers, artists, and intellectuals during the 1920s known as the Lost Generation. Instead, it brought them a renewed sense of militancy and affirmation. By the summer of 1932, even the "golden boy" of the Lost Generation, F. Scott Fitzgerald, had declared that "to bring on the revolution, it may be necessary to work within the Communist party."

Few Americans remained members of the Communist party for long, however. Most writers rebelled at demands to hew to a shifting party line, and many abandoned communism by the end of the decade upon learning that Soviet leader Josef Stalin practiced a tyranny more horrible than that of the Russian czars.

LITERATURE AND THE DEPRESSION Among the writers who addressed themes of social significance during the 1930s, two deserve special notice: John Steinbeck and Richard Wright. To capture the ordeal of the Depression in *The Grapes of Wrath* (1939), Steinbeck traveled with displaced "Okies" driven from the Dust Bowl to chase the false rumor that good jobs were to be had for the taking in the fields of California's Central Valley.

This firsthand experience allowed Steinbeck to create a vivid tale of the Joad family's gritty struggle for survival. "Rich fellas come up an' they die, an' their kids ain't no good an' they die out," says Ma Joad. "But we keep a'comin'. We're the people that live. They can't wipe us out; they can't lick us. We'll go on forever, Pa, cause we're the people." To Steinbeck, the solidarity of struggling people was the theme of the Depression. As Tom Joad promises, "Wherever there's a fight so hungry people can eat, I'll be there."

Among the most talented novelists to emerge in the 1930s was Richard Wright. The grandson of former slaves and the son of a Mississippi sharecropper who deserted his family, Wright ended his formal schooling with the ninth grade (as valedictorian of his class). He then worked in Memphis and devoured books he borrowed on a white friend's library card, all the while saving to go north. In Chicago, his period as a Communist, from 1934 to 1944, gave him an intellectual framework for his powerful novels centered on the quest for social justice.

Native Son (1940), Wright's masterpiece, focuses on the forgotten Americans at the bottom of the heap. It's the story of twenty-year-old Bigger Thomas, a black pool shark and petty thief imprisoned in a Chicago ghetto by virtue of his birth. "Bigger, sometimes I wonder why I birthed you," his God-fearing mother tells him. "Honest, you the most no-countest man I ever seen in all my life." Bigger fears and envies whites. "Every time I get to thinking about me being black and they being white, me being here and they being there," he explains, "I feel like something awful's going to happen to me."

And something awful does happen. An accidental murder and its cover-up lead him to more heinous crimes, all of which, Wright suggests, resulted from the racism in American society. "I just can't get used to it," Bigger tells one of his poolroom buddies. "I swear to God I can't. . . . Every time I think about it [white oppression] I feel like somebody's poking a red-hot iron down my throat."

At Bigger's murder trial, his attorney, Mr. Max, pleads for African Americans in general: "They are not simply twelve million people; in reality they constitute a separate nation, stunted, stripped and held captive *within* this nation." Many of them are overflowing with "balked longing for some kind of fulfilment and exultation"; and their seething futility is "what makes our future seem a looming image of violence."

POPULAR CULTURE While many writers and artists dealt with the suffering and social tensions aroused by the Great Depression, the more popular cultural outlets, such as radio programs and movies, provided a welcome escape. In 1930, more than 10 million families owned a radio; by the end of the decade, the number had tripled.

Movies were transformed by the introduction of sound. The "talkies" made movies the most popular form of entertainment during the 1930s, and the introduction of double features in 1931 and the construction of outdoor drive-in theaters in 1933 boosted interest and attendance. More than 60 percent of the population—70 million people—paid a quarter to see at least one movie each week.

The movies rarely dealt directly with hard times. People wanted to be entertained and uplifted. In *Stand Up and Cheer!* (1934), featuring child star Shirley Temple, President Roosevelt appoints a Broadway producer to his cabinet as

***A Paramount Picture* (1934)** The glamor of actress Claudette Colbert's Cleopatra is contrasted with the exhaustion of the theater-goers in this painting by Reginald Marsh. The growing popularity of movies offered an escape from the daily challenges of the Great Depression, although Marsh's work suggests it was fleeting at best.

Secretary of Amusement. His goal is to use entertainment to distract people from the ravages of the Depression.

Most feature films transported viewers into the escapist realms of adventure, spectacle, and fantasy. *Gone with the Wind* (1939), based on Margaret

Mitchell's Pulitzer Prize-winning novel, was a good example, as were *The Wizard of Oz* (1939) and Walt Disney's Mickey Mouse cartoons. Movie-goers also relished shoot-'em-up gangster films, extravagant musicals (especially those starring dancers Fred Astaire and Ginger Rogers), "screwball" romantic comedies like *It Happened One Night* (1934), *My Man Godfrey* (1936), and *Mister Deeds Goes to Town* (1936), and horror films such as *Dracula* (1931), *Frankenstein* (1931), *The Mummy* (1932), *King Kong* (1933), *The Invisible Man* (1933), and *Werewolf of London* (1935).

Perhaps the best way to escape the Depression was to watch the zany comedies of the Marx Brothers. As one Hollywood official explained, the movies of the 1930s were intended to "laugh the big bad wolf of the depression out of the public mind." *The Cocoanuts* (1929), *Animal Crackers* (1930), *Monkey Business* (1931), *Horse Feathers* (1932), and *Duck Soup* (1933) introduced movie-goers to the anarchic antics of Chico, Groucho, Harpo, and Zeppo Marx, who combined slapstick humor with verbal wit to create plotless masterpieces of irreverent satire.

CRITICS ASSAULT THE NEW DEAL

For all their criticisms of New Deal programs, Native Americans and African Americans still voted in large majorities for Franklin Roosevelt. Other New Deal critics, however, hated Roosevelt and despised his policies. Many Republican business executives were so angered by the president's promotion of a welfare state and support for labor unions that they refused to use his name, calling him instead "that man in the White House."

HUEY LONG Others criticized Roosevelt for not doing enough to help the common people. The most potent of the president's "populist" opponents was Huey Pierce Long Jr., the flamboyant Democratic senator from Louisiana. A short, colorful man with wild, curly hair, Long was a classic demagogue, a theatrical politician who appealed to the raw emotions of the masses (populism). The swaggering son of a backwoods farmer, he sported pink suits and pastel shirts, red ties, and two-toned shoes. Long, known as "Kingfish," claimed to be leading a crusade to serve the poor, arguing that Louisiana would be a place where "every man [is] a king, but no one wears a crown."

First as Louisiana's governor, then as its powerful U.S. senator, Long came to view the state as his personal empire. Reporters called him the "dictator of Louisiana." True, he reduced state taxes, improved roads and schools, built charity hospitals, and provided better public services. But in the process, he used bribery, intimidation, and blackmail to get his way.

In 1933, Long arrived in Washington as a supporter of Roosevelt and the New Deal, but he quickly grew suspicious of the NRA's efforts to cooperate with Big Business. Having developed presidential aspirations, he also grew jealous of Roosevelt's popularity.

To launch his presidential candidacy, Long devised a simplistic plan that he called the Share-the-Wealth Society. Long wanted to raise taxes on the wealthiest Americans and redistribute the money to "the people"— giving every poor family $5,000 and every wage worker an annual income of $2,500, providing pensions to retirees, reducing working hours, paying bonuses to military veterans, and enabling every qualified student to attend college. It did not matter that his plan would have spent far more money than his proposed taxes would have raised. As he told a group of Iowa farmers, "Maybe somebody says I don't understand it [government finance]. Well, you don't have to. Just shut your damn eyes and believe it. That's all."

Huey Long As the powerful governor of Louisiana, Long was a shrewd lawyer and consummate "wheeler-dealer" politician.

By early 1935, Long claimed to have enough support to unseat Roosevelt: "He's a phony. . . . He's scared of me. I can outpromise him, and he knows it. People will believe me, and they won't believe him." Long's antics led Roosevelt to declare that the Louisiana senator was "one of the two most dangerous men in the country." (The other was General Douglas MacArthur.)

THE TOWNSEND PLAN Another critic of Roosevelt who championed a form of populist capitalism was Francis E. Townsend, a retired California doctor. Shocked by the sight of three elderly women digging through garbage cans for food scraps, he began promoting the Townsend Recovery Plan in 1934. He wanted the federal government to pay $200 a month to every American over age sixty who agreed to quit working. The recipients would have to spend the money each month.

Townsend claimed that his plan would create jobs for young people by giving older people the means to retire, and it would energize the economy by enabling retirees to buy more products. But like Long's Share-the-Wealth scheme, the numbers in Townsend's plan did not add up. It would have paid retirees, only 9 percent of the population, more than half the total national income.

Townsend, like Long, didn't care about his plan's cost. Not surprisingly, it attracted great support among Americans sixty years and older. Advocates flooded the White House with letters urging Roosevelt to enact it.

FATHER COUGHLIN A third outspoken critic of FDR and the New Deal was Father Charles E. Coughlin, a Canadian-born Roman Catholic "radio priest" in Detroit, Michigan. In fiery weekly broadcasts that attracted as many as 40 million listeners nationwide, he assailed President Roosevelt as "anti-God" and claimed that the New Deal was a Communist conspiracy. Coughlin wanted to put all banks, utilities, oil companies, and "our God-given natural resources" under government control.

During the 1930s, as Fascism and Nazism gained power in Europe, Coughlin became rabidly anti-Semitic, claiming that Roosevelt was a tool of

Promoters of demagogic capitalism Dr. Francis E. Townsend, Rev. Gerald L.K. Smith, and Rev. Charles E. Coughlin (left to right) attend the Townsend Recovery Plan convention in Cleveland, Ohio.

"international Jewish bankers" and relabeling the New Deal the "Jew Deal." He praised Adolf Hitler and the Nazis for killing Jews because they were all Communists. During the 1940 presidential campaign, Coughlin gave a Nazi salute and bragged, "When we get through with the Jews in America, they'll think the treatment they received in Germany was nothing."

Such threats finally galvanized groups across the country, both Jewish and non-Jewish. They exerted enough pressure to force radio stations to drop Coughlin's weekly broadcast. By late 1940, his radio show went off the air.

In the mid-thirties, however, Coughlin was at the peak of his influence, and, along with Francis Townsend and Huey Long, they formed a powerful threat to Roosevelt's reelection. A 1935 poll showed that Long could draw more than 5 million votes as a third-party candidate for president, perhaps enough to prevent Roosevelt's reelection. General Hugh S. Johnson, head of the NRA, warned corporate executives, "You can laugh at Father Coughlin. You can snort at Huey Long—but this country was never under a greater menace."

Roosevelt decided to "steal the thunder" from his three most visible critics by instituting an array of new programs. "I'm fighting Communism, Huey Longism, Coughlinism, Townsendism," he told a reporter in early 1935. He explained that he needed "to save our system, the capitalist system" from such "crackpot ideas."

Opposition from the Court

The growing opposition to the New Deal came from all directions. By the mid-1930s, businesses were filing lawsuits against various elements of the New Deal, and some of them made their way to the U.S. Supreme Court.

On May 27, 1935, the Court killed the National Industrial Recovery Act (NIRA) by a unanimous vote. In *Schechter Poultry Corporation v. United States*, the justices ruled that Congress had given too much authority to the president when the National Recovery Administration (NRA) brought business and labor leaders together to create "codes of fair competition" for their industries—an activity that violated federal anti-trust laws.

On January 6, 1936, in *United States v. Butler*, the Supreme Court declared the Agricultural Adjustment Act's tax on "middle men," the companies that processed food crops and warehoused commodities like cotton, unconstitutional. In response, the Roosevelt administration passed the Agricultural Adjustment Act of 1938, which reestablished the earlier crop-reduction payment programs but left out the tax on processors. Although the AAA helped boost the overall farm economy, conservatives criticized the sweeping powers of the new program.

By the end of its 1936 term, the Supreme Court had ruled against New Deal programs in seven of nine major cases. Similar conservative judicial reasoning, Roosevelt warned, might endanger other New Deal programs—if he did not prevent it.

THE SECOND NEW DEAL

To rescue his legislative program from judicial and political challenges, President Roosevelt launched in January 1935 the second, more radical phase of the New Deal, explaining that "social justice . . . has become a definite goal" of his administration. In his effort to undermine Long's appeal, the president called on Congress to pass legislation that included another federal construction program to employ the jobless; banking reforms; higher taxes on the wealthy; and "social security" programs to protect people during unemployment, old age, and illness. Roosevelt's closest aide, Harry L. Hopkins, told the cabinet: "Boys—this is our hour. We've got to get everything we want—a [public] works program, social security, wages and hours, everything—now or never."

THE WPA In the first three months of 1935, dubbed the Second Hundred Days, Roosevelt convinced Congress to pass most of the **Second New Deal**'s "must" legislation. The results of the Second New Deal (1935-1938) would change the face of American life.

The first major initiative was the $4.8 billion Emergency Relief Appropriation Act. The largest peacetime spending bill in history to that point, it included an array of job programs managed by a new agency, the **Works Progress Administration** (WPA).

The WPA quickly became the nation's largest employer, hiring an average of 2 million people annually over four years. WPA workers built New York's LaGuardia Airport; restored the St. Louis riverfront; and employed a wide range of writers, artists, actors, and musicians in new cultural programs: the Federal Theatre Project, the Federal Art Project, the Federal Music Project, and the Federal Writers' Project.

The National Youth Administration (NYA), also under the WPA, provided part-time employment to students and aided jobless youths. Two future presidents were among the beneficiaries: Twenty-seven-year-old Lyndon B. Johnson directed an NYA program in Texas, and Richard M. Nixon, a Duke University law student, found work through the NYA at 35¢ an hour. The WPA helped some 9 million people before it expired in 1943.

Federal art project A group of WPA artists at work on *Building the Transcontinental Railroad*, a mural celebrating the contributions of foreign newcomers that appears in the immigrants' dining hall on Ellis Island, outside New York City.

THE WAGNER ACT Another major element of the Second New Deal was the National Labor Relations Act, often called the **Wagner Act** in honor of the New York senator, Robert Wagner, who drafted it and convinced Roosevelt to support it. The Wagner Act guaranteed workers the right to organize unions and bargain directly with management about wages and other issues. It also created a National Labor Relations Board to oversee union activities and ensure that management bargained with them in good faith.

SOCIAL SECURITY The Great Depression hit the oldest Americans and those with disabilities especially hard. To address these problems, FDR proposed the **Social Security Act** of 1935. Social Security, he announced, was the "cornerstone" and "supreme achievement" of the New Deal.

The basic concept of government assistance to the elderly was not new. Progressives during the early 1900s had proposed a federal system of social security for the aged, poor, disabled, and unemployed, and other nations had already enacted such programs. The hardships caused by the Great Depression

Social Security A poster distributed by the government to educate the public about the new Social Security Act.

revived the idea, and Roosevelt masterfully guided the legislation through Congress.

The Social Security Act, designed by Secretary of Labor Frances Coralie Perkins, the first woman cabinet member in history, included three major provisions. Its centerpiece was a federal retirement fund for people over sixty-five. Beginning in January 1937, workers and employers contributed payroll taxes to establish the fund, and the first payments were made to recipients. Most of the collected taxes funded pension payments to retirees; the rest went into a trust fund for the future.

Roosevelt stressed that Social Security would not guarantee everyone a comfortable retirement. Rather, it would supplement other sources of income and protect the elderly. Not until the 1950s did voters and politicians come to view Social Security as the *primary* source of retirement income for working-class Americans.

The Social Security Act also set up a shared federal–state unemployment-insurance program, financed by a payroll tax paid by employers. In addition, it committed the national government to a broad range of social-welfare activities based upon the assumption that "unemployables"—people who were unable to work—would remain a state responsibility while the national government would provide work relief for the able-bodied. To that end, the Social Security Act provided federal funding for three state-administered programs—old-age assistance, aid to dependent children, and aid for the blind—and further aid for maternal, child-welfare, and public health services.

When compared with similar programs in Europe, the U.S. Social Security system was—and remains—conservative. It is the only government-managed retirement program in the world financed by taxes on the earnings of workers; most other countries fund such programs out of general government revenues.

The Social Security payroll tax was also a regressive tax because it used a single withholding tax *rate* for everyone, regardless of income level. It thus pinched the poor more than the rich and hurt efforts to revive the economy because it removed from circulation a significant amount of money. In addition, the Social Security system, at the insistence of southern Democrats, *excluded* nearly half the national workforce, some 9.5 million workers who most needed it: low-paid farm laborers, domestic workers (maids and cooks), and the self-employed, a disproportionate percentage of whom were African Americans.

Treasury officials cited a practical reason for this exclusion: how could they collect Social Security taxes from people earning "irregular" wages paid in cash rather than through a weekly payroll system. Others, however, argued that the exclusion was made at the insistence of powerful southern Democrats in Congress afraid of the federal government gaining influence in the South through such "welfare" programs.

Roosevelt regretted the Social Security Act's limitations, but he saw them as necessary compromises to gain congressional approval and withstand court challenges. As he told an aide who criticized funding the program out of employee contributions:

> I guess you're right on the economics, but those taxes were never a problem of economics. They are politics all the way through. We put those payroll contributions there so as to give the contributors a moral, legal, and political right to collect their pensions and their unemployment benefits. With those taxes in there, no damn politician can ever scrap my Social Security program.

FDR also preferred that workers fund their own Social Security pensions because he wanted Americans to view their retirement checks as an *entitlement*—as something that they had paid for and deserved.

Conservatives condemned the Social Security Act as another "tyrannical" expansion of government power. The head of the National Association of Manufacturers told Congress that Social Security would lead to "ultimate socialist control of life and industry." Former president Herbert Hoover refused to apply for a Social Security card because of his opposition to the "radical" program. He received a Social Security number anyway.

TAXING THE RICH Another major bill in the second phase of the New Deal was the Revenue Act of 1935, sometimes called the "Wealth-Tax Act" but popularly known as the "soak-the-rich" tax. It raised tax rates on annual income above $50,000, in part because of stories that many wealthy Americans were not paying taxes. The powerful banker J. P. Morgan, for example, confessed to a Senate committee that he had created fictitious sales of stock to his wife that enabled him to pay no taxes.

Wealthy Americans fumed over Roosevelt's tax and spending policies. Newspaper tycoon William Randolph Hearst growled that the wealth tax was "essentially communism." Roosevelt countered, stressing that "I am fighting communism. . . . I want to save our system, the capitalistic system." Yet he added that saving capitalism and "rebalancing" its essential elements required a more equal "distribution of wealth."

A NEW DIRECTION FOR UNIONS The New Deal reinvigorated the labor union movement. When the National Industrial Recovery Act (NIRA) demanded that industry fairness codes affirm workers' rights to organize, unionists quickly translated it to mean "the president wants you to join the union." John L. Lewis, head of the United Mine Workers (UMW), was among the first to capitalize on the pro-union spirit of the NIRA. He rebuilt the UMW from 150,000 members to 500,000 within a year.

Encouraged by Lewis's success, Sidney Hillman of the Amalgamated Clothing Workers and David Dubinsky of the International Ladies Garment Workers organized clothing industry workers into an industrial union (composed of all types of workers, skilled and unskilled). Opposing them were the smaller craft unions (composed of skilled male workers only, with each union serving just one trade).

In 1935, with the passage of the Wagner Act, industrial unions formed a Committee for Industrial Organization (CIO) to represent their interests. In 1936, the American Federation of Labor (AFL) expelled the CIO unions, which then formed a permanent structure of their own called the Congress of Industrial Organizations (also known by the initials CIO). The rivalry spurred both groups to greater efforts.

The Congress of Industrial Organizations focused on organizing the automobile and steel industries. Until the Supreme Court upheld the Wagner Act in 1937, however, companies used various forms of intimidation to fight the unions. Early in 1937, automobile workers tried a new tactic, the "sit-down strike," in which they refused to leave a workplace until employers had granted them collective-bargaining rights.

Led by the fiery Walter Reuther, thousands of employees at the General Motors plant in Flint, Michigan, stopped production and locked themselves in the plant. "She's ours," yelled one worker participating in the sit-down strike. Company officials responded by turning off the heat to the plant, called in police to harass the strikers with tear gas and cut off their food supply, and threatened to fire the workers. They also pleaded with President Roosevelt to dispatch federal troops. He refused but expressed his displeasure with the strike.

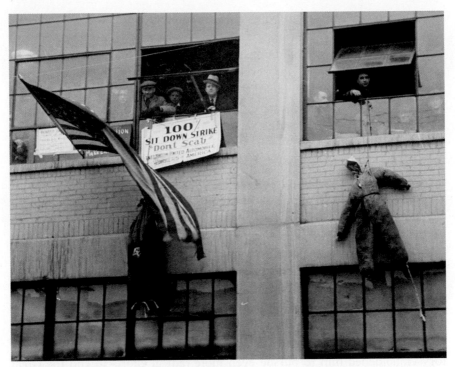

"100 Sit Down Strike – 'Don't Scab'" Unionized automobile workers, striking in 1937, hang effigies of stool pigeons (police informants) from the windows of their factory.

The standoff lasted more than a month before the company relented and signed a contract recognizing the United Automobile Workers (UAW) as a legitimate union. Dubbed the "strike heard round the world," the successful takeover of automobile plants inspired workers and led many to join unions. In the year following the strike, the UAW's membership soared from 30,000 to 500,000.

Roosevelt's Second Term

On June 27, 1936, Franklin Delano Roosevelt accepted the Democratic party's nomination for a second term as president. The Republicans chose Governor Alfred M. Landon of Kansas, a progressive who had endorsed many New Deal programs. "We cannot go back to the days before the depression," Landon scolded conservative Republicans. "We must go forward, facing our new problems."

The Republicans hoped that the followers of Huey Long, Charles E. Coughlin, Francis E. Townsend, and other Roosevelt critics would combine to draw enough Democratic votes away from the president to give Landon a winning margin. That possibility faded, however, when an assassin shot and killed the forty-two-year-old Long in 1935.

In the 1936 election, Roosevelt carried every state except Maine and Vermont, with a popular vote of 27.7 million to Landon's 16.7 million, the largest margin of victory to that point. Democrats would also dominate the new Congress, by 77 to 19 in the Senate and 328 to 107 in the House.

Roosevelt had forged a new electoral coalition that would affect national politics for years to come. While holding the support of most traditional Democrats, North and South, he made strong gains in the West. In the northern cities, he held on to the ethnic groups helped by New Deal welfare policies. Many middle-class voters flocked to support him, as did intellectuals stirred by the ferment of new ideas. The revived labor union movement also threw its support to Roosevelt, and, in the most meaningful shift of all, a majority of African Americans voted for a Democratic president. "My friends, go home and turn Lincoln's picture to the wall," a Pittsburgh journalist told black voters. "That debt has been paid in full."

THE COURT-PACKING PLAN President Roosevelt's landslide victory emboldened him to pursue even more radical efforts to end the Great Depression. One major roadblock stood in the way: the conservative Supreme Court. In Roosevelt's view, it had become an outdated "horse-and-buggy" Court made up of "nine old men" (average age: seventy-one) determined to thwart Roosevelt's attempts to expand executive authority to deal with the economic crisis.

Lawsuits challenging the constitutionality of the Social Security and Wagner Acts were pending. Given the Court's conservative bent and its earlier anti–New Deal rulings, Roosevelt feared that the Second New Deal was in danger of being nullified by Republican judges.

For that reason, he hatched a clumsy plan to "reform" the Supreme Court by enlarging it. Congress, not the Constitution, determines the size of the Court, which over the years had numbered between six and ten justices. In 1937, the number was nine. On February 5, 1937, Roosevelt asked Congress to name up to six new justices, one for each of the current justices over seventy years old, explaining that the aging members of the Court were falling behind in their work and needed help.

The **"Court-packing" plan**, as opponents labeled the plan, backfired, however, and ignited a profound debate among the three branches of government—executive, legislative, and judicial. For the next 168 days, the nation was preoccupied with the constitutionality of Roosevelt's proposal. In the end, both Republicans and Democrats decided that the Court-packing scheme was too manipulative and far too political.

As it turned out, several Supreme Court decisions during the spring of 1937 *upheld* disputed provisions of the Wagner and Social Security Acts. In addition, a conservative justice resigned, and Roosevelt replaced him with a New Dealer, Senator Hugo Black of Alabama.

Still, Roosevelt insisted on forcing his Court-packing bill through Congress. The Senate Judiciary Committee described it as "a measure which should be so emphatically rejected that its parallel will never again be presented to the free representatives of the free people of America." On July 22, 1937, the Senate overwhelmingly voted it down.

It was the worst political blunder and greatest humiliation of Roosevelt's career. The episode fractured the Democratic party and damaged the president's prestige, but the bill's defeat preserved the institutional integrity of the Supreme Court.

A SLUMPING ECONOMY During 1935 and 1936, the economy finally began showing signs of revival. By the spring of 1937, industrial output had risen above the 1929 level before the stock market crash. In 1937, however, President Roosevelt, worried about federal budget deficits and rising inflation, ordered sharp cuts in government spending. The economy stalled, then slid into a slump nearly as deep as that of 1929 after the collapse on Wall Street. In only three months, unemployment rose by 2 million. When the spring of 1938 failed to bring recovery, Roosevelt reversed himself and asked Congress for a new federal spending program. Congress approved $3.3 billion in new expenditures. The increase in government spending helped, but only during the Second World War would employment again reach pre-1929 levels.

The Court-packing fight, the sit-down strikes, and the 1937 recession all undercut Roosevelt's prestige and power. When the 1937 congressional session ended, the only major New Deal initiatives were the Wagner-Steagall National Housing Act and the Bankhead-Jones Farm Tenant Act. The Housing Act, developed by Senator Robert F. Wagner, set up the United States Housing Authority within the Department of Interior. It extended long-term loans to cities to build high-rise public housing projects in blighted neighborhoods and provide subsidized rents for low-income residents. Later, during the Second World War, it would finance housing for employees working in new defense plants.

The Farm Tenant Act created the Farm Security Administration (FSA), which provided loans to keep farmers from losing their land to bankruptcy. It also made loans to tenant farmers to enable them to purchase farms. In the end, however, the FSA did little more than tide a few farmers over during difficult times. A more effective answer to the sluggish economy eventually arrived in the form of national mobilization for war, which landed many struggling tenant farmers in military service or the defense industry, broadened their horizons, and taught them new skills.

In 1938, Congress enacted the Fair Labor Standards Act. It replaced many of the provisions that had been in the NIRA, which were deemed unconstitutional. Like the NIRA, it established a minimum wage of 40¢ an hour and a maximum workweek of forty hours. The act, which applied only to businesses engaged in *interstate* commerce, also prohibited the employment of children under the age of sixteen.

SETBACKS FOR THE PRESIDENT During the late 1930s, Democrats in Congress increasingly split into two factions, with conservative southerners on one side and liberal northerners on the other. Many southern Democrats balked at the party's growing dependence on the votes of northern union members and African Americans. Senator Ellison "Cotton Ed" Smith of South Carolina and several other southern delegates walked out of the 1936 Democratic party convention, with Smith declaring that he would not support any party that views "the Negro as a political and social equal." Other critics believed that President Roosevelt was exercising too much power and spending too much money. Some southern Democrats began to work with conservative Republicans to block proposed New Deal programs.

The congressional elections of November 1938 handed the administration another setback when the Democrats lost 7 seats in the Senate and 80 in the House. In his State of the Union message in 1939, Roosevelt for the first time spoke of the need "to *preserve* our reforms" rather than add to them. The conservative coalition of Republicans and southern Democrats had stalemated him.

A HALFWAY REVOLUTION The New Deal's political momentum petered out in 1939 just as a new world war was erupting in Europe and Asia. What, then, was its impact? In hindsight, it had more energy than coherence. Many New Deal programs failed or were poorly conceived and implemented. But several programs changed life for the better: Social Security, federal regulation of stock markets and banks, minimum wage levels for workers, federally insured bank accounts, and government-sanctioned labor unions.

The greatest triumph of the New Deal, however, was its demonstration that American democracy could cope with the collapse of capitalism. A self-proclaimed "preacher President," Franklin Roosevelt raised the nation's spirits and its income through his relentless optimism and unprecedented activism. As a CCC worker recalled late in life, Roosevelt "restored a sense of confidence and morale and hope—hope being the greatest of all." New Deal programs provided stability for tens of millions of people. "We aren't on relief anymore," one woman noted with pride. "My husband is working for the government."

The greatest failure of the New Deal was its inability to restore prosperity and end record levels of unemployment. In 1939, an estimated 10 million Americans—nearly 17 percent of the workforce—remained jobless. Only the Second World War would finally produce full employment.

Roosevelt was an idealist without illusions. Energetic pragmatism was his greatest strength—and weakness. He admitted that he often acted out of conflicting convictions. "I am a juggler," he explained. "I never let my right hand know what my left hand does." He sharply increased the regulatory powers of the federal government and laid the foundation for what would become an expanding system of social welfare programs.

The result was both revolutionary and conservative. New Deal initiatives left a legacy of unprecedented innovations: a joint federal-state system of unemployment insurance; a compulsory, federally administered retirement system; financial support for families with dependent children; maternal and child-care programs; and several public health programs. The New Deal also improved working conditions and raised wage levels for millions.

Roosevelt had sought to preserve the basic capitalist economic structure while providing protection to the most vulnerable. In this sense, the New Deal represented a "halfway revolution" that permanently altered the nation's social and political landscape. "During the ten years between 1929 and 1939," marveled an appreciative social worker in 1940, "more progress was made in public welfare and relief than in the three hundred years after this country was first settled." In a time of peril, Roosevelt created for Americans a more secure future.

CHAPTER REVIEW

SUMMARY

- **The First New Deal**   During his early months in office, Franklin Roosevelt pushed through Congress the *First New Deal (1933–1935)*, which propped up the banking industry with the *Federal Deposit Insurance Corporation (1933)*, provided short-term emergency work relief and promoted industrial recovery with the *National Recovery Administration (1933)*, raised agricultural prices with the *Agricultural Adjustment Act (1933)*, and enforced new laws and regulations on Wall Street with the *Securities and Exchange Commission (1934)*. Most of the early New Deal programs helped end the economy's downward spiral but still left millions unemployed and mired in poverty, despite the earnest efforts of First Lady Eleanor Roosevelt, who became justly famous for her strenuous efforts to help the poor, minorities, and refugees.

- **New Deal under Fire**   The Supreme Court ruled that many of the First New Deal programs were unconstitutional violations of private property and states' rights. Conservatives criticized the New Deal for expanding the scope and reach of the federal government so much that it was steering the nation toward socialism. The "radio priest," Father Charles E. Coughlin, charged that the New Deal was a Jewish-atheist-Communist conspiracy. Other critics did not think New Deal reforms went far enough. Senator Huey Long of Louisiana and Dr. Francis Townsend of California proposed radical plans to reshape the distribution of wealth from the rich to the poor. African Americans criticized the widespread racial discrimination in New Deal policies and agencies.

- **The Second New Deal and the New Deal's Legacy**   Roosevelt responded to the criticism and continuing economic hardship with a *Second New Deal (1935–1938)*, which sought to reshape the nation's social structure by expanding the role of the federal government. Many of the programs making up the Second New Deal, such as the *Works Progress Administration*, *Social Security*, and the *Wagner Act*, aimed to achieve greater social justice by establishing new regulatory agencies and laying the foundation of a federal social welfare system. Frustrated by the Supreme Court's opposition to the First New Deal, Roosevelt proposed his *Court-packing scheme (1937)*, but it was rejected by the Senate. Support for the New Deal began to lose steam in the late 1930s amid the lingering effects of the Great Depression. However, the New Deal established the idea that the federal government should provide at least a minimal quality of life for all Americans, and it provided people with some security against a future crisis, reaffirming for millions a faith in American capitalism.

CHRONOLOGY

November 1932	Franklin D. Roosevelt is elected president
March 1933	Congress passes the Emergency Banking Relief Act
	Congress establishes the Civilian Conservation Corps
May 1933	Congress creates the Tennessee Valley Authority and the Agricultural Adjustment Act
June 1933	Congress establishes the Federal Deposit Insurance Corporation (Glass-Steagall Banking Act) and passes the National Industrial Recovery Act
December 1933	Prohibition repealed with the passage of the Twenty-First Amendment to the Constitution
May 1935	Supreme Court finds the National Industrial Recovery Act unconstitutional
1935	President Roosevelt creates the Works Progress Administration
1936	President Roosevelt is reelected in a landslide
1937	Social Security taxes and payments begin

KEY TERMS

First New Deal (1933–1935) p. 1170

Federal Deposit Insurance Corporation (FDIC) (1933) p. 1171

Securities and Exchange Commission (1934) p. 1172

National Recovery Administration (NRA) (1933) p. 1176

Agricultural Adjustment Act (1933) p. 1177

Dust Bowl p. 1177

Second New Deal (1935–1938) p. 1196

Works Progress Administration (WPA) (1935) p. 1196

Wagner Act (1935) p. 1197

Social Security Act (1935) p. 1197

Court-packing plan (1937) p. 1202

 INQUIZITIVE

Go to InQuizitive to see what you've learned—and learn what you've missed—with personalized feedback along the way.

26 The Second World War

1933–1945

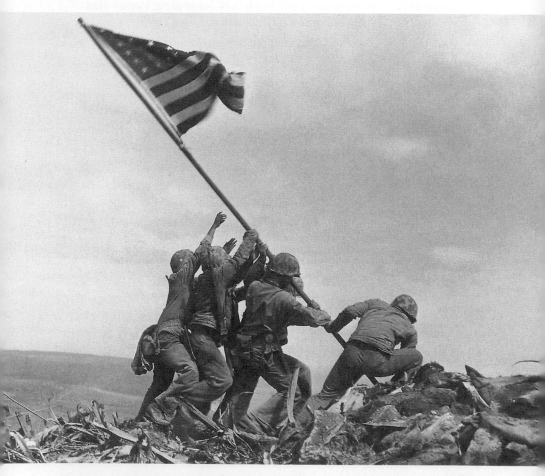

***Raising the Flag on Iwo Jima* (February 23, 1945)** Five members of the United States Marine Corps raise the U.S. flag on Mount Suribachi, during the Battle of Iwo Jima. Three of them would die within days after this photograph was taken. The image earned photographer Joe Rosenthal the Pulitzer Prize. A bronze statue of this scene is the centerpiece of the Marine Corps War Memorial in Virginia.

When Franklin Roosevelt became president in 1933, he shared with most Americans a determination to stay out of international disputes. While the United States had become deeply involved in global trade during the twenties, it had remained aloof from global conflicts. So-called isolationists insisted that there was no justification for America to become embroiled in international affairs, much less another major war. With each passing year during the 1930s, however, Germany, Italy, and Japan threatened the peace and stability of Europe and Asia.

Roosevelt strove to keep the United States out of what he called the "spreading epidemic of world lawlessness," as fascist dictatorships in Germany and Italy and ultranationalist militarists in Japan violated international law by invading neighboring countries. By the end of the decade, Roosevelt had decided that the only way for the United States to avoid another war was to offer all possible assistance to Great Britain, France, and China.

Roosevelt's efforts to stop "aggressor nations" ignited a fierce debate between isolationists and interventionists that ended suddenly on December 7, 1941, when Japan staged a surprise attack against U.S. military bases at Pearl Harbor in Hawaii. America was again involved in a world war. It would become the most significant event of the twentieth century, engulfing five continents and leaving few people untouched.

The Japanese attack unified the country as never before. Men and women rushed to join the armed forces. Eventually, 16.4 million Americans would serve in the military during the war, including 350,000 women. The massive

focus questions

1. How did German and Japanese actions lead to the outbreak of war in Europe and Asia?

2. How did President Roosevelt and Congress respond to the outbreak of wars in Europe and Asia between 1933 and 1941?

3. What were the effects of the Second World War on American society?

4. What major factors enabled the United States and its allies to win the war in Europe?

5. How were the Japanese defeated in the war in the Pacific?

6. How did President Roosevelt and the Allies work to shape the postwar world?

government spending required to wage total war boosted industrial production and wrenched the economy out of the Great Depression.

The United States and its allies emerged victorious from the costliest and most destructive war in history. More than 50 million people were killed in the war between 1939 and 1945—perhaps 60 percent of them civilians, including millions of Jews and other ethnic and social minorities in Nazi death camps and Soviet concentration camps.

The scope and scale of the Second World War transformed America's role in the world. Isolationism gave way to internationalism. By 1945, America was the world's most powerful nation, with new international interests and responsibilities. Instead of bringing peace, however, the end of the fighting led to a new "cold war" between two former allies, the United States and the Soviet Union.

THE RISE OF FASCISM IN EUROPE

In 1917, Woodrow Wilson had led the United States into the Great War to make the world "safe for democracy." In fact, though, democracy was in retreat after 1919, while Soviet communism was on the march. So, too, was **fascism**, a radical form of totalitarian government in which a dictator uses propaganda and brute force to seize control of all aspects of national life—the economy, the armed forces, the legal and educational systems, and the press. Fascism in Germany and Italy thrived on a violent ultranationalist patriotism and almost hysterical emotionalism built upon claims of racial superiority and the simmering resentments that grew out of defeat in the Great War.

At the same time, halfway around the world, the Japanese government fell under the control of expansionists eager to conquer China and most of Asia. Japanese leaders were convinced that theirs was a "master race" with a mission to lead a resurgent Asia, just as Adolf Hitler claimed that Germany's mission was to use its supposed racial supremacy to dominate Europe. By 1941, there would be only a dozen or so democratic nations left on earth.

ITALY AND GERMANY In 1922, Benito Mussolini and 40,000 of his black-shirted supporters seized control of Italy, taking advantage of a government incapable of dealing with widespread unemployment, runaway inflation, mass strikes, and fears of communism. By 1925, Mussolini was wielding dictatorial power as "Il Duce" (the Leader). He called his version of antisocialist totalitarian nationalism *fascism*. He eliminated all political parties except the Fascists and ordered his political opponents murdered. There was something clownish about the strutting, chest-thumping Mussolini, who claimed that "my animal instincts are always right," when in fact he was at best a mediocre statesman.

There was nothing amusing, however, about his German counterpart, the Austrian-born Adolf Hitler, whom Mussolini privately described as "an aggressive little man . . . probably a liar, and certainly mad."

Hitler's transformation during the 1920s from social misfit to head of the National Socialist German Workers' (Nazi) party startled the world and led many to underestimate the man and his appeal. As late as 1930, a German magazine editor dismissed Hitler as a "half-insane rascal," a "pathetic dunderhead," and a "nowhere fool" whose Nazi organization had "no future at all."

Yet Hitler used his talents at demagoguery, lying, and showmanship to organize a grassroots movement through nativist appeals to the masses.

Fascist propaganda Benito Mussolini's headquarters in Rome's Palazzo Braschi, which bore an oversized reproduction of his head.

Hitler and the Nazis claimed that they represented a German "master race" whose "purity and strength" were threatened by liberals and other "inferior" peoples: Jews, socialists, Romani (gypsies), Communists, and homosexuals. "Democracy must be destroyed," he shouted.

Hitler promised to make Germany strong again by renouncing the Versailles treaty, defying the limits on its armed forces, and establishing a Greater German Empire that would give the nation what Hitler called "living space" to expand, dominate "lesser" races, and rid the continent of Jews. He was appointed chancellor on January 30, 1933.

Like Mussolini, Hitler was idolized by the masses. He declared himself absolute leader, or *Führer*, and in 1934 became Germany's president and supreme commander of the armed forces. All the while, he was imposing a totalitarian regime. He banned all political parties except the Nazis, had his opponents jailed or killed, created a secret police force (the *Gestapo)*, and stripped people of voting rights. There would be no more elections, unions,

Adolf Hitler Hitler performs the Nazi salute at a rally. The giant banners, triumphant music, powerful oratory, and expansive parades were all designed to stir excitement and allegiance among Nazis.

or strikes. All non-German books were burned, and the Nazis scapegoated innocent Jews as the cause of most of Germany's problems.

Hitler's Nazi police state employed tyranny and terrorism, propaganda and censorship to impose absolute control over Germany. Two million brown-shirted thugs ("storm troopers") fanned out across the nation, burning books and persecuting, imprisoning, and murdering Communists, Jews, Gypsies—and their sympathizers.

Most Germans gloried in Hitler's ruthless aggressiveness in crushing all opposition. At a famous rally in Nuremburg, his supporters screamed: "We want one leader! Nothing for us! Everything for Germany!"

THE EXPANDING AXIS As the 1930s unfolded, a catastrophic series of events sent the world hurtling toward disaster. In 1931–1932, some 10,000 Japanese troops had occupied Manchuria, in northeast China. It was a territory rich in raw materials; mineral deposits, including iron ore and coal; and farmland needed for Japanese expansion. At the time, China was fragmented by civil war between Communists led by Mao Zedong and Nationalists led by Chiang Kai-shek. The Japanese took advantage of China's weakness to proclaim Manchuria's independence, renaming it the "Republic of Manchukuo."

While Japan was expanding its control in Asia, Mussolini was on the march. In 1935, he launched a reconquest of Ethiopia, a nation in eastern Africa that Italy had controlled until 1896. When the League of Nations retaliated by imposing economic sanctions on Italy, Mussolini expressed surprise that European leaders would prefer a "horde of barbarian Negroes" in Ethiopia over Italy, the "mother of civilization."

In 1935, Hitler, in flagrant violation of the Versailles treaty, began rebuilding Germany's armed forces. He reinstated compulsory military service and started building an air force. The next year, he sent 35,000 soldiers into the Rhineland, the demilitarized buffer zone between France and Germany. In a staged vote, 99 percent of the Germans living in the Rhineland approved Hitler's action. The failure of France and Great Britain to counter these moves convinced Hitler that the western democracies were cowards and would not try to stop him.

The year 1936 also witnessed the outbreak of the Spanish Civil War, which began when Spanish troops (the Nationalists) loyal to General Francisco Franco, with the support of the Roman Catholic Church, revolted against the fragile new democratic government (the Republicans). Hitler and Mussolini rushed troops (called "volunteers" to disguise their purpose), warplanes, and military and financial aid to support Franco's fascist insurgency. Some 2,800 American volunteers joined the Abraham Lincoln Battalion in defense of Spain's republican government, supported by weapons from the Soviet Union.

While peace in Europe was unraveling, the Japanese government fell under the control of aggressive militarists. On July 7, 1937, Japanese and Chinese soldiers clashed at China's Marco Polo Bridge, near Beijing. The incident quickly escalated into the Sino-Japanese War.

By December, the Japanese had captured the Nationalist Chinese capital of Nanjing. They looted the city and murdered and tortured as many as 300,000 civilians in what came to be called the Rape of Nanjing. Thereafter, the Sino-Japanese War bogged down into a stalemate.

FROM ISOLATIONISM TO INTERVENTION

Most Americans responded to the mounting foreign crises by deepening their commitment to isolationism. In his 1933 inaugural address, President Roosevelt announced that he would continue to promote what Woodrow Wilson had earlier called "the good neighbor policy" in the Western Hemisphere, declaring that no nation "has the right to intervene in the internal or external affairs of another."

The nation's isolationist mood was reinforced by a Senate inquiry into the role of bankers and businesses in the American government's decision to enter the Great War. Chaired by Senator Gerald P. Nye of North Dakota, the "Nye Committee" concluded that weapons makers and bankers (the "merchants of death") had spurred U.S. intervention in 1917 and were continuing to "help frighten nations into military activity."

U.S. NEUTRALITY In 1935, *Christian Century* magazine declared that "ninety-nine Americans out of a hundred would today regard as an imbecile anyone who might suggest that, in the event of another European war, the United States should again participate in it."

Such isolationism led President Roosevelt to sign the first of several **"neutrality laws"** to help avoid the supposed mistakes that had led the nation into the Great War. The Neutrality Act of 1935 prohibited American manufacturers from selling weapons to nations at war ("belligerents") and banned citizens from traveling on ships owned by belligerents. In 1936, Congress revised the Neutrality Act by banning loans to warring nations.

Roosevelt, however, was not so sure that the United States could or should remain neutral. In October 1937, he delivered a speech in Chicago, the

Neutrality A 1938 cartoon shows U.S. foreign policy entangled by the serpent of isolationism.

heartland of isolationism, in which he called for international cooperation to "quarantine the aggressors." But his appeal fell flat as isolationists warned he would get America embroiled in another war.

The Neutrality Act of 1937 allowed Roosevelt to sell nonmilitary goods to warring nations on a "cash-and-carry" basis—that is, a nation would have to pay cash and then carry the U.S.-made goods in its own ships. This would preserve America's profitable trade with warring nations without running the risk of being drawn into the fighting.

THE AXIS ALLIANCE In 1937, Japan joined Germany and Italy in establishing the Rome-Berlin-Tokyo **"Axis" alliance** because they claimed that all other nations would be forced to revolve around the "axis" created by those three dominant nations. Hitler and Mussolini vowed to create a "new order in Europe," while Japanese imperialists pursued their "divine right" to control east Asia by creating what they called the Greater East Asia Co-Prosperity Sphere.

ANSCHLUSS Hitler's madness broke over Europe in dark waves. In March 1938, he forced the *Anschluss* (union) of Austria with Germany. His triumphant return to his native country delighted crowds waving Nazi flags and tossing flowers. Soon, "Jews not Wanted" signs appeared in Austrian cities. When Mussolini congratulated Hitler for his daring move, the German dictator told his Italian partner that he would "never forget him for this. Never, never, never—whatever happens."

A month later, after arresting more than 70,000 anti-Nazis, German leaders announced that 99.75 percent of Austrian voters had "approved" the forced union with Germany. (In fact, it was a sham election, since some 400,000 Austrians, mostly liberals and Jews, were prevented from voting.)

Soon the Nazi government in Austria began arresting or murdering opponents and imprisoning or exiling Jews, including the famed psychiatrist Sigmund Freud.

Again, no nation stepped up to oppose Hitler, in part because it was so hard to assess the German leader's motives, predict his moves, and understand his ambition—or his lunacy.

THE MUNICH PACT (1938) Hitler turned next to the Sudeten territory (Sudetenland), a mountainous region in western Czechoslovakia along the German border where more than 3 million ethnic Germans lived. It was also where the Czechs had positioned their defensive positions in the event of a war with Germany. Hitler threatened to ignite a European war unless the Sudetenland was ceded to Germany. In response, timid British and French leaders tried to "appease" Hitler, hoping that if they agreed to his demands for the Sudeten territory he would stop his aggressions.

On September 30, 1938, the British prime minister, Neville Chamberlain, and the French prime minister, Édouard Daladier, joined Mussolini and Hitler in signing the notorious Munich Pact, which transferred the Sudetenland to Germany. In Prague, the capital, Czechs listened to the official announcement of the Munich Pact with the excruciating sadness of people too weak to preserve their own independence. As pawns in the chess game of European politics, the Czechs now faced a grim future. President Roosevelt privately grumbled that Britain and France had left Czechoslovakia "to paddle its own canoe" and predicted that they would "wash the blood from their Judas Iscariot hands."

The naive Chamberlain claimed that the Munich treaty had provided "peace for our time. Peace with honor." Winston Churchill, a member of the British Parliament who would become prime minister in May 1940, strongly disagreed. In a speech to the House of Commons, he claimed that "England has been offered a choice between war and shame. She has chosen shame, and will get war. . . . This is only the beginning of the reckoning."

Churchill was right. Hitler never intended to honor the Munich Pact. Although the Nazi tyrant had promised that the Sudetenland would be his last territorial demand, he scrapped his pledge in March 1939 and sent German tanks and soldiers to conquer the remainder of the multinational and multiethnic Czech Republic. The European democracies, having shrunk their armies after the Great War, continued to cower in the face of his seemingly unstoppable military advances.

After German troops seized Czechoslovakia on March 15, 1939, Hitler called it "the greatest day of my life." He immediately set about oppressing the 263,000 Jews living in Czechoslovakia, lumping them together with "thieves, criminals, swindlers, insane people, and alcoholics." By the end of May, the Nazis were filling prisons with Czechs who resisted or resented the German occupation. Hitler's conquest of Czechoslovakia convinced Roosevelt that fascism and Nazism must be stopped. Hitler and Mussolini were "madmen" who "respect force and force alone." Throughout late 1938 and 1939, Roosevelt tried to persuade Congress to increase military spending in anticipation of a possible war.

THE CONQUEST OF POLAND In 1939, Hitler, having decided that he had "the world in my pocket," turned to Poland, Germany's eastern neighbor. Conquering Poland would give the German army a clear path to invade the Soviet Union, especially the fertile Ukraine region, where much of the world's grains were grown.

To ensure that the Soviets did not interfere, Hitler camouflaged his intentions. On August 23, 1939, he shocked the world by signing the Nazi-Soviet Non-Aggression Pact with Josef Stalin, the brutish, anti-fascist Soviet premier.

Stalin had become the Soviet leader after Vladimir Lenin's death in 1924. Soon after, he had launched a Great Purge, in which some 8 million "critics" of his iron-fisted rule were executed and millions more exiled to forced labor camps. Two thirds of the Communist party leadership and some 35,000 army officers were victims of Stalin's reign of terror.

The announcement of the Nazi-Soviet treaty surprised a world that had assumed fascism and communism to be mortal enemies. Stalin and Hitler agreed to divide northern and eastern Europe between them. The Germans took most of Poland, and the Soviet

Josef Stalin Brutal leader of the Soviet Union who rose to power after the death of Vladimir Lenin.

Union claimed a "sphere of interest" in Estonia, Latvia, Finland, and a portion of Lithuania.

Just nine days later, at dawn on September 1, an estimated 1.5 million German troops invaded Poland from the north, south, and west. Hitler ordered them "to kill without mercy men, women, and children of the Polish race or language." He also directed that all terminally ill patients in German hospitals be killed to make room for soldiers wounded in Poland.

The invasion of Poland was the final straw for the western democracies. On September 3, Great Britain and France declared war against Germany. The nations making up the British Empire and Commonwealth—Canada, India, Australia, New Zealand—joined the war as Americans watched in horror. "This nation," declared Franklin Roosevelt, "will remain a neutral nation, but I cannot ask that every American remain neutral in thought as well. Even a neutral cannot be asked to close his mind or conscience."

Sixteen days after German troops stormed across the Polish border, the Soviet Union invaded Poland from the east. Pressed from all sides, 700,000 poorly equipped Polish soldiers surrendered after a few weeks. On October 6, 1939, the Nazis and Soviets divided Poland between them.

Hitler's goal was to obliterate Polish civilization, especially the Jewish population, and to Germanize the country. For his part, Stalin wanted to recapture Polish territory lost during the Great War. Over the next five years, millions of Poles were arrested, deported, enslaved, and murdered. In April and May 1940, the Russians executed some 22,000 Polish military officers to ensure that its conquered neighbor would never mount a rebellion.

In late November 1939, the Soviets invaded neighboring Finland, leading President Roosevelt to condemn their "wanton disregard for law." Outnumbered five to one, Finnish troops held off the invaders for three months before being forced to negotiate a treaty that gave the Soviet Union a tenth of Finland.

REVISING THE NEUTRALITY ACT In September 1939, President Roosevelt decided that the United States must do more to stop "aggressor" nations. He summoned Congress into special session to revise the Neutrality Act. "I regret that Congress passed the Act," the president said. "I regret equally that I signed the Act."

The Neutrality Act of 1939 allowed Britain and France to send freighters to the United States to bring back American military supplies. It was, said Roosevelt, the best way "to keep us out of war." Public opinion supported such measures as long as other nations did the fighting.

WAR IN EUROPE The war in Europe settled into a three-month stalemate during early 1940, as Hitler's generals waited out the winter. Then, at dawn on April 9, Germany attacked again, invading Denmark and landing along the Norwegian coast. German paratroopers, the first used in warfare, seized Norway's airports. Denmark fell in a day, Norway within a few weeks. On May 10, German forces invaded the Low Countries—Belgium, Luxembourg, and the Netherlands (Holland). Luxembourg fell the first day, the Netherlands three days later. Belgium held out until May 28.

A few days later, German tanks roared into northern France. "The fight beginning today," Hitler declared, "decides the fate of the German nation for the next thousand years!" His blitzkrieg ("lightning war") strategy centered on speed. Columns of tanks, motorized artillery, and truck-borne infantry, all supported by warplanes and paratroopers, moved so fast they stunned their opponents. Winston Churchill called the Allied performance "a colossal military disaster."

A British force sent to help the Belgians and French fled along with French troops toward the coast, with the Germans in hot pursuit. On May 26, Churchill organized a desperate weeklong evacuation of British, Belgian,

Canadian, and French soldiers from the beaches at Dunkirk. Despite attacks by German warplanes, some 338,000 soldiers escaped in 700 warships and an array of privately-owned vessels volunteered for the emergency: fishing trawlers, barges, yachts, and other pleasure craft. The fleeing troops left behind vast stockpiles of vehicles, weaponry, and ammunition. "Wars are not won by evacuations," observed Prime Minister Churchill, "but there was a victory inside this deliverance."

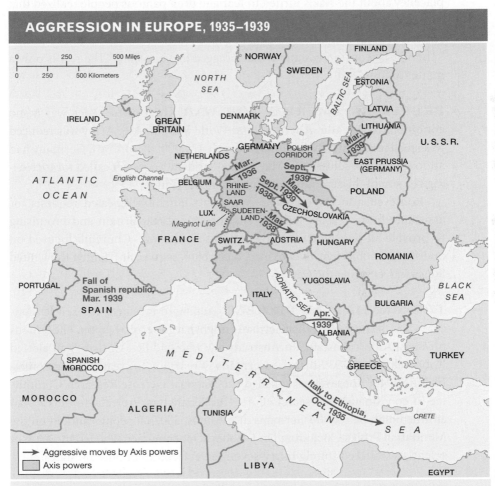

AGGRESSION IN EUROPE, 1935–1939

■ Keeping in mind the terms of the Treaty of Versailles ending the First World War, explain why Hitler began his campaign of expansion by invading the Rhineland and the Sudetenland.

■ Why did the German attack on Poland begin the Second World War, whereas Hitler's previous invasions of Austria and Czechoslovakia did not?

While the evacuation was unfolding, German forces decimated the remaining French armies. Tens of thousands of panicked refugees and soldiers clogged the roads to Paris. Mussolini also declared war on France and Great Britain, which he dismissed as "the reactionary democracies of the West."

On June 14, 1940, German soldiers marched unopposed through the streets of Paris. Eight days later, French leaders officially surrendered, whereupon the Germans established a puppet fascist French government in the city of Vichy.

The rapid fall of France astonished the world. In the United States, complacency about the Nazis turned to fear and even panic as people realized that the Germans, who now ruled most of western Europe, could eventually assault America. Great Britain stood alone against Hitler's relentless military power. "The war is won," an ecstatic Hitler bragged to Mussolini. "The rest is only a matter of time."

PREPARING AMERICA FOR WAR The United States was in no condition to wage war. After the First World War, the U.S. Army was reduced to a small force; by 1939, it numbered only 175,000. By contrast, Germany had almost 5 million soldiers. In May 1940, President Roosevelt called for increasing the size of the army and adding 50,000 warplanes.

Roosevelt also responded to Winston Churchill's repeated requests for assistance by increasing military shipments to Great Britain and promising to provide all possible "aid to the Allies short of war." Churchill focused on one strategic objective: to convince, coax, bluff, seduce, or frighten the United States into entering the war.

THE MANHATTAN PROJECT Adding to President Roosevelt's concerns was the possibility that Germany might have a secret weapon. The famous physicist Albert Einstein, an Austrian Jew who had fled Nazism, had alerted Roosevelt in late 1939 that the Germans were trying to create atomic bombs. In June 1940, Roosevelt established the National Defense Research Committee to coordinate a top-secret effort—the Manhattan Project—to develop an atomic bomb before the Germans did. Almost 200,000 people worked on the Manhattan Project, including Dr. J. Robert Oppenheimer, who led the team of scientists scattered among thirty-seven secret facilities in thirteen states.

THE BATTLE OF BRITAIN Having conquered western Europe, Hitler began preparing to invade Great Britain ("Operation Sea Lion"). He launched the Battle of Britain, as the Germans sought to destroy the Royal Air Force (RAF). The Nazis deployed some 2,500 warplanes, outnumbering the

RAF two to one. "Never has a nation been so naked before its foes," Winston Churchill admitted.

Churchill became the symbol of Britain's determination to stop Hitler. With his bulldog face, ever-present cigar, and "V for Victory" gesture, he urged the citizenry to make the defense of their homeland "their finest hour." He breathed defiance as the British built fortifications, laid mines, dug trenches, and mobilized for war. The British, Churchill pledged, would confront Hitler's invaders with "blood, toil, tears, and sweat." They would "never surrender."

In July and August 1940, the German air force (*Luftwaffe*) launched raids against military targets across southeast England. RAF pilots employed radar, a secret new technology, to fend off the assault, ultimately destroying 1,700 German warplanes.

Winston Churchill Prime Minister of Great Britain during the Second World War.

Hitler then ordered his bombers to target civilians and cities (especially London) in night raids designed to terrorize civilians and force a surrender. In what came to be called "the Blitz" during September and October 1940, German bombers destroyed a million homes and killed 40,000 civilians. "The last three nights in London," reported the U.S. ambassador to Great Britain on September 10, "have been simply hell."

The Blitz, however, enraged rather than demoralized the British. A London newspaper headline summarized the nation's courage and mood: "Is That the Best You Can Do, Adolf?" The British success in the air proved decisive. Hitler scrapped his invasion plans and turned his attention to the Soviet Union. It was the first battle he had lost, and it was Britain's finest hour.

"**ALL AID SHORT OF WAR**" During the Battle of Britain, Franklin Roosevelt began an urgent and eloquent campaign to convince Americans that isolationism was impractical and even dangerous. His phrase, "all aid short of war," became the label for his efforts to help Great Britain.

The London "Blitz" An aerial photograph of London set aflame by German bombing raids in 1940. Winston Churchill responded, "We shall never surrender."

Roosevelt was especially concerned about a German invasion of the British Isles. "It is now most urgent," Prime Minister Churchill cabled Roosevelt, "that you let us have the destroyers" needed to stop such an invasion.

To address the challenge, Roosevelt and Churchill negotiated a trade on September 2, 1940, called the Destroyers for Bases Agreement, by which fifty old U.S. warships went to the British Royal Navy in return for allowing the United States to build military bases on British island colonies in the Caribbean.

Two weeks later, on September 16, 1940, a reluctant Congress approved the first peacetime conscription (military draft) in American history. The Selective Training and Service Act, passed by a single vote, required all 16 million men ages twenty-one to thirty-five to register for the draft at one of 6,500 local draft boards. (The minimum age was later reduced to eighteen and the maximum increased to forty-five.)

A SAVAGE DEBATE The world crisis transformed Franklin Roosevelt. Having been stalemated for much of his second term by congressional opposition to the New Deal, he was revitalized by the need to stop Nazism. Yet his efforts outraged isolationists. A prominent Democrat later remembered that the dispute between isolationists and so-called interventionists was "the most savage political debate during my lifetime."

Isolationists, mostly midwestern and western Republicans, formed the America First Committee to oppose "military preparedness." Charles Lindbergh, the first man to fly solo across the Atlantic Ocean, led the effort. Openly sympathetic to Nazism and fascism, he charged that Roosevelt's efforts to help Britain were driven by Jews who owned "our motion pictures, our press, our radio, and our government." Were it not for the Jews in America, Lindbergh claimed, "we would not be on the verge of war today." He assured Americans that Britain was doomed and that they should join hands with Hitler: "Democracy as we know it is a thing of the past," and "one of the first steps must be to disenfranchise the Negro."

ROOSEVELT'S THIRD TERM Charles Lindbergh and other isolationists sought to make the 1940 presidential campaign a debate about the war. The Republicans nominated Wendell L. Willkie of Indiana, a plainspoken corporate lawyer and former Democrat who had voted for FDR in 1932.

Willkie called Roosevelt a "warmonger" and predicted that "if you re-elect him, you may expect war in April, 1941." Roosevelt responded that he had "said this before, but I shall say it again and again and again: Your boys are not going to be sent into any foreign wars." In November 1940, Roosevelt won an unprecedented third term by 27 million votes to Willkie's 22 million and by an even more decisive margin, 449 to 82, in the electoral college. Winston Churchill wrote Roosevelt that he had "prayed for your success and I am truly thankful for it."

THE LEND-LEASE ACT Once reelected, Roosevelt found an ingenious way to provide more aid to Britain, whose cash was running out. The **Lend-Lease Act** (officially "An Act to Promote the Defense of the United States"), introduced in Congress on January 10, 1941, allowed the president to lend or lease military equipment to "any country whose defense the President deems vital to the defense of the United States." It was a bold challenge to the isolationists. As Senator Hiram Johnson of California claimed, "This bill is war."

Roosevelt told critics that "no nation can appease the Nazis. No man can turn a tiger into a kitten by stroking it." The United States, he added, would provide everything the British needed while doing the same for China in its war against Japan, all in an effort to keep Americans from going to war themselves. Churchill shored up the president's efforts by announcing that Britain did not need American troops to defeat Hitler: "Give us the tools and we will

Lend-Lease Act Members of the isolationist "Mother's Crusade," urging defeat of the lend-lease program, kneel in prayer in front of the Capitol in Washington, D.C. They feared the program aiding America's allies would bring the United States into the wars in Europe and Asia.

finish the job." In early March, 1941, Congress approved the Lend-Lease Act. "Let not the dictators of Europe or Asia doubt our unanimity now," Roosevelt declared.

Between 1941 and 1945, the Lend-Lease program would ship $50 billion worth of supplies to Great Britain, the Soviet Union, France, China, and other Allied nations. Churchill called it the most generous "act in the history of any nation."

GERMANY INVADES THE SOVIET UNION While Americans continued to debate President Roosevelt's efforts to help Great Britain, the European war expanded. In the spring of 1941, German troops joined Italian armies in Libya, forcing the British army in North Africa to withdraw to Egypt. In April 1941, Nazi armies overwhelmed Yugoslavia and Greece. With Hungary, Romania, and Bulgaria also under Nazi control, Hitler ruled most of Europe. His ambition was unbounded, however, and he remained dangerously unpredictable.

On June 22, 1941, Hitler launched "Operation Barbarossa," a shocking invasion of the Soviet Union, his supposed ally. His objective was to destroy communism (his long-standing obsession), enslave the vast population of the Soviet Union, open up new lands for German settlement, and exploit Russia's considerable natural resources.

Hitler's decision was the defining moment of the European war. The 3 million German soldiers sent to the Soviet Union would be worn down and thrown back. At first, however, the invasion seemed a great success, as entire Soviet armies and cities were destroyed. During the second half of 1941, an estimated 3 million Soviet soldiers—50 percent of the Soviet army—were captured. For four months, the Soviets retreated in the face of the German blitzkrieg.

During the summer of 1941, German forces surrounded Leningrad (now called St. Petersburg) and lay siege to the city. Food and supplies became scarce; hunger alone would kill 800,000 Russians. Desperate people ate cats, dogs, rats, and even sawdust. As a bitterly cold winter set in, corpses were left to freeze in the snow. Still, Leningrad held out and became known as the city that refused to die. By December 1941, other German armies had reached the suburbs of Moscow, 1,000 miles east of Berlin.

To American isolationists, Germany's invasion of Russia confirmed that the United States should stay out of the war and let the two dictatorships bleed each other to death. Roosevelt, however, insisted on including the Soviet Union in the Lend-Lease agreement. He and Churchill were determined to keep the Russians fighting Hitler so that the Nazis could not concentrate on Great Britain. In 1941 alone, America sent thousands of trucks, tanks, guns, and warplanes to the Soviet Union, along with food (especially Spam) and enough blankets, shoes, and boots to clothe every Soviet soldier.

Gradually, Josef Stalin slowed the Nazi advance by forcing the Russian people to fight—or be killed. During the Battle of Moscow, Soviet defenders executed 8,000 civilians charged with "cowardice." Stalin ordered that Soviet soldiers who surrendered be classified as traitors. In 1941, when the Germans captured Stalin's eldest son, Yakov, Stalin had his son's wife arrested, separated from her three-year-old daughter, and imprisoned for two years as punishment for her husband's "cowardice" in surrendering. "There are no prisoners of war," Stalin explained, "only traitors to their homeland." While still a prisoner-of-war, Yakov committed suicide in 1943 by throwing himself onto an electric fence.

By the winter of 1941–1942, Hitler's generals were learning the same bitter lesson that the Russians had taught Napoléon and the French in 1812: invading armies must contend not only with Russia's ferocious fighters and enormous population but also vast distances, deep snow, and subzero temperatures.

THE ATLANTIC CHARTER By late summer 1941, the United States was no longer a neutral nation. In August, Roosevelt and Churchill met on a warship off the Canadian coast and drew up a joint statement of "common principles" known as the **Atlantic Charter**. The agreement pledged that after the "final destruction of the Nazi tyranny," the victors would promote the self-determination of all peoples, economic cooperation, freedom of the seas, and a new multination system of international security to be called the United Nations. Within weeks, eleven anti-Axis nations, including the Soviet Union, had endorsed the Atlantic Charter.

WORLD WAR II MILITARY ALLIANCES, 1942

- ■ What was the Atlantic Charter?
- ■ Compare and contrast the political/military alliances in the First World War with those in the Second World War.
- ■ How were the German armies able to seize most of Europe so quickly?

WAR IN THE ATLANTIC No sooner had Franklin Roosevelt signed the Atlantic Charter than U.S. warships came under fire. On September 4, 1941, the *Greer* was tracking a German submarine ("U-boat") off the coast of Iceland and sharing the information with British warplanes when it was attacked. In response, Roosevelt began an undeclared war in the Atlantic by ordering warships to protect shipping convoys all the way to Iceland.

Six weeks later, on October 17, 1941, a German U-boat sank the U.S. warship *Kearny*. Eleven sailors died. "The shooting has started," Roosevelt reported, "and history has recorded who fired the first shot." Two weeks later, the *Reuben James* was torpedoed and sunk while escorting a convoy near Iceland, with a loss of 115 seamen.

The attacks spurred Congress to change the 1939 Neutrality Act by allowing freighters and oil tankers to be armed and to enter combat zones and the ports of nations at war ("belligerents"). Step by step, the United States was engaging in naval warfare against Nazi Germany. Still, Americans hoped to avoid all-out war.

THE STORM IN THE PACIFIC

In 1940, Japan and the United States had begun to move closer to war. The Japanese had built airfields in French Indochina (now Cambodia, Laos, and Vietnam). The United States responded with the Export Control Act of July 2, 1940, which authorized President Roosevelt to restrict the export of military supplies and other strategic materials to Japan. Three weeks later, on July 26, Roosevelt ordered that all Japanese assets in the United States be frozen and that oil shipments be stopped.

THE TRIPARTITE PACT On September 27, 1940, the Imperial Japanese government signed a Tripartite Pact with Nazi Germany and fascist Italy, by which each pledged to declare war on any nation that attacked any of them. Roosevelt called the pact an "unholy alliance" designed to "dominate and enslave the entire human race." Several weeks later, the United States expanded its trade embargo against Japan to include iron ore, copper, and brass, deliberately leaving oil as the remaining bargaining chip in the ongoing tension between the two nations, for it was the commodity Japan most needed to sustain its war against China.

In July 1941, Japan announced that it was taking complete control of French Indochina and thereby gaining access to the raw materials denied it by the United States. Roosevelt responded by restricting oil exports to Japan. *Time* magazine claimed that Roosevelt was "waging the first great undeclared war in U.S. history."

THE ATTACK ON PEARL HARBOR On October 16, 1941, Hideki Tōjō became the Japanese prime minister. He ordered a fleet of Japanese warships to prepare for a surprise attack on Hawaii's Pearl Harbor, the most important U.S. military base in the Pacific. The Japanese naval commander, Admiral Isoroku Yamamoto, knew that his country could not defeat the United States in a long war. Its only hope was "to decide the fate of the war on the very first day" by launching a "fatal attack."

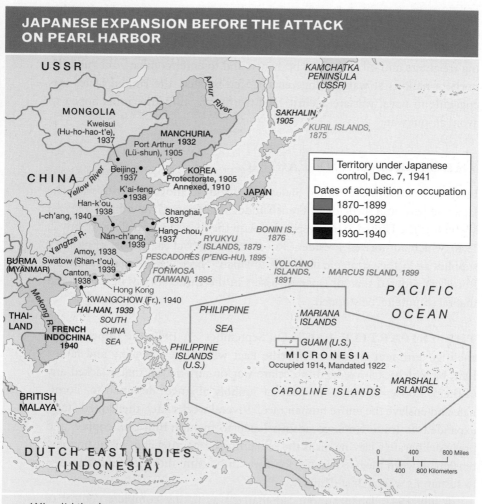

JAPANESE EXPANSION BEFORE THE ATTACK ON PEARL HARBOR

Legend:
- Territory under Japanese control, Dec. 7, 1941
- Dates of acquisition or occupation
  - 1870–1899
  - 1900–1929
  - 1930–1940

- Why did the Japanese want to control French Indochina and the Dutch East Indies?
- Why did Japan sign the Tripartite Pact with Germany and Italy?

On November 5, 1941, the Japanese asked the Roosevelt administration to end its embargo or "face conflict." Secretary of State Cordell Hull responded on November 26 that Japan must remove its troops from China before the United States would lift its embargo. The Japanese government then secretly ordered a fleet of warships to begin steaming toward Hawaii. By this time, political and military leaders on both sides considered war inevitable. Yet Hull continued to meet with Japanese diplomats in Washington, privately dismissing them as being as "crooked as a barrel of fish hooks."

Roosevelt and others expected the Japanese to strike Singapore or the Philippines. The U.S. Navy Department sent an urgent message to its commanders in the Pacific: "Negotiations with Japan . . . have ceased, and an aggressive move by Japan is expected within the next few days."

Early Sunday morning, December 7, 1941, Japanese planes began bombing the unsuspecting U.S. fleet at **Pearl Harbor**. Of the eight battleships, all were sunk or disabled, along with eleven other ships and 180 U.S. warplanes. The raid, which lasted less than two hours, killed more than 2,400 servicemen (mostly sailors) and civilians, and wounded nearly 1,200 more. At the same time, the Japanese assaulted U.S. military facilities in the Philippines and on Guam and Wake Islands in the Pacific, as well as British bases in Singapore, Hong Kong, and Malaya.

The shocking attack on Pearl Harbor fell short in two important ways. First, the bombers ignored the maintenance facilities and oil storage tanks that supported the U.S. fleet, without which the surviving ships might have been forced back to the West Coast. Second, the Japanese missed the U.S. aircraft carriers that had left port a few days earlier. In the naval war to come, aircraft carriers, not battleships, would prove to be decisive.

In a larger sense, the attack on Pearl Harbor was a spectacular miscalculation, for it destroyed the American isolationist movement. As the Japanese admiral who planned the attack said, "I fear that we have only succeeded in awakening a sleeping tiger." After learning of the Japanese attack, Winston Churchill, who desperately wanted the United States to enter the war, wrote that he "slept the sleep of the saved and thankful."

At half past noon on December 8, President Roosevelt delivered his war message to Congress: "Yesterday, December 7, 1941—a date which will live in infamy—the United States of America was suddenly and deliberately attacked by naval and air forces of the Empire of Japan." He asked Congress to declare a "state of war." The Senate approved the resolution twenty-five minutes after Roosevelt finished speaking; the House followed immediately thereafter.

Three days later, on December 11, Germany and Italy declared war on what Hitler called the "half Judaized and the other half Negrified" United States.

Explosion of the USS *Shaw* The destroyer exploded after being hit by Japanese warplanes at Pearl Harbor. It was repaired shortly thereafter and went on to earn eleven battle stars in the Pacific campaign.

After learning of the attack on Pearl Harbor, Hitler shouted that "it is impossible for us to lose the war." The separate wars in Asia, Europe, and Africa had now become one global conflict. Roosevelt told the American people in a radio address that "we are going to win, and we are going to win the peace that follows." Privately, however, he knew that it would be a long, tough war against the "forces of savagery and barbarism."

ARSENAL OF DEMOCRACY

Waging war against Germany and Japan required harnessing all of America's population and industrial capacity. On December 18, 1941, Congress passed the War Powers Act, which gave the president far-reaching authority to reorganize government agencies and create new ones, regulate business and industry, and even censor mail and other forms of communication.

Millions of Americans were soon leaving civilian life and donning military uniforms. The average U.S. soldier or sailor was twenty-six years old, stood five feet eight, and weighed 144 pounds, an inch taller and eight pounds heavier than the typical recruit in the First World War. Only one in ten had attended college, and only one in four had graduated from high school.

Among those who enlisted after the attack on Pearl Harbor were all nine sons of Hiram and Elizabeth Bond, from Fond du Lac, Wisconsin. The Bond brothers survived the war but not without some close calls. One spent the rest of his life with a limp because of a German bullet in his hip. Another was shot in the thigh and hip before being captured by German soldiers in France. Still another, Russell Bond, served as a radio operator in the Army Air Corps (there was no separate air force during the Second World War). Flying in a bomber from England to Germany and back, he wrote, "was no picnic." After one mission, his B-24 Liberator returned with 1,800 holes from German anti-aircraft guns and fighter planes. None of the Bond brothers thought of themselves as heroes. Every young man, it seemed, recalled wife Marilyn Bond, "went into the service. It was just to keep our country safe, so that's what they did."

MILITARY PRODUCTION After the attack on Pearl Harbor, President Roosevelt told Congress that the nation's "powerful enemies must be outfought and outproduced." In 1940, Adolf Hitler had scoffed at the idea that the United States could produce 50,000 warplanes a year, claiming that America was nothing but "beauty queens, millionaires, and Hollywood." By the end of 1942, however, U.S. war production exceeded the *combined* output of Germany, Japan, and Italy.

The **War Production Board**, created by Roosevelt in 1942, directed the conversion of industries to war production. In 1941, more than 3 million automobiles were manufactured; only 139 were built during the next four years, as automobile plants were reorganized to produce huge numbers of tanks, jeeps, trucks, and warplanes. "Something is happening that Hitler doesn't understand," announced *Time* magazine in 1942. "It is the Miracle of production."

War Production Board This 1942 poster features caricatures of Mussolini, Hitler, and Tōjō, who—according to the poster—will fall on their "axis" if Americans continued their relentless production of military equipment.

The Roosevelt administration transformed the nation's war economy into the world's most efficient military machine. By 1945, America would be manufacturing half the goods produced in the world. Factories, many running twenty-four hours a day, seven days a week, produced 300,000 warplanes, 89,000 tanks, 3 million machine guns, and 7 million rifles.

FINANCING THE WAR To cover the war's huge cost (more than $3 trillion in today's values), Congress passed the Revenue Act of 1942 (Victory Tax), which required most workers to begin paying taxes. In 1939, only about 4 million people (about 5 percent of the workforce) earned enough to file tax returns; by the end of the war, 90 percent of workers were paying income tax. Tax revenues covered about 45 percent of military costs from 1939 to 1946; the government borrowed the rest, mostly by selling $185 billion worth of government war bonds, which paid interest to purchasers. By the end of the war, the national debt was six times what it had been at the start.

The size of the federal government soared. More than a dozen new federal agencies managed the war effort, and the number of civilian federal workers quadrupled to 4 million.

Jobs were suddenly plentiful, as millions quit work to join the military. The unemployment rate plummeted from 14 percent in 1940 to 2 percent in 1943. People who had long lived on the margins of the economic system, especially women, now entered the labor force in large numbers.

For most civilians, especially those who had lost their jobs and homes in the Depression, the war spelled a better life. Some 24 million Americans moved during the war to take advantage of new job opportunities in different parts of the country. Many headed to the West Coast, where shipyards and airplane factories were hiring nonstop.

ECONOMIC CONTROLS The United States not only had to equip and feed its military forces but also needed to provide massive amounts of food, clothing, and weapons to its allies. This created shortages at home that caused sharp price increases in consumer goods. In 1942, Congress ordered the Office of Price Administration to set price ceilings. With prices frozen, basic goods had to be allocated through rationing, with coupons doled out for limited amounts of sugar, coffee, gasoline, automobile tires, and meat.

The government urged every family to become a "fighting unit on the home front." Posters featured slogans such as "Save Your Stuff to Make Us Tough," "Use it up, wear it out, make it do, or do without," and "Save Your Scraps to Beat the Japs." People collected scrap metal, tin foil, rubber, and cardboard for military use.

Businesses and workers often grumbled about the wage and price controls, but the system succeeded. By the end of the war, consumer prices had risen about 31 percent, far less than the increase of 62 percent during the First World War.

A CONSERVATIVE BACKLASH For all of the patriotism inspired by the war effort, criticism of government actions such as rationing increased with each passing year. In the 1942 congressional elections, Republicans gained forty-six seats in the House and nine in the Senate. During the 1940s, a coalition of conservatives from both parties dismantled "nonessential" New Deal agencies such as the Work Projects Administration (originally the Works Progress Administration), the National Youth Administration, and the Civilian Conservation Corps.

Organized labor, despite substantial gains in membership and power during the war, felt the impact of the conservative trend. In the spring of 1943, when 400,000 coal miners went on strike demanding a $2-a-day wage increase, conservatives in Congress passed, over Roosevelt's veto, the Smith-Connally War Labor Disputes Act, which authorized the government to seize plants and mines and keep them operating if workers went on strike.

THE DISRUPTIVE EFFECTS OF WORLD WAR

The Second World War transformed domestic life. Housewives went to work as welders and riveters (workers who connected sheets of metal together with metal pins) at aircraft factories and defense plants. Some 3.5 million rural southerners left farms for cities outside the South. The federal government paid for a national day-care program for young children to enable their mothers to work full-time. The dramatic changes affected many areas of social life, and their impact would last long after the war's end.

WOMEN IN THE WAR The war marked a watershed in the status of women. Nearly 350,000 women served in the U.S. armed forces. They enlisted in the **Women's Army Corps (WAC)**; the navy's equivalent, called the Women Accepted for Volunteer Emergency Service (WAVES); and in the Marine Corps, the Coast Guard, and the Army Air Force.

With millions of men going into military service, more than 8 million women entered the civilian workforce. To help recruit women for traditionally male jobs, the government launched a promotional campaign featuring the story of "Rosie the Riveter," a woman named Rosina Bonavita, who excelled as a worker at an airplane factory.

Women of the workforce, 1942 At the Douglas Aircraft Company in Long Beach, California, three women assemble the tail section of a Boeing B-17 Flying Fortress bomber.

Many men opposed women taking traditionally male jobs. A disgruntled male legislator asked: "Who will do the cooking, the washing, the mending, the humble homey tasks to which every woman has devoted herself; who will rear and nurture the children?" Many women, however, were eager to escape the grinding routines of domestic life and earn good wages. A female welder remembered that her wartime job "was the first time I had a chance to get out of the kitchen and work in industry and make a few bucks. This was something I had never dreamed would happen."

AFRICAN AMERICANS DURING THE WAR Although Americans found themselves fighting the racial bigotry celebrated by fascism and Nazism, the war did not end racism in the United States. The Red Cross, for example, initially refused to accept blood donated by African Americans, and the president of North American Aviation announced that "we will not employ Negroes." Black workers were often limited to the lowest-paid, lowest-skilled jobs.

Some courageous black leaders fought back. In 1941, A. Philip Randolph, head of the Brotherhood of Sleeping Car Porters, planned a march on Washington, D.C., to demand an end to racial discrimination in defense industries. To fend off the march, the Roosevelt administration struck a bargain. Randolph called off the demonstration in return for a presidential order requiring equal treatment in the hiring of workers.

Throughout the war, African Americans noted the irony of the United States fighting racism abroad while tolerating it at home. "The army is about to take me to fight for democracy," a black draftee said, "but I would [rather] fight for democracy right here." During the summer of 1943 alone, there were 274 race-related incidents in almost fifty cities. In Detroit, racial tensions escalated into a full-fledged riot. Fighting raged for two days until federal troops arrived. Twenty-five blacks and nine whites were killed, and more than 700 people were injured.

More than a half-million African Americans left the South for better opportunities during the war years, and more than a million blacks joined

Fighting for equal treatment A. Philip Randolph (center), president of the Brotherhood of Sleeping Car Porters, stands alongside other members of the group.

Bigotry at home During the Detroit Riots of 1943, police officers do nothing when a white thug hits a black man.

the industrial workforce for the first time. Lured by jobs and higher wages in plants and factories retooled for military production, African Americans from Texas, Oklahoma, Arkansas, and Louisiana headed north and west, where the dramatic expansion of defense-related jobs had significant effects on the region's population. During the war years, the number of African Americans rose sharply in western cities such as Seattle, Portland, and Los Angeles.

The war also provided a boon to southern textile mills by requiring millions of uniforms and blankets. Manufacturing jobs led thousands of "dirt poor" sharecroppers and tenant farmers to pursue the steady work offered in new mills and factories. Sixty of the nation's 100 army camps were in southern states, further transforming local economies. During the war, the U.S. rural population decreased by 20 percent.

RACIAL TENSION IN THE MILITARY The most volatile social issue ignited by the war was African American participation in the military.

Although the armed forces were still racially segregated in 1941, African Americans rushed to enlist after the attack on Pearl Harbor. As Joe Louis, the heavyweight boxing champion, explained, "Lots of things [are] wrong with America, but Hitler ain't going to fix them." Altogether, about a million African Americans—men and women—served in the armed forces during the war.

Black soldiers and sailors were initially excluded from combat units. They loaded ships, drove trucks, dug latrines, and handled supplies and mail. Black officers could not command white soldiers or sailors. Henry L. Stimson, the secretary of war, claimed that "leadership is not embedded in the negro race." Military bases had segregated facilities to prevent the "intermingling" of "colored and white" troops.

In late 1944, however, the need for more troops led the government to revisit its racial policies. General Dwight Eisenhower, commander of U.S. forces in Europe, agreed to let black volunteers fight in all-black fifty-man

Tuskegee Airmen The Tuskegee Airmen were the first African American military pilots. Here, the first graduates are reviewed at Tuskegee, Alabama, in 1941.

platoons commanded by white officers. A black officer said the decision was "the greatest" for African Americans "since enactment of the constitutional amendments following the Civil War."

Black soldiers became known as fierce fighters. The same was true of some 600 African American pilots trained in Tuskegee, Alabama. The **Tuskegee Airmen** flew more than 15,000 missions, and their undeniable excellence spurred military and civilian leaders to desegregate the armed forces after the war. At war's end, however, the U.S. Army reimposed segregation. It would be several more years before the military was truly integrated.

MEXICAN AMERICANS AND THE WAR As rural dwellers moved west, many farm counties experienced a labor shortage. In an ironic about-face, local and federal authorities who before the war had forced migrant laborers back across the Mexican border now recruited them to harvest crops on American farms. The Mexican government would not consent to provide the laborers, however, until the United States promised to ensure them decent working and living conditions.

The result was the creation in 1942 of the Emergency Farm Labor Program, soon dubbed the **bracero program** (for a Spanish word meaning manual laborer). Under the program, Mexico agreed to provide about 70,000 seasonal farmworkers on year-long contracts between 1942–1945. (At least that many

Off to court Latinos dressed in zoot suits are loaded onto a Los Angeles County Sheriff's bus for a court appearance in June 1943.

more crossed the border as undocumented workers.) They were not considered immigrants since they were supposed to return to Mexico when the war ended. The success of the program led to its extension after the war, and the annual numbers soared.

Even though some 300,000 Mexican Americans served in the war and earned a higher percentage of Congressional Medals of Honor than any other minority group, racial prejudice against Mexicans and other Latinos persisted. In southern California, for example, there was constant conflict between white servicemen and Mexican American gang members and teenage "zoot-suiters." (Zoot suits were flamboyant clothing worn by some young Mexican American men.) In 1943, several thousand off-duty sailors and soldiers, joined by hundreds of whites, rampaged through Los Angeles, assaulting Mexicans and other people of color. The weeklong violence came to be called the "Zoot Suit Riots."

NATIVE AMERICANS IN THE MILITARY Native Americans supported the war effort more fully than any other group. Almost a third of

Navajo code talkers The complex Navajo language made it impossible for the Germans and Japanese to decode American messages. Here, a code talker relays messages for U.S. Marines in the Battle of Bougainville in the South Pacific in 1943.

eligible Native American men served in the armed forces. Unlike their African American counterparts, Indian servicemen were integrated into regular units with whites. Many others worked in defense-related industries, and thousands of Indian women volunteered as nurses or joined the WAVES. As was the case with African Americans, Native Americans benefited from the experiences afforded by the war by gaining vocational skills they would transfer to civilian jobs after the war.

Why did so many Native Americans fight for a nation that had stripped them of their land and ravaged their heritage? Some felt that they had no choice. Mobilization for the war ended many New Deal programs that had provided them with jobs. At the same time, many viewed the Nazis and Japanese as threats to their own homeland.

Whatever their motivations, Indians distinguished themselves in the military. Perhaps their most distinctive role was serving as "code talkers." As had occurred during the First World War, every military branch used Native Americans, especially Navajos, to encode and decipher messages using Indian languages unknown to the Germans and Japanese.

DISCRIMINATION AGAINST JAPANESE AMERICANS After Pearl Harbor, widespread fear of a Japanese attack on the U.S. mainland fueled a hunger for vengeance against the Nisei—people of Japanese descent living in the United States. "A Jap's a Jap," declared Lieutenant General John L. DeWitt, head of West Coast defense efforts. "It makes no difference whether he's an American [citizen] or not." Storefront signs appeared declaring, "No Japs Wanted." Banks stopped cashing the checks of Japanese Americans, and grocers refused to sell them food.

Such bigotry helps explain why the U.S. government sponsored one of the worst violations of civil liberties in history when armed soldiers forcibly removed more than 112,000 Nisei from their homes and transported them to ten "**war relocation camps**." These were hastily constructed tent cities in remote areas that were essentially internment camps guarded by sentry towers and soldiers with machine guns.

President Roosevelt initiated the incarceration of Japanese Americans, 70 percent of whom were already U.S. citizens, when he issued Executive Order 9066 on February 19, 1942. There were no trials, no "due process," no concerns about violations of civil rights. Roosevelt called the program a "military necessity," although not a single incident of espionage involving Japanese Americans was proved. Only later did government documents reveal that the motive for the mass removal of Japanese Americans was to quell fears among the general public after the attack on Pearl Harbor.

A farewell to civil rights American troops escorted Japanese Americans by gunpoint to remote war relocation camps, some of which were horse-racing tracks, whose stables served as housing.

On Evacuation Day, Burt Wilson, a white schoolboy in Sacramento, California, was baffled as soldiers ushered the Nisei children out of his school:

> We wondered what had happened. They took somebody out of eighth grade, a boy named Sammy, who drew wonderful cartoons. He was my friend, and one day he was there and the next day he was gone. And that was very difficult for us to understand because we didn't see Sammy or any Japanese American—at least I didn't—as the enemy.

Some 39,000 Japanese Americans served in the U.S. armed forces during the war, and others worked as interpreters and translators. All were victims of racial and fear-based prejudice.

Not until 1983 did the U.S. government acknowledge the injustice of the incarceration policy. Five years later, the Civil Liberties Act granted those Nisei still living $20,000 each in compensation, a minor sum relative to what they had lost during four years of confinement. "The internment of Americans of Japanese ancestry," explained President George H. W. Bush in 1991, "was a great injustice, and it will never be repeated."

THE ALLIED DRIVE TOWARD BERLIN

By mid-1942, U.S. naval forces had become increasingly successful at destroying German U-boats off the Atlantic coast. Up to that point, German submarines had sunk hundreds of Allied cargo vessels, killing 2,500 sailors. Stopping the submarine attacks was important because the Grand Alliance—Great Britain, the United States, and the Soviet Union—called for the defeat of Germany first. Defeating the Japanese could wait.

WAR AIMS AND STRATEGY

A major consideration for Allied military strategy was the clash of massive armies on the vast Eastern Front in the Soviet Union. The Soviet population—by far—bore the brunt of the war against the Nazis, leading Josef Stalin to insist that the Americans and British attack the Germans in western Europe, thereby forcing Hitler to pull units away from the Russian Front.

Meanwhile, with most of the German army deployed on the Russian Front, the British and American air forces, flying from bases in England, would bomb military and industrial targets in German-occupied western Europe, and in Germany itself, while making plans to attack Nazi troops in North Africa, Italy, and France.

Franklin Roosevelt and Winston Churchill agreed that they needed to create a second front in western Europe, but they could not agree on the timing or location of an invasion. U.S. planners wanted to attack the Germans in France before the end of 1942. The British, however, were wary of moving too fast. An Allied defeat on the French coast, Churchill warned, was "the only way in which we could possibly lose this war." Finally, Roosevelt decided to accept Churchill's proposal for a joint Anglo-American invasion of North Africa, which was then controlled by German and Italian armies not nearly as strong as those in Europe.

THE NORTH AFRICA CAMPAIGN On November 8, 1942, the Americans and British landed 100,000 troops in Morocco and Algeria on the North African coast ("Operation Torch"). U.S. general Dwight D. Eisenhower led the assault. After the Americans lost badly in early battles, Eisenhower,

Major General George S. Patton   Patton commanded the U.S. invasion of Sicily, the largest amphibious action in the war up to that point. He believed that war "brings out all that is best in men."

soon known as "Ike," found a brilliant field commander in General George Patton, who said he loved war "more than my life."

Brimming with bravado, Patton showed American troops how to fight a modern war of speed and daring. On May 12, 1943, some 250,000 Germans and Italians surrendered, leaving North Africa in Allied control. The "continent had been redeemed," said Winston Churchill.

THE CASABLANCA CONFERENCE Five months earlier, in January 1943, Franklin Roosevelt, Winston Churchill, and the Anglo-American military chiefs met at a seaside resort near Casablanca in French Morocco. It was a historic occasion for Roosevelt. No U.S. president had ever flown abroad while in office, and none had ever visited Africa. Stalin chose to stay in the Soviet Union, but he again urged the Allies to invade Nazi-controlled western Europe to relieve the pressure on the Russians.

At the conference, the British convinced the Americans to assault the Italian island of Sicily. Roosevelt and Churchill also decided to step up the bombing of Germany and to increase shipments of military supplies to the Soviet Union and the Nationalist Chinese forces fighting the Japanese.

Before leaving the conference, Roosevelt announced, with Churchill's blessing, that the war would end only with the "unconditional surrender" of all enemy nations. This decision was designed to ease Soviet suspicions that the Americans and British might negotiate separately with Hitler to end the war in western Europe. The announcement also reflected Roosevelt's determination that "every person in Germany should realize that this time Germany is a defeated nation."

Whatever its impact on Soviet morale or enemy resistance, however, the decision to require unconditional surrender ensured the destruction of Germany and Japan that would create power vacuums along the western and eastern borders of the Soviet Union.

THE BATTLE OF THE ATLANTIC While fighting raged in North Africa, the Battle of the Atlantic reached its climax. Great Britain desperately needed more food and military supplies from the United States, but German submarines were sinking British vessels faster than shipyards could replace them. By July 1942, some 230 Allied ships and almost 5 million tons of war supplies had been lost. "The only thing that ever frightened me during the war," recalled Churchill, "was the U-boat peril."

By the end of 1942, however, the British and Americans had cracked the German naval radio codes, enabling Allied convoys to steer clear of U-boats or hunt them down with warplanes (called "subchasers") and anti-submarine weapons deployed on warships. New technology also helped, as sonar and radar allowed Allied ships to track submarines. In May 1943, the Allies destroyed fifty U-boats. Thereafter, Allied shipping losses fell significantly— just as hundreds of thousands of American troops and equipment were being transported across the Atlantic.

SICILY AND ITALY On July 10, 1943, following the Allied victory in North Africa, about 250,000 British and American troops landed on the coast of Sicily. General Eisenhower called it the "first page of the liberation of the European continent." The island was in Allied hands by August 17, bringing to an end Benito Mussolini's twenty years of fascist rule in Italy.

On July 25, 1943, the Italian king had dismissed Mussolini as prime minister and had him arrested. The new Italian government then startled the Allies when it offered to switch sides in the war. Hitler responded by sending German armies into Italy.

The Italian campaign thereafter became a series of stalemated battles. Winter came early to southern Italy, making life even more miserable for the soldiers. The Germans positioned themselves behind formidable defenses and rugged terrain that enabled them to slow the Allied advance to a crawl. "Italy was one hill after another," said a U.S. soldier, "and when it was wet, you were either going up too slow or down too fast, but always the mud. And every hill had a German [machine] gun on it." Allied casualties soared.

By February 1944, the two sides were, in the words of U.S. commander Mark W. Clark, like "two boxers in the ring, both about to collapse." Mussolini, plucked from prison by a daring German airborne commando raid, became head of a fascist government in northern Italy as Allied forces finally took control of the rest of the country. On June 4, 1944, the U.S. Fifth Army entered Rome, just two days before D-day on the coast of France. "We were woken by trucks moving through the street," one overjoyed Italian remembered. "At first I thought it was the Germans, but then I heard American accents. . . . By dawn people were lining the streets. I cried."

THE TEHRAN CONFERENCE Late in the fall of 1943, in Tehran, Iran, Winston Churchill and Franklin Roosevelt had their first joint meeting with Josef Stalin. Their discussions focused on the planned invasion of Nazi-controlled France and a simultaneous Russian offensive across eastern Europe. The three leaders agreed to create an international organization—the United Nations—to maintain peace after the war. By the end of the conference, Roosevelt told a cabinet officer that he had grown to like Stalin and had forged a close working relationship with the Soviet leader. Stalin knew this, too, for he had told his secret police to bug Roosevelt's rooms.

Upon arriving back in the United States, Roosevelt confided to Churchill his distrust of Stalin, saying that it was a "ticklish" business keeping the "Russians cozy with us" because of the tension between communism and capitalism. As General Eisenhower stressed, however, the fate of Britain and the United States depended on the Soviets' survival as an ally. "The prize we seek," he said in 1942, "is to keep 8 million Russians [soldiers] in the war."

THE STRATEGIC BOMBING OF EUROPE Months of preparation went into the Allied invasion of German-occupied France. While waiting for D-day (the day the invasion would begin), the U.S. Army Air Force tried to pound Germany into submission. Although the air offensive, while killing 350,000 civilians, failed to shatter German morale or war-related production, it did force the Germans to commit precious resources to air-raid defense and eventually wore down their air force. With Allied air supremacy assured by 1944, the much-anticipated invasion of Hitler's "Fortress Europe" could move forward.

PLANNING AN INVASION In early 1944, Dwight D. Eisenhower arrived in London with a new title: Supreme Commander of the Allied Expeditionary Force (AEF). He faced the daunting task of planning **Operation Overlord**, the daring assault on Hitler's "Atlantic Wall," an array of mines, machine guns, barbed wire, and jagged obstacles along the French coastline. The planned invasion gave Churchill nightmares: "When I think of the beaches . . . choked with the flower of American and British youth . . . I see the tides running red with their blood. I have my doubts. I have my doubts."

For months, Eisenhower, neither an experienced strategist nor a combat commander, dedicated himself to planning the risky invasion and managing the complex political and military rivalries among the Allied leaders. Well-organized and efficient, he was a high-energy perfectionist, impatient and often short-tempered with his staff. He attended to every detail, including the amassing of 5 million tons of military equipment and munitions and thousands of warplanes and ships.

The seaborne invasion would be the greatest gamble and most complex military operation in history. "I am very uneasy about the whole operation," admitted Sir Alan Brooke, head of British forces. "It may well be the most ghastly disaster of the whole war." Eisenhower was so concerned that he carried in his wallet a note to be circulated if the Allies failed. It read: "If any blame or fault attaches to the attempt, it is mine alone."

D-DAY AND AFTER Operation Overlord succeeded in part because it surprised the Germans. The Allies positioned British decoy troops and made misleading public statements to fool the Nazis into believing that the invasion would come at Pas-de-Calais, on the French-Belgian border, where the English Channel was narrowest. Instead, the landings would actually occur along 50 miles of shoreline in northern Normandy, a French coastal region almost 200 miles south.

On the blustery evening of June 5, 1944, General Eisenhower visited some of the 16,000 U.S. paratroopers preparing to drop behind German lines. The soldiers, noticing Eisenhower's concerned demeanor, tried to lift his spirits. "Now quit worrying, General," one of them said, "we'll take care of this thing for you." A sergeant said, "We ain't worried. It's Hitler's turn to worry."

After the planes took off, Eisenhower confided to an aide: "I hope to God I know what I'm doing." Others were concerned too. As he got into bed that night, Winston Churchill, with tears running down his cheeks, asked his wife:

General Dwight Eisenhower Eisenhower visiting with U.S. paratroopers before they began the night assault in Operation Overlord.

"Do you know that by the time you wake up in the morning, 20,000 men may have been killed?"

As the planes carrying the paratroopers arrived over coastal France, thick clouds and German anti-aircraft fire disrupted the formations. Some soldiers were dropped miles from their landing sites, some were dropped far out at sea, and some were dropped so low that their parachutes never opened. Yet those among the U.S. 82nd and 101st Airborne Divisions who landed safely outfought three German divisions during the night and prepared the way for the main invasion by destroying bridges and capturing artillery positions and key road junctions.

Donald Burgett, a nineteen-year-old paratrooper in the 101st Airborne Division, recalled dropping into France in the dark of night and being alone: "My throat went dry and I swallowed, but nothing went down. My heart pounded, sending blood throbbing through my temples and causing a weak-feeling in the pit of my stomach." But he had no time for fear. As he stumbled upon others who had survived the landing, they soon found themselves embroiled in combat.

THE NORMANDY LANDINGS As the gray, misty light of dawn broke on D-day, June 6, 1944, the biggest invasion fleet in history—some 5,300 Allied ships carrying 370,000 soldiers and sailors—filled the horizon off the

The landing at Normandy D-Day, June 6, 1944. Before they could huddle under a seawall and begin to dislodge the Nazi defenders, U.S. soldiers on Omaha Beach had to cross a fifty-yard stretch that exposed them to machine guns housed in concrete bunkers.

Normandy coast. Sleepy German soldiers awoke to the breathtaking array of ships. "I saw an armada like a plague of locusts," said a German officer. "The number of ships was uncountable."

Eisenhower was lucky on D-day, for the Germans misinterpreted the Normandy landings as a diversion for the "real" attack at Pas-de-Calais. It helped that the German commander, Field Marshal Erwin Rommel, assuming that the weather was too rough for an invasion, had gone home to Germany to celebrate his wife's June 6 birthday. "How stupid of me," Rommel said when he heard the news. "How stupid of me!" By one in the afternoon, he was racing back to France.

When Hitler learned of the Allied landings, he boasted that "the news couldn't be better. As long as they [the Allied armies] were in Britain, we couldn't get at them. Now we have them where we can destroy them." In the United States, word that the long-anticipated liberation of Nazi Europe had begun captured the nation's attention. Businesses closed, church bells tolled, and people prayed in the streets.

During the first day of Operation Overlord, foul weather and rough seas caused injuries and seasickness and capsized dozens of the boxy, flat-bottomed landing craft. More than 1,000 soldiers, weighed down by seventy pounds of equipment, drowned as they stepped into water above their heads. Some of the landing craft delivered their often seasick troops to the wrong locations. "We have landed in the wrong place," shouted fifty-six-year-old Brigadier General Theodore Roosevelt Jr. (son of the former president), who would receive the Medal of Honor for his courage that day. "But we will start the war from here."

The noise was deafening as shells exploded across the beaches and in the surf. Bodies piled up amid wrenching cries for help. "As our boat touched sand and the ramp went down," Private Harry Parley remembered, "I became a visitor to Hell."

The first U.S. units ashore at Omaha Beach, beneath 130-foot-tall cliffs defended by German machine guns and mortars, lost more than 90 percent of their men. Officers struggled to rally the troops. "Two kinds of men are staying on this beach," shouted cigar-smoking Colonel George Taylor. "The dead and those who are going to die. Get up! Move in! Goddammit! Move in and die! Get the hell out of here!"

Inch by inch, U.S. troops pushed across the beaches and up the cliffs. By nightfall, 170,000 Allied soldiers—57,000 of them Americans—were scattered across fifty miles of the windswept Normandy coastline. So too were the bodies of 10,724 dead or wounded Allied soldiers.

On June 13, a week after the Normandy landings, Erwin Rommel, the German commander, told his wife that the "battle is not going at all well for us." Within three weeks, the Allies had landed more than a million troops, 566,000 tons of supplies, and 171,000 vehicles. "Whether the enemy can still be stopped at this point is questionable," German army headquarters near Paris warned Hitler. "The enemy air superiority is terrific and smothers almost every one of our movements. . . . Losses in men and equipment are extraordinary."

Operation Overlord was the greatest seaborne invasion in the history of warfare, but it was small when compared with the offensive launched by the Soviet army a few weeks later. Between June and August 1944, the Soviets killed, wounded, or captured more German soldiers (350,000) than were stationed in all of western Europe.

Still, the Normandy invasion was a turning point in the war. With the beachhead secured, the Allied leaders knew that final victory was just a matter of time, as Hitler's armies were caught between the Soviets advancing from the east and the Allied forces from the west and south. "What a plan!" Churchill exclaimed to the British Parliament.

THE LIBERATION OF PARIS It would take seven more weeks and 37,000 more lives for the Allied troops to gain control of Normandy. The Germans lost more than twice that many, and some 19,000 French civilians were killed. Then, on July 25, American armies headed east from Normandy toward Paris. On August 15, a joint American-French force landed on the Mediterranean coast and raced up the Rhone Valley in eastern France.

German resistance collapsed after only ten weeks. On D-day, one German unit, the 21st Panzer Division, boasted 12,000 men and 127 tanks; ten weeks

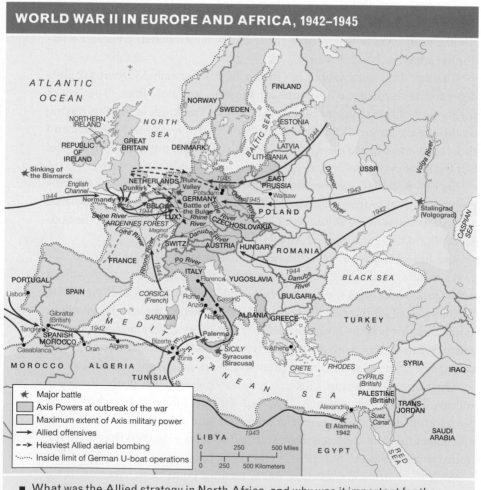

WORLD WAR II IN EUROPE AND AFRICA, 1942–1945

Legend:
- ★ Major battle
- Axis Powers at outbreak of the war
- Maximum extent of Axis military power
- → Allied offensives
- --→ Heaviest Allied aerial bombing
- ······ Inside limit of German U-boat operations

- What was the Allied strategy in North Africa, and why was it important for the invasion of Italy?
- Why did Eisenhower's D-day plan succeed?
- What was the role of strategic bombing in the war? Was it effective?

later, having retreated across France, it had just 300 men and 10 tanks left. A division of the Free French Resistance, aided by American units, liberated Paris on August 25. As U.S. soldiers marched through the cheering crowds, a reporter said that he had never "seen in any place such joy as radiated from the people of Paris this morning."

By mid-September, most of France and Belgium had been cleared of German troops. Meanwhile, the Soviet army moved relentlessly westward along a 1,200-mile front, pushing the fleeing Germans out of Russia. Between D-day and the end of the war in Europe a year later, 1.2 million German soldiers were killed or wounded.

ROOSEVELT'S FOURTH TERM In 1944, war or no war, the calendar required another presidential election. This time the Republicans nominated New York governor Thomas E. Dewey, who argued that it was time for a younger man to replace the "tired" Democratic leader.

Franklin Roosevelt was not only tired; he was seriously ill. In March, the president's physician had said that Roosevelt would not survive another four years in office. The next day, the president, determined to guide the nation to victory and create a stable postwar world, announced that he would accept his party's nomination for a fourth term. The public knew nothing about his failing health. On November 7, 1944, Roosevelt won yet again, this time by a popular vote of 25.6 million to 22 million and an electoral vote of 432 to 99.

THE RACE TO BERLIN By the time Franklin Roosevelt was reelected, Allied armies were approaching the German border from the east and the west. Winston Churchill was worried that if the Soviets arrived first in Berlin, the German capital, Josef Stalin would control the postwar map of Europe. Churchill urged Eisenhower to beat the Soviets to Berlin. Eisenhower, however, decided it was not worth the estimated 100,000 American casualties such an operation would cost.

GERMAN COUNTERATTACK: THE BATTLE OF THE BULGE As the Anglo-American armies approached the German border in mid-December 1944, a desperate Hitler sprang a surprise. He dispatched most of his army's reserves and 1,800 tanks to the Ardennes Forest in Belgium, where they launched a counterattack intended to split the Allied advance and retake the Belgian port of Antwerp. "This battle is to decide whether we shall live or die," Hitler told his officers. "The battle must be fought with brutality, and all resistance must be broken in a wave of terror."

Battle of the Bulge Two U.S. soldiers stand out sharply against snow-covered ground and a night sky alight with a barrage of artillery fire.

The Battle of the Bulge involved a million combatants and almost changed the course of the war. Initially, the counterattack surprised Allied commanders, punched a hole in the overstretched Allied lines, and drove the British and U.S. forces back fifty miles, thus creating the "bulge" on the map that gave the battle its name. Eight days of bad weather complicated matters, as frigid temperatures, blinding snow, winter fog, and thick clouds prevented Allied warplanes from supporting the troops.

General Eisenhower remained calm. He saw the massive assault as "an opportunity" to destroy much of the German army. The heaviest fighting centered on Bastogne, where seven key roads converged. There, some 18,000 U.S. infantry and paratroopers found themselves hopelessly surrounded. For more than a week, as they ran low on supplies, they held off a much larger force of Germans as General George S. Patton's Third Army, some ninety miles away, raced to the rescue with 250,000 soldiers. Patton, too, saw the German counterattack as an opportunity to shorten the war. Hitler, he claimed, "had stuck his head into a meat grinder, and this time I've got the handle."

On December 22, the German commander encircling Bastogne sent his American counterpart, General Anthony McAuliffe, a demand to surrender within two hours or be "annihilated." McAuliffe's one-word reply ("Nuts!") confused the Germans. An American officer then explained to the German representative that "Nuts" meant the same as "Go to Hell." And, he added, "we will kill every goddamned German who tries to break into the city."

The weather cleared the next morning, enabling U.S. planes to bring desperately needed supplies to the units trapped in Bastogne. A few days later, the advance guard of Patton's relief force arrived. Bastogne was no longer surrounded. For three more weeks, the Germans repeatedly tried to take the town, but without success. Throughout the region, wave after wave of American and British warplanes assaulted German forces in what one observer called "a great slaughter."

Hitler's great gamble had failed. The Germans at the Battle of the Bulge lost more than 100,000 men—killed, wounded, or captured. American casualties were also high—81,000—but it was clear that Germany was teetering toward defeat. "Now," Patton wrote in his diary, "we are going to attack until the war is over."

THE YALTA CONFERENCE As the Allied armies converged on Berlin, Josef Stalin hosted Franklin Roosevelt and Winston Churchill at the **Yalta Conference** (February 4–11, 1945) in Crimea, a seaside resort on the Black Sea. The "Big Three" agreed that, once Germany surrendered, the Soviets would occupy eastern Germany, and the Americans and British would control western Germany. Berlin, the German capital within the Soviet zone, would be subject to joint occupation.

Stalin's goals were to retrieve former Russian territory transferred to Poland after the First World War and impose Soviet control over eastern and central Europe. Churchill and Roosevelt urged Stalin to allow Poland, then occupied by the Red Army, to become a self-governing democracy. Stalin refused, explaining that Soviet control of Poland was more important to him than participation in the United Nations, Roosevelt's proposed international peacekeeping organization.

Stalin also knew that the Americans needed Soviet support in the ongoing war with Japan. Military analysts estimated that Japan could hold out for eighteen months after the defeat of Germany unless the Soviets joined the war in Asia. Stalin agreed to do so, but the price was high: he demanded territories from Japan and China.

As a face-saving gesture, Roosevelt and Churchill convinced Stalin to sign the Yalta Declaration of Liberated Europe, which called for free and open

The Yalta Conference Churchill, Roosevelt, and Stalin (with their respective foreign ministers behind them) confer on plans for the postwar world in February 1945.

elections in the liberated nations of eastern Europe. Nevertheless, Stalin would fail to live up to his promises. When the Soviet Red Army "liberated" Hungary, Romania, Bulgaria, Czechoslovakia, Poland, and eastern Germany, it plundered and sent back to Russia anything of economic value, dismantling thousands of factories and mills and rebuilding them in the Soviet Union. To ensure control over eastern Europe, the Soviets shipped off to prison anyone who questioned the new Communist governments they created.

At Yalta, the three leaders agreed to hold organizational meetings for the United Nations beginning on April 25, 1945. Like Woodrow Wilson, Roosevelt was determined to replace America's "outdated" isolationism with an engaged internationalism. But to get Stalin's approval of the UN, Roosevelt gave in to the Soviet leader's demands for territory held by Japan in northeast Asia.

Admiral William D. Leahy, the president's chief of staff, complained to Roosevelt that the agreement's language on Poland was "so elastic that the Russians can stretch it all the way from Yalta to Washington without ever technically breaking it." Some blamed Roosevelt's unwillingness to force Stalin to create democracies in the liberated nations on his declining health. (He would die in a few weeks.)

But even a robust Roosevelt could not have dislodged the Soviet army from its control of eastern Europe. The course of the war shaped the outcome at Yalta, and the United States had no real leverage. As a U.S. diplomat admitted, "Stalin held all the cards." Roosevelt agreed. "I didn't say the result was good," Roosevelt said after returning from the Yalta Conference. "I said it was the best I can do for Poland at this time."

DEATH OF A PRESIDENT By early 1945, Nazi Germany was on the verge of defeat, but sixty-three-year-old Franklin Roosevelt would not live to join the victory celebrations.

In the spring of 1945, he went to the "Little White House" in Warm Springs, Georgia. On April 12, 1945, just eighty-two days into his fourth term, he complained of a headache but seemed to be in good spirits. It was nearly lunchtime when he said to an artist painting his portrait, "Now we've got just about 15 minutes more to work." Then, while reading some documents, Roosevelt groaned, saying that he had "terrific pain" in the back of his head. He slumped over, fell into a coma, and died two hours later.

On hand to witness the president's death was Lucy Mercer Rutherford, the woman with whom Roosevelt had an affair thirty years before. Eleanor Roosevelt was in Washington, D.C., when Franklin died, unaware of the president's guest. Although Franklin had promised in 1918 to end all communications with Mercer, he had in fact secretly stayed in touch, even enabling her to attend his presidential inauguration in 1933.

Roosevelt's death shocked and saddened the world. Even his sharpest critics were devastated. Ohio senator Robert Taft, known as "Mr. Republican," said, "The President's death removes the greatest figure of our time at the very climax of his career. . . . He dies a hero of the war, for he literally worked himself to death in the service of the American people."

Children took Roosevelt's death especially hard. It was "catastrophic" news for twelve-year-old Burt Wilson of Sacramento, California. "My parents were Republicans and hated Roosevelt, but I loved him. And most of us kids loved him, I believe, because he was the face of America that was saying, 'Hey, things are going to get better.'"

THE COLLAPSE OF NAZISM Adolf Hitler's Nazi empire collapsed less than a month later. In Berlin on April 28, as Soviet troops entered the German capital, Hitler married his mistress, Eva Braun, in an underground bunker. That same day, Italian freedom fighters captured Mussolini. Despite his plea to "Let me live, and I will give you an empire," Mussolini and his mistress were shot and hung by their heels from a girder above a Milan gas station. On April 30, Hitler and his wife retired to their underground bedroom, where she poisoned herself and he put a bullet in his head. Their bodies were taken outside, doused with gasoline, and burned.

On May 2, Berlin fell. Axis forces in Italy surrendered the same day. Five days later, on May 7, the chief of staff of the German armed forces agreed to unconditional surrender. So ended the Nazi domination of Europe, just over twelve years after Hitler had proclaimed his "Thousand-Year Reich."

On May 8, V-E day ("Victory in Europe") generated massive celebrations. In Paris, an American bomber pilot flew his plane through the arch of the Eiffel Tower. In New York City, 500,000 people celebrated in the streets. The elation,

May 8, 1945 The celebration in New York City's Times Square on V-E day.

however, was tempered by the ongoing war against Japan and the immense challenges of helping Europe rebuild. The German economy had to be revived, a new democratic government had to be formed, and millions of displaced Europeans had to be clothed, housed, and fed.

THE HOLOCAUST The end of the war in Europe revealed to the world the horrific extent of the **Holocaust**, Hitler's systematic program to destroy Jews, whom he hated and blamed for most of Germany's problems. In 1941, a German soldier wrote his wife: "The Jews are being completely exterminated." He reminded her not to tell their son about such atrocities.

It took longer for the rest of the world to learn of the Holocaust. Reports of the Nazis' methodical slaughter of Jews had appeared as early as 1942, but the ghastly stories of millions killed in gas chambers seemed beyond belief until the Allied armies liberated the death camps in central and eastern Europe. There the Germans had imposed their "Final Solution": the wholesale extermination of at least 6 million Jews, and many millions more non-Jewish peoples deemed unworthy of living within the German Reich.

The Allied troops were shocked at what they discovered in the extermination camps, where as many as 24,000 Jews a day had been killed. Bodies were piled as high as buildings; survivors were living skeletons. General Eisenhower reported that the "things I saw beggar description." Everywhere, the "starvation, cruelty, and bestiality were so overpowering as to leave me a bit sick. In one room, where they were piled up twenty or thirty naked men, killed by starvation, [General] George Patton would not even enter. He said that he would get sick if he did so. I made the visit deliberately, in

Holocaust survivors American troops liberate survivors of the Mauthausen concentration camp in Austria in May 1945. The Nazis tattooed the prisoners with identification numbers on their wrists or chests, as seen on the man at left.

order to be in a position to give first-hand evidence of these things if ever, in the future, there develops a tendency to charge these allegations merely to 'propaganda.'"

American government officials had dragged their feet in acknowledging the Holocaust for fear that relief efforts for Jewish refugees might stir up anti-Semitism at home. At the same time, several key figures in the State Department proved to be anti-Semitic themselves, and they balked at bringing more refugees to America. Under pressure from Jewish groups and his wife, President Roosevelt had created a War Refugee Board early in 1944 to save European Jews at risk of extermination. The War Refugee Board managed to rescue about 200,000 European Jews and some 20,000 other refugees. But the administration refused appeals from Jewish leaders to bomb the concentration camp at Auschwitz, arguing that doing so would kill many Jews, be ineffective (the Nazis would simply build another one), and distract resources from the priority of defeating Hitler's war machine. In 1944, Winston Churchill called the Holocaust the "most horrible crime ever committed in the history of the world." He did not know at the time that Stalin's death camps had killed more people than Hitler's.

THE PACIFIC WAR

For months after the attack on Pearl Harbor at the end of 1941, the news from the Pacific was "all bad," as President Roosevelt acknowledged. With stunning speed, the Japanese had captured numerous territories in Asia, including the British colonies of Hong Kong, Burma, Malaya, and Singapore, and the French colony of Indochina.

THE PHILIPPINES In the Philippines, U.S. forces and their Filipino allies were overwhelmed. On April 10, 1942, the Japanese gathered some 12,000 captured American troops along with 66,000 Filipinos and forced them to march sixty-five miles in six days up the Bataan peninsula. Already underfed and ravaged by disease, the prisoners were brutalized in what came to be known as the Bataan Death March. Those who fell out of line were bayoneted or shot. Others were beaten, stabbed, or shot for no reason. More than 10,000 prisoners died along the way. News of the Bataan Death March outraged Americans and contributed to the Pacific war's emotional intensity and mutual atrocities.

By the summer of 1942, Japan was on the verge of assaulting Australia when its naval leaders succumbed to what one admiral called "victory disease." Intoxicated with easy victories and lusting for more, they pushed into the South Pacific, intending to isolate Australia and strike again at Hawaii.

CORAL SEA AND MIDWAY During the spring of 1942, U.S. forces in the Pacific finally had some success. In the Battle of the Coral Sea (May 2–6), U.S. warplanes forced a Japanese fleet headed toward the island of New Guinea to turn back after sinking an aircraft carrier and destroying seventy planes.

A few weeks later, Admiral Yamamoto steered his main Japanese fleet of eighty-six warships and 700 warplanes toward Midway, the westernmost of Hawaii's inhabited islands, from which he hoped to strike Pearl Harbor again. This time, however, the Japanese were the ones who were surprised. In a crucial breakthrough, Americans had cracked the Japanese military radio code, allowing Admiral Chester Nimitz, commander of the U.S. central Pacific fleet, to learn where Yamamoto's fleet was heading.

The Japanese hit Midway hard on June 4, 1942, but at the cost of about a third of their warplanes. American planes then struck back, crippling the Japanese fleet.

The **Battle of Midway** was the first major defeat for the Japanese navy in 350 years and a turning point of the Pacific war. The American victory blunted Japan's military momentum, eliminated the threat to Hawaii, and bought time for the United States to organize its massive industrial productivity for a wider war.

MACARTHUR'S PACIFIC STRATEGY American and Australian forces were jointly under the command of General Douglas MacArthur, an egotistical military genius who irritated his superiors with his "unpleasant personality" and constant self-promotion. MacArthur had retired in 1937 but was called back into service in mid-1941. In 1942, he assumed command of the Allied forces in the southwest Pacific.

On August 7, 1942, some 19,000 U.S. Marines landed on Guadalcanal Island, where the Japanese had an air base. Savage fighting lasted through February 1943, but it resulted in the Japanese army's first defeat, with a loss of 20,000 men compared to 1,752 Americans. Said a U.S. Marine, "These people refuse to surrender."

The suicidal intensity of the Japanese led MacArthur and Admiral Chester Nimitz to adopt a "leapfrogging" or "island-hopping" strategy whereby they liberated the most important islands and bypassed the others, leaving isolated Japanese bases to "wither on the vine," as Nimitz put it.

BATTLES IN THE CENTRAL PACIFIC   On June 15, 1944, U.S. forces liberated Tinian, Guam, and Saipan in the Mariana Islands. Saipan was strategically important because it allowed new B-29 Superfortress bombers, the largest in the war, to strike Japan itself. The struggle for Saipan lasted three weeks. Some 20,000 Japanese were killed compared to 3,500 Americans. But 7,000 more Japanese soldiers committed suicide upon the order of their commanding general, who killed himself with his sword.

General MacArthur's forces invaded the Philippines on October 20. The Japanese, knowing that the loss of the Philippines would cut them off from essential raw materials, brought in warships from three directions.

The four battles fought in the Philippine Sea from October 23 to October 26, 1944, known collectively as the Battle of Leyte Gulf, marked the largest naval engagement in history and the worst Japanese defeat of the war. Some 216 U.S. warships converged to engage 64 Japanese ships. By the end of the battle's last day, thirty-six Japanese warships, including four aircraft carriers, had been destroyed.

The Battle of Leyte Gulf included the first Japanese *kamikaze* ("divine wind") attacks, in which pilots deliberately crashed their bomb-laden planes

General Douglas MacArthur MacArthur theatrically coming ashore at the island of Leyte in the Philippines, October 1944. Preoccupied with publicity, he staged the walk ashore several times to get the best shot on film.

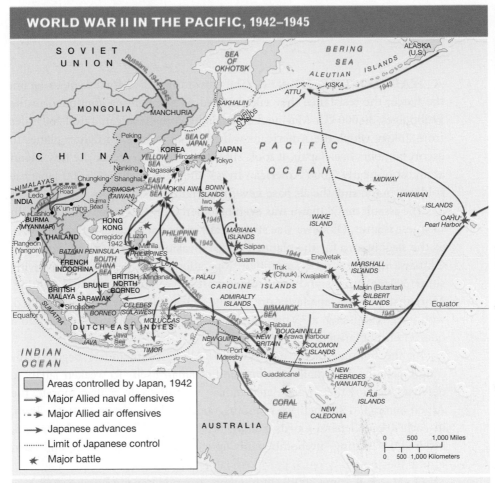

WORLD WAR II IN THE PACIFIC, 1942–1945

- Areas controlled by Japan, 1942
- Major Allied naval offensives
- Major Allied air offensives
- Japanese advances
- Limit of Japanese control
- Major battle

- What was MacArthur's "leapfrogging" strategy? Why were the battles in the Marianas a major turning point in the war?
- What was the significance of the Battle of Leyte Gulf?
- How did the battle at Okinawa affect both Japanese and American military strategists?

into American warships. From the fall of 1944 to the war's end in the summer of 1945, an estimated 4,000 kamikaze pilots died on suicide missions. "Kamikazes just poured at us, again and again," a sailor remembered. "It scared the shit out of us."

As MacArthur waded ashore with the U.S. troops liberating the Philippines, he reminded reporters of his 1942 pledge—"I shall return"—when he was evacuated in the face of the Japanese invasion. Now he announced: "People of the Philippines, I have returned! The hour of your redemption is here. . . . Rally to me."

A WAR TO THE DEATH The closer the Allied forces got to Japan, the fiercer the resistance they encountered. While fighting continued in the Philippines, 30,000 U.S. Marines landed on Iwo Jima, a volcanic atoll 760 miles from Tokyo, which the Americans wanted as an airbase for fighter planes to escort bombers over Japan. It took almost six weeks to secure the tiny island at a cost of nearly 7,000 American lives—and 21,000 of the 22,000 Japanese soldiers. In the end, the air base never materialized.

The assault on Okinawa was even bloodier. Only 360 miles from the main Japanese islands, Okinawa was strategically important because it would serve as the staging area for the planned Allied invasion of Japan. The conquest of Okinawa was the largest amphibious operation of the Pacific war, involving some 300,000 troops and requiring almost three months of brutal fighting. More than 150,000 Japanese were killed; some 49,000 Americans were killed, wounded, or missing, a 35 percent casualty rate. A third of U.S. pilots and a quarter of submariners lost their lives.

As the fighting raged on Okinawa, Allied commanders began planning Operation Downfall—the invasion of Japan itself. To weaken Japanese defenses, destroy their war-related industries, and erode civilian morale, the Allied command stepped up bombing raids in the summer of 1944. Then, in early 1945, General Curtis Lemay, head of the U.S. Bomber Command, ordered devastating "firebomb" raids upon Japanese cities: "Bomb and burn 'em till they quit."

On March 9, some 300 B-29 bombers dropped napalm bombs on Tokyo. The attack incinerated sixteen square miles of the city and killed some 100,000 people while rendering a million people homeless. By then, American military leaders had lost all moral qualms about targeting civilians. The kamikaze attacks, the Japanese savagery toward prisoners of war, the burning of Manila that killed 100,000 civilians, and the brutal treatment of Chinese civilians had eroded almost all sympathy.

By August 1945, sixty-six Japanese cities had been firebombed. Secretary of War Henry Stimson called the lack of public outcry in the United States over the raids "appalling."

THE ATOMIC BOMB Still, the Japanese refused to surrender. In early 1945, Harry S. Truman, the vice president who became president upon Roosevelt's death on April 12, learned of the first successful test of an atomic bomb in New Mexico. Now that military planners knew the bomb would work, they selected two Japanese cities as targets. The first was **Hiroshima**, a port city and army headquarters in southern Japan. On July 25, 1945, Truman, who knew nothing about the devastating effects of radiation poisoning, ordered that the atomic bomb be dropped if Japan did not surrender before August 3.

Although an intense debate emerged over the decision (General Eisenhower argued that the "Japanese were ready to surrender," and he "hated to see our country be the first to use such a weapon"), Truman later recalled, "We faced half a million casualties trying to take Japan by land. It was either that or the atom bomb, and I didn't hesitate a minute, and I've never lost any sleep over it since."

To Truman and others, the use of atomic bombs seemed a logical next step to end the war. As it turned out, scientists greatly underestimated the bomb's power. Their prediction that 20,000 people would be killed proved much too low.

In mid-July 1945, the Allied leaders met in Potsdam, Germany, near Berlin. Josef Stalin demanded, according to Truman, that the United States and Great Britain "recognize the new puppet governments" the Soviets had created in Romania, Bulgaria, and Hungary. Truman responded that the United States would do so only after the Soviets allowed "free access" to them and adopted "democratic" processes. Until that happened, America would veto efforts to allow such Soviet-dominated nations to participate in the new United Nations.

The conference deadlocked over the issue of Soviet control of eastern Europe. The allies did issue the Potsdam Declaration, which demanded that Japan surrender by August 3 or face "prompt and utter destruction." Truman left Potsdam optimistic about postwar relations with the Soviet Union. "I can deal with Stalin," he wrote. "He is honest—but smart as hell." (Truman would soon change his mind about Stalin's honesty.)

The aftermath of Little Boy This image shows the wasteland that remained after the atomic bomb "Little Boy" decimated Hiroshima, Japan, on August 6, 1945.

The deadline calling for Japan's surrender passed, and on August 6, 1945, a B-29 bomber piloted by Colonel Paul Tibbets (the plane was named *Enola*

Bombing of Nagasaki A 52,000 foot tall mushroom cloud enveloped the city of Nagasaki after the atomic bombing on August 9, 1945.

Gay after Tibbets' mother) took off at 2 A.M. from the island of Tinian, headed for Hiroshima. At 8:15 A.M., flying at 31,600 feet, the bombardier aboard the *Enola Gay* released the five-ton, ten-foot-long uranium bomb nicknamed "Little Boy."

Forty-three seconds later, the bomb exploded at an altitude of 1,900 feet, creating a blinding flash of light followed by a fireball towering to 40,000 feet. The tail gunner on the *Enola Gay* described the scene: "It's like bubbling molasses down there . . . the mushroom is spreading out . . . fires are springing up everywhere . . . it's like a peep into hell."

The bomb's shock wave and firestorm initially killed some 78,000 people, including thousands of Japanese soldiers and twenty-three American prisoners of war. By the end of the year, the death toll would reach 140,000, as more people died of injuries or radiation poisoning. In addition, the bomb destroyed 76,000 buildings.

President Truman was returning from the Potsdam conference when news arrived that the atomic bomb had been dropped. "This is the greatest thing in history!" he repeatedly exclaimed. In the United States, Americans greeted the news with similar joy. "No tears of sympathy will be shed in America for the Japanese people," the *Omaha World-Herald* predicted. "Had they possessed a comparable weapon at Pearl Harbor, would they have hesitated to use it?" Others reacted by pointing to the implications of atomic warfare. "Yesterday," journalist Hanson Baldwin wrote in the *New York Times*, "we clinched victory in the Pacific, but we sowed the whirlwind."

Two days after the Hiroshima bombing, an opportunistic Soviet Union entered the war in the Pacific by sending hundreds of thousands of troops into Japanese-occupied Manchuria, along the border between China and the Soviet Union. Truman and his aides, frustrated by the refusal of Japanese leaders to surrender and fearful that the Soviet Union's entry would complicate negotiations, ordered a second atomic bomb ("Fat Man") to be dropped.

On August 9, the city of Nagasaki, a shipbuilding center, experienced the same nuclear devastation that had destroyed Hiroshima. An estimated 71,000 people were killed in the city of some 240,000 residents. Five days later, on August 14, 1945, the Japanese emperor accepted the terms of surrender. The formal surrender ceremony occurred on an American warship in Tokyo Bay on September 2, 1945, a date quickly known as V-J Day.

A New Age Is Born

Thus ended the costliest war in history. Including deaths from war-related disease and famine, some 50 million civilians and 22 million combatants had died.

The Second World War was more costly for the United States than any other foreign war: 292,000 combat deaths and 114,000 noncombat deaths among soldiers, sailors, airmen, and marines. A million more were wounded, with half of them seriously disabled.

In proportion to its population, however, the United States suffered far fewer losses than did the other major Allies or their enemies. For every American killed in the Second World War, for example, some fifty-nine Soviets died.

The war was the pivotal event of the turbulent twentieth century. It engulfed five continents, leveled cities, reshaped societies, transformed international relations, and destroyed German and Italian fascism and Japanese militarism. It set in motion the fall of China to communism in 1949 and the outbreak of the Korean War a year later. Colonial empires in Africa and Asia rapidly crumbled as the conflict unleashed independence movements. The Soviet Union emerged as a new global superpower, while the United States, as Winston Churchill told the House of Commons, stood "at the summit of the world."

WHY DID THE ALLIES WIN? Many factors contributed to the Allied victory. Franklin Roosevelt and Winston Churchill were better at coordinating military efforts and maintaining national morale than were Hitler, Mussolini, and the Japanese emperor, Hirohito. By 1944, Hitler had grown increasingly unstable and more withdrawn, especially after a failed attempt by high-ranking officers to assassinate him that July by placing a bomb under his desk. The blast shattered Hitler's eardrums, riddled his body with wooden splinters, and caused a nervous breakdown that left him paranoid, anxious, and addicted to cocaine injections.

In the end, however, what turned the tide was the awesome productivity of American industry and the ability of the Soviet Union to absorb the massive German invasion and push the Nazis back to Berlin. By the end of the war, Japan had run out of food and Germany had run out of fuel. By contrast, the United States was churning out more of everything. As early as 1942, just a few weeks after the Japanese attack on Pearl Harbor, Fritz Todt, a Nazi engineer, told Hitler that the war against the United States was already lost because of America's ability to outproduce all the other warring nations combined.

A TRANSFORMATIONAL WAR The Second World War shattered the old world order and created a new international system. Nations such as France, Germany, Great Britain, and Japan were left devastated or impoverished.

Henry Luce, publisher of *Time* magazine, said that the war had demonstrated the "moral and practical bankruptcy of all forms of Isolationism." Internationalism was now dominant, and most Americans acknowledged that the United States had profound responsibilities for global stability and security. It had emerged from the war with the most powerful military in the world—and as the only nation with atomic weapons.

The expansion of the federal government spurred by the war effort continued after 1945, and presidential authority increased enormously at the expense of congressional and state power. The war also ended the Great Depression and launched a long period of unprecedented prosperity and global economic domination.

Big businesses grew into gigantic corporations as a result of huge government contracts for military weapons and supplies. New technologies and products developed for military purposes—radar, computers, electronics, plastics and synthetics, jet engines, rockets, atomic energy—transformed the private sector, as did new consumer products generated from war-related innovations. And the opportunities created for women as well as African Americans, Mexican Americans, and other minorities set in motion social changes that would culminate in the civil rights movement of the 1960s and the feminist movement of the 1970s.

In August 1945, President Truman announced that the United States had "emerged from this war the most powerful nation in this world—the most powerful nation, perhaps, in all history." But the Soviet Union, despite its human losses and physical destruction, had gained much new territory, built massive armed forces, and enhanced its international influence, making it the greatest power in Eurasia. A little over a century after Frenchman Alexis de Tocqueville had predicted that Europe would eventually be overshadowed by the United States and Russia, his prophecy had come to pass.

CHAPTER REVIEW

SUMMARY

- **Fascism and the Start of the War** In Italy, Benito Mussolini and his Fascist party assumed control in 1922 by promising law and order. Adolf Hitler rearmed Germany in defiance of the Treaty of Versailles. By March 1939, Nazi Germany had annexed Austria and seized Czechoslovakia. Hitler then invaded Poland with the *blitzkrieg* strategy after signing a non-aggression pact with the Soviet Union. The British and French governments declared war.

- **America Goes to War** The United States issued *neutrality laws (1935–1939)* to avoid being drawn into wars in Europe and Asia, but after the fall of France in 1940, President Roosevelt accelerated military aid to Great Britain through the *Lend-Lease Act (1941)*. In 1941, the United States and Great Britain signed the *Atlantic Charter*. After Japan joined with Germany and Italy to form the *Axis alliance,* Roosevelt froze Japanese assets in the United States and restricted oil exports to Japan, which led the frustrated Japanese government to launch a surprise attack at *Pearl Harbor (1941)* in Hawaii.

- **The Second World War and American Society** The war had profound social effects. Americans—white, black, and brown—enlisted in the military, went to work in defense plants, and migrated west to take jobs in factories. Farmers recovered, supported by Mexican labor through the *bracero program (1942–1945)*. The federal government, through agencies such as the *War Production Board*, took control of managing the economy. Many women took nontraditional jobs, including service in the military. More than 150,000 joined in the *Women's Army Corps (WAC)*. About a million African Americans joined the military in segregated units, the most famous of which was the *Tuskegee Airmen*. More than 100,000 Japanese Americans were forcibly interned in *war relocation camps*.

- **Road to Allied Victory in Europe** By 1943, the Allies had defeated the German and Italian armies occupying North Africa. From there, they launched attacks on Sicily and then the mainland of Italy. *Operation Overlord*, the invasion of Western Europe, began June 6, 1944. German resistance slowly crumbled. The "Big Three"—Roosevelt, Churchill, and Stalin—met at the *Yalta Conference* in February 1945, where they decided that a conquered Germany would be divided into four occupation zones. In May, Soviet forces captured Berlin, and Germany surrendered. After the war, Allied forces discovered the extent of the *Holocaust*—the Nazis' systematic effort to exterminate European Jews and other minority groups.

- **The Pacific War** The Japanese advance across the Pacific was halted in June 1942 at the *Battle of Midway*. Fierce Japanese resistance at Iwo Jima and Okinawa, and Japan's refusal to surrender after the firebombing of Tokyo, led the new president, Harry S. Truman, to order the use of atomic bombs on the cities of *Hiroshima* and Nagasaki in August 1945.

- **Postwar World** The Soviet Union and United States emerged from the war as global superpowers, with the United States possessing the world's strongest economy. The opportunities for women and minorities during the war also increased their aspirations and would contribute to the emergence of the civil rights and feminist movements.

CHRONOLOGY

1933	Adolf Hitler becomes chancellor of Germany
1937	War between China and Japan begins
September 1939	German troops invade Poland
1940	Battle of Britain
June 1941	Germany invades Soviet Union
August 1941	United States and Great Britain sign the Atlantic Charter
December 7, 1941	Japanese launch surprise attack at Pearl Harbor, Hawaii
June 1942	Battle of Midway
June 6, 1944	D-day
February 1945	Yalta Conference
April 1945	Roosevelt dies; Hitler commits suicide
May 7–8, 1945	Nazi Germany surrenders; V-E day
August 1945	Atomic bombs dropped on Hiroshima and Nagasaki
September 2, 1945	Japan surrenders

KEY TERMS

fascism p. 1210

neutrality laws p. 1214

Axis alliance p. 1215

Lend-Lease Act (1941) p. 1223

Atlantic Charter (1941) p. 1226

Pearl Harbor (1941) p. 1229

War Production Board p. 1231

Women's Army Corps p. 1233

Tuskegee Airmen p. 1238

bracero program (1942-1945) p. 1238

war relocation camps p. 1240

Operation Overlord p. 1246

Yalta Conference (1945) p. 1253

Holocaust p. 1256

Battle of Midway (1942) p. 1259

Hiroshima (1945) p. 1263

 INQUIZITIVE

Go to InQuizitive to see what you've learned—and learn what you've missed—with personalized feedback along the way.

part seven

THE AMERICAN AGE

As the Second World War was ending in 1945, President Franklin D. Roosevelt, like Woodrow Wilson before him, staked his hopes for a peaceful future on a new international organization.

On April 25, 1945, two weeks after Roosevelt's death and two weeks before the German surrender, delegates from fifty nations met in San Francisco to draw up the Charter of the United Nations. It gave the UN Security Council "primary responsibility for the maintenance of international peace and security." The Security Council included five *permanent* members: the United States, the Soviet Union (replaced by the Russian Federation in 1991), Great Britain, France, and the Republic of China (replaced by the People's Republic of China in 1971). Each could *veto* any proposed action by the United Nations.

It soon became evident, however, that the United States and the Soviet Union had such intense differences of opinion about international policies that the United Nations was largely impotent in dealing with the emerging cold war between the competing ideologies of communism and capitalism.

The United States emerged from the Second World War as the dominant nation. It was the world's preeminent military and economic power, and the only nation with atomic weapons. While much of Europe, Asia, and Africa struggled to recover from the war's destruction, the United States emerged from the conflict with its economic infrastructure intact and operating at peak efficiency. Jobs were available for the taking. By 1955, the United States, with only 6 percent of the world's population, was producing half the world's goods.

However, the deepening cold war between democratic and Communist nations cast a cloud over the postwar world. The tense ideological contest with the Soviet Union produced numerous crises and sparked a witch hunt for Communists in the United States. After 1945, Republican and Democratic presidents sought to "contain" the spread of communism; this bedrock assumption embroiled the United States in costly wars in Korea and in Southeast Asia.

A backlash against the Vietnam War (1964–1973) inflamed a rebellious countercultural movement in which young idealists opposed to the war also provided much of the energy for many overdue social reforms. An array of social justice and liberation movements emerged during the sixties, including racial and ethnic equality, gay rights (known as LGBTQ rights since the 1990s), feminism, and environmentalism. The anti-war movement destroyed Lyndon Johnson's presidency in 1968 and provoked a conservative counterattack by Republicans. President Richard Nixon's paranoid reaction to his critics led to the Watergate affair and the destruction of his presidency.

Through all this turmoil, however, the expanding role of the federal government that Franklin Roosevelt and his New Deal programs had initiated remained essentially intact. With only a few exceptions, both Republicans and Democrats after 1945 acknowledged that the federal government must assume greater responsibility for the welfare of individuals. Yet by the late 1980s this fragile consensus on public policy collapsed amid stunning international developments and social changes at home. The implosion and dissolution of the Soviet Union in 1989 left the United States as the world's only superpower, lowered the threat of nuclear war, and reduced public interest in foreign affairs.

Numerous ethnic, nationalist, and separatist conflicts, however, brought constant international instability. The United States found itself drawn into political and military crises in Bosnia, Somalia, Afghanistan, Iraq, Ukraine, and Syria.

Throughout the 1990s, the United States waged a difficult struggle against many groups engaged in organized terrorism. The challenges of tracking the movements of foreign terrorists became tragically evident in 2001. At 8:46 on the morning of September 11, 2001, the world watched in horror as hijacked commercial airplanes slammed into the World Trade Center in New York City and the Pentagon Washington, D.C.

Officials identified the hijackers as members of al Qaeda (Arabic for "the Base"), a well-financed network of Islamic terrorists led by a wealthy Saudi renegade, Osama bin Laden. President George W. Bush responded by declaring a "war on terror." With the passage of the so-called Patriot Act, Congress gave the president authority to track down and imprison terrorists at home and abroad. Militarily, the war on terror began with assaults first on terrorist bases in Afghanistan and then on Saddam Hussein's dictatorship in Iraq (Operation Iraqi Freedom).

Frustrated by the expense and casualties of the ongoing wars in Iraq and Afghanistan, American voters elected Democrat Barack Obama in the 2008 presidential contest. He pledged to end the wars, create a national health-care system directed at the growing numbers of uninsured, unite the polarized nation, and provide jobs to the unemployed. As the first African American U.S. president, Obama symbolized the societal changes transforming national life.

Upon taking office, President Obama inherited the worst economic slowdown since the Great Depression. What came to be called the Great Recession dominated both terms of his presidency. For all its economic power and military might, the United States in the twenty-first century has not eliminated the threat of terrorism or unlocked the mystery of sustaining prosperity and reducing economic inequality.

That many Americans did not share in the economic recovery and were frustrated by the continuing influx of immigrants, especially Mexicans, helps explain the remarkable presidential candidacy of brash real-estate developer Donald Trump. As a self-described "disruptive" political force, he seized control of the 2016 presidential campaign by turning conventional assumptions of America's role abroad and its priorities at home topsy-turvy.

27 The Cold War and the Fair Deal

1945–1952

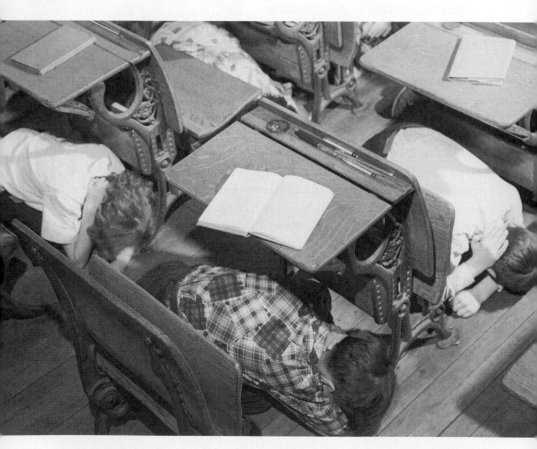

Duck and cover A "duck-and-cover" air-raid drill in 1951 that was commonplace in schools during the cold war. The drills began in 1949, when the Soviet Union set off its first nuclear weapon. Pictured above are schoolchildren practicing ducking and covering in February 1951.

No sooner did the Second World War end than a tense cold war erupted between communism and capitalism, totalitarianism and democracy. For over forty years after 1945, the Soviet Union and the United States engaged in a relentless war of words as each sought to gain influence around the world for its way of life. The awkward wartime alliance between the United States and the Soviet Union collapsed during the spring and summer of 1945. With the elimination of German Nazism, the two nations became fierce rivals who could not bridge their ideological differences over basic issues such as human rights, individual liberties, democratic elections, and religious freedom. As President Harry Truman said, the most important issue facing the postwar world was the choice between "tyranny or freedom."

Mutual suspicion and a race to gain influence over "nonaligned" nations in Asia, Africa, the Middle East, and Central and South America further distanced the two former allies. The defeat of Japan and Germany had created power vacuums in Europe and Asia that sucked the Soviet Union and the United States into a contest for global influence and control.

The postwar era also brought anti-colonial liberation movements that would soon strip Great Britain, France, the Netherlands, and the United States of their global empires. The emergence of Communist China (the People's Republic) in 1949 further complicated global politics and cold war dynamics.

In the unstable postwar world, international tensions shaped domestic politics and foreign relations. The advent of atomic weapons made the very idea of warfare unthinkably horrific, which in turn made national leaders more cautious so as not to trigger a third world war.

focus questions

1. Why and how did the cold war between the United States and the Soviet Union develop?

2. What was the impact of U.S. efforts to contain the Soviet Union and the growth of global communism during Harry Truman's presidency?

3. How did Truman expand the New Deal? How effective was his Fair Deal agenda?

4. What were the major international developments during 1949–1950, and how did they alter U.S. foreign policy?

5. How did the Red Scare emerge? How did it impact American politics and society?

TRUMAN AND THE COLD WAR

In April 1945, less than three months after Harry S. Truman had begun his new role as vice president, Eleanor Roosevelt calmly informed him, "Harry, the President is dead." When Truman asked how he could help her, the First Lady replied: "Is there anything we can do for *you*? For you are the one in trouble now." Truman was largely unknown outside of Washington. What everyone did know, however, was that he was not Franklin Delano Roosevelt. Truman had no wealthy family, had not traveled the world, and had not attended Harvard or Columbia like Roosevelt. In fact, he had not attended any college.

Born in 1884 in western Missouri, Truman grew up in Independence, near Kansas City. During the First World War, he served in France as captain of an artillery battery. Afterward, he and a partner started a clothing business, but it failed in the recession of 1922, leaving him in debt for twenty years. Truman then entered politics as a Democrat. In 1934, Missouri sent him to the U.S. Senate.

On his first full day as president, Truman was awestruck. "Boys, if you ever pray, pray for me now," he told reporters. "I don't know whether you fellows ever had a load of hay fall on you, but when they told me yesterday what had happened, I felt like the moon, the stars and all the planets had fallen on me."

An unreflective man rarely troubled by doubts or moral ambiguities, Truman was famously short-tempered, profane, and dismissive. His press conferences were punctuated by confrontations. ("If you ask smart-aleck questions, I'll give you smart-aleck answers.") He called publisher William Randolph Hearst "the number one whore monger of our time," columnist Westbrook Pegler "the greatest character assassin in the United States," and Richard Nixon "a shifty-eyed goddamned liar." The president's behavior, said the *Chicago Tribune*, called into question his "mental competence and emotional stability."

Harry S. Truman The successor to Franklin Roosevelt who led the United States out of the Second World War and into the cold war.

Although Washington politicos had low expectations for the new president, Truman did better than anyone expected. He rose above his limitations and never pretended to be something he was not. During a visit in 1952, British leader Winston Churchill confessed to Truman that initially he had held him "in very low regard. I loathed your taking the place of Franklin Roosevelt. I misjudged you badly. Since that time, you, more than any other man, have saved Western civilization."

ORIGINS OF THE COLD WAR Historians have long debated the unanswerable question: Was the United States or the Soviet Union more responsible for the onset of the cold war? The conventional view argues that the Soviets, led by Josef Stalin, set out to dominate the globe after 1945. The United States had no choice but to defend democratic capitalist values.

Historians critical of this explanation insist that the United States unnecessarily antagonized the Soviet Union. Instead of continuing Franklin Roosevelt's collaborative efforts with the Soviets, Truman pursued a confrontational foreign policy that focused on stopping the spread of communism, a policy that only aggravated tensions. For example, the United States in 1947 and 1948 secretly intervened in elections in France and Italy to ensure that Communist candidates were defeated. American agents gave bags of money to anti-Communist candidates, provided campaign advisers, and publicly threatened to cut off aid to the governments if Communists were elected.

In retrospect, the onset of the cold war seems to have been an unavoidable result of the ideological competition between democratic capitalism and totalitarian communism and their opposing views of what the postwar world should become. America's commitment to free-enterprise capitalism, political self-determination, and religious freedom conflicted with the Soviet Union's preference for controlling its neighbors, ideological conformity, and prohibiting religious practices.

Insecurity drove much of Soviet behavior. Russia, after all, had been invaded by Germany twice in the first half of the twentieth century, and some 23 million people died as a result. Soviet leaders were determined to dominate nations on their borders and in their region, just as the United States had been doing for decades in Central and South America.

The people of Eastern Europe were caught in the middle, and the cold war soon came to dominate global politics. We are still living in its shadow.

CONFLICTS WITH THE SOVIETS The wartime military alliance against Nazism disintegrated after 1945 as the Soviet Union violated the promises it had made at the Yalta Conference. The USSR imposed military control and a Communist political system on the nations of Eastern Europe that it had liberated from Nazi control. On May 12, 1945, four days after victory in Europe, Winston Churchill asked Truman: "What is to happen about [Eastern] Europe? An **iron curtain** is drawn down upon [the Russian] front. We do not know what is going on behind [it]." Churchill and Truman wanted to lift the iron curtain and help those nations develop democratic governments. Events during the second half of 1945, however, dashed those expectations.

Beginning in the spring of 1945 and continuing for the next two years, the Soviet Union systematically imprisoned half the European continent and installed puppet governments across Central and Eastern Europe (Albania, Bulgaria, Czechoslovakia, East Germany, Hungary, Poland, Romania, and Yugoslavia). The Soviets eliminated all political parties except the Communists; created secret police forces; took control of intellectual and cultural life, including the mass media; and organized a process of ethnic cleansing whereby whole populations—12 million Germans, as well as Poles and Hungarians—were relocated, usually to West Germany or to prisons. Anyone who opposed the Soviet-installed regimes was exiled, silenced, imprisoned, or executed.

Stalin's promise at the Yalta Conference to allow open elections in the nations controlled by Soviet armies had turned out to be a lie. In a fit of candor, he admitted that "a freely elected government in any of these countries would be anti-Soviet, and that we cannot allow."

U.S. Secretary of State James F. Byrnes tried to use America's monopoly on the atomic bomb to pressure the Soviets. In April 1945, he suggested to President Truman that nuclear weapons "might well put us in position to dictate our own terms [with the Soviets] at the end of the war." The Soviets, however, paid little attention, in part because their spies had kept them informed of what U.S. scientists had been doing and in part because they were developing their own atomic bombs.

In April, a few days before the opening of the conference to organize the United Nations, Truman met with Soviet foreign minister Vyacheslav Molotov. Truman directed Molotov to tell Stalin that the United States expected the Soviet leader to live up to his agreements. "I have never been talked to like that in my life," Molotov angrily replied. "Carry out your agreements," Truman snapped, "and you won't get talked to like that."

That July, when Truman met Stalin at the Potsdam conference, he wrote that he had never seen "such pig-headed people as are the Russians." He later acknowledged that they broke their promises "as soon as the unconscionable Russian Dictator [Stalin] returned to Moscow!" Truman added, with a note of embarrassment, "And I liked the little son of a bitch."

THE CONTAINMENT POLICY

In February 1946, Stalin had proclaimed the superiority of the Soviet Communist system of government and declared that peace was impossible "under the present capitalist development of the world economy." By the beginning of 1947, relations with the Soviet Union had grown ice cold. Stalin's provocative statement against capitalism led the State Department to ask for an analysis of Soviet communism from George Frost Kennan, the best-informed expert on the Soviet Union, who was then working in the U.S. embassy in Moscow.

Kennan responded on February 22, 1946, with a 5,000-word "Long Telegram." He predicted that the Soviets would never embrace a "permanent happy coexistence" of the socialist and capitalist worlds.

Kennan explained that the Soviet Union was founded on a rigid ideology (Marxism-Leninism), which saw a fundamental global conflict between Communist and capitalist nations. The Soviets, he said, were "fanatically" committed to perpetual tension and conflict. Kennan implied that Franklin Roosevelt had mistakenly assumed that his personal diplomacy with Stalin would ensure that the Soviets behaved.

The Soviet goal, according to Kennan, was to build military strength while subverting the stability of capitalist democracies. He recommended that American policy focus on the strategic **containment** of Soviet expansionism. That could best be achieved through patient, persistent, tactical efforts to undermine the appeal of Soviet communism. Kennan highlighted the economic power of capitalist democracies as their greatest asset in thwarting Soviet expansion. Creating "unalterable counterforce" to Communist expansionism, Kennan

George F. Kennan A specialist in the history and behavior of the Soviet Union, diplomat George Kennan developed the rationale for containment at the heart of the Truman Doctrine.

predicted, would eventually cause "either the breakup or the gradual mellowing of Soviet power" because communism was inherently unstable and would eventually collapse.

New secretary of state George C. Marshall, the distinguished commander of the U.S. armed forces during the war, was so impressed by Kennan's analysis that he put him in charge of the State Department's Policy Planning office. No other diplomat at the time forecast so accurately what would happen to the Soviet Union some forty years later.

But how were the United States and its allies to *contain* the Soviet Union's expansionist tendencies? How should the United States respond to Soviet aggression? Kennan left the task of containing communism to Truman and his advisers, most of whom, unlike Kennan, considered containment to be as much a *military* doctrine as a *political* strategy. As Truman insisted, the Soviets understood only one language: military power.

In 1946, civil war broke out in Greece between the monarchy backed by the British and a Communist-led insurgency supported by the Soviets. On February 21, 1947, the British informed the U.S. government that they could no longer provide economic and military aid to Greece and would withdraw their 40,000 troops in five weeks. Truman quickly conferred with congressional leaders. One of them, Republican senator Arthur Vandenberg of Michigan, warned the president that he would need to "scare the hell out of the American people" about the menace of communism to gain public support for any new aid program.

THE TRUMAN DOCTRINE On March 12, 1947, President Truman gave a national radio speech in which he asked Congress to provide $400 million for economic and military assistance to Greece and Turkey. More important, he announced what came to be known as the **Truman Doctrine**, which would guide American foreign policy for the next two decades. To ensure congressional support, the president exaggerated the danger of a Communist takeover in Greece. Like a row of dominoes, Truman predicted, the fall of Greece would topple the other nations of the eastern Mediterranean, then Western Europe. To prevent such a catastrophe, he said, the United States must "support free peoples who are resisting attempted subjugation by armed minorities or by outside pressures."

In this single sentence, Truman in essence was declaring war on communism everywhere. In his view, shared by later presidents, the assumptions of the "domino theory" made an aggressive containment strategy a necessity.

Truman's speech generated widespread public support. The *New York Times* said that his message was clear: "The epoch of isolation is ended. It is being replaced by an epoch of American responsibility." At the State Department, Secretary Marshall announced that "we are now concerned with the peace of the entire world."

Still, the secretary of state and others privately feared that Truman's speech was unnecessarily provocative. Marshall believed that the president was overstating the Soviet threat. Others expressed concern about the scope and vagueness of the Truman Doctrine. Bernard Baruch, a prominent political adviser, charged that Truman's speech represented a "declaration of . . . an ideological or religious war" against the Soviet Union.

George Kennan similarly cringed at the president's "grandiose" commitment to contain communism *everywhere*. In Kennan's view, Truman's "militarized view of the Cold War" was an open-ended ideological confrontation rather than a *policy* with an accompanying program of steps capable of implementation. Efforts to contain communism needed to be selective rather than universal, political and economic rather than military. The United States could not intervene in every "hot spot" around the world.

Walter Lippmann, the nation's leading political journalist, characterized Truman's policy of global anti-communism as a "strategic monstrosity" that would entangle the United States in endless international disputes and force it to partner with right-wing dictatorships—as turned out to be the case.

Truman and his advisers rejected such concerns. In 1947, Congress approved the president's request for aid to Greece and Turkey.

THE MARSHALL PLAN In the spring of 1947, most postwar European governments remained insolvent, shattered, and desperate, and political unrest was growing. By 1947, Socialist and Communist parties were forming in many European nations, including Italy, France, and Belgium. The crises among these struggling democracies required bold action.

The United States stepped into the breach. In May 1947, Secretary of State Marshall, building upon suggestions from George Kennan and others, called for a massive U.S. program to provide financial and technical assistance to rescue Europe, including the Soviet Union.

What came to be known as the **Marshall Plan** was intended to reconstruct the European economy, neutralize Communist insurgencies, and build up foreign markets for U.S. products. As Truman said, "the American [capitalist] system can survive only if it is part of a world system." The Marshall Plan was about more than economics, however. It was part of Truman's effort to contain the expansionist tendencies of the Soviet Union by reestablishing a strong Western Europe anchored in American values.

"It's the same thing" The Marshall Plan, which distributed massive amounts of economic aid throughout postwar Europe, is represented in this 1949 cartoon as a modern tractor driven by a prosperous farmer. In the foreground, a poor, overworked man is yoked to an old-fashioned "Soviet" plow, forced to go over the ground of the "Marshal Stalin Plan," while Stalin himself tries to persuade others that "it's the same thing without mechanical problems."

In December 1947, Truman submitted Marshall's proposal to Congress, saying that "if Europe fails to recover" from the war's devastation, voters might be won over by Communist parties, which would deal a "shattering blow to peace and stability."

Initially, Republican critics dismissed the Marshall Plan as "New Dealism" for Europe, a "costly boondoggle" that smacked of socialism. However, two months later, on February 25, 1948, a Communist-led coup in Czechoslovakia, the last nation in Eastern Europe with a democratic government, ensured the Marshall Plan's passage.

From 1948 until 1951, the Marshall Plan provided $13 billion to sixteen European nations. The Soviet Union, however, refused to participate and forced the Eastern European countries under its control—Albania, Bulgaria, Poland, Romania, Yugoslavia—to refuse as well.

The Marshall Plan (officially called the European Recovery Plan) worked as hoped. By 1951, Western Europe's industrial production had soared to 40 percent above prewar levels, and its farm output was larger than ever. England's *Economist* magazine called the Marshall Plan "an act without peer." It became the most successful peacetime diplomatic initiative in history.

DIVIDED GERMANY Although the Marshall Plan drew the nations of Western Europe closer together, it increased tensions with the Soviet Union. The breakdown of the wartime alliance between the United States and the Soviet Union also left the problem of postwar Germany unsettled. In 1945, Berlin, the German capital, had been divided into four sectors, or zones, each governed by one of the four principal allied nations—the United States, France, Great Britain, and the Soviet Union.

The German economy continued to languish, requiring the U.S. Army to provide food and supplies to millions of civilians. Slowly, the Allied occupation zones evolved into functioning governments. In 1948, the British, French, and Americans united their three administrative zones into one and developed a common currency for West Germany and West Berlin, a city of 2.5 million people, which was more than 100 miles inside the Soviet occupation zone of East Germany. The West Germans also organized state governments and began drafting a federal constitution.

The political unification and economic recovery of West Germany infuriated Stalin, and the status of divided Berlin had become a powder keg. In March 1948, Stalin prevented the new West German currency from being used in Berlin. Then, on June 23, he stopped all road and rail traffic into West Berlin, hoping to force the United States and its allies to leave the divided city.

Americans interpreted Stalin's blockade as a tipping point in the cold war. "When Berlin falls," predicted General Lucius D. Clay, the U.S. Army commander in Germany, "western Germany will be next. Communism will run rampant." The United States thus faced a dilemma: risk a third world war by using force to break the Soviet blockade or begin a humiliating retreat from West Berlin.

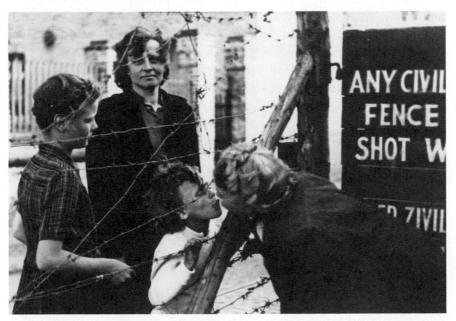

Family reunion A girl gives her grandmother a kiss through the barbed wire fence that divided the Dutch-German frontier in 1947.

Through the iron curtain German children greet a U.S. cargo plane as it flies into West Berlin to drop off much-needed food and supplies.

Truman was firm: "We stay in Berlin—period." The United States announced an embargo against all goods exported from Soviet-controlled eastern Germany and began organizing a massive airlift to provide food and supplies to West Berliners.

By October 1948, U.S. and British air forces were flying in 7,000 tons of food, fuel, medicine, coal, and equipment to Berlin each day. To support the airlift and prepare for a possible war, thousands of former military pilots were called back into service. Truman revived the military draft, and Congress provided emergency funds to increase military spending. The world watched as the two superpowers teetered on the edge of conflict.

For all the threats and harsh words, however, the **Berlin airlift** went on for 321 days without shots being fired. Finally, on May 12, 1949, the Soviets lifted their blockade, in part because bad Russian harvests had made them desperate for food grown in western Germany.

The Berlin airlift was the first major "victory" for the West in the cold war, and the unprecedented efforts of the United States and Great Britain to supply West Berliners transformed most of them into devoted allies. In May 1949, the Federal Republic of Germany (West Germany) was founded. In October, the Soviet-controlled German Democratic Republic (East Germany) came into being.

FORMING ALLIANCES The Soviet blockade of Berlin convinced the United States and its allies that they needed to act together to stop further Communist expansion into Western Europe. On April 4, 1949, representatives of twelve nations signed the North Atlantic Treaty: the United States, Great Britain, France, Belgium, the Netherlands, Luxembourg, Canada, Denmark, Iceland, Italy, Norway, and Portugal. Greece and Turkey joined the alliance in 1952, West Germany in 1955, and Spain in 1982.

THE OCCUPATION OF GERMANY AND AUSTRIA

French zone	U.S. zone
British zone	Soviet zone

- How did the Allies decide to divide postwar Germany at the Yalta Conference?
- What was the "iron curtain"?
- Why did the Allies airlift supplies to West Berlin?

The **North Atlantic Treaty Organization (NATO)**, the largest defensive alliance in the world, declared that an attack against any of the members would be an attack against all. The creation of NATO marked the high point of efforts to contain Soviet expansion. By joining NATO, the United States committed itself to go to war on behalf of its allies. Isolationism was dead.

REORGANIZING THE MILITARY The onset of the cold war and the emergence of nuclear weapons led President Truman to sign the **National Security Act** (1947), which reorganized the armed forces and intelligence agencies. It created a Department of Defense led by a new cabinet officer, the secretary of defense; a Joint Chiefs of Staff to oversee the three military branches—the army, navy, and the newly created air force; and established the National Security Council (NSC), a group of top specialists in international relations appointed to advise the president. The act also established the Central Intelligence Agency (CIA) to coordinate global intelligence-gathering activities. The following year, the NSC gave the CIA permission to launch covert operations abroad to undermine governments that threatened American interests.

A JEWISH NATION: ISRAEL At the same time that the United States was forming new alliances, it was helping to form a new nation. Palestine, the biblical Holy Land, had been a British protectorate since 1919. For hundreds of years, Jews throughout the world had dreamed of returning to their ancestral homeland of Israel and its ancient capital Zion, a part of Jerusalem. Many Zionists—Jews who wanted a separate Jewish nation—had migrated there. More arrived during and after the Nazi persecution of European Jews. Hitler's effort to exterminate Jews convinced many that their only hope for a secure future was to create their own nation.

Late in 1947, the United Nations voted to divide ("partition") Palestine into separate Jewish and Arab states. The Jews agreed to the partition, but the Arabs opposed it. Palestine was their ancestral home, too; Jerusalem was as holy to Muslims and Christians as it was to Jews.

Arabs viewed the creation of a Jewish nation in Palestine as an act of war, and they attacked Israel in early 1948. Hundreds were killed before the Haganah (Jewish militia) won control of most of Palestine. When British oversight of Palestine officially expired on May 14, 1948, David Ben-Gurion, the Jewish leader in Palestine, proclaimed Israel's independence. President Truman officially recognized the new Israeli nation within minutes, as did the Soviet Union.

One million Jews, most of them European immigrants, now had their own nation. Early the next morning, however, the Arab League nations—Lebanon,

Syria, Iraq, Jordan, and Egypt—invaded Israel. Mediators from the United Nations gradually worked out a truce, restoring an unstable peace by May 11, 1949, when Israel joined the United Nations. Israel kept all its conquered territories, including the whole Palestine coast.

The Palestinian Arabs lost everything. Most became stateless refugees who scattered into neighboring Lebanon, Jordan, and Egypt. Stored-up resentments and sporadic warfare between Israel and the Arab states have festered since, complicating U.S. foreign policy, which has tried to maintain friendships with both sides but has usually tilted toward Israel.

EXPANDING THE NEW DEAL

For the most part, Republicans and Democrats in Congress cooperated with President Truman on domestic issues. However, Truman faced widespread opposition on issues related to the cold war. Senator Claude Pepper, a liberal Democrat from Florida, insisted that if Franklin Roosevelt were still alive, "we'd be getting on better with Russia." Republican senator Robert A. Taft of Ohio accused Truman of "appeasing Russia, a policy which has sacrificed throughout Eastern Europe and Asia the freedom of many nations and millions of people." The cost-cutting Republicans in Congress hoped that they could end the New Deal as the Second World War drew to a close.

FROM WAR TO PEACE In September 1945, Truman called Congress into a special emergency session at which he presented a twenty-one-point program to guide the nation's "reconversion" from wartime back to peacetime. His greatest challenge was to ensure that the peacetime economy absorbed the millions of men and women who had served in the armed forces and were now seeking civilian jobs.

That would not be easy. The day after the war in Asia ended, the Springfield Armory, which had made weapons for the army, fired every worker. Other military-dependent companies also announced layoffs. The nation faced a crisis as some 12 million men and women in uniform left military service and returned to an economy careening into recession.

Fears of massive unemployment in defense-related industries prompted concerns about another depression. A *New York Times* headline predicted: "5,000,000 EXPECTED TO LOSE ARMS JOBS!" Truman called for unemployment insurance to cover more workers, a higher minimum wage, construction of massive public-housing projects, regional development projects to put military veterans to work, and much more.

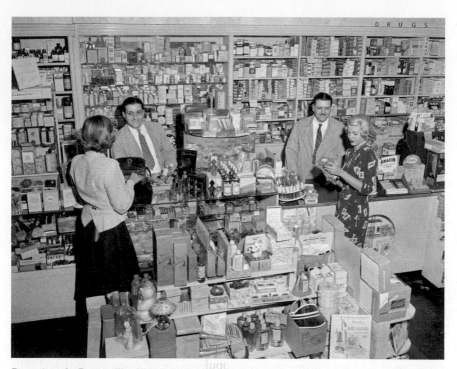

Drugstore in Bronxville, NY America quickly demobilized after the long war effort, turning its attention to the pursuit of abundance.

A powerful Republican congressman, Joseph W. Martin, was left speechless by the scope of Truman's proposals. "Not even President Roosevelt," he gasped, "ever asked for so much at one sitting."

Truman's primary goal was to "prevent prolonged unemployment" while avoiding the "bitter mistakes" that had produced wild price inflation and a recession after the First World War. He also wanted to retain, for a while, the wartime controls on wages, prices, and rents, as well as the rationing of scarce food items. Most of all, he wanted to ensure that military veterans found civilian jobs. Truman called on Congress to *guarantee* every American a job.

Congress refused to go that far. Instead, it approved the Employment Act of 1946, which called on the federal government "to promote maximum employment, production, and purchasing power." Liberals were disappointed by Truman's inability to win over skeptical legislators. "Alas for Truman," said the *New Republic*, there was "no bugle note in his voice" to rally public opinion. "What one misses," said journalist Max Lerner, "is the confident sense of direction that Roosevelt gave, despite all the contradictions of his policy."

Throughout 1946, Republicans and conservative southern Democrats in Congress balked at Truman's efforts to revive or expand New Deal programs. The Great Depression was over, critics stressed. Different times demanded different programs—or none at all.

The end of the war caused short-term economic problems. The federal government immediately canceled 100,000 contracts for military supplies and equipment. Many women who had been recruited to work in wartime defense industries were shoved out as men took off uniforms and looked for jobs. At a shipyard in California, a foreman gathered women workers and told them to welcome the troop ships as they pulled into port from Asia. The next day, the women were laid off to make room for male veterans.

Still, several shock absorbers cushioned the economic impact of demobilization. They included federal unemployment insurance (and other Social Security benefits) and the Servicemen's Readjustment Act of 1944, known as the GI Bill of Rights, under which the federal government provided $13 billion for veterans to use for education, vocational training, medical treatment, unemployment insurance, and loans for building houses and starting new businesses.

Veterans eagerly returned to colleges, jobs, wives and husbands, and babies. Marriage rates soared. So, too, did population growth, which had dropped off sharply in the 1930s. Americans born during the postwar period (roughly 1946–1964) composed the "baby boom generation," a disproportionately large group that would shape the nation's social and cultural life throughout the second half of the twentieth century and after.

WAGES, PRICES, AND LABOR UNREST The most acute economic problem Harry Truman faced was the postwar spike in prices for consumer goods. During the war, the government had frozen wages and prices and banned strikes by labor unions. Truman's decision in June 1946 to remove wartime controls on wages and consumer prices caused consumer prices to spike, which led labor unions to demand pay increases. When management balked at providing higher wages, more than 4,000 strikes at automobile plants, steel mills, coal mines, and railroads erupted in 1945–1946, involving some 5 million workers. Never before or since had so many employees walked off the job in one year.

Truman grew frustrated with the stubbornness of both management and labor leaders. He took federal control of the coal mines, whereupon the mine owners agreed to union demands. In May 1946, Truman threatened to use soldiers to operate the trains and to draft striking railroad workers into the military if they did not go back to work, for the entire national rail system had been forced to shut down. In a speech to Congress, Truman declared that "this is no longer a dispute between labor and management. It has now become a strike against the United States government itself." His threat, probably unconstitutional, did the trick, but it embittered many union members who had long voted Democratic.

The backlash over postwar inflation led Truman to restore government controls on particular consumer items such as meat. This only led to more complaints. Ranchers were so upset that they refused to sell their cattle for slaughter. Suddenly, there was a "beefsteak" crisis as consumers complained that the supply of food was worse than it had been during the war. *Time* magazine's Washington-based political reporter alerted his editor that Truman was so unpopular "he could not carry Missouri now."

POLITICAL COOPERATION AND CONFLICT During the congressional election campaigns in 1946, Republicans adopted a simple, four-word slogan: "Had Enough? Vote Republican!" Using loudspeakers, Republicans drove through city streets saying, "Ladies, if you want meat, vote Republican." A union leader tagged Truman "the No. 1 Strikebreaker," while much of the public, upset by the unions, price increases, food shortages, and scarcity of automobiles and affordable housing, blamed the strikes on the White House.

Labor unions had emerged from the war with more power than ever, for blue-collar workers were essential to military victory. The National Labor Relations Act (NLRA) of 1935 had also helped ensure the rights of workers to form and join unions. As a consequence, by 1945 some 14.5 million workers, more than a third of the workforce, were unionized. Members had tended to vote Democratic, but not in the 1946 elections, for union members viewed Truman as their enemy. Their votes gave the Republicans majorities in both houses of Congress for the first time since 1928. Even many Democrats had soured on Truman, circulating a slogan that expressed their frustration: "I'm just Mild about Harry."

Tired of strikes and labor unrest, the Republican Congress that convened in early 1947 sought to curb the power of unions by passing the **Taft-Hartley Labor Act** (officially called the Labor-Management Relations Act). The law gutted many of the provisions of the NLRA by allowing employers to campaign against efforts to form unions and outlawed unions from coercing workers to join or refusing to negotiate grievances.

The Taft-Hartley Act also required union leaders to take "loyalty oaths" declaring that they were not members of the Communist party, banned strikes by federal government employees, and imposed a "cooling-off" period of eighty days on any strike that the president deemed dangerous to the public welfare. Yet the most troubling element of the new bill for unions was a provision that allowed state legislatures to pass "right-to-work" laws that ended the practice of forcing all workers to join a union once a majority voted to unionize. William Green, the president of the American Federation of Labor (AFL) proclaimed that the true purpose of the Taft-Hartley Act was "to destroy unions and to wreck collective bargaining."

Truman vetoed the Taft-Hartley Act, denouncing it as "bad for labor, bad for management, and bad for the country." Working-class Democrats were delighted. Many unionists who had voted Republican in 1946 now returned to the Democrats. Journalist James Wechsler reported that "Mr. Truman has reached the crucial fork in the road and turned unmistakably to the left."

Congress, however, overturned the president's veto, and Taft-Hartley became law, largely because southern Democrats overwhelmingly supported it. Southern conservatives adamantly opposed the formation of unions. They feared that unions would disrupt the profitability of the southern textile industry and exert pressure against the tradition of racial segregation.

Vance Muse, a prominent Texas business executive, lobbyist, and white supremacist, hated unions because they encouraged workers to organize across racial lines. His own grandson described him as "a white supremacist, an anti-Semite, and a Communist-baiter, a man who beat on labor unions not on behalf of working people, as he said, but because he was paid to do so." Without the right-to-work provisions of the Taft-Hartley Act, Muse warned, "white women and white men will be forced into organizations with black African apes whom they will have to call 'brother' or lose their jobs."

The number of strikes dropped sharply as a result of the Taft-Hartley Act, and representatives of management and labor learned to work together. By 1954, fifteen state legislatures, mainly in the South and West, had used the Taft-Hartley Act to pass right-to-work laws. Those states thereafter recruited industries to relocate because of their low wages and nonunion policies. As the Republicans celebrated, however, they did not realize that the Taft-Hartley Act would cause most union members to vote Democratic in 1948.

CIVIL RIGHTS AMID A CHANGING SOCIETY President Truman was also forced to confront the bigotry faced by returning African American soldiers. When one black veteran arrived home in a uniform decorated with combat medals, a white neighbor yelled, "Don't you forget . . . that you're still a nigger." Another black veteran was yanked off a bus in South Carolina and beaten so badly that he was blinded.

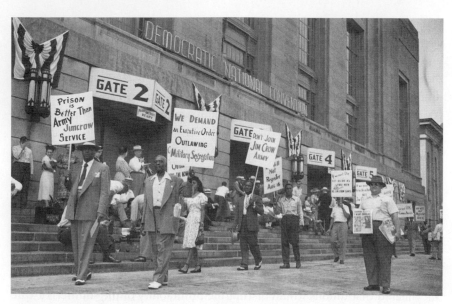

Fight for desegregation Demonstrators led by activist A. Philip Randolph (left) picket the Democratic National Convention on July 12, 1948, calling for racial integration of the armed forces.

The Second World War had changed America's racial landscape in important ways, however. As a *New York Times* editorial explained in early 1946, "This is a particularly good time to campaign against the evils of bigotry, prejudice, and race hatred because we have witnessed the defeat of enemies who tried to found a mastery of the world upon such cruel and fallacious policy."

African Americans had fought to overthrow the Nazi regime of government-sponsored racism, and many returning black veterans were unwilling to put up with racial abuse at home. The cold war also gave political leaders added incentive to improve race relations. The Soviets often compared racism in the United States to the Nazis' brutalization of Jewish people. In the ideological contest against capitalism, Communists highlighted examples of racism to win influence among newly emerging African nations.

Black veterans who spoke out often risked their lives. In 1946, a white mob in rural Georgia gunned down two African American couples. One of the murderers explained that George Dorsey, one of the victims, was "a good nigger" until he went into the army. "But when he came out, he thought he was as good as any white people."

In the fall of 1946, a delegation of civil rights activists urged President Truman to condemn the Ku Klux Klan and the lynching of African Americans.

The delegation graphically described incidents of torture and intimidation against blacks in the South. Truman was horrified: "My God! I had no idea that it was as terrible as that! We've got to do something."

Truman thereupon appointed a Commission on Civil Rights. A year later, with the president's endorsement, the Commission issued a report, *To Secure These Rights*, which called for a federal anti-lynching bill, abolition of the poll tax designed to keep poor black people from voting, a voting rights act, an end to racial segregation in the armed forces, and a ban on racial segregation in public transportation.

Southern Democrats were furious. A Mississippi congressman claimed that Truman "had seen fit to run a political dagger into our backs." A South Carolina legislator said his friends and neighbors were now "more afraid of Truman than of Russia." South Carolina governor J. Strom Thurmond warned Truman that the southern Democratic vote was no longer "in the bag." Thurmond would soon leave the party to form the Dixiecrats.

On July 26, 1948, Truman took a bolder step by banning racial discrimination throughout the federal government. Four days later, he issued an executive order ending racial segregation in the armed forces. Desegregating the military was, Truman claimed, "the greatest thing that ever happened to America." White southerners disagreed. Democratic congressman Mendel Rivers of South Carolina boasted that Truman "is a dead bird" as far as being reelected. "We in the South are going to see to that."

JACKIE ROBINSON Meanwhile, racial segregation was being dismantled in a much more public area: professional baseball. In April 1947, the Brooklyn Dodgers roster included the first African American to play major league baseball: Jack Roosevelt "Jackie" Robinson. He was born in 1919 in a Georgia sharecropper's cabin, the grandson of slaves. Six months later, his father left, never to return. Robinson's mother moved the family to Pasadena, California, where he became a marvelous all-around athlete. At UCLA, Robinson was the first athlete in school history to letter in four sports: baseball, basketball, football, and track. After serving in the army during World War II, he began playing professional baseball in the so-called Negro Leagues. Major league scouts reported that he could play in the big leagues.

At that point, Branch Rickey, president and general manager of the Brooklyn Dodgers, interviewed Robinson for three hours on August 28, 1945. Rickey asked Robinson if he could face racial abuse without losing his temper. Robinson was shocked: "Are you looking for a Negro who is afraid to fight back?" Rickey replied that he needed a "Negro player" with "guts enough *not* to fight back." Robinson assured him he was the best candidate to integrate

Jackie Robinson Robinson's unfaltering courage and superior athletic skills prompted the integration of sports, drawing African American and Latino spectators to the games. Here, he greets his Dominican fans at Trujillo High School in Santo Domingo.

baseball. After signing Robinson to a contract for $600 a month, Rickey explained to his critics that he had found a terrific player of incomparable courage capable of looking the other way when provoked. And Robinson was often provoked.

Soon after Robinson arrived for preseason practice, many of his white teammates refused to take the field with him. Manager Leo Durocher told the team, "I don't care if the guy is yellow or black, or if he has stripes . . . I'm the manager of this team, and I say he plays."

During the 1947 season, teammates and opposing players viciously baited Robinson. Pitchers hit him, baserunners spiked him, and spectators booed him and even threatened to kill him. Hotels refused him rooms, and restaurants denied him service. Hate mail arrived by the bucketful. One sportswriter called Robinson "the loneliest man I have ever seen in sports."

On the other hand, black spectators loved Robinson's courageous example and turned out in droves to watch him play. A headline in a Boston newspaper expressed the prevailing sentiment: "Triumph of Whole Race Seen in Jackie's Debut in Major League Ball."

As time passed, Robinson won over many fans and players with his courage, wit, grit, and talent. Sportswriter Red Smith observed that Robinson was an example of "the unconquerable doing the impossible." During his first season with the Dodgers, Robinson led the National League in stolen bases and was named Rookie of the Year. Between 1949 and 1954, he had a batting average of .327, among the best in baseball. Robinson's very presence on the field forced spectators sitting in racially divided bleachers to confront the hypocritical reality of segregation. Other teams soon began signing black players. In 1947, Robinson was voted the second most popular American, behind singer Bing Crosby. "My life," Robinson remembered, "produced understanding among whites, and it gave black people the idea that if I could do it, they could do it, too, that blackness wasn't subservient to anything."

MEXICAN AMERICANS AND CIVIL RIGHTS In the Far West, Mexican Americans (often grouped with other Spanish-speaking immigrants as *Hispanics* or *Latinos*) continued to experience ethnic prejudice. Schools in Arizona, New Mexico, Texas, and California routinely segregated Mexican American children from whites. The 500,000 Latino military veterans were especially frustrated that their efforts in the war did not bring equality at home. They were frequently denied access to educational, medical, and housing benefits available to white veterans. Some mortuaries even denied funeral services to Mexican Americans killed in combat. As a funeral director in Texas explained, "the Anglo people would not stand for it."

To fight such treatment, Mexican American veterans led by Dr. Hector Perez Garcia, a U.S. Army major who had served as a combat surgeon, organized the GI Forum in Texas in 1948. Soon there were branches across the nation.

Garcia, born in Mexico in 1914 and raised in Texas, stressed the importance of formal education. At a time when Mexican Americans in Texas averaged no more than a third-grade education, Garcia and five of his siblings had completed medical school. Yet upon his return from the war, he encountered "discrimination everywhere. We had no opportunities. We had to pay [poll taxes] to vote. We had segregated schools. We were not allowed to go into public places."

Garcia and the GI Forum initially focused on veterans' issues but soon expanded the organization's scope to include fostering equal treatment for all people. The GI Forum lobbied to end poll taxes, sued for the right of Latinos to serve on juries, and developed schools for jobless veterans. In 1984, Garcia received the Presidential Medal of Freedom, the nation's highest civilian honor.

SHAPING THE FAIR DEAL During 1947, after less than three years in the White House, President Truman had yet to shake the widespread impression that he was not up to the job. Critics proclaimed, "To err is Truman." The editors of *Time* magazine reflected the national sentiment when they wrote, "Mr. Truman has often faced his responsibilities with a cheerful, dogged courage. But his performance was almost invariably awkward, uninspired, and above all, mediocre." Voters, they added, believed that Truman "means well, but he doesn't do well."

Most political analysts assumed that the president would lose the next election. "Never was there such a mess," Truman told his mother. "The President," predicted the *United States News*, "is a one-termer." When asked how he planned to deal with an Eightieth Congress dominated by Republicans, Truman said he intended to do "as I damn please for the next two years and to hell with them."

Truman, too, feared that he would not be reelected. In July 1947, he met with Dwight D. Eisenhower. Worried that General Douglas MacArthur might be the Republican presidential nominee in 1948, Truman urged Eisenhower to run as the Democratic nominee and even offered to be his vice-presidential running mate. Eisenhower declined, explaining that he was going to become president of Columbia University in New York City.

With Truman's popularity sinking, the Democratic party was about to split in two. While southern conservatives resented the president's outspoken support of civil rights, the left wing of the party resented the firing of Secretary of Commerce Henry A. Wallace for criticizing the administration's anti-Soviet policies. "Getting tough [with the Soviet Union]," Wallace had argued, "never brought anything real and lasting—whether for schoolyard bullies or world powers. The tougher we get, the tougher the Russians will get."

Wallace had said that the United States had "no more business in the *political affairs* of Eastern Europe than Russia has in the *political affairs* of Latin America." The danger of another world war, he said, "is much less from communism than it is from [American] imperialism." Wallace's comments so outraged the leaders of the State Department that Truman fired him, even though the president had preapproved his controversial remarks.

Despite the gloomy predictions for 1948, Truman mounted an energetic reelection campaign. His first step was to shore up the major elements of the New Deal coalition of working-class voters: farmers, labor unionists, and African Americans.

In his 1948 State of the Union message, Truman announced that the programs he would later call his **Fair Deal** would build upon the efforts of Roosevelt's New Deal. The first goal, Truman said, was to ensure civil rights for everyone. He added proposals to increase federal aid to education, expand unemployment and retirement benefits, create a comprehensive system of national health insurance, enable more rural people to connect to electricity, and increase the minimum wage.

THE ELECTION OF 1948 The Republican-controlled Congress dismissed President Truman's proposals, an action it would later regret. At the Republican convention, moderate New York governor Thomas E. Dewey, who had lost to Roosevelt in 1944, won the presidential nomination on the third ballot. While the party's platform endorsed most New Deal reforms and approved the administration's bipartisan foreign policy, Dewey promised to run things more efficiently and promote civil rights for all.

In July, glum Democrats gathered in Philadelphia. A reporter wrote that they behaved "as though they [had] accepted an invitation to a funeral." At the convention, some party leaders, including Franklin Roosevelt's son James, a California congressman, tried again to convince Dwight Eisenhower to accept the Democratic nomination. The popular war hero declined.

Delegates who expected to do little more than go through the motions of nominating Truman were doubly surprised, first by the battle on the convention floor over civil rights and then by Truman's endorsement of civil rights in his acceptance speech. Liberal Democrats led by Minnesota's Hubert Humphrey commended Truman "for his courageous stand" and declared that the "time has arrived for the Democratic party to get out of the shadow of civil rights." White delegates from Alabama and Mississippi walked out in protest. The solidly Democratic South had fractured over race.

On July 17, a group of rebellious southern Democrats assembled at their own convention in Birmingham, Alabama. While waving Confederate flags and singing "Dixie," they nominated South Carolina's segregationist governor, Strom Thurmond, on a States' Rights Democratic party ticket, whose members were quickly dubbed the "**Dixiecrats**." Thurmond was a cocky white supremacist who had secretly fathered a child with a black housekeeper. He later paid hush money to his biracial daughter, denounced Truman's civil rights initiatives, and championed states' rights against federal efforts to change the tradition of white supremacy in the South. He warned that there were "not enough troops in the U.S. Army to force the Southern people to . . . admit the Negro race into our theaters, into our swimming pools, into our homes and into our churches."

On July 23, the left wing of the Democratic party gathered in Philadelphia to form a new Progressive third party and nominate for president Henry A. Wallace, FDR's former vice president, whom Truman had fired as secretary of

Birth of the Dixiecrats Alabama delegates stand to boo Truman's call for civil rights before they walked out of the 1948 Democratic National Convention.

commerce. Wallace charged that both major parties were recklessly provoking a confrontation with the Soviet Union.

The splits in the Democratic ranks seemed to spell doom for Truman, but he refused to give in. He aroused the faithful by promising, "I will win this election and make the Republicans like it!" He pledged to bring Congress into special session and demand that it confront the housing crisis and boost the minimum wage.

Within days, Truman set out on a 22,000-mile "whistle-stop" train tour, making 271 speeches scolding the "do-nothing" Republicans. The plain-talking president attracted huge crowds. The Republicans, he charged, "have the propaganda and the money, but we have the people, and the people have the votes. *That's* why we're going to win." Friendly audiences loved his fighting spirit and dogged courage, shouting, "Pour it on, Harry!" and "Give 'em hell, Harry." Truman responded: "I don't give 'em hell. I just tell the truth and they think it's hell."

The polls predicted a sure win for Dewey, but on Election Day Truman pulled off the biggest upset ever, taking 24.2 million votes (49.5 percent) to Dewey's 22 million (45.1 percent) and winning a thumping margin of 303 to

THE ELECTION OF 1948

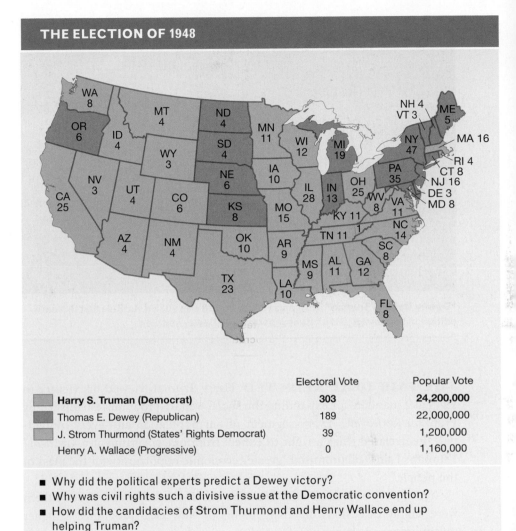

	Electoral Vote	Popular Vote
Harry S. Truman (Democrat)	**303**	**24,200,000**
Thomas E. Dewey (Republican)	189	22,000,000
J. Strom Thurmond (States' Rights Democrat)	39	1,200,000
Henry A. Wallace (Progressive)	0	1,160,000

- Why did the political experts predict a Dewey victory?
- Why was civil rights such a divisive issue at the Democratic convention?
- How did the candidacies of Strom Thurmond and Henry Wallace end up helping Truman?

189 in the electoral college. Democrats also regained control of both houses of Congress. Thurmond and Wallace each received more than a million votes. The president was helped by black voters who, angered by the Dixiecrats, turned out in record numbers to support him, while the Progressive party's radicalism made it hard for Republicans to tag Truman as a communist sympathizer. Thurmond carried only four southern states (South Carolina, Mississippi, Alabama, and Louisiana).

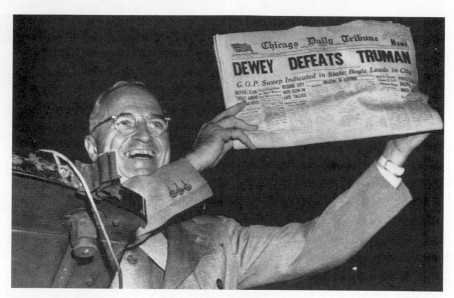

"Dewey Defeats Truman" Truman's victory in 1948 was such a surprise that this early edition of the *Chicago Daily Tribune* reported that Dewey had won.

THE FAIR DEAL REJECTED Harry Truman viewed his victory in 1948 as a mandate for expanding the social welfare programs established by Franklin Roosevelt. "Every segment of our population and every individual," he declared, "has a right to expect from our government a *fair deal.*" Truman's Fair Deal promised "greater economic opportunity for the mass of the people."

Yet there was little new in Truman's Fair Deal proposals. Most of them were simply extensions or enlargements of New Deal programs: a higher minimum wage, expansion of Social Security coverage to 10 million workers not included in the original 1935 bill, and a large slum-clearance and public-housing program.

Despite enjoying Democratic majorities in Congress, however, Truman ran up against the same alliance of conservative southern Democrats and Republicans who had worked against Roosevelt in the late 1930s. The bipartisan coalition rejected several civil rights bills, national health insurance, federal aid to education, and a new approach to subsidizing farmers. It also turned down Truman's requested repeal of the anti-union Taft-Hartley Act.

Yet the Fair Deal was not a complete failure. It laid the foundation for programs that the next generation of reformers would promote.

THE COLD WAR HEATS UP

Global concerns during Harry Truman's second term would again distract him from domestic issues. In his 1949 inaugural address, Truman called for a vigilant anti-Communist foreign policy resting on three pillars: the United Nations, the Marshall Plan, and NATO. None of them could help resolve the civil war in China, however.

"LOSING" CHINA One of the thorniest postwar problems, the Chinese civil war, was fast coming to a head. Chinese Nationalists, led by Chiang Kai-shek, had been fighting Mao Zedong and the Communists since the 1920s. After the Second World War, the Communists won over most of the peasants. By the end of 1949, the Nationalist government had fled to the island of Formosa, which it renamed Taiwan.

President Truman's critics—mostly Republicans—asked, "Who lost China to communism?" What they did not explain was how Truman could have prevented a Communist victory without a massive U.S. military intervention, which would have been risky, unpopular, and expensive. After 1949, the United States continued to recognize the Nationalist government on the island

Mao Zedong Chairman of the Chinese Communist Party and the founder of the People's Republic of China.

of Taiwan as the official government of China, delaying formal relations with the People's Republic of China ("Red China") for thirty years.

THE SOVIETS DEVELOP ATOMIC BOMBS As the Communists were gaining control of China in 1949, news that the Soviets had detonated a nuclear weapon led Truman to accelerate the design of a hydrogen "super-bomb," a weapon far more powerful than the atomic bombs dropped on Japan. That the Soviets now possessed atomic weapons intensified every cold war confrontation. "There is only one thing worse than one nation having an atomic bomb," said Nobel Prize–winning physicist Harold C. Urey, who helped develop the first atomic bomb. "That's two nations having it."

NSC-68 In January 1950, President Truman grew so concerned about the Soviets possessing atomic weapons that he asked the National Security Council to assess America's readiness to contain communism. Four months later, the Council submitted a top-secret report, *NSC-68*, which called for an even more

Shelter for sale On display in a 1950s showroom is a basement fallout shelter, complete with a television, library, and exercise bike, intended to help a family survive a nuclear attack.

robust effort and revealed the major assumptions that would guide U.S. for-eign policy for the next twenty years: "The issues that face us are momentous, involving the fulfillment or destruction not only of this Republic but of civili-zation itself."

NSC-68 endorsed George Kennan's containment strategy. But where he had focused on political and economic counterpressure, the report called for a massive military buildup and "a policy of calculated and gradual coercion" against Soviet expansionism—everywhere.

Paul Nitze, Kennan's successor as director of policy planning for the State Department, wrote *NSC-68*. He claimed that the Soviets were becoming increasingly "reckless" and would invade Western Europe by 1954, by which time they would have enough nuclear weapons to destroy the United States. *NSC-68* became the guidebook for future American policy, especially as the United States became involved in an unexpected conflict in Korea that turned the cold war into a hot war.

WAR IN KOREA

By the mid-1950s, tensions between the United States and the Soviet Union in Europe had temporarily eased as a result of the "balance of terror" created by both sides having atomic weapons. In Asia, however, the situation remained turbulent. Communists had gained control of mainland China and were threatening to destroy the Chinese Nationalists, who had taken refuge on the island of Taiwan.

Japan, meanwhile, was experiencing a dramatic recovery from the devasta-tion caused by the Second World War. Douglas MacArthur showed deft leader-ship as the consul in charge of U.S.-occupied Japan. He oversaw the disarming of the Japanese military, the drafting of a democratic constitution, and the nation's economic recovery, all of which were turning Japan into America's friend.

To the east, however, tensions between North and South Korea threatened to erupt into civil war. The Japanese had occupied the Korean Peninsula since 1910, but after they were defeated and withdrew in 1945, the victorious Allies had faced the difficult task of creating an independent Korean nation.

A DIVIDED KOREA Complicating that effort was the presence of Soviet troops in northern Korea. They had accepted the surrender of Japanese forces above the 38th parallel, which divides the Korean Peninsula, while U.S. forces had overseen the surrender south of the line. The Soviets quickly organized a Communist government, the Democratic People's Republic of Korea (North Korea). The Americans countered by helping to establish a democratic government in the more populous south, the Republic of Korea (South Korea). By the end of 1948, Soviet and U.S. forces had withdrawn, and some 2 million North Koreans had fled to South Korea.

WAR ERUPTS On January 12, 1950, Secretary of State Dean Acheson gave a speech in which he said he was often asked, "Has the State Department got an Asian policy?" He stressed that the United States had assumed "the necessity of . . . the military defense of Japan." Acheson then added that America had created a "defensive perimeter" running along the Aleutian Islands off the coast of Alaska to Japan to the Ryukyu Islands to the Philippines. Where "other areas in the Pacific are concerned," Acheson added, "it must be clear that no person can guarantee these areas against military attack."

Acheson's statement came back to haunt him. On June 24, 1950, he telephoned President Truman to report, "The North Koreans have invaded South Korea." With the encouragement of the Soviet Union and Communist China, the Soviet-equipped North Korean People's Army—135,000 strong—had forced the South Korean defenders into a headlong retreat. Within three days, Seoul, the South Korean capital, was captured, and only 22,000 of the 100,000 South Korean soldiers were still capable of combat. People then and since have argued that Acheson's clumsy reference to the limits of the "defensive perimeter" in Asia may have convinced the North Koreans and Soviets that the United States would not resist an invasion of South Korea.

When reporters asked Truman how he would respond, the president declared: "By God, I'm going to let them have it!" Without consulting the Joint Chiefs of Staff or Congress, he decided to wage war through the backing of the United Nations rather than by seeking a declaration of war from Congress, which the Constitution requires. He feared that a congressional debate would take so long that, once finished, it might then be too late to stop the Communists from seizing control of South Korea.

An emergency meeting of the UN Security Council in late June 1950 censured the North Korean "breach of peace." By sheer coincidence, the Soviet delegate, who held a veto power, was at the time boycotting the council because it would not seat Communist China in place of Nationalist China. On June 27, the Security Council called on UN members to "furnish such assistance to the Republic of Korea as may be necessary to repel the armed attack and to restore international peace and security in the area."

Truman then ordered U.S. air, naval, and ground forces into action and appointed seventy-year-old Douglas MacArthur supreme commander of the UN forces. The attack on South Korea, Truman said, made "it plain beyond all doubt that the international Communist movement is prepared to use armed

Fight and flight U.S. soldiers and Korean civilian refugees march into the Nakdong River region in the south.

invasion to conquer independent nations." Truman's decisive steps gained strong bipartisan approval, but neither the nation nor the administration were united on the objectives of the war or how it was to be conducted.

The Korean conflict was the first military action authorized by the United Nations, and some twenty other nations participated along with the United States. For the first time, soldiers fought under an international flag. America provided the largest contingent by far, some 330,000 troops. The defense of South Korea set a worrisome precedent: war by order of a president—rather than by a vote of Congress. Truman dodged the issue by calling the conflict a "police action" rather than a war. Critics labeled it "Mr. Truman's War."

TURNING THE TABLES The Korean War featured brutal combat in terrible conditions punctuated by heavy casualties and widespread destruction. For the first three months, the fighting went badly for the Republic of Korea (ROK) and the UN forces. By September 1950, South Korean troops were barely hanging on at Pusan, at the southern tip of the Korean Peninsula.

Then, in a brilliant maneuver on September 15, General MacArthur staged a surprise amphibious landing behind the North Korean lines at Inchŏn, the port city for Seoul, some 150 miles north of Pusan. United Nations' troops drove a wedge through the North Korean army. Days later, South Korean troops recaptured Seoul.

At that point, an overconfident MacArthur hatched a grandiose plan to rid North Korea of the "red menace," even if this meant expanding the war into China. Truman foolishly approved MacArthur's request to advance into North Korea so as to destroy its armies and enable the unification of the Koreas.

THE KOREAN WAR, 1950 AND 1950–1953

■ How did the surrender of the Japanese in Korea during 1945 set up the conflict between Soviet-influenced North Korea and U.S.-influenced South Korea?

■ What was General MacArthur's strategy for winning the Korean conflict?

■ Why did President Truman remove General MacArthur from command?

THE CHINESE INTERVENE By October 1950, UN forces were about to capture the North Korean capital, P'yŏngyang. President Truman, concerned that General MacArthur's move would provoke Communist China to enter the war, repeatedly asked the U.S. commander to meet with him, only to be rebuffed. Finally, the president flew 7,000 miles to Wake Island to meet with MacArthur, who contemptuously refused to salute his commander in chief.

At the meeting on October 15, MacArthur dismissed Chinese threats to intervene, even though they had massed troops on the Korean border. That same day, the Chinese Communist government announced that it "cannot stand idly by" as its North Korean allies were humiliated. On October 20, UN forces entered the North Korean capital, and six days later, advance units reached Ch'osan on the Yalu River, North Korea's border with China.

MacArthur predicted total victory by Christmas. He could not have been more wrong. On the night of November 25, some 500,000 Chinese "volunteers" crossed into Korea and surprised MacArthur, sending the U.S. forces in retreat. MacArthur called for more troops and suggested that atomic weapons be used. Truman wrote in his diary that it "looks like World War III is here."

By January 15, the Communist Chinese and North Koreans had recaptured Seoul, the South Korean capital. "We ran like antelopes," said one American soldier. "We lost everything we had." What had started as a defensive war against North Korean aggression had become an unlimited war against the North Koreans and China's People's Liberation Army.

MACARTHUR CROSSES THE LINE In late 1950, the UN forces rallied. By January 1951, they had secured their lines below Seoul and launched a counterattack.

When President Truman began negotiations with North Korea to restore the prewar boundary, General MacArthur undermined him by issuing an ultimatum for China to make peace or suffer an attack. On April 5, on the floor of Congress, the Republican minority leader read a letter from MacArthur that criticized the president and said that "there is no substitute for victory." Such open insubordination left Truman only two choices: He could accept MacArthur's aggressive demands, or fire him. Secretary of State Dean Acheson warned Truman that "if you relieve MacArthur, you will have the biggest fight of your administration."

SACKING A HERO On April 11, 1951, Truman removed MacArthur and replaced him with General Matthew B. Ridgway, who better understood how to conduct a modern war in pursuit of limited objectives. "I believe that we must try to limit the war to Korea," Truman explained to the nation.

Firing of MacArthur In this 1951 cartoon by L. J. Roche, President Truman, Secretary of State Dean Acheson, and the Pentagon dance in the public's proverbial frying pan for the removal of General MacArthur as supreme commander of UN forces in Korea.

"A number of events have made it evident that General MacArthur did not agree with that policy. I have therefore considered it essential to relieve General MacArthur so that there would be no doubt or confusion as to the real purpose and aim of our policy."

Truman's sacking of MacArthur, the army's only five-star general, divided the nation. "Seldom had a more unpopular man fired a more popular one," *Time* magazine reported. Senator Joseph McCarthy called the president a "son of a bitch," and an editorial in the *Chicago Tribune* demanded that Truman "be impeached and convicted." Sixty-six percent of Americans initially opposed Truman's decision.

Douglas MacArthur was greeted by adoring crowds upon his return to the United States, but Truman stood firm: "I fired him because he wouldn't respect the authority of the President. I didn't fire him because he was a dumb son of a bitch, although he was, but that's not against the law for generals. If it was, half to three-quarters of them would be in jail." That all of the top military leaders supported Truman's decision deflated much of the criticism. "Why, hell, if MacArthur had had his way," the president warned, "he'd have had us in the Third World War and blown up two-thirds of the world."

A CEASE-FIRE On June 24, 1951, the Soviet representative at the United Nations proposed a cease-fire in Korea along the 38th parallel, the original dividing line between North and South. Secretary of State Acheson accepted the cease-fire (armistice) with the consent of the United Nations. China and North Korea responded favorably.

Truce talks that started on July 10, 1951, dragged on for two years while sporadic fighting continued. The chief snags were exchanges of prisoners (many captured North Korean and Chinese soldiers did not want to go home) and South Korea's insistence on unification of the two Koreas.

By the time a truce was reached, on July 27, 1953, Truman had retired and Dwight D. Eisenhower was president. No peace treaty was ever signed, and Korea, like Germany, remained divided. The inconclusive war cost the United States more than 33,000 battle deaths and 103,000 wounded or missing. South Korean casualties were about 2 million, and North Korean and Chinese casualties were an estimated 3 million.

THE IMPACT OF THE KOREAN WAR Harry Truman's assumption that Stalin and the Soviets were behind the invasion of South Korea led him to deepen the American commitment to stop communism. Fearful that the Soviets would use the Korean conflict as a diversion to invade Western Europe, he ordered a major expansion of U.S. military forces around the world. Truman also increased assistance to French troops fighting a Communist independence movement in the French colony of Indochina (which included Vietnam), starting America's military involvement in Southeast Asia.

ANOTHER RED SCARE

The Korean War sparked another Red Scare at home, as the **House Committee on Un-American Activities (HUAC)** had claimed that Communist agents were actively trying to subvert the federal government.

On March 21, 1947, President Truman sought to blunt conservative Republicans' attacks on the patriotism of left-wing Democrats by signing an executive order (known as the Loyalty Order). It required all 2 million federal government workers to undergo a background investigation to ensure they had no ties to Communists or other "subversive" groups.

Truman was responding to pressure from FBI director J. Edgar Hoover and Attorney General Tom Clark, both of whom believed that there were numerous spies working inside the federal government. Truman was also eager to reduce criticism that he was not doing enough to ensure that Soviet sympathizers were not working in government.

Privately, however, Truman thought that concerns about Communist subversives were exaggerated. As he wrote to Pennsylvania governor George Earle, "I am of the opinion that the country is perfectly safe so far as Communism is concerned." By early 1951, the federal Civil Service Commission had cleared more than 3 million government workers, while only 378 had been dismissed for doubtful loyalty. In 1953, President Eisenhower revoked the Loyalty Order.

THE HOLLYWOOD TEN Charges that the Hollywood movie industry was a "hotbed of communism" led the HUAC to launch a full-blown investigation. The committee subpoenaed dozens of actors, producers, and directors to testify at hearings held in Los Angeles in October 1947. Ten witnesses refused to testify, arguing that the questioning violated their First Amendment rights. When asked if he were a member of the Communist party, screenwriter Ring Lardner Jr. replied: "I could answer, but I would hate myself in the morning." Another member of the so-called Hollywood Ten, screenwriter Dalton Trumbo, shouted as he left the hearings, "This is the beginning of an American concentration camp." All ten were cited for contempt of Congress, given prison terms, and blacklisted (banned) from the film industry.

The witch hunt launched by the HUAC inspired Arthur Miller, who himself was blacklisted, to write *The Crucible*, an award-winning play produced in 1953. His dramatic account of the witch trials in Salem, Massachusetts, at the end of the seventeenth century, was intended to alert audiences to the dangers of anti-Communist hysteria.

The Red Scare and Hollywood Several courageous movie stars attended the HUAC hearings to support their friends and colleagues who were accused of being Communists. Left to right: Danny Kaye, June Havoc, Humphrey Bogart, and Lauren Bacall (seated).

ALGER HISS The spy case most damaging to the Truman administration involved Alger Hiss, president of the Carnegie Endowment for International Peace. Whittaker Chambers, a former Soviet spy who reversed himself and became an informer testifying against supposed Communists in the government, told the HUAC in 1948 that Hiss had given him secret documents ten years earlier, when Chambers was spying for the Soviets and Hiss was working in the State Department. Hiss sued Chambers for libel, and Chambers produced microfilm of the State Department documents that he said Hiss had passed to him. Although Hiss denied the accusation, he was convicted in 1950. The charge was perjury, but he was convicted of lying about espionage, for which he could not be tried because the statute of limitations on the crime had expired.

More cases of Communist infiltration surfaced. In 1949, eleven top leaders of the Communist party of the United States were convicted under the Smith Act of 1940, which outlawed any conspiracy to advocate the overthrow of the government. The Supreme Court upheld the law under the doctrine of a "clear and present danger," which overrode the right to free speech.

ATOMIC SPYING In 1950, the FBI unearthed a spy network involving American and British Communists who had secretly passed information about the development of the atomic bomb to the Soviet Union. The disclosure led to the arrest of Klaus Fuchs, a German-born English nuclear physicist who had worked in the United States and helped to develop the atomic bomb.

As it turned out, a New York couple, former Communists Julius and Ethel Rosenberg, were part of the same Soviet spy ring. Their claims of innocence were undercut by Ethel's brother, who admitted he was a spy along with his sister and brother-in-law.

The convictions of Fuchs and the Rosenbergs fueled Republican charges that Truman's administration was not doing enough to hunt down Communist agents. The case, called the crime of the century by J. Edgar Hoover, also heightened fears that a vast Soviet network of spies and sympathizers was operating in the United States. Irving Kaufman, the federal judge who sentenced the Rosenbergs to death, explained that "plain, deliberate murder is dwarfed . . . by comparison with the crime you have committed." They were the first Americans executed for spying.

McCARTHY'S WITCH HUNT Evidence of Soviet spying encouraged some to exploit fears of the Communist menace. Early in 1950, a little-known Republican senator, Joseph R. McCarthy of Wisconsin, surfaced as the most ruthless manipulator of anti-Communist anxieties.

Joseph R. McCarthy The crusading senator who was determined to "sweep" Communists out of the federal government.

McCarthy, eager to attract media attention through his "bare-knuckle," red-baiting tactics, delivered a fiery speech in Wheeling, West Virginia, on February 9, 1950, in which he charged that the State Department was infested with Communists. He claimed to have their names, although he never provided them.

McCarthy's stunt got him what he wanted most: publicity. As the *New York Times* said, "It is difficult, if not impossible, to ignore charges made by Senator McCarthy just because they are usually proved exaggerated or false." During the next four years, McCarthy made more irresponsible accusations, initially against many Democrats, whom he smeared as "dupes" or "fellow travelers" of the "Commies," then, unbelievably, against officers in the U.S. Army.

McCarthy enjoyed the backing of fellow Republicans eager to hurt Democrats in the 1950 congressional elections by claiming they were not being tough enough in fighting communism. Senator Lyndon B. Johnson of Texas said McCarthy was "the sorriest senator" in Washington. "But he's riding high now, he's got people scared to death."

By the summer of 1951, however, **McCarthyism** spun out of control when the zealous senator accused George Marshall, the former secretary of state and war hero, of "being an instrument of the Communist conspiracy." Concerns about truth or fair play did not faze McCarthy; his goal was to create a reign of terror. President Truman called him a "pathological character assassin."

For all his boasting, McCarthy never uncovered a single Communist agent within the federal government. Yet his smear campaign, which tarnished many reputations and had a chilling effect on free speech, went largely unchallenged until the end of the Korean War. During the Red Scare, thousands of left-wing activists were blacklisted from employment because of past political associations, real or rumored. Movies with titles like "I Married a Communist" fed the hysteria, and magazine stories warned of "a Red under every bed."

THE McCARRAN ACT Fears of Soviet spies working with American sympathizers led Congress in 1950 to pass, over President Truman's veto, the McCarran Internal Security Act, which made it unlawful "to combine, conspire, or agree with any other person to perform any act which would substantially contribute to . . . the establishment of a totalitarian dictatorship." The legislation, proposed by Nevada Democratic senator Pat McCarran, required Communist organizations to register with the Justice Department. Immigrants who had belonged to totalitarian parties in their home countries were barred from entering the United States, and during any future national emergencies, Communists were to be herded into concentration camps. The McCarran Internal Security Act, Truman said in his veto message, would "put the government into the business of thought control."

Concerns about Communist infiltration also shaped immigration policy. In 1952, Senator McCarran pushed through the Immigration and Nationality Act of 1952 (the McCarran-Walter Act). While reducing the number of

McCarran-Walter Act The German-born wife and daughter of an American GI are interrogated by immigration inspectors at Ellis Island after being detained under the McCarran-Walter Act.

immigrants admitted each year, it renewed the national origins quota system established by the Immigration Act of 1924, which favored newcomers from northern and western Europe. As a result, the act allocated 85 percent of the 154,277 annual visas to people from northern and Western European nations. It also introduced a system of preferences based on skills and family ties and removed the ban on Asian immigrants. Yet the number of Asians allowed into the United States remained small (only 100 a year). Finally, it barred suspected "subversives" and the "immoral," including gays and lesbians. Truman vetoed the bill, but Congress overrode him again.

THE RED SCARE AND THE COLD WAR The Red Scare ended up violating the civil liberties of innocent people. President Truman may have erred in 1947 by creating a government loyalty program that aggravated the anti-Communist hysteria. He also overstretched resources when he pledged to contain communism everywhere. Containment's chief theorist, George F. Kennan, later confessed that he had failed to clarify the limits of the containment policy and to stress that the United States needed to prioritize its responses to Soviet adventurism.

A COLD WAR GOVERNMENT Having taken on global burdens after the Second World War, the United States became committed to a large military establishment, along with shadowy new government agencies such as the National Security Council (NSC), the National Security Agency (NSA), and the Central Intelligence Agency (CIA).

The federal government—and the presidency—grew larger, more powerful, and more secretive, fueled by the actions of both major political parties as well as by the intense lobbying efforts of what Dwight D. Eisenhower would later call the *military-industrial complex*—defense contractors, lobbyists, and influential legislators.

Fears of communism and concerns about a Soviet spy network in the United States mushroomed into politically motivated paranoia. Long-standing anti-Semitism fed the hysteria; indeed, many Communist sympathizers were Jews from Eastern Europe.

The Red Scare also provided a powerful tool for Republicans to claim that Democrats were soft on communism and to encourage widespread conformity of thought and behavior. By 1950, it had become dangerous to criticize anything associated with the American way of life.

ASSESSING HARRY TRUMAN On March 30, 1952, Harry Truman announced that he would not seek another presidential term, in part because it was unlikely he could win. Fewer than 25 percent of voters surveyed thought he was doing a good job, the lowest presidential approval rating in history. The unrelenting war against communism, at home and abroad, led people to question Truman's strategy. Negotiations to end the war in Korea had bogged down, the "red-baiting" of McCarthyism was expanding, and conservative southern Democrats had defeated most of his Fair Deal proposals. The war had also brought higher taxes and higher prices for consumers, many of whom blamed the president. Only years later would the American people (and historians) fully appreciate how effectively Truman had dealt with so many complex problems.

To the end of his presidency, Truman viewed himself as an ordinary person operating in extraordinary times. "I have tried my best to give the nation everything I have in me," Truman told reporters at one of his last press conferences. "There are a great many people . . . who could have done the job better than I did it. But I had the job and had to do it." At the end of one difficult day in the White House, Truman growled: "They [his critics] talk about the power of the President, how I can just push a button to get things done. Why, I spend most of my time kissing somebody's ass."

By the time he left the White House in early 1953, the cold war had become an accepted part of the American way of life. But fears about the spread of communism were counterbalanced by the joys of unexpected prosperity. Toward the end of Truman's presidency, the economy began to grow at the fastest rate in history, transforming social and cultural life and becoming the marvel of the world.

CHAPTER REVIEW

SUMMARY

- **The Cold War** The cold war was an ideological contest between the Western democracies (especially the United States) and Communist countries. At the end of the Second World War, the Soviet Union established puppet governments in the Eastern European countries it occupied behind an *iron curtain* of totalitarian control and secrecy.

- **Containment** President Truman responded to the Soviet occupation of Eastern Europe with the policy of *containment*. With the *Truman Doctrine (1947)*, he proposed giving economic and military aid to countries facing Communist insurgencies. He also convinced Congress to approve the *National Security Act*, which reorganized the U.S. armed forces and created the Central Intelligence Agency. With the *Marshall Plan (1948)*, Truman offered redevelopment aid to all European nations. In 1949, the United States became a founding member of the *North Atlantic Treaty Organization* (*NATO*).

- **Truman's Fair Deal** Truman's proposed *Fair Deal (1949)* would have expanded the New Deal despite intense Republican opposition in Congress. Truman could not stop the *Taft-Hartley Act (1947)*, a Republican-backed measure to curb the power of labor unions. Truman was more successful in expanding Social Security, desegregating the military, and banning racial discrimination in the hiring of federal employees. After winning a second term in 1948, he proposed a civil rights bill, national health insurance, federal aid to education, and new farm subsidies. Despite the Democrats' majority in Congress, however, conservative Republicans and southern Democrats (*Dixiecrats*) joined forces to defeat these initiatives.

- **The Korean War** Containment policies proved less effective in East Asia, as Communists won a long civil war in China in 1949 and ignited a war in Korea. In 1950, Truman authorized *NSC-68* in response—a comprehensive blueprint for foreign and defense policies that called for a dramatic increase in military spending and nuclear arms. When North Korean troops invaded South Korea in June 1950, Truman quickly decided to go to war under the auspices of the United Nations. A truce was concluded in July 1953 and established a demilitarized zone in Korea.

- **The Red Scare** The onset of the cold war inflamed another Red Scare. Investigations by the *House Committee on Un-American Activities (HUAC)* sought to find "subversives" within the federal government. Starting in 1950, Senator Joseph R. McCarthy exploited fears of Soviet spies infiltrating the highest levels of the U.S. government. *McCarthyism* flourished in the short term because the threat of a world dominated by Communist governments seemed all too real.

CHRONOLOGY

November 1946	Republicans win control of both houses of Congress
February 1946	George Kennan urges a containment policy toward the Soviet Union
March 1947	The Truman Doctrine promises financial and military assistance to countries resisting Communist takeover
May 1947	The Marshall plan calls for massive financial assistance to European nations
June 1947	Congress passes the Taft-Hartley Labor Act
July 1947	National Security Council (NSC) is established
May 1948	Israel is proclaimed an independent nation
July 1948	Truman's executive order ends segregation in the U.S. armed forces
October 1948	United States and Great Britain begin airlifting supplies to West Berlin
November 1948	Truman defeats Dewey in the presidential election
April 1949	North Atlantic Treaty Organization (NATO) is created
October 1949	China "falls" to communism
February 1950	Senator Joseph McCarthy begins his crusade against suspected Communists in the federal government
June 1950	United States and other UN members go to war in Korea

KEY TERMS

iron curtain p. 1278

containment p. 1279

Truman Doctrine (1947) p. 1280

Marshall Plan (1948) p. 1281

Berlin airlift (1948–1949) p. 1284

North Atlantic Treaty Organization (NATO) p. 1286

National Security Act p. 1286

Taft-Hartley Labor Act (1947) p. 1290

Fair Deal (1949) p. 1296

Dixiecrats p. 1297

NSC-68 (1950) p. 1302

House Committee on Un-American Activities (HUAC) p. 1309

McCarthyism p. 1312

 INQUIZITIVE

Go to InQuizitive to see what you've learned—and learn what you've missed—with personalized feedback along the way.

28 America in the Fifties

The art of consumerism The United States experienced unprecedented prosperity after the Second World War, enabling many Americans in the 1950s to engage in carefree consumption—and personal indebtedness.

In the summer of 1959, a survey revealed that most Americans believed that a nuclear holocaust was "likely." To highlight the possibility, newlyweds Melvin and Maria Mininson spent their two-week honeymoon in an underground bomb shelter in their Miami backyard. *Life* magazine showcased their 18-by-24-foot "fallout" shelter twelve feet underground. Weighing twenty tons, the steel and concrete bunker held enough food and water to survive an atomic attack.

The image of newlyweds seeking sheltered security in a new age of nuclear terror symbolized America in the 1950s. The deepening cold war with the Soviet Union cast a frightening shadow over the nation's traditionally sunny optimism.

Still, most Americans had emerged from the Second World War proud of their country's military strength, international stature, and industrial might. As the editors of *Fortune* magazine proclaimed in 1946, "This is a dream era. . . . The Great American Boom is on."

So it was, at least for white, middle-class Americans. During the late 1940s and throughout the 1950s, the United States enjoyed unprecedented economic growth, and surveys suggested that most people were content. Divorce and homicide rates fell, and people lived longer, on average, thanks in part to medical breakthroughs, including new antibiotics and the vaccine invented by Dr. Jonas Salk that ended the menace of polio.

The idealized image of America in the fifties as an innocent, prosperous nation awash in good times and enlivened by teenage energies contains a kernel of truth. But life was actually much more complicated—even contradictory and hypocritical at times.

focus questions

1. What were President Eisenhower's political philosophy and priorities?

2. What factors contributed to America's postwar prosperity? To what extent did all benefit from it?

3. What were the criticisms of postwar society and culture? What were the various forms of dissent and anxiety?

4. What were the goals and strategies of the civil rights movement? What was its impact?

5. What were President Eisenhower's foreign policy priorities? What was his influence on global affairs?

MODERATE REPUBLICANISM

Dwight David Eisenhower dominated politics during the 1950s. He was the nation's most famous figure, a model of moderation, modesty, stability, and optimism, celebrated for his genial personality and irresistible grin. He was a soldier who hated war, a politician who hated politics. If forced to choose, he preferred golf over governance. Committed to what he called **moderate Republicanism**, Eisenhower promised to restore the authority of state and local governments and restrain the federal government from engaging in political and social "engineering." In the process, he sought to renew traditional virtues and inspire Americans with a vision of a brighter future.

"TIME FOR A CHANGE" By 1952, the Truman administration was the target of growing public criticism. The conflict in Korea had stalled, the economy was sputtering, and President Truman was put on the defensive by the disclosure that corrupt lobbyists had rigged military contracts during the Korean conflict. The scandal led him to fire nearly 250 Internal Revenue Service employees, but doubts lingered that he would ever finish the housecleaning. Critics charged that the slogan for his administration was "plunder at home, blunder abroad."

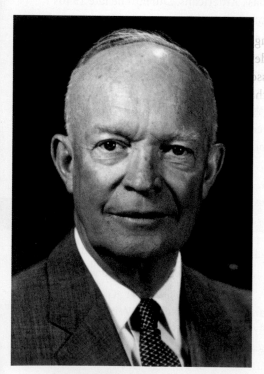

Dwight D. Eisenhower His many supporters wore "I Like Ike" hats, pins, and even nylon stockings, speaking to the consumer culture's impact on politics.

Public sentiment turned toward Republicans. Beginning in the late 1940s, both Republican and Democratic leaders, including Truman, recruited Eisenhower to be their presidential candidate. Eisenhower, known as "Ike," had displayed remarkable organizational and diplomatic skill in coordinating the Allied invasion of Nazi-controlled Europe. In 1952, after serving as president of Columbia University, he had moved to Paris to become supreme commander of NATO forces in Europe. His decision to run for president as a Republican was wildly popular. Bumper stickers announced, "I Like Ike."

At the 1952 Republican presidential convention, Eisenhower was nominated on the first ballot. Republican leaders then tried to reassure party conservatives by balancing the ticket with a youthful running mate: Richard M. Nixon, a thirty-nine-year-old California senator known for his shrewd opportunism and combative temperament. Nixon was an aggressive anti-Communist; his dogged pursuit of the Alger Hiss spying case had brought him national prominence.

The Republican platform declared that the Democratic emphasis on containing communism was "negative, futile, and misguided." If elected, Eisenhower would bring "genuine independence" to the oppressed people of Eastern Europe.

THE ELECTION OF 1952 The presidential campaign featured contrasting personalities. Dwight Eisenhower was an international figure and a man of readily acknowledged decency and integrity. He pledged to clean up "the mess in Washington" and to travel to Korea to secure "an early and honorable" end to the prolonged conflict.

Illinois governor Adlai Stevenson, the Democratic candidate, was virtually unknown outside his home state. Although brilliant and witty, he came across as more an aloof intellectual than a leader. Republicans labeled him an "egghead" (meant to suggest a balding professor with more intellect than common sense). Even Harry Truman grumbled that Stevenson "was too busy making up his mind whether he had to go to the bathroom or not."

Stevenson was outmatched. On election night, Eisenhower triumphed in a landslide, gathering nearly 34 million votes to Stevenson's 27 million. The electoral vote was more lopsided: 442 to 89. Stevenson even failed to win his home state of Illinois. More important, by securing four southern states, Eisenhower had cracked the solidly Democratic South.

Yet voters liked Eisenhower more than they liked other Republican candidates. In the 1952 election, Democrats kept control of most governorships, lost control in the House by only eight seats, and broke even in the Senate.

A "MIDDLE WAY" PRESIDENCY Dwight Eisenhower was the first professional soldier elected president since Ulysses S. Grant in 1868. During his campaign, he appealed to the "middle-of-the-road voter." Once elected, he promised to pursue a "middle way" between conservatism and liberalism. He was a pragmatist who liked to be called a "responsible progressive." Rather than dismantle all the New Deal and Fair Deal programs, he wanted to end the "excesses" that had resulted from twenty years of Democratic control of the White House.

Eisenhower pledged to shrink the federal bureaucracy and make it more efficient while restoring the balance between the executive and legislative

THE ELECTION OF 1952

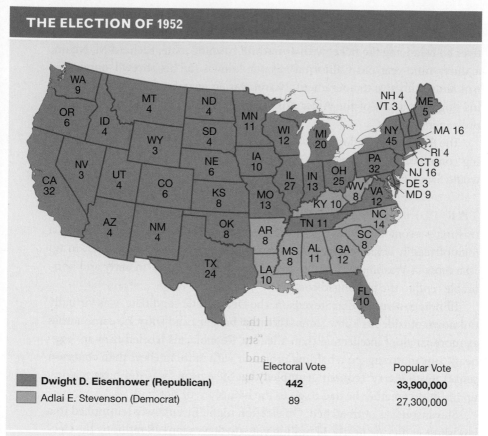

	Electoral Vote	Popular Vote
Dwight D. Eisenhower (Republican)	**442**	**33,900,000**
Adlai E. Stevenson (Democrat)	89	27,300,000

- Why was the contest between Adlai Stevenson and Dwight D. Eisenhower so lopsided?
- Why was Eisenhower's victory in several southern states remarkable?

branches. He also promised to reduce the national debt, cut military expenses, balance the federal budget, and trim taxes. At the same time, however, he insisted that workers had a right to form unions and bargain with management. He added that employees needed to be paid enough to afford the comforts of a good life. "We all—workers and farmers, foremen and financiers, technicians and builders—all must produce, produce more, and produce yet more," he said. Peace would be maintained "not by weapons of war but by wheat and cotton, by milk and wool, by meat and by timber and by rice." He hated the arms race because "every gun that is made, every warship launched, every rocket fired signifies, in the final sense, a theft from those who hunger and are not fed, those who are cold and are not clothed."

Eisenhower's cautious personality and genial public face fit the prevailing mood of most voters. He inspired trust, sought consensus, and avoided confrontation. He also championed the nineteenth-century view that Congress should make policy and the president should carry it out. Like Calvin Coolidge, Eisenhower said his administration searched for "things it can stop doing rather than new things for it to do."

"DYNAMIC CONSERVATISM" AT HOME President Eisenhower labeled his domestic program "dynamic conservatism," by which he meant being "conservative when it comes to money and liberal when it comes to human beings." He kept intact the basic structure of the New Deal, even convincing Congress to establish a federal Department of Health, Education, and Welfare and to extend Social Security benefits to millions of workers formerly excluded: white-collar professionals, housekeepers and sales clerks, farmworkers, and members of the armed forces. Eisenhower also approved increases in the minimum wage and additional public-housing projects for low-income occupants.

Conservative Republicans charged that he was being too liberal. He told his brother Edgar in 1954 that if the "stupid" right wing of the Republican party tried "to abolish Social Security and eliminate labor laws and farm programs, you would not hear of that party again in our political history."

TRANSPORTATION IMPROVEMENTS Under Eisenhower, the federal government launched two huge construction projects: the St. Lawrence Seaway and the Interstate Highway System, both of which resembled the public works projects constructed under the New Deal during the 1930s. The St. Lawrence Seaway project (in partnership with Canada) opened the Great Lakes to oceangoing ships.

The **Federal-Aid Highway Act** (1956) created a network of interstate highways to serve the needs of commerce and defense, as well as the public. The $32 billion interstate highway system, funded largely by federal gasoline taxes, took twenty-five years to construct and was the largest federal project in history. It stretched for 47,000 miles and required 55,512 bridges.

Highway construction generated what economists call "multiplier effects." It created jobs; stimulated economic growth; and spurred the tourism, motor hotel ("motel"), billboard, fast-food, and long-haul trucking industries. Interstates transformed the way people traveled and where they lived, while creating a new form of middle-class leisure—the family vacation by car. In 1956, writer Bernard De Voto exclaimed that "a new highway is not only a measure of progress, but a true index of our culture."

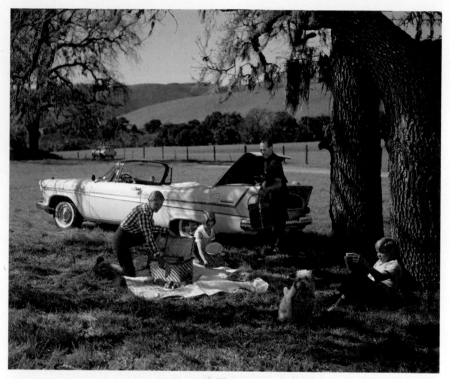

1950s car culture In this 1958 advertisement for Plymouth Belvedere convertibles, a family get ready to enjoy a picnic lunch in the countryside.

THE CAR CULTURE "The American," novelist William Faulkner observed in 1948, "really loves nothing but his automobile." Thanks to the highway system, said President Eisenhower, cars would provide "greater convenience, greater happiness, and greater standards of living." In 1948, only 60 percent of families owned a car; by 1955, some 90 percent owned a car, and many households had two.

Americans had always cherished personal freedom and mobility, rugged individualism, and masculine force. Automobiles embodied all these qualities and more. Cars were much more than a form of transportation; they provided social status, freedom, and a wider range of choices—where to travel, where to work and live, where to seek pleasure and recreation. The car culture prompted the creation of "convenience stores," drive-in movies, and fast-food restaurants. Even more important, the interstate highway system and the car culture weakened public transit systems (buses and subways), accelerated the movement of white people from cities to suburbs, and caused a surge in environmental pollution.

THE END OF McCARTHYISM Republicans thought their presidential victory in 1952 would curb the efforts of Wisconsin senator Joseph R. McCarthy to ferret out Communist spies in the federal government. Instead, the publicity-seeking senator's behavior grew even more outlandish, in part because reporters loved his theatrics and in part because he became a master at telling outrageous lies. President Eisenhower despised McCarthy but refused to criticize him in public, explaining that he did not want to "get into a pissing contest with that skunk."

McCarthy finally committed political suicide when he made the absurd charge that the U.S. Army was soft on communism. For thirty-six days in the spring of 1954, the Army-McCarthy hearings provided television viewers with a fantastic spectacle. The unkempt McCarthy was at his worst, browbeating high-ranking officers, shamelessly promoting himself, and producing little evidence to back up his charges. "You are a disgrace to the uniform," he told General Ralph Zwicker. "You're shielding Communist conspirators. You're not fit to be an officer. You're ignorant. You are going to be put on public display."

McCarthy was finally outwitted by the deliberate, reasoned counterattacks of the army's legal counsel, Joseph Welch. When McCarthy tried to smear one of Welch's associates, the attorney exploded: "Until this moment, Senator, I think I never really gauged your cruelty or your recklessness. . . . Have you no sense of decency, sir, at long last?" When the audience burst into applause, the confused senator was reduced to whispering, "What did I do?"

On December 2, 1954, the Senate voted 67 to 22 to "condemn" McCarthy. Soon thereafter, his influence collapsed. His crusade against Communists had catapulted him into the limelight and captured the nation's attention, but he had trampled upon civil liberties. His rapid demise helped the Democrats capture control of both houses of Congress in the 1954 elections. In 1957, at the age of forty-eight, he died of liver inflammation brought on by years of alcohol abuse.

A People of Plenty

What most distinguished the United States from the rest of the world after the Second World War was what one journalist called America's "screwball materialism." The economy soared to record heights as businesses shifted from wartime production to the construction of new housing and the manufacture of mass-produced consumer goods. The quarter century from 1948 to 1973 witnessed the greatest economic growth in history. In 1957, *U.S. News and World Report* magazine declared that "never had so many people, anywhere, been so well off."

POSTWAR PROSPERITY

Several factors led to the nation's extraordinary prosperity. First, huge federal expenditures during the Second World War and Korean War propelled the economy out of the Great Depression. Unemployment was virtually nonexistent. High government spending continued in the 1950s, thanks to the construction of highways, bridges, airports, and ports, and the global arms race. The military budget after 1945 represented 60 percent of the national budget and was by far the single most important stimulant to the economy.

The superior productivity of American industries also contributed to economic growth. No sooner was the war over than the government transferred many federal defense plants to civilian owners who retooled them for peacetime manufacturing. Military-related research helped stimulate new glamour industries: chemicals (including plastics), electronics, and aviation. By 1957, the aircraft industry was the nation's largest employer.

The economy also benefited from the emergence of new technologies, including the first generation of computers. Factories and industries became

Postwar consumerism Booming chain stores, such as the Super Giant Supermarket shown above, began to dot the suburbs in the fifties, offering an outlet for the consumerism of the postwar years.

increasingly automated. At the same time, the oil boom in Texas, Wyoming, and Oklahoma continued to provide low-cost fuel to heat buildings and power cars and trucks.

Another reason for the record-breaking economic growth was the lack of foreign competition. Most of the other major industrial nations—Great Britain, France, Germany, Japan, and the Soviet Union—had been physically devastated during the Second World War, leaving American manufacturers with a virtual monopoly on international trade that lasted well into the 1950s.

THE CONSUMER CULTURE

What differentiated the postwar era from earlier periods of prosperity was the large number of people who shared in the rising standard of living. *Consumerism* became America's secular religion.

Most Americans had money to spend during the fifties, and they did so with gusto. Between 1947 and 1960, the average income for the working class increased by as much as it had in the previous *fifty* years. More and more blue-collar Americans, especially unionized automotive and steel workers, moved into the middle class. George Meany, the leading union spokesman during the 1950s, declared in 1955 that his members "never had it so good." A marketing consultant stressed that the new economy required "that we convert the buying and use of goods into [religious] rituals, that we seek our spiritual satisfaction, our ego satisfaction, in consumption."

A BUYING SPREE Innovations in financing made it easier to buy things. The first credit card appeared in 1949; soon, "buying with plastic" had become the new norm. Personal indebtedness doubled, and frugality became unpatriotic. As television personality Hugh Downs remembered, "those were exciting days . . . of hope and optimism . . . when the sky was the limit."

What most Americans wanted to buy was a new house. In 1945, only 40 percent of Americans owned homes; by 1960, the number had increased to 60 percent. New homes featured the latest electrical appliances—refrigerators, dishwashers, washing machines, vacuum cleaners, electric mixers, carving knives, even shoe polishers.

The use of electricity tripled, in part because of the popularity of television, which displaced listening to the radio and going to the movies as the most popular way to spend free time. Between 1946 and 1960, the number of homes with TV sets soared from 8,000 to 46 million. In 1954, grocery stores began selling frozen "TV dinners" to be heated and consumed while watching popular shows such as *Father Knows Best, I Love Lucy, Leave It to Beaver*, and

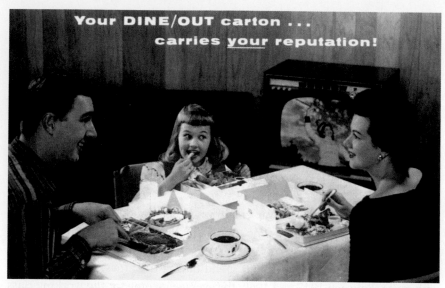

Family, modified The dynamics of American family life changed with the onslaught of new products. In this 1959 advertisement for TV dinners, a family eats out of disposable containers in front of the television.

The Adventures of Ozzie and Harriet, all of which idealized the child-centered world of suburban white families.

The popularity of television provided a powerful medium for advertisers to promote a new phase of the consumer culture that reshaped the contours of postwar life: the nature of work, where people lived and traveled, how they interacted, and what they valued. It also affected class structure, race relations, and gender roles. Jack Metzgar, the son of a Pennsylvania steelworker, remembered that in 1946 "we did not have a car, a television set, or a refrigerator. By 1952, we had all those things."

THE GI BILL OF RIGHTS As World War II came to an end, fear that a sudden influx of veterans into the workforce would produce widespread unemployment led Congress to pass the Servicemen's Readjustment Act, nicknamed the **GI Bill of Rights,** passed in 1944. ("GI" meant "government issue," a phrase stamped on military uniforms and equipment that became slang for "serviceman.")

The GI Bill's package of benefits for veterans included unemployment pay for one year, preference to those applying for federal government jobs, loans for home construction or starting a business, access to government hospitals, and generous subsidies for education. Some 5 million veterans bought homes with the assistance of GI Bill mortgage loans, which required no down payment. Almost 8 million took advantage of GI Bill benefits to attend college or enroll in job-training programs.

Before the Second World War, about 160,000 Americans had graduated from college each year. By 1950, the figure had risen to 500,000. In 1949, veterans accounted for 40 percent of college enrollments, and the United States could boast the world's best-educated workforce, largely because of the GI Bill. For African American veterans, however, most colleges and universities remained racially segregated and refused to admit blacks; those that did often discriminated against them.

African American students at white colleges or universities were barred from playing on athletic teams, attending social events, and joining fraternities or sororities. Even with the GI Bill's subsidized mortgages, black veterans were often prevented from buying homes in white neighborhoods. Although women veterans were eligible for the GI Bill, there were so few of them that the program had the unintended effect of widening the income gap between men and women, since the much more numerous male veterans had greater access to education and housing.

COOLING THE SUBURBAN FRONTIER The second half of the twentieth century brought a mass migration to a new frontier—the suburbs. An acute postwar housing shortage sparked the escape from inner cities to the sprawling suburbs emerging in the countryside, just outside of city or town limits. Of the 13 million homes built between 1948 and 1958, more than 11 million were in the suburbs. Many among the exploding middle-class white population moved to what were called the Sun Belt states—California, Arizona, Florida, Texas—as well as to the Southeast, where rapid population growth and new highways generated an economic boom.

The first air-conditioning system was designed in 1902 by inventor Willis Carrier. The earliest home unit was installed in 1914, but it utilized hazardous chemicals and was too bulky, noisy, and expensive to become widely applicable. Advances in technology eventually produced the more convenient window air conditioner in the late 1930s, though it remained too costly for most residents.

Most Americans first encountered air conditioning while sitting in movie theaters and walking through department stores. In 1951, inexpensive window units were invented, and soon thousands of homes featured dripping, humming metal boxes hanging out bedroom windows.

As air conditioning became common across the Sun Belt, the appeal of living in warmer climates soared. California led the way. In 1940, it was the fifth most-populous state; by 1963, it held first place. And, by 1960, for the first time since the Civil War, more people moved into the South than moved out.

SUBURBAN CULTURE Suburbia met an acute need (affordable housing) and fulfilled a common dream—personal freedom and family security within commuting distance of cities. In the half century after the Second World War, the suburban "good life" included a big home with a big yard on a big lot accessed by a big car—or two. By 1970, more people lived in suburbs than in cities.

A brassy New York real estate developer, William Levitt, led the suburban revolution. Between 1947 and 1951, on 6,000 acres of Long Island farmland east of New York City, he built 17,447 small (750 square feet), sturdy, two-bedroom homes to house more than 82,000 mostly lower-middle-class people. Levitt believed he was enabling the American dream. "No man who owns his own lot and his own house can be a communist," he said.

The planned community, called Levittown, included schools, parks, swimming pools, shopping centers, and playing fields. The look-alike houses came in three styles—the Cape Cod, the Rancher, and the Colonial. All sold for the same low price—$6,990, with no down payments for veterans—and featured the same floor plan and accessories. Each had a living room with a picture window and a television set, a bathroom, two bedrooms, and a kitchen equipped with an electric refrigerator, oven, and washing machine. Homeowners were required to cut their grass once a week and prohibited from hanging laundry on outside clotheslines on weekends.

When the first houses in Levittown went on sale, people, especially military veterans, stood in long lines to buy one. Levitt soon built three more Levittowns in Pennsylvania, New Jersey, and Puerto Rico. They and other planned suburban communities benefited greatly from government assistance. Federal and state tax codes favored homeowners over renters, and local governments paid for the infrastructure the subdivisions required: roads, water and sewer lines, fire and police protection. By insuring loans for up to 95 percent of the value of a house, the Federal Housing Administration (FHA) made it easy for builders to construct low-cost homes and for people to purchase them.

Levittown Identical mass-produced houses in Levittown, New York, and other suburbs across the country provided veterans and their families with affordable homes.

Initially, the contracts for houses in Levittown specifically excluded "members of other than the Caucasian race." When asked about this "racial covenant,"

Levitt blamed prevailing prejudices: "If we sell one house to a Negro family, then 90 to 95 percent of our white customers will not buy into the community." His policy was: "We can solve a housing problem or we can try to solve a racial problem. But we can't combine the two." It wasn't long, however, before the U.S. Supreme Court ruled in *Shelley v. Kraemer* (1948) that such racial restrictions were illegal.

The Court ruling, however, did not end segregated housing practices; it simply made them more discreet. In 1953, when the original Levittown's population reached 70,000, it was the largest community in the nation without an African American resident. Although Jewish himself, Levitt discouraged Jews from living in his communities. "As a Jew," he explained, "I have no room in my heart for racial prejudice. But the plain fact is that most whites prefer not to live in mixed communities. This attitude may be wrong morally, and someday it may change. I hope it will."

Other developers soon mimicked Levitt's efforts, building all-white suburban communities with rustic names such as Lakewood, Streamwood, Elmwood, Cedar Hill, Park Forest, and Deer Park. In 1955, *House and Garden* magazine declared that suburbia had become the "national way of life." By 1960, however, only 5 percent of African Americans lived in suburbs.

PEOPLE OF COLOR ON THE MOVE The mass migration of rural southern blacks to the urban North, Midwest, and West after the Second World War was much larger than the migration after the First World War, and its social consequences were even more dramatic. After 1945, more than 5 million blacks left the South in search of better jobs and housing, higher wages, and greater civil rights.

By 1960, for the first time in history, more African Americans were living in urban areas than in rural areas. As blacks moved into cities, however, many white residents left for the suburbs. Between 1950 and 1960, some 3.6 million whites left the nation's largest cities for suburban neighborhoods ("white flight"), while 4.5 million blacks moved into the cities.

Through organizations such as the National Association for the Advancement of Colored People (NAACP), the Congress of Racial Equality (CORE), and the National Urban League, African Americans sought to change the hearts and minds of their white neighbors. However, for all the racism that black migrants encountered, most of them preferred their new lives to the enforced segregation and often violent abuse in the South.

Just as African Americans were on the move, so, too, were Mexicans and Puerto Ricans. Congress renewed the bracero program, begun during the Second World War, which enabled Mexicans to work as wage laborers

The Second Great Migration African American families, such as the New Jersey–bound family pictured here, moved to northern urban centers in droves following the end of World War II.

in the United States, often as migrant farmworkers. Mexicans streamed across the nation's southwest border. By 1960, Los Angeles had the largest concentration of Mexican Americans in the nation.

Mexican Americans, Puerto Ricans, and other Latinos who served in the military also benefited from the GI Bill. Many of them—and their families—were able to relocate to the mainland United States because of the educational and housing programs provided veterans through the federal government. Between 1940 and 1960, nearly a million Puerto Ricans, mostly small farmers and agricultural workers, moved into American cities, especially New York City. By the late 1960s, more Puerto Ricans (who enjoy dual citizenship of the Commonwealth of Puerto Rico and the United States) lived in New York City than in San Juan, the capital of Puerto Rico.

SHIFTING WOMEN'S ROLES During the Second World War, millions of women had assumed traditionally male jobs in factories and mills. After the war, the influx of men returning to the civilian workforce led many employers to push working women back into traditional homemaking roles. A 1945 article in *House Beautiful* magazine informed women that the returning war veteran was "head man again. . . . Your part in the remaking of this man is to fit his home to him, understanding why he wants it this way, forgetting your own preferences."

Advertisements in popular magazines often targeted middle-class women, depicting them happily bound to the house, at work in the kitchen in dresses adorned with jewelry (usually pearl necklaces) and high heels, conversing with children, serving dinner, cleaning, and otherwise displaying the joy of a spotless home or the latest kitchen appliance.

The prevailing images of middle-class life featured tree-lined suburban streets, kids riding their bikes through beautiful neighborhoods, and women as devoted servants to their husbands. Idealized images of "the happy homemaker" and suburban life in popular television programs like *The Donna Reed Show* or *Leave It to Beaver* also supported the cold war propaganda campaign to portray the superiority of capitalism, democracy, freedom, and religion over communism. Russian women were depicted toiling at menial work in drab factories or on government-managed farms.

During the 1950s, the U.S. marriage rate reached an all-time high, and the average age of marriage for women plummeted to nineteen. There was enormous social pressure on teenaged girls to get married quickly; if a woman wasn't engaged or married by her early twenties, she was in danger of becoming an "old maid." In 1956, one fourth of white college women wed while still

The new household A Tupperware party in a middle-class suburban home.

Hollywood homemakers TV shows, movies, and plays in the fifties were outlets for homemakers' anxieties and fantasies. Left: *Leave It to Beaver* (1957) was a popular comedy about a young boy and his happy-go-lucky family living in suburban America. Right: Domestic bliss was out of reach for African American female characters. In the award-winning Broadway production of *Porgy and Bess* (1959), Dorothy Dandridge plays an addict so lost in the vice of New Orleans that even her self-sacrificing disabled lover (Sidney Poitier) cannot save her.

enrolled in school, and most dropped out before receiving a degree. A common joke was that women went to college to get an "M.R.S. degree"—that is, a husband. Female college students were encouraged to take such courses as home economics, interior decoration, and family finance. Lynn White, president of Mills College, argued that "the curriculum for female students should prepare women to foster the intellectual and emotional life of her family and community."

Despite this "modern" version of the nineteenth century's cult of domesticity, many women did work outside the home. In 1950, women comprised 29 percent of the workforce, and that percentage rose steadily throughout the decade. Some 70 percent of employed women worked in clerical positions—as secretaries, bank tellers, or sales clerks—or on assembly lines or in the service industry (waitresses, laundresses, housekeepers). Less than 15 percent were employed in a professional capacity (teachers, nurses, accountants, social workers). Women represented only 3.5 percent of attorneys and 6 percent of physicians. African American and other women of color had even fewer vocational choices and were mostly delegated to low-paying service jobs such as housekeepers and cooks.

THE CHILD-CENTERED FIFTIES With the war over, millions of military veterans eagerly returned to civilian life and growing families. The record number of Americans born during the postwar period (roughly 1941–1964) composed what came to be known as the "**baby boom** generation," which would shape the nation's social and cultural life throughout the second half of the twentieth century and after.

The fifties was the ideal decade to be a child because there were so many of them. Social life became centered on the needs of children. Between 1946 and 1964, the birth of 76 million Americans reversed a century-long decline in the nation's birthrate and created a demographic upheaval whose repercussions are still being felt. The baby boom peaked in 1957, when a record 4.3 million births occurred. From 1940 to 1960, the number of families with three children doubled, and the number with four quadrupled.

Postwar babies initially created a surge in demand for diapers, washing machines, and baby food, then required the construction of thousands of new schools—and the hiring of teachers to staff them. Children's needs drove much of the economy's growth, creating a huge market for toys, candy, gum, records, clothes, and other items. In 1958, *Life* magazine reported that four-year-olds were causing a "backlog of business orders that will take two decades to fulfill."

That so many women were having babies and raising children necessarily shaped societal attitudes toward them—and vice versa. A special issue of *Life* in 1956 featured the "ideal" middle-class woman: a thirty-two-year-old "pretty and popular" white suburban housewife, mother of four, who had married at age sixteen. She was described as an excellent wife, mother, volunteer, and "home manager." She made her own clothes, hosted dozens of dinner parties each year, sang in her church choir, and was devoted to her husband. "In her daily round," *Life* reported, "she attends club or charity meetings, drives the children to school, does the weekly grocery shopping, makes ceramics, and is planning to study French."

The soaring birthrate reinforced the notion that a woman's place was in the home. "Of all the accomplishments of the American woman," *Life* proclaimed, "the one she brings off with the most spectacular success is having babies."

A Religious Nation

After the Second World War, Americans joined churches and synagogues in record numbers. In 1940, less than half the adult population belonged to a church; by 1960, more than 65 percent were members of churches or synagogues. The cold war provided a stimulant to Christian evangelism. A godly nation, it was assumed, would better withstand the march of "godless" communism.

Roadside service Drive-in churches offered members the comfort of listening to Sunday Mass from their cars. Here, the pastor of New York's Tremont Methodist Church greets a member of his four-wheeled congregation.

President Eisenhower promoted a patriotic religious crusade. "Recognition of the Supreme Being," he declared, "is the first, the most basic, expression of Americanism. Without God, there could be no American form of government, nor an American way of life." In 1954, Congress added the phrase "[one nation] under God" to the Pledge of Allegiance. In 1956, it made the statement "In God We Trust" the nation's official motto, and Eisenhower ordered it displayed on all currency. "Today in the United States," *Time* magazine claimed in 1954, "the Christian faith is back at the center of things." The prevailing tone of the religious revival was upbeat and soothing. As the Protestant Council of New York City explained to its radio and television presenters, their on-air broadcasts "should project love, joy, courage, hope, faith, trust in God, goodwill. . . . In a very real sense we are 'selling' religion, the good news of the Gospel."

The best salesman for this "good news" was the Reverend Norman Vincent Peale. No speaker was more in demand, and no writer was more widely read. Peale's book *The Power of Positive Thinking* (1952) was a phenomenal best seller—and for good reason. It offered a simple how-to course in personal happiness, which Peale called Practical Christianity. "Flush out all depressing, negative, and tired thoughts," he advised. "Start thinking faith, enthusiasm, and joy." By following this simple formula, he pledged, each American could become "a more popular, esteemed, and well-liked individual." At the height of Peale's popularity, he was reaching 30 million people each week through radio, television, and his weekly newspaper columns.

CRACKS IN THE PICTURE WINDOW

In contrast to the "happy days" image of the fifties, there was also anxiety, dissent, and diversity. In *The Affluent Society* (1958), economist John Kenneth Galbraith attacked the prevailing notion that sustained economic growth was solving social problems. He reminded readers that the nation had yet to eradicate poverty, especially among minorities in inner cities; female-led households; Mexican American migrant farmworkers; Native Americans; and rural southerners, both black and white.

POVERTY AMID PROSPERITY Uncritical praise for the "throwaway" culture of consumption masked the nation's chronic poverty amid its mythic plenty. In 1959, a quarter of the population had *no* financial assets, and more than half had no savings accounts or credit cards. Poverty afflicted nearly half of African Americans, compared to only a quarter of whites. At least 40 million people had incomes below the poverty line during the 1950s.

The "promised land" in the North was not perfect. Because those who left the South were often undereducated, poor, and black, they were regularly denied access to good jobs, good schools, and good housing. Although states in the North, Midwest, and Far West were not as blatantly discriminatory as in the South, African Americans still encountered racism and discrimination.

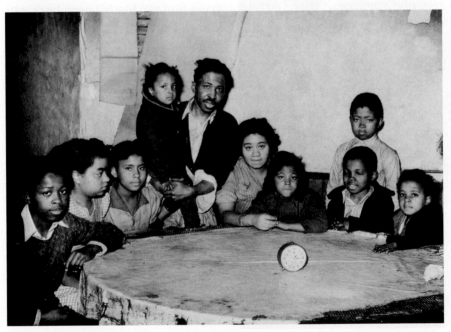

Family on relief Many African American families who migrated from the South to the Midwest became a part of the marginalized population in Chicago, dependent on public housing and experiencing the North's forms of racism.

LITERATURE AS SOCIAL CRITICISM Many critics, writers, and artists rejected America's social complacency and worship of consumerism. Playwright Thornton Wilder labeled young adults of the fifties the "Silent Generation" because of their self-centered outlook, and writer Norman Mailer said the 1950s was "one of the worst decades in the history of man" because so many Americans embraced a bland conformity. The most powerful novels of the postwar period emphasized the individual's struggle for survival amid the smothering forces of mass society. Books such as James Jones's *From Here to Eternity* (1951), Ralph Ellison's *Invisible Man* (1952), Saul Bellow's *Seize the Day* (1956), J. D. Salinger's *Catcher in the Rye* (1951), William Styron's *Lie Down in Darkness* (1951), and John Updike's *Rabbit, Run* (1961) feature restless, tormented souls who can find neither contentment nor respect in a superficial world.

The upper-middle-class white suburbs and the culture of comfortable conformity were frequent literary targets. John Cheever set most of his short stories in suburban neighborhoods—"cesspools of conformity." The typical suburban dweller, one critic charged in 1956, "buys the right car, keeps his lawn like his neighbor's, eats crunchy breakfast cereal, and votes Republican."

In his vicious satire of affluent suburbia, *The Crack in the Picture Window* (1956), John Keats charged that "miles of identical boxes are spreading like gangrene" across the nation, producing "haggard" businessmen, "tense and anxious" housewives, and "the gimme kids" who, after unwrapping the last Christmas gift, "look up and ask whether that is all." He dismissed Levittowns as residential "developments conceived in error, nurtured by greed, corroding everything they touch. They destroy established cities and trade patterns, pose dangerous problems for the areas they invade, and actually drive mad myriads of housewives shut up in them."

Ralph Ellison Ellison is best remembered for his 1952 novel *Invisible Man*.

THE BEATS A small but highly controversial group of young writers, poets, painters, and musicians rejected the consumer culture and the traditional responsibilities of middle-class life. They were known as the **Beats**. To be "beat" was likened to being "upbeat" and even "beatific," as well as being "on the beat" in "real cool" jazz music. But the Beats also liked the name because it implied "weariness," being "exhausted" or "beaten down," qualities which none of them actually exhibited.

Jack Kerouac, Allen Ginsberg, William Burroughs, Neal and Carolyn Cassady, Gary Snyder, Joyce Johnson, Diane Di Prima, and other Beats rebelled against conventional literary and artistic expression and excelled at often purposeless and even criminal behavior. In nurturing their alienation from mainstream life, the mostly male Beats were nomadic seekers, restless and tormented souls who stole cars and cash and sought solace in booze, mind-altering drugs, carefree sex, and various forms of risk-taking behavior. A drunk Burroughs, for example, tried to shoot an apple off his wife's head and missed, killing her instantly.

Intensely self-absorbed to the point of ruthlessness, the Beats celebrated lives of breathtaking risk, fueled by feverish spontaneity and raw energy. They pursued communal alcohol- and drug-induced ecstasies and sexual excesses. Carolyn Cassady once happened upon husband Neal in bed with his first wife and Allen Ginsberg; later, she agreed to her husband's request that she have an affair with his best friend, Jack Kerouac.

The Beats emerged from the bohemian underground in New York City's Greenwich Village. They wanted their art and literature to change consciousness rather than address social ills. Ginsberg called them "angelheaded hipsters burning for the ancient heavenly connection." An anarchic boys club, the

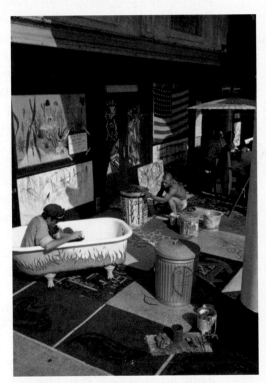

Art ache The Beat community fostered a frenzied desire to experience life in all its intensity and spontaneity, including the cultural realm. In this 1959 photograph, poet Tex Kleen reads verse in a bathtub at Venice Beach, California, while artist Mad Mike paints trash cans.

Beats were masters at outrageous behavior: they viewed getting high as first-class trips and women as second-class accessories; they were serial misogynists. Carolyn Cassady said that "the boys didn't know where they were going. . . . They just knew they wanted to *go*."

During three feverish weeks, Kerouac typed nonstop on a continuous roll of teletype paper the manuscript of his remarkable novel *On the Road* (1957), an account of a series of frenzied cross-country trips he and others made between 1948 and 1950.

Kerouac and the Beats were, at heart, outlandish romantics searching for an authentic sense of self in a nation absorbed in consumerism, conformism, and anti-communism. The Beats were as much a social force as they were a cultural movement. Many Beats, notably Allen Ginsberg and his life-long partner, poet Peter Orlovsky, were gay or bisexual during an era when homosexuality continued to be scorned as "deviant" behavior. Ginsberg and Orlovsky termed their relationship a marriage, and by doing so the two men were social pioneers, the first gay "married" couple that many people had ever encountered. They remained partners for more than forty years, until Ginsberg's death in 1997.

Ginsberg's provocative jazzed-up prose-poem, "Howl," which applauded the defiant alienation of the Beats, openly celebrated erotic homosexuality. It was so stippled with vivid sexual references that copies of the poem were impounded by United States Customs agents and its publisher, poet Lawrence Ferlinghetti, was charged with obscenity. After a long trial, Ferlinghetti was acquitted after the judge ruled that the poem was neither obscene nor without "redeeming social importance." Thereafter, "Howl" served as a manifesto for the sexual revolution.

The raucous rebelliousness of the Beats set the stage for the more widespread youth revolt of the 1960s and the flowering of the hippies.

ROCK 'N' ROLL The millions of children making up the first wave of baby boomers became adolescents in the late 1950s. People began calling them teenagers, and a distinctive teen subculture began to emerge, as did a wave of juvenile delinquency. By 1956, more than a million teens were being arrested each year. One contributing factor was access to automobiles, which enabled them to escape parental control and, in the words of one journalist, provided "a private lounge for drinking and for petting [embracing and kissing] or sex episodes."

Many blamed teen delinquency on rock 'n' roll, a new form of music. Alan Freed, a Cleveland disc jockey, coined the term *rock 'n' roll* in 1951. He had noticed that white teenagers buying rhythm and blues (R&B) records preferred the livelier recordings by African Americans and Latino Americans.

Freed began playing R&B records on his radio show, but he called the music rock 'n' roll (a phrase used in African American communities to refer to dancing and sex). By 1954, Freed had moved to New York City, where his program helped bridge the gap between "white" and "black" music.

African American singers such as Chuck Berry, Little Richard, and Ray Charles, along with Latino American performers such as Ritchie Valens (Richard Valenzuela), captivated young, white, middle-class audiences. At the same time, Sam Phillips, a disk jockey in Memphis, Tennessee, was searching for a particular type of pop singer. "If I could find a white man with a Negro sound," Phillips said, "I could make a billion dollars."

He found him in Elvis Presley, the lanky son of poor Mississippi farmers. In 1956, the twenty-one-year-old Presley, by then a regional star famous for his long, unruly hair, sullen yet sensual sneer, and swiveling hips, released his smash-hit recording "Heartbreak Hotel." Over the next two years, he emerged as the most popular musician in American history, carrying rock 'n' roll across the race barrier and assaulting the bland conformity of fifties culture. Presley's gyrating performances (his nickname was "Elvis the Pelvis") and incomparable voice drove young people wild and earned him millions of fans. His movements, said one music critic, "suggest, in a word, sex."

Cultural conservatives urged parents to destroy Presley's records. A Roman Catholic official denounced Presley as a symptom of a teenage "creed of dishonesty, violence, lust and degeneration." Patriotic groups claimed that rock 'n' roll music was part of a Communist plot to corrupt America's youth. Writing in the *New York Times*, a psychiatrist characterized it as a "communicable disease." A U.S. Senate subcommittee warned that Presley was threatening "to rock-n-roll the juvenile world into open revolt against society. The gangster of tomorrow is the Elvis Presley type of today."

Yet rock 'n' roll flourished in part because it was so controversial. It gave teenagers a sense of belonging to a tribal social group. More important, it brought together, on equal terms, musicians (and their audiences) of varied races and backgrounds.

Elvis Presley Star-struck girls grab at him from all angles, but the "King of Rock and Roll" stays cool while performing in Miami in 1956.

THE CIVIL RIGHTS MOVEMENT

Soon after the cold war began, Soviet diplomats began to use America's widespread racial discrimination against African Americans as a propaganda tool to illustrate the defects of the American way of life. Under the Jim Crow system in southern states, blacks still risked being lynched if they registered to vote. They were forced to use separate facilities—water fountains, restrooms, hotels, theaters, parks—and attend segregated schools. In the North, discrimination was not officially sanctioned by local and state laws as it was in the South, but it was equally real, especially in housing and employment. President Eisenhower had an opportunity to exercise transformational leadership in race relations; his unwillingness to do so was his greatest failure. As *Time* magazine noted in 1958, Eisenhower "overlooked the fact that the U.S. needed [his] moral leadership in fighting segregation."

EISENHOWER AND RACE Eisenhower had entered the White House committed to civil rights in principle, and he pushed for improvements in some areas. During his first three years, public facilities (parks, playgrounds, libraries, restaurants) in Washington, D.C., were desegregated, and he intervened to end discrimination at military bases in Virginia and South Carolina. Beyond that, however, he refused to make civil rights for African Americans a moral crusade. Pushing too hard, he believed, would "raise tempers and increase prejudices."

Two aspects of Eisenhower's political philosophy limited his commitment to racial equality: his preference for state or local action over federal involvement and his doubt that laws could change attitudes. His passivity meant that governmental leadership on civil rights would come from the judiciary more than from the executive or legislative branches.

In 1953, Eisenhower appointed Republican Earl Warren, former governor of California, as chief justice of the U.S. Supreme Court, a decision he later said was the "biggest damn fool mistake I ever made." Warren, who had seemed safely conservative while in elected office, displayed a social conscience and a streak of libertarianism on the bench. Under his leadership (1953–1969), the Supreme Court became a powerful force for social and political change.

AFRICAN AMERICAN ACTIVISM The most-crucial leaders of the civil rights movement came from those whose rights were most often violated: African Americans, Latino Americans, Asian Americans, and other people of color. Courageous blacks led what would become the most important social movement in twentieth-century America. They fought in the courts, at the ballot box, and in the streets.

Fountains of truth An Alabama motel offers its white patrons chilled water from a cooler, while its African American guests are limited to a simple drinking fountain.

Although many African Americans had moved to the North and West, a majority remained in the South, where they still faced a rigidly segregated society. In the 1952 presidential election, for example, only 20 percent of eligible African Americans were registered to vote. And although the public schools, especially in the South, were supposedly racially separate but equal in quality, many all-black schools were actually underfunded, understaffed, and overcrowded.

In the mid-1930s, the National Association for the Advancement of Colored People (NAACP) challenged the **separate-but-equal** judicial doctrine that had preserved racial segregation since the *Plessy* decision by the Supreme Court in 1896. It took almost fifteen years, however, to convince the courts that racial segregation must end. Finally, in *Sweatt v. Painter* (1950), the Supreme Court ruled that a separate black law school in Texas was *not* equal in quality to the state's whites-only schools. The Court ordered Texas to remedy the situation. It was the first step toward dismantling America's tradition of racial segregation.

THE *BROWN* DECISION By the early 1950s, people were challenging state laws requiring racial segregation in the public schools. Five such cases, from Kansas, Delaware, South Carolina, Virginia, and the District of Columbia—usually cited by reference to the first, ***Brown v. Board of Education*** of Topeka, Kansas*—went to the Supreme Court in 1952. President Eisenhower gutlessly told the attorney general that he hoped the justices would postpone dealing with the case "until the next Administration took over." When it became obvious that the Court was moving forward, Eisenhower urged Chief Justice Warren to side with segregationists. Warren was not swayed: "You mind your business," he told the president, "and I'll mind mine."

Warren wrote the pathbreaking opinion, delivered on May 17, 1954, in which the Court declared that "in the field of public education the doctrine of 'separate but equal' has no place." The justices used a variety of sociological and psychological findings to show that even if racially separate schools were equal in quality, the very practice of separating students by race caused feelings of inferiority among black children. A year later, the Court directed that racial *integration* should move forward "with all deliberate speed."

Eisenhower refused to endorse or enforce the Court's ruling. He grumbled in private "that the Supreme Court decision set back progress in the South at least fifteen years." Anyone who thinks "you can do these things by force is just plain nuts," he said. He even refused to condemn the lynching of fourteen-year-old Emmett Till, an African American whose mutilated body was found in a Mississippi River after he had supposedly whistled at a white woman.

While token racial integration began as early as 1954 in northern states and the border states of Kentucky and Missouri, hostility mounted in the Lower South and Virginia. The Alabama State Senate and the Virginia legislature

Separate, but not equal African American children pose outside their separate-but-unequal schoolhouse in Selma, Alabama, in 1965.

both passed resolutions "nullifying" the Supreme Court's decision, arguing that racial integration was an issue of states' rights. Arkansas governor Orval Faubus insisted that the "federal government is a creature of the states. . . . We must either choose to defend our rights or else surrender."

In 1954, Harry F. Byrd, a Virginia senator and former governor, called for "**massive resistance**" against federal efforts to enforce integration in the South. Senator James O. Eastland of Mississippi, a state where African Americans made up 45 percent of the population, pledged that "integration will never come to Mississippi." A plantation owner and notorious racist whose father had lynched a black couple, Eastland denounced the *Brown* decision as an "illegal, immoral, and sinful doctrine." He told the Senate that "the Negro race is an inferior race" and that the South was determined to maintain white supremacy.

The grassroots opposition among southern whites to the *Brown* case was led by newly formed Citizens' Councils, middle-class versions of the Ku Klux Klan that spread quickly and eventually enrolled 250,000 members. The Councils, which used economic coercion against blacks who crossed racial boundaries, grew so powerful in some communities that membership became almost a necessity for an aspiring white politician.

One hundred one members of Congress signed a Declaration of Constitutional Principles ("Southern Manifesto") in 1956, deploring the *Brown* decision as "a clear abuse of judicial power" that had created an "explosive and dangerous condition" in the South. Only three southern Democrats refused to sign. One of them, Senator Lyndon B. Johnson of Texas, would become president seven years later. In six southern states at the end of 1956, two years after the *Brown* ruling, no black children attended school with whites. By 1960, only 765 of 6,676 school districts in the South had desegregated.

THE MONTGOMERY BUS BOYCOTT While mobilizing white resistance, the *Brown* case also inspired many black (and white) activists by suggesting that the federal government was finally beginning to confront racial discrimination. Yet the essential role played by the NAACP and the courts in the civil rights movement often overshadows the courageous contributions of individual African Americans who took great risks to challenge segregation.

For example, in Montgomery, Alabama, on December 1, 1955, Mrs. Rosa Parks, a forty-two-year-old seamstress who was a determined activist for racial justice, boarded the Cleveland Avenue bus and sat in the third row. As white passengers boarded, the driver, James Blake, told Parks she had to move to the back, as the city required blacks to do. She refused. Blake then demanded, "Why don't you stand up?" Parks calmly replied, "I don't think I should have to

Rosa Parks Parks is fingerprinted by a Montgomery policeman on February 22, 1956, along with about 100 others who joined the bus boycott.

stand up." When the driver told her that "niggers must move back" or he would have her arrested, she replied, "You may do that." Parks recalled that she was "tired of giving in." Police then arrested her. In holding her ground, Parks had unwittingly launched the modern civil rights movement.

The next night, black community leaders met at Dexter Avenue Baptist Church to organize a long-planned boycott of the city's bus system, most of whose riders were African Americans. Student and faculty volunteers from Alabama State University stayed up all night to distribute 35,000 flyers denouncing the arrest of Rosa Parks and urging support for the **Montgomery bus boycott**.

MARTIN LUTHER KING JR In the Dexter Avenue church's twenty-six-year-old pastor, Martin Luther King Jr., the boycott movement found a brave and charismatic leader. The grandson of a slave and son of a prominent minister, King was an eloquent speaker. "We must use the weapon of love," he told supporters. "We must realize so many people are taught to hate us that they are not totally responsible for their hate."

To his foes, King warned, "We will soon wear you down by our capacity to suffer, and in winning our freedom we will so appeal to your heart and conscience that we will win you in the process." He preached **nonviolent civil disobedience**, the tactic of defying unjust laws through peaceful actions, but he also valued militancy, for without crisis and confrontation there would be no progress.

The Montgomery bus boycott was a stunning success. For 381 days, African Americans, women and men, organized carpools, used black-owned taxis, hitchhiked, or simply walked. White supporters also provided rides. The unprecedented mass protest infuriated many whites; police harassed and ticketed black carpools, and white thugs attacked black pedestrians. Ku Klux Klan members burned black churches and bombed houses. King himself was arrested twice.

On December 20, 1956, the Montgomery boycotters won a federal case they had initiated against racial segregation on public buses. The Supreme Court affirmed that "the separate but equal doctrine can no longer be safely followed as a correct statement of the law." The next day, King and other African Americans boarded the city buses. They showed that well-coordinated, nonviolent black activism could trigger major changes. Among African Americans,

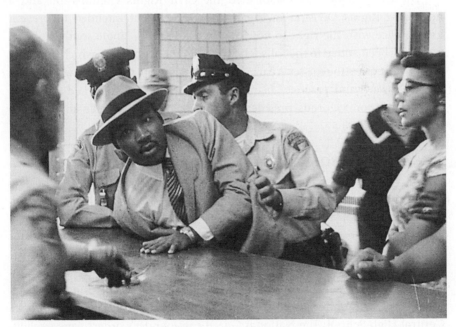

Civil disobedience Martin Luther King Jr. is arrested for "loitering" in 1958. He was arrested thirty times for defying racist laws.

hope replaced resignation, and action supplanted passivity. The boycott also catapulted King into the national spotlight.

And what of Rosa Parks? She and her husband lost their jobs. Hate mail, death threats, and firebombings forced them to leave Alabama eight months after her arrest. They moved to Detroit, where they remained fully engaged in the evolving civil rights movement. "Freedom fighters never retire," she explained.

THE CIVIL RIGHTS ACTS OF 1957 AND 1960 In 1956, hoping to exploit divisions between northern and southern Democrats and reclaim some of the black vote for Republicans, congressional leaders agreed to support what became the Civil Rights Act of 1957.

The first civil rights law passed since 1875, it finally got through the Senate, after a year's delay, with the help of majority leader Lyndon B. Johnson, a Texas Democrat who knew that he could never be elected president if he was viewed as just another racist white southerner. The bill was intended to ensure that all Americans, regardless of race or ethnicity, were allowed to vote. Johnson won southern acceptance of the bill by watering down its enforcement provisions. Eisenhower reassured Johnson that the final version represented "the mildest civil rights bill possible."

The Civil Rights Act established the Civil Rights Commission and a new Civil Rights Division in the Justice Department intended to prevent interference with the right to vote. Yet by 1959, not a single southern black voter had been added to the rolls. The Civil Rights Act of 1960, which provided for federal courts to register African Americans to vote in districts where there was a "pattern and practice" of racial discrimination, also lacked teeth and depended upon vigorous presidential enforcement to achieve any tangible results.

DESEGREGATION IN LITTLE ROCK A few weeks after the Civil Rights Act of 1957 was passed, Arkansas's Democratic governor, Orval Eugene Faubus, a rabid segregationist, called a special session of the state legislature. He asked the legislators to pass a series of bills designed to give him sweeping powers to close public schools threatened with integration and to transfer funds from public schools facing federally enforced integration to private "segregation academies."

In the fall of 1957, Faubus defied a federal court order by using the state's National Guard to prevent nine black students from enrolling at Little Rock's Central High School. The National Guard commander's orders were explicit: "No niggers in the building." When one of the students, fifteen-year-old Elizabeth Eckford, tried to enter the school, National Guardsmen barred the

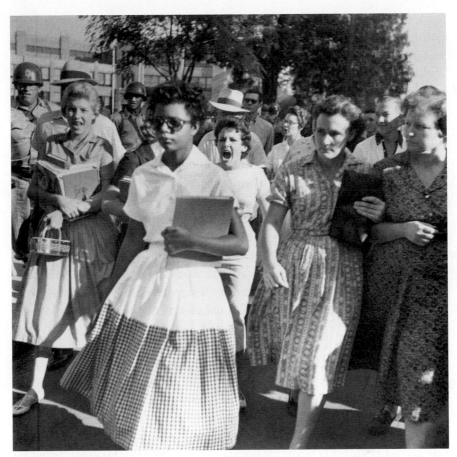

"Lynch her!" A determined Elizabeth Eckford endures the hostile screams of future classmates as she enters Central High School in Little Rock, Arkansas.

door. All alone, she headed back to the bus stop, only to be confronted by a mob of jeering white mothers and schoolgirls shrieking, "Lynch her! Lynch her!" Eckford recalled, "They moved closer and closer. . . . I tried to see a friendly face somewhere in the crowd—someone who maybe could help. I looked into the face of an old woman and it seemed a kind face, but when I looked at her again, she spat at me."

The mayor of Little Rock frantically called the White House "pleading" for federal troops. At that point, President Eisenhower, who had resisted all appeals for federal action, reluctantly dispatched 1,000 army paratroopers to protect the brave black students as they entered the school. "Mob rule," he told the nation, "cannot be allowed to overrule the decisions of our courts."

It was the first time since the 1870s that federal troops had been sent to the South to protect African Americans. Dunbar Ogden, a Presbyterian minister in Little Rock, found a ray of hope in the ugly confrontation: "This may be looked back upon by future historians as the turning point—for good—of race relations in this country."

With television cameras sending dramatic images across the country, paratroopers used bayonets and rifle butts to disperse the angry crowd. The nine black students attended their first classes with soldiers patrolling the halls.

The soldiers stayed in Little Rock through the school year. To a man, unyielding southern governors and congressmen furiously lashed out at Eisenhower, charging that he was violating states' rights. The president had "lit the fires of hate," claimed Senator James Eastland. Eisenhower, who had grown up in an all-white Kansas town and spent his military career in a segregated army, stressed that his use of federal troops had little to do with "the integration or segregation question" and everything to do with maintaining law and order. Although Eisenhower favored equality of opportunity, he explained to an aide that equality did not mean "that a Negro should court my daughter."

In Eisenhower's view, the gleaming bayonets in Little Rock showed that the United States was a government of law, that the Constitution remained the supreme law of the land, and that the U.S. Supreme Court was the final interpreter of the Constitution. Martin Luther King Jr. forced the president out of his comfort zone. He told Eisenhower that the "overwhelming majority of southerners, Negro and white, stand behind your resolute action to restore law and order in Little Rock." Many southern politicians, however, called for the president's impeachment and removal.

In the summer of 1958, Governor Faubus closed the Little Rock high schools rather than allow racial integration. The governor of Virginia did the same. Their actions led Jonathan Daniels, editor of the Raleigh (North Carolina) News & Observer, to write that closing public schools is "something beyond secession from the Union; [it] is secession from civilization."

Court proceedings in Arkansas dragged into 1959 before the schools reopened. Resistance to integration in Virginia collapsed when state and federal courts struck down state laws that had cut off funds to integrated public schools. Thereafter, massive resistance to racial integration was confined mostly to the Lower South, where five states—from South Carolina westward through Louisiana—still opposed even token integration. Not a single pupil in those states attended an integrated school. Faubus went on to serve six terms as governor of Arkansas.

SOUTHERN CHRISTIAN LEADERSHIP CONFERENCE After Little Rock, progress toward greater civil rights seemed agonizingly slow. Frustrated African Americans began blaming the NAACP for relying too much on the courts.

The widespread sense of disappointment gave Martin Luther King's nonviolent civil rights movement even greater visibility. As King explained, "We were confronted with blasted hopes, and the dark shadow of a deep disappointment settled upon us. So we had no alternative except that of preparing for direct action, whereby we would present our very bodies as a means of laying our case before the conscience of the local and national community."

On January 10, 1957, King invited about sixty black ministers and leaders to Ebenezer Church in Atlanta. Their goal was to form an organization to promote nonviolent civil disobedience as a method of desegregating bus systems across the South. A new organization soon emerged: the **Southern Christian Leadership Conference (SCLC)**, with King as its president. Unlike the NAACP, which recruited individual members, SCLC coordinated activities on behalf of a cluster of organizations, mostly individual churches or community groups. Because King pushed for direct action, only a few African American ministers were initially willing to affiliate with SCLC, for fear of a white backlash.

King persisted, however, and over time SCLC grew into a powerful organization. The activists knew that violence awaited them. Roy Wilkins, head of the NAACP, noted that "the Negro citizen has come to the point where he is not afraid of violence. He no longer shrinks back. He will assert himself, and if violence comes, so be it."

Thus began the second phase of the civil rights movement. It would come to fruition in the 1960s as African American activists showed the courage to resist injustice, the power to love everyone, and the strength to endure discouragement and opposition. They did so without the president's support. As Wilkins asserted: "President Eisenhower was a fine general and a good, decent man, but if he had fought World War II the way he fought for civil rights, we would all be speaking German today."

FOREIGN POLICY IN THE FIFTIES

The Truman administration's commitment to contain communism focused on the Soviet threat to Western Europe. During the 1950s, the Eisenhower administration, especially Secretary of State John Foster Dulles, determined that containment was no longer enough; instead, the United States must develop a "dynamic" foreign policy that would "roll back" communism around the world.

Dulles's goal was to "liberate" people under Communist rule rather than merely contain its expansion. "For us," he said, "there are two kinds of people in the world. There are those who are Christians and support free enterprise, and there are the others." He soon discovered, however, that the complexities of world affairs and the realities of Soviet and Communist Chinese power made his moral commitment to manage the destiny of the world unrealistic—and costly.

CONCLUDING AN ARMISTICE In Korea, President Eisenhower faced three choices: increase the war effort, continue the military stalemate, or pursue a negotiated settlement. Eisenhower chose the third option, but he first had to convince John Foster Dulles that negotiations were warranted. In April 1953, Eisenhower told Dulles that he was not willing to prolong the military effort, but he was comfortable using the threat of nuclear weapons to reach a settlement.

In May, Eisenhower took the bold step of intensifying the aerial bombardment of North Korea. He let it be known that he would use nuclear weapons if a truce were not forthcoming. Thereafter, negotiations moved quickly toward an armistice (cease-fire agreement) on July 26, 1953. It ended "all acts of armed force" and reaffirmed the historical border between the two Koreas just above the 38th parallel until both sides could arrive at a "final peaceful settlement." Other factors in bringing about the armistice were China's rising military losses in the conflict and the spirit of uncertainty felt by Soviet Communists after the death of Josef Stalin on March 5, 1953.

The Korean War was the first in which helicopters were used in combat, and it ushered in the era of jet fighters. It transformed the United States into the world's police officer by convincing American political and military leaders that communism was indeed a global threat. Within a few years, the United States would create scores of permanent military bases around the world and organize a national security apparatus in Washington to manage its new responsibilities—not the least of which was a growing stockpile of nuclear weaponry.

DULLES AND MASSIVE RETALIATION Like Woodrow Wilson, Secretary of State Dulles was a Presbyterian minister's son. He believed that the United States was "born with a sense of destiny and mission" to defeat communism. (His British counterparts, however, were not impressed with his sermonizing monologues, calling them "dull, duller, Dulles.")

Dulles (and Eisenhower) insisted that containing communism was immoral because it did nothing to free people from oppression. America, he argued, should work toward the liberation of the "captive peoples" of Eastern Europe and China. When State Department analyst George F. Kennan, architect of the containment doctrine, dismissed Dulles's rhetoric as lunacy, Dulles fired him.

Eisenhower, however, understood Kennan's objections. He stressed that the so-called liberation doctrine would not involve military force. Instead, he would promote the removal of Communist control "by every peaceful means, but only by peaceful means." Yet he did nothing to temper Dulles's rhetoric and praised his secretary of state's moral fervor.

Dulles and Eisenhower knew they could not win a ground war against the Soviet Union or Communist China, whose armies had millions more soldiers than did the United States. Nor could the administration afford—politically or financially—to sustain military expenditures at the levels required during the Korean War. So they crafted a strategy that came to be called "**massive retaliation**," which meant using the threat of nuclear warfare to prevent Communist aggression. The strategy, they argued, would provide a "maximum deterrent at bearable cost," or "more bang for the buck."

Massive retaliation had major weaknesses, however. By the mid-1950s, both the United States and Soviet Union had developed hydrogen bombs that were 750 times as powerful as the atomic bombs dropped on Japan in 1945. A single hydrogen bomb would have a devastating global impact, yet war planners envisioned using hundreds of them. "The necessary art," Dulles explained, was in the *brinkmanship*, "the ability to get to the verge without getting into war. . . . If you are scared to go to the brink, you are lost." The *Milwaukee Journal* found Dulles's brinkmanship strategy terrifying: "It is like saying that the closer you get to war the better you serve peace. It is like saying that the destiny of the human race is something to gamble with."

THE CIA'S FOREIGN INTERVENTIONS While publicly promoting the liberation of Communist nations and massive retaliation as a strategy against the Soviets, President Eisenhower and Secretary of State Dulles were secretly using the **Central Intelligence Agency (CIA)** to manipulate world politics in covert ways that produced unintended consequences—all of them bad.

The anti-colonial independence movements unleashed by the Second World War led to nationalist groups around the globe revolting against British and French rule. In May 1951, the Iran parliament seized control of the nation's British-run oil industry. The following year, prime minister Moham-

"Don't Be Afraid—I Can Always Pull You Back" Secretary of State John Foster Dulles pushed America to the brink of war as a means of creating diplomatic leverage.

med Mossadegh cut diplomatic ties with Great Britain and insisted that Iran, not Britain, should own, sell, and profit from Iranian oil. Dulles predicted that Iran was on the verge of falling under Communist control. The CIA and the British intelligence service, MI6, then launched Operation Ajax to oust Mossadegh.

The CIA bribed Iranian army officers and hired Iranian agents to arrest Mossadegh, who was then convicted of high treason. Thereafter, in return for access to Iranian oil, the U.S. government provided massive support for the anti-Communist (and increasingly authoritarian) regime of the shah (king) of Iran, Mohammad Reza Pahlavi, who seized power. The Iranians would not forget that the Americans had put the hated shah in power.

The success of the CIA-engineered coup emboldened Eisenhower to authorize other secret operations to undermine "unfriendly" government regimes, even if it meant aligning with corrupt dictatorships. In 1954, the target was Guatemala, a poor Central American country led by Colonel Jacobo Arbenz Guzman. Arbenz's decision to take over U.S.-owned property and industries convinced Dulles that Guatemala was falling victim to "international communism." Dulles persuaded Eisenhower to approve a CIA operation to organize a secret Guatemalan army in Honduras.

On June 18, 1954, aided by CIA-piloted warplanes, 150 paid "liberators" forced Arbenz Guzman into exile in Mexico. The United States then installed a new ruler in Guatemala who eliminated all political opposition.

By secretly overthrowing elected governments to ensure that they did not join the Soviet bloc, however, the CIA destabilized Iran and Guatemala and created resentments in the Middle East and Central America that would eventually come back to haunt the United States.

INDOCHINA During the 1950s, the United States also became embroiled in Southeast Asia. Indochina, created by French imperialists in the nineteenth century out of the old kingdoms of Cambodia, Laos, and Vietnam, offered a distinctive case of anti-colonial nationalism. During the Second World War, after Japanese troops had occupied the region, the Viet Minh (League for the Independence of Vietnam) waged a guerrilla resistance movement led by Ho Chi Minh, a seasoned revolutionary and passionate nationalist.

"Uncle Ho," a wispy man weighing barely 100 pounds, had a single goal for his country: independence. At the end of the war against Japan, the Viet Minh controlled part of northern Vietnam. On September 2, 1945, Ho Chi Minh proclaimed the creation of a Democratic Republic of Vietnam, with its capital in Hanoi.

The French, like the Americans would later, underestimated the determination of the Vietnamese nationalists to maintain their independence. In 1946, the First Indochina War erupted when Ho's fighters resisted French

Ho Chi Minh Though a ruthless leader, he cultivated a public image of himself as the humble, gentle Uncle Ho, a man of the people.

efforts to restore the colonial regime. French forces quickly regained control of the cities, while the Viet Minh controlled the countryside. Ho predicted that his forces would absorb more losses, but the French would give in first.

When the Korean War ended, the United States continued its efforts to strengthen French control of Vietnam. By the end of 1953, the Eisenhower administration was paying nearly 80 percent of the cost of the French military effort.

In December 1953, some 12,000 French soldiers parachuted into **Dien Bien Phu**, a cluster of villages in a valley ringed by mountains in northwestern Vietnam. Their plan was to lure Viet Minh guerrillas into the open and then overwhelm them with superior firepower. The French assumed that the surrounding forested hills were impassable. Their strategy, however, backfired.

Slowly, more than 55,000 Viet Minh fighters took up positions atop the ridges overlooking the French base. They then laboriously dug trenches and tunnels down into the valley. By March 1954, the French found themselves surrounded.

Dien Bien Phu Viet Minh soldiers march French captives to a prisoner-of-war camp in Dien Bien Phu on May 7, 1954.

As the weeks passed, the French government pleaded with the United States to relieve the pressure on Dien Bien Phu. The National Security Council—John Foster Dulles, Vice President Nixon, and the chairman of the Joint Chiefs of Staff—urged President Eisenhower to use atomic bombs to aid the French. Eisenhower snapped back: "You boys must be crazy. We can't use those awful things against Asians for the second time in less than ten years. My God!"

The president opposed U.S. intervention unless the British joined the effort. When they refused, Eisenhower told the French that U.S. military action was "politically impossible." On May 7, 1954, the Viet Minh fighters overwhelmed the last French resistance. The catastrophic defeat signaled the end of French colonial rule in Asia.

On July 20, 1954, representatives of France, Britain, the Soviet Union, the People's Republic of China, and the Viet Minh signed the Geneva Accords,

POSTWAR ALLIANCES: THE FAR EAST

USSR

SEA OF OKHOTSK

MONGOLIA

MANCHURIA

NORTH KOREA

SEA OF JAPAN

JAPAN

SOUTH KOREA

0   250   1,000 Miles
0   250   1,000 Kilometers

CHINA

BONIN ISLANDS

INDIA

HONG KONG (G.B.)

REPUBLIC OF CHINA (TAIWAN)

IWO JIMA

PACIFIC OCEAN

BURMA (MYANMAR)

Hanoi

LAOS

EAST PAKISTAN

NORTH VIETNAM

PHILIPPINE SEA

MARIANA ISLANDS

BAY OF BENGAL

THAILAND

SOUTH CHINA SEA

PHILIPPINES

GUAM (U.S.)

CAMBODIA

SOUTH VIETNAM

MALAYSIA

CAROLINE ISLANDS (U.S. Trust)

SUMATRA

NEW GUINEA

BORNEO

SULAWESI (CELEBES)

WEST IRIAN
To Indonesia 1963

TRUST TERR. OF NEW GUINEA (Aust.)

INDIAN OCEAN

INDONESIA

JAVA

TIMOR

TERR. OF PAPUA (Aust.)

CORAL SEA

☐ Nations having bilateral defense treaties with the U.S.

☐ Members of SEATO

☐ Communist bloc

AUSTRALIA

- How did the United States become increasingly involved in Vietnam during the fifties?
- Why did the installation of Ngo Dinh Diem by the French and the Americans backfire and generate more conflict in Vietnam?

which gave Laos and Cambodia their independence and divided Vietnam at the 17th parallel of latitude. The Viet Minh Communists were given control in the North, with the French remaining south of the line until nationwide elections in 1956. Ho Chi Minh took charge of the government in North Vietnam, executing thousands of Vietnamese he deemed opponents.

In South Vietnam, power gravitated to a new premier chosen by the French at American urging: Ngo Dinh Diem, a Catholic nationalist who had opposed both the French and the Viet Minh. In 1954, Eisenhower began providing military and economic aid to Diem. Yet Diem's autocratic efforts to eliminate all opposition played into the hands of the Communists, who found eager recruits among the discontented South Vietnamese. By 1957, Communist guerrillas known as the **Viet Cong** were launching attacks on the Diem government. As the warfare intensified, the Eisenhower administration concluded that its only option was to "sink or swim with Diem."

Eisenhower had used what he called the **"falling-domino" theory** to explain why the United States needed to fight communism in Vietnam: "You have a row of dominos set up, you knock over the first one, and what will happen to the last one is the certainty that it will go over very quickly." If South Vietnam were to fall to communism, he predicted, the rest of Southeast Asia would soon follow.

The domino analogy assumed that communism was a global movement directed by Soviet leaders in Moscow. Yet anti-colonial insurgencies resulted more from nationalist motives than Communist ideology. The domino analogy thus informed policy decisions to the point that the United States had to police the entire world. As a consequence, *every* insurgency mushroomed into a strategic crisis.

Reelection and Foreign Crises

As a new presidential campaign unfolded in 1956, Dwight Eisenhower still enjoyed widespread public support. But his health was beginning to deteriorate. In September 1955, he suffered a heart attack, the first of three major illnesses that would affect the rest of his presidency.

The Republicans eagerly renominated Eisenhower and Vice President Richard Nixon. The party platform endorsed Eisenhower's moderate Republicanism, meaning balanced budgets, reduced government intervention in the economy, and an internationalist foreign policy. The Democrats turned again to the liberal Illinois leader, Adlai Stevenson.

REPRESSION IN HUNGARY During the last week of the presidential campaign, fighting erupted along the Suez Canal in Egypt and in the streets of Budapest, Hungary. On October 23, 1956, Hungarian nationalists, encouraged by American propaganda broadcasts through Radio Free Europe, revolted against Communist troops. The Soviets responded by killing 2,000 Hungarian freedom fighters and forcing nearly 200,000 more to flee before installing a new puppet government. The revolution had been smothered in twelve days.

Eisenhower's strategy in dealing with such crises was, as he later said, "Take a hard line—and bluff." Although he avoided war over Hungary, Eisenhower had allowed administration officials, especially Secretary of State Dulles, to make reckless pledges about "rolling back" communism and "liberating" Eastern Europe.

In Hungary, the Soviets called the administration's bluff. The Hungarian freedom fighters, having been led to expect U.S. support, paid with their lives. Richard Nixon cynically reassured Eisenhower that the Soviet crackdown would be beneficial in showing the world the ruthlessness of communism. The president felt guilty about failing to support the rebels, but Dulles showed little concern, reminding the president that "we always have been against violent rebellion."

THE SUEZ WAR President Eisenhower was more successful in handling an unexpected crisis in Egypt. In 1952, Egyptian army officer Gamal Abdel Nasser had overthrown King Farouk and set out to become the leader of the Arab world. To do so, he promised to destroy the new Israeli nation, created in 1948, and to end British and French imperialism in the region. Nasser, with Soviet support, first sought to take control of the Suez Canal, the internationally managed waterway in Egypt connecting the Mediterranean and the Red Sea flowing into the Indian Ocean.

The canal had opened in 1869 as a joint French–Egyptian venture. From 1882 on, British troops had protected it as the British Empire's "lifeline" to oil in the Middle East and to India and its other Asian colonies. When Nasser's regime pressed for the withdrawal of the British forces, an Anglo-Egyptian treaty provided for their withdrawal within twenty months.

In 1955, Nasser, adept at playing both sides, announced a huge arms deal with the Soviet Union. The United States countered by offering to help Egypt finance a massive hydroelectric dam at Aswan on the Nile River. In 1956, after Nasser increased trade with the Soviet bloc and recognized the People's Republic of China, John Foster Dulles abruptly canceled the Aswan Dam offer.

Unable to retaliate directly against the United States, Nasser seized control of the French-owned Suez Canal Company and denied Israel-bound ships access through the canal. For Egyptians, this was their declaration of independence from European colonialism. The British and French were furious, for two thirds of Europe's oil came through the canal, but they needed a pretext for military action. Israel soon provided one.

On September 30, 1956, Israeli, British, and French officials secretly hatched a full-scale invasion plan: Israel would attack Egypt from the east and race west to the Suez Canal. The French and British would then send troops to the canal zone, posing as peacekeepers.

On October 29, 1956, Israeli paratroopers dropped into Egypt. The British and French then issued an ultimatum demanding that the fighting cease. When Egypt rejected the ultimatum, British warplanes began bombing Egyptian airfields. On November 5, British and French soldiers invaded the canal zone. Nasser responded by sinking all forty international ships then in the Suez Canal. A few days later, Anglo-French commandos and paratroopers took control of the canal.

Eisenhower was furious that the three nations had attacked Egypt without informing the American government. He resolved to put a stop to the invasion, for he believed the Egyptians had the right to control the Suez Canal, since it was entirely within their boundaries. "How could we possibly support Britain and France," he asked, "if in doing so we lose the whole Arab world?"

Eisenhower demanded that the British and French withdraw and that the Israelis evacuate the Sinai Peninsula—or face severe economic sanctions. The three aggressor nations grudgingly complied on November 7.

The Suez debacle led to the resignation of Prime Minister Anthony Eden in Great Britain and hastened the process of independence among its remaining colonies. But perhaps its major result was that the British government realized the risk of acting independently of the United States. Egypt reopened the Suez Canal, and, as Eisenhower had predicted, operated it in a professional, nonpolitical manner.

The **Suez crisis** and the Hungarian revolt led Democrat Adlai Stevenson to declare the Eisenhower administration's foreign policy "bankrupt." Most Americans, however, reasoned that the crises actually affirmed the nation's status as *the* global superpower. Voters handed Eisenhower an even more lopsided victory than the one in 1952. Eisenhower carried all but seven states and won the electoral vote 457 to 73. His decisive victory, however, failed to swing a congressional majority for his party in either house.

SPUTNIK   On October 4, 1957, the Soviets shocked the world when they announced the launch of the first communications satellite, called *Sputnik* ("traveling companion"). Americans panicked, believing that if the Soviets could put a satellite in orbit, they could also fire a rocket with a nuclear warhead across the Pacific Ocean and detonate it on the West Coast. Senator Lyndon B. Johnson warned that the Russians would soon be "dropping bombs on us from space like kids dropping rocks on cars from freeway overpasses."

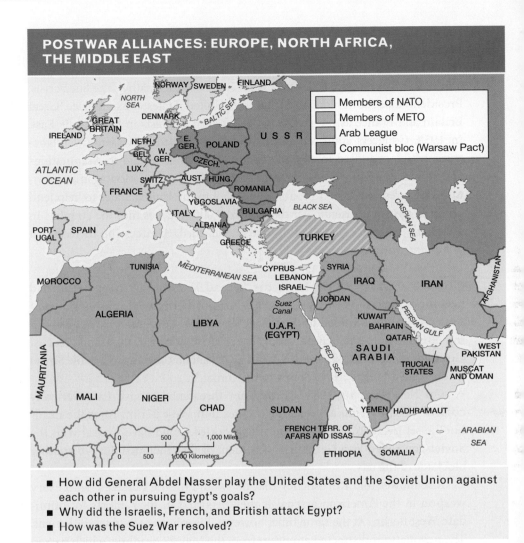

POSTWAR ALLIANCES: EUROPE, NORTH AFRICA, THE MIDDLE EAST

- How did General Abdel Nasser play the United States and the Soviet Union against each other in pursuing Egypt's goals?
- Why did the Israelis, French, and British attack Egypt?
- How was the Suez War resolved?

The Soviet success in space also dealt a severe blow to the prestige of American science and technology and changed the military balance of power. Democrats charged that the Soviets had "humiliated" the United States and opened a congressional investigation to assess the new threat.

"*Sputnik*-mania" led the United States to increase defense spending and enhance science education. In 1958, Congress created the National Aeronautics and Space Administration (NASA) to coordinate research and development related to outer space. The same year, Congress, with President Eisenhower's support, enacted the National Defense Education Act (NDEA), which authorized large federal grants to colleges and universities to enhance education and research in mathematics, science, and modern languages, as well as for student loans and fellowships.

THE EISENHOWER DOCTRINE In the aftermath of the Suez crisis, President Eisenhower decided that the United States must replace Great Britain and France as the guarantor of Western interests in the Middle East. In 1958, Congress approved what came to be called the Eisenhower Doctrine, which promised to extend economic and military aid to Arab nations and to use armed force if necessary to assist any such nation against Communist aggression. When Lebanon appealed to the United States to help fend off an insurgency, Eisenhower dispatched 5,000 marines into the country. In October 1958, once the situation had stabilized, U.S. forces (up to 15,000 at one point) withdrew.

CRISIS IN BERLIN Since the Second World War, West Berlin had become an oasis of Western democracy and prosperity, while East Berlin continued to be administered by the Soviet Union. West Berlin served as an enticing alternative to life behind the iron curtain. Each year, thousands of East Germans escaped to West Berlin. Nikita Khrushchev, the unpredictable Soviet leader, called West Berlin a "bone in my throat."

On November 10, 1958, Khrushchev threatened to give East Germany control of East Berlin and of the air lanes into West Berlin. After the deadline he set (May 27, 1959), Western authorities would have to deal with the Soviet-controlled East German government or face the possibility of another blockade of the city.

Eisenhower told Khrushchev that he "would hit the Russians" with every weapon in the American arsenal if they persisted in their efforts to intimidate West Berlin. At the same time, however, Eisenhower sought a settlement. The negotiations distracted attention from the May 27 deadline, which passed almost unnoticed. In September 1959, Khrushchev and Eisenhower agreed to a summit meeting.

THE U-2 SUMMIT The summit meeting literally crashed and burned, however, when on Sunday morning, May 1, 1960, a Soviet rocket brought down a U.S. spy plane (called the U-2) flying at 70,000 feet over the Soviet Union. Khrushchev, embarrassed by the ability of U.S. spy planes to enter Soviet airspace, then sprang a trap on Eisenhower. The Soviets announced only that the plane had been shot down. The U.S. government, not realizing that the Soviets had captured the pilot, lied about the incident and claimed that it was missing a weather-monitoring plane over Turkey. Khrushchev then announced that the Soviets had American pilot Francis Gary Powers "alive and kicking" and also had the photographs Powers had taken of Soviet military installations.

On May 11, Eisenhower took personal responsibility for the spying program, explaining that such illegally obtained intelligence information was crucial to national security. At the testy summit in Paris five days later, Khrushchev lectured Eisenhower for forty-five minutes before walking out because the U.S. president refused to apologize. Later, in 1962, Powers would be exchanged for a captured Soviet spy.

Nikita Khrushchev A fiery speaker, the Soviet premier addresses journalists at a press conference in 1959.

COMMUNIST CUBA President Eisenhower's greatest embarrassment was Fidel Castro's new Communist regime in Cuba, which came to power on January 1, 1959, after two years of guerrilla warfare against the U.S.-supported dictator, Fulgencio Batista. The bearded, cigar-smoking Castro embraced Soviet support as he systematically imprisoned hundreds of opponents, canceled elections, and staged public executions. A CIA agent predicted, "We're going to take care of Castro just like we took care of Arbenz [in Guatemala]." The Soviets warned that American intervention in Cuba would trigger a military response.

One of Eisenhower's last acts as president, on January 3, 1961, was to suspend diplomatic relations with Cuba. He also authorized a secret CIA operation to train a force of Cuban refugees to oust Castro, but the final decision on the use of the invasion force would rest with the next president, John F. Kennedy.

EVALUATING THE EISENHOWER PRESIDENCY

During President Eisenhower's second term, Congress added Alaska and Hawaii as the forty-ninth and fiftieth states (1959), while the nation experienced its worst economic slump since the Great Depression. Volatile issues such as civil rights, defense policy, and corrupt aides compounded the administration's troubles. The president's desire to avoid divisive issues led him at

Fidel Castro Castro became Cuba's Communist premier in 1959 after overthrowing the Batista regime.

times to value harmony and popularity over justice. One observer called the Eisenhower years "the time of the great postponement."

Opinion of Eisenhower's presidency has improved with time, however. He presided with steady self-confidence over a prosperous nation. In dealing with crises, he displayed good judgment and firmness of purpose. He fulfilled his pledge to end the war in Korea, refused to intervene militarily in Indochina, and maintained the peace in the face of explosive global tensions.

Eisenhower's greatest decisions were the wars he chose to avoid. After the truce in Korea, not a single American soldier died in combat during his two administrations, something no president since has achieved. For the most part, he acted with poise, restraint, and intelligence in managing an increasingly complex cold war.

If Eisenhower refused to take the lead in addressing social and racial problems, he did balance the budget while sustaining the major reforms of the New Deal. If he tolerated unemployment of as much as 7 percent, he saw to it that inflation remained minimal. Even Adlai Stevenson admitted that Ike's victory in 1952 had been good for America. "I like Ike, too," he said.

Still, it is fair to ask what might have happened if Eisenhower had invested his enormous prestige and popularity in the civil rights movement. Because he did not, his successors were forced to try to improve race relations in a much more volatile political and social climate.

Eisenhower's January 17, 1961, farewell address focused on the threat posed to government integrity by "an immense military establishment and a large arms industry." It was striking for Eisenhower, a celebrated military leader, to highlight the dangers of a large "military-industrial complex" exerting "unwarranted influence" in Congress and the White House.

Eisenhower confessed that his greatest disappointment was that he could affirm only that "war has been avoided," not that "a lasting peace is in sight." Eisenhower, who never promoted warfare as an instrument of foreign policy, pledged to "do anything to achieve peace within honorable means. I'll travel anywhere. I'll talk to anyone." His successors would not be as successful in keeping war at bay.

CHAPTER REVIEW

Summary

- **Eisenhower's Dynamic Conservatism**   President Eisenhower promoted *moderate Republicanism*, or "dynamic conservatism." While critical of excessive government spending on social programs, he expanded Social Security coverage and launched ambitious public works programs, such as the *Federal-Aid Highway Act (1956)*. Interstate highways helped stimulate the rise of *suburbia*, which transformed social life for many Americans and contributed to a declining quality of life in inner cities. The need for more housing in the fifties was in part a function of the *baby boom*.

- **Growth of the U.S. Economy**   High levels of federal spending continued during the postwar period. The *GI Bill of Rights (1944)* boosted home buying and helped many veterans attend college and enter the middle class. Consumer demand for homes, cars, and household goods fueled the economy.

- **Critics of Mainstream Culture**   The *Beats* and many other writers and artists rejected what they claimed was the suffocating conformity of middle-class life. Adolescents rebelled through acts of juvenile delinquency and a new form of sexually provocative music called rock 'n' roll. Pockets of chronic poverty persisted despite record-breaking economic growth, and people of color did not prosper to the extent that white Americans did.

- **Civil Rights Movement**   During the early 1950s, the NAACP mounted legal challenges to states that refused to create racially segregated public schools. In *Brown v. Board of Education (1954)*, the U.S. Supreme Court nullified the *separate-but-equal* doctrine. Many white southerners adopted a strategy of *massive resistance* against court-ordered desegregation. In response, civil rights activists used *nonviolent civil disobedience* to force local and state officials to allow integration, as demonstrated in the *Montgomery bus* **boycott** *(1955–1956)* in Alabama and the forced desegregation of public schools in Little Rock, Arkansas. Martin Luther King Jr. organized the *Southern Christian Leadership Conference (SCLC)* after white violence against activists in Little Rock. In 1957, Congress passed a Civil Rights Act intended to stop discrimination against black voters in the South, but it was rarely enforced.

- **American Foreign Policy in the 1950s**   Eisenhower's first major foreign-policy accomplishment was to end the fighting in Korea. Thereafter, he kept the United States out of war and relied on secret *Central Intelligence Agency (CIA)* intervention, financial and military aid, and threats of *massive retaliation* to stem the spread of communism. Eisenhower's belief in the *falling-domino theory* deepened U.S. support for the government in South Vietnam in its war with North Vietnam and the Communist *Viet Cong* insurgents. In 1956, Eisenhower opposed the invasion of Egypt by Israeli, French, and British forces determined to take control of the strategic Suez Canal. The *Suez crisis (1956)* was resolved when the invaders withdrew from Egypt in response to U.S. pressure.

CHRONOLOGY

1944	Congress passes the GI Bill of Rights
1951	Alan Freed coins the term *rock 'n' roll*
1952	Eisenhower wins the presidency
July 1953	Armistice is reached in Korea
1954	Supreme Court decides *Brown v. Board of Education of Topeka, Kansas*
July 1954	Geneva Accords adopted
December 1955	Montgomery, Alabama, bus boycott begins
1956	Congress passes the Federal-Aid Highway Act
	Soviets suppress Hungarian revolt
1957	Federal troops sent to protect students attempting to integrate Central High School in Little Rock, Arkansas
	Soviet Union launches *Sputnik* satellite
1960	U-2 Incident

KEY TERMS

moderate Republicanism p. 1320

Federal-Aid Highway Act (1956) p. 1323

GI Bill of Rights (1944) p. 1328

suburbia p. 1330

baby boom p. 1335

Beats p. 1339

separate-but-equal p. 1343

Brown v. Board of Education (1954) p. 1343

massive resistance p. 1345

Montgomery bus boycott (1955–1956) p. 1346

nonviolent civil disobedience p. 1347

Southern Christian Leadership Conference (SCLC) p. 1351

massive retaliation p. 1353

Central Intelligence Agency (CIA) p. 1353

Dien Bien Phu (1954) p. 1355

Viet Cong p. 1358

falling-domino theory p. 1358

Suez crisis p. 1360

 INQUIZITIVE

Go to InQuizitive to see what you've learned—and learn what you've missed—with personalized feedback along the way.

29 A New Frontier and a Great Society

1960–1968

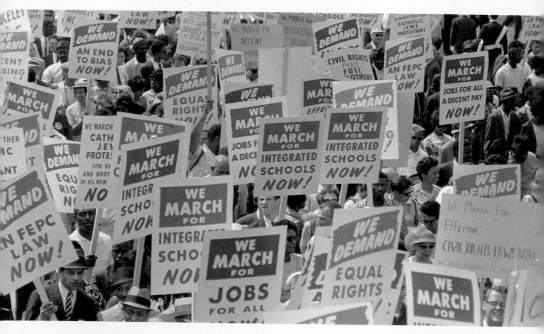

March on Washington Marchers hold aloft picket signs calling for "INTEGRATED SCHOOLS NOW!," "EQUAL RIGHTS," "JOBS FOR ALL," and "CIVIL RIGHTS LAWS NOW." They were among the more than 250,000 people who joined the March on Washington for Jobs and Freedom on August 28, 1963. The march was televised extensively, and was host to Martin Luther King Jr.'s landmark "I Have a Dream" speech. At the time, it was the largest protest ever held in the nation's capital.

For those who considered the fifties dull, the following decade provided a striking contrast. The 1960s were years of extraordinary social turbulence and liberal activism, tragic assassinations and painful trauma, cultural conflict and youth rebellion, civil rights and civil unrest. Assassins killed four of the most important leaders of the time: John F. Kennedy, Malcolm X, Martin Luther King Jr., and Robert F. Kennedy.

The "politics of expectation" that a British journalist said shone brightly in John Kennedy's short tenure as president did not die with him in November 1963. Instead, his idealistic commitment to improving America's quality of life—for everyone—was given new meaning by his successor, Texan Lyndon B. Johnson, whose war on poverty and Great Society programs outstripped Franklin Roosevelt's New Deal in their scope and promises.

Johnson's energy and legislative savvy resulted in a blizzard of new programs as many social issues that had been ignored or postponed for decades—civil rights for people of color, equality for women, gay and lesbian rights, medical insurance, federal aid to the poor—forced their way to the forefront of national concerns.

In the end, however, Johnson promised too much. The Great Society programs fell victim to unrealistic hopes, poor execution, and the nation's expanding involvement in Vietnam. The deeply entrenched assumptions of the cold war led the nation into the longest, most controversial, and least successful war in its history.

focus questions

1. How did President John F. Kennedy try to contain communism abroad and pursue civil rights and other social programs at home?

2. What were the strategies and achievements of the civil rights movement in the 1960s? What divisions emerged among its activists?

3. What were President Lyndon B. Johnson's major war on poverty and Great Society initiatives? How did they impact American society?

4. What were Kennedy's and Johnson's motivations for deepening America's military involvement in the Vietnam War?

5. What issues propelled Richard Nixon to victory in the 1968 presidential election?

THE NEW FRONTIER

In his 1960 speech accepting the Democratic presidential nomination, John F. Kennedy (JFK) showcased the muscular language that would characterize his campaign and his presidency: "We stand today on the edge of a **New Frontier**—the frontier of unknown opportunities and perils—a frontier of unfulfilled hopes and threats." He wanted Americans to explore "science and space, unsolved problems of peace and war, unconquered pockets of ignorance and prejudice, unanswered questions of poverty and surplus."

Kennedy and his staff fastened upon the frontier metaphor as the label for their proposed domestic program because they believed Americans had always been eager to conquer and exploit new frontiers. Kennedy promised to get the country "moving again" and to be more aggressive in waging the cold war with the Soviet Union than Dwight Eisenhower had been.

KENNEDY VERSUS NIXON In 1960, the presidential election featured two candidates—Vice President Richard M. Nixon and Massachusetts senator John F. Kennedy—of similar ages and life experiences. Both were elected to Congress in 1946, both were Navy veterans, and both preferred foreign affairs over domestic issues.

But in fact, they were more different than alike. Although Nixon was Dwight Eisenhower's vice president for two terms, Eisenhower had grave misgivings about him. When asked by reporters to name a single major accomplishment of his vice president, Ike replied: "If you give me a week, I might think of one."

The two Republican leaders had long had a testy relationship. Nixon once called Eisenhower "a goddamned old fool," while the president dismissed his vice president as a man who couldn't "think of anything but politics." On more than one occasion, Eisenhower had sought to dump Nixon in favor of other Republicans whom he respected.

A native of California, the forty-seven-year-old Nixon was the son of a shopkeeper. All his life he had fought to be a success, first as an attorney, then as a congressman. He had come to Washington after the Second World War eager to reverse the tide of New Deal liberalism. His visibility among Republicans rose when he led the anti-Communist hearings in Congress during the McCarthy hysteria.

Nixon—graceless, awkward, and stiff—proved to be one of the most complicated political figures in American history. By 1960, he had become known as "Tricky Dick," a cunning deceiver who concealed his real ideas and bigoted attitudes. Kennedy told an aide that "Nixon doesn't know who he is . . . so

The Kennedy–Nixon debates Nixon's decision to debate his less prominent opponent on television backfired.

every time he makes a speech he has to decide which Nixon he is, and that will be very exhausting."

The forty-three-year-old Kennedy had not distinguished himself in the House or the Senate. More pragmatic than principled, more personality than character, he was handsome, articulate, and blessed with youthful energy and wit. Kennedy lit up a room with his smile and zest for life. Coolly analytical and dangerously self-absorbed, he was a contradictory and elusive political celebrity.

But this much is certain about the 35th president: Kennedy had a bright, agile mind; a Harvard education; a record of heroism in the Second World War; a rich and powerful Roman Catholic family; and a beautiful and accomplished young wife. In the words of a southern senator, Kennedy combined "the best qualities of Elvis Presley and Franklin D. Roosevelt"—a combination that played well in the first-ever televised presidential debate.

Some 70 million people tuned in to watch the debate. They saw an uncomfortable Nixon, ill with a virus and perspiring heavily; he looked pale and haggard, and as a number of viewers described, even somewhat menacing. By contrast, Kennedy looked tanned and confident. He offered crisp answers that made him appear qualified for the nation's highest office. The morning after the debate, his approval ratings skyrocketed. The *Chicago Daily News* asked, "Was Nixon Sabotaged by TV Makeup Artists?"

Kennedy's political rise owed much to the public relations campaign engineered by his father, Joseph, a self-made tycoon with a genius for promotion who believed that *image* was much more important than substance. "Can't you get it into your head," he told his son John, "that it's not important what you *really* are? The only important thing is what people *think* you are." The elder Kennedy hired talented writers to produce his son's two books, paid a publisher to print them, purchased thousands of copies to make them "best sellers," and helped engineer his son's elections to the House and Senate.

John Kennedy was a relentless presidential campaigner, traveling 65,000 miles, visiting twenty-five states, and making more than 350 speeches. In an address to Protestant ministers in Texas, he neutralized concerns about his being a Roman Catholic by stressing that the pope would never "tell the President—should he be a Catholic—how to act."

Kennedy emphasized that he was tired of reading about what Soviet and Cuban leaders were doing. He wanted to read about what the U.S. president was doing to combat communism. "The enemy," Kennedy said in 1960, "is the Communist system itself—implacable, insatiable, increasing in its drive for world domination." He saw the cold war as a "struggle for supremacy between two conflicting ideologies: freedom under God versus ruthless, godless tyranny."

Although Kennedy worked to increase voter registration among African Americans, his response to the growing civil rights movement was ambivalent. Like Eisenhower, Kennedy believed racial unrest needed to be handled with caution. To him, racial justice was less an urgent moral crusade than a potential barrier to his election. He understood the injustices of bigotry and segregation, but he needed the votes of southern whites to win the presidency.

During the campaign, Kennedy won the hearts of many black voters by helping to get Martin Luther King Jr. discharged from a Georgia prison after King had been convicted of trespassing in an all-white restaurant in a downtown department store, where he and members of the Student Nonviolent Coordinating Committee (SNCC) had organized a sit-in. Kennedy's efforts led King's father to change his opinion on the election. "I had expected to vote against Senator Kennedy because of his religion," the elder Reverend King explained. "Now he can be my president, Catholic or whatever he is." On the Sunday before Election Day, a million leaflets describing Kennedy's effort

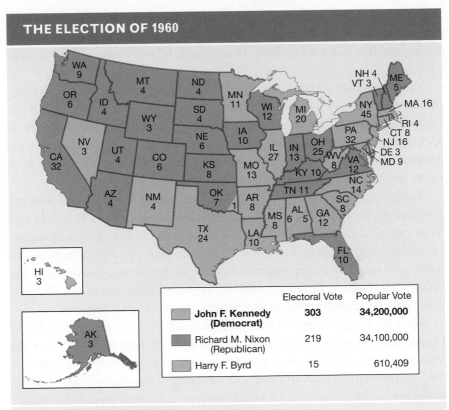

THE ELECTION OF 1960

		Electoral Vote	Popular Vote
	John F. Kennedy (Democrat)	**303**	**34,200,000**
	Richard M. Nixon (Republican)	219	34,100,000
	Harry F. Byrd	15	610,409

- How did the election of 1960 represent a sea change in American presidential politics?
- How did John F. Kennedy win the election in spite of winning fewer states than Richard M. Nixon?

to release King from prison were distributed in African American churches across the nation.

In November, Kennedy and his running mate, Texas senator Lyndon B. Johnson, won one of the closest presidential elections in history. Their margin was only 118,574 votes out of more than 68 million cast, a record turnout. Nixon won more states, but Kennedy captured 70 percent of the black vote, which proved decisive in at least three key states. Nixon convinced himself that the Democrats had stolen the election through chicanery in Illinois and Texas, but recounts confirmed Kennedy's victory.

A VIGOROUS NEW ADMINISTRATION John F. Kennedy was the youngest person and the first Roman Catholic elected president. At times, he seemed self-assured to the point of cockiness. "Sure it's a big job," he told a reporter. "But I don't know anybody who can do it any better than I can." That he had been elected by the narrowest of margins and had no working majority in Congress did not faze him. In his mind, he was destined to be a great president.

Kennedy's inauguration ceremony on a cold, sunny, blustery January day introduced the nation to his distinctive elegance and flair. In his speech, he focused almost entirely on foreign affairs. He accepted the responsibility of "defending freedom in its hour of maximum danger" and promised to keep America strong while seeking to reduce friction with the Soviet Union: "Let us never negotiate out of fear, but let us never fear to negotiate."

Kennedy claimed "that the torch has been passed to a new generation of Americans—born in this century, tempered by war, disciplined by a hard and bitter peace," and he dazzled listeners with uplifting words: "Let every nation know, whether it wishes us well or ill, that we shall pay any price, bear any burden, meet any hardship, support any friend, oppose any foe, to assure the survival and success of liberty. And so, my fellow Americans: ask not what your country can do for you—ask what *you* can do for your country."

Such steely optimism heralded a presidency of fresh promise and new beginnings. Yet much of the glamour surrounding Kennedy was cosmetic. Despite his athletic interests and robust appearance, he suffered from serious medical problems: Addison's disease (a withering of the adrenal glands), venereal disease, chronic back pain, and fierce fevers. He took powerful prescription medicines or injections daily to manage a degenerative bone disease, to deal with anxiety, to help him sleep, and to control his allergies. (The medications gave Kennedy the perpetual tan that the public interpreted as a sign of good health.) Kennedy and his associates also hid both his physical ailments and his often reckless sexual dalliances in the White House with a galaxy of women, including actress Marilyn Monroe and Judith Campbell Exner, the girlfriend of a Chicago mob boss.

Kennedy represented a new wave of political figures who had fought in the Second World War. Known as the "pragmatic generation," they were decisive, bold, and prized courage and conviction in the face of the cold war and the threat of nuclear conflict. With at times an almost dismissive arrogance, Kennedy frequently complained about "academics" who criticized statesmen without exercising responsibility themselves. In the White House, he observed, he and others could not afford to be professorial. The Oval Office was "where decisions have to be made."

Kennedy appointed his younger brother Robert ("Bobby") as attorney general even though he had never tried a case or even practiced law. The *New York Times* called the younger Kennedy's qualifications "insufficient," and the *Wall*

Jack and Jackie Young, dashing, wealthy, and culturally sophisticated, the Kennedys were instant celebrities. Women imitated the First Lady's famous hairdo, while men admired JFK's effortless "cool" and youthful energy.

Street Journal predicted he would be an "unmitigated disaster." The president, however, assured skeptics that his brother could learn "on the job."

A BALKY CONGRESS President Kennedy had a difficult time launching his New Frontier domestic program. Conservative southern Democrats joined with Republicans in blocking efforts to increase federal aid to education, provide medical insurance for the aged, and establish a cabinet-level department of urban affairs and housing to address inner-city poverty. In his first year, Kennedy submitted 355 legislative requests; Congress approved only half of them. He complained that he "couldn't get a Mother's Day resolution through the goddamned Congress."

Legislators did approve increasing the minimum wage; a Housing Act that earmarked nearly $5 billion for new public-housing projects in poverty-stricken inner-city areas; the Peace Corps, which recruited idealistic young volunteers who would provide educational and technical service abroad; and the Alliance for Progress, a financial assistance program to Latin American countries intended to blunt the appeal of communism. In 1963, Kennedy also signed the Equal Pay Act, which required that women performing the same jobs as men be paid the same. But his efforts to provide more assistance for educational programs and for medical care for the elderly never got out of committees.

News that the Soviets had launched the first manned space flight in 1961 prompted Kennedy's greatest legislative success. He convinced Congress to commit $40 billion to put an American on the moon within ten years. (The goal was achieved in 1969.) Former president Eisenhower said that Kennedy's "race to the moon for national prestige is nuts." But Vice President Lyndon Johnson assured the president that "dramatic accomplishments in space are being increasingly identified as a major indicator of world leadership." Kennedy explained that he had decided to shoot for the moon not because it is "easy, but because it is hard, because that goal will serve to organize and measure the best of our energies and skills."

JFK AND CIVIL RIGHTS   The most important developments in domestic life during the sixties occurred in civil rights. Throughout the South, racial segregation remained firmly in place. Signs outside public restrooms distinguished between "whites" and "colored"; restaurants declared "Colored Not Allowed," or "Colored Served Only in Rear." Stores prohibited African Americans from trying on clothes before buying them. Despite the *Brown v. Board of Education* ruling in 1954, many public schools across the South remained segregated and unequal in quality.

Like Franklin D. Roosevelt and Dwight Eisenhower, President Kennedy celebrated racial equality but did little to promote it until forced to do so. Knowing that challenging the segregated South was a political land mine, Kennedy was reluctant to anger conservative southern Democrats on this explosive issue. Both he and his brother Bobby, his closest adviser, had to be dragged into supporting the civil rights movement. After appointing Harris Wofford, a white law professor and campaigner for racial equality, as the special presidential assistant for civil rights, President Kennedy told him "to make substantial headway against . . . the nonsense of racial discrimination," but to do so with "minimum civil rights legislation [and] maximum Executive action." Such an approach led Martin Luther King Jr. to comment that Kennedy had great political skill but no "moral passion" about the need to end racial injustice.

CATASTROPHE IN CUBA   Kennedy's performance in foreign relations was spectacularly mixed. Although he had told a reporter that he wanted to "break out of the confines of the cold war," he quickly found himself reinforcing its ideological assumptions. While still a senator, Kennedy had blasted President Eisenhower for not being tough enough with the Soviets and for allowing Fidel Castro and his Communist followers to take over Cuba, just ninety miles from the southern tip of Florida.

Soon after his inauguration, Kennedy learned that Eisenhower had approved a secret CIA operation to train some 1,400 anti-Castro Cubans to invade their homeland in hopes of triggering a mass uprising against Castro. U.S. military leaders assured Kennedy that the invasion plan, called Operation Trinidad, was feasible; CIA analysts and the Joint Chiefs of Staff naively predicted that news of the invasion would inspire anti-Castro Cubans to rebel. Secretary of Defense Robert McNamara, National Security Advisor McGeorge Bundy, and Bobby Kennedy endorsed the plan, as did the new president.

The covert operation, however, was a total failure. Its assumptions were flawed, its strategy faulty, its tactics bungled, and the forces and weapons used inadequate.

The ragtag group of Miami-based Cuban exiles, trained by the CIA and transported on American ships, landed before dawn at the **Bay of Pigs** on Cuba's south shore on April 17, 1961. Having been tipped off by spies, Castro had 20,000 soldiers waiting. Kennedy panicked when he realized the operation

Walk of shame Captured anti-Castro Cubans after the failed invasion at the Bay of Pigs.

was failing and he refused pleas from the rebels for support from U.S. warplanes that Kennedy had promised. General Lyman Lemnitzer, chair of the Joint Chiefs of Staff, said that Kennedy's "pulling out the rug [on the Cuban invaders] was . . . absolutely reprehensible, almost criminal." More than a hundred of the invaders were killed and more than 1,200 were captured. (Kennedy later paid $53 million to ransom the captured rebels.)

The failed operation humiliated Kennedy and elevated Castro in the eyes of the world. A *New York Times* columnist reported that the Americans "looked like fools to our friends, rascals to our enemies, and incompetents to the rest." In Moscow, Nikita Khrushchev asked if Kennedy could "really be that indecisive?"

To his credit, Kennedy admitted that the Bay of Pigs invasion was a "colossal mistake." Only later did he learn that the planners had assumed that he would commit American forces if the invasion effort failed. He said that after the initial disastrous reports from the Bay of Pigs, "we all looked at each other and asked, 'How could we have been so stupid?'"

Afterward, Kennedy met with Eisenhower and discussed the Bay of Pigs fiasco. The former president recalled that Kennedy seemed "more than a little bewildered." The new president admitted that "you don't know how tough this job is until you have it." In reference to the failed invasion, Eisenhower told Kennedy that there was "only one thing to do when you go into this kind of thing. It must be a success."

THE VIENNA SUMMIT Just weeks after the Bay of Pigs invasion, President Kennedy met Soviet premier Khrushchev at a summit conference in Vienna, Austria. Khrushchev badgered Kennedy, bragged about the superiority of communism, and threatened to take full control of Berlin, the divided city inside Communist East Germany. Kennedy confided to a journalist that the summit "was awful. Worst thing of my life. He rolled right over me—he thinks I'm a fool—he thinks I'm weak. . . . He treated me like a little boy." When asked what he planned to do next, Kennedy replied: "I have to confront them [the Soviets] someplace to show that we're tough."

The first thing Kennedy did upon returning to the White House was to request an estimate of how many Americans might be killed in a nuclear war with the Soviet Union. The answer was chilling: 70 million. Kennedy, desperate not to appear weak in the face of Khrushchev's aggressive actions in Germany, asked Congress for additional spending on defense and called up 156,000 members of the Army Reserve and National Guard to protect West Berlin. He also ordered an armed military convoy to travel from West Germany across East Germany to West Berlin to show the Soviets that he would use force to

Severed ties Two West Berliners climb the newly constructed Berlin Wall to talk with a family member at an open window.

protect the city. "West Berlin," he declared, "has become . . . the great testing place of Western courage and will."

The Soviets responded on August 13, 1961. They stopped all traffic between East and West Berlin and began erecting the twenty-seven-mile-long **Berlin Wall** to separate East and West Berlin, where thousands of refugees were fleeing communism each week. For the United States, the wall became a powerful propaganda weapon in the cold war. As Kennedy said, "Freedom has many difficulties and democracy is not perfect, but we have never had to put up a wall to keep our people in."

The Berlin Wall demonstrated the Soviets' willingness to challenge American resolve in Europe. In response, Kennedy gave a televised address alerting the nation to the significance of the Berlin crisis. Then, he and Secretary of Defense Robert McNamara embarked upon the most intensive arms race in history. The administration increased the number of nuclear missiles fivefold, added 300,000 troops to the armed forces, and created the U.S. Special Forces (Green Berets), an elite group of commandos who specialized in guerrilla warfare and could provide a "more flexible response" to hot spots around the world.

In contrast to the Eisenhower–Dulles emphasis on "massive retaliation," Kennedy sought more military flexibility: "We intend to have a wider choice than humiliation or all-out war." He and McNamara also launched a civil defense program focused on the construction of nuclear fallout shelters. Secretly, they commissioned an analysis of the implications of launching a full-scale nuclear strike against the Soviet Union in response to any effort to invade West Berlin.

THE CUBAN MISSILE CRISIS In the fall of 1962, Nikita Khrushchev and the Soviets decided to challenge President Kennedy again. To protect Communist Cuba and show critics at home that he was not afraid of the Americans, Khrushchev approved the secret installation of Soviet missiles on the island nation. The Soviets felt justified in doing so because Kennedy, after the Bay of Pigs invasion, had ordered that U.S. missiles with nuclear warheads be installed in Turkey, along the Soviet border.

On October 16, 1962, Kennedy learned that photos taken by U.S. spy planes showed some forty Soviet missile sites and twenty-five jet bombers in Cuba. "We have some big trouble," he alerted his brother Bobby by phone. Somehow, the president had to convince the Soviets to remove the missiles. But how? As the air force chief of staff told Kennedy, "You're in a pretty bad fix, Mr. President."

Over the next thirteen days, Kennedy and the National Security Council (NSC) considered several possible responses. The world held its breath as the NSC discussed the unthinkable possibility of a nuclear exchange with the Soviets. The commander of the U.S. Marines at one point reminded the group that the missiles in Cuba were not a true strategic threat; the Soviet Union, he said, "has a hell of a lot better way to attack us than to attack us from Cuba." Secretary of Defense Robert McNamara agreed, noting that "it makes no difference whether you are killed by a missile fired from the Soviet Union or from Cuba."

Eventually, the NSC fastened on two options: (1) a "surgical" air strike on the missiles, followed, if necessary, by an invasion, or (2) a naval blockade of Cuba in which U.S. warships would stop Soviet vessels and search them for missiles. Although most of the military advisers supported the first option, Kennedy chose the blockade, prompting a general to shout, "You're screwed! You're screwed!"

Kennedy had been burned by overconfident military advisers during the Bay of Pigs operation, and he was not going to let it happen again. He also feared that an American attack on Cuba would give the Soviets an excuse to take control of West Berlin.

On October 22, Kennedy delivered a televised speech of the "highest national urgency," announcing that the U.S. Navy was establishing a "quarantine" of Cuba to prevent Soviet ships from delivering more weapons to the island nation. Kennedy added that he had "directed the armed forces to prepare for any eventuality." He closed by urging the Soviets to "move the world back from the abyss of destruction." Tensions grew, and some 200,000 U.S. soldiers made their way to southern Florida.

Khrushchev replied that Soviet ships would ignore the quarantine and accused Kennedy of "an act of aggression propelling humankind into the abyss of a world nuclear-missile war." Despite such rhetoric, however, on Wednesday, October 24, five Soviet ships, presumably with more missiles aboard, stopped well short of the quarantine line.

Two days later, Khrushchev, knowing that the United States enjoyed a 5 to 1 advantage in nuclear weapons, offered a deal. Neither he nor Kennedy wanted to be the first to launch nuclear missiles. The Soviets would agree to remove the missiles already in Cuba in return for a *public* pledge by the United States never to invade Cuba—and a *secret* agreement to remove U.S. missiles from Turkey. Kennedy agreed. Secretary of State Dean Rusk stressed to a newscaster, "Remember, when you report this, [say] that eyeball to eyeball, they [the Soviets] blinked first."

In the aftermath of the **Cuban missile crisis**, cold war tensions subsided, in part because of several symbolic steps: an agreement to sell the Soviet Union surplus American wheat, the installation of a "hotline" telephone between

The Cuban missile crisis Photographs taken from a U.S. surveillance plane on October 14, 1962, revealed both Soviet missile launchers and missile shelters near San Cristóbal, Cuba.

Washington and Moscow to provide instant contact between the heads of government, and the removal of U.S. missiles from Turkey, Italy, and Britain.

"PEACE FOR ALL TIME" Approaching the brink of nuclear war convinced President Kennedy and others in the administration to soften their cold war rhetoric and pursue other ways to reduce the threat of atomic warfare. Kennedy told an audience at American University on June 10, 1963, that his new goal was "not merely peace in our time, but peace for all time."

Soon thereafter, the president began discussions with Soviet and British leaders to reduce the risk of nuclear war. The discussions resulted in the Limited Nuclear Test Ban Treaty, ratified in September 1963, which banned the testing of nuclear weapons in the atmosphere. It was the first joint agreement of the cold war and an important move toward improved relations with the Soviet Union. As Kennedy put it, using an ancient Chinese proverb: "A journey of a thousand miles begins with one step."

VIETNAM As tensions with the Soviet Union eased, events in Southeast Asia were moving toward what would become the greatest American foreign-policy calamity of the century. Throughout the 1950s, U.S. officials increasingly came to view the preservation of anticommunist South Vietnam as the critical test of American willpower in the cold war. As a senator in 1956, John F. Kennedy described South Vietnam as the "cornerstone of the free world in Southeast Asia."

Yet the situation in South Vietnam had worsened under the corrupt leadership of Premier Ngo Dinh Diem and his family. Diem had backed away from promised social and economic reforms, and his repressive tactics, directed not only against Communists but also against the Buddhist majority and other critics, played into the hands of his enemies.

President Eisenhower had provided more than $1 billion in aid to Diem's government during the late fifties. Kennedy sent even more weapons, money, and some 16,000 military "advisers" to South Vietnam to help shore up the government. (They were called advisers to avoid the impression that U.S. soldiers were doing the fighting.) "If I tried to pull out," Kennedy explained, "we would have another Joe McCarthy red scare on our hands," with Republicans accusing him of "losing" Vietnam to communism. To withdraw "would be a great mistake."

In the countryside of South Vietnam, the National Liberation Front (NLF), a left-wing nationalist movement backed by Communist North Vietnam, had launched a violent insurgency in which guerrilla fighters known as the Viet Cong (VC) were winning the fight against the South Vietnamese government. American military advisers began relocating Vietnamese peasants to "strategic hamlets"—new villages ringed by barbed wire—where the VC could not receive assistance.

By the fall of 1963, Kennedy acknowledged that Diem was "out of touch with his people" and had to be removed. On November 1, Vietnamese generals, with the approval of U.S. officials, seized control of the Saigon government. They then took a step that Kennedy had neither intended nor expected: they murdered Diem and his brother on November 2, 1963.

The rebel generals soon began fighting one another, leaving Vietnam even more vulnerable to the Communist insurgency during 1964. Thereafter, South Vietnam essentially became an American colony. The United States put Vietnamese generals in power, gave them orders, and provided massive financial support, much of which was diverted into the hands of corrupt politicians and their families.

Just weeks before Kennedy was assassinated in November 1963, he developed doubts about the ability of the United States to prop up the South Vietnamese government. "In the final analysis," he told aides, "it's their war. . . . We can help them as advisers but they have to win it." Yet only a week later, in a televised interview, Kennedy reiterated the domino theory endorsed by Presidents Truman and Eisenhower, saying that if South Vietnam fell to communism, the rest of Southeast Asia would follow. He stressed that "we should stay [in South Vietnam]. We should use our influence in as effective a way as we can, but we should not withdraw."

KENNEDY'S ASSASSINATION   What Kennedy would have done in Vietnam has remained a matter of endless discussion, because his presidency suffered an untimely end. At noon on November 22, 1963, while riding in an open car through Dallas, Texas, he was shot and killed by Lee Harvey Oswald, a twenty-four-year-old ex-Marine turned Communist. Oswald idolized Fidel Castro and hated the United States. As he fled after shooting Kennedy, he also killed a Dallas policeman.

Kennedy seemed to have had a premonition of his death. "We're heading into nut country today," he warned his wife that morning. "But Jackie, if somebody wants to shoot me from a window with a rifle, nobody can stop it, so why worry about it?"

Debate still swirls about whether Oswald, who had lived in the Soviet Union and had met with officials in Cuba, acted alone or as part of a conspiracy, because he did not live long enough to tell his story. As he was being transported to a court hearing, Jack Ruby, a Dallas nightclub owner distraught over Kennedy's death, shot and killed Oswald as a nationwide television audience watched.

Kennedy's assassination and heartrending funeral enshrined the president in the public imagination as a martyred leader cut down in the prime of life. He came to have a stronger reputation after his death than he enjoyed in life.

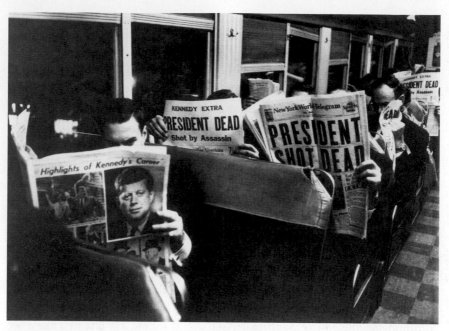

"President Shot Dead" Commuters react to the news of President Kennedy's assassination on November 22, 1963.

"That debonair touch, that shock of chestnut hair, that beguiling grin, that shattering understatement—these are what we shall remember," wrote newspaper columnist Mary McGrory.

Kennedy's thousand-day presidency had flamed up and out like a comet hitting the earth's atmosphere. Yet all the transformational events of the later 1960s—the Vietnam War, the civil rights revolution, and the youth rebellion— were set in motion during his brief time in the White House. With his death, Americans wept in the streets, and the world was on edge as the nation buried its fallen president. Roy Wilkins, a prominent civil rights leader, noted that "the bullet that killed Kennedy paralyzed the civil rights movement" as the world welcomed a new and very different president, Lyndon Johnson.

CIVIL RIGHTS TRIUMPHANT

During the sixties, Martin Luther King Jr. remained the face and heart of the civil rights movement. He was an uplifting example of fortitude and dignity in confronting brutality and oppression, and he had an astonishing capacity for forgiveness and a deep understanding of the dynamics of political power and social change. Yet he was also immensely complicated and contradictory, even hypocritical, as the FBI discovered by subjecting him to relentless electronic surveillance and even blackmail.

King was neither a genius nor a saint, but his shortcomings pale when compared to his achievements. He was an inspiring example of courage, conviction, and dignity in the face of often violent prejudice and persecution. With the help of those he led, King changed the trajectory of American history—for the better. Alas, like the Kennedy brothers, he did not live to see the promised land made possible by his actions.

SIT-INS The civil rights movement gained momentum when four African American college students sat down and ordered coffee and doughnuts at an "all-white" Woolworth's lunch counter in Greensboro, North Carolina, on February 1, 1960. The clerk refused to serve them, explaining that blacks had to eat standing up or take their food outside.

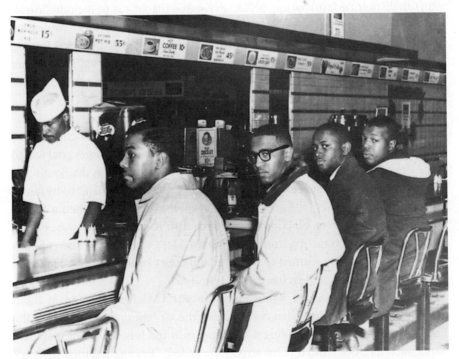

Civil rights and its peaceful warriors Joseph McNeil, Franklin McCain, Billy Smith, and Clarence Henderson (listed from left) await service on day two of their sit-in at the Woolworth's in Greensboro, North Carolina. A painful irony of the Jim Crow system was how African Americans could work at diners but not eat there.

The Greensboro Four, as the students came to be called, waited forty-five minutes and then returned the next day with two dozen more students. As they sat for hours, fruitlessly waiting to be served, some read Bibles; others read Henry David Thoreau's famous essay on civil disobedience. They returned every day for a week, patiently tolerating the hostility of white hooligans.

Within two months, similar sit-ins—involving 50,000 blacks and whites, men and women, young and old—had occurred in more than 100 cities. Black comedian Dick Gregory participated in several sit-ins. When the managers told him, "We don't serve Negroes," he replied: "No problem, I don't eat Negroes." Some 3,600 people were arrested nationwide, but the sit-ins worked. By the end of July 1960, officials in Greensboro lifted the whites-only policy. The civil rights movement had found an effective new, nonviolent tactic against segregation.

In April 1960, some 200 student activists, black and white, converged in Raleigh, North Carolina, to form the **Student Nonviolent Coordinating Committee** (**SNCC**—pronounced "snick"). Their goal was to intensify the effort to dismantle segregation. SNCC expanded the sit-ins to include "kneel-ins" at all-white churches and "wade-ins" at segregated public swimming pools. In many communities, demonstrators were pelted with rocks, burned with cigarettes, and even killed by white racists. As a Florida hog farmer named Holstead "Hoss" Manucy told a journalist, "I ain't got no bad habits. Don't smoke. Don't cuss. My only bad habit is fightin' niggahs."

FREEDOM RIDES In 1961, civil rights leaders decided to focus on integrating public transportation, namely buses and trains. Their larger goal was to force President Kennedy to embrace the cause of civil rights in the South. On May 4, the New York–based Congress of Racial Equality (CORE), led by James Farmer, decided to put "the civil rights movement on wheels" when a courageous group of eighteen black and white **Freedom Riders**, as they were called, boarded two buses traveling from Washington, D.C., through the Lower South to New Orleans. They wanted to test a federal court ruling that banned racial segregation on buses and trains, and in terminals.

On May 14, a mob of white racists in rural Alabama, many of them members of the Ku Klux Klan, surrounded the Greyhound bus carrying the Freedom Riders. After throwing a firebomb into the bus, the Klan members barricaded its door. "Burn them alive," one yelled. "Fry the damned niggers." The riders were able to escape the bus, only to be battered with metal pipes, chains, and clubs.

A few hours later, Freedom Riders on a second bus were beaten after entering whites-only waiting rooms at a terminal in Birmingham, Alabama. The

Freedom Riders On May 14, 1961, a white mob in Alabama assaulted a Freedom Bus, flinging fire bombs into its windows and beating the activists as they emerged. Here, the Freedom Riders sit outside the burnt shell of their bus.

police, it turned out, had encouraged the beatings. The brutality, displayed on television, caused national outrage. The Freedom Riders wanted to continue their trip, but the bus drivers refused out of fear for their safety.

When Diane Nash, a black college student and SNCC leader in Nashville, Tennessee, heard about the violence in Birmingham, she recruited new riders. President Kennedy called her, warning that she could "get killed if you do this." Her response: "It doesn't matter if we're killed. Others will come—others will come."

On May 17, Nash and ten other students took a bus to Birmingham, where they were arrested. While in jail, they sang "freedom songs": "We'll Never Turn Back," "Ain't Gonna Let Nobody Turn Me Around," "We Shall Overcome." Their joyous rebelliousness so frustrated Eugene "Bull" Connor, the city's racist police chief, that he drove them in the middle of the night to the Tennessee state line and dropped them off to walk. Instead of going back to Nashville, however, the students returned to Birmingham.

To President Kennedy, the Freedom Riders were a "pain in the ass." He called them "publicity seekers" who were threatening to embarrass him and the United States on the eve of his summit meeting with Soviet leader Nikita Khrushchev.

Kennedy ordered Harris Wofford, his special assistant on civil rights, to end the freedom rides: "Can't you get your goddamned friends off those buses? Stop them!"

When Kennedy suggested to several civil rights leaders that they allow things to "cool off," James Farmer replied that blacks had been "cooling off for a hundred years. . . . If we got any cooler, we'd be in the deep freeze."

The activists finally forced the president to provide another bus, which enabled them to renew the journey to New Orleans. When the new group of riders reached Montgomery, the capital of Alabama, white racists attacked them. The next night, civil rights activists, including Martin Luther King Jr., gathered at a Montgomery church to honor the Freedom Riders. But their meeting was interrupted by a mob of whites armed with rocks and fire bombs.

Ministers made frantic appeals to the White House. Kennedy responded by urging the Alabama governor to intervene. After midnight, national guardsmen arrived. The Freedom Riders continued into Mississippi, where they were jailed. They never made it to New Orleans.

Still, their courage and principled resistance—along with that of federal judges whose rulings supported integration efforts—prompted the Interstate Commerce Commission (ICC) in September 1961 to order that all interstate transportation facilities be integrated. Equally important, the Freedom Riders kindled the rapid growth of civil rights groups. The freedom rides were a crucial turning point in the civil rights movement.

Despite the court rulings, white segregationists remained violently opposed to racial equality. In Birmingham in September 1962, King was speaking at the meeting of the Southern Christian Leadership Conference when a white member of the American Nazi party jumped to the stage and punched him in the face. King simply dropped his hands and allowed the man to hit him again. "Don't touch him," King yelled. "We have to pray for him." King was determined, as an aide said, to "love segregation to death." His home was bombed three times, and he was arrested fourteen times, yet he kept telling people to use "the weapon of nonviolence, the breastplate of righteousness, the armor of truth, and just keep marching."

JAMES MEREDITH In the fall of 1962, James Meredith, an African American student and air force veteran whose grandfather had been a slave, tried to enroll at the all-white University of Mississippi in Oxford. Ross Barnett, the governor of Mississippi, refused to allow Meredith to register. Breathing defiance, Barnett vowed "to rot in jail" rather than "let one Negro ever darken the sacred threshold of our white schools."

U.S. Attorney General Robert F. Kennedy dispatched federal marshals to enforce the law, but when they were assaulted by a white mob shouting "Go to Hell, JFK," the president sent National Guard troops. Their arrival ignited rioting that left two dead and dozens injured. Once the violence subsided, Meredith was registered at the university. "Only in America," a reporter noted, "would the federal government send thousands of troops to enforce the right of an otherwise obscure citizen to attend a particular university."

BIRMINGHAM In early 1963, in conjunction with the celebration of the 100th anniversary of Abraham Lincoln's Emancipation Proclamation, Martin Luther King Jr. organized a massive series of demonstrations in Birmingham. Alabama was now led by George Wallace, an openly racist governor who had vowed to protect "segregation now, segregation tomorrow, segregation forever!"

King knew that weeks of public demonstrations would likely provoke violence and result in thousands of arrests, but a victory in Birmingham, he felt, would "break the back of segregation all over the nation" by revealing southern "brutality openly—in the light of day—with the rest of the world looking on" through television cameras.

The Birmingham campaign began with sit-ins at restaurants, picket lines at segregated businesses, and a march on city hall. The police arrested and

Bull's dogs Eugene "Bull" Connor ordered Birmingham police to unleash their dogs and nightsticks on civil rights demonstrators in May 1963.

jailed hundreds of activists. Each day, however, more demonstrators, black and white, joined the efforts. As thousands of demonstrators marched through Birmingham streets on May 7, the all-white police force led by "Bull" Connor used snarling dogs, tear gas, electric cattle prods, and high-pressure fire hoses on the protesters. Millions of Americans were outraged when they saw the ugly confrontations on television. "The civil rights movement," President Kennedy observed, "owes Bull Connor as much as it owes Abraham Lincoln." It also owed a lot to the power of television.

More than 3,000 demonstrators were arrested, including King and several white ministers, both men and women. In his cell, King wrote a "Letter from Birmingham Jail," a stirring defense of **nonviolent civil disobedience** that has become a classic document of the civil rights movement. "One who breaks an unjust law," King stressed, "must do so openly, lovingly, and with a willingness to *accept the penalty.*" In a reference to President Kennedy's timid support, King wrote that the most perplexing foe of equal justice was not the southern white bigot but "the white moderate, who is more devoted to 'order' than to justice . . . who constantly says, 'I agree with you in the goal you seek, but I cannot agree with your methods.'"

King's efforts prevailed when Birmingham officials finally agreed to end their segregationist practices. But throughout 1963, whites in the Lower South continued to defy efforts at racial integration, while black and white activists organized demonstrations across the nation. By 1963, Alabama was the only state where black and white students did not attend the same schools or colleges. On June 11, 1963, Alabama governor George Wallace theatrically blocked the door at the University of Alabama as African American students tried to register for classes. Wallace finally stepped aside in the face of insistent federal marshals.

That night, President Kennedy finally decided he needed to lead. In a hastily arranged televised speech, he announced that he would soon submit to Congress a major new civil rights bill that would remove race as a consideration "in American life or law." He stressed that "a great change is at hand," and he was determined to make "that change, that [civil rights] revolution," peaceful and constructive. "We are confronted primarily with a moral issue," the president said in language King had been urging him to invoke for years. "It is as old as the Scriptures and is as clear as the American Constitution. The heart of the question is whether all Americans are to be afforded equal rights and equal opportunities." He asked "every American, regardless of where he lives," to "stop and examine his conscience," for America, "for all its hopes and all its boasts, will not be fully free until all its citizens are free."

That same night, in Mississippi, a thirty-seven-year-old African American activist, Medgar Evers, listened to the president's speech in his car. Kennedy's remarks so excited him that he turned around and went home so that he could discuss the speech with his children. When Evers arrived at his house in Jackson at midnight, he was shot by a white racist lying in ambush. He died before reaching a hospital.

The killing of Medgar Evers led President Kennedy to host his first meeting of civil rights leaders in the White House.

"I HAVE A DREAM!" For weeks, southern Democrats in the House of Representatives blocked President Kennedy's civil rights bill. The standoff led African American leaders to take a bold step. On August 28, some 250,000 blacks and whites, many of them schoolchildren brought in on buses, marched arm in arm down the Mall in Washington, D.C., chanting "Equality Now!" and singing "We Shall Overcome."

The **March on Washington** for Jobs and Freedom was the largest political demonstration in American history. "When you looked at the crowd," remembered a U.S. Park Service ranger, "you didn't see blacks or whites. You saw

"I Have a Dream," August 28, 1963 Protesters in the massive March on Washington make their way to the Lincoln Memorial, where Martin Luther King Jr. delivered his now-famous speech.

America." For almost six hours, prominent entertainers sang protest songs, and civil rights activists gave speeches calling for racial justice.

Then something remarkable happened. On the steps of the Lincoln Memorial, thirty-four-year-old Martin Luther King Jr. came to the podium. He started awkwardly. Noticing his nervousness, someone urged him to "tell 'em about the dream, Martin."

As if suddenly inspired, King set aside his prepared remarks and delivered an extraordinary sermon in the form of a speech, using righteousness and passion to inspire his listeners to action. He started slowly and picked up speed, as if he were speaking at a revival, giving poetic voice to the hopes of millions as he stressed the "fierce urgency of now" and the unstoppable power of "meeting physical force with soul force."

King then shared his dream for an America in which equality would be realized:

> In spite of the difficulties and frustrations of the moment, I still have a *dream*. It is a *dream* deeply rooted in the American dream. I have a *dream* that one day this nation will rise up and live out the true meaning of its creed: 'We hold these truths to be self-evident; that all men are created equal.' I have a *dream* that one day . . . the sons of former slaves and the sons of former slaveowners will be able to sit together at the table of brotherhood.

King summoned the nation to justice: "So let freedom ring!" he shouted, for "when we allow freedom to ring from every town and every hamlet, from every state and every city, we will be able to speed up the day when *all* God's children—black men and white men, Jews and Gentiles, Protestants and Catholics—will be able to join hands and sing in the words of the old Negro spiritual, *Free at last, free at last, thank God Almighty, we are free at last!*"

As King finished, there was a startling hush, then a deafening ovation. The crowd spontaneously joined hands and began singing "We Shall Overcome." "I have never been so proud to be a Negro," said baseball superstar Jackie Robinson. "I have never been so proud to be an American." President Kennedy, who had tried to convince organizers to call off the march, was watching on TV at the White House, just a mile away. As King spoke, the president told an aide that "he's damn good."

But King's dream remained just that—a dream deferred. Eighteen days later, four Klansmen in Birmingham detonated a bomb in a black church, killing four young girls. The murders sparked a new wave of indignation across the country and the world. The editors of the *Milwaukee Sentinel* stressed that the bombing "should serve to goad the conscience. The deaths . . . in a sense are on the hands of each of us."

THE WARREN COURT The civil rights movement depended as much on the courts as it did on the leadership of Martin Luther King, Rosa Parks, James Farmer, Diane Nash, and others. Federal judges kept forcing states and localities to integrate schools and other public places. Under Chief Justice Earl Warren, the U.S. Supreme Court also made landmark decisions in other areas of American life.

In 1962, the Court ruled in *Engel v. Vitale* that a school prayer adopted by the New York State Board of Regents violated the constitutional prohibition against government-supported religion. In *Gideon v. Wainwright* (1963), the Court required that every felony defendant be provided a lawyer regardless of the defendant's ability to pay. In 1964, the Court ruled in *Escobedo v. Illinois* that a person accused of a crime must be allowed to consult a lawyer before being interrogated by police.

Two years later, in *Miranda v. Arizona* (1966), the Court ordered that an accused person in police custody must be informed of certain basic rights: the right to remain silent; the right to know that anything said to authorities can be used against the individual in court; and the right to have a defense attorney present during interrogation.

FREEDOM SUMMER During late 1963 and throughout 1964, the civil rights movement continued to grow. Racism, however, remained entrenched in the Lower South. White officials kept African Americans from voting by charging them poll taxes, forcing them to take difficult literacy tests, making the application process inconvenient, and intimidating them through arson, beatings, and lynchings.

In early 1964, Robert "Bob" Moses, a black New Yorker who had resigned from the SCLC to head the Student Nonviolent Coordinating Committee (SNCC) office in Mississippi, decided it would take "an army" to force the state to give voting rights to black people. So he set about recruiting black and white volunteers who would live with rural African Americans, teach them in "freedom schools," and help them register to vote.

Most of the recruits for what came to be called Freedom Summer were idealistic white college students, many of them Jewish. Mississippi's white leaders prepared for "the nigger-Communist invasion" by doubling the state police force and stockpiling tear gas, electric cattle prods, and shotguns.

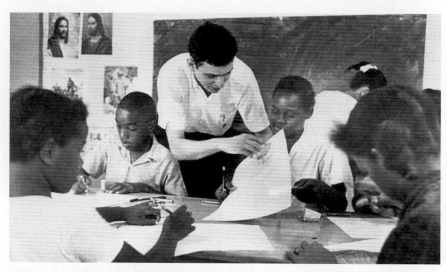

A freedom school in Jackson, Mississippi A volunteer from Brooklyn, New York, instructs young black students on the arts, African American history, and civil rights at a freedom school as part of the "Mississippi Summer Project" in August 1964.

In mid-June, the volunteer activists met at an Ohio college to learn about southern racial history, nonviolent civil disobedience, and the likely abuses they would suffer. On the final evening of training, Moses pleaded with anyone who feared heading to Mississippi to go home; several did. The next day, the volunteers boarded buses and headed south.

In all, forty-one freedom schools taught thousands of Mississippi children math, writing, and history. They also tutored black adults about the complicated process of voter registration. Stokely Carmichael, an African American student from Trinidad who had recently graduated from Howard University, wrote that black Mississippians "took us in, fed us, instructed and protected us, and ultimately civilized, educated, and inspired the smartassed college students."

Forty-six-year-old Fannie Lou Hamer was one of the local black activists who worked with the SNCC volunteers during Freedom Summer. The youngest in a household of twenty children, she had spent most of her life working on local cotton plantations. During the Freedom Summer of 1963 and after, she led gatherings of volunteers in freedom songs and excelled as a lay preacher. "God is not pleased," she said, "at all the murdering, and all the brutality, and all the killings for no reason at all. God is not pleased at the Negro children in the State of Mississippi, suffering from malnutrition. God is not pleased because we have to go raggedy each day. God is not pleased because we have to go to the field and work from ten to eleven hours for three lousy dollars."

The Ku Klux Klan, local police, and other white racists harassed, arrested, and assaulted many of the volunteers. But the worst incident occurred June 21, 1964, just two days after Congress approved the Civil Rights Act, when three young SNCC workers—James Earl Chaney, Andrew Goodman, and Michael "Mickey" Schwerner—disappeared after going to investigate the burning of an African American church. Their decomposed, bullet-riddled bodies were found two months later buried in a dam at a cattle pond. They had been abducted and murdered by Klan members. While searching for the missing men, authorities found the bodies of eight black men in rivers and swamps who also had been killed. The murders, said one volunteer, were "the end of innocence," after which "things could never be the same." A growing number of black activists began to call into question Martin Luther King's nonviolent strategy.

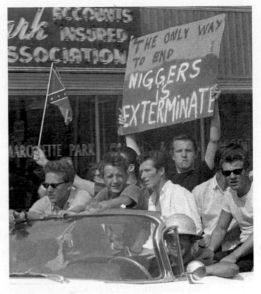

White terror Young men cruise through a riot zone in Chicago in 1966, brandishing a Confederate flag and racist signs.

BLACK POWER Racism was not limited to the South. By the mid-1960s, about 70 percent of the nation's African Americans were living in blighted urban areas, and many young blacks were losing faith in the strategy of Christian nonviolence. Inner-city poverty and frustration cried out for its own social justice movement.

The fragmentation of the civil rights movement was tragically evident on August 11, 1965, when Watts, the largest black neighborhood in Los Angeles, exploded in rioting and looting that left 34 dead, almost 4,000 in jail, and widespread property damage. Dozens of other cities experienced similar riots in the summer of 1966. Between 1965 and 1968, nearly 300 racial uprisings rocked urban America.

The violence revealed the growing civil war within the civil rights movement. As Gil Scott-Heron, a black musician, sang: "We are tired of praying and marching and thinking and learning / Brothers want to start cutting and shooting and stealing and burning." What came to be called "black power" began to compete with the integrationist, nonviolent philosophy espoused by Martin Luther King and the SCLC.

MALCOLM X The most visible spokesman for the **Black Power movement** was Malcolm X, born in 1925 in Omaha, Nebraska, as Malcolm Little. His father, a Baptist minister, and his West Indian mother, had supported Marcus Garvey's crusade for black nationalism in the 1920s, and their home was burned to the ground by white racists because of their affiliation. His father was killed when Malcolm was six, perhaps by white supremacists. Afterward, Malcolm's mother suffered a breakdown and was institutionalized for the rest of her life. Young Malcolm was placed in foster care, but after being expelled from school in the ninth grade, he drifted from Detroit to New York City to Boston.

By age nineteen, Malcolm, now known as Detroit Red, had become a thief, drug dealer, and pimp. He spent seven years in Massachusetts prisons, where he joined a small Chicago-based religious sect, the Nation of Islam (NOI), whose members were called Black Muslims. The organization had little to do with Islam and everything to do with its domineering leader, Elijah Muhammad. Muhammad dismissed whites as "devils" and championed black nationalism, racial pride, self-respect, and self-discipline. By 1953, a year after leaving prison, Malcolm Little was calling himself Malcolm X in tribute to his lost African name, and he had become a full-time NOI minister famous for electrifying speeches attacking white racism and black powerlessness.

Malcolm X dismissed Martin Luther King and other mainstream civil rights leaders as "nothing but modern Uncle Toms" who "keep you and me in check, keep us under control, keep us passive and peaceful and nonviolent." He insisted that there "was no such thing as a nonviolent revolution." His militant speeches inspired thousands of mostly urban blacks to join the Nation of Islam.

Malcolm X expressed the emotions and frustrations of the inner-city African American working poor. Yet at the peak of his influence, and just as he was moderating his militant message, he became embroiled in a conflict with Elijah Muhammad that proved fatal. NOI assassins killed Malcolm X in Manhattan on February 21, 1965.

Malcolm X The Black Power movement's most influential spokesman.

Black militancy did not end with Malcolm X, however. By 1966, "black power" had become a rallying cry for many young militants. When Stokely Carmichael became head of the Student Nonviolent Coordinating Committee (SNCC), he ousted whites from the organization. "When you talk of black power," Carmichael shouted, "you talk of bringing this country to its knees, of building a movement that will smash everything Western civilization has created." Having been beaten by whites and having seen fellow volunteers killed, Carmichael rejected the nonviolent philosophy of the civil rights movement.

THE BLACK PANTHER PARTY Carmichael and other firebrands spoke to the seething rage of the young black underclass. Soon he would move on to the Black Panther Party for Self Defense (BPP), a group of black revolutionaries founded in 1966 by Huey P. Newton and Bobby Seale in Oakland, California. Newton and Seale, both college-educated, were community workers in a federal anti-poverty program. They decided to form a militant self-defense organization (the BPP) after San Francisco police killed Matthew Johnson, an unarmed black teen. The BPP called for an end to "police terrorism," full employment for African Americans, decent housing, and the release of all "black men" from prison.

Wearing black berets, leather coats, and sunglasses and armed with rifles and shotguns, cartridge belts, a menacing swagger, and a clenched fist black power salute, Black Panthers rejected the integrationist philosophy of Dr. Martin Luther King Jr. in favor of revolutionary violence. "We do not believe in passive and nonviolent tactics," Newton explained. "They haven't worked for us black people. They are bankrupt" in the inner cities of America. "Force, guns, and arms are the real political arena." The "racist" police "in our communities are not there to protect us. They are here to contain us, to oppress us, to brutalize us."

The Black Panthers intended to "police the police" in their communities while addressing the pressing needs of their inner-city neighborhoods. They sought to become self-governing communities. To that end, they organized Free Breakfast for Children programs, offered job-training programs, and created free community health clinics. Soon, more than forty Black Panther chapters emerged in cities across America: New York, Los Angeles, Chicago, Boston, Philadelphia, and Seattle, among others.

The Black Panthers insisted that they had a right to defend themselves from police harassment and brutality. A gun battle with police in which an officer was shot and killed landed Newton in jail. Between 1967 and 1969, nine police officers and ten Black Panthers were killed in shootouts. FBI Director J. Edgar Hoover labeled the Black Panthers terrorists who constituted the "greatest threat to the internal security of the country." To meet that threat of "black nationalist hate groups," he organized a comprehensive program to undermine the Black Panther party. The efforts of the FBI, along with infighting and drug abuse among the members, destroyed the Black Panthers by 1982.

For all their violent and self-destructive behavior, the Black Panthers infused the civil rights movement with powerful insights and constructive beliefs. They affirmed that the necessary first step for African Americans seeking true equality was first to learn to love oneself and then to love and protect each other, regardless of age, gender, or sexual preference.

Audre Lorde, a powerful New York writer, the child of West Indian immigrants who described herself as a black lesbian feminist, mother, warrior, and poet, credited the Black Panthers with helping to expand the civil rights movement to include other "disenfranchised" groups such as women and gays/lesbians. Huey Newton, for example, urged the BPP "to form a working coalition with the Gay Liberation and Women's Liberation groups."

Lorde emphatically agreed, noting that people "don't lead single-issue lives." Creating a truly powerful movement for social change thus required connecting across difference to link organizations that speak to different constituencies. Activists must learn "how to take our differences and make them strengths."

The men who founded the Black Panther party proclaimed themselves "the cream of Black Manhood" who would protect and defend "our Black community." Initially, the role of female Panthers was to "stand behind black men" and be supportive. Yet despite such masculine bravado, the majority of Black Panthers were women. "The women who were drawn to the Black Panther Party were all feminists," explained Ericka Huggins, a leader of the organization. By 1969, the Black Panther Party newspaper declared that men and women were now equal members of the organization and instructed male members to treat women as equals.

Alabama-born Angela Davis, a Phi Beta Kappa graduate of Brandeis University who earned a doctoral degree in philosophy from Humboldt University in Germany and taught at the University of California at Los Angeles (UCLA), was a radical feminist aligned with SNCC, the Black Panthers, and the Communist Party. California governor Ronald Reagan ordered the Board of Regents to fire Davis for using "inflammatory language," for she repeatedly referred to police officers as "pigs."

A formidable speaker, Davis became an outspoken activist for an array of causes. She opposed the Vietnam War, racism, sexism, and the "prison-industrial complex." She also supported gay/lesbian rights and other social justice movements. "I am no longer accepting the things I cannot change," she declared. "I am changing the things I cannot accept."

Panther power Black Panthers issue a black power salute outside a San Francisco Liberation School, where activists raised awareness and appreciation of African American history, a topic often ignored by white, mainstream curricula.

THE EFFECT OF BLACK POWER Although widely covered in the media, the Black Power movement never attracted more than a small minority of African Americans. Still, it forced Martin Luther King and others to shift the focus of the civil rights movement from the rural South to inner-city neighborhoods in the North and West.

The time had come, King declared while launching his "Poor People's Campaign" in December 1967, for radical new measures "to provide jobs and income for the poor." Yet as he and others stressed, the war in Vietnam was stealing funds from federal programs serving the poor, and black soldiers were dying in disproportionate numbers in Southeast Asia.

The Black Power movement also motivated African Americans to push for black studies programs in schools and colleges, the celebration of African cultural and artistic traditions, the organizing of inner-city voters to elect black mayors, laws forcing landlords to treat blacks fairly, and the creation of grassroots organizations and community centers in black neighborhoods. As an NOI minister, Malcolm X had insisted that blacks call themselves *African Americans* as a symbol of pride and as a spur to learn more about their history.

THE GREAT SOCIETY

Stronger federal support for civil rights came from an unlikely source: the white Texan who succeeded John F. Kennedy in the White House. Lyndon B. Johnson, known as "LBJ," took the presidential oath on board the plane that brought Kennedy's body back to Washington from Dallas.

Johnson, who was fifty-five years old and stood six feet, four inches tall, had risen to be one of the most powerful Democratic leaders ever in the Senate during his twenty-six years in Washington. Now, this legislative magician was the first southern president since Woodrow Wilson.

Johnson's transition to the presidency was not easy. The Kennedy brothers despised him and his hardscrabble background. JFK had warned aides that Johnson was "a very insecure, sensitive man with a huge ego," and he had directed them to "kiss his ass from one end of Washington to the other." Not surprisingly, Johnson had come to hate the Kennedys.

The oath of office Less than ninety minutes after John Kennedy's death, Lyndon Johnson took the presidential oath aboard Air Force One between his wife, Lady Bird (left), and Jacqueline Kennedy (right), before flying out of Dallas for Washington, D.C.

Like Kennedy, Johnson was one of the most complex men to occupy the White House. Unlike Kennedy, however, Johnson's was a rags-to-riches story. He had worked his way out of rural Texas poverty during the Great Depression to become one of the Senate's dominant figures.

LBJ's personality largely shaped his successes and failures. His ego and insecurities were as massive as his vanity and ambition. He could not stand being alone, and he insisted on always being the center of attention. At press conferences, he referred to "my Vietnam policy," "my Security Council," "my Cabinet," "my legislation," and "my boys" fighting in Southeast Asia.

George Reedy, his press secretary, described Johnson as a "man of too many paradoxes." Ruthless and often bullying, needy and warmhearted, Johnson was a crude idealist and brutal optimist so thin-skinned that he took all criticism personally. In his vengeful view, people were either with him or against him, and he was rabidly impatient with anyone who dissented or diverged from his agenda.

In essence, psychologists believed, Johnson suffered from narcissism and bipolar disorder. Being respected was not enough; he needed to be adored. Famous for his dramatic mood swings and coarse behavior, he often berated his aides with cutting profanity and belittling humor. "There's only two kinds at the White House," he told the staff. "There's elephants and there's pissants. And I'm the only elephant." Reedy described Johnson as "a miserable person— a bully, sadist, lout, and egoist."

Most of all, Johnson yearned to be recognized as a transformational leader. And, like the Kennedy brothers, he had a weakness for attractive women. He often bragged about how many women he had bedded, and when aides mentioned Kennedy's escapades, Johnson would claim that he had "had more women by accident than Kennedy ever had on purpose." Early in his presidency, LBJ alerted reporters that they should ignore him "coming in and out of a few women's bedrooms while in the White House." His long-suffering wife, Claudia "Lady Bird" Johnson, explained that "Lyndon loved the human race, and half of the human race are women."

Johnson wanted to be the greatest American president, the one who did the most good for the most people by creating the most new programs. Those who dismissed him as a traditional southern conservative failed to appreciate his genuine compassion for the poor and his embrace of civil rights. "I'm going to be the best friend the Negro ever had," Johnson bragged.

His commitment to civil rights was in part motivated by politics, in part by his desire to bring the South into the mainstream of American life, and in part by his life experiences. His first teaching job was at an elementary school in Texas that served Mexican American children. His experiences created in him a lifelong desire to help "those poor little kids. I saw hunger in their eyes and pain in their bodies. Those little brown bodies had so little and needed so much."

POLITICS AND POVERTY

Lyndon Johnson maneuvered legislation through Congress better than any president in history. In 1964, he took advantage of widespread public support in the aftermath of Kennedy's death to push through Congress the fallen president's stalled measures for tax reductions and civil rights. He later said that he wanted to take Kennedy's incomplete program "and turn it into a martyr's cause."

The Revenue Act of 1964 provided a 20 percent reduction in tax rates. (The top rate was then a whopping 91 percent, compared to 37 today.) It was intended to give consumers more money to spend so as to boost economic growth and create new jobs—and it worked. Unemployment fell from 5.2 percent in 1964, to 4.5 percent in 1965, and to 3.8 percent in 1966.

THE CIVIL RIGHTS ACT Long thwarted by southern Democrats in Congress, the **Civil Rights Act of 1964** finally became law on July 2. It guaranteed equal treatment for *all* Americans and outlawed discrimination in public places on the basis of race, sex, or national origin. It also prohibited discrimination in the buying, selling, and renting of housing, as well as in the hiring and firing of employees.

Johnson pursued its passage with an urgent sense of purpose. He lobbied key legislators one-on-one over drinks and cigarettes in his office, his outsized presence intimidating any opposition. One senator who survived the "Johnson treatment" said that the president would "twist your arm off at the shoulder and beat your head with it" if you did not agree to vote as he wanted.

Soon after becoming president, Johnson hosted Georgia senator Richard Russell, his close friend and an arch-segregationist. Over lunch, the president warned Russell that "you've got to get out of my way. I'm going to run over you" to pass the Civil Rights Act. "You may do that," Russell replied. "But by God, it's going to cost you the South and cost you the election of 1964." Johnson answered: "If that's the price I've got to pay, I'll pay it gladly." Soon thereafter, Johnson told Congress that "we have talked long enough in this country about equal rights. . . . It is time now to write the next chapter, and to write it in the book of law." He added that it would be the best way to honor Kennedy's memory.

People from all walks of life helped Johnson convince Congress to pass the Civil Rights Act—Senator Hubert Humphrey, congressional committee chairs (both Republicans and Democrats), labor unions, church leaders, and civil rights organizations. Their efforts produced what is arguably the most important piece of legislation in the twentieth century. The passage of the Civil Rights Act marked one of those extraordinary moments when the ideals of democracy, equal opportunity, and human dignity were affirmed.

The Civil Rights Act dealt a major blow to racial segregation while giving the federal government new powers to bring lawsuits against organizations or businesses that violated constitutional rights. It also established the Equal Employment Opportunities Commission to ensure that employers treated job applicants equally, regardless of race, gender, or national origin.

Down with segregation A worker removes a sign from a public restroom at Montgomery Municipal Airport that reads: "WHITE MEN."

On the night after signing the bill, Johnson predicted that "we have just delivered the South to the Republican party for a long time to come." He feared that his commitment to civil rights would cost him the election of 1964.

A WAR ON POVERTY In addition to fulfilling President Kennedy's legislative priorities that had stalled in Congress, Lyndon Johnson launched an elaborate legislative program of his own, declaring "unconditional war on poverty in America." Americans had "rediscovered" poverty in 1962 when social critic Michael Harrington published a powerful exposé, *The Other America*, in which he revealed that more than 40 million people were mired in an invisible "culture of poverty." Poverty led to poor housing conditions, which in turn led to poor health, poor attendance at school or work, alcohol and drug abuse, unwanted pregnancies, and single-parent families. Harrington added that poverty was much more extensive than people realized because much of it was hidden from view in isolated rural areas or inner-city slums. He pushed for a "comprehensive assault on poverty."

Kennedy had read Harrington's book and had asked his advisers in the fall of 1963, just before his assassination, to investigate the problem and suggest solutions. Upon becoming president, Johnson announced that he wanted an anti-poverty legislative package "with real impact." He was determined to

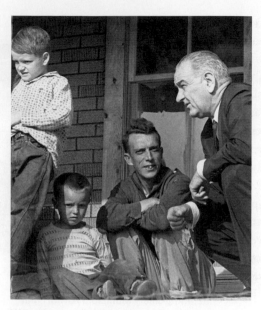

War on poverty In 1964, President Johnson visited Tom Fletcher, a father of eight children living in a tar-paper shack in rural Kentucky. Fletcher became a "poster father" for the war on poverty, although his life benefited little from its programs.

help the "one-fifth of all American families with incomes too small to even meet their basic needs." Money for the program would come from the tax revenues generated by corporate profits made possible by the tax reduction of 1964, which had led to one of the longest sustained economic booms in history.

Johnson knew that the "war" on poverty would be long and costly. He did not expect to "wipe out poverty" in "my lifetime. But we can minimize it, moderate it, and in time eliminate it." He pledged that his war on poverty would not be "a struggle to support people" by giving them handouts but by opening "the door of opportunity" for them.

The **Economic Opportunity Act** of 1964 was the primary weapon in Johnson's war on poverty. It created an Office of Economic Opportunity (OEO) to administer eleven new community-based programs, many of which still exist. They included a Job Corps training program for the long-term unemployed; an Upward Bound program to excite inner-city youth about attending college; a Head Start educational program for disadvantaged preschoolers; a Legal Services Corporation to provide legal assistance for low-income Americans; financial-aid programs for low-income college students; grants to small farmers and rural businesses; loans to businesses that hired the chronically unemployed; the Volunteers in Service to America program (VISTA) to combat inner-city poverty; and the Community Action Program, which would allow the poor "maximum feasible participation" in organizing and directing their own neighborhood programs. In 1964, Congress also approved the Food Stamp Act to help the poor afford groceries.

THE ELECTION OF 1964 President Johnson's successes aroused a conservative Republican counterattack. Arizona senator Barry Goldwater, a wealthy department-store owner, emerged as the square-jawed, blunt-talking leader of the growing right wing of the Republican party. He was one of only six Republican senators to vote against the Civil Rights Act and warned that the bill would lead to a "federal police state."

In his best-selling book *The Conscience of a Conservative* (1960), Goldwater had called for ending the income tax and drastically reducing federal entitlement programs such as Social Security. Conservatives controlled the Republican National Convention when it gathered in San Francisco in the early summer of 1964, and they ensured Goldwater's nomination. "I would remind you," Goldwater told the delegates, "that extremism in the defense of liberty is no vice." He later explained that his objective was like that of Calvin Coolidge in the 1920s: "to reduce the size of government. Not to pass laws, but repeal them."

Goldwater was refreshingly candid. A rugged outdoorsman, he was quick to smile and easy to like, but he was out of his depth as a presidential candidate. He frightened many voters by urging wholesale bombing of North Vietnam and suggesting the use of atomic weapons. He criticized Johnson's war on poverty as a waste of money, told students that the federal government should not provide assistance for education, and opposed the nuclear test ban treaty. To Republican campaign buttons that claimed, "In your heart, you know he's right," Democrats responded, "In your guts, you know he's nuts."

Johnson, by comparison, portrayed himself as a responsible centrist. He chose as his running mate Hubert H. Humphrey of Minnesota, a prominent liberal senator who had long promoted civil rights, and pledged that he was "not about to send American boys nine or ten thousand miles from home to do what Asian boys ought to be doing for themselves."

The election was not close. Johnson won 61 percent of the popular vote and dominated the electoral vote, 486 to 52. Goldwater captured only Arizona and five states in the Lower South. In the Senate, the Democrats increased their majority by two (68 to 32) and in the House by thirty-seven (295 to 140).

But Goldwater's success in the Lower South accelerated the region's shift to the Republican party, and his candidacy proved to be a turning point in the development of the national conservative movement by inspiring a generation of young activists and the formation of conservative organizations that would transform the dynamics of American politics during the 1970s and 1980s. Their success would culminate in the presidency of Ronald Reagan, the Hollywood actor who co-chaired the "California for Goldwater" campaign in 1964.

The Great Society

Lyndon Johnson misread his lopsided victory in 1964 as a mandate for massive changes. He knew, however, that his popularity could quickly fade. "Every day I'm in office," he told his aides, "I'm going to lose votes. I'm going to alienate somebody. . . . We've got to get this legislation fast. You've got to get it during my honeymoon."

As Johnson's war on poverty gathered momentum, his ambitions grew. He resolved to finish FDR's New Deal by creating what he called the **Great Society**. In May 1964, he announced his intention to develop an array of programs designed to "move not only toward the rich society and the powerful society, but upward to the Great Society" which would end poverty and racial injustice and provide "abundance and liberty for all."

Johnson viewed the federal government as the magical lever for raising the quality of life for all Americans. "Hell, we're the richest country in the world, the most powerful," Johnson told an aide. "We can do it all."

Soon, Johnson was working to gain congressional approval for dozens of new bills and federal programs. He eventually convinced the Democrat-controlled Congress to approve a torrent of legislative requests focused on education, health care, civil rights, urban renewal, rural poverty, transportation, and even cultural offerings such as government-funded public television and radio programming. The Great Society also featured dozens of initiatives to enhance the environment, including an Air Quality Act, a Wilderness Act, an Endangered Species Act, a Scenic Rivers Act, and a National Trails Act.

HEALTH INSURANCE, HOUSING DEVELOPMENT, AND HIGHER EDUCATION Lyndon Johnson's first priorities among his Great Society programs were federal health insurance and aid for young people to pursue higher education—all liberal proposals that had first been suggested by President Truman in 1945 but were rejected by conservative southern Democrats and Republicans in Congress. For twenty years, the steadfast opposition of the American Medical Association (AMA) had stalled a comprehensive medical-insurance program. Now that Johnson and the Democrats had the votes, however, the AMA joined Republicans in supporting a bill serving only those over age sixty-five.

The act created not just a **Medicare** health insurance program for the elderly but also a **Medicaid** program of federal grants to states to help cover medical expenses for the poor of all ages. Johnson signed the bill on July 30, 1965, in Independence, Missouri, with eighty-one-year-old Harry Truman looking on.

The Higher Education Act of 1965 increased federal grants to universities, created scholarships for low-income students, provided low-interest loans for students, and established a National Teachers Corps. "Every child," Johnson asserted, "must be encouraged to get as much education as he has the ability to take."

The momentum generated by the Higher Education and Medicare Acts helped carry many more Great Society bills through Congress. Among them was the Appalachian Regional Development Act of 1966, which allocated $1 billion for programs in impoverished mountain areas. The Housing and Urban Development Act of 1965 provided $3 billion for urban renewal projects in inner cities. Funds to help low-income families pay their rent followed in 1966, and the same year a new Department of Housing and Urban Development was established, headed by Robert C. Weaver, the first African American cabinet member.

THE IMMIGRATION ACT Little noticed in the stream of Great Society legislation was the Immigration and Nationality Services Act of 1965 (also called the **Hart-Celler Act**), which Johnson signed in a ceremony at the base of the Statue of Liberty in New York Harbor. It was the most sweeping revision in immigration policies in decades, and both Democrats and Republicans supported it. In his speech, Johnson stressed that the law would redress the wrong done to those "from southern and eastern Europe" and the "developing continents" of Asia, Africa, and Latin America.

The old system, dating to 1924, greatly favored immigrants from Great Britain and the countries of western and northern Europe over those from southern and Eastern Europe, Asia, and Africa. The new law ended discriminatory national-origins quotas and created hemispheric ceilings on visas issued: 170,000 for persons from outside the Western Hemisphere, 120,000 for persons from within. It also stipulated that no more than 20,000 people could come from any one country each year.

The 290,000 immigrants admitted annually were to be accepted under seven "preference" quotas. First and second preferences—40 percent of the total—were provided for unmarried adult sons and daughters of citizens and documented immigrants. (Spouses, minor children, and parents of citizens were not counted in the quotas.) The third preference, 10 percent, went to "members of the professions and scientists and artists of exceptional ability." The fourth, 10 percent, went to adult married children of U.S. citizens, and the fifth, 24 percent, to brothers and sisters of citizens. The sixth, 10 percent, was for "skilled labor in great demand" and "unskilled workers in occupations for which labor is in short supply." The final preference, 6 percent, was for refugees from political tyranny.

Johnson explained that the new law "repairs a deep and painful flaw in the fabric of American life. . . . The days of unlimited immigration are past. But those who come will come because of what they are—not because of the land from which they sprung."

Johnson's insistence that the new law was not "revolutionary" has been proven wrong. During the 1960s and since, European immigrants dropped to less than 10 percent of the total. Asians and Latin Americans became the largest cohort of new Americans. More than 80 million immigrants have come to America since 1965, most of them from Mexico, the Philippines, Cuba, South Korea, China, and Taiwan.

VOTING RIGHTS LEGISLATION Building upon the successes of Freedom Summer, Martin Luther King Jr. organized an effort in early 1965 to register the 3 million unregistered African American voters in the South. On February 6, the White House announced that it would urge Congress to enact a voting rights bill.

Activists converged on Selma, Alabama, where only 250 of the 15,000 blacks of voting age were registered voters. King told his staff on February 10 that to get the voting rights bill passed, "we need to make a dramatic" statement. That drama occurred three weeks later.

On Sunday, March 7, hundreds of black and white civil rights activists assembled near the Edmund Pettus Bridge to begin a fifty-four-mile march to the state capitol in Montgomery. Before reaching the bridge, however, the marchers were assaulted by state troopers and local police using billy clubs, tear gas, and bullwhips. In what came to be called "Bloody Sunday," the violence was televised for all to see. Fifty marchers were hospitalized.

King, torn between congressional appeals to call off the march and the demands of militants that it continue, announced that a second march would be held. A federal judge agreed to allow the marchers to continue once President Johnson agreed to provide soldiers and federal marshals for their protection.

By March 25, when the demonstrators reached Montgomery, some 25,000 people were with them. King delivered a rousing address in which he said, "the battle is in our hands. And we can answer with creative nonviolence the call to higher ground to which the new directions of our struggle summons us."

Several days earlier, President Johnson had urged Congress to "overcome the crippling legacy of bigotry and injustice" by making the cause of civil rights "our cause too." He concluded by slowly speaking the words of the movement's hymn: "And we *shall* overcome."

Voting Rights Act of 1965 President Johnson gifts the Reverend Martin Luther King Jr. with a souvenir pen—one of those used to sign the bill into law.

The resulting **Voting Rights Act of 1965** was a momentous legislative accomplishment. It ensured *all* citizens the right to vote and authorized Attorney General Nicholas Katzenbach to send federal officials to register voters in areas that had long experienced racial discrimination. The act banned the various methods, like requiring literacy tests, that local officials had used to keep black and Latino citizens from voting.

By the end of the year, some 250,000 African Americans were newly registered to vote in several southern states. By 1968, an estimated 53 percent of blacks in Alabama were registered, compared to only 14 percent in 1960. In this respect, the Voting Rights Act was even more important than the Civil Rights Act because it empowered black voters in the South, thereby transforming the white-dominated politics in the region and making possible the election of black public officials. Yet by enabling southern blacks—most of whom preferred Democratic candidates—to vote, it also helped turn the once-solidly Democratic South into a Republican stronghold, as many white voters switched parties.

THE GREAT SOCIETY IN PRACTICE Lyndon B. Johnson sought to give Americans a sense of forward movement in troubled times and show them that he could create a "great society" whereby people would be "more concerned with the quality of their goals than the quantity of their goods." Franklin Roosevelt passed fifteen major bills in his First Hundred Days, Johnson told an aide in 1966, whereas he had "passed two hundred in the last two years." A *New York Times* columnist joked that LBJ was "getting everything through the Congress but the abolition of the Republican party, and he hasn't tried that yet."

The scope of Lyndon Johnson's Great Society programs exceeded Franklin Roosevelt's New Deal in part because of the nation's booming prosperity during the mid-1960s. "This country," Johnson proclaimed, "is rich enough to do anything it has the guts to do and the vision to do and the will to do."

That proved *not* to be the case, however. As *Time* magazine reported, "No matter how much Lyndon gets, he asks for more." Soon there was no more money to spend. In 1966, Johnson warned that if taxes were not raised, the economy would suffer a "ruinous spiral of inflation" and "brutally higher interest rates."

The Great Society and war on poverty did not end urban blight or rural poverty or stubborn social problems, in part because the Vietnam War soon took priority and siphoned away funding, and in part because neither Johnson nor his congressional supporters understood the complexity of chronic poverty.

The Great Society programs did lead to several triumphs since their enactment, however. Infant mortality has dropped, college completion rates have soared, malnutrition has virtually disappeared, and far fewer elderly Americans live below the poverty line and without access to health care. The federal guarantee of civil rights and voting rights remains in place. Medicare and Medicaid have become two of the most appreciated—and expensive—government programs. Consumers now have a federal agency protecting them. Head Start programs providing preschool enrichment activities for poor students have produced long-term benefits. The federal food stamp program has improved the nutrition and health of children living in poverty. Finally, scholarships for low-income college students have made access to higher education possible for millions.

Several of Johnson's most ambitious programs, however, were ill-conceived. Others were vastly underfunded, and many were mismanaged and even corrupt. Some of the problems they were meant to address actually worsened. Medicare, for example, removed incentives for hospitals to control costs, thereby contributing to skyrocketing medical bills. In addition, food stamp fraud occurred as people took advantage of a program intended to ensure healthy nutrition. A final example has been the challenge of single-parent households. In 1960, about 5 percent of children were born to single mothers. Today, the number has soared to 40 percent, in part because of federal programs that provide child support.

Overall, Great Society programs helped reduce poverty from 19 percent in 1964 to 10 percent in 1973, but it did so largely by providing federal welfare payments, not by finding people jobs. In 1966, middle-class resentment over the cost and excesses of the Great Society programs generated a conservative backlash that fueled a Republican resurgence. In the congressional elections of 1966, only thirty-eight of the seventy-one Democrats elected to the House in 1964 won reelection.

THE TRAGEDY OF VIETNAM

In foreign affairs, Lyndon Johnson was, like Woodrow Wilson, a novice. He admitted that he was "not temperamentally equipped to be commander in chief." And, again like Wilson, his presidency would become a victim of his crusading idealism.

In early 1965, LBJ confided to friends that the "Vietnam thing" was "wearing him down." As racial violence erupted in America's cities, the war in Vietnam reached new levels of intensity and destruction. Using weapons and supplies from China and the Soviet Union, North Vietnam provided massive support to the Viet Cong—the guerrillas fighting in South Vietnam to overthrow the U.S.-backed government.

Johnson inherited a long-standing U.S. commitment to prevent a Communist takeover in Vietnam. Beginning with Harry S. Truman, U.S. presidents had done just enough to avoid being charged with having "lost" Vietnam. Johnson initially sought to do the same.

U.S. air strikes Sustained bombing of Vietnam left thirty- to fifty-foot-wide craters still visible today.

Johnson, however, soon came to doubt that South Vietnam was worth more extensive military involvement. In May 1964, he told his national security adviser, McGeorge Bundy: "It looks to me like we are getting into another Korea. . . . I don't think it's worth fighting for. And I don't think we can get out. It's just the biggest damned mess that I ever saw." Yet Johnson's fear of appearing weak outweighed his misgivings.

ESCALATION IN VIETNAM The official justification for the military *escalation*—a Defense Department term—was the **Tonkin Gulf Resolution**, passed by the Senate on August 7, 1964. On that day, President Johnson, unknowingly acting on false information provided by Secretary of Defense Robert McNamara, reported that on August 2 and 4, North Vietnamese torpedo boats had attacked two U.S. warships in the Gulf of Tonkin, off the coast of North Vietnam. He called it "naked aggression on the high seas." As it turned out, however, the American vessels had actually fired first in support of South Vietnamese attacks against two North Vietnamese islands—attacks planned by American advisers. (Whether the American warships were actually fired upon remains in dispute).

The Tonkin Gulf Resolution empowered Johnson to "take all necessary measures" to protect U.S. forces and "prevent further aggression." Only two senators voted against the resolution. Johnson interpreted the support as equivalent to a congressional declaration of war, since it allowed him to wage war as he saw fit.

It would be no small war, however. Soon after the landslide victory over Barry Goldwater in November 1964, Johnson committed America to full-scale war in Vietnam. On February 5, 1965, Viet Cong guerrillas attacked a U.S. military base near Pleiku, in South Vietnam, killing and wounding more than 100 Americans. More attacks led Johnson to approve Operation Rolling Thunder, the first sustained U.S. bombing of North Vietnam. Thereafter, there were essentially two fronts in the war: one, in North Vietnam, where U.S. warplanes conducted a massive bombing campaign, and the other, in South Vietnam, where nearly all the ground combat occurred.

In March 1965, the U.S. commander, General William C. Westmoreland, greeted the first American combat troops in Vietnam. His strategy was focused on waging a war of attrition, using overwhelming U.S. firepower to produce so many casualties that the Viet Cong and North Vietnamese would give up.

Soon, U.S. forces launched "search and destroy" operations against VC guerrillas throughout South Vietnam. But the Viet Cong, made up of both men and women, wore no uniforms and dissolved by day into the villages, hiding among civilians. Their elusiveness exasperated American soldiers, most

VIETNAM, 1966

CHINA

Red River

NORTH VIETNAM

Dien Bien Phu

Hanoi   Haiphong

GULF OF TONKIN

HAI-NAN

SOUTH CHINA SEA

Mekong R.

Vinh

LAOS

Vientiane

Demarcation Line of 1954

Udon Thani

Hue

THAILAND

Ho Chi Minh Trail

Mekong River

Da Nang

Chu Lai   My Lai

Quang Ngai

Ubon Ratchathani

Kon Tum

An Khe

Ta Khli

Pleiku   Qui Nhon

SOUTH VIETNAM

CAMBODIA

Nha Trang

Cam Ranh Bay

Bangkok

Bien Hoa

Phnom Penh

Saigon

Tan Son Nhut

GULF OF THAILAND

Can Tho

SOUTH CHINA SEA

■ Major U.S. military bases

| 0 | 100 | 200 Miles |
| 0 | 100 | 200 Kilometers |

- Why did the United States intervene militarily in South Vietnam?
- What was the Tet offensive?

of whom were not trained for such unconventional warfare in Vietnam's dense jungles and intense heat and humidity.

The escalating war brought rising U.S. casualties (the number of killed, wounded, and missing), which were announced each week on television news programs. Criticism of the war grew, but LBJ stood firm. "We will not be defeated," he told the nation. "We will not grow tired. We will not withdraw."

Johnson viewed the war as a test of his manliness. He vowed to an aide that he was not going to let a "raggedy-ass little fourth-rate country" like North Vietnam push him around.

Yet LBJ greatly underestimated the tenacity and ingenuity of the North Vietnamese. On July 20, 1965, Secretary McNamara told Johnson that "the situation in South Vietnam is worse than a year ago (when it was worse than the year before that)." The South Vietnamese army seemed inept, and the U.S. bombing campaign was ineffective.

McNamara posed three options: (1) "cut our losses and withdraw"; (2) "continue about the present level"; or, (3) "expand promptly and substantially the U.S. pressure." LBJ chose the third option, and the American buildup in Vietnam began. By the end of 1965, there were 184,000 U.S. troops in Vietnam; in 1966, there were 385,000; by 1969, at the height of the war effort, 542,000.

What the public did not know was that Johnson never thought the war was winnable. He told Lady Bird in July 1965 that escalating the war was "like being in an airplane and I have to choose between crashing the plane or jumping out. I do not have a parachute."

THE CONTEXT FOR POLICY President Johnson's decision to "Americanize" the war flowed directly from the assumptions that had long guided U.S. foreign policy during the cold war. The commitment to contain the spread of communism guided Johnson as well. "Why are we in Vietnam?" the president asked during a speech in 1965. "We are there because we have a promise to keep. . . . To leave Vietnam to its fate would shake the confidence of all these people in the value of American commitment." What Johnson did not say was that he dreaded being blamed for "losing Vietnam" to communism.

Johnson's military advisers also believed that U.S. military force would defeat the Viet Cong. Yet the president insisted that the American war effort not reach levels that would cause the Chinese or Soviets to become involved—which meant, as it turned out, that a military victory was never possible. The United States was not fighting to "win" but to prevent the North Vietnamese and Viet Cong from winning and, eventually, to force them to sign a negotiated settlement. This meant that the United States would have to maintain a military presence as long as the enemy retained the will to fight.

RESISTANCE GROWS As the war ground on, opposition grew fierce. In 1965, college campuses began hosting "teach-ins" critical of the war effort. Professors would gather with students to discuss "a better policy" in Vietnam. In April 1965, some 20,000 students converged on Washington, D.C., where they picketed the White House before moving to the Washington Monument, where they carried signs saying: GET OUT OF SAIGON AND INTO SELMA, FREEDOM NOW IN VIETNAM, WAR ON POVERTY NOT PEOPLE. The crowd then went to the Capitol, where it demanded that Congress "end, not extend, the war in Vietnam."

The following year, Senator J. William Fulbright of Arkansas, chairman of the Senate Foreign Relations Committee, began congressional investigations into American policy in Vietnam. George F. Kennan, the former State Department diplomat who had inspired the containment policy, told the committee that the containment doctrine was appropriate for Europe but not for Southeast Asia, which he did not consider a region vital to American security. Johnson labeled his political critics and anti-war protesters "Communists" and used government agencies to punish them.

Still, the resistance grew. By 1967, anti-war demonstrations were commonplace. Americans began dividing into "hawks" who supported the war and "doves" who opposed it. Nightly television accounts of the fighting—Vietnam was the first war to receive extended television coverage and hence was dubbed the "living-room war"—called into question the accuracy of statements by military and government officials claiming the Americans were winning. Journalists called it a "credibility crisis." But Johnson insisted that there would be no withdrawal from Vietnam.

As American military involvement deepened and criticism of the war mounted, Johnson grew more frustrated and depressed. "I can't get out [of Vietnam]. I can't finish it with what

Whose war? President Johnson lowers his head in disappointment as he listens to a commander's report from Vietnam.

I got. So what the hell can I do?" His wife recalled that Vietnam became a "hell of a thorn stuck in his throat. It wouldn't come up; it wouldn't go down. . . . It was pure hell." White House aides became so concerned about Johnson's mental stability that they consulted psychiatrists.

Johnson became preoccupied with the day-to-day conduct of the war, insisting on giving the final approval to bombing targets, fretting over logistical details, demanding information about enemy movements. As Westmoreland requested more and more soldiers, Johnson found it impossible to turn him down, explaining that doing so would be like "hearing the call from the Alamo for help and answering that we're not coming." Yet spending so much time dealing with the war was bitterly frustrating to Johnson. How could he be expected to win the war on poverty if the war kept siphoning away the nation's resources?

THE TET OFFENSIVE On January 31, 1968, the first day of the Vietnamese New Year (Tet), some 70,000 Viet Cong and North Vietnamese troops unleashed surprise attacks on U.S. and South Vietnamese forces throughout South Vietnam. Within a few days, American firepower turned the tables, but the damage had been done.

Although General Westmoreland proclaimed the **Tet offensive** a major defeat for the Viet Cong, its *political* impact in the United States was dramatic; it decisively turned Americans against the war. The scope and intensity of the Tet offensive contradicted upbeat claims by U.S. commanders. "What the hell is going on?" CBS newscaster Walter Cronkite demanded. "I thought we were winning this war." After the Tet offensive, Johnson's popularity plummeted, as did his own confidence in his Vietnam policy.

Equally disturbing to LBJ was Westmoreland's unexpected request for more than 200,000 additional U.S. troops. The request stunned Clark Clifford, who had replaced Robert McNamara as defense secretary. He told the president that the military leaders "don't know what they're talking about." Instead of winning the war, he added, the United States had become mired in a sinkhole with "no end in sight."

Civil rights leaders and social activists felt betrayed as federal funds earmarked for the war on poverty were gobbled up by the war. By 1967, the United States was spending some $2 billion each month in Vietnam, about $322,000 for every VC killed. Anti-poverty programs at home received only $53 per person. Martin Luther King Jr. pointed out that "the bombs in Vietnam explode at home—they destroy the hopes and possibilities for a decent America."

Senator Eugene McCarthy of Minnesota took advantage of the consternation caused by the Tet offensive to ramp up his anti-war challenge to Johnson in the Democratic primaries. With students rallying to his "Dump Johnson" candidacy, McCarthy polled a stunning 42 percent of the vote to Johnson's 48 percent in New Hampshire's March primary. "Dove bites Hawk," a reporter quipped.

McCarthy's success in New Hampshire convinced Robert F. Kennedy, now a New York senator, to launch his own challenge to Johnson's reelection. That members of his own party were opposing his reelection devastated Johnson.

The growing opposition to the Vietnam war was even a worse blow. During a private meeting with military leaders, the president acknowledged that "the country is demoralized. . . . Most of the press is against us. . . . We have no support for the war." Johnson had also grown concerned about his own health. Lady Bird told him to think about retiring after one term.

On March 31, 1968, Johnson appeared on national television to announce a limited halt to the bombing of North Vietnam to enable a negotiated cease-fire agreement with the Communists. Then, he made an astounding announcement: "I shall not seek, and I will not accept, the nomination of my party for another term as your President." As his daughter explained, the "agony of Vietnam" had engulfed her father.

Johnson had become a tragic victim of his grandiose ambitions. By promising far more than he could accomplish, he raised false hopes, stoked resentments, and fractured society. Although U.S. troops would remain in Vietnam for five more years, the quest for military victory ended with Johnson's presidency. The problem with Johnson's attempt to fight a limited war in Vietnam was that the Vietnamese Communists fought an absolute war in defense of their country. Among other things, the war revealed that the capabilities of the United States, including its military power, were limited; the nation could not simply have its way around the world.

Now there were three candidates for the Democratic nomination: McCarthy, Kennedy, and Vice President Hubert Humphrey. Many anti-war Democrats expected McCarthy to drop out in favor of Kennedy, but the Minnesota senator, buoyed by his success and convinced of his moral superiority, refused to leave the race. For his part, Kennedy, with his long hair and boyish faith, appealed to the idealism of America's youth: "Some men see things as they are and ask, why? I dream things that never were and say, why not?"

THE TURMOIL OF THE SIXTIES

By the late 1960s, traditional notions of authority were under attack. The spirit of resistance was especially evident among disaffected youth who called into question not only the Vietnam War and the credibility of the Johnson administration but virtually every aspect of mainstream life, including the traditional family structure, the middle-class work ethic, universities, religion, and the nonviolent integrationist philosophy underpinning the civil rights movement. Many alienated young Americans, often lumped together as "hippies," felt that they were part of "the Revolution," a magical force that would overthrow a corrupt and outdated way of life.

1968: A TRAUMATIC YEAR All the turbulent elements affecting American life came to a head in 1968, the most traumatic year in a traumatic decade. As *Time* magazine reported, "Nineteen sixty-eight was a knife blade that severed past from future." It was "one tragic, surprising, and perplexing thing after another."

On April 4, James Earl Ray, a petty thief, drifter, and white racist, shot and killed Martin Luther King Jr. as the African American leader stood outside the Lorraine Motel in Memphis, Tennessee. Ray had earlier vowed that he was going "to get the big nigger."

King's murder ignited a wave of violence. Riots erupted in more than 100 cities, but the damage was especially devastating in Chicago, Baltimore, and Washington. Forty-six people were killed, all but five of them black. Some 20,000 army soldiers and 34,000 National Guard troops eventually helped stop the violence across the country, and 21,000 people were arrested.

The night that King died, Robert Kennedy was in Indianapolis, Indiana. Upon hearing the news, he stood on a flatbed truck to speak to a grieving crowd of African Americans. "Those of you who are black can be filled with hatred, with bitterness and a desire for revenge," he said. "We can move toward further polarization. Or we can make an effort, as Dr. King did, to understand, to reconcile ourselves and to love."

Two months after King's death, after midnight on June 6, 1968, Kennedy appeared at the Ambassador Hotel in Los Angeles to celebrate his victory over Eugene McCarthy in the California presidential primary. Kennedy closed his remarks by pledging that "we can end the divisions within the United States, end the violence."

After the applause subsided, Kennedy walked through the hotel kitchen on his way to the press room for interviews. Along the way, a Jordanian Arab named Sirhan Sirhan, resentful of the senator's strong support of Israel, pulled out a pistol and fired eight shots, hitting Kennedy in the head and wounding three others. Kennedy died the next morning. Only forty-two years old, he was buried beside his brother John in Arlington National Cemetery outside of Washington, D.C.

The assassinations of the Kennedys, Martin Luther King, and Malcolm X came to frame the sixties. With their deaths, a wealth of idealism died too—the idealism that Bobby Kennedy had hoped would put a fragmented America back together again. Having lost the leading voices for real change, a growing number of young people lost hope in democracy and turned to radicalism and violence—or dropped out of society.

CHICAGO AND MIAMI In August 1968, the nation's social unrest came to a head at the **Chicago Democratic National Convention**, where delegates gathered to nominate Johnson's faithful vice president, Hubert H. Humphrey, as the party's candidate for president. LBJ had endorsed Humphrey as his successor despite criticizing him in private as "all heart and no balls."

Outside the Chicago convention hall, almost 20,000 police officers and National Guard soldiers confronted thousands of anti-war protesters who taunted the police with obscenities. Richard J. Daley, Chicago's gruff Democratic mayor, warned that he would not tolerate disruptions. Nonetheless, riots broke out and were televised nationwide. As police used tear gas and clubs to pummel the demonstrators, others chanted, "The whole world is watching." The *New York Times* reported, "Those were our children in the streets, and the Chicago police beat them up." Nationally, the Democratic party began to fragment as a result of the chaos in Chicago.

Three weeks earlier, the Republicans had gathered in Miami Beach to nominate Richard Nixon. In 1962, after losing the California governor's race, Nixon had vowed never again to run for public office. By 1968, however, he had changed his mind and become a self-appointed spokesman for the values of "middle America." He and the Republicans claimed they would "end the war" in Vietnam and "win the peace" while bringing law and order to the nation's streets.

Nixon appealed to what he called the "**silent majority**" of working- and middle-class Americans who viewed the "rabble rousing" protesters with contempt. In accepting the nomination, Nixon pledged to listen to "the voice of the great majority of Americans, the forgotten Americans, the non-shouters, the non-demonstrators, that are not racists or sick, that are not guilty of the crime that plagues the land."

Former Alabama governor George Wallace, an outspoken segregationist, ran on the American Independent party ticket. Wallace mounted a crusade on behalf of "common folks" against blacks, political elites, and "little pinkos." He promised to get tough on "scummy anarchists" and bring stability to the nation. He appealed even more forcefully than Nixon to working-class voters' disgust with anti-war protesters, the mushrooming federal welfare system, the growth of the federal government, forced racial integration, and rioting in the inner cities.

Wallace displayed a savage wit, once saying that the "only four-letter words that hippies did not know were w-o-r-k and s-o-a-p." He predicted that on Election Day, the nation would realize that "there are a lot of rednecks in this country." His candidacy generated considerable appeal outside his native South, especially among white working-class communities. Wallace hoped to deny Humphrey and Nixon an electoral majority and throw the choice into the House of Representatives, which would have provided a fitting climax to a chaotic year.

Nixon resolved to do anything to win, including violating the Logan Act, which prohibits private citizens from communicating with foreign governments about controversial issues. Just weeks before the election, Nixon ordered an aide to "monkey wrench" President Johnson's last-minute efforts to end the Vietnam War. Nixon used an intermediary to let South Vietnamese leaders know they should stall the ongoing negotiations because Nixon, if elected, would provide them better terms.

When Johnson learned, through CIA surveillance, of Nixon's efforts to subvert the negotiations, he was furious, shouting that the Republican presidential candidate had committed "treason." But he did not have enough proof to share with the public.

While it remains an open question whether Johnson could have negotiated a deal to end the war before the election, Nixon's most recent biographer, John A. Farrell, concluded that "of all of Richard Nixon's actions in a lifetime of politics, this was the most reprehensible," for he chose winning an election over the possibility of ending a war. In what one journalist called an "uncommon act of political decency," Humphrey decided not to make Nixon's efforts to sabotage the peace a last-minute election issue.

NIXON TRIUMPHANT On November 5, 1968, voters gave Richard Nixon what he had been lusting for since 1960. When the ballots were counted, he and Governor Spiro Agnew of Maryland, his acid-tongued running mate, eked out a narrow victory of some 500,000 votes, a margin of about 1 percentage point. The electoral vote was more decisive: 301 for Nixon and 191 for Hubert Humphrey; the 46 electoral votes for George Wallace all came from the Lower South.

Embedded in the election returns was a sobering development for Democrats. White wage workers, the backbone of the party since FDR and the New Deal, were shifting to the Republicans. Both Ohio and New Jersey, traditional

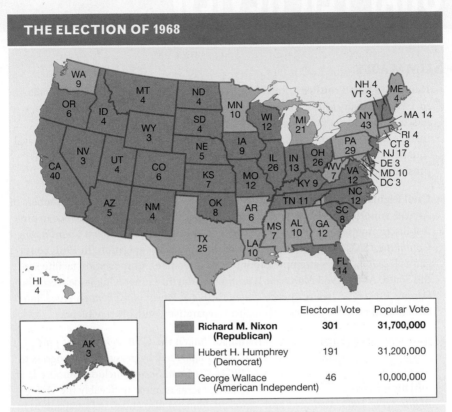

THE ELECTION OF 1968

		Electoral Vote	Popular Vote
Richard M. Nixon (Republican)		**301**	**31,700,000**
Hubert H. Humphrey (Democrat)		191	31,200,000
George Wallace (American Independent)		46	10,000,000

- How did the riots at the Chicago Democratic National Convention affect the 1968 presidential campaign?
- What does the electoral map reveal about the support for each of the three major candidates?
- How was Richard Nixon able to win enough electoral votes in such a close, three-way presidential race?
- What was George Wallace's appeal to 10 million voters?

Democratic strongholds, went for Nixon. And more southern whites voted Republican than Democrat, a trend that has continued to this day.

So at the end of 1968, the century's most turbulent year, a divided society looked to Richard Nixon to fulfill his promises to bring "peace with honor" in Vietnam and to "bring us together" as a nation. Nixon privately admitted that he was a polarizing figure. In his first week in the White House, he told an aide that "I've got to put on my nice-guy hat . . . but let me make it clear that's not my nature."

CHAPTER REVIEW

SUMMARY

- **Kennedy's New Frontier**   President John F. Kennedy promised a *New Frontier* in 1961, but many of his domestic policies stalled in Congress. The *Bay of Pigs* fiasco led the Soviet premier, Nikita Khrushchev, to erect the *Berlin Wall* and install nuclear-armed missiles in Cuba. In October 1962, Kennedy ordered a naval "quarantine" of Cuba that led Khrushchev to withdraw the missiles. During his presidency, Kennedy deepened America's commitment in Vietnam.

- **Civil Rights' Achievements**   At the beginning of the decade, growing numbers of African Americans and whites staged acts of nonviolent civil disobedience to protest discrimination. In 1960, activists formed the *Student Nonviolent Coordinating Committee (SNCC)* to intensify efforts to dismantle desegregation. In 1961, courageous *Freedom Riders* attempted to integrate interstate transportation facilities in the South. At the 1963 *March on Washington,* Martin Luther King Jr. delivered his famous "I Have a Dream" speech. Later, the *Black Power movement* emerged and emphasized militancy, black nationalism, separatism, and, often, violence.

- **Johnson's Great Society**   Lyndon Johnson forced the *Civil Rights Act of 1964* through Congress and then declared "war" on poverty by persuading Congress to pass the *Economic Opportunity Act (1964)*. His *Great Society* included hundreds of initiatives to expand federal social-welfare programs, most noticeably the *Voting Rights Act of 1965, Medicare,* and *Medicaid.* Johnson also ended national quotas in immigration law through the *Immigration and Nationality Services Act of 1965.*

- **The Vietnam War**   The *Tonkin Gulf Resolution (1964)* gave the administration the power to wage war in Southeast Asia without a congressional declaration of war. During early 1965, the United States began escalating its role in Vietnam. By 1968, more than 500,000 U.S. military personnel were in South Vietnam. Claims that the Americans were winning were upended by the *Tet offensive (1968)*. Its initial success led many Americans to decide that the war could not be won. Resistance to "Johnson's War" thereafter steadily increased.

- **1968 Presidential Election**   Frustrated by his failures in Vietnam and aware that he had lost public support, Johnson chose not to seek reelection in 1968. Anti-war Democrats rallied around senators Eugene McCarthy and Robert Kennedy. In April, Martin Luther King Jr. was assassinated, setting off riots in inner-city neighborhoods across the country. Two months later, Robert Kennedy was assassinated. Ultimately, the Democrats selected Johnson's loyal vice president, Hubert Humphrey, as their nominee, provoking angry protests by anti-war demonstrators at the *1968 Chicago Democratic National Convention*. As they had in 1960, the Republicans nominated Richard Nixon, who claimed to represent the *silent majority*. In the end, Nixon narrowly bested Humphrey.

Chronology

Key Terms

 INQUIZITIVE

Go to InQuizitive to see what you've learned—and learn what you've missed—with personalized feedback along the way.

30 Rebellion and Reaction

1960s and 1970s

Rebels with a cause Established in 1967, the Vietnam Veterans Against the War (VVAW) grew quickly during the sixties and early seventies. Here, a former Marine throws his service jacket and medals onto the Capitol steps on April 23, 1971, as part of a protest against the U.S. invasion of Laos.

As Richard M. Nixon entered the White House in early 1969, the nation's social fabric was in tatters. The traumatic events of 1968 had revealed how deeply divided American society had become and how difficult a task Nixon faced in carrying out his campaign pledge to restore social harmony.

Ironically, many of the forces that had contributed to the complacent prosperity of the fifties—the baby boom, the cold war, and the growing consumer culture—helped generate the social upheaval of the sixties and early seventies. The civil rights movement inspired efforts to ensure equal treatment for other minorities, from African Americans to women, gays and lesbians, bisexuals, Native Americans, Latinos, and people with disabilities. At the same time, intense opposition to the Vietnam War helped launch an unprecedented countercultural "youth revolt" that encompassed a unique blend of idealism, opportunism, and goofiness.

Despite Nixon's promise to restore the public's faith in the integrity of its leaders, he ended up aggravating the growing cynicism about the motives and methods of government officials. During 1973 and 1974, the Watergate scandal resulted in the greatest constitutional crisis since the impeachment of President Andrew Johnson in 1868, and it ended with the first resignation of a U.S. president.

focus questions

1. How did the origins of the youth revolt shape the New Left and the counterculture?

2. How did the youth revolt and early civil rights movement influence other protest movements? How did new protest movements affect social attitudes and public policy?

3. How did the political environment of the late sixties influence Richard Nixon's election strategy and domestic policy?

4. How and why did Nixon change military and political strategies to end America's involvement in the Vietnam War?

5. What was the international strategy brought about by Nixon's and Kissinger's diplomacy and foreign policy during the 1970s?

6. How did the Watergate scandal unfold? What was its political significance?

"Forever Young": The Youth Revolt

The Greensboro sit-ins in 1960 not only launched a decade of civil rights activism but also signaled an end to the complacency that had characterized the fifties. Rennie Davis, a sophomore at Ohio's Oberlin College in 1960, remembered that the Greensboro student activists inspired him and many others: "Here were four students from Greensboro who were suddenly all over *Life* magazine. There was a feeling that they were us and we were them, and a recognition that they were expressing something we were feeling as well."

The sit-ins, marches, protests, and sacrifices associated with the civil rights movement inspired other groups—women, Native Americans, Latinos, gays, lesbians, bisexuals, and people with disabilities—to demand justice, freedom, and equality. Many idealistic young people decided that they could no longer ignore the widespread injustice and inequality staining the American dream.

A full-fledged youth revolt erupted. "Your sons and your daughters are beyond your command," sang Bob Dylan in "The Times They Are a-Changin'." By 1970, more than half of Americans were under thirty. These baby boomers, who unlike their parents had experienced neither an economic depression nor a major war, were now attending colleges and universities in record numbers; enrollment quadrupled between 1945 and 1970.

Many universities had become gigantic institutions dependent upon huge research contracts from corporations and the federal government, especially the Defense Department. As these "multiversities" grew larger and more bureaucratic, they became targets for students wary of what President Dwight D. Eisenhower had labeled "the military-industrial complex." As criticism of U.S. military involvement in Vietnam mounted, disillusioned young people flowed into two distinct yet frequently overlapping movements: the New Left and the counterculture.

THE NEW LEFT The political arm of the youth revolt originated in 1959 with the formation of Students for a Democratic Society (SDS). Three years later, in 1962, Tom Hayden and Alan Haber, two University of Michigan students, convened a meeting of sixty SDS activists at Port Huron, Michigan. Their goal was ambitious: to quit reading history in order to *make* history, and to remake the United States into a more democratic society. Several participants were the children of former leftists or Communists; even more were Jewish.

At the gathering, Hayden, a veteran of the civil rights struggle in the South, drafted an impassioned document known as the "Port Huron Statement."

The manifesto began: "We are the people of this generation, bred in at least moderate comfort, housed in universities, looking uncomfortably to the world we inherit." Only by giving "power to the people," the manifesto insisted, could America restore its founding principles. Inspired by African American civil rights activists, Hayden declared that college campuses would become the crossroads of social change. College students would snatch "control of the educational process from the administrative bureaucracy."

Hayden and other members of SDS adopted the term **New Left** to distinguish their efforts at grassroots democracy from those of the "Old Left" of the 1930s, which had embraced an orthodox Marxism. Hayden's revolution would be energized by hope and change, not abstract theories. Within a few years, more than 1,000 campuses hosted SDS chapters, and the organization began publishing its own underground newspaper, *The Rag*.

In the fall of 1964, students at the University of California at Berkeley took Hayden's New Left program to heart. Several had spent the summer working with the Student Nonviolent Coordinating Committee's (SNCC) voter-registration project in Mississippi (freedom summer), where three volunteers had been killed by Klansmen and many others had been arrested or harassed. When the university's chancellor announced that campus political

The free-speech movement Mario Savio, a founder of the free-speech movement, speaks at a rally at the University of California at Berkeley.

demonstrations were banned, thousands of students staged a sit-in. After a thirty-two-hour standoff, the administration relented. Student groups then formed the free-speech movement (FSM).

Led by Mario Savio, who had participated in Freedom Summer in Mississippi, the FSM initially protested on behalf of students' rights, but it quickly mounted more general criticisms of the university and what Savio called the "depersonalized, unresponsive bureaucracy" stifling free speech on many campuses. In 1964, Savio led hundreds of students into Sproul Hall, UC Berkeley's administration building, and organized another sit-in. At 4 A.M., 600 state police arrested the protesters.

A few hours later, some 7,000 students filled Sproul Plaza, circulating leaflets and joining folk singer Joan Baez in singing "We Shall Overcome." Finally, the university's president gave in and revoked the ban on political demonstrations.

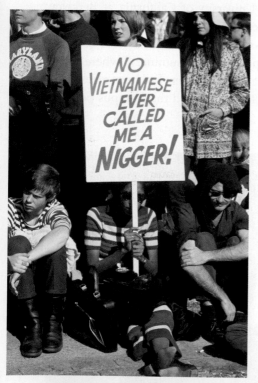

All that rises must converge This protester's sign at a Washington, D.C. demonstration bridged the civil rights and anti-war movements, which pursued many of the same racial and political goals.

ANTI-WAR PROTESTS By 1965, the growing U.S. involvement in Vietnam had changed the New Left's agenda as millions of young men suddenly faced the prospect of being drafted to fight in the increasingly unpopular conflict.

The Vietnam War was primarily a poor man's fight. Most college students were able to postpone military service until they received their degree or reached the age of twenty-four. From 1965 through 1966, college students made up only 2 percent of military inductees. African Americans and Latinos were twice as likely to be drafted as whites.

As the war dragged on, opposition to U.S. involvement exploded. Some 200,000 young men ignored their draft notices, and some 4,000 served prison sentences for doing so. Another 56,000 qualified for conscientious objector (CO) status, meaning that they presented evidence to officials authenticating their moral, ethical, or religious opposition to war and/or the military. If granted, a CO had to perform alternative civilian service, often in hospitals or clinics. Others defied the draft by burning their draft cards while shouting "Hell No, We Won't Go!" Still others fled to Canada or Sweden to avoid military service or found creative ways to flunk the physical examination. Whatever the method, many college students succeeded in avoiding military service. Of the 1,200 men in Harvard's class of 1970, only 56 served in the military, and just 2 of them went to Vietnam.

RISING VIOLENCE Throughout 1967 and 1968, the anti-war move-ment grew more violent as inner-city neighborhoods in Cleveland, Detroit, Newark, and other large urban areas exploded in flames fanned by racial injus-tice. Frustration over discrimination in employment and housing, as well as staggering rates of joblessness among inner-city African American youths, ignited the rage. "There was a sense everywhere, in 1968," journalist Garry Wills wrote, "that things were giving way."

During the eventful spring of 1968—when Lyndon Johnson announced that he would not run for reelection and Martin Luther King Jr. and Robert F. Kennedy were assassinated—campus unrest boiled over. The turmoil reached a climax at Columbia University, where SDS student radicals and black militants occupied the president's office and classroom buildings. They renamed the administration building Malcolm X Hall.

Mark Rudd, the campus SDS leader, called his parents to report, "We took a building." His father, Jacob Rudd, a retired army officer and a real estate investor, replied, "Well, give it back." After a failed attempt to nego-tiate an end to the takeover, the uni-versity's president canceled classes and called in the New York City police. More than 100 students were injured, 700 were arrested, and the leaders of the uprising were expelled. Pres-ident Nixon declared that the rebel-lion was "the first major skirmish in a revolutionary struggle to seize the universities."

Columbia riots Mark Rudd, leader of SDS at Columbia University, speaks to the media during student protests on campus in April 1968.

Part of the problem with SDS and other militant organizations was that they were much more effective at criticizing the status quo than they were at creating a blueprint for an alternative future. "If there is a road to power," SDS president Todd Gitlin acknowledged, "we have no map for it."

The events at Columbia inspired similar clashes at Harvard, Cornell, and San Francisco State, among others. Vice President Spiro Agnew dismissed the young militants as "impudent snobs who characterize themselves as intellectuals" and condemned the "circuit-riding, Hanoi-visiting . . . caterwauling, riot-inciting, burn-America-down" anti-war protesters, whom he labeled "thieves and traitors" and "nattering nabobs of negativism."

THE WEATHER UNDERGROUND A small group of extremists calling themselves the Revolutionary Youth Movement (RYM) emerged during the summer of 1969. They wanted to move political radicalism from "protest to resistance." At the SDS convention in Chicago on June 18, 1969, RYM members distributed a position paper titled "You don't need a weatherman / To know which way the wind blows," a line from Bob Dylan's 1965 song "Subterranean Homesick Blues."

The document called for a "white fighting force" to ally with the Black Panthers and others to destroy "U.S. imperialism and achieve a classless world: world communism." By embracing revolutionary violence, however, the so-called Weathermen essentially committed suicide. They killed SDS by abandoning the pacifist principles that had given the movement moral legitimacy.

Members of the Weather Underground took to the streets of Chicago in October 1969 to assault police and trash the city. Their goal was "to lead white kids into armed revolution." Almost 300 were arrested. During the so-called Days of Rage between September 1969 and May 1970, 250 draft board offices, ROTC buildings (for military training on university campuses), federal government facilities, and corporate headquarters were bombed. In March 1970, three members of the Weather Underground in New York City died when a bomb they were making exploded prematurely.

The Weathermen and other radical groups were forced underground by the aggressive efforts of federal law enforcement agencies. Their momentum diminished once President Nixon ended the draft and withdrew U.S. troops from Vietnam. Mark Rudd, who became one of the Weathermen organizers, later confessed that they intended to destroy SDS "because it wasn't revolutionary enough for us. I am not proud of this history."

Rudd's conversion to revolutionary violence, he explained, "had something to do with an exaggerated sense of my own importance. I wanted to prove myself as a man—a motive exploited by all armies and terrorist groups." Rudd later regretted his embrace of revolutionary violence, calling the intentional destruction of SDS by the Weathermen a "crime." It weakened "the larger anti-war movement and demoralized many good people." Blowing things up "got us isolated" by the media and "smashed" by the FBI.

THE COUNTERCULTURE Looking back over the 1960s, Tom Hayden, the founder of SDS, recalled that most rebellious young Americans "were not narrowly political. Most were not so interested in attaining [elected] office but in changing lifestyles." Hayden acknowledged that the shocking events of 1968 led disaffected young rebels—so-called hippies—to embrace the **counterculture**, an unorganized rebellion against mainstream institutions, values, and behavior that focused more on cultural change than political activism. (The term was coined by Theodore Roszak in his 1969 book, *The Making of a Counter Culture*.)

In pursuing personal liberation, hippies strove to exceed limits, trespass across boundaries, and heighten sensibilities. They rejected the pursuit of wealth and careers and embraced plain living, authenticity, friendship, peace, and, especially, *freedom*. In a 1967 cover story, the editors of *Time* magazine suggested that "in their independence of material possessions and their emphasis on peacefulness and honesty, hippies lead considerably more virtuous lives than the great majority of their fellow citizens. . . . In the end, it may be that the hippies have not so much dropped out of American society as given it something to think about."

Both the counterculture and the New Left rejected the status quo, but most hippies preferred to "drop out" of mainstream society rather than try to change the political system. Their preferred slogan was "Make Love, Not War." Like the Beats of the fifties, hippies created their own subculture that promoted freedom from all traditional constraints. In all their technicolor variety, they were defiant, innocent, egalitarian, optimistic, and indulgent as they rejected the authority of the nation's core institutions: the family, government, political parties, corporations, the military, and colleges and universities. The "idea was to liberate yourself from the confining conventions of life and to celebrate the irrational side of your nature, kind of let yourself go," explained a student at the University of Chicago. "Do Your Own Thing" became their unofficial motto.

The counterculture lifestyle included an array of popular ideals and activities: peace, love, harmony, rock music, mystical religions, mind-altering drugs, casual sex, yoga, vegetarianism, organic food, and communal living. Hippie fashion featured rebelliously long hair for both women and men and

Flower power Hippies let loose at a 1967 love-in, one of many such gatherings that celebrated world peace, free love, and nontheological spirituality, often as a gesture of protest.

casual clothing that was striking, unusual, or, God forbid, comfortable: flowing cotton dresses, granny gowns, ragged bell-bottom blue jeans, tie-dyed T-shirts, love beads, Tibetan bells, peace symbols, black boots, and sandals. Young men grew beards and women stopped wearing makeup as badges of difference (or indifference).

Underground newspapers celebrating the aimless questing of the counterculture appeared in every large city, many of them with defiant names such as *Fuck You: A Magazine of the Arts*. A hippie magazine called *Avatar* asked, "Who is the underground?" Its answer: "You are, if you think, dream, work, and build towards the improvements and changes in your life, your social and personal environments, towards the expectations of a better existence. . . . Think, look around, maybe in a mirror, maybe inside."

DO YOUR OWN THING The countercultural rebels were primarily middle-class whites alienated by the Vietnam War, racism, political corruption, and parental authority. In their view, a superficial materialism had settled over mainstream life, which they defied by embracing the pathway to freedom popularized by former Harvard clinical psychology professor Timothy Leary: "Tune in, turn on, drop out."

Leary, the self-styled high priest of the psychedelic revolution, had been dismissed by Harvard in 1963 for using students in experiments with hallucinatory drugs (one high student tried to eat the bark off a tree). In 1966, Leary formed the League of Spiritual Discovery (LSD) to lobby for decriminalization of mind-altering drugs. He promised his mostly young supporters that "proper drugs and rock music can make everybody young forever." He assured audiences that he had "a blueprint [for a new mind-altering religion], and we're going to change society in the next ten years."

Leary's crusade on behalf of expanded consciousness frightened most Americans, for LSD ruined many young people, some of whom committed suicide under its influence. President Richard Nixon called Leary "the most dangerous man in America." Leary responded by announcing his candidacy for the governorship of California, Nixon's home state. John Lennon of the Beatles wrote his campaign song, "Come Together."

Soon thereafter, however, Leary was forced to give up politics and psychedelics for a long prison sentence, having been convicted in California of possessing marijuana. The judge called him "an insidious menace" to society and a "pleasure–seeking, irresponsible, Madison Avenue advocate of the free use of LSD." Six months later, however, prisoner Leary pulled off a dramatic penitentiary escape and with the help of friends left the country. He was ultimately captured in Afghanistan and returned to prison in California, where he was a jailmate of mass murderer Charles Manson.

"EIGHT MILES HIGH" As Leary hoped, illegal drugs—marijuana, amphetamines, cocaine, peyote, hashish, heroin, and LSD, the "Acid Test"— became commonplace within the counterculture. Said SDS veteran Todd Gitlin, "More and more, to get access to youth culture" in the late 1960s, "you had to get high." The Byrds sang about getting "Eight Miles High," and Bob Dylan proclaimed that "everybody must get stoned!"

Getting stoned was one of the favorite activities of the millions who participated in the 1967 "Summer of Love," a series of nationwide events protesting the Vietnam War and celebrating the youth revolt. The initial event was actually held in the spring, on April 15, when a peace march in New York City attracted 300,000 participants, the most ever assembled for a single event up to that time.

The most publicized activity of the Summer of Love occurred in San Francisco, where more than 100,000 hippies ("flower children") converged in search of tribal intimacy. As author P. J. O'Rourke recalled, "You name it and I believed it" that summer. "I believed love was all you need. . . . I believed drugs could make you a better person. I believed I could hitchhike to California with

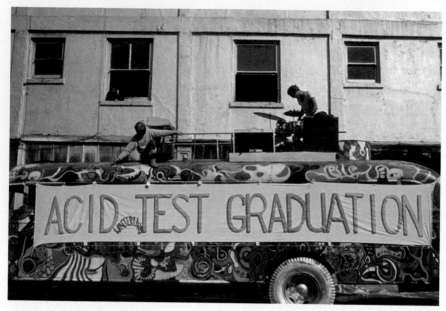

Acid Test Author Ken Kesey and his posse, the Merry Pranksters, held Acid Test Graduation parties throughout the San Francisco area that celebrated the psychedelic drug LSD (also known as "acid").

35 cents and people would be glad to feed me. . . . I believed the Age of Aquarius was about to happen. . . . With the exception of anything my parents said, I believed everything."

The loosely organized "Council for the Summer of Love" intended the gathering to be the first step in a grassroots revolution opposing the war in Vietnam by celebrating "hippiedom" and other alternative lifestyles.

That summer, the Beatles unwittingly provided the Summer of Love with its anthem when they issued one of their all-time best-selling songs, "All You Need Is Love"—a number-one hit worldwide.

THE YIPPIES The countercultural alternative to SDS and the New Left was the Youth International party, better known as the Yippies, founded in New York City on December 31, 1967, by two irreverent pranksters, Jerry Rubin and Abbie Hoffman. The Yippies were countercultural comedians bent on thumbing their noses at the "absurdity" of conventional laws and behavior and mocking capitalism and the consumer culture. Utterly alienated from mainstream life, they wanted "to offer the people an alternative lifestyle. Something to do other than conform or die." Their notion of community was modeled after their often superficial understanding of Native Americans: "a whole bunch of people living together, having children, none of them married."

Hoffman explained that their "conception of revolution is that it's fun." They wanted to form an alliance between hippies and Weathermen, a "blending of pot and politics," and overthrow the power structure. Rubin claimed that "the first part of the Yippie program is to kill your parents," since they are "our first oppressors." He added that the use of "psychedelic" drugs "signifies the total end of the Protestant ethic: screw work, we want to know ourselves." The Yippie platform called for peace in Vietnam, absolute personal freedom, free birth control and abortions, and legalization of marijuana and LSD. Hoffman had no interest in making the Yippies a traditional political organization. "We shall not defeat *Amerika* by organizing a political party," he declared. "We shall do it by building a new nation—a nation as rugged as the marijuana leaf."

The anarchistic Yippies organized marijuana "smoke-ins," threw pies at political figures, nominated a squealing pig for the presidency, urged voters to cast their ballots for "None of the Above," and threatened to put LSD in Chicago's water supply during the 1968 Democratic National Convention. When asked what being a Yippie meant, Hoffman replied, "Energy–fun–fierceness– exclamation point!"

COMMUNES For some, the counterculture involved experimenting with alternative living arrangements, especially "intentional communities" or "communes." Communal living in urban areas such as San Francisco's Haight-Ashbury district, New York's Greenwich Village, Chicago's Uptown, and Atlanta's 14th Street neighborhood were popular for a time, as were rural communes. Thousands of hippie romantics flocked to the countryside, eager to live in harmony with nature, coexist in love and openness, deepen their sense of self, and forge authentic community ties. "Out here," one of the rural communalists reflected, "we've got the earth and ourselves and God above. . . . We came for simplicity and to rediscover God."

Yet all but a handful of the back-to-the-land experiments collapsed within a few months or years. Almost none of the participants knew how to sustain a farm, and many were unwilling to do the hard work that living off the land required. "The hippies will not change America," a journalist predicted, "because change means pain, and the hippie subculture is rooted in the pleasure principle."

Little house on the commune This photograph of the members of the Family of the Mystic Arts commune in Oregon appeared on the cover of *Life* magazine's July 18, 1969, edition.

In 1968, *Newsweek* magazine reported "Trouble in Hippieland," noting that most flower children were "seriously disturbed youngsters" incapable of sustaining an alternative to mainstream life. In a candid reflection, a young hippie confessed that "we are so stupid, so unable to cope with anything practical." A resident of Paper Farm in northern California, which started in 1968 and collapsed a year later, said of its participants: "They had no commitment to the land—a big problem. All would take food from the land, but few would tend it. . . . We were entirely open. We did not say no [to anyone]. We felt this would make for a more dynamic group. But we got a lot of sick people."

WOODSTOCK The sixties counterculture thrived on music—initially folk "protest" songs and later psychedelic rock music. During the early sixties, Pete Seeger; Joan Baez; Peter, Paul, and Mary; and Bob Dylan, among others, produced powerful songs intended to spur social reform. In Dylan's "The Times They Are a-Changin'," he warns: "There's a battle outside and it's ragin' / It'll soon shake your windows and rattle your walls / For the times, they are a-changin'."

Within a few years, however, the hippies' favorite performers were those under the influence of mind-altering drugs, especially the San Francisco–based "acid rock" bands: Jefferson Airplane, Big Brother and the Holding Company, and the Grateful Dead. "Rock 'n roll was the tribal telegraph," remembered Jann Wenner, founder of *Rolling Stone* magazine.

Huge outdoor concerts—music-infused psychedelic picnics—were wildly popular. The largest and most publicized was the sprawling Woodstock Music and Art Fair ("Aquarian Exposition"). In mid-August 1969, more than 400,000 mostly young people converged on a 600-acre farm near the tiny rural town of Bethel, New York, for what was billed as the world's "largest happening," three days "of peace and music."

The festival boasted an all-star cast of musicians, among them Jimi Hendrix; Jefferson Airplane; Janis Joplin; Santana; the Who; Joan Baez; and Crosby, Stills and Nash. For three days amid heat, rain storms, and rivers of mud, the assembled flower children "grooved" on music, beer and booze, cheap marijuana, and casual sex. Baez described Woodstock as a "technicolor, mud-splattered reflection of the 1960s."

Woodstock's carefree "spirit of love" was short-lived, however. Just four months later, when other concert promoters tried to replicate the experience at the Altamont Speedway Free Festival near San Francisco, the counterculture fell victim to the criminal culture.

The Rolling Stones foolishly hired the Hells Angels motorcycle gang to provide "security" for their show. During the band's performance of "Under My Thumb," a drunken Hells Angel stabbed

Bob Dylan Born Robert Allen Zimmerman in northern Minnesota, Dylan helped transform the New York folk music scene, penning the anti-war movement anthem "Blowin' in the Wind."

to death an eighteen-year-old African American man wielding a gun in front of the stage. Three other spectators were killed that night. Much of the vitality and innocence of the counterculture died with them.

After 1969, the hippie phenomenon began to fade as the spirit of liberation ran up against the hard realities of poverty, drug addiction, crime, and mental and physical illness among the flower children. Yet strands of the counterculture survive in the popularity of ecology; yoga; meditation; "health foods" and organic farming; food co-ops; craft guilds; and digital social media promoting connectedness, sharing, and collaboration.

Social Activism Spreads

The same liberationist ideals that prompted young people to revolt against mainstream values and protest against the Vietnam War led many of them to embrace other causes. The civil rights movement inspired women, Latinos, and Native Americans, gays and lesbians, the elderly, and people with physical and mental disabilities to demand equal opportunities and equal rights. Still others joined the emerging environmental movement or groups working on behalf of consumers.

THE NEW FEMINISM

The first wave of the women's movement in the late nineteenth and early twentieth centuries had focused on gaining the right to vote. The second wave of the feminist movement, in the sixties and seventies, challenged the conventional ideal of female domesticity and worked to ensure that women gained equal treatment in the workplace.

Many women in the early 1960s, however, did not view gender equality as possible or even desirable. In 1962, more than two thirds of women surveyed agreed that the most important family decisions "should be made by the man of the house." Although the Equal Pay Act of 1963 had made it illegal to pay women less than men for doing the same job, discrimination and harassment continued. Women, who were 51 percent of the nation's population and held 37 percent of the jobs, were paid 42 percent less than men on average.

Betty Friedan, a forty-two-year-old mother of three from Peoria, Illinois, who supplemented her husband's income by writing articles for women's magazines, emerged as one of the leaders of the postwar **women's movement**. As a brilliant student at all-female Smith College in Massachusetts, she had edited the campus newspaper, arguing for non-intervention in the Second World War and unionization for the campus housekeepers. After the war, she worked as a journalist for progressive publications promoting labor unions. In her articles, Friedan called for equal pay for equal work and an end to gender and race-based discrimination in hiring and housing. Then, in 1963, she published her searing first book, *The Feminine Mystique*, which helped launch the second phase of the feminist movement. Rarely has a single book exercised such a transformational influence.

Friedan argued that her generation of upper- and middle-class college-educated white mothers and wives (she did not discuss working-class women, women of color, or women without husbands or suburban homes) had actually lost ground after the Second World War, when many left wartime employment and settled in suburbia as full-time wives and mothers, only to suffer from the "happy homemaker" syndrome that undermined their intellectual capacity and public aspirations. Suburban women of privilege, like herself, Friedan observed, "seemed suddenly incapable of any ambition, any vision, any passion, except the pursuit of a wedding ring."

She blamed the "enforced domesticity" of postwar America on a massive propaganda campaign by advertisers and women's magazines that brainwashed women to embrace the "feminine mystique," in which fulfillment came only with marriage and motherhood. Women, Friedan claimed, "were being duped into believing homemaking was their natural destiny."

The Feminine Mystique, an immediate best seller, forever changed American society by defining "the problem that has no name." Friedan inspired many well-educated, unfulfilled middle- and upper-class white women who felt trapped by household drudgery.

Moreover, Friedan discovered that there were far more women working outside the home than she had assumed. Many were frustrated by the

Betty Friedan Author of *The Feminine Mystique* and the first president of NOW.

demands of holding "two full-time jobs instead of just one—underpaid clerical worker and unpaid housekeeper." Perhaps most important, Friedan helped empower women to achieve their "full human capacities"—in the home, in schools, in offices, on college campuses, and in politics.

In 1966, Friedan and other activists founded the National Organization for Women (NOW) to serve as the NAACP for women. They chose the acronym NOW because it was part of a popular civil rights chant: "What do you want?" protesters yelled. "FREEDOM!" "When do you want it?" "NOW!"

NOW promoted "true equality for all women in America . . . as part of the worldwide revolution of human rights now taking place." It sought to end gender discrimination in the workplace and spearheaded efforts to legalize abortion and obtain federal and state support for child-care centers. Change came slowly, however. By 1970, there was still only one woman in the U.S. Senate, ten in the House of Representatives, and none on the Supreme Court or in the president's cabinet.

GLORIA STEINEM The women's movement received a boost from the energetic leadership provided by Gloria Steinem, who founded, with others, *Ms.* magazine in 1971. It was the first feminist periodical with a national readership.

Its first edition of 300,000 copies sold out in eight days, and at the end of the first year it enjoyed half a million subscribers. By writing scores of hard-hitting essays in *Ms.* and other national magazines, Steinem expanded the scope of feminism beyond what Betty Friedan and others had started.

Born in Toledo, Ohio, in 1934, Steinem grew up in a poor, dysfunctional family. By age ten, she became her family's primary caregiver. Gloria did not spend a full year in school until she was twelve, but by then she was reading a book a day on her own. To supplement her family's meager finances, she performed as a tap dancer and sales clerk before she earned a scholarship to Smith College, where she majored in government and political affairs. She graduated with honors in 1956 and earned a two-year fellowship for study in India.

Upon her return to America, Steinem began a career as a hard-nosed freelance investigative journalist living in New York City. In 1963, *Show* magazine hired her to go undercover as a scantily-clad Playboy "Bunny" at the New York City Playboy Club. The resulting article ("I Was a Playboy Bunny") detailed the degrading treatment and inequitable wages she and others received as sex objects wearing rabbit ears and cottontails. It also made Steinem famous. In 1968, she helped found *New York* magazine, which enabled her, the only woman on the staff, to write about political topics and progressive social issues.

A year later, in 1969, Steinem attended an event in Greenwich Village sponsored by the Redstockings, a radical feminist group, at which women stood and recounted their experience with abortion. Having had an illegal abortion in London at age twenty-two on her way to India, Steinem stood and told her story to the group of strangers. "Why should each of us," she asked, "be made to feel criminal or alone?"

That event proved to be life-changing, as Steinem sensed "a great blinding lightbulb" coming on in her head. She committed herself that night to advancing the women's liberation movement through advocacy journalism that gave voice to the voiceless. She resolved to engage in "outrageous acts and everyday rebellions."

Steinem thereafter became a prolific writer, fundraiser, and speaker, addressing numerous rallies, sit-ins, demonstrations, corporations, and organizations. She donated half her speaking fees to women's organizations and insisted on sharing the lectern with at least one woman of color to demonstrate that the women's liberation movement encompassed many diverse feminisms. "For twenty years," she recalled, "not a week went by when I wasn't on a plane" headed to give another public address.

Steinem soon became the public face and voice of the women's liberation movement, its celebrity diva and the icon of feminism. She was usually the first choice of reporters eager for provocative interviews and comments. As feminist scholar Rebecca Traister explained, Steinem was "young and white and pretty, and she looked great on magazine covers. I'm not deriding her. She tells this story about herself." Steinem testified before a Senate committee in 1970 on behalf of the Equal Rights Amendment, and co-founded the Women's Action Alliance, and the National Women's Political Caucus in 1971.

Steinem then joined forces with fellow journalists Patricia Carbine and Letty Cottin Pogrebin to launch *Ms.* magazine in December 1971 because there was "nothing for women to read that was controlled by women." The masthead of the first issue listed the editors alphabetically so as not to imply a hierarchy, because hierarchies were male and hence undesirable. The first issue included stories titled "Sisterhood," "Raising Kids without Sex Roles," and "Women Tell the Truth about Their Abortions." Just a few months later, *Ms.* shocked the publishing world in 1972 when it revealed the names of women who admitted to having had an abortion when the procedure was still illegal in most states.

Unlike other women's magazines, *Ms.* focused on controversial topics such as gender bias, sexual harassment, abortion, pornography, workplace equality, same-sex marriage, and college curricula. "We need Women's Studies courses just as much as Black Studies," Steinem insisted in 1971.

INNER TURMOIL Like every other movement for social justice, the feminist movement experienced internal tensions. Betty Friedan, famous for her prickly claim to the leadership spotlight of the feminist movement, grew jealous of Steinem's celebrity status and her hip glamour. Steinem had become famous for her tinted aviator glasses, belted mini-dresses, backless blouses, long brown hair streaked with signature blond highlights, white lipstick, and romances with powerful men. More important, Friedan accused Steinem and others of practicing a "female chauvinism" that was "corrupting our movement for equality." She bristled at Steinem's dismissal of conventional marriage as a form of "prostitution." Steinem replied that she was puzzled by Friedan's broadside. Male critics had long "falsely" accused her of liking men too much, yet now Friedan was falsely accusing her "of not liking them enough."

Other criticisms were more worrisome. The much-celebrated African American writer Alice Walker, an early *Ms.* contributor, resigned from the staff because the magazine covers featured too many whites and not enough blacks. Steinem persevered in the face of attacks from all sides. She was a gifted conciliator who always sought common ground in dealing with her critics.

FEMINIST VICTORIES In the early 1970s, she joined members of Congress, the Supreme Court, and NOW in advancing the cause of gender equality. A major victory occurred with the Congressional passage of Title IX of the Educational Amendments of 1972. It barred gender discrimination in any "education program or activity receiving federal financial assistance." Most notably applied to athletics, Title IX spurred female participation in high school sports to increase nearly tenfold and to almost double at the college level.

In large part because of the efforts of Steinem and other women activists, members of Congress, the Supreme Court, and NOW advanced the cause of gender equality. Title IX of the Educational Amendments of 1972 barred gender discrimination in any "education program or activity receiving federal financial assistance." Most notably applied to athletics, Title IX spurred female participation in high school sports to increase nearly tenfold and to almost double at the college level.

The women's movement also convinced Congress to approve overwhelmingly an equal-rights amendment (ERA) to the U.S. Constitution, which, if ratified by the states, would have required equal treatment for women throughout society and politics. By mid-1973, twenty-eight states had approved the amendment, ten short of the thirty-eight needed for approval.

In 1973, the Supreme Court, in its *Roe v. Wade* decision, struck down state laws forbidding abortions during the first three months of pregnancy. The Court ruled that women have a fundamental "right to choose" whether to bear a child or not, since pregnancy necessarily affects a woman's health and well-being. The *Roe v. Wade* decision, and the ensuing success of NOW's efforts to liberalize local and state abortion laws, generated a powerful conservative backlash, especially among Roman Catholics and evangelical Protestants, who mounted a "right-to-life" crusade that helped fuel the conservative political resurgence in the seventies and thereafter.

RADICAL FEMINISM During the late sixties, a new wave of younger, more-militant feminists emerged. They sought "women's liberation" from all forms of sexism (also called "male chauvinism" or "male oppression").

Many of the new feminists, often called "women's libbers," were veterans of the civil rights and anti-war movements. Having come to realize that male revolutionaries could be sexists, too, the women began meeting in small groups to discuss their opposition to the war and racism, only to discover at such "consciousness-raising" sessions that what bound them together was their shared grievances as women in a "man's world."

Gaining true liberation, many of them decided, required exercising "sexual politics" whereby women would organize their own political movement. Writer Robin Morgan captured this newly politicized feminism in the slogan, "The personal is political," a radical notion that Betty Friedan rejected. When

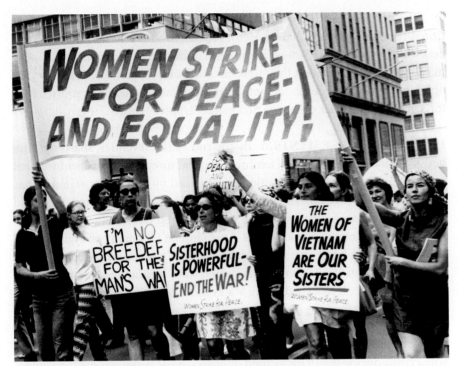

What women want The Women's Strike for Equality brought tens of thousands of women together on August 26, 1970, to march for gender equality and celebrate the fiftieth anniversary of the Nineteenth Amendment.

lesbians and bisexual women demanded a public role in the feminist movement, Friedan deplored the "lavender menace" of lesbianism as a divisive distraction that would only enrage their homophobic opponents. By 1973, however, NOW had endorsed gay and lesbian rights.

Friedan failed to dampen or deflect the younger generation of women activists, just as Martin Luther King Jr. had failed to suppress the Black Power movement. The goal of the women's liberation movement, said Susan Brownmiller, was to "go beyond a simple concept of equality. NOW's emphasis on legislative change left the radicals cold."

For women to be truly equal, many new feminists believed, *every* aspect of society needed to be transformed: child rearing, entertainment, domestic duties, business, and the arts. In pursuit of their goal, they took direct action, such as picketing the 1968 Miss America Pageant, burning copies of *Playboy* and other men's magazines, and tossing their bras and high-heeled shoes into "freedom cans."

They also formed radical organizations like WITCH (Women's International Terrorist Conspiracy from Hell), WRAP (Women's Radical Action Project), Keep on Truckin' Sisters, Radicalesbians, and the Redstockings, whose manifesto proclaimed that they were tired of being exploited by men "as sex objects, breeders, domestic servants, and cheap labor." Members sported buttons proclaiming their collective nickname: "Uppity Women."

FRACTURED FEMINISM By the end of the seventies, sharp disputes between moderate and radical feminists had fractured the women's movement in ways similar to the fragmentation experienced by civil rights organizations a decade earlier. The movement's failure to broaden its appeal much beyond white middle class heterosexual women also caused reform efforts to stall.

Ratification of the Equal Rights Amendment ("Equality of rights under the law shall not be denied or abridged by the United States or by any State on account of sex") was stymied in several state legislatures by conservative groups. By 1982, it had died, three states short of ratification. Conservatives saw the defeat of the ERA as a triumph. They drew much of their strength from the backlash against changing social attitudes about women's roles.

Yet the successes of the women's movement endured. The women fighting for equal rights during the 1970s focused on several basic issues: gender discrimination in the workplace; equal pay for equal work; an equal chance at jobs traditionally reserved for men; the availability of high-quality, government-subsidized child-care centers; and easier access to birth-control devices, prenatal care, and abortion. Feminists also helped win improvements in divorce laws. In 1970, only forty percent of women favored fighting for equal rights; by 2013, the number was 82 percent.

Conservative women speak
The anti-feminist campaign, STOP ERA ("Stop Taking Our Privileges, Equal Rights Amendment"), found its most outspoken activist in Phyllis Schlafly, a constitutional lawyer and staunch conservative.

Feminists called attention to issues long hidden or ignored. In 1970, for example, 36 percent of the nation's "poor" families were headed by women, as were most urban families dependent on federal welfare services. Nearly 3 million poor children needed access to day-care centers, but there were places for only 530,000.

The feminist movement helped women achieve mass entry into the labor market and enjoy steady improvements toward equal pay and treatment. In 1960, some 38 percent of women were working outside the home; by 1980, an estimated 52 percent were doing so.

Their growing presence in the labor force brought women a greater share of economic and political influence. By 1976, more than half of married women, and nine of ten female college graduates, were employed outside the home, a development that one economist called "the single most outstanding phenomenon of this century." Women also enrolled in graduate and professional schools in record numbers. During the 1970s, women began winning elected offices at the local, state, and national levels.

Birth control To spread the word about birth-control options, Planned Parenthood in 1967 displayed posters like this one in New York City buses.

THE SEXUAL REVOLUTION AND THE PILL The feminist movement coincided with the so-called sexual revolution. Americans became more tolerant of premarital sex, and women became more sexually active. Between 1960 and 1975, the number of college women engaging in heterosexual sexual intercourse doubled, to 50 percent.

Enabling this change, in large part, was the birth-control pill, approved for public use by the Food and Drug Administration in 1960. Widespread access to the pill gave women a greater sense of sexual freedom and led to more-open discussion of birth control, reproduction, and sexuality in general.

Although the pill contributed to a rise in sexually transmitted diseases, many women viewed it as an inexpensive, nonintrusive way to gain better control over their bodies, their careers, and their futures.

Latino Rights

The activism of student revolts, the civil rights movement, and the crusade for women's rights soon spread to other marginalized groups. The word *Latino*, referring to people who trace their ancestry to Spanish-speaking Latin America, came into use after 1945 in conjunction with growing efforts to promote economic and social justice.

Labor shortages during the Second World War had led defense industries to offer Latino Americans their first significant access to skilled-labor jobs. And as with African Americans, service in the military helped to heighten an American identity among Latino Americans and increase their desire for equal rights and social opportunities.

Social equality, however, remained elusive for people of color. Latino Americans still faced widespread discrimination in hiring, housing, and education after the war. Latino American activists denounced segregation; called for improved public schools; and struggled to increase their political influence, economic opportunities, and visibility in the curricula of schools and colleges.

Latino civil rights leaders faced an awkward dilemma: what should they do about the stream of undocumented Mexicans flowing across the border into the United States? Many Latino Americans argued that their hopes for economic advancement and social equality were threatened by the influx of Mexican laborers willing to accept low-paying jobs. In 1964, Latino American leaders helped end the *bracero* program, which trucked in contract day laborers from Mexico during harvest season.

THE UNITED FARM WORKERS In 1965, Latino American workers formed their own civil rights organization, the **United Farm Workers (UFW)**. Its founder was the charismatic Cesar Chavez. Born in 1927 in Yuma, Arizona, the son of Mexican immigrants, Chavez spent his youth shuttling with his family to various farm camps. The family often earned only a dollar a day as fruit pickers. Chavez and his siblings went barefoot and attended 40 different schools. During the Second World War, he served in the U.S. Navy. Afterward, he was a migrant laborer and community organizer focused on registering Latinos to vote.

In 1962 Chavez formed the Farm Workers' Association. Like the earlier farm Alliances, it was more than a union. It was *La Causa*, a broad social movement intended to enhance the solidarity and dignity of migrant farm workers. By 1965, he and Dolores Huerta converted the Farm Workers' Association into the United Farm Workers (UFW), a union for migrant lettuce workers and grape pickers, many of them undocumented immigrants who could be deported at any time. Over the next ten years, Chavez led some of the poorest workers in the nation in a series of nonviolent protest marches, staged hunger strikes, and managed nationwide boycotts. Workers were spellbound by his humility, his integrity, and his sincere dedication to improving the quality of their lives.

The United Farm Workers gained national attention in September 1965 when it joined with Filipino migrant workers in organizing a strike (*la huelga*) against grape growers in California's San Joaquin Valley. Their grievance

Cesar Chavez The usually energetic Chavez is visibly weakened from what would be a twenty-five-day hunger strike in support of the United Farm Workers Union in March 1968. Robert F. Kennedy, a great admirer of Chavez, is seated to his right.

focused on wages; they earned about $1,350 a year. As Huerta explained, "We have to get farmworkers the same type of benefits, the same type of wages, and the respect that they deserve because they do the most sacred work of all. They feed our nation every day."

Chavez's relentless energy and deep Catholic faith, his insistence upon nonviolent tactics, his reliance upon college-student volunteers, his skillful alliance with organized labor and religious groups, and his simple lifestyle attracted popular support in a strike that would last five years.

In 1968, Chavez began a twenty-five-day hunger strike to raise national attention for his efforts. On the day he broke his fast, the first to greet him was Robert F. Kennedy, then campaigning for the Democratic presidential nomination. "The world must know, from this time forward, that the migrant farm worker, the Mexican-American, is coming into his own rights," Kennedy declared, adding that the farmworkers were gaining "a special kind of citizenship. . . . You are winning it for yourselves—and therefore no one can ever take it away."

Finally, in 1970, the grape growers agreed to raise wages, offer health benefits, and improve working conditions. Chavez then turned his attention to political activism, organizing voter registration drives and advocating laws to protect the civil rights of migrant workers.

As Chavez recognized, the chief strength of the Latino rights movement lay less in the tactics of sit-ins and protest marches than in the rapid growth of the Latino American population. From 1970 to 2019, their numbers grew from 9 million (4.8 percent of the total population) to 60 million, making them the nation's largest ethnic group (17 percent). The increased population of Latinos in key electoral states has given them significant political clout.

NATIVE AMERICANS' QUEST FOR EQUALITY

American Indians—many of whom began calling themselves *Native Americans*—also emerged as a political force in the late 1960s. Two conditions combined to make Indian rights a priority. First, many whites felt guilty for the destructive actions of their ancestors toward a people who had, after all, been here first. Second, Indian unemployment was ten times the national rate, life expectancy was twenty years lower than the national average, and the suicide rate was a hundred times higher than the rate for whites.

Although President Lyndon Johnson attempted to funnel federal anti-poverty-program funds to reservations, many Native American activists grew impatient with the pace of change. Those promoting "**Red Power**" organized protests and demonstrations against local, state, and federal agencies.

On November 20, 1969, fourteen Red Power activists occupied Alcatraz Island near San Francisco. Over the next several months, hundreds of others, mostly students, joined them. The Nixon administration responded by cutting off electrical service and telephone lines. Stranded without power and fresh water, most of the protesters left the island. Finally, on June 11, 1971, the government removed the remaining fifteen Native Americans.

In 1968, the year before the Alcatraz occupation, George Mitchell and Dennis Banks, two Chippewas (or Ojibwas) living in Minneapolis, founded the American Indian Movement (AIM). In October 1972, AIM organized the Trail of Broken Treaties caravan, which traveled by bus and car from the West Coast to Washington, D.C., to draw attention to the federal government's broken promises. When Nixon administration officials refused to meet with them, the protesters barged into the offices of the Bureau of Indian Affairs. The sit-in ended when government negotiators agreed to renew discussions of Native American grievances.

In 1973, AIM led 200 Sioux in the occupation of the tiny South Dakota village of Wounded Knee, where the U.S. Seventh Cavalry had massacred an entire Sioux village in 1890. Newly outraged by the light sentences given a group of local whites who had killed a Sioux just a year earlier, the organizers sought to draw attention to the plight of Native Americans and took eleven hostages.

Standoff at Wounded Knee After occupying Wounded Knee and taking eleven hostages, members of the American Indian Movement and the Oglala Sioux stand guard outside of the town's Sacred Heart Catholic Church.

Federal marshals and FBI agents surrounded the encampment. When AIM leaders tried to bring in food and supplies, a shoot-out erupted, with two activists killed and a U.S. Marshal shot and paralyzed. The confrontation ended with a government promise to reexamine Indian treaty rights.

Indian protesters subsequently discovered a more effective tactic: they went into federal courts armed with copies of old treaties and demanded that the documents become the basis for financial restitution for the lands taken from them. In Alaska, Maine, South Carolina, and Massachusetts, the groups won substantial settlements that officially recognized their tribal rights and helped to upgrade the standard of living on several reservations.

GAY AND LESBIAN RIGHTS

The liberationist impulses of the sixties also encouraged gay, lesbian, and transgender people, long defamed as sinful or mentally unbalanced, to assert their right to be treated as equals. Throughout the 1960s, this population continued to encounter social and institutional discrimination. Many local ordinances and state laws deemed non-heterosexual behavior a vice crime, meaning an activity deemed illegal because it "offended" the moral standards of the community.

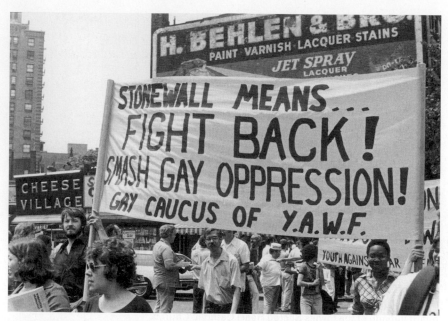

Gay/lesbian pride in the seventies Activists march in the Annual Gay Pride Day demonstration, commemorating the fifth anniversary of the Stonewall riots that sparked what became the modern LGBTQ (lesbian, gay, bisexual, transgender, and queer) rights movement in the United States.

On Saturday night, June 28, 1969, New York City vice police raided the Stonewall Inn, a popular gay bar in Greenwich Village. The patrons, led by transgender women of color, drag queens, and street people, fought back, and the struggle spilled outside, forcing the outnumbered police to take shelter inside the bar. One participant described the rioting as "a public assertion of real anger by gay people that was just electric."

The **Stonewall riots** lasted five days, during which the Stonewall Inn burned down. When the turmoil ended, gays had forged a sense of solidarity embodied in two new organizations, the Gay Liberation Front and the Gay Activists' Alliance, both of which focused on ending discrimination and harassment against gay, lesbian, bisexual, and transgender people.

As news of the Stonewall rebellion spread, the gay rights movement grew. By 1973, almost 800 organizations supporting sexual orientation and gender identification rights had emerged. That year, the American Psychiatric Association removed homosexuality from its official diagnostic manual of mental disorders. Colleges and universities began offering courses and majors in gay/lesbian studies (what would come to be called queer studies), and groups began pushing for official government recognition of same-sex marriages. As with the civil rights and women's movements, however, the campaign for gay/lesbian rights soon suffered from internal divisions and a conservative counterattack.

Nixon and the Revival of Conservatism

The turmoil of the sixties spawned a cultural backlash from what President Richard Nixon called the "great silent majority" of middle-class Americans who had propelled him to victory in 1968. Elected as the representative of middle America, his voters were fed up with liberal politics, hippies, radical feminism, gay and lesbian rights, and **affirmative-action** programs that gave preferential treatment to people of color and women to atone for past injustices.

THE CONSERVATIVE BACKLASH Alabama's Democratic governor, George Wallace, led the conservative white backlash against the counterculture. "Liberals, intellectuals, and long hairs," he shouted, "have run the country for too long." He repeatedly attacked "welfare queens," unmarried African American mothers he claimed "were breeding children as a cash crop" to receive federal child-support checks. Wallace became the voice for many working-class whites fed up with political liberalism and social radicalism.

All in the Family, the most popular television show in the 1970s, showcased the decade's culture wars. In the much-celebrated sitcom, the Bunker family lived in a working-class suburb of New York City. Semiliterate Archie Bunker (played by Carroll O'Connor), a Polish American loading-dock worker, was the gruff but lovable head of the family, a proud Republican, Nixon supporter, and talkative member of the silent majority who railed against blacks, Jews, Italians, gays, feminists, hippies, and liberals (including his live-in daughter and her hippie husband). At one point, he said: "I ain't no bigot. I'm the first guy to say, 'It ain't your fault that youse are colored.'"

The producer of the series, Norman Lear, sought to provoke viewers to question their own prejudices. In fact, however, many of the 50 million people watching each Saturday night identified *with* Archie's values.

RICHARD NIXON Richard Nixon courted working- and middle-class whites who feared that America was being corrupted by permissiveness, anarchy, and the tyranny of the rebellious minority. He explicitly appealed to voters "who did not break the law, people who pay their taxes and go to work, people who send their children to school, who go to their churches, people who are not haters, people who love this country." Above all, he promised to restore "law and order," by which he meant using brute force against African Americans protesting in the streets, and "cracking down" on anti-war protesters, civil rights demonstrators, and activists who challenged traditional gender roles.

In 1952, Senator Robert A. Taft of Ohio, known as "Mr. Republican," had characterized young Senator Nixon as a "little man in a big hurry" with "a mean and vindictive streak." A grocer's son from Whittier, California, Nixon was a humorless man of fierce ambition and extraordinary perseverance. Raised in a family that struggled with poverty, he had to claw and struggle to the top, and he nursed a deep resentment of people who had enjoyed an easier time (the "moneyed class").

Like Lyndon Johnson, Nixon was a paradoxical character, an introvert operating in the extroverted vocation of politics. He was smart, cunning, and doggedly determined to succeed in politics. Cold and calculating, he divided the world into enemies and friends and allowed his paranoia and vengefulness to isolate him from political reality—and from his family. He and his wife, Pat, had separate bedrooms for most of their marriage. He even wrote sterile memos to her with the salutation, "To Mrs. Nixon, from the President."

Prone to eruptions of ferocious temper, Nixon was also famously hard to get to know. Republican senator Barry Goldwater described Nixon as "the most complete loner I've ever known." White House staffers reported that even the family dog, an Irish setter, avoided Nixon.

Nixon displayed violent mood swings (punctuated by alcohol abuse), raging temper tantrums, profanity, and anti-Semitic outbursts. He was driven as much by anger and resentment as by civic duty. Critics nicknamed him "Tricky Dick" because he excelled at deceit. In his speech accepting the Republican nomination in 1968, Nixon pledged "to find the truth, to speak the truth, and live with the truth." In fact, however, he often did the opposite. One of his presidential aides admitted that "we did often lie, mislead, deceive, try to use [the media], and to con them."

NIXON'S APPOINTMENTS In his first term, Nixon selected for his cabinet and staff only white men who would blindly carry out his orders. John Mitchell, the gruff attorney general who had been a senior partner in Nixon's New York law firm, was his closest confidant. H. R. (Bob) Haldeman, a former advertising executive, served as chief of staff. Nixon called him his "chief executioner." As Haldeman explained, "Every President needs a son of a bitch, and I'm Nixon's." John Ehrlichman, a Seattle attorney and college schoolmate of

Haldeman, was chief domestic-policy adviser. John W. Dean III, an associate deputy in the office of the U.S. Attorney General, became the White House legal counsel.

Nixon tapped as secretary of state his friend William Rogers, who had served as attorney general under Dwight D. Eisenhower. The president, however, virtually ignored Rogers while forging an unlikely partnership with Dr. Henry Kissinger, a brilliant German-born Jew and Harvard political scientist who had become the nation's leading foreign-policy expert. Kissinger's thick accent, owlish appearance, and outsized ego had helped to make him an international celebrity, courted by presidents of both parties. In 1969, Nixon named Kissinger his national security adviser, and in 1973 Kissinger became secretary of state, although in private Nixon called him "my Jew-boy."

Both Nixon and Kissinger were outsiders who preferred operating in secret; both were insecure and even paranoid at times; and both mistrusted and envied the other's power and prestige. Nixon would eventually tire of Kissinger's efforts at self-promotion and frequent threats to resign.

For his part, Kissinger lavished praise on Nixon in public, but in private he dismissed the president as an insecure man with a "meatball mind" who went on frequent stress-induced drinking binges. (To his aides, Kissinger frequently referred to Nixon as "our drunken friend.") Yet for all their differences, they worked well together, in part because they both loved intrigue, power politics, and diplomatic flexibility, and in part because of their shared vision of a multipolar world order that was beginning to replace the bipolar cold war.

THE SOUTHERN STRATEGY A major reason for Nixon's election victories in 1968 and 1972 was his shrewd southern strategy, designed to win over white southern Democrats angered by the civil rights revolution. The majority of white southern voters were religious and patriotic, fervently anti-Communist and anti-union, and skeptical of social-welfare programs benefiting people of color.

For a century, whites in the South had steadfastly voted for Democrats. This trend reflected lingering resentments, dating to the Civil War and Reconstruction, against Abraham Lincoln and his Republican successors for imposing northern ways of life on the South, including racial integration. During the late 1960s and 1970s, however, a surging economy and a spurt of population growth began to transform the South.

Between 1970 and 1990, the South's population grew by 40 percent, a rate of more than twice the national average. The region's warm climate, low cost of living, absence of labor unions, low taxes, and government incentives for economic development convinced waves of businesses to relocate there. During the 1970s, the rate of job growth in the South was seven times greater than in New York and Pennsylvania.

Southern "redneck" culture suddenly became the rage as the nation embraced stock car racing, cowboy boots, pickup trucks, barbecue, and country music. Rapid population growth—and the continuing spread of air-conditioning—brought the sunbelt states of the South, the Southwest, and California more congressional seats and more electoral votes. Every president elected between 1964 and 2008 had roots in the Sun Belt.

Nixon's favorite singer, country star Merle Haggard, crooned in his smash hit, "Okie from Muskogee": "We don't smoke marijuana in Muskogee / We don't take our trips on LSD / We don't burn our draft cards down on Main Street / We like livin' right and bein' free." Haggard's conservative working-class fans bristled at anti-war protesters, hippies, rising taxes, social-welfare programs, and civil rights activism. The alienation of many blue-collar whites from the Democratic party, the demographic changes transforming sunbelt states, and the white backlash against court-ordered integration created a fertile opportunity to gain southern votes that the Republican party eagerly exploited.

In the 1968 presidential campaign, Nixon won over traditionally Democratic white working-class voters. He cleverly "played the race card," assuring white conservatives that he would appoint justices to the Supreme Court who would undermine federal enforcement of civil rights laws, such as mandatory school busing to achieve racial integration and affirmative-action programs that gave women and people of color priority in hiring decisions and the awarding of government contracts. Nixon also appealed to the economic concerns of middle-class southern whites by promising lower tax rates and less government regulation.

In the 1972 election, Nixon easily carried every southern state. The Republican takeover of the Solid South was the greatest political realignment since Franklin D. Roosevelt's election in 1932. It was also an unlikely coalition, for it brought together traditional "country club" Republicans—corporate executives, financiers, and investors—with poor, rural, fundamentalist southerners who had always voted for segregationist Democrats. What they shared was a simmering hatred for what the Democratic party had become.

NIXON'S DOMESTIC AGENDA Richard Nixon shared with his predecessors John Kennedy and Lyndon Johnson an urge to increase presidential power. All three believed that the presidency had become the central source of governmental action, that foreign policy should be managed from the White House rather than the State Department, and that the president had the authority to wage war without a congressional declaration of war.

Nixon was less a rigid conservative ideologue than a crafty politician. Forced to deal with a Congress controlled by Democrats, he chose his battles carefully and showed surprising flexibility, leading journalist Tom Wicker to describe him as "at once liberal and conservative, generous and begrudging, cynical and idealistic, choleric and calm, resentful and forgiving."

Nixon focused during his first term on developing policies and programs that would please conservatives and ensure his reelection. To recruit conservative Democrats, he touted his New Federalism, which sent federal money to state and local governments to spend as they saw fit. He also disbanded the core agency of Lyndon Johnson's war on poverty—the Office of Economic Opportunity—and cut funding to several Great Society programs.

At the same time, Democrats in Congress passed significant legislation that Nixon signed: the right of eighteen-year-olds to vote in national elections (1970) and in all elections under the Twenty-Sixth Amendment (1971); increases in Social Security benefits and food-stamp funding; the Occupational Safety and Health Act (1970) to ensure safer workplace environments; and the Federal Election Campaign Act (1971), which modified the rules governing corporate financial donations to political campaigns.

NIXON AND CIVIL RIGHTS During his first term, President Nixon followed through on campaign pledges to blunt the momentum of the civil rights movement. He appointed no African Americans to his cabinet and refused to meet with the all-Democratic Congressional Black Caucus. "We've had enough social programs: forced integration, education, housing," he told his chief of staff. "People don't want more [people] on welfare. They don't want to help the working poor, and our mood needs to be harder on this, not softer."

He also launched a concerted effort to block congressional renewal of the Voting Rights Act of 1965 and to delay implementation of federal court orders requiring the racial desegregation of school districts in Mississippi. Sixty-five lawyers in the Justice Department signed a letter protesting Nixon's

Off to school Because of violent protests by whites against forced desegregation, school buses in Boston were escorted by police in 1974.

stance. The Democratic-controlled Congress extended the Voting Rights Act over Nixon's veto.

The Supreme Court also thwarted Nixon's efforts to slow desegregation. In its first decision under the new chief justice, Warren Burger—a Nixon appointee—the Court ordered the racial integration of the Mississippi public schools in *Alexander v. Holmes County Board of Education* (1969). During Nixon's first term, more schools were desegregated under court order than in all the Kennedy–Johnson years combined.

The Burger Court also ruled unanimously in *Swann v. Charlotte-Mecklenburg Board of Education* (1971) that school systems must bus students out of their neighborhoods if necessary to achieve racially integrated schools. Protests over busing erupted in the North, the Midwest, and the Southwest, as white families denounced the destruction of "the neighborhood school." Angry white parents in Pontiac, Michigan, were so determined to stop mandatory busing that they boycotted the schools and firebombed ten empty school buses.

NIXON AND ENVIRONMENTAL PROTECTION During the seventies, dramatic increases in the price of oil and gasoline fueled a major energy crisis. Natural resources grew limited—and increasingly precious. Nixon recognized that the public mood had shifted in favor of greater federal environmental protections, especially after two widely publicized environmental events in 1969.

Environmental awareness An Earth Day demonstration dramatizing the dangers of air pollution, April 1972.

The first was a massive oil spill off the coast of Santa Barbara, California, when a slick of crude oil contaminated 200 miles of California beaches, killing thousands of sea birds and marine animals. Six months later, on June 22, 1969, the Cuyahoga River, an eighty-mile-long stream that slices through Cleveland, Ohio, spontaneously caught fire. Fouled with oil and grease, bubbling with subsurface gases, and littered with debris, the river burned for five days.

The images of the burning river helped raise environmental awareness. A 1969 survey of college campuses by the *New York Times* revealed that many young people were transferring their idealism from the anti-war movement to the environmental movement.

Nixon knew that if he vetoed legislative efforts to improve environmental quality, the Democratic majorities in Congress would overrule him, so he chose not to stand in the way. Soon after becoming president, Nixon told John Ehrlichman, "Just keep me out of trouble on environmental issues."

In late 1969, he signed the amended Endangered Species Preservation Act and the National Environmental Policy Act. The latter became effective on January 1, 1970, the year that environmental groups established an annual Earth Day celebration. In 1970, Nixon signed an executive order that created two federal agencies, the **Environmental Protection Agency (EPA)** and the National Oceanic and Atmospheric Administration (NOAA), and signed the Clean Air Act. Two years later, he vetoed a new clean water act, only to see Congress override him. He also undermined many new environmental laws by refusing to spend money appropriated by Congress to fund them.

"**STAGFLATION**" The major domestic development during the Nixon administration was a floundering economy. The accumulated expense of the Vietnam War and the Great Society programs helped quadruple the annual inflation rate from 3 percent in 1967 to 12 percent in 1974. Meanwhile, unemployment, at only 3.3 percent when Nixon took office, hit 6 percent by the end of 1970.

Economists coined the term "**stagflation**" to describe the simultaneous problems of stalled economic growth (stagnation), rising inflation, and high unemployment. Consumer prices usually rose with a rapidly growing economy and rising employment. This was just the reverse, and there were no easy ways to fight the unusual combination of recession and inflation.

Stagflation had at least three causes. First, the Johnson administration had financed both the Great Society social-welfare programs and the Vietnam War without a major tax increase, thereby generating large federal deficits, a major expansion of the money supply, and price inflation. Second, U.S. companies were facing stiff competition from West Germany, Japan, and other emerging international industrial powers. Third, America's prosperity since 1945 had resulted in part from the ready availability of cheap sources of energy. No other nation was more dependent upon the automobile, and no other nation was more wasteful in its use of fossil fuels. During the seventies, however, oil and gasoline became scarcer and costlier. High energy prices and oil shortages took their toll on the economy.

It was oil that complicated U.S. foreign policies in the Middle East. The longstanding American commitment to the security of Israel clashed with

Arab countries determined to engineer the Jewish nation's destruction. In late May 1967, Israeli intelligence services discovered that Egypt, Jordan, Iraq, and Palestinian forces were preparing an attack. On June 5, Israeli forces launched a surprise preemptive air strike, destroying most of Egypt's and Syria's warplanes. Israeli tanks and infantry then captured the Gaza Strip, much of Egypt's Sinai Peninsula, the West Bank of the Jordan River, and East Jerusalem.

After just six days of fighting, the Arab nations requested a cease fire, which the United Nations helped to negotiate. Egypt, Syria, and Jordan had suffered more than 18,000 killed or wounded, compared with only 700 casualties for Israel.

The lopsided Six-Day War had long-range consequences, as the Israelis took control of strategic Syrian and Egyptian territories that almost doubled the nation's size. More important, the war launched a new phase in the perennial conflict between Israel and the nation-less Palestinians. The brief conflict uprooted hundreds of thousands of Palestinian refugees and brought more than one million Palestinians in the occupied territories under Israeli rule.

In 1973, tensions between Israel and its Arab neighbors again boiled over, and the United States was caught in the crossfire. When Egypt and Syria attacked Israel on Yom Kippur, the holiest day on the Jewish calendar, President Nixon sent massive aid to Israel. In response, the Arab members of the Organization of Petroleum Exporting Countries (OPEC) convinced the group to cut off oil shipments to America.

President Nixon warned Americans that the nation was facing "the most acute shortage of energy since World War II." He asked commercial airlines to reduce flights, lowered the speed limit on federal highways from 70 to 55, halted plans to convert electricity-generating plants from coal to oil, and urged all Americans to conserve energy.

The Arab oil embargo caused gasoline shortages and skyrocketing prices. Motorists suddenly faced mile-long lines at gas stations. "These people are like animals foraging for food," said a gas station owner. "If I can't sell them gas, they threaten to beat you up, wreck

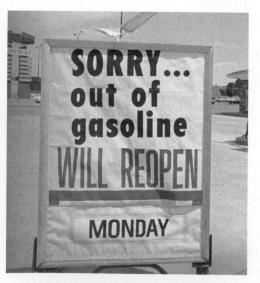

Oil crisis, 1973 The embargo of imported Arab oil forced the rationing of gasoline. Gas stations, such as this one in Colorado, closed on Sundays to conserve supplies.

your station, or run you over with a car." To manage the crisis, the federal government created a gas-rationing program: service stations would be open on alternate days to drivers with license plates ending in odd or even numbers.

Another condition leading to stagflation was people flooding into the workforce—mainly baby boomers and women. From 1965 to 1980, the number of people seeking work grew by almost 30 million, but there weren't enough new jobs to keep up with demand, so many were left unemployed.

The Nixon administration responded erratically and ineffectively to the stagflation crisis. First, the president sought to reduce the federal deficit by raising taxes and cutting the budget. When the Democratic Congress refused to cooperate, he encouraged the Federal Reserve Board to reduce the nation's money supply by raising interest rates. The stock market immediately nosedived, and the economy plunged into the "Nixon recession."

In 1969, when asked about the possibility of imposing government caps on wages and prices, Nixon had been clear: "Oh, my God, no! . . . We'll never go to controls." In 1971, however, he reversed himself and froze wages and prices for ninety days, arguing that doing so would generate a "new prosperity: more jobs, more incomes, more profits, without inflation and without war." But the economy remained sluggish.

"Peace with Honor": Ending the Vietnam War

Since 1945, the United States had lost its monopoly on nuclear weapons, its overwhelming economic dominance, and much of its geopolitical influence. The rapid rise of competing power centers in Europe, China, and Japan further complicated international relations and the cold war.

Richard Nixon and Henry Kissinger developed a comprehensive plan for a new world order that would defuse the cold war by pursuing peaceful coexistence with the Soviets and Chinese. Preoccupied with secrecy, they bypassed the State Department and Congress between 1969 and 1973 in their efforts to take advantage of shifting world events.

Their immediate task was to end the war in Vietnam. Until all troops had returned home, the social harmony that Nixon had promised would remain elusive. Privately, he had decided by 1969 that "there's no way to win the war," so he sought what he and Kissinger called "peace with honor." That is, the United States needed to withdraw in a way that upheld the credibility of its military alliances around the world. Peace, however, was long in coming, not honorable, and shockingly brief.

GRADUAL WITHDRAWAL (1969–1973) The Vietnam policy implemented by Nixon and Kissinger moved along three fronts in 1969. First, U.S. negotiators in Paris demanded the withdrawal of Viet Cong forces from South Vietnam and the preservation of the U.S.-backed government of President Nguyen Van Thieu. The North Vietnamese and Viet Cong negotiators insisted on retaining a Communist military presence in the south and reunifying the Vietnamese people under a government dominated by the Communists. Hidden from public awareness and from America's South Vietnamese allies were secret meetings between Kissinger and the North Vietnamese.

On the second front, Nixon sought to steadily reduce the number of U.S. troops in Vietnam, justifying the reduction as the natural result of "**Vietnamization**"—the equipping and training of South Vietnamese soldiers and pilots to assume the burden of combat. The president began withdrawing U.S. troops while expanding the bombing of North Vietnam to buy time for the transition. From a peak of 560,000 American troops in January 1969, only 50,000 remained in Vietnam by 1973.

In 1969, Nixon also established a draft lottery whereby the birthdates of nineteen-year-old men were randomly selected and assigned a number between 1 and 366. Those with low lottery numbers would be the first drafted into military service. The lottery system eliminated many inequities and clarified the likelihood of being drafted. Four years later, in 1973, the president ended the draft by creating an all-volunteer military.

These initiatives, coupled with the troop withdrawals, defused the anti-war movement, and opinion polls showed strong support for Nixon's war policies. "We've got those liberal bastards on the run now," the president gloated.

On the third front, Nixon and Kissinger greatly intensified the bombing of North Vietnam in hopes of pressuring the Communist leaders to end the war. Kissinger felt that "a fourth-rate power" like North Vietnam must have a "breaking point." Nixon agreed, suggesting that they let the North Vietnamese leaders know that he was so "obsessed about Communism" that he might use the "nuclear button" if necessary.

In March 1969, Nixon approved a secret fourteen-month-long bombing campaign aimed at Vietnamese forces using neighboring Cambodia as a base for raids into South Vietnam. The total tonnage of bombs dropped was four times that dropped on Japan during the Second World War. Still, Hanoi's leaders did not flinch.

Then, over a year later, on April 30, 1970, Nixon announced a U.S. military incursion into "neutral" Cambodia to "clean out" hidden Communist military bases. Privately, Nixon told Kissinger, who endorsed the decision, "If this doesn't work, it'll be your ass, Henry." Nixon knew that sending troops into

Cambodia would reignite the anti-war movement. Secretary of State William Rogers predicted that "this will make the [anti-war] students puke."

DIVISIONS AT HOME Strident public opposition to the war and Nixon's slow withdrawal of combat forces devastated the military's morale and reputation. "No one wants to be the last grunt to die in this lousy war," said one soldier. Between 1969 and 1971, there were 730 reported fragging incidents (efforts by troops to kill or injure their officers). In 1971, four times as many troops were hospitalized for drug overdoses as for combat-related wounds.

Revelations of atrocities committed by U.S. soldiers caused even the staunchest supporters of the war to wince. Late in 1969, the story of the My Lai Massacre exposed the country to the tale of William L. "Rusty" Calley, a twenty-six-year-old army lieutenant who ordered the murder of 347 Vietnamese civilians in the village of My Lai in 1968. One soldier described it as "point-blank murder, and I was standing there watching it."

Newsmagazines published gruesome photos of the massacre, and Americans debated the issues it raised. A father in northern California grumbled that Calley "would have been a hero" in the Second World War. His son shot back: "Yeah, if you were a Nazi." Twenty-five army officers were charged with complicity in the massacre and subsequent cover-up, but only Calley was convicted. Nixon later granted him parole.

The escalation of the air war in Vietnam and the extension of the war into Cambodia triggered widespread anti-war demonstrations. The president, however, was unmoved. "As far as this kind of activity is concerned," he gruffly explained, "we expect it; however, under no circumstances will I be affected whatever by it."

The news of the secret Cambodian incursion set off explosive demonstrations on college campuses. At Kent State University, the Ohio National Guard mobilized on May 4. As protesters hurled insults and rocks at

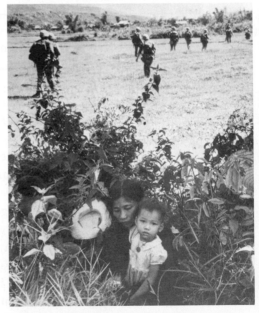

Hidden A Vietnamese mother hides with her child in the bushes near My Lai in 1968 after U.S. soldiers murdered Vietnamese villagers.

Shooting at Kent State Mary Ann Vecchio, a teenage runaway participating in the anti-war demonstration, decries the killing of a Kent State student after the National Guard fired into the crowd.

them, the poorly trained guardsmen panicked and opened fire. Four people, all bystanders, were killed, and thirteen students were wounded. Four of Kissinger's aides resigned in protest. Over 200 State Department staffers sent a petition to Secretary of State Rogers protesting the expansion of the war. Nixon responded to such insubordination by demanding that "all those sons of bitches are fired."

The killings at Kent State added new fury to the anti-war and anti-Nixon movements. That spring, demonstrations occurred on more than 350 campuses.

A presidential commission charged with investigating the shootings concluded that they were "unnecessary and unwarranted." Not all agreed. A resident of Kent told a reporter that "anyone who appears on the streets of a city like Kent with long hair, dirty clothes, or barefooted deserves to be shot. . . . It would have been better if the Guard had shot the whole lot of them."

Singer Neil Young had a different view. Shortly after the killings, he composed a song called "Ohio":

Tin soldiers and Nixon's coming.

We're finally on our own.

This summer I hear the drumming.

Four dead in Ohio.

The Ohio governor banned radio stations from playing the song, which only made it more popular.

Eleven days after the Kent State tragedy, on May 15, Mississippi highway patrolmen riddled a dormitory at predominantly black Jackson State College with 460 bullets, killing two students and wounding twelve. The tragedy was brought on by chronic tensions between white police and black students. "We weren't thinking about Vietnam," explained one of the Jackson State students. We were thinking about a racist governor and racist whites yelling things and throwing things at us from their cars." Charles Evers, mayor of a nearby town, said: "If Jackson State had been a white campus, not a single bullet would have been fired."

In New York City, anti-war demonstrators were attacked by conservative "hard-hat" construction workers, many of them shouting "All the way, USA" and "America: Love It or Leave It." They forced the protesters to disperse, then marched on City Hall to raise the U.S. flag, which had been lowered to half-staff in mourning for the Kent State victims.

In June 1971, the *New York Times* began publishing excerpts from *The History of the U.S. Decision-Making Process of Vietnam Policy*, a secret Defense Department study commissioned by Robert McNamara before his resignation as secretary of defense in 1968. The so-called Pentagon Papers, leaked to the press by Daniel Ellsberg, a former Marine and Defense Department official, confirmed what many critics of the war had long suspected: Congress and the public had not received the full story about the Gulf of Tonkin incident of 1964. Plans for the U.S. entry into the war were being drawn up even as President Johnson was promising that combat troops would never be sent to Vietnam.

Although the Pentagon Papers dealt with events only up to 1965, the Nixon administration blocked their publication, arguing that their release would endanger national security and prolong the war. By a vote of 6 to 3, the Supreme Court ruled against the government. Newspapers began publishing the documents the next day. A furious Nixon ordered the FBI to find out who had leaked the Pentagon Papers. When the agency identified Ellsberg as the culprit, the president launched a crusade to destroy him, including a botched effort to break into his psychiatrist's office.

WAR WITHOUT END   In the summer of 1972, Henry Kissinger renewed private meetings with the North Vietnamese negotiators in Paris. He dropped his insistence upon the removal of all North Vietnamese troops from South Vietnam before the withdrawal of the remaining U.S. troops. On October 26, a week before the U.S. presidential election, a jubilant Kissinger announced that "Peace is at hand."

As it turned out, however, this was a cynical ploy to win votes for Nixon's reelection bid. Several days earlier, the Thieu regime in South Vietnam had rejected the Kissinger plan for a cease-fire, fearful that allowing North Vietnamese troops to remain in the south would guarantee a Communist victory. The peace talks broke off on December 16, and two days later the newly reelected Nixon ordered massive bombings of Hanoi and Haiphong, the two largest cities in North Vietnam. Nixon told Kissinger that he now would "stop at nothing to bring the enemy to his knees. . . . We have the power. The only question is whether we have the will to use that power. What distinguishes me from Johnson is that I have the will in spades."

The so-called Christmas bombings and the simultaneous U.S. decision to place explosive underwater mines in North Vietnam's Haiphong harbor to prevent ships from offloading their cargoes aroused worldwide protests. Yet the talks in Paris soon resumed, and on January 27, 1973, the United States, North and South Vietnam, and the Viet Cong signed an "agreement on ending the war and restoring peace in Vietnam," known as the Paris Peace Accords.

In fact, however, the agreement was a carefully disguised surrender that enabled the United States to end its combat role. While Nixon and Kissinger claimed that the bombings had brought North Vietnam to its senses, in truth the North Vietnamese never altered their basic stance; they kept 150,000 troops in South Vietnam and remained committed to the reunification of Vietnam under one government. What had changed was the willingness of the South Vietnamese leaders, who had not been allowed to participate in the negotiations, to accept the agreement on the basis of Nixon's personal promise that the United States would respond "with full force" to any Communist violation of the agreement.

Between the time Nixon took office in 1969 and the signing of the Paris Peace Accords in 1973, another 20,000 American troops had died; the morale of the U.S. military had been shattered and millions of Southeast Asians had been killed, wounded, or displaced. Fighting soon broke out again in both Vietnam and Cambodia. In the end, the diplomatic efforts gained nothing the president could not have accomplished in 1969 by ending the war on similar terms.

THE COLLAPSE OF SOUTH VIETNAM On March 29, 1973, the last U.S. combat troops left Vietnam. The same day, the North Vietnamese released almost 600 U.S. prisoners of war. Within months, however, the cease-fire collapsed, the war resumed, and Communist forces gained the upper hand. In Cambodia (renamed the Khmer Republic after a 1970 military coup) and Laos, where fighting had been sporadic, a Communist victory seemed inevitable.

In 1975, the North Vietnamese launched a full-scale invasion of South Vietnam, sending the country into headlong panic. President Thieu appealed to Washington for the U.S. assistance promised in the Paris Peace Accords. But Congress, weary of spending dollars and lives in Vietnam, refused. On April 21, Thieu resigned and flew to Taiwan.

In the end, "peace with honor" had given the United States just enough time to remove itself before the collapse of the South Vietnamese government. On April 30, 1975, Americans watched on television as North Vietnamese tanks rolled into Saigon, soon to be renamed Ho Chi Minh City, and military helicopters airlifted U.S. embassy and South Vietnamese officials and their families to warships offshore.

Leave with honor Hundreds of thousands of terrified South Vietnamese tried to flee the Communist forces with evacuating Americans. Here, a U.S. official punches a Vietnamese man trying to join his family in an overflowing airplane at Nha Trang.

The longest, most controversial, and least successful war in American history to that point was finally over. It left a bitter legacy. During the period of U.S. involvement, the combined death count for combatants and civilians reached nearly 2 million. North Vietnam absorbed incredible losses—some 600,000 soldiers and countless civilians. South Vietnam lost 240,000 soldiers, and more than 500,000 Vietnamese became refugees in the United States. More than 58,000 Americans died; another 300,000 were wounded, 2,500 were declared missing, and almost 100,000 returned missing one or more limbs. The United States spent more than $699 billion on the war.

The Vietnam War was the defining life event for the baby boomers, the generation that provided most of the U.S. troops as well as most of the anti-war protesters. The controversial war divided them in ways that would be felt for years. The "loss" of the war, combined with news of atrocities committed by American soldiers, eroded respect for the military so thoroughly that many young people came to regard military service as corrupting and dishonorable.

Vietnam veterans (average age nineteen, compared to twenty-six in the Second World War) had "lost" a war in which their country had lost interest. When they returned, many found even their families unwilling to talk about what the soldiers had experienced, or they themselves were embarrassed about their involvement in the war. "I went over there thinking I was doing something right and came back a bum," said Larry Langowski from Illinois. "I came back decked with medals on my uniform, and I got spit on by a hippie girl."

The Vietnam War, initially described as a crusade for democratic ideals, revealed that America's form of democracy was not easily transferable to regions of the world that lacked democratic traditions. And, as critics noted, imposed democracy is not democratic. Fought to contain the spread of communism, the war instead fragmented the national consensus that had governed U.S. foreign affairs since 1947, when President Truman developed policies to contain communism around the world.

As opposition to the war undermined Lyndon B. Johnson's presidency, it also created enduring fractures within the Democratic party. Said George McGovern, the anti-war senator and 1972 Democratic presidential nominee, "The Vietnam tragedy is at the root of the confusion and division of the Democratic party. It tore up our souls."

Not only had a decade of American effort in Vietnam proved costly and futile, but the Khmer Rouge, the insurgent Cambodian Communist movement, had also won a resounding victory over the U.S.-backed Khmer Republic, plunging the country into a horrific bloodbath. The maniacal Khmer Rouge leaders renamed the country Kampuchea and organized a campaign to destroy all their opponents, killing almost a third of the total population.

THE NIXON DOCTRINE AND A THAWING COLD WAR

Richard Nixon greatly preferred foreign policy to domestic policy (which he compared to building "sewer projects"), and his greatest successes were in international relations. Nixon was an expert in foreign affairs, and he benefited greatly from the strategic vision of Henry Kissinger. Their grand design for U.S. foreign policy after the Vietnam War centered on developing friendly relations with the Soviet Union and Communist China.

THE CIA IN CHILE Henry Kissinger pressed for a return to an Eisenhower-era approach to foreign policy that entailed using the Central Intelligence Agency (CIA) to pursue America's strategic interests covertly while reducing large-scale military interventions.

Since Fidel Castro and his supporters gained control of Cuba in 1959, American presidents had been determined to prevent any more Communist insurgencies in the Western Hemisphere. In 1970, Salvador Allende, a Socialist party leader, friend of Castro, and critic of the United States, was a leading presidential candidate in Chile. Kissinger and President Nixon knew that, if elected, Allende planned to take control of Chilean industries owned by U.S. corporations, just as Fidel Castro had done after seizing power in Cuba in 1959.

Nixon urged the CIA to do anything to prevent an Allende presidency. Although CIA agents provided campaign funds to his opponents, Allende was democratically elected on October 24, 1970. The CIA then encouraged Chilean military leaders to oust him. In September 1973, the army took control, Allende either committed suicide or was murdered, and General Augusto Pinochet, a ruthless dictator supposedly friendly to the United States, declared himself head of the government. Within a few months, Pinochet had taken over dozens of U.S.-owned businesses in Chile and executed thousands of political opponents. It was yet another example of the United States being so obsessed by anti-communism and protecting American business interests that it was willing to interfere in the democratic process of other nations. Kissinger, now secretary of state, told Nixon that the CIA "didn't do it," but "we helped" put Pinochet in office by creating the conditions that made the coup possible.

THE NIXON DOCTRINE In July 1969, while announcing the first troop withdrawals from Vietnam, President Nixon unveiled what came to be called the Nixon Doctrine. Unlike John F. Kennedy, who had declared that the United States would "pay any price, bear any burden" to win the cold war, Nixon explained that "America cannot—and will not—conceive *all* the plans, design *all* the programs, execute *all* the decisions, and undertake *all* the defense of the free nations of the world." Under the Nixon Doctrine, the United States would support "proxy warfare," providing weapons and money to fend off Communist insurgencies, but not American troops.

At the same time, Nixon announced that he would pursue partnerships with Communist countries in areas of mutual interest. That Nixon, with his history of rabid anti-communism, would embrace such a policy of **détente** (a French word meaning "easing of relations") shocked many and demonstrated yet again his pragmatic flexibility.

THE PEOPLE'S REPUBLIC OF CHINA Richard Nixon had an exquisite gift for doing the unexpected. In 1971, Nixon sent Henry Kissinger on a secret trip to Beijing to explore the possibility of U.S. recognition of Communist China, the most populous nation in the world, with over 800 million people. Kissinger was flabbergasted. He told his staff that "our leader has taken leave of reality. He thinks this is the moment to establish normal relations with Communist China."

Since 1949, when Mao Zedong's revolutionary movement established control, the United States, with Richard Nixon's hearty support, had refused even to recognize the People's Republic of China, preferring to regard Chiang Kai-shek's exiled regime on Taiwan as the legitimate Chinese government.

Nixon goes to China President Nixon and Chinese premier Zhou Enlai toast each other at a farewell banquet in Shanghai celebrating the historic visit.

Now, however, the time seemed ripe for a bold renewal of ties. Both the United States and Communist China were exhausted from domestic strife (anti-war protests in America, the Cultural Revolution in China), and both were eager to resist Soviet expansionism. Nixon also relished the shock effect of his action, which he told senior aide John Ehrlichman would "discombobulate" the "goddamned liberals."

Nixon's bombshell announcement on July 15, 1971, that Kissinger had just returned from Beijing and that the president himself would be going to China the following year, sent shock waves around the world. Nixon became the first U.S. president to use the term *People's Republic of China*, a symbolic step in normalizing relations. The Nationalist Chinese on Taiwan felt betrayed, and the Japanese, historic enemies of China, were furious. In October 1971, the United Nations voted to admit the People's Republic of China and expel Taiwan.

On February 21, 1972, during the "week that changed the world," Nixon arrived in Beijing. Americans watched on television as the president shook hands and drank toasts with Prime Minister Zhou Enlai and Communist party Chairman Mao Zedong. In one simple but astonishing stroke, Nixon and Kissinger had ended two decades of diplomatic isolation of the People's Republic of China.

During the president's week-long visit, the two nations agreed to scientific and cultural exchanges, steps toward resuming trade, and the eventual reunification of Taiwan with the mainland. A year later, "liaison offices" that served as unofficial embassies were established in Washington and Beijing. In 1979, diplomatic recognition was officially formalized.

As a conservative anti-Communist, Nixon had accomplished a diplomatic feat that his Democratic predecessors could not have attempted for fear of being branded "soft" on communism. Nixon's and Kissinger's bold move gave them leverage with the Soviet Union, which was understandably nervous about a U.S.–Chinese alliance.

EMBRACING THE SOVIET UNION China welcomed the breakthrough because of tensions with the Soviet Union, with which it shared a long but contested border. By 1972, the Chinese had become more fearful of the Soviet Union than of the United States.

The Soviets were also eager to ease tensions with the Americans. In 1972, President Nixon again surprised the world by announcing that he would visit Moscow for discussions with Leonid Brezhnev, the Soviet premier. The high drama of the China visit was repeated in Moscow, with toasts and dinners attended by world leaders who had previously regarded each other as incarnations of evil.

Nixon and Brezhnev signed the pathbreaking **Strategic Arms Limitation Treaty (SALT I)**, which negotiators had been working on since 1969. The agreement did not end the nuclear arms race, but it did limit the number of missiles with nuclear warheads and prohibited the construction of missile-defense systems. The Moscow summit also produced new trade agreements, including an arrangement whereby the United States sold almost a quarter of its wheat crop to the Soviets at a favorable price.

The summit resulted in a dramatic easing of tensions. As Nixon told Congress upon his return, "never before have two adversaries, so deeply divided by conflicting ideologies and political rivalries, been able to limit the armaments upon which their survival depends."

The agreements with China and the Soviet Union represented monumental changes in the global order. Over time, détente with the Soviet Union would help end the cold war by lowering Soviet hostility to Western influences, which in turn slowly eroded Communist rule from the inside.

SHUTTLE DIPLOMACY The Nixon–Kissinger initiatives in the Middle East were less dramatic and less conclusive than those in China and the Soviet Union, but they showed that the United States at last recognized the legitimacy of Arab interests in the region and its own dependence upon Middle Eastern oil.

On October 6, 1973, Syria and Egypt, backed by Saudi Arabia and armed with Soviet weapons, attacked Israel, igniting what became the Yom Kippur War. It created the most dangerous confrontation between the United States and the Soviet Union since the Cuban missile crisis.

When the Israeli army, with weapons supplied by the United States, launched a fierce counterattack that appeared likely to overwhelm Egypt, the Soviets threatened to intervene militarily. Nixon, whose presidency was increasingly at risk because of the Watergate investigations, was bedridden because he was drunk, according to Henry Kissinger and other aides, so Kissinger, as secretary of state, presided over a National Security Council meeting that placed America's military forces on full alert.

On October 20, Kissinger flew to Moscow to meet with Soviet premier Brezhnev. Kissinger skillfully negotiated a cease-fire agreement and exerted pressure on the Israelis to prevent them from taking additional Arab territory, and in an attempt to broker a lasting settlement, he made numerous flights among the capitals of the Middle East. His "shuttle diplomacy" won acclaim from all sides, although he failed to find a comprehensive formula for peace. He did, however, lay the groundwork for an important treaty between Israel and Egypt in 1977.

WATERGATE

Nixon's foreign policy achievements allowed him to stage the presidential campaign of 1972 as a triumphal procession. Early on, the main threat to his reelection came from George Wallace, who had the potential as a third-party candidate to deprive the Republicans of conservative southern votes and thereby throw the election to the Democrats. That threat ended, however, on May 15, 1972, when Wallace was shot in an assassination attempt. Although he survived, he was left paralyzed below the waist and had to withdraw from the campaign. Nixon ordered aides to plant a false story that Democrats had orchestrated Wallace's assassination.

Meanwhile, the Democrats nominated Senator George McGovern of South Dakota, an anti-war liberal. "George is the most decent man in the Senate," Robert Kennedy had said. "As a matter of fact, he is the only decent man."

Decency does not win elections, however. McGovern was a poor campaigner, and many dismissed him as a left-wing extremist. Nixon also defused the Vietnam War as the central issue in the campaign, emphasizing that he had brought more than 500,000 troops home from Vietnam.

Nixon won the greatest victory of any Republican presidential candidate in history, capturing 520 electoral votes to only 17 for McGovern. The popular vote was equally decisive: 46 million to 28 million, a proportion of the total vote (60.8 percent) second only to Lyndon Johnson's victory over Barry Goldwater in 1964. The only downside for the Republicans was that the Democrats maintained control of Congress.

For all of Nixon's abilities and accomplishments, however, he remained chronically insecure. He began keeping a secret "enemies list" and approved plans to break into the offices of some of his opponents. Little did he know that such behavior would bring him crashing down.

"**DIRTY TRICKS**" By the spring of 1972, Nixon aide John Ehrlichman was overseeing a secret team of agents who performed various acts of partisan sabotage, such as falsely accusing Democratic senators Hubert H. Humphrey and Henry Jackson of sexual improprieties, forging press releases, setting off stink bombs at Democratic campaign events, and planting spies on George McGovern's campaign plane. Charles "Chuck" Colson, one of the most active "dirty tricksters," admitted that "we did a hell of a lot of things and never got caught."

But others were caught. On June 17, 1972, police in Washington, D.C., nabbed five burglars breaking into the Democratic National Committee headquarters in the **Watergate** hotel-apartment-office complex. The burglars were all former CIA agents; four were Miami-based Cuban exiles, and the other, James W. McCord, was the Nixon campaign's security director. Two others were also arrested—Gordon Liddy and E. Howard Hunt—who were directing the break-in from a hotel across the street. The police found wads of hundred-dollar bills on the burglars. When the bungled break-in was first reported, McGovern's complaints about it seemed like sour grapes from a candidate running far behind in the polls.

Nixon and his staff did their best to dismiss the incident as a "third-rate burglary." The president denied any involvement, but he was lying; he told

Alexander Haig, then his national security adviser, that "we will cover up [the Watergate burglary] until hell freezes over."

To protect Nixon, White House aides secretly provided $350,000 in "hush money" to the jailed burglars, only to learn that it was not enough—they wanted $1 million. Nixon and his aides also discussed using the CIA to derail the Justice Department's investigation of the burglary. Bob Haldeman, Nixon's chief of staff, told the FBI to quit investigating the incident, falsely claiming that it involved a super-secret CIA operation. Meanwhile, White House spokesmen lied to journalists and destroyed evidence.

Nixon encouraged the cover-up, stressing that his "main concern is to keep the White House out of it." In August 1972, he told reporters that his own investigation into the Watergate incident had confirmed that no one in the White House or the administration was involved—when in fact, there was no such investigation.

UNCOVERING THE COVER-UP During the trial of the accused Watergate burglars in January 1973, relentless questioning by federal judge John J. Sirica, a Nixon supporter and hard-nosed jurist with the nickname "Maximum John" because of his reputation for issuing harsh sentences, led one of the accused to tell the full story. James W. McCord, security chief of the Committee to Re-Elect the President (CREEP), was the first in what would become a long line of informers to reveal the systematic efforts of Nixon and his aides to create an "imperial presidency." By the time of the Watergate break-in, money to finance such dirty tricks was being illegally collected through CREEP and controlled by the White House staff.

The trail of evidence was pursued first by Sirica, then by a grand jury, and finally by a Senate committee headed by Democrat Samuel J. Ervin Jr. of North Carolina. The investigations led directly to what White House legal counsel John Dean called a "cancer close to the Presidency." By this point, Nixon was using his presidential powers to block the investigation. He ordered the CIA to keep the FBI off the case and coached his aides on how to lie under oath. Most alarming, as it turned out, the Watergate burglary was merely part of a larger pattern of corruption and criminality sanctioned by the White House.

The cover-up crumbled as people involved began to cooperate with prosecutors. James McCord admitted to Sirica that the White House had provided the burglars hush money and that witnesses had lied at the trial. He then named names before the Ervin committee. Other White House aides also confessed their roles in the burglary and cover-up.

At the same time, two reporters for the *Washington Post*, Carl Bernstein and Bob Woodward, relentlessly pursued the story, eventually making it a compelling topic of national conversation. Still, Nixon continued to lie, telling

Americans that he condemned "any attempt to cover up this case."

The cover-up unraveled further in 1973 when L. Patrick Gray, acting director of the FBI, resigned after confessing that he had destroyed incriminating documents at the behest of the president. On April 30, Ehrlichman and Haldeman also resigned (they would later serve time in prison), as did Attorney General Richard Kleindienst. A few days later, Nixon nervously assured the public in a television address, "I am not a crook."

John Ehrlichman Ehrlichman, aide to President Nixon, addresses the Senate Watergate committee on July 24, 1973.

Then John Dean, the White House legal counsel whom Nixon had dismissed because of his cooperation with prosecutors, shocked the nation. He told the Ervin committee that there had been a White House cover-up approved by the president himself.

Nixon thereafter behaved like a cornered lion. He refused to provide Senator Ervin's committee with documents it requested, citing "executive privilege" to protect national security. Then, in another shocking disclosure, a White House aide told the committee that Nixon had installed a secret taping system in the White House, meaning that many of the conversations about the Watergate burglary and cover-up had been recorded.

The bombshell news set off a legal battle for the "Nixon tapes." Harvard law professor Archibald Cox, whom Nixon's new attorney general, Elliot Richardson, had appointed as special prosecutor to investigate the Watergate case, took the president to court in October 1973 to obtain the tapes. Nixon refused to release the recordings and ordered Cox fired.

On October 20, in what became known as the "Saturday Night Massacre," Richardson and his deputy, William Ruckelshaus, resigned rather than fire Cox. (Solicitor General Robert Bork finally fired him.) Cox's dismissal produced a firestorm of public indignation. Numerous newspapers and magazines, as well as a growing chorus of legislators, called for the president to resign or be impeached for obstructing justice. A Gallup poll revealed that Nixon's approval rating had plunged to 17 percent, the lowest in presidential history.

The new special prosecutor, Leon Jaworski, a prominent Texas attorney, also took the president to court. In March 1974, the Watergate grand jury indicted Ehrlichman, Haldeman, and former attorney general John Mitchell for obstruction of justice and named Nixon an "unindicted co-conspirator."

On April 30, Nixon, still refusing to turn over the tapes, released 1,254 pages of transcribed recordings that he had edited himself, often substituting the phrase "expletive deleted" for his vulgar language and anti-Semitic rants. ("People said my language was bad," Nixon later rationalized, "but Jesus, you should have heard LBJ!"). The transcripts revealed a president whose conversations were so petty, self-serving, bigoted, and profane that they degraded the stature of the office. At one point in the transcripts, the president told his aides to have frequent memory lapses when testifying.

By the summer of 1974, Nixon was in full retreat. He became alternately combative, melancholy, and petty, and his efforts to orchestrate the cover-up obsessed, unbalanced, and unhinged him. Henry Kissinger found him increasingly unstable and drinking heavily. After meeting with the president, Senator Barry Goldwater reported that Nixon "jabbered incessantly, often incoherently." He seemed "to be cracking."

On July 24, 1974, the Supreme Court ruled unanimously that the president must surrender *all* the tape recordings. A few days later, the House Judiciary Committee voted to recommend three articles of impeachment: obstruction of justice through the payment of hush money to witnesses and the withholding of evidence; abuse of power through the use of federal agencies to deprive citizens of their constitutional rights; and defiance of Congress by withholding the tapes. The president, chief of staff Alexander Haig confided to White House aides, was "guilty as hell." He then told Nixon that he did not "see how we can survive this one."

Before the House of Representatives could vote on impeachment, Nixon grudgingly handed over the tapes. The drama continued, however, when investigators learned that segments of several recordings were missing, including eighteen minutes of a conversation in June 1972 during which Nixon first mentioned the Watergate burglary.

The president's loyal secretary took the blame for the erasure, claiming that she had accidentally pushed the wrong

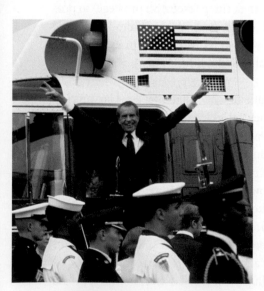

V for "Victory" Before boarding the White House helicopter following his resignation, Nixon flashes a bright smile and his trademark V-sign to the world on August 9, 1974.

button, but technical experts later concluded that the missing segments had been intentionally deleted. The other recordings, however, provided more than enough evidence of Nixon's involvement in the cover-up. At one point, he had yelled at aides who were asking what they and others should say to Watergate investigators: "I don't give a shit what happens. I want you all to stonewall it, let them plead the Fifth Amendment, cover up or anything else."

The incriminating recordings led Republican leaders to urge the embattled president to quit rather than face an impeachment trial in the Senate. "There are only so many lies you can take and now there has been one too many," Senator Barry Goldwater concluded. "Nixon should get his ass out of the White House—today."

On August 9, 1974, Nixon did just that. He resigned from office, the only president to do so.

Nixon had begun his presidency hoping to heal a fractured America. Now he left the White House for a self-imposed exile at his home in San Clemente, California, having deeply wounded the nation. A London newspaper explained that America had digressed "from George Washington, who could not tell a lie, to Richard Nixon, who could not tell the truth."

Nixon never understood why the Watergate affair could have ended his presidency; in his view, his only mistake was getting caught. Nixon claimed that a president's actions could not be "illegal." He was wrong. The Watergate affair's clearest lesson was that not even a president is above the law. But while the system worked by calling a president to justice, many Americans lost faith in the credibility of elected officials. The *New York Times* reported that people "think and feel differently from what they once did" as a result of the Watergate crisis. "They ask questions, they reject assumptions, they doubt what they are told."

WATERGATE AND THE PRESIDENCY If there was a silver lining in the dark cloud of Watergate, it was the vigor and resilience of the institutions that had brought a rogue president to justice—the press, Congress, the courts, and public opinion.

In the aftermath of the scandal, Congress passed several pieces of legislation designed to curb executive power. Nervous about possible efforts to renew military assistance to South Vietnam, the Democratic Congress passed the **War Powers Act** (1973), which requires a president to inform Congress within forty-eight hours if U.S. troops are deployed in combat abroad and to withdraw them after sixty days unless Congress specifically approves their stay.

Then, to correct abuses in the use of campaign funds, Congress enacted legislation in 1974 that set new ceilings on political campaign contributions and expenditures. And in reaction to the Nixon claim of "executive privilege" as a means of withholding evidence, Congress strengthened the 1966 Freedom of Information Act to require prompt responses to requests for information from government files and to place on government agencies the burden of proof for classifying information as secret.

AN UNELECTED PRESIDENT During Richard Nixon's last year in office, the Watergate crisis so dominated national politics that major domestic and foreign problems received little attention.

Vice President Spiro Agnew had himself been forced to resign in October 1973 for accepting bribes from Maryland contractors before and during his term in office. The vice president at the time of Nixon's resignation was Gerald Rudolph Ford, a square-jawed, plain-speaking former House minority leader from Michigan whom Nixon had appointed to succeed Agnew under the provisions of the Twenty-Fifth Amendment.

On August 9, 1974, Ford, an honest and decent man who held a law degree from Yale, was sworn in as the nation's chief executive, the only person in history to serve as both vice president and president without having been elected to those

Gerald Ford The 38th president is pictured listening apprehensively to reports of rising rates of unemployment and inflation in 1974.

offices. "I am acutely aware that you have not elected me as your President by your ballots," Ford said in a televised address. "So I ask you to confirm me as your President with your prayers." He then assured the nation that "our long national nightmare [Watergate] is over."

But less than a month after taking office, Ford reopened the wounds of Watergate by issuing Nixon a "full, free, and absolute pardon" for any crimes he may have committed while in office.

Ford's pardon unleashed a storm of controversy. "Jail Ford!" yelled protesters outside the White House. A House subcommittee grilled the new president, wanting to know whether Nixon had made a secret deal for the pardon. Ford vigorously denied the charge, but others wondered why he had pardoned someone who had not been charged with a crime. The *Washington Post* declared that Ford's decision was "nothing less than the continuation of a cover-up," while the *New York Times* dismissed the pardon as "profoundly unwise, divisive, and unjust."

The controversial pardon hobbled Ford's presidency. Doing what he had thought was the right thing made him suspect in the eyes of many voters. His approval rating plummeted from 71 percent to 49 percent in one day, the steepest drop ever recorded. His press secretary resigned in protest of the "Nixon pardon."

THE FORD YEARS As president, Gerald Ford adopted the posture he had developed as minority leader in the House of Representatives: naysaying head of the opposition who believed the federal government exercised too much power. In his first fifteen months as president, Ford vetoed thirty-nine bills passed by the Democratic-controlled Congress, outstripping Herbert Hoover's all-time veto record in less than half the time.

By far the most important issue during Ford's brief presidency was the struggling economy. In the fall of 1974, the nation entered its deepest recession since the Great Depression. Unemployment jumped to 9 percent in 1975, the rate of inflation reached double digits, and the federal budget deficit soon hit a record. Ford announced that inflation had become "Public Enemy No. 1," but instead of taking bold action, he launched a timid public relations campaign featuring lapel buttons that simply read WIN, symbolizing the administration's determination to "Whip Inflation Now."

The WIN buttons became a national joke and a symbol of Ford's ineffectiveness in the fight against stagflation. He later admitted that they were a failed "gimmick."

In his State of the Union address in 1975, Ford conceded that "the state of the union is not good." The economic recession was now his greatest concern, not inflation. In March 1975, Ford signed a tax reduction bill that failed to stimulate economic growth. The federal budget deficit grew from $53 billion in 1975 to $74 billion in 1976.

Whip Inflation Now! Initial excitement about the program, which was ultimately unsuccessful, generated great quantities of WIN-themed collectibles. These items included stickers, buttons, clothing, and even earrings.

In foreign policy, Ford retained Henry Kissinger as secretary of state (while stripping him of his dual role as national security adviser). He continued to pursue Nixon's goals of stability in the Middle East, friendly relations with China, and détente with the Soviet Union. Kissinger's tireless Middle East diplomacy produced an important agreement: Israel promised to return to Egypt most of the Sinai territory captured in the 1967 war, and the two nations agreed to rely on diplomacy rather than force to settle future disagreements.

These limited but significant achievements, however, were drowned in the criticism over the collapse of the South Vietnamese government in the face of the North Vietnamese invasion. At the same time, conservative Republicans led by Ronald Reagan lambasted Ford and Kissinger for their policy of détente toward the Soviet Union. Reagan argued that the efforts of Nixon, Kissinger, and Ford were helping to ensure the continued existence of the Soviet Union rather than accelerating its self-destruction.

THE ELECTION OF 1976 Both political parties were in disarray as they prepared for the 1976 presidential election. Gerald Ford had to fend off a challenge from the darling of the Republican party's growing conservative wing, Ronald Reagan, a former two-term California governor and Hollywood actor. Richard Nixon told Ford that "Reagan was a lightweight and not someone to be considered seriously or feared."

The Democrats chose a little-known candidate: James "Jimmy" Carter Jr., who had served one term as governor of Georgia. When Carter told his mother he was running for president, she replied: "President of *what*?" Tip O'Neill, the Democratic Speaker of the House, dismissed Carter as "a complete unknown."

Yet Carter did have several assets. A former naval officer and engineer turned peanut farmer, he was one of several Democratic southern governors who sought to move their party away from its traditional "tax and spend" liberalism. The federal government, he charged, was a "horrible, bloated, confused . . . bureaucratic mess." The Great Society social-welfare programs created by LBJ were a "failure" that were in "urgent need of a complete overhaul."

Carter capitalized on post-Watergate cynicism about Washington politicos by promising that he would "never tell a lie to the American people." He also trumpeted his status as a political "outsider," and reporters covering the campaign marveled at a Southern Baptist candidate who was a "born again" Christian.

A poll found that voters viewed Ford as "a nice guy," but "not . . . very smart about the issues the country is facing." Ford reinforced that impression during a televised debate with Carter when he mistakenly claimed that "there is no Soviet domination of Eastern Europe."

Carter revived the New Deal voting alliance of southern whites, blacks, urban labor unionists, and ethnic groups like Jews and Latinos to eke out a narrow win, receiving 41 million votes to Ford's 39 million. A heavy turnout of African Americans in the South enabled Carter to sweep every state in the region except Virginia. He also benefited from the appeal of Walter F. Mondale, his liberal running mate and a favorite among blue-collar workers and the urban poor. Ford was the first president to lose his bid for reelection since Herbert Hoover in 1932.

The most significant story of the election, however, was the low voter turnout. Almost half the eligible voters chose to sit out the election, the lowest turnout since the Second World War.

In explaining why he had not voted, one man noted that he was "a three-time loser. In 1964 I voted for the peace candidate—Johnson—and got war. In '68 I voted for the law-and-order candidate—and got crime. In '72 I voted for Nixon again, and we got Watergate." Such an alienated voter was not a good omen for a new Democratic president about to begin his first term as head of the nation.

CHAPTER REVIEW

SUMMARY

- **Youth Revolt** Civil rights activism inspired a heightened interest in social causes during the 1960s, especially among the young. Students for a Democratic Society (SDS) embodied the *New Left* ideology, and their ideas and tactics spread to many campuses. By 1970, a distinctive *counterculture* had emerged among disaffected youth ("hippies").

- **The Inspirational Effects of the Civil Rights Movement** The civil rights movement and the youth revolt inspired many social reform movements, including the *women's movement*, the *Red Power* movement among Native Americans, and the *United Farm Workers (UFW)*. The *Stonewall riots* in New York City in 1969 triggered a militant new era for gay and lesbian rights.

- **Reaction and Domestic Agenda** Richard Nixon's southern strategy drew conservative southern white Democrats to the Republican party. As president, he sought to slow the momentum of the civil rights movement, including *affirmative-action* programs. Congress overrode his veto of the Voting Rights Act of 1968. Nixon did grudgingly support new federal environmental policies, such as the creation of the *Environmental Protection Agency (EPA)* in 1970. During Nixon's second term, the economy struggled with *stagflation*. In a landmark decision, the Supreme Court in *Roe v. Wade* (1973) struck down state laws forbidding abortions during the first three months of pregnancy.

- **End of the Vietnam War** In 1968, Nixon campaigned for the presidency pledging to secure "peace with honor" in Vietnam, but years would pass before the war ended. Nixon implemented the *Vietnamization* strategy, which involved increasing economic and military aid to the South Vietnamese, reducing U.S. ground forces, and escalating the bombing of North Vietnam (and Cambodia), all while attempting to negotiate a cease-fire agreement with North Vietnamese diplomats. The publication of the Pentagon Papers in 1971 and the intense bombing of North Vietnam in December 1972 aroused more protests, but a month after the bombings began, North and South Vietnam agreed to a cease-fire called the Paris Peace Accords. In November 1973, Congress passed the *War Powers Act*, which requires the president to notify Congress within 48 hours of committing armed forces to military action and forbids armed forces from remaining for more than 60 days without Congressional approval or a declaration of war.

- **Détente** Nixon's greatest accomplishments were in foreign policy. He opened diplomatic relations with Communist China and pursued *détente* with the Soviet Union, focusing on areas of shared agreement with the 1972 *Strategic Arms Limitation Treaty (SALT I)* treaty. He and Henry Kissinger also helped ease tensions in the Middle East.

- **Watergate** During the 1972 presidential campaign, burglars were caught breaking into the Democratic party's national campaign headquarters at the *Watergate* complex in Washington, D.C. Nixon tried to block congressional investigations, which eventually led to calls for his impeachment for obstruction of justice. Nixon resigned in 1974 and was succeeded by Vice President Gerald Ford.

Chronology

1965	Vietnam War expands
1966	National Organization for Women (NOW) founded
1967	Six-Day War in Middle East
1968	Richard M. Nixon elected president
1969	Stonewall riots in New York City
	Woodstock music festival attracts 400,000 people
1970	EPA created and Clean Air Act passed
	Shooting of students at Kent State University
1971	Ratification of the Twenty-Sixth Amendment
	Nixon begins withdrawing troops from Vietnam
1972	Nixon wins reelection and visits Communist China
	Nixon visits USSR and signs SALT I treaty
1972–1974	Watergate scandal unfolds
1973	Cease-fire declared in Vietnam War
	Nixon ends the military draft
	Supreme Court overturns anti-abortion laws in *Roe v. Wade*
	Congress passes War Powers Act
1974	Gerald Ford becomes president after Nixon's resignation
1975	Saigon falls to the North Vietnamese
1976	Democrat Jimmy Carter defeats Gerald Ford

Key Terms

New Left p. 1427

counterculture p. 1431

women's movement p. 1438

Roe v. Wade (1973) p. 1442

United Farm Workers (UFW) p. 1446

Red Power p. 1448

Stonewall riots (1969) p. 1450

affirmative action p. 1451

Environmental Protection Agency (EPA) (1970) p. 1457

stagflation p. 1457

Vietnamization p. 1460

détente p. 1468

Strategic Arms Limitation Treaty (SALT I) p. 1469

Watergate (1972–1974) p. 1471

War Powers Act (1973) p. 1475

 INQUIZITIVE

Go to InQuizitive to see what you've learned—and learn what you've missed—with personalized feedback along the way.

31 Conservative Revival

1977–1990

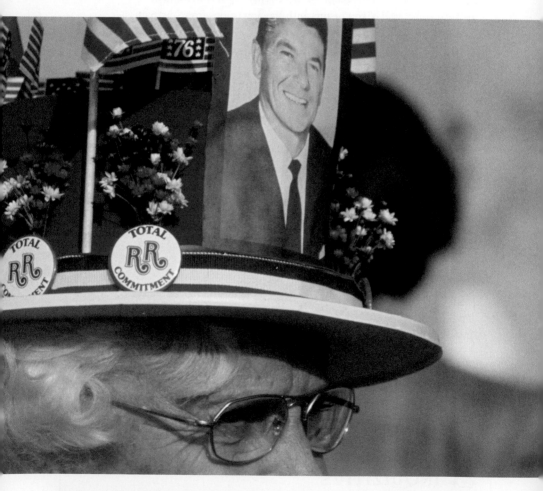

Feels good to be Right This proud Republican lets her hat adorned with campaign buttons speak for her at the 1980 Republican National Convention. Held in Detroit, Michigan, the convention nominated former California governor Ronald Reagan, who promised to "make America great again."

D uring the 1970s, the United States lost much of its self-confidence as it confronted difficult lessons about the limits of its power and financial resources and the pitfalls of greed and corruption. The failed Vietnam War; the Watergate scandal; and the spike in oil prices, interest rates, and consumer prices frustrated Americans. For a country accustomed to economic growth and carefree consumerism, the persistence of stagflation and gasoline shortages was exasperating. In July 1976, as the United States celebrated the bicentennial of its independence from Great Britain, many people were downsizing their expectations of the American dream.

Jimmy Carter, the first president from the Lower South, took office in 1977 promising a government that would be "competent" as well as "decent, open, fair, and compassionate." After four years, however, Carter had little to show for his efforts. The economy remained sluggish, consumer prices continued to increase, and failed efforts to free Americans held hostage in Iran prompted critics, including Democrats, to denounce Carter's administration as indecisive and inept. In the end, Carter's inability to mobilize support for an ill-fated energy program and his call for "a time of national austerity" revealed both his clumsy legislative skills and his misreading of the public mood.

The Republicans capitalized on public frustration by electing Ronald Reagan president in 1980. The new president promised to revive the capitalist spirit, restore national pride, and regain international respect. He did all of

focus questions

1. Why did Jimmy Carter have such limited success as president?

2. What factors led to the election of Ronald Reagan, the rise of the conservative movement, and the resurgence of the Republican party?

3. What is "Reaganomics"? What were its effects on American society and the economy?

4. How did Reagan's Soviet strategy help end the cold war?

5. What social and economic issues and innovations emerged during the 1980s?

6. What was the impact of the end of the cold war and the efforts of President George H. W. Bush to create a post–cold war foreign policy?

that and more, as he inspired a conservative resurgence, helped raise morale, and accelerated the forces that would cause the collapse of the Soviet Union and bring an end to the cold war.

THE CARTER PRESIDENCY

James ("Jimmy") Earl Carter Jr. won the 1976 election because he convinced voters that he was a man of pure motives, a born-again Christian who would restore integrity and honesty to the presidency. A former Georgia governor (1971–1975), he represented a new generation of moderate southern Democrats who were committed to restraining "big-government" spending. In his inaugural address, Carter confessed that he had no grand "vision." Unlike his predecessors, he highlighted America's limitations rather than its potential: "We have learned that 'more' is not necessarily 'better,' that even our great nation has its recognized limits, and that we can neither answer all questions nor solve all problems."

Carter later admitted that his remarks about dialing back national expectations were "politically unpopular," for "Americans were not accustomed to limits—on natural resources . . . or on the power of our country to . . . control international events."

JIMMY WHO?

Jimmy Carter's public modesty masked a complex and, at times, contradictory personality. No modern president was as openly committed to his Christian faith as Carter. At the same time, few presidents were as tough on others as Carter was.

Carter, who came out of nowhere to win the presidency ("Jimmy Who?"), displayed an "almost arrogant self-confidence," as *Time* magazine described it. All his life he had shown a fierce determination to succeed and he expected those around him to show the same tenacity. "I am pretty rigid," Carter admitted. Carter and his closest aides ("the Georgia Mafia") arrived in Washington, D.C., convinced that they would clean up the "mess" made by politicos and bureaucrats within the federal government. Congress, Carter noted in his diary, "was disgusting." Yet his naive dismissal of Congress would prove to be his downfall.

Carter wanted to be a "strong, aggressive president," an incorruptible outsider who would make the federal government run more smoothly at less expense to taxpayers by eliminating waste and providing expert management. Yet he could not inspire people. Democratic senator Eugene McCarthy described Carter as an "oratorical mortician," while a journalist stressed that "there's no music in him." He was, as he acknowledged, a manager rather than a visionary.

In 1977, Carter faced formidable challenges. Americans expected him to restore U.S. stature abroad, cure the stubborn economic recession, and reduce both unemployment and inflation at a time when industrial economies around the world were struggling.

Carter was also expected to lift the national spirit in the wake of the Watergate scandal. Meeting such daunting expectations would be miraculous, and Carter displayed a sunburst smile and flinty willpower, but he was no miracle worker.

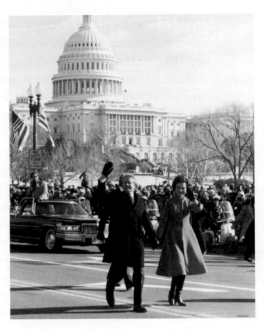

The Carters After his inauguration in 1977, President Jimmy Carter forgoes the traditional limousine and walks down Pennsylvania Avenue with his wife, Rosalynn.

EARLY SUCCESS During the first two years of his presidency, Carter enjoyed several successes, both symbolic and real. To demonstrate his frugality, he took the symbolic step of selling the presidential yacht, cut the White House staff by a third, told cabinet officers to give up their government cars, and installed solar panels on the White House roof to draw attention to the nation's need to become energy independent. His administration included more African Americans and women than any before.

More tangibly, Carter fulfilled a campaign pledge by offering amnesty (forgiveness) to the thousands of young men who had fled the country rather than serve in Vietnam. He also reorganized the executive branch and reduced government bureaucracy.

Carter pushed several significant environmental initiatives through the Democratic-controlled Congress, including stricter controls over the stripmining of coal, the creation of a $1.6 billion "Superfund" to clean up toxic chemical waste sites, and a bill protecting more than 100 million acres of Alaskan land from development. He also deregulated the trucking, airline, and financial industries in an effort to restore competition. At the end of his first 100 days in office, Carter enjoyed a 75 percent public approval rating.

CARTER'S LIMITATIONS Jimmy Carter's successes were short-lived, however. By nature, he was less a compelling leader than a compulsive microman-ager (he even insisted on scheduling the use of the White House tennis court).

For his first two years in the White House, Carter chose to serve as his own chief of staff, with disastrous results, for he was so busy with mundane activities that he failed to establish an uplifting vision for the nation's future. Instead of focusing on a few priorities, he tried to do too much too fast, and his inexperi-enced team of senior aides was often more a burden than a blessing. The chief of staff he finally appointed, Hamilton Jordan, spent much of his time drink-ing, chasing women, and alienating members of Congress. Worst of all, the self-proclaimed "outsider" president saw little need to consult with Democratic leaders, which helps explain why many of his legislative requests got nowhere.

Ultimately, Carter's inability to revive the economy crippled his presidency. He first attacked unemployment, authorizing some $14 billion in federal spending to trigger job growth while cutting taxes by $34 billion. His actions helped generate new jobs but also caused a spike in consumer prices from 5 percent when he took office to as much as 13 percent during 1980. The result was a deepening recession and rising unemployment.

Liberal Democrats complained that Carter was doing nothing to address spreading poverty and inner-city decline. He responded with a lecture that sounded more like a conservative Republican president: "Government cannot solve our problems. It cannot eliminate poverty, or provide a bountiful econ-omy, or reduce inflation, or save our cities, or cure illiteracy, or provide energy."

Carter was also hampered by the worsening global "energy crisis." He claimed that America was the "most wasteful nation on earth." Since the Arab oil embargo in 1973, the price of imported oil had doubled, while U.S. dependence on foreign oil had grown from 35 to 50 percent of its annual needs. In April 1977, Carter presented Congress with a comprehensive energy proposal designed to cut oil consumption. Legislators, however, turned down most of the bill's key elements when the National Energy Bill was finally passed in 1978.

In 1979, the energy crisis grew more troublesome when Islamic funda-mentalists assumed power in oil-rich Iran. They shut off the supply of Iranian oil to the United States, creating gasoline shortages and higher prices. Warning that the "growing scarcity in energy" would paralyze the U.S. economy, Carter asked Congress for a more comprehensive energy bill, but again the legislators rejected its conservation measures.

A "CRISIS OF CONFIDENCE" By July 1979, President Carter had grown so discouraged with both public and private efforts to reduce U.S. oil consumption that for eleven days he holed up at Camp David, the presidential retreat in the Maryland mountains. There he met privately with some 150 representatives from business, labor, education, politics, religion, even psychiatrists—all the while keeping the media at bay.

On July 15, he returned to the White House and delivered a televised speech in which he sounded more like an angry preacher than a president. He declared that a "crisis of confidence" was paralyzing the nation. The people had lost confidence in his leadership, and America had become rudderless, with no "sense of purpose" other than "to worship self-indulgence and consumption." He repeatedly blamed the citizenry for the nation's problems. "All the legislation in the world can't fix what's wrong with America," Carter stressed. Americans had become preoccupied with "owning and consuming things" at the expense of "hard work, strong families, close-knit communities, and our faith in God."

The nation was at a crossroads, Carter concluded. Americans could choose continued self-indulgence and political stalemate, or they could revive traditional values such as thrift, mutual aid, simple living, and spirituality. "We can take the first step down that path as we begin to solve our energy problem. Energy will be the immediate test of our ability to unite this nation."

Carter failed that test, however. An Arizona newspaper grumbled that "the nation did not tune in Carter to hear a sermon. It . . . wanted answers. It did not get them." Even Democrats lambasted the speech. Arkansas governor Bill Clinton said that Carter was behaving more like a "17th century New England Puritan than a 20th century Southern Baptist."

It did not help when, two days after the speech, Carter asked more than thirty government officials, including his entire cabinet, to resign. He accepted the resignations of five cabinet officers. In doing so, he reinforced the public image of a White House out of control.

Carter's inept legislative relations ensured that his energy proposals got nowhere in Congress. By the fall of 1979, his poll ratings were among the lowest in history. Former president Gerald Ford observed that if Nixon had created "an imperial presidency," Carter had fashioned "an imperiled presidency."

CARTER'S FOREIGN POLICY

Carter's greatest success was facilitating a 1978 peace agreement between Prime Minister Menachem Begin of Israel and President Anwar Sadat of Egypt. When the two foreign leaders, bitter enemies, arrived in September at Camp David, Maryland, they refused to be in the same room together. After twelve days, however, Carter's patience paid off when the parties signed two landmark treaties, thereafter called the **Camp David Accords.**

The Camp David Accords Egyptian president Anwar el-Sadat (left), Jimmy Carter (center), and Israeli prime minister Menachem Begin (right) at the announcement of the Camp David Accords, September 1978.

The first provided the framework for an eventual peace treaty. The Israelis pledged to end their military occupation of the Sinai region of Egypt, and the Egyptians promised to restore Israeli access to the Suez Canal. The second treaty called for a comprehensive settlement based on Israel's willingness to allow the Palestinians living in the Israeli-controlled West Bank and Gaza Strip to govern themselves.

Sadat's willingness to recognize the legitimacy of the Israeli nation and sign the two treaties sparked violent protests across the Arab world. The Arab League, representing twenty-two Arab nations, expelled Egypt and announced an economic boycott, and the Israelis later backtracked on their initial willingness to have the Palestinian authority replace Israeli security forces in the occupied territories. Sadat, however, paid the highest price, as Islamist extremists assassinated him in 1981. Still, Carter's diplomacy made war between Israel and the Arab world less likely.

HUMAN RIGHTS Carter stumbled again, however, when he vowed that "the soul of our foreign policy" should be an absolute "commitment to human rights" abroad, drawing a direct contrast between his international "idealism" and the geopolitical "realism" practiced by Richard Nixon and Henry Kissinger. Carter created an Office of Human Rights within the State Department and selectively cut off financial assistance to some repressive governments. "America did not invent human rights," he stressed. "In a very real sense, human rights invented America."

Critics noted that the United States had its own human rights issues, including the plight of Native Americans and African Americans, and that Carter ignored abuses by key allies, such as the shah of Iran. Others asserted that the president's definition of human rights was so vague and sweeping that few nations could meet its benchmark. Critics on the right argued that the president was sacrificing America's global interests to promote an impossible standard of international moral purity, while critics on the left highlighted his seeming hypocrisy in pursuing human rights in a few nations but not everywhere.

THE PANAMA CANAL Similarly, Carter's decision to turn over control of the ten-mile-wide Panama Canal Zone to the Panamanian government aroused intense criticism. He argued that Panama's deep resentment of America for taking control of the Canal Zone during the presidency of Theodore Roosevelt left him no choice.

Conservatives blasted Carter's "giveaway." In Ronald Reagan's view, "We bought it, we paid for it, it's ours." Legal scholars and the Panamanian government disagreed, however. No Panamanian had signed the 1903 document granting the United States perpetual control of the strategic waterway. The new agreement called for the Canal Zone to be transferred to Panama at the end of 1999. Carter said the exchange reflected the American belief that "fairness, not force, should lie at the heart of our dealings with the world."

AFGHANISTAN In late December 1979, President Carter faced another crisis when 100,000 Soviet soldiers invaded Afghanistan, a remote, mountainous country where a faltering Communist government was being challenged by Islamist *jihadists* ("holy warriors") and ethnic warlords. It was the first Soviet army deployment outside Europe since the Second World War, and the invaders soon found themselves mired in what some called the Soviet Vietnam.

Carter responded with a series of steps in response to the Soviet invasion. In January 1980, he refused to sign a Strategic Arms Limitation Talks (SALT II) treaty with the Soviets, suspended U.S. grain shipments to the Soviet Union, began using the CIA to supply Afghan "freedom fighters" with weapons, requested large increases in U.S. military spending, required all nineteen-year-old men to register for the military draft, and called for an international boycott of the 1980 Olympic Games, which were to be held that summer in Moscow. Some sixty nations joined the United States in the boycott. Still, the Soviets persisted in their Afghan intervention for nine years before giving up. It ultimately cost 15,000 Soviet lives.

The Soviet invasion of Afghanistan also prompted Carter to announce what came to be called the Carter Doctrine, in which he threatened to use military force to prevent any nation from gaining control of the Persian Gulf waterways, through which most of the oil from the Middle East made its way to foreign ports.

CRISIS IN IRAN Then came the **Iranian hostage crisis**, a series of dramatic events that illustrated the inability of the United States to control world affairs.

In January 1979, Islamist revolutionaries had ousted the pro-American government led by the hated ruler of Iran, Shah Mohammad Reza Pahlavi. The rebel leaders executed hundreds of the shah's former officials. Thousands more Iranians were imprisoned, tortured, or executed for refusing to

A king's ransom An Iranian militant holds a group of U.S. embassy staff members hostage in Tehran, Iran, in 1979.

abide by strict Islamist social codes. The turmoil led to a sharp drop in oil production, driving up gasoline prices worldwide. By the spring of 1979, Americans were again waiting in long lines for limited amounts of high-priced gasoline.

In October, the Carter administration allowed the deposed shah to come to the United States to receive medical treatment for cancer. The president's "humanitarian" decision enraged Iranian revolutionaries. On November 4, 1979, a frenzied mob stormed the U.S. embassy in Tehran and seized sixty-six diplomats, Marines, and staff, including fifty-two American citizens. Iranian leader Ayatollah Ruhollah Khomeini demanded the return of the shah (and all his wealth) in exchange for the release of the hostages. Nightly television coverage in the United States generated a near obsession with the fate of the hostages.

Angry Americans, including many in Congress, demanded a military response. Carter appealed to the United Nations, but Khomeini scoffed at UN efforts to end the crisis. Carter then froze all Iranian financial assets in America and asked Europe to join in a trade embargo of Iran. But because America's allies were not willing to lose access to Iranian oil, the trade restrictions were only partially effective.

As the crisis continued and gasoline prices rose to record levels, Carter authorized a risky rescue attempt by U.S. commandos on April 24, 1980. (His secretary of state, Cyrus Vance, resigned in protest because he thought the military action would be counterproductive.) As it turned out, the raid had to be aborted when several helicopters developed mechanical problems; it ended with the loss of eight U.S. soldiers when a helicopter collided with a transport plane in the Iranian desert.

For fourteen months, the Iranian hostage crisis paralyzed Carter's ability to lead. For many, the prolonged standoff became a symbol of his failed presidency. A Democrat in Congress reported that Carter "hasn't a single friend up here. Not one soul."

Ayatollah Khomeini Religious figure and leader of the Iranian Revolution who overthrew the Iranian monarchy in 1979.

The Iranian crisis finally ended after 444 days, on January 20, 1981, when Carter, just hours before leaving office, released several billion dollars of Iranian assets to ransom the hostages.

THE RISE OF RONALD REAGAN

No sooner had Jimmy Carter been elected in 1976 than conservative Republicans (the "New Right") began working to ensure that he would not win a second term. Their plans centered on the tall, square-shouldered, plain-speaking Ronald Reagan—the handsome actor, two-term California governor, and prominent political commentator. Reagan was not a deep thinker, but he was a superb reader of the public mood, an outspoken patriot, and a committed champion of conservative principles.

THE ACTOR TURNED PRESIDENT

Born in Tampico, Illinois, in 1911, the son of an often-drunk, Irish Catholic shoe salesman and a devout, Bible-quoting mother, Ronald Reagan earned

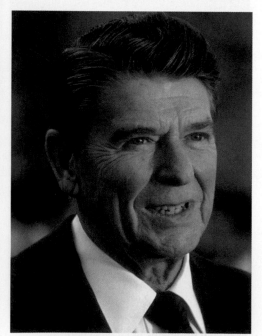

Ronald Reagan The "Great Communicator" flashes his charming, trademark smile.

a football scholarship to attend tiny Eureka College during the Great Depression; he washed dishes in the dining hall to pay for his meals. After graduation, Reagan worked as a radio sportscaster before starting a movie career in Hollywood. He served three years in the army during the Second World War, making training films. At that time, as he recalled, he was a Democrat, "a New Dealer to the core."

After the war, Reagan became president of the acting profession's union, the Screen Actors Guild (SAG), where he honed his negotiating skills and fended off Communist efforts to infiltrate the union. Reagan supported Democrat Harry S. Truman in the 1948 presidential election, but during the fifties he decided that federal taxes were too high. In 1960, he campaigned as a Democrat for Richard Nixon, and two years later he joined the Republican party, explaining that he "didn't leave the Democratic party, the Democratic party left me."

Reagan achieved political stardom in 1964 when he delivered a rousing speech on national television on behalf of Barry Goldwater's presidential candidacy. Wealthy admirers convinced him to run for governor of California in 1966, and he won by a landslide.

As the Republican presidential nominee in 1980, Reagan set about contrasting his optimistic vision of America's future with Jimmy Carter's bleak outlook and "mediocre leadership." Reagan insisted that there was "nothing wrong with the American people" and that there were "simple answers" to the complex problems facing the country, although they were not *easy* answers. He pledged to slash many social-welfare programs, increase military spending to "win" the cold war, dismantle the "bloated" federal bureaucracy, restore states' rights, reduce taxes and government regulation of businesses, and appoint conservative judges to the federal courts. He also promised to affirm old-time religious values by banning abortions and reinstituting prayer in public schools.

Reagan's popularity resulted in part from his skill as a speaker (journalists dubbed him the "Great Communicator") and his commitment to a few basic principles and simple themes. Blessed with a reassuring baritone voice and a wealth of entertaining stories, he rejected Carter's assumption that Americans needed "to start getting along with less, to accept a decline in our standard of living."

THE RISE OF THE NEW RIGHT

By 1980, an increase in the number of senior citizens, a group that tends to be more politically and socially conservative, and the steady migration of people—especially older Americans—to the conservative Sun Belt states were shifting the political balance of power. Fully 90 percent of the nation's population growth during the 1980s occurred in southern or western sunbelt states, while the Northeast and industrial states of the Midwest—Ohio, Michigan, Illinois, Pennsylvania, and West Virginia (called the Rust Belt)—experienced economic decline, factory closings, and population losses.

A related development was a growing tax revolt. As consumer prices and home values rose, so did property taxes. In California, Ronald Reagan's home state, skyrocketing property taxes threatened to force many working-class people from their homes. This spurred efforts to cut back on the size and cost of government to enable reductions in property taxes. In June 1978, tax rebels, with Reagan's support, succeeded in putting an initiative known as Proposition 13 on the state ballot. An overwhelming majority of voters approved the measure, which slashed property taxes by 57 percent and amended the state constitution to make it more difficult to raise taxes. The "Prop 13" tax revolt soon spread across the nation, leading the *New York Times* to call it a "modern Boston Tea Party."

THE CHRISTIAN RIGHT Conservatives promoting a faith-based political agenda formed the strongest grassroots movement of the late twentieth century. By the 1980s, Catholic conservatives and Protestant evangelicals owned television and radio stations, operated their own schools and universities, and organized megachurches from which televangelists such as the Reverend Jerry Falwell launched a cultural crusade against the "demonic" forces of liberalism at home and communism abroad.

In 1979, Falwell formed the **Moral Majority** (later renamed the Liberty Alliance) to campaign for the political and social goals of the Christian Right: The economy should operate without "interference" by the government, which should be reduced in size; the Supreme Court decision in *Roe v. Wade* (1973) legalizing abortion should be reversed; Darwinian evolution should be replaced in school textbooks by the biblical story of creation; daily prayer should return to public schools; women should submit to their husbands; and communism should be opposed as a form of pagan totalitarianism.

Look on the Right side The rise of the Religious Right brought protests against Supreme Court rulings that reinforced the separation of church and state. Here, in a 1984 rally organized by the Moral Majority, students chant "Kids want to pray!" in support of an amendment to reinstate prayer in public schools. (The effort failed.)

That Ronald Reagan became the hero of the Christian Right was a tribute to his political skills, for he rarely attended church and had no strong religious affiliations. Jimmy Carter, though famous as a born-again Baptist Sunday-school teacher, lost the support of religious conservatives because he was not willing to ban abortions or restore prayers in public schools. His push for state ratification of the Equal Rights Amendment (ERA) also cost him votes among conservatives.

ANTI-FEMINIST BACKLASH By the late 1970s, a well-organized, well-financed backlash against the feminist movement reinforced the rise of the New Right. Activists like Republican Phyllis Schlafly, a conservative Catholic attorney from Illinois, stopped the ERA from being ratified by the required thirty-eight states. Schlafly's STOP (Stop Taking Our Privileges) ERA organization warned that the ERA would allow husbands to abandon their wives, force women into military service, and give gay "perverts" the right to marry. She and others stressed that the gender equality promised by the proposed amendment violated biblical teachings about women's "God-given" roles as nurturers and helpmates.

Many of Schlafly's supporters also participated in the growing anti-abortion, or "pro-life," movement. The emotional intensity of the issue made it a powerful political force.

FINANCING CONSERVATISM The business community had also become a source of conservative activism. In 1972, leaders of the nation's largest corporations formed the Business Roundtable to promote their interests in Congress. Within a few years, many of them had created political action committees (PACs) to distribute money to pro-business political candidates. Corporate donations also helped fund conservative "think tanks," such as the American Enterprise Institute, the Cato Institute, and the Heritage Foundation. By 1980, the conservative insurgency had become a powerful political force.

THE ELECTION OF 1980 Ronald Reagan's supporters loved his simple solutions and genial, upbeat personality, and they responded passionately to his recurring question: "Are you better off than you were four years ago?" Their answer was a resounding "No!" Jimmy Carter had not been able to gain the release of the Americans held hostage in Iran, nor had he improved the economy. His approval ratings had sunk below those of Richard Nixon.

On Election Day, Reagan swept to a lopsided victory, with 489 electoral votes to 49 for Carter, who carried only six states. (It was the second worst defeat for an incumbent president in the twentieth century, behind William Howard Taft in 1912). The popular vote was 44 million (51 percent) for Reagan to Carter's 35 million (41 percent), with 7 percent going to John Anderson, a moderate Republican who ran as an independent. Reagan's victory signaled a major realignment of voters in which many so-called Reagan Democrats— conservative white southern Protestants and blue-collar northern Catholics— crossed over to the Republican party.

THE REAGAN REVOLUTION

Democrats who dismissed sixty-nine-year-old Ronald Reagan, the oldest man to assume the presidency, as a mental lightweight underrated him. Few people in public life had Reagan's presence—or confidence. His ability to revitalize the American dream won him the 1980 and 1984 presidential elections and ensured the victory of his anointed successor, Vice President George H. W. Bush, in 1988. Reagan's actions and beliefs set the tone for the decade's political and economic life.

REAGAN'S FIRST TERM

"Fellow conservatives," President Reagan said in a speech in 1981, "our moment has arrived." In his inaugural address, he promised to help Americans "renew our faith and hope" in their nation as a "shining city on a hill" for the rest of the world to emulate.

Reagan succeeded where Carter failed for three main reasons. First, he focused on a few priorities like slowing the rate of inflation, lowering tax rates, reducing the scope of the federal government, increasing military spending, and conducting an anti-Soviet foreign policy.

Second, he was a shrewd negotiator with congressional leaders and foreign heads of state. He also recognized early on that governing a representative democracy requires compromises. He thus combined the passion of a revolutionary with the pragmatism of a diplomat.

Third, Reagan's infectious optimism, like that of Franklin Roosevelt before him, gave people a sense of common purpose and renewed confidence. "We have every right," he stressed, "to dream heroic dreams."

Reagan's first step as president was to freeze federal hiring. "Government," he declared, "is not the solution to our problems. Government *is* the problem." To drive home that theme, he ordered that the portrait of Harry Truman in the Cabinet Room be replaced with one of Calvin Coolidge, the

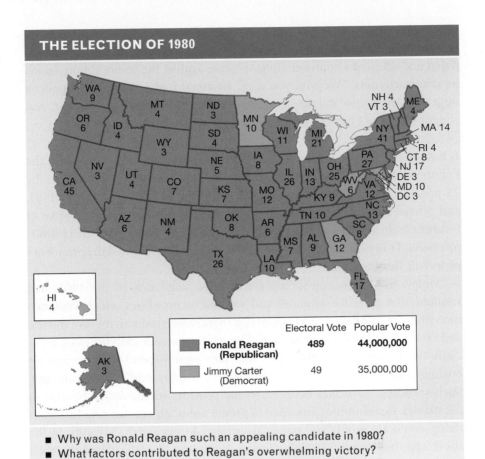

THE ELECTION OF 1980

		Electoral Vote	Popular Vote
Ronald Reagan (Republican)		489	44,000,000
Jimmy Carter (Democrat)		49	35,000,000

■ Why was Ronald Reagan such an appealing candidate in 1980?
■ What factors contributed to Reagan's overwhelming victory?

most anti-government president of the twentieth century—and, like Reagan, a man who loved afternoon naps.

Public affection for Reagan spiked just two months into his presidency when an emotionally disturbed man fired six shots at the president, one of which punctured a lung and lodged near his heart. Reagan told doctors as they prepared for life-saving surgery, "Please tell me you're Republicans." Reagan's gritty response to the assassination attempt created an outpouring of support that gave his presidency added momentum. The Democratic Speaker of the House, Tip O'Neill, told colleagues that Reagan "has become a hero. We can't argue with a man as popular as he is."

Reagan inherited an economy in shambles. The annual rate of inflation had reached 13 percent, and unemployment hovered at 7.5 percent. At the same time, the cold war was heating up again. The Soviet Union had placed missiles with nuclear weapons in the nations of central and Eastern Europe under its control—which threatened the entire continent. Reagan refused to be intimidated and adopted a confrontational posture against the Soviet Union, which he summarized as, "We win, you lose." He convinced Congress to support a huge increase in the military budget, deployed U.S. missiles in Europe, and sought to root out Communist insurgencies in Central America.

REAGANOMICS On August 1, 1981, President Reagan signed the Economic Recovery Tax Act (ERTA), which cut personal income taxes by 25 percent, lowered the maximum tax rate from 70 to 50 percent for 1982, and offered a broad array of tax concessions. The bill was the centerpiece of Reagan's "common sense" economic plan. While theorists called the philosophy behind the plan supply-side economics, journalists dubbed the president's proposals **Reaganomics**.

Simply put, Reaganomics argued that the stagflation of the 1970s had resulted from excessive corporate and personal income taxes, which weakened incentives for individuals and businesses to increase productivity, save money, and reinvest in economic expansion. The solution was to slash tax rates, especially on the wealthy, in the belief that they would spend their savings on business expansion and consumer goods (the "supply side" of the economy). Such spending, advocates believed, would provide "trickle down" benefits to the masses. Reaganomics promised to produce enough new tax revenues from rising corporate profits and personal incomes to pay for the tax cuts. In the short term, however, ERTA did not work as planned. The federal budget deficit grew, and by November 1981, the economy was officially in recession.

MANAGING THE BUDGET To offset the loss of government tax revenues, David Stockman, President Reagan's budget director, proposed sharp reductions in federal spending, including Social Security and Medicare, the two most expensive—and most popular—federal social-welfare programs. Liberal Democrats howled, and Reagan responded that he was committed to maintaining the "safety net" of government services for the "truly needy." According to Stockman, Reagan was "too kind, gentle, and sentimental" to make the drastic cuts needed to balance the budget.

The Reagan administration also continued huge federal subsidies to corporations and agribusinesses—what critics called "welfare for the rich." In the end, Reagan never dismantled the major New Deal programs that he had savagely criticized. Conservative political columnist George Will explained Reagan's failure to make substantial cuts in federal spending by noting that "Americans are conservative. What they want to conserve is the New Deal."

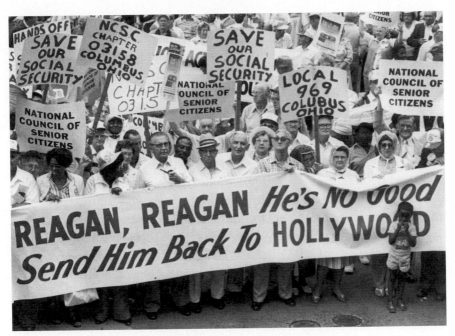

A miss for Reaganomics More than 5,000 senior citizens staged a demonstration in downtown Detroit against Reagan's decision to make cuts in Social Security and other federal programs supporting the elderly in 1982.

Within a year, Stockman realized that the actual cuts in domestic spending had fallen far short of what the president had promised. Massive increases in military spending complicated the situation. Over the next five years, the administration would spend $1.2 *trillion* on military expenses, the highest amount ever. Something had to give.

In the summer of 1981, Stockman warned that "we're heading for a crash landing on the budget. We're facing potential deficit numbers so big that they could wreck the president's entire economic program." The fast-growing federal deficit, which had helped trigger the worst recession since the 1930s, was Reagan's greatest failure. During 1982, an estimated 10 million Americans, more than ten percent of the workforce, were jobless. "The stench of failure hangs over Ronald Reagan's White House," declared the *New York Times*.

Stockman and other aides finally convinced the president that the government needed "revenue enhancements" (tax increases). With Reagan's support, Congress passed a tax bill in 1982 that would raise almost $100 billion, but the economic slump persisted. In the 1982 congressional midterm elections, Democrats picked up twenty-six seats in the House of Representatives.

Over time, however, Reagan's determination to "stay the course" began to pay off. By the summer of 1983, a robust economic recovery was underway, in part because of increased government spending and lower interest rates, and in part because of lower tax rates. Inflation subsided, as did unemployment. Reaganomics was not helping to balance the budget as promised, however. In fact, the federal deficits had grown larger—so much so that the president had run up an accumulated debt larger than that of all his predecessors combined.

REAGAN'S ANTI-LIBERALISM During Ronald Reagan's presidency, organized labor suffered severe setbacks. In 1981, he fired 11,359 members of the Professional Air Traffic Controllers Organization who had participated in an illegal strike intended to shut down air travel. (Air traffic controllers were deemed essential to public safety and therefore were prohibited from striking by the Taft-Hartley Act of 1947.) Reagan's actions broke the political power of the American Federation of Labor–Congress of Industrial Organizations (AFL-CIO), the national confederation of labor unions that traditionally supported Democratic candidates. Although record numbers of jobs were created during the 1980s, union membership steadily dropped. By 1987, unions represented only 17 percent of the nation's full-time workers, down from 24 percent in 1979.

Reagan also opposed the Equal Rights Amendment, abortion rights, and proposals by women's rights organizations to require comparable pay for jobs of comparable worth. In affirming his conservative credentials, he cut funds for civil rights enforcement and the Equal Employment Opportunity Commission, and he opposed renewal of the Voting Rights Act of 1965.

Sandra Day O'Connor Her Supreme Court confirmation hearing in September 1981 was picketed by conservatives who decried her pro-abortion stance.

He did name Sandra Day O'Connor, an Arizona judge, as the first woman Supreme Court justice in 1981, despite the Religious Right's objections that O'Connor supported abortion rights for women. O'Connor gained the support of both Democrats and Republicans, and she was confirmed by a vote of 99–0 in the U.S. Senate. She would serve on the Supreme Court for a quarter of a century, and was quite often considered to be an important "swing vote" on many major cases.

THE ELECTION OF 1984 By 1983, Reagan's supply-side economics was at last working as advertised—except for the growing federal budget deficit, which had always been a sore subject to fiscal conservatives. Reporters began to speak of the "Reagan Revolution." In 1984, the slogan at the Republican National Convention was, "America is back and standing tall."

The Democrats' presidential nominee, Walter Mondale, Jimmy Carter's vice president, was endorsed by the AFL-CIO, the National Organization for Women (NOW), and many prominent African Americans. He made history by choosing as his running mate Geraldine Ferraro, a New York congresswoman.

A bit of frankness in Mondale's acceptance speech ended up hurting his campaign. "Mr. Reagan will raise taxes [to reduce budget deficits], and so will I," he told the convention. "He won't tell you. I just did." Reagan responded by vowing never to approve another tax increase (a promise he could not keep). Reagan also repeated a theme he had used against Carter: "It's morning again in America," and record numbers of Americans were finding jobs. In the end, Reagan took 59 percent of the popular vote and lost only Minnesota (Mondale's home state) and the District of Columbia. It was the worst defeat ever for a Democratic candidate.

REAGAN'S SECOND TERM

Spurred by his landslide reelection, Ronald Reagan called for "a Second American Revolution of hope and opportunity." Through much of 1985, he drummed up support for a tax-simplification plan. After vigorous debate, Congress passed a comprehensive Tax Reform Act in 1986. It cut the number of federal tax brackets from fourteen to two and reduced rates from the maximum of 50 percent to 15 and 28 percent—the lowest since Calvin Coolidge was president in the 1920s.

REAGAN'S HALF-HEARTED REVOLUTION Although Ronald Reagan had promised to "curb the size and influence of the federal establishment," the number of federal employees actually *grew* during his two terms as president. Neither Social Security nor Medicare, the two largest federal social programs, was overhauled, and the federal agencies that Reagan had threatened to abolish, such as the Department of Education, not only survived but saw their budgets grow.

The federal deficit almost tripled during Reagan's two terms. He blamed Congress for the problem, "since only Congress can spend money," but the legislators essentially approved the budgets Reagan submitted to them. As Dick

Cheney, a future Republican vice president, quipped, "Reagan showed that deficits don't matter."

The cost of Social Security, the most expensive "entitlement" program, grew by 27 percent under Reagan, as some 6,000 people each day turned sixty-five years old. Moreover, he failed to fulfill his campaign promises to the Religious Right, such as reinstituting daily prayer in public schools and banning abortion. Reagan did follow through on his pledge to reshape the federal court system. He appointed 368 mostly conservative judges, including Supreme Court justices Antonin Scalia and Anthony Kennedy, along with Sandra Day O'Connor.

Reagan also ended the prolonged period of stagflation and set in motion what economists called the "Great Expansion," an unprecedented twenty-year burst of productivity and prosperity. True, Reagan's presidency left the nation with a massive debt burden that would cause major problems, but the Great Communicator also renewed the nation's strength, self-confidence, and soaring sense of possibilities.

Over two terms, Ronald Reagan became a transformational president. While restoring the stature of the presidency and reviving the economy, he upended political life by accelerating the nation's shift toward conservatism and by revitalizing the Republican party. He put the Democrats on the defensive and forced conventional New Deal liberalism into a panicked retreat. For the next twenty years or so, Reagan's anti-government, anti-tax conservative agenda would dominate the national political landscape.

An Anti-Soviet Foreign Policy

To end the cold war, President Reagan promoted what he called his "peace through strength" strategy. Through a series of bold steps, he would eventually build up the U.S. military to the point that it would overwhelm the Soviet Union, both financially and militarily.

What came to be called the Reagan Doctrine pledged to combat Soviet adventurism throughout the world, even if it meant partnering with brutal dictatorships. Reagan believed that aggressive CIA-led efforts to stymie Soviet expansionism would eventually cause the unstable Soviet system to implode "on the ash heap of history."

A MASSIVE DEFENSE BUILDUP Ronald Reagan long believed that Richard Nixon and Gerald Ford (who followed Henry Kissinger's advice) had been too soft on the Soviets. Kissinger's emphasis on détente, Reagan said, had been a "one-way street" favoring the Soviets. Reagan wanted to reduce the risk of nuclear war by convincing the Soviets that they could not win such a conflict.

To do so, he and Secretary of Defense Caspar Weinberger embarked upon a major buildup of nuclear and conventional weapons. Defense spending came to represent a fourth of all federal government expenditures. To critics who complained about the spending, Reagan replied, "It will break the Soviets." It did.

"STAR WARS" On March 23, 1983, two weeks after denouncing the Soviet Union as "the focus of evil in the modern world," Reagan escalated the nuclear arms race when he announced that he was authorizing the Defense Department to develop a **Strategic Defense Initiative (SDI).** The complex antimissile defense system featured satellites equipped with laser weapons that would "intercept and destroy" Soviet missiles in flight before they could harm the United States. The program was controversial because it relied upon untested technology and violated a 1972 U.S.–Soviet treaty banning such antimissile defensive systems.

Despite skepticism among journalists, scientists, and even government officials that such an expensive defense system (dubbed "Star Wars" by the media) could be built, Congress approved the first stage of funding, eventually

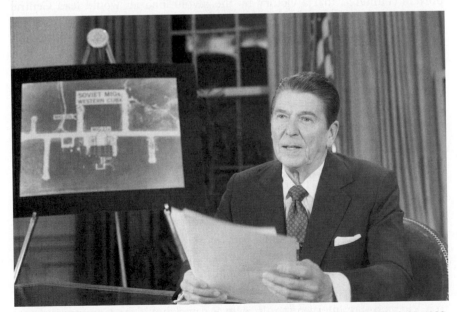

Strategic Defense Initiative President Reagan addresses the nation on March 23, 1983, promoting the development of a space-age shield to intercept Soviet missiles.

allocating $30 billion to the program. Although SDI was never implemented, it did force the Soviets to launch an expensive research and development effort of their own, which helped bankrupt their economy. As a Soviet foreign minister later admitted, Reagan's commitment to SDI "made us realize we were in a very dangerous spot."

CONFRONTING THE EVIL EMPIRE President Reagan also expressed resolve in the face of "Communist aggression anywhere in the world." When the Polish Communist government declared martial law during the winter of 1981, Reagan imposed economic sanctions and worked behind the scenes to support the Polish protest movement, Solidarity, which sought independence from Soviet control.

COMMUNIST INSURGENCIES IN CENTRAL AMERICA President Reagan's foremost international concern was Central America. The tiny nation of El Salvador was caught up in a brutal struggle between Communist-supported revolutionaries and the right-wing military government, which received U.S. economic and military assistance. Critics argued that U.S. involvement ensured that the revolutionary forces would gain favor among the people by capitalizing on "anti-Yankee" sentiment. Reagan's supporters countered that a victory by the revolutionaries would lead Central America into the Communist camp (a new "domino" theory). By 1984, the U.S.-backed government of President José Napoleón Duarte had brought some stability to El Salvador.

More troubling to Reagan was the situation in Nicaragua. The State Department claimed that the Cuban-sponsored Sandinista socialist government, which had seized power in 1979, was sending arms to leftist Salvadoran rebels. In response, the Reagan administration ordered the CIA to train, equip, and finance anti-Communist Nicaraguans, or Contras (short for *contrarevolucionarios*, or "counterrevolutionaries"), who staged attacks on Sandinista bases.

In supporting these "freedom fighters," Reagan sought to impede the traffic in arms to Salvadoran rebels and to replace the Sandinistas with a democratic government friendly to the United States. Yet his anti-Communist interventionism fostered a prolonged civil war that killed tens of thousands of Nicaraguans on both sides. Critics of American involvement accused the Contras of being right-wing fanatics who killed indiscriminately. They also feared that the United States might eventually commit its own combat forces, leading to a Vietnam-like intervention. Reagan warned that if the Communists prevailed in Central America, "our credibility would collapse, our alliances would crumble, and the safety of our homeland would be jeopardized."

STRIFE IN THE MIDDLE EAST The Middle East remained a tinderbox of conflict during the 1980s. In September 1980, the Iraqi despot, Saddam Hussein, had attacked his neighbor, Iran. The brutal war involved the extensive use of chemical weapons and generated hundreds of thousands of casualties on both sides, but showed no sign of ending. In 1984, both sides began to attack oil tankers in the Persian Gulf, a major source of the world's oil. Nor was any cease-fire imminent in Afghanistan, where Soviet occupation forces had bogged down as badly as the Americans had in Vietnam.

American administrations continued to consider Israel the strongest and most reliable ally in the volatile Middle East, while still seeking to encourage moderate Arab groups. But the forces of moderation were dealt a blow during the mid-1970s when Lebanon, long an enclave of peace, collapsed into an anarchy of warring groups. The most powerful of the rival factions was the Palestine Liberation Organization (PLO). Founded in 1964, the PLO sought the "liberation of Palestine" from Israeli control through armed struggle, with much of its violence aimed at Israeli civilians on Lebanon's southern border.

In 1982, Israeli forces pushed the PLO from southern Lebanon north to Beirut, where they began shelling PLO strongholds. The United States sent a special ambassador to negotiate a settlement. Israeli troops moved into Beirut and looked the other way when Christian militiamen slaughtered Muslim women and children in Palestinian refugee camps. French, Italian, and U.S. forces then moved into Lebanon as "peacekeepers," but in such small numbers they became targets themselves. Islamists resentful of Western troops in their homeland constantly harassed them. American warships and planes responded by bombing Muslim positions in the highlands behind Beirut.

By 1983, Israel had driven the PLO from Beirut, but the city became increasingly unstable. In April, Islamist suicide bombers drove a truck laden with explosives into the U.S.-embassy compound in Beirut, detonated it, and killed forty people, including seventeen Americans. On October 23, 1983, an Islamist suicide bomber attacked U.S. Marine headquarters at the Beirut airport; the explosion left 241 Americans and 58 French dead. In early 1984, Reagan announced that the Marines remaining in Lebanon would be redeployed to warships offshore. The Israeli forces pulled back to southern Lebanon, while the Syrians remained in eastern Lebanon. Peaceful coexistence in the region proved to be an elusive dream.

U.S. INTERVENTION IN GRENADA Fortune, as it happened, presented Ronald Reagan the chance for an easy triumph closer to home that eclipsed news of the debacle in Lebanon. On the tiny Caribbean island of Grenada, whose population of 91,000 made it the smallest independent country in the Western Hemisphere, a leftist government had recruited Cuban workers to build a new airfield and signed military agreements with Communist countries. In October 1983, a radical military council seized power and killed the prime minister. Appeals from neighboring islands convinced Reagan to send 1,900 Marines to invade Grenada, depose the new military government, and evacuate a small group of American students at the country's medical school. The UN General Assembly condemned the U.S. invasion, but it was popular among Grenadians and their neighbors and in the United States (The date of the invasion is now a national holiday in Grenada, called Thanksgiving Day.). The decisive move served as notice to Latin American revolutionaries that Reagan might use military force elsewhere in the region.

THE IRAN-CONTRA AFFAIR During the fall of 1986, Democrats regained control of the Senate and picked up six seats in the House, increasing their already comfortable margin to 259–176. The election results meant that Reagan would face a Democrat-led Congress during the last two years of his presidency.

Worse for the administration were reports that surfaced in late 1986 finding the United States had been secretly selling arms to U.S.-hating Iran in the hope of securing the release of American hostages held in Lebanon by extremist groups sympathetic to Iran. Such action contradicted Reagan's insistence that his administration would never negotiate with terrorists. The disclosures angered America's allies as well as many Americans who vividly remembered the 1979 Iranian hostage situation.

Over the next several months, revelations emerged about a complicated series of covert activities carried out by administration officials. At the center of

Iran-Contra hearings Admiral John Poindexter listens warily to a question from the congressional investigation committee on July 21, 1987.

what came to be called the **Iran-Contra affair** was U.S. Marine Corps lieutenant colonel Oliver North, a National Security Council aide who specialized in counterterrorism. Working from the basement of the White House, North had secretly sold military supplies to Iran and used the proceeds to support the Contra rebels in Nicaragua at a time when Congress had banned such aid.

North's activities, it turned out, had been approved by national security adviser Robert McFarlane; McFarlane's successor, Admiral John Poindexter; and CIA director William Casey. After information about the secret dealings surfaced, North and others erased incriminating computer files and destroyed documents. McFarlane attempted suicide before being convicted of withholding information from Congress. Poindexter resigned, and North, described by the White House as a "loose cannon," was fired.

Facing a barrage of criticism, Reagan appointed a commission, led by former Republican senator John Tower, to investigate the scandal. The Tower Commission issued a devastating report early in 1987 that placed much of the responsibility for the Iran-Contra affair on Reagan's loose management style. When asked if he had known of Colonel North's illegal actions, the president simply replied, "I don't remember." During the spring and summer of 1987, a joint House-Senate committee held hearings into the Iran-Contra affair. In his testimony, North claimed that he thought "he had received authority from the President."

The Iran-Contra cover-up In Paul Szep's 1987 cartoon, political figures including President Reagan, Robert McFarlane, Lieutenant Colonel Oliver North, and Iran's Ayatollah Khomeini attempt to deflect blame for the Iran-Contra affair.

The investigations led to six indictments in 1988. A jury found North guilty of three minor charges but innocent of nine more serious counts because he had acted as an agent of higher-ups. An appellate court later overturned his conviction. Of those involved, only John Poindexter received a jail sentence—six months for obstructing justice and lying to Congress.

A HISTORIC TREATY The most notable achievement at the end of Reagan's second term was a surprising arms-reduction agreement with the Soviet government. Under Mikhail Gorbachev, who came to power in 1985, the Soviets pursued three dramatic initiatives. They renewed the policy of détente, encouraging a reduction of tensions with the United States, so that they could subsequently reduce military spending and focus on more-pressing problems, chiefly an inefficient economy and a losing war in Afghanistan.

Gorbachev also instituted what he called *perestroika* (restructuring) to make the Soviet government bureaucracy more efficient. Third, he encouraged *glasnost* (openness), a radical reappraisal of the Soviet system that allowed for open debate and shared information. In the end, however, the forces of modernization that Gorbachev helped unleash would end up dismantling the Soviet Union.

Mikhail Gorbachev Deputy chairman, and later, president of the Soviet Union.

THE REYKJAVIK SUMMIT In October 1986, Ronald Reagan and Mikhail Gorbachev met for the first time in Reykjavik, Iceland, to discuss ways to reduce the threat of nuclear war. At one point, Reagan shocked Gorbachev and the Soviets by saying, "It would be fine with me if we eliminated all nuclear weapons." Equally shocking was Gorbachev's reply: "We can do that."

By the end of the meeting, however, the two sides remained far apart, and Gorbachev privately called Reagan a "feebleminded cave man." The main sticking point was Reagan's refusal to abandon the Strategic Defense Initiative (SDI, or "Star Wars").

THE INF TREATY The logjam in the disarmament negotiations suddenly broke in 1987, when Mikhail Gorbachev announced that he was willing to consider mutual reductions in nuclear weaponry. A member of the Soviet negotiating team acknowledged Ronald Reagan's role in the breakthrough. The U.S. president, he explained, "takes you by the arm, walks you to the cliff's edge, and invites you to step forward for the good of humanity."

After nine months of negotiations, Reagan and Gorbachev met in Washington, D.C., on December 9, 1987, and signed the **Intermediate-Range Nuclear Forces (INF) Treaty**, an agreement to eliminate intermediate-range (300- to 3,000-mile) missiles. The treaty marked the first time that the two nations had agreed to destroy a whole class of weapons systems and produced the most sweeping cuts in nuclear weaponry in history.

REAGAN'S GLOBAL LEGACY Ronald Reagan achieved the unthinkable by helping to end the cold war. Although his massive defense buildup almost bankrupted the United States, it forced Gorbachev to the bargaining table. By negotiating the nuclear disarmament treaty and lighting the fuse of democratic freedom in Soviet-controlled East Germany, Hungary, Poland, and Czechoslovakia, Reagan set in motion events that would lead to the collapse of the Soviet Union.

In June 1987, Reagan visited the Berlin Wall in East Germany and, in a dramatic speech, called upon the Soviet Union to allow greater freedom within the countries under its control. "General Secretary Gorbachev, if you seek peace, if you seek prosperity for the Soviet Union and Eastern Europe, if you seek liberalization: Come here to this gate! Mr. Gorbachev, open this gate! Mr. Gorbachev, tear down this wall!" It was great theater and good politics.

THE CHANGING ECONOMIC AND SOCIAL LANDSCAPE

During the 1980s, the U.S. economy went through a wrenching transformation. The nations most devastated by the Second World War—France, Germany, the Soviet Union, Japan, and China—had now developed formidable economies with higher levels of productivity than in the United States. Increasingly more U.S. companies shifted their production overseas to take advantage of lower labor costs, accelerating the transition of the economy from its once-dominant industrial base to a more services-oriented approach. Driving these changes were the computer revolution and the development of the internet.

THE COMPUTER REVOLUTION The idea of a programmable machine that would rapidly perform mental tasks had been around since the eighteenth century, but it took the Second World War to gather the intellectual and financial resources needed to create such a "computer."

In 1946, a team of engineers at the University of Pennsylvania developed ENIAC (electronic numerical integrator and computer), the first all-purpose, all-electronic digital computer. It required 18,000 vacuum tubes to operate and an entire room to house it. The following year, researchers at Bell Telephone Laboratories invented the transistor, which replaced the bulky vacuum tubes and enabled much smaller, yet more-powerful, computers—as well as being the foundation for new devices such as hearing aids and transistor radios.

The next major breakthrough was the invention in 1971 of the **microprocessor**—virtually a tiny computer on a silicon chip. The microprocessor chip revolutionized computing by allowing for the storage of far more data in much smaller machines.

The microchip made possible the personal computer. In 1975, an engineer named Ed Roberts developed the Altair 8800, the prototype of the personal

"Introducing Macintosh. For the rest of us." Personal computers are introduced to the masses in this 1980s Apple advertisement.

computer. Its potential excited a Harvard University sophomore named Bill Gates, who improved the software of the Altair 8800, dropped out of college, and formed a company called Microsoft.

During the 1980s, IBM (International Business Machines), using a microprocessor made by the Intel Corporation and an operating system provided by Microsoft, helped transform the personal computer into a mass consumer product. In 1963, a half-million computer chips were sold worldwide; by 1970, the number was 300 million.

Computer chips transformed a variety of electronic products—televisions, calculators, wristwatches, clocks, ovens, phones, laptops, and automobiles—while facilitating efforts to land astronauts on the moon and launch satellites into space. The development of the internet, email, and cell-phone technology during the 1980s and '90s allowed for instantaneous communication, thereby accelerating the globalization of the economy and dramatically increasing productivity in the workplace.

CAREFREE CONSUMERS AND THE STOCK MARKET PLUNGE In the late 1970s, Jimmy Carter had urged Americans to lead simpler lives, reduce energy use, and invest more time in faith and family. During the 1980s, Ronald Reagan reduced tax rates so people would have more money to spend. Americans preferred Reagan's emphasis on prosperity to Carter's focus on propriety.

Reagan, however, succeeded too well in shifting the public mood back to the "bigger is better" tradition of heedless consumerism. During the "age of Reagan," advertisements celebrated instant gratification. Many consumers went on self-indulgent spending sprees, and the more they bought, the more they wanted. As the stock market soared, the number of multimillionaires working on Wall Street and in the financial industry mushroomed as income inequality in the United States widened. The national economy during the 1980s shifted from manufacturing to service industries, where wages were lower (a process known as "deindustrialization"). Most new jobs created during the 1980s paid only the minimum wage.

Yet affluent Americans showed little concern about those struggling to make ends meet. The money fever was contagious. Compulsive shoppers donned T-shirts proclaiming: "Born to Shop." By 1988, some 110 million Americans had an average of seven credit cards each. Money—lots of it—came to define the American dream. In the hit movie *Wall Street* (1987), the high-flying land developer and corporate raider Gordon Gekko, played by actor Michael Douglas, announced, "Greed . . . is good. Greed is right."

During the 1980s, many Americans began spending more than they earned. All categories of debt dramatically increased. Americans in the 1960s had saved, on average, 10 percent of their income; in 1987, the figure was less than 4 percent. The federal debt more than tripled, from $908 billion in 1980 to $2.9 trillion at the end of the 1989 fiscal year.

On October 19, 1987, the bill collector suddenly arrived at the nation's doorstep. On that "Black Monday," the stock market experienced a tidal wave of selling reminiscent of the 1929 crash, as investors worried that the United States would never address its massive budget deficits. The Dow Jones Industrial Average plummeted 22.6 percent, nearly doubling the 12.8 percent fall on October 28, 1929. Wall Street's selling frenzy sent stock prices plummeting in Tokyo, London, Paris, and Toronto.

In the aftermath of Black Monday, fears of an impending recession led business leaders and economists to attack President Reagan for allowing such huge budget deficits. He responded by agreeing to work with Congress to develop a deficit-reduction package. For the first time, Reagan indicated a willingness to increase taxes to help reduce the deficit. The eventual compromise plan, however, was so modest that it did little to restore investor confidence.

Black Monday A 508-point plunge devastated the stock market on October 19, 1987, and sent traders on the floor of the New York Stock Exchange into a panic-selling frenzy.

THE POOR Despite unprecedented prosperity in the eighties, homelessness became an acute social issue. An estimated 400,000 people were dispossessed by the end of the decade. Several factors had led to a shortage of low-cost housing. The government had given up on building public housing, urban-renewal programs had demolished blighted areas but provided no housing for those who were displaced, and owners had abandoned unprofitable buildings in poor inner-city neighborhoods or converted them into expensive condominiums for high-income city dwellers, a process called gentrification.

In addition, the working poor during the 1980s saw their incomes decline at the same time that the Reagan administration was making deep cuts in federal social welfare programs. By 1983, over 15 percent of adults were living below the poverty line, even though half of them lived in households where at least one person worked. Still another factor affecting the homelessness epidemic was the unintended effects of new medications that allowed some patients to be discharged from mental institutions. Once released, many of them ended up on the sidewalks of America, homeless and without care, because promised mental-health services failed to materialize. Between 1982 and 1985, federal programs targeted to the poor were reduced by $57 billion.

The culture of homelessness often sent victims on a downward spiral. Drug and alcohol abuse were rampant among the homeless. In Los Angeles County, for example, there were 400,000 cocaine addicts and 200,000 other drug addicts in need of treatment by the late 1980s. An estimated 100,000 of them were homeless or poor. Nationwide, a quarter of the homeless (about 100,000 people) had spent time in mental institutions, and some 40 percent had spent time in jail.

THE AIDS EPIDEMIC Still another group of outcasts included those suffering from a new disease called AIDS (acquired immunodeficiency syndrome). At the beginning of the 1980s, public health officials had reported that gay men and intravenous drug users were especially at risk for developing AIDS. People contracted the human immunodeficiency virus (HIV), which causes AIDS, through contact with the blood or body fluids of an infected person. Those infected with the virus showed signs of extreme fatigue, developed a strange combination of infections, and soon died.

The Reagan administration showed little interest in AIDS in part because it was viewed as a "gay" disease. Reagan himself did not specifically mention AIDS in public until 1985, even though some 5,000 Americans had died of the

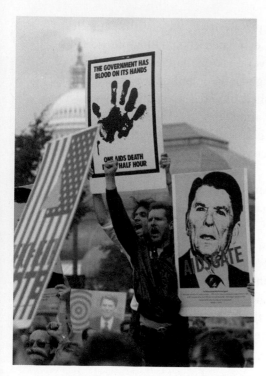

Act Up! Members of the influential AIDS activist group Act Up! demonstrate for increased availability of life-saving medication.

disease. Patrick Buchanan, who served as Reagan's director of communications, said that gays had "declared war on nature, and now nature is extracting an awful retribution." Buchanan and others convinced Reagan not to engage in the **HIV/AIDS** issue. In part because of federal government indifference, by 2001, 774,467 persons had contracted AIDS in the United States, and 448,060 of them had died. The disease had become the leading cause of death among men ages twenty-five to forty-four.

Frustrated by the lack of concern shown by the Reagan administration, activists founded the AIDS Coalition to Unleash Power (ACT UP) in 1987. It has since become the most effective voice for fighting AIDS. In large part because of its advocacy, the number of newly reported AIDS cases has significantly declined from nearly 200,000 a year in 1988 to 40,000 in 2016.

THE PRESIDENCY OF GEORGE H. W. BUSH

In his farewell address in January 1989, Ronald Reagan said with a smile, "My friends, we did it. We . . . made a difference." Over his two terms, Reagan had become a transformational president. While restoring the stature of the presidency, helping to defuse the cold war, and reviving the economy, he had accelerated the nation's shift toward conservatism and rejuvenated the Republican party after the Watergate scandal.

He would be a tough act to follow. His two-term vice president, George H. W. Bush, won the Republican presidential nomination in 1988 because he pledged to create an ethical government, be a more "hands-on" president than Reagan, and promote "a more compassionate conservatism." It was time to deal more seriously with the thorny problems of inner-city poverty, homelessness, and drug abuse.

Born into a prominent New England family, the son of a U.S. senator, George H. W. Bush had, at the age of eighteen, enlisted in the U.S. Navy at the start of the Second World War, becoming the youngest combat pilot to have flown in the U.S. military. After his distinguished military service, Bush graduated from Yale University and became a wealthy oil executive in Texas before entering government service. He served first as a member of the U.S. House of Representatives and then as U.S. ambassador to the United Nations. He was elected chair of the Republican National Committee, became a diplomat in China, and was appointed director of the CIA before becoming Reagan's loyal vice president.

In all those roles, Bush had displayed intelligence, integrity, and courage, but he lacked Reagan's charm and eloquence. One Democrat described Bush as being born "with a silver foot in his mouth."

George H. W. Bush His son, George W. Bush, would also serve as president, making them the second father-son presidential duo in history (the first was John Adams and John Quincy Adams).

A centrist Republican, Bush stressed that he would be a different president than Reagan, more compassionate, more progressive, less ideological. He promised to use the White House to fight bigotry, illiteracy, and homelessness. "I want a kinder, gentler nation," Bush said in accepting the Republican nomination. Yet his most memorable line in his speech was a defiant statement ruling out tax increases: "The Congress will push me to raise taxes, and I'll say no, and they'll push, and I'll say no, and they'll push again. And I'll say to them: Read my lips. No new taxes."

In the end, Bush won decisively over the Democratic nominee, Massachusetts governor Michael Dukakis. Dukakis carried only ten states plus the District of Columbia. Bush won with a margin of about 54 percent to 46 percent in the popular vote and 426 to 111 in the electoral college, but the Democrats retained control of the House and Senate.

As the new president, George H. W. Bush felt the need to show that he was his own man, not a Reagan clone. To that end, he replaced Calvin

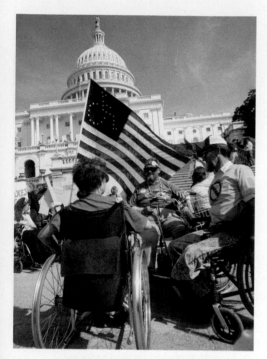

Americans with Disabilities Act
People congregated in front of the Capitol to demonstrate their support for the ADA. Someone holds up an American flag whose stars are in the shape of the International Symbol of Access.

Coolidge's portrait in the White House with one of Theodore Roosevelt, and he ordered all Reagan appointees to submit their resignation. Bush ended support for the Contras in Nicaragua and abandoned Reagan's unworkable "Star Wars" missile defense program.

Yet, for the most part, Bush sought to consolidate the initiatives that Reagan had put in place rather than launch his own array of programs and policies. "We don't need to remake society," he announced. As an example of his compassionate conservatism, Bush supported the Democratic-proposed Americans with Disabilities Act (1990), long-proposed legislation that strengthened the civil rights of those who are physically or mentally disabled in areas such as employment, public transportation, and housing. The ADA also required organizations to provide amenities such as mechanized doors, wheelchair ramps, and elevators to ensure that people with physical disabilities could more easily access facilities.

IMMIGRATION ACT OF 1990 On November 29, 1990, President Bush signed the bipartisan Immigration Act of 1990, which amended the Immigration and Nationality Act of 1965. It initially increased the total number of immigrants allowed each year to 700,000 between 1992 and 1994, and then the number would be capped at an annual 675,000 thereafter. Most of the visas would still be allocated to family members of American citizens, but the bill added other preferences: people of "extraordinary ability" or "special skills," or with professional degrees in law, medicine, accounting, engineering, and other fields, all designed to attract the "best and the brightest" in the global labor market. Foreign workers in such specialized fields would receive an H1-B work visa. In addition, the amendment introduced a "diversity lottery" system

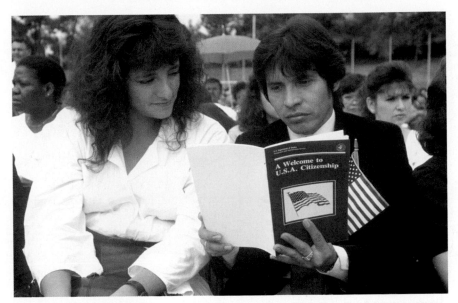

Immigration Act of 1990 New citizens wait to be sworn in at a United States Citizenship Ceremony in Los Angeles, California.

to assign visas to immigrants randomly, regardless of their country of origin. The act also lifted the ban on "suspected homosexual" immigrants.

In signing the legislation, President Bush described it as the most comprehensive revision of immigration laws in decades and applauded its emphasis on ensuring greater diversity among immigrants being welcomed into the United States. He added that he was "also pleased to note that this Act facilitates immigration not just in numerical terms, but also in terms of basic entry rights of those beyond our borders." The new immigration act had a greater impact than its proponents imagined. During the 1990s, more immigrants entered the country than in any previous decade.

THE FEDERAL DEBT AND RECESSION The biggest problem facing the Bush administration was the huge national debt, which stood at $2.6 trillion in 1989, nearly three times its 1980 level. President Bush's pledge not to increase taxes made it all the more difficult to reduce the deficit or trim the debt. Likewise, Bush was not willing to make substantial spending cuts to defense or social-welfare programs like Social Security, Medicare, and food stamps. As a result, by 1990 the country faced "a fiscal mess."

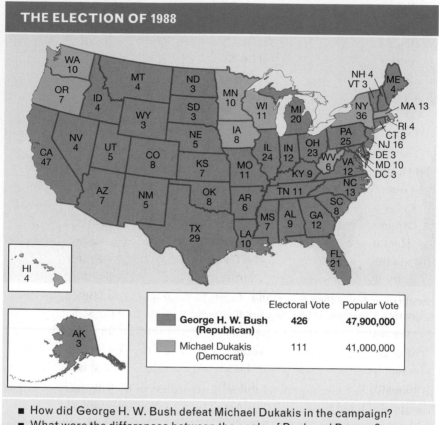

THE ELECTION OF 1988

	Electoral Vote	Popular Vote
George H. W. Bush (Republican)	426	47,900,000
Michael Dukakis (Democrat)	111	41,000,000

- How did George H. W. Bush defeat Michael Dukakis in the campaign?
- What were the differences between the goals of Bush and Reagan?

During the summer of 1990, Bush proposed several tax increases, which he had sworn to avoid. His reversal set off a revolt among conservative Republicans. A Republican-aligned newspaper expressed its views with a banner headline: "READ MY LIPS: I LIED."

Congressional Republicans were so angry that they joined with Democrats in nixing Bush's budget proposal. With Congress and the White House unable to reach agreement, the federal government shut down. The public was furious, and its anger forced Bush to sign a resolution that reopened government offices. To do so, however, he had to agree to a new budget drafted by Democrats. It replaced his proposed gasoline tax with an increase in the top income tax rate, from 28 to 31 percent. Only a fourth of Republicans supported the idea, but the Democrats marshaled enough votes for it to become law in October 1990.

The budget fiasco and tax increase created a lasting divide between congressional Republicans and President Bush. Even more worrisome was that the economy barely grew during the first three years of the Bush administration— the worst record since the end of the Second World War. By 1991, the economy was in a recession, the unemployment rate had spiked to 8 percent, and public disapproval of the president had risen accordingly.

THE DEMOCRACY MOVEMENT ABROAD George H. W. Bush entered the White House with more foreign-policy experience than most presidents, and, like Nixon, he preferred to deal with international relations rather than domestic problems, especially since the Democrats controlled Congress.

In the Soviet Union, with his nation's economy failing, Mikhail Gorbachev accelerated the implementation of policies designed to democratize Soviet life. His foreign policy sought harmony and trade with the West, staking his nation's future on cooperation and trade with its cold war enemies.

Early in 1989, Soviet troops left Afghanistan. Gorbachev then renounced the history of Soviet intervention in the internal affairs of other Communist countries. His foreign minister, Eduard Shevardnadze, told the Soviet legislature that the nations of Eastern Europe had "absolute freedom" to choose their own form of government. Soon thereafter, Communist regimes in Eastern Europe were toppled, first in Poland and Hungary, then in Czechoslovakia and Bulgaria. In Romania, the people joined the army in a bloody uprising against Nicolae Ceauşescu, the country's brutal dictator. He and his wife were captured and tried, then executed on Christmas Day. Although the new democratic governments faced immense economic and social challenges, Europe had been born anew.

THE DESTRUCTION OF THE BERLIN WALL The most spectacular event in the collapse of the Soviet empire came on November 9, 1989, when tens of thousands of East Germans gathered at the Berlin Wall and demanded that the border guards open the gates to West Berlin to allow them to flee. The guards reluctantly did so, and soon Germans on both sides began tearing the wall down. What Germans called the "peaceful revolution" had occurred with dramatic suddenness. With the borders to West Germany now fully open, the Communist government of East Germany collapsed. On October 3, 1990, the five states of East Germany would be united with West Germany.

On December 3, 1989, Bush and Gorbachev met on a ship off the coast of Malta, an island in the Mediterranean. After Gorbachev declared that the Soviet Union no longer regarded "the United States as an adversary," Bush announced that "We stand at the threshold of a brand new era of U.S.-Soviet relations." The cold war was over.

COMMUNIST COUP FAILS The reform impulse sped out of control within the Soviet Union itself, however. Gorbachev had proven unusually adept at political restructuring and building a presidential system that gave him, if anything, increased powers. His skills, however, could not salvage an antiquated economy that resisted change. In addition, as various Soviet states sought their independence, hardline Communist leaders questioned Gorbachev's leadership.

Gorbachev's popularity shrank in the Soviet Union as it grew abroad. On August 18, 1991, a group of "old guard" political and military leaders accosted him at his vacation retreat in Crimea and demanded that he proclaim a state of emergency and transfer his powers to them so that they could restore the supremacy of the Communist party. He replied, "Go to hell," whereupon he was placed under house arrest.

The coup, however, was poorly planned and clumsily implemented. The plotters failed to arrest popular leaders such as Boris Yeltsin, the feisty president of the Russian Republic. They also neglected to close airports or cut off telephone and television communications, and they were opposed by key elements of the military and KGB (the Soviet secret police).

A hammer to the Soviet empire
A West German demonstrator pounds away at the Berlin Wall on November 11, 1989, while East German border guards look on. Two days later, all the crossings between East and West Germany were opened.

On August 20, President Bush responded favorably to Yeltsin's request for support and persuaded other leaders to join him in refusing to recognize the new Soviet government. The next day, word began to seep out that the plotters were fleeing. Several committed suicide, and a freed Gorbachev ordered the others arrested. Although Gorbachev reclaimed the title of president, he was forced to resign as head of the Communist party and admit that he had made a mistake in appointing the men who had turned against him. Yeltsin emerged as the most popular political figure in the country.

What had begun as a reactionary coup turned into a powerful accelerant for the "Soviet Disunion," as one journalist termed it. Most of the fifteen republics proclaimed their independence from Russia, with the Baltic states of Latvia, Lithuania, and Estonia regaining the status of independent nations. The Communist party was dismantled, prompting celebrating crowds to topple statues of Lenin and other Communist heroes. On December 25, 1991, the Soviet flag was lowered from the Kremlin for the last time. The cold war had ended with the dismemberment of the Soviet Union and its fifteen republics.

U.S. INVASION OF PANAMA The end of the cold war and implosion of the Soviet Union did not spell the end of international tensions, however. Before the close of 1989, U.S. troops were engaged in battle in Panama.

In 1983, General Manuel Noriega had become the ruthless leader of the Panamanian Defense Forces, which made him head of the government in fact if not in title. In 1988, federal grand juries in Florida indicted Noriega and fifteen others on charges of conspiring with Colombia's drug lords to ship cocaine through Panama to the United States. The next year, the Panamanian president tried to fire Noriega, but the National Assembly ousted the president and named Noriega "maximum leader." The legislators then declared Panama "in a state of war" with the United States.

On December 16, 1989, Noriega's henchmen killed a U.S. Marine in Panama, and brutally beat another and assaulted his wife. President Bush thereupon ordered a military invasion (Operation Just Cause) to capture Noriega and install a government to be headed by Guillermo Endara, who had won the presidency in an election that was nullified by Noriega.

Early on December 20, U.S. troops, including "a sky full of paratroopers," struck at strategic targets. Panamanian forces surrendered within hours, but Noriega took refuge in a Catholic church. Knowing that the Panamanian dictator loved opera music, the U.S. forces surrounding his refuge used loudspeakers to blast nerve-shattering rock music at Noriega day and night. Their favorite selection was a Linda Ronstadt song titled, "You're No Good." An exasperated Noriega finally gave himself up and was whisked to a Miami jail cell.

Twenty-three U.S. servicemen were killed in Operation Just Cause; estimates of Panamanian casualties were as high as 4,000, including civilians. In April 1992, Noriega was convicted in the United States on eight counts of racketeering and trafficking in illegal drugs. A *New York Times* correspondent wrote that Bush's Panama operation revealed him to be "a man capable of bold action."

THE GULF WAR On August 2, 1990, Saddam Hussein, dictator of Iraq, focused U.S. attention back upon the Middle East when his army suddenly invaded its tiny neighbor, Kuwait. The assault was justified, he claimed,

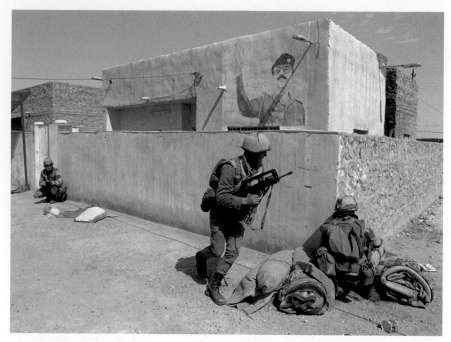

Operation Desert Storm Allied soldiers patrol the southern Iraqi town of Salman on February 27, 1991. On the side of a building is a propaganda mural of dictator Saddam Hussein in military uniform.

because Kuwait had increased its oil production, contrary to agreements with the Organization of the Petroleum Exporting Countries (OPEC). The resulting drop in global oil prices offended the Iraqi regime, which was deeply in debt and heavily dependent upon oil revenues.

President Bush condemned Iraq's "naked aggression" and dispatched warplanes and troops to Saudi Arabia, on the southern border of Iraq and Kuwait. British forces soon joined in, as did Arab units from Egypt, Morocco, Syria, Oman, the United Arab Emirates, and Qatar. Iraq refused to yield, and on January 12, 1991, Congress authorized the use of U.S. armed forces.

Four days later, U.S. armed forces and those from thirty-three other nations, including ten Islamic countries, launched **Operation Desert Storm** against Iraq. During the next six weeks, Iraqi soldiers surrendered by the thousands, and on February 28, Bush called for a cease-fire. The Iraqis accepted. There were 137 American fatalities; the lowest estimate of Iraqi deaths, civilian and military, was 100,000. Although coalition forces occupied about a fifth of Iraq, Hussein's tyrannical regime remained intact.

The decision to stop the fighting short of toppling Hussein contradicted Bush's earlier pledge to oust the Iraqi leader ("regime change"): "We need a surrender—we need Saddam out." Yet he had decided that the sight of Allied forces pummeling a defenseless Iraq would have alienated much of the Arab world.

What came to be called the First Gulf War was thus a triumph without victory. Hussein had been defeated, but he remained in power. The consequences of the brief but intense war would be played out in the future, as Arabs humiliated by the American triumph began plotting revenge that would spiral into a global war of terrorism.

BUSH'S "NEW WORLD ORDER" The disintegration of the Soviet Union suddenly made containment of Communism, the bedrock of U.S. foreign policy for more than four decades, irrelevant. For all its potential horrors, the cold war had brought a wary stability; the two superpowers, the United States and the Soviet Union, had restrained themselves from an all-out nuclear war. Now the world would witness a growing number of unresolved crises and unstable regimes, some of which had access to weapons of mass destruction—nuclear as well as chemical and biological.

Bush faced an unexpected challenge for the 1992 Republican presidential nomination from Patrick Buchanan, the conservative commentator and former White House aide, who adopted the slogan "America First" and called on Bush to "bring home the boys."

The excitement over the victory in the Gulf War also gave way to anxiety over the depressed economy. Bush tried a clumsy balancing act, acknowledging that "people are hurting" while telling Americans that "this is a good time to buy a car." By the summer of 1992, as Bush prepared to launch his campaign for a second term, his public approval rating had plummeted from it post–Gulf War highs to 29 percent.

THE ELECTION OF 1992 At the 1992 Republican National Convention, Patrick Buchanan, who had won about a third of the votes in the party's primaries, blasted Bush for breaking his pledge not to raise taxes and for becoming the "biggest spender in American history." Rush Limbaugh, the popular conservative Republican radio commentator, showed equal disdain for Bush, charging that he had "compromised his promises and beliefs on nearly every important principle he articulated." According to Limbaugh, Bush had "rolled over for the liberals," and the result was a failed presidency.

As the 1992 election unfolded, however, Bush's real problem proved to be his failure to improve the economy. In reflection of the high unemployment rate, a popular bumper sticker reflected the public's frustration: "Saddam Hussein still has his job. What about you?"

In contrast, the Democrats presented an image of moderate forces in control. For several years, the Democratic Leadership Council, led by Arkansas governor William Jefferson Clinton, had been pushing the party from the liberal left to the center. He called for reforming the welfare system and endorsed the death penalty.

Born in 1946 in Hope, Arkansas, Bill Clinton was a brilliant student who attended Georgetown University in Washington, D.C., won a Rhodes Scholarship to Oxford University, and earned a law degree from Yale University, where he met his future wife, Hillary Rodham. Clinton returned to Arkansas and won election as the state's attorney general. By 1979, at age thirty-two, he was the youngest governor in the country. He served three more terms as "boy governor" and emerged as a dynamic leader of the **New Democrats**," who were committed to winning back the middle-class whites ("Reagan Democrats") who had voted Republican during the 1980s.

In seeking the Democratic nomination, Clinton promised to cut the defense budget, provide tax relief, and create a massive economic aid package to help the former republics of the Soviet Union forge democratic societies. Witty, intelligent, optimistic, and charismatic, with an in-depth knowledge of public policy, Clinton reminded many of John F. Kennedy, his boyhood hero.

Bill Clinton and Al Gore After winning the presidential election, the Democratic candidates celebrate in Clinton's hometown of Little Rock, Arkansas, on November 3, 1992.

But beneath Clinton's charisma and expertise were several flaws. The *New York Times* explained that Clinton was "emotionally needy, indecisive, and undisciplined." He had also earned a well-deserved reputation for half-truths, exaggerations, and talking out of both sides of his mouth. Clinton used opinion polls to shape his stances on issues, pandered to special-interest groups, and flip-flopped on controversial subjects, leading critics to label him "Slick Willie."

Even more enticing to the media were charges that Clinton was a chronic adulterer, a pot smoker, and that he had manipulated the Reserve Officers' Training Corps (ROTC) program during the Vietnam War to avoid military service in a discreet way so as "to maintain my political viability." Clinton's evasive denials could not dispel lingering mistrust.

After a series of closely contested primaries, Clinton won the Democratic nomination and promised to restore the "hopes of the forgotten middle class." He chose Senator Albert "Al" Gore Jr. of Tennessee as his running mate. The Clinton-Gore team hammered Bush on economic issues. Clinton pledged that, if elected, he would cut the federal budget deficit in half in four years while reducing taxes on middle-class Americans.

The 1992 campaign also featured a third-party candidate, H. Ross Perot, a puckish Texas billionaire who found a large audience ("Perotistas") for his criticism of Reaganomics as "voodoo economics" (a phrase originally used by Bush in the 1980 Republican primary before he was named the vice-presidential candidate). Perot appealed to those fed up with government "gridlock" created by the polarization of the two major parties. As the CEO of a high-tech company, Perot initially won support for a unique proposal: an electronic town hall that would enable voters to express their preferences for major policies through instantaneous digital polling.

As political experts predicted, Perot's on-again, off-again candidacy helped elect Bill Clinton by drawing Republican votes away from Bush. Clinton won only 43 percent of the popular vote but garnered 370 electoral votes. Bush received 168 electoral votes and 39 percent of the vote. Perot won 19 percent of the popular vote, more than any third-party candidate since Theodore Roosevelt ran as a Progressive in 1912.

As 1992 came to an end, Bill Clinton, the New Democrat, prepared to lead the United States. "The urgent question of our time," he said, "is whether we can make change our friend and not our enemy." Clinton would embrace unexpected changes while ushering America into the twenty-first century.

CHAPTER REVIEW

SUMMARY

- **The Carter Presidency**   While Jimmy Carter had some notable achievements, such as the *Camp David Accords (1978)*, his administration suffered from legislative inexperience, a deepening economic recession, soaring inflation, and the *Iranian hostage crisis (1979)*.

- **The Rise of Conservatism**   The Republican insurgency, beginning with Reagan's election, was dominated by Christian conservatives like those who made up the *Moral Majority*. The migration of older Americans and others to conservative southern and western states increased the voting power of the so-called Sun Belt.

- **Reaganomics**   Reagan introduced a "supply-side" economic philosophy, commonly called *Reaganomics*, that championed tax cuts for the rich, reductions in government regulations, cuts to social-welfare programs, and increased defense spending. Reagan was unable to cut domestic spending, however, and the tax cuts failed to pay for themselves as promised. The result was a dramatic increase in the national debt.

- **The End of the Cold War**   Reagan's military buildup, including the *Strategic Defense Initiative (SDI) (1983)*, helped force the Soviets to the negotiating table to conclude the *Intermediate-Range Nuclear Forces (INF) Treaty (1987)*—the beginning of the end of the cold war. But Reagan's foreign-policy efforts were tarnished by the *Iran-Contra affair (1987)*, in which members of his administration sold American-made armaments to Iran in exchange for Iranian influence to secure the release of American hostages held in Lebanon.

- **America in the 1980s**   Americans in the eighties not only experienced unprecedented prosperity but also rising poverty and homelessness. Conservatives condemned (and dismissed) *HIV/AIDS* as a "gay" disease. The development of the *microprocessor* paved the way for the computer revolution. Consumerism flourished resulting in massive public and private debt. Two major initiatives in 1990 transformed the quality of life for many: the Immigration Act and the Americans with Disabilities Act (ADA).

- **A New World Order**   Republican George H. W. Bush won the presidency in 1988. At the end of the 1980s, democratic political movements emerged across Eastern Europe. In the Soviet Union, Mikhail Gorbachev's steps to restructure the economy (*perestroika*) and promote more open policies (*glasnost*) led to further reform and the collapse of the Soviet empire. But new trouble spots quickly emerged. Iraq, led by Saddam Hussein, invaded neighboring Kuwait in 1990. President Bush ordered American-led allied forces to launch *Operation Desert Storm*, and the Iraqis surrendered within six weeks. Despite the success of the first Gulf War, the sluggish economy and President Bush's decision to raise taxes led to his defeat by Democrat Bill Clinton in 1992.

CHRONOLOGY

1978	President Carter helps negotiate the Camp David Accords
November 1979	Iranian hostage crisis
1980	Ronald Reagan elected president
1981	President Reagan enacts major tax cuts
1983	President Reagan authorizes development of the Strategic Defense Initiative (SDI)
1987	Reagan delivers his famous Berlin Wall speech; stock market crashes on Black Monday
1988	George H. W. Bush is elected president
November 1989	Berlin Wall is torn down
December 1989	U.S. troops invade Panama and capture Manuel Noriega
1991	Iraq forced from Kuwait in the First Gulf War
	Breakup of the USSR
1992	Bill Clinton is elected president

KEY TERMS

Camp David Accords (1978) p. 1487

Iranian hostage crisis (1979) p. 1490

Moral Majority p. 1494

Reaganomics p. 1498

Strategic Defense Initiative (SDI) (1983) p. 1503

Iran-Contra affair (1987) p. 1506

perestroika p. 1508

glasnost p. 1508

Intermediate-Range Nuclear Forces (INF) Treaty (1987) p. 1509

microprocessor p. 1510

HIV/AIDS p. 1514

Operation Desert Storm (1991) p. 1522

New Democrats p. 1524

 INQUIZITIVE

Go to InQuizitive to see what you've learned—and learn what you've missed—with personalized feedback along the way.

32

Twenty-First-Century America

1993–Present

March for Our Lives Throngs of people on Pennsylvania Avenue hold up home-made signs in support of gun control at the student-led rally on Saturday, March 24, 2018 after another tragic school shooting. Some 800 sister events to the Washington, D.C. rally took place in the United States and across the world. Two of the signs read: LOVE OVER LEAD and KIDS OVER CAMPAIGN DONATIONS.

The United States entered the final decade of the twentieth century triumphant. American persistence in the cold war had brought about the collapse of the Soviet Union and the birth of democracy and capitalism in Eastern Europe. During the 1990s, the U.S. economy became the marvel of the world, as remarkable gains in productivity boosted by new digital technologies led to the greatest prosperity in modern history.

Yet America's sense of physical security and material comfort was soon shattered by terrorist assaults on New York City and Washington, D.C., in 2001. The attacks killed thousands and raised a new level of fear about national security, personal safety, and civil liberties.

In leading the fight against global terrorism, the United States became embroiled in long, costly, and controversial wars in Iraq and Afghanistan. Opposition to those wars would provide much of the momentum for Democrat Barack Obama's election in 2008 as the nation's first African American president. Obama entered the White House at the same time that the United States and Europe were experiencing the Great Recession, a prolonged economic downturn that threatened the global banking system, caused widespread unemployment, and ignited social unrest and political tensions.

focus questions

1. What were the major population trends (demographics) in the United States during the twenty-first century? How did they influence the nation's politics?

2. What were the accomplishments and setbacks of Bill Clinton's presidency?

3. What was the impact of global terrorism during the presidency of George W. Bush? How effective was his "war on terror"?

4. What were the issues and developments during Bush's second term that helped lead to Barack Obama's historic victory in the 2008 presidential election?

5. What were President Obama's priorities at home and abroad? How effective were his efforts to pursue them?

6. What were the factors that led to Donald Trump's 2016 presidential election and how would you assess his early presidency?

Eight years later, those political tensions gave rise to an unconventional populist Republican presidential candidate, billionaire New York real-estate developer Donald Trump. In 2016, he would surprise mainstream Republican leaders, pundits, pollsters and the American electorate by winning the Republican nomination and then narrowly defeating Democrat Hillary Clinton in the general election.

AMERICA'S CHANGING POPULATION

The United States in the twenty-first century experienced dramatic social changes. By 2019, America's population had surpassed 330 million, more than 80 percent of whom lived in cities or suburbs.

Even more important, the nation's racial and ethnic composition was changing rapidly in ways that would reshape society and politics. In 1980, the national population was 80 percent white. By 2019, that percentage had fallen below 60 percent. Latinos in 2019 represented 19 percent of the population, African Americans 13 percent, Asians about 5 percent, and Native Americans 1 percent. The growth among those four groups was increasing twice as fast as it had during the 1980s. In 2005, Latinos surpassed African Americans as the nation's largest minority group (and salsa replaced ketchup as the nation's top condiment). Latinos were two-thirds of the population of Miami, nearly half of Los Angeles, and over one-fifth of New York City and Chicago.

Yet the fastest-growing group in the United States was composed of the nearly 10 million people who described themselves as "multiracial," and who represented more than 3 percent of the population.

This dramatic change in the nation's ethnic mix resulted from an immigration surge during the late twentieth and early twenty-first centuries. In 1996, immigration reached its highest level since before the First World War. By 2019, the United States had more foreign-born residents than ever—more than 46 million, 11 million of whom were undocumented immigrants (formerly classified as "illegal aliens"). In the first decade of the twenty-first century, the United States became home to more than twice as many immigrants as in *all* other countries combined. And for the first time, the majority of immigrants to America came not from Europe but from other parts of the world: Asia, Latin America, and Africa. Mexicans made up the largest share of Latinos, followed by Puerto Ricans and Cubans. Asian Americans increased their numbers at a faster rate than any other ethnic group, largely because of a surge in Chinese immigrants.

In 1980, Latinos lived mainly in five states: California, Arizona, New Mexico, Texas, and Florida. By 2019, every state had a rapidly growing Latino population. Demographers projected that by 2044, whites would become a minority in the United States.

Immigration also had potent political effects, as almost 1 million Latinos reached voting age each year. In 1980, six Latino Americans served in Congress. By 2010, there were more than five times as many. In 1992, Latinos constituted only 2 percent of American voters; by 2019, they were nearly 13 percent.

By 2016, only 23 percent of baby boomers born during and after the Second World War considered the surge in American diversity a "change for the better." They worried that Latinos would never truly assimilate into mainstream American culture but would constitute a permanent underclass of people tied closely to their ancestral homelands.

Yet such concerns were countered by growing evidence during the twenty-first century that Latinos were successfully integrating into American society and embracing its ideals. High school graduation and college-enrollment rates among Latinos rose, teen pregnancy fell, and more and more used English as their primary language. In recent years, more than a quarter of Latino marriages involved a non-Latino partner.

Far from being a disaster, the growing Latino population provided the nation in the new century with a surge of youthful energy and vitality—and demonstrated such traditional American attributes as self-reliance, rugged individualism, thrift, close family ties, strong religious beliefs, support for the military, and an ethic of hard work.

The nation's African American population also experienced significant changes in the early twenty-first century. In a reverse of the Great Migration of the 1920s and after, a steady stream of young blacks moved out of rust belt states like Michigan and Illinois to the South. Atlanta replaced Chicago as the metro area with the largest population of African Americans. By 2010, some 57 percent of African Americans lived in the states of the former Confederacy, the highest percentage in fifty years.

The Clinton Presidency (1993–2001)

Bill Clinton brought to the White House extraordinary gifts—and robust weaknesses. At forty-six years old, he was the third-youngest president in history. Like Ronald Reagan, Clinton charmed people, and his speeches inspired them. Wickedly smart and politically shrewd, he embraced politics as a civic duty and painstakingly learned the details of major policies and programs while mastering the personal touch.

While graced with charm and a common touch, Clinton was also prone to self-absorption, self-deception, and self-inflicted wounds. Susceptible to flattery with a compulsion to please and be loved, he often decided his stances on issues by studying focus-group interviews and public-opinion surveys. He at times seemed less a president than a flawed good ol' boy capable of self-righteousness and shameless misbehavior.

In sum, Clinton was a bundle of warring impulses whose faults often confounded his talents. Yet he displayed legendary energy and "slick" resilience—his nicknames were "Slick Willie" and the "Comeback Kid"—and he seemed to thrive amid controversy and setbacks. One of his advisers predicted that Clinton would make every mistake possible, "but he will only make it once."

Clinton's inexperience in international affairs and congressional maneuvering led to several missteps in his first year as president. Like George H. W. Bush before him, he reneged on several campaign promises. In a bruising battle with Congress, he was forced to abandon his proposed middle-class tax cut in order to keep another campaign promise to reduce the federal deficit. Then he dropped his promise to allow gays, lesbians, and bisexuals to serve openly in the armed forces after military commanders expressed strong opposition. He later announced an ambiguous policy called "don't ask, don't tell" (DADT), which allowed gays, lesbians, and bisexuals to serve in the military but only if they kept their sexual orientation secret (DADT did not mention transgender service members). "I got the worst of both worlds," Clinton later confessed. "I lost the fight, and the gay community was highly critical of me for the compromise."

THE ECONOMY As a candidate, Bill Clinton had pledged to reduce the federal deficit without damaging the economy or hurting the nation's most vulnerable people. To this end, he proposed $241 billion in higher taxes for corporations and for the wealthiest individuals over four years, and $255 billion in spending cuts over the same period. The hotly contested bill passed the Democratic-controlled Congress by the slimmest of margins: 218 to 216 in the House and 51 to 50 in the Senate, with Vice President Al Gore providing the tie-breaking vote.

For virtually the first time since 1945, Congress had passed a major bill without a single Republican vote, a troubling indication of the nation's growing partisan divide. Clinton's deficit-reduction effort worked as planned, however. It led to lower interest rates, which, along with low energy prices, helped spur economic growth.

Equally difficult was gaining congressional approval of the **North American Free Trade Agreement (NAFTA)**, which the Bush administration had negotiated with Canada and Mexico. In 1994, Clinton urged Congress to approve NAFTA, which would make North America the largest free-trade zone in the world. Opponents favored tariffs to discourage the importation of cheaper foreign products, especially from Mexico. Yet Clinton prevailed with solid Republican support. A sizable minority of Democrats, mostly labor unionists and southerners, opposed NAFTA, fearing that textile mills would lose business (and millions of jobs) to "cheap labor" countries—as they did.

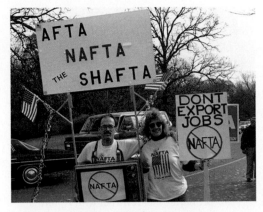

NAFTA protesters Protesters going to a rally against NAFTA, the controversial free-trade agreement for North America.

HEALTH-CARE REFORM Clinton's primary public-policy initiative was an ambitious plan to overhaul the nation's health-care system. "If I don't get health care," he declared, "I'll wish I didn't run for president." Public support for government-administered health insurance had increased as medical costs skyrocketed and some 37 million Americans, most of them poor or unemployed, went without coverage.

The Clinton administration argued that providing medical insurance to everyone, regardless of income, would reduce the costs of health care, but critics questioned the savings—and the ability of the federal government to manage such a huge program. The grand plan, known as the Health Security Act, called for large corporations to pay most of the medical insurance expenses of their employees and required small businesses to form "health alliances" so that they, too, could provide subsidized health insurance to their workers.

By the summer of 1994, Clinton's plan, developed by a task force headed by First Lady Hillary Rodham Clinton, was doomed, in part because the president opposed any changes and in part because, as one of Hillary Clinton's aides confessed, the "ludicrously complex report . . . had something in it to piss everybody off. So by the time it goes up to the Hill, it's dead on arrival." Congress voted down the bill in August 1994, and the controversial Clinton health plan turned many away from the Democratic party.

LANDSLIDE REPUBLICAN VICTORY The health-care disaster and the growing federal budget deficit played a dramatic role in the 1994 midterm elections. In the most stunning congressional victory of the twentieth century,

Newt Gingrich Joined by 160 of his fellow House Republicans, Gingrich promotes the Contract with America in April 1995.

the Republicans captured both houses of Congress for the first time since 1953 and won thirty-two governorships, including those in the most populous states of California, New York, and Texas, where George W. Bush, son of the former president and a future president himself, won handily.

The Republican victory was led by a combative Georgia conservative named Newton ("Newt") Leroy Gingrich. In early 1995, he became the first Republican Speaker of the House in forty-two years. Gingrich, a former history professor with a lust for controversy and an unruly ego, was a superb tactician who had helped mobilize conservatives associated with the Christian Coalition.

The Christian Coalition, organized by television evangelist Pat Robertson in 1989 to replace Jerry Falwell's Moral Majority (which had disbanded that year), was pro–school prayer, anti-abortion, anti-feminist, and anti–LGBTQ (lesbian, gay, bisexual, transgender, queer) rights. In many respects, the Religious Right took control of the political and social landscape in the nineties.

In 1994, Gingrich and other Republican candidates rallied conservative voters by lambasting Bill Clinton as "the enemy of normal Americans" and promised to bring forward a **Contract with America**, a pledge to dismantle the "corrupt liberal welfare state" created by Democrats. The ten-point, anti-big-government "contract" promised a smaller federal government by reducing taxes and regulations, requiring term limits for members of Congress, slashing social-welfare programs, and passing a constitutional amendment requiring a balanced federal budget. As Texan Tom DeLay, a leading House Republican, explained, "You've got to understand, we are ideologues. We have an agenda. We have a philosophy."

Yet the much-trumpeted Contract with America quickly fizzled. The conservatives pushed too hard and too fast, realizing too late that their slim majority in Congress could not launch a revolution.

Gingrich's heavy-handed methods contributed to the disintegration of the Contract with America. He was too ambitious, too abrasive, too divisive. When Clinton refused to go along with Republican demands for a balanced-budget pledge, Gingrich twice shut down the federal government during the fall of 1995, sending 800,000 employees home and closing national parks, Social

Security offices, and other agencies. The tactic backfired. By 1996, Republicans had abandoned their Contract with America.

THE SUPREME COURT AND RACE The conservative mood also revealed itself in Supreme Court rulings that undermined affirmative-action programs, which gave African American students special consideration in college admissions and financial-aid awards. Between 1970 and 1977, African American enrollment in colleges and universities doubled, even as white students and their parents complained about "reverse discrimination."

Two major 1996 rulings affected affirmative action in college admissions. In *Hopwood v. Texas*, a federal court ruled that race could not be used as a consideration for admission. Later that year, California voters passed Proposition 209 (also known as the California Civil Rights Initiative, or CCRI), which ruled out preferential treatment (affirmative action) in government hiring, government contracting, and public schools and colleges based on race, sex, ethnicity, or national origin.

Similar complaints were directed against affirmative-action programs that awarded government contracts to businesses owned by women and people of color. In 1995, the Court in *Adarand Constructors v. Peña* declared that affirmative-action programs had to be "narrowly tailored" to serve a "compelling national interest." The implication of such vague language was clear: the mostly conservative justices on the Court had come to share the growing public suspicion of the legitimacy of programs designed to benefit a particular race, gender, or ethnic group.

LEGISLATIVE BREAKTHROUGH After the surprising 1994 Republican takeover of Congress, Bill Clinton shrewdly resolved to reinforce his claim that he was a "centrist." He co-opted much of the energy of the conservative movement by announcing that "the era of big government is over" and by reforming the federal system of welfare payments to the poor.

Late in the summer of 1996, the Republican-controlled Congress passed a comprehensive welfare-reform measure, the **Personal Responsibility and Work Opportunity Act of 1996 (PRWOA)**. It abolished the Aid to Families with Dependent Children (AFDC) program, which had provided poor families almost $8,000 a year, and replaced it with the Temporary Assistance for Needy Families program, which limited the duration of welfare payments to two years in an effort to encourage unemployed people—including immigrants—to get self-supporting jobs.

President Clinton privately called the new measure "a decent welfare bill wrapped in a sack of s–t," but he signed it anyway to help ensure his reelection.

Liberal Democrats bitterly criticized Clinton's "welfare reform" deal. Yet it was a statistical success. Both the number of welfare recipients and poverty rates declined during the late 1990s, leading the editors of the left-leaning *New Republic* to report that the PRWOA had "worked much as its designers had hoped."

THE 1996 CAMPAIGN The Republican takeover of Congress in 1994 gave the party hope that it could prevent President Clinton's reelection. After clinching the GOP presidential nomination in 1996, Senate majority leader Bob Dole resigned his seat to devote his attention to the campaign. Clinton, however, maintained a large lead in the polls.

Concern about Dole's age (73) and his gruff personality, as well as tensions between economic and social conservatives over volatile issues such as abortion and gun control, hampered Dole's efforts to generate widespread support, especially among independent voters. Dole portrayed himself as a pragmatist willing to "downsize government, [but] not devastate it," as he said in May 1995. Clinton, however, framed the election as a stark choice between Dole's desire to build a bridge to the past and Clinton's promise to build a bridge to the future.

On November 5, 1996, Clinton won with an electoral vote victory of 379 to 159 and 49 percent of the popular vote. Dole received 41 percent of the popular vote. Third-party candidate Ross Perot got 8 percent.

THE "NEW ECONOMY" Bill Clinton's presidency benefited from a prolonged period of unprecedented prosperity. During his last three years in office (1998–2000), the federal government generated unheard-of budget *surpluses*. What came to be called the "new economy" featured high-flying electronics, computer, software, telecommunications (cell phones, cable TV, etc.), and e-commerce internet firms called "dot-com" companies.

These dynamic tech enterprises helped the U.S. economy set records in every area: low inflation, low unemployment, corporate profits, and personal fortunes. Alan Greenspan, the Federal Reserve Board chairman, suggested that "we have moved beyond history" into an economy that seemed only to grow. He would be proven wrong.

GLOBALIZATION Another feature of the new economy was **globalization**. The end of the cold war and the disintegration of the Soviet Union opened many opportunities for U.S. companies in international trade. In addition, new globe-spanning communication technologies and massive new container-carrying ships and cargo jets shortened time and distance, enabling multinational companies to conduct more business abroad.

Bill Clinton accelerated the process of globalization. "The global economy," he said, "is giving more of our own people, and billions around the world, the chance to work and live and raise their families with dignity." He especially welcomed the World Wide Web, which opened the internet to everyone, and, by doing so, greatly accelerated U.S. dominance of the international economy.

By 2000, more than a third of the production of U.S. multinational companies was occurring abroad, compared with 9 percent in 1980. In 1970, there were 7,000 American multinational companies; by 2000, there were 63,000. Many pursued controversial *outsourcing* strategies—moving their production "offshore" to nations such as Mexico and China to take advantage of lower labor costs and fewer workplace and environmental regulations. At the same time, many European and Asian companies, especially automobile manufacturers, built large plants in the United States to reduce the shipping expenses required to get their products to American markets.

FOREIGN POLICY IN THE NINETIES

Unlike George H. W. Bush, Bill Clinton had little interest in global politics. Untrained and inexperienced in international relations, he sought to create opportunities around the world for U.S. business expansion. Yet, as international analyst Leslie Gelb cautioned Clinton, "A foreign economic policy is not a foreign policy, and it is not a national security strategy." Events soon forced Clinton to intervene to help foreign nations in crisis.

THE MIDDLE EAST During the 1990s, the Middle East remained a region fractured by ethnic and religious conflict and stubbornly composed of authoritarian regimes. President Clinton continued George H. W. Bush's policy of orchestrating patient negotiations between the Arabs and the Israelis. A new development was the inclusion of the Palestine Liberation Organization (PLO) in the discussions.

In 1993, secret talks between Israeli and Palestinian representatives resulted in a draft agreement that provided for the restoration of Palestinian self-rule in the occupied Gaza Strip and in Jericho, in the West Bank, in a "land for peace" exchange as outlined in United Nations Security Council resolutions. A formal signing occurred at the White House on September 13, 1993.

However, the Middle East peace process suffered a terrible blow in early November 1995, when Israeli prime minister Yitzhak Rabin was assassinated by a countryman because of his efforts to negotiate with the Palestinians. Seven months later, conservative hard-liner Benjamin Netanyahu narrowly defeated the U.S.–backed Shimon Peres in the Israeli national elections. Nevertheless,

Clinton and the Middle East President Clinton presides as Israeli prime minister Yitzhak Rabin (left) and PLO leader Yasir Arafat (right) agree to a pathbreaking peace accord between Israel and the Palestinians, September 1993.

in October 1998, Clinton brought Yasir Arafat, Netanyahu, and King Hussein of Jordan together to reach an agreement. Under the Wye River Accords, Israel agreed to surrender land in return for security guarantees by the Palestinians.

THE BALKANS President Clinton also felt compelled to address turmoil in the Eastern European nations recently freed from Soviet domination. In 1991, Yugoslavia had disintegrated into ethnic warfare as four of its six multiethnic republics declared their independence. Serb minorities, backed by the new Republic of Serbia, stirred up civil wars in neighboring Croatia and Bosnia. In Bosnia, the conflict involved systematic efforts to eliminate Muslims. Clinton decided that the situation was "intolerable" because the massacres of thousands of people "tore at the very fabric" of human decency. He ordered food and medical supplies sent to Bosnian Muslims and dispatched warplanes to stop the massacres.

In 1995, U.S. negotiators finally persuaded the foreign ministers of Croatia, Bosnia, and Yugoslavia (by then a loose federation of the Republics of Serbia and Montenegro) to agree to a comprehensive peace plan. Bosnia would remain a single nation divided into two states: a Muslim-Croat federation controlling 51 percent of the territory, and a Bosnian-Serb republic controlling the rest. To enforce the agreement, 60,000 NATO peacekeeping troops were dispatched to Bosnia.

In 1998, the Balkan tinderbox flared up again, this time in the Yugo-slav province of Kosovo, long considered sacred ground by Christian Serbs, although 90 percent of the 2 million Kosovars were in fact Albanian Muslims. In 1998, Yugoslav president Slobodan Milošević began a program of "**ethnic cleansing**" whereby Yugoslav forces burned Albanian villages, murdered men, raped women, and displaced hundreds of thousands of Muslim Kosovars.

On March 24, 1999, NATO, relying heavily upon U.S. military support, launched air strikes against Yugoslavian military targets. After seventy-two days of bombardment, Milošević sued for peace on NATO's terms, in part because his Russian allies had abandoned him. An agreement was reached on June 3, 1999, and Clinton pledged extensive U.S. aid to help the Yugoslavs rebuild.

THE SCANDAL MACHINE

For a time, Bill Clinton's preoccupation with foreign crises helped deflect attention from a growing number of investigations into his personal conduct. During his first term, he was dogged by old charges about investments he and his wife had made in Whitewater, a planned resort development in Arkansas. The project turned out to be a fraud and a failure, and people accused the Clintons of conspiring with the developer. In 1994, Kenneth Starr, a former judge and a conservative Republican, was appointed by a panel of three federal judges to investigate the Whitewater case.

Starr found no evidence that the Clintons were involved in the Whitewater fraud, but he soon happened upon evidence of a White House sex scandal. For years, rumors had circulated about the president's dalliances. James Carville, Clinton's political consultant, once asked Clinton about his sexual risk-taking. "Well," Clinton replied, "they haven't caught me." He spoke too soon.

MONICAGATE Between 1995 and 1997, President Clinton had engaged in a sexual affair with an unpaid, twenty-two-year-old White House intern, Monica Lewinsky. More disturbing, he had pressed her to lie about their rela-tionship, even under oath. Clinton initially denied the affair, telling the nation in late January 1998 that "I did not have sexual relations with that woman, Miss Lewinsky."

Yet the scandal would not disappear, and for the next thirteen months, the media circus surrounding the "Monicagate" or "Zippergate" affair cap-tured public attention like a daily soap opera. (Since the Watergate affair in 1973–1974, journalists have routinely attached the suffix "-gate" to scandals.) Other women stepped forward to claim that Clinton had engaged in improper relations with them, charges that the president denied.

The First Lady, Hillary Clinton, grimly stood by her husband, declaring that the rumors were the result of a "vast right-wing conspiracy." With the economy booming, Clinton's public approval ratings actually rose during 1998. In August, however, the scandal revived when Lewinsky provided a federal grand jury with a detailed account of her relationship with the president.

Soon thereafter, Clinton became the first president to testify before a grand jury. On August 17, he admitted having "inappropriate, intimate physical contact" with Lewinsky, and he acknowledged that it was "wrong." He also admitted that he had misled the American people. The president insisted, however, that he had done nothing illegal.

Public reaction was mixed. A majority expressed sympathy for Clinton because of his humiliation and because the Lewinsky affair was a private act of consensual sex. Others, however, were eager to see the president resign. Republicans were convinced they could impeach him.

THE IMPEACHMENT OF CLINTON On September 9, 1998, Special Prosecutor Kenneth Starr submitted to Congress thirty-six boxes of documents that included graphic accounts of the president's encounters with Monica Lewinsky. The report claimed that there was "substantial and creditable" evidence of presidential wrongdoing (perjury, obstructing justice, and abuse of power).

The Starr report prompted the Republican-dominated House of Representatives on October 8 to begin a wide-ranging impeachment inquiry, which led Bill Clinton to claim that he was the victim of a rogue prosecutor run amok. "When this thing is over," Clinton said, "there's only going to be one of us left standing. And it's going to be me."

On December 19, 1998, William Jefferson Clinton was impeached (charged with "high crimes and misdemeanors") by the House of Representatives. The House accused Clinton of obstructing justice and lying under oath to a federal grand jury. He was the first elected president to be impeached. (Andrew Johnson was not elected; he became president upon the assassination of Abraham Lincoln.)

House Speaker Newt Gingrich led the impeachment effort, even though he himself was, at the time, secretly engaged in a longstanding affair with a congressional staff member. (Gingrich resigned as speaker in November 1998 and left both the House and his wife, escaping with his new wife from elected office altogether.) Journalists began calling Clinton's Senate trial the "soap opera" impeachment after Gingrich's successor as Speaker, Robert Livingston of Louisiana, suddenly resigned after admitting that he, too, had engaged in adulterous affairs.

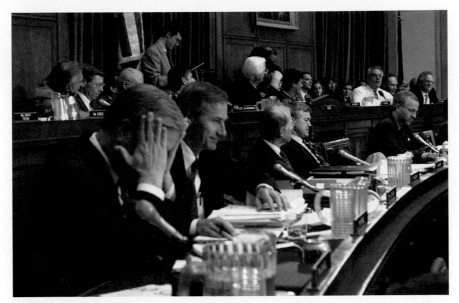

Impeachment Representative Edward Pease, a member of the House Judiciary Committee, covers his face during the vote on the third of four articles of impeachment charging President Clinton with "high crimes and misdemeanors" in December 1998.

The Senate impeachment trial began on January 7, 1999. Five weeks later, on February 12, Clinton was acquitted, largely on a party-line vote. A majority of senators, Democrats and a few Republicans (55–45), decided that Clinton had not committed the "high crimes and misdemeanors" required to remove a president from office.

Most Americans agreed. As historian Steven Gillon observed, "The only thing most Americans disliked more than a devious middle-aged man lying about sex was moralizing, self-righteous hypocrites telling other people how to lead their lives."

Although the impeachment effort failed, the scandal tainted Clinton's final eighteen months in office.

ASSESSING THE CLINTON PRESIDENCY For all his faults, Bill Clinton presided over an unprecedented period of prosperity (115 consecutive months of economic growth and the lowest unemployment rate in 30 years), generated record budget surpluses, and passed a welfare-reform measure with support from both parties. In the process, he revitalized the Democratic party by moving it from the left to the "vital center" of the political spectrum. Clinton also helped bring peace and stability to the Balkans.

At times, however, his boundless self-confidence led to arrogant reckless-ness. He debased the presidency with his sexual escapades, and his effort to bring health insurance to the uninsured was a clumsy failure. Yet in 2000, his last year in office, his public approval rating was 65 percent, the highest end-of-term rating since President Dwight D. Eisenhower. Bill Clinton's popularity was not enough, however, to ensure the election of his vice president, Al Gore, as his successor.

A Chaotic Start to a New Century

Wild celebrations ushered in the year 2000, and Americans led the cheering. The cold war was over, the United States was the world's only superpower, and the high-tech American economy dominated global trade. But the joyous mood did not last. Powerful and unstable forces were emerging, the most dan-gerous of which were sophisticated global networks of Islamist terrorists eager to disrupt and destroy American values and institutions.

A Disputed Election

The presidential election of 2000 proved to be one of the closest and most con-troversial in history. The two major-party candidates, Vice President Albert Gore Jr., the Democrat, and Texas governor George W. Bush, son of the former Republican president, offered contrasting views on the role of the federal gov-ernment, tax cuts, environmental policies, and the best way to preserve Social Security and Medicare.

Gore, a Tennessee native and Harvard graduate whose father had been a U.S. senator, favored an active federal government that would do more to protect the environment.

Bush, on the other hand, campaigned on a theme of "compassionate con-servatism." He also promised to restore "honor and dignity" to the White House after the Clinton scandal, and he proposed transferring power from the federal government to the states. A born-again Christian and former alco-holic with degrees from Yale University and Harvard Business School, he also urged a more "humble" foreign policy that would end U.S. efforts at "nation-building," whereby American officials sought to install democratic govern-ments in undemocratic societies.

The November election results created high drama. The television net-works initially reported that Gore had narrowly won the state of Florida and its decisive twenty-five electoral votes. Later in the evening, however, they

THE ELECTION OF 2000

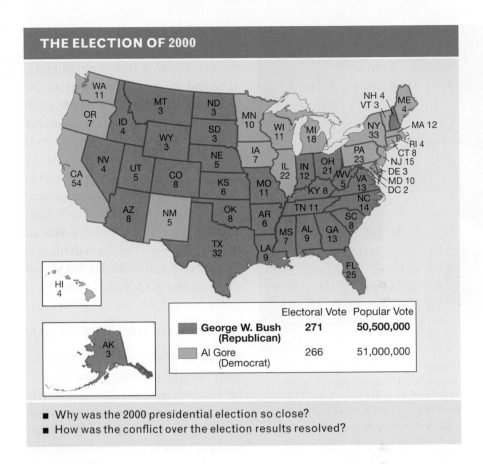

		Electoral Vote	Popular Vote
▮	**George W. Bush (Republican)**	271	**50,500,000**
▮	Al Gore (Democrat)	266	51,000,000

- Why was the 2000 presidential election so close?
- How was the conflict over the election results resolved?

reversed themselves, saying that Florida was too close to call. In the chaotic early-morning hours, the networks declared that Bush had been elected president. The final tally showed Bush with a razor-thin lead, but Florida law required a recount. For the first time in 125 years, the results of a presidential election remained in doubt for weeks.

As a painstaking hand recount proceeded, the two sides sparred in court, each accusing the other of trying to steal the election. The drama lasted for five weeks, until, on December 12, a divided U.S. Supreme Court ruled 5–4 that the recount be halted. Bush was declared the winner in Florida by 537 votes. Gore had amassed a 540,000-vote lead nationwide, but losing Florida meant he lost the electoral college tally by two votes. Although Gore "strongly disagreed" with the Supreme Court's decision, he asked voters to rally around Bush and move forward. "Partisan rancor," he urged, "must be put aside."

The ferocious sparring between the two national parties was not put aside, however, in part because Bush chose as key advisers men known for

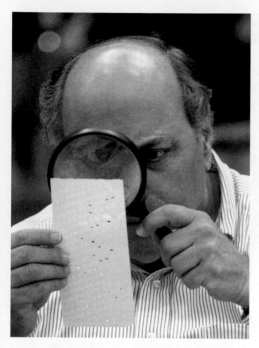

The recount In yet another recount, Judge Robert Rosenberg examines a ballot with a magnifying glass. That Florida's voting machines were so unreliable introduced doubt about the legitimacy of the close results in the November 2000 election.

their strong ideological convictions. One of them, hawkish Richard "Dick" Cheney, a former Wyoming congressman and influential member of the Nixon, Ford, and George H. W. Bush administrations, quickly became the most powerful vice president in modern history. The secretive Cheney used his long experience with government bureaucracy to fill the administration with like-minded associates who helped him control the flow of information to the president. He became a domineering influence on the inexperienced Bush.

A CHANGE OF DIRECTION

George W. Bush had promised to cut taxes for the wealthy, increase military spending, and eliminate overly strict environmental regulations. First, however, he had to deal with a sputtering economy, which in March 2001 was in recession for the first time in more than a decade. Bush decided that cutting taxes was the best way to boost economic growth and to generate jobs for the growing number of unemployed. On June 7, 2001, he signed the Economic Growth and Tax Relief Act, which cut $1.35 trillion in taxes.

Instead of paying for themselves in renewed economic growth, however, the tax cuts led to a sharp drop in federal revenue, producing in turn a fast-growing budget deficit as the Clinton surpluses were quickly used up. Huge increases in the costs of Medicare and Medicaid resulting from the aging of the baby boom generation contributed to the deficit, as did military expenditures caused by an unexpected war against terrorism.

Islamist militants around the world bitterly resented what they viewed as the "imperial" globalization of U.S. culture and power. With increasing frequency, they used terrorism, including suicide bombings, to gain notoriety, exact vengeance, and generate fear and insecurity.

Throughout the 1990s, the United States had fought a losing struggle against global terrorist groups. The ineffectiveness of U.S. intelligence agencies in tracking the movements and intentions of militant extremists became tragically evident in the late summer of 2001.

9/11—A NEW DAY OF INFAMY Early on the morning of September 11, 2001, Islamist terrorists hijacked a U.S. airliner in Boston. They flew it to New York City, where at 8:44 A.M. they slammed the fuel-laden jet into the north tower of the World Trade Center in the heart of the nation's financial district. The twin towers, each 110 stories tall and filled with Wall Street investment companies, had been viewed as the cathedrals of capitalism, and now they were being toppled. Eighteen minutes after the first tower was hit, a second hijacked jumbo jet crashed into the Trade Center's south tower.

The two skyscrapers, filled with 50,000 workers, burned fiercely. The televised images were heartbreaking. Hundreds of trapped occupants, many of

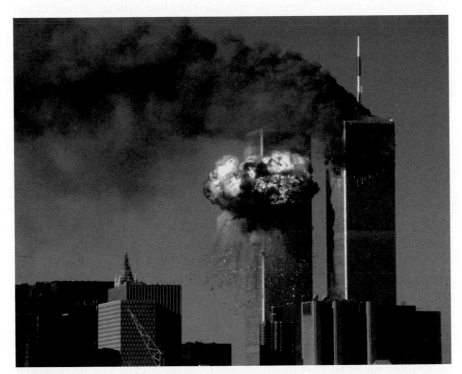

September 11 Smoke pours out of the north tower of the World Trade Center as the south tower bursts into flames after being struck by a second hijacked airplane. Both iconic buildings would collapse within an hour.

them on fire, saw no choice but to jump to their deaths. One couple held hands as they plummeted to the ground.

The mammoth steel structures quickly collapsed from the intense inferno, destroying surrounding buildings and killing nearly 3,000 people, including more than 400 firefighters, police officers, and emergency responders. One of the dead, the Reverend Mychal Judge, was a fire department chaplain who was killed by falling debris as he administered last rites to an injured fireman. The southern end of Manhattan—"ground zero"—became a hellish scene of raging fires, twisted steel, broken concrete, suffocating smoke, wailing sirens, blood-covered streets, victims in agony, and thousands of panicked people fleeing the island.

While the catastrophic drama in New York City was unfolding, a third hijacked plane crashed into the Pentagon in Washington, D.C. A fourth hijacked airliner, most likely aimed toward the White House, missed its mark when passengers—who had heard reports of the earlier hijackings via cell phones—assaulted the knife-wielding hijackers to prevent the plane from being used as a weapon. During the struggle, the plane went out of control and plummeted into the ground near Shanksville, Pennsylvania, killing all aboard.

Within hours of the hijackings, the nineteen dead terrorists, fifteen of them from Saudi Arabia, were identified as members of al Qaeda (Arabic for "the Base"), a well-financed network of Islamist extremists led by a wealthy Saudi renegade, Osama bin Laden. Years before, bin Laden had declared *jihad* ("holy war") on the United States, Israel, and the Saudi monarchy in his effort to create a single Islamist caliphate ("global empire"). He used remote bases in Sudan and Afghanistan as training centers for jihadist fighters recruited from around the world. Collaborating with bin Laden's terrorist network was Afghanistan's ruling Taliban, a coalition of ultraconservative Islamists who provided bin Laden a safe haven.

The governments of Islamic nations condemned the 9/11 attacks, but al Qaeda was not a nation. Instead it was a new and extremely dangerous type of organization—a shadowy virtual terrorist state, borderless yet global in its reach, and populated by Islamist zealots from across the world. As religious terrorists, they were the products of failed societies that bred their anger and their hatred of the West—and of America in particular because of its steadfast support of Israel. As a Pakistani newspaper asserted, "September 11 was not a mindless terrorism for terrorism's sake. It was reaction and revenge, even retribution" for America's pro-Israeli policies in the Middle East. They viewed themselves as God's people doing holy work. Killing "infidels" (Americans and their allies) was a sacred act that would earn heavenly rewards. Bin Laden told his followers that it was their religious duty "to kill the Americans and their allies, civilian and military, in any country."

THE "WAR ON TERROR"

The 9/11 assault on the United States, like the Japanese attack on Pearl Harbor on December 7, 1941, changed the course of modern life. Many Americans were initially paralyzed by grief, confusion, and fear. "We felt so secure, so self-confident behind our oceans and our armaments," noted a magazine editor. "Now the assault on our heartland has punctured the illusion that we are invulnerable."

As the shock wore off, however, Americans were consumed by blinding anger and a feverish quest for retaliation and revenge, the same emotions that had propelled the terrorists. As a journalist wrote in *Time* magazine, "A day cannot live in infamy without the nourishment of rage. Let's have rage . . . a purple American fury."

George W. Bush suddenly found his presidential voice and purpose as he forged a coalition of allied nations committed to a global **war on terror** "to answer these attacks and rid the world of evil. . . . We will not waver, we will not tire, we will not falter, and we will not fail." He warned other nations that they needed to make a grave decision: "either you are with us or you are with the terrorists." The war, Bush stressed, would begin with al Qaeda but would "not end until every terrorist group of global reach has been found, stopped, and defeated."

War fever President George W. Bush addresses members of the Special Forces in July 2002 as part of an appeal to Congress to increase defense spending after the September 11 terrorist attacks.

A wave of patriotic fervor swept the nation after Bush's declaration of war. In just 48 hours, Walmart sold more than 300,000 U.S. flags. People formed long lines to donate blood, and many men and women signed up for military service.

President Bush led the military campaign to ferret out the al Qaeda terrorists and destroy their networks and infrastructure. That required ousting the Taliban movement, for it hosted al Qaeda. Bush demanded that Afghanistan's Taliban government surrender the al Qaeda terrorists or risk military attack. The Taliban refused, and on October 7, 2001, the United States and its allies launched an invasion of Afghanistan dubbed Operation Enduring Freedom. Bush pledged that American forces would stay until they finished the job. (The war is now in its eighteenth year.)

On December 9, the Taliban regime collapsed, and the United States inherited a failed nation. Afghanistan was a desperately poor country with a dysfunctional and corrupt government and inhabited by a largely rural population whose life expectancy was forty-seven and literacy rate was thirty-eight percent. The United States proved unable to improve the Islamic nation's quality of life, and, as a result, the war in Afghanistan transitioned into a high-stakes manhunt for the elusive Osama bin Laden.

As former president Bill Clinton noted, however, "Getting Osama bin Laden is the beginning, not the end, of this process." A veteran of the Second World War, Paul Fussell, a literary historian, also worried about the long-term

The Taliban A young woman shows her face in public for the first time in five years after Northern Alliance troops capture Kabul, the capital of Afghanistan, in November 2001. The strict sharia law enforced by the Taliban required that women be covered from head to foot.

effects of the terrorist attacks. "If we go into Afghanistan, when do we get out? It seems to me this will be another South Korea: We will keep troops [there] forever." Little did he know that his prediction would come true.

FIGHTING TERROR AT HOME While the fighting continued in Afghanistan, officials in Washington worried that terrorists might attack the United States with biological, chemical, or even nuclear weapons. To address the threat and help restore public confidence, President Bush exercised extraordinary executive powers as commander in chief. Without congressional approval, he established the Office of Homeland Security and gave it sweeping authority to spy on Americans. Another new federal agency, the Transportation Security Administration (TSA), assumed responsibility for screening airline passengers for weapons and bombs.

At the same time, Bush and a supportive Congress created the **USA Patriot Act**, which gave government agencies the right to eavesdrop on confidential conversations between prison inmates and their lawyers, and permitted suspected terrorists to be tried in secret military courts. Civil liberties groups voiced concerns that the measures jeopardized constitutional rights and protections, but most people supported them.

What the public did not know was that Vice President Cheney, Secretary of Defense Donald Rumsfeld, and other so-called neoconservatives ("neocons") in the Departments of State and Defense had convinced Bush to authorize the use of torture ("enhanced interrogation techniques") in interviewing captured terrorist suspects. Such tactics violated international law and compromised human rights. When asked about this approach, Cheney scoffed that America sometimes had to work "the dark side": "We've got to spend time in the shadows in the intelligence world."

THE BUSH DOCTRINE In the fall of 2002, George Bush unveiled a dramatic new national security policy. The **Bush Doctrine** said that the growing menace posed by "shadowy networks" of terrorist groups and unstable rogue nations with "**weapons of mass destruction**" (often referred to as WMDs), required the United States at times to use *preemptive* military action and to act unilaterally [alone] if necessary to defuse threats. "If we wait for threats to fully materialize," or wait for allies to join America, he explained, "we will have waited too long. In the world we have entered, the only path to safety is the path of action. And this nation will act."

The sweeping Bush Doctrine promised to "extend the benefits of freedom across the globe . . . for all peoples everywhere" without mentioning the potential human and financial cost of such an open-ended commitment.

THE SECOND IRAQ WAR During 2002 and 2003, Iraq emerged as the focus of the Bush administration's policy of preemptive military action. Vice President Cheney, Secretary of Defense Rumsfeld, and Deputy Defense Secretary Paul Wolfowitz urged the president to use U.S. power to reshape the world in America's image. This included sponsoring "regime change" in authoritarian nations lacking "political and economic freedom" so as to create a new world order "friendly to our security, our prosperity, and our principles." They convinced Bush that the dictatorial Iraqi regime of Saddam Hussein represented a "grave and gathering danger" because of its supposed possession of biological and chemical weapons of mass destruction.

On March 17, 2003, Bush issued Hussein an ultimatum: leave Iraq within forty-eight hours or face a United States–led invasion. Hussein refused. Two days later, on March 19, American and British forces attacked Iraq. They did so, according to Bush, because Saddam "promotes international terror" and "seeks nuclear weapons." Bush and his advisers, especially Secretary of Defense Rumsfeld, claimed that American forces would quickly topple Hussein and usher in a new era of U.S.-style democracy in Iraq.

The Second Iraq War began with a massive bombing campaign, followed by a fast-moving invasion from bases in Kuwait. On April 9, after three weeks of intense fighting, U.S. forces captured Baghdad, the capital of Iraq. Hussein's regime and his demoralized army collapsed a week later.

The six-week war was ferociously efficient: among the 300,000 allied troops less than 200 were killed compared to more than 2,000 Iraqi combat deaths; civilian casualties (the administration termed them "enemy non-combatants") numbered in the tens of thousands. President Bush staged a celebration onboard a U.S. aircraft carrier at which he announced victory under a massive banner proclaiming "MISSION ACCOMPLISHED."

But the president, as he later admitted, spoke too soon; the initial military triumph carried with it the seeds of deception and disaster, as no weapons of mass destruction were to be found in Iraq. Bush said that the absence of WMDs left him with a "sickening feeling," for he knew that his primary justification for the war had evaporated.

REBUILDING IRAQ It proved far easier to defeat the Iraqi army than to rebuild Iraq in America's image. Unprepared U.S. officials faced the daunting task of installing a democratic government in a nation fractured by religious feuds, and with ethnic tensions made worse by the breakdown in law and order caused by the allied invasion. U.S. troops liberated millions from the tyrannical authority of Hussein's government, but few of them seemed grateful. Large parts of the war-torn country fell into civil war as sectarian tribalism replaced the dictatorship. As a result of the U.S. invasion, the entire Middle East was further destabilized.

Rather than reducing the number of Islamist terrorists, the U.S. intervention in Iraq served to increase them. And soon Iraq became a quagmire for American forces reminiscent of the Vietnam War. Within weeks of the U.S. invasion, vengeful Islamist radicals streamed into Iraq to wage a campaign of terror, sabotage, and suicide bombings.

Bush's macho reaction—"Bring 'em on!"—revealed how uninformed he was about the fast-deteriorating situation. The leader of the new Iraqi government, Prime Minister Nouri al-Maliki, quickly imposed his own authoritarian government on the fractured nation. As head of the Shiite-dominated regime, he discriminated against the Sunnis, the Kurds, and other ethnic and religious minorities. Soon the chaotic conflict had grown beyond America's capacity to control or end.

Bush and his key aides greatly underestimated the difficulty and expense of occupying, pacifying, and reconstructing postwar Iraq. By the fall of 2003, Bush admitted that substantial numbers of American troops (around 150,000) would have to remain in Iraq much longer than anticipated. He also acknowledged that rebuilding Iraq would take years and cost almost a trillion dollars.

Americans grew more and more dismayed as the number of casualties and the expense of the military occupation in Iraq soared. The nation became more alienated from the Iraqi intervention when journalists revealed graphic pictures of U.S. soldiers abusing and torturing Arab detainees in the Abu Ghraib prison near Baghdad. "When you lose the moral high ground," an army general observed, "you lose it all." By 2004, a Republican journalist dismissed Bush's Middle East strategy as "shiftless, reactive, irrelevantly grandiose; our war aims undefined; our preparations insufficient; our civil defense neglected."

Regardless, President Bush still insisted that a democratic Iraq would bring stability to the Middle East and blunt the momentum of Islamist terrorism. Yet even though Saddam Hussein was captured in December 2003 and later hanged, Iraq seemed less secure than ever.

By the beginning of 2004, some 1,000 Americans had died in the conflict, more than 10,000 had been wounded, and many other veterans of the conflict suffered from post–traumatic stress disorder (PTSD). The ethnic and religious tensions only worsened as Sunni jihadists allied with al Qaeda to undermine the new Iraqi government and assault U.S. forces.

The U.S. effort in Iraq was the wrong war in the wrong place fought in the wrong way. It forced Bush to spend government funds at a rate faster than any president since Lyndon Johnson, and it distracted attention from the revival of the Taliban and other terrorist groups in Afghanistan. Journalist Roger Cohen

Freedom for whom? The American torture of Iraqis in Abu Ghraib prison only exacerbated the anger and humiliation that Iraqis experienced since the First Gulf War. In response to America's incessant promises of peace and autonomy, a Baghdad mural fires back: "That Freedom for B[u]sh."

distilled perhaps the most important lesson from the wars in Iraq and Afghanistan when he said that the American ideal of democracy "can still resonate" with people around the world, but U.S. leaders "must embody it rather than impose it."

THE ELECTION OF 2004 Growing concern about Iraq complicated George W. Bush's campaign for a second presidential term in 2004. The Democratic nominee, Senator John Kerry of Massachusetts, condemned Bush for misleading the nation about weapons of mass destruction and for his slipshod handling of the reconstruction of postwar Iraq. Kerry also highlighted the Bush administration's record budget deficits. Bush countered that the tortuous efforts to create a democratic government in Iraq would enhance America's long-term security.

On Election Day, November 2, 2004, exit polls suggested a Kerry victory, but in the end the election hinged on the crucial swing state of Ohio, where late returns tipped the balance toward Bush, even as rumors of electoral "irregularities" began to circulate. Nevertheless, Kerry conceded. "The outcome," he stressed, "should be decided by voters, not a protracted legal battle."

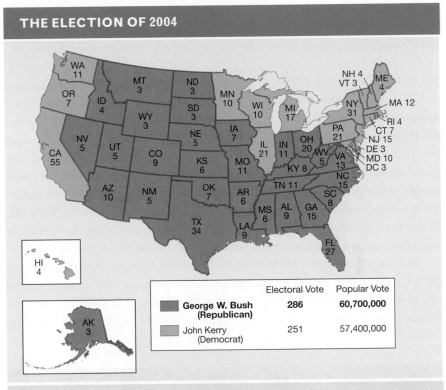

THE ELECTION OF 2004

	Electoral Vote	Popular Vote
George W. Bush (Republican)	286	60,700,000
John Kerry (Democrat)	251	57,400,000

■ How did the war in Iraq polarize American politics?

■ In what ways did the election of 2004 give Republicans a mandate for change?

By winning Ohio, Bush captured 286 electoral votes to Kerry's 251. Yet in some respects, the election was not so close. Bush received 3.5 million more votes nationwide than Kerry, and Republicans increased their majorities in both houses of Congress. Bush pledged to bring democracy and stability to Iraq, trim the federal deficit, pass a major energy bill, create more jobs, and privatize Social Security funds by investing them in the stock market. "I earned capital in the campaign, political capital, and now I intend to spend it," he told reporters.

SECOND-TERM BLUES

George Bush's second term was beset by thorny political problems, a sluggish economy, and continuing turmoil in Iraq. In 2005, he pushed through Congress an energy bill and the Central American Free Trade Agreement (CAFTA). But his effort to enable individuals to invest their accumulated Social Security pension funds themselves went nowhere, and soaring budget deficits made many fiscal conservatives feel betrayed by the supposedly "conservative" Bush.

HURRICANE KATRINA In late August 2005, President Bush's eroding public support suffered another blow in the form of a natural disaster. When killer-hurricane Katrina slammed into the Gulf coast, it devastated large areas of Alabama, Mississippi, and Louisiana. Katrina left more than 1,500 dead and many thousands more homeless and hopeless, especially in New Orleans. Local officials and the Federal Emergency Management Agency (FEMA) were caught unprepared, and confusion and incompetence abounded. President Bush seemed listless, confused, and tone-deaf as the storm took its tragic toll. In the face of blistering criticism, he accepted responsibility for the balky federal response and accepted the resignation of the FEMA director.

The backlash over the federal response to Katrina contributed to a devastating defeat for Republicans in the November 2006 congressional elections. The Democrats won control of the House of Representatives, the Senate, and a majority of governorships and state legislatures. The elec-

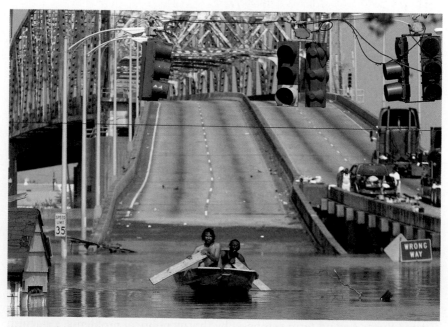

The aftermath of Hurricane Katrina Two men use boards to paddle through high water in flood-devastated New Orleans.

tion also included a significant milestone: Californian Nancy Pelosi, leader of the Democrats in the House of Representatives, became the highest-ranking woman in the history of the U.S. Congress upon her election as House Speaker in January 2007.

THE "SURGE" IN IRAQ George W. Bush bore the brunt of public indignation over the bungled response to Katrina. He also received the blame for the costs and casualties of the unending war in Iraq, where the violence increased throughout the fall of 2006. Bush eventually responded to declining public and political support by creating the Iraq Study Group, a bipartisan task force that surprised the president by issuing a report recommending the withdrawal of combat forces from a "grave and deteriorating Iraq" by the spring of 2008.

Nancy Pelosi The first female Speaker of the House at a news conference on Capitol Hill in 2007.

Bush disagreed with those who urged a phased withdrawal. On January 10, 2007, he announced that he was sending a "surge" of 20,000 (eventually 30,000) more troops to Iraq, bringing the total to almost 170,000. From a military perspective, the military surge succeeded. By the fall of 2008, violence in Iraq had declined dramatically, and the U.S.-supported Iraqi government had grown in stature and confidence.

The U.S. general who masterminded the increase in troops admitted that the gains were "fragile and reversible," however. As the number of U.S. combat deaths in Iraq passed 4,000, Bush acknowledged that the conflict was "longer and harder and more costly than we anticipated." By 2008, more than 60 percent of Americans believed the Iraqi invasion had been a mistake and that the conflict had become a war without end.

ECONOMIC SHOCK After the intense but brief 2001 recession, the boom/bust economy had begun another period of prolonged expansion. Between 1997 and 2006, home prices in the United States rose 85 percent, leading to a frenzy of irresponsible mortgage lending—whereby homebuyers were often freed from making down payments or demonstrating

credit-worthiness—and a debt-financed consumer spending spree. Tens of millions of people bought houses they could not afford, refinanced their mortgages, or tapped home-equity loans to make discretionary purchases.

Then in 2007, the huge housing-price bubble burst and home values and real-estate sales began a sharp decline. The loss of trillions of dollars in home values set off a seismic shock across the economy, as record numbers of borrowers defaulted on their mortgage payments. Foreclosures and bankruptcies soared, and banks lost billions, first on the shaky mortgages, then on other categories of overleveraged debt: credit cards, car loans, student loans, and commercial mortgage-backed securities.

The economy fell into a recession in 2008, and some of the nation's most prestigious banks, investment firms, and insurance companies went belly up. Neither politicians nor government regulators were prepared for the financial calamity that quickly threatened to turn into a depression. The price of food and gasoline spiked. Unemployment soared. What had begun as a sharp decline in home prices became a global economic meltdown.

The economic crisis demanded decisive action to stem the panic and restore confidence. On October 3, 2008, President Bush signed into law the Troubled Asset Relief Program (TARP), which called for the Treasury Department to spend $700 billion to keep big banks and other large financial institutions afloat since they were deemed "too big to fail." Treasury Secretary Hank Paulson, the former head of Goldman Sachs (a leading global investment bank), was made so nervous by the near meltdown of the world financial system that he regularly left emergency meetings to vomit in the hallway. "To protect free-enterprise capitalism," he reflected, "I had become the treasury secretary who would forever be associated with government intervention and bank bail-outs."

Yet given its ambitious goal, the TARP program did little to restore confidence in an economy headed into free fall. In early October, stock markets around the world began to crash with the onset of what came to be called the **Great Recession**, which technically lasted from December 2007 to January 2009 and forced almost 9 million people out of work. Federal Reserve chairman Ben Bernanke called it "the worst financial crisis in modern history."

The effects of the Great Recession lasted long thereafter. The economic recovery that began in June 2009 would be the weakest since the end of the Second World War. Between 2009 and 2013, economic growth averaged just 2.2 percent, barely half the 4.2 percent average of the seven previous recoveries.

Why was the recovery so tepid? Consumers were burdened by too much household debt, businesses were unable or unwilling to make new capital investments, and the damaged financial system continued to stifle commercial and personal loans.

Taken together, the wars in Afghanistan and Iraq, coupled with a slumping economy, shattered public support for the Bush administration. During Bush's last year in office, his approval rating was an abysmal 25 percent, just one point higher than Richard Nixon's during the Watergate investigations. Alan Brinkley, a distinguished political historian, noted in 2008 that presidential scholars were deeming Bush "the most disastrous president in our history." Bush's failed presidency weakened the Republican party, strained the nation's military, eroded American prestige abroad, and created the largest budget deficits in history by cutting taxes while increasing spending.

A HISTORIC NEW PRESIDENCY

Democrats were excited about the possibility of regaining the White House in 2008. The early front-runner for their party's nomination was New York senator Hillary Rodham Clinton, the spouse of ex-president Bill Clinton, who enjoyed the support of the most powerful Democratic leaders. Like her husband, she displayed an impressive command of policy issues and mobilized a well-funded campaign team. Moreover, as the first woman with a serious chance of gaining the presidency, she had widespread support among voters eager for female leadership.

In the end, however, an overconfident Clinton lost the nomination to Barack Obama of Illinois, a little-known first-term senator. Young, handsome, and intelligent, a vibrant mixture of idealism and pragmatism, coolness and passion, Obama was an inspiring speaker who promised a vague "politics of hope," the "energy of change," and the revival of bipartisanship. In early June 2008, he gained enough delegates to secure the nomination, with Senator Joseph Biden of Delaware as his running mate.

Obama, the first African American presidential nominee of either party, was the biracial son of a white mother from Kansas and a black father from Kenya who left the household and returned to Africa when Barack was a toddler. Obama eventually graduated from Columbia University before earning a law degree from Harvard. The forty-seven-year-old senator presented himself as a leader who could inspire, unite, and forge collaborations across the partisan divide.

Candidate Obama radiated poise, confidence, and energy. He promised to end the wars in Afghanistan and Iraq, stop the use of torture in the war on terror, reduce nuclear weapons, tighten regulation of the banking industry, secure the border with Mexico, enable a path to citizenship for undocumented immigrants, and provide medical coverage to the millions of uninsured.

Barack Obama The president-elect and his family wave to supporters in Chicago's Grant Park.

Obama and his strategists mastered the use of social media to organize rock-concert-like campaign rallies and turned his vitality and political inexperience into strengths at a time when voter disgust with politics was widespread.

By contrast, his Republican opponent, seventy-two-year-old Arizona senator John McCain, was the oldest presidential candidate in history. A twenty-five-year veteran of Congress, McCain had developed a reputation as a bipartisan "maverick" willing to work with Democrats to achieve legislative goals. His impolitic and unpredictable running mate, former Alaska governor Sarah Palin, did not help McCain's chances when she revealed to a reporter that she could not recall reading any newspapers or magazines.

On November 4, 2008, Obama made history by becoming the first person of color to be elected president. He won the popular vote by 53 percent to 46 percent, and the electoral college 365 to 173. He also helped the Democrats win solid majorities in both houses of Congress.

Obama considered his election a "defining moment" in political history. "It's been a long time coming, but tonight . . . change has come to America." He urged Americans to "resist the temptation to fall back on the same partisanship and pettiness and immaturity that has poisoned our politics for so long." It was one of those uplifting sentiments that sounded great but had no chance of unifying America's polarized electorate.

OBAMA'S FIRST TERM In his 2009 inaugural address, President Obama acknowledged that America was in a crisis forged by a staggering number of challenges. The new administration inherited two unpopular wars, rising unemployment, and a staggering national debt. The economy was the weakest it had been in eighty years, and health care was too costly for most Americans. Worst of all, he observed, was the "sapping of confidence across our land—a nagging fear that America's decline is inevitable, and that the next generation must lower its sights."

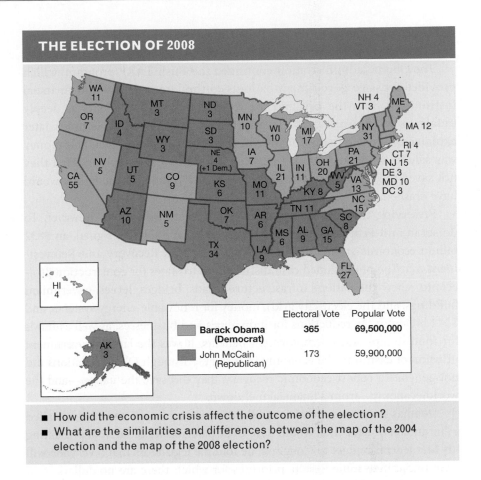

THE ELECTION OF 2008

	Electoral Vote	Popular Vote
Barack Obama (Democrat)	365	69,500,000
John McCain (Republican)	173	59,900,000

- How did the economic crisis affect the outcome of the election?
- What are the similarities and differences between the map of the 2004 election and the map of the 2008 election?

Yet the new president pledged to lead the nation out of the paralyzing sense of crisis. To do so, he promised to inaugurate "a new politics for a new time"— without explaining what that meant or how he planned to implement it. In the end, Obama would prove to be more inspirational than effective as the nation's chief executive.

Obama's most pressing challenge was to keep the Great Recession from becoming a prolonged depression. Unemployment had passed 8 percent and was still rising. The financial sector remained paralyzed, and public confidence in the economy had plummeted.

One visible sign of the Great Recession's effects was the sharp decline in Mexicans emigrating to the United States. In 2000, some 700,000 Mexicans had crossed the Rio Grande, but by 2010, the number had dropped to less than 150,000, as it became easier for people to improve their quality of life in Mexico and harder to do so in the United States. By 2014, some experts believed that more Mexicans were leaving the United States than entering it.

The Obama administration continued the Bush TARP program, which provided massive government bailouts to the largest banks and financial institutions. Both the Left and the Right attacked the bailouts as deeply unfair to most Americans. Treasury Secretary Timothy Geithner later explained, "We had to do whatever we could to help people feel their money was safe in the [banking] system, even if it made us unpopular." Had they not saved the big banks, Obama and Geithner argued, the economy would have crashed.

Preserving the banking system did not create many jobs, however. To do so, in mid-February 2009, Congress passed, and Obama signed, an $832 billion economic-stimulus bill called the American Recovery and Reinvestment Act. The bill included cash distributions to states for construction projects to renew the nation's infrastructure (roads, bridges, levees, government buildings, and the electricity grid), money for renewable-energy systems, and $212 billion in tax reductions for individuals and businesses, as well as funds for food stamps and unemployment benefits. It was the largest government infusion of cash into the economy in history. Although Obama's actions did not generate a robust economic recovery, they did save the nation—and the world economy—from a financial meltdown.

Obama's strenuous efforts to avoid a depression also created what he called a "mountain of debt" that would have to be paid sooner or later. In presenting his first federal budget to Congress, he told the legislators that "everyone will have to sacrifice some worthy priorities for which there are no dollars. And that includes me."

HEALTH-CARE REFORM From his first day in office, Barack Obama stressed his intention to reform a health-care system that was "bankrupting families, bankrupting businesses, and bankrupting our government at the state and federal level." The United States was the only developed nation without a national health-care program. Since 1970, the proportion of people uninsured had been steadily rising, as had health-care costs. In 2010, roughly 50 million Americans (16 percent of the population), most of them poor, young, people of color, or part-time workers or self-employed, had no health insurance.

The president's goal in creating the Patient Protection and **Affordable Care Act (ACA)**, which critics labeled "**Obamacare**," was to make health insurance more affordable and health care accessible to everyone.

The $940 billion law, proposed in 2009 and debated for a year, centered on the so-called individual mandate, which required uninsured adults to purchase an approved private insurance policy through state-run exchanges (websites where people could shop for insurance), or pay a tax penalty. Low-income Americans could receive federal subsidies to help pay for their coverage, and insurance companies could no longer deny coverage to people with preexisting illnesses. Employers who did not offer health insurance would have to pay higher taxes, and drug companies and manufacturers of medical devices would have to pay annual government fees. Everyone would pay higher Medicare payroll taxes to help fund the changes, but eventually, the theory went, with more people insured, rates would go down.

The idea of forcing people to buy health insurance flew in the face of such ideals as individual freedom and personal responsibility. Critics questioned not only the individual mandate but the administration's projections that the program would reduce federal expenditures over the long haul.

Republicans mobilized to defeat the ACA, but it passed with narrow party-line majorities in both houses of Congress. Obama signed it into law on March 23, 2010. Its complex provisions, to be implemented over a four-year period, would bring health insurance to a promised 32 million people, half of whom would be covered by expanded Medicaid and the other half by the individual mandate. In the end, about half those numbers enrolled. In its scope and goals, the ACA was a landmark in the history of health and social welfare—as well as in the expansion of the federal government.

OBAMACARE AND THE COURTS No sooner had President Obama pushed his health-care plan through Congress, than Republicans began challenging its constitutionality. On June 28, 2012, in *National Federation of Independent Business v. Sebelius*, the Supreme Court ruled 5–4 that most of the new law was constitutional. Even more surprising was that the chief justice, John G. Roberts, a philosophical conservative who had never before voted with the four "liberal" justices on the Court, cast the deciding vote. Roberts upheld the ACA's individual mandate that required people to buy private health insurance or pay a penalty tax, arguing that it was within Congress's power

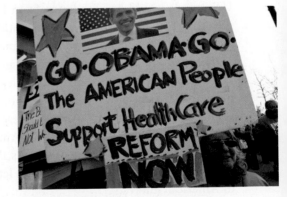

Go Obama Go A Democrat holds up a sign in support of the Affordable Care Act, more commonly known as Obamacare, in a march in Washington, D.C., in 2010.

to impose taxes as outlined in Article 1 of the Constitution. The verdict led the *New York Times* to predict that the ruling "may secure Obama's place in history."

REGULATING WALL STREET The near collapse of the nation's financial system beginning in 2008 prompted calls for overhauling the financial regulatory system. On July 21, 2010, Obama signed the Wall Street Reform and Consumer Protection Act, also called the Dodd-Frank bill after its two congressional sponsors. The 2,319-page law required government agencies to exercise greater oversight over complex new financial transactions and protected consumers from unfair practices in loans and credit cards by establishing the Consumer Financial Protection Bureau.

FOREIGN AFFAIRS

President Obama had more success in dealing with foreign affairs than in reviving the American economy. What journalists came to call the Obama Doctrine was much like the Nixon Doctrine, stressing that the United States could not afford to police the world.

THE OBAMA DOCTRINE The loosely defined Obama Doctrine grew out of efforts to end the costly wars in Iraq and Afghanistan. In essence, the president wanted to replace confrontation and military intervention with a stance of cooperation and negotiation.

On February 27, 2009, President Obama announced that all 142,000 U.S. troops would be withdrawn from Iraq by the end of 2011, as the Iraqi government and the Bush administration had agreed in 2008. True to his word, the last U.S. combat troops left Iraq in December 2011. Their departure marked the end of a bitterly divisive war that had raged for nearly nine years, killed more than 110,000 Iraqis, and left the nation shattered and unstable, despite Obama's claim that the U.S. forces were "leaving behind a sovereign, stable, and self-reliant Iraq with a representative government."

The war had cost more than 4,500 American lives, 30,000 wounded (many grievously so), and $2 trillion. Perhaps the greatest embarrassment was that the Iraqi government the United States left in power was inept and unfriendly to American interests.

The long and chaotic war was an expensive mistake. As it turned out, there were no weapons of mass destruction, as the Bush administration had contended, nor was there a direct link between the al Qaeda terrorists and Saddam Hussein. Al Qaeda, in fact, did not arrive in Iraq until after the American

Home from Iraq U.S. troops returned from Iraq to few celebrations.

invasion. "The first Iraq war, in which I led a tank platoon, was necessary," said John Nagel, a retired army officer. "This one was not."

American efforts at nation building had failed. Obama's hopes that the United States could avoid fighting in the Middle East and that the Iraqis could sustain a stable government in the face of terrorist incursions and sectarian fighting proved fruitless. Iraq's woeful government and constant sectarian strife required continued infusions of U.S. military assistance, daily bombing raids, and massive economic aid.

"SURGE" IN AFGHANISTAN At the same time that President Obama was ending U.S. military involvement in Iraq, he dispatched 21,000 additional troops to Afghanistan and changed the U.S. commander on the ground in what had become America's longest war. While doing so, however, he narrowed the focus of the U.S. mission to suppressing terrorists rather than transforming the strife-torn country into a stable capitalist democracy.

The surge worked as hoped. By the summer of 2011, Obama announced that the "tide of war was receding" and that the United States had largely achieved its goals, setting in motion a substantial withdrawal of forces that lasted until 2014. "We will not try to make Afghanistan a perfect place," Obama said. "We will not police its streets or patrol its mountains indefinitely. That is the responsibility of the Afghan government."

Since then, however, the situation has deteriorated, and substantial American forces remain in place. The Taliban have increased the amount of territory they control, and the Afghan government continues to be ineffective, unstable, and corrupt.

THE DEATH OF OSAMA BIN LADEN Ever since the attacks of 9/11, Osama bin Laden, tall and thin with a scraggly beard, had eluded an intensive manhunt. In August 2010, however, U.S. intelligence analysts discovered his sanctuary in a walled residential compound outside of Abbottabad, Pakistan. On May 1, 2011, President Obama authorized a daring night raid by a U.S. Navy SEAL team transported by helicopters from Afghanistan. After a brief firefight, the SEALs killed bin Laden. His death was a watershed moment, but it did not spell the end of Islamist terrorism.

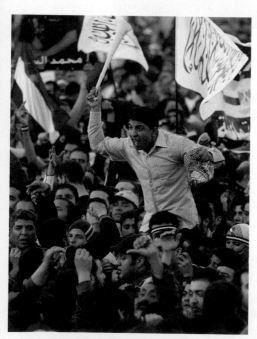

Arab Awakening Thousands of protesters converge in Cairo's Tahrir Square to call for an end to Mubarak's rule in the Middle East.

THE "ARAB AWAKENING" In late 2010 and early 2011, spontaneous uprisings erupted throughout much of the Arab world as long-oppressed peoples rose up against authoritarian regimes. Young idealists inspired by the hope of democracy and connected by social media forced corrupt tyrants from power. The essentially leaderless uprisings seemed to herald a new era in the Middle East.

Yet building new democratic governments proved much harder than expected. The Middle East had no models of open societies to follow, and the essential elements of democratic governance had to be established from scratch. As a result, the grassroots revolutionary movements in most Arab nations stalled by 2014. Egypt reverted to an even harsher authoritarian government, Libya lapsed into chaos, and Yemen exploded in civil war.

LIBYA OUSTS GADDAFI The pro-democracy turmoil in North Africa engulfed oil-rich Libya, long governed by Colonel Muammar Gaddafi, the Arab world's most violent dictator. Anti-government demonstrations began on February 15, 2011, prompting Gaddafi to order Libyan soldiers and mercenaries (paid foreign soldiers) to suppress the rebellious "rats." By the end of February, what began as a peaceful pro-democratic uprising had turned into a full-scale civil war that provided the first real test of the Obama Doctrine.

True to his word, the president refused to act alone in helping the Libyan rebels. Instead, he encouraged European allies to take the lead. On March 19, France and Great Britain, with American support, began bombing Gaddafi's military strongholds. In late August, rebel forces captured the capital of Tripoli, ending Gaddafi's forty-two-year dictatorship. On October 20, rebel fighters killed Gaddafi, but stability remained elusive.

THE CUBAN THAW At the end of 2014, President Obama surprised the world by announcing that the United States and Cuba would restore normal relations after more than fifty years of bitter hostility. As a first step, Obama relaxed restrictions on American tourists visiting Cuba. Six months later, in mid-2015, the two nations reestablished embassies in each other's capital cities.

The powerful Cuban community in south Florida fiercely criticized Obama's decision, and congressional Republicans threatened to block the appointment of a U.S. ambassador to Cuba because of its Communist government. But the president insisted that isolating Cuba had not worked. "Americans and Cubans alike are ready to move forward," he said in July 2015. "I believe it's time for Congress to do the same."

Polarized Politics

Barack Obama had campaigned in 2008 on the promise of bringing dramatic change while reducing the partisan warfare between the two national parties. By the end of his first year in office, however, a Gallup poll found that he had become the most polarizing president in modern history. In part, the partisan civil war resulted from Obama's detached style. Like Jimmy Carter, he did not like to lobby and horse-trade his way to legislative approval. Republican senator John McCain quipped that Obama preferred "leading from behind." Even Democrats criticized his "aloofness."

Yet the standoff with Congress was not solely his fault. His Republican opponents refused to negotiate with him. Senate Minority Leader Mitch McConnell made no effort to disguise his overarching goal: "The single most important thing we want to achieve is for President Obama to be a one-term president."

American political culture had become so polarized that it resembled two separate nations. Each party had its own cable-news station and rabidly partisan commentators, its own newspapers, its own think tanks, and its own billionaire donors. Governing, Obama quickly discovered, is far more difficult than campaigning.

THE TEA PARTY No sooner was Barack Obama sworn in than grassroots conservatives mobilized against the "tax-and-spend" liberalism he represented in their eyes. In January 2009, a New York stock trader named Graham Makohoniuk urged people to send tea bags to their congressional representatives to symbolize the Boston Tea Party of 1773, when American colonists protested against British tax policies.

Within a year or so, the revolt against big government had become a national **Tea Party** movement, with chapters in all fifty states. The Tea Party was not so much a cohesive political organization as it was an attitude and an ideology, a collection of self-described "disaffected," "angry," and "very conservative" activists, mostly white, male, married, middle-class Republicans over forty-five years of age who had grown incensed by the corporate bailouts and unprecedented federal government spending (by both Bush and Obama)

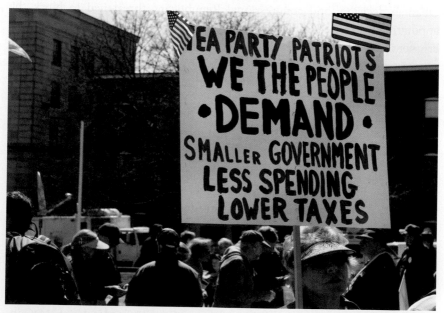

The Tea Party movement Tea Party supporters gather outside the New Hampshire Statehouse for a tax-day rally.

to check the Great Recession. Tea Party members tended to focus more on bloated governments and reckless spending than on religious or cultu. ·l issues such as abortion or LGBTQ rights.

To the anti-tax rebels, the bailouts were a form of "crony capitalism" whereby the political "elite" rewarded big companies that had funded their campaigns, colluding for power and profit at the expense of common folk. Tea Party members demanded a radically smaller federal government (although most of them supported Social Security and Medicare, the most expensive federal social programs). Democrats, including Obama, initially dismissed the Tea Party as a fringe group, but the 2010 election results proved it had become a fast-brewing political force, mobilizing almost 25 percent of voters.

Democratic House and Senate candidates (as well as moderate Republicans), including many long-serving leaders, were defeated in droves when conservative Republicans, many of them aligned with the Tea Party, gained sixty-three seats to recapture control of the House of Representatives. They won a near majority in the Senate as well. It was the most lopsided midterm election since 1938.

Still, mainstream Republicans remained wary of the Tea Partiers, for they seemed determined to embroil the party in perpetual civil war. "If the Republicans don't come through on their promises," threatened Colleen Conley of Rhode Island, "maybe the party needs to be blown up." Her take-no-prisoners outlook galvanized Congressman Mike Pence of Indiana: "There will be no compromise on stopping runaway spending, deficits, and debt. There will be no compromise on repealing Obamacare."

OCCUPY WALL STREET The emergence of the Tea Party was mirrored on the left by the Occupy Wall Street (OWS) movement, mobilized in the fall of 2011 when a call went out over the internet to "Occupy Wall Street. Bring tent." Dozens, then hundreds, then thousands of people, many of them unemployed young adults, converged on Zuccotti Park in lower Manhattan to "occupy" Wall Street, protesting the "tyrannical" power of major banks and investment companies.

The protesters described themselves as the voice of the 99 percent of Americans who were being victimized by the 1 percent—the wealthiest and most politically connected Americans. Economic inequality had become a chasm during the twenty-first century, with the rich getting much richer and the working poor seeing their quality of life stagnate. Unlike the Tea Party, however, OWS did not have staying power. Within a year, its energies and visibility had waned, in part because of mass arrests and in part because

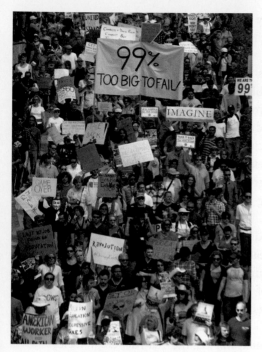

Occupy Wall Street The Manhattan-born grassroots movement grew rapidly from rallies to massive marches in financial districts nationwide, like this demonstration in Los Angeles.

it was an intentionally "leaderless" movement more interested in saying what it was against than explaining what it was for.

Bold Decisions

For all the political sniping, however, attitudes toward some hot-button cultural values were slowly changing. In December 2010, Congress repealed the "don't ask, don't tell" (DADT) military policy that, since 1993, had resulted in some 9,500 gays and lesbians being discharged from the armed forces. A year later, a report by army officers concluded that the repeal "had no overall negative impact on military readiness or its component dimensions, including cohesion, recruitment, retention, assaults, harassment, or morale." In June 2016, the Pentagon would lift the ban on transgender people serving openly in the U.S. military.

MARRIAGE EQUALITY In May 2012, President Obama became the first sitting president to support the right of gay and lesbian couples to marry. That his statement came a day after the North Carolina legislature voted to ban all rights for couples of the same sex, illustrated how incendiary the issue was. While asserting that it was the "right" thing to do, Obama knew that endorsing **marriage equality** had powerful political implications. The LGBTQ community would come to play an energetic role in the 2012 presidential election, and the youth vote—the under-thirty electorate who most supported marriage equality—would be crucial. No sooner had Obama made his announcement than polls showed that American voters were, for the first time, evenly split on the charged issue, with Democrats and independent voters providing the bulk of support for marriage equality.

THE DREAM ACT AND DACA In 2012, the Census Bureau reported that 39.5 million residents, some 13 percent of the total population, had been born outside the United States. In June 2012, Obama again bypassed the Republican-controlled Congress and issued an executive order called the Development, Relief and Education for Alien Minors Act (soon labeled the DREAM Act) that allowed 1.5 million undocumented immigrants (Dreamers) brought to the United States as children (under the age of sixteen) to remain as residents and pursue formal citizenship. The policy had been debated in Congress since 2001 but had never been passed. Obama decided to break the legislative logjam by using an executive order to implement the policy. His unanticipated decision thrilled Latino supporters who were discouraged by his failure to convince Congress to support more-comprehensive immigration reform.

The DREAM Act, however, had unexpected consequences. It excited masses of Central Americans willing to endure enormous risks to migrate to America. Panicked parents in El Salvador, Guatemala, and Honduras, worried about widespread drug-related gang violence, sent their children through Mexico to the United States in hopes of connecting with relatives and being granted citizenship. At the same time, the Obama administration was deporting record numbers of undocumented immigrants (more than 2 million by the end of 2014), some of whom had been working in the nation for decades,

Refugees from gangland Braving hundreds of miles on foot, Honduran and Salvadorian children are sent off by their parents for a better life in the United States, away from the drug-dealing violence of Central America. Here, border guards stop a group of child refugees in Granjeno, Texas.

in what was called the "great expulsion." Obama, called the "Deporter in Chief" by critics, claimed that he was only following the laws written by anti-immigration Republicans.

At the same time, however, Obama continued to use his administrative authority to address the growing issue of undocumented immigrant children. On June 15, 2012, Janet Napolitano, Secretary of Homeland Security, announced a new agency policy called Deferred Action for Childhood Arrivals (DACA). An exercise of prosecutorial discretion, DACA provided temporary relief from deportation ("deferred action") to undocumented immigrants brought to the United States as children. DACA enabled almost 800,000 eligible young adults to work lawfully, attend school, and pursue their dreams without the threat of deportation. However, as an administrative policy DACA did not provide permanent legal status to individuals and had to be renewed every two years (the policy would be rescinded by the Trump administration in 2017).

THE SUPREME COURT IN THE TWENTY-FIRST CENTURY

The Supreme Court surprised observers in 2013 by overturning the Defense of Marriage Act (DOMA) of 1996, which had denied gay and lesbian couples who married in states allowing such unions the right to federal benefits. In *United States v. Windsor* (2013), the Court voted 5–4 that the federal government could not withhold spousal benefits from gay and lesbian couples who had been legally married. But the justices did not rule that same-sex marriage was a right guaranteed under the Constitution. That issue would have to be resolved by a future Court. In the meantime, each state could decide whether to allow such marriages. During 2014, however, federal courts repeatedly overturned state laws banning same-sex marriages.

While the Supreme Court disappointed social conservatives with its *Windsor* decision, its five conservative justices continued to restrict the powers of the federal government. In June 2013, in *Shelby County v. Holder*, the Court gutted key provisions of the 1965 Voting Rights Act (VRA), which had outlawed discrimination toward voters "on account of race or color." The majority opinion declared that in five of the six southern states originally covered by the VRA, black voter turnout now exceeded white turnout. To the judges, this seemed to prove that there was no evidence of continuing racial discrimination. Today's laws "must be justified by current needs," Chief Justice John Roberts wrote.

Soon after the Court's ruling, counties and states in the South pushed through new laws that had the effect of making voting more difficult for people of color, poor people, and immigrants by reducing voting hours or requiring that driver's licenses or other government-issued identification cards be shown on voting days. That there was in fact little evidence of voter fraud to justify such new restrictions led critics to charge that the new requirements were in fact intended to suppress Democratic votes.

THE 2012 ELECTION The 2012 presidential election would be the most expensive election ever, in part because the Supreme Court had ruled in *Citizens United v. Federal Elections Committee* (2010) that corporations could spend as much as they wanted in support of candidates.

Mitt Romney, a corporate executive who served as governor of Massachusetts (2003–2007), emerged as the Republican nominee. The main question for Romney was whether the Religious Right would allow him, a Mormon, to sidestep volatile social issues such as abortion, LGBTQ rights, and school prayer; the question for President Obama was whether he could overcome his failure to restore prosperity.

Two factors hurt Romney's candidacy. The first was his decision to please right-wing voters by opposing immigration reforms that might allow undocumented immigrants a pathway to citizenship. The second was the disclosure of a recording in which he had privately told a group of wealthy contributors that he "did not care" about the 47 percent of Americans who failed "to take personal responsibility and care for their lives." The Obama campaign seized on the impolitic statement and demonized Romney as an uncaring elitist. On Election Day, Obama won with 66 million votes to Romney's 61 million, and 332 electoral votes to 206.

Nearly 60 percent of white voters chose Romney. But the nation's fastest-growing groups—Latinos, Asian Americans, and African Americans—voted overwhelmingly for Obama, as did college-educated women. David Frum, a prominent Republican speechwriter and columnist, confessed that his party was becoming "increasingly isolated and estranged from modern America."

BLACK LIVES MATTER Many people of color also felt more "isolated and estranged" in twenty-first-century America. In 2013, a Florida jury of six women acquitted George Zimmerman, a white Latino man on "neighborhood watch" who the year before had shot and killed Trayvon Martin, an unarmed seventeen-year-old African American. Zimmerman claimed that Martin had assaulted him and that he had used his pistol in self-defense.

Zimmerman's acquittal set off a firestorm of protest around the country. In 2013, three African American activists—Alicia Garza, Patrisse

Cullors, and Opal Tometi—created a civil rights organization called Black Lives Matter to address mounting evidence that African Americans were being treated unfairly by law enforcement officers and the judicial system. In 2012, 31 percent of people killed by police were African American (often unarmed), even though blacks made up just 13 percent of the total population.

Using social media as their primary recruiting tool, Garza, Cullors, Tometi, and others generated widespread support. Black Lives Matter, the organizers explained, "is an ideological and political intervention in a world where Black lives are systematically and intentionally targeted for demise. It is an affirmation of Black folks' humanity, our contributions to this society, and our resilience in the face of deadly oppression."

The Black Lives Matter movement gained added urgency on August 9, 2014, when Michael Brown, an unarmed black teenager, was shot and killed by a white police officer in Ferguson, Missouri, a St. Louis suburb. The failure of a grand jury to indict the police officer prompted civil unrest and organized protests around the country. In the process, the phrase "Black Lives Matter" became a rallying cry for millions of Americans who had grown convinced

Black Lives Matter The founders of the movement stand with arms linked at a protest in Cleveland, Ohio. Left to right: Opal Tometi, Alicia Garza, and Patrisse Cullors.

that police brutality against people of color had become commonplace. "We have made enormous progress in race relations over the course of the past several decades," President Obama said in response to the Missouri case. "But what is also true is that there are still problems, and communities of color aren't just making these problems up."

OBAMACARE ON THE DEFENSIVE President Obama's proudest achievement, the Affordable Care Act, was so massive and complicated that it took four years before it was ready to roll out. In the fall of 2013, the federal online health insurance "exchange," where people without insurance could sign up, opened with great fanfare. Obama assured Americans that using the online registration system would be "real simple."

It was not. On October 1, millions tried to sign up; only six succeeded. The website had never been properly tested, and it was hobbled with technical glitches. It also became evident that Obama had misled the nation when he told voters that if they liked their current health-insurance plan, they could, under Obamacare, "keep that insurance. Period. End of story." As it turned out, many saw their policies canceled by insurers.

Eventually, the ACA website was fixed, and by August 2014, more than 9 million people, well above the original target number, had signed up for health insurance. "The Affordable Care Act is here to stay," Obama said. But public skepticism about the government's ability to manage the program continued.

NEW GLOBAL CHALLENGES IN AN AGE OF INSECURITY

In 2013, the United States held its first high-level talks with Iran since 1979, when Iranian militants had taken U.S. embassy employees in Tehran hostage. On November 23, Secretary of State John Kerry reached a multinational agreement with Iran to scale back its nuclear development program for six months as a first step toward a more comprehensive agreement not to develop nuclear weapons.

At the same time, an increasingly bloody civil war in Syria was beginning to have major international repercussions. U.S. intelligence analysts confirmed that the Syrian government, ruled by dictator Bashar al-Assad, had used chemical weapons to kill 1,400 people, many of them children.

President Obama had repeatedly warned that the use of weapons of mass destruction was a "red line" that would trigger international military intervention of "enormous consequences." In late August, he (and the French government) hesitantly began preparing for a military strike, against Syria, but his failure to follow through led his former secretary of defense, Leon Panetta, to argue that backing off the threat "was a blow to American credibility. When the president as commander in chief draws a red line, it is critical that he act if the line is crossed."

On September 9, Kerry defused the crisis by signing an agreement with Russia to dispose of Syria's chemical weapons. By the end of October, the chemical weapon stockpiles had supposedly been destroyed or dismantled, but the civil war raged on.

RUSSIA'S ANNEXATION OF CRIMEA For nearly a quarter of a century, Russian president Vladimir Putin had viewed the disintegration of the Soviet Union as the "greatest geopolitical catastrophe of the century." To restore Russian influence over its neighbors and to divide NATO and the European Union, he used economic and political pressure to coerce the republics of the former Soviet Union.

On February 27, 2013, Putin sent troops into Crimea, a part of Ukraine, a former Soviet republic. A week later, the Crimean parliament voted to become part of the Russian Federation. Putin, claiming that Crimea had "always been an inseparable part of Russia," made the illegal annexation official by positioning Russian troops there, even though he denied their presence.

The speed and ruthlessness with which Putin seized control of Crimea, mobilized 40,000 Russian troops on the Ukrainian border, and cut off Ukraine's access to Russian natural gas surprised President Obama and European leaders. It may not have been the start of a new cold war, but it put an end to hope that Russia would become a cordial partner of the United States and the European democracies. By 2014, Putin was displaying a raw and resentful anti-Americanism.

In response, the United States and the European Union organized diplomatic efforts to de-escalate the crisis. They refused to recognize the annexation of Crimea and announced economic sanctions against Russia while pledging financial assistance to Ukraine. By a vote of 100–11, the United Nations General Assembly also opposed the annexation.

In April 2014, heavily armed pro-Russian separatists, as many as a third of whom were Russian soldiers and agents, seized control of several cities in eastern Ukraine. They declared a "people's republic" and called for secession.

After a Malaysian passenger jet flying across eastern Ukraine was shot down by a Russian-made rocket in July 2014, killing all 298 on board, the

United States and its allies slammed Russia with more economic sanctions. But Putin showed no sign of backing away. In fact, his popularity in Russia soared, leaving the United States once again in the position of trying to contain Russia's expansionist ambitions.

THE BURDENS OF LEADERSHIP Rarely are presidents more popular than on their first day in office. To govern requires making decisions, and decisions in democratic nations inevitably produce disappointments, disagreements, and criticism.

During his presidency, Barack Obama discovered how hard it was to lead the world's economic and military superpower in the post–cold war era. He struggled to stabilize a cluster of unstable nations—Iraq, Afghanistan, Libya, Ukraine, and Syria—that craved U.S. resources but resented American meddling.

Overall, Obama adopted a posture of restraint in world affairs. He was determined to "avoid stupid errors," wind down the wars in Iraq and Afghanistan, and reduce the use of U.S. military power abroad.

Yet he and others were naive to think that the United States could avoid the burdens of being the only superpower in a post–cold war world of growing anarchy and violence. Democratic senator Diane Feinstein of California wondered in September 2014 if Obama had become "too cautious" about the use of force in world affairs.

ISLAMISTS ON THE MOVE Unexpected events during the summer of 2014 gave Barack Obama the opportunity to take decisive action. In June, the volatile Middle East took a sudden turn for the worse when Sunni jihadists who had been fighting in Syria invaded northern Iraq and announced the creation of their own caliphate (Islamic-controlled region), called the Islamic State (ISIS). Originally a small Iraqi affiliate of al Qaeda that specialized in suicide bombings, ISIS quickly emerged as the largest, best-financed, most heavily armed, and most brutal of the jihadist terrorist groups.

ISIS represented both the culmination of decades of Arab Islamist rage against Europe and the United States and the collapse of effective government and security in Syria and Iraq. Once American forces left Iraq and Sunnis grew frustrated with the Shiite-dominated government, ISIS swept in. Sadistic ISIS fighters seized huge tracts of territory in Syria and Iraq while enslaving, terrorizing, raping, massacring, crucifying, or beheading thousands of men, women, and children belonging to religious minorities, including Christians.

In August 2014, after ISIS terrorists gruesomely beheaded two captured Americans, Obama ordered systematic airstrikes, first in Iraq and later in

Syria, as ISIS fighters assaulted Christians, Yazidis, and Kurds in the region. If George W. Bush had plunged U.S. power too deeply into Iraq, Obama seemed to have withdrawn U.S. power too quickly. One overreached, the other undershot.

THE AGE OF GRIDLOCK

American politics has always been chaotic and combative; its raucous energy is one of its great strengths. During Barack Obama's two terms as president, however, both parties rejected "compromise" and "moderation" as legitimate political tools. Republican efforts to reject any and all proposals from the Obama White House meant stalemate had become the controlling political principle.

Intense partisanship dominated the 2014 congressional elections, when Republicans gained control of the Senate for the first time since 2006. They also strengthened their hold on the House, added governorships, and tightened their control of state legislatures. Republicans campaigned on a single theme: the "failure" of President Obama and the "disaster" of Obamacare.

Political moderates became a dying breed. By late 2014, the percentage of voters who described themselves as liberals or conservatives had doubled since 1994, and more than twice as many Democratic and Republican voters as in 1994 had a "very unfavorable" view of the other party. Congress included mostly Republicans on the far right, Democrats on the far left, and hardly anyone in the middle. "That alignment," said Gerald Seib of the *Wall Street Journal*, created a Congress "that does less, and does it less well, than any time in memory."

Voters hoping for a more energetic and engaged Obama after his reelection were disappointed. He seemed disheartened by the "gap between the magnitude of our challenges and the smallness of our politics" and blamed Republicans for stalemating his second term. But the president was not blameless. As Ian Bremmer, a political scientist specializing in foreign policy, said, "George W. Bush was a leader who didn't like to think. Barack Obama is a thinker who doesn't like to lead."

RENEWED ENERGY Yet during the summer of 2015, in the sunset of his presidency, Obama regained his energy. He also benefited from two surprising U.S. Supreme Court rulings.

For years, Republicans had waged all-out war on the Affordable Care Act. Unable to halt the implementation of the new program in Congress, critics turned again to the courts to challenge the health-care law. The claim raised in *King v. Burwell* (2015)—that individuals who purchase insurance on the federal government's health-care exchange are not entitled to the tax subsidies available to those purchasing on state exchanges—would, if accepted by the Court, have greatly weakened ACA.

In a surprising 6–3 decision, the Supreme Court saved the controversial law. Chief Justice John Roberts explained in the majority opinion that the sloppy language in the original legislation should not be used to destroy the program. "Congress passed the Affordable Care Act to improve health insurance markets, not to destroy them," Roberts stressed. "If at all possible, we must interpret the Act in a way that is consistent with the former, and avoids the latter."

Just a day after announcing the *King v. Burwell* decision, the Supreme Court issued another bombshell ruling when it announced a 5–4 decision in *Obergefell v. Hodges* (2015), which banned states from preventing marriages between same-sex couples. The landmark decision infuriated the Religious Right. Rick Scarborough, a Baptist minister in Texas, vowed that he and others

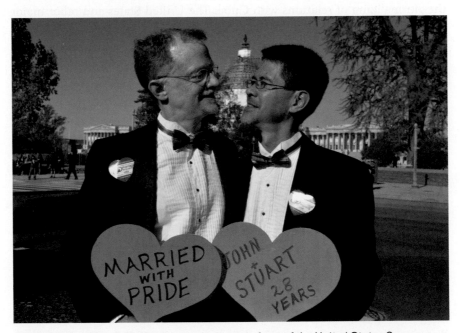

Married with pride A California couple poses in front of the United States Supreme Court building in Washington, D.C., while the justices hear arguments on the constitutional right for same-sex couples to wed in April 2015. On June 26, 2015, in a landmark 5–4 decision, the Court ruled in favor of upholding marriage equality in all fifty states.

would "denounce this practice in our [religious] services, we will not teach it in our schools, we will refuse to officiate at this type of wedding, and we will not accept any encroachments on our First Amendment rights."

Yet the Supreme Court's affirmation of same-sex marriage reflected the profound change in public attitudes toward lesbian, gay, and LGBTQ rights writ large, during the early twenty-first century. In 2008, presidential candidate Barack Obama had felt the need to disavow support for marriage equality. By 2012, he had reversed himself by embracing the right to marriage between same-sex couples. His change of mind reflected a resurgent social transformation in American life. Cultural diversity, like Obamacare, was here to stay. Obama had appointed two women to the U.S. Supreme Court, including the first Latina justice. He also ended the ban on lesbian, gay, and bisexual people serving openly in the military.

The momentum of the Court decisions in June 2015 bolstered Obama's efforts in foreign policy. In his 2009 inaugural address, he had vowed to international enemies that "we will extend a hand if you are willing to unclench your fist." That effort finally paid off in 2015, and not only with the normalizing of relations with Cuba. The United States and other major world powers (Russia, China, Germany, Britain, France, and the European Union) announced a draft treaty with Iran intended to thwart its efforts to develop a nuclear weapon. In exchange for ending the international trade embargo against Iran, the agreement called for the Iranians to dismantle much of their nuclear program and allow for international inspectors to confirm their actions. Obama warned congressional critics that any attempt to veto the treaty (called the Joint Comprehensive Plan of Action) would mean "a greater chance of war in the Middle East." In July 2015 the Iran nuclear deal was formalized, despite strident opposition from Israel, the nation most threatened by Iran.

THE "ANGRY" 2016 ELECTION

In 1780, future president John Adams proclaimed that "division of the republic into two great parties, each arranged under its leader. . . . is to be dreaded as the greatest political evil under our Constitution." His fears were well founded. Because of over-the-top partisanship, many party followers—even young people—distrust, disdain, or even smear the opposition party. They do not acknowledge its legitimacy, much less respect it.

A study commissioned by the Pew Foundation found that 38 percent of Democrats and 43 percent of Republicans display a "very unfavorable" view of the other party, triple the numbers from just twenty years before. People with strong political views today tend to believe that the opposition has no redeeming virtues. Politics has devolved into an "us versus them" zero-sum game, a death match between good and evil energized by mutual contempt. There is no room for compromise or bargaining because there are few negotiable principles, just intense team loyalties.

Embedded in the 2017 Pew survey on the partisan divide, however, is a surprising and perhaps encouraging trend: record numbers of Americans are declaring their independence and rejecting both the Republican and Democratic parties. In fact, there are more independents than Democrats or Republicans. Independent voters tend to be closer on economic issues to Republicans and closer to Democrats on social issues, and their growing numbers represent a direct reaction against the unprecedented polarization of the two parties.

THE 2016 PRESIDENTIAL PRIMARIES The ferocious polarization of American society and politics was on full display during the 2016 presidential campaign. The contest featured a seething sense of anger at the federal government among voters furious at cultural liberalism, bureaucratic incompetence, and the self-serving focus of party leaders. "Both parties have failed us," observed a lifelong conservative.

Surveys showed that Americans were more divided about partisan politics than they were about race, class, gender, and age. Republicans self-identify as conservative, and 87 percent of them are non-Hispanic whites, with an average age of fifty. Over half of Democrats call themselves liberals. They are more racially diverse than ever before and less likely to belong to a church or synagogue or to have "old-fashioned values about family and marriage."

The *emotional* discord of growing partisanship is revealed in a single data point: in 1960, only 5 percent of Republicans and 4 percent of Democrats said they would oppose their child marrying someone with the opposing party affiliation. A 2010 survey found that 49 percent of Republicans said they would resist their child marrying a Democrat, and 33 percent of Democrats said they would oppose their child marrying a Republican.

As the 2016 presidential campaign began, many working-class whites felt left behind by the economic recovery. Some had seen their factory jobs go offshore through globalization. Others had seen their wages stagnate, their prospects diminished, their hopes crushed. Although unemployment nationally was low, about one-third of U.S. adults faced financial insecurity in 2016 and often struggled to pay unexpected expenses. Three in ten adults saw their monthly incomes fluctuate—often because of unstable work schedules—and that caused about one in ten Americans to miss bill payments.

Many blamed their troubles on an economic system that favored the wealthy, government-subsidized minorities, low-wage immigrant labor, and the political elite. Their shared anxieties and resentments had coalesced into a grassroots, mostly white nationalist backlash against the multiculturalism evident during Obama's presidency.

CLINTON VERSUS SANDERS A handful of Democrats emerged as presidential candidates in 2015, but the race soon narrowed to two: Hillary Rodham Clinton, the former First Lady who had served as a U.S. senator from New York and as secretary of state in the Obama administration, and seventy-four-year-old Vermont senator Bernie Sanders. The policy-fluent Clinton, a supreme political insider, represented the party establishment, but she was more admired than loved by most Democrats. Sanders, a rumpled, white-haired socialist and grandfather of seven, surprisingly appealed most to younger, progressive Democrats who viewed Clinton as too conservative and too scripted. "She tries so hard to be real she just seems false," said an Ohio college student.

Sanders portrayed Clinton as a fraud who claimed to be a friend of the common folk but actually preferred hobnobbing with the rich and famous, and who promised to protect American jobs while supporting free-trade pacts that shut down plants and factories. In a series of bruising primaries, Clinton emerged on top and became the first female major-party nominee in history.

Democratic campaigns, 2016 Democrats in the 2016 primary election had two very different candidates to choose between. (Left) Hillary Rodham Clinton, the first woman to be nominated by a major political party, was saddled with a long history of establishment politics. (Right) Bernie Sanders, in contrast, was viewed as an outsider who represented a progressive, socialist platform.

TRUMP THE OUTSIDER The Republican contest was more a carnival than a campaign. Seventeen aspirants competed for the nomination—governors, senators, corporate executives—but one was unique: New Yorker Donald Trump, a billionaire real estate developer and reality-television star with a genius for self-promotion and a habit of stretching the truth or dismissing it altogether. He had never held elected office but, unlike the other candidates, had national name recognition.

Trump's unconventional campaign infuriated many mainstream Republicans. *National Review*, a leading conservative magazine, focused its January 2016 issue on a symposium titled "Against Trump." The editors explained that "Donald Trump is a menace to American conservatism who would take the work of generations and trample it underfoot in behalf of a populism as heedless and as crude as the Donald himself." Yet such criticism only increased Trump's popularity among disaffected Republicans and those attracted to the Tea Party.

The wealthiest of the contenders and the only one who refused to disclose his tax returns, Trump was an unrelenting dynamo, a charismatic if sometimes crude and impulsive showman possessed of the ruthless skill to skewer his opponents and the mainstream media. He was both volatile and competitive, always on the go, and, like Bill Clinton, eager to be both loved and adored.

Trump positioned himself as an "outsider" who promised to "drain the swamp" of corruption created by political insiders in Washington, D.C. He skillfully exploited the emotions of people who were "mad as hell" about being left behind by the economic recovery and resentful of "unregulated immigration." Trump promised to end Obama's DACA policy protecting so-called immigrants, and he campaigned ferociously against "career politicians," Washington bureaucrats, and liberal journalists whose attacks against him he dismissed as "fake news."

"MAKE AMERICA GREAT AGAIN" Americans had never seen a candidate as unconventional, unpredictable, and inexplicable as Donald John Trump, yet his entertaining shoot-from-the-hip candor and combativeness appealed to voters fed up with conventional politics and to journalists eager to cover his latest controversial statement.

Born in 1946 in Queens, a borough of New York City, Trump attended Fordham University for two years before transferring to the Wharton School of Business at the University of Pennsylvania, where he earned a degree in economics in 1968. Trump then parlayed a large loan from his wealthy father into a successful real estate development business, called the Trump Organization.

Thereafter, Trump expanded his business empire into the casino gambling industry and later acquired numerous golf resorts around the world. All the while, he focused on building the Trump brand, despite his own business failures and bankruptcies. Trump's visibility earned him a starring role in a popular NBC television reality series called *The Apprentice*, in which contestants vied for a management position within the Trump Organization.

A master at the use of social media, especially late-night Twitter rants, candidate Trump fed upon and reinforced the anger felt by many Americans left out of the economic recovery. He was one of the few candidates to embrace those living in the left-behind parts of the country, including people suffering from the opioid drug epidemic, declining manufacturing jobs, and the rising cost of health care.

More people were living in poverty in 2016 than ever before. Many of them had grown up assuming that America was the most powerful and prosperous nation on earth, famous for the upward mobility it provided its citizens. Now they worried that was no longer true. For adults in their thirties, the chance of earning more than their parents over their lifetimes dropped to 50 percent from 90 percent just two generations earlier. The American middle class, once the envy of the world, was no longer the world's richest. For these reasons and

Republican rally Donning his "Make America Great Again" baseball cap, Donald Trump speaks at a rally in Orlando, Florida, six days before the presidential election.

others, many working-class Americans and farmers were angry; they wanted someone to blame and that someone was the party in power: Democrats.

Trump appealed directly to such disgruntled voters, many of them independents or members of the Tea Party. He depicted a declining America besieged by cheap Chinese imports, Muslim terrorists, and illegal immigrants ("bad dudes") and poorly led by self-serving liberal "elites" who championed unconstrained diversity at the expense of national security.

Trump vowed to "Make America Great Again." He promised to end Obamacare, cut taxes, abandon the "unfair" NAFTA and TPP (Trans-Pacific Partnership) trade deals, reverse the Obama administration's environmental protections, increase funding for the military, and appoint only "the best people" to his administration. Most of all, he repeatedly lashed out at "illegal immigrants," promising to build a towering, "beautiful" wall along the entire border with Mexico, from the Pacific Ocean to the Gulf of Mexico—and vowed to make the Mexican government pay for it.

Trump offered simplistic solutions to complex problems. On the campaign trail, he preferred spontaneous remarks over prepared speeches, and he became famous for his exaggerations, half-truths, outright falsehoods, and praise for white supremacists and foreign dictators.

Trump overflowed with confidence as he was swept along by a tidal wave of populist rage. "I alone can fix" America's problems, he shouted, claiming that he was the best, the smartest, and the toughest candidate.

Trump was like a whirlwind, capturing daily headlines and building grass-roots support. He focused on the fears and prejudices of his supporters ("Trumpsters"), especially working-class whites in the South and the crucial Midwest "rust belt" states—Ohio, Michigan, Pennsylvania, West Virginia, and Wisconsin. "I love the poorly educated," he proudly affirmed. "The hell with political correctness." As a Trump supporter in New Hampshire explained, "he tells us what we all think but are afraid to say." The "country's spiraling downwards, people are not getting pay raises, and we're not the superpower we think we are."

Trump's nontraditional campaign also benefited from the surging influence of social media such as Twitter and Facebook. People could now discuss politics in an unmediated way, reading and expressing themselves in the language of resentment not allowed on television or in newspapers.

To the surprise of pundits and the chagrin of party leaders, Trump won the Republican nomination in July 2016. The raucous outsider and his populist insurgency had overturned the party establishment and fractured the conservative movement. Many leading Republicans, including former presidents George H. W. Bush and George W. Bush, and former presidential nominees John McCain and Mitt Romney, were so alienated by Trump's boorish behavior and disrespectful treatment that they refused to attend the Republican nominating convention or to campaign for him.

Such opposition within his own party never fazed Trump. In fact, he loved the challenge of running against two parties, for he knew his supporters were passionately committed to him. "I could stand in the middle of Fifth Avenue and shoot somebody, and I wouldn't lose [my] voters," Trump boasted.

A CAMPAIGN LIKE NO OTHER The 2016 contest between Donald Trump and Hillary Clinton was more memorable for its drama and insults than its issues or proposals. Trump dismissed "crooked Hillary" as a "nasty woman," calling her the "most corrupt person ever to seek the presidency." He lampooned her as a creature of the Washington and Wall Street elite who masqueraded as a friend of the people while raking in millions of dollars for the Clinton Foundation. If elected president, he promised, he would "put her in jail," leading his supporters to wear T-shirts saying, "Lock Her Up."

For her part, Clinton dismissed Trump as unfit for the highest office in the land, labeling him as dangerous, unpredictable, and lacking the temperament demanded of the U.S. president. She hurt her cause when, in a fit of frustration, she claimed that "you could put half of Trump's supporters into what I call the 'basket of deplorables.'"

The fall campaign featured one startling surprise after another. On October 7, 2016, just two days before the candidates' second televised debate, the *Washington Post* released a videotape from 2005 that showed a married Trump lewdly describing his unsolicited kissing and groping of women he had just met. "You know I'm automatically attracted to beautiful women," he bragged. "I just start kissing them. It's like a magnet. Just kiss. I don't even wait [to be asked]. And when you're a star [like me], they let you do it. You can do anything [to them]." A media furor ensued, but Trump barreled on, dismissing his comments as simply "locker room banter" that he claimed all men engage in.

Hillary Clinton confronted her own scandals. In March 2015, the *New York Times* reported that Clinton, as secretary of state between 2009 and 2013, had used her family's email server for official communications rather than the State Department server. Doing so violated departmental protocols, created a security risk that confidential ("classified") diplomatic emails might be hacked by foreign agents, and prevented the State Department from archiving her 62,000 messages. After an exhaustive investigation, the FBI director, James B. Comey, concluded publicly that Clinton had been "extremely careless" in handling her email, but saw no point in prosecuting her. Republican critics used the issue to call into question Clinton's honesty and reliability. Trump charged that Clinton's use of a personal email server was "worse than Watergate."

Then came more surprises. During the summer of 2016, agents of the Russian government "hacked" the email system of the Democratic National Committee and forwarded the data to WikiLeaks, which collaborated with Russian agents to release tens of thousands of confidential messages intended to embarrass and distract the Clinton campaign and thereby help to elect Trump.

On October 28, 2016, just eleven days before the presidential election, FBI director Comey violated long-standing FBI practices to keep the bureau out of national elections when he informed Congress that "in connection with an unrelated case, the FBI has learned of the existence of emails that appear pertinent to the investigation" of Clinton's use of her personal email server when serving as secretary of state.

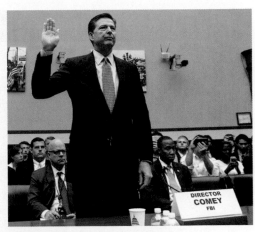

James Comey in Congress FBI Director James Comey swears an oath before the House Oversight Committee on July 7, 2016, two days after announcing that he would not recommend pressing criminal charges against Hillary Clinton, after all.

This revelation hit the Clinton campaign like a bomb. It raised new questions about her presidential fitness and revealed that the ongoing investigation into her emails would last beyond Election Day. Clinton would later claim that Comey's "October surprise" cost her the election.

Clinton's loss to Trump on November 8 surprised virtually everyone. All major polls had predicted a narrow Democratic victory. Yet Trump won 309 electoral votes to her 228. True, Clinton attracted 3 million more votes out of the 136 million cast, but she lost by 78,000 votes the crucial swing states of Michigan, Ohio, Pennsylvania, and Wisconsin, whose electoral votes decided the winner. The Trump victory meant that Republicans would control all three branches of the federal government, 32 state legislatures, and 33 governorships. The liberalism promoted by the Democratic party was sent reeling.

Clinton's failure to attract white working-class and lower middle-class males in the rust belt states was her downfall, along with the fact that fewer than expected Democrat-leaning minority voters went to the polls. Fewer than 500 counties voted for Clinton, but those counties accounted for two-thirds of the nation's economic wealth. The more than 2,600 counties that went for Trump accounted for the remaining third.

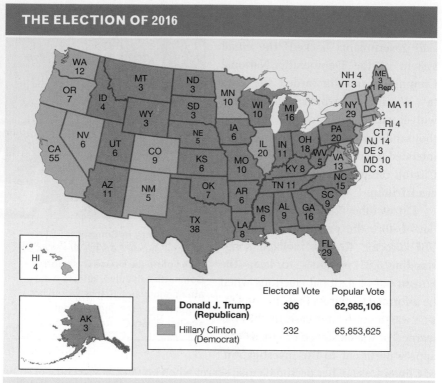

THE ELECTION OF 2016

		Electoral Vote	Popular Vote
	Donald J. Trump (Republican)	306	62,985,106
	Hillary Clinton (Democrat)	232	65,853,625

- What are some of the factors that may have changed the course of the election?
- What does the map reveal, or conceal, about the disconnect between the popular vote and the electoral college?

A sense of having lost ground economically was the most important factor motivating Trump voters in those counties. In 2016, the average annual income of an American worker was $44,500, not much more than the average in 1979, when accounting for inflation. Nearly 80 percent of Americans claim they live from paycheck to paycheck, saving little for the future. Yes, the overall economy keeps growing, but the profits are going to a small minority. Economic inequality has never been more acute.

Clinton not only failed to attract such working-class voters, she also was a lackluster defender of more government as the solution to the nation's problems. She also struggled to articulate a unifying vision or fashion a compelling explanation for why she should be president. At the close of her campaign, she could only offer a limp promise: "I'm not him." Shannon Goodin, a twenty-four-year-old first-time voter in Michigan, explained that Trump won her vote by being a "big poster child for change." She added that traditional "politicians don't appeal to us. Clinton would go out of her way to appeal to minorities, immigrants, but she didn't really care for everyday Americans."

A POPULIST PRESIDENT

President-elect Trump could claim several firsts. He was the first president never to have served in the military or to have held public office, and at seventy-one, he was the oldest president on Inauguration Day.

Yet Trump was also the most unpopular new president in history. His 40 percent approval rate upon taking office was the lowest ever. A majority of Americans voted against him, and no sooner was he elected than his opponents mobilized to contest his presidency. In more than 50 cities and towns, demonstrators took to the streets, stopping traffic and chanting, "We reject the president-elect!"

The grassroots opposition to President Trump soon had a name—The Resistance—and it quickly became a significant political force. Women upset by Trump's election organized mass demonstrations the day after the presidential inauguration on behalf of women's rights, immigrants and refugees, improved health care, reproductive rights, LGBTQ rights, racial equality, freedom of religion, and workers' rights. At the Women's March on Washington, D.C., which included a half a million protesters, twice the number of those who attended Trump's inauguration, feminist leader Gloria Steinem directed her comments at the newly installed president: "Our Constitution does not begin with 'I, the President.' It begins with, 'We, the People.'"

Trump, whom more than a dozen women had accused of sexual misconduct, also fell afoul of the Me Too crusade against widespread sexual assault and abuse. Started in 2007 by Tarana Burke, an African American civil rights activist, the small Me Too organization suddenly gained national support in October 2017 when dozens of actresses and female staffers accused Harvey Weinstein, a prominent movie producer, of rape, sexual assault, and sexual abuse over many years.

Me Too The creator of the movement Tarana Burke (center) and others lead the #MeToo Women's March in Los Angeles on November 12, 2017.

Women's March on Washington On January 21, 2017, demonstrators flooded the National Mall in support of women's rights and reproductive justice, health-care and immigration reform, racial justice, LGBTQ rights, and other interconnected issues. The Washington demonstration was grounded in the nonviolent ideology of the civil rights movement, and went down as the largest coordinated protest in U.S. history; along with hundreds of global counterparts, it drew 5 million participants.

The widely publicized scandal prompted a wave of similar allegations against powerful men—politicians, CEOs, actors, sports stars, and celebrities of all sorts. Growing numbers of women and men came forward to share on social media under the hashtag MeToo their own experiences of sexual assault, harassment, or rape.

A CHAOTIC FIRST 100 DAYS Trump's supporters were enthusiastic about a future of unconventional presidential action designed to end their alienation and nurture their bitterness. In his inaugural address, Trump assured the nation that his swearing-in ceremony would be "remembered as the day the people became the rulers of this nation again." He told his ecstatic followers that "you will never be ignored again," for he intended to uproot the political "establishment." An unapologetic and aggressive hypernationalism would be the theme of his administration: "From this day forward, it is going to be only America first—America first." In December 2015, Florida

Republican Jeb Bush made a prediction about then candidate Donald Trump. "Donald, you know, is great at the one-liners," Bush quipped. "But, he's a chaos candidate. And he'd be a chaos president."

Indeed, chaos characterized Trump's presidency. He forged an unstable cabinet dominated by family members and wealthy loyalist ideologues, bankers, businessmen, and billionaires, mostly older white men with little government experience. Some of his closest aides, such as Steve Bannon, his chief strategist, and senior policy adviser Stephen Miller, were leaders of "alt-right" (alternative right), hypernationalist organizations that promoted white supremacy, anti-immigrant nativism, and America-first trade policies while rejecting multiculturalism and political correctness.

An unprecedented number of Trump's cabinet members and senior aides did not last long in their new government jobs. The president's national security adviser, Michael Flynn, a former army general who had led the Defense Intelligence Agency before being fired by President Obama, was forced to resign after lying to Vice President Mike Pence and the FBI about secret conversations he had with the Russian ambassador about lifting U.S. sanctions. He had also violated protocols and laws by failing to disclose huge payments in 2015 from foreign companies linked to Russia and Turkey.

In 2017, Flynn offered to testify to congressional committees investigating Russian efforts to influence the 2016 presidential election in exchange for immunity from prosecution. Even more worrisome for the Trump administration was news that the FBI was investigating the possibility that people associated with the Trump campaign had secretly collaborated with Russia to torpedo Hillary Clinton's campaign.

Trump vigorously denied that he or his campaign staff ever "colluded" with Russian officials to benefit his election, and rejected any suggestion that his new administration was anything but perfect. As journalist Timothy Noah explained, however, "the Trump administration in its infancy [was] creating enough blunders, scandals, and controversies to strain the resources" of the White House press corps.

AN ACTIVIST PRESIDENT To generate momentum for his presidency, Donald Trump in his first year declared a freeze on most federal hiring, cut aid payments to foreign governments, pressured several U.S. companies to abandon plans to build plants or factories overseas, curbed federal efforts to constrict the coal industry, and signed thirty-two executive orders *removing* protections for consumers, food safety, internet privacy, transgender Americans, and victims of sexual abuse.

ABANDONING THE CLIMATE COMMITMENT On June 1, 2017, President Trump announced that the U.S., the world's second largest polluter, would cease all participation in the 2015 Paris Climate Agreement addressing climate change. He claimed that the agreement, signed by 195 nations, imposed grossly unfair environmental standards on American businesses and workers. He vowed to stand with the people of the United States against what he called a "draconian" international deal. Trump's withdrawal from the global climate agreement represented his most sweeping assertion of an "America First" foreign policy. Others disagreed. "Removing the United States from the Paris agreement is a reckless and indefensible action," asserted Al Gore, the former vice president who has become an evangelist for fighting climate change. "It undermines America's standing in the world and threatens to damage humanity's ability to solve the climate crisis in time."

BANNING MUSLIMS OR SECURING THE BORDERS? Trump's most controversial executive order was a temporary ban on immigrants and refugees from seven nations with large Muslim populations. The resistance to Trump's proposal was immediate and widespread. Tens of thousands of Americans organized protests at airports across the nation while lawyers for various organizations filed suits to stop the executive order from taking effect.

Within days, federal judges dismissed the travel ban as an unconstitutional targeting of a particular religious group. A furious Trump scorned the "ridiculous" ruling and pledged to overturn it. The pro-Trump editors of the *Wall Street Journal* described the immigration order as "so poorly explained and prepared for, that it has produced fear and confusion at airports, an immediate legal defeat, and political fury at home and abroad."

Yet Trump persisted in his efforts to stop people from entering the United States from the seven targeted nations. On March 6, 2017, he issued a revised executive order, but it too was staunchly opposed and rejected by federal judges as discriminatory. In mid-2018, the U.S. Supreme Court by a 5-4 vote in *Trump v. Hawaii* approved a revised ban on immigrants from seven Muslim nations because the president deemed them terrorist risks. Speaking for the majority, Chief Justice John Roberts acknowledged that the court had "no view on the soundness of the policy," but insisted that the president had the authority to impose such a ban for national security reasons. In her dissenting opinion, Justice Sonia Sotomayor argued that any "reasonable observer" would conclude that the travel ban was "motivated by anti-Muslim animus."

A similar battle with the courts greeted Trump's announcement reversing Barack Obama's decision in 2016 to allow transgender people to serve openly in the military. The United States "will not accept or allow" transgender people

Muslim Ban A crowd of protesters gather at the Los Angeles International Airport on January 29, 2017, speaking out against President Trump's executive order to ban immigrants from certain Muslim-majority countries from entering the United States.

in the military "in any capacity," Trump tweeted in July 2017, without having consulted with his defense secretary, James Mattis. He added that the military "cannot be burdened with the tremendous medical costs and disruption that transgender in the military would entail."

Congressman Ted Lieu of California, himself a military veteran, was one of many legislators and military leaders who opposed the new policy affecting some 15,000 personnel. "We're discriminating against people who want to sacrifice for their country. What's worse, we're doing it for no measurable reason." Lawsuits filed in several federal courts delayed implementation of the ban. In issuing an injunction against the ban, U.S. District Court Judge Colleen Kollar-Kotelly found "absolutely no support for the claim that the ongoing service of transgender people would have any negative effects on the military."

A CONSERVATIVE COURT Trump's greatest success early in his presidency was the appointment of a conservative justice to the Supreme Court. Although most Democrats opposed the nomination of Neil Gorsuch, a federal court of appeals judge with a sterling reputation, the Republican majority revised the Senate filibuster rules to ensure his confirmation. In 2018, President Trump seized the opportunity presented by the retirement announcement of

"RESIST" Thousands of New Yorkers took to the streets of Time Square in July 2017 to oppose banning transgender people from military service. Many of them hold up "Resist" signs decorated in the same color scheme as the Transgender Pride Flag.

Justice Anthony Kennedy to nominate another conservative Republican judge, Brett Kavanaugh, to be confirmed by the Senate.

REPEALING OBAMACARE Eventually, Trump could not govern simply by issuing executive orders; he had to negotiate the passage of legislation. Throughout the presidential campaign, candidate Trump had lambasted Obamacare, promising to replace it "on day one" with a much better healthcare program "at a tiny fraction of the cost, and it is going to be so easy." To that end, he and House speaker Paul Ryan unveiled in early 2017 the American Health Care Act (AHCA). It would have removed many of the pillars of Obamacare, including phasing out Medicaid subsidies that had enabled millions of people to gain coverage for the first time.

Yet surveys showed that only 17 percent of voters liked the new bill. For that reason and others, Trump and Ryan could not get the Republican majority in the House to support "Trumpcare." The Republican leadership in Congress withdrew the AHCA without a formal vote. Trump, the self-described wizard at "deal-making," had been unable to strike a deal with members of his

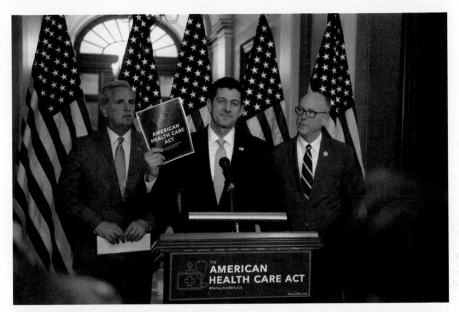

Trumpcare Speaker of the House Paul Ryan holds up a copy of the American Health Care Act on March 7, 2017. The Republican's bill to replace the Affordable Care Act was supremely unpopular.

own party. He admitted to being surprised "that health care could be so complicated," but he remained committed to the repeal of Obamacare.

BUILDING A WALL Trump's other showcase campaign promise proved equally difficult to implement: building a "huge" wall along the 2,000 mile-long Mexican border and forcing Mexico to pay for it. In late April 2017, the president acknowledged that he could not convince Congress to finance the wall. In 2018, Congress approved limited funds for a small portion of the wall Trump had demanded. Rebuffed by Capitol Hill, Trump redirected his efforts toward federal enforcement. He vowed to triple the number of Immigration and Customs Enforcement (ICE) officers and expand the Border Patrol.

FORGING FOREIGN POLICIES In foreign affairs, Donald Trump's early actions were equally minimal, in part because he had so little preparation for global leadership. Other than hosting several foreign dignitaries, talking tough toward rogue nations North Korea and Iran, and twice launching a volley of cruise missiles at Syrian air bases in retaliation for chemical attacks by the Syrian government on its own civilians, the president's view of America's role in the world remained confusing.

In 2013, for example, when Syria had first used chemical weapons against its opponents, killing a thousand people, Trump had urged President Obama: "Do not attack Syria. There is no upside and tremendous downside." Similarly, during his campaign against Clinton, he had told Reuters news service that "we should not be focusing on Syria. You're going to end up in World War III over Syria if we listen to Hillary Clinton." He saw no need to explain his change of heart as president.

THE 100-DAY MARK

By the end of his first 100 days in office, President Trump was floundering as a result of self-inflicted wounds, missteps, contradictions, and his naive understanding of the political process. At times, his administration seemed overwhelmed. Of the 556 executive branch positions requiring Senate confirmation, Trump had filled only a few dozen by the summer of 2017, in part because he insisted on personally approving every nominee to ensure their personal loyalty to him.

Candidate Trump had promised ten significant pieces of legislation by the end of April 2017. In fact, however, he had no major legislation to his credit and the lowest public approval rating (37 percent) of any first-term president.

In an early assessment of the Trump presidency, Jennifer Rubin, a conservative columnist, saw "nothing much of substance" accomplished because of "an unhinged president, too many weak aides, and an administration that cannot control itself." Trump, in her view, had overpromised and underdelivered. He had become "all flash and big talk."

Trump confessed to a Reuters reporter that he was not enjoying his presidential duties: "I loved my previous life. I had so many things going." Being president, however, was much "more work than in my previous life. I thought it would be easier."

LEGAL ISSUES Nothing was easy for the Trump administration, however. In May 2017, the president stunned the nation by firing James Comey, the FBI director, who was leading the agency's investigation into contacts between Trump campaign officials and Russia. White House aides initially claimed that Trump had acted on the advice of the deputy attorney general, only to have the president contradict them the next day when he acknowledged that he had grown frustrated by Comey's Russia investigation.

Only days later, the *New York Times* reported that Comey had created detailed summaries of his meetings with the president, one of which revealed that Trump on February 14 had urged the FBI director to drop the investigation into Michael Flynn's illegal interactions with Russian officials, pressuring him to "let this go." Trump denied the story, but on the face of it, the revelation suggested that the president may have engaged in obstruction of justice, a criminal offense.

On May 18, 2017, after Jeff Sessions, the attorney general, had recused himself because of his own contacts with Russian officials during the 2016 campaign, Rod Rosenstein, the deputy attorney general, appointed a special counsel, Robert Mueller III. A former FBI director held in high esteem by both Democrats and Republicans, Mueller was asked to lead a criminal investigation into Russian involvement in the 2016 campaign.

Trump's response to the investigation was consistently combative. On May 18, he tweeted that his administration was the victim of the greatest "witch hunt" in history. Almost every day, he attacked the media, calling its critical stories about him and his administration "fake news." Witch hunt or not, Trump faced the prospect of a prolonged criminal investigation shrouding the White House and playing havoc with his efforts to fulfill his campaign promises.

Equally challenging to the new president was the constant turnover within the senior administration. By early 2018, nearly half of Trump's inner circle of aides and cabinet members had resigned or been fired. The departed included the secretary of state; the secretary of human services; the secretary of veterans affairs; the national security adviser and deputy national security adviser; the FBI director; the chief strategist; the chief of staff and deputy chief of staff; the chief economic adviser; the administrator of the Environmental Protection Agency; the press secretary; and several members of his personal legal team.

In just eight months, Trump appointed six communications directors, one of whom lasted only eleven days. General John Kelly, Trump's second chief of staff, joked that "I did something wrong and God punished me, I guess," for leaving the Department of Homeland Security to run the White House staff.

TAX REFORM VICTORY President Trump finally achieved a major legislative victory with the passage of a comprehensive tax cut at the end of 2017. It was one of his primary campaign promises and marked the first major reduction in federal taxes in more than thirty years.

On December 22, 2017, the president signed the Tax Cuts and Jobs Act, which the Republican-controlled Congress passed without a single Democratic vote. In the belief that lower business taxes would boost economic growth, it cut the corporate tax rate from 35 percent to 21 percent, beginning in 2018. The bill lowered income tax rates overall, doubled the standard deduction, and eliminated personal exemptions.

It also repealed the individual mandate at the center of Obamacare (the Affordable Care Act). Analysts predicted that this would lead to 13 million fewer persons covered by health insurance, mostly young adults likely to opt out. With fewer healthy adults in the ACA pool, those still enrolled would pay higher insurance costs, which would lead still more people to drop their coverage.

The Congressional Budget Office estimated that the Trump tax cut would add $1.455 trillion to the national debt over ten years. Republicans, who for decades had stressed the importance of reducing the federal deficit and balancing budgets, abandoned such priorities in approving the tax cut without any offsetting spending cuts. Just seven months after the tax cut was implemented, the Federal Reserve Bank of San Francisco announced that Trump's key piece of legislation would trigger much less economic growth than anticipated—and perhaps none at all, for it appeared as the economy was already robust.

A UNIQUE PRESIDENCY As Donald Trump entered his second year as president, he remained the most unique person ever to occupy the Oval Office. His intentionally disruptive behavior continued to entertain and perplex observers while roiling financial markets. He often seemed angry and isolated; he lashed out at friends and enemies and was exasperated by daily leaks from his staff to the press.

In March 2018, Trump abruptly announced punitive tariffs on imported steel and aluminum, catching his aides and fellow Republicans off guard and infuriating America's most reliable trading partners, who predicted a no-win, tit-for-tat, retaliatory trade war resulting from his actions. His own economic adviser, who resigned in protest, dismissed the tariffs as "obviously stupid." Trump, however, responded that "trade wars are good, and easy to win," which stunned economists and Republicans in Congress. Over a hundred Republicans in the House of Representatives urged the president to reconsider launching a trade war, claiming that no nation wins such vengeful efforts.

Just weeks later, on May 8, 2018, President Trump again angered America's western European allies when he announced that the U.S. would withdraw from the Joint Comprehensive Plan of Action (JCPA) agreement with Iran and reinstitute economic sanctions. It was Trump's most consequential foreign policy action, and it baffled observers, since the United Nations had verified that Iran was abiding by the agreement. Trump's withdrawal from the JCPA called into question the U.S. government's commitment to other treaties around the

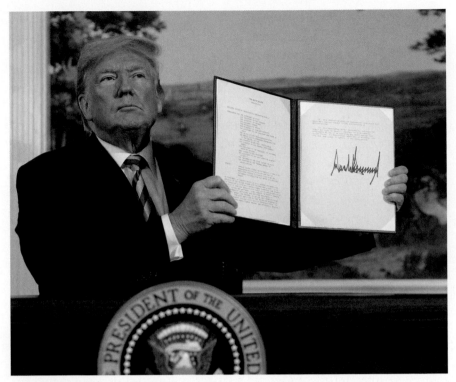

"Iran Deal" withdrawal President Trump displays his signature on a document reinstituting sanctions against Iran after withdrawing the United States from the Joint Comprehensive Plan of Action in May 2018.

world. Britain, France, and Germany admonished Trump and vowed to honor the deal.

Soon after, Trump again surprised the world when he announced that he and North Korean leader Kim Jong-un would hold a summit meeting to discuss the future of nuclear weapons in the Communist nation. On June 12, the two leaders met in Singapore and announced that discussions would continue "to work toward complete denuclearization of the Korean Peninsula." Ten days later, President Trump claimed that North Korea had begun to dismantle its nuclear test sites, only to be contradicted by his secretary of defense, James Mattis, who said there was no evidence of North Korea taking any concrete steps to denuclearize.

Also in June 2018 the Trump administration ignited a firestorm of criticism over its zero-tolerance policy on undocumented immigrants crossing into the United States from Mexico, many of them coming from strife-torn

North Korea summit President Trump poses alongside North Korean leader Kim Jong-un at a photo session during their one-on-one summit in Singapore.

Central America. The Department of Homeland Security and the U.S. Border Patrol began separating hundreds of detainee parents from their children while the parents, many of them seeking asylum from political tyranny at home, were being prosecuted and potentially deported. The new policy required the separation of children from their undocumented immigrant parents, which led scores of business executives to demand that the "zero tolerance" program be stopped. "This is not who we are as a country," said Tim Cook, the CEO of Apple. If he were president, "my goal would be to monopolize the world's talent" by recruiting *more* immigrants.

When congressional Republicans condemned the "zero tolerance" approach to detainees, President Trump reversed himself on June 20, 2018, signing an executive order meant to end the separation of families at the border.

This much seemed certain as 2018 unfolded: Donald Trump would continue to please and irritate Americans with his efforts to stop the flow of "illegal immigrants" into the country, his strong criticism of America's allies and his praise of tyrants and dictators, his changing stances toward rogue nations

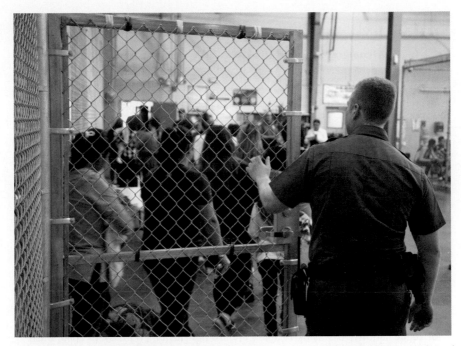

Families separated at the border U.S. Border Patrol agents detain undocumented asylum seekers in steel cages at the Central Processing Center in McAllen, Texas in June 2018. Two thousand children were separated from their parents during a six-week period under the Trump administration.

like North Korea, and his decision to withdraw the United States from some of its major treaty commitments like the JCPA and NAFTA.

Yet amid all fury and furor of the Trump White House, the president continued to enjoy intense support among his "base"—those loyal voters who carried him into office. They seemed uninterested in the ongoing investigations and the drama surrounding the White House. And the president—a man celebrated for his resilience—seemed determined to fend off all challenges by staying on the offensive, persistently dismissing his critics, while continuing to promote populist ideas and policies that his base strongly supported. What the future of his presidency would hold remained predictably unpredictable.

CHAPTER REVIEW

SUMMARY

- **Changing Demographics**   From 1980 to 2019, the population of the United States grew by 40 percent, reaching 330 million. A wave of immigration from Latin America allowed Latinos to surpass African Americans as the nation's largest minority. By 2018, the U.S. population included more foreign-born and first-generation residents than ever.

- **Divided Government**   Just two years after the election of "New Democrat" Bill Clinton in 1992, Republican Speaker of the House Newt Gingrich crafted his *Contract with America* and achieved a Republican landslide victory in the midterm elections of 1994. Despite the bipartisan success of the *North American Free Trade Agreement (NAFTA)* and the *Personal Responsibility and Work Opportunity Act of 1996*—and a prosperous, high-tech "new economy" that helped balance the federal budget—Clinton's private life produced a sex scandal that resulted in impeachment.

- **Global Terrorism**   The 9/11 attacks led President George W. Bush to declare a *war on terror* that commenced with the U.S. invasion of Afghanistan to capture Osama bin Laden and oust the Islamist Taliban government. The *Bush Doctrine* declared America's right to initiate preemptive military strikes against terrorists or rogue nations possessing *weapons of mass destruction (WMDs)*. In 2003, Bush invoked this doctrine against Saddam Hussein, the leader of Iraq. The ensuing Second Iraq War removed Hussein from power but turned up no WMDs.

- **A Historic Election**   The 2008 presidential primary campaigns featured Democratic senators Hillary Rodham Clinton, the first formidable female candidate, and Barack Obama, the first truly contending African American candidate, as well as Republican senator John McCain, the oldest candidate in history. Obama won his party's nomination and went on to take the election in large part due to public dismay about the *Great Recession (2007–2009)*.

- **Obama's Priorities**   Obama's first priority was to shore up the failing economy, which he attempted through controversial Wall Street "bailouts" and a huge "economic stimulus" package. Yet the recovery remained slow and unequal, widening the economic divide and spawning the short-lived Occupy Wall Street movement. The *Affordable Care Act (ACA)* incited increasingly bitter opposition from the conservative *Tea Party*. Obama was more successful in winning public support to reduce American military deployment abroad, remove all combat troops from Iraq in 2011, and downsize their presence in Afghanistan.

- **A Populist President**   The election of Donald Trump in 2016 in part reflected how divided American society had become over the last four decades. His promise to "Make America Great Again" appealed to voters who felt alienated as American society moved toward becoming part of an interconnected, global world. Efforts early in his administration to enact policies to limit immigration, protect jobs, and pull out of various treaties with other nations were met with strong resistance. Eventually, the new president would be able to claim some victories: tax reform, rolling back environmental regulations, and the appointment of two conservative U.S. Supreme Court justices.

CHRONOLOGY

1992	Bill Clinton elected president
1993	Congress passes NAFTA
1994	The Contract with America
1998	President Clinton impeached and acquitted
2000	George W. Bush elected after controversial recount
September 11, 2001	Terrorists attack New York City and Washington, D.C.
October 2001	Operation Enduring Freedom begins in Afghanistan
March 2003	Iraq War begins
2007	Global financial markets collapse; Great Recession begins
2009	Barack Obama elected nation's first black president
	American Recovery and Investment Act
2010	Congress passes the Affordable Care Act (Obamacare)
May 2011	Al Qaeda leader Osama bin Laden killed
2016	Donald Trump elected president

KEY TERMS

North American Free Trade Agreement (NAFTA) p. 1532

Contract with America p. 1534

Personal Responsibility and Work Opportunity Act of 1996 (PRWOA) p. 1535

globalization p. 1536

ethnic cleansing p. 1539

war on terror p. 1547

USA Patriot Act (2001) p. 1549

Bush Doctrine p. 1549

weapons of mass destruction (WMDs) p. 1549

Great Recession (2007–2009) p. 1556

Affordable Care Act (ACA—also called Obamacare) p. 1560

Tea Party p. 1566

marriage equality p. 1568

 INQUIZITIVE

Go to InQuizitive to see what you've learned—and learn what you've missed—with personalized feedback along the way.

GLOSSARY

1968 Chicago Democratic National Convention Held August 26–29 in Chicago, Illinois, the event was infamously tumultuous. Inside the International Amphitheatre, the Democratic Party fought over its direction on Vietnam, while outside tens of thousands of Vietnam War protestors clashed with police.

36°30' According to the Missouri Compromise, any part of the Louisiana Purchase north of this line (Missouri's southern border) was to be excluded from slavery.

54th Massachusetts Regiment After President Abraham Lincoln's Emancipation Proclamation, the Union army organized all black military units, which white officers led. The 54th Massachusetts Regiment was one of the first of such units to be organized.

Abigail Adams (1744–1818) As the wife of John Adams, she endured long periods of separation from him while he served in many political roles. During these times apart, she wrote often to her husband, and their correspondence has provided a detailed portrait of life during the Revolutionary War.

abolition In the early 1830s, the anti-slavery movement shifted its goal from the gradual end of slavery to the immediate end or abolition of slavery.

John Adams (1735–1826) He was a signer of the Declaration of Independence and a delegate to the First and Second Continental Congresses. A member of the Federalist Party, he served as the first vice president and the second president of the United States. As president, he passed the Alien and Sedition Acts and endured a stormy relationship with France, which included the XYZ affair.

John Quincy Adams (1767–1848) As secretary of state, he urged President Monroe to issue the Monroe Doctrine, which incorporated his belief in an expanded use of federal powers. As the sixth president, Adams's nationalism and praise of European leaders caused a split in his party, causing some Republicans to leave and form the Democrat party.

Samuel Adams (1722–1803) A genius of revolutionary agitation, he believed that English Parliament had no right to legislate for the colonies. He organized the Sons of Liberty as well as protests in Boston against the British.

Jane Addams (1860–1935) She founded and ran of one of the best known settlement houses, the Hull House. Active in the peace and suffragist movements, she established child care for working mothers, health clinics, job training, and other social programs.

affirmative action Programs designed to give preferential treatment to women and people of color as compensation for past injustices.

Affordable Care Act (ACA) (2010) Vast health-care reform initiative signed into law and championed by President Obama, and widely criticized by Republicans, that aims to make health insurance more affordable and make health care accessible to everyone, regardless of income or prior medical conditions.

Agricultural Adjustment Act (1933) Legislation that paid farmers to produce less in order to raise crop prices for all; the AAA was later declared unconstitutional by the U.S. Supreme Court in the case of *United States v. Butler* (1936).

Emilio Aguinaldo (1869?–1964) He was a leader in the Filipino struggle for independence. During the war of 1898, Commodore George Dewey brought Aguinaldo back to the Philippines from exile to help fight the Spanish. However, after the Spanish surrendered to Americans, America annexed the Philippines and Aguinaldo fought against the American military until he was captured in 1901.

Battle of the Alamo Siege in the Texas War for Independence of 1836, in which the San Antonio mission fell to the Mexicans. Davy Crockett and Jim Bowie were among the courageous defenders.

Albany Plan of Union (1754) A failed proposal by the seven northern colonies in anticipation of the French and Indian War, urging the unification of the colonies under one Crown-appointed president.

Alien and Sedition Acts of 1798 Four measures passed during the undeclared war with France that limited the freedoms of speech and press and restricted the liberty of noncitizens.

alliance with France Critical diplomatic, military, and economic alliance between France and the newly independent United States, codified by the Treaty of Amity and Commerce and the Treaty of Alliance (1778).

Allied Powers The nations fighting the Central Powers during the First World War, including France, Great Britain, and Russia; later joined by Italy and, after Russia quit the war in 1917, the United States.

American Anti-Imperialist League Coalition of anti-imperialist groups united in 1899 to protest American territorial expansion, especially in the Philippine Islands; its membership included prominent politicians, industrialists, labor leaders, and social reformers.

American Colonization Society Established in 1817, an organization whose mission was to return freed slaves to Africa.

American Federation of Labor Founded in 1881 as a national federation of trade unions made up of skilled workers.

American Indian Movement (AIM) Fed up with the poor conditions on Indian reservations and the federal government's unwillingness to help, Native Americans founded the American Indian Movement (AIM) in 1963. In 1973, AIM led 200 Sioux in the occupation of Wounded Knee. After a ten-week standoff with the federal authorities, the government agreed to reexamine Indian treaty rights and the occupation ended.

American Recovery and Reinvestment Act Hoping to restart the weak economy, President Obama signed this $787-billion economic stimulus bill in February of 2009. The bill included cash distributions to states, funds for food stamps, unemployment benefits, construction projects to renew the nation's infrastructure, funds for renewable-energy systems, and tax reductions.

American System Economic plan championed by Henry Clay of Kentucky that called for federal tariffs on imports, a strong national bank, and federally financed internal improvements—roads, bridges, canals—all intended to strengthen the national economy and end American dependence on Great Britain.

American Tobacco Company Business founded in 1890 by North Carolina's James Buchanan Duke, who combined the major tobacco manufacturers of the time, ultimately controlling 90 percent of the country's cigarette production.

Anaconda Plan The Union's primary war strategy calling for a naval blockade of major southern seaports and then dividing the Confederacy by gaining control of the Tennessee, Cumberland, and Mississippi Rivers.

Annapolis Convention In 1786, all thirteen colonies were invited to a convention in Annapolis to discuss commercial problems, but only representatives from five states attended. However, the convention was not a complete failure because the delegates decided to have another convention in order to write the constitution.

Battle of Antietam (1862) Turning-point battle near Sharpsburg, Maryland, leaving over 20,000 soldiers dead or wounded, in which Union forces halted a Confederate invasion of the North.

anti-Federalists Opponents of the Constitution as an infringement on individual and states' rights, whose criticism led to the addition of a Bill of Rights to the document. Many anti-Federalists later joined Thomas Jefferson's Democratic-Republican party.

Anti-Masonic party This party grew out of popular hostility toward the Masonic fraternal order and entered the presidential election of 1832 as a third party. It was the first party to run as a third party in a presidential election as well as the first to hold a nomination convention and announce a party platform.

Appomattox Court House Virginia village where Confederate general Robert E. Lee surrendered to Union general Ulysses S. Grant on April 9, 1865.

Arab Awakening A wave of spontaneous democratic uprisings that spread throughout the Arab world beginning in 2011, in which long-oppressed peoples demanded basic liberties from generations-old authoritarian regimes.

Armory Show A divisive and sensational art exhibition in 1913 that introduced European-inspired modernism to American audiences.

Benedict Arnold (1741–1801) A traitorous American commander who planned to sell out the American garrison at West Point to the British; his plot was discovered before it could be executed and he joined the British army.

Articles of Confederation The first form of government for the United States, ratified by the original thirteen states in 1781; weak in central authority, it was replaced by the U.S. Constitution in 1789.

Atlanta Compromise (1895) A speech by Booker T. Washington that called for the black community to strive for economic prosperity before attempting political and social equality.

Atlantic Charter (1941) Joint statement crafted by Franklin D. Roosevelt and British prime minister Winston Churchill that listed the war goals of the Allied Powers.

Crispus Attucks (1723–1770) During the Boston Massacre, he was supposedly at the head of the crowd of hecklers who baited the British troops. He was killed when the British troops fired on the crowd.

Stephen F. Austin (1793–1836) He established the first colony of Americans in Texas, which eventually attracted 2,000 people.

Axis alliance Military alliance formed in 1937 by the three major fascist powers: Germany, Italy, and Japan.

Aztec Empire Mesoamerican people who were conquered by the Spanish under Hernando Cortés, 1519–1528.

baby boom Markedly high birth rate in the years following World War II, leading to the biggest demographic "bubble" in U.S. history.

Bacon's Rebellion Unsuccessful 1676 revolt led by planter Nathaniel Bacon against Virginia governor William Berkeley's administration, which, Bacon charged, had failed to protect settlers from Indian raids.

Bank of the United States (1791) National bank responsible for holding and transferring federal government funds, making business loans, and issuing a national currency.

Bank War Political struggle in the early 1830s between President Jackson and financier Nicholas Biddle over the renewing of the Second Bank's charter.

Barbary pirates North Africans who waged war (1801–1805) on the United States after President Thomas Jefferson refused to pay tribute (a bribe) to protect American ships.

Bay of Pigs Failed CIA operation that, in April 1961, deployed a band of Cuban rebels to overthrow Fidel Castro's Communist regime.

Battle of the Bulge On December 16, 1944, the German army launched a counterattack against the Allied forces, which pushed them back. However, the Allies were eventually able to recover and break through the German lines. This defeat was a great blow to the Nazi's morale and their army's strength. The battle used up the last of Hitler's reserve units and opened a route into Germany's heartland.

Bear Flag Republic On June 14, 1846, a group of Americans in California captured Sonoma from the Mexican army and declared it the Republic of California whose flag featured a grizzly bear. In July, the commodore of the U.S. Pacific Fleet landed troops on California's shores and declared it part of the United States.

Beats Group of bohemian, downtown New York writers, artists, and musicians who flouted convention in favor of liberated forms of self-expression.

beatnik A name referring to almost any young rebel who openly dissented from the middle-class life. The name itself stems from the Beats.

Berlin airlift (1948–1949) Effort by the United States and Great Britain to deliver massive amounts of food and supplies flown to West Berlin in response to the Soviet land blockade of the city.

Berlin Wall Twenty-seven-mile-long concrete wall constructed in 1961 by East German authorities to stop the flow of East Germans fleeing to West Berlin.

Bessemer converter Apparatus that blasts air through molten iron to produce steel in very large quantities.

Nicholas Biddle (1786–1844) He was the president of the second Bank of the United States. In response to President Andrew Jackson's attacks on the bank, Biddle curtailed the bank's loans and exchanged its paper currency for gold and silver. In response, state banks began printing paper without restraint and lent it to speculators, causing a binge in speculating and an enormous increase in debt.

Bill of Rights First ten amendments to the U.S. Constitution, adopted in 1791 to guarantee individual rights and to help secure ratification of the Constitution by the states.

Osama bin Laden (1957–2011) The Saudi-born leader of al Qaeda, whose members attacked America on September 11, 2001. Years before the attack, he had declared *jihad* (holy war) on the United States, Israel, and the Saudi monarchy. In Afghanistan, the Taliban leaders gave bin Laden a safe haven in exchange for aid in fighting the Northern Alliance, who were rebels opposed to the Taliban. Following the Taliban's refusal to turn over bin Laden to the United States, America and a multinational coalition invaded Afghanistan and overthrew the Taliban. In May 2011, bin Laden was shot and killed by American special forces during a covert operation in Pakistan.

birth rate Proportion of births per 1,000 of the total population.

black codes Laws passed in southern states to restrict the rights of former slaves; to combat the codes, Congress passed the Civil Rights Act of 1866 and the Fourteenth Amendment and set up military governments in southern states that refused to ratify the amendment.

Black nationalism A cultural and political movement in the 1920s spearheaded by Marcus Garvey that exalted blackness, black cultural expression, and black exclusiveness.

Black Power movement Militant form of civil rights protest focused on urban communities in the North and led by Malcolm X that grew as a response to impatience with the nonviolent tactics of Martin Luther King Jr.

James Gillepsie Blaine (1830–1893) As a Republican congressman from Maine, he developed close ties with business leaders, which contributed to him losing the presidential election of 1884. He later opposed President Cleveland's efforts to reduce tariffs, which became a significant issue in the 1888 presidential election. Blaine served as secretary of state under President Benjamin Harrison.

Bleeding Kansas (1856) A series of violent conflicts in the Kansas Territory between anti-slavery and pro-slavery factions over the status of slavery.

blitzkrieg (1940) The German "lightning war" strategy characterized by swift, well-organized attacks using infantry, tanks, and warplanes.

Bolsheviks Under the leadership of Vladimir Lenin, this Marxist party led the November 1917 revolution against the newly formed provisional government in Russia. After seizing control, the Bolsheviks negotiated a peace treaty with Germany, the Treaty of Brest-Litovsk, and ended their participation in World War I.

Bonus Expeditionary Force (1932) Protest march in Washington, D.C., by thousands of World War I veterans and their families, calling for immediate payment of their service bonuses certificates; violence ensued when President Herbert Hoover ordered their tent villages cleared.

boomtown Town, often in the West, that developed rapidly due to the sudden influx of wealth and work opportunities; often male-dominated with a substantial immigrant population.

Daniel Boone (1734–1820) He found and expanded a trail into Kentucky, which pioneers used to reach and settle the area.

John Wilkes Booth (1838?–1865) He assassinated President Abraham Lincoln at the Ford's Theater on April 14, 1865. He was pursued and killed.

Boston Massacre Violent confrontation between British soldiers and a Boston mob on March 5, 1770, in which five colonists were killed.

Boston Tea Party Demonstration against the Tea Act of 1773 in which the Sons of Liberty, dressed as Indians, dumped hundreds of chests of British-owned tea into Boston Harbor.

Bourbons In post–Civil War southern politics, the opponents of the Redeemers were called Bourbons. They were known for having forgotten nothing and learned nothing from the ordeal of the Civil War.

bracero program (1942) System created in 1942 that permitted seasonal farm workers from Mexico to work in the United States on year-long contracts.

Joseph Brant (1742?–1807) Mohawk leader who led the Iroquois against the Americans in the Revolutionary War.

brinksmanship Secretary of State John Foster Dulles believed that communism could be contained by bringing America to the brink of war with an aggressive Communist nation. He believed that the aggressor would back down when confronted with the prospect of receiving a mass retaliation from a country with nuclear weapons.

John Brown (1800–1859) In response to a pro-slavery mob's sacking of the free-state town of Lawrence, Kansas, Brown went to the pro-slavery settlement of Pottawatomie, Kansas, which led to a guerrilla war in the Kansas territory. In 1859, he attempted to raid the federal arsenal at Harpers Ferry, hoping to use the stolen weapons to arm slaves, but he was captured and executed.

Brown v. Board of Education **(1954)** Landmark Supreme Court case that struck down racial segregation in public schools and declared "separate-but-equal" unconstitutional.

William Jennings Bryan (1860–1925) He delivered the pro-silver "cross of gold" speech at the 1896 Democratic Convention and won his party's nomination for president. Disappointed pro-gold Democrats chose to walk out of the convention and nominate their own candidate, which split the Democratic party and cost them the White House. Bryan's loss also crippled the Populist movement that had endorsed him.

"Bull Moose" Progressive party *See* Progressive party

Battles of (First and Second Manassas) Bull Run First land engagement of the Civil War took place on July 21, 1861, at Manassas Junction, Virginia, at which surprised Union troops quickly retreated; one year later, on August 29–30, Confederates captured the federal supply depot and forced Union troops back to Washington.

Martin Van Buren (1782–1862) During President Jackson's first term, he served as secretary of state and minister to London. In 1836, Van Buren was elected president, and he inherited a financial crisis. He believed that the government should not continue to keep its deposits in state banks and set up an independent Treasury, which was approved by Congress after several years of political maneuvering.

General John Burgoyne (1722–1792) He was the commander of Britain's northern forces during the Revolutionary War. He and most of his troops surrendered to the Americans at the Battle of Saratoga.

burial mounds A funeral tradition, practiced in the Mississippi and Ohio Valleys by the Adena-Hopewell cultures, of erecting massive mounds of earth over graves, often in the designs of serpents and other animals.

burned-over district Area of western New York strongly influenced by the revivalist fervor of the Second Great Awakening; Disciples of Christ and Mormons are among the many sects that trace their roots to the phenomenon.

Aaron Burr (1756–1836) Even though he was Thomas Jefferson's vice president, he lost favor with Jefferson's Republican supporters. He sought to work with the Federalists and run as their candidate for the governor of New York. Alexander Hamilton opposed Burr's candidacy and his stinging remarks on the subject led to Burr challenging him to duel in which Hamilton was killed.

George H. W. Bush (1924–) He served as vice president during the Reagan administration and then won the presidential election of 1988. His presidency was marked by raised taxes in the face of the federal deficit, the creation of the Office of National Drug Control Policy, and military activity abroad, including the invasion of Panama and Operation Desert Storm in Kuwait. He lost the 1992 presidential election to Bill Clinton.

George W. Bush (1946–) In the 2000 presidential election, Texas governor George W. Bush won as the Republican nominee against Democratic nominee Vice President Al Gore. After the September 11 terrorist attacks, he launched his "war on terrorism." President Bush adopted the Bush Doctrine, and United States invaded Afghanistan and Iraq with unclear outcomes leaving the countries divided. In September 2008, the nation's economy nose-dived as a credit crunch spiraled into a global economic meltdown. Bush signed into law the bank bailout fund called Troubled Asset Relief Program (TARP), but the economy did not improve.

Bush v. Gore (2000) The close 2000 presidential election came down to Florida's decisive twenty-five electoral votes. The final tally in Florida gave Bush a slight lead, but it was so small that a recount was required by state law. While the votes were being recounted, a legal battle was being waged to stop the recount. Finally, the case, *Bush v. Gore*, was presented to the Supreme Court who ruled 5–4 to stop the recount and Bush was declared the winner.

Bush Doctrine National security policy launched in 2002 by which the Bush administration claimed the right to launch preemptive military attacks against perceived enemies, particularly outlaw nations or terrorist organizations believed to possess weapons of mass destruction.

buying (stock) on margin The investment practice of making a small down payment (the "margin") on a stock and borrowing the rest of the money needed for the purchase from a broker who held the stock as security against a down market. If the stock's value declined and the buyer failed to meet a margin call for more funds, the broker could sell the stock to cover his loan.

Cahokia The largest chiefdom and city of the Mississippian Indian culture located in present-day Illinois, and the site of a sophisticated farming settlement that supported up to 15,000 inhabitants.

John C. Calhoun (1782–1850) He served in both the House of Representatives and the Senate for South Carolina before becoming secretary of war under President Monroe and then John Quincy Adams's vice president. Though he started his political career as an advocate of a strong national government, he eventually believed that states' rights, limited central government, and the power of nullification were necessary to preserve the Union.

California gold rush (1849) A massive migration of gold hunters, mostly men, who transformed the economy of California after gold was discovered in the foothills of northern California.

Camp David Accords (1978) Peace agreement between Prime Minister Menachem Begin of Israel and President Anwar Sadat of Egypt, the first Arab head of state to officially recognize the state of Israel.

"Scarface" Al Capone (1899–1947) The most successful gangster of the Prohibition era whose Chicago-based criminal empire included bootlegging, prostitution, and gambling.

Andrew Carnegie (1835–1919) A steel magnate who believed that the general public benefited from big business even if these companies employed harsh business practices. This philosophy became deeply ingrained in the conventional wisdom of some Americans. After retiring, he devoted himself to philanthropy in hopes of promoting social welfare and world peace.

Carnegie Steel Company Corporation under the leadership of Andrew Carnegie that came to dominate the American steel industry.

Carolina colonies English proprietary colonies comprised of North and South Carolina, whose semitropical climate made them profitable centers of rice, timber, and tar production.

carpetbaggers Northern emigrants who participated in the Republican governments of the reconstructed South.

Jimmy Carter (1924–) Elected president in 1976, Jimmy Carter was an outsider to Washington. He created the departments of Energy and Education and signed into law several environmental initiatives. In 1978, he successfully brokered a peace agreement between Israel and Egypt called the Camp David Accords. However, his unwillingness to make deals with legislators caused other bills to be either gutted or stalled in Congress. His administration was plagued with a series of crises: a recession and increased inflation, a fuel shortage, the Soviet invasion of Afghanistan, and the overthrow of the Shah of Iran, leading to the Iran Hostage Crisis. Carter struggled to get the hostages released and was unable to do so until after he lost the 1980 election to Ronald Reagan. He was awarded the Nobel Peace Prize in 2002 for his efforts to further peace and democratic elections around the world.

Jacques Cartier (1491–1557) He led the first French effort to colonize North America and explored the Gulf of St. Lawrence, reaching as far as present day Montreal on the St. Lawrence River.

Fidel Castro (1926–) In 1959, his Communist regime came to power in Cuba after two years of guerrilla warfare against the dictator Fulgenico Batista. He enacted land redistribution programs and nationalized all foreign-owned property. The latter action as well as his political trials and summary executions damaged relations between Cuba and America. Castro was turned down when he asked for loans from the United States. However, he did receive aid from the Soviet Union.

Central Intelligence Agency (CIA) Intelligence-gathering government agency founded in 1947; under President Eisenhower's orders, secretly undermined elected governments deemed susceptible to communism.

Central Powers One of the two sides during the First World War, including Germany, Austria-Hungary, the Ottoman Empire (Turkey), and Bulgaria.

Carrie Chapman Catt (1859–1947) She was a leader of a new generation of activists in the women's suffrage movement who carried on the work started by Elizabeth Cady Stanton and Susan B. Anthony.

Cesar Chavez (1927–1993) He founded the United Farm Workers (UFW) in 1962 and worked to organize migrant farm workers. In 1965, the UFW joined Filipino farm workers striking against corporate grape farmers in California's San Joaquin Valley. In 1970, the strike and a consumer boycott on grapes compelled the farmers to formally recognize the UFW. As the result of Chavez's efforts, wages and working conditions improved for migrant workers. In 1975, the California state legislature passed a bill that required growers to bargain collectively with representatives of the farm workers.

child labor The practice of sending children to work in mines, mills, and factories, often in unsafe conditions; widespread among poor families in the late nineteenth century.

Chinese Exclusion Act (1882) Federal law that barred Chinese laborers from immigrating to America.

Church of Jesus Christ of Latter-day Saints / Mormons Founded in 1830 by Joseph Smith, the sect was a product of the intense revivalism of the burned-over district of New York; Smith's successor Brigham Young led 15,000 followers to Utah in 1847 to escape persecution.

Winston Churchill (1874–1965) The British prime minister who led the country during the Second World War. Along with Roosevelt and Stalin, he helped shape the postwar world at the Yalta Conference. He also coined the term "iron curtain," which he used in his famous "The Sinews of Peace" speech.

citizen-soldiers Part-time nonprofessional soldiers, mostly poor farmers or recent immigrants who had been indentured servants, who played an important role in the Revolutionary War.

"city machines" Local political party officials used these organizations to dispense patronage and favoritism amongst voters and businesses to ensure their loyal support to the political party.

Civil Rights Act of 1957 First federal civil rights law since Reconstruction; established the Civil Rights Commission and the Civil Rights Division of the Department of Justice.

Civil Rights Act of 1964 Legislation that outlawed discrimination in public accommodations and employment, passed at the urging of President Lyndon B. Johnson.

civil service reform An extended effort led by political reformers to end the patronage system; led to the Pendleton Act (1883), which called for government positions to be awarded based on merit rather than party loyalty.

Henry Clay (1777–1852) In the first half of the nineteenth century, he was the foremost spokesman for the American system. As Speaker of the House in the 1820s, he promoted economic nationalism, "market revolution," and the rapid development of western states and territories. A broker of compromise, he formulated the "second" Missouri Compromise and the Compromise of 1850. In 1824, Clay supported John Quincy Adams, who won the presidency and appointed Clay to secretary of state. Andrew Jackson claimed that Clay had entered into a "corrupt bargain" with Adams for his own selfish gains.

Clayton Anti-Trust Act (1914) Legislation that served to enhance the Sherman Anti-Trust Act (1890) by clarifying what constituted "monopolistic" activities and declaring that labor unions were not to be viewed as "monopolies in restraint of trade."

Bill Clinton (1946–) The governor of Arkansas won the 1992 presidential election against President George H. W. Bush. In his first term, he pushed through Congress a tax increase, an economic stimulus package, the adoption of the North America Free Trade Agreement, welfare reform, a raise in the minimum wage, and improved public access to health insurance. His administration also negotiated the Oslo Accord and the Dayton Accords. After his re-election in 1996, he was involved in two high-profile scandals: his investment in the fraudulent Whitewater Development Corporation (but no evidence was found of him being involved in any wrong-doing) and his sexual affair with a White House intern. His attempt to cover up the affair led to a vote in Congress on whether or not to begin an impeachment inquiry. The House of Representatives voted to impeach Clinton, but the Senate found him not guilty.

Hillary Rodham Clinton (1947–) In the 2008 presidential election, Senator Hillary Clinton, the spouse of former President Bill Clinton, initially was the front-runner for the Democratic nomination, which made her the first woman with a serious chance to win the presidency. However, Senator Barack Obama's Internet-based and grassroots-orientated campaign garnered him enough delegates to win the nomination. After Obama became president, she was appointed secretary of state. In 2016, Clinton ran again and won the Democratic nomination for the presidency. Although she won the popular vote, she lost the election to Donald Trump.

clipper ships Tall, slender, mid-nineteenth-century sailing ships that were favored over older merchant ships for their speed, but ultimately gave way to steamships because they lacked cargo space.

Coercive Acts (1774) Four parliamentary measures that required the colonies to pay for the Boston Tea Party's damages, imposed a military government, disallowed colonial trials of British soldiers, and forced the quartering of troops in private homes.

coffin ships Irish immigrants fleeing the potato famine had to endure a six-week journey across the Atlantic to reach America. During these voyages, thousands of passengers died of disease and starvation, which led to the ships being called "coffin ships."

cold war A state of political and ideological conflict between nations, primarily the United States, representing western-democratic nations, and the Soviet Union, representing Marxist-communist nations, marked by propaganda, threats, and other hostilities falling short of direct open warfare between the United States and Soviet Union.

Columbian Exchange The transfer of biological and social elements, such as plants, animals, people, diseases, and cultural practices, among Europe, the Americas, and Africa in the wake of Christopher Columbus's voyages to the "New World."

Christopher Columbus (1451–1506) The Italian sailor who persuaded King Ferdinad and Queen Isabella of Spain to fund his expedition across the Atlantic to discover a new trade route to Asia. Instead of arriving at China or Japan, he reached the Bahamas in 1492.

James B. Comey (1960–) FBI director fired by President Donald Trump in 2017.

Committee of Correspondence Group organized by Samuel Adams in retaliation for the *Gaspée* incident to address American grievances, assert American rights, and form a network of rebellion.

Committee on Public Information During the First World War, this committee produced war propaganda that conveyed the Allies' war aims to Americans as well as attempted to weaken the enemy's morale.

Committee to Re-elect the President (CREEP) During Nixon's presidency, his administration engaged in a number of immoral acts, such as attempting to steal information and falsely accusing political appointments of sexual improprieties. These acts were funded by money illegally collected through CREEP.

Common Sense (1776) Popular pamphlet written by Thomas Paine attacking British principles of hereditary rule and monarchical government, and advocating a declaration of American independence.

Compromise of 1850 A package of five bills presented to the Congress by Henry Clay intended to avoid secession or civil war by reducing tensions between North and South over the status of slavery.

Compromise of 1877 Deal made by a special congressional commission on March 2, 1877, to resolve the disputed presidential election of 1876; Republican Rutherford B. Hayes, who had lost the popular vote, was declared the winner in exchange for the withdrawal of federal troops from the South, marking the end of Reconstruction.

Comstock Lode Mine in eastern Nevada acquired by Canadian fur trapper Henry Comstock that between 1860 and 1880 yielded almost $1 billion worth of gold and silver.

Conestoga wagons These large horse-drawn wagons were used to carry people or heavy freight long distances, including from the East to the western frontier settlements.

Congressional Reconstruction Phase of Reconstruction directed by Radical Republicans through the passage of three laws: the Military Reconstruction Act, the Command of the Army Act, and the Tenure of Office Act.

conquistadores Spanish term for "conquerors," applied to Spanish and Portuguese soldiers who conquered lands held by indigenous peoples in central and southern America as well as the current states of Texas, New Mexico, Arizona, and California.

consumer culture A society in which mass production and consumption of nationally advertised products comes to dictate much of social life and status.

containment U.S. cold war strategy that sought to prevent global Soviet expansion and influence through political, economic, and, if necessary, military pressure as a means of combating the spread of communism.

Continental army Army authorized by the Continental Congress, 1775–1784, to fight the British; commanded by General George Washington.

Contract with America A list of conservative promises in response to the supposed liberalism of the Clinton administration, that was drafted by Speaker of the House Newt Gingrich and other congressional Republicans as the GOP platform for the 1994 midterm elections. More a campaign tactic than a practical program, few of its proposed items ever became law.

contrabands Slaves who sought refuge in Union military camps or who lived in areas of the Confederacy under Union control.

Contras The Reagan administration ordered the CIA to train and supply guerrilla bands of anti-Communist Nicaraguans called Contras. They were fighting the Sandinista government that had recently come to power in Nicaragua. The State Department believed that the Sandinista government was supplying the leftist Salvadoran rebels with Soviet and Cuban arms. A cease-fire agreement between the Contras and Sandinistas was signed in 1988.

Calvin Coolidge (1872–1933) After President Harding's death, his vice president, Calvin Coolidge, assumed the presidency. Coolidge believed that the nation's welfare was tied to the success of Big Business, and he worked to end government regulation of business and industry as well as reduce taxes. In particular, he focused on the nation's industrial development.

Copperhead Democrats Democrats in northern states who opposed the Civil War and argued for an immediate peace settlement with the Confederates; Republicans labeled them "Copperheads," because they wore copper coins on their lapels.

Hernán Cortés (1485–1547) The Spanish conquistador who conquered the Aztec Empire and set the precedent for other plundering conquistadores.

General Charles Cornwallis (1738–1805) He was in charge of British troops in the South during the Revolutionary War. His surrender to George Washington at the Battle of Yorktown ended the Revolutionary War.

Corps of Discovery Meriwether Lewis and William Clark led this group of men on an expedition of the newly purchased Louisiana territory, which took them from Missouri to Oregon. As they traveled, they kept detailed journals and drew maps of the previously unexplored territory. Their reports attracted traders and trappers to the region and gave the United States a claim to the Oregon country by right of discovery and exploration.

corrupt bargain Scandal in which presidential candidate and Speaker of the House Henry Clay secured John Quincy Adams's victory over Andrew Jackson in the 1824 election, supposedly in exchange for Clay being named secretary of state.

cotton White fibers harvested from cotton plants, spun into yarn, and woven into textiles that made comfortable, easy-to-clean products, especially clothing; the most valuable cash crop driving the economy in the United States and Great Britain during the nineteenth century.

cotton gin Hand-operated machine invented by Eli Whitney in the late eighteenth century that quickly removed seeds from cotton bolls, enabling the mass production of cotton in nineteenth-century America.

Cotton Kingdom Cotton-producing region, relying predominantly on slave labor, that spanned from North Carolina west to Louisiana and reached as far north as southern Illinois.

counterculture Unorganized youth rebellion against mainstream institutions, values, and behavior that more often focused on cultural rather than political activism.

Court-packing scheme President Franklin D. Roosevelt's failed 1937 attempt to increase the number of U.S. Supreme Court justices from nine to fifteen in order to save his Second New Deal programs from constitutional challenges.

covenant theory A Puritan concept that believed true Christians could enter a voluntary union for the common worship of God. Taking the idea one step further, the union could also be used for the purposes of establishing governments.

crop-lien system Credit system used by sharecroppers and share tenants who pledged a portion ("share") of their future crop to local merchants or land owners in exchange for farming supplies and food.

"Cross of Gold" Speech In the 1896 election, the Democratic Party split over the issue of whether to use gold or silver to back American currency. Significant to this division was the pro-silver "Cross of Gold" speech that William Jennings Bryan delivered at the Democratic convention, which was so well received that Bryan won the nomination to be their presidential candidate. Disappointed pro-gold Democrats chose to walk out of the convention and nominate their own candidate.

Cuban missile crisis Thirteen-day U.S.-Soviet standoff in October 1962, sparked by the discovery of Soviet missile sites in Cuba; the crisis was the closest the world has come to nuclear war since 1945.

cult of domesticity A pervasive nineteenth-century ideology that urged women to celebrate their role as manager of the household and nurturer of the children.

George A. Custer (1839–1876) He was a reckless and glory-seeking Lieutenant Colonel of the U.S. Army who fought the Sioux Indians in the Great Sioux War. In 1876, he and his detachment of soldiers were entirely wiped out in the Battle of Little Bighorn.

Dartmouth College v. Woodward (1819) Supreme Court ruling that enlarged the definition of *contract* to put corporations beyond the reach of the states that chartered them.

Daughters of Liberty Colonial women who protested the British government's tax policies by boycotting British products, such as clothing, and who wove their own fabric, or "homespun."

Dawes Severalty Act (1887) Federal legislation that divided ancestral Native American lands among the heads of each Indian family in an attempt to "Americanize" Indians by forcing them to become farmers working individual plots of land.

D-day June 6, 1944, when an Allied amphibious assault landed on the Normandy coast and established a foothold in Europe from which Hitler's defenses could not recover.

Jefferson Davis (1808–1889) He was the president of the Confederacy during the Civil War. When the Confederacy's defeat seemed invitable in early 1865, he refused to surrender. Union forces captured him in May of that year.

Bartolomé de Las Casas (1484–1566) A Catholic missionary who renounced the Spanish practice of coercively converting Indians and advocated their better treatment. In 1552, he wrote *A Brief Relation of the Destruction of the Indies*, which described the Spanish's cruel treatment of the Indians.

death rate Proportion of deaths per 1,000 of the total population; also called *mortality rate*.

Eugene V. Debs (1855–1926) Founder of the American Railway Union, which he organized against the Pullman Palace Car Company during the Pullman strike. Later he organized the Social Democratic party, which eventually became the Socialist Party of America. In the 1912 presidential election, he ran as the Socialist party's candidate and received more than 900,000 votes.

Declaration of Independence Formal statement, principally drafted by Thomas Jefferson and adopted by the Second Continental Congress on July 4, 1776, that officially announced the thirteen colonies' break with Great Britain.

Declaration of Rights and Sentiments Document based on the Declaration of Independence that called for gender equality, written primarily by Elizabeth Cady Stanton and signed by Seneca Falls Convention delegates in 1848.

Declaratory Act Following the repeal of the Stamp Act in 1766, Parliament passed this act which asserted Parliament's full power to make laws binding the colonies "in all cases whatsoever."

Deism Enlightenment thought applied to religion, emphasizing reason, morality, and natural law rather than scriptural authority or an ever-present God intervening in human life.

détente Period of improving relations between the United States and Communist nations, particularly China and the Soviet Union, during the Nixon administration.

George Dewey (1837–1917) On April 30, 1898, Commodore George Dewey's small U.S. naval squadron defeated the Spanish warships in Manila Bay in the Philippines. This quick victory aroused expansionist fever in the United States.

John Dewey (1859–1952) He is an important philosopher of pragmatism. However, he preferred to use the term *instrumentalism*, because he saw ideas as instruments of action.

Ngo Dinh Diem (1901–1963) Following the Geneva Accords, the French, with the support of America, forced the Vietnamese emperor to accept Dinh Diem as the new premier of South Vietnam. President Eisenhower sent advisors to train Diem's police and army. In return, the United States expected Diem to enact democratic reforms and distribute land to the peasants. Instead, he suppressed his political opponents, did little or no land distribution, and let corruption grow. In 1956, he refused to participate in elections to reunify Vietnam. Eventually, he ousted the emperor and declared himself president.

Distribution Act (1836) Law requiring the distribution of the federal budget surplus to the states, creating chaos among state banks that had become dependent on such federal funds.

Dorothea Lynde Dix (1802–1887) She was an important figure in increasing the public's awareness of the plight of the mentally ill. After a two-year investigation of the treatment of the mentally ill in Massachusetts, she presented her findings and won the support of leading reformers. She eventually convinced twenty states to reform their treatment of the mentally ill.

Dixiecrats Breakaway faction of southern Democrats who defected from the national Democratic party in 1948 to protest the party's increased support for civil rights and to nominate their own segregationist candidates for elective office.

dollar diplomacy Practice advocated by President Theodore Roosevelt in which the U.S. government fostered American investments in less developed nations and then used U.S. military force to protect those investments

Donner party Forty-seven surviving members of a group of migrants to California were forced to resort to cannibalism to survive a brutal winter trapped in the Sierra Nevadas, 1846–1847; highest death toll of any group traveling the Overland Trail.

Stephen A. Douglas (1812–1861) As a senator from Illinois, he authored the Kansas-Nebraska Act. Running for senatorial reelection in 1858, he engaged Abraham Lincoln in a series of public debates about slavery in the territories. Even though Douglas won the election, the debates gave Lincoln a national reputation.

Frederick Douglass (1818–1895) He escaped from slavery and become an eloquent speaker and writer against the institution. In 1845, he published his autobiography entitled *Narrative of the Life of Frederick Douglass* and two years later he founded an abolitionist newspaper for blacks called the *North Star*.

dot-coms In the late 1990s, the stock market soared to new heights and defied the predictions of experts that the economy could not sustain such a performance. Much of the economic success was based on dot-com enterprises, which were firms specializing in computers, software, telecommunications, and the internet. However, many of the companies' stock market values were driven higher and higher by speculation instead of financial success. Eventually the stock market bubble burst.

***Dred Scott v. Sandford* (1857)** U.S. Supreme Court ruling that slaves were not U.S. citizens and therefore could not sue for their freedom and that Congress could not prohibit slavery in the western territories.

W. E. B. Du Bois (1868–1963) He criticized Booker T. Washington's views on civil rights as being accommodationist. He advocated "ceaseless agitation" for civil rights and the immediate end to segregation and an enforcement of laws to protect civil rights and equality. He promoted an education for African Americans that would nurture bold leaders who were willing to challenge discrimination in politics.

John Foster Dulles (1888–1959) As President Eisenhower's secretary of state, he institutionalized the policy of containment and introduced the strategy of deterrence.

He believed in using brinkmanship to halt the spread of communism. He attempted to employ it in Indochina, which led to the United States' involvement in Vietnam.

Dust Bowl Vast area of the Midwest where windstorms blew away millions of tons of top-soil from parched farmland after a long drought in the 1930s, causing great social distress and a massive migration of farm families.

Eastern Woodlands Peoples Various Native American peoples, particularly the Algonquian, Iroquoian, and Muskogean regional groups, who once dominated the Atlantic seaboard from Maine to Louisiana.

Peggy Eaton (1796–1879) The wife of John Eaton, President Jackson's secretary of war, was the daughter of a tavern owner with an unsavory past. Supposedly her first husband had committed suicide after learning that she was having an affair with John Eaton. The wives of members of Jackson's cabinet snubbed her because of her lowly origins and past, resulting in a scandal known as the Eaton Affair.

Economic Opportunity Act (1964) Key legislation in President Johnson's "War on Poverty" which created the Office of Economic Opportunity and programs like Head Start and work-study.

Jonathan Edwards (1703–1758) New England Congregationalist minister who began a religious revival in his Northampton church and was an important figure in the Great Awakening.

election of 1800 Presidential election between Thomas Jefferson and John Adams; resulted in the first Democratic-Republican party victory after the Federalist administrations of George Washington and John Adams.

election campaign of 1828 Bitter presidential contest between Democrat Andrew Jackson and National Republican John Quincy Adams (running for reelection), resulting in Jackson's victory.

election of 1864 Abraham Lincoln's successful reelection campaign, capitalizing on Union military successes in Georgia, to defeat Democratic opponent, former general George B. McClellan, who ran on a peace platform.

election of 1912 The presidential election of 1912 featured four candidates: Wilson, Taft, Roosevelt, and Debs. Each candidate believed in the basic assumptions of progressive politics, but each had a different view on how progressive ideals should be implemented through policy. In the end, Taft and Roosevelt split the Republican party votes and Wilson emerged as the winner.

Queen Elizabeth I of England (1533–1603) The protestant daughter of Henry VIII, she was Queen of England from 1558–1603 and played a major role in the Protestant Reformation. During her long reign, the doctrines and services of the Church of England were defined and the Spanish Armada was defeated.

General Dwight D. Eisenhower (1890–1969) During the Second World War, he commanded the Allied Forces landing in Africa and was the supreme Allied commander as well as planner for Operation Overlord. In 1952, he was elected president on his popularity as a war hero and his promises to clean up Washington. His administration sought to cut the nation's domestic programs and budget, ended the fighting in Korea, and institutionalized the policies of containment and deterrence. He established the Eisenhower doctrine, which promised to aid any nation against aggression by a Communist nation.

Ellis Island Reception center in New York Harbor through which most European immigrants to America were processed from 1892 to 1954.

Emancipation Proclamation (1862) Military order issued by President Abraham Lincoln that freed slaves in areas still controlled by the Confederacy but did not free the 500,000 slaves in the four border states that remained in the Union.

Embargo Act (1807) A law promoted by President Thomas Jefferson prohibiting American ships from leaving for foreign ports, in order to safeguard them from British and French attacks. This ban on American exports proved disastrous to the U.S. economy.

Ralph Waldo Emerson (1803–1882) As a leader of the transcendentalist movement, he wrote poems, essays, and speeches that discussed the sacredness of nature, optimism, self-reliance, and the unlimited potential of the individual. He wanted to transcend the limitations of inherited conventions and rationalism to reach the inner recesses of the self.

encomienda A land-grant system under which Spanish army officers (*conquistadores*) were awarded large parcels of land taken from Native Americans.

Enlightenment A revolution in thought begun in Europe in the seventeenth century that emphasized reason and science over the authority and myths of traditional religion.

enumerated goods According to the Navigation Act, these particular goods, like tobacco or cotton, could only be shipped to England or other English colonies.

Environmental Protection Agency (EPA) (1970) Federal environmental agency created by Nixon to appease the demands of congressional Democrats for a federal environmental watchdog agency.

Erie Canal (1825) Most important and profitable of the barge canals of the 1820s and 1830s; stretched from Buffalo to Albany, New York, connecting the Great Lakes to the East Coast and making New York City the nation's largest port.

ethnic cleansing The systematic removal of an ethnic group from a territory through violence or intimidation in order to create a homogenous society; the term was popularized by the Yugoslav policy brutally targeting Albanian Muslims in Kosovo.

Exodusters African Americans who migrated west from the South in search of a haven from racism and poverty after the collapse of Radical Republican rule.

Fair Deal (1949) President Truman's proposals to build upon the New Deal with national health insurance, the repeal of the Taft-Hartley Act, new civil rights legislation, and other initiatives; most were rejected by the Republican-controlled Congress.

Fair Employment Practices Commission Created in 1941 by executive order, the FEPC sought to eliminate racial discrimination in jobs; it possessed little power but represented a step toward civil rights for African Americans.

falling-domino theory Theory that if one country fell to communism, its neighboring countries would follow suit.

Farmers' Alliances Like the Granger movement, these organizations sought to address the issues of small farming communities; however Alliances emphasized more political action and called for the creation of a Third Party to advocate their concerns.

fascism A radical form of totalitarian government that emerged in Italy and Germany in the 1920s in which a dictator uses propaganda and brute force to seize control of all aspects of national life.

Federal-Aid Highway Act (1956) Largest federal project in U.S. history that created a national network of interstate highways and was the largest federal project in history.

Federal Deposit Insurance Corporation (1933) Independent government agency, established to prevent bank panics, which guarantees the safety of deposits in citizens' savings accounts.

Federal Reserve Act (1913) Legislation passed by Congress to create a new national banking system in order to regulate the nation's currency supply and ensure the stability and integrity of member banks who made up the Federal Reserve System across the nation.

Federal Trade Commission (1914) Independent agency created by the Wilson administration that replaced the Bureau of Corporations as an even more powerful tool to combat unfair trade practices and monopolies.

Federal Writers' Project During the Great Depression, this project provided writers, such as Ralph Ellison, Richard Wright, and Saul Bellow, with work, which gave them employment and a chance to develop as artists.

federalism Concept of dividing governmental authority between the national government and the states.

The Federalist Papers Collection of eighty-five essays, published widely in newspapers in 1787 and 1788, written by Alexander Hamilton, James Madison, and John Jay in support of adopting the proposed U.S. Constitution.

Federalists Proponents of a centralized federal system and the ratification of the Constitution. Most Federalists were relatively young, educated men who supported a broad interpretation of the Constitution whenever national interest dictated such flexibility. Notable Federalists included Alexander Hamilton and John Jay.

Geraldine Ferraro (1935–) In the 1984 presidential election, Democratic nominee, Walter Mondale, chose her as his running mate. As a member of the U.S. House of Representatives from New York, she was the first woman to be a vice-presidential nominee for a major political party. However, she was placed on the defensive because of her husband's complicated business dealings.

field hands Slaves who toiled in the cotton or cane fields in organized work gangs.

Fifteenth Amendment (1870) This amendment forbids states to deny any person the right to vote on grounds of "race, color or pervious condition of servitude." Former Confederate states were required to ratify this amendment before they could be readmitted to the Union.

"final solution" The Nazi party's systematic murder of some 6 million Jews along with more than a million other people including, but not limited to, gypsies, homosexuals, and handicap individuals.

First New Deal (1933–1935) Franklin D. Roosevelt's ambitious first-term cluster of economic and social programs designed to combat the Great Depression.

First Red Scare (1919–1920) Outbreak of anti-Communist hysteria that included the arrest without warrants of thousands of suspected radicals, most of whom (mainly Russian immigrants) were deported.

flappers Young women of the 1920s whose rebellion against prewar standards of femininity included wearing shorter dresses, bobbing their hair, dancing to jazz music, driving cars, smoking cigarettes, and indulging in illegal drinking and gambling.

Food Administration After America's entry into World War I, the economy of the home front needed to be reorganized to provide the most efficient means of conducting the war. The Food Administration was a part of this effort. Under the leadership of Herbert Hoover, the organization sought to increase agricultural production while reducing civilian consumption of foodstuffs.

Force Bill (1833) Legislation, sparked by the Nullification Crisis in South Carolina, that authorized the president's use of the army to compel states to comply with federal law.

Gerald Ford (1913–2006) He was appointed to the vice presidency under President Nixon after the resignation of Spiro Agnew, and assumed the presidency after President Nixon's resignation. He resisted congressional pressure to both reduce taxes and increase federal spending, which sent the American economy into the deepest recession since the Great Depression. Ford retained Kissinger as his secretary of state and continued Nixon's foreign policy goals. He was heavily criticized following the collapse of South Vietnam.

Fort Laramie Treaty (1851) Restricted the Plains Indians from using the Overland Trail and permitted the building of government forts.

Fort Necessity After attacking a group of French soldiers, George Washington constructed and took shelter in this fort from vengeful French troops. Washington eventually surrendered to them after a day-long battle. This conflict was a significant event in igniting the French and Indian War.

Fort Sumter First battle of the Civil War, in which the federal fort in Charleston (South Carolina) Harbor was captured by the Confederates on April 14, 1861, after two days of shelling.

"forty-niners" Speculators who went to northern California following the discovery of gold in 1848; the first of several years of large-scale migration was 1849.

Fourteen Points (1918) President Woodrow Wilson's proposed plan for the peace agreement after the First World War that included the creation of a "league of nations" intended to keep the peace.

Fourteenth Amendment (1866) Guaranteed rights of citizenship to former slaves, in words similar to those of the Civil Rights Act of 1866.

Franciscan Missions In 1769, Franciscan missioners accompanied Spanish soldiers to California and over the next fifty years established a chain of missions from San Diego to San Francisco. At these missions, friars sought to convert Indians to Catholicism and make them members of the Spanish empire. The friars stripped the Indians of their native heritage and used soldiers to enforce their will.

Benjamin Franklin (1706–1790) A Boston-born American, who epitomized the Enlightenment for many Americans and Europeans, Franklin's wide range of interests led him to become a publisher, inventor, and statesman. As the latter, he contributed to the writing of the Declaration of Independence, served as the minister to France during the Revolutionary War, and was a delegate to the Constitutional Convention.

Free-Soil party A political coalition created in 1848 that opposed the expansion of slavery into the new western territories.

Freedmen's Bureau Reconstruction agency established in 1865 to protect the legal rights of former slaves and to assist with their education, jobs, health care, and landowning.

Freedom Riders Activists who, beginning in 1961, traveled by bus through the South to test federal court rulings that banned segregation on buses and trains.

John C. Frémont "the Pathfinder" (1813–1890) He was an explorer and surveyor who helped inspire Americans living in California to rebel against the Mexican government and declare independence.

French and Indian War (Seven Years' War) (1756–1763) The last—and the most important—of four colonial wars fought between England and France for control of North America east of the Mississippi River.

French Revolution Revolutionary movement beginning in 1789 that overthrew the monarchy and transformed France into an unstable republic before Napoleon Bonaparte assumed power in 1799.

Sigmund Freud (1865–1939) He was the founder of psychoanalysis, which suggested that human behavior was motivated by unconscious and irrational forces. By the 1920s, his ideas were being discussed more openly in America.

frontier revivals Religious revival movement within the Second Great Awakening, that took place in frontier churches in western territories and states in the early nineteenth century.

Fugitive Slave Act (1850) Part of the Compromise of 1850, a provision that authorized federal officials to help capture and then return escaped slaves to their owners without trials.

fundamentalism Anti-modernist Protestant movement started in the early twentieth century that proclaimed the literal truth of the Bible; the name came from *The Fundamentals*, published by conservative leaders.

William Lloyd Garrison (1805–1879) In 1831, he started the anti-slavery newspaper *Liberator* and helped start the New England Anti-Slavery Society. Two years later, he assisted Arthur and Lewis Tappan in the founding of the American Anti-Slavery Society. He and his followers believed that America had been thoroughly corrupted and needed a wide range of reforms, embracing abolition, temperance, pacifism, and women's rights.

Marcus Garvey (1887–1940) He was the leading spokesman for Negro Nationalism, which exalted blackness, black cultural expression, and black exclusiveness. He called upon African Americans to liberate themselves from the surrounding white culture and create their own businesses, cultural centers, and newspapers. He was also the founder of the Universal Negro Improvement Association.

Citizen Genet (1763–1834) As the ambassador to the United States from the new French Republic, he engaged American privateers to attack British ships and conspired with frontiersmen and land speculators to organize an attack on Spanish Florida and Louisiana. His actions and the French radicals excessive actions against their enemies in the new French Republic caused the French Revolution to lose support among Americans.

Geneva Accords In 1954, the Geneva Accords were signed, which ended French colonial rule in Indochina. The agreement created the independent nations of Laos and Cambodia and divided Vietnam along the 17th parallel until an election in 1956 would reunify the country.

Battle of Gettysburg (1863) A monumental three-day battle in southern Pennsylvania, widely considered a turning point in the war, in which Union forces successfully countered a second Confederate invasion of the North.

Ghost Dance movement A spiritual and political movement among Native Americans whose followers performed a ceremonial "ghost dance" intended to connect the living with the dead and make the Indians bulletproof in battles to restore their homelands.

GI Bill of Rights (1944) Provided unemployment, education, and financial benefits for World War II veterans to ease their transition back to the civilian world.

***Gibbons v. Ogden* (1824)** Supreme Court case that gave the federal government the power to regulate interstate commerce.

Newt Gingrich (1943–) He led the Republican insurgency in Congress in the mid 1990s through mobilizing religious and social conservatives. Along with other Republican congressmen, he created the Contract with America, which was a ten-point anti-big government program. However, the program fizzled out after many of its bills were not passed by Congress.

Gilded Age (1860–1896) An era of dramatic industrial and urban growth characterized by widespread political corruption and loose government oversight of corporations.

The Gilded Age Mark Twain and Charles Dudley Warner's 1873 novel, the title of which became the popular name for the period from the end of the Civil War to the turn of the century.

glasnost Russian term for "openness"; applied to the loosening of censorship in the Soviet Union under Mikhail Gorbachev.

globalization An important, and controversial, transformation of the world economy whereby the Internet helped revolutionize global commerce by creating an international marketplace for goods and services. Led by the growing number of multinational companies and the Americanization of many foreign consumer cultures, with companies like McDonald's and Starbucks appearing in all of the major cities of the world.

Glorious Revolution (1688) Successful coup, instigated by a group of English aristocrats, which overthrew King James II and instated William of Orange and Mary, his English wife, to the British throne.

Barry Goldwater (1909–1998) A leader of the Republican right whose book, *The Conscience of a Conservative*, was highly influential to that segment of the party. He proposed eliminating the income tax and overhauling Social Security. In 1964, he ran as the Republican presidential candidate and lost to President Johnson. He campaigned against Johnson's war on poverty, the tradition of New Deal, the nuclear test ban and the Civil Rights Act of 1964 and advocated the wholesale bombing of North Vietnam.

Samuel Gompers (1850–1924) He served as the president of the American Federation of Labor from its inception until his death. He focused on achieving concrete economic gains such as higher wages, shorter hours, and better working conditions.

"good neighbor" policy Proclaimed by President Franklin D. Roosevelt in his first inaugural address in 1933, it sought improved diplomatic relations between the United States and its Latin American neighbors.

Mikhail Gorbachev (1931–) In the late 1980s, Soviet leader Mikhail Gorbachev attempted to reform the Soviet Union through his programs of *perestroika* and *glasnost* and pursued a renewal of détente with America, signing new arms-control agreements with President Reagan. Gorbachev allowed the velvet revolutions of Eastern Europe to occur without outside interference. Eventually the political, social, and economic upheaval he had unleashed would lead to the break-up of the Soviet Union.

Albert Gore Jr. (1948–) He served as a senator of Tennessee and then as President Clinton's vice president. In the 2000 presidential election, he was the Democratic candidate against Governor George W. Bush. The close election came down to Florida's electoral votes. While the votes were being recounted as required by state law, a legal battle was being waged to stop the recount. Finally, the case, *Bush v. Gore*, was presented to the Supreme Court who ruled 5–4 to stop the recount and Bush was declared the winner.

Jay Gould (1836–1892) As one of the biggest railroad robber barons, he was infamous for buying rundown railroads, making cosmetic improvements and then reselling them for a profit. He used corporate funds for personal investments and to bribe politicians and judges.

gradualism This strategy for ending slavery involved promoting the banning of slavery in the new western territories and encouraging the release of slaves from slavery. Supporters of this method believed that it would bring about the gradual end of slavery.

Granger movement Began by offering social and educational activities for isolated farmers and their families and later started to promote "cooperatives" where farmers could join together to buy, store, and sell their crops to avoid the high fees charged by brokers and other middle-men.

Ulysses S. Grant (1822–1885) After distinguishing himself in the western theater of the Civil War, he was appointed general in chief of the Union army in 1864. Afterward, he defeated General Robert E. Lee through a policy of aggressive attrition. Lee surrendered to Grant on April 9th, 1865 at the Appomattox Court House. His presidential tenure suffered from scandals and fiscal problems, including the debate on whether or not greenbacks, paper money, should be removed from circulation.

Great Awakening Fervent religious revival movement that swept the thirteen colonies from the 1720s through the 1740s.

Great Compromise (Connecticut Compromise) Mediated the differences between the New Jersey and Virginia delegations to the Constitutional Convention by providing for a bicameral legislature, the upper house of which would have equal representation and the lower house of which would be apportioned by population.

Great Depression (1929–1941) Worst economic downturn in American history; it was spurred by the stock market crash in the fall of 1929 and lasted until the Second World War.

Great Migration Mass exodus of African Americans from the rural South to the Northeast and Midwest during and after the First World War.

Great Railroad Strike of 1877 A series of demonstrations, some violent, held nationwide in support of striking railroad workers in Martinsburg, West Virginia, who refused to work due to wage cuts.

Great Recession (2007–2009) Massive, prolonged economic downturn sparked by the collapse of the housing market and the financial institutions holding unpaid mortgages; it lasted from December 2007 to January 2009 and resulted in 9 million Americans losing their jobs.

Great Sioux War Conflict between Sioux and Cheyenne Indians and federal troops over lands in the Dakotas in the mid-1870s.

Great Society Term coined by President Lyndon B. Johnson in his 1965 State of the Union address, in which he proposed legislation to address problems of voting rights, poverty, diseases, education, immigration, and the environment.

Horace Greeley (1811–1872) In reaction to Radical Reconstruction and corruption in President Ulysses S. Grant's administration, a group of Republicans broke from the party to form the Liberal Republicans. In 1872, the Liberal Republicans chose Horace Greeley as their presidential candidate who ran on a platform of favoring civil service reform and condemning the Republican's Reconstruction policy.

greenbacks Paper money issued during the Civil War. After the war ended, a debate emerged on whether or not to remove the paper currency from circulation and revert back to hard-money currency (gold coins). Opponents of hard-money feared that eliminating the greenbacks would shrink the money supply, which would lower crop prices and make it more difficult to repay long-term debts. President Ulysses S. Grant, as well as hard-currency advocates, believed that gold coins were morally preferable to paper currency.

Greenback party Formed in 1876 in reaction to economic depression, the party favored issuance of unsecured paper money to help farmers repay debts; the movement for free coinage of silver took the place of the greenback movement by the 1880s.

General Nathanael Greene (1742–1786) He was appointed by Congress to command the American army fighting in the South during the Revolutionary War. Using his patience and his skills of managing men, saving supplies, and avoiding needless risks, he waged a successful war of attrition against the British.

Sarah Grimké (1792–1873) and **Angelina Grimké (1805–1879)** These two sisters gave anti-slavery speeches to crowds of mixed gender that caused some people to condemn them for engaging in unfeminine activities. In 1840, William Lloyd Garrison convinced the Anti-Slavery Society to allow women equal participation in the organization.

Half-Way Covenant Allowed baptized children of church members to be admitted to a "halfway" membership in the church and secure baptism for their own children in turn, but allowed them neither a vote in the church, nor communion.

Alexander Hamilton (1755–1804) His belief in a strong federal government led him to become a leader of the Federalists. As the first secretary of the Treasury, he laid the foundation for American capitalism through his creation of a federal budget, funded debt, a federal tax system, a national bank, a customs service, and a coast guard. His "Reports on Public Credit" and "Reports on Manufactures" outlined his vision for economic development and government finances. He died in a duel against Aaron Burr.

Alexander Hamilton's economic reforms Various measures designed to strengthen the nation's economy and generate federal revenue through the promotion of new industries, the adoption of new tax policies, the payment of war debts, and the establishment of a national bank.

Warren G. Harding (1865–1923) In the 1920 presidential election, he was the Republican nominee who promised Americans a "return to normalcy." Once in office, Harding's administration dismantled many of the social and economic components of progressivism and pursued a pro-business agenda. Harding appointed four pro-business Supreme Court Justices, cut taxes, increased tariffs, and promoted a lenient attitude towards regulation of corporations. However, he did speak out against racism and ended the exclusion of African Americans from federal positions.

Harlem Renaissance The nation's first self-conscious black literary and artistic movement; it was centered in New York City's Harlem district, which had a largely black population in the wake of the Great Migration from the South.

Hartford Convention A series of secret meetings in December 1814 and January 1815 at which New England Federalists protested American involvement in the War of 1812 and discussed several constitutional amendments, including limiting each president to one term, designed to weaken the dominant Republican party.

Haymarket riot (1886) Violent uprising in Haymarket Square, Chicago, where police clashed with labor demonstrators in the aftermath of a bombing.

headright A land-grant policy that promised fifty acres to any colonist who could afford passage to Virginia, as well as fifty more for any accompanying servants. The head-right policy was eventually expanded to include any colonists—and was also adopted in other colonies.

Patrick Henry (1736–1799) He inspired the Virginia Resolves, which declared that Englishmen could only be taxed by their elected representatives. In March of 1775, he met with other colonial leaders to discuss the goals of the upcoming Continental Congress and famously declared "Give me liberty or give me death." During the ratification process of the U.S. Constitution, he became one of the leaders of the anti-federalists.

Hessians German mercenary soldiers who are paid by the royal government to fight alongside the British army.

Hiroshima (1945) Japanese port city that was the first target of the newly developed atomic bomb on August 6, 1945. Most of the city was destroyed.

Alger Hiss (1904–1996) During the second Red Scare he had served in several government departments and was accused of being a spy for the Soviet Union and was convicted of lying about espionage. The case was politically damaging to the Truman administration because the president called the charges against Hiss a "red herring."

Adolph Hitler (1889–1945) The leader of the Nazis who advocated a violent anti-Semitic, anti-Marxist, pan-German ideology. He started World War II in Europe and orchestrated the systematic murder of some 6 million Jews along with more than a million others.

HIV/AIDS Human immunodeficiency virus (HIV) transmitted via the bodily fluids of infected persons to cause acquired immunodeficiency syndrome (AIDS), an often-fatal disease of the immune system when it appeared in the 1980s.

holding company A corporation established to own and manage other companies' stock rather than to produce goods and services itself.

Holocaust Systematic racist attempt by the Nazis to exterminate all Jews in Europe, resulting in the murder of more than 6 million Jews and more than 5 million other "undesirables."

Homestead Act (1862) Legislation granting "homesteads" of 160 acres of government-owned land to settlers who agreed to work the land for at least five years.

Homestead Steel strike (1892) Labor conflict at the Homestead steel mill near Pittsburgh, Pennsylvania, culminating in a battle between strikers and private security agents hired by the factory's management.

Herbert Hoover (1874–1964) Prior to becoming president, Hoover served as the secretary of commerce in both the Harding and Coolidge administrations. As president during the Great Depression, he believed that the nation's business structure was sound and sought to revive the economy through boosting the nation's confidence. He also tried to restart the economy with government constructions projects, lower taxes and new federal loan programs, but nothing worked.

horizontal integration The process by which a corporation acquires or merges with its competitors.

horse A tall, four-legged mammal (*Equus caballus*), domesticated and bred since prehistoric times for carrying riders and pulling heavy loads. The Spanish introduced horses to the Americas, eventually transforming many Native American cultures.

House Committee on Un-American Activities (HUAC) Committee of the U.S. House of Representatives formed in 1938; it was originally tasked with investigating Nazi subversion during the Second World War and later shifted its focus to rooting out Communists in the government and the motion-picture industry.

Sam Houston (1793–1863) During Texas's fight for independence from Mexico, Sam Houston was the commander in chief of the Texas forces, and he led the attack that captured General Antonio López de Santa Anna. After Texas gained its independence, he was named its first president.

How the Other Half Lives In this book, early muckraking journalist Jacob Riis exposed the slum conditions in New York City.

General William Howe (1729–1814) As the commander of the British army in the Revolutionary War, he seized New York City from Washington's army, but failed to capture it. He missed several more opportunities to quickly end the rebellion, and he resigned his command after the British defeat at Saratoga.

Saddam Hussein (1937–2006) The former dictator of Iraq who became the head of state in 1979. In 1980, he invaded Iran and started the eight-year-long Iran-Iraq War. In 1990, he invaded Kuwait, which caused the Gulf War of 1991. In 2003, he was overthrown and captured when the United States invaded. He was sentenced to death by hanging in 2006.

Anne Hutchinson (1591–1643) The articulate, strong-willed, and intelligent wife of a prominent Boston merchant, who espoused her belief in direct divine revelation.

She quarreled with Puritan leaders over her beliefs; and they banished her from the colony.

Immigration Act of 1924 Federal legislation intended to favor northern and western European immigrants over those from southern and eastern Europe by restricting the number of immigrants from any one European country to 2 percent of the total number of immigrants per year, with an overall limit of slightly over 150,000 new arrivals per year.

Immigration and Nationality Services Act of 1965 (Hart-Cellar Act) Legislation that abolished discriminatory quotas based upon immigrants' national origin and treated all nationalities and races equally.

impeachment A formal misconduct charge made against a public official, usually the president, by the House of Representatives. The official's removal from office requires a separate process in the form of a trial facilitated by the Senate. A guilty verdict from two-thirds of the participating senators leads to a conviction.

imperialism The use of diplomatic or military force to extend a nation's power and enhance its economic interests, often by acquiring territory or colonies and justifying such behavior with assumptions of racial superiority.

indentured servants Settlers who consented to work for a defined period of labor (often four to seven years) in exchange for having their passage to the New World paid by their "master."

Independent Treasury Act (1840) System created by President Martin Van Buren and approved by Congress in 1840 whereby the federal government moved its funds from favored state banks to the U.S. Treasury, whose financial transactions could only be in gold or silver coins of paper currency backed by gold or silver.

"Indian New Deal" This phrase refers to the reforms implemented for Native Americans during the New Deal era. John Collier, the commissioner of the Bureau of Indian Affairs (BIA), increased the access Native Americans had to relief programs and employed more Native Americans at the BIA. He worked to pass the Indian Reorganization Act. However, the version of the act passed by Congress was a much-diluted version of Collier's original proposal and did not greatly improve the lives of Native Americans.

Indian Removal Act (1830) Law permitting the forced relocation of Indians to federal lands west of the Mississippi River in exchange for the land they occupied in the East and South.

Indian wars Bloody conflicts between U.S. soldiers and Native Americans that raged in the West from the early 1860s to the late 1870s, sparked by American settlers moving into ancestral Indian lands.

Indochina This area of Southeast Asia consists of Laos, Cambodia, and Vietnam and was once controlled by France as a colony. After the Viet Minh defeated the French, the Geneva Accords were signed, which ended French colonial rule. The agreement created the independent nations of Laos and Cambodia and divided Vietnam along the 17th parallel until an election would reunify the country. Fearing a Communist take over, the United States government began intervening in the region during the Truman administration, which led to President Johnson's full-scale military involvement in Vietnam.

industrialization Major shift in the nineteenth century from handmade manufacturing to mass production in mills and factories using water-, coal-, and steam-powered machinery.

Industrial Revolution Major shift in the nineteenth century from hand-made manufacturing to mass production in mills and factories using water-, coal-, and steam-powered machinery.

industrial war A new concept of war enabled by industrialization that developed from the early 1800s through the Atomic Age. New technologies, including automatic weaponry, forms of transportation like the railroad and airplane, and communication technologies such as the telegraph and telephone, enabled nations to equip large, mass-conscripted armies with chemical and automatic weapons to decimate opposing armies in a "total war."

Industrial Workers of the World (IWW) A radical union organized in Chicago in 1905, nicknamed the Wobblies; its opposition to World War I led to its destruction by the federal government under the Espionage Act.

infectious diseases Also called contagious diseases, illnesses that can pass from one person to another by way of invasive biological organisms able to reproduce in the bodily tissues of their hosts. Europeans unwittingly brought many such diseases to the Americas, devastating the Native American peoples.

The Influence of Sea Power upon History, 1660–1783 **(1890)** Historical work in which Rear Admiral Alfred Thayer Mahan argues that a nation's greatness and prosperity comes from the power of its navy; the book helped bolster imperialist sentiment in the United States in the late nineteenth century.

Intermediate-Range Nuclear Forces (INF) Treaty (1987) Agreement signed by U.S. president Ronald Reagan and Soviet premier Mikhail Gorbachev to eliminate the deployment of intermediate-range missiles with nuclear warheads.

internal improvements Construction of roads, bridges, canals, harbors, and other infrastructural projects intended to facilitate the flow of goods and people.

internationalists Prior to the United States' entry in World War II, internationalists believed that America's national security depended on aiding Britain in its struggle against Germany.

Interstate Commerce Commission (ICC) (1887) An independent federal agency established to oversee businesses engaged in interstate trade, especially railroads, but whose regulatory power was limited when tested in the courts.

interstate highway system In the late 1950s, construction began on a national network of interstate superhighways for the purpose of commerce and defense. The interstate highways would enable the rapid movement of military convoys and the evacuation of cities after a nuclear attack.

Iran-Contra affair (1987) Reagan administration scandal over the secret, unlawful U.S. sale of arms to Iran in partial exchange for the release of hostages in Lebanon; the arms money in turn was used illegally to aid Nicaraguan right-wing insurgents, the Contras.

Iranian hostage crisis (1979) Storming of the U.S. embassy in Tehran by Iranian revolutionaries, who held fifty-two Americans hostage for 444 days, despite President Carter's appeals for their release as well as a botched rescue attempt.

Irish Potato Famine In 1845, an epidemic of potato rot brought a famine to rural Ireland that killed over 1 million peasants and instigated a huge increase in the number of Irish immigrating to America. By 1850, the Irish made up 43 percent of the foreign-born population in the United States; and in the 1850s, they made up over half the population of New York City and Boston.

iron curtain Term coined by Winston Churchill to describe the cold war divide between western Europe and the Soviet Union's Eastern European satellites.

Iroquois League An alliance of the Iroquois tribes, originally formed sometime between 1450 and 1600, that used their combined strength to pressure Europeans to work with them in the fur trade and to wage war across what is today eastern North America.

Andrew Jackson (1767–1837) As a major general in the Tennessee militia, he had a number of military successes. As president, he worked to enable the "common man" to play a greater role in the political arena. He vetoed the re-chartering of the Second National Bank and reduced federal spending. When South Carolina nullified the Tariffs of 1828 and 1832, Jackson requested that Congress pass a "force bill" that would authorize him to use the army to compel the state to comply with the tariffs. He forced eastern Indians to move west of the Mississippi River so their lands could be used by white settlers. Groups of those who opposed Jackson come together to form a new political party called the Whigs.

Thomas "Stonewall" Jackson (1824–1863) A Confederate general who was known for his fearlessness in leading rapid marches, bold flanking movements, and furious assaults. He earned his nickname at the Battle of the First Bull Run for standing courageously against Union fire. During the battle of Chancellorsville, his own men accidentally mortally wounded him.

William James (1842–1910) He was the founder of Pragmatism and one of the fathers of modern psychology. He believed that ideas gained their validity not from their inherent truth, but from their social consequences and practical application.

Jay's Treaty (1794) Agreement between Britain and the United States, negotiated by Chief Justice John Jay, that settled disputes over trade, prewar debts owed to British merchants, British-occupied forts in American territory, and the seizure of American ships and cargo.

Jazz Age Term coined by writer F. Scott Fitzgerald to characterize the spirit of rebellion and spontaneity among young Americans in the 1920s, a spirit epitomized by the hugely popular jazz music of the era.

Thomas Jefferson (1743–1826) He was a plantation owner, author, the drafter of the Declaration Independence, ambassador to France, leader of the Republican party, secretary of state, and the third president of the United States. As president, he purchased the Louisiana territory from France, withheld appointments made by President Adams leading to *Marybury v. Madison*, outlawed foreign slave trade, and was committed to a "wise and frugal" government.

Jeffersonian Republicans Political party founded by Thomas Jefferson in opposition to the Federalist party led by Alexander Hamilton and John Adams; also known as the Democratic-Republican party.

Jesuits A religious order founded in 1540 by Ignatius Loyola. They sought to counter the spread of Protestantism during the Protestant Reformation and spread the Catholic faith through work as missionaries. Roughly 3,500 served in New Spain and New France.

"Jim Crow" laws In the New South, these laws mandated the separation of races in various public places that served as a way for the ruling whites to impose their will on all areas of black life.

Andrew Johnson (1808–1875) He was elevated to the presidency after Abraham Lincoln's assassination. In order to restore the Union after the Civil War, he issued an amnesty proclamation and required former Confederate states to ratify the Thirteenth Amendment. After disagreements over the power to restore states rights, the Radical Republicans attempted to impeach Johnson but fell short on the required number of votes needed to remove him from office.

Lyndon B. Johnson (1908–1973) Former member of the House of Representatives and the former Majority Leader of the Senate, Vice President Lyndon B. Johnson assumed the presidency after President Kennedy's assassination. During his presidency, he passed the Civil Rights Act of 1964, declared a "war on poverty" promoting his own social program called the Great Society, and signed the Immigration and Nationality Service Act of 1965. Johnson greatly increased America's role in Vietnam.

Johnson's Restoration Plan Plan to require southern states to ratify the Thirteenth Amendment, disqualify wealthy ex-Confederates from voting, and appoint a Unionist governor.

joint-stock companies Businesses owned by investors, who purchase shares of companies' stocks and share all the profits and losses.

Kansas-Nebraska Act (1854) Controversial legislation that created two new territories taken from Native Americans, Kansas and Nebraska, where residents would vote to decide whether slavery would be allowed (popular sovereignty).

Florence Kelley (1859–1932) As the head of the National Consumer's League, she led the crusade to promote state laws to regulate the number of working hours imposed on women who were wives and mothers.

George F. Kennan (1904–2005) While working as an American diplomat, he devised the strategy of containment, which called for the halting of Soviet expansion. It became America's choice strategy throughout the cold war.

John F. Kennedy (1917–1963) He was elected president in 1960. Despite the difficulties he had in getting his legislation through Congress, he established the Alliance for Progress programs to help Latin America, the Peace Corps, the Trade Expansion Act of 1962, and funding for urban renewal projects and the space program. His foreign political involvement included the failed Bay of Pigs invasion and the missile crisis in Cuba, as well as support of local governments in Indochina. In 1963, he was assassinated by Lee Harvey Oswald in Dallas, Texas.

Kent State During the spring of 1970, students on college campuses across the country protested the expansion of the Vietnam War into Cambodia. At Kent State University, the National Guard attempted to quell the rioting students. The guardsmen panicked and shot at rock-throwing demonstrators. Four student bystanders were killed.

Kentucky and Virginia Resolutions (1798–1799) Passed in response to the Alien and Sedition Acts, the resolutions advanced the state-compact theory that held states could nullify an act of Congress if they deemed it unconstitutional.

Francis Scott Key (1779–1843) During the War of 1812, he watched British forces bombard Fort McHenry, but fail to take it. Seeing the American flag still flying over the fort at dawn inspired him to write "The Star-Spangled Banner," which became the American national anthem.

Martin Luther King Jr. (1929–1968) A central leader of the civil rights movement, he urged people to use nonviolent civil disobedience to demand their rights and bring about change. He successfully led the Montgomery bus boycott. While in jail for his role in demonstrations, he wrote his famous "Letter from Birmingham City Jail," in which he defended his strategy of nonviolent protest. In 1963, he delivered his famous "I Have a Dream Speech" from the steps of the Lincoln Memorial as a part of the March on Washington. A year later, he was awarded the Nobel Peace Prize. In 1968, he was assassinated.

King Philip's War A bloody, three-year war in New England (1675–1676), resulting from the escalation of tensions between Indians and English settlers; the defeat of the Indians led to broadened freedoms for the settlers and their dispossessing the region's Indians of most of their land.

King William's War (War of the League of Augsburg) First (1689–1697) of four colonial wars between England and France.

Henry Kissinger (1923–) He served as the secretary of state and national security advisor in the Nixon administration. He negotiated with North Vietnam for an end to the Vietnam War, but the cease-fire did not last; South Vietnam fell to North Vietnam. He helped organize Nixon's historic trips to China and the Soviet Union. In the Middle East, he negotiated a cease-fire between Israel and its neighbors following the Yom

Kippur War and solidified Israel's promise to return to Egypt most of the land it had taken during the 1967 war.

Knights of Labor A national labor organization with a broad reform platform; reached peak membership in the 1880s.

Know-Nothings Nativist, anti-Catholic third party organized in 1854 in reaction to large-scale German and Irish immigration.

Ku Klux Klan Organized in Pulaski, Tennessee, in 1866 to terrorize former slaves who voted and held political offices during Reconstruction; a revived organization in the 1910s and 1920s stressed white, Anglo-Saxon, fundamentalist Protestant supremacy; the Klan revived a third time to fight the civil rights movement of the 1950s and 1960s in the South.

Marquis de Lafayette (1757–1834) A wealthy French idealist excited by the American cause, he offered to serve in Washington's army for free in exchange for being named a major general. He overcame Washington's initial skepticism to become one of his most trusted aides.

laissez-faire An economic doctrine holding that businesses and individuals should be able to pursue their economic interests without government interference.

Land Ordinance of 1785 Directed surveying of the Northwest Territory into townships of thirty-six sections (square miles) each, the sale of the sixteenth section of which was to be used to finance public education.

League of Nations Organization of nations formed in the aftermath of the First World War to mediate disputes and maintain international peace; despite President Wilson's intense lobbying for the League of Nations, Congress did not ratify the treaty and the United States failed to join.

Mary Elizabeth Lease (1850–1933) She was a leader of the farm protest movement who advocated violence if change could not be obtained at the ballot box. She believed that the urban-industrial East was the enemy of the working class.

Robert E. Lee (1807–1870) Even though he had served in the United States Army for thirty years, he chose to fight on the side of the Confederacy. Lee was excellent at using his field commanders and his soldiers respected him. However, General Ulysses S. Grant eventually wore down his army, and Lee surrendered to Grant at the Appomattox Court House on April 9, 1865.

Lend-Lease Act (1941) Legislation that allowed the president to lend or lease military equipment to any country whose own defense was deemed vital to the defense of the United States.

Levittown First low-cost, mass-produced development of suburban tract housing built by William Levitt on Long Island, New York, in 1947.

Lewis and Clark expedition (1804–1806) Led by Meriwether Lewis and William Clark, a mission to the Pacific coast commissioned for the purposes of scientific and geographical exploration

Battle of Lexington and Concord The first shots fired in the Revolutionary War, on April 19, 1775, near Boston; approximately 100 Minutemen and 250 British soldiers were killed.

Liberator William Lloyd Garrison started this anti-slavery newspaper in 1831 in which he renounced gradualism and called for abolition.

Queen Liliuokalani (1838–1917) In 1891, she ascended to the throne of the Hawaiian royal family and tried to eliminate white control of the Hawaiian government. Two years later, Hawaii's white population revolted and seized power with the support of American Marines.

Abraham Lincoln (1809–1865) Shortly after he was elected president in 1860, southern states began seceding from the Union, and in April of 1861 he declared war on the seceding states. On January 1, 1863, Lincoln signed the Emancipation Proclamation. At the end of the war, he favored a reconstruction strategy for the former Confederate states that did not radically alter southern social and economic life. He was assassinated by John Wilkes Booth at Ford's Theater on April 14, 1865.

Lincoln-Douglas debates (1858) During the Illinois race between Republican Abraham Lincoln and Democrat Stephen A. Douglas for a seat in the U.S. Senate, a series of seven dramatic debates focusing on the issue of slavery in the territories.

John Locke (1632–1704) An English philosopher whose ideas were influential during the Enlightenment. He argued in his *Essay on Human Understanding* (1690) that humanity is largely the product of the environment, the mind being a blank tablet, *tabula rasa*, on which experience is written.

Henry Cabot Lodge (1850–1924) He was the chairman of the Senate Foreign Relations Committee who favored limiting America's involvement in the League of Nations' covenant and sought to amend the Treaty of Versailles.

de Lôme letter (1898) Private correspondence written by the Spanish ambassador to the U.S., Depuy de Lôme, that described President McKinley as "weak"; the letter was stolen by Cuban revolutionaries and published in the *New York Journal*, deepening American resentment of Spain and moving the two countries closer to war in Cuba.

Lone Star Republic After winning independence from Mexico, Texas became its own nation that was called the Lone Star Republic. In 1836, Texans drafted a constitution, legalized slavery, banned free blacks, named Sam Houston president, and voted for the annexation to the United States. However, quarrels over adding a slave state and fears of instigating a war with Mexico delayed Texas's entrance into the Union until December 29, 1845.

Huey P. Long (1893–1935) He began his political career in Louisiana where he developed a reputation for being an unscrupulous reformer. As a U.S. senator, he became a critic of President Roosevelt's New Deal Plan and offered his alternative called the Share-the-Wealth program. He was assassinated in 1935.

Lost Cause narrative Southern whites' view of secession as a noble "lost cause." A revisionist version of history that glamorized plantation culture and insisted that the Civil War had little to do with slavery and everything to do with a defense of states' rights from the Republican party and the "War of Northern Aggression."

Lost Generation Label given to modernist writers and authors, such as F. Scott Fitzgerald and Ernest Hemingway, who had lost faith in the values and institutions of Western civilization in the aftermath of the Great War.

Louisiana Purchase (1803) President Thomas Jefferson's purchase of the Louisiana Territory from France for $15 million, doubling the size of U.S. territory.

Lowell system Model New England factory communities that during the first half of the nineteenth century provided employees, mostly young women, with meals, a boardinghouse, and moral discipline, as well as educational and cultural opportunities.

Loyalists Colonists who remained loyal to Great Britain before and during the Revolutionary War.

Lusitania British ocean liner torpedoed and sunk by a German U-boat in 1915; the deaths of nearly 1,200 of its civilian passengers, including many Americans, caused international outrage.

Martin Luther (1483–1546) A German monk who founded the Lutheran church. He protested abuses in the Catholic Church by posting his Ninety-five Theses, which began the Protestant Reformation.

General Douglas MacArthur (1880–1964) During World War II, he and Admiral Chester Nimitz dislodged the Japanese military from the Pacific Islands they had occupied. Following the war, he was in charge of the occupation of Japan. After North Korea invaded South Korea, Truman sent the U.S. military to defend South Korea under the command of MacArthur. Later in the war, Truman expressed his willingness to negotiate the restoration of prewar boundaries which MacArthur attempted to undermine. Truman fired MacArthur for his open insubordination.

James Madison (1751–1836) He participated in the Constitutional Convention during which he proposed the Virginia Plan. He believed in a strong federal government and was a leader of the Federalists. However, he also presented to Congress the Bill of Rights and drafted the Virginia Resolutions. As secretary of state, he withheld a commission for William Marbury, which led to the landmark *Marbury v. Madison* decision. During his presidency, he declared war on Britain in response to violations of American shipping rights, which started the War of 1812.

U.S. battleship *Maine* American warship that exploded in the Cuban port of Havana on January 25, 1898; though later discovered to be the result of an accident, the destruction of the *Maine* was attributed by war-hungry Americans to Spain, contributing to the onset of the War of 1898.

maize (corn) The primary grain crop in Mesoamerica yielding small kernels often ground into cornmeal. Easy to grow in a broad range of conditions, it enabled a global population explosion after being brought to Europe, Africa, and Asia.

Malcolm X (1925–1964) The most articulate spokesman for black power. Originally the chief disciple of Elijah Muhammad, the black Muslim leader in the United States, Malcolm X broke away and founded his own organization committed to establishing relations between African Americans and the nonwhite peoples of the world. Near the end of his life, he began to preach a biracial message of social change. In 1964, he was assassinated by members of a rival group of black Muslims.

Manchuria incident The northeast region of Manchuria was an area contested between China and Russia. In 1931, the Japanese claimed that they needed to protect their extensive investments in the area and moved their army into Manchuria. They quickly conquered the region and set up their own puppet empire. China asked both the United States and the League of Nations for help and neither responded.

manifest destiny The widespread belief that America was "destined" by God to expand westward across the continent into lands claimed by Native Americans as well as European nations.

Horace Mann (1796–1859) He believed the public school system was the best way to achieve social stability and equal opportunity. As a reformer of education, he sponsored a state board of education, the first state-supported "normal" school for training teachers, a state association for teachers, the minimum school year of six months, and led the drive for a statewide school system.

***Marbury v. Madison* (1803)** First Supreme Court decision to declare a federal law—the Judiciary Act of 1801—unconstitutional.

March on Washington Civil rights demonstration on August 28, 1963, on the National Mall, where Martin Luther King Jr. gave his famous "I Have a Dream" speech.

March to the Sea (1864) The Union army's devastating march through Georgia from Atlanta to Savannah led by General William T. Sherman, intended to demoralize civilians and destroy the resources the Confederate army needed to fight.

market-based economy Large-scale manufacturing and commercial agriculture that emerged in America during the first half of the nineteenth century, displacing much of the premarket subsistence and barter-based economy and producing boom-and-bust cycles while raising the American standard of living.

marriage equality The legal right for gay and lesbian couples to marry; it became the most divisive issue in the culture wars of the early 2010s as more and more court rulings affirmed this right in states and municipalities across the United States. The 2015 Supreme Court case *Obergefell v. Hodges* affirmed the right to same-sex marriage, also known as marriage equality, nationally.

George C. Marshall (1880–1959) As the chairman of the Joint Chiefs of Staff, he orchestrated the Allied victories over Germany and Japan in the Second World War. In 1947, he became President Truman's secretary of state and proposed the massive reconstruction program for western Europe called the Marshall Plan.

Chief Justice John Marshall (1755–1835) During his long tenure as chief justice of the supreme court (1801–1835), he established the foundations for American jurisprudence, the authority of the Supreme Court, and the constitutional supremacy of the national government over states.

Marshall Plan (1948) Secretary of State George C. Marshall's post–World War II program providing massive U.S. financial and technical assistance to war-torn European countries.

Massachusetts Bay Colony English colony founded by English Puritans in 1630 as a haven for persecuted Congregationalists.

massive resistance White rallying cry disrupting federal efforts to enforce racial integration in the South.

massive retaliation Strategy that used the threat of nuclear warfare as a means of combating the global spread of communism.

Mayflower Compact A formal agreement signed by the Separatist colonists aboard the *Mayflower* in 1620 to abide by laws made by leaders of their own choosing.

Senator Joseph R. McCarthy (1908–1957) In 1950, this senator became the shrewdest and most ruthless exploiter of America's anxiety of communism. He claimed that the United States government was full of Communists and led a witch hunt to find them, but he was never able to uncover a single communist agent.

McCarthyism Anti-Communist hysteria led by Senator Joseph McCarthy's "witch hunts" attacking the loyalty of politicians, federal employees, and public figures, despite a lack of evidence.

George B. McClellan (1826–1885) In 1861, President Abraham Lincoln appointed him head of the Army of the Potomac and, later, general in chief of the U.S. Army. He built his army into well trained and powerful force. After failing to achieve a decisive victory against the Confederacy, he was removed from command in 1862.

Cyrus Hall McCormick (1809–1884) In 1831, he invented a mechanical reaper to harvest wheat, which transformed the scale of agriculture. By hand a farmer could only harvest a half an acre a day, while the McCormick reaper allowed two people to harvest twelve acres of wheat a day.

McCormick reaper Mechanical reaper invented by Cyrus Hall McCormick in 1831 that dramatically increased the production of wheat.

McCulloch v. Maryland (1819) Supreme Court ruling that prohibited states from taxing the Bank of the United States.

William McKinley (1843–1901) As a congressman, he was responsible for the McKinley Tariff of 1890, which raised the duties on manufactured products to their highest level ever. Voters disliked the tariff and McKinley, as well as other Republicans, lost his seat in Congress the next election. However, he won the presidential election of 1896 and raised the tariffs again. In 1898, he annexed Hawaii and declared war on Spain. The war concluded with the Treaty of Paris, which gave America control over Puerto Rico, Guam, and the Philippines. Soon America was fighting Filipinos, who were seeking independence for their country. In 1901, McKinley was assassinated.

Robert McNamara (1916–) He was the secretary of defense for both President Kennedy and President Johnson and a supporter of America's involvement in Vietnam.

Medicare and Medicaid Health-care programs designed to aid the elderly and disadvantaged, respectively, as part of President Johnson's Great Society initiative.

Andrew W. Mellon (1855–1937) As President Harding's secretary of the Treasury, he sought to generate economic growth through reducing government spending and lowering taxes. However, he insisted that the tax reductions mainly go to the rich because he believed the wealthy would reinvest their money. In order to bring greater efficiency and nonpartisanship to the government's budget process, he persuaded Congress to created a new Bureau of the Budget and a General Accounting Office.

mercantilism Policy of Great Britain and other imperial powers of regulating the economies of colonies to benefit the mother country.

James Meredith (1933–) In 1962, the governor of Mississippi defied a Supreme Court ruling and refused to allow James Meredith, an African American, to enroll at the University of Mississippi. Federal marshals were sent to enforce the law which led to clashes between a white mob and the marshals. Federal troops intervened and two people were killed and many others were injured. A few days later, Meredith was able to register at the university.

Merrimack* (ship renamed the *Virginia*) and the *Monitor First engagement between ironclad ships; fought at Hampton Roads, Virginia, on March 9, 1862.

Metacomet or King Philip (?–1676) The chief of the Wampanoages, who the colonists called King Philip. He resented English efforts to convert Indians to Christianity and waged a war against the English colonists in which he was killed.

Mexica Otherwise known as "Aztecs," a Mesoamerican people of northern Mexico who founded the vast Aztec Empire in the fourteenth century, later conquered by the Spanish under Hernán Cortés in 1521.

microprocessor An electronic circuit printed on a small silicon chip; a major technological breakthrough in 1971, it paved the way for the development of the personal computer.

Middle Passage The hellish and often deadly middle leg of the transatlantic "Triangular Trade" in which European ships carried manufactured goods to Africa, then transported enslaved Africans to the Americas and the Caribbean, and finally conveyed American agricultural products back to Europe; from the late sixteenth to the early nineteenth centuries, some 12 million Africans were transported via the Middle Passage, unknown millions more dying en route.

Battle of Midway A 1942 battle that proved to be a turning point in the Pacific front during World War II; it was the Japanese navy's first major defeat in 350 years.

militant nonviolence After the success of the Montgomery bus boycott, people were inspired by Martin Luther King Jr.'s use of this nonviolent form of protest. Throughout the civil rights movement, demonstrators used this method of protest to challenge racial segregation in the South.

Militia Act (1862) Congressional measure that permitted freed slaves to serve as laborers or soldiers in the United States Army.

Ho Chi Minh (1890–1969) He was the Vietnamese communist resistance leader who drove the French and the United States out of Vietnam. After the Geneva Accords divided the region into four countries, he controlled North Vietnam, and ultimately became the leader of all of Vietnam at the conclusion of the Vietnam War.

minstrelsy A form of entertainment that was popular from the 1830s to the 1870s. The performances featured white performers who were made up as African Americans or blackface. They performed banjo and fiddle music, "shuffle" dances and lowbrow humor that reinforced racial stereotypes.

Minutemen Special units organized by the militia to be ready for quick mobilization.

Miranda v. Arizona **(1966)** U.S. Supreme Court decision required police to advise persons in custody of their rights to legal counsel and against self-incrimination.

Mississippi Plan (1890) Series of state constitutional amendments that sought to severely disenfranchise black voters and were quickly adopted by other southern states.

Missouri Compromise (1820) Legislative decision to admit Missouri as a slave state and abolish slavery in the area west of the Mississippi River and north of the parallel 36°30′.

Model T Ford Henry Ford developed this model of car so that it was affordable for everyone. Its success led to an increase in the production of automobiles which stimulated other related industries such steel, oil, and rubber. The mass use of automobiles increased the speed goods could be transported, encouraged urban sprawl, and sparked real estate booms in California and Florida.

moderate Republicanism Promise to curb federal government and restore state and local government authority, spearheaded by President Eisenhower.

modernism An early-twentieth-century intellectual and artistic movement that rejected traditional notions of reality and adopted radical new forms of artistic expression.

money problem Late-nineteenth-century national debate over the nature of U.S. currency; supporters of a fixed gold standard were generally money lenders, and thus preferred to keep the value of money high, while supporters of silver (and gold) coinage were debtors, they owed money, so they wanted to keep the value of money low by increasing the currency supply (inflation).

monopoly A corporation so large that it effectively controls the entire market for its products or services.

James Monroe (1758–1831) He served as secretary of state and war under President Madison and was elected president. As the latter, he signed the Transcontinental Treaty with Spain which gave the United States Florida and expanded the Louisiana territory's western border to the Pacific coast. In 1823, he established the Monroe Doctrine. This foreign policy proclaimed the American continents were no longer open to colonization and America would be neutral in European affairs.

Monroe Doctrine (1823) U.S. foreign policy that barred further colonization in the Western Hemisphere by European powers and pledged that there would be no American interference with any existing European colonies.

Montgomery bus boycott (1955–1956) Boycott of bus system in Montgomery, Alabama, organized by civil rights activists after the arrest of Rosa Parks.

Moral Majority Televangelist Jerry Falwell's political lobbying organization, the name of which became synonymous with the Religious Right—conservative evangelical Protestants who helped ensure President Ronald Reagan's 1980 victory.

J. Pierpont Morgan (1837–1913) As a powerful investment banker, he would acquire, reorganize, and consolidate companies into giant trusts. His biggest achievement was the consolidation of the steel industry into the United States Steel Corporation, which was the first billion-dollar corporation.

J. Pierpont Morgan and Company An investment bank under the leadership of J. Pierpont Morgan that bought or merged unrelated American companies, often using capital acquired from European investors.

Mormons Members of the Church of Jesus Christ of Latter-day Saints, which dismissed other Christian denominations, emphasizing universal salvation and a modest lifestyle; Mormons were often persecuted for their secrecy and clannishness.

Morrill Land Grant College Act (1862) Federal statute that allowed for the creation of land-grant colleges and universities, which were founded to provide technical education in agriculture, mining, and industry.

Samuel F. B. Morse (1791–1872) In 1832, he invented the telegraph and revolutionized the speed of communication.

mountain men Inspired by the fur trade, these men left civilization to work as trappers and reverted to a primitive existence in the wilderness. They were the first white people to find routes through the Rocky Mountains, and they pioneered trails that settlers later used to reach the Oregon country and California in the 1840s.

muckrakers Writers who exposed corruption and abuses in politics, business, consumer safety, working conditions, and more, spurring public interest in progressive reforms.

Mugwumps Reformers who bolted from the Republican party in 1884 to support Democratic Grover Cleveland for president over Republican James G. Blaine, whose secret dealings on behalf of railroad companies had brought charges of corruption.

mulattoes Mixed-race people who constituted most of the South's free black population.

Benito Mussolini (1883–1945) The Italian founder of the Fascist party who came to power in Italy in 1922 and allied himself with Adolf Hitler and the Axis powers during the Second World War.

National Association for the Advancement of Colored People (NAACP) Organization founded in 1910 by black activists and white progressives that promoted education as a means of combating social problems and focused on legal action to secure the civil rights supposedly guaranteed by the Fourteenth and Fifteenth Amendments.

National Banking Act (1863) The U.S. Congress created a national banking system to finance the enormous expense of the Civil War. It enabled loans to the government and established a single national currency, including the issuance of paper money ("greenbacks").

National Industrial Recovery Act (1933) Passed on the last of the Hundred Days; it created public-works jobs through the Federal Emergency Relief Administration and established a system of self-regulation for industry through the National Recovery Administration, which was ruled unconstitutional in 1935.

National Labor Union (NLU) A federation of labor and reform leaders established in 1866 to advocate for new state and local laws to improve working conditions.

National Recovery Administration (NRA) (1933) Controversial federal agency that brought together business and labor leaders to create "codes of fair competition" and "fair labor" policies, including a national minimum wage.

National Security Act (1947) Congressional legislation that created the Department of Defense, the National Security Council, and the Central Intelligence Agency.

National Socialist German Workers' Party (Nazi) Founded in the 1920s, this party gained control over Germany under the leadership of Adolf Hitler in 1933 and continued in power until Germany's defeat at the end of the Second World War. It advocated a violent anti-Semitic, anti-Marxist, pan-German ideology. The Nazi party perpetrated the Holocaust.

National Trades' Unions Formed in 1834 to organize all local trade unions into a stronger national association, only to be dissolved amid the economic depression during the late 1830s.

nativism Reactionary conservative movement characterized by heightened nationalism, anti-immigrant sentiment, and the enactment of laws setting stricter regulations on immigration.

nativists Members of a reactionary conservative movement characterized by heightened nationalism, anti-immigrant sentiment, and the enactment of laws setting stricter regulations on immigration.

natural rights An individual's basic rights that should not be violated by any government or community.

Navigation Acts (1650–1775) Restrictions passed by the British Parliament to control colonial trade and bolster the mercantile system.

Negrophobia A violent new wave of racism that spread in the late nineteenth century largely spurred by white resentment for African American financial success and growing political influence.

neutrality laws Series of laws passed by Congress aimed at avoiding entering a Second World War; these included the Neutrality Act of 1935, which banned loans to warring nations.

new conservatism The political philosophy of those who led the conservative insurgency of the early 1980s. This brand of conservatism was personified in Ronald Reagan who believed in less government, supply-side economics, and "family values."

New Democrats Centrist ("moderate") Democrats led by President Bill Clinton that emerged in the late 1980s and early 1990s to challenge the "liberal" direction of the party.

"new economy" Period of sustained economic prosperity during the nineties marked by budget surpluses, the explosion of dot.com industries, low inflation, and low unemployment.

New France The name used for the area of North America that was colonized by the French. Unlike Spanish or English colonies, New France had a small number of colonists, which forced them to initially seek good relations with the indigenous people they encountered.

New Freedom Program championed in 1912 by the Woodrow Wilson campaign that aimed to restore competition in the economy by eliminating all trusts rather than simply regulating them.

New Frontier Proposed domestic program championed by the incoming Kennedy administration in 1961 that aimed to jump-start the economy and trigger social progress.

new immigrants Wave of newcomers from southern and eastern Europe, including many Jews, who became a majority among immigrants to America after 1890.

New Jersey Plan The delegations to the Constitutional Convention were divided between two plans on how to structure the government: New Jersey wanted one legislative body with equal representation for each state.

New Left Term coined by the Students for a Democratic Society to distinguish their efforts at grassroots democracy from those of the 1930s Old Left, which had embraced orthodox Marxism.

New Mexico A U.S. territory and later a state in the American Southwest, originally established by the Spanish, who settled there in the sixteenth century, founded Catholic missions, and exploited the region's indigenous peoples.

New Nationalism Platform of the Progressive party and slogan of former President Theodore Roosevelt in the presidential campaign of 1912; stressed government activism, including regulation of trusts, conservation, and recall of state court decisions that had nullified progressive programs.

"New Negro" In the 1920s, a slow and steady growth of black political influence occurred in northern cities where African Americans were freer to speak and act. This political activity created a spirit of protest that expressed itself culturally in the Harlem Renaissance and politically in "new Negro" nationalism.

New Netherland Dutch colony conquered by the English in 1667 and out of which four new colonies were created—New York, New Jersey, Pennsylvania, and Delaware.

Battle of New Orleans (1815) Final major battle in the War of 1812, in which the Americans under General Andrew Jackson unexpectedly and decisively countered the British attempt to seize the port of New Orleans, Louisiana.

New South *Atlanta Constitution* editor Henry W. Grady's 1886 term for the prosperous post–Civil War South: democratic, industrial, urban, and free of nostalgia for the defeated plantation South.

New York Journal In the late 1890s, William Randolph Hearst's *New York Journal* and its rival, the *New York World*, printed sensationalism on the Cuban revolution as part of their heated competition for readership. The *New York Journal* printed a negative letter from the Spanish ambassador about President McKinley and inflammatory coverage of the sinking of the *Maine* in Havana Harbor. These two events roused the American public's outcry against Spain.

New York World In the late 1890s, Joseph Pulitzer's *New York World* and its rival, the *New York Journal*, printed sensationalism on the Cuban revolution as part of their heated competition for readership.

Admiral Chester Nimitz (1885–1966) During the Second World War, he was the commander of central Pacific. Along with General Douglas MacArthur, he dislodged the Japanese military from the Pacific Islands they had occupied.

Nineteenth Amendment (1920) Constitutional amendment that granted women the right to vote.

Richard M. Nixon (1913–1994) He first came to national prominence as a congress-man involved in the investigation of Alger Hiss, and later served as vice president during the Eisenhower administration. After being elected president in 1968, he slowed the federal enforcement of civil rights and appointed pro-Southern justices to the Supreme Court. He began a program of Vietnamization of the war. In 1973, America, North and South Vietnam, and the Viet Cong agreed to end the war and the United States withdrew. However, the cease-fire was broken, and the South Vietnam fell to North Vietnam. In 1970, Nixon declared that America was no longer the world's policeman and he would seek some partnerships with Communist countries, historically traveling to China and the Soviet Union. In 1972, he was reelected, but the Watergate scandal erupted shortly after his victory; he resigned the presidency under threat of impeachment.

No Child Left Behind President George W. Bush's education reform plan that required states to set and meet learning standards for students and make sure that all students were "proficient" in reading and writing by 2014. States had to submit annual reports of students' standardized test scores. Teachers were required to be "proficient" in their subject area. Schools who failed to show progress would face sanctions. States criticized the lack of funding for remedial programs and noted that poor school districts would find it very difficult to meet the new guidelines.

nonviolent civil disobedience Tactic of defying unjust laws through peaceful actions championed by Dr. Martin Luther King Jr.

Lord North (1732–1792) The first minister of King George III's cabinet whose efforts to subdue the colonies only brought them closer to revolution. He helped bring about the Tea Act of 1773, which led to the Boston Tea Party. In an effort to discipline Boston, he wrote, and Parliament passed, four acts that galvanized colonial resistance.

North American Free Trade Agreement (NAFTA) (1994) Agreement eliminating trade barriers that was signed by the United States, Canada, and Mexico, making North America the largest free-trade zone in the world.

North Atlantic Treaty Organization (NATO) Defensive alliance founded in 1949 by ten western European nations, the United States, and Canada to deter Soviet expansion in Europe.

Northwest Ordinance (1787) Land policy for new western territories in the Ohio Valley that established the terms and conditions for self-government and statehood while also banning slavery from the region.

NSC-68 (1950) Top-secret policy paper approved by President Truman that outlined a militaristic approach to combating the spread of global communism.

nullification The right claimed by some states to veto a federal law deemed unconstitutional.

Nuremberg trials At the site of the annual Nazi party rallies, twenty-one major German offenders faced an international military tribunal for Nazi atrocities. After a ten-month trial, the court acquitted three and sentenced eleven to death, three to life imprisonment, and four to shorter terms.

Barack Obama (1961–) In the 2008 presidential election, Senator Barack Obama mounted an innovative Internet based and grassroots orientated campaign. As the nation's economy nose-dived in the fall of 2008, Obama linked the Republican economic philosophy with the country's dismal financial state and promoted a message of "change" and "politics of hope," which resonated with voters. He decisively won the presidency and became America's first person of color to be elected president. In 2012, Obama successfully won re-election to serve as president for a second term.

Occupy Wall Street A grassroots movement protesting a capitalist system that fostered social and economic inequality. Begun in Zuccotti Park, New York City, during 2011, the movement spread rapidly across the nation, triggering a national conversation about income inequality and protests of the government's "bailouts" of the banks and corporations allegedly responsible for the Great Recession.

Sandra Day O'Connor (1930–) She was the first woman to serve on the Supreme Court of the United States and was appointed by President Reagan. Reagan's critics charged that her appointment was a token gesture and not a sign of any real commitment to gender equality.

Ohio gang In order to escape the pressures of the White House, President Harding met with a group of people, called the "Ohio gang," in a house on K Street in Washington D.C. Members of this gang were given low-level positions in the American government and they used their White House connection to "line their pockets" by granting government contracts without bidding, which led to a series of scandals, most notably the Teapot Dome Scandal.

Old Southwest Region covering western Georgia, Alabama, Mississippi, Louisiana, Arkansas, and Texas, where low land prices and fertile soil attracted hundreds of thousands of settlers after the American Revolution.

Frederick Law Olmsted (1822–1903) In 1858, he constructed New York's Central Park, which led to a growth in the movement to create urban parks. He went on to design parks for Boston, Brooklyn, Chicago, Philadelphia, San Francisco, and many other cities.

Open Door policy (1899) Official U.S. insistence that Chinese trade would be open to all nations; Secretary of State John Hay unilaterally announced the policy in hopes of protecting the Chinese market for U.S. exports.

open range Informal system of governing property on the frontier in which small ranchers could graze their cattle anywhere on unfenced lands; brought to an end by the introduction of barbed wire, a low-cost way to fence off one's land.

open shop Business policy of not requiring union membership as a condition of employment; such a policy, where legal, has the effect of weakening unions and diminishing workers' rights.

Operation Desert Shield After Saddam Hussein invaded Kuwait in 1990, President George H. W. Bush sent American military forces to Saudi Arabia on a strictly defensive mission. They were soon joined by a multinational coalition. When the coalition's mission changed to the retaking of Kuwait, the operation was renamed Desert Storm.

Operation Desert Storm (1991) Assault by American-led multinational forces that quickly defeated Iraqi forces under Saddam Hussein in the First Gulf War, ending the Iraqi occupation of Kuwait.

Operation Overlord The Allies' assault on Hitler's "Atlantic Wall," a seemingly impregnable series of fortifications and minefields along the French coastline that German forces had created using captive Europeans for laborers.

J. Robert Oppenheimer (1904–1967) He led the group of physicists at the laboratory in Los Alamos, New Mexico, who constructed the first atomic bomb.

Oregon Country The Convention of 1818 between Britain and the United States established the Oregon Country as being west of the crest of the Rocky Mountains and the two countries were to jointly occupy it. In 1824, the United States and Russia signed a treaty that established the line of 54°40′ as the southern boundary of Russia's territorial claim in North America. A similar agreement between Britain and Russia finally gave the Oregon Country clearly defined boarders, but it remained under joint British and American control.

Oregon fever The lure of fertile land and economic opportunities in the Oregon Country that drew thousands of settlers westward, beginning in the late 1830s.

Osceola (1804?–1838) He was the leader of the Seminole nation who resisted the federal Indian removal policy through a protracted guerilla war. In 1837, he was treacherously seized under a flag of truce and imprisoned at Fort Moultrie, where he was left to die.

Overland Trails Trail routes followed by wagon trains bearing settlers and trade goods from Missouri to the Oregon Country, California, and New Mexico, beginning in the 1840s.

Pacific Railway Act (1862) Congress provided funding for a transcontinental railroad from Nebraska west to California.

A. Mitchell Palmer (1872–1936) As the attorney general, he played an active role in the government's response to the Red Scare. After several bombings across America, including one at Palmer's home, he and other Americans became convinced that there was a well-organized Communist terror campaign at work. The federal government launched a campaign of raids, deportations, and collecting files on radical individuals.

Panic of 1819 A financial panic that began a three-year-long economic crisis triggered by a reduced demand of American imports, declining land values, and reckless practices by local and state banks.

Panic of 1837 A financial calamity in the United States brought on by a dramatic slowdown in the British economy and falling cotton prices, failed crops, high inflation, and reckless state banks.

Panic of 1873 A financial calamity in the United States brought on by a dramatic slowdown in the British economy and exacerbated by falling cotton prices, failed crops, high inflation, and reckless state banks.

Panic of 1893 A major collapse in the national economy after several major railroad companies declared bankruptcy, leading to a severe depression and several violent clashes between workers and management.

panning A method of mining that used a large metal pan to sift gold dust and nuggets from riverbeds during the California gold rush of 1849.

Rosa Parks (1913–2005) In 1955, she refused to give up her seat to a white man on a city bus in Montgomery, Alabama, which a local ordinance required of blacks. She was arrested for disobeying the ordinance. In response, black community leaders organized the Montgomery bus boycott.

Parliament Legislature of Great Britain, composed of the House of Commons, whose members are elected, and the House of Lords, whose members are either hereditary or appointed.

party "boss" A powerful political leader who controlled a "machine" of associates and operatives to promote both individual and party interests, often using informal tactics such as intimidation or the patronage system.

paternalism A moral position developed during the first half of the nineteenth century which claimed that slaves were deprived of liberty for their own "good." Such a rationalization was adopted by some slave owners to justify slavery.

Patriots Colonists who rebelled against British authority before and during the Revolutionary War.

patronage An informal system (sometimes called the "spoils system") used by politicians to reward their supporters with government appointments or contracts.

Alice Paul (1885–1977) She was a leader of the women's suffrage movement and head of the Congressional Committee of National Women Suffrage Association. She instructed female suffrage activists to use more militant tactics, such as picketing state legislatures, chaining themselves to public buildings, inciting police to arrest them, and undertaking hunger strikes.

Norman Vincent Peale (1898–1993) He was a champion of the upbeat and feel-good theology that was popular in the 1950s religious revival. He advocated getting rid of any depressing or negative thoughts and replacing them with "faith, enthusiasm and joy," which would make an individual popular and well liked.

Pearl Harbor (1941) Surprise Japanese attack on the U.S. fleet at Pearl Harbor on December 7, which prompted the immediate American entry into the war.

peculiar institution A phrase used by whites in the antebellum South to refer to slavery without using the word slavery.

Pentagon Papers Informal name for the Defense Department's secret history of the Vietnam conflict; leaked to the press by former official Daniel Ellsberg and published in the *New York Times* in 1971.

People's party (Populists) Political party largely made up of farmers from the South and West that struggled to gain political influence from the East. Populists advocated a variety of reforms, including free coinage of silver, a progressive income tax, postal savings banks, regulation of railroads, and direct election of U.S. senators.

Pequot War Massacre in 1637 and subsequent dissolution of the Pequot Nation by Puritan settlers, who seized the Indians' lands.

perestroika Russian term for "economic restructuring"; applied to Mikhail Gorbachev's series of political and economic reforms that included shifting a centrally planned Commmunist economy to a mixed economy allowing for capitalism.

Commodore Matthew Perry (1794–1858) In 1854, he negotiated the Treaty of Kanagawa, which was the first step in starting a political and commercial relationship between the United States and Japan.

John J. Pershing United States general sent by President Wilson to put down attacks on the Mexican border led by Francisco "Pancho" Villa.

Personal Responsibility and Work Opportunity Act of 1996 (PRWOA) Comprehensive welfare-reform measure, passed by a Republican Congress and signed by President Clinton, that aimed to decrease the size of the "welfare state" by limiting the amount of government aid provided the unemployed so as to encourage recipients to find jobs.

"pet banks" During President Andrew Jackson's fight with the national bank, Jackson resolved to remove all federal deposits from it. To comply with Jackson's demands, Secretary of the Treasury Taney continued to draw on government's accounts in the national bank, but deposit all new federal receipts in state banks. The state banks that received these deposits were called "pet banks."

Pilgrims Puritan Separatists who broke completely with the Church of England and sailed to the New World aboard the *Mayflower*, founding Plymouth Colony on Cape Cod in 1620.

Dien Bien Phu Cluster of Vietnamese villages and site of a major Vietnamese victory over the French in the First Indochina War.

Gifford Pinchot (1865–1946) As the head of the Division of Forestry, he implemented a conservation policy that entailed the scientific management of natural resources to serve the public interest. His work helped start the conservation movement.

Elizabeth Lucas Pinckney (1722? –1793) One of the most enterprising horticulturists in colonial America, she began managing her family's three plantations in South Carolina at the age of sixteen. She had tremendous success growing indigo, which led to many other plantations growing the crop as well.

Pinckney's Treaty Treaty with Spain negotiated by Thomas Pinckney in 1795; established United States boundaries at the Mississippi River and the 31st parallel and allowed open transportation on the Mississippi.

Francisco Pizarro (1478?–1541) In 1531, he lead his Spanish soldiers to Peru and conquered the Inca Empire.

plain white folk Yeoman farmers who lived and worked on their own small farms, growing a food and cash crops to trade for necessities.

plantation mistress Matriarch of a planter's household, responsible for supervising the domestic aspects of the estate.

planters Owners of large farms in the South that were worked by twenty or more slaves and supervised by overseers.

political "machine" A network of political activists and elected officials, usually controlled by a powerful "boss," that attempts to manipulate local politics

James Knox Polk "Young Hickory" (1795–1849) As president, his chief concern was the expansion of the United States. Shortly, after taking office, Mexico broke off relations with the United States over the annexation of Texas. Polk declared war on Mexico and sought to subvert Mexican authority in California. The United States defeated Mexico; and the two nations signed the Treaty of Guadalupe Hidalgo in which Mexico gave up any claims on Texas north of the Rio Grande River and ceded New Mexico and California to the United States.

Pontiac's Rebellion (1763) An Indian attack on British forts and settlements after France ceded to the British its territory east of the Mississippi River, as part of the Treaty of Paris, without consulting France's Indian allies.

popular sovereignty Legal concept by which the white male settlers in a new U.S. territory would vote to decide whether or not to permit slavery.

Populist/People's party Political success of Farmers' Alliance candidates encouraged the formation in 1892 of the People's party (later renamed the Populist party); active until 1912, it advocated a variety of reform issues, including free coinage of silver, income tax, postal savings, regulation of railroads, and direct election of U.S. senators.

Pottawatomie Massacre In retaliation for the "sack of Lawrence," John Brown and his abolitionist cohorts hacked five men to death in the pro-slavery settlement of Pottawatomie, Kansas, on May 24, 1856, triggering a guerrilla war in the Kansas Territory that cost 200 settler lives.

Powhatan Confederacy An alliance of several powerful Algonquian tribes under the leadership of Chief Powhatan, organized into thirty chiefdoms along much of the Atlantic coast in the late sixteenth and early seventeenth centuries.

Chief Powhatan Wahunsonacock He was called Powhatan by the English after the name of his tribe, and was the powerful, charismatic chief of numerous Algonquian-speaking towns in eastern Virginia representing over 10,000 Indians.

pragmatism William James founded this philosophy in the early 1900s. Pragmatists believed that ideas gained their validity not from their inherent truth, but from their social consequences and practical application.

professions Occupations requiring specialized knowledge of some field; the Industrial Revolution and its new organization of labor created an array of professions in the nineteenth century.

Progressive party In the 1912 election, Theodore Roosevelt was unable to secure the Republican nomination for president. He left the Republican party and formed his own party of progressive Republicans, called the "Bull Moose" party (later Progressive party). Roosevelt and Taft split the Republican vote, which allowed Democrat Woodrow Wilson to win.

progressivism A sometimes grassroots and sometimes elite-driven national movement for social and political reforms that called for more government regulation of business, supported by elements of both major political parties during the Progressive Era (1890–1920).

Prohibition National ban on the manufacture and sale of alcohol that lasted from 1920 to 1933, though the law was widely violated and proved too difficult to enforce effectively.

proprietary colonies A colony owned by an individual, rather than a joint-stock company.

Protestant Reformation Sixteenth-century religious movement initiated by Martin Luther, a German monk whose public criticism of corruption in the Roman Catholic Church, and whose teaching that Christians can communicate directly with God, gained a wide following.

pueblos The Spanish term for the adobe cliff dwellings of the indigenous people of the southwestern United States.

Pullman strike (1894) A national strike by the American Railway Union, whose members shut down major railways in sympathy with striking workers in Pullman, Illinois; ended with intervention of federal troops.

Puritans English religious dissenters who sought to "purify" the Church of England of its Catholic practices.

Quakers George Fox founded the Quaker religion in 1647. They rejected the use of formal sacraments and ministry, refused to take oaths and embraced pacifism. Fleeing persecution, they settled and established the colony of Pennsylvania.

race-based slavery Institution that uses racial characteristics and myths to justify enslaving a people.

Radical Republicans Senators and congressmen who, strictly identifying the Civil War with the abolitionist cause, sought swift emancipation of the slaves, punishment of the rebels, and tight controls over the former Confederate states after the war.

railroads Steam-powered vehicles that improved passenger transportation, quickened western settlement, and enabled commercial agriculture in the nineteenth century.

Raleigh's Roanoke Island Colony English expedition of 117 settlers, including Virginia Dare, the first English child born in the New World; colony disappeared from Roanoke Island in the Outer Banks sometime between 1587 and 1590.

A. Philip Randolph (1889–1979) He was the head of the Brotherhood of Sleeping Car Porters who planned a march on Washington D.C. to demand an end to racial discrimination in the defense industries. To stop the march, the Roosevelt administration negotiated an agreement with the Randolph group. The demonstration would be called off and an executive order would be issued that forbid discrimination in defense work and training programs and set up the Fair Employment Practices Committee.

range wars In the late 1800s, conflicting claims over land and water rights triggered violent disputes between farmers and ranchers in parts of the western United States.

Ronald Reagan (1911–2004) In 1980, the former actor and governor of California was elected president. In office, he reduced social spending, cut taxes, and increased defense spending. During his presidency, the federal debt tripled, the federal deficit rose, programs such as housing and school lunches were cut, and the HIV/AIDS crisis grew to prominence in the United States. He signed an arms-control treaty with the Soviet Union in 1987, authorized covert CIA operations in Central America, and in 1986 the Iran-Contra scandal was revealed.

Reaganomics President Reagan's "supply-side" economic philosophy combining tax cuts with the goals of decreased government spending, reduced regulation of business, and a balanced budget.

Reconstruction Finance Corporation (1932) Federal program established under President Hoover to loan money to banks and other corporations to help them avoid bankruptcy.

Red Power Activism by militant Native American groups to protest living conditions on Indian reservations through demonstrations, legal action, and, at times, violence.

First Red Scare Fear among many Americans after the First World War of Communists in particular and noncitizens in general, it was a reaction to the Russian Revolution, mail bombs, strikes, and riots.

redeemers Post–Civil War Democratic leaders who supposedly saved the South from Yankee domination and preserved the primarily rural economy.

Dr. Walter Reed (1851–1902) His work on yellow fever in Cuba led to the discovery that the fever was carried by mosquitoes. This understanding helped develop more effective controls of the worldwide disease.

reform Darwinism A social philosophy developed by Lester Frank War that challenged the ruthlessness of social Darwinism by asserting that humans were not passive pawns of evolutionary forces. Instead, people could actively shape the process of evolutionary social development through cooperation, innovation, and planning.

Reformation European religious movement that challenged the Catholic Church and resulted in the beginnings of Protestant Christianity. During this period, Catholics and Protestants persecuted, imprisoned, tortured, and killed each other in large numbers.

religious right Christian conservatives with a faith-based political agenda that includes prohibition of abortion and allowing prayer in public schools.

reparations As a part of the Treaty of Versailles, Germany was required to confess its responsibility for the First World War and make payments to the victors for the entire expense of the war. These two requirements created a deep bitterness among Germans.

Report on Manufactures First Secretary of the Treasury Alexander Hamilton's 1791 analysis that accurately foretold the future of American industry and proposed tariffs and subsidies to promote it.

republican ideology Political belief in representative democracy in which citizens govern themselves by electing representatives, or legislators, to make key decisions on the citizens' behalf.

republican simplicity Deliberate attitude of humility and frugality, as opposed to monarchical pomp and ceremony, adopted by Thomas Jefferson in his presidency.

Republicans First used during the early nineteenth century to describe supporters of a strict interpretation of the Constitution, which they believed would safeguard individual freedoms and states' rights from the threats posed by a strong central government. The idealist Republican vision of sustaining an agrarian-oriented union was developed largely by Thomas Jefferson.

return to normalcy Campaign promise of Republican presidential candidate Warren G. Harding in 1920, meant to contrast with Woodrow Wilson's progressivism and internationalism.

Paul Revere (1735–1818) On the night of April 18, 1775, British soldiers marched toward Concord to arrest American Revolutionary leaders and seize their depot of supplies. Paul Revere famously rode through the night and raised the alarm about the approaching British troops.

Roaring Twenties The 1920s, an era of social and intellectual revolution in which young people experimented with new forms of recreation and sexuality. The Eastern, urban cultural shift clashed with conservative and insular Midwestern America, which increased the tensions between the two regions.

Jackie Robinson (1919–1972) In 1947, he became the first African American to play major league baseball. He won over fans and players and stimulated the integration of other professional sports.

rock-and-roll music Alan Freed, a disc jockey, noticed white teenagers were buying rhythm and blues records that had been only purchased by African Americans and Hispanic Americans. Freed began playing these records, but called them rock-and-roll records as a way to overcome the racial barrier. As the popularity of the music genre increased, it helped bridge the gap between "white" and "black" music.

John D. Rockefeller (1839–1937) In 1870, he founded the Standard Oil Company of Ohio, which was his first step in creating his vast oil empire. He perfected the idea of a holding company.

Roe v. Wade **(1973)** Landmark Supreme Court decision striking down state laws that banned abortions during the first trimester of pregnancy.

Roman Catholicism The Christian faith and religious practices of the Roman Catholic Church, which exerted great political, economic, and social influence on much of Western Europe and, through the Spanish and Portuguese Empires, on the Americas.

Romanticism Philosophical, literary, and artistic movement of the nineteenth century that was largely a reaction to the rationalism of the previous century; Romantics valued emotion, mysticism, and individualism.

Eleanor Roosevelt (1884–1962) She redefined the role of the presidential spouse and was the first woman to address a national political convention, write a nationally syndicated column and hold regular press conferences. She travelled throughout the nation to promote the New Deal, women's causes, organized labor, and meet with African American leaders.

Franklin Delano Roosevelt (1882–1945) Elected during the Great Depression, Roosevelt sought to help struggling Americans through his New Deal programs that created employment and social programs, such as Social Security. After the bombing of Pearl Harbor, he declared war on Japan and Germany and led the country through most of the Second World War before dying of cerebral hemorrhage.

Theodore Roosevelt (1858–1919) As the assistant secretary of the navy, he supported expansionism, American imperialism, and war with Spain. He led the Rough Riders in Cuba during the war of 1898 and used the notoriety of this military campaign for political gain. As President McKinley's vice president, he succeeded McKinley after his assassination. His forceful foreign policy became known as "big stick diplomacy." Domestically, his policies on natural resources helped start the conservation movement. Unable to win the Republican nomination for president in 1912, he formed his own party of progressive Republicans called the "Bull Moose" party.

religious Right Christian conservatives with a faith-based political agenda that includes allowing prayer in public schools and prohibition of abortion.

Roosevelt Corollary (1904) President Theodore Roosevelt's revision of the Monroe Doctrine (1823) in which he argued that the United States could use military force in Central and South American nations to prevent European nations from intervening in the Western Hemisphere.

Rough Riders The First U.S. Volunteer Cavalry, led in the War of 1898 by Theodore Roosevelt; they were victorious in their only engagement, the Battle of San Juan Hill near Santiago, Cuba, and Roosevelt was celebrated as a national hero, bolstering his political career.

Royal Proclamation of 1763 Proclamation drawing a boundary along the Appalachian Mountains from Canada to Georgia in order to minimize occurrences of settler–Indian violence; colonists were forbidden to go west of the line.

Rust Belt Parts of the midwestern and northeastern United States marked by industrial decline and falling populations during the second half of the twentieth century, exemplified by steel-manufacturing cities in Ohio and Pennsylvania.

Nicola Sacco (1891–1927) In 1920, he and Bartolomeo Vanzetti were Italian immigrants who were arrested for stealing $16,000 and killing a paymaster and his guard. Their trial took place during a time of numerous bombings by anarchists and their judge was openly prejudicial; many liberals and radicals believe that their conviction was based on their political ideas and ethnic origin rather than the evidence against them.

Sacco and Vanzetti case (1921) Trial of two Italian immigrants that occurred at the height of Italian immigration and against the backdrop of numerous terror attacks by anarchists; despite a lack of clear evidence, the two defendants, both self-professed anarchists, were convicted of murder and were executed in 1927.

saloons Bars or taverns where mostly men would gather to drink, eat, relax, play games, and, often, to discuss politics.

salutary neglect Informal British policy during the first half of the eighteenth century that allowed the American colonies considerable freedom to pursue their economic and political interests in exchange for colonial obedience.

Sand Creek Massacre (1864) Colonel Chivington's unprovoked slaughter of the Cheyennes and Arapahos in Colorado, initially reported as a justified battle but soon exposed for the despicable massacre it was.

Sandinista Cuban-sponsored government that came to power in Nicaragua after toppling a corrupt dictator. The State Department believed that the Sandinistas were supplying the leftist Salvadoran rebels with Cuban and Soviet arms. In response, the Reagan administration ordered the CIA to train and supply guerrilla bands of anti-Communist Nicaraguans called Contras. A cease-fire agreement between the Contras and Sandinistas was signed in 1988.

Sandlot Incident Violence occurring during the Great Railroad Strike of 1877, when mobs of frustrated working-class whites in San Francisco attacked Chinese immigrants, blaming them for economic hardship.

General Antonio López de Santa Anna (1794–1876) In 1834, he seized political power in Mexico and became a dictator. In 1835, Texans rebelled against him and he led his army to Texas to crush their rebellion. He captured the mission called the Alamo and killed all of its defenders, which inspired Texans to continue resistance and Americans to volunteer to fight for Texas. The Texans captured Santa Anna during a surprise attack and he bought his freedom by signing a treaty recognizing Texas's independence.

Battles of Saratoga Decisive defeat of 5,000 British troops under General John Burgoyne in several battles near Saratoga, New York, in October 1777; the American victory helped convince France to enter the war on the side of the Patriots.

scalawags White southern Republicans—some former Unionists—who served in Reconstruction governments.

Phyllis Schlafly (1924–2016) A right-wing Republican activist who spearheaded the anti-feminism movement. She believed feminists were "anti-family, anti-children, and pro-abortion." She worked against the equal-rights amendment for women and civil rights protection for gays.

Scopes Trial Highly publicized 1925 trial of a high school teacher in Tennessee for violating a state law that prohibited the teaching of evolution; the trial was seen as the climax of the fundamentalist war on Darwinism.

Winfield Scott (1786–1866) During the Mexican War, he was the American general who captured Mexico City, which ended the war. Using his popularity from his military success, he ran as a Whig party candidate for President.

Sears, Roebuck and Company By the end of the nineteenth century, this company dominated the mail-order industry and helped create a truly national market. Its mail-order catalog and low prices allowed people living in rural areas and small towns to buy products that were previously too expensive or available only to city dwellers.

secession Shortly after President Abraham Lincoln was elected, southern states began dissolving their ties with the United States because they believed Lincoln and the Republican party were a threat to slavery.

Second Bank of the United States (B.U.S) Established in 1816 after the first national bank's charter expired; it stabilized the economy by creating a sound national currency, by making loans to farmers, small manufacturers, and entrepreneurs, and by regulating the ability of state banks to issue their own paper currency.

Second Great Awakening Religious revival movement that arose in reaction to the growth of secularism and rationalist religion; spurred the growth of the Baptist and Methodist churches.

Second Industrial Revolution Beginning in the late nineteenth century, a wave of technological innovations, especially in iron and steel production, steam and electrical power, and telegraphic communications, all of which spurred industrial development and urban growth.

Second New Deal (1935–1938) Expansive cluster of legislation proposed by President Roosevelt that established new regulatory agencies, strengthened the rights of workers to organize unions, and laid the foundation of a federal social welfare system through the creation of Social Security.

second two-party system The political party system in the United States between 1828 and 1854, consisting of Andrew Jackson's Democratic Party and Henry Clay's Whig Party. The first two party system consisted of the Federalist and Democratic-Republican Parties.

Securities and Exchange Commission (1934) Federal agency established to regulate the issuance and trading of stocks and bonds in an effort to avoid financial panics and stock market "crashes."

Seneca Falls Convention (1848) Convention organized by feminists Lucretia Mott and Elizabeth Cady Stanton to promote women's rights and issue the pathbreaking Declaration of Sentiments.

separate but equal Principle underlying legal racial segregation, which was upheld in *Plessy v. Ferguson* (1896) and struck down in *Brown v. Board of Education* (1954).

separation of powers Strict division of the powers of government among three separate branches (executive, legislative, and judicial) which, in turn, check and balance each other.

September 11 On September 11, 2001, Islamic terrorists, who were members of the al Qaeda terrorist organization, hijacked four commercial airliners. Two were flown into the World Trade Center, a third into the Pentagon, and a fourth plane was brought down in Pennsylvania. In response, President George W. Bush launched his "war on terrorism." His administration assembled an international coalition to fight terrorism, which invaded Afghanistan after the country's government would not turn over Osama bin Laden. Bush and Congress passed the U.S.A. Patriot Act, which allowed government agencies to try suspected terrorists in secret military courts and eavesdrop on confidential conversations.

settlement houses Product of the late nineteenth-century movement to offer a broad array of social services in urban immigrant neighborhoods; Chicago's Hull House was one of hundreds of settlement houses that operated by the early twentieth century.

Seventeenth Amendment (1913) Constitutional amendment that provided for the direct election of senators rather than the traditional practice allowing state legislatures to name them.

Shakers Founded by Mother Ann Lee Stanley in England, the United Society of Believers in Christ's Second Appearing settled in Watervliet, New York, in 1774 and subsequently established eighteen additional communes in the Northeast, Indiana, and Kentucky.

share tenants Poor farmers who rented land to farm in exchange for a substantial share of the crop, though they would often have their own horse or mule, tools, and line of credit with a nearby store.

sharecroppers Poor, mostly black farmers who would work an owner's land in return for shelter, seed, fertilizer, mules, supplies, and food, as well as a substantial share of the crop produced.

Share-the-Wealth program Huey Long offered this program as an alternative to the New Deal. The program proposed to confiscate large personal fortunes, which would be used to guarantee every poor family a cash grant of $5,000 and every worker an annual income of $2,500. This program promised to provide pensions, reduce working hours, pay veterans' bonuses, and ensures a college education to every qualified student.

Shays's Rebellion (1786–1787) Storming of the Massachusetts federal arsenal by Daniel Shays and 1,200 armed farmers seeking debt relief from the state legislature through issuance of paper currency and lower taxes.

silent majority Term popularized by President Richard Nixon to describe the great majority of American voters who did not express their political opinions publicly—"the non-demonstrators."

Sixteenth Amendment (1913) Constitutional amendment that authorized the federal income tax.

slave codes Ordinances passed by a colony or state to regulate the behavior of slaves, often including brutal punishments for infractions.

Alfred E. Smith (1873–1944) In the 1928 presidential election, he won the Democratic nomination, but failed to win the presidency. Rural voters distrusted him for being Catholic and the son of Irish immigrants as well as his anti-Prohibition stance.

Captain John Smith (1580–1631) A swashbuckling soldier of fortune with rare powers of leadership and self-promotion, he was appointed to the resident council to manage Jamestown.

Joseph Smith (1805–1844) In 1823, he claimed that the Angel Moroni showed him the location of several gold tablets on which the Book of Mormon was written. Using the Book of Mormon as his gospel, he founded the Church of Jesus Christ of Latter-day Saints, or Mormons. In 1839, they settled in Commerce, Illinois, to avoid persecution. In 1844, Joseph and his brother were arrested and jailed for ordering the destruction of a newspaper that opposed them. While in jail, an anti-Mormon mob stormed the jail and killed both of them.

social Darwinism The application of Charles Darwin's theory of evolutionary natural selection to human society; Social Darwinists used the concept of "survival of the fittest" to justify class distinctions, explain poverty, and oppose government intervention in the economy.

social gospel Protestant movement that stressed the Christian obligation to address the mounting social problems caused by urbanization and industrialization.

social justice An important part of the Progressive's agenda, social justice sought to solve social problems through reform and regulation. Methods used to bring about social justice ranged from the founding of charities to the legislation of a ban on child labor.

Social Security Act (1935) Legislation enacted to provide federal assistance to retired workers through tax-funded pension payments and benefit payments to the unemployed and disabled.

Sons of Liberty First organized by Samuel Adams in the 1770s, groups of colonists dedicated to militant resistance against British control of the colonies.

Hernando de Soto (1500?–1542) A conquistador who explored the west coast of Florida, western North Carolina, and along the Arkansas river from 1539 till his death in 1542.

Southern Christian Leadership Conference (SCLC) Civil rights organization formed by Dr. Martin Luther King Jr., that championed nonviolent direct action as a means of ending segregation.

"southern strategy" This strategy was a major reason for Richard Nixon's victory in the 1968 presidential election. To gain support in the South, Nixon assured southern conservatives that he would slow the federal enforcement of civil rights laws and appoint pro-southern justices to the Supreme Court. As president, Nixon fulfilled these promises.

Spanish Armada A massive Spanish fleet of 130 warships that was defeated at Plymouth in 1588 by the English navy during the reign of Queen Elizabeth I.

Spanish flu Unprecedentedly lethal influenza epidemic of 1918 that killed more than 22 million people worldwide.

Herbert Spencer (1820–1903) As the first major proponent of social Darwinism, he argued that human society and institutions are subject to the process of natural selection and that society naturally evolves for the better. He was against any form of government interference with the evolution of society, like business regulations, because it would help the "unfit" to survive.

spirituals Songs with religious messages sung by slaves to help ease the strain of field labor and to voice their suffering at the hands of their masters and overseers.

spoils system The term—meaning the filling of federal government jobs with persons loyal to the party of the president—originated in Andrew Jackson's first term; the system was replaced in the Progressive Era by civil service.

Square Deal Roosevelt's progressive agenda of the "Three C's": control of corporations, conservation of natural resources, and consumer protection.

stagflation Term coined by economists during the Nixon presidency to describe the unprecedented situation of stagnant economic growth and consumer price inflation occurring at the same time.

Joseph Stalin (1879–1953) The Bolshevik leader who succeeded Lenin as the leader of the Soviet Union in 1924 and ruled the country until his death. During his totalitarian rule of the Soviet Union, he used purges and a system of forced labor camps to maintain control over the country, and claimed vast areas of Eastern Europe for Soviet domination.

Stalwarts Conservative Republican party faction during the presidency of Rutherford B. Hayes, 1877–1881; led by Senator Roscoe B. Conkling of New York, Stalwarts opposed civil service reform and favored a third term for President Ulysses S. Grant.

Stamp Act (1765) Act of Parliament requiring that all printed materials (e.g., newspapers, bonds, and even playing cards) in the American colonies use paper with an official tax stamp in order to pay for British military protection of the colonies.

Stamp Act Congress Twenty-seven delegates from nine of the colonies met from October 7 to 25, 1765 and wrote a Declaration of the Rights and Grievances of the Colonies, a petition to the King and a petition to Parliament for the repeal of the Stamp Act.

Standard Oil Company Corporation under the leadership of John D. Rockefeller that attempted to dominate the entire oil industry through horizontal and vertical integration.

Elizabeth Cady Stanton (1815–1902) A prominent reformer and advocate for the rights of women, she helped organize the Seneca Falls Convention to discuss women's rights. The convention was the first of its kind and produced the Declaration of Sentiments, which proclaimed the equality of men and women.

staple crop A profitable market crop, such as cotton, tobacco, or rice that predominates in a given region.

state constitutions Charters that define the relationship between the state government and local governments and individuals, and also protects their rights from violation by the national government.

steamboats Ships and boats powered by wood-fired steam engines. First used in the early nineteenth century, they made two-way traffic possible in eastern river systems, creating a transcontinental market and an agricultural empire.

Thaddeus Stevens (1792–1868) As one of the leaders of the Radical Republicans, he argued that the former Confederate states should be viewed as conquered provinces, which were subject to the demands of the conquerors. He believed that all of Southern society needed to be changed, and he supported the abolition of slavery and racial equality.

Adlai E. Stevenson (1900–1965) In the 1952 and 1956 presidential elections, he was the Democratic nominee who lost to Dwight Eisenhower. He was also the U.S. Ambassador to the United Nations and is remembered for his famous speech in 1962 before the UN Security Council that unequivocally demonstrated that the Soviet Union had built nuclear missile bases in Cuba.

Stonewall riots (1969) Violent clashes between police and lesbian, gay, bisexual, transgender, and queer (LGBTQ) patrons of New York City's Stonewall Inn, seen as the starting point of the modern LGBTQ rights movement.

Stono Rebellion (1739) A slave uprising in South Carolina that was brutally quashed, leading to executions as well as a severe tightening of the slave code.

Strategic Arms Limitation Talks (SALT I) (1972) Agreement signed by President Nixon and Secretary Brezhnev prohibiting the development of missile defense systems in the United States and Soviet Union and limiting the quantity of nuclear warheads for both.

Strategic Defense Initiative (SDI) (1983) Ronald Reagan's proposed space-based antimissile defense system, dubbed "Star Wars" by the media, that aroused great controversy and escalated the arms race between the United States and the Soviet Union.

Levi Strauss (1829–1902) A Jewish tailor who followed miners to California during the gold rush and began making durable work pants that were later dubbed blue jeans or Levi's.

Student Nonviolent Coordinating Committee (SNCC) Interracial organization formed in 1960 with the goal of intensifying the effort to end racial segregation.

Students for a Democratic Society (SDS) Major organization of the New Left, founded at the University of Michigan in 1960 by Tom Hayden and Al Haber.

suburbia Communities formed from mass migration of middle-class whites from urban centers.

Suez crisis (1956) British, French, and Israeli attack on Egypt after Nasser's seizure of the Suez Canal; President Eisenhower interceded to demand the withdrawal of the British, French, and Israeli forces from the Sinai Peninsula and the canal.

Sun Belt The label for an arc that stretched from the Carolinas to California. During the postwar era, much of the urban population growth occurred in this area.

"surge" In early 2007, President Bush decided he would send a "surge" of new troops to Iraq and implement a new strategy. U.S. forces would shift their focus from offensive operations to the protection of Iraqi civilians from attacks by terrorist insurgents and sectarian militias. While the "surge" reduced the violence in Iraq, Iraqi leaders were still unable to develop a self-sustaining democracy.

Taft-Hartley Labor Act (1947) Congressional legislation that banned "unfair labor practices" by labor unions, required union leaders to sign anti-Communist "loyalty oaths," and prohibited federal employees from going on strike.

Taliban A coalition of ultraconservative Islamists who rose to power in Afghanistan after the Soviets withdrew. The Taliban leaders gave Osama bin Laden a safe haven in their country in exchange for aid in fighting the Northern Alliance, who were rebels opposed to the Taliban. After they refused to turn bin Laden over to the United States, America invaded Afghanistan.

Tammany Hall The "city machine" used by "Boss" Tweed to dominate politics in New York City until his arrest in 1871.

tariff A tax on goods imported from other nations, typically used to protect home industries from foreign competitors and to generate revenue for the federal government.

Tariff of 1816 A cluster of taxes on imports passed by Congress to protect America's emerging iron and textile industries from British competition.

Tariff of 1832 This tariff act reduced the duties on many items, but the tariffs on cloth and iron remained high. South Carolina nullified it along with the tariff of 1828. President Andrew Jackson sent federal troops to the state and asked Congress to grant him the authority to enforce the tariffs. Henry Clay presented a plan of gradually reducing the tariffs until 1842, which Congress passed and ended the crisis.

Tariff of Abominations (1828) Tax on imported goods, including British cloth and clothing, that strengthened New England textile companies but hurt southern consumers, who experienced a decrease in British demand for raw cotton grown in the South.

tariff reform (1887) Effort led by the Democratic party to reduce taxes on imported goods, which Republicans argued were needed to protect American industries from foreign competition.

Troubled Asset Relief Program (TARP) In 2008 President George W. Bush signed into law the bank bailout fund called Troubled Asset Relief Program (TARP), which required the Treasury Department to spend $700 billion to keep banks and other financial institutions from collapsing.

Zachary Taylor (1784–1850) During the Mexican War, he scored two quick victories against Mexico, which made him very popular in America. He used his popularity from his military victories to be elected president as a member of the Whig party, but died before he could complete his term.

Taylorism Labor system based on detailed study of work tasks, championed by Frederick Winslow Taylor, intended to maximize efficiency and profits for employers.

Tea Party Right-wing populist movement, largely made up of middle-class, white male conservatives, that emerged as a response to the expansion of the federal government under the Obama administration.

Teapot Dome Affair (1923) Harding administration scandal in which Secretary of the Interior Albert B. Fall profited from secret leasing of government oil reserves in Wyoming to private oil companies.

Tecumseh (1768–1813) He was a leader of the Shawnee tribe who tried to unite all Indians into a confederation that could defend their hunting grounds. He believed that no land cessions could be made without the consent of all the tribes since they held the land in common. His beliefs and leadership made him seem dangerous to the American government and they waged war on him and his tribe. He was killed at the Battle of the Thames.

Tecumseh's Indian Confederacy A group of Native Americans under leadership of Shawnee leader Tecumseh and his prophet brother Tenskwatawa; its mission of fighting off American expansion was thwarted in the Battle of Tippecanoe (1811), when the confederacy fell apart.

telegraph system System of electronic communication invented by Samuel F. B. Morse that could be transmitted instantaneously across great distances (first used in the 1840s).

Teller Amendment Addition to the congressional war resolution of April 20, 1898, which marked the U.S. entry into the war with Spain; the amendment declared that the United States' goal in entering the war was to ensure Cuba's independence, not to annex Cuba as a territory.

temperance A widespread reform movement, led by militant Christians, focused on reducing the use of alcoholic beverages.

tenements Shabby, low-cost inner-city apartment buildings that housed the urban poor in cramped, unventilated apartments.

Tenochtitlán The capital city of the Aztec Empire. The city was built on marshy islands on the western side of Lake Tetzcoco, which is the site of present-day Mexico City.

Tet offensive (1968) Surprise attack by Viet Cong guerrillas and the North Vietnamese army on U.S. and South Vietnamese forces that shocked the American public and led to widespread sentiment against the war.

Texas Revolution (1835–1836) Conflict between Texas colonists and the Mexican government that resulted in the creation of the separate Republic of Texas in 1836.

textile industry Commercial production of thread, fabric, and clothing from raw cotton in mills in New England during the first half of the nineteenth century, and later in the South in the late nineteenth century.

Thirteenth Amendment (1865) Amendment to the U. S. Constitution that freed all slaves in the United States.

Battle of Tippecanoe (1811) Battle in northern Indiana between U.S. troops and Native American warriors led by Tenskwatawa, the brother of Tecumseh, who had organized an anti-American Indian confederacy to fight American efforts to settle on Indian lands.

tobacco A cash crop grown in the Caribbean as well as the Virginia and Maryland colonies, made increasingly profitable by the rapidly growing popularity of smoking in Europe after the voyages of Columbus.

Gulf of Tonkin incident On August 2 and 4 of 1964, North Vietnamese vessels attacked two American destroyers in the Gulf of Tonkin off the coast of North Vietnam. President Johnson described the attacks as unprovoked. In reality, the U.S. ships were monitoring South Vietnamese attacks on North Vietnamese islands that America advisors had planned. The incident spurred the Tonkin Gulf resolution.

Tonkin Gulf Resolution Congressional action that granted the president unlimited authority to defend U.S. forces abroad, passed in August 1964 after an allegedly unprovoked attack on American warships off the coast of North Vietnam.

Tories Term used by Patriots to refer to Loyalists, or colonists who supported the Crown after the Declaration of Independence.

Townshend Acts Parliamentary measures to extract more revenue from the colonies; the Revenue Act of 1767, which taxed tea, paper, and other colonial imports, was one of the most notorious of these policies.

Trail of Tears (1832–1840) The Cherokees' 800-mile journey from the southern Appalachians to Indian Territory (in present-day Oklahoma); 4,000 people died along the way.

transcendentalism Philosophy of a small group of New England writers and thinkers who advocated personal spirituality, self-reliance, social reform, and harmony with nature.

Transcontinental railroad First line across the continent from Omaha, Nebraska, to Sacramento, California, established in 1869 with the linkage of the Union Pacific and Central Pacific railroads at Promontory, Utah.

Transcontinental Treaty (1819) (Adams-Onís Treaty) Treaty between Spain and the United States that clarified the boundaries of the Louisiana Purchase and arranged the transfer of Florida to the United States in exchange for cash.

Treaty of Ghent Agreement between Great Britain and the United States that ended the War of 1812, signed on December 24, 1814.

Treaty of Guadalupe Hidalgo (1848) Treaty between United States and Mexico that ended the Mexican-American War.

Treaty of Paris (1763) Settlement between Great Britain and France that ended the French and Indian War.

Treaty of Versailles Peace treaty that ended the First World War, forcing Germany to dismantle its military, pay immense war reparations, and give up its colonies around the world.

trench warfare A form of prolonged combat between the entrenched positions of opposing armies, often with little tactical movement.

Battle of Trenton A surprising and pivotal victory for General Washington and American forces in December 1776 that resulted in major British and Hessian losses.

triangular trade A network of trade in which exports from one region were sold to another region, which sent its exports to a third region, which exported its own goods back to the first country or colony.

Harry S. Truman (1884–1972) As President Roosevelt's vice president, he succeeded him after his death near the end of the Second World War. After the war, Truman wrestled with the inflation of both prices and wages, worked with Congress to pass the National Security Act, and banned racial discrimination in the hiring of federal employees and ended racial segregation in the armed forces. In foreign affairs, he established the Truman Doctrine to contain communism, developed the Marshall Plan to rebuild Europe, and sent the U.S. military to defend South Korea after North Korea invaded.

Truman Doctrine (1947) President Truman's program of "containing" communism in Eastern Europe and providing economic and military aid to any nations at risk of Communist takeover.

Donald J. Trump (1946–) The 45th President of the United States.

trust A business arrangement that gives a person or corporation (the "trustee") the legal power to manage another person's money or another company without owning those entities outright.

Sojourner Truth (1797?–1883) She was born into slavery, but New York State freed her in 1827. She spent the 1840s and 1850s travelling across the country and speaking to audiences about her experiences as slave and asking them to support abolition and women's rights.

Harriet Tubman (1820–1913) She was born a slave, but escaped to the North. She then returned to the South nineteen times and guided 300 slaves to freedom.

Frederick Jackson Turner An influential historian who authored the "Frontier Thesis" in 1893, arguing that the existence of an alluring frontier and the experience of persistent westward expansion informed the nation's democratic politics, unfettered economy, and rugged individualism.

Nat Turner (1800–1831) He was the leader of the only slave revolt to get past the planning stages. In August of 1831, the revolt began with the slaves killing the members of Turner's master's household. Then they attacked other neighboring farmhouses and recruited more slaves until the militia crushed the revolt. At least fifty-five whites were killed during the uprising and seventeen slaves were hanged afterwards.

Nat Turner's Rebellion (1831) Insurrection in rural Virginia led by black overseer Nat Turner, who killed slave owners and their families; in turn, federal troops indiscriminately killed hundreds of slaves in the process of putting down Turner and his rebels.

Tuskegee Airmen U.S. Army Air Corps unit of African American pilots whose combat success spurred military and civilian leaders to desegregate the armed forces after the war.

Mark Twain (1835–1910) Born Samuel Langhorne Clemens in Missouri, he became a popular humorous writer and lecturer and established himself as one of the great American satirists and authors. His two greatest books, *The Adventures of Tom Sawyer* and *The Adventures of Huckleberry Finn*, drew heavily on his childhood in Missouri.

"Boss" Tweed (1823–1878) An infamous political boss in New York City, Tweed used his "city machine," the Tammany Hall ring, to rule, plunder and sometimes improve the city's government. His political domination of New York City ended with his arrest in 1871 and conviction in 1873.

Twenty-first Amendment (1933) Repealed prohibition on the manufacture, sale, and transportation of alcoholic beverages, effectively nullifying the Eighteenth Amendment.

two-party system Domination of national politics by two major political parties, such as the Whigs and Democrats during the 1830s and 1840s.

U-boat German military submarine (*Unterseeboot*) used during the First World War to attack enemy naval vessels as well as merchant ships of enemy and neutral nations.

Underground Railroad A secret system of routes and safe houses through which runaway slaves were led to freedom in the North.

Unitarians Members of the liberal New England Congregationalist offshoot, often well-educated and wealthy, who profess the oneness of God and the goodness of rational man.

United Farm Workers (UFW) Organization formed in 1965 to represent the interests of Mexican American migrant workers.

United Nations Security Council A major agency within the United Nations which remains in permanent session and has the responsibility of maintaining international peace and security. Originally, it consisted of five permanent members, (United States, Soviet Union, Britain, France, and the Republic of China), and six members elected to two-year terms. After 1965, the number of rotating members was increased to ten. In 1971, the Republic of China was replaced with the People's Republic of China and the Soviet Union was replaced by the Russian Federation in 1991.

Universalists Members of a New England religious movement, often from the working class, who believed in a merciful God and universal salvation.

USA Patriot Act (2001) Wide-reaching Congressional legislation, triggered by the war on terror, which gave government agencies the right to eavesdrop on confidential conversations between prison inmates and their lawyers and permitted suspected terrorists to be tried in secret military courts.

utopian communities Ideal communities that offered innovative social and economic relationships to those who were interested in achieving salvation.

Valley Forge American military encampment near Philadelphia, where more than 3,500 soldiers deserted or died from cold and hunger in the winter of 1777–1778.

Cornelius Vanderbilt (1794–1877) In the 1860s, he consolidated several separate railroad companies into one vast entity, New York Central Railroad.

Bartolomeo Vanzetti (1888–1927) In 1920, he and Nicola Sacco were Italian immigrants who were arrested for stealing $16,000 and killing a paymaster and his guard. Their trial took place during a time of numerous bombings by anarchists and their judge was openly prejudicial. Many liberals and radicals believe that their conviction was based on their political ideas and ethnic origin rather than the evidence against them.

vertical integration The process by which a corporation gains control of all aspects of the resources and processes needed to produce and sell a product.

Amerigo Vespucci (1455–1512) Italian explorer who reached the New World in 1499 and was the first to suggest that South America was a new continent. Afterward, European mapmakers used a variant of his first name, America, to label the New World.

Battle of Vicksburg (1863) A protracted battle in northern Mississippi in which Union forces under Ulysses Grant besieged the last major Confederate fortress on the Mississippi River, forcing the inhabitants into starvation and then submission.

Viet Cong Communist guerrillas in Vietnam who launched attacks on the Diem government.

Vietnamization Nixon-era policy of equipping and training South Vietnamese forces to take over the burden of combat from U.S. troops.

Vikings Norse people from Scandinavia who sailed to Newfoundland about a.d. 1001.

Francisco Pancho Villa (1877–1923) While the leader of one of the competing factions in the Mexican civil war, he provoked the United States into intervening. He hoped attacking the United States would help him build a reputation as an opponent of the United States, which would increase his popularity and discredit Mexican President Carranza.

Virginia Company A joint stock enterprise that King James I chartered in 1606. The company was to spread Christianity in the New World as well as find ways to make a profit in it.

Virginia Plan The delegations to the Constitutional Convention were divided between two plans on how to structure the government: Virginia called for a strong central government and a two-house legislature apportioned by population.

Virginia Statute of Religious Freedom A Virginia law, drafted by Thomas Jefferson in 1777 and enacted in 1786, that guarantees freedom of, and from, religion.

virtual representation The idea that the American colonies, although they had no actual representative in Parliament, were "virtually" represented by all members of Parliament.

Voting Rights Act of 1965 Legislation ensuring that all Americans were able to vote; the law ended literacy tests and other means of restricting voting rights.

Wagner Act (1935) Legislation that guaranteed workers the right to organize unions, granted them direct bargaining power, and barred employers from interfering with union activities.

George Wallace (1919–1998) An outspoken defender of segregation. As the governor of Alabama, he once attempted to block African American students from enrolling at the University of Alabama. He ran as the presidential candidate for the American Independent party in 1968, appealing to voters who were concerned about rioting anti-war protestors, the welfare system, and the growth of the federal government.

war hawks In 1811, congressional members from the southern and western districts who clamored for a war to seize Canada and Florida were dubbed "war hawks."

War of 1812 (1812–1815) Conflict fought in North America and at sea between Great Britain and the United States over American shipping rights and British efforts to spur Indian attacks on American settlements. Canadians and Native Americans also fought in the war.

war on terror Global crusade to root out anti-American, anti-Western Islamist terrorist cells launched by President George W. Bush as a response to the 9/11 attacks.

War Powers Act (1973) Legislation requiring the president to inform Congress within 48 hours of the deployment of U.S. troops abroad and to withdraw them after 60 days unless Congress approves their continued deployment.

War Production Board Federal agency created by President Roosevelt in 1942 that converted America's industrial output to war production.

war relocation camps Detention camps housing thousands of Japanese Americans from the West Coast who were forcibly interned from 1942 until the end of the Second World War.

Warren Court The U.S. Supreme Court under Chief Justice Earl Warren, 1953–1969, decided such landmark cases as *Brown v. Board of Education* (school desegregation), *Baker v. Carr* (legislative redistricting), and *Gideon v. Wainwright* and *Miranda v. Arizona* (rights of criminal defendants).

Booker T. Washington (1856–1915) He founded a leading college for African Americans in Tuskegee, Alabama, and become the foremost black educator in America by the 1890s. He believed that the African American community should establish an economic base for its advancement before striving for social equality. His critics charged that his philosophy sacrificed educational and civil rights for dubious social acceptance and economic opportunities.

George Washington (1732–1799) In 1775, the Continental Congress named him the commander in chief of the Continental Army which defeated the British in the American Revolution. He had previously served as an officer in the French and Indian War. In 1787, he was the presiding officer over the Constitutional Convention, but participated little in the debates. In 1789, the Electoral College chose Washington to be the nation's first president. Washington faced the nation's first foreign and domestic crises, maintaining the United States' neutrality in foreign affairs. After two terms in office, Washington chose to step down; and the power of the presidency was peacefully passed to John Adams.

Watergate (1972–1974) Scandal that exposed the criminality and corruption of the Nixon administration and ultimately led to President Nixon's resignation in 1974.

weapons of mass destruction (WMDs) Radioactive, chemical, or biological weapons capable of unleashing mass death and damage. The Bush administration believed Saddam Hussein to possess such weapons, which it used to justify the second U.S invasion of Iraq during the War on Terror following the 9/11 terrorist bombings.

Daniel Webster (1782–1852) As a representative from New Hampshire, he led the New Federalists in opposition to the moving of the second national bank from Boston to Philadelphia. Later, he served as representative and a senator for Massachusetts and emerged as a champion of a stronger national government. He also switched from opposing to supporting tariffs because New England had built up its manufactures with the understanding tariffs would protect them from foreign competitors.

Webster-Ashburton Treaty Settlement in 1842 of U.S.–Canadian border disputes in Maine, New York, Vermont, and in the Wisconsin Territory (now northern Minnesota).

Webster-Hayne debate U.S. Senate debate of January 1830 between Daniel Webster of Massachusetts and Robert Hayne of South Carolina over nullification and states' rights.

Western Front The contested frontier between the Central and Allied Powers that ran along northern France and across Belgium.

Whig party Political party founded in 1834 in opposition to the Jacksonian Democrats; Whigs supported federal funding for internal improvements, a national bank, and high tariffs on imported goods.

Whigs Another name for revolutionary Patriots.

Whiskey Rebellion (1794) Violent protest by western Pennsylvania farmers against the federal excise tax on corn whiskey, put down by a federal army.

Eli Whitney (1765–1825) He invented the cotton gin which could separate cotton from its seeds. One machine operator could separate fifty times more cotton than worker could by hand, which led to an increase in cotton production and prices. These increases gave planters a new profitable use for slavery and a lucrative slave trade emerged from the coastal South to the Southwest.

Wilderness Road Originally an Indian path through the Cumberland Gap, it was used by over 300,000 settlers who migrated westward to Kentucky in the last quarter of the eighteenth century.

Roger Williams (1603–1683) Puritan who believed that the purity of the church required a complete separation between church and state and freedom from coercion in matters of faith. In 1636, he established the town of Providence, the first permanent settlement in Rhode Island and the first to allow religious freedom in America.

Wendell L. Willkie (1892–1944) In the 1940 presidential election, he was the Republican nominee who ran against President Roosevelt. He supported aid to the Allies and criticized the New Deal programs. Voters looked at the increasingly dangerous world situation and chose to keep President Roosevelt in office for a third term.

Wilmot Proviso (1846) Proposal by Congressman David Wilmot, a Pennsylvania Democrat, to prohibit slavery in any land acquired in the Mexican-American War.

Woodrow Wilson (1856–1924) In the 1912 presidential election, Woodrow Wilson ran under the slogan of New Freedom, which promised to improve of the banking system, lower tariffs, and break up monopolies. At the beginning of the First World War, Wilson kept America neutral, but provided the Allies with credit for purchases of supplies; however, the sinking of U.S. merchant ships and the Zimmerman telegram caused him to ask Congress to declare war on Germany. Wilson supported the entry of America into the League of Nations and the ratification of the Treaty of Versailles, but Congress would not approve the entry or ratification.

John Winthrop Puritan leader and Governor of the Massachusetts Bay Colony who resolved to use the colony as a refuge for persecuted Puritans and as an instrument of building a "wilderness Zion" in America.

women's suffrage Movement to give women the right to vote through a constitutional amendment, spearheaded by Susan B. Anthony and Elizabeth Cady Stanton's National Woman Suffrage Association.

Women Accepted for Voluntary Emergency Services (WAVES) During the Second World War, the increased demand for labor shook up old prejudices about gender roles in the workplace and in the military. Nearly 200,000 women served in the Women's Army Corps or its naval equivalent, Women Accepted for Volunteer Emergency Service (WAVES).

Women's Army Corps Women's branch of the United States Army; by the end of the Second World War nearly 150,000 women had served in the WAC.

women's movement Wave of activism sparked by Betty Friedan's *The Feminine Mystique* (1963); it argued for equal rights for women and fought against the cult of domesticity of the 1950s that limited women's roles to the home as wife, mother, and housewife.

women's work The traditional term referring to routine tasks in the house, garden, and fields performed by women. The sphere of women's occupations expanded in the colonies to include medicine, shopkeeping, upholstering, and the operation of inns and taverns.

Woodstock In 1969, roughly a half a million young people converged on a farm near Bethel, New York, for a three-day music festival that was an expression of the flower children's free spirit.

Works Progress Administration (1935) Government agency established to manage several federal job programs created under the New Deal; the WPA became the largest employer in the nation.

Battle of Wounded Knee Last incident of the Indians Wars took place in 1890 in the Dakota Territory, where the U.S. Cavalry killed over 200 Sioux men, women, and children who were in the process of surrender.

XYZ affair French foreign minister Tallyrand's three anonymous agents demanded payments to stop French plundering of American ships in 1797; refusal to pay the bribe led to two years of sea war with France (1798–1800).

Yalta Conference (1945) Meeting of the "Big Three" Allied leaders, Franklin D. Roosevelt, Winston Churchill, and Joseph Stalin, to discuss how to divide control of postwar Germany and Eastern Europe

yellow journalism A type of news reporting, epitomized in the 1890s by the newspaper empires of William Randolph Hearst and Joseph Pulitzer, that intentionally manipulates public opinion through sensational headlines, illustrations, and articles about both real and invented events.

yeomen Small landowners (the majority of white families in the South) who farmed their own land and usually did not own slaves.

Battle of Yorktown Last major battle of the Revolutionary War; General Cornwallis along with over 7,000 British troops surrendered to George Washington at Yorktown, Virginia, on October 17, 1781.

Brigham Young (1801–1877) Following Joseph Smith's death, he became the leader of the Mormons and promised Illinois officials that the Mormons would leave the state. In 1846, he led the Mormons to Utah and settled near the Salt Lake. After the United States gained Utah as part of the Treaty of Guadalupe Hidalgo, he became the governor of the territory and kept the Mormons virtually independent of federal authority.

youth culture The youth of the 1950s had more money and free time than any previous generation which allowed a distinct youth culture to emerge. A market emerged for products and activities that were specifically for young people such as transistor radios, rock records, *Seventeen* magazine, and Pat Boone movies.

Zimmermann telegram Message sent by a German official to the Mexican government in 1917 urging an invasion of the United States; the telegram was intercepted by British intelligence agents and angered Americans, many of whom called for war against Germany.

APPENDIX

THE DECLARATION OF INDEPENDENCE (1776)

When in the Course of human events, it becomes necessary for one people to dissolve the political bands which have connected them with another, and to assume among the powers of the earth, the separate and equal station to which the Laws of Nature and of Nature's God entitle them, a decent respect to the opinions of mankind requires that they should declare the causes which impel them to the separation.

We hold these truths to be self-evident, that all men are created equal, that they are endowed by their Creator with certain unalienable Rights, that among these are Life, Liberty and the pursuit of Happiness. —That to secure these rights, Governments are instituted among Men, deriving their just powers from the consent of the governed, —That whenever any Form of Government becomes destructive of these ends, it is the Right of the People to alter or to abolish it, and to institute new Government, laying its foundation on such principles and organizing its powers in such form, as to them shall seem most likely to effect their Safety and Happiness. Prudence, indeed, will dictate that Governments long established should not be changed for light and transient causes; and accordingly all experience hath shewn, that mankind are more disposed to suffer, while evils are sufferable, than to right themselves by abolishing the forms to which they are accustomed. But when a long train of abuses and usurpations, pursuing invariably the same Object evinces a design to reduce them under absolute Despotism, it is their right, it is their duty, to throw off such Government, and to provide new Guards for their future security.—Such has been the patient sufferance of these Colonies; and such is now the necessity which constrains them to alter their former Systems of Government. The history of the present King of Great Britain is a history of repeated injuries and usurpations, all having in direct object the establishment of an absolute Tyranny over these States. To prove this, let Facts be submitted to a candid world.

He has refused his Assent to Laws, the most wholesome and necessary for the public good.

He has forbidden his Governors to pass Laws of immediate and pressing importance, unless suspended in their operation till his Assent should be obtained; and when so suspended, he has utterly neglected to attend to them.

He has refused to pass other Laws for the accommodation of large districts of people, unless those people would relinquish the right of Representation in the Legislature, a right inestimable to them and formidable to tyrants only.

He has called together legislative bodies at places unusual, uncomfortable, and distant from the depository of their public Records, for the sole purpose of fatiguing them into compliance with his measures.

He has dissolved Representative Houses repeatedly, for opposing with manly firmness his invasions on the rights of the people.

He has refused for a long time, after such dissolutions, to cause others to be elected; whereby the Legislative powers, incapable of Annihilation, have returned to the People at large for their exercise; the State remaining in the mean time exposed to all the dangers of invasion from without, and convulsions within.

He has endeavoured to prevent the population of these States; for that purpose obstructing the Laws for Naturalization of Foreigners; refusing to pass others to encourage their migrations hither, and raising the conditions of new Appropriations of Lands.

He has obstructed the Administration of Justice, by refusing his Assent to Laws for establishing Judiciary powers.

He has made Judges dependent on his Will alone, for the tenure of their offices, and the amount and payment of their salaries.

He has erected a multitude of New Offices, and sent hither swarms of Officers to harrass our people, and eat out their substance.

He has kept among us, in times of peace, Standing Armies without the Consent of our legislatures.

He has affected to render the Military independent of and superior to the Civil power.

He has combined with others to subject us to a jurisdiction foreign to our constitution, and unacknowledged by our laws; giving his Assent to their Acts of pretended Legislation:

For quartering large bodies of armed troops among us:

For protecting them, by a mock Trial, from punishment for any Murders which they should commit on the Inhabitants of these States:

For cutting off our Trade with all parts of the world:

For imposing Taxes on us without our Consent:

For depriving us in many cases, of the benefits of Trial by Jury:

For transporting us beyond Seas to be tried for pretended offences

For abolishing the free System of English Laws in a neighbouring Province, establishing therein an Arbitrary government, and enlarging its Boundaries so as to render it at once an example and fit instrument for introducing the same absolute rule into these Colonies:

For taking away our Charters, abolishing our most valuable Laws, and altering fundamentally the Forms of our Governments:

For suspending our own Legislatures, and declaring themselves invested with power to legislate for us in all cases whatsoever.

He has abdicated Government here, by declaring us out of his Protection and waging War against us.

He has plundered our seas, ravaged our Coasts, burnt our towns, and destroyed the lives of our people.

He is at this time transporting large Armies of foreign Mercenaries to compleat the works of death, desolation and tyranny, already begun with circumstances of Cruelty & perfidy scarcely paralleled in the most barbarous ages, and totally unworthy the Head of a civilized nation.

He has constrained our fellow Citizens taken Captive on the high Seas to bear Arms against their Country, to become the executioners of their friends and Brethren, or to fall themselves by their Hands.

He has excited domestic insurrections amongst us, and has endeavoured to bring on the inhabitants of our frontiers, the merciless Indian Savages, whose known rule of warfare, is an undistinguished destruction of all ages, sexes and conditions.

In every stage of these Oppressions We have Petitioned for Redress in the most humble terms: Our repeated Petitions have been answered only by repeated injury. A Prince whose character is thus marked by every act which may define a Tyrant, is unfit to be the ruler of a free people.

Nor have We been wanting in attentions to our Brittish brethren. We have warned them from time to time of attempts by their legislature to extend an unwarrantable jurisdiction over us. We have reminded them of the circumstances of our emigration and settlement here. We have appealed to their native justice and magnanimity, and we have conjured them by the ties of our common kindred to disavow these usurpations, which, would inevitably interrupt our connections and correspondence. They too have been deaf to the voice of justice and of consanguinity. We must, therefore, acquiesce in the necessity, which denounces our Separation, and hold them, as we hold the rest of mankind, Enemies in War, in Peace Friends.

We, therefore, the Representatives of the united States of America, in General Congress, Assembled, appealing to the Supreme Judge of the world for the rectitude of our intentions, do, in the Name, and by Authority of the good People of these Colonies, solemnly publish and declare, That these United Colonies are, and of Right ought to be Free and Independent States; that they are Absolved from all Allegiance to the British Crown, and that all political connection between them and the State of Great Britain, is and ought to be totally dissolved; and that as Free and Independent States, they have full Power to levy War, conclude Peace, contract Alliances, establish Commerce, and to do all other Acts and Things which Independent States may of right do. And for the support of this Declaration, with a firm reliance on the protection of divine Providence, we mutually pledge to each other our Lives, our Fortunes and our sacred Honor.

Georgia
Button Gwinnett
Lyman Hall
George Walton

North Carolina
William Hooper
Joseph Hewes
John Penn

South Carolina
Edward Rutledge
Thomas Heyward, Jr.
Thomas Lynch, Jr.
Arthur Middleton

Massachusetts
John Hancock

Maryland
Samuel Chase
William Paca
Thomas Stone
Charles Carroll of
   Carrollton

Virginia
George Wythe
Richard Henry Lee
Thomas Jefferson
Benjamin Harrison
Thomas Nelson, Jr.
Francis Lightfoot Lee
Carter Braxton

Pennsylvania
Robert Morris
Benjamin Rush
Benjamin Franklin
John Morton
George Clymer
James Smith
George Taylor
James Wilson
George Ross

Delaware
Caesar Rodney
George Read
Thomas McKean

New York
William Floyd
Philip Livingston
Francis Lewis
Lewis Morris

New Jersey
Richard Stockton
John Witherspoon
Francis Hopkinson
John Hart
Abraham Clark

New Hampshire
Josiah Bartlett
William Whipple

Massachusetts
Samuel Adams
John Adams
Robert Treat Paine
Elbridge Gerry

Rhode Island
Stephen Hopkins
William Ellery

Connecticut
Roger Sherman
Samuel Huntington
William Williams
Oliver Wolcott

New Hampshire
Matthew Thornton

ARTICLES OF CONFEDERATION (1787)

To ALL TO WHOM these Presents shall come, we the undersigned Delegates of the States affixed to our Names send greeting.

Whereas the Delegates of the United States of America in Congress assembled did on the fifteenth day of November in the Year of our Lord One Thousand Seven Hundred and Seventy-seven, and in the Second Year of the Independence of America agree to certain articles of Confederation and perpetual Union between the States of Newhampshire, Massachusetts-bay, Rhodeisland and Providence Plantations, Connecticut, New York, New Jersey, Pennsylvania, Delaware, Maryland, Virginia, North-Carolina, South-Carolina and Georgia in the Words following, viz.

Articles of Confederation and perpetual Union between the States of Newhampshire, Massachusetts-bay, Rhodeisland and Providence Plantations, Connecticut, New-York, New-Jersey, Pennsylvania, Delaware, Maryland, Virginia, North-Carolina, South-Carolina and Georgia.

ARTICLE I. The stile of this confederacy shall be "The United States of America."

ARTICLE II. Each State retains its sovereignty, freedom and independence, and every power, jurisdiction and right, which is not by this confederation expressly delegated to the United States, in Congress assembled.

ARTICLE III. The said States hereby severally enter into a firm league of friendship with each other, for their common defence, the security of their liberties, and their mutual and general welfare, binding themselves to assist each other, against all force offered to, or attacks made upon them, or any of them, on account of religion, sovereignty, trade or any other pretence whatever.

ARTICLE IV. The better to secure and perpetuate mutual friendship and intercourse among the people of the different States in this Union, the free inhabitants of each of these States, paupers, vagabonds and fugitives from justice excepted, shall be entitled to all privileges and immunities of free citizens in the several States; and the people of each State shall have free ingress and regress to and from any other State, and shall enjoy therein all the privileges of trade and commerce, subject to the same duties, impositions and restrictions as the inhabitants thereof respectively, provided that such restrictions shall not extend so far as to prevent the removal of property imported into any State, to any other State of which the owner is an inhabitant; provided also that no imposition, duties or restriction shall be laid by any State, on the property of the United States, or either of them.

If any person guilty of, or charged with treason, felony, or other high misdemeanor in any State, shall flee from justice, and be found in any of the United States, he shall upon demand of the Governor or Executive power, of the State from which he fled, be delivered up and removed to the State having jurisdiction of his offence.

Full faith and credit shall be given in each of these States to the records, acts and judicial proceedings of the courts and magistrates of every other State.

ARTICLE V. For the more convenient management of the general interests of the United States, delegates shall be annually appointed in such manner as the legislature of each State shall direct, to meet in Congress on the first Monday in November, in every year, with a power reserved to each State, to recall its delegates, or any of them, at any time within the year, and to send others in their stead, for the remainder of the year.

No State shall be represented in Congress by less than two, nor by more than seven members; and no person shall be capable of being a delegate for more than three years in any term of six years; nor shall any person, being a delegate, be capable of holding any office under the United States, for which he, or another for his benefit receives any salary, fees or emolument of any kind.

Each State shall maintain its own delegates in a meeting of the States, and while they act as members of the committee of the States.

In determining questions in the United States, in Congress assembled, each State shall have one vote.

Freedom of speech and debate in Congress shall not be impeached or questioned in any court, or place out of Congress, and the members of Congress shall be protected in their persons from arrests and imprisonments, during the time of their going to and from, and attendance on Congress, except for treason, felony, or breach of the peace.

ARTICLE VI. No State without the consent of the United States in Congress assembled, shall send any embassy to, or receive any embassy from, or enter into any conference, agreement, alliance or treaty with any king, prince or state; nor shall any person holding any office of profit or trust under the United States, or any of them, accept of any present, emolument, office or title of any kind whatever from any king, prince or foreign state; nor shall the United States in Congress assembled, or any of them, grant any title of nobility.

No two or more States shall enter into any treaty, confederation or alliance whatever between them, without the consent of the United States in Congress assembled, specifying accurately the purposes for which the same is to be entered into, and how long it shall continue.

No State shall lay any imposts or duties, which may interfere with any stipulations in treaties, entered into by the United States in Congress assembled, with any king, prince or state, in pursuance of any treaties already proposed by Congress, to the courts of France and Spain.

No vessels of war shall be kept up in time of peace by any State, except such number only, as shall be deemed necessary by the United States in Congress assembled, for the defence of such State, or its trade; nor shall any body of forces be kept up by any State, in time of peace, except such number only, as in the judgment of the United States, in Congress assembled, shall be deemed requisite to garrison the forts necessary for the defence of such State; but every State shall always keep up a well regulated and disciplined militia, sufficiently armed and accoutred, and shall provide and constantly have ready for use, in public stores, a due number of field pieces and tents, and a proper quantity of arms, ammunition and camp equipage.

No State shall engage in any war without the consent of the United States in Congress assembled, unless such State be actually invaded by enemies, or shall have received certain advice of a resolution being formed by some nation of Indians to invade such State, and the danger is so imminent as not to admit of a delay, till the United States in Congress assembled can be consulted: nor shall any State grant commissions to any ships or vessels of war, nor letters of marque or reprisal, except it be after a declaration of war by the United States in Congress assembled, and then only against the kingdom or state and the subjects thereof, against which war has been so declared, and under such regulations as shall be established by the United States in Congress assembled, unless such State be infested by pirates, in which case vessels of war may be fitted out for that occasion, and kept so long as the danger shall continue, or until the United States in Congress assembled shall determine otherwise.

ARTICLE VII. When land-forces are raised by any State of the common defence, all officers of or under the rank of colonel, shall be appointed by the Legislature of each State respectively by whom such forces shall be raised, or in such manner as such State shall direct, and all vacancies shall be filled up by the State which first made the appointment.

ARTICLE VIII. All charges of war, and all other expenses that shall be incurred for the common defence or general welfare, and allowed by the United States in Congress assembled, shall be defrayed out of a common treasury, which shall be supplied by the several States, in proportion to the value of all land within each State, granted to or surveyed for any person, as such land and the buildings and improvements thereon shall be estimated according to such mode as the United States in Congress assembled, shall from time to time direct and appoint.

The taxes for paying that proportion shall be laid and levied by the authority and direction of the Legislatures of the several States within the time agreed upon by the United States in Congress assembled.

ARTICLE IX. The United States in Congress assembled, shall have the sole and exclusive right and power of determining on peace and war, except in the cases mentioned in the sixth article—of sending and receiving ambassadors— entering into treaties and alliances, provided that no treaty of commerce shall be made whereby the legislative power of the respective States shall be restrained from imposing such imposts and duties on foreigners, as their own people are subjected to, or from prohibiting the exportation or importation of and species of goods or commodities whatsoever—of establishing rules for deciding in all cases, what captures on land or water shall be legal, and in what manner prizes taken by land or naval forces in the service of the United States shall be divided or appropriated—of granting letters of marque and reprisal in times of peace—appointing courts for the trial of piracies and felonies committed on the high seas and establishing courts for receiving and determining finally appeals in all cases of captures, provided that no member of Congress shall be appointed a judge of any of the said courts.

The United States in Congress assembled shall also be the last resort on appeal in all disputes and differences now subsisting or that hereafter may arise between two or more States concerning boundary, jurisdiction or any other cause whatever; which authority shall always be exercised in the manner following. Whenever the legislative or executive authority or lawful agent of any State in controversy with another shall present a petition to Congress, stating the matter in question and praying for a hearing, notice thereof shall be given by order of Congress to the legislative or executive authority of the other State in controversy, and a day assigned for the appearance of the parties by their lawful agents, who shall then be directed to appoint by joint consent, commissioners or judges to constitute a court for hearing and determining the matter in question: but if they cannot agree, Congress shall name three persons out of each of the United States, and from the list of such persons each party shall alternately strike out one, the petitioners beginning, until the number shall be reduced to thirteen; and from that number not less than seven, nor more than nine names as Congress shall direct, shall in the presence of Congress be drawn out by lot, and the persons whose names shall be so drawn or any five of them, shall be commissioners or judges, to hear and finally determine the controversy, so always as a major part of the judges who shall hear the cause shall agree in the determination: and if either party shall neglect to attend at the day appointed, without reasons, which Congress shall judge sufficient, or being present shall refuse to strike, the Congress shall proceed to nominate three persons out of each State, and the Secretary of Congress shall strike in behalf of such party absent or refusing; and the judgment and sentence of the court to be appointed, in the manner before prescribed, shall be final and conclusive; and if any of the parties shall refuse to submit to the authority of such court, or to appear or defend their claim or cause, the court shall nevertheless proceed to pronounce sentence, or judgment, which shall in like manner be final and decisive, the judgment or sentence and other proceedings being in either case transmitted to Congress, and lodged among the acts of Congress for the security of the parties concerned: provided that every commissioner, before he sits in judgment, shall take an oath to be administered by one of the judges of the supreme or superior court of the State where the case shall be tried, "well and truly to hear and determine the matter in question, according to the best of his judgment, without favour, affection or hope of reward:" provided also that no State shall be deprived of territory for the benefit of the United States.

All controversies concerning the private right of soil claimed under different grants of two or more States, whose jurisdiction as they may respect such lands, and the states which passed such grants are adjusted, the said grants or either of them being at the same time claimed to have originated antecedent to such settlement of jurisdiction, shall on the petition of either party to the Congress of the United States, be finally determined as near as may be in the same manner as is before prescribed for deciding disputes respecting territorial jurisdiction between different States.

The United States in Congress assembled shall also have the sole and exclusive right and power of regulating the alloy and value of coin struck by their own authority, or by that of the respective States—fixing the standard of weights and measures throughout the United States—regulating the trade and managing all affairs with the Indians, not members of any of the States, provided that the legislative right of any State within its own limits be not infringed or violated—establishing and regulating post-offices from one State to another, throughout all of the United States, and exacting such postage on the papers passing thro' the same as may be requisite to defray the expenses of the said office—appointing all officers of the land forces, in the service of the United States, excepting regimental officers—appointing all the officers of the naval forces, and commissioning all officers whatever in the service of the United States—making rules for the government and regulation of the said land and naval forces, and directing their operations.

The United States in Congress assembled shall have authority to appoint a committee, to sit in the recess of Congress, to be denominated "a Committee of the States," and to consist of one delegate from each State; and to appoint such other committees and civil officers as may be necessary for managing the general affairs of the United States under their direction—to appoint one of their number to preside, provided that no person be allowed to serve in the office of president more than one year in any term of three years; to ascertain the necessary sums of money to be raised for the service of the United States, and to appropriate and apply the same for defraying the public expenses—to borrow money, or emit bills on the credit of the United States, transmitting every half year to the respective States an account of the sums of money so borrowed or emitted,—to build and equip a navy—to agree upon the number of land forces, and to make requisitions from each State for its quota, in proportion to the number of white inhabitants in such State; which requisition shall be binding, and thereupon the Legislature of each State shall appoint the regimental officers, raise the men and cloath, arm and equip them in a soldier like manner, at the expense of the United States; and the officers and men so cloathed, armed and equipped shall march to the place appointed, and within the time agreed on by the United States in Congress assembled: but if the United States in Congress assembled shall, on consideration of circumstances judge proper that any State should not raise men, or should raise a smaller number of men than the quota thereof, such extra number shall be raised, officered, cloathed, armed and equipped in the same manner as the quota of such State, unless the legislature of such State shall judge that such extra number cannot be safely spared out of the same, in which case they shall raise officer, cloath, arm and equip as many of such extra number as they judge can be safely spared. And the officers and men so cloathed, armed and equipped, shall march to the place appointed, and within the time agreed on by the United States in Congress assembled.

The United States in Congress assembled shall never engage in a war, nor grant letters of marque and reprisal in time of peace, nor enter into any treaties or alliances, nor coin money, nor regulate the value thereof, nor ascertain the sums and expenses necessary for the defence and welfare of the United States, or any of them, nor emit bills, nor borrow money on the credit of the United States, nor appropriate money, nor agree upon the number of vessels to be built or purchased, or the number of land or sea forces to be raised, nor appoint a commander in chief of the army or navy, unless nine States assent to the same: nor shall a question on any other point, except for adjourning from day to day be determined, unless by the votes of a majority of the United States in Congress assembled.

The Congress of the United States shall have power to adjourn to any time within the year, and to any place within the United States, so that no period of adjournment be for a longer duration than the space of six months, and shall publish the journal of their proceedings monthly, except such parts thereof relating to treaties, alliances or military operations, as in their judgment require secresy; and the yeas and nays of the delegates of each State on any question shall be entered on the Journal, when it is desired by any delegate; and the delegates of a State, or any of them, at his or their request shall be furnished with a transcript of the said journal, except such parts as are above excepted, to lay before the Legislatures of the several States.

Article X. The committee of the States, or any nine of them, shall be authorized to execute, in the recess of Congress, such of the powers of Congress as the United States in Congress assembled, by the consent of nine States, shall from time to time think expedient to vest them with; provided that no power be delegated to the said committee, for the exercise of which, by the articles of confederation, the voice of nine States in the Congress of the United States assembled is requisite.

Article XI. Canada acceding to this confederation, and joining in the measures of the United States, shall be admitted into, and entitled to all the advantages of this Union: but no other colony shall be admitted into the same, unless such admission be agreed to by nine States.

Article XII. All bills of credit emitted, monies borrowed and debts contracted by, or under the authority of Congress, before the assembling of the United States, in pursuance of the present confederation, shall be deemed and considered as a charge against the United States, for payment and satisfaction whereof the said United States, and the public faith are hereby solemnly pledged.

Article XIII. Every State shall abide by the determinations of the United States in Congress assembled, on all questions which by this confederation are submitted to them. And the articles of this confederation shall be inviolably observed by every State, and the Union shall be perpetual; nor shall any alteration at any time hereafter be made in any of them; unless such alteration be agreed to in a Congress of the United States, and be afterwards confirmed by the Legislatures of every State.

And whereas it has pleased the Great Governor of the world to incline the hearts of the Legislatures we respectively represent in Congress, to approve of, and to authorize us to ratify the said articles of confederation and perpetual union. Know ye that we the undersigned delegates, by virtue of the power and authority to us given for that purpose, do by these presents, in the name and in behalf of our respective constituents, fully and entirely ratify and confirm each and every of the said articles of confederation and perpetual union, and all and singular the matters and things therein contained: and we do further solemnly plight and engage the faith of our respective constituents, that they shall abide by the determinations of the United States in Congress assembled, on all questions, which by the said confederation are submitted to them. And that the articles thereof shall be inviolably observed by the States we respectively represent, and that the Union shall be perpetual.

In witness thereof we have hereunto set our hands in Congress. Done at Philadelphia in the State of Pennsylvania the ninth day of July in the year of our Lord one thousand seven hundred and seventy-eight, and in the third year of the independence of America.

THE CONSTITUTION OF THE UNITED STATES (1787)

We the People of the United States, in Order to form a more perfect Union, establish Justice, insure domestic Tranquility, provide for the common defence, promote the general Welfare, and secure the Blessings of Liberty to ourselves and our Posterity, do ordain and establish this Constitution for the United States of America.

ARTICLE. I.

SECTION. 1. All legislative Powers herein granted shall be vested in a Congress of the United States, which shall consist of a Senate and House of Representatives.

SECTION. 2. The House of Representatives shall be composed of Members chosen every second Year by the People of the several States, and the Electors in each State shall have the Qualifications requisite for Electors of the most numerous Branch of the State Legislature.

No Person shall be a Representative who shall not have attained to the Age of twenty five Years, and been seven Years a Citizen of the United States, and who shall not, when elected, be an Inhabitant of that State in which he shall be chosen.

Representatives and direct Taxes shall be apportioned among the several States which may be included within this Union, according to their respective Numbers, which shall be determined by adding to the whole Number of free Persons, including those bound to Service for a Term of Years, and excluding Indians not taxed, three fifths of all other Persons. The actual Enumeration shall be made within three Years after the first Meeting of the Congress of the United States, and within every subsequent Term of ten Years, in such Manner as they shall by Law direct. The Number of Representatives shall not exceed one for every thirty Thousand, but each State shall have at Least one Representative; and until such enumeration shall be made, the State of New Hampshire shall be entitled to chuse three, Massachusetts eight, Rhode-Island and Providence Plantations one, Connecticut five, New-York six, New Jersey four, Pennsylvania eight, Delaware one, Maryland six, Virginia ten, North Carolina five, South Carolina five, and Georgia three.

When vacancies happen in the Representation from any State, the Executive Authority thereof shall issue Writs of Election to fill such Vacancies.

The House of Representatives shall chuse their Speaker and other Officers; and shall have the sole Power of Impeachment.

SECTION. 3. The Senate of the United States shall be composed of two Senators from each State, chosen by the Legislature thereof for six Years; and each Senator shall have one Vote.

Immediately after they shall be assembled in Consequence of the first Election, they shall be divided as equally as may be into three Classes. The Seats of the Senators of the first Class shall be vacated at the Expiration of the second Year, of the second Class at the Expiration of the fourth Year, and of the third Class at the Expiration of the sixth Year, so that one third may be chosen every second Year; and if Vacancies happen by Resignation, or otherwise, during the Recess of the Legislature of any State, the Executive thereof may make temporary Appointments until the next Meeting of the Legislature, which shall then fill such Vacancies.

No Person shall be a Senator who shall not have attained to the Age of thirty Years, and been nine Years a Citizen of the United States, and who shall not, when elected, be an Inhabitant of that State for which he shall be chosen.

The Vice President of the United States shall be President of the Senate, but shall have no Vote, unless they be equally divided.

The Senate shall chuse their other Officers, and also a President pro tempore, in the Absence of the Vice President, or when he shall exercise the Office of President of the United States.

The Senate shall have the sole Power to try all Impeachments. When sitting for that Purpose, they shall be on Oath or Affirmation. When the President of the United States is tried, the Chief Justice shall preside: And no Person shall be convicted without the Concurrence of two thirds of the Members present.

Judgment in Cases of Impeachment shall not extend further than to removal from Office, and disqualification to hold and enjoy any Office of honor, Trust or Profit under the United States: but the Party convicted shall nevertheless be liable and subject to Indictment, Trial, Judgment and Punishment, according to Law.

SECTION. 4. The Times, Places and Manner of holding Elections for Senators and Representatives, shall be prescribed in each State by the Legislature thereof; but the Congress may at any time by Law make or alter such Regulations, except as to the Places of chusing Senators.

The Congress shall assemble at least once in every Year, and such Meeting shall be on the first Monday in December, unless they shall by Law appoint a different Day.

SECTION. 5. Each House shall be the Judge of the Elections, Returns and Qualifications of its own Members, and a Majority of each shall constitute a Quorum to do Business; but a smaller Number may adjourn from day to day, and may be authorized to compel the Attendance of absent Members, in such Manner, and under such Penalties as each House may provide.

Each House may determine the Rules of its Proceedings, punish its Members for disorderly Behaviour, and, with the Concurrence of two thirds, expel a Member.

Each House shall keep a Journal of its Proceedings, and from time to time publish the same, excepting such Parts as may in their Judgment require Secrecy; and the Yeas and Nays of the Members of either House on any question shall, at the Desire of one fifth of those Present, be entered on the Journal.

Neither House, during the Session of Congress, shall, without the Consent of the other, adjourn for more than three days, nor to any other Place than that in which the two Houses shall be sitting.

SECTION. 6. The Senators and Representatives shall receive a Compensation for their Services, to be ascertained by Law, and paid out of the Treasury of the United States. They shall in all Cases, except Treason, Felony and Breach of the Peace, be privileged from Arrest during their Attendance at the Session of their respective Houses, and in going to and returning from the same; and for any Speech or Debate in either House, they shall not be questioned in any other Place.

No Senator or Representative shall, during the Time for which he was elected, be appointed to any civil Office under the Authority of the United States, which shall have been created, or the Emoluments whereof shall have been encreased during such time; and no Person holding any Office under the United States, shall be a Member of either House during his Continuance in Office.

SECTION. 7. All Bills for raising Revenue shall originate in the House of Representatives; but the Senate may propose or concur with Amendments as on other Bills.

Every Bill which shall have passed the House of Representatives and the Senate shall, before it become a Law, be presented to the President of the United States; If he approve he shall sign it, but if not he shall return it, with his

Objections to that House in which it shall have originated, who shall enter the Objections at large on their Journal, and proceed to reconsider it. If after such Reconsideration two thirds of that House shall agree to pass the Bill, it shall be sent, together with the Objections, to the other House, by which it shall likewise be reconsidered, and if approved by two thirds of that House, it shall become a Law. But in all such Cases the Votes of both Houses shall be determined by yeas and Nays, and the Names of the Persons voting for and against the Bill shall be entered on the Journal of each House respectively. If any Bill shall not be returned by the President within ten Days (Sundays excepted) after it shall have been presented to him, the Same shall be a Law, in like Manner as if he had signed it, unless the Congress by their Adjournment prevent its Return, in which Case it shall not be a Law.

Every Order, Resolution, or Vote to which the Concurrence of the Senate and House of Representatives may be necessary (except on a question of Adjournment) shall be presented to the President of the United States; and before the Same shall take Effect, shall be approved by him, or being disapproved by him, shall be repassed by two thirds of the Senate and House of Representatives, according to the Rules and Limitations prescribed in the Case of a Bill.

SECTION. 8. The Congress shall have Power To lay and collect Taxes, Duties, Imposts and Excises, to pay the Debts and provide for the common Defence and general Welfare of the United States; but all Duties, Imposts and Excises shall be uniform throughout the United States;

To borrow Money on the credit of the United States;

To regulate Commerce with foreign Nations, and among the several States, and with the Indian Tribes;

To establish an uniform Rule of Naturalization, and uniform Laws on the subject of Bankruptcies throughout the United States;

To coin Money, regulate the Value thereof, and of foreign Coin, and fix the Standard of Weights and Measures;

To provide for the Punishment of counterfeiting the Securities and current Coin of the United States;

To establish Post Offices and post Roads;

To promote the Progress of Science and useful Arts, by securing for limited Times to Authors and Inventors the exclusive Right to their respective Writings and Discoveries;

To constitute Tribunals inferior to the supreme Court;

To define and punish Piracies and Felonies committed on the high Seas, and Offences against the Law of Nations;

To declare War, grant Letters of Marque and Reprisal, and make Rules concerning Captures on Land and Water;

To raise and support Armies, but no Appropriation of Money to that Use shall be for a longer Term than two Years;

To provide and maintain a Navy;

To make Rules for the Government and Regulation of the land and naval Forces;

To provide for calling forth the Militia to execute the Laws of the Union, suppress Insurrections and repel Invasions;

To provide for organizing, arming, and disciplining, the Militia, and for governing such Part of them as may be employed in the Service of the United States, reserving to the States respectively, the Appointment of the Officers, and the Authority of training the Militia according to the discipline prescribed by Congress;

To exercise exclusive Legislation in all Cases whatsoever, over such District (not exceeding ten Miles square) as may, by Cession of particular States, and the Acceptance of Congress, become the Seat of the Government of the United States, and to exercise like Authority over all Places purchased by the Consent of the Legislature of the State in which the Same shall be, for the Erection of Forts, Magazines, Arsenals, dock-Yards, and other needful Buildings;—And

To make all Laws which shall be necessary and proper for carrying into Execution the foregoing Powers, and all other Powers vested by this Constitution in the Government of the United States, or in any Department or Officer thereof.

SECTION. 9. The Migration or Importation of such Persons as any of the States now existing shall think proper to admit, shall not be prohibited by the Congress prior to the Year one thousand eight hundred and eight, but a Tax or duty may be imposed on such Importation, not exceeding ten dollars for each Person.

The Privilege of the Writ of Habeas Corpus shall not be suspended, unless when in Cases of Rebellion or Invasion the public Safety may require it.

No Bill of Attainder or ex post facto Law shall be passed.

No Capitation, or other direct, Tax shall be laid, unless in Proportion to the Census or enumeration herein before directed to be taken.

No Tax or Duty shall be laid on Articles exported from any State.

No Preference shall be given by any Regulation of Commerce or Revenue to the Ports of one State over those of another; nor shall Vessels bound to, or from, one State, be obliged to enter, clear, or pay Duties in another.

No Money shall be drawn from the Treasury, but in Consequence of Appropriations made by Law; and a regular Statement and Account of the Receipts and Expenditures of all public Money shall be published from time to time.

No Title of Nobility shall be granted by the United States: And no Person holding any Office of Profit or Trust under them, shall, without the Consent of the Congress, accept of any present, Emolument, Office, or Title, of any kind whatever, from any King, Prince, or foreign State.

SECTION. 10. No State shall enter into any Treaty, Alliance, or Confederation; grant Letters of Marque and Reprisal; coin Money; emit Bills of Credit; make any Thing but gold and silver Coin a Tender in Payment of Debts; pass any Bill of Attainder, ex post facto Law, or Law impairing the Obligation of Contracts, or grant any Title of Nobility.

No State shall, without the Consent of the Congress, lay any Imposts or Duties on Imports or Exports, except what may be absolutely necessary for executing it's inspection Laws: and the net Produce of all Duties and Imposts, laid by any State on Imports or Exports, shall be for the Use of the Treasury of the United States; and all such Laws shall be subject to the Revision and Controul of the Congress.

No State shall, without the Consent of Congress, lay any Duty of Tonnage, keep Troops, or Ships of War in time of Peace, enter into any Agreement or Compact with another State, or with a foreign Power, or engage in War, unless actually invaded, or in such imminent Danger as will not admit of delay.

ARTICLE. II.

SECTION. 1. The executive Power shall be vested in a President of the United States of America. He shall hold his Office during the Term of four Years, and, together with the Vice President, chosen for the same Term, be elected, as follows:

Each State shall appoint, in such Manner as the Legislature thereof may direct, a Number of Electors, equal to the whole Number of Senators and Representatives to which the State may be entitled in the Congress: but no Senator or Representative, or Person holding an Office of Trust or Profit under the United States, shall be appointed an Elector.

The Electors shall meet in their respective States, and vote by Ballot for two Persons, of whom one at least shall not be an Inhabitant of the same State with themselves. And they shall make a List of all the Persons voted for, and of the Number of Votes for each; which List they shall sign and certify, and transmit sealed to the Seat of the Government of the United States, directed to the President of the Senate. The President of the Senate shall, in the Presence of the Senate and House of Representatives, open all the Certificates, and the Votes shall then be counted. The Person having the greatest Number of Votes shall be the President, if such Number be a Majority of the whole Number of Electors appointed; and if there be more than one who have such Majority, and have an equal Number of Votes, then the House of Representatives shall immediately chuse by Ballot one of them for President; and if no Person have a Majority, then from the five highest on the List the said House shall in like Manner chuse the President. But in chusing the President, the Votes shall be taken by States, the Representation from each State having one Vote; A quorum for this purpose shall consist of a Member or Members from two thirds of the States, and a Majority of all the States shall be necessary to a Choice. In every Case, after the Choice of the President, the Person having the greatest Number of Votes of the Electors shall be the Vice President. But if there should remain two or more who have equal Votes, the Senate shall chuse from them by Ballot the Vice President.

The Congress may determine the Time of chusing the Electors, and the Day on which they shall give their Votes; which Day shall be the same throughout the United States.

No Person except a natural born Citizen, or a Citizen of the United States, at the time of the Adoption of this Constitution, shall be eligible to the Office of President; neither shall any Person be eligible to that Office who shall not have attained to the Age of thirty five Years, and been fourteen Years a Resident within the United States.

In Case of the Removal of the President from Office, or of his Death, Resignation, or Inability to discharge the Powers and Duties of the said Office, the Same shall devolve on the Vice President, and the Congress may by Law provide for the Case of Removal, Death, Resignation or Inability, both of the President and Vice President, declaring what Officer shall then act as President, and such Officer shall act accordingly, until the Disability be removed, or a President shall be elected.

The President shall, at stated Times, receive for his Services, a Compensation, which shall neither be increased nor diminished during the Period for which he shall have been elected, and he shall not receive within that Period any other Emolument from the United States, or any of them.

Before he enter on the Execution of his Office, he shall take the following Oath or Affirmation:—"I do solemnly swear (or affirm) that I will faithfully execute the Office of President of the United States, and will to the best of my Ability, preserve, protect and defend the Constitution of the United States."

SECTION. 2. The President shall be Commander in Chief of the Army and Navy of the United States, and of the Militia of the several States, when called into the actual Service of the United States; he may require the Opinion, in writing, of the principal Officer in each of the executive Departments, upon any Subject relating to the Duties of their respective Offices, and he shall have Power to grant Reprieves and Pardons for Offences against the United States, except in Cases of Impeachment.

He shall have Power, by and with the Advice and Consent of the Senate, to make Treaties, provided two thirds of the Senators present concur; and he shall nominate, and by and with the Advice and Consent of the Senate, shall appoint Ambassadors, other public Ministers and Consuls, Judges of the supreme Court, and all other Officers of the United States, whose Appointments are not herein otherwise provided for, and which shall be established by Law: but the Congress may by Law vest the Appointment of such inferior Officers, as they think proper, in the President alone, in the Courts of Law, or in the Heads of Departments.

The President shall have Power to fill up all Vacancies that may happen during the Recess of the Senate, by granting Commissions which shall expire at the End of their next Session.

SECTION. 3. He shall from time to time give to the Congress Information of the State of the Union, and recommend to their Consideration such Measures as he shall judge necessary and expedient; he may, on extraordinary Occasions, convene both Houses, or either of them, and in Case of Disagreement between them, with Respect to the Time of Adjournment, he may adjourn them to such Time as he shall think proper; he shall receive Ambassadors and other public Ministers; he shall take Care that the Laws be faithfully executed, and shall Commission all the Officers of the United States.

SECTION. 4. The President, Vice President and all civil Officers of the United States, shall be removed from Office on Impeachment for, and Conviction of, Treason, Bribery, or other high Crimes and Misdemeanors.

Article. III.

SECTION. 1. The judicial Power of the United States shall be vested in one supreme Court, and in such inferior Courts as the Congress may from time to time ordain and establish. The Judges, both of the supreme and inferior Courts, shall hold their Offices during good Behaviour, and shall, at stated Times, receive for their Services a Compensation, which shall not be diminished during their Continuance in Office.

SECTION. 2. The judicial Power shall extend to all Cases, in Law and Equity, arising under this Constitution, the Laws of the United States, and Treaties made, or which shall be made, under their Authority;—to all Cases affecting Ambassadors, other public Ministers and Consuls;—to all Cases of admiralty and maritime Jurisdiction;—to Controversies to which the United States shall be a Party;—to Controversies between two or more States;—between a State and Citizens of another State,—between Citizens of different States,—between Citizens of the same State claiming Lands under Grants of different States, and between a State, or the Citizens thereof, and foreign States, Citizens or Subjects.

In all Cases affecting Ambassadors, other public Ministers and Consuls, and those in which a State shall be Party, the supreme Court shall have original Jurisdiction. In all the other Cases before mentioned, the supreme Court shall have appellate Jurisdiction, both as to Law and Fact, with such Exceptions, and under such Regulations as the Congress shall make.

The Trial of all Crimes, except in Cases of Impeachment, shall be by Jury; and such Trial shall be held in the State where the said Crimes shall have been committed; but when not committed within any State, the Trial shall be at such Place or Places as the Congress may by Law have directed.

SECTION. 3. Treason against the United States, shall consist only in levying War against them, or in adhering to their Enemies, giving them Aid and Comfort. No Person shall be convicted of Treason unless on the Testimony of two Witnesses to the same overt Act, or on Confession in open Court.

The Congress shall have Power to declare the Punishment of Treason, but no Attainder of Treason shall work Corruption of Blood, or Forfeiture except during the Life of the Person attainted.

ARTICLE. IV.

SECTION. 1. Full Faith and Credit shall be given in each State to the public Acts, Records, and judicial Proceedings of every other State. And the Congress may by general Laws prescribe the Manner in which such Acts, Records and Proceedings shall be proved, and the Effect thereof.

SECTION. 2. The Citizens of each State shall be entitled to all Privileges and Immunities of Citizens in the several States.

A Person charged in any State with Treason, Felony, or other Crime, who shall flee from Justice, and be found in another State, shall on Demand of the executive Authority of the State from which he fled, be delivered up, to be removed to the State having Jurisdiction of the Crime.

No Person held to Service or Labour in one State, under the Laws thereof, escaping into another, shall, in Consequence of any Law or Regulation therein, be discharged from such Service or Labour, but shall be delivered up on Claim of the Party to whom such Service or Labour may be due.

SECTION. 3. New States may be admitted by the Congress into this Union; but no new State shall be formed or erected within the Jurisdiction of any other State; nor any State be formed by the Junction of two or more States, or Parts of States, without the Consent of the Legislatures of the States concerned as well as of the Congress.

The Congress shall have Power to dispose of and make all needful Rules and Regulations respecting the Territory or other Property belonging to the United States; and nothing in this Constitution shall be so construed as to Prejudice any Claims of the United States, or of any particular States.

SECTION. 4. The United States shall guarantee to every State in this Union a Republican Form of Government, and shall protect each of them against Invasion; and on Application of the Legislature, or of the Executive (when the Legislature cannot be convened), against domestic Violence.

ARTICLE. V.

The Congress, whenever two thirds of both Houses shall deem it necessary, shall propose Amendments to this Constitution, or, on the Application of the Legislatures of two thirds of the several States, shall call a Convention for proposing Amendments, which, in either Case, shall be valid to all Intents and Purposes, as Part of this Constitution, when ratified by the Legislatures of three fourths of the several States, or by Conventions in three fourths thereof, as the one or the other Mode of Ratification may be proposed by the Congress; Provided that no Amendment which may be made prior to the Year One thousand eight hundred and eight shall in any Manner affect the first and fourth Clauses in the Ninth Section of the first Article; and that no State, without its Consent, shall be deprived of its equal Suffrage in the Senate.

ARTICLE. VI.

All Debts contracted and Engagements entered into, before the Adoption of this Constitution, shall be as valid against the United States under this Constitution, as under the Confederation.

This Constitution, and the Laws of the United States which shall be made in Pursuance thereof; and all Treaties made, or which shall be made, under the Authority of the United States, shall be the supreme Law of the Land; and the Judges in every State shall be bound thereby, any Thing in the Constitution or Laws of any State to the Contrary notwithstanding.

The Senators and Representatives before mentioned, and the Members of the several State Legislatures, and all executive and judicial Officers, both of the United States and of the several States, shall be bound by Oath or Affirmation, to support this Constitution; but no religious Test shall ever be required as a Qualification to any Office or public Trust under the United States.

ARTICLE. VII.

The Ratification of the Conventions of nine States, shall be sufficient for the Establishment of this Constitution between the States so ratifying the Same.

The Word, "the," being interlined between the seventh and eighth Lines of the first Page, the Word "Thirty" being partly written on an Erazure in the fifteenth Line of the first Page, The Words "is tried" being interlined between the thirty second and thirty third Lines of the first Page and the Word "the" being interlined between the forty third and forty fourth Lines of the second Page.

Attest William Jackson Secretary

Done in Convention by the Unanimous Consent of the States present the Seventeenth Day of September in the Year of our Lord one thousand seven hundred and Eighty seven and of the Independance of the United States of America the Twelfth In witness whereof We have hereunto subscribed our Names,

G°. Washington
Presidt and deputy from Virginia

Delaware	Geo: Read Gunning Bedford jun John Dickinson Richard Bassett Jaco: Broom	**New Hampshire**	John Langdon Nicholas Gilman
		Massachusetts	Nathaniel Gorham Rufus King
Maryland	James McHenry Dan of St Thos. Jenifer Danl. Carrol	**Connecticut**	Wm. Saml. Johnson Roger Sherman
		New York	Alexander Hamilton
Virginia	John Blair James Madison Jr.		
North Carolina	Wm. Blount Richd. Dobbs Spaight Hu Williamson	**New Jersey**	Wil: Livingston David Brearley Wm. Paterson Jona: Dayton
South Carolina	J. Rutledge Charles Cotesworth Pinckney Charles Pinckney Pierce Butler	**Pennsylvania**	B Franklin Thomas Mifflin Robt. Morris Geo. Clymer Thos. FitzSimons Jared Ingersoll James Wilson Gouv Morris
Georgia	William Few Abr Baldwin		

Amendments to the Constitution

The Bill of Rights: A Transcription

THE PREAMBLE TO THE BILL OF RIGHTS Congress of the United States begun and held at the City of New-York, on Wednesday the fourth of March, one thousand seven hundred and eighty nine.

THE Conventions of a number of the States, having at the time of their adopting the Constitution, expressed a desire, in order to prevent misconstruction or abuse of its powers, that further declaratory and restrictive clauses should be added: And as extending the ground of public confidence in the Government, will best ensure the beneficent ends of its institution.

RESOLVED by the Senate and House of Representatives of the United States of America, in Congress assembled, two thirds of both Houses concurring, that the following Articles be proposed to the Legislatures of the several States, as amendments to the Constitution of the United States, all, or any of which Articles, when ratified by three fourths of the said Legislatures, to be valid to all intents and purposes, as part of the said Constitution; viz.

ARTICLES in addition to, and Amendment of the Constitution of the United States of America, proposed by Congress, and ratified by the Legislatures of the several States, pursuant to the fifth Article of the original Constitution.

Note: The first ten amendments to the Constitution were ratified December 15, 1791, and form what is known as the "Bill of Rights."

Amendment I

Congress shall make no law respecting an establishment of religion, or prohibiting the free exercise thereof; or abridging the freedom of speech, or of the press; or the right of the people peaceably to assemble, and to petition the Government for a redress of grievances.

Amendment II

A well regulated Militia, being necessary to the security of a free State, the right of the people to keep and bear Arms, shall not be infringed.

AMENDMENT III

No Soldier shall, in time of peace be quartered in any house, without the consent of the Owner, nor in time of war, but in a manner to be prescribed by law.

AMENDMENT IV

The right of the people to be secure in their persons, houses, papers, and effects, against unreasonable searches and seizures, shall not be violated, and no Warrants shall issue, but upon probable cause, supported by Oath or affirmation, and particularly describing the place to be searched, and the persons or things to be seized.

AMENDMENT V

No person shall be held to answer for a capital, or otherwise infamous crime, unless on a presentment or indictment of a Grand Jury, except in cases arising in the land or naval forces, or in the Militia, when in actual service in time of War or public danger; nor shall any person be subject for the same offence to be twice put in jeopardy of life or limb; nor shall be compelled in any criminal case to be a witness against himself, nor be deprived of life, liberty, or property, without due process of law; nor shall private property be taken for public use, without just compensation.

AMENDMENT VI

In all criminal prosecutions, the accused shall enjoy the right to a speedy and public trial, by an impartial jury of the State and district wherein the crime shall have been committed, which district shall have been previously ascertained by law, and to be informed of the nature and cause of the accusation; to be confronted with the witnesses against him; to have compulsory process for obtaining witnesses in his favor, and to have the Assistance of Counsel for his defence.

AMENDMENT VII

In Suits at common law, where the value in controversy shall exceed twenty dollars, the right of trial by jury shall be preserved, and no fact tried by a jury, shall be otherwise re-examined in any Court of the United States, than according to the rules of the common law.

Amendment VIII

Excessive bail shall not be required, nor excessive fines imposed, nor cruel and unusual punishments inflicted.

Amendment IX

The enumeration in the Constitution, of certain rights, shall not be construed to deny or disparage others retained by the people.

Amendment X

The powers not delegated to the United States by the Constitution, nor prohibited by it to the States, are reserved to the States respectively, or to the people.

Amendment XI

Passed by Congress March 4, 1794. Ratified February 7, 1795.

Note: Article III, section 2, of the Constitution was modified by amendment 11.

The Judicial power of the United States shall not be construed to extend to any suit in law or equity, commenced or prosecuted against one of the United States by Citizens of another State, or by Citizens or Subjects of any Foreign State.

Amendment XII

Passed by Congress December 9, 1803. Ratified June 15, 1804.

Note: A portion of Article II, section 1 of the Constitution was superseded by the 12th amendment.

The Electors shall meet in their respective states and vote by ballot for President and Vice-President, one of whom, at least, shall not be an inhabitant of the same state with themselves; they shall name in their ballots the person voted for as President, and in distinct ballots the person voted for as Vice-President, and they shall make distinct lists of all persons voted for as President, and of all persons voted for as Vice-President, and of the number of votes for each, which lists they shall sign and certify, and transmit sealed to the seat of the government of the United States, directed to the President of the Senate; — the President of the Senate shall, in the presence of the Senate and House of Representatives, open all the certificates and the votes shall then be counted; — The person having the greatest number of votes for President, shall be the President, if such number be a majority of the whole number of Electors appointed; and if no person have such majority, then from the persons having the highest numbers not exceeding three on the list of those voted for as President, the House of Representatives shall choose immediately, by ballot, the President. But in choosing the President, the votes shall be taken by states, the representation from each state having one vote; a quorum for this purpose shall consist of a member or members from two-thirds of the states, and a majority of all the states shall be necessary to a choice. [And if the House of Representatives shall not choose a President whenever the right of choice shall devolve upon them, before the fourth day of March next following, then the Vice-President shall act as President, as in case of the death or other constitutional disability of the President. —]* The person having the greatest number of votes as Vice-President, shall be the Vice-President, if such number be a majority of the whole number of Electors appointed, and if no person have a majority, then from the two highest numbers on the list, the Senate shall choose the Vice-President; a quorum for the purpose shall consist of two-thirds of the whole number of Senators, and a majority of the whole number shall be necessary to a choice. But no person constitutionally ineligible to the office of President shall be eligible to that of Vice-President of the United States.

AMENDMENT XIII

Passed by Congress January 31, 1865. Ratified December 6, 1865.

Note: A portion of Article IV, section 2, of the Constitution was superseded by the 13th amendment.

SECTION 1. Neither slavery nor involuntary servitude, except as a punishment for crime whereof the party shall have been duly convicted, shall exist within the United States, or any place subject to their jurisdiction.

SECTION 2. Congress shall have power to enforce this article by appropriate legislation.

Superseded by section 3 of the 20th amendment.

AMENDMENT XIV

Passed by Congress June 13, 1866. Ratified July 9, 1868.

Note: Article I, section 2, of the Constitution was modified by section 2 of the 14th amendment.

SECTION 1. All persons born or naturalized in the United States, and subject to the jurisdiction thereof, are citizens of the United States and of the State wherein they reside. No State shall make or enforce any law which shall abridge the privileges or immunities of citizens of the United States; nor shall any State deprive any person of life, liberty, or property, without due process of law; nor deny to any person within its jurisdiction the equal protection of the laws.

SECTION 2. Representatives shall be apportioned among the several States according to their respective numbers, counting the whole number of persons in each State, excluding Indians not taxed. But when the right to vote at any election for the choice of electors for President and Vice-President of the United States, Representatives in Congress, the Executive and Judicial officers of a State, or the members of the Legislature thereof, is denied to any of the male inhabitants of such State, being twenty-one years of age,* and citizens of the United States, or in any way abridged, except for participation in rebellion, or other crime, the basis of representation therein shall be reduced in the proportion which the number of such male citizens shall bear to the whole number of male citizens twenty-one years of age in such State.

SECTION 3. No person shall be a Senator or Representative in Congress, or elector of President and Vice-President, or hold any office, civil or military, under the United States, or under any State, who, having previously taken an oath, as a member of Congress, or as an officer of the United States, or as a member of any State legislature, or as an executive or judicial officer of any State, to support the Constitution of the United States, shall have engaged in insurrection or rebellion against the same, or given aid or comfort to the enemies thereof. But Congress may by a vote of two-thirds of each House, remove such disability.

SECTION 4. The validity of the public debt of the United States, authorized by law, including debts incurred for payment of pensions and bounties for services in suppressing insurrection or rebellion, shall not be

---

Changed by section 1 of the 26th amendment.

questioned. But neither the United States nor any State shall assume or pay any debt or obligation incurred in aid of insurrection or rebellion against the United States, or any claim for the loss or emancipation of any slave; but all such debts, obligations and claims shall be held illegal and void.

SECTION 5. The Congress shall have the power to enforce, by appropriate legislation, the provisions of this article.

AMENDMENT XV

Passed by Congress February 26, 1869. Ratified February 3, 1870.

SECTION 1. The right of citizens of the United States to vote shall not be denied or abridged by the United States or by any State on account of race, color, or previous condition of servitude—

SECTION 2. The Congress shall have the power to enforce this article by appropriate legislation.

AMENDMENT XVI

Passed by Congress July 2, 1909. Ratified February 3, 1913.

Note: Article I, section 9, of the Constitution was modified by amendment 16.

The Congress shall have power to lay and collect taxes on incomes, from whatever source derived, without apportionment among the several States, and without regard to any census or enumeration.

AMENDMENT XVII

Passed by Congress May 13, 1912. Ratified April 8, 1913.

Note: Article I, section 3, of the Constitution was modified by the 17th amendment.

The Senate of the United States shall be composed of two Senators from each State, elected by the people thereof, for six years; and each Senator shall have one vote. The electors in each State shall have the qualifications requisite for electors of the most numerous branch of the State legislatures.

When vacancies happen in the representation of any State in the Senate, the executive authority of such State shall issue writs of election to fill such vacancies: *Provided*, That the legislature of any State may empower the executive thereof to make temporary appointments until the people fill the vacancies by election as the legislature may direct.

This amendment shall not be so construed as to affect the election or term of any Senator chosen before it becomes valid as part of the Constitution.

AMENDMENT XVIII

Passed by Congress December 18, 1917. Ratified January 16, 1919. Repealed by amendment 21.

SECTION 1. After one year from the ratification of this article the manufacture, sale, or transportation of intoxicating liquors within, the importation thereof into, or the exportation thereof from the United States and all territory subject to the jurisdiction thereof for beverage purposes is hereby prohibited.

SECTION 2. The Congress and the several States shall have concurrent power to enforce this article by appropriate legislation.

SECTION 3. This article shall be inoperative unless it shall have been ratified as an amendment to the Constitution by the legislatures of the several States, as provided in the Constitution, within seven years from the date of the submission hereof to the States by the Congress.

AMENDMENT XIX

Passed by Congress June 4, 1919. Ratified August 18, 1920.

The right of citizens of the United States to vote shall not be denied or abridged by the United States or by any State on account of sex.

Congress shall have power to enforce this article by appropriate legislation.

AMENDMENT XX

Passed by Congress March 2, 1932. Ratified January 23, 1933.

Note: Article I, section 4, of the Constitution was modified by section 2 of this amendment. In addition, a portion of the 12th amendment was superseded by section 3.

SECTION 1. The terms of the President and the Vice President shall end at noon on the 20th day of January, and the terms of Senators and Representatives at noon on the 3rd day of January, of the years in which such terms would have ended if this article had not been ratified; and the terms of their successors shall then begin.

SECTION 2. The Congress shall assemble at least once in every year, and such meeting shall begin at noon on the 3d day of January, unless they shall by law appoint a different day.

SECTION 3. If, at the time fixed for the beginning of the term of the President, the President elect shall have died, the Vice President elect shall become President. If a President shall not have been chosen before the time fixed for the beginning of his term, or if the President elect shall have failed to qualify, then the Vice President elect shall act as President until a President shall have qualified; and the Congress may by law provide for the case wherein neither a President elect nor a Vice President shall have qualified, declaring who shall then act as President, or the manner in which one who is to act shall be selected, and such person shall act accordingly until a President or Vice President shall have qualified.

SECTION 4. The Congress may by law provide for the case of the death of any of the persons from whom the House of Representatives may choose a President whenever the right of choice shall have devolved upon them, and for the case of the death of any of the persons from whom the Senate may choose a Vice President whenever the right of choice shall have devolved upon them.

SECTION 5. Sections 1 and 2 shall take effect on the 15th day of October following the ratification of this article.

SECTION 6. This article shall be inoperative unless it shall have been ratified as an amendment to the Constitution by the legislatures of three-fourths of the several States within seven years from the date of its submission.

AMENDMENT XXI

Passed by Congress February 20, 1933. Ratified December 5, 1933.

SECTION 1. The eighteenth article of amendment to the Constitution of the United States is hereby repealed.

SECTION 2. The transportation or importation into any State, Territory, or Possession of the United States for delivery or use therein of intoxicating liquors, in violation of the laws thereof, is hereby prohibited.

SECTION 3. This article shall be inoperative unless it shall have been ratified as an amendment to the Constitution by conventions in the several States, as provided in the Constitution, within seven years from the date of the submission hereof to the States by the Congress.

Amendment XXII

Passed by Congress March 21, 1947. Ratified February 27, 1951.

SECTION 1. No person shall be elected to the office of the President more than twice, and no person who has held the office of President, or acted as President, for more than two years of a term to which some other person was elected President shall be elected to the office of President more than once. But this Article shall not apply to any person holding the office of President when this Article was proposed by Congress, and shall not prevent any person who may be holding the office of President, or acting as President, during the term within which this Article becomes operative from holding the office of President or acting as President during the remainder of such term.

SECTION 2. This article shall be inoperative unless it shall have been ratified as an amendment to the Constitution by the legislatures of three-fourths of the several States within seven years from the date of its submission to the States by the Congress.

Amendment XXIII

Passed by Congress June 16, 1960. Ratified March 29, 1961.

SECTION 1. The District constituting the seat of Government of the United States shall appoint in such manner as Congress may direct:
 A number of electors of President and Vice President equal to the whole number of Senators and Representatives in Congress to which the District would be entitled if it were a State, but in no event more than the least populous State; they shall be in addition to those appointed by the States, but they shall be

considered, for the purposes of the election of President and Vice President, to be electors appointed by a State; and they shall meet in the District and perform such duties as provided by the twelfth article of amendment.

SECTION 2. The Congress shall have power to enforce this article by appropriate legislation.

AMENDMENT XXIV

Passed by Congress August 27, 1962. Ratified January 23, 1964.

SECTION 1. The right of citizens of the United States to vote in any primary or other election for President or Vice President, for electors for President or Vice President, or for Senator or Representative in Congress, shall not be denied or abridged by the United States or any State by reason of failure to pay poll tax or other tax.

SECTION 2. The Congress shall have power to enforce this article by appropriate legislation.

AMENDMENT XXV

Passed by Congress July 6, 1965. Ratified February 10, 1967.

Note: Article II, section 1, of the Constitution was affected by the 25th amendment.

SECTION 1. In case of the removal of the President from office or of his death or resignation, the Vice President shall become President.

SECTION 2. Whenever there is a vacancy in the office of the Vice President, the President shall nominate a Vice President who shall take office upon confirmation by a majority vote of both Houses of Congress.

SECTION 3. Whenever the President transmits to the President pro tempore of the Senate and the Speaker of the House of Representatives his written declaration that he is unable to discharge the powers and duties of his office, and until he transmits to them a written declaration to the contrary, such powers and duties shall be discharged by the Vice President as Acting President.

SECTION 4. Whenever the Vice President and a majority of either the principal officers of the executive departments or of such other body as Congress may by law provide, transmit to the President pro tempore of the Senate and the Speaker of the House of Representatives their written declaration that the President is unable to discharge the powers and duties of his office, the Vice President shall immediately assume the powers and duties of the office as Acting President.

Thereafter, when the President transmits to the President pro tempore of the Senate and the Speaker of the House of Representatives his written declaration that no inability exists, he shall resume the powers and duties of his office unless the Vice President and a majority of either the principal officers of the executive department or of such other body as Congress may by law provide, transmit within four days to the President pro tempore of the Senate and the Speaker of the House of Representatives their written declaration that the President is unable to discharge the powers and duties of his office. Thereupon Congress shall decide the issue, assembling within forty-eight hours for that purpose if not in session. If the Congress, within twenty-one days after receipt of the latter written declaration, or, if Congress is not in session, within twenty-one days after Congress is required to assemble, determines by two-thirds vote of both Houses that the President is unable to discharge the powers and duties of his office, the Vice President shall continue to discharge the same as Acting President; otherwise, the President shall resume the powers and duties of his office.

AMENDMENT XXVI

Passed by Congress March 23, 1971. Ratified July 1, 1971.

Note: Amendment 14, section 2, of the Constitution was modified by section 1 of the 26th amendment.

SECTION 1. The right of citizens of the United States, who are eighteen years of age or older, to vote shall not be denied or abridged by the United States or by any State on account of age.

SECTION 2. The Congress shall have power to enforce this article by appropriate legislation.

AMENDMENT XXVII

Originally proposed Sept. 25, 1789. Ratified May 7, 1992.

No law, varying the compensation for the services of the Senators and Representatives, shall take effect, until an election of representatives shall have intervened.

PRESIDENTIAL ELECTIONS

Year	Number of States	Candidates	Parties	Popular Vote	% of Popular Vote	Electoral Vote	% Voter Participation
1789	11	**GEORGE WASHINGTON**	No party			69	
		John Adams	designations			34	
		Other candidates				35	
1792	15	**GEORGE WASHINGTON**	No party			132	
		John Adams	designations			77	
		George Clinton				50	
		Other candidates				5	
1796	16	**JOHN ADAMS**	Federalist			71	
		Thomas Jefferson	Democratic-Republican			68	
		Thomas Pinckney	Federalist			59	
		Aaron Burr	Democratic-Republican			30	
		Other candidates				48	
1800	16	**THOMAS JEFFERSON**	Democratic-Republican			73	
		Aaron Burr	Democratic-Republican			73	
		John Adams	Federalist			65	
		Charles C. Pinckney	Federalist			64	
		John Jay	Federalist			1	
1804	17	**THOMAS JEFFERSON**	Democratic-Republican			162	
		Charles C. Pinckney	Federalist			14	

Year	Number of States	Candidates	Parties	Popular Vote	% of Popular Vote	Electoral Vote	% Voter Participation
1808	17	**JAMES MADISON**	Democratic-Republican			122	
		Charles C. Pinckney	Federalist			47	
		George Clinton	Democratic-Republican			6	
1812	18	**JAMES MADISON**	Democratic-Republican			128	
		DeWitt Clinton	Federalist			89	
1816	19	**JAMES MONROE**	Democratic-Republican			183	
		Rufus King	Federalist			34	
1820	24	**JAMES MONROE**	Democratic-Republican			231	
		John Quincy Adams	Independent			1	
1824	24	**JOHN QUINCY ADAMS**	Democratic-Republican	108,740	30.5	84	26.9
		Andrew Jackson	Democratic-Republican	153,544	43.1	99	
		Henry Clay	Democratic-Republican	47,136	13.2	37	
		William H. Crawford	Democratic-Republican	46,618	13.1	41	
1828	24	**ANDREW JACKSON**	Democratic	647,286	56.0	178	57.6
		John Quincy Adams	National-Republican	508,064	44.0	83	

Year	Number of States	Candidates	Parties	Popular Vote	% of Popular Vote	Electoral Vote	% Voter Participation
1832	24	**ANDREW JACKSON**	Democratic	688,242	54.5	219	55.4
		Henry Clay	National-Republican	473,462	37.5	49	
		William Wirt	Anti-Masonic	101,051	8.0	7	
		John Floyd	Democratic			11	
1836	26	**MARTIN VAN BUREN**	Democratic	765,483	50.9	170	57.8
		William H. Harrison	Whig			73	
		Hugh L. White	Whig	739,795	49.1	26	
		Daniel Webster	Whig			14	
		W. P. Mangum	Whig			11	
1840	26	**WILLIAM H. HARRISON**	Whig	1,274,624	53.1	234	80.2
		Martin Van Buren	Democratic	1,127,781	46.9	60	
1844	26	**JAMES K. POLK**	Democratic	1,338,464	49.6	170	78.9
		Henry Clay	Whig	1,300,097	48.1	105	
		James G. Birney	Liberty	62,300	2.3		
1848	30	**ZACHARY TAYLOR**	Whig	1,360,967	47.4	163	72.7
		Lewis Cass	Democratic	1,222,342	42.5	127	
		Martin Van Buren	Free Soil	291,263	10.1		
1852	31	**FRANKLIN PIERCE**	Democratic	1,601,117	50.9	254	69.6
		Winfield Scott	Whig	1,385,453	44.1	42	
		John P. Hale	Free Soil	155,825	5.0		
1856	31	**JAMES BUCHANAN**	Democratic	1,832,955	45.3	174	78.9
		John C. Frémont	Republican	1,339,932	33.1	114	
		Millard Fillmore	American	871,731	21.6	8	

Year	Number of States	Candidates	Parties	Popular Vote	% of Popular Vote	Electoral Vote	% Voter Participation
1860	33	**ABRAHAM LINCOLN**	Republican	1,865,593	39.8	180	81.2
		Stephen A. Douglas	Democratic	1,382,713	29.5	12	
		John C. Breckinridge	Democratic	848,356	18.1	72	
		John Bell	Constitutional Union	592,906	12.6	39	
1864	36	**ABRAHAM LINCOLN**	Republican	2,206,938	55.0	212	73.8
		George B. McClellan	Democratic	1,803,787	45.0	21	
1868	37	**ULYSSES S. GRANT**	Republican	3,013,421	52.7	214	78.1
		Horatio Seymour	Democratic	2,706,829	47.3	80	
1872	37	**ULYSSES S. GRANT**	Republican	3,596,745	55.6	286	71.3
		Horace Greeley	Democratic	2,843,446	43.9	66	
1876	38	Rutherford B. Hayes	Republican	4,036,572	48.0	185	81.8
		Samuel J. Tilden	Democratic	4,284,020	51.0	184	
1880	38	**JAMES A. GARFIELD**	Republican	4,453,295	48.5	214	79.4
		Winfield S. Hancock	Democratic	4,414,082	48.1	155	
		James B. Weaver	Greenback-Labor	308,578	3.4		
1884	38	**GROVER CLEVELAND**	Democratic	4,879,507	48.5	219	77.5
		James G. Blaine	Republican	4,850,293	48.2	182	
		Benjamin F. Butler	Greenback-Labor	175,370	1.8		
		John P. St. John	Prohibition	150,369	1.5		
1888	38	**BENJAMIN HARRISON**	Republican	5,477,129	47.9	233	79.3
		Grover Cleveland	Democratic	5,537,857	48.6	168	
		Clinton B. Fisk	Prohibition	249,506	2.2		
		Anson J. Streeter	Union Labor	146,935	1.3		

Year	Number of States	Candidates	Parties	Popular Vote	% of Popular Vote	Electoral Vote	% Voter Participation
1892	44	**GROVER CLEVELAND**	Democratic	5,555,426	46.1	277	74.7
		Benjamin Harrison	Republican	5,182,690	43.0	145	
		James B. Weaver	People's	1,029,846	8.5	22	
		John Bidwell	Prohibition	264,133	2.2		
1896	45	**WILLIAM MCKINLEY**	Republican	7,102,246	51.1	271	79.3
		William J. Bryan	Democratic	6,492,559	47.7	176	
1900	45	**WILLIAM MCKINLEY**	Republican	7,218,491	51.7	292	73.2
		William J. Bryan	Democratic; Populist	6,356,734	45.5	155	
		John C. Wooley	Prohibition	208,914	1.5		
1904	45	**THEODORE ROOSEVELT**	Republican	7,628,461	57.4	336	65.2
		Alton B. Parker	Democratic	5,084,223	37.6	140	
		Eugene V. Debs	Socialist	402,283	3.0		
		Silas C. Swallow	Prohibition	258,536	1.9		
1908	46	**WILLIAM H. TAFT**	Republican	7,675,320	51.6	321	65.4
		William J. Bryan	Democratic	6,412,294	43.1	162	
		Eugene V. Debs	Socialist	420,793	2.8		
		Eugene W. Chafin	Prohibition	253,840	1.7		
1912	48	**WOODROW WILSON**	Democratic	6,296,547	41.9	435	58.8
		Theodore Roosevelt	Progressive	4,118,571	27.4	88	
		William H. Taft	Republican	3,486,720	23.2	8	
		Eugene V. Debs	Socialist	900,672	6.0		
		Eugene W. Chafin	Prohibition	206,275	1.4		

Year	Number of States	Candidates	Parties	Popular Vote	% of Popular Vote	Electoral Vote	% Voter Participation
1916	48	**WOODROW WILSON**	Democratic	9,127,695	49.4	277	61.6
		Charles E. Hughes	Republican	8,533,507	46.2	254	
		A. L. Benson	Socialist	585,113	3.2		
		J. Frank Hanly	Prohibition	220,506	1.2		
1920	48	**WARREN G. HARDING**	Republican	16,143,407	60.4	404	49.2
		James M. Cox	Democratic	9,130,328	34.2	127	
		Eugene V. Debs	Socialist	919,799	3.4		
		P. P. Christensen	Farmer-Labor	265,411	1.0		
1924	48	**CALVIN COOLIDGE**	Republican	15,718,211	54.0	382	48.9
		John W. Davis	Democratic	8,385,283	28.8	136	
		Robert M. La Follette	Progressive	4,831,289	16.6	13	
1928	48	**HERBERT C. HOOVER**	Republican	21,391,993	58.2	444	56.9
		Alfred E. Smith	Democratic	15,016,169	40.9	87	
1932	48	**FRANKLIN D. ROOSEVELT**	Democratic	22,809,638	57.4	472	56.9
		Herbert C. Hoover	Republican	15,758,901	39.7	59	
		Norman Thomas	Socialist	881,951	2.2		
1936	48	**FRANKLIN D. ROOSEVELT**	Democratic	27,752,869	60.8	523	61.0
		Alfred M. Landon	Republican	16,674,665	36.5	8	
		William Lemke	Union	882,479	1.9		
1940	48	**FRANKLIN D. ROOSEVELT**	Democratic	27,307,819	54.8	449	62.5
		Wendell L. Willkie	Republican	22,321,018	44.8	82	
1944	48	**FRANKLIN D. ROOSEVELT**	Democratic	25,606,585	53.5	432	55.9
		Thomas E. Dewey	Republican	22,014,745	46.0	99	

Year	Number of States	Candidates	Parties	Popular Vote	% of Popular Vote	Electoral Vote	% Voter Participation
1948	48	**HARRY S. TRUMAN**	Democratic	24,179,345	49.6	303	53.0
		Thomas E. Dewey	Republican	21,991,291	45.1	189	
		J. Strom Thurmond	States' Rights	1,176,125	2.4	39	
		Henry A. Wallace	Progressive	1,157,326	2.4		
1952	48	**DWIGHT D. EISENHOWER**	Republican	33,936,234	55.1	442	63.3
		Adlai E. Stevenson	Democratic	27,314,992	44.4	89	
1956	48	**DWIGHT D. EISENHOWER**	Republican	35,590,472	57.6	457	60.6
		Adlai E. Stevenson	Democratic	26,022,752	42.1	73	
1960	50	**JOHN F. KENNEDY**	Democratic	34,226,731	49.7	303	62.8
		Richard M. Nixon	Republican	34,108,157	49.5	219	
1964	50	**LYNDON B. JOHNSON**	Democratic	43,129,566	61.1	486	61.9
		Barry M. Goldwater	Republican	27,178,188	38.5	52	
1968	50	**RICHARD M. NIXON**	Republican	31,785,480	43.4	301	60.9
		Hubert H. Humphrey	Democratic	31,275,166	42.7	191	
		George C. Wallace	American Independent	9,906,473	13.5	46	
1972	50	**RICHARD M. NIXON**	Republican	47,169,911	60.7	520	55.2
		George S. McGovern	Democratic	29,170,383	37.5	17	
		John G. Schmitz	American	1,099,482	1.4		
1976	50	**JIMMY CARTER**	Democratic	40,830,763	50.1	297	53.5
		Gerald R. Ford	Republican	39,147,793	48.0	240	

Year	Number of States	Candidates	Parties	Popular Vote	% Popular Vote	Electoral Vote	% Voter Participation
1980	50	**RONALD REAGAN**	Republican	43,901,812	50.7	489	52.6
		Jimmy Carter	Democratic	35,483,820	41.0	49	
		John B. Anderson	Independent	5,719,437	6.6		
		Ed Clark	Libertarian	921,188	1.1		
1984	50	**RONALD REAGAN**	Republican	54,451,521	58.8	525	53.1
		Walter F. Mondale	Democratic	37,565,334	40.6	13	
1988	50	**GEORGE H. W. BUSH**	Republican	47,917,341	53.4	426	50.1
		Michael Dukakis	Democratic	41,013,030	45.6	111	
1992	50	**BILL CLINTON**	Democratic	44,908,254	43.0	370	55.0
		George H. W. Bush	Republican	39,102,343	37.4	168	
		H. Ross Perot	Independent	19,741,065	18.9		
1996	50	**BILL CLINTON**	Democratic	47,401,185	49.0	379	49.0
		Bob Dole	Republican	39,197,469	41.0	159	
		H. Ross Perot	Independent	8,085,295	8.0		
2000	50	**GEORGE W. BUSH**	Republican	50,455,156	47.9	271	50.4
		Al Gore	Democrat	50,997,335	48.4	266	
		Ralph Nader	Green	2,882,897	2.7		
2004	50	**GEORGE W. BUSH**	Republican	62,040,610	50.7	286	60.7
		John F. Kerry	Democrat	59,028,444	48.3	251	
2008	50	**BARACK OBAMA**	Democrat	69,456,897	52.9	365	63.0
		John McCain	Republican	59,934,814	45.7	173	
2012	50	**BARACK OBAMA**	Democrat	65,915,795	51.1	332	57.5
		Mitt Romney	Republican	60,933,504	47.2	206	
2016	50	**DONALD TRUMP**	Republican	62,979,636	46.1	304	60.2
		Hillary Rodham Clinton	Democrat	65,844,610	48.2	227	
		Gary Johnson	Libertarian	4,489,235	3.3		
		Jill Stein	Green	1,457,226	1.1		

Candidates receiving less than 1 percent of the popular vote have been omitted. Thus the percentage of popular vote given for any election year may not total 100 percent.

Before the passage of the Twelfth Amendment in 1804, the electoral college voted for two presidential candidates; the runner-up became vice president.

ADMISSION OF STATES

Order of Admission	State	Date of Admission	Order of Admission	State	Date of Admission
1	Delaware	December 7, 1787	26	Michigan	January 26, 1837
2	Pennsylvania	December 12, 1787	27	Florida	March 3, 1845
3	New Jersey	December 18, 1787	28	Texas	December 29, 1845
4	Georgia	January 2, 1788	29	Iowa	December 28, 1846
5	Connecticut	January 9, 1788	30	Wisconsin	May 29, 1848
6	Massachusetts	February 7, 1788	31	California	September 9, 1850
7	Maryland	April 28, 1788	32	Minnesota	May 11, 1858
8	South Carolina	May 23, 1788	33	Oregon	February 14, 1859
9	New Hampshire	June 21, 1788	34	Kansas	January 29, 1861
10	Virginia	June 25, 1788	35	West Virginia	June 30, 1863
11	New York	July 26, 1788	36	Nevada	October 31, 1864
12	North Carolina	November 21, 1789	37	Nebraska	March 1, 1867
13	Rhode Island	May 29, 1790	38	Colorado	August 1, 1876
14	Vermont	March 4, 1791	39	North Dakota	November 2, 1889
15	Kentucky	June 1, 1792	40	South Dakota	November 2, 1889
16	Tennessee	June 1, 1796	41	Montana	November 8, 1889
17	Ohio	March 1, 1803	42	Washington	November 11, 1889
18	Louisiana	April 30, 1812	43	Idaho	July 3, 1890
19	Indiana	December 11, 1816	44	Wyoming	July 10, 1890
20	Mississippi	December 10, 1817	45	Utah	January 4, 1896
21	Illinois	December 3, 1818	46	Oklahoma	November 16, 1907
22	Alabama	December 14, 1819	47	New Mexico	January 6, 1912
23	Maine	March 15, 1820	48	Arizona	February 14, 1912
24	Missouri	August 10, 1821	49	Alaska	January 3, 1959
25	Arkansas	June 15, 1836	50	Hawaii	August 21, 1959

POPULATION OF THE UNITED STATES

Year	Number of States	Population	% Increase	Population per Square Mile
1790	13	3,929,214		4.5
1800	16	5,308,483	35.1	6.1
1810	17	7,239,881	36.4	4.3
1820	23	9,638,453	33.1	5.5
1830	24	12,866,020	33.5	7.4
1840	26	17,069,453	32.7	9.8
1850	31	23,191,876	35.9	7.9
1860	33	31,443,321	35.6	10.6
1870	37	39,818,449	26.6	13.4
1880	38	50,155,783	26.0	16.9
1890	44	62,947,714	25.5	21.1
1900	45	75,994,575	20.7	25.6
1910	46	91,972,266	21.0	31.0
1920	48	105,710,620	14.9	35.6
1930	48	122,775,046	16.1	41.2
1940	48	131,669,275	7.2	44.2
1950	48	150,697,361	14.5	50.7
1960	50	179,323,175	19.0	50.6
1970	50	203,235,298	13.3	57.5
1980	50	226,504,825	11.4	64.0
1985	50	237,839,000	5.0	67.2
1990	50	250,122,000	5.2	70.6
1995	50	263,411,707	5.3	74.4
2000	50	281,421,906	6.8	77.0
2005	50	296,410,404	5.3	77.9
2010	50	308,745,538	9.7	87.4
2015	50	321,931,311	4.3	91.1

LEGAL IMMIGRATION TO THE UNITED STATES, FISCAL YEARS 1820–2016**

Year	Number	Year	Number	Year	Number	Year	Number
1820–1989	**55,457,531**	**1871–80**	**2,812,191**	**1921–30**	**4,107,209**	**1971–80**	**4,493,314**
1820	8,385	1871	321,350	1921	805,228	1971	370,478
1821–30	**143,439**	1872	404,806	1922	309,556	1972	384,685
1821	9,127	1873	459,803	1923	522,919	1973	400,063
1822	6,911	1874	313,339	1924	706,896	1974	394,861
1823	6,354	1875	227,498	1925	294,314	1975	386,914
1824	7,912	1876	169,986	1926	304,488	1976	398,613
1825	10,199	1877	141,857	1927	335,175		103,676
1826	10,837	1878	138,469	1928	307,255	1977	462,315
1827	18,875	1879	177,826	1929	279,678	1978	601,442
1828	27,382	1880	457,257	1930	241,700	1979	460,348
1829	22,520	**1881–90**	**5,246,613**	**1931–40**	**528,431**	1980	530,639
1830	23,322	1881	669,431	1931	97,139	**1981–90**	**7,338,062**
1831–40	**599,125**	1882	788,992	1932	35,576	1981	596,600
1831	22,633	1883	603,322	1933	23,068	1982	594,131
1832	60,482	1884	518,592	1934	29,470	1983	559,763
1833	58,640	1885	395,346	1935	34,956	1984	543,903
1834	65,365	1886	334,203	1936	36,329	1985	570,009
1835	45,374	1887	490,109	1937	50,244	1986	601,708
1836	76,242	1888	546,889	1938	67,895	1987	601,516
1837	79,340	1889	444,427	1939	82,998	1988	643,025
1838	38,914	1890	455,302	1940	70,756	1989	1,090,924
1839	68,069	**1891–1900**	**3,687,564**	**1941–50**	**1,035,039**	1990	1,536,483
1840	84,066	1891	560,319	1941	51,776	**1991–2000**	**9,090,857**
1841–50	**1,713,251**	1892	579,663	1942	28,781	1991	1,827,167
1841	80,289	1893	439,730	1943	23,725	1992	973,977
1842	104,565	1894	285,631	1944	28,551	1993	904,292
		1895	258,536	1945	38,119	1994	804,416
		1896	343,267	1946	108,721		

Year	Number	Year	Number	Year	Number	Year	Number
1843	52,496	1897	230,832	1947	147,292	1995	720,461
1844	78,615	1898	229,299	1948	170,570	1996	915,900
1845	114,371	1899	311,715	1949	188,317	1997	798,378
1846	154,416	1900	448,572	1950	249,187	1998	660,477
1847	234,968					1999	644,787
1848	226,527	**1901–10**	**8,795,386**	**1951–60**	**2,515,479**	2000	841,002
1849	297,024	1901	487,918	1951	205,717		
1850	369,980	1902	648,743	1952	265,520	**2001–10**	**10,503,454**
		1903	857,046	1953	170,434	2001	1,058,902
1851–60	**2,598,214**	1904	812,870	1954	208,177	2002	1,059,356
1851	379,466	1905	1,026,499	1955	237,790	2003	705,827
1852	371,603	1906	1,100,735	1956	321,625	2004	957,883
1853	368,645	1907	1,285,349	1957	326,867	2005	1,122,373
1854	427,833	1908	782,870	1958	253,265	2006	1,266,129
1855	200,877	1909	751,786	1959	260,686	2007	1,052,415
1856	200,436	1910	1,041,570	1960	265,398	2008	1,107,126
1857	251,306					2009	1,130,818
1858	123,126	**1911–20**	**5,735,811**	**1961–70**	**3,321,677**	2010	1,042,625
1859	121,282	1911	878,587	1961	271,344		
1860	153,640	1912	838,172	1962	283,763	**2011–15**	**5,356,671**
		1913	1,197,892	1963	306,260	2011	1,062,040
1861–70	**2,314,824**	1914	1,218,480	1964	292,248	2012	1,031,631
1861	91,918	1915	326,700	1965	296,697	2013	523,000
1862	91,985	1916	298,826	1966	323,040	2014	1,360,000
1863	176,282	1917	295,403	1967	361,972	2015	1,380,000
1864	193,418	1918	110,618	1968	454,448		
1865	248,120	1919	141,132	1969	358,579		
1866	318,568	1920	430,001	1970	373,326		
1867	315,722						
1868	138,840						
1869	352,768						
1870	387,203						

Source: U.S. Department of Homeland Security.

IMMIGRATION BY REGION AND SELECTED COUNTRY OF LAST RESIDENCE, FISCAL YEARS 1820–2015

Region and country of last residence	1820 to 1829	1830 to 1839	1840 to 1849	1850 to 1859	1860 to 1869	1870 to 1879	1880 to 1889	1890 to 1899
Total	128,502	538,381	1,427,337	2,814,554	2,081,261	2,742,137	5,248,568	3,694,294
Europe	99,272	422,771	1,369,259	2,619,680	1,877,726	2,251,878	4,638,677	3,576,411
Austria-Hungary	—	—	—	—	3,375	60,127	314,787	534,059
Austria	—	—	—	—	2,700	54,529	204,805	268,218
Hungary	—	—	—	—	483	5,598	109,982	203,350
Belgium	28	20	3,996	5,765	5,785	6,991	18,738	19,642
Bulgaria	—	—	—	—	—	—	—	52
*Former Czechoslovakia	—	—	—	—	—	—	—	—
Denmark	173	927	671	3,227	13,553	29,278	85,342	56,671
Finland	—	—	—	—	—	—	—	—
France	7,694	39,330	75,300	81,778	35,938	71,901	48,193	35,616
Germany	5,753	124,726	385,434	976,072	723,734	751,769	1,445,181	579,072
Greece	17	49	17	32	51	209	1,807	12,732
Ireland	51,617	170,672	656,145	1,029,486	427,419	422,264	674,061	405,710
Italy	430	2,225	1,476	8,643	9,853	46,296	267,660	603,761
Netherlands	1,105	1,377	7,624	11,122	8,387	14,267	52,715	29,349
Norway-Sweden	91	1,149	12,389	22,202	82,937	178,823	586,441	334,058
Norway	—	—	—	—	16,068	88,644	185,111	96,810
Sweden	—	—	—	—	24,224	90,179	401,330	237,248
Poland	19	366	105	1,087	1,886	11,016	42,910	107,793
Portugal	177	820	196	1,299	2,083	13,971	15,186	25,874
Romania	—	—	—	—	—	—	5,842	6,808
Russia	86	280	520	423	1,670	35,177	182,698	450,101
Spain	2,595	2,010	1,916	8,795	6,966	5,540	3,995	9,189
Switzerland	3,148	4,430	4,819	24,423	21,124	25,212	81,151	37,020
United Kingdom	26,336	74,350	218,572	445,322	532,956	578,447	810,900	328,759
*Former Yugoslavia	—	—	—	—	—	—	—	—
Other Europe	3	40	79	4	9	590	1,070	145

Asia	34	55	121	36,080	54,408	134,128	71,151	61,285
China	3	8	32	35,933	54,028	133,139	65,797	15,268
Hong Kong	—	—	—	42	50	166	247	102
India	9	38	33	—	—	—	—	102
Iran	—	—	—	—	—	—	—	—
*Israel	—	—	—	—	—	—	—	—
Japan	—	—	—	—	138	193	1,583	13,998
Jordan	—	—	—	—	—	—	—	—
*Korea	—	—	—	—	—	—	—	—
Philippines	—	—	—	—	—	—	—	—
Syria	—	—	—	—	—	—	—	—
Taiwan	—	—	—	—	—	382	2,478	27,510
Turkey	19	8	45	94	129	—	—	—
Vietnam	—	—	—	—	—	—	—	—
Other Asia	3	1	11	11	63	248	1,046	4,407
North America	9,655	31,905	50,516	84,145	130,292	345,010	524,826	37,350
Canada and Newfoundland	2,297	11,875	34,285	64,171	117,978	324,310	492,865	3,098
Mexico	3,835	7,187	3,069	3,446	1,957	5,133	2,405	734
Caribbean	3,061	11,792	11,803	12,447	8,751	14,285	27,323	31,480
Cuba	—	—	—	—	—	—	—	—
Dominican Republic	—	—	—	—	—	—	—	—
Haiti	—	—	—	—	—	—	—	—
Jamaica	—	—	—	—	—	—	—	—
Other Caribbean	3,061	11,792	11,803	12,447	8,751	14,285	27,323	31,480
Central America	57	94	297	512	70	173	279	649
Belize	—	—	—	—	—	—	—	—
Costa Rica	—	—	—	—	—	—	—	—
El Salvador	—	—	—	—	—	—	—	—
Guatemala	—	—	—	—	—	—	—	—
Honduras	—	—	—	—	—	—	—	—
Nicaragua	—	—	—	—	—	—	—	—
Panama	—	—	—	—	—	—	—	—
Other Central America	57	94	297	512	70	173	279	649
South America	405	957	1,062	3,569	1,536	1,109	1,954	1,389
Argentina	—	—	—	—	—	—	—	—
Bolivia	—	—	—	—	—	—	—	—

Region and country of last residence	1820 to 1829	1830 to 1839	1840 to 1849	1850 to 1859	1860 to 1869	1870 to 1879	1880 to 1889	1890 to 1899
Brazil	—	—	—	—	—	—	—	—
Chile	—	—	—	—	—	—	—	—
Colombia	—	—	—	—	—	—	—	—
Ecuador	—	—	—	—	—	—	—	—
Guyana	—	—	—	—	—	—	—	—
Paraguay	—	—	—	—	—	—	—	—
Peru	—	—	—	—	—	—	—	—
Suriname	—	—	—	—	—	—	—	—
Uruguay	—	—	—	—	—	—	—	—
Venezuela	—	—	—	—	—	—	—	—
Other South America	405	957	1,062	3,569	1,536	1,109	1,954	1,389
Other America	—	—	—	—	—	—	—	—
Africa	15	50	61	84	407	371	763	432
Egypt	—	—	—	—	4	29	145	51
Ethiopia	—	—	—	—	—	—	—	—
Liberia	1	8	5	7	43	52	21	9
Morocco	—	—	—	—	—	—	—	—
South Africa	—	—	—	—	35	48	23	9
Other Africa	14	42	56	77	325	242	574	363
Oceania	3	7	14	166	187	9,996	12,361	4,704
Australia	2	1	2	15	—	8,930	7,250	3,098
New Zealand	—	—	—	—	—	39	21	12
Other Oceania	1	6	12	151	187	1,027	5,090	1,594
Not Specified	19,523	83,593	7,366	74,399	18,241	754	790	14,112

Region and country of last residence	1900 to 1909	1910 to 1919	1920 to 1929	1930 to 1939	1940 to 1949	1950 to 1959	1960 to 1969	1980 to 1989
Total	8,202,388	6,347,380	4,295,510	699,375	856,608	2,499,268	3,213,749	6,244,379
Europe	7,572,569	4,985,411	2,560,340	444,399	472,524	1,404,973	1,133,443	668,866
Austria-Hungary	2,001,376	1,154,727	60,891	12,531	13,574	113,015	27,590	20,437
Austria	532,416	589,174	31,392	5,307	8,393	81,354	17,571	15,374
Hungary	685,567	565,553	29,499	7,224	5,181	31,661	10,019	5,063
Belgium	37,429	32,574	21,511	4,013	12,473	18,885	9,647	7,028
Bulgaria	34,651	27,180	2,824	1,062	449	97	598	1,124
*Former Czechoslovakia	—	—	101,182	17,757	8,475	1,624	2,758	5,678
Denmark	61,227	45,830	34,406	3,470	4,549	10,918	9,797	4,847
Finland	—	—	16,922	2,438	2,230	4,923	4,310	2,569
France	67,735	60,335	54,842	13,761	36,954	50,113	46,975	32,066
Germany	328,722	174,227	386,634	119,107	119,506	576,905	209,616	85,752
Greece	145,402	198,108	60,774	10,599	8,605	45,153	74,173	37,729
Ireland	344,940	166,445	202,854	28,195	15,701	47,189	37,788	22,210
Italy	1,930,475	1,229,916	528,133	85,053	50,509	184,576	200,111	55,562
Netherlands	42,463	46,065	29,397	7,791	13,877	46,703	37,150	11,234
Norway-Sweden	426,981	192,445	170,329	13,452	17,326	44,224	36,150	13,941
Norway	182,542	79,488	70,327	6,901	8,326	22,806	17,371	3,835
Sweden	244,439	112,957	100,002	6,551	9,000	21,418	18,779	10,106
Poland	—	—	223,316	25,555	7,577	6,465	55,742	63,483
Portugal	65,154	82,489	44,829	3,518	6,765	13,928	70,568	42,685
Romania	57,322	13,566	67,810	5,264	1,254	914	2,339	24,753
Russia	1,501,301	1,106,998	61,604	2,463	605	453	2,329	33,311
Spain	24,818	53,262	47,109	3,669	2,774	6,880	40,793	22,783
Switzerland	32,541	22,839	31,772	5,990	9,904	17,577	19,193	8,316
United Kingdom	469,518	371,878	341,552	61,813	131,794	195,709	220,213	153,644
*Former Yugoslavia	—	—	49,215	6,920	2,039	6,966	17,990	16,267
Other Europe	514	269,736	22,434	9,978	5,584	11,756	6,845	3,447
Asia	299,836	20,916	126,740	19,231	34,532	135,844	358,605	2,391,356
China	19,884	—	30,648	5,874	16,072	8,836	14,060	170,897
Hong Kong	—	—	—	—	—	13,781	67,047	112,132
India	3,026	3,478	2,076	554	1,692	1,850	18,638	231,649
Iran	—	—	208	198	1,144	3,195	9,059	98,141
*Israel	—	—	—	—	98	21,376	30,911	43,669

Region and country of last residence	1900 to 1909	1910 to 1919	1920 to 1929	1930 to 1939	1940 to 1949	1950 to 1959	1960 to 1969	1980 to 1989
Japan	139,712	77,125	42,057	2,683	1,557	40,651	40,956	44,150
Jordan	—	—	—	—	—	4,899	9,230	28,928
*Korea	—	—	—	—	83	4,845	27,048	322,708
Philippines	—	—	5,307	391	4,099	17,245	70,660	502,056
Syria	—	—	—	2,188	1,179	1,091	2,432	14,534
Taiwan	—	—	—	—	—	721	15,657	119,051
Turkey	127,999	160,717	40,450	1,327	754	2,980	9,464	19,208
Vietnam	—	—	—	—	—	290	2,949	200,632
Other Asia	9,215	7,500	5,994	6,016	7,854	14,084	40,494	483,601
North America	277,809	1,070,539	1,591,278	230,319	328,435	921,610	1,674,172	2,695,329
Canada and Newfoundland	123,067	708,715	949,286	162,703	160,911	353,169	433,128	156,313
Mexico	31,188	185,334	498,945	32,709	56,158	273,847	441,824	1,009,586
Caribbean	100,960	120,860	83,482	18,052	46,194	115,661	427,235	790,109
Cuba	—	—	12,769	10,641	25,976	73,221	202,030	132,552
Dominican Republic	—	—	—	1,026	4,802	10,219	83,552	221,552
Haiti	—	—	—	156	823	3,787	28,992	121,406
Jamaica	—	—	—	—	—	7,397	62,218	193,874
Other Caribbean	100,960	120,860	70,713	6,229	14,593	21,037	50,443	120,725
Central America	7,341	15,692	16,511	6,840	20,135	40,201	98,560	339,376
Belize	77	40	285	193	433	1,133	4,185	14,964
Costa Rica	—	—	—	431	1,965	4,044	17,975	25,017
El Salvador	—	—	—	597	4,885	5,094	14,405	137,418
Guatemala	—	—	—	423	1,303	4,197	14,357	58,847
Honduras	—	—	—	679	1,874	5,320	15,078	39,071
Nicaragua	—	—	—	405	4,393	7,812	10,383	31,102
Panama	—	—	—	1,452	5,282	12,601	22,177	32,957
Other Central America	7,264	15,652	16,226	2,660	—	—	—	—

South America	15,253	39,938	43,025	9,990	19,662	78,418	250,754	399,862
Argentina	—	—	—	1,067	3,108	16,346	49,384	23,442
Bolivia	—	—	—	50	893	2,759	6,205	9,798
Brazil	—	—	4,627	1,468	3,653	11,547	29,238	22,944
Chile	—	—	—	347	1,320	4,669	12,384	19,749
Colombia	—	—	—	1,027	3,454	15,567	68,371	105,494
Ecuador	—	—	—	244	2,207	8,574	34,107	48,015
Guyana	—	—	—	131	596	1,131	4,546	85,886
Paraguay	—	—	—	33	85	576	1,249	3,518
Peru	—	—	—	321	1,273	5,980	19,783	49,958
Suriname	—	—	—	25	130	299	612	1,357
Uruguay	—	—	—	112	754	1,026	4,089	7,235
Venezuela	—	—	—	1,155	2,182	9,927	20,758	22,405
Other South America	15,253	39,938	38,398	4,010	7	17	28	61
Other America	—	—	29	25	25,375	60,314	22,671	83
Africa	6,326	8,867	6,362	2,120	6,720	13,016	23,780	141,990
Egypt	—	—	1,063	781	1,613	1,996	5,581	26,744
Ethiopia	—	—	—	10	28	302	804	12,927
Liberia	—	—	—	35	37	289	841	6,420
Morocco	—	—	—	73	879	2,703	2,880	3,471
South Africa	—	—	—	312	1,022	2,278	4,360	15,505
Other Africa	6,326	8,867	5,299	909	3,141	5,448	9,314	76,923
Oceania	12,355	12,339	9,860	3,306	14,262	11,353	23,630	41,432
Australia	11,191	11,280	8,404	2,260	11,201	8,275	14,986	16,901
New Zealand	—	—	935	790	2,351	1,799	3,775	6,129
Other Oceania	1,164	1,059	521	256	710	1,279	4,869	18,402
Not Specified	33,493	488	930	—	135	12,472	119	305,406

Region and country of last residence	1990 to 1999	2000 to 2009	2010	2011	2012	2013	2014	2015	2016
Total	9,775,398	10,299,430	1,042,625	1,062,040	1,031,631	990,553	1,016,518	1,051,031	1,183,505
Europe	1,348,612	1,349,609	95,429	90,712	86,956	91,095	87,790	90,789	98,043
Austria-Hungary	27,529	33,929	4,325	4,703	3,208	2,061	2,058	2,965	2,620
Austria	18,234	21,151	3,319	3,654	2,199	1,053	1,088	1,928	1,621
Hungary	9,295	12,778	1,006	1,049	1,009	1,008	970	1,037	999
Belgium	7,077	8,157	732	700	698	803	775	809	821
Bulgaria	16,948	40,003	2,465	2,549	2,322	2,720	2,886	2,585	2,560
*Former Czechoslovakia	8,970	18,691	1,510	1,374	1,316	1,258	1,168	1,236	1,299
Denmark	6,189	6,049	545	473	492	546	533	634	562
Finland	3,970	3,970	414	398	373	360	368	397	512
France	35,945	45,637	4,339	3,967	4,201	4,668	4,544	5,034	5,473
Germany	92,207	122,373	7,929	7,072	6,732	6,880	6,387	5,965	5,895
Greece	25,403	16,841	966	1,196	1,264	1,526	1,388	1,330	1,664
Ireland	65,384	15,642	1,610	1,533	1,694	1,765	1,721	1,798	1,895
Italy	75,992	28,329	2,956	2,670	2,946	3,233	3,647	3,829	4,385
Netherlands	13,345	17,351	1,520	1,258	1,294	1,376	1,373	1,505	1,550
Norway-Sweden	17,825	19,382	1,662	1,530	1,441	1,665	1,479	1,551	1,729
Norway	5,211	4,599	363	405	314	389	332	357	404
Sweden	12,614	14,783	1,299	1,125	1,127	1,276	1,147	1,194	1,325
Poland	172,249	117,921	7,391	6,634	6,024	6,073	5,437	4,921	5,287
Portugal	25,497	11,479	759	878	837	917	920	869	1,017
Romania	48,136	52,154	3,735	3,679	3,477	3,475	3,022	3,160	3,322
Russia	433,427	167,152	7,502	8,548	10,114	10,154	9,455	9,030	9,280
Spain	18,443	17,695	2,040	2,319	2,316	2,970	3,341	3,707	4,018
Switzerland	11,768	12,173	868	861	916	1,040	888	1,007	1,090
United Kingdom	156,182	171,979	14,781	13,443	13,938	15,321	14,395	14,653	14,887
*Former Yugoslavia	57,039	131,831	4,772	4,611	4,488	4,445	4,321	4,721	5,392
Other Europe	29,087	290,871	22,608	20,316	16,865	17,839	17,684	19,083	22,785

Asia	2,859,899	3,470,835	410,209	438,580	389,301	419,382	405,854	442,854
China	342,058	591,711	67,634	83,603	68,410	72,492	70,977	77,658
Hong Kong	116,894	57,583	3,263	3,149	2,614	2,515	2,426	2,982
India	352,528	590,464	66,185	66,331	65,506	74,451	61,380	61,691
Iran	76,899	76,755	9,078	9,015	9,658	8,894	9,074	9,596
*Israel	41,340	54,081	5,172	4,389	4,555	4,251	4,324	4,652
Japan	66,582	84,552	7,100	6,751	6,383	5,980	5,808	5,709
Jordan	42,755	53,550	9,327	8,211	5,949	9,028	7,835	7,345
*Korea	179,770	209,758	22,022	22,748	22,937	20,313	16,976	21,329
Philippines	534,338	545,463	56,399	55,251	52,955	48,633	54,307	50,609
Syria	22,906	30,807	7,424	7,983	3,999	4,677	5,459	3,800
Taiwan	132,647	92,657	6,785	6,206	5,336	4,712	4,814	5,062
Turkey	38,687	48,394	7,435	9,040	7,189	7,248	8,762	8,635
Vietnam	275,379	289,616	30,065	33,486	26,578	29,825	30,332	40,412
Other Asia	637,116	745,444	112,320	122,417	107,232	126,363	123,380	143,374
North America	5,137,743	4,441,529	426,981	423,277	399,380	400,102	439,228	502,639
Canada and Newfoundland	194,788	236,349	19,491	19,506	20,489	17,670	19,309	19,349
Mexico	2,757,418	1,704,166	138,717	142,823	134,198	133,107	157,227	172,726
Caribbean	1,004,687	1,053,357	139,389	133,012	121,349	133,550	146,086	180,479
Cuba	159,037	271,742	33,372	36,261	31,343	46,505	54,178	66,120
Dominican Republic	359,818	291,492	53,890	46,036	41,487	44,550	50,382	60,613
Haiti	177,446	203,827	22,336	21,802	20,083	15,107	16,787	23,185
Jamaica	177,143	172,523	19,439	19,298	19,052	18,804	17,362	22,833
Other Caribbean	181,243	113,773	10,352	9,615	9,384	8,584	7,377	7,728
Central America	610,189	591,130	43,597	43,249	44,056	43,638	46,556	54,512
Belize	12,600	9,682	997	933	969	823	804	878
Costa Rica	17,054	21,571	2,306	2,230	2,232	2,018	2,121	2,295
El Salvador	273,017	251,237	18,547	18,477	18,015	18,964	18,699	21,268
Guatemala	126,043	156,992	10,263	10,795	9,829	9,871	11,466	12,548
Honduras	72,880	63,513	6,381	6,053	8,795	8,025	9,071	12,996

Region and country of last residence	1990 to 1999	2000 to 2009	2010	2011	2012	2013	2014	2015	2016
Nicaragua	80,446	70,015	3,476	3,314	2,943	2,940	2,773	3,262	3,397
Panama	28,149	18,120	1,627	1,447	1,363	1,276	1,164	1,133	1,130
Other Central America	—								—
South America	570,624	856,508	85,783	84,687	77,748	79,287	72,135	70,049	75,571
Argentina	30,065	47,955	4,312	4,335	4,218	4,227	3,757	3,542	3,783
Bolivia	18,111	21,921	2,211	2,113	1,920	2,005	1,663	1,549	1,481
Brazil	50,744	115,404	12,057	11,643	11,248	10,772	10,246	11,247	13,528
Chile	18,200	19,792	1,940	1,854	1,628	1,751	1,591	1,620	1,711
Colombia	137,985	236,570	21,861	22,130	20,272	20,611	17,614	16,509	16,830
Ecuador	81,358	107,977	11,463	11,068	9,284	10,553	10,871	9,816	10,779
Guyana	74,407	70,373	6,441	6,288	5,282	5,564	6,031	5,313	4,909
Paraguay	6,082	4,623	449	501	454	437	363	353	400
Peru	110,117	137,614	14,063	13,836	12,414	12,370	10,450	9,973	10,519
Suriname	2,285	2,363	202	167	216	170	160	116	130
Uruguay	6,062	9,827	1,286	1,521	1,348	1,314	1,098	1,023	911
Venezuela	35,180	82,087	9,497	9,229	9,464	9,512	8,289	8,985	10,590
Other South America	28	19	1	2	—	1	2	3	—
Other America	37	19	4	—	—	1	2	1	2
Africa	346,416	759,734	98,246	97,429	103,685	94,589	94,834	98,677	110,754
Egypt	44,604	81,564	9,822	9,096	10,172	10,719	12,043	13,907	13,367
Ethiopia	40,097	87,207	13,853	13,985	15,400	13,484	12,926	12,566	13,699
Liberia	13,587	23,316	2,924	3,117	3,451	3,036	3,681	3,580	3,545
Morocco	15,768	40,844	4,847	4,249	3,534	3,202	3,495	3,569	4,447
South Africa	21,964	32,221	2,705	2,754	2,960	2,693	2,871	3,298	3,441
Other Africa	210,396	494,582	64,095	64,228	68,168	61,455	59,818	61,757	72,255
Oceania	56,800	65,793	5,946	5,825	5,573	6,061	5,980	6,227	6,489
Australia	24,288	32,728	3,077	3,062	3,146	3,529	3,582	3,795	4,173
New Zealand	8,600	12,495	1,046	1,006	980	1,027	941	978	939
Other Oceania	23,912	20,570	1,823	1,757	1,447	1,505	1,457	1,454	1,377
Not Specified	25,928	211,930	5,814	6,217	9,265	10,127	8,430	10,256	22,726

—Represents zero or not available. *Note that a) Korea split into North Korea and South Korea in 1945; b) Czechoslovakia separated into the Czech Republic and the Slovak Republic in 1993; c) Former Yugoslavia, beginning in the 1990s, broke into the six nations of Serbia, Montenegro, Slovenia, Croatia, Macedonia, and Kosovo; d) and due to the way United States immigration statistics are recognized and collected, immigrants from the Occupied Palestinian Territories are grouped together with immigrants from Israel. **This data tracks the number of people who are annually granted legal permanent residence.

PRESIDENTS, VICE PRESIDENTS,
AND SECRETARIES OF STATE

	President	Vice President	Secretary of State
1.	George Washington, Federalist 1789	John Adams, Federalist 1789	Thomas Jefferson 1789 Edmund Randolph 1794 Timothy Pickering 1795
2.	John Adams, Federalist 1797	Thomas Jefferson, Dem.-Rep. 1797	Timothy Pickering 1797 John Marshall 1800
3.	Thomas Jefferson, Dem.-Rep. 1801	Aaron Burr, Dem.-Rep. 1801 George Clinton, Dem.-Rep. 1805	James Madison 1801
4.	James Madison, Dem.-Rep. 1809	George Clinton, Dem.-Rep. 1809 Elbridge Gerry, Dem.-Rep. 1813	Robert Smith 1809 James Monroe 1811
5.	James Monroe, Dem.-Rep. 1817	Daniel D. Tompkins, Dem.-Rep. 1817	John Q. Adams 1817
6.	John Quincy Adams, Dem.-Rep. 1825	John C. Calhoun, Dem.-Rep. 1825	Henry Clay 1825
7.	Andrew Jackson, Democratic 1829	John C. Calhoun, Democratic 1829 Martin Van Buren, Democratic 1833	Martin Van Buren 1829 Edward Livingston 1831 Louis McLane 1833 John Forsyth 1834
8.	Martin Van Buren, Democratic 1837	Richard M. Johnson, Democratic 1837	John Forsyth 1837
9.	William H. Harrison, Whig 1841	John Tyler, Whig 1841	Daniel Webster 1841

President	Vice President	Secretary of State
10. John Tyler, Whig and Democratic 1841	None	Daniel Webster 1841 Hugh S. Legaré 1843 Abel P. Upshur 1843 John C. Calhoun 1844
11. James K. Polk, Democratic 1845	George M. Dallas, Democratic 1845	James Buchanan 1845
12. Zachary Taylor, Whig 1849	Millard Fillmore, Whig 1848	John M. Clayton 1849
13. Millard Fillmore, Whig 1850	None	Daniel Webster 1850 Edward Everett 1852
14. Franklin Pierce, Democratic 1853	William R. King, Democratic 1853	William L. Marcy 1853
15. James Buchanan, Democratic 1857	John C. Breckinridge, Democratic 1857	Lewis Cass 1857 Jeremiah S. Black 1860
16. Abraham Lincoln, Republican 1861	Hannibal Hamlin, Republican 1861 Andrew Johnson, Unionist 1865	William H. Seward 1861
17. Andrew Johnson, Unionist 1865	None	William H. Seward 1865
18. Ulysses S. Grant, Republican 1869	Schuyler Colfax, Republican 1869 Henry Wilson, Republican 1873	Elihu B. Washburne 1869 Hamilton Fish 1869
19. Rutherford B. Hayes, Republican 1877	William A. Wheeler, Republican 1877	William M. Evarts 1877

	President	Vice President	Secretary of State
20.	James A. Garfield, Republican 1881	Chester A. Arthur, Republican 1881	James G. Blaine 1881
21.	Chester A. Arthur, Republican 1881	None	Frederick T. Frelinghuysen 1881
22.	Grover Cleveland, Democratic 1885	Thomas A. Hendricks, Democratic 1885	Thomas F. Bayard 1885
23.	Benjamin Harrison, Republican 1889	Levi P. Morton, Republican 1889	James G. Blaine 1889 John W. Foster 1892
24.	Grover Cleveland, Democratic 1893	Adlai E. Stevenson, Democratic 1893	Walter Q. Gresham 1893 Richard Olney 1895
25.	William McKinley, Republican 1897	Garret A. Hobart, Republican 1897 Theodore Roosevelt, Republican 1901	John Sherman 1897 William R. Day 1898 John Hay 1898
26.	Theodore Roosevelt, Republican 1901	Charles Fairbanks, Republican 1905	John Hay 1901 Elihu Root 1905 Robert Bacon 1909
27.	William H. Taft, Republican 1909	James S. Sherman, Republican 1909	Philander C. Knox 1909
28.	Woodrow Wilson, Democratic 1913	Thomas R. Marshall, Democratic 1913	William J. Bryan 1913 Robert Lansing 1915 Bainbridge Colby 1920
29.	Warren G. Harding, Republican 1921	Calvin Coolidge, Republican 1921	Charles E. Hughes 1921
30.	Calvin Coolidge, Republican 1923	Charles G. Dawes, Republican 1925	Charles E. Hughes 1923 Frank B. Kellogg 1925

	President	Vice President	Secretary of State
31.	Herbert Hoover, Republican 1929	Charles Curtis, Republican 1929	Henry L. Stimson 1929
32.	Franklin D. Roosevelt, Democratic 1933	John Nance Garner, Democratic 1933 Henry A. Wallace, Democratic 1941 Harry S. Truman, Democratic 1945	Cordell Hull 1933 Edward R. Stettinius, Jr. 1944
33.	Harry S. Truman, Democratic 1945	Alben W. Barkley, Democratic 1949	Edward R. Stettinius, Jr. 1945 James F. Byrnes 1945 George C. Marshall 1947 Dean G. Acheson 1949
34.	Dwight D. Eisenhower, Republican 1953	Richard M. Nixon, Republican 1953	John F. Dulles 1953 Christian A. Herter 1959
35.	John F. Kennedy, Democratic 1961	Lyndon B. Johnson, Democratic 1961	Dean Rusk 1961
36.	Lyndon B. Johnson, Democratic 1963	Hubert H. Humphrey, Democratic 1965	Dean Rusk 1963
37.	Richard M. Nixon, Republican 1969	Spiro T. Agnew, Republican 1969 Gerald R. Ford, Republican 1973	William P. Rogers 1969 Henry Kissinger 1973
38.	Gerald R. Ford, Republican 1974	Nelson Rockefeller, Republican 1974	Henry Kissinger 1974
39.	Jimmy Carter, Democratic 1977	Walter Mondale, Democratic 1977	Cyrus Vance 1977 Edmund Muskie 1980

	President	Vice President	Secretary of State
40.	Ronald Reagan, Republican 1981	George H. W. Bush, Republican 1981	Alexander Haig 1981 George Schultz 1982
41.	George H. W. Bush, Republican 1989	J. Danforth Quayle, Republican 1989	James A. Baker 1989 Lawrence Eagleburger 1992
42.	William J. Clinton, Democratic 1993	Albert Gore, Jr., Democratic 1993	Warren Christopher 1993 Madeleine Albright 1997
43.	George W. Bush, Republican 2001	Richard B. Cheney, Republican 2001	Colin L. Powell 2001 Condoleezza Rice 2005
44.	Barack Obama, Democratic 2009	Joseph R. Biden, Democratic 2009	Hillary Rodham Clinton 2009 John Kerry 2013
45.	Donald J. Trump, Republican 2017	Michael R. Pence, Republican 2017	Rex W. Tillerson 2017 Michael R. Pompeo 2018

FURTHER READINGS

CHAPTER 16

The most comprehensive treatment of Reconstruction is ˉric Foner's *Reconstruction: America's Unfinished Revolution, 1863–1877* (1988). A good brief history is Alan Guelzo's *Reconstruction: A Concise History* (2018). On Andrew Johnson, see Hans L. Trefousse's *Andrew Johnson: A Biography* (1989) and David D. Stewart's *Impeached: The Trial of Andrew Johnson and the Fight for Lincoln's Legacy* (2009).

Scholars have been sympathetic to the aims and motives of the Radical Republicans. See, for instance, Herman Belz's *Reconstructing the Union: Theory and Policy during the Civil War* (1969) and Richard Nelson Current's *Those Terrible Carpetbaggers: A Reinterpretation* (1988). The ideology of the Radicals is explored in Michael Les Benedict's *A Compromise of Principle: Congressional Republicans and Reconstruction, 1863–1869* (1974). On the black political leaders, see Phillip Dray's *Capitol Men: The Epic Story of Reconstruction through the Lives of the First Black Congressmen* (2008).

The intransigence of southern white attitudes is examined in Michael Perman's *Reunion without Compromise: The South and Reconstruction, 1865–1868* (1973) and Dan T. Carter's *When the War Was Over: The Failure of Self-Reconstruction in the South, 1865–1867* (1985). Allen W. Trelease's *White Terror: The Ku Klux Klan Conspiracy and Southern Reconstruction* (1971) covers the various organizations that practiced vigilante tactics. On the massacre of African Americans, see Charles Lane's *The Day Freedom Died: The Colfax Massacre, the Supreme Court, and the Betrayal of Reconstruction* (2008).

The difficulties former slaves had in adjusting to the new labor system are documented in James L. Roark's *Masters without Slaves: Southern Planters in the Civil War and Reconstruction* (1977). Books on southern politics during Reconstruction include Michael Perman's *The Road to Redemption: Southern Politics, 1869–1879* (1984), Terry L. Seip's *The South Returns to Congress: Men,*

Economic Measures, and Intersectional Relationships, 1868–1879 (1983), and Mark W. Summers's *Railroads, Reconstruction, and the Gospel of Prosperity: Aid under the Radical Republicans, 1865–1877* (1984).

Numerous works study the freed blacks' experience in the South. Start with Leon F. Litwack's *Been in the Storm So Long: The Aftermath of Slavery* (1979). The Freedmen's Bureau is explored in William S. McFeely's *Yankee Stepfather: General O. O. Howard and the Freedmen* (1968). The situation of freed slave women is in the focus of Jacqueline Jones's *Labor of Love, Labor of Sorrow: Black Women, Work and the Family, from Slavery to the Present* (1985).

The politics of corruption outside the South is depicted in William S. McFeely's *Grant: A Biography* (1981). The best recent biography of the 18th president is Ron Chernow's *Grant* (2017). The political maneuvers of the election of 1876 and the resultant crisis and compromise are explained in Michael Holt's *By One Vote: The Disputed Presidential Election of 1876* (2008).

CHAPTER 17

For masterly syntheses of post–Civil War industrial development, see Walter Licht's *Industrializing America: The Nineteenth Century* (1995) and Maury Klein's *The Genesis of Industrial America, 1870–1920* (2007). On the growth of railroads, see Richard White's *Railroaded: The Transcontinentals and the Making of Modern America* (2011) and Albro Martin's *Railroad Triumphant: The Growth, Rejection, and Rebirth of a Vital American Force* (1992).

On entrepreneurship in the iron and steel sector, and Thomas J. Misa's *A Nation of Steel: The Making of Modern America, 1865–1925* (1995). The best biographies of the leading business tycoons are Ron Chernow's *Titan: The Life of John D. Rockefeller, Sr.* (1998), David Nasaw's *Andrew Carnegie* (2006), and Jean Strouse's *Morgan: American Financier* (1999). Nathan Rosenberg's *Technology and American Economic Growth* (1972) documents the growth of invention during the period.

For an overview of the struggle of workers to organize unions, see Philip Bray's *There Is Power in a Union: The Epic Story of Labor in America* (2010). On the 1877 railroad strike, see David O. Stowell's *Streets, Railroad, and the Great Strike of 1877* (1999). For the role of women in the changing workplace, see Alice Kessler-Harris's *Out to Work: A History of Wage-Earning Women in the United States* (1982) and Susan E. Kennedy's *If All We Did Was to Weep at Home: A History of White Working-Class Women in American* (1979). On Mother Jones, see Elliott J. Gorn's *Mother Jones: The Most Dangerous Woman in America* (2001). To trace the rise of socialism among organized workers, see Nick Salvatore's *Eugene V. Debs: Citizen and Socialist* (1982) and Patrick Renshaw's *The Wobblies: The Story of the IWW* (1999). The key strikes are discussed in Paul Arvich's *The Haymarket Tragedy* (1984), W. F. Burns's *The Pullman Boycott: A Complete History of the Railroad Strike* (2015), and Paul Krause's *The Battle for Homestead, 1880–1892: Politics, Culture, and Steel* (1992).

CHAPTER 18

The classic study of the emergence of the New South remains C. Vann Woodward's *Origins of the New South, 1877–1913* (1951). A more recent treatment of southern society after the end of Reconstruction is Edward L. Ayers's *Southern Crossing: A History of the American South, 1877–1906* (1995). A thorough survey of industrialization in the South is James C. Cobb's *Industrialization and Southern Society, 1877–1984* (1984). On southern efforts to rationalize their defeat, see Edward H. Bonekemper's *The Myth of the Lost Cause: Why the South Fought the Civil War and the North Won* (2015).

On race relations, see Howard N. Rabinowitz's *Race Relations in the Urban South, 1865–1890* (1978). Leon F. Litwack's *Trouble in Mind: Black Southerners in the Age of Jim Crow* (1998) treats the rise of legal segregation, while Michael Perman's *Struggle for Mastery: Disfranchisement in the South, 1888–1908* (2001) surveys efforts to keep African Americans from voting. An award-winning study of white women and the race issue is Glenda Elizabeth Gilmore's *Gender and Jim Crow: Women and the Politics of White Supremacy in North Carolina, 1896–1920* (1996). On W. E. B. Du Bois, see David Levering Lewis's *W. E. B. Du Bois: Biography of a Race, 1868–1919* (1993). On Booker T. Washington, see Robert J. Norrell's *Up from History: The Life of Booker T. Washington* (2009).

For stimulating reinterpretations of the frontier and the development of the West, see William Cronon's *Nature's Metropolis: Chicago and the Great West* (1991), Patricia Nelson Limerick's *The Legacy of Conquest: The Unbroken Past of the American West* (1987), Richard White's *"It's Your Misfortune and None of My Own": A New History of the American West* (1991), and Walter Nugent's *Into the West: The Story of Its People* (1999). An excellent overview is James M. McPherson's *Into the West: From Reconstruction to the Final Days of the American Frontier* (2006).

The role of African Americans in western settlement is the focus of William Loren Katz's *The Black West: A Documentary and Pictorial History of the African American Role in the Westward Expansion of the United States,* rev. ed. (2005), and Nell Irvin Painter's *Exodusters: Black Migration to Kansas after Reconstruction* (1977).

The role of women in the West is the focus of Cathy Lucetti and Carol Olwell's *Women of the West* (2017) and Glenda Riley's *Women and Nature: Saving the Wild West* (1999).

The best account of the conflicts between Indians and whites is Robert M. Utley's *The Indian Frontier of the American West, 1846–1890* (1984). For the Sand Creek massacre, see Ari Kellman's *A Misplaced Massacre: Struggling over the Memory of Sand Creek* (2013). On the Battle of the Little Bighorn, see Nathaniel Philbrick's *The Last Stand: Custer, Sitting Bull, and the Battle of the Little Bighorn* (2010). On Crazy Horse, see Thomas Powers's *The Killing of Crazy Horse* (2010).

For a presentation of the Native American side of the story, see Peter Nabokov's *Native American Testimony: A Chronicle of Indian-White Relations from Prophecy to the Present, 1492–2000,* rev. ed. (1999). On the demise of the buffalo herds, see Andrew C. Isenberg's *The Destruction of the Bison: An Environmental History, 1750–1920* (2000).

CHAPTER 19

For a survey of urbanization, see David R. Goldfield's *Urban America: A History* (1989). Gunther Barth discusses the emergence of a new post-Civil War urban culture in *City People: The Rise of Modern City Culture in Nineteenth-Century America* (1980). John Bodnar offers a synthesis of the urban immigrant experience in *The Transplanted: A History of Immigrants in Urban America* (1985). See also Roger Daniels's *Guarding the Golden Door: American Immigration Policy and Immigrants since 1882* (2004). Walter Nugent's *Crossings: The Great Transatlantic Migrations, 1870–1914* (1992) provides a wealth of demographic information and insight. Efforts to stop Chinese immigration are detailed in Erika Lee's *At America's Gates: Chinese Immigration during the Exclusion Era* (2003).

On urban environments and sanitary reforms, see Martin V. Melosi's *The Sanitary City: Urban Infrastructure in America from Colonial Times to the Present* (2000), Joel A. Tarr's *The Search for the Ultimate Sink: Urban Pollution in Historical Perspective* (1996), and Suellen Hoy's *Chasing Dirt: The American Pursuit of Cleanliness* (1995).

For the growth of urban leisure and sports, see Roy Rosenzweig's *Eight Hours for What We Will: Workers and Leisure in an Industrial City, 1870–1920* (1983) and Steven A. Riess's *City Games: The Evolution of American Urban Society and the Rise of Sports* (1989). Saloon culture is examined in Madelon

Powers's *Faces along the Bar: Lore and Order in the Workingman's Saloon, 1870–1920* (1998).

On the impact of Darwin's theory of evolution, see Barry Werth's *Banquet at Delmonico's: Great Minds, the Gilded Age, and the Triumph of Evolution in America* (2009). On the rise of realism in thought and the arts during the second half of the nineteenth century, see David E. Shi's *Facing Facts: Realism in American Thought and Culture, 1850–1920* (1995). The rise of pragmatism is the focus of Louis Menand's *The Metaphysical Club: A Story of Ideas in America* (2001).

Helpful overviews of the Gilded Age are Alex Axelrod's *The Gilded Age, 1876–1912* (2017), Sean Cashman's *America in the Gilded Age: From the Death of Lincoln to the Rise of Theodore Roosevelt* (1984), and Richard White's *The Republic for Which It Stands: The U.S. during Reconstruction and the Gilded Age* (2017). Nell Irvin Painter's *Standing at Armageddon: The United States, 1877–1919* (1987) focuses on the experience of the working class.

For a stimulating overview of the political, social, and economic trends during the Gilded Age, see Jack Beatty's *Age of Betrayal: The Triumph of Money in America, 1865–1900* (2007). On the development of city rings and bosses, see Kenneth D. Ackerman's *Boss Tweed: The Rise and Fall of the Corrupt Pol Who Conceived the Soul of Modern New York* (2005). Excellent presidential biographies include Hans L. Trefousse's *Rutherford B. Hayes* (2002), Zachary Karabell's *Chester Alan Arthur* (2004), Henry F. Graff's *Grover Cleveland* (2002), and Kevin Phillips's *William McKinley* (2003). On the political culture of the Gilded Age, see Charles Calhoun's *Minority Victory: Gilded Age Politics and the Front Porch Campaign of 1888* (2008).

Balanced accounts of Populism can be found in Charles Postel's *The Populist Vision* (2007) and Michael McGerr's *A Fierce Discontent: The Rise and Fall of the Progressive Movement, 1870–1920* (2005). The election of 1896 is the focus of R. Hal Williams's *Realigning America: McKinley, Bryan, and the Remarkable Election of 1896* (2010). On the role of religion in the agrarian protest movements, see Joe Creech's *Righteous Indignation: Religion and the Populist Revolution* (2006). The best biography of Bryan is Michael Kazin's *A Godly Hero: The Life of William Jennings Bryan* (2006).

CHAPTER 20

An excellent survey of the diplomacy of the era is Charles S. Campbell's *The Transformation of American Foreign Relations, 1865–1900* (1976). For background on the events of the 1890s, see David Healy's *U.S. Expansionism: The Imperialist Urge in the 1890s* (1970). The dispute over American policy in

Hawaii is covered in Thomas J. Osborne's *"Empire Can Wait": American Opposition to Hawaiian Annexation, 1893–1898* (1981).

Ivan Musicant's *Empire by Default: The Spanish-American War and the Dawn of the American Century* (1998) is the most comprehensive volume on the conflict. A colorful treatment of the powerful men promoting war is Evan Thomas's *The War Lovers: Roosevelt, Lodge, Mahan, and the Rush to Empire, 1898* (2010). For the war's aftermath in the Philippines, see Stuart Creighton Miller's *"Benevolent Assimilation": The American Conquest of the Philippines, 1899–1903* (1982). On the Philippine-American War, see David J. Silbey's *A War of Frontier and Empire: The Philippine-American War, 1899–1902* (2007).

A good introduction to American interest in China is Michael H. Hunt's *The Making of a Special Relationship: The United States and China to 1914* (1983). John Taliaferro's *All the Great Prizes: The Life of John Hay* (2013) examines the role of this key secretary of state in forming policy.

For U.S. policy in the Caribbean and Central America, see Walter LaFeber's *Inevitable Revolutions: The United States in Central America,* 2nd ed. (1993). David McCullough's *The Path between the Seas: The Creation of the Panama Canal, 1870–1914* (1977) presents an admiring account of how the United States secured the Panama Canal. A more sober assessment is Julie Greene's *The Canal Builders: Making America's Empire at the Panama Canal* (2009). For a detailed treatment of Theodore Roosevelt's diplomacy as president, see James Bradley's *The Imperial Cruise: A Secret History of Empire and War* (2009).

CHAPTER 21

Splendid analyses of progressivism can be found in John Whiteclay Chambers II's *The Tyranny of Change: America in the Progressive Era, 1890–1920,* rev. ed. (2000), Steven J. Diner's *A Very Different Age: Americans of the Progressive Era* (1997), Maureen A. Flanagan's *America Reformed: Progressives and Progressivisms, 1890–1920* (2006), Michael McGerr's *A Fierce Discontent: The Rise and Fall of the Progressive Movement in America* (2003) and David Traxel's *Crusader Nation: The United States in Peace and the Great War, 1898–1920* (2006). On Ida Tarbell and the muckrakers, see Steve Weinberg's *Taking on the Trust: The Epic Battle of Ida Tarbell and John D. Rockefeller* (2008).

The evolution of government policy toward business is examined in Martin J. Sklar's *The Corporate Reconstruction of American Capitalism, 1890–1916: The Market, the Law, and Politics* (1988). Mina Carson's *Settlement Folk: Social Thought and the American Settlement Movement,*

1885–1930 (1990) examines the social problems in the cities. Robert Kanigel's *The One Best Way: Frederick Winslow Taylor and the Enigma of Efficiency* (1997) highlights the role of efficiency and expertise in the Progressive Era.

An excellent study of the role of women in progressivism's emphasis on social justice is Kathryn Kish Sklar's *Florence Kelley and the Nation's Work: The Rise of Women's Political Culture, 1830–1900* (1995). On the tragic fire at the Triangle Shirtwaist Company, see David Von Drehle's *Triangle: The Fire That Changed America* (2003). The best study of the settlement house movement is Jean Bethke Elshtain's *Jane Addams and the Dream of American Democracy: A Life* (2002).

On Theodore Roosevelt and the conservation movement, see Douglas Brinkley's *The Wilderness Warrior: Theodore Roosevelt and the Crusade for America* (2009) For insights into Republicans and Progressivism, see Michael Wolraich's *Unreasonable Men: Theodore Roosevelt and the Republican Rebels Who Created Progressive Politics* (2014). The immensely important election of 1912 is covered in James Chace's *1912: Wilson, Roosevelt, Taft, and Debs—The Election That Changed the Country* (2004) and Sidney M. Milkis's *TR, the Progressive Party, and the Transformation of Democracy* (2009). Excellent biographies include Kathleen Dalton's *Theodore Roosevelt: A Strenuous Life* (2002) and Patricia O'Toole's *The Moralist: Woodrow Wilson and the World He Made* (2019). The racial blind spot of Progressivism is in the focus of David W. Southern's *The Progressive Era and Race: Reform and Reaction, 1900–1917* (2006).

CHAPTER 22

A lucid overview of international events in the early twentieth century is Robert H. Ferrell's *Woodrow Wilson and World War I, 1917–1921* (1985). For a vivid account of U.S. intervention in Mexico, see Frederick Katz's *The Life and Times of Pancho Villa* (1999). On Wilson's stance toward the European war, see Robert W. Tucker's *Woodrow Wilson and the Great War: Reconsidering America's Neutrality, 1914–1917* (2007). An excellent biography is John Milton Cooper Jr.'s *Woodrow Wilson: A Biography* (2010).

For the European experience in the Great War, see Adam Hochschild's *To End All Wars: A Story of Loyalty and Rebellion, 1914–1918* (2011), Margaret MacMillan's *The War That Ended Peace* (2013), and William Philpott's *Attrition: Fighting the First World War* (2015). Edward M. Coffman's *The War to End All Wars: The American Military Experience in World War I* (1968) is a detailed presentation of America's military involvement. See also Peter Hart's *The Great War: A Combat History of World War I* (2015) and Gary Mead's *The Doughboys: America and the First World War* (2000).

For a survey of the impact of the war on the home front, see Meirion Harries and Susie Harries's *The Last Days of Innocence: America at War, 1917-1918* (1997). Maurine Weiner Greenwald's *Women, War, and Work: The Impact of World War I on Women Workers in the United States* (1980) discusses the role of women in the war effort while Sara Hunter Graham's *Woman Suffrage and the New Democracy* (1996) traces the movement during the war to give women the vote. Ronald Schaffer's *America in the Great War: The Rise of the War Welfare State* (1991) shows the effect of war mobilization on business organization. Richard Polenberg's *Fighting Faiths: The Abrams Case, the Supreme Court, and Free Speech* (1987) examines the prosecution of a case under the 1918 Sedition Act. See also Ernest Freeberg's *Democracy's Prisoner: Eugene V. Debs, the Great War, and the Right to Dissent* (2009).

How American diplomacy fared in the making of peace has received considerable attention. Thomas J. Knock connects domestic affairs and foreign relations in his explanation of Wilson's peacemaking in *To End All Wars: Woodrow Wilson and the Quest for a New World Order* (1992). See also John Milton Cooper Jr.'s *Breaking the Heart of the World: Woodrow Wilson and the Fight for the League of Nations* (2002), Charles L. Mee's *1919 Versailles: The End of the War to End All Wars* (2014), G.J. Meyers's *The World Remade: America in World War I* (2018), and Adam Tooze's *The Deluge: The Great War, America, and the Remaking of the Global Order* (2014).

The problems of the immediate postwar years are chronicled by a number of historians. The best overview is Ann Hagedorn's *Savage Peace: Hope and Fear in America, 1919* (2007). On the Spanish flu, see John M. Barry's *The Great Influenza: The Epic Story of the Deadliest Plague in History* (2004). Labor tensions are examined in David E. Brody's *Labor in Crisis: The Steel Strike of 1919* (1965) and Francis Russell's *A City in Terror: Calvin Coolidge and the 1919 Boston Police Strike* (1975). On racial strife, see Jan Voogd's *Race Riots and Resistance: The Red Summer of 1919* (2008). The fear of Communists is analyzed in Robert K. Murray's *Red Scare: A Study in National Hysteria, 1919-1920* (1955).

CHAPTER 23

For a lively survey of the social and cultural changes during the interwar period, start with William E. Leuchtenburg's *The Perils of Prosperity, 1914-32*, 2nd ed. (1993). Even more comprehensive is Michael E. Parrish's *Anxious Decades: America in Prosperity and Depression, 1920-1941* (1992). The best introduction to the culture of the 1920s remains Roderick Nash's *The Nervous*

Generation: American Thought, 1917–1930 (1990). See also Lynn Dumenil's *The Modern Temper: American Culture and Society in the 1920s* (1995).

The impact of woman suffrage is treated in Kristi Anderson's *After Suffrage: Women in Partisan and Electoral Politics before the New Deal* (1996). The best study of the birth-control movement is Ellen Chesler's *Woman of Valor: Margaret Sanger and the Birth Control Movement in America* (1992).

On the African American migration from the South, see James N. Gregory's *The Southern Diaspora: How the Great Migrations of Black and White Southerners Transformed America* (2005). See Charles Flint Kellogg's *NAACP: A History of the National Association for the Advancement of Colored People* (1967) for his analysis of the pioneering court cases against racial discrimination. Nathan Irvin Huggins's *Harlem Renaissance* (1971) assesses the cultural impact of the Great Migration on New York City.

On the radio craze, see Alfred Balk's *The Rise of Radio* (2005). For the automobile culture, see Richard Snow's *I Invented the Modern Age: The Rise of Henry Ford* (2014). On the emergence of airplanes, see Dan Hampton's *The Flight* (2017) and Mike Campbell's *Amelia Earhart* (2016) and Keith O'Brien's *Fly Girls* (2018).

The emergence of jazz is documented in Burton W. Peretti's *The Creation of Jazz: Music, Race, and Culture in Urban America* (1992). Scientific breakthroughs are analyzed in Manjit Kumar's *Quantum: Einstein, Bohr, and the Great Debate about the Nature of Reality* (2010). See also Steven Gimbel's *Einstein: His Space and Times* (2015). The best overviews of cultural modernism in Europe are Ann L. Ardis's *Modernism and Cultural Conflict, 1880–1922* (2008) and Peter Gay's *Modernism: The Lure of Heresy from Baudelaire to Beckett and Beyond* (2009). On southern modernism, see Daniel Joseph Singal's *The War Within: From Victorian to Modernist Thought in the South, 1919–1945* (1982). Stanley Coben's *Rebellion against Victorianism: The Impetus for Cultural Change in 1920s America* (1991) surveys the appeal of modernism among writers, artists, and intellectuals. See also Charles J. Shindo's *1927 and the Rise of Modern America* (2010).

CHAPTER 24

On Harding, see Robert K. Murray's *The Harding Era: Warren G. Harding and His Administration* (1969) and Charles L. Mee's *The Ohio Gang: The World of Warren G. Harding* (2014). See Nan Britton's account of her affair with Harding, *The President's Daughter* (2008). On Coolidge, see Amith Shlaes's *Coolidge*

(2013). On Hoover, see Martin L. Fausold's *The Presidency of Herbert C. Hoover* (1985). The influential secretary of the Treasury during the 1920s is ably analyzed in David Cannadine's *Mellon: An American Life* (2006).

John Higham's *Strangers in the Land: Patterns of American Nativism, 1860–1925*, 2nd ed. (2002) details the story of immigration restriction. The controversial Sacco and Vanzetti case is the focus of Moshik Temkin's *The Sacco-Vanzetti Affair: America on Trial* (2009). For analysis of the revival of Klan activity, see Linda Gordon's *The Second Coming of the KKK* (2017) and Thomas R. Pegram's *One Hundred Percent American: The Rebirth and Decline of the Ku Klux Klan in the 1920s* (2011). The best analysis of the Scopes trial is Edward J. Larson's *Summer for the Gods: The Scopes Trial and America's Continuing Debate over Science and Religion* (1997). On Prohibition, see Daniel Okrent's *Last Call: The Rise and Fall of Prohibition* (2011). For the story of the invention of the airplane, see David McCullough's *The Wright Brothers* (2015).

On the stock market crash in 1929, see Maury Klein's *Rainbow's End: The Crash of 1929* (2000). Overviews of the depressed economy are found in Charles P. Kindleberger's *The World in Depression, 1929–1939*, rev. and enlarged ed. (1986) and Peter Fearon's *War, Prosperity, and Depression: The U.S. Economy, 1917–1945* (1987). On the removal of the Bonus Army, see Paul Dickson and Thomas B. Allen's *The Bonus Army: An American Epic* (2004).

CHAPTER 25

Two excellent overviews of the New Deal are Ira Katznelson's *Fear Itself: The New Deal and the Origins of Our Time* (2013) and David M. Kennedy's *Freedom from Fear: The American People in Depression and War, 1929–1945* (1999). A lively biography of Roosevelt is H. W. Brands's *Traitor to His Class: The Privileged Life and Radical Presidency of Franklin Delano Roosevelt* (2009). The Roosevelt marriage is well described in Hazel Rowley's *Franklin and Eleanor: An Extraordinary Marriage* (2011).

The busy first year of the New Deal is ably detailed in Anthony J. Badger's *FDR: The First Hundred Days* (2008). Perhaps the most successful of the early New Deal programs is the focus of Neil M. Maher's *Nature's New Deal: The Civilian Conservation Corps and the Roots of the American Environmental Movement* (2008). On the political opponents of the New Deal, see Alan Brinkley's *Voices of Protest: Huey Long, Father Coughlin, and the Great Depression* (1982). Roosevelt's battle with the Supreme Court is detailed in Jeff Shesol's *Supreme Power: Franklin Roosevelt vs. The Supreme Court* (2010).

The actual effects of the New Deal on the economy are detailed in Elliot A. Rosen's *Roosevelt, the Great Depression, and the Economics of Recovery* (2005).

Critical assessments of Roosevelt and the New Deal are Burton Folsom's *New Deal or Raw Deal* (2009) and Amity Schlaes's *The Forgotten Man: A New History of the Great Depression* (2008). James N. Gregory's *American Exodus: The Dust Bowl Migration and Okie Culture in California* (1989) describes the migratory movement. The dramatic Scottsboro court case is the focus of James Goodman's *Stories of Scottsboro* (1995). On the environmental and human causes of the dust bowl, see Donald Worster, *Dust Bowl: The Southern Plains in the 1930s* (1979). On cultural life during the 1930s, see Morris Dickstein's *Dancing in the Dark: A Cultural History of the Great Depression* (2009).

The best overview of diplomacy between the world wars remains Selig Adler's *The Uncertain Giant, 1921–1941: American Foreign Policy between the Wars* (1965). Robert Dallek's *Franklin D. Roosevelt and American Foreign Policy, 1932–1945* (1979) provides a judicious assessment of Roosevelt's foreign policy initiatives during the 1930s.

On Roosevelt's war of words with isolationists, see Lynne Olsen's *Those Angry Days: Roosevelt, Lindbergh, and America's Fight over World War II, 1939–1942* (2013), David Kaiser's *No End Save Victory: How FDR Led the Nation into War* (2014), and Nicholas Wapshott's *The Sphinx: Franklin Roosevelt, the Isolationists, and the Road to World War II* (2015). See also David Reynolds's *From Munich to Pearl Harbor: Roosevelt's America and the Origins of the Second World War* (2001). For the Japanese perspective, see Eri Hotta's *Japan 1941: Countdown to Infamy* (2014). On the surprise attack on Pearl Harbor, see Gordon W. Prange's *Pearl Harbor: The Verdict of History* (1986).

CHAPTER 26

For a sweeping survey of the Second World War, consult Anthony Roberts's *The Storm of War: A New History of the Second World War* (2011). A detailed treatment of U.S. involvement is Rick Atkinson's multivolume Pulitzer prize–winning series, *An Army at Dawn* (2007), *The Day of Battle* (2008), and *The Guns at Last Light* (2013). Roosevelt's wartime leadership is analyzed in Eric Larrabee's *Commander in Chief: Franklin Delano Roosevelt, His Lieutenants, and Their War* (1987).

Books on specific European campaigns include Anthony Beevor's *D-Day: The Battle for Normandy* (2010) and Charles B. MacDonald's *A Time for*

Trumpets: The Untold Story of the Battle of the Bulge (1985). On the Allied commander, see Carlo D'Este's *Eisenhower: A Soldier's Life* (2002). Richard Overy assesses the controversial role of air power in *The Bombing War: Europe, 1939–1945* (2013).

For the war in the Far East, see John Costello's *The Pacific War, 1941–1945* (1981), Ronald H. Spector's *Eagle against the Sun: The American War with Japan* (1985), John W. Dower's award-winning *War without Mercy: Race and Power in the Pacific War* (1986), and Dan van der Vat's *The Pacific Campaign: The U.S.-Japanese Naval War, 1941–1945* (1991).

An excellent overview of the war's effects on the home front is Michael C. C. Adams's *The Best War Ever: America and World War II* (1994). On the transformation to the wartime economy, see Arthur Herman's *Freedom's Forge: How American Business Produced Victory in World War II* (2012) and Maury Klein's *A Call to Arms* (2013). Susan M. Hartmann's *The Home Front and Beyond: American Women in the 1940s* (1982) treats the new working environment for women. Kenneth D. Rose tells the story of problems on the home front in *Myth and the Greatest Generation: A Social History of Americans in World War II* (2008). Neil A. Wynn looks at the participation of blacks in *The Afro-American and the Second World War* (1976). The story of the oppression of Japanese Americans is told in Greg Robinson's *A Tragedy for Democracy: Japanese Confinement in North America* (2009).

On the development of the atomic bomb, see Jim Baggott's *The First War of Physics: The Secret History of the Atomic Bomb* (2010). The devastation caused by the atomic bomb is the focus of Paul Ham's *Hiroshima Nagasaki: The Real Story of the Atomic Bombings* (2015) and Susan Southard's *Nagasaki: Life after Nuclear War* (2015). For the controversy over America's policies towards the Holocaust, see Richard Breitman and Alan J. Lichtman's *FDR and the Jews* (2013).

A detailed introduction to U.S. diplomacy during the conflict can be found in Gaddis Smith's *American Diplomacy during the Second World War, 1941–1945* (1985). To understand the role that Roosevelt played in policy making, consult Warren F. Kimball's *The Juggler: Franklin Roosevelt as Wartime Statesman* (1991). The most important wartime summit meeting is assessed in S. M. Plokhy's *Yalta: The Price of Peace* (2010). The issues and events that led to the deployment of atomic weapons are addressed in Martin J. Sherwin's *A World Destroyed: The Atomic Bomb and the Grand Alliance* (1975). See also Michael Dobbs's *Six Months in 1945: FDR, Stalin, Churchill, and Truman—From World War to Cold War* (2013).

CHAPTER 27

The cold war remains a hotly debated topic. The traditional interpretation is best reflected in John Lewis Gaddis's *The Cold War: A New History* (2005). Both superpowers, Gaddis argues, were responsible for causing the cold war, but the Soviet Union was more culpable. The revisionist perspective is represented by Gar Alperovitz's *Atomic Diplomacy: Hiroshima and Potsdam: The Use of the Atomic Bomb and the American Confrontation with Soviet Power*, 2nd ed. (1994). Also see H. W. Brands's *The Devil We Knew: Americans and the Cold War* (1993), Melvyn P. Leffler's *For the Soul of Mankind: The United States, the Soviet Union, and the Cold War* (2007), Ralph Levering's *The Cold War: A Post-Cold War History* (2016), and Odd Arne Westad's *The Cold War: A World History* (2017). On the architect of the containment strategy, see John L. Gaddis, *George F. Kennan: An American Life* (2011). For the Marshall Plan, see Benn Steil's *The Marshall Plan: Dawn of the Cold War* (2018).

Frank Constigliola assesses Franklin Roosevelt's role in the start of the cold war in *Roosevelt's Lost Alliances: How Personal Politics Helped Start the Cold War* (2013). Arnold A. Offner indicts Truman for clumsy statesmanship in *Another Such Victory: President Truman and the Cold War, 1945–1953* (2002). For a positive assessment of Truman's leadership, see Alonzo L. Hamby's *Beyond the New Deal: Harry S. Truman and American Liberalism* (1973) and Robert Dallek's *The Lost Peace: Leadership in a Time of Horror and Hope, 1945–1953* (2010).

The domestic policies of Truman's Fair Deal are treated in William C. Berman's *The Politics of Civil Rights in the Truman Administration* (1970), Richard M. Dalfiume's *Desegregation of the U.S. Armed Forces: Fighting on Two Fronts, 1939–1953* (1969), and Maeva Marcus's *Truman and the Steel Seizure Case: The Limits of Presidential Power* (1977). The most comprehensive biography of Truman is David McCullough's *Truman* (1992).

For an introduction to the tensions in Asia, see Akira Iriye's *The Cold War in Asia: A Historical Introduction* (1974). For the Korean conflict, see Callum A. MacDonald's *Korea: The War before Vietnam* (1986) and Max Hasting's *The Korean War* (1987).

The anti-Communist crusade is surveyed in David Caute's *The Great Fear: The Anti-Communist Purge under Truman and Eisenhower* (1978) and M. Stanton Evans's *Blacklisted by History: The Untold Story of Joseph McCarthy* (2009). Arthur Herman's *Joseph McCarthy: Reexamining the Life and Legacy of America's Most Hated Senator* (2000) covers McCarthy himself. For a well-documented account of how the cold war was sustained by superpatriotism, intolerance, and suspicion, see Stephen J. Whitfield's *The Culture of the Cold War*, 2nd ed. (1996).

CHAPTER 28

Two excellent overviews of social and cultural trends in the postwar era are William H. Chafe's *The Unfinished Journey: America since World War II*, 6th ed. (2006), William Hitchcock's *The Age of Eisenhower: American and the World in the 1950s* (2018), and William E. Leuchtenburg's *A Troubled Feast: America since 1945*, rev. ed. (1979). For insights into the cultural life of the 1950s, see Jeffrey Hart's *When the Going Was Good! American Life in the Fifties* (1982) and David Halberstam's *The Fifties* (1993).

The baby boom generation and its impact are vividly described in Paul C. Light's *Baby Boomers* (1988). The emergence of the television industry is discussed in Erik Barnouw's *Tube of Plenty: The Evolution of American Television*, 2nd rev. ed. (1990), and Ella Taylor's *Prime-Time Families: Television Culture in Postwar America* (1989).

On the process of suburban development, see Kenneth T. Jackson's *Crabgrass Frontier: The Suburbanization of the United States* (1985). Equally good is Tom Martinson's *American Dreamscape: The Pursuit of Happiness in Postwar Suburbia* (2000).

The middle-class ideal of family life in the 1950s is examined in Elaine Tyler May's *Homeward Bound: American Families in the Cold War Era*, rev. ed. (2008). Thorough accounts of women's issues are found in Wini Breines's *Young, White, and Miserable: Growing Up Female in the Fifties* (1992). For an overview of the resurgence of religion in the 1950s, see George M. Marsden's *Religion and American Culture*, 2nd ed. (2000).

The origins and growth of rock and roll are surveyed in Carl Belz's *The Story of Rock*, 2nd ed. (1972). The colorful Beats are brought to life in Steven Watson's *The Birth of the Beat Generation: Visionaries, Rebels, and Hipsters, 1944–1960* (1995) and Dennis McNally's *Desolate Angel: Jack Kerouac, the Beat Generation, and America* (2003).

Scholarship on the Eisenhower years is extensive. Balanced treatments include Jim Newton's *Eisenhower: The White House Years* (2012) and Jean Edward Smith's *Eisenhower in War and Peace* (2012). For the manner in which Eisenhower conducted foreign policy, see Evan Thomas's *Ike's Bluff: President Eisenhower's Secret Battle to Save the World* (2012).

The best overview of American foreign policy since 1945 is Stephen E. Ambrose and Douglas G. Brinkley's *Rise to Globalism: American Foreign Policy since 1938* 9th ed. (2011). For the buildup of U.S. involvement in Indochina, consult Fredrik Logevall's *Embers of War: The Fall of an Empire and the Making of America's Vietnam* (2012). The Cold War strategy of the Eisenhower administration is the focus of Chris Tudda's *The Truth Is Our Weapon: The Rhetorical Diplomacy of Dwight D. Eisenhower and John Foster Dulles* (2006). To learn about the CIA's secret activities in Iran, see Ervand Abrahamian's *The Coup: 1953, the CIA, and the Roots of Modern U.S.-Iranian Relations* (2013). On the Suez Crisis, see Alex von Tunzelmann's *Blood and Sand: Suez, Hungary, and the Crisis that Shook the World* (2017).

The impact of the Supreme Court during the 1950s is the focus of Archibald Cox's *The Warren Court: Constitutional Decision as an Instrument of Reform* (1968). A masterly study of the important Warren Court decision on school desegregation is James T. Patterson's *Brown v. Board of Education: A Civil Rights Milestone and Its Troubled Legacy* (2001).

For the story of the early years of the civil rights movement, see Taylor Branch's *Parting the Waters: America in the King Years, 1954–1963* (1988), Robert Weisbrot's *Freedom Bound: A History of America's Civil Rights Movement* (1990), and David A. Nicholas's *A Matter of Justice: Eisenhower and the Beginning of the Civil Rights Revolution* (2007). On Rosa Parks, see Jeanne Theoharis's *The Rebellious Life of Mrs. Rosa Parks* (2013). On the testy relationship of Eisenhower and his vice president, Richard Nixon, see Jeffrey Frank's *Ike and Dick: Portrait of a Strange Political Marriage* (2013).

CHAPTER 29

A superb analysis of John Kennedy's life is Thomas C. Reeves's *A Question of Character: A Life of John F. Kennedy* (1991). The 1960 campaign is detailed in Gary A. Donaldson's *The First Modern Campaign: Kennedy, Nixon, and the Election of 1960* (2007). The best study of the Kennedy administration's domestic policies is Irving Bernstein's *Promises Kept: John F. Kennedy's New Frontier* (1991). See also Robert Dallek's *Camelot's Court: Inside the Kennedy White House* (2013), Thurston Clarke's *JFK's Last Hundred Days* (2013), and Ira Stoll's *JFK, Conservative* (2013). For details on the still swirling conspiracy theories about the assassination, see David W. Belin's *Final Disclosure: The Full Truth about the Assassination of President Kennedy* (1988).

On Barry Goldwater and the rise of modern conservatism, see Rick Perlstein's *Before the Storm: Barry Goldwater and the Unmaking of the American Consensus*

(2009). On LBJ, see the magisterial multivolume biography by Robert Caro's titled *The Years of Lyndon Johnson* (1990–2013). On the Johnson administration, see Vaughn Davis Bornet's *The Presidency of Lyndon B. Johnson* (1984). For an insider's perspective, see Joseph A. Califano's *The Triumph and Tragedy of Lyndon Johnson* (2015). For the inside story of Johnson's White House, see Joshua Zeitz's *Building the Great Society: Inside Lyndon Johnson's White House* (2018). Also insightful is Randall B. Woods's *Prisoners of Hope: Lyndon B. Johnson, the Great Society, and the Limits of Liberalism* (2016).

Among the works that interpret Johnson's social policies during the 1960s, John E. Schwarz's *America's Hidden Success: A Reassessment of Twenty Years of Public Policy* (1983) offers a glowing endorsement of Democratic programs. For a contrasting perspective, see Charles Murray's *Losing Ground: American Social Policy, 1950–1980* (1994). Also see Martha J. Bailey and Sheldon Danzinger's *Legacies of the War on Poverty* (2015).

On foreign policy, see *Kennedy's Quest for Victory: American Foreign Policy, 1961–1963* (1989), edited by Thomas G. Paterson, and Patrick J. Sloyan's *The Politics of Deception* (2015). To learn more about Kennedy's problems in Cuba, see Mark J. White's *Missiles in Cuba: Kennedy, Khrushchev, Castro and the 1962 Crisis* (1997). See also Aleksandr Fursenko and Timothy Naftali's *"One Hell of a Gamble": Khrushchev, Castro and Kennedy, 1958–1964* (1997).

American involvement in Vietnam has received voluminous treatment from all political perspectives. For an excellent overview, see Larry Berman's *Planning a Tragedy: The Americanization of the War in Vietnam* (1983) and *Lyndon Johnson's War: The Road to Stalemate in Vietnam* (1989), as well as Stanley Karnow's *Vietnam: A History*, 2nd rev. ed. (1997). An analysis of policy making concerning the Vietnam War is David M. Barrett's *Uncertain Warriors: Lyndon Johnson and His Vietnam Advisors* (1993). A fine account of the military involvement is Robert D. Schulzinger's *A Time for War: The United States and Vietnam, 1941–1975* (1997). On the legacy of the Vietnam War, see Arnold R. Isaacs's *Vietnam Shadows: The War, Its Ghosts, and Its Legacy* (1997).

Many scholars have dealt with various aspects of the civil rights movement and race relations in the 1960s. See especially Carl M. Brauer's *John F. Kennedy and the Second Reconstruction* (1977), David J. Garrow's *Bearing the Cross: Martin Luther King, Jr., and the Southern Christian Leadership Conference* (1986), and Adam Fairclough's *To Redeem the Soul of America: The Southern Christian Leadership Conference and Martin Luther King, Jr.* (1987). William H. Chafe's *Civilities and Civil Rights: Greensboro, North Carolina, and the Black Struggle for Freedom* (1980) details the original sit-ins. An award-winning study of racial and economic inequality in a representative American city is Thomas J. Sugrue's *The Origins of the Urban Crisis: Race and Inequality in Postwar Detroit* (1996).

CHAPTER 30

An engaging overview of the cultural trends of the 1960s is Maurice Isserman and Michael Kazin's *America Divided: The Civil War of the 1960s*, 3rd ed. (2007). The New Left is assessed in Irwin Unger's *The Movement: A History of the American New Left, 1959–1972* (1974). On the Students for a Democratic Society, see Kirkpatrick Sale's *SDS* (1973) and Allen J. Matusow's *The Unraveling of America: A History of Liberalism in the 1960s* (1984). Also useful are Todd Gitlin's *The Sixties: Years of Hope, Days of Rage*, rev. ed. (1993) and Bryan Burrough's *Days of Rage* (2015). For a focused study, see James T. Patterson's *The Eve of Destruction: How 1965 Transformed America* (2013). On the popularity of folk music and the role of Greenwich Village, see Stephen Petrus and Ronald D. Cohen's *Folk City* (2015).

For insights into the black power movement, see Peniel E. Joseph's *Stokely: A Life* (2014), and Joshua Bloom and Waldo E. Martin Jr.'s *Black against Empire: The History and Politics of the Black Panther Party* (2013).

Two influential assessments of the counterculture by sympathetic commentators are Theodore Roszak's *The Making of a Counter-Culture: Reflections on the Technocratic Society and Its Youthful Opposition* (1969) and Charles A. Reich's *The Greening of America: How the Youth Revolution Is Trying to Make America Livable* (1970). A good scholarly analysis that takes the hippies seriously is Timothy Miller's *The Hippies and American Values* (1991). A more recent assessment of the "culture wars" since the Sixties is Andrew Hartman's *A War for the Soul of America* (2015).

The best study of the women's liberation movement is Ruth Rosen's *The World Split Open: How the Modern Women's Movement Changed America*, rev. ed. (2006). On Betty Friedan, see Daniel Horowitz's *Betty Friedan and the Making of the Feminine Mystique* (2000). For the point of view of a militant feminist, see Vivian Gornick, *Essays in Feminism* (1978). On the gay liberation movement, see Jim Downs's *Stand by Me: The Forgotten History of Gay Liberation* (2016). The Stonewall riots are featured in Ann Bausum's *Stonewall: Breaking Out in the Fight for Gay Rights* (2016). See also Joanne Meyerowitz's *How Sex Changed: A History of Transexuality in the United States* (2004), Vicki L. Eklors's *Queer America: A People's LGBT History of the*

United States (2011), and Julia Seranos's *Outspoken: A Decade of Transgender Activism* (2016).

The union organizing efforts of Cesar Chavez are detailed in Ronald B. Taylor's *Chavez and the Farm Workers* (1975). See also Miriam Pawel's *The Crusades of Cesar Chavez: A Biography* (2014). The struggles of Native Americans for recognition and power are sympathetically described in Stan Steiner's *The New Indians* (1968).

The best overview of the 1970s and 1980s is James T. Patterson's *Restless Giant: The United States from Watergate to Bush v. Gore* (2005). On Nixon, see Melvin Small's thorough analysis in *The Presidency of Richard Nixon* (1999). A good slim biography is Elizabeth Drew's *Richard M. Nixon* (2007). A massive biography is Evan Thomas's *Being Nixon* (2015). An especially critical approach is Tim Weiner's *One Man Against the World: The Tragedy of Richard Nixon* (2015). For an overview of the Watergate scandal, see Stanley I. Kutler's *The Wars of Watergate: The Last Crisis of Richard Nixon* (1990). For the way the Republicans handled foreign affairs, consult Tad Szulc's *The Illusion of Peace: Foreign Policy in the Nixon Years* (1978). The Nixon White House tapes make for fascinating reading. See *The Nixon Tapes* (2014), ed. by Douglas Brinkley and Luke Nichter. Rick Perlstein traces the effects of Nixon's career on the Republican party and the conservative movement in two compelling books: *Nixonland: The Rise of a President and the Fracturing of America* (2007) and *The Invisible Bridge: The Fall of Nixon and the Rise of Reagan* (2014).

The Communist takeover of Vietnam and the end of American involvement there are traced in Larry Berman's *No Peace, No Honor: Nixon, Kissinger, and Betrayal in Vietnam* (2001). William Shawcross's *Sideshow: Kissinger, Nixon and the Destruction of Cambodia*, rev. ed. (2002), deals with the broadening of the war, while Larry Berman's *Planning a Tragedy: The Americanization of the War in Vietnam* (1982) assesses the final impact of U.S. involvement. The most comprehensive treatment of the anti-war movement is Tom Wells's *The War Within: America's Battle over Vietnam* (1994).

A comprehensive treatment of the Ford administration is contained in John Robert Greene's *The Presidency of Gerald R. Ford* (1995). The best overview of the Carter administration is Burton I. Kaufman's *The Presidency of James Earl Carter, Jr.*, 2nd rev. ed. (2006). A work more sympathetic to the Carter administration is John Dumbrell's *The Carter Presidency: A Re-evaluation*, 2nd ed. (1995). Gaddis Smith's *Morality, Reason, and Power: American Diplomacy in the Carter Years* (1986) provides an overview. Background on how the Middle East came to dominate much of American policy is found in William B. Quandt's *Decade of Decisions: American Policy toward the Arab-Israeli Conflict, 1967–1976* (1977). For a biography of Carter, see Randall Balmer, *Redeemer: The Life of Jimmy Carter* (2014).

CHAPTER 31

The rise of modern political conservatism is well told in Patrick Allitt's *The Conservatives: Ideas and Personalities throughout American History* (2009) and Michael Schaller's *Right Turn: American Life in the Reagan-Bush Era, 1980–1992* (2007).

On Reagan, see John Patrick Diggins's *Ronald Reagan: Fate, Freedom, and the Making of History* (2007), Richard Reeves's *President Reagan: The Triumph of Imagination* (2005), Sean Wilentz's *The Age of Reagan: A History, 1974–2008* (2008), and Thomas C. Reed's *The Reagan Enigma: 1964–1980* (2015). The best political analysis is Robert M. Collins's *Transforming America: Politics and Culture during the Reagan Years* (2007). For insights into the 1980 election, see Andrew E. Busch's *Reagan's Victory: The Presidential Election of 1980 and the Rise of the Right* (2005). On Reaganomics, see David A. Stockman's *The Triumph of Politics: Why the Reagan Revolution Failed* (1986).

For Reagan's foreign policy in Central America, see James Chace's *Endless War: How We Got Involved in Central America—and What Can Be Done* (1984) and Walter LaFeber's *Inevitable Revolutions: The United States in Central America*, 2nd ed. (1993). On Reagan's second term, see Jane Mayer and Doyle McManus's *Landslide: The Unmaking of the President, 1984–1988* (1988). For a masterly work on the Iran-Contra affair, see Theodore Draper's *A Very Thin Line: The Iran Contra Affairs* (1991). Several collections of essays include varying assessments of the Reagan years. Among these are *The Reagan Revolution?* (1988), edited by B. B. Kymlicka and Jean V. Matthews; *The Reagan Presidency: An Incomplete Revolution?* (1990), edited by Dilys M. Hill, Raymond A. Moore, and Phil Williams; and *Looking Back on the Reagan Presidency* (1990), edited by Larry Berman.

The 41st president is the focus of Timothy Naftali's *George H. W. Bush* (2007). The best biography is Jon Meacham's *Destiny and Power: The American Odyssey of George Herbert Walker Bush* (2015). On the 1988 campaign, see Sidney Blumenthal's *Pledging Allegiance: The Last Campaign of the Cold War* (1990). For a social history of the decade, see John Ehrman's *The Eighties: America in the Age of Reagan* (2005). On the Persian Gulf conflict, see Lester H. Brune's *America and the Iraqi Crisis, 1990–1992: Origins and Aftermath* (1993). For the end of the Cold War, see Jeffrey Engel's *When the World Seemed New: George H. W. Bush and the End of the Cold War* (2017).

Chapter 32

Analysis of the Clinton years can be found in Joe Klein's *The Natural: The Misunderstood Presidency of Bill Clinton* (2002). More recent biographies include John F. Harris's *The Survivor: Bill Clinton in the White House* (2006) and Patrick J. Maney's *Bill Clinton: New Gilded Age President* (2016) Clinton's impeachment is assessed in Richard A. Posner's *An Affair of State: The Investigation, Impeachment, and Trial of President Clinton* (1999). The conflict between Clinton and Newt Gingrich is explained in Elizabeth Drew's *The Struggle between Gingrich and the Clinton White House* (1996).

On changing demographic trends, see Sam Roberts's *Who We Are Now: The Changing Face of America in the Twenty-First Century* (2004). For a textured account of the exploding Latino culture, see Roberto Suro's *Strangers among Us: How Latino Immigration Is Transforming America* (1998). On social and cultural life in the 1990s, see Haynes Johnson's *The Best of Times: America in the Clinton Years* (2001). Economic and technological changes are assessed in Daniel T. Rogers's *Age of Fracture* (2011). The onset and growth of the AIDS epidemic are traced in *And the Band Played On: Politics, People, and the AIDS Epidemic,* 20th anniversary ed. (2007), by Randy Shilts.

On the religious right, see George M. Marsden's *Understanding Fundamentalism and Evangelicalism,* new ed. (2006) and Ralph E. Reed's *Politically Incorrect: The Emerging Faith Factor in American Politics* (1994).

On the invention of the computer and the Internet, see Paul E. Ceruzzi's *A History of Modern Computing,* 2nd ed. (2003), Janet Abbate's *Inventing the Internet* (1999), and Michael Lewis, *The New New Thing: A Silicon Valley Story* (1999). The booming economy of the 1990s is well analyzed in Joseph E. Stiglitz's *The Roaring Nineties: A New History of the World's Most Prosperous Decade* (2003).

For further treatment of the end of the cold war, see Michael R. Beschloss and Strobe Talbott's *At the Highest Levels: The Inside Story of the End of the Cold War* (1993) and Richard Crockatt's *The Fifty Years War: The United States and the Soviet Union in World Politics, 1941–1991* (1995).

On the transformation of American foreign policy, see James Mann's *Rise of the Vulcans: The History of Bush's War Cabinet* (2004), Claes G. Ryn's *America the Virtuous: The Crisis of Democracy and the Quest for Empire* (2003), and Stephen M. Walt's *Taming American Power: The Global Response to U.S. Primacy* (2005).

The disputed 2000 presidential election is the focus of Jeffrey Toobin's *Too Close to Call: The Thirty-Six-Day Battle to Decide the 2000 Election* (2001).

On the Bush presidency, see *The Presidency of George W. Bush: A First Historical Assessment*, edited by Julian E. Zelizer (2010) and Jean Edward Smith's *Bush* (2017). See also Fred H. Israel and Jonathan Mann's *The Election of 2000 and the Administration of George W. Bush* (2003). Also see Dick Cheney's illuminating, if self-serving, account of his service as Bush's vice president in *In My Time: A Personal and Political Memoir* (2011). For Bush's memoirs, see *Decision Points* (2010).

On the attacks of September 11, 2001, and their aftermath, see *The Age of Terror: America and the World after September 11*, edited by Strobe Talbott and Nayan Chanda (2001). For a devastating account of the Bush administration by a White House insider, see Scott McClellan's *What Happened: Inside the Bush White House and Washington's Culture of Deception* (2008).

On the historic 2008 election, see Michael Nelson's *The Elections of 2008* (2009). The best biography of Obama is David Maraniss's *Barack Obama: The Story* (2012). See also David Garrow's *Rising Star: The Making of Barack Obama* (2017) and Pete Souza's *Shade: A Tale of Two Presidents* (2018). A conservative critique is provided in Edward Klein's *The Amateur: Barack Obama in the White House* (2012). For insiders' accounts of the Obama administration, see David Axelrod's *Believer: My Forty Years in Politics* (2015) and Ben Rhodes's *The World As It Is: A Memoir of the Obama White House* (2018). The best overviews of the Obama presidency are Peter Baker's *Obama: The Call of History* (2017), and Mark Greenburg and Ken Burns's *Obama: The Historic Presidency of Barack Obama* (2017).

The Great Recession is explained in Alan S. Blinder's *After the Music Stopped: The Financial Crisis, the Response, and the Work Ahead* (2013) and Adam Toozes's *Crashed: How a Decade of Financial Crises Changed the World* (2018). The recession's effects on modern politics are the focus of John B. Judis's *The Populist Explosion: How the Great Recession Transformed American and European Politics* (2016). The Tea Party movement is assessed in Theda Skocpol and Vanessa Williamson's *The Tea Party and the Remaking of Republican Conservatism* (2012) and Elizabeth Price Foley's *The Tea Party: Three Principles* (2012). The polarization of politics is the focus of Russell Muirhead's *The Promise of Party in a Polarized Age* (2015). The partisan gridlock in Congress is analyzed in Thomas E. Mann and Norman J. Ornstein's *The Broken Branch: How Congress Is Failing America and How to Get it Back on Track* (2012). The tension between the conservative majority on the U.S. Supreme Court and the Obama administration is examined in Jeffrey Toobin's *The Oath: The Obama White House and the Supreme Court* (2012). On the growing economic inequality in America, see Joseph Stiglitz's *The Price of Inequality: How Today's Divided Society Endangers Our Future* (2013).

The emergence of Islamist radicalism is explained in Michael Weiss and Hassan Hassan's *ISIS: Inside the Army of Terror* (2015) and Jesssica Stern and J. M. Berger's *ISIS: The State of Terror* (2015). The conflicts in the Middle East are the focus of Dominic Tierney's *The Right Way to Lose a War: America in an Age of Unwinnable Conflicts* (2015).

The dramatic presidential election of 2016 is assessed in James W. Ceaser and Andrew E. Busch's *Defying the Odds: The 2016 Elections and American Politics* (2017), Larry Sabato and Kyle Kondik's *Trumped: The 2016 Election That Broke All the Rules* (2017), and Doug Wead's *Game of Thorns: The Inside Story of Hillary Clinton's Failed Campaign and Donald Trump's Winning Strategy* (2017). Donald Trump explained the purpose of his candidacy in *Great Again: How to Fix Our Crippled America* (2016). Hillary Clinton's assessed her election loss in *What Happened* (2017). For the emergence of populism, see Salena Zito and Brad Todd's *The Great Revolt: Inside the Populist Coalition Reshaping American Politics* (2018).

Inside looks at the chaotic Trump White House include James Comey's *A Higher Loyalty: Truth, Lies, and Leadership* (2018), and Bob Woodward's *Fear: Trump in the White House* (2018).

PHOTO CREDITS

CHAPTER 16: p. 728: Smithsonian American Art Museum, Washington, DC/Art Resource; p. 731: GRANGER — All rights reserved; p. 734: Sarin Images/GRANGER — All rights reserved; p. 735: © CORBIS/Corbis via Getty Images; p. 736: Bettmann/Corbis/Getty Images; p. 737: © Maryann Groves/ North Wind Picture Archives; p. 742: Library of Congress; p. 745: Library of Congress; p. 747: Library of Congress; p. 749: GRANGER — All rights reserved; p. 750: Library of Congress; p. 751: GRANGER — All rights reserved; p. 753: Bettmann/Corbis/Getty Images; p. 754: GRANGER — All rights reserved; p. 756: Library of Congress; p. 758: Library of Congress; p. 766: GRANGER — All rights reserved.

PART V: p. 777: PhotoQuest/Getty Images; p. 778: David J. & Janice L. Frent Collection/Corbis/ Getty Images

CHAPTER 17: p. 780: GRANGER — All rights reserved; p. 784: GRANGER — All rights reserved; p. 785: GRANGER — All rights reserved; p. 791: Bettmann/Corbis/Getty Images; p. 792: National Archives; p. 796: Wikimedia, pd; p. 797: American Petroleum Institute Historical Photo Collection; National Museum of American History, Smithsonian Institution; p. 798: Sarin Images/ GRANGER — All rights reserved; p. 800: Sarin Images/GRANGER — All rights reserved; p. 801: GRANGER — All rights reserved; p. 803: Special Collections Research Center, Swem Library, College of William & Mary; p. 804: Private Collection/Peter Newark American Pictures/Bridgeman Images; p. 806: © Museum of the City of New York, USA/Bridgeman Images; p. 807: Archives and Special Collections, Vassar College Library, 08.07.05; p. 809: Ludlow Santo Domingo Library; p. 810: GRANGER — All rights reserved; p. 812: Bettmann/Corbis/Getty Images; p. 813: Private Collection/Peter Newark American Pictures/Bridgeman Images; p. 816: T.V. Powderly Photographic Collection, The American Catholic History Research Center and University Archives (ACUA), The Catholic University of America, Washington, D.C.; p. 817: Library of Congress; p. 824: PhotoQuest/ Getty Images; p. 825: Photosearch/Stringer/Getty Images.

CHAPTER 18: p. 832: GRANGER — All rights reserved; p. 836: The New York Public Library/Art Resource, NY; p. 838: Library of Congress; p. 844: Corbis/Getty Images; p. 845: Corbis/Getty Images; p. 847: Special Collections, University of Chicago Library; p. 848: Library of Congress; p. 849: Science Source; p. 854: Kansas State Historical Society; p. 856: National Archives; p. 858: Corbis/Getty Images; p. 862: Library of Congress; p. 863: Glasshouse Images/Alamy Stock Photo; p. 868: Library of Congress; p. 870: Corbis/Getty Images; p. 872: Library of Congress; p. 876: Chinese workers who were returned to Rock Springs to work after the 1885 massacre, Wyoming State Archives Photo Collection, #11821, Wyoming State Archives.

CHAPTER 19: p. 880: National Gallery of Art, Washington DC, USA/Bridgeman Images; p. 884: Bettmann/Corbis/Getty Images; p. 886: William Williams Papers, Manuscripts and Archives Division, The New York Public Library, Astor, Lenox and Tilden Foundations, Art Resource, NY; p. 889: GRANGER — All rights reserved; p. 890: Bettmann/Corbis/Getty Images; p. 891: Library of Congress; p. 892: © Museum of the City of New York, USA/Bridgeman Images; p. 893: Bettmann/Corbis/Getty

Images; **p. 897:** Cleveland Museum of Art/Hinman B. Hurlbut Collection/Bridgeman Images; **p. 899:** Library of Congress; **p. 902:** Library of Congress; **p. 905:** Library of Congress; **p. 907:** Bettmann/Corbis/Getty Images; **p. 911:** GRANGER — All rights reserved; **p. 912:** Wikimedia, pd; **p. 913:** Bettmann/Corbis/Getty Images; **p. 915:** Library of Congress; **p. 919:** Kansas State Historical Society; **p. 920:** Nebraska State Historical Society; **p. 921:** GRANGER — All rights reserved; **p. 922 (both):** David J. & Janice L. Frent Collection/Getty Images; **p. 923:** Bettmann/Corbis/Getty Images.

PART VI: **p. 931:** Bettmann/Corbis/Getty Images; **p. 933:** From the Collections of The Henry Ford Museum.

CHAPTER 20: **p. 934:** Courtesy Frederic Remington Art Museum, Ogdensburg, New York; **p. 939:** GRANGER — All rights reserved; **p. 940:** Hawaiian Legacy Archive/agefotostock; **p. 942:** Wikimedia, pd; **p. 945:** Corbis/Getty Images; **p. 947:** Bettmann/Corbis/Getty Images; **p. 952:** National Archives; **p. 953:** Interim Archives/Getty Images; **p. 956:** GRANGER — All rights reserved; **p. 958:** Bettmann/Corbis/Getty Images; **p. 961:** GRANGER — All rights reserved; **p. 964:** Bettmann/Corbis/Getty Images; **p. 966:** National Archives; **p. 968:** GRANGER — All rights reserved.

CHAPTER 21: **p. 972:** Sarin Images/GRANGER — All rights reserved; **p. 976:** The Museum of the City of New York/Art Resource, NY; **p. 977:** Pictorial Press Ltd/Alamy Stock Photo; **p. 980:** AP Photos; **p. 981:** Library of Congress; **p. 986:** Wikimedia, pd; **p. 988:** Corbis/Getty Images; **p. 989:** Library of Congress; **p. 990:** Library of Congress; **p. 993:** Library of Congress; **p. 995 (top):** Collection of the New-York Historical Society, USA/Bridgeman Images; **(bottom):** Library of Congress; **p. 997:** NYPL/Art Resource, NY; **p. 998:** GRANGER — All rights reserved; **p. 999:** Everett/Shutterstock; **p. 1001:** Library of Congress; **p. 1003:** Library of Congress; **p. 1004:** Donald C. & Elizabeth M. Dickinson Research Center, National Cowboy & Western Heritage Museum; **p. 1006:** Library of Congress; **p. 1014:** Corbis/Getty Images; **p. 1015:** GRANGER — All rights reserved.

CHAPTER 22: **p. 1020:** Library of Congress; **p. 1026:** GRANGER — All rights reserved; **p. 1028:** Galerie Bilderwelt/Getty Images; **p. 1030:** GRANGER — All rights reserved; **p. 1034:** Bettmann/Corbis/Getty Images; **p. 1038:** Library of Congress; **p. 1039:** Bettmann/Corbis/Getty Images; **p. 1040:** Library of Congress; **p. 1043:** Library of Congress; **p. 1045:** Library of Congress; **p. 1047:** Bettmann/Corbis/Getty Images; **p. 1051:** Bettmann/Corbis/Getty Images; **p. 1052:** US Army Signal Corps/Education Images/UIG via Getty Images; **p. 1053:** National Archives; **p. 1055:** GRANGER — All rights reserved; **p. 1057:** GRANGER — All rights reserved; **p. 1065:** Bettmann/Corbis/Getty Images; **p. 1066:** Bettmann/Corbis/Getty Images; **p. 1067:** Library of Congress; **p. 1068:** Bettmann/Corbis/Getty Images.

CHAPTER 23: **p. 1074:** GRANGER — All rights reserved; **p. 1078:** GRANGER — All rights reserved; **p. 1080:** GRANGER — All rights reserved; **p. 1082:** © CORBIS/Corbis via Getty Images; **p. 1083:** Hulton Archive/Getty Images; **p. 1085:** Schlesinger Library, Radcliffe Institute, Harvard University/Bridgeman Images; **p. 1086:** From the Collections of The Henry Ford Museum; **p. 1088:** Bettmann/Corbis/Getty Images; **p. 1090:** Bettmann/Corbis/Getty Images; **p. 1092:** Wikimedia, pd; **p. 1093:** GRANGER — All rights reserved; **p. 1094:** George Rinhart/Corbis via Getty Images; **p. 1096:** Snark/Art Resource, NY; **p. 1098:** (2018) The Jacob and Gwendolyn Knight Lawrence Foundation, Seattle/Artists Rights Society (ARS), New York. GRANGER — All rights reserved; **p. 1100:** Alfred Eisenstaedt/The LIFE Picture Collection/Getty Images; **p. 1101 (left):** © 2018 Heirs of Aaron Douglas/Licensed by VAGA at Artists Rights Society (ARS), NY; **(right):** Andrew Herman, photographer. Federal Art Project, pd, Photographic Division collection, Archives of American Art, Smithsonian Institution; **p. 1102:** AP Photo/File; **p. 1104:** Ferdinand Schmutzer/Wikimedia, pd; **p. 1107:** Max Weber (American, born Russia, 1881-1961). Russian Ballet, 1916. Oil on canvas, 30 x 36 in. (76.2 x 91.4 cm). Brooklyn Museum, Bequest of Edith and Milton Lowenthal, 1992.11.29.

CHAPTER 24: **p. 1114:** © CORBIS/Corbis via Getty Images; **p. 1116:** GRANGER — All rights reserved; **p. 1118:** Bettmann/Corbis/Getty Images; **p. 1120:** Bettmann/Corbis/Getty Images; **p. 1124:**

Everett Collection Inc/Alamy Stock Photo; **p. 1127:** Hulton-Deutsch Collection/Getty Images; **p. 1133:** Library of Congress/Corbis/VCG via Getty Images; **p. 1140:** Sarin Images/GRANGER — All rights reserved; **p. 1142:** Library of Congress; **p. 1146:** Kirn Vintage Stock/Corbis via Getty Images; **p. 1147:** The Frent Collection/Getty Images; **p. 1148:** Herbert Hoover Presidential Library; **p. 1151:** AP Photo; **p. 1155:** Library of Congress/Corbis/VCG via Getty Images; **p. 1157:** Bettmann/Corbis/Getty Images; **p. 1160:** Photo 12/Alamy Stock Photo.

CHAPTER 25: p. 1166: GRANGER — All rights reserved; **p. 1170:** Corbis/Getty Images; **p. 1172:** GRANGER — All rights reserved; **p. 1174:** Bettmann/Corbis/Getty Images; **p. 1178:** Library of Congress; **p. 1179:** Berenice Abbot/Getty Images; **p. 1181:** Everett Collection Historical/Alamy Stock Photo; **p. 1182:** Franklin D. Roosevelt Presidential Library & Museum; **p. 1183:** Franklin D. Roosevelt Presidential Library & Museum; **p. 1186:** Margaret Bourke-White/Time & Life Pictures/Getty Images; **p. 1187:** Bettmann/Corbis/Getty Images; **p. 1188:** George Rinhart/Corbis via Getty Images; **p. 1191:** © 2018 Estate of Reginald Marsh/Arts Students League, New York/Artists Rights Society (ARS), New York. *A Paramount Picture*, 1934 (tempera on masonite), Marsh, Reginald (1898-1954)/Cleveland Museum of Art, OH, USA/Leonard C. Hanna, Jr. Fund/Bridgeman Images; **p. 1193:** Bettmann/Corbis/Getty Images; **p. 1194:** Bettmann/Corbis/Getty Images; **p. 1197:** The Art Archive/Shutterstock; **p. 1198:** Library of Congress; **p. 1201:** Time Life Pictures/Pictures Inc./The LIFE Picture Collection/Getty Images.

CHAPTER 26: p. 1208: AP Photo/Joe Rosenthal; **p. 1211:** Imagno/Getty Images; **p. 1212:** Hugo Jaeger/Getty Images; **p. 1214:** GRANGER — All rights reserved; **p. 1217:** AF archive/Alamy Stock Photo; **p. 1221:** Library of Congress; **p. 1222:** ullstein bild/GRANGER — All rights reserved; **p. 1224:** Bettmann/Corbis/Getty Images; **p. 1230:** National Archives; **p. 1231:** National Archives; **p. 1234:** Library of Congress; **p. 1235:** Everett Collection/SuperStock; **p. 1236:** GRANGER — All rights reserved; **p. 1237:** AP Photo/U.S. Army Signal Corps; **p. 1238:** Library of Congress; **p. 1239:** Bettmann/Corbis/Getty Images; **p. 1241:** National Archives; **p. 1243:** AP Photo; **p. 1247:** National Archives; **p. 1248:** Lt. Handford/IWM via Getty Images; **p. 1252:** © Robert Hunt Library/Mary Evans; **p. 1254:** HIP/Art Resource, NY; **p. 1256:** Herbert Gehr/The LIFE Picture Collection/Getty Images; **p. 1257:** Gamma-Keystone/Getty Images; **p. 1260:** National Archives; **p. 1263:** Bettmann/Corbis/Getty Images; **p. 1264:** John van Hasselt/Sygma via Getty Images.

PART VII: p. 1271: Eugene Gordon/The New York Historical Society/Getty Images; **p. 1273:** STR/Reuters/Newscom.

CHAPTER 27: p. 1274: Bettmann/Corbis/Getty Images; **p. 1276:** Bettmann/Corbis/Getty Images; **p. 1279:** AP Photo/John Rooney; **p. 1282:** A 1949 Herblock Cartoon, © The Herb Block Foundation; **p. 1283:** © Hulton-Deutsch Collection/CORBIS/Corbis via Getty Images; **p. 1284:** Bettmann/Corbis/Getty Images; **p. 1288:** ClassicStock/Alamy Stock Photo; **p. 1292:** Bettmann/Corbis/Getty Images; **p. 1294:** Bettmann/Corbis/Getty Images; **p. 1298:** Francis Miller/The LIFE Picture Collection/Getty Images; **p. 1300:** Bettmann/Corbis/Getty Images; **p. 1301:** Sovfoto/Universal Images Group/Shutterstock; **p. 1302:** Pictorial Parade/Getty Images; **p. 1305:** Bettmann/Corbis/Getty Images; **p. 1308:** Sarin Images/GRANGER — All rights reserved; **p. 1310:** Martha Holmes/The LIFE Picture Collection/Getty Images; **p. 1312:** Private Collection/J. T. Vintage/Bridgeman Images; **p. 1313:** GRANGER — All rights reserved.

CHAPTER 28: p. 1318: GraphicaArtis/Getty Images; **p. 1320:** Corbis/Getty Images; **p. 1324:** Tom Kelley/Getty Images; **p. 1326:** John Dominis//Time Life Pictures/Getty Images; **p. 1328:** Heritage Image Partnership Ltd/Alamy Stock Photo; **p. 1330:** Hulton Archives/Getty Images; **p. 1332:** Library of Congress; **p. 1333:** Harvard Art Museums/Fogg Museum, Transfer from the Carpenter Center for the Visual Arts, American Professional Photographers Collection, 4.2002.3. Photo: Imaging Department © President and Fellows of Harvard College; **p. 1334 (left):** Everett Collection Historical/Alamy Stock Photo; **(right):** Mondadori via Getty Images; **p. 1336:** Three Lions/Getty Images; **p. 1337:** Mondadori Portfolio via Getty Images; **p. 1338:** David Attie/Getty Images; **p. 1339:** Allan Grant/The LIFE Picture

Collection/Getty Images; **p. 1341:** Don Wright/The LIFE Images Collection via Getty Images; **p. 1343:** Elliott Erwitt/Magnum Photos; **p. 1344:** Bruce Davidson/Magnum Photos; **p. 1346:** GRANGER — All rights reserved; **p. 1347:** Charles Moore/Getty Images; **p. 1349:** Bettmann/Corbis/Getty Images; **p. 1354:** A 1956 Herblock Cartoon, © Herb Block Foundation; **p. 1355:** Bettmann/Corbis/Getty Images; **p. 1356:** AFP/Getty Images; **p. 1363:** Howard Sochurek/The LIFE Picture Collection/Getty Images; **p. 1364:** Sovfoto/Universal Images Group/Shutterstock.

CHAPTER 29: p. 1368: Library of Congress; **p. 1371:** GRANGER — All rights reserved; **p. 1375:** Bettmann/Corbis/Getty Images; **p. 1377:** GRANGER — All rights reserved; **p. 1379:** Bettmann/Corbis/Getty Images; **p. 1381:** National Archives; **p. 1384:** Carl Mydans/The LIFE Picture Collection/Getty Images; **p. 1385:** GRANGER — All rights reserved; **p. 1387:** GRANGER — All rights reserved; **p. 1389:** AP Photo/Bill Hudson; **p. 1391:** Kurt Severin/Getty Images; **p. 1394:** AP Photo/BH; **p. 1395:** AP Photo; **p. 1396:** Bettmann/Corbis/Getty Images; **p. 1399:** Bettmann/Corbis/Getty Images; **p. 1400:** National Archives; **p. 1403:** AP Photo; **p. 1404:** Everett Collection Historical/Alamy Stock Photo; **p. 1409:** PhotoQuest/Getty Images; **p. 1411:** © Tim Page/CORBIS/Corbis via Getty Images; **p. 1415:** Jack Kightlinger, Lyndon Baines Johnson Library and Museum.

CHAPTER 30: p. 1424: Bettmann/Corbis/Getty Images; **p. 1427:** Ted Streshinsky Photographic Archive/Getty Images; **p. 1428:** Leif Skoogfors/Corbis Historical/Getty Images; **p. 1429:** AP Photo; **p. 1432:** Henry Diltz/Corbis via Getty Images; **p. 1434:** Ted Streshinsky Photographic Archive/Getty Images; **p. 1436:** John Olson/The LIFE Picture Collection/Getty Images; **p. 1437:** Michael Ochs Archive/Getty Images; **p. 1439:** © Globe Photos/ZUMAPRESS.com; **p. 1443:** Eugene Gordon/The New York Historical Society/Getty Images; **p. 1444:** Bettmann/Corbis/Getty Images; **p. 1445:** H. William Tetlow/Fox Photos/Getty Images; **p. 1447:** Michael Rougier/The LIFE Picture Collection/Getty Images; **p. 1449:** Bettmann/Corbis/Getty Images; **p. 1450:** Fred W. McDarrah/Getty Images; **p. 1455:** Lee Lockwood/The LIFE Images Collection/Getty Images; **p. 1456:** AP Photo; **p. 1458:** Bettmann/Corbis/Getty Images; **p. 1461:** Bettmann/Corbis/Getty Images; **p. 1462:** Howard Ruffner/Getty Images; **p. 1465:** Bettmann/Corbis/Getty Images; **p. 1468:** John Dominis/The LIFE Picture Collection/Getty Images; **p. 1473:** AP Photo; **p. 1474:** Bettmann/Corbis/Getty Images; **p. 1476:** Dirck Halstead/The LIFE Images Collection/Getty Images; **p. 1477:** Gerald R. Ford Presidential Museum, Grand Rapids, MI.

CHAPTER 31: p. 1482: © Wally McNamee/CORBIS/Corbis via Getty Images; **p. 1485:** © CORBIS/Corbis via Getty Images; **p. 1488:** AP Photo/stf; **p. 1490:** Mohsen Shandiz/Sygma via Getty Images; **p. 1491:** Bettmann/Corbis/Getty Images; **p. 1492:** Francois LOCHON/Gamma-Rapho via Getty Images; **p. 1494:** Bettmann/Corbis/Getty Images; **p. 1499:** Bettmann/Corbis/Getty Images; **p. 1500:** Wally McNamee/Corbis/Getty Images; **p. 1503:** National Archives; **p. 1506:** Bettmann/Corbis/Getty Images; **p. 1507:** © Paul Szep; **p. 1508:** Peter Turnley/Corbis/VCG via Getty Images; **p. 1510:** Image Courtesy of The Advertising Archives; **p. 1512:** AP Photo/Peter Morgan, File; **p. 1514:** AP Photo/Marcy Nighswander; **p. 1515:** © Wally McNamee/CORBIS/Corbis via Getty Images; **p. 1516:** AP Photo/Jeff Markowitz; **p. 1517:** Visions of America/UIG via Getty Images; **p. 1520:** STR/Reuters/Newscom; **p. 1522:** MIKE NELSON/AFP/Getty Images; **p. 1524:** AP Photo/Susan Ragan.

CHAPTER 32: p. 1528: AP Photo/Alex Brandon; **p. 1533:** AP Photo/James Finley; **p. 1534:** Richard Ellis/AFP/Getty Images; **p. 1538:** AP Photo/Ron Edmonds; **p. 1541:** AP Photo/Doug Mills; **p. 1544:** Robert King/Newsmakers/Getty Images; **p. 1545:** STR/Reuters/Newscom; **p. 1547:** Kevin Lamarque/Reuters/Newscom; **p. 1548:** Yannis Behrakis/Reuters/Newscom; **p. 1552:** Ali Jasim/Reuters/Newscom; **p. 1554:** Mario Tama/Getty Images; **p. 1555:** AP Photo/Pablo Martinez Monsivais; **p. 1558:** AP Photo/Jae C. Hong, file; **p. 1561:** Jewel Samad/AFP/Getty Images; **p. 1563:** AP Photo/Erich Schlegel, File; **p. 1564:** Jeff J Mitchell/Getty Images; **p. 1566:** Darren McCollester/Getty Images; **p. 1568:** AP Photo/Ringo H.W. Chiu; **p. 1569:** AP Photo/Eric Gay; **p. 1572:** Ben Baker/Redux; **p. 1577:** Mladen Antonov/AFP/Getty Images; **p. 1580 (left):** Spencer Platt/Getty

Images; **(right):** David McNew/Getty Images; **p. 1582:** The Photo Access/Alamy Stock Photo; **p. 1585:** Xinhua/Bao Dandan via Getty Images; **p. 1587:** MediaPunch/Shutterstock; **p. 1588:** Amy Sussman/Shutterstock; **p. 1591:** Brian van der Brug/LA Times via Getty Images; **p. 1592:** Michael Nigro/Pacific Press/LightRocket via Getty Images; **p. 1593:** Jeff Malet Photography/Newscom; **p. 1597:** Shutterstock; **p. 1598:** Yonhap News/YNA/Newscom; **p. 1599:** U.S. Border Patrol/Handout/ Anadolu Agency/Getty Images.

INDEX

Page numbers in *italics* refer to illustrations.